EDUCATION IN THE UNITED STATES
A DOCUMENTARY HISTORY

SOL COHEN is Associate Professor of Education in the
Graduate School of Education at the University of
California, Los Angeles. He received his Ph.D. in 1964
from Columbia University where he was a Romiett
Stevens Scholar and Alumni Fellow at Teachers
College. He is the author of *Progressive and Urban
School Reform* (1965) and has contributed numerous
articles to scholarly journals and encyclopedias.
Professor Cohen has also been a Visiting Scholar at
the University of London Institute of Education.

EDUCATION IN THE UNITED STATES
A DOCUMENTARY HISTORY

Edited by
SOL COHEN

UNIVERSITY OF
CALIFORNIA
LOS ANGELES

VOLUME 1

Random House New York

Reference Series Editors:

Fred L. Israel
William P. Hansen

Acknowledgments for use of material covered by
Copyright Conventions appear on pages 3395–99.

Art spots courtesy of Dover Pictorial Archives

FIRST EDITION

9 8 7 6 5 4 3 2 1

*Education in the United States: A Documentary
History is now exclusively published and distributed
by*   *Greenwood Press, Inc.*
      51 Riverside Avenue
       Westport, Ct. 06880
ISBN 0-313-20141-2 SET
0-313-20142-0 v.1
0-313-20143-9 v.2
0-313-20144-7 v.3
0-313-20145-5 v. 4
0-313-20146-3 v.5

Designed by Marsha Picker
for computer typesetting by Volt Information Sciences, Inc.

PREFACE

> That education should be regulated by law and should be an affair of state is
> not to be denied, but what should be the character of this . . . education, and
> how young persons should be educated, are questions which remain to be
> considered. As things are, there is disagreement about these subjects. For
> mankind are by no means agreed about the things to be taught, whether we
> look to virtue or the best life. Neither is it clear whether education is more
> concerned with intellectual or with moral virtue. The existing practice is
> perplexing; no one knows on what principle we should proceed—should the
> useful in life, or should virtue, or should the higher knowledge, be the aim of
> our training . . . Again, about the means there is no agreement; for different
> persons, starting with different ideas about the nature of virtue, naturally
> disagree about the practice of it .
>
> Aristotle, The Politics

So Aristotle summarized the situation in Athens some 2400 years
ago. Such is the case today with American education, and the widespread interest in
the subject is in part a reflection of our bewilderment. There is in American
education a definite absence of a general purpose and aim—for teacher and student
alike. This is where the history of American education has a contribution to make.

The study of the history of American education should help make us conscious
of our educational origins and provide a diary of the long journey we have travelled
to get where we are educationally. Furthermore, it should give us the equivalent of
a memory and so help in locating ourselves more accurately in the present. For, as
Professor Franklin Le Van Baumer put it, in a different but related context, we
think and behave the way we do because we have traversed this road and not some
other.

The history of American education should also enable us to draw upon the
discourse that has gone on about education through the centuries. The plethora of
ideas, practices, ideals in the history of education, many of which run opposite to
either our present practices or our future aspirations, might give us a salutary
shock. That is to say, historical example should force us to think about, though not
necessarily to change, our course of action; should compel us to test the validity and
cogency of our educational ideas. Study of the history of education should throw
some light on the nature of schools and education; on education and the school's
limitations and potentialities. It can perhaps suggest more intelligent ways of
handling contemporary educational problems. Finally, the rich heritage of the
history of American education should help equip those who study it to transcend
the provincialisms of time and space and point of view, and help equip those who
study it for more informed decision making, not only in the field of education but
also in the broader area of public policy. It is probably a sense of this extraordinary
fruitfulness that has elicited the widespread dissatisfaction in recent years with
traditional versions of the history of American education.

Since it was first introduced as a specialty in American teacher-training
institutions more than three quarters of a century ago, the history of American
education has always had a promising though unfulfilled future. Unfortunately, too

much of the literature on the subject has been parochial, anachronistic, or out of touch with main currents of contemporary scholarship. This was the gist of three important essays which broke new ground in the late 50's and early 60's: The Fund for the Advancement of Education's *The Role of Education in American History;* Bernard Bailyn's, *Education In the Forming of American Society,* and Lawrence A. Cremin's *The Wonderful World of Ellwood Patterson Cubberley: An Essay In the Historiography of American Education.*[1]

In 1953 the Ford Foundation's Fund for the Advancement of Education appointed a prestigious committee of historians to study the historiography of American education. Their call for action was published four years later. The committee was unanimous in its contention that, relative to its importance in the development of the nation, the history of education in America had been shamefully neglected by American historians. The consequences of this neglect were serious, affecting adversely the planning of curricula, the formulation of policy, and the administration of educational agencies in the continuing crisis of American education.[2] The committee urged historians to devote themselves to close monographic study of the role of education, formal and informal, in American history. It called for a new history of American education that would break from particularized and narrow institutional history and concern itself with the broader subject of the impact of education upon society. The committee urged historians to investigate the influence of education upon such matters as economic development, the building of new communities on the frontier, social mobility, assimilation of immigrants, and the development of political values and institutions, among other topics.

In his seminal essay, the first fruit of the Fund's call, Professor Bailyn brought together two papers; the first, a lengthy critique of American educational historiography; the second, a trenchant revisionist interpretation of colonial educational history. At a time of deep public concern over the schools, Bailyn charged, "the role of education in American history is obscure. We have almost no historical leverage on the problems of American education."[3] The men who have taught the history of education—and written the textbooks—Bailyn continued, have viewed the subject not as an aspect of American history writ large, but rather as a device for communicating an appropriate ideology to a newly self-conscious profession. As a consequence, the history of American education suffers not so much from neglect as from distortion. The result has been a "foreshortened chronicle of pedagogical institutions so caught up in anachronisms as to make (historical) explanation impossible."[4] As a corrective to this myopic point of view, Bailyn urged

---

[1] Fund for the Advancement of Education, *The Role of Education in American History* (New York, 1957); Fund for the Advancement of Education, Committee on the Role of Education in American History, *Education and American History* (New York, 1965); Bernard Bailyn, *Education In The Forming of American Society* (Chapel Hill, 1960); Lawrence A. Cremin, *The Wonderful World of Ellwood Patterson Cubberley: An Essay In The Historiography of American Education* (New York, 1965). See also Bailyn's "Education as a Discipline: Some Historical Notes," in John Walton and James L. Kuethe, eds., *The Discipline of Education* (Madison, 1963), and Wilson Smith, "The New Historian of American Education," *Harvard Educational Review,* vol. xxxi (Spring 1961).

[2] *Education and American History,* p. 4.

[3] *Education In The Forming of American Society,* p. 4.

[4] *Ibid.* p. 5.

in a widely quoted dictum that historians think of education not only as formal pedagogy but rather as the entire process by which a culture transmits itself across the generations.

Lawrence Cremin continued the historiographical dialogue in his essay on Cubberley. Like a number of other early American educational historians, Cubberley had little professional training in history. His major area of training (and expertise) was not history but school administration. But he worked within a fairly well-formulated tradition. As a former public school superintendent, Cubberley found especially congenial the accounts of schools and schoolmen written by pioneer school administrators like Henry Barnard, James Wickersham, George Martin, and the Reverend A. D. Mayo, to whom educational history was the history of the public school realizing itself over time: "The moral of educational history is the common school triumphant, and with it, the Republic."[5] Activists all, they believed that a recital of past victories would unite and inspire a new profession. Cubberley stayed in this tradition with his extremely influential *Public Education in the United States* (1919). While acknowledging Cubberley's astounding industry and his service to the teaching profession, Cremin concludes that Cubberley's version of the American educational past had helped to produce a generation of schoolmen unable to comprehend—much less contend with—the great educational controversies which beset America in the decades following World War II. In his assessment of Cubberley's work, Cremin agreed with Bailyn that Cubberley committed many sins against Clio. Cremin closed his essay by suggesting some possible directions which a revitalized American educational history might take. Cremin saw special promise in efforts to assimilate history of American education to the model provided by social and cultural history. He urged historians to examine informal education, that is, to examine the educational activities and effects of churches, libraries, museums, the mass media, and to bring revisionist interpretations characteristic of the field of history in general to bear on educational questions, and to place educational history in a comparative perspective.

Few fields of recent scholarship have been so transformed as the historical study of American education. The past decade has witnessed a surge of writing on the history of American education, broadly conceived, closely allied with the fields of social and intellectual history, imaginative and mature in its use of the tools and apparatus of historical scholarship. Bailyn's *Education in the Forming of American Society* (1960) and Cremin's Bancroft Prize-winning *The Transformation of the School: Progressivism In American Education, 1876-1957* (1961) have provided the models. Bailyn and Cremin in the past decade have been followed or accompanied by many others. The new historians of education, whether on school of education faculties or history faculties, have eschewed writing about the public school as if it were unequivocally progressive and historically inevitable. They are now seeking to analyze educational adaptation to social change, and to emphasize the relation of pedagogical ideas and practices to social, economic, and political contexts. They are demonstrating how methods and insights borrowed from the social sciences can provide significant new approaches. Furthermore, they are bringing to their enterprise an awareness of the racial, ethnic and religious conflict with which our educational history is permeated, as well as an awareness of the complex interplay between schools and society. There is, of course, a danger in the

---

[5] Cremin, *op. cit.*, pp. 17, 25.

work of some of the new historians of American education, a tendency to polarize and simplify, and to drift toward conspiratorial interpretations of events. But most, in Bailyn's words, seek simply "to see education in its elaborate, intricate involvement with the rest of society." It is in this spirit that the following volumes were prepared, and not with an eye to demonstrating the validity of this or that interpretation.

This five-volume work attempts to bring together the most significant documents in the field of American education, extending from the 16th- and 17th-century English and European background to the earliest colonial beginnings to the present, and to locate them in their historical context. Each book is prefaced with an historical overview. Here, inevitably a point of view emerges, but an effort has been made to be catholic in the selection of documents. The documents are organized according to chronological periods within topical chapters. The periodization followed is flexible rather than rigid. Thus, in some cases, documents which are thematically relevant have been included in a given period even though they may not fall, chronologically, strictly within it. As a rule, the documents are of relatively substantial length rather than fragmentary units. But exigencies of space force excerpts or emendations. If, as is usually the case, the document has been extracted from a larger whole, an effort has been made to faithfully represent the author's view. The text of each document usually represents the usage of the source from which it was reproduced, but a few minor changes have been made in the interests of readability.

There are already available some excellent collections of source materials, but these are limited in one respect or another. Thus, for example, E. W. Knight's five-volume *Documentary History of Education in the South Before 1860* (1945) is confined to one region, while Richard Hofstadter and Wilson Smith's *American Higher Education: A Documentary History* (1961) is confined to one stage of education. This collection attempts to be comprehensive. One might argue that not every document of significance in the educational history of the United States is included, but for breadth and variety of reference material this is perhaps a more comprehensive and a better balanced collection than that of any predecessor—filling in lacuna especially in topics such as regionalism, religion, minorities, and overseas influences on and foreign commentary about American education, aspects of the history of American education which are usually overlooked or neglected in such collections. Because this work deals with so many central aspects of American life and character: marriage and the family, child welfare and child raising, immigration, religion, politics, psychology, law, race, the media, and economics, as well as education, it is hoped that it will be of use to those professionals or laymen interested in American social and intellectual history in general, as well as those interested in education specifically. The index, hopefully, will facilitate its use.

In the preparation of these volumes, the editor is under obligation to many people and many institutions. Especially helpful were the staffs at the libraries of UCLA, the University of London, and the British Museum. The editor is also indebted to the indispensable help of his assistants: Miss Laurie Lieberman, and Misters Nicholas Beck, Ralph Bregman and Perry Bloom, as well as the staff of the Communications Processing Center at the UCLA Graduate School of Education. A University of California Research Committee grant also helped. The project was substantially completed while the editor was on sabbatical leave from UCLA as Visiting Scholar at the University of London Institute of Education.

VOLUME I
CONTENTS

PROVINCIALS

NEGROES, INDIANS, AND GERMAN IMMIGRANTS

VOLUME II
CONTENTS

BOOK TWO   The Shaping of American Education, 1789–1895

VOLUME III
CONTENTS

VOLUME IV
CONTENTS

VOLUME V
CONTENTS

BOOK ONE

The Planting, 1607–1789

"Wee shall be as a Citty Upon a Hill, the eies of all people are upon us; soe that if wee shall deale falsely with our god in this work wee have undertaken and soe cause him to withdrawe his present help from us, wee shall be made a story and a by-word through the world."

John Winthrop

a. The colonies established along the Atlantic seaboard during the early decades of the 17th century were essentially a new frontier of Western European civilization, bound in innumerable ways to the traditions, customs, ideas and institutions of the Old World. The men who dominated the early colonial ventures remained essentially English and European in temper and outlook, and assumed that their culture would be transmitted through old and familiar means. Vigorous efforts were made to maintain the civilization they knew. As they struggled to subdue a raw continent, however, the colonists did not hesitate to modify the original inheritance to meet new needs.

A critical problem, and one the colonies regarded with the gravest concern, was the transmission of culture to the young. It is as part of the story of the threat of a breakdown of those social mechanisms that had supported culture that the history of American education in the colonial period may best be understood. In the course of adjustment to a new environment the familiar English and continental patterns of education were altered. Though many elements survived, by 1789 education in America was rather different from what most colonists in the early 17th century had anticipated. On many points the expectations of the first generation of settlers had been frustrated. How? What notions and traditions did the colonists start with? What was reproduced in the New World? What was modified or altered? What was wholly new? The answers to these questions provide us with the necessary background for understanding the history of American education in the colonial period.

b. Colonial educational ideals were derived from two traditions—the ethical and religious tradition of the Reformation, and the humanist tradition of the Renaissance. The Reformation had a profound impact on education in England. Until the 1530's, all Englishmen were Catholic, their church an integral part of a united Christendom ruled by the Pope. Then within a period of about thirty years, England became a Protestant country. The Reformation in England produced no dominating religious leader to match Luther or Calvin. Rather it took place from the top down, beginning under Edward VIII in the 1530's and completed under Queen Elizabeth around 1559. By then the Church of England or the Anglican Church became the Established Church. The consequences for education were profound. Many monastery schools, chantries, and colleges were suppressed. On the other hand, to help strengthen the new religious establishment and protect it from dissident minorities—Catholics on the right, and Puritans and other Calvinists on the left—many schools were re-founded. There was also a flourish of new schools and colleges, organized now on principles and curricula geared to Reformation doctrine. There were other critical developments on the continent as well as in England.

The Reformation encouraged the right of private judgment especially with regard to interpretation of Scripture. Luther, for example, wrote eloquently of the need to spread education so that ordinary folk might have access to the Scriptures in their native tongue. Under the stimulus of Luther and Philip Melancthon, his faithful lieutenant, several of the German states and free cities issued civil codes for the conduct of schools—notably Wurttemberg in 1559, and Saxony in 1580. In the Netherlands, the Synod of Dort in 1618 provided for the establishment of schools for the poor. But the plea for literacy in the vernacular was voiced most clearly in the Dutchman Erasmus' *Exhortation to Diligent Study of the Scripture*, a plea perhaps best heeded in England. Thus in 1525, Tyndale produced the first English translation of the *New Testament*. Coverdale's translation of the Bible followed a decade later, then Mathew's Bible in 1537, and Cranmer's Great Bible in 1540. All were superceded, of course, in 1611 with the publication of The Authorized Version, the King James Bible. Not only was the Bible to be taught in school and pulpit, but it was also to be the centre of family life. Indeed, a point so obvious as to be frequently overlooked or neglected—the Bible in its various versions, together with devotional works like Bunyan's *Pilgrim's Progress*, were the principal sources of education in England during the 16th and 17th centuries. Thanks to the development of printing, by the mid-17th century the English had become, in the words of John Richard Green, "the people of a book, and that book was the Bible."

For Protestants, all knowledge and learning had as their be-all and end-all the glory of God. Indeed, all human activity was to be regulated to this purpose. The end of all learning and eloquence, said Erasmus, for example, is to know God and honour him. But there was in Protestant thought an intimate connection between piety and intellect. The search for sanctity, the quest for salvation was uppermost, but salvation required learning, in pursuit of which all were supposed to join regardless of natural ability or worldly circumstance. The importance of capturing the minds of the young in order to advance Protestantism was recognized on the Continent by Luther in Germany, John Calvin in Geneva, John Knox in Scotland, (no less than by the Jesuits, who turned to education to defend Catholicism, as we shall see later). As the Reformation swept through northern and western Germany, then Switzerland and England, the reorganization of schools and education became a touchstone, an indispensable aspect of the establishment of a Protestant state.

Man's relation to God was a matter of great urgency to all Englishmen in the 16th and 17th centuries. But perhaps it was the Puritans who inherited in greatest measure the Scholastic impulse to rationalize faith and the belief that learning has a high and vital place in religion. But not the medieval learning. The colonists were heirs not only of the Reformation with its stress on the Bible; they were Renaissance humanists as well. After all, Latin, Greek, and Hebrew were the "holy" languages which enabled men to get a closer acquaintance with the Bible.

c. The Renaissance as a period in European history extended from the 14th century to the 17th century. Beginning in Italy, thence travelling north to Germany and France and the Low Countries, the Renaissance reached England at the turn of the 15th century, somewhat before the Reformation. The Renaissance signified the "rebirth" or "recovery" of letters, that is of ancient Latin texts unknown or undervalued in previous centuries, of more accurate and elegant Latinity, and of the renewed study of Greek. In the Middle Ages the staples of instruction were the works of Aristotle and various commentaries on the Bible and the Church Fathers. For the scholastic philosophy and logic, and the religious texts and glosses of the Middle Ages, men of the early Renaissance substituted Latin and Greek literature, rhetoric, history and moral philosophy. These were the humanistic studies. Paul Oskar Kristeller describes humanism best: "By humanism we mean merely the general tendency of the age to attach the greatest importance to classical studies, and to consider classical antiquity as the common standard and model by which to guide all cultural activities." Perhaps the chief fact to remember about humanism for the history of education is its reliance upon Latin and Greek (and less, Hebrew), as the chief instruments of pedagogy.

The critical date for the Renaissance in England is perhaps 1496–97 when John Colet returned from Italy and delivered his famous Oxford lectures on Paul's *Epistle to the Romans*. Cambridge caught up with the new learning somewhat later. Erasmus' sojourn at Cambridge from 1511–14 had much to do with it. Indeed Erasmus is, with another non-Englishman, the Spaniard Vives, along with Thomas More, Thomas Linacre, William Grocyn, and Colet, one of the central figures, if not the central figure of the English Renaissance. As Professor R. R. Bolgar asserts, Erasmus "is the greatest man we come across in the history of education." A prolific writer, Erasmus was the leader in introducing the cultivation of classical languages into the schools of England. As Erasmus put it in *De Ratione Studii*, "Language thus claims the first place in the order of studies and from the outset should include both Greek and Latin . . . within these two literatures are contained all the knowledge which we recognize as of vital importance to mankind." Earlier, the Italian humanists Vergerius and Bruni had made essentially the same point.

But Erasmus was also convinced that the character of education had to be ultimately Christian. As a Christian Humanist, Erasmus believed not only in the renewed study of classical antiquity, of the classics of Latin and Greek, but of the patristic writings, and of the Bible, from the most authoritative sources. He also believed in a subject matter that was at once classical and Christian—the "pietas litterata." Thus the Reformation and Renaissance fused into one broad movement of reformation in church and state.

Indeed, devotion to the study of the classics was part and parcel of Protestant and Catholic education alike in 16th century Europe. For the Jesuits too turned to the classical languages and literatures to cleanse and spread the Catholic faith and combat Protestantism. The founding of the Society of Jesus under the leadership of Ignatius Loyola, confirmed by papal bull in 1540, is a milestone in the history of European humanist education. The famous *Ratio Studiorum*, issued to the Society in 1599, became the official Jesuit pedagogical guide down to the temporary suppression of the Society in 1773. The quickened interest in education in Catholic lands was expressed also through the founding of several newer teaching orders such as the Fathers of the Oratory and the Institute of the Brothers of the Christian Schools. Thus not only humanistic education, but the long established principle of the Roman Catholic Church that education is properly a function of the church was embedded even more firmly in Western education by the Protestant Reformation and the Catholic Counter-Reformation. The vast majority of Christians agreed that education should be religious, and that it should be humanistic, they disagreed only as to the specific doctrines of the religion to be taught and as to the relative role to be played by church and state in education.

Protestant doctrines and polity, exhortations to "search the Scriptures," demanded not only a learned ministry but a literate laity. Sixteenth century schools in England were of two principal kinds—ABC or elementary schools, called "petty schools," and grammar schools. As a rule, pupils entered petty school at the age of four. It was the place for learning the Catechism and Primer, for familiarizing children with Anglican doctrines. But first children learned the alphabet, then reading and writing, and perhaps arithmetic. More serious mental training was reserved for the grammar school. Everywhere in Protestant Europe the Renaissance saw a flourish of new schools carrying the standards of the humanistic tradition. With Luther's encouragement, Philip Melancthon planned humanist schools for Saxony, Calvin organized a model Academy in Geneva, Johan Sturm organized the *gymnasium* in Strassberg, and in England the Latin grammar school became the principal carrier of the new learning.

In the 16th century in England great grammar schools like St. Paul's were refounded with humanist curricula, and new grammar schools like Eton, Winchester, and Merchant Taylor's were established under humanist control. Colet's Statutes of 1518 for St. Paul's, a model humanist school, provides the best picture we have of the ideals and practices of Tudor grammar school education. As Colet put it: "I would they were taught always in good literature both Latin and Greek, and good authors such as have the very Roman eloquence joined with wisdom, especially Christian authors that wrote their wisdom in clear and chaste Latin." The basis of the grammar school curriculum was, of course, Latin. Canterbury School regulations (1541) even make the speaking of English an offense. Schools had to use an official Latin grammar—William Lily's. In some grammar schools like St. Paul's, Eton, and Winchester, Greek was taught. In a very few Elizabethan grammar schools, like Westminster and York, Hebrew found a place. Games and sport also occupied a prominent place in English grammar school life. But of course the major concern was to permeate the schools with Christian principle. For example, the aim of St. Paul's, to quote Colet's Statutes again, was "especially to increase knowledge and Worshipping of God and Our Lord Christ Jesus and good Christian life and manners in the children." Girls were to receive some education but not very much. There was little opportunity for higher education for girls in schools as such. The education of girls took place mainly in the home; in wealthy homes by tutor or governess; in middle class homes and amongst the poor—the girls mother was usually the only teacher. But there is plenty of evidence of educated women in England in the 16th century. Lady Jane Grey, Mary Tudor, and Elizabeth were all, for example, accomplished linguists. Vives and other humanists called for the education of women, and some, like Vives, tutored them.

At the university level, one effect of the Renaissance in England was the foundation of new colleges with humanist curricula; like Corpus Christi and Christ Church at Oxford, and Trinity, St. John's College and Emmanuel College at Cambridge. Indeed, as early as the mid-16th century humanists were in control of Oxford and Cambridge. The founding of Trinity College in 1546 with its several fellows in Greek along with the regius professorships in Greek, Hebrew, and civil law, established earlier by Henry VIII, finally set the seal upon the transition from the medieval to the humanistic tradition. The study of the classical languages and literatures of Latin and Greek, and to a lesser extent, Hebrew, had become the staples of higher education. Latin poets, orators, and historians, Greek authors, the Old Testament and the New, replaced Aristotle and logic and dialectic at the heart of the university curriculum. To the medieval ideal of a thorough training in logic and training for the priesthood or for the law, was added the renaissance ideal of a training no less thorough in Latin and Greek, in what the humanists called "bonnae litterae" or polite letters, for personal development and for training for service to the state, or for the practical affairs of life.

By the 17th century, the chief aim of English schooling was no longer simply to train students for the ministry or the law, or to train them in the classics, but also to train young men to be gentlemen. As evidence, witness the popularity of the "courtesy" writers and other theorists of the education of gentlemen, as for example, Erasmus' model of a Christian Prince or Castiglione's Courtier. And one may trace Erasmus' influence on Sir Thomas Elyot's *The Boke Named The Governour* (1531), probably the first major treatise on the humanist point of view in education to appear in the English language, as well as on Roger Ascham's *The Scholemaster* (1570), and Henry Peacham's, *The Compleat Gentleman* (1622). All were concerned with education for civility as well as education for piety and learning. The same trinity of intentions were continued at the first colleges to be established in the American colonies; Harvard, and William and Mary College. The colonists were disciples of Vives, Erasmus, Elyot, Colet, and Castiglione.

The triumph of humanism in the 16th century as the dominant educational movement in Europe led to a frantic search for methods of instruction other than memorization and drill. During the 16th and 17th centuries the quest for a more appropriate pedagogical method occupied a great number of educators, including the Jesuits, the Abbe de Saint Cyran at the "Litle Schools" of Port Royal, August Francke, the German pietist, and Johan Amos Comenius, the great Moravian Bishop. For information about teaching and grammar schools in England in the 16th and 17th centuries, the most obvious sources are Richard Mulcaster, John Brinsley, Edmund Coote and Charles Hoole, all practicing schoolmasters. Mulcaster urged that instruction should be adapted to the pupil's interests and capacities and that better use should be made of physical activity, music, drawing and games. Coote and Hoole called for the use of English in the study of all school subjects, the grading of subject matter, and the division of pupils into classes by ability.

The teaching profession in England in this period was closely regulated by the Anglican church. Schoolmasters had to swear allegiance to the Act of Supremacy and the Thirty-Nine articles of the church, and secure license from the Bishop of the diocese in which they taught. Religious training of a uniform kind was also enforced on schools. This chiefly took the form of authorized manuals of religious instruction: the Primer for young children and the Catechism for older ones. This uniformity of religious instruction was reinforced by the compulsory use of the Royal Grammar; i.e., the Latin Grammar compiled about 1515 by William Lily and his collaborator, Erasmus, for St. Paul's. Its sole use had been commanded by proclamation of Henry VIII in 1542. There was also compulsory bible study and church attendance. One consequence was that for some 200 v⌐ ⌐s Catholics were driven to defy the law and educate their children in secret or send them to schools maintained by English Catholics abroad or to Jesuit seminaries on the continent.

d. As the 17th century progressed, Christian humanism was increasingly challenged by the rise of science. In this domain, by far the most important advance was in astronomy. The revelations of Copernicus, Kepler, and Galileo, among others, not only disturbed religious faith, but also shook the absolute authority of the classics and the traditional humanistic disciplines. It was in the field of astronomy, especially, that the discoveries were made which had the most shattering impact upon ideas and beliefs long accepted as eternal verities. To most Englishmen of the early 17th century, the earth had held the place of honor in the universe, centrally fixed and immovable. Around it, the universe was believed to revolve in a series of concentric crystalline spheres, extending from the sublunary region through the moon and the planets to the Empyraean Heaven, the abode of God and the elect. This Christianized Ptolemaic system was kept in motion by God with the aid of a working force of occult spirits.

Then in 1543 Copernicus produced his *On the Revolution of the Heavenly Orbs*, in which he argued that the earth was but another planet revolving in circles around the sun. In the early years of the 17th century, Kepler, by altering the planetary orbits from circles to ellipses, removed the mathematical difficulties that had marred the Corpernican system, while Galileo established the science of dynamics on an experimental and mathematical basis, while lending further scientific support to Copernicus in his *Two Chief Systems of the World*. In 1687 Sir Isaac Newton's

Principia Mathematica appeared, combining the law of inertia with the law of gravity to demonstrate that the intricate exploration of the universe could be reduced to the simply expressed principle that each particle of matter behaved as though it attracted every other particle with a force inversely proportional to the square of the distance between them. The law of gravity held mathematically accountable the moon, the sun, and the planets, as well as the tides and the formerly mystifying appearances of comets.

The crowning scientific achievements of Galileo and Newton were effected by application of a method that was a radical departure from previous practice. Aristotle had been concerned with final purposes and had attributed to everything a "nature" which explained its actions. Galileo, on the other hand, did not concern himself with final causes and purposes. He carried on experiments, and he accepted the results, whether or not they accorded with any prior religious or logical system. Newton concluded of principles like gravity and inertia: "These principles I consider not as occult qualities, supposed to result from the specific forms of things, but as general laws of nature by which the things themselves are formed . . ." The Scientist changed man's picture of himself and the world. Men, in Raleigh's words, were no longer persuaded that God "hath shut up all the light of learning within the Lanthorn of Aristotle's brains." Natural law now became the master key to the universe, Englishmen strove earnestly to keep abreast of the revolutionary new findings and even to add contributions of their own. Thus in 1662, the Royal Society of London was organized to "improve the knowledge of natural things," and stimulate and co-ordinate scientific efforts in England. At Oxford and Cambridge even earlier there were opportunities for studying the theories of Copernicus, Ramus, and Descartes. The invention of printing forced the pace of change in science as in every field of learning.

Inevitably the educational system of England was also in the 17th century undergoing challenges triggered by the rise of science. As early as 1570, Sir Humphrey Gilbert proposed a "Queen Elizabeth's Academy" with an enlarged curriculum, the subjects to be taught in English. The so-called "Commonwealth" educators (1640–1666) like John Durie, Sir William Petty, Samuel Hartlib, and even John Milton, more the devoted humanist than the others, sought reforms in the schools to make them teach practical skills, useful knowledge, and applied science. The so-called dissenting academies in England were especially hospitable in the 17th century to the new science, the practical subjects, and modern languages.

The outstanding propagandist for science in the 17th century was, of course, Francis Bacon, not a scientist himself but a master of popularizing the value of science through his writings and his influential position as lord chancellor in England. In his *Advancement of Learning*, Bacon put forward the claims of science as a new method of inquiry, and experimental method as the chief basis for acquiring knowledge that would be exact, reliable, and useful. In his *Novum Organum*, Bacon described in detail the inductive method whereby authoritative knowledge could be obtained. Bacon ridiculed the authority of Aristotle, proposing instead that man's senses were the only reliable criteria of truth. Once he purged himself of all "idols," Bacon taught, man could by patient observation and experiment arrive at knowledge based on evidence.

If Bacon was the high priest of "realistic" educational theory, Comenius was the outstanding educationist who applied the doctrines of sense realism to pedagogical methods and to subject matter. Comenius was extremely popular in England, his pedagogical ideas widely disseminated through the efforts of Samuel Hartlib and his circle. His application in *The Great Didactic* of the inductive method to the education of children appears strikingly modern: appeal to the child's sense experience; recognize the stages of a child's development; in the teaching of language take care to start with things; in teaching, proceed from the known to the unknown, and from the simple to the complex. Perhaps his most successful attempt to translate theory into practice was through textbooks like *Orbis Pictus,* his most popular text, designed to improve language teaching by utilizing pictures accompanied by explanatory sentences in Latin and in the vernacular. Later in the 17th century another enormously influential critic of the schools, John Locke, made his appearance. Locke has been called the father of the Enlightenment in educational thought. His *Essay Concerning Human Understanding* appeared in 1690 and laid the psychological groundwork for modern educational theory. His *Some Thoughts Concerning Education,* which appeared in 1693, applied his theories to education. It took half a century of insistent propaganda to diffuse the notion that childhood is a stage of development with its own rhythm of development and its own pedagogical needs. But after Locke, the ground was laid for the doctrines of innate human goodness and perfectability that received their most influential formulation by Rousseau and other French writers on education in the latter part of the 18th century.

   e. Nevertheless, the society the settlers of America had left in England had long depended on forms of education which were, in Bernard Bailyn's words, "largely instinctive and traditional, little articulated and little formalized." The family, patriarchal, hierarchical in organization, like the organization of society, served, in the first place, as the central agency in the socialization of the child. English writers of the late 16th and early 17th centuries agreed that the father's unchallenged rule was the sole assurance of a proper discharge of the family's social obligations. Nor were they loathe to reinforce theories of absolute monarchy with parallels between family and Kingdom, and father and King, and the necessity for hierarchy in the family and the social order in general. The family, as one writer put it, "is a school wherein the first principles and grounds of government and subjection are learned." Even Erasmus stressed parental responsibility for the early education of children. To help guide the family in its responsibilities many pocket-size manuals came off the new printing presses in increasing numbers in the 16th century.

  Another commonly held notion was that the family or household served as the principal educator of the child. That is, the family's educational responsibility was not restricted to elementary socialization. Within the family, with the aid of books such as Edmund Coote's *The English Schoolmaister* (1596), or Hugh Rhodes' *The Book of Nurture,* or a simple hornbook, or ABC primer, or the Bible itself, reading was usually taught and practiced, as well as skills that provided at least the first step in vocational training. Indeed in a great many cases, as among the agricultural laboring population and small tradesmen who together comprised the overwhelming majority of the English population at this time, the family provided all the vocational instruction necessary for mature life. The family's role in this training was extended and formalized in a most important institution of education, apprenticeship. What might be termed the technical education of the time was provided by the apprenticeship system. Nor was apprenticeship limited to training in a craft. As regularized in the Statute of Artificers, passed by the Elizabethan Parliament in 1563, a master was expected to see to the literacy of his charges, he was expected and required by law to bring them up in a good Christian cultivation, and to see to their proper deportment. He frequently contracted to provide them with training in skills such as casting accounts besides.

Apprenticeship of course was never simply an educational instrument, however. A master taking on a young boy expected his charge to work as well as to learn. The indenture always provided that the apprenticeship would obey and serve his master for a specified time, usually seven years, and was restricted to parents who held a freehold of some value. Furthermore, parents usually paid a fee at the signing of indentures. The usual age for apprenticeship was twelve.

What family and apprenticeship left undone by way of informal education, the local community and church most often completed. Anglicans in the 16th and 17th centuries held to the view that education as such was not a function of the state. Traditionally the role of the state in the education of the young was relatively passive and indirect. This is one difference between the Lutheran, Calvinist, and Anglican Reformations. The latter were reluctant to use the secular arm of the state for example to impose compulsory schooling. In England there was no Saxony Plan, no Calvin, no John Knox. Schools were usually provided by religious groups, private endowments, guilds, and other private entities. Church and charitable organizations were especially concerned with the education of the poor. The Society for the Promotion of Christian Knowledge (1699), the first national body in England to organize schools catering for the children or the poor, frequently fed and clothed as well as catechised poor children. An important exception to this policy of *laissez-faire* was a series of laws passed by Parliament in the late 16th century having to do with the problem of poor relief, culminating in the so-called "Poor Law" of 1601.

     f. By way of summary it should be pointed out that, as Lawrence A. Cremin puts it, English culture was but one version of a more general Western European culture: it shared a common heritage with the Dutch, Spanish, French, and Italian cultures, and it remained in continuing contact with them. Thus the Englishmen who came to America carried Bibles, and the writings of Augustine, the poetry of Virgil, and the letters of Cicero, all of which Europeans revered in common. Furthermore, the colonists brought as part of their literary culture treatises by Erasmus a Dutchman, Vives a Spaniard, Castiglione an Italian, Montaigne a Frenchman, and a host of other Renaissance and Reformation figures from the Continent as well as from England. There was nothing particularly "pure" about the English tradition, and a good deal of the cosmopolitan thought that marked Renaissance Europe was simply carried over to the colonies. It should also be pointed out that English culture was itself changing and in turmoil during the 16th and 17th centuries, as witness the struggles between Protestant and Catholic, Anglican and Puritan, scientist and humanist. Finally, almost as soon as certain cultural and social forms were planted in the New World, they began to change in response to the unique social and physical conditions of the New World.

    II   **a.** All the colonies established in the New World were concerned with the threat of barbarism, that children would grow up wild and illiterate. The emphasis on reading the Bible and cultivating learning and civility were shared to some degree by all Protestant sects. But the pattern of colonial education from the beginning varied considerably according to local custom and circumstance, patterns of settlement, and even geography. Indeed it may be said that education in the colonies early took on regional characteristics. It may also be said that the New England colonies put into effect at an early date and maintained fairly consistently in the colonial period an ambitious school system, more widely available and of higher quality than anywhere else in the colonies.

Religion was the heart of the matter, the most pervasive influence in colonial New England. In the 17th century, Puritanism was a militant faith, full of vigor and strength. Never were a people more sure of having been on the right track. "That which is our greatest comfort, and means of defense above all others," Francis Higginson wrote in the earliest days, in *New England's Plantation*, "is, that we have here the true Religion and holy Ordinances of Almighty God taught among us. . . . Thus we doubt not but God will be with us, and if God be with us, who can be against us?" Theirs would be a society dedicated to the glory of God. The Lord had called them to this remote place to complete the Protestant Reformation and lead the way for all mankind. To the 17th century Puritan, the ideal society was the society of believers governed by an hierarchy of the elect. From its inception, the Massachusetts Bay Colony effectively joined Church and State into a unified theocracy, which from the outset considered education to be a public responsibility, the chief aim of which was to produce pious and learned and well-mannered Christians.

The search for sanctity, the quest for salvation, was uppermost. But salvation required learning, in pursuit of which all were supposed to join regardless of natural ability or worldly circumstance. The Puritans inherited in greater measure than any other Protestant group the Scholastic impulse to rationalize faith and the Reformation belief that learning has a high and vital place in religion. Though the intellectual leaders of the colonies made much in their writings of the religious aspect of life and thus were children of the Protestant Reformation, they were just as truly children of the Renaissance humanism of the 15th and 16th centuries. When the colonists came to America the study of the classical languages and literatures of Greek and Latin had become the staples of English and continental higher education. There was almost complete agreement on the importance of classical learning among colonial intellectuals for those who would become leaders in church and state. Many of the earliest Puritan leaders had been grounded in the classics in the grammar schools or dissenting academies or universities of England and they moved promptly to establish similar institutions with similar curricula in America.

"How hard will it be for one brought up among books and learned men to live in a barbarous place where there is no learning and less civility," wrote one of John Winthrop's friends on the eve of his departure from England. The answer of Winthrop and the other emigrants was to take along books and to build schools. Nothing so clearly illustrates the Puritan determination to create a New Zion as their zeal for education. In the face of tremendous obstacles—the bitter environment and an ocean's distance from centers of learning—New England's cultural achievement was extraordinary. A decade had not passed after the founding of Massachusetts Bay Colony before a Latin grammar school and a college had been founded. Not many years passed before statutes were enacted which had as their purpose the attainment of universal literacy and the establishment of a colony-wide system of schools. In 1636 Harvard was founded. At about the same time, so was the Boston Latin Grammar School. When the Puritans created schools, they did so remembering education in England. Harvard was based on Emmanuel College, Cambridge. The Classical curriculum of the Boston Latin Grammar School also followed English precedent. (And the colonial dame schools resembled those in countless villages in England.) Before 1647, eleven of the sixty towns in New

England had voluntarily established, and were supporting by various means—subscription, land rentals, tuition, endowment—grammar schools.

Still, as Bernard Bailyn points out in his provocative essay on education in the colonial period, *Education In The Forming of American Society*, the family was expected to carry the greatest educational burden. The family, the patrilineal group of extended kinship gathered into a single household, not the school, served as the central agency for education. It was, in the first place, the primary agent in the socialization of the child. But the family's educational role was not restricted to elementary socialization. Within these kinship groupings, skills that provided at least the first steps in literacy as well as in vocational training were taught and practiced. In a great many cases, the family provided all the vocational instruction necessary for mature life. The family's role in vocational training was extended and formalized in a most important institution of education: apprenticeship. This was a typical English method of bringing up male children to be useful. Nor was apprenticeship limited to training in a craft. A master was expected to see to the literacy of his charges, he was expected and required by law to bring them up in good Christian cultivation, and to see to their proper deportment. He frequently contracted to provide them with training in such skills as casting accounts besides. Further, most of the learned professions too, rested upon apprenticeship rather than formal training. What family and apprenticeship left undone by way of informal education the local community and church most often completed. Traditionally, as we have seen, the role of the State in the education of the young was passive and indirect.

Within a short time it became clear that the family was failing in some of its more obvious functions. Seventeenth century laws and admonitions relating to family life are poignant. Massachusetts and Connecticut passed laws demanding filial obedience from children and specifying harsh penalties for contempt and abuse of parents. Meanwhile, laws passed in 1642 and 1647 in the Massachusetts Bay Colony signaled the opening of a second line of defense: the deliberate use of schools and education to shore up the social order.

Only a few years' experience had shown that *laissez-faire* in education was a failure. Parents would not or could not be depended upon to do their duty; they would have to be forced to by law. The Massachusetts School Law of 1642 was one of a series of expediencies aimed at stemming the tide of ignorance and civil disorder: parents and masters were to be compelled to see to it that their children and apprentices were taught to read and understand the principles of religion and the laws of the country, and also some definite calling or trade. The Statute of 1642 in effect required compulsory education, but contained no provisions with respect to compulsory school attendance, while the entire responsibility for the education of children was placed upon parents and masters. It soon became apparent that schools would have to be established if children and youth were to receive the amount and kind of education deemed essential. Five years later, in 1647, the Massachusetts Bay Colony enacted the famous "Old Deluder Satan" Law. The Law of 1647 stipulated that all towns of fifty or more families would be required to provide someone to teach "all such children as shall resort to him to read and write." Towns of 100 or more families were to set up a grammar school, the master thereof to prepare children for the college. Fines were to be exacted by the selectmen for failure to comply. It was left to the towns to choose the means of supporting the school. Connecticut and New Hampshire soon followed Massachusetts' example.

The Law of 1647 is a significant statute in several respects. Assuming a determinative role in education was a novel move by the State, passing the burden of management and finance onto the towns was a shrewd one, with important ramifications. For example, in its periodic meetings, the town handled the school in just the same manner that it did any public business. Thus the school could not escape the impact of ordinary town politics and financial pressures. In the matter of educational finance, too, the settlers had to alter traditional forms. Everywhere the original reliance was on private benefaction, and everywhere, in the first few years, private donations were made in the familiar manner. But it quickly became apparent that such benefaction would not satisfy the need. Sufficient funds were not forthcoming and those that appeared failed to produce the expected yield. The solution that emerged by the mid-17th century in New England was the pooling of community resources in the form of general taxation, though this practice did not, of course, appear everywhere. Since support for schools and even colleges came usually not from an automatic yield from secure investment, but from the repeated acts of current donation, whether in the form of taxes, or of individual, family, or community gifts, the autonomy that comes from an independent, reliable, self-perpetuating income was lacking. Dependent for support upon "gifts," education in New England in the colonial period came within direct control not of those responsible for instruction, but of those who created and financed educational institutions; American education would always be sensitive to community pressure, to the pressure of funding and sustaining groups.

That many New England towns were taxing themselves to provide a part of the cost of maintaining schools is clear from the record. It is equally clear that the picture sometimes drawn of every New England town, with a public school free and open to all, is without foundation in fact. To be sure, for example, the Massachusetts schools were in some key respects "public." The initiative was taken by citizens in town meetings. The towns in their corporate character voted to have schools. But public support was not compulsory; few schools in the 17th century were completely free. Indeed, enforcement of the school laws was by no means easy. In time, some towns, because of the dispersion of population, experimented with the "moving school," in which the schoolmaster moved from one district in the town to another, spending a few weeks in one or a few months in the other, depending, as a rule, upon the amount of taxes each district had paid into the town treasury for school purposes. Quite a few towns simply gave up the attempt to keep a school open and paid the fine for non-compliance of the law. Further, Protestant piety inevitably permeated the teachings of the schools.

Even as religion permeated the Puritan's life, so religion was to permeate his schools. Life on earth was, after all, but a preparation for eternity. The teacher was of utmost importance to this end. Not only did he have the duty of imparting the rudiments of knowledge to children, but he also had the sacred responsibility of caring for the souls of his charges. Cotton Mather refers to the teacher as the "tutelar angel" of the children. The chief concern of the teacher is to make his children "wise unto salvation." When Ezekiel Cheever died in 1708, after having schooled New England's sons for 70 years, Mather eulogized him in these words: "He so constantly prayed with us every day, and catechised us every week, and let fall such holy counsels upon us—he took so many occasions to make speeches unto us, that should make us afraid of sin and of incurring the fearful judgments of God by sin, that I do propose him for imitation." The fear of God had to be imparted to the hearts of children. This is the point of Michael Wigglesworth's *Day of Doom*, a grim 17th century description of judgment day, which reserved for children the "easiest room in hell." In "Adam's Fall We Sinned All" begins the most famous of American readers, the *New England Primer*, the chief staple of instruction in the lower schools. John Cotton's catechism, *Spiritual Milk for Boston Babes in Either England* (1656), was also popular in the 17th century. Furthermore, Latin grammar schools stressed religious instruction as well as classical studies and grammar. In short, evangelical religion permeated Puritan education, it even led them into a vain and tragic effort to educate the Indian, an effort described below.

b. The educational ideals and practices of the Southern colonists were only slightly changed by transit to America. By and large the Englishmen who migrated to Virginia had no quarrel with the Anglican Church. Although religious, they were prompted with no thoughts of founding a religious utopia. And indeed, the transplanted Anglican Church never really thrived in the South. It was never liberally supported, and it did not draw out of England any large number of outstanding intellectual leaders. The clergy played no such important role in the cultural life of the South as did the clergy in New England.

Nevertheless, the Protestant theory of education as essential to a godly life was shared by Anglicans who migrated to the Southern colonies. Almost universally the church, the family, and philanthropy continued to be looked upon as the agencies which should play a large part in the establishment, control, and maintenance of educational programs. In 1671, more than 60 years after the founding of Virginia, Governor Berkeley, in answer to a query from the Board of Trade as to what course was taken about education in the colony, replied: "The same that is taken in England out of towns; every man according to his own ability instructing his children." This is not to imply there was a lack of interest in education and schooling.

In the South too, there was persistent concern lest the children grow up wild. But facts of geography and environment and economics militated against the establishment of town school systems. For example, New Englanders settled in towns round the numerous harbors and quickly adopted an urban existence. Compactness made possible the town meetings, the town church, and the town school. While in the South, tobacco was king. Tobacco cultivation required large tracts of land, thus enforcing ruralness and militating against urban development. The plantation life of the Southern colonies with its scattered population, made the establishment of town schools unfeasible. Further, the ideal which shaped educational theory and practice in the South was that of reproducing the life of the English country gentleman. A planter aristocracy amply able to educate its own youth was little disposed to champion the cause of popular education. Education remained the province of tutors, privately endowed schools, religious charities, and private philanthropy.

The great families of Virginia—the Byrds, Carters, Masons, Lees, and Fitzhughs—were as greatly concerned with education as the Mather's or Winthrop's of New England. William Byrd, because he believed that a gentleman and a Christian should also be a learned man, set himself a discipline of study that would have shamed a cloistered monk. Often he arose at dawn to read Hebrew, Greek or Latin; occasionally he read French or Italian to keep up with the modern tongues. Wealthy Southerners built up extensive libraries, secured indentured servants like John Harrower and learned tutors like Philip Vickers Fithian to educate their children. Some planters left endowments in their wills for the establishment of schools, as for example, the wills of Virginians Benjamin Syms in 1634 and Thomas Eaton in 1659. A few planters sent their children to the New England Colonies, or on the hazardous trip to England for their schooling; some headmasters of schools in England thought it worth their while to advertise in Virginia newspapers. It was not until 1693, when the College of William and Mary was finally founded, that Southern youth could secure a higher education on home soil. In fact, within a decade after the first settlers stepped ashore at Jamestown (1607), a movement was under way to found a college in the colony. As early as 1619 the Crown appropriated 9,000 acres for a seminary to be known as Henrico College, only to have an Indian massacre in 1622 eliminate many friends of the proposed institution. In 1660 the Virginia Assembly voted to create a college, but circumstances were not propitious, and the Crown refused to cooperate. Finally in 1693 the Crown acceded to Virginia's request for a college charter. The college finally opened five years later.

Almost the only general educational legislation of the Virginia colony, for example, dealt with the apprenticeship of special classes of children—paupers and orphans and illegitimate children, applying and extending precedents established in the English Poor Laws. Such was the Virginia educational legislation of 1642 and 1646 that conferred upon justices of the peace the power to bind out and apprentice children. The other Southern colonies eventually followed the patterns that Virginia had set. Again, the lack of educational legislation did not indicate lack of concern on the part of the Southern colonists. For the most part, well-to-do parents and masters relied on their own resources for the education of their children; the poor relied on church and charity. Many children were educated in community schools, the so-called "old field schools." Occasionally, bequests, gifts, and other endowments led to the establishment of quasi-public schools like the Free School at Charleston, South Carolina, established in 1712. Two other interesting experiments in philanthropy and education in the south in the colonial period may be mentioned—the Bethesda Orphan House in Georgia and the Winyaw Indigo Society School in South Carolina. Dr. Thomas Bray and his associates in Maryland and Virginia also worked to found libraries and schools and to spread religious literacy. But the nearest equivalent of a general system of education in the South before the Revolution were the schools subsidized by the Society for the Propagation of the Gospel in Foreign Parts (SPG). This organization, established in England in 1701 as the overseas arm of the Anglican church, was active in promoting religious education in all the Southern colonies except Virginia. It was virtually the sole educator of the Negro in the South.

c. Anglicans, Puritans, Indians, and Negroes were not the only ones who participated in the colonial enterprise. In greater or lesser numbers Dutch came to New Netherlands, Finns and Swedes to settlements along the Delaware, Scots-Irish and Germans to Pennsylvania, Swiss to North Carolina, and French Huguenots to South Carolina. Most subscribed to one or another form of Protestantism. Catholics settled in Maryland (and of course, earlier, there were Catholic Spaniards in Florida and the Southwest, and Catholic French in the transAppalachian hinterland). There were also among the non-British immigrants from Europe a few Jews of Dutch, Spanish, or Portuguese origin. By the Revolution there were Jews in all thirteen colonies.

In the middle colonies of Pennsylvania, New York, New Jersey, and Delaware, educational developments were greatly influenced by the great ethnic and religious diversity characteristic of these colonies. The middle colonies were settled by people from many religious sects and many nations. Each of the national and religious groups dispersed through the middle colonies hoped to perpetuate its own culture and traditions. The governments of Pennsylvania and New York, for example, encouraged philanthropic societies and religious groups to establish schools, but never attempted to impose on their diverse populations through schools the sort of religious and social orthodoxy that was required by New England theocracy.

This is not to say that the Dutch in New York and the Quakers in Pennsylvania did not make serious efforts to promote education by public authority. The leaders of the Dutch Reformed Church had much the same outlook on education as the Puritans. Thus in 1649 the Nine Tribunes of New Netherlands complained of the need for good teachers "so that the youth in so wild a country where there are so many dissolute people may first of all be well instructed and indoctrinated not only in reading and writing, but in knowledge and fear of the Lord." Indeed ten years earlier, Adam Roelantsen had opened the first elementary school in the colony. And by 1652, a grammar school was in operation. Still the heterogeneity of the population critically influenced educational progress. The population of New Netherland was drawn from many countries. It is said that in 1644 eighteen languages were spoken in or near New Amsterdam, although Dutch was the one in most common use. English settlers, however, were in a majority on Long Island, and on the Delaware the Swedes predominated. French, Walloons, Norwegians, Danes, Irish, Scotch, and Germans added to the cosmopolitan character of the colony. Religious sects were even more numerous than national or ethnic groups. The colony from the beginning followed, for the most part, the same liberal policy with respect to religious refugees that had been followed in Holland, which, after gaining independence from Spanish control, had provided asylum to many persecuted religious sects of Europe. In spite of Stuyvesant's bigotry and bullying, French Huguenots, Baptists, Quakers, Presbyterians, Lutherans, Mennonites and Jews found in New Netherland greater tolerance than was generally the case in the Old World (or in New England).

As in the homeland, so in New Netherland, the school and the church were closely knit together throughout its history. The Classis of Amsterdam, representing the Dutch Reformed Church, exercised considerable authority in the educational affairs of New Netherland. But, in New Netherland as in the Massachusetts Bay Colony, the formal obligation to provide schools rested upon the state authorities, or upon the Dutch West India Company, which represented the state. One of the last ordinances of the Dutch government in America required that children be publicly catechised on Wednesday and Sunday by the schoolmasters and the ministers. As mentioned earlier, some parish schools were established by the Company before the English occupation in 1644; until the mid-18th century, the Dutch Reformed Church maintained schools in New York.

Under the English, religion ceased to be a powerful factor in the educational history of colonial New York. The Dutch were Calvinists, and like Calvinists elsewhere, they displayed some interest in maintaining schools. After the English took over, an attempt was made to make the Church of England the State Church, but with little success. Other religious groups were too numerous—Quakers, Anabaptists, Presbyterians, some Jews. It is paradoxical that at a time when one of the chief purposes of education was to serve religious ends, this multiplicity of religious faiths practically precluded any cooperative or colony-wide action in the maintenance of schools. Following the English practice, the colonial government of New York engaged in few educational activities other than providing for the general oversight of poor children and apprentices, and asserting its right with respect to the licensing of teachers. The government, however, did encourage the work of the Society for the Propagation of the Gospel in Foreign Parts. The Society, until it withdrew during the Revolution, found New York a fertile field for missionary and educational work. But the denominations were also active in establishing schools. Notable among these was the "lay college" conducted by William Tennent as a training school for Presbyterian ministers at Neshaminy, New Jersey. Catholic schools were also conducted in New York as well as Maryland in the 17th century.

Though Quakers were regarded as religious and social radicals, their views on the subject of education were fairly radical also. William Penn was fully aware of the importance of education to the State as well as to the individual. As early as 1682, Penn was proposing a colony-wide system of schools under the control and supervision of public authority. But such plans foundered due to the ever-increasing religious and ethnic diversity of the colony. The Pennsylvania legislature did pass acts in the early 18th century making it possible for the various religious groups to own property for educational purposes. This was particularly helpful to the foreign-language sects who could now feel free to develop their schools. Prominent among these were Nazareth Hall (established by the Moravians in 1759), the Moravian School of Christopher Dock, and the Lutheran schools promoted by Henry Muhlenberg. Even earlier, in 1689, the Friends' Public School, now known as William Penn Charter School, was opened in Philadelphia. Lutherans and Scots-Irish were also enterprising in setting up schools. Except for the religious affiliations and language of instruction, the schools of the various denominations were much alike. But as long as they could, the various denominations held to their own vernacular languages.

III a. The cities of America have always fascinated European visitors. In the mid-18th century astonishment and approval animated most of them at their first sight of any of the five metropolises of the English colonies: Boston, Philadelphia, Newport, New York, and Charleston. They would hardly have been prepared for what they saw as they sailed into any of the five harbors. Not a wilderness of tall trees, fierce animals and red savages, but rather rising centers of civilization, cities as busy, as large and sightly as any but the great capitals of Europe. By 1760, the population of the colonies was about 1,600,000. Philadelphia led the way with 23,000, New York 18,000, Boston 16,000, Charleston 8,000 and Newport 7,500. The steady stream of immigration, improved transportation and communication, physical expansion and economic prosperity, taken in conjunction with the maturing effect of a century of town life, presaged rapid and profound changes in the cultural and intellectual life of the colonies. In no place was the change more drastic than in New England.

By the opening of the 18th century, New England society was taking on a purpose and a form very different from that of the original design. As the century progressed, commerce and business swept to the fore. As economic interests assumed a new importance, there was a subtle but relentless shift from a religious to a more secular outlook on life. Piety was still important, but in the 18th century God was required more and more to share the stage with Locke's philosophy and Newton's science. The year John Winthrop sailed to Massachusetts (1630) was the same year Galileo completed his *Dialogues of the Two Chief Systems of the World*. In fact, the English settlement of America took place during the century when modern science emerged to reshape the thought of Western civilization. Even ministers like Cotton Mather celebrated the new sciences as a revelation of the work of God. Many Americans strove earnestly to keep abreast of the revolutionary new findings (almanacs, for example, quickly acquired an important function as an instrument of informal education in colonial America, especially in the field of science), and even, like Benjamin Franklin, botanist John Bartram, and astronomer David Rittenhouse, to mention a few, to add contributions of their own. Although Calvinism in the 18th century found an extremely forceful spokesman in Jonathan Edwards, the chief figure of the first sustained wave of religious revivalism in America known as the Great Awakening, its course as the dominant intellectual force in New England was run. The New Englander was changing from Puritan to Yankee. It was only natural that certain modifications should have taken place with respect to both the purpose of education and the means of its diffusion.

The 18th century was a period of very swift economic and social change, change at a pace with which the traditional educational system could not keep up. The development of commerce and trade made special demands on education. For example, New England needed navigators to chart courses for its ships, surveyors to lay out lands bought by prosperous merchants, bookkeepers and scribes to keep the records of its countinghouses and shops. In search of training for these occupations, few turned to the town Latin Grammar School. There was no place in these schools for technical, business, or commercial education. Indeed, there was no place in the Latin Grammar School for those "polite accomplishments," like music, dancing, or French so dear to the sons and daughters of the rising middle class. The educational opportunities afforded by the Latin Grammar Schools were too narrow and restricted to meet the needs of a large element of the population. Youths who wanted to engage in one or another of the business enterprises of the day or who desired a certain refinement of taste had to seek it elsewhere. Eighteenth century colonials did just that, in the private venture or "English" school, and then later in the academy.

In the 18th century the rising merchant and trading classes began to press for an education more appropriate to their interests, an education more useful and utilitarian than that of the Christian Scholar and Gentleman. Trade, commerce, and business required skills in modern languages, navigation, surveying, accounting. The emerging city life and greater affluence and leisure created demands for the arts of polite society. The Latin Grammar Schools were circumscribed in content and aim by the humanistic tradition of classical scholarship (and college entrance requirements). The private venture schools, the "English" schools, best described in the accounts of Robert F. Seybolt, helped meet the needs of the time. The advertisements that appeared widely in the newspapers of Boston, Philadelphia, Baltimore, and Charleston reveal the range and extent of subjects offered, almost all of a secular nature. From 1733 more than 400 advertisements relating to English schools and schoolmasters appeared in the *South Carolina Gazette* alone.

The private venture schools taught the "accomplishments" which the new leisure and affluence seemed to require: for boys, fencing, dancing, horsemanship; for girls, French, needlework, dancing, drawing, and vocal and instrumental music. The private venture schools taught as well the business and commercial subjects like surveying, navigation, bookkeeping, Italian, Portuguese, and Spanish. Unhindered by tradition, free to experiment, offering whatever was needed to whomever would pay for it in day schools, evening schools, early morning schools, even in correspondence schools, offering group or tutorial instruction, to girls as well as boys, they offered the most popular instruction of the secondary grade of the 18th century, and after incorporation into the Academy, the most popular into the 19th century.

The appearance of private venture or English schools had further ramifications. The emergence of the private schools marked the definite transfer, for example, of vocational education from the family and apprenticeship to the school. The transfer of vocational training from the family and apprenticeship, where a trade, a skill, a craft, could retain its "mystery," into a world of publicly available schools marks the beginning of the end in America of certain restrictive practices by which control of education and apprenticeship, and hence recruitment into the trades of an orderly society, had been maintained. It was an early indication that America was going to be an open, fluid, mobile society, in which the lines of social stratification would be soft and penetrable; the schools would provide opportunity for careers.

b. If the gap left by the town schools was to be filled, however, what was needed was no fly-by-night institution, but one able to command private or public support and to survive the death or departure of masters. In the latter half of the 18th century, the private English schools gave way to the academies, which were usually incorporated and founded on a more permanent basis. The father of the academy movement and the apostle of practicality was Benjamin Franklin. But his influence has been much more pervasive. Franklin's own life-long efforts at gaining an education have come to symbolize a characteristic American commitment to self-improvement through self-culture. "The doors of wisdom are never shut," Poor Richard once remarked. Franklin has become the American success symbol for the immigrant arriving in a new world of opportunity, seeking his fortune in a society where talent and industry were rewarded more than birth and privilege. Possessed of a consistently positive attitude to life, ready to learn from experience, able to improvise and adapt, Franklin epitomized much that became the American ethos of self-help, rugged individualism, and inevitable success.

It is worthy of note that Franklin's life nearly spanned the entire 18th century, the Age of Reason, the Age of Enlightenment. Franklin, in his wide-ranging scientific interests, in his concern for self-improvement, in his faith in progress through the application of human intelligence and energy, was the embodiment of the Age of Enlightenment. His *Autobiography* is too well known to require explication. Suffice to say it has the qualities of a folk myth; the story of the poor boy who lands in Philadelphia with three rolls in his pocket, and the "emergence from poverty and obscurity" to a "state of influence and some degree of reputation in the world." The *Autobiography* is a moral fable which has grasped the imagination of America. It is a secular *Pilgrim's Progress*, in which our hero wins salvation not through a spiritual pilgrimage, but through the practice of the homely virtues of thrift, industry, frugality, sobriety, honesty, and moderation. The moral is obvious and was well-suited to the New Man and the New Society emerging in America.

As a school reformer, Franklin cast aside two traditional guides to education— academic custom and religious orthodoxy. In 1749, in his "Proposals Relating to the Education of Youth in Pennsylvania," Franlin put forward his plan for the establishment of an academy. Up to then the educational fashion in secondary education in the colonies had hardly changed through the decades. But Franklin spoke for the awakening middle class. The new school's character was to be utilitarian and secular in tone and content; the technical and vocational educational education long taught by private masters or under contract through apprenticeship was to be formalized and institutionalized. Franklin had no quarrel with the classical subjects as such, only their monopoly on education. Nor did Franklin have any quarrel with religion as such. But, as Poor Richard advises, "God helps those that help themselves." Franklin and his Puritan contemporaries also differed sharply in their conception of the child to be educated. To Jonathan Edwards, for example, in words redolent of Wigglesworth's *Day of Doom* almost a century earlier, sin was "bound up in the heart of a child"; children had to be "saved." To Franklin, the child was neither sinful nor good, but, following the environmentalism of John Locke, impressionable.

Under ideal conditions, said Franklin, students would be "taught everything that is useful, and everything that is ornamental; regard being had to the several professions for which they are intended." In a sense the curriculum of the academy was an effort to combine the values and contents of the Latin schools and the English schools into one institution; the academy was to have a Latin Department and an English Department. Of course the Proposals were utilitarian. But it was no narrow utilitarianism Franklin had in mind. He wanted subjects and instruction that trained not for limited goals, not for close-bound predetermined careers, but for the broadest possible range of enterprise. What lay behind his interest in libraries, Junto, self-improvement, the Academy, was the hope that America would be a mobile, fluid society where one's life was not fully cast at birth. That opportunities beyond expectations of birth lay about and could be reached by effort and education.

But Franklin's efforts to educate the next generation were not limited to the youth of Philadelphia. In a revealing but little known episode, Franklin also turned to the schools to help assimilate non-English, non-Protestant immigrants. Fearful that German Catholic newcomers to Pennsylvania might make common cause with the "Papists" on the Western frontier, Franklin kept a close and anxious eye on the refugees. When the Germans were reluctant to heed his appeal to take up arms against the French and Indians, Franklin turned on them. He was especially antipathetic towards the German language schools. "Why should the Palatine Boors be suffered to swarm into our Settlements, and by herding together, establish their Language and Manners to the Exclusion of ours?" To help "anglify" them, with the Rev. Michael Schlatter, and William Smith, he was instrumental in forming the Society for the Relief and Instruction of Poor Germans, whose purpose was to establish charity or free English schools among the German settlers. Though the Germans, led by the talented Christopher Saur, organized a formidable opposition, Franklin and his associates nevertheless pushed ahead with their plan. By April, 1755, they had four charity schools open and planned six more. But by 1758, Smith's Germanophobia had become unpalatable for Franklin, and the latter withdrew all interest in the project. By 1761 the project had been abandoned. Thus the first, but not the last, deliberate attempt to use schools to Americanize immigrants, ended in fiasco.

       c. Franklin's Philadelphia Academy was opened in 1751. By 1775 it had fallen into the hands of a conservative elite, whose cultural ties were closer to London than to Philadelphia. Franklin then severed his relations with it, asserting that it "was no longer concerned with education for such a country as ours." Franklin failed then in his attempt to institutionalize his experiences. Yet, the Academy marked the beginning of a significant new movement in American secondary education. Beginning in New England with the chartering of Phillips

Academy in Andover, Massachusetts, in 1780 and Phillips Exeter Academy in Exeter, New Hampshire, in 1781, the academy movement spread South and West, until a peak was reached around 1850. The Academy was to be the dominant form of secondary school in America until the Civil War. The academies helped bring into American secondary education the study of English literature, modern languages, the social studies, and technical and business subjects, none of which were being developed in the Latin schools. Many academies were truly comprehensive. Some had a four-year "classical" course to prepare for the university, a three-year course to prepare for business and commerce, and a one-year teacher training course to provide teachers for the lower schools. A few of the early academies accepted girls; some were open to girls only, the so-called "female seminaries." Despite the academy's adaptability, however, it in turn would fail to meet the needs of the 19th century; the Age of Jackson would demand public secondary education, *gratis*, for all its sons and daughters.

      d. The main purpose in establishing the early colleges, of course, was to provide the churches with a learned ministry. On a gate in the Harvard Yard is engraved the opening statement of *New England's First Fruits*, the first commencement program, so to speak, of the college, published in 1643. It reads:

> After God had carried us safe to *New England*, and wee had builded our houses, provided necessaries for our livli-hood, rear'd convenient places for Gods worship, and settled the Civill Government: One of the next things we longed for, and looked after was to advance *Learning* and perpetuate it to Posterity; dreading to leave an illiterate Ministry to the Churches, when our present Ministers shall lie in the Dust.

Piety was the major concern of the colonial college. Again to use Harvard as an example, its first laws declared that every student was to be plainly instructed that the "maine end of his life and studies" was "to know God and Jesus Christ . . . and therefore to lay Christ in the bottom, as the only foundation of all sound knowledge and learning." But neither Harvard nor William and Mary nor Yale, founded in 1701, were conceived solely as religious seminaries. They were concerned with the advancement and perpetuation of learning and civility as well as the training of ministers. Harvard's purpose, expressed in the Charter of 1650, was "The advancement and education of youth in all manner of good literature Artes and Sciences" (*sic*). The College of William and Mary was established so that the youth of Virginia could be educated in "good letters and Manners," the churches supplied with ministers, and the Indians instructed in Christianity. Their course of study was the liberal education of the time, modeled on the arts courses at Cambridge University. The course of study was, of course, based upon Latin, which was presumed to have been mastered in the grammar school.

      The college entrance requirements of the colonial colleges give a fairly good idea of what the Latin grammar schools were supposed to do. In 1642 Harvard required its freshman students to be able to understand and read at sight some Latin author of the difficulty of Cicero, be able to speak Latin in prose and poetry, and be able to decline Greek nouns and conjugate Greek verbs. A hundred years later, the Harvard requirements had not changed substantially. The entrance requirements of other colonial colleges were similar to that of Harvard. Yale followed Harvard's lead almost exactly until 1745 when, in addition to the classics, it began to require "understanding of the rules of common arithmetic." Princeton's requirements in 1748 were about the same as those of Harvard in 1642. The universal requirement was ability to read Latin. Little wonder, then, that the grammar schools concentrated on the study of Latin and, to a lesser extent, the study of Greek.

At the Boston Latin School at the beginning of the 18th century the course was seven years in length, the boys beginning at the age of seven or eight years. The common method of instruction was memorization of the lessons by the pupil followed by recitation in the presence of the schoolmaster. During the first three years students learned by heart an "Accidence" or beginning Latin Book, together with a Latin-English phrasebook and vocabulary, and read and parsed Latin sentences in such Latin readers as Cato's *Distichs*, the *Colloquies* of Corderius (a 16th century Humanist), and Aesop's *Fables*. In the fourth year they read Erasmus, Aesop, Ovid, and studied Latin grammar, most likely taught from Lily, supplemented by Comenius' *Orbis Pictus*. In the fifth year they continued Erasmus and Ovid, and took up Cicero's *Letters* along with practice in composition and verse making in Latin. The sixth year was devoted to Cicero's *De Officiis*, Vergil's *Aeneid*, Ovid's *Metamorphoses*, Thomas Godwyn's history of Rome, and the beginning of Greek and rhetoric. In the final year the program ranged over a wide list of Latin and Greek authors including Cicero, Vergil, Horace, Juvenal, Homer, Isocrates, and Hesiod. Students also read the New Testament in Greek. Some students could probably begin Hebrew as well. Considerable attention was given to writing Latin dialogues, verses, and compositions, and translating Greek sentences into Latin. This was a stiff and formidable program of studies, probably matched by only a few other schools in the colonies, but it represents what was meant at that time by a grammar school.

In the colonial period, child labor was more than acceptable. If necessity justified the labor of young children, religion sanctified it. From an early age, children were warned that idleness destroyed souls and undermined the social system. Children began to work at an early age. In their teens, boys did the work of men, girls of women. There was little enough time for the schooling of children, yet it couldn't be ignored. The high rate of child mortality impressed the religious with the need for children to learn to read as early as possible, so they might be "saved." To learn to read then was the first and greatest task set school children of the colonial period. The hornbook, a small wooden paddle-shaped instrument with a sheet of paper pasted on, containing the alphabet, numerals, the Lord's Prayer and a catechism, was the first "book" put into the hands of little children. A "primer" came after the hornbook. There were many different primers in use at different times. But the one most commonly used in early American schools was the *New England Primer*, containing a rhymed alphabet, the commandments, a catechism, and other religious material. The child was then ready to proceed to the reading of the Psalter or Book of Psalms or the New Testament or the Bible. Towards the end of the 18th century, spelling and reading books were available which contained less religious content, as for example the very popular Thomas Dilworth, *A New Guide to the English Tongue*, published in 1740.

The youngest children, sometimes as young as three and four, learned to read in a so-called "dame school." It had long been the custom in England for some woman in the community to gather a few children into her home and to teach them, for a small fee, their ABC's and the rudiments of reading while she carried on the routine work of the household. The dame school was early transplanted to the New England colonies. The curriculum of the dame school was a simple matter. Pupils were taught their ABC's, a little spelling, the rudiments of reading, and moral and religious precepts. Girls were frequently taught sewing and knitting. Writing and counting, which required special teaching ability and special equipment, was usually taught in a separate writing school, or in the town primary school, or in an "old field" school. Both boys and girls attended the dame school and the writing school. The boys, after having learned to read a little, could go on to the writing school or the Latin grammar school. But for girls, the dame school usually marked the end of formal education unless, perchance, some member of the family or a private tutor carried them farther along the road of learning.

Few girls were able to secure a higher education in the colonial period. When the English colonists settled in America they brought with them the custom and traditions of England respecting the status of women. By and large the English held that women's sphere was in the home, bearing and rearing children, carrying on domestic duties. Every good home was a training school in which daughters were instructed by mothers in domestic occupations. Some girls were apprenticed to be taught the art of spinning, knitting or sewing, and sometimes reading, writing and religion.

In fact, however, women entered occupations outside the home, especially in the larger cities where they could even be found as shopkeepers and tavern keepers. But with the notable exception of the Quakers, the colonists looked with scant favor on intellectual pursuits for the female sex. For example, take the comments of Governor Winthrop with respect to Mistress Hopkins, the studious wife of the Governor of Hartford Colony. In his *Journal* under date of 1645, Winthrop sets down that this unfortunate lady had "fallen into a sad infirmity, the loss of her understanding and reason . . . by occasion of giving herself wholly to reading and writing. . . ." Yale in 1783 examined Lucinda Foote, age 12, and found her "fully qualified, except in regard to sex, to be received as a pupil of the freshman class." The general prejudice against women who possessed wit and learning must have bitterly annoyed 17th century poet Anne Bradstreet. She writes in "The Prologue":

> I am obnoxious to each carping tongue
> Who says my hand a needle better fits,
> A Poets pen all scorn I should thus wrong,
> For such despite they cast on Female wits:
> If what I do prove well, it won't advance,
> They'll say its stolen, or else it was by chance.

If the school doors to higher education were largely barred, still a few talented women like Mistress Bradstreet and Phyllis Wheatley persevered and left their mark on the intellectual and cultural life of the time.

In the colonial period, securing qualified teachers was a constant problem. In a raw community like early colonial America, the opportunities for a man of learning outside the realm of teaching were too great to leave many first-rate men available for an ill-compensated, low-status position. The teachers who conducted colonial schools ranged from untutored and frequently unlettered housewives who maintained the aforementioned dame schools in their kitchens to cultured university graduates who presided over the better grammar schools. Everywhere, there was much concern over the qualifications of teachers. In New England teachers were approved by town meetings, selectmen, school committees, or ministers; in the middle colonies they were issued certificates by royal governors, royal proprietors, and religious groups; in the South they were certified by governors, parish officials, and religious agencies. Where the Church of England was established, teachers often had to be certified by the Bishop of London; under Dutch rule in New York the certifying agency was the governor by authority of the Classis of Amsterdam or the Dutch West India Company.

The three most common requirements of teachers were that they be religiously orthodox, loyal to the civil government, and morally acceptable. Intellectual qualifications were less commonly specified, though most grammar schools assumed an acquaintance with the classical languages and literature, if not possession of a college degree. For example, a law of Massachusetts in 1654 required that the overseers of Harvard and the selectmen of the towns ensure that no teachers were appointed who were "unsound in the faith or scandalous in their lives." While the colonies were subject to the crown and Parliament of England, teachers were required to be loyal to England and take oaths of allegiance to the crown. When the Revolution broke out, many of the legislatures quickly moved to pass laws requiring teachers to sign oaths of allegiance to the newly established states. Such laws were passed by Massachusetts in 1776, New Jersey in 1777, and Pennsylvania in 1778. The Quaker meeting in Philadelphia in 1779 protested the Pennsylvania oath law, however, and were able to achieve the revocation of a fine levied upon a Quaker schoolmaster who had refused to sign the oath of allegiance on grounds of conscientious objection to the taking of oaths.

Of course, there were some good teachers, men like Cheever, Elijah Corlet, Anthony Benezet, Christopher Dock, and Francis Pastorius, most of them to be found in grammar schools. The Society for the Propagation of the Gospel imposed qualifications on its teachers. And the teachers of Friends' schools, as of Puritan schools, were generally of good repute. Most often, however, teachers possessed few qualifications and less sense of vocation. By and large, communities had to accept the fact that a permanent and qualified schoolmaster was all but impossible to find and employed briefly a series of ambitious young men who were on their way to other careers—perhaps in the ministry or law. In some towns, ministers doubled as schoolmasters, or the schoolmaster doubled as a local man of all work. Men permanently fixed in the role of schoolmaster in the colonial period seemed to have been of indifferent quality and extraordinarily ill-suited for the job. Still, it's difficult to generalize. Most teachers were humble folk who left little information about themselves and attracted little attention from others.

It's not surprising then that so little allowance was made for childhood as a unique period by schoolmasters of the time. The boys sat long hours on hard benches with little attention to comfort, relaxation, or play. Discipline was likely to be severe with heavy emphasis on corporal punishment, or as was often stated "without respect to person." Nevertheless, even in the early years, coercive and narrow approaches to education did not meet with universal approval. In Pennsylvania, William Penn complained that 17th century schooling tended to produce scholars rather than men, and because of its emphasis on memorizing material from books failed to use adequately either the children's own common sense or the lessons of nature, a concern shared by Christopher Dock, the 18th century schoolmaster of German Pennsylvania, whose *Schulordnung* was one of the first books published in America to deal with methods of schoolkeeping. The Society for the Propagation of the Gospel in 1706 enjoined its schoolmasters to use "all kind and gentle methods of Government of their scholars." Even Puritan Cotton Mather claimed that he would avoid a "fierce, crabbed usage of children," and that children ought to understand what they memorized. These isolated criticisms were forerunners of the more optimistic attitudes which under the influence of Locke and Rousseau came to characterize much of late 18th century educational thought.

IV **a.** The colonists spoke of the country as a "wilderness" inhabited by savages, or as a "virgin land" as though it were a vacant tract without human interest or history. Puritan John Winthrop in 1629 declared that most land in America was *vacuum domicilium;* i.e., legally, wasteland. The Puritans described the Indian as a lazy, treacherous savage. Yet nothing is so frequently recorded in the earliest chronicles as the warmth of the reception accorded these first colonists by the Indians. And in the beginning, Virginians were interested in "trade, traffic and commerce" with the Indians. Yet it was apparently the colonists' divine duty to take the Indians' lands, even destroy him: save the Indian and you saved one of Satan's victims; destroy the Indian and you destroyed one of Satan's disciples. Colonists who were setting out to build their new society could find a place in it for the Indian only if he surrendered his tribal heritage or if he were out of the way or dead. Not all colonists felt this way, however. Many Puritans and Quakers were sympathetically disposed towards the Indians. Benjamin Franklin once wrote: "Savages we call them, because their manners differ from ours, which we think the Perfection of Civility: they think the same of theirs."

The colonists, in their greed for land, viewed the Indian as a barrier to be removed. On the other hand, a broad spirit of Christianity, as well as a desire to gain the Indian as an ally, also instilled in the colonists a desire to convert and assimilate the Indian. Concern for the education of the Indian appeared early in the history of the English colonies in the New World. Several colonial charters stressed the education of the Indian as a primary aim of colonization. As soon as the English reached America, they turned their attention to the needs of the natives' souls. Although not as effective as the Spanish colonists to the South, the English were by no means laggard in launching missionary experiments. In both Virginia and Massachusetts, large sums were donated for both secular and religious instruction. An elaborate plan for missionary activity in Virginia included the building of a college for Indians at Henrico. The scheme went up in smoke, however, with the Massacre of 1622, which ended all but scattered missionary efforts in Virginia for the remainder of the century.

Perhaps no other region did as well as New England in its attempts to educate the Indians. In New England as early as the 1630's money had been sent for missionary work among the Indians. In 1636 Plymouth Colony enacted laws to provide for the preaching of the Gospel among the Indians. Relations between Indian and Puritan were relatively cordial until the Pequot War of 1636. The power of that warlike tribe was completely broken, its survivors sold into bondage or slavery or distributed among the friendly tribes. It was from these captives that the indefatigable John Eliot of Massachusetts selected a bond servant from whom he began to learn the Algonquin language. In 1646 Eliot began systematically to preach to the Indians in their own language, and began translating the Old and New Testaments into Algonquin. In 1651, Eliot founded Natick, a Christian-Indian town, the progenitor of the idea of the reservation system. There he conducted a school for some 145 Indians, "setting up a lecture among them in logick and theology once every fortnight." For Eliot, civilization and Christianity and learning must go hand-in-hand. The Indians were to learn the liberal arts and "civility" as well as Calvinism, so as to become as much like their English and Puritan neighbors as possible. By 1674 there were some fourteen "Praying Indian" towns in the Bay jurisdiction. How ironic that the Indian was to be segregated in order to prepare him for assimilation.

Eliot's utopias were hardly more fanciful than the Indian College set up by President Dunster at Harvard, or Thomas Mayhew's missions on Martha's Vineyard and Nantucket, or the earlier effort to set up a seminary for Indians at Henrico by the Virginia Company. In all cases, the lasting results were minimal, and by the time of his death in 1690, Eliot realized that he had failed completely. The failures of the missionary movement owed something to Indian uprising, to the Indian's lack of interest in the white men's ways, and to his justified suspicion of their intentions. On the other hand, the missionary purpose was often in conflict with the designs of other colonists on the Indians. Traders, soldiers, and colonial officials often resisted and undermined missionary endeavors.

b. Education occasioned even fewer contacts between Indians and whites in the 18th century. The aggressive Anglican missionary organization, the Society for the Propagation of the Gospel in Foreign Parts, launched new efforts to convert Indians in South Carolina and New York. And the Anglican Society for Propagating Christian Knowledge supported a number of missions to the Indians, notably the work of David Brainerd among the Delawares and Susquehannas.

John Eliot had his successor in Congregationalist minister Eleazar Wheelock of Connecticut. The Christianizing of the Indian, to Wheelock, was an obligation imposed from heaven on God's covenant people. Wheelock's idea was to train Indians in boarding schools far removed from the tribal environment and return them to their brethren as missionaries and instructors. His chief school, Moor's Charity School, was located in Lebanon, Connecticut. The school was opened in 1754, and by 1765 its enrolment included 29 Indian boys, 10 Indian girls and 7 white boys. The boys were taught the three R's, also Greek and Latin, and of course religion. The girls were taught the three R's and housekeeping. The girls too were to be missionaries. When the Iroquois withdrew support for his efforts, Wheelock moved to New Hampshire where he founded Dartmouth College for the education of "youths of the Indian tribes in this land in reading, writing, and all parts of learning which shall appear necessary and expedient, for civilizing and Christianizing the children of pagans, as well as in all liberal arts and sciences, and also of English youths and others."

Only this last phrase in the foregoing statement of purpose was to be achieved. The hostile relations between whites and Indians ran counter to the peaceful pursuits of the church and the school. A long and devastating series of wars, at first between the English colonists and the French, later between the Americans and the British in Canada, drew Indian tribes into diplomatic and military alliances that militated against the presence of missionaries and schoolmasters among them. Not until the conclusion of the frontier wars with the American victory over the northwest tribes in the War of 1812 was a peaceful status established sufficient to encourage sustained missionary and educational endeavors. In the colonial period then, with a few exceptions, it may be said that the principal modes of contact between whites and Indians were trade and warfare. Missionaries could rarely bridge the chasm of mistrust and hostility that resulted from wars, massacres, and broken promises. It is little wonder that attempts to win converts and to assimilate the Indian should fail.

c. Within 12 years of its founding a new racial element had come to the first English settlement. In late August of 1619, a Dutch frigate landed a cargo of 10 Negroes at Jamestown, Virginia. These first Jamestown Negroes were not slaves, nor were they free, they were indentured servants. By 1700, however, indentured servitude was no longer the preferred labor base in the plantation colonies. It had been superseded by slavery. Indeed, from the 1680's on, the more prosperous planters had begun to import Negro slaves in increasing numbers. Labor had always been a problem in the southern colony, and the Africans met the demand for labor at a cheap enough price to produce tobacco profitably.

Although there were slaves everywhere in the colonies north of Maryland by the late 17th century, they were few and not considered a problem. But by 1715, one-fourth of Virginia's population were Negro slaves; five-eighths of the population of South Carolina were Negro slaves. The conditions of living for the slaves, children as well as adults, varied enormously, according to place, master, kind of work. Generalizations are difficult to make. But masters had virtually complete legal carte-blanche. The situation of the slave family amply illustrates the slave's predicament. In a legal sense, the slave family did not exist. Although marriage was sometimes sanctified by a religious ceremony and respected by slaves themselves, it was not protected by the hands of law. Masters could sunder husband and wife, parents and children, as they wished. Slaves of the same family were kept together or separated as the interests or whims of the master dictated.

From the beginning the question of Negro education was perplexing to the South. Little argument was needed to convince slave owners that slaves who had some conception of modern civilization and understanding of the language of their owners would be more valuable than ignorant men with whom one couldn't communicate. But could slaves be enlightened without developing in them a rebellious spirit? If slaves were converted to Christianity, did they then inherit a claim to freedom? Were they not easier to exploit, more docile and pliant if they were uneducated? The majority of Southerners finally saw it this way. But in the beginning some masters acquiesced in the enlightenment of their slaves. Especially active in the education of the Negro in the South were the clergymen of the Society for the Propagation of the Gospel in Foreign Parts (SPG). Their main interest was in the propagation of the Gospel to the heathen, but also in teaching them the rudiments of the three R's.

The SPG was chartered in England in 1701 "for the purpose of providing the ministrations of religion for our countrymen in the Colonies, and of bringing the surrounding heathen to the knowledge of the truth." The Reverend James Blair became the Bishop of London's Commissary for Virginia and the Reverend Thomas Bray for Maryland. By the late 17th century, the SPG was active in the Carolinas, Maryland and Georgia, as well as New York. The activities of the SPG were discontinued in America with the Revolution. But prior to its discontinuation much of the money expended by the organization had been used for work in the American colonies, with Negroes and Indians being special objects of its solicitude. The missionaries sent by the SPG to the Southern colonies and to New York (Elias Neau was only the first of a series of catechists for New York Negroes) often complained about problems of health and the high rate of mortality, the troubles caused by dissenters, as well as officials and slave owners who distrusted them and their educational works. Their teaching was rudimentary and partisan, and their schools not everywhere popular, but for a long time the SPG was the only organization that made any pretense at operating a centrally administered school system for Negroes in English-speaking America.

Slavery likewise had an early beginning in the middle colonies and New England. Long before the English took the New Netherlands in 1664, the Dutch had established slavery. When in 1681 and 1682 William Penn received the land grants that eventually became Pennsylvania and Delaware, he found that Negroes were already located in that region and that he had to recognize slavery as a matter of course. The New England colonies had their early Negro inhabitants too, dating from within ten years after the Massachusetts Bay Company made its first settlement. Although New England's Negroes were often termed "servants," they were, as historian Benjamin Quarles points out, in most instances slaves. But, by whatever term he was designated, the Negro was to be found in every one of the thirteen mainland colonies, his presence in each dating invariably from its first years of settlement.

The farther North one went though, the smaller was the slave population. For example, New England's slaves in the colonial period never numbered more than 2 per cent of the total population. There was also more opposition to slavery in the middle colonies and in New England then in the South. Thus Puritan judge Samuel Sewall early condemned slavery. Puritan minister Cotton Mather insisted that masters treat their slaves "according to the rules of humanity." The Puritans were also among the first to encourage the religious instruction of Negroes. As early as 1674, John Eliot urged masters to allow their slaves to be educated, offering to instruct the latter once a week. Cotton Mather, in 1717, actually established a catechetical school for Negroes and Indians. Most of these early ventures were short-lived, but some masters continued to instruct their own slaves. Quakers were good friends of the slave. In 1688 the Germantown, Pennsylvania, Quakers issued the first group protest against slavery in America. From 1754 to his death in 1772 Quaker teacher John Woolman tried to persuade Friends to emancipate their slaves. The benevolent Quaker schoolmaster Anthony Benezet established a night school for Negroes in 1750 and devoted the rest of his life to the education of Negroes.

d. The numbers of both Black slaves and freemen increased dramatically throughout the 18th century. In 1700 there were approximately 25,000 Negro slaves in the colonies, or about one in every ten inhabitants. Seventy-five years later there were about 500,000 slaves, or one Negro in every five inhabitants of the colonies. There were slaves north and south of the Mason-Dixon line, most of them in the South, however, where in fact the slave population exceeded the free population. As the number of slaves in the southern colonies increased, their lives were increasingly hedged with restrictions. Missionaries still kept school for slaves but the trend was against any kind of education. In 1740, after a slave rebellion, South Carolina made it a crime to teach a slave to write. Similar legislation was enacted in Georgia in 1770, and following a rebellion scare in South Carolina in 1800, meetings of slaves "for purposes of mental instruction in a confined or secret place" were outlawed. For the time being, however, these laws were not copied in other slave states.

In the North, in the 18th century, slaves comprised about 14 per cent of the New York population, with other figures ranging from eight percent in New Jersey to three percent in Connecticut and Pennsylvania. There were also a small number of free Negroes especially in the northern colonies. Released from slavery as a reward for services, or allowed to purchase their freedom, they might be found scattered through colonial towns engaged in trades and common labor. A large addition to their ranks resulted from the War for Independence. Some blacks won freedom through service in the armies; others obtained it on the basis of the principles of natural right and human equality that were used to help justify the war; it was difficult to square the principles of the Declaration of Independence with the perpetuation of human bondage. Washington and John Randolph of

Virginia freed their slaves. Most of the Founding Fathers looked forward to the day when the curse would be forever erased from the land, though prejudice and economic interest would long make the dream utopian.

After the Revolution, many northern states made provision for the freedom of slaves; by 1830, less than one percent of the 125,000 northern blacks were slaves. Bondage had become a *peculiar* institution, retained alone in the southern states. In any case, rarely was any special obligation assumed on behalf of Negro children. Private philanthropic and religious schools were the principal recourse for Black children since the states and other governing agencies assumed a policy of *laissez-faire* in the matter of Negro education. The Philadelphia Society for Free Instruction of Colored People, founded in 1789, encouraged and coordinated Quaker instruction of black children in towns like Baltimore, Providence, Newport, and Burlington, New Jersey. Schools for Negroes were established by the New York African Free Society in 1786. And the abolitionist societies of northern towns and states typically turned to education once emancipation statutes had been enacted. These philanthropic organizations, usually led by influential whites, sometimes succeeded in obtaining intermittent public support for their schools. In addition, black parents, despite limited resources, participated in the founding of schools for their children in Washington, D. C., Philadelphia, New Orleans, and Charleston. Even with all these efforts most free black children in the 18th century grew up without formal instruction. The magnitude of the task far exceeded the resources devoted to it. Yet, toward the end of the colonial period, an increasing number of slaves were literate. Some, who served New York and New Jersey masters, learned to speak Dutch and soon became multilingual. A few Negroes, like Captain Paul Cuffe, became prosperous. And against tremendous odds, a few others, like poets Phyllis Wheatley and Jupiter Hammon, and mathematician Benjamin Banneker, made names for themselves.

V **a.** American schools were products as much of necessity, reflecting political, economic, social, and cultural conditions of the New World, as of theory, reflecting ties to the Old World. This was the case even in higher education. In Europe a "liberal education" was the property of an exclusive few. In 17th and 18th century England, the Bachelor of Arts degree could under Parliamentary authority be awarded only by Oxford and Cambridge. This ancient clerical and aristocratic monopoly of degree-granting (and therefore of political and ecclesiastical preferment) had helped preserve the learned tradition and helped produce many of the finest fruits of European thought. But their ancient walls were doubly confining—they isolated the inmates from the outside community, while they separated those on the outside from the University's wisdom. Efforts to found additional degree-granting institutions were repeatedly defeated. The monopoly of Oxford and Cambridge was to be complete until London University was founded in 1827. In America there was to be no such monopoly in higher education.

The most important factor in the diffusion of collegiate education in America was religious denominationalism. The first three colonial colleges—Harvard in 1636, William and Mary in 1693, and Yale in 1701—were founded to support the established church of their particular colonies, and these were the only colonial colleges until 1746. Not until the mid-18th century and the "Great Awakening," inspired by the preaching of men like Gilbert Tennent, George Whitefield, and Jonathan Edwards, with its aroused religious enthusiasm and sharpened sectarian zeal did the rash of colleges appear. The Great Awakening led to splits in the Congregational, Presbyterian, and Baptist groups. By the time of the Revolution, nearly every major Christian sect had a collegiate institution of its own; New-Side Presbyterians founded Princeton (1746), Revivalist Baptists founded Rhode Island College, later Brown (1764), Dutch Reformed Revivalists founded Queens College, later Rutgers, (1776), a Congregational minister, Eleazar Wheelock, transformed an Indian missionary school into Dartmouth (1769), and Anglicans and Presbyterians worked together to found King's College, later Columbia University (1754). The College of Philadelphia, later the University of Pennsylvania (1755) was founded under interdenominational auspices.

American legal vagueness, as Daniel Boorstin points out, also helped break up educational monopolies. Although the origins of Oxbridge are shrouded in medieval mists, their control over higher learning in England came from their clear legal monopoly. Oxford in 1571 and Cambridge in 1573 had received charters of incorporation and held, for all England, the exclusive power to grant degrees. It was different in America. The legal powers of the different colonial governments, especially their powers to create corporations and to establish monopolies, were varied, fluid and uncertain. The American legal situation was vague; the vagueness proved fertile. According to English law, a group of individuals could not act as a corporation, unless granted this privilege by King or Parliament. Who, if anyone, in the American colonies, possessed this important power to create corporations? There were several kinds of colony: charter, royal, and proprietary, each with a different legal character, none with any explicit delegation of right to incorporate. Add to this the many uncertainties over the relative legal powers of the colonial governors versus the colonial legislatures and of all the colonial governments as against the power of London, and the picture is one of uncharted legal terrain in which "many disorderly, inconsistent, and unpredictable institutions sprouted." Before the outbreak of the Revolution, nine colonial colleges were already granting degrees.

One significant outcome of the proliferation of colleges was the fostering of religious tolerance. Thus, the following note, necessitated by the interdenominational politics of New Jersey, was struck in the Princeton charter—students could not be excluded from or discriminated against in the college because of their religion. Other colleges soon followed suit. Another significant and largely unintended outcome of the proliferation of colleges during the last half of the 18th century was the emergence of a degree of interdenominational sponsorship. In those colonies that had a mixture of denominations, it became difficult to maintain complete sectarian control. Thus, although the president of King's College (Columbia) was required by charter to be an Anglican, its first board of trustees included the pastors of the four non-Anglican denominations in New York City. When its president, Samuel Johnson, first advertised the opening of the college and set forth its plan of studies, it was with the assurance that "there is no intention to impose on the scholars, the peculiar tenets of any particular set of Christians." The ideal of the sectarian college died hard, however, witness President Thomas Clap of Yale's "The Religious Constitution of Colleges," a systematic defense of the idea that a college should be organized and vigorously controlled by a single sect. In fact, it was Clap's ideal, by and large, rather than that of his opponents, that was to prevail in the closing decades of the 18th and the opening decades of the 19th centuries in the great majority of American colleges.

It is still widely believed that Harvard and the other early colleges were established as theological seminaries, with the exclusive object of training a ministry. There can be no doubt that the maintenance of the Puritan tradition of a learned ministry was an important object, but it was also believed that the collegiate education proper for a minister should be the same as for an educated layman. For example, the Puritan founders expected their colleges would produce not only ministers but Christian gentlemen trained to be civic leaders. Harvard's charter of 1650 referred to "the advancement of all good literature arts and sciences" as well as to "the education of the English and Indian Youth of this Country in Knowledge: and Godliness" (sic). The first charter of Yale (1701) referred to the school as one in which the youth of Connecticut would be instructed in the arts and sciences so as to be "fitted for Publick employment both in Church and Civil State" (sic). William and Mary's charter (1693) expresses the hope that it will educate ministers, but also that it will educate youth "in good Letters and Manners" (as well as propagate Christianity among the Indians).

In practically every respect the colonial colleges attempted to duplicate the conditions of the colleges of the ancient universities of England. They carried on with the classical curriculum; they were residential colleges in the English fashion; their bodies of rules were patterned from the customs of Cambridge or Oxford. In one major respect it proved to be difficult to reproduce the conditions of Old World universities. The colleges in America ceased practically from the beginning to be a body of self-governing scholars and fell under the control of non-resident laymen. This was almost inevitable. American colleges and universities were staffed for generations not by mature scholars but mainly by young and transient tutors, and community leaders were reluctant to drop their reins of control. This reluctance was manifested, for example, in the Constitution of Harvard with its creation of a Board of Overseers for the college.

b. Though the grip of the classics and of religion was to be retained until well into the 19th century, nevertheless the curriculum of the colonial colleges did respond to new conditions. Even ministers, as mentioned earlier, in colonial New England were eager, with Cotton Mather, a Fellow of the Royal Society, to celebrate the new science as the revelation of the work of God. And science early found a home in the colonial college. By the mid-18th century, instruction in Locke, Newton, and Copernicus could be had at Yale. The early laws of King's College played up its offerings in "The mathematical and experimental philosophy." In 1772, John Witherspoon, promoting the College of New Jersey (Princeton), dwelt with pride upon its scientific offerings. By 1766, two-thirds of the colonial colleges were supporting professorships of mathematics and natural philosophy. The new spirit was also evident in the increasingly political content of moral philosophy courses in 18th-century colleges and in demands for curriculum changes which, for example, if Thomas Jefferson had had his way, would have allowed the students of William and Mary by 1779 to study modern languages, law and medicine, as well as the traditional disciplines. The new spirit was also evident in the interests of student organizations, like Phi Beta Kappa, which began to make their appearance in the late 18th century.

On the eve of the Revolution then, the English colonies in the New World were supporting nine colleges. It might be well to be reminded, however, that the scale is small. The largest graduating class at Harvard before the Revolution—the class of 1771—counted only 63 graduates. William and Mary in 1779 had only six instructors. One obvious effect of the dispersion and the proliferation of colleges was to diffuse learning widely in the terms of place and social class, and to increase the number of college degrees. Whether the colonies needed nine colleges, whether the colonial colleges were simply distributing to the many what in England was reserved for the privileged few, or whether they were issuing an inflated currency are other questions. The proliferation of colleges certainly hurt the older, better-established colleges, which were weakened by the diffusion of the country's educational energies—a circumstance foreseen by the overseers of Harvard as early as 1762, when they protested against the premature proposal of a new college in Hampshire County. Still, the colonial pattern of the dispersion of higher education was never to be broken. From time to time, after the Revolution, grandiose hopes were expressed for a model national university to be supported by Congress and situated in the national capital, on which the intellectual resources of the nation could be concentrated. All such plans were defeated. From the start, American colleges would be more anxious to spread than to deepen the higher learning.

VI **a.** "The American war is over," Benjamin Rush wrote in 1787. "But this is far from being the case with the American revolution. On the contrary, nothing but the first act of the great drama is closed. It remains yet to establish and perfect our new forms of government, and to prepare the principles, morals, and manners of our citizens for perfection." The war transformed the meaning of the colonial experience. For in severing the political ties to England, it hastened the need for that rethinking and recasting of American education that was already under way but not yet completed. When the war ended Americans turned with renewed zeal to the subject of education. Nor is this surprising. This was the Age of Enlightenment, when society was discovering how to reorder itself in accordance with the laws of nature. Newtonian science revealed an orderly, intelligible, mathematically accountable universe. The Newtonian universe was self-evidently the handiwork, not of a fearful God of Wrath, but rather of a rational Creator, whose intentions were to be discovered through an examination of his works. Furthermore, all men were equally the creatures of this benevolent God. Man possessed the God-given power of intelligence sufficient to enable him to reorder society so as to protect him in his natural progress. America, after its stunning victory in the War of Independence, seemed to be an especially felicitous environment for a society founded upon reason and education.

Near the end of the Colonial period, the young French emigre Hector St. Jean de Crevecoeur, sensing that a new people had evolved in the American colonies, commented exuberantly on the American melting pot out of which came a new man; an American, changed and different from the Englishman, Dutchman, Frenchman, German, or Jew who had arrived as an immigrant. But if theory led to optimism, the exigencies of the time fostered apprehension. In the post-war period, the new nation was faced with the enormous uncertainties of peace and independence. Gradually, as Americans began to assess the implications of their Revolution, the euphoria of the triumph receded before a wave of doubts about the future. The ebullient new Republic had neither reigning house nor landed aristocracy and a bad record of mob violence and political instability. Just as the Puritans feared failure in their errand into the wilderness, so many leaders of the infant nation feared failure in their experiment in republicanism. What could unify such a widely scattered and diverse people? The answer seemed to lie in the deliberate casting off of Old World cultural ties and the construction of a distinctive American way of life. High priority was accorded the role of the schools and a "wider diffusion of knowledge among the people." Madison warned that "a people who mean to be their own governors must arm themselves with the power which knowledge gives." Washington agreed that "in proportion as the structure of a government gives force to a public opinion, it is essential that public opinion be enlightened."

The fear of political and social contamination from the Old World, with its corrupt monarchies, aristocracies, and churches, and the desire to preserve the American character in a Protestant and republican image were reflected in the repeatedly expressed hope that Americans would no longer send their children to Europe for an education. Good patriots agreed that to send American youth abroad would be a humiliating acknowledgment of ignorance or inferiority. Washington, in a plan endorsed, unsuccessfully, by all of his successors in the presidency up to Jackson, repeatedly urged the creation of a national university. Nevertheless, the new national government undertook to further education in significant ways. Thus the Land Ordinance of 1785 reserved one lot in each township for support of the public schools, while the Northwest Ordinance of 1787 decreed that "religion, morality, and knowledge being necessary to good government and the happiness of mankind, schools and the means of education shall forever be encouraged." The Land Ordinance of 1785 set precedents which were followed in virtually all subsequent government grants of land to territories and states for educational purposes. Meanwhile in the South and Southwest, liberal educational theorists, influenced by the Enlightenment, hoped to rescue the collegiate system from sectarianism, and, taking advantage of the fact that a system of private sectarian colleges had not yet been established, they founded state institutions. The University of Georgia was founded in 1785; it was soon followed by the University of North Carolina in 1789 and the University of Tennessee in 1794, and the South Carolina College (later the University of South Carolina) in 1801. Still later Jefferson, disappointed at the development of his alma mater, William and Mary, planned what was expected to be the most ambitious of the state institutions, the University of Virginia. The state university idea spread rapidly westward, though its full flowering did not come until after the Civil War.

b. In the early federal era, many leaders of the infant nation—Benjamin Rush, Samuel Smith, Robert Coram, Samuel Knox, Noah Webster and others—issued widely discussed plans for the development of a uniform, national system of education, one that would be "best adapted to the genius of the Government of the United States." The traditional classical education was to be discarded in favor of an education that would be utilitarian, and "republican." Perhaps the most significant feature of the various plans was their concern that popular education must have a predominantly political aim. "The business of education," wrote Benjamin Rush in 1786, "acquires new complexion by the independence of our country. It become us, therefore, to examine our former habits upon this subject, and in laying the foundations for nurseries of wise and good men, to adapt our modes of teaching to the peculiar form of our government." The new nation required an education to produce a citizen who would function as a "republican machine." Rush urged the establishment of one general and uniform national system of education that would "render the mass of the people more homogeneous, and thereby fit them more easily for uniform and peaceable government." This must be done if republican government were to endure. Schoolbooks, strongly colored by religion in the colonial period, were at the beginning of the national period rededicated to patriotic virtues. The *New England*

Primer, after the Revolution, added this rhyme: "Queens and Kings are gaudy things." Noah Webster, the most successful schoolbook writer of his time, wished to inculcate patriotism through uniformity in spelling and pronunciation and all textbooks of instruction. "Begin with the infant in his cradle," he admonished in the preface of his reader, *An American Selection of Lessons In Reading and Speaking,* "let the first word he lisps be 'Washington.'" Later, in the 19th century, the *McGuffey Readers* would assume the task of defining and inculcating Americanism.

One of the earliest plans for a republican education was Thomas Jefferson's "Bill For The More General Diffusion of Knowledge" presented to the Virginia Assembly in 1779. Jefferson, like Rush and Washington and Madison, proclaimed that the key to Republican government lay in the diffusion of knowledge among the people. Jefferson proposed the establishment of a system of elementary and grammar schools, wholly under the auspices of the civil authority, and supported wholly by public funds. Thus Jefferson hoped to deliver the *coup-de-grace* to the principle of "voluntarism" in education. All free children were to be entitled to free tuition for at least three years and as much longer at private expense as their parents wished and could afford. Annually there would be a competition to select a few poor boys for further education at the grammar schools, and then at William and Mary College, to be made into a public institution also. By this means, Jefferson asserted, "twenty of the best geniuses will be raked from the rubbish annually."

What Jefferson's intentions were regarding the extension of educational opportunity is a subject of some disagreement among historians. No doubt Jefferson wished to broaden the base of recruitment of leadership cadres. But no doubt he also suspected that "the natural aristocracy of talents and virtues" was a small one, and could be found for the most part among families of means; a free public education would be extended to a minute aristocracy of talent from among the poor. While the poor were to be carefully screened, and only the most talented would be sent on to higher education at the public expense, the wealthy, on the other hand, were of course able to send their children for as much schooling as they desired or could afford without any regard to talent. The majority of students in the grammar schools and William and Mary would continue to be the sons of planters and professionals who had long enjoyed a monopoly of formal education. Vernon Parrington once said that Jefferson had an aristocratic head set on a plebeian frame. In this bill, Jefferson's aristocratic head was dominant. Jefferson deviated from his proclaimed principles in one other regard. All teachers would have to "give assurance of fidelity to the Commonwealth." And as founder of the University of Virginia, Jefferson would use political tests in the hiring of faculty and prescribe the textbooks to be used in the classroom—students would have to be protected from Federalist doctrine. Like Rush, Jefferson would have liked to diffuse only knowledge which would produce safe political views.

Nevertheless, the various plans for a national system of education are, on the whole, informed by a generous view of mankind. Human capabilities, the possibilities of social and individual improvement, the great power of nurture over nature—these articles of 18th-century Enlightenment faith directed the founders to think expansively. On the other hand, they were fearful of the breakdown of social and political controls. Their commitment to enlightened public opinion was hedged round with apprehension that the Republic might founder on too much liberty and freedom. Many of the Founding Fathers, not content with the unconscious and haphazard socialization provided by the family, press, community, or informal associations, sought deliberately to form a patriotic character in the schools. The new republic was a great experiment in freedom. Yet to make this experiment work required political indoctrination. Thus the Founding Fathers raised a problem still troubling American education. Can one train a citizen to think critically, but be patriotic above all?

c. Jefferson's "Bill" was never enacted. Indeed, none of the proposals of the Founding Fathers became operational. The Revolution had a disastrous effect upon all colonial educational institutions. Even on the eve of the Revolution, with the exception of New England, there was no public provision for education anywhere in the American colonies. Charity schools conducted by the religious denominations were the common institutions of elementary education. The situation deteriorated after the Revolution. The Constitution was silent on education; the responsibilities for the establishment of schools remained vested in each of the individual States of the Union. State constitutions characteristically required their legislatures to support education, though they rarely stipulated the means to be followed. Provisions on education were included in six of the eleven new state constitutions. Most, like Pennsylvania, acknowledged a duty to promote education, but little more. As the early constitutions were revised toward the end of the century, some provisions were made for the education of the poor. Thus the second constitution of Pennsylvania (1790) asked the legislature to provide free education for the poor. The States characteristically delegated substantial educational powers to local school districts. The great qualitative variations that have developed since in American public schools reflect, among other things, the local school district's ability to support schools. In the early national period then, schools in all regions of the country fared badly. The country was poor and debt-ridden, still overwhelmingly agricultural and, indeed, sparsely settled. As late as 1800 the population of the country was only about 4,000,000. As late as 1820, only 13 cities in the country contained over 8,000 inhabitants; only about 5% of the population lived in these cities. The overwhelming majority of Americans lived in isolated villages and farms, learning what they had to in the family, the field, the church.

d. If schooling suffered in the Revolutionary period, there were developments in the field of religious freedom through the separation of church and state which would subsequently have great bearing on education. The founding fathers were, generally speaking, devoutly religious men, but few were orthodox trinitarian Christians. Most viewed religion as a private matter, and they vested their faith in natural religion, with its reliance upon observation over revelation, and with its elevation of science over Biblical fiat as the most authoritative source for an understanding of God's nature and purposes. They were not aggressive deists, nor were they actively anticlerical. They were sure that human liberty was ultimately founded upon a belief in God and that churches performed a necessary social as well as religious function. But they tended to distrust organized religion especially where it was supported by the State. They knew that an endless variety of religious beliefs existed in the world, and like Franklin, Jefferson, and Madison, they doubted any one of them could claim to be the true religion. Even in Puritan Massachusetts, by the late 18th century the upper classes were won to the religion of the Enlightenment. Indeed the falling away from the original orthodoxy was early lamented by New England ministers. The congregational form of church organization permitted each individual congregation to conduct its own affairs and many of them, notably in eastern Massachusetts, drifted towards Unitarian liberalism.

Still, at the outbreak of the Revolution, with the exception of Rhode Island and the middle colonies, the rest of the thirteen colonies had established churches. In

Massachusetts, Connecticut, and New Hampshire the Congregational church was established. The Church of England was established in all the colonies south of Pennsylvania and its ministers paid as other officers of the state. Teachers in these colonies were required to hold appropriate certification from the church through the permission of the Bishop of London or other ecclesiastical authority in England or his representative in America. Anglicans such as Jefferson and Madison, however, were opposed to the union of church and state as an infringement of religious liberty. The Anglican Church, weakened during the war by its English connection, was finally disestablished in the southern states during the Revolutionary Era. On the other hand, many of the Congregational Churches of New England remained state-supported well into the 19th century. The Constitution, meanwhile, was notably silent on the subject of religion. But the first amendment went beyond silence to delcare that "Congress shall make no law respecting an establishment of religion, or prohibiting the free exercise thereof," a guarantee which subsequently would have great impact on American education.

VII By 1789, education in America was a rather different process from what anyone in the early 17th century would have expected. On several points there had been departures from precedent, the first important one being the increasingly important role played by colonial (as opposed to English) government in the promoting, supervising, and financing of schools. This trend, however, was reversed in the latter part of the 18th century as local governments retreated to a position of a neutral arbiter in the face of the increasing diversity of ethnic, class, sectional, and religious interests—a process confirmed by the Revolution, despite the Founding Fathers' dreams of a truly "national" education. A second important change was the gradual shifting of responsibility for education from informal agencies (home and family, church, community, apprenticeship) to formal ones (schools and colleges). A third departure was the increasing sensitivity of educational institutions themselves to community pressure at all levels. From the beginning, especially in New England and the middle colonies, sectional and religious diversity fostered the decentralization of schools, and education became entangled with other political, economic, and social business on the agenda of town and district and other local governments.

American education thus responded to American needs. As the country passed out of the colonial into the early national period, schools gradually receded in character from English or European models, and emphasized more and more distinctively American characteristics. By 1789, as Professor Bailyn has noted, American education had been cast loose from its old moorings. There was much confusion and debate over the nature, methods, extent and goals of education. Many kinds of schools were educating the American people; town schools, endowed schools, denominational schools, private schools, public schools. There were religious schools and secular schools, classical schools and vocational schools. The picture is one of tremendous fragmentation, of diversity and variety in support, in sponsorship, in state participation, as well as in the forms educational institutions assumed.

By the end of the colonial period, education was no longer dedicated exclusively to the classics and religion. This did not however herald a decline of interest in education. What occurred in the 18th century was not so much a decline of interest in education as a reordering or shift in educational priorities. New courses in surveying, navigation, and French seemed to many colonists of more relevance than the study of Latin and Greek. Further, the layman with his interests in the more practical pursuits of life was beginning to charge the schools with a great variety of responsibilities. Education had become an instrument to achieve a wide range of social and economic as well as religious goals. It had become all things to all men: knowledge of the world, virtue, manners, piety, business and professional skills. It was to serve the ends of individual self-improvement, economic development, social betterment, and moral and ethical training. There was little consensus about what American education ought to be. Yet, while acknowledging the complexity of the subject, it is possible to discern in the history of American education in the colonial period at least several persistent themes: one, the desire to popularize education with respect to access, substance, and control, a commitment which early and decisively became the single most characteristic commitment of American education; and two, the desire to extend education for a variety of social as well as pedagogical purposes.

American education then passed on into the 19th century as it had developed in the colonial period, with the original inheritance called into question, challenged, altered. A process whose origins lay in the half-instinctive workings of a homogeneous, integrated society was transformed in the New World. By 1789, the homogeneous, integrated education of a homogeneous, integrated society had been shattered into multiplicity. The whole process of education was no longer instinctive or reliable; it had become controversial, self-conscious, and a matter of deliberate will and effort. This picture of fast-paced educational change can however be overdrawn. The patterns of education throughout the colonial period still bore considerable resemblance to those of England. The household remained the single most fundamental unit of social organization in the 18th century, and for the vast majority of Americans, the decisive agency of deliberate cultural transmission. The educative influence of the church persisted throughout the colonial period, though with abated power and in somewhat different form. Home instruction, dame schools, and "hornbooks" played an important part in primary education on both sides of the ocean. Colonial grammar schools and colleges in the late 18th century still attempted to reproduce the curriculum and spirit of their English counterparts.

Perhaps this latter point should be emphasized. That is, to the picture of the emergence of several distinctively American patterns of education at least one very important caveat must be entered—the persistence of classical education through a period of fast-paced change. The colonial colleges, the great grammar schools, and even the academies continued to stress Latin and Greek throughout the 18th century. Many of the Founding Fathers had been brought up on a classical education (27 of the signers of the Declaration of Independence had college degrees from Europe or America) and could not discard it; their writings and speeches are permeated with classical learning. In 1789 John Adams wrote to Benjamin Rush: "I should as soon think of closing all my window-shutters to enable me to see, as of banishing the classics to improve Republican ideas." Indeed, as late as 1816 when Horace Mann entered Brown University he had to clear almost the same Latin and Greek hurdles as did a freshman at Harvard in the 1630's. The classics then were apparently relevant to the cultural and civic needs of the New World, serving in Bacon's term "for delight, for ornament, and for ability." Finally, deficient as colonial schools may seem in retrospect, as Professor Cremin demonstrates in *American Education: The Colonial Experience, 1607-1783*, they nevertheless helped to create and maintain a level of literacy which compares very well with England in the 17th and 18th centuries.

1

THE
EUROPEAN
HERITAGE

The Renaissance

VERGERIUS DESCRIBES A LIBERAL EDUCATION (c. 1392) From Petrus Paulus Vergerius, *De Ingenuis Moribus,* as quoted in W. H. Woodward, ed., *Vittorino da Feltre and Other Humanist Educators* (Cambridge, Mass., 1897), pp. 96-97, 102-09.

Your grandfather, Francesco I., a man distinguished for his capacity in affairs and for his sound judgment, was in the habit of saying that a parent owes three duties to his children. The first of these is to bestow upon them names of which they need not feel ashamed. For not seldom, out of caprice, or even indifference, or perhaps from a wish to perpetuate a family name, a father in naming his child inflicts upon him a misfortune which clings to him for life. The second obligation is this: to provide that his child be brought up in a city of distinction, for this not only concerns his future self-respect, but is closely connected with the third and most important care which is due from father to son. This is the duty of seeing that he be trained in sound learning. For no wealth, no possible security against the future, can be compared with the gift of an education in grave and liberal studies. By them a man may win distinction for the most modest name, and bring honour to the city of his birth however obscure it may be. But we must remember that whilst a man may escape from the burden of an unlucky name, or from the contempt attaching to a city of no repute, by changing the one or quitting the other, he can never remedy the neglect of early education. The foundation, therefore, of this last must be laid in the first years of life, the disposition moulded whilst it is susceptible and the mind trained whilst it is retentive.

This duty, common indeed to all parents, is specially incumbent upon such as hold high station. For the lives of men of position are passed, as it were, in public view; and are fairly expected to serve as witness to personal merit and capacity on part of those who occupy such exceptional place amongst their fellow men. You therefore, Ubertinus, the bearer of an illustrious name, the representative of a house for many generations sovereign in our ancient and most learned city of Padua, are peculiarly concerned in attaining this excellence in learning of which we speak. Our name, our birthplace, are not of our own choice. Progress in learning, on the other hand, as in character, depends largely on ourselves, and brings with it its own abiding reward. But I know that I am urging one who needs no spur. Can I say more than this?—continue as you have begun; let the promise of the future be consistent with your performance in the past.

To you, therefore, I have addressed this tractate upon the principles of Learning and of Conduct: by which I intend the subjects and the manner of study in which youth may be best exercised, and the actions which it behoves them to pursue, or to avoid, in the course of their daily life. Although addressed to you, it is intended for all who, blessed by nature with quickened minds and lofty aims, desire to shew by their lives their gratitude for such gifts. For no liberal mind will readily sink into mere sloth or become absorbed in the meaner side of existence.

*   *   *

We call those studies *liberal* which are worthy of a free man; those studies by which we attain and practise virtue and wisdom; that education which calls forth, trains and develops those highest gifts of body and of mind which ennoble men, and which are rightly judged to rank next in dignity to virtue only. For to a vulgar temper gain and pleasure are the one aim of existence, to a lofty nature, moral worth and fame. It is, then, of the highest importance that even from infancy this aim, this effort, should constantly be kept alive in growing minds. For I may affirm with fullest conviction that we shall not have attained wisdom in our later years unless in our earliest we have sincerely entered on its search. Nor may we for a moment admit, with the unthinking crowd, that those who give early promise fail in subsequent fulfilment. This may, partly from physical causes, happen in exceptional cases. But there is no doubt that nature has endowed some children with so keen, so ready an intelligence, that without serious effort they attain to a notable power of reasoning and conversing upon grave and lofty subjects, and by aid of right guidance and sound learning reach in manhood the highest distinction. On the other hand, children of modest powers demand even more attention, that their natural defects may be supplied by art. But all alike must in those early years, 'Dum faciles animi juvenum, dum mobilis aetas,' whilst the mind is supple, be inured to the toil and effort of learning. Not that education, in the broad sense, is exclusively the concern of youth. Did not Cato think it honourable to learn Greek in later life? Did not Socrates, greatest of philosophers, compel his aged fingers to the lute?

Our youth of to-day, it is to be feared, is backward to learn; studies are accounted irksome. Boys hardly weaned begin to claim their own way, at a time when every art should be employed to bring them under control and attract them to grave studies. The Master must judge how far he can rely upon emulation, rewards, encouragement; how far he must have recourse to sterner measures. Too much leniency is objectionable; so also is too great severity, for we must avoid all that terrifies a boy. In certain temperaments—those in which a dark complexion denotes a quiet but strong personality—restraint must be cautiously applied. Boys of this type are mostly highly gifted and can bear a gentle hand. Not seldom it happens that a finely tempered nature is thwarted by circumstances, such as poverty at home, which compels a promising youth to forsake learning for trade: though, on the other hand, poverty is less dangerous to lofty instincts than great wealth. Or again, parents encourage their sons to follow a career traditional in their family, which may divert them from liberal studies: and the customary pursuits of the city in which we dwell exercise a decided influence on our choice. So that we may say that a perfectly unbiassed decision in these matters is seldom possible, except to certain select natures, who by favour of the gods, as the poets have it, are unconsciously brought to choose the right path in life. The myth of Hercules, who, in the solitude of his wanderings, learned to accept the strenuous life and to reject the way of self-indulgence, and so attain the highest, is the significant setting of this profound truth. For us it is the best that can befall, that either the circumstances of our life, or the guidance and exhortations of those in charge of us, should mould our natures whilst they are still plastic.

In your own case, Ubertinus, you had before you the choice of training in Arms or in Letters. Either holds a place of distinction amongst the pursuits which appeal to men of noble spirit; either leads to fame and honour in the world. It would have been natural that you, the scion of a House ennobled by its prowess in arms, should have been content to accept your father's permission to devote yourself wholly to that discipline. But to your great credit you elected to become proficient in both alike: to add to the career of arms traditional in your family, an equal success in that other great discipline of mind and character, the study of Literature.

There was courage in your choice. For we cannot deny that there is still a horde—as I must call them—of people who, like Licinius the Emperor, denounce learning and the Arts as a danger to the State and hateful in themselves. In reality the very opposite is the truth. However, as we look back upon history we cannot deny that learning by no means expels wickedness, but may be indeed an additional instrument for evil in the hands of the corrupt. To a man of virtuous instincts knowledge is a help and an adornment; to a Claudius or a Nero it was a means of refinement in cruelty or in folly. On the other hand, your grandfather, Jacopo da Carrara, who, though a patron of learning, was not himself versed in Letters, died regretting that opportunity of acquiring a knowledge of higher studies had not been given him in youth; which shews us that, although we may in old age long for it, only in early years can we be sure of attaining that learning which we desire. So that it is no light motive to youthful diligence that we thereby provide ourselves with precious advantages against on-coming age, a spring of interest for a leisured life, a recreation for a busy one. Consider the necessity of the literary art to one immersed in reading and speculation: and its importance to one absorbed in affairs. To be able to speak and write with elegance is no slight advantage in negotiation, whether in public or private concerns. Especially in administration of the State, when intervals of rest and privacy are accorded to a prince, how must he value those means of occupying them wisely which the knowledge of literature affords to him! Think of Domitian: son of Vespasian though he was, and brother of Titus, he was driven to occupy his leisure by killing flies! What a warning is here conveyed of the critical judgments which posterity passes upon Princes! They live in a light in which nothing can long remain hid. Contrast with this the saying of Scipio: 'Never am I less idle, less solitary, than when to outward seeming I am doing nothing or am alone': evidence of a noble temper, worthy to be placed beside that recorded practice of Cato, who, amid the tedious business of the Senate, could withdraw himself from outward distractions and find himself truly alone in the companionship of his books.

Indeed the power which good books have of diverting our thoughts from unworthy or distressing themes is another support to my argument for the study of letters. Add to this their helpfulness on those occasions when we find ourselves alone, without companions and without preoccupations—what can we do better than gather our books around us? In them we see unfolded before us vast stores of knowledge, for our delight, it may be, or for our inspiration. In them are contained the records of the great achievements of men; the wonders of Nature; the works of Providence in the past, the key to her secrets of the future. And, most important of all, this Knowledge is not liable to decay. With a picture, an inscription, a coin, books share a kind of immortality. In all these memory is, as it were, made permanent; although, in its freedom from accidental risks, Literature surpasses every other form of record.

Literature indeed exhibits not facts alone, but thoughts, and their expression. Provided such thoughts be worthy, and worthily expressed, we feel assured that they will not die: although I do not think that thoughts without style will be likely to attract much notice or secure a sure survival. What greater charm can life offer than this power of making the past, the present, and even the future, our own by means of literature? How bright a household is the family of books! we may cry, with Cicero. In their company is no noise, no greed, no self-will: at a word they speak to you, at a word they are still: to all our requests their response is ever ready and to the point. Books indeed are a higher—a wider, more tenacious—memory, a store-house which is the common property of us all.

I attach great weight to the duty of handing down this priceless treasure to our sons unimpaired by any carelessness on our part. How many are the gaps which the ignorance of past ages has wilfully caused in the long and noble roll of writers! Books—in part or in their entirety—have been allowed to perish. What remains of others is often sorely corrupt, mutilated, or imperfect. It is hard that no slight portion of the history of Rome is only to be known through the labours of one writing in the Greek language: it is still worse that this same noble tongue, once well nigh the daily speech of our race, as familiar as the Latin language itself, is on the point of perishing even amongst its own sons, and to us Italians is already utterly lost, unless we except one or two who in our time are tardily endeavouring to rescue something—if it be only a mere echo of it—from oblivion.

We come now to the consideration of the various subjects which may rightly be included under the name of 'Liberal Studies.' Amongst these I accord the first place to History, on grounds both of its attractiveness and of its utility, qualities which appeal equally to the scholar and to the statesman. Next in importance ranks Moral Philosophy, which indeed is, in a peculiar sense, a 'Liberal Art,' in that its purpose is to teach men the secret of true freedom. History, then, gives us the concrete examples of the precepts inculcated by philosophy. The one shews what men should do, the other what men have said and done in the past, and what practical lessons we may draw therefrom for the present day. I would indicate as the third main branch of study, Eloquence, which indeed holds a place of distinction amongst the refined Arts. By philosophy we learn the essential truth of things, which by eloquence we so exhibit in orderly adornment as to bring conviction to differing minds. And history provides the light of experience—a cumulative wisdom fit to supplement the force of reason and the persuasion of eloquence. For we allow that soundness of judgment, wisdom of speech, integrity of conduct are the marks of a truly liberal temper.

We are told that the Greeks devised for their sons a course of training in four subjects: letters, gymnastic, music and drawing. Now, of these drawing has no place amongst our liberal studies; except in so far as it is identical with writing, (which is in reality one side of the art of Drawing), it belongs to the Painter's profession: the Greeks, as an art-loving people, attached to it an exceptional value.

The Art of Letters, however, rests upon a different footing. It is a study adapted to all times and to all circumstances, to the investigation of fresh knowledge or to the re-casting and application of old. Hence the importance of grammar and of the rules of composition must be recognised at the outset, as the foundation on which the whole study of Literature must rest: and closely associated with these rudiments, the art of Disputation or Logical argument. The function of this is to enable us to discern fallacy from truth in discussion. Logic, indeed, as setting forth the true method of learning, is the guide to the acquisition of knowledge in whatever subject. Rhetoric comes next, and is strictly speaking the formal study by which we attain the art of eloquence; which, as we have just stated, takes the third place amongst the studies specially important in public life. It is now, indeed, fallen from its old renown and is well nigh a lost art. In the Law-Court, in the Council, in the popular Assembly, in exposition, in persuasion, in debate, eloquence finds no place now-a-days: speed, brevity, homeliness are the only qualities desired. Oratory, in which our forefathers gained so great glory for themselves and for their language, is despised: but our youth, if they would earn the repute of true education, must emulate their ancestors in this accomplishment.

After Eloquence we place Poetry and the Poetic Art, which though not without their value in daily life and as an aid to oratory, have nevertheless their main concern for the leisure side of existence.

As to Music, the Greeks refused the title of 'Educated' to anyone who could not sing or play. Socrates set an example to the Athenian youth, by himself learning to play in his old age; urging the pursuit of music not as a sensuous indulgence, but as an aid to the inner harmony of the soul. In so far as it is taught as a healthy recreation for the moral and spiritual nature, music is a truly liberal art, and, both as regards its theory and its practice, should find a place in education.

Arithmetic, which treats of the properties of numbers, Geometry, which treats of the properties of dimensions, lines, surfaces, and solid bodies, are weighty studies because they possess a peculiar element of certainty. The science of the Stars, their motions, magnitudes and distances, lifts us into the clear calm of the upper air. There we may contemplate the fixed stars, or the conjunctions of the planets, and predict the eclipses of the sun and the moon. The knowledge of Nature—animate and inanimate—the laws and the properties of things in heaven and in earth, their causes, mutations and effects, especially the explanation of their wonders (as they are popularly supposed) by the unravelling of their causes—this is a most delightful, and at the same time most profitable, study for youth. With these may be joined investigations concerning the weights of bodies, and those relative to the subject which mathematicians call 'Perspective.'

I may here glance for a moment at the three great professional Disciplines: Medicine, Law, Theology. Medicine, which is applied science, has undoubtedly much that makes it attractive to a student. But it cannot be described as a Liberal study. Law, which is based upon moral philosophy, is undoubtedly held in high respect. Regarding Law as a subject of study, such respect is entirely deserved: but Law as practised becomes a mere trade. Theology, on the other hand, treats of themes removed from our senses, and attainable only by pure intelligence.

The principal 'Disciplines' have now been reviewed. It must not be supposed that a liberal education requires acquaintance with them all: for a thorough mastery of even one of them might fairly be the achievement of a lifetime. Most of us, too, must learn to be content with modest capacity as with modest fortune. Perhaps we do wisely to pursue that study which we find most suited to our intelligence and our tastes, though it is true that we cannot rightly understand one subject unless we can perceive its relation to the rest. The choice of studies will depend to some extent upon the character of individual minds. For whilst one boy seizes rapidly the point of which he is in search and states it ably, another, working far more slowly, has yet the sounder judgment and so detects the weak spot in his rival's conclusions. The former, perhaps, will succeed in poetry, or in the abstract sciences; the latter in real studies and practical pursuits. Or a boy may be apt in thinking, but slow in expressing himself; to him the study of Rhetoric and Logic will be of much value. Where the power of talk alone is remarkable I hardly know what advice to give. Some minds are strong on the side of memory: these should be apt for history. But it is of importance to remember that in comparison with intelligence memory is of little worth, though intelligence without memory is, so far as education is concerned, of none at all. For we are not able to give evidence that we know a thing unless we can reproduce it.

Again, some minds have peculiar power in dealing with abstract truths, but are defective on the side of the particular and the concrete, and so make good progress in mathematics and in metaphysic. Those of just opposite temper are apt in Natural Science and in practical affairs. And the natural bent should be recognized and followed in education. Let the boy of limited capacity work only at that subject in which he shews he can attain some result.

LIONARDO BRUNI ON THE STUDY OF LITERATURE (c. 1405)   From W. H. Woodward, ed., *Vittorino da Feltre and Other Humanist Educators* (Cambridge, Mass., 1897), pp. 123-32.

Lionardo D'Arezzo Concerning the Study of Literature,—A Letter Addressed to the Illustrious Lady, Baptista Malatesta.

I am led to address this Tractate to you, Illustrious Lady, by the high repute which attaches to your name in the field of learning; and I offer it, partly as an expression of my homage to distinction already attained, partly as an encouragement to further effort. Were it necessary I might urge you by brilliant instances from antiquity: Cornelia, the daughter of Scipio, whose Epistles survived for centuries as models of style; Sappho, the poetess, held in so great honour for the exuberance of her poetic art; Aspasia, whose learning and eloquence made her not unworthy of the intimacy of Socrates. Upon these, the most distinguished of a long range of great names, I would have you fix your mind; for an intelligence such as your own can be satisfied with nothing less than the best. You yourself, indeed, may hope to win a fame higher even than theirs. For they lived in days when learning was no rare attainment, and therefore they enjoyed no unique renown. Whilst, alas, upon such times are we fallen that a learned man seems well-nigh a portent, and erudition in a woman is a thing utterly unknown. For true learning has almost died away amongst us. True learning, I say: not a mere acquaintance with that vulgar, threadbare jargon which satisfies those who devote themselves to Theology, but sound learning in its proper and legitimate sense, viz., the knowledge of realities— Facts and Principles—united to a perfect familiarity with Letters and the art of expression. Now this combination we find in Lactantius, in Augustine, or in Jerome; each of them at once a great theologian and profoundly versed in literature. But turn from them to their successors of to-day: how must we blush for their ignorance of the whole field of Letters!

This leads me to press home this truth—though in your case it is unnecessary— that the foundations of all true learning must be laid in the sound and thorough knowledge of Latin: which implies study marked by a broad spirit, accurate scholarship, and careful attention to details. Unless this solid basis be secured it is useless to attempt to rear an enduring edifice. Without it the great monuments of literature are unintelligible, and the art of composition impossible. To attain this essential knowledge we must never relax our careful attention to the grammar of the language, but perpetually confirm and extend our acquaintance with it until it is thoroughly our own. We may gain much from Servius, Donatus and Priscian, but more by careful observation in our own reading, in which we must note attentively vocabulary and inflexions, figures of speech and metaphors, and all the devices of style, such as rhythm, or antithesis, by which fine taste is exhibited. To this end we must be supremely careful in our choice of authors, lest an inartistic and debased style infect our own writing and degrade our taste; which danger is best avoided by bringing a keen, critical sense to bear upon select works, observing the sense of each passage, the structure of the sentence, the force of every word down to the least important particle. In this way our reading reacts directly upon our style.

You may naturally turn first to Christian writers, foremost amongst whom, with marked distinction, stands Lactantius, by common consent the finest stylist of the post-classical period. Especially do I commend to your study his works, 'Adversus falsam Religionem,' 'De via Dei,' and 'De opificio hominis.' After Lactantius your choice may lie between Augustine, Jerome, Ambrose, and Cyprian; should you desire to read Gregory of Nazianzen, Chrysostom, and Basil, be careful as to the accuracy of the translations you adopt. Of the classical authors Cicero will be your constant pleasure: how unapproachable in wealth of ideas and of language, in force of style, indeed, in all that can attract in a writer! Next to him ranks Vergil, the glory and the delight of our national literature. Livy and Sallust, and then the chief poets, follow in order. The usage of these authors will serve you as your test of correctness in choice of vocabulary and of constructions. . . .

But the wider question now confronts us, that of the subject matter of our studies, that which I have already called the realities of fact and principle, as distinct from literary form. Here, as before, I am contemplating a student of keen and lofty aspiration to whom nothing that is worthy in any learned discipline is without its interest. But it is necessary to exercise discrimination. In some branches of knowledge I would rather restrain the ardour of the learner, in others, again, encourage it to the uttermost. Thus there are certain subjects in which, whilst a modest proficiency is on all accounts to be desired, a minute knowledge and excessive devotion seem to be a vain display. For instance, subtleties of Arithmetic and Geometry are not worthy to absorb a cultivated mind, and the same must be said of Astrology. You will be surprised to find me suggesting (though with much more hesitation) that the great and complex art of Rhetoric should be placed in the same category. My chief reason is the obvious one, that I have in view the cultivation most fitting to a woman. To her neither the intricacies of debate nor the oratorical artifices of action and delivery are of the least practical use, if indeed they are not positively unbecoming. Rhetoric in all its forms,—public discussion, forensic argument, logical fence, and the like—lies absolutely outside the province of woman.

Moreover, the cultivated Christian lady has no need . . . to confine herself to ecclesiastical writers. Morals, indeed, have been treated of by the noblest intellects of Greece and Rome. What they have left to us upon Continence, Temperance, Modesty, Justice, Courage, Greatness of Soul, demands your sincere respect. You must enter into such questions as the sufficiency of Virtue to Happiness; or whether, if Happiness consist in Virtue, it can be destroyed by torture, imprisonment or exile; whether, admitting that these may prevent a man from being happy, they can be further said to make him miserable. Again, does Happiness consist (with Epicurus) in the presence of pleasure and the absence of pain: or (with Xenophon) in the consciousness of uprightness: or (with Aristotle) in the practice of Virtue? These inquiries are, of all others, most worthy to be pursued by men and women alike; they are fit material for formal discussion and for literary exercise. Let religion and morals, therefore, hold the first place in the education of a Christian lady.

But we must not forget that true distinction is to be gained by a wide and varied range of such studies as conduce to the profitable enjoyment of life, in which, however, we must observe due proportion in the attention and time we devote to them.

First amongst such studies I place History: a subject which must not on any account be neglected by one who aspires to true cultivation. For it is our duty to understand the origins of our own history and its development; and the achievements of Peoples and of Kings.

For the careful study of the past enlarges our foresight in contemporary affairs and affords to citizens and to monarchs lessons of incitement or warning in the ordering of public policy. From History, also, we draw our store of examples of moral precepts.

In the monuments of ancient literature which have come down to us History holds a position of great distinction. We specially prize such authors as Livy, Sallust and Curtius; and, perhaps even above these, Julius Caesar; the style of whose Commentaries, so elegant and so limpid, entitles them to our warm admiration. Such writers are fully within the comprehension of a studious lady. For, after all, History is an easy subject: there is nothing in its study subtle or complex. It consists in the narration of the simplest matters of fact which, once grasped, are readily retained in the memory.

The great Orators of antiquity must by all means be included. Nowhere do we find the virtues more warmly extolled, the vices so fiercely decried. From them we may learn, also, how to express consolation, encouragement, disuasion or advice.

❖   ❖   ❖

Familiarity with the great poets of antiquity is [also] essential to any claim to true education. For in their writings we find deep speculations upon Nature, and upon the Causes and Origins of things, which must carry weight with us both from their antiquity and from their authorship. Besides these, many important truths upon matters of daily life are suggested or illustrated. All this is expressed with such grace and dignity as demands our admiration. . . .

We know, however, that in certain quarters—where all knowledge and appreciation of Letters is wanting—this whole branch of Literature, marked as it is by something of the Divine, and fit, therefore, for the highest place, is decried as unworthy of study. But when we remember the value of the best poetry, its charm of form and the variety and interest of its subject-matter, when we consider the ease with which from our childhood up it can be committed to memory, when we recall the peculiar affinity of rhythm and metre to our emotions and our intelligence, we must conclude that Nature herself is against such headlong critics. . . . Plato and Aristotle studied the poets, and I decline to admit that in practical wisdom or in moral earnestness they yield to our modern critics. They were not Christians, indeed, but consistency of life and abhorrence of evil existed before Christianity and are independent of it.

To sum up what I have endeavoured to set forth. That high standard of education to which I referred at the outset is only to be reached by one who has seen many things and read much. Poet, Orator, Historian, and the rest, all must be studied, each must contribute a share. Our learning thus becomes full, ready, varied and elegant, available for action or for discourse in all subjects. But to enable us to make effectual use of what we know we must add to our knowledge the power of expression. These two sides of learning, indeed, should not be separated: they afford mutual aid and distinction. Proficiency in literary form, not accompanied by broad acquaintance with facts and truths, is a barren attainment; whilst information, however vast, which lacks all grace of expression would seem to be put under a bushel or partly thrown away. Indeed, one may fairly ask what advantage it is to possess profound and varied learning if one cannot convey it in language worthy of the subject. Where, however, this double capacity exists—breadth of learning and grace of style—we allow the highest title to distinction and to abiding fame. If we review the great names of ancient literature, Plato, Democritus, Aristotle, Theophrastus, Varro, Cicero, Seneca, Augustine, Jerome, Lactantius, we shall find it hard to say whether we admire more their attainments or their literary power.

But my last word must be this. The intelligence that aspires to the best must aim at both. In doing so, all sources of profitable learning will in due proportion claim your study. None have more urgent claim than the subjects and authors which treat of Religion and of our duties in the world; and it is because they assist and illustrate these supreme studies that I press upon your attention the works of the most approved poets, historians and orators of the past.

GUARINO ON TEACHING THE CLASSICAL AUTHORS (1459)   From Battista Guarino, "Upon the Method of Teaching and of Reading the Classical Authors," as quoted in W. H. Woodward, ed., *Vittorino da Feltre and Other Humanist Educators* (Cambridge, Mass., 1897) pp. 162-164, 166-168.

Let me, at the outset, begin with a caution. No master can endow a careless and indifferent nature with the true passion for learning. That a young man must acquire for himself. But once the taste begins to develope, then in Ovid's words 'the more we drink, the more we thirst.' For when the mind has begun to enjoy the pleasures of learning the passion for fuller and deeper knowledge will grow from day to day. But there can be no proficiency in studies unless there be first the desire to excel. Wherefore let a young man set forward eagerly in quest of those true, honourable, and enduring treasures of the mind which neither disease nor death has power to destroy. Riches, which adventurers seek by land and sea, too often win men to pleasure rather than to learning; for self-indulgence is a snare from whose enticements it is the bounden duty of parents to wean their children, by kind word, or by severity if need arise. Perchance then in later years the echo of a father's wise advice may linger and may avail in the hour of temptation.

In the choice of a Master we ought to remember that his position should carry with it something of the authority of a father: for unless respect be paid to the man and to his office regard will not be had to his words. Our forefathers were certainly right in basing the relation of teacher and pupil upon the foundation of filial reverence on the one part and fatherly affection on the other. Thus the instinct of

Alexander of Macedon was a sound one which led him to say that, whilst he owed to his father Philip the gift of life, he owed to his tutor Aristotle an equal debt, namely, the knowledge how to use it. Care must be taken therefore from the outset to avoid a wrong choice of master: one, for instance, who is ill-bred, or ill-educated. Such a one may by bad teaching waste precious years of a boy's life; not only is nothing rightly learnt, but much of that which passes as instruction needs to be undone again, as Timotheus said long ago. Faults, moreover, imbibed in early years, as Horace reminds us, are by no means easy to eradicate. Next, the master must not be prone to flogging as an inducement to learning. It is an indignity to a free-born youth, and its infliction renders learning itself repulsive, and the mere dread of it provokes to unworthy evasions on the part of timorous boys. The scholar is thus morally and intellectually injured, the master is deceived, and the discipline altogether fails of its purpose. The habitual instrument of the teacher must be kindness, though punishment should be retained as it were in the background as a final resource. In the case of elder boys, emulation and the sense of shame, which shrinks from the discredit of failure, may be relied upon. I advise also that boys, at this stage, work two together with a view to encouraging a healthy spirit of rivalry between them, from which much benefit may be expected. Large classes should be discouraged, especially for beginners, for though a fair average excellence may be apparently secured, thorough grounding, which is so important, is impossible. In the case of more advanced pupils, however, numbers tend rather to stimulate the teacher.

As regards the course of study. From the first, stress must be laid upon distinct and sustained enunciation, both in speaking and in reading. But at the same time utterance must be perfectly natural; if affected or exaggerated the effect is unpleasing. The foundation of education must be laid in Grammar. Unless this be thoroughly learnt subsequent progress is uncertain,—a house built upon treacherous ground. Hence let the knowledge of nouns and verbs be secured early, as the starting point for the rest. The master will employ the devices of repetition, examination, and the correction of erroneous inflexions purposely introduced.

Grammar falls into two parts. The first treats of the rules which govern the use of the different Parts of Speech, and is called therefore 'Methodice,' the second includes the study of continuous prose, especially of historical narrative[1], and is called 'Historice.'

Now these Rules can be most satisfactorily learnt from the Compendium[2] written by my father which briefly sets out the more important laws of composition. In using this or a similar text-book the pupil must be practised both in written and in oral exercises. Only by rapid practice in oral composition can fluency and readiness be gained. And this will be further secured if the class is accustomed to speak in Latin. Certain general Rules of a crucial nature must be early learnt, and constantly practised, by the whole class. Such are those by which we recognise the differences between active, passive and deponent verbs, or between those of transitive or intransitive meaning. It is most important that each boy be required to form examples in illustration of the main rules of accidence and syntax, not only with accuracy but also with a certain propriety of style, as for instance with due attention to the order of words in the sentence. In this way the habit of sound and

[1] This would take the form of Delectus, Extracts, or continuous reading of an easy historical author in Greek or Latin.

[2] The *Regulae Guarini*, a very popular manual of accidence, intended to be learnt by heart.

tasteful composition is imbibed during the earliest stages of education. A master who is properly qualified for his work will be careful to use only such transcripts of texts as can be relied upon for accuracy and completeness. The work just referred to has been much disfigured by additions and alterations due to the ignorance or conceit of the would-be emendator. As examples of what I mean you may turn to the rule as to the formation of the comparative of adjectives of the second declension where an inept correction is added in some copies ('vowel before a vowel' is turned into 'vowel before -us'); and in another place the spelling 'Tydites' is substituted for my father's (and, of course, the correct) form 'Tydides.'

*　　*　　*

I have said that ability to write Latin verse is one of the essential marks of an educated person. I wish now to indicate a second, which is of at least equal importance, namely, familiarity with the language and literature of Greece. The time has come when we must speak with no uncertain voice upon this vital requirement of scholarship. I am well aware that those who are ignorant of the Greek tongue decry its necessity, for reasons which are sufficiently evident. But I can allow no doubt to remain as to my own conviction that without a knowledge of Greek Latin scholarship itself is, in any real sense, impossible. I might point to the vast number of words derived or borrowed from the Greek, and the questions which arise in connection with them; such as the quantity of the vowel sounds, the use of the diphthongs, obscure orthographies and etymologies. Vergil's allusion to the Avernian Lake:

> 'O'er that dread space no flying thing
> Unjeoparded could ply its wing,'

is wholly missed by one who is ignorant of the relation between the name of the lake and the Greek word $o\rho\nu\iota\varsigma$. Or again the lines of Ovid,

> 'Quae quia nascuntur dura vivacia caute
> Agrestes aconita vocant,'

is unintelligible unless we can associate 'cautes' with the Greek ($\alpha\kappa o\nu\eta$). So too the name *Ciris* ($\kappa\epsilon\iota\rho\omega$), and the full force of *Aphrodite* ($\alpha\phi\rho\omega\nu$) are but vaguely understood without a clear perception of their Greek etymologies. The Greek grammar, again, can alone explain the unusual case-endings which are met with in the declension of certain nouns, mostly proper names, which retain their foreign shape; such as 'Dido' and 'Mantus.' Nor are these exceptional forms confined to the poetic use. But I turn to the authority of the great Latins themselves, to Cicero, Quintilian, Cato and Horace: they are unanimous in proclaiming the close dependence of the Roman speech and Roman literature upon the Greek, and in urging by example as well as by precept the constant study of the older language. To quote Horace alone:

> 'Do you, my friends, from Greece your models draw,
> And day and night to con them be your law.'

And again,

> 'To Greece, that cared for nought but fame, the Muse
> Gave genius, and a tongue the gods might use.'

In such company I do not fear to urge the same contention.

Were we, indeed, to follow Quintilian, we should even begin with Greek in preference to Latin. But this is practically impossible, when we consider that Greek must be for us, almost of necessity, a learned and not a colloquial language; and that Latin itself needs much more elaborate and careful teaching than was requisite to a Roman of the imperial epoch. On the other hand, I have myself known not a few pupils of my father—he was, as you know, a scholar of equal distinction in either language—who, after gaining a thorough mastery of Latin, could then in a single year make such progress with Greek that they translated accurately entire works of ordinary difficulty from that language into good readable Latin *at sight*. Now proficiency of this degree can only be attained by careful and systematic teaching of the rudiments of the Grammar, as they are laid down in such a manual as the well-known Ἐρωτήματα of Manuel Chrysoloras, or in the abridgement which my father drew up of the original work of his beloved master. In using such a text-book the greatest attention must be paid to the verb, the regular form, with its scheme of moods and tenses; then the irregular verbs must be equally mastered. When the forms of noun and verb can be immediately distinguished, and each inflexion of voice, mood and tense recognised,—and this can only be tested by constant *viva voce* exercises—then a beginning should be made with simple narrative prose. At this stage all authors whose subject matter requires close thought should be avoided, for the entire attention must be concentrated upon vocabulary and grammatical structure. Only when some degree of freedom in these latter respects has been secured should the master introduce books of increasing difficulty.

Our scholar should make his first acquaintance with the Poets through Homer, the sovereign master of them all. For from Homer our own poets, notably Vergil, drew their inspiration; and in reading the *Iliad* or the *Odyssey* no small part of our pleasure is derived from the constant parallels we meet with. Indeed in them we see as in a mirror the form and manner of the *Aeneid* figured roughly before us, the incidents, not less than the simile or epithet which describe them, are, one might say, all there. In the same way, in his minor works Vergil has borrowed from Theocritus or Hesiod. After Homer has been attempted the way lies open to the other Heroic poets and to the Dramatists.

In reading of this wider range a large increase of vocabulary is gained, and in this the memory will be greatly assisted by the practice of making notes, which should be methodically arranged afterwards. The rules of Accentuation should now be learnt and their application observed after the same method. It is very important that regular exercises in elementary composition be required from the first, and this partly as an aid to construing. The scholar will now shortly be able to render a Latin author into Greek, a practice which compels us, as nothing else does, to realise the appropriateness of the writer's language, and its dignity of style, whilst at the same time it gives us increased freedom in handling it. For though delicate shades of meaning or beauties of expression may be overlooked by a casual reader they cannot escape a faithful translator.

ERASMUS ON THE RIGHT METHOD OF INSTRUCTION (1511) From *De Ratione Studii*, as quoted in W. H. Woodward, ed. and trans., *Desiderius Erasmus Concerning the Aim and Method of Education* (Cambridge, Mass., 1904), pp. 162-63, 166-67, 177-78.

Thought and Expression Form the Two-fold
Material of Instruction

All knowledge falls into one of two divisions: the knowledge of "truths" and the knowledge of "words": and if the former is first in importance the latter is acquired first in order of time. They are not to be commended who, in their anxiety to increase their store of truths, neglect the necessary art of expressing them. For ideas are only intelligible to us by means of the words which describe them; wherefore defective knowledge of language reacts upon our apprehension of the truths expressed. We often find that no one is so apt to lose himself in verbal arguments as the man who boasts that facts, not words, are the only things that interest him. This goes to prove that true education includes what is best in both kinds of knowledge, taught, I must add, under the best guidance. For, remembering how difficult it is to eradicate early impressions, we should aim from the first at learning what need never be unlearnt, and that only.

Expression Claims the First Place in Point of Time.
Both the Greek and Latin Languages Needful to
the Educated Man

Language thus claims the first place in the order of studies and from the outset should include both Greek and Latin. The argument for this is two-fold. First, that within these two literatures are contained all the knowledge which we recognise as of vital importance to mankind. Secondly, that the natural affinity of the two tongues renders it more profitable to study them side by side than apart. Latin particularly gains by this method. Quintilian advised that a beginning should be made with Greek before systematic work in Latin is taken in hand. Of course he regarded proficiency in both as essential. The elements, therefore, of Greek and Latin should be acquired early, and should a thoroughly skilled master not be available, then—but only then—let the learner fall back upon self-teaching by means of the study of classical masterpieces.

*   *   *

Instruction Generally: Choice of Subjects of
Instruction. The Range of Study Necessary to
a Well-Read Master

This brings me to treat of the art of instruction generally, though it seems a mere impertinence in me to handle afresh a subject which has been made so conspicuously his own by the great Quintilian.

As regards the choice of *material*, it is essential that from the outset the child be made acquainted only with the best that is available. This implies that the Master is competent to recognise the best in the mass of erudition open to him, which in turn signifies that he has read far more widely than the range of authors to be taught by him. This applies even to the tutor of beginners. The Master should, therefore, acquaint himself with authors of every type, with a view to contents rather than to style; and the better to classify what he reads he must adopt the system of classifying his matter by means of note-books, upon the plan suggested by me in *De Copia*. As examples of the authors I refer to I put Pliny first, then Macrobius, Aulus Gellius, and, in Greek, Athenaeus. Indeed to lay in a store of ancient wisdom the studious master must go straight to the Greeks: to Plato, Aristotle, Theophrastus and Plotinus; to Origen, Chrysostom, Basil. Of the Latin Fathers, Ambrosius will be found most fertile in classical allusions. Jerome has the greatest command of Holy Scripture. I cannot, however, enumerate the entire extent of reading which a competent knowledge of antiquity demands. I can only indicate a few directions which study ought to take.

For the right understanding of the poets, the *Legends* of Gods and Heroes must be mastered: Homer, Hesiod, Ovid, and the Italian Boccaccio should be read for this. A knowledge of *Geography* is of prime importance, for the study both of ancient poets and of historians. Pomponius Mela makes a useful compendium; Pliny and Ptolemy are learned and elaborate writers; Strabo is something more than a geographer. This subject includes two parts, a knowledge, first, of the names, ancient and modern, of mountains, rivers, cities; secondly, of names of trees, plants, animals, of dress, appliances, precious stones, in which the average writer of to-day shews a strange ignorance. Here we gain help from the works which have come down to us upon agriculture, architecture, the art of war, cookery, precious stones, and natural history. We can make good use, in the same subject, of etymology (the name "unicorn" is an example). Or again we can trace word-change in names through modern Greek, or Italian and Spanish (Tiber, now "Tevere," is an example). I may say that modern French has wandered too far from its classical mother-speech to be of much help to us in recognising and identifying ancient names.

*　　*　　*

Progress in Classical Knowledge Depends upon
the Learning and the Skill of the Master

What has been laid down above as the function of the schoolmaster implies, I allow, that he be a person of no slight learning and experience. But, given these qualities, I have no doubt that the class will speedily absorb the kind of knowledge which I have indicated. The first steps may be slow and laborious, but exercise and right instruction make progress certain. I only stipulate that the material selected be of sound classical excellence (nothing mediaeval), and the method skilfully adapted to the growing comprehension; the teacher forcing nothing, but working forward gradually from the broader aspects of his subject to the more minute. Success then is assured. One further counsel, however. The master must not omit to set as an exercise the reproduction of what he has given to the class. It involves time and trouble to the teacher, I know well, but it is essential. A literal reproduction of the matter taught is, of course, not required, but the substance of it presented in the pupil's own way. Personally I disapprove of the practice of taking down a lecture just as it is delivered. For this prevents reliance upon memory which should, as time goes on; need less and less of that external aid which note-taking supplies.

Conclusion

Such weight do I ascribe to right method in instruction—and I include herein choice of material as well as of modes of imparting it—that I undertake by its means to carry forward youths of merely average intelligence to a creditable standard of scholarship, and of conversation also, in Latin and Greek, at an age when, under the common schoolmaster of to-day, the same youths would be just stammering through their Primer. With the foundations thus rightly laid a boy may confidently look forward to success in the higher range of learning. He will, when he looks back, admit that the essential condition of his attainment was the care which was devoted to the beginnings of his education.

ERASMUS ON THE EDUCATION OF A CHRISTIAN PRINCE (1516)
From Erasmus, *The Education of a Christian Prince*, L. K. Born, trans. (New York, 1936), pp. 140-48.

The more difficult it is to change your choice, the more circumspectly should your candidate be chosen, or else the rashness of a single hour may spread its retributions over a lifetime. There is no choice, however, in the case of hereditary succession of princes. This was the usual practice with various barbarian nations of old, as Aristotle tells us, and it is also almost universally accepted in our own times. Under that condition, the chief hope for a good prince is from his education, which should be especially looked to. In this way the interest in his education will compensate for the loss of the right of election. Hence, from the very cradle, as it were, the mind of the future prince, while still open and unmolded, must be filled with salutary thoughts. Then the seeds of morality must be sown in the virgin soil of his spirit so that little by little they may grow and mature through age and experience, to remain firmly implanted throughout the course of life. Nothing remains so deeply and tenaciously rooted as those things learned in the first years. What is absorbed in those years is of prime importance to all, especially in the case of a prince.

When there is no opportunity to choose the prince, care should be exercised in the same manner in choosing the tutor to the future prince. That a prince be born of worthy character we must beseech the gods above; that a prince born of good parts may not go amiss, or that one of mediocre accomplishments may be bettered through education is mainly within our province. It was formerly the custom to decree statues, arches, and honorary titles to those deserving honor from the state. None is more worthy of this honor than he who labors faithfully and zealously in the proper training of the prince, and looks not to personal emolument but rather to the welfare of his country. A country owes everything to a good prince; him it owes to the man who made him such by his moral principles. There is no better time to shape and improve a prince than when he does not yet realize himself a prince. This time must be diligently employed, not only to the end that for a while he may be kept away from base associations, but also that he may be imbued with certain definite moral principles. If diligent parents raise with great care a boy who is destined to inherit only an acre or two, think how much interest and concern should be given to the education of one who will succeed not to a single dwelling, but to so many peoples, to so many cities, yea, to the world, either as a good man for the common gain of all, or an evil one, to the great ruination of all! It is a great and glorious thing to rule an empire well, but none-the-less glorious to pass it on to no worse a ruler: nay, rather it is the main task of a good prince to see that he does not become a bad one. So conduct your rule as if this were your aim: "My equal shall never succeed me!" In the meantime, raise your children for future rule as if it were your desire to be succeeded by a better prince. There can be no more splendid commendation of a worthy prince than to say that he left such a successor to the state, that he himself seemed average by comparison. His own glory cannot be more truly shown than to be so obscured. The worst possible praise is that a ruler who was intolerable during his life is longingly missed as a good and beneficial prince each time a worse man ascends the throne. Let the good and wise prince always so educate his children that he seems ever to have remembered that they were born for the state and are being educated for the state, not for his own fancy. Concern for the state must always be superior to the personal feelings of the parent. However many statues he may set up, however many massive works he may erect, a prince can have no more excellent monument to his worth than a son, splendid in every way, who is like his excellent father in his outstanding deeds. He does not die, who leaves a living likeness of himself! The prince should choose for this duty teachers from among all the number of his subjects—or even summon from every direction men of good character, unquestioned principles, serious, of long experience and not merely learned in theories—to whom advancing years provide deep respect; purity of life, prestige; sociability and an affable manner, love and friendship. Thus a tender young spirit may not be cut by the severity of its training and learn to hate worthiness before it knows it; nor on the other hand, debased by the unseasoned indulgence of its tutor, slip back where it should not. In the education of anyone, but especially in the case of a prince, the teacher must adopt a mid-course; he should be stern enough to suppress the wild pranks of youth, yet have a friendly understanding to lessen and temper the severity of his restraint. Such a man should the future prince's tutor be (as Seneca elaborately sets forth), that he can scold without railing, praise without flattering, be revered for his stainless life, and loved for his pleasing manner.

Some princes exercise themselves greatly over the proper care of a beautiful horse, or a bird, or a dog, yet consider it a matter of no importance to whom they entrust the training of their son. Him they often put in the hands of such teachers as no common citizen with any sense at all would want in charge of his sons. Of what consequence is it to have begot a son for the throne, unless you educate him for his rule? Neither is the young prince to be given to any sort of nurse, but only to those of stainless character, who have been previously instructed in their duties and are well trained. He should not be allowed to associate with whatever playmates appear, but only with those boys of good and modest character; he should be reared and trained most carefully and as becomes a gentleman. That whole crowd of wantons, hard drinkers, filthy-tongued fellows, especially flatterers, must be kept far from his sight and hearing while his mind is not yet fortified with precepts to the contrary. Since the natures of so many men are inclined towards the ways of evil, there is no nature so happily born that it cannot be corrupted by wrong training.

What do you expect except a great fund of evil in a prince, who, regardless of his native character (and a long line of ancestors does not necessarily furnish a mind, as it does a kingdom), is beset from his very cradle by the most inane opinions; is raised in the circle of senseless women; grows to boyhood among naughty girls, abandoned playfellows, and the most abject flatterers, among buffoons and mimes, drinkers and gamesters, and worse than stupid and worthless creators of wanton pleasures. In the company of all of these he hears nothing, learns nothing, absorbs nothing except pleasures, amusements, arrogance, haughtiness, greed, petulance, and tyranny—and from this school he will soon progress to the government of his kingdom! Although each one of all the great arts is very difficult, there is none finer nor more difficult than that of ruling well. Why in the case of this one thing alone do we feel the need of no training, but deem it sufficient to have been born for it? To what end except tyranny do they devote themselves as men, who as boys played at nothing except as tyrants?

*   *   *

Whoever will undertake the task of educating the prince, let him ponder again and again the fact that he is undertaking a duty by no means slight. Just as it is the greatest of all [duties], so is it beset with the most trials. In the first place, he should have an attitude of mind befitting his undertaking; he should not contemplate the number of priestly benefices he can gain as a result, but rather in what way he can repay the hopes of his country entrusted to him by giving it a prince heedful of his country's needs. Think, you who would teach, how much you owe your country, which has entrusted the source of its fortunes to you! It rests with you whether you are going to turn out a power for good in your country or visit it with a scourge and plague.

The teacher, into whose care the state has given its prince, shall give much careful thought to discover his leanings. Sometimes, too, at this early age it can be discovered by certain signs whether the prince is more prone to petulance or arrogance, to a desire for popularity or a thirst for fame, to licentiousness or dicing or greed, to defense or war, to rashness or tyranny. When he has found the prince's weak spot, there he should strengthen him with goodly doctrines and suitable teachings and try to lead into better ways a spirit still prone to follow. On the other hand, if he finds a nature prone to the good things of life, or at any rate to only those vices which are readily turned to virtue, e.g., ambition and prodigality, he should work the harder and assist advantages of nature with refinement. It is not enough just to hand out precepts to restrain the prince from vices or to incite him to a better course—they must be impressed, crammed in, inculcated, and in one way and another be kept before him, now by a suggestive thought, now by a fable, now by analogy, now by example, now by maxims, now by a proverb. They should be engraved on rings, painted in pictures, appended to the wreaths of honor, and, by using any other means by which that age can be interested, kept always before him. The deeds of famous men fire the minds of noble youths, but the opinions with which they become imbued is a matter of far greater importance, for from these sources the whole scheme of life is developed. In the case of a mere boy, we must immediately be on guard, to see that he gets only the virtuous and helpful ideas and that he be fortified as by certain efficacious drugs against the poisoned opinions of the common people. But if the prince happens to be somewhat tinged with the thoughts of the common people, then the first effort must be to rid him of them little by little, to weed out the seeds of trouble and replace them by wholesome ones. As Aristo says in Seneca, "It is no use to teach a crazy man how to speak, how to act, how to conduct himself in public, how alone, until you have driven out the root of the malady." Just so is it fruitless to attempt advice on the theory of governing, until you have freed the prince's mind from those most common yet most truly false opinions of the common people. There is no chance for the tutor to avoid or shrink his responsibility if he unfortunately encounters a headstrong and untractable nature. There is no beast so wild, so terrible, that the skill and endurance of his trainer will not tame him. Why should the tutor judge any man to be so coarse and so forsaken that he will not be corrected by painstaking instruction?

*   *   *

When the little fellow has listened with pleasure to Aesop's fable of the lion and the mouse or of the dove and the ant, and when he has finished his laugh, then the teacher should point out the new moral: the first fable teaches the prince to despise no one, but to seek zealously to win to himself by kindnesses the heart of even the lowest peasant, for no one is so weak but that on occasion he may be a friend to help you, or an enemy to harm you, even though you be the most powerful. When he has had his fun out of the eagle, queen of the birds, that was almost completely done for by the beetle, the teacher should again point out the meaning: not even the most powerful prince can afford to provoke or overlook even the humblest enemy. Often those who can inflict no harm by physical strength can do much by the machinations of their minds. When he has learned with pleasure the story of Phaeton, the teacher should show that he represents a prince, who while still headstrong with the ardor of youth, but with no supporting wisdom, seized the reins of government and turned everything into ruin for himself and the whole world. When he has finished the story of the Cyclops who was blinded by Ulysses, the teacher should say in conclusion that the prince who has great strength of body, but not of mind, is like Polyphemus.

Who has not heard with interest of the government of the bees and ants? When temptations begin to descend into the youthful heart of the prince, then his tutor should point out such of these stories as belong in his education. He should tell him that the king never flies far away, has wings smaller in proportion to the size of its body than the others, and that he alone has no sting. From this the tutor should point out that it is the part of a good prince always to remain within the limits of his realm; his reputation for clemency should be his special form of praise. The same idea should be carried on throughout.

*   *   *

Before all else the story of Christ must be firmly rooted in the mind of the prince. He should drink deeply of His teachings, gathered in handy texts, and then later from those very fountains themselves, whence he may drink more purely and more effectively. He should be taught that the teachings of Christ apply to no one more than to the prince.

The great mass of people are swayed by false opinions and are no different from those in Plato's cave, who took the empty shadows as the real things. It is the part of a good prince to admire none of the things that the common people consider of great consequence, but to judge all things on their own merits as "good" or "bad." But nothing is truly "bad" unless joined with base infamy. Nothing is really "good" unless associated with moral integrity.

Therefore, the tutor should first see that his pupil loves and honors virtue as the finest quality of all, the most felicitous, the most fitting a prince; and that he loathes and shuns moral turpitude as the foulest and most terrible of things.

ERASMUS ON THE EDUCATION OF YOUNG CHILDREN (1529) From *De Pueris Instituendis* as quoted in W. H. Woodward, ed. and trans., *Desiderius Erasmus Concerning the Aim and Method of Education* (Cambridge, Mass., 1904), pp. 180-84, 186-87, 191-92, 195-96, 222.

The Argument at Large

I desire to urge upon you, Illustrious Duke, to take into your early and serious consideration the future nurture and training of the son lately born to you. For, with Chrysippus, I contend that the young child must be led to sound learning whilst his wit is yet unwarped, his age tender, his mind flexible and tenacious. In manhood we remember nothing so well as the truths which we imbibed in our youth. Wherefore I beg you to put aside all idle chatter which would persuade you that this early childhood is unmeet for the discipline and the effort of studies.

The arguments which I shall enlarge upon are the following. First, the beginnings of learning are the work of memory, which in young children is most tenacious. Next, as nature has implanted in us the instinct to seek for knowledge, can we be too early in obeying her behest? Thirdly, there are not a few things which it imports greatly that we should know well, and which we can learn far more readily in our tender years. I speak of the elements of Letters, Grammar, and the fables and stories found in the ancient Poets. Fourthly, since children, as all agree, are fit to acquire manners, why may they not acquire the rudiments of learning? And seeing that they must needs be busy about something, what else can be better approved? For how much wiser to amuse their hours with Letters, than to see them frittered away in aimless trifling!

It is, however, objected, first, that such knowledge as can be thus early got is of slight value. But even so, why despise it, if so be it serve as the foundation for much greater things? For if in early childhood a boy acquire such useful elements he will be free to apply his youth to higher knowledge, to the saving of his time. Moreover, whilst he is thus occupied in sound learning he will perforce be kept from some of the temptations which befall youth, seeing that nothing engages the whole mind more than studies. And this I count a high gain in such times as ours.

Next, it is urged that by such application health may be somewhat endangered. Supposing this to be true, still the compensation is great, for by discipline the mind gains far more in alertness and in vigour than the body is ever likely to lose. Watchfulness, however, will prevent any such risk as is imagined. Also, for this tender age you will employ a teacher who will win and not drive, just as you will choose such subjects as are pleasant and attractive, in which the young mind will find recreation rather than toil.

Furthermore, I bid you remember that a man ignorant of Letters is no man at all, that human life is a fleeting thing, that youth is easily enticed into sin, that early manhood is absorbed by clashing interests, that old age is unproductive, and that few reach it. How then can you allow your child, in whom you yourself live again, to lose even one of those precious years in which he may begin to acquire those means whereby he may elevate his whole life and keep at arm's length temptation and evil?

✻   ✻   ✻

The Supreme Importance of Education to Human Well-being

To dumb creatures Mother Nature has given an innate power or instinct, whereby they may in great part attain to their right capacities. But Providence in granting to man alone the privilege of reason has thrown the burden of development of the human being upon training. Well, therefore, has it been said that the first means, the second, and the third means to happiness is right training or education. Sound education is the condition of real wisdom. And if an education which is soundly planned and carefully carried out is the very fount of all human excellence, so, on the other hand, careless and unworthy training is the true source of folly and vice. This capacity for training is, indeed, the chief aptitude which has been bestowed upon humanity. Unto the animals nature has given swiftness of foot or of wing, keenness of sight, strength or size of frame, and various weapons of defence. To Man, instead of physical powers, is given a mind apt for training; in this single gift all others are comprised, for him, at least, who turns it to due profit. We see that where native instinct is strong—as in squirrels or bees—capacity for being taught is wanting. Man, lacking instinct, can do little or nothing of innate power; scarce can he eat, or walk, or speak, unless he be guided thereto. How then can we expect that he should become competent to the duties of life unless straightway and with much diligence he be brought under the discipline of a worthy education? Let me enforce this by the well-known story of Lycurgus, who, to convince the Spartans, brought out two hounds, one of good mettle, but untrained and therefore useless in the field, and the other poorly bred and well-drilled at his work; "Nature," he said, "may be strong, yet Education is more powerful still."

✻   ✻   ✻

Reason the True Mark of Man

Now it is the possession of Reason which constitutes a Man. If trees or wild beasts grow, men, believe me, are fashioned. Men in olden time who led their life in forests, driven by the mere needs and desires of their natures, guided by no laws, with no ordering in communities, are to be judged rather as savage beasts than as men. For Reason, the mark of humanity, has no place where all is determined by appetite. It is beyond dispute that a man not instructed through reason in philosophy and sound learning is a creature lower than a brute, seeing that there is no beast more wild or more harmful than a man who is driven hither and thither by ambition, or desire, anger or envy, or lawless temper. Therefore do I conclude that he that provides not that his own son may presently be instructed in the best learning is neither a man nor the son of a man. Would it not be a horror to look upon a human soul clad in the form of a beast, as Circe is fabled to have done by her spells? But is it not worse that a father should see his own image slowly but surely becoming the dwelling-place of a brute's nature? It is said a bear's cub is at birth but an ill-formed lump which by a long process of licking is brought into shape. Nature, in giving you a son, presents you, let me say, a rude, unformed creature, which it is your part to fashion so that it may become indeed a man. If this fashioning be neglected you have but an animal still: if it be contrived earnestly and wisely, you have, I had almost said, what may prove a being not far from a God.

✳   ✳   ✳

The Three Factors in Individual Progress: Nature, Method, Practice

Can anything be more deplorable than to have to admit that, whilst an unreasoning animal performs by instinct its duty towards its offspring, Man, the creature of Reason, is blind to what he owes to Nature, to parental responsibility, and to God? But I will now consider definitely the three conditions which determine individual progress. They are Nature, Training and Practice. By Nature, I mean, partly, innate capacity for being trained, partly, native bent towards excellence. By Training, I mean the skilled application of instruction and guidance. By Practice, the free exercise on our own part of that activity which has been implanted by Nature and is furthered by Training. Nature without skilled Training must be imperfect, and Practice without the method which Training supplies leads to hopeless confusion.

The Error of Those Who Think That Experience Gives All the Education That Men Need

They err, therefore, who affirm that wisdom is won by handling affairs and by contact with life, without aid from the teaching of philosophy. Tell me, can a man run his best in the dark? Or, can a gladiator conquer if he be blindfold? The precepts of philosophy—which is knowledge applied to life—are, as it were, the eyes of the mind, and lighten us to the consciousness of what we may do and may not do. A long and manifold experience is, beyond doubt, of great profit, but only to such as by the wisdom of learning have acquired an intelligent and informed judgment. Besides, philosophy teaches us more in one year than our own individual experience can teach us in thirty.

Individuality of the Child; its Recognition by the Teacher; its Importance in Determining the Choice of Subjects to be Taught

By the nature of a man we mean, as a rule, that which is common to Man as such: the characteristic, namely, of being guided by Reason. But we may mean something less broad than this: the characteristic peculiar to each personality, which we may call individuality. Thus one child may shew a native bent to Mathematics, another to Divinity, another to Rhetoric, or Poetry, another to War. So strongly disposed are certain types of mind to certain studies that they cannot be won to others; the very attempt in that direction sets up a positive repulsion. I was once very intimate with a student, who, having attained a high level in Greek and Latin scholarship, and in some other of the liberal arts, was sent by his patron the Archbishop to the University to study Law. But this discipline he found wholly repugnant to his nature. "I am," he told me, "so averse to the Law that when I force myself to its study I feel as if a sword were being driven through my heart." Minds of that strong determination ought not to be forced against their instinct; it is almost as though we should train a cow to box or a donkey to play the violin.

The Master will be wise to observe such natural inclination, such individuality, in the early stages of child life, since we learn most easily the things which conform to it. It is not, I believe, a vain thing to try and infer from the face and bearing of a boy what disposition he will show. Nature has not omitted to give us marks for our guidance in this respect. Aristotle wrote a work on physiognomy; and Vergil bids us recognise the differences which distinguish one type of cattle from another in regard to the uses to which we may put them. However, I am personally of opinion that where the method is sound, where teaching and practice go hand in hand, any discipline may ordinarily be acquired by the flexible intellect of man. What, indeed, should be beyond his powers when, as we are told, an elephant has been trained to walk a tightrope?

Conclusion

Now I have done. I make my appeal to that practical wisdom which you have always exhibited in affairs. Consider how dear a possession is your son; how many-sided is learning; how exacting its pursuit, and how honourable! Think how instinctive is the child's wish to learn, how plastic his mind, how responsive to judicious training, if only he be entrusted to instructors at once sympathetic and skilled to ease the first steps in knowledge. Let me recall to you the durability of early impressions, made upon the unformed mind, as compared with those acquired in later life. You know also how hard it is to overtake time lost; how wise, in all things, to begin our tasks in season; how great is the power of persistence in accumulating what we prize; how fleeting a thing is the life of man, how busy is youth, how inapt for learning is age. In face, then, of all these serious facts you will not suffer, I do not say seven years, but three days even, of your son's life to pass, before you take into earnest consideration his nurture and future education.

VIVES ON DIFFERENCES AMONG STUDENTS (1531)   From Foster Watson, ed. and trans., *Vives: On Education, A Translation of the* De Trandendis Disciplinis *of Juan Luis Vives* (Cambridge, Mass., 1913), pp. 72-80.

Let a school be established in every township, and let there be received into it as teachers men who are of ascertained learning, uprightness and prudence. Let their salary be paid to them from the public treasury. Let boys and youths learn from these men those arts which are suited to their age and tastes; but let their training for service to their country and their whole education in civil life be given by wise old men, as formerly at Rome. For, as it is recorded by Plutarch in his *Problems*, "the ancients considered it an honourable thing to educate their relatives and friends." If any youths, on account of alertness of wit and goodness, are quick at their studies, when the transition stage from boyhood to youth has been reached, when their minds are now strengthened by right opinions about affairs, and are now prepared and fortified, let these be sent under auspicious circumstances to the Academy. And if anyone is sent earlier, because it is thought that he cannot be conveniently taught at home, let him go with a tutor whom he can reverence as his father; on the other hand, let the tutor show himself worthy of reverence by his practical wisdom and ability, and worthy of love by his kindness, but let him beware above all, to the utmost of his power, not to bring upon himself the dislike of his charge. Now let us go on to speak about the instruction itself.

When a boy is taken to school, let the father know what he ought to consider as the fruit of studious labour; surely, not honour or money, but the culture of the mind—a thing of exceeding great and incomparable value—that the youth may become more learned and more virtuous through sound teaching. Therefore if he brought with him to the school any baser idea, let him return home persuaded that he now expects higher and greater things of his son. Let the boy be taken under the condition that he is to be tried for some months; for when this is done in the case of men-servants and women-servants, and those who place plates and dishes on the table, how absurd it is that it should not be done in the case of those who can only become learned at so much greater cost both to themselves and others. In determining the instruction to be given to each person, the disposition is to be regarded; the close consideration of this subject belongs to psychological inquiry. I will therefore borrow some remarks from the treatise I have written on this subject (*de Anima*). Natural powers of the mind are: sharpness in observing, capacity for comprehending, power in comparing and judging. . . .

Some scholars find the first beginnings of things easy but soon are perplexed, over whose mental eye, as it were, a kind of mist spreads while they are working, which was not present when they came new and fresh to the work. Others, eager and strong, most happily continue steadfastly. Some accept as joined those things which they see together; some analyse things into their separate parts by a close examination, which is called subtlety. There are some who at the right moment, by their concentration, strike at the root of things, hasten on through many fields of knowledge and do not stop to rest; others linger and, as it were, leave their footprints behind. There are some, free and unrestrained, who quickly pursue what they want, e.g. men of well-balanced powers, whose minds are endowed with such vigour that they see at a glance through everything needed, and have it ready to hand, . . .

As to mental material (or content), some persons are exceedingly clever in things which are done by the hands. . . . Such boys you always see painting, building, weaving, and they do all these things so well, and with such great pleasure that you would think they had learnt them a long time. Others are devoted to the more sublime matters of judgment and reason, incited by a greater and higher mental impulse, and from their boyhood they perform those manual arts ineptly, yet they understand already every word which they hear, and promptly and quickly discover the reason for a thing. A very few are good at both activities, though there are some of this kind. Some are suited to a particular branch of learning, e.g. poets who find themselves embarrassed in attempting fluent prose. I have known men who could narrate most wittily, yet in their reasoning were most absurd. Of rare quality are those who are equally capable in all the material of the mind, not only in hand-activities, but also in those which require a special intellectual activity; Plutarch has shown that the mind of Cicero was of this quality.

✳   ✳   ✳

Morals also change the natural disposition in many ways, for the constitution of the body has a great influence on the strength of the mind and it is from the body that the passions take their rise. But the ground of morals is twofold, for they spring either from the nature of the body or from habit. Some have easily aroused feelings, others more tranquil ones; and in the latter, all affections, as it were by turns, rule and then have their fling. In the original feelings arising from the constitution of the body some are inclined to what is good, others to evil. In some men, certain feelings occupy the kingdom of the whole mind to such a degree that they drag to themselves everything that enters the mind. Just as when the stomach is diseased it turns whatever comes into it into noxious humours, so those minds which are ashamed to learn in the presence of witnesses are twisted aside to pride, arrogance or ostentation. Wisely did Bion say that Pride is an impediment to great achievements. Such students give way to lust or evil desires, or to depraved ideas or sinister interpretations. Some have minds partly right, but suddenly a feeling rises up unexpectedly which lays its hand upon them and compels them to turn from the right way. Some are simple, upright, good; some crafty and crooked; some who constantly hide themselves; some who, on the contrary, always push themselves forward. With some minds, fear only effects anything; with others, kindness. Some minds are sensible, sober and temperate; others insane and furious, and this either habitually or at intervals. Some are gentle, others fierce and eager; some even are of an unbridled nature. Some sustain the movements of their minds by just and great undertakings, and these we call manly; others by slight enterprises or none at all, and are turned aside by a slight whiff of air: these are called childish and fickle. O admirable Author of such great variety! Thou Who alone hast created these conditions of mind, alone knowest the causes. There are indeed other differences of minds, but this treatment suffices for the present.

VIVES ON THE INSTRUCTION OF WOMEN (1540) From *The Instruction of a Christian Woman,* as quoted in Foster Watson, ed., *Vives and the Renascence Education of Women* (London, 1912), pp. 32-38.

The Preface of the Most Famous Clerk Maister Ludovic Vives, upon his Book, called the Instruction of a Christian Woman, unto the Most Gracious Princess, Catharine Queen of England.

I have been moved partly by the holiness and goodness of your living, partly by the favour, love and zeal that your Grace beareth toward holy study and learning, to write some thing unto your good grace, of the information and bringing up of a Christian woman: a matter never yet entreated of any man, among so great plenty and variety of wits and writers. For Xenophon and Aristotle, giving rules of housekeeping, and Plato making precepts of ordering the common weal, spake many things appertaining unto the woman's office and duty: and S. Cyprian, S. Hierome (Jerome), S. Ambrose, and S. Augustine, have entreated of Maids and Widows, but in such wise, that they appear rather to exhort and counsel them unto some kind of living, than to instruct and teach them. They spend all their speech in the lauds and praises of chastity, which is a goodly thing, and fitted for those great witted and holy men: how be it they write but few precepts and rules how to live: supposing it to be better, to exhort them unto the best, and help them up to the highest, than to inform and teach the lower things.

But I will let pass all such exhortations because everybody shall pick out the ways of living, out of these men's authority, rather than of my fantasy: and I will compile rules of living. Therefore in the first book, I will begin at the beginning of a woman's life, and lead her forth unto the time of marriage. In the second from marriage unto widowhood, how she ought to pass the time of her life well and virtuously with her husband. In the last book, I inform and teach the widowhood. And because the matter could not be otherwise handled, there be many things told in the first book, pertaining unto wives and widows: and much in the second, belonging unto unmarried women: and some in the third pertaining unto all, lest a maid should think that she need to read but only the first book, or a wife the second, or a widow the third. I will that every of them shall read all. In which I have been more short than many would I should have been. Notwithstanding, who so considereth well the cause of mine intent, and taketh good heed shall find it done not without skill. For in giving precepts, a man ought specially to be brief, lest he sooner dull the wits of the readers, than teach them with long babbling. And precepts ought to be such, that every body may soon con them, and bear [them] easily in mind. Nor we should not be ignorant of the laws that Christ and his disciples, Peter, Paul, James, John and Jude taught us: where we may see that they give us the divine precepts brief and shortly. For who can bear in remembrance those laws, which they bear not well in mind, that have spent their whole life in study of them? And therefore have I neither thrust in many examples, nor gone out of my matter to entreat generally of vice and virtue, which were a large field to walk in, to the end that my book might be not onely read without tediousness: but also be read often. Moreover, though the precepts for men be innumerable: women yet may be informed with few words. For men must be occupied both at home and abroad, both in their own matters and for the common weal. Therefore it cannot be declared in few books, but in many and long, how they shall handle themselves, in so many and divers things. As for a woman, she hath no charge to see to, but her honesty and chastity. Wherefore when she is informed of that, she is sufficiently appointed. Wherefore their wickedness is the more cursed and detestable, that go about to perish that one treasure of women: as though a man had but one eye, and another would go about to put it out. Some write filthy and bawdy rimes, which men I cannot see what honest excuse they can lay for themselves; but that their corrupt mind swelled with poison, can breathe none other thing but venom, to destroy them that are near unto it. But they call themselves lovers, and I believe they be so indeed: yea, and blind and mad, too, withal. And though thou love, canst thou not obtain thine own, except thou infect all other[s]?

Therefore in my mind no man was ever banished more rightfully than was Ovid, at leastwise, if he was banished for writing the Craft of Love. For other[s] write wanton and naughty ballads, but this worshipful Artificer, must make rules in God's name, and precepts of his unthriftiness, a Schoolmaister of bawdry, and a common corrupter of virtue. Now I doubt not but some will think my precepts over sore and sharp. Howbeit, the nature of all things is such that the way of virtue is easy and large unto good men, and the way of vice contrary, strait and rough. But unto ill men, neither the way that they go in is pleasant, nor the way of virtue large and easy enough: and seeing it is so, it is better to assent unto good men than ill: and rather to reckon the bad folks' opinion false, than the good men's. Pythagoras the philosopher and other of his school, in the description of this letter Y. say, that when a man is past the first difficulty of virtue, all after is easy and plain.

Plato giveth counsel to choose the best way in living: which way, use and custom shall also make pleasant. Our Lord in the Gospel saith, that the way into the kingdom of heaven is strait, not because it is so indeed, but because few go it, except a man would count his words false, when he saith: My yoke is sweet, and my burthen light. Or else where he promiseth, that there is no man that forgoeth any thing for his sake, but he shall have far more for it again: yea, and that in this life. And what was meant thereby, but the pleasures of virtue? Therefore I see unto whom my precepts shall seem rigorous and sharp: that is, to young men that be ignorant, wanton and unthrifty: which cannot once bear the sight of a good woman.

It is no news, that ill folk hate them that advise them well. St. Jerome writeth of himself unto the holy maid Demetrias in this wise: "More than thirty years ago, I wrote a book *Of Virginity*, in the which I must needs speak against vice, and patefy the traps of the devil for the instruction of the maid that I taught, the which writing may be agrieved withal: when every one taketh the matter, as said by himself, and will not hear me, as an exhorter and counsellor; but loatheth me as an accuser and rebuker of his doing." Thus saith he: "Lo, what manner of men we shall displease with teaching them virtuously. Verily such as it were a shame and rebuke to please: but sad men, chaste maids, virtuous wives, wise widows, and finally, all that are true Christian people, not only in name but also in deed and with their hearts, will stand on our part: which know and agree all in this, that nothing can be more mild and gentle than the precepts of our Faith, from the which Christ grant us never to decline our mind and purpose, one hair's breadth." I have put in remembrance of their duty the good and holy women, but slightly: other[s] now and then, I take up sharply: because I saw that onely teaching availeth but a little, unto those that struggle with the Leader, and must be drawn. Therefore have I spoken sometime the more plainly, that they might see the filthiness of their conditions (as it were) painted in a table, to the intent that they should be ashamed, and at last, leave their shameful deeds. And also that good women should be gladder to see themselves out of those vices, and labour more to be further from them, and to enter into the habitacle [? tabernacle] of virtue. For I had leaver as S. Jerome counselleth, adventure my shamefastness a little while, than jeopard my matter: so yet that I would not fall into any uncleanliness, which were the greatest shame that can be for him that should be a teacher of chastity: wherefore oftentimes the reader must understand more in sentence, than I speak in words. And this work (most excellent and gracious Queen) I offer unto you in like manner, as if a painter would bring unto you your own visage and image, most cunningly painted. For like as in that portraiture you might see your bodily similitude: so in these books shall you see the resemblance of your mind and goodness; because that you have been both maid, wife and widow, and so you have been handled yourself in all the order and course of your life, that whatsoever you did might be an example unto other to live after. But you had leaver the virtues to be praised, than yourself: howbeit no man can praise the virtues of women, but he must needs comprehend you in the same praise, howbeit your mind ought to be obeyed. Therefore you shall understand, that many like unto you be praised here by name expressly: but yourself spoken of continually, though you be not named. For virtues can never be praised, but they must needs be praised withal, that be excellent in them, though their name be not spoken of. Also your dearest daughter Mary, shall read these instructions of mine, and follow in living. Which she must needs do, if she order herself after the example that she hath at home with her, of your virtue and wisdom. Nor there is no doubt, but she will do after them, and except she alone of all other, disappoint and beguile every man's opinion, she must needs be both very good and holy, that is come of you, and noble King Henry the Eight[h], such a couple of mates, that your honour and virtue pass all crafts of praising. Therefore all other women shall have an example of your life and deeds: and by these books that I have dedicated unto your name, they shall have rules and precepts to live by: and so shall they be bounden unto your goodness, both for that, which itself hath done in giving example: and that it hath been the occasion of my writing. And so I pray God give your good Grace long well to fare.

CASTIGLIONE DEPICTS THE EDUCATION OF A COURTIER (1561) From Castiglione, *The Book of the Courtier,* Ernest Rhys, trans. (London, 1928), pp. 15-21.

The First Booke of the Courtier of Counte Baldesser Castilio, unto Maister Alfonsus Ariosto.

I have a long time douted with my self (moste loving M. Alphonsus) whiche of the two were harder for me, either to denie you the thing that you have with such instance many times required of me, or to take it in hand: because on the one side mee thought it a verie hard matter to denie any thing, especially the request being honest, to the person whom I love dearely, and of whom I perceive my selfe dearly beloved. Againe, on the other side, to undertake an enterprise which I doe not know my selfe able to bring to an ende, I judged it uncomly for him that weyeth due reproofes so much as they ought to bee weyed.

At length, after much debating, I have determined to proove in this behalfe, what ayde that affection and great desire to please can bring unto my diligence, which in other things is woont to encrease the labour of men.

You then require me to write, (what is to my thinking) the trade and maner of courtiers, which is most convenient for a gentleman that liveth in the Court of Princes, by the which he may have the knowledge how to serve them perfitely in every fasonable matter, and obtaine therby favour of them, and praise of other men.

Finally of what sort hee ought to bee that deserveth to be called so perfit a Courtier, that there be no want in him:

Wherefore I considering this kinde of request (say) that in case it shoulde not appeare to my selfe a greater blame, to have you esteeme me to be of small friendship, than all other men of little wisdom, I would have ridde my hands of this labour, for feare least I should be counted rash of al such as knowe, what a hard matter it is, among such diversitie of maners, that are used in the Courts of Christendome, to picke out the perfectest trade and way, and (as it were) the floure of this Courtiership. Bicause use maketh us many times to delite in, and to set little by the selfe same things: whereby sometime it proceedeth that maners, garments, customes, and fashions, which at somtime have ben in price, become not regarded, and contrariwise, the not regarded, become of price.

Therefore it is manifestly to be discerned, that use hath greater force than reason, to bring up new inventions among us, and to abolish the olde, of the which who so goeth about to judge the perfection, is oftentimes deceived.

For which consideration, perceiving this and many other lettes, in the matter propounded for me to write upon, I am constreined to make a peece of an excuse, and to open plainely that this error (if it may be termed an errour) is common to us both, that if any blame happen to me about it, it may be partned with you. For it ought to bee reckned a no lesse offence in you, to lay upon me a burthen that passeth my strength, than in me to take it upon me.

Let us therefore at length settle our selves to beginne that that is our purpose and drift, and (if be it possible) let us fashion such a Courtier, as the Prince that shall be worthie to have him in his service, although his state be but small, may notwithstanding be called a mighty Lord.

We wil not in these books follow any certaine order or rule of appointed preceptes, the which for the most part is woont to bee observed in teaching of any thing whatsoever it bee: But after the manner of men of olde time, renuing a gratefull memorie: we will repeate certaine reasonings that were debated in times past, betweene men very excellent for that purpose. And although I was not there present, but at the time when they were debated, it was my chaunce to be in Englande, yet soone after my returne, I heard them of a person that faithfully reported them unto me. And I will endevour my selfe, for so much as my memory will serve me, to call them particularly to remembrance, that you may see, what men worthy great commendation, and unto whose judgement a man may in every point give an undoubted credite, have judged and beleeved in this matter.

Neither shall we swarve from the purpose to arrive in good order at the ende, unto the which all our communication is directed, if we disclose the cause of the reasonings that hereafter follow. As every man knoweth, the little Citie of Urbin is situated upon the side of the Appennine (in a manner) in the middes of Italy, towards the Goulfe of Venice. The which for all it is placed among hilles, and those not so pleasant as perhappes some other that we behold in many places, yet in this point the Element hath beene favourable unto it, that all about, the Countrey is verie plentifull and full of fruites: so that beside the holesomnes of ayre, it is verie aboundant and stored with all thinges necessarie for the life of man. But among the greatest felicities that man can reckon to have, I count this the chiefe, that now a long time it hath alwaies bene governed with very good princes, in the common calamities of the wars of Italie it remained also a season without any at all.

But without searching further of this, we may make a good proofe with the famous memorie of Duke Fridericke, who in his daies was the light of Italy. Neither do wee want true and very large testimonies yet remaning of his wisedome, courtesie, justice, liberalitie, of his invincible courage and policy of warre. And of this doe his so manye victories make proofe, chiefly his conquering of places impugnable, so sodaine readines in setting forward to give battaile, his putting to flight sundrie times with a small number, very great and puissant armies, and never sustained losse in anye conflict. So that we may, not without cause, compare him to many famous men of olde time.

This man among his other deedes praise-worthie, in the hard and sharpe situation of Urbin buylt a Palace, to the opinion of many men, the fairest that was to bee found in all Italie and so furnished it with all necessarie implementes belonging thereto, that it appeared not a Palace, but a Citie in forme of a Palace, and that not onelye with ordinarye matters, as Silver plate, hangings for Chambers of very rich cloth of Golde, of Silke and other like, but also for sightlines: and to decke it out withall, placed there a wondrous number of auncient Images, of Marble and Mettall, very excellent paintings and Instruments of Musicke of all sortes, and nothing would he have there but what was most rare and excellent.

To this with verie great charges hee gathered together a great number of most excellent and rare bookes, in Greeke, Latin, and Hebrue, the which all hee garnished with gold and silver, esteeming this to be the chiefest ornament of his great Palace.

This Duke then following the course of nature, when he was threescore and five yeares of age, as he had lived, so did he end his lyfe with glorie. And left Duke after him a child of ten yeres having no more male, and without mother, who hight Guidubaldo.

This childe, as of the state, so did it appeare also that he was heire of all his fathers vertues: and sodainly with a marveilous towardnes, began to promise so much of himselfe, as a man would not have thought possible to bee hoped of a man mortall. So that the opinion of men was, that of all Duke Frederickes notable deedes, there was none greater than that he begat such a sonn. But fortune envying this so great vertue, with all her might gainstood this so glorious a beginning, in such wise that before Duke Guidubaldo was xx. yeares of age, he fell sicke of the goute, the which encreasing upon him with most bitter paines, in a short time so nummed him of all his members, that hee coulde neither stand on foote, nor move himselfe. And in this manner was one of the best favoured, and towardliest personages in the world, deformed and marred in his greene age. And beside, not satisfied with this, fortune was so contrarie to him in al his purposes, that verye seldome he brought to passe any thing to his mind. And for all hee had in him most wise counsaile and an invincible courage, yet it seemed that whatsoever he tooke in hand, both in feats of armes, and in everye other thing small or great, it came alwaies to ill sucesse.

And of this make proofe his manye and diverse calamities, which hee alwaies bare out with such stoutnesse of courage, that vertue never yeelded to fortune. But with a bold stomacke despising her stormes, lived with great dignitie and estimation among all men: in sicknesse, as one that was sounde, and in adversitie, as one that was most fortunate. So that for all hee was thus diseased in his bodie he served in time of warre with most honourable entertainement under the most famous kings of Naples, Alphonsus and Ferdinande the yonger. Afterward with Pope Alexander the sixt, with the Lordes of Venice and Florence.

And when Julius the second was created Pope, hee was then made General Capitaine of the Church: at which time proceeding in his accustomed usage, hee set his delight above all thinges to have his house furnished with most noble and valiant Gentlemen, with whom hee lived verie familiarly, enjoying their conversation.

Wherein the pleasure which hee gave unto other men was no lesse, than that he received of other, because hee was verie well seene in both toongs, and togither with a loving behaviour and pleasantnesse hee had also accompanied the knowledge of infinite things. And beside this, the greatnesse of his courage so quickned him, that where hee was not in case with his person to practise the feates of Chivalrie, as he had done long before, yet did he take verie great delight to beholde them in other men, and with his wordes sometime correcting, and otherwhile praising every man according to his deserts, he declared evidently how great a judgement hee had in those matters.

And upon this at Tilt, at Tourney, in playing at all sorts of weapon, also in inventing devices in pastimes, in Musicke, finally in all exercises meete for noble Gentlemen, every man strived to shew himselfe such a one, as might deserve to bee judged worthie of so noble assembly.

Therefore were all the houres of the day divided into honourable and pleasant exercises, as well of the bodie, as of the minde. But because the Duke used continually, by reason of his infirmitie, soone after Supper to goe to his rest, everie man ordinarily, at that houre drew where the Dutchesse was, the Ladie Elizabeth Gonzaga, where also continually was the Ladie Emilia Pia, who for that shee was indued with so lively a wit and judgement, as you know, seemed the maistresse and ringleader of all the company, and that everie man at her received understanding and courage.

There was then to bee heard pleasant communications and merie conceites, and in everie mans countenance a man might perceive painted a loving jocundnesse. So that this house truely might wel be called the very Mansion place of mirth and joy. And I beleeve it was never so tasted in other place, what manner a thing the sweete conversation is that is occasioned of an amiable and loving company, as it was once there.

For leaving apart what honour it was to all us to serve such a Lorde, as hee whom I declared unto you right now, everye man conceived in his minde an high contentation every time we came into the Dutchesse sight. And it appeared that this was a chaine that kept all linked together in love, in such wise that there was never agreement of wil or hartie love greater betweene brethren, than there was betweene us all.

The like was betweene the woman, with whom we had such free and honest conversation, that everye man might commune, sitte, dallye, and laugh with whom hee had lusted.

But such was the respect which we bore to the Dutchesse will, that the selfe same libertie was a very great bridle. Neither was there any that thought it not the greatest pleasure he could have in the world, to please her, and the greatest griefe to offend her.

For this respect were there most honest conditions coupled with wondrous great libertie, and devises of pastimes, and laughing matters tempred in her sight, beside most witty jestes, with so comely and grave a Majestie, that the verye sober moode and greatnes that did knit together all the actes, woordes and gestures of the

Dutchesse in jesting and laughing, made them all that had never seene her in their lyfe before, to count her a verie great Ladie.

And all that came in her presence, having this respect fixed in their breast, it seemed shee had made them to her becke.

So that everie man enforced himselfe to followe this trade, taking (as it were) a rule and ensample of faire conditions at the presence of so great and so vertuous a Ladie. Whose most excellent qualities I entend not now to expresse, for it is neither my purpose, and againe they are well ynough knowne to the world, and much better than I am able either with tongue, or with pen to indite.

And such as would perhaps have lien hid a space, fortune, as shee that wondreth at so rare vertues, hath thought good with manye adversities and temptations of miseries to disclose them, to make triall thereby that in the tender breast of a woman, in companie with singular beautie, there can dwel wisedome, and stoutnes of courage and all other vertues that in grave men themselves are most seldome.

But leaving this apart, I say that the maner of the gentlemen in the house was immediately after supper to assemble together where the Dutchesse was. Where among other recreations, musicke and dauncing, which they used continually, sometime they propounded feate questions, otherwhile they invented certayne wittye sportes and pastimes at the device sometime of one sometime of another, in the which under sundry coverts oftentimes the standers by opened subtilly their immaginations unto whome they thought best.

At other times there arose other disputations of divers matters, or else jeastings with prompt inventions. Many times they fell into purposes, (as we now a daies terme them) where in this kinde of talke and debating of matters, there was wonderous great pleasure on al sides: Because (as I have said) the house was replenished with most noble wittes.

MONTAIGNE ON THE EDUCATION OF CHILDREN (1580)   From *Of the Education of Children,* as quoted in *The Essays of Montaigne,* George B. Ives, trans. (Cambridge, Mass., 1925), pp. 199-201, 205-06, 213-15, 219-21.

Some one who had read the preceding pages said to me the other day, at my house, that I ought to have enlarged a little on the subject of the education of children. Well, madame, if I have any competence on that subject, I can make no better use of it than to make a present of it to the little man who threatens soon to make a happy exit from you (you are too noble by nature to begin otherwise than with a boy); for, having had so large a part in the arrangement of your marriage, I have some right and interest in the greatness and prosperity of all that comes from it; besides that, the long-standing claim that you have upon my service well constrains me to desire honour, good, and profit for whatever concerns you. But, really, I know nothing of this matter except that the greatest and most weighty difficulty in human knowledge seems to lie at that point where it deals with the nurture and education of children. Just as in agriculture the methods that precede planting are certain and easy, and the same with planting itself; but after what is planted has taken on life, there is a great variety of methods, and much difficulty in raising it; in like manner with men, there is little skill in planting them, but after they are born, we have a varied burden, full of toil and anxiety, in training and nurturing them. The display of their inclinations is so slight and so obscure at that tender age, the promises so uncertain and so deceitful, that it is difficult to base on them sure judgements. Look at Cymon, look at Themistocles, and a thousand others, how inconsistent they were with themselves. The young of bears and dogs show their native inclination; but men, being cast forthwith into the midst of usages, opinions, and laws, are easily changed or disguised. Yet it is hard to overcome the natural propensities; whence it happens that, for lack of having fitly chosen their path, we often labour to no purpose, and employ much of our life in training children to things in which they can not find a footing. Howbeit, in this difficulty my judgement is to direct them always to the best and most profitable things, and that we should pay little heed to the slight conjectures and prognostications that we derive from the impulses of their childhood. Plato even, in his Republic, seems to me to give them too much authority.

Learning is a noble adornment, madame, and a marvellously useful tool, notably to persons raised to such a degree of fortune as you are. In fact, it is of no true use in mean and low hands. It is much more proud to lend its resources to conduct a war, to rule a people, to cultivate the friendship of a prince or a foreign nation, than to draft a dialectical argument, or to argue an appeal, or concoct a mixture for pills. And so, madame, because I believe that you will not forget this portion of the education of your children, you who have tasted its delights and who are of a lettered race,—for we have still the writings of those former Comtes de Foix from whom monsieur le comte, your husband, and you are both descended; and François, Monsieur de Candale, your uncle, gives birth every day to other writings which will extend the knowledge of this quality of your family to many ages,—I desire to tell you of one single idea of mine regarding this, which is contrary to the common wont; it is all that I can offer for your service in this matter.

The office of the tutor whom you will give him—upon the choice of whom the whole result of his education depends—has many other important duties; but I do not touch on those, because I am unable to contribute there any thing of value; and upon this one point, about which I take upon myself to give him advice, he will believe me so far as he shall see reason so to do. For a child of good family, who seeks letters and learning, not for profit (for so base an object is unworthy of the grace and favour of the Muses, and, too, it concerns and depends upon others), and not so much for external benefits as for those peculiar to himself, and to enrich and adorn himself inwardly, being desirous to turn out a man of ability rather than a learned man, I should wish, moreover, that care should be taken to select a guide whose head is very sound rather than very full; and that, while both qualities should be required, good morals and understanding, rather than book-knowledge, should be the more so; and that he should carry himself in his office in a novel way. They are always bawling into our ears as if pouring into a tunnel; and our business is simply to repeat what they tell us. I would have him amend this state of things, and that from the outset, according to the ability of the mind he has to deal with, he should begin to exercise it, making it examine things, choose among them, and distinguish them by itself; sometimes breaking out the path for it, sometimes letting it break it out. I would not have him alone think and speak: I would have him listen while his pupil takes his turn at speaking.

Now, in this study, all that presents itself to our eyes serves as a book to learn from: the mischief of a page, the stupidity of a servant, a remark at table, are so many new subjects.

For this reason, intercourse with men is wonderfully proper for it, and travel in foreign countries, not simply to bring back, after the manner of our French nobility, the number of feet of the Santa Rotonda, or the elegance of Signora Livia's drawers; or, like others, how much longer or broader the face of Nero is in some old ruin, than it is on some equally old coin; but chiefly to bring back the characteristics of those nations and their manner of living, and to rub and file our wits against those of others. I would have him begin to be taken about in his tender years, and especially, to kill two birds with one stone, among the neighbouring nations whose languages are most unlike ours, to which the tongue can not be wonted unless you train it in good season. And also, it is an opinion accepted by every one that it is not well to bring up a child in the lap of his parents: their natural affection softens and relaxes them too much, even the wisest; they are capable neither of punishing his faults nor of allowing him to be nurtured roughly, as he should be, and at haphazard; they could not endure his returning sweating and dusty from his exercises, taking hot or cold drinks, or to see him on a restive horse, or facing a skilful fencer, foil in hand, or his first arquebus. But there is no escape: he who would make of him a man of worth must doubtless not spare him in those early years, and must often run counter to the rules of medicine.

It is not enough to strengthen his mind—we must strengthen his muscles also. The mind is too hard pressed if it be not supported, and has too much to do to discharge alone two functions. I know how mine labours in company with so tender, so sensitive a body, which lets itself so greatly depend upon it; and I often observe in my reading that my masters, in their writings, pass off as due to magnanimity and high spirit, examples which usually belong more to thickness of skin and hardness of bone. I have seen men, women, and children of such nature that a flogging is less to them than a fillip to me; who neither cry out nor scowl under the blows that are given to them. When athletes are like philosophers in patience, it is strength of nerve rather than of mind. Now, accustomedness to labour is accustomedness to pain. . . . He must be practised in the discomfort and severity of action, to train him for the discomfort and severity of dislocation, of the colic, of the cautery, and of prison, and of torture. For even he may fall into the clutches of these last, which, according to the times, seize upon good men as well as bad. We are experiencing this. He who rebels against the laws renders the best men liable to whippings and the rope.

✳   ✳   ✳

Among the liberal arts, let us begin with the art that liberates us. They all help somewhat in the instruction of our life and in its employment, as all other things help somewhat. But let us choose that one which helps directly and professedly. If we could confine the appurtenances of our lives within their due and natural limits, we should find that the greater number of the branches of knowledge that are in use are outside of our use, and that even in those which are [adapted to our use] there are breadths and depths which we should do well to let alone, and, following the teaching of Socrates, limit our course of study in those branches where usefulness is lacking.

After he has been taught what helps to make him wiser and better, then let his tutor enlighten him as to what logic is, and physics, and geometry, and rhetoric; and the branch of learning that he shall choose when his judgement is formed, he will very soon master. Let his lesson be given sometimes by talk, sometimes by books; sometimes his tutor will supply him with the very author suitable for that part of his instruction; sometimes he will give him the marrow and substance of the book all prepared. And if he be not himself sufficiently familiar with books to find in them the many admirable passages they contain fit for his purpose, some man of letters can be joined with him, who, whenever there is need, can supply him with such provisions as he may require, to deal out and dispense to his nursling. And who can doubt that this method of instruction is easier and more natural than that of Gaza? In that are thorny and disagreeable precepts and idle and bloodless words, in which there is nothing to catch hold of, nothing that awakens the mind. In this other method the mind finds a place to browse and to pasture on. This fruit is incomparably greater, and yet it will be sooner ripe.

*   *   *

For all that, I would not have the boy confined. I would not have him given over to the brooding melancholy of a passionate schoolmaster. I would not spoil his mind by keeping it in torture and at work, as others do, fourteen or fifteen hours a day, like a porter. Nor should I think it well, if, from an unsocial and pensive disposition, he were addicted to an unwise application to the study of books, that he should be encouraged therein; it unfits boys for social intercourse and diverts them from better occupations. And how many men have I seen in my time, stultified by a reckless greediness of learning! Carneades was so besotted with it that he had no time to attend to his hair and his nails. Nor would I have his good manners spoilt by others' clownishness and rudeness. French discretion was long ago proverbial as a discretion which took root early but had little hold. In truth, we still see that there is nothing so charming as the young French children; but commonly they disappoint the hopes conceived of them, and as grown men, no excellence is seen in them. I have heard it maintained by men of understanding that it is these schools to which they are sent, of which there are so many, that brutify them thus.

To our pupil, a closet, a garden, table and bed, solitude, company, morning and evening—all hours will be alike to him, every place his study: for philosophy, which, as the moulder of opinions and manners, will be his principal lesson, has this privilege of entering into every thing. Isocrates the orator being urged at a banquet to talk about his art, every one thought he was right in replying: "It is not the time now for what I can do; and I can not do that for which it is now the time." For to offer harangues or rhetorical discussions to a company assembled for merry-making and feasting would be too discordant a combination; and one might say as much of all the other kinds of learning. But, as for philosophy, in those parts where she treats of man, and of his duties and functions, it has been the universal opinion of all wise men that the charm of her conversation is such that she should not be denied admission to either banquets or games; and Plato, having bidden her to his Banquet, we see how she discourses to the company in a pleasant fashion, adapted to the time and place, although it is one of his loftiest and most salutary treatises.

*   *   *

Thus, doubtless, he will have not so many holidays as the others; but as the steps that we take in walking in a gallery tire us less, although there may be three times as many, than those we take on some highway, so our lessons, coming about as if by accident, without set obligation of time and place, and being mingled with all our acts, will flow on without making themselves felt. Even games and bodily exercises will be a part of his study: running, wrestling, music, dancing, hunting, the management of horses and the use of weapons. I would have his exterior agreeableness and social demeanour and his personal bearing shape themselves at the same time with his inner being. It is not a spirit, it is not a body that we are training: it is a man; we must not separate them. And, as Plato says, we must not train one of them without the other, but drive them side by side, like a pair of horses fastened to the same pole. And, listening to him, does he not seem to allot more time and care to the exercises of the body, and to judge that the mind may be exercised at the same time, and not the opposite? Meanwhile, this instruction should be carried on with grave gentleness, not as it is. Instead of inviting children to study, they bring them, in truth, nothing but fear and cruelty. Away with violence and compulsion; there is nothing, in my opinion, which so debases and stupefies a well-born nature. If you wish him to fear disgrace and punishment, do not harden him to them; harden him to sweat and cold, to the wind, to the sun, and to the chances which he ought to despise; take from him all sensitiveness and fastidious-ness about his clothing and his bed, about eating and drinking; accustom him to every thing; let him not be a pretty boy and effeminate, but sturdy and vigorous. In youth, in middle age, and in old age, I have always believed and thought this. But, among other things, this method of government of the greater part of our schools has always offended me. Failure would perchance be less harmful in the direction of indulgence. They are veritable prisons.

The Reformations

LUTHER ON THE ESTABLISHMENT OF SCHOOLS IN GERMANY
(**1524**)   From F.V.N. Painter, ed., *Luther on Education* (Philadelphia, 1899), pp. 169-71, 179-88, 206-09.

Letter to the Mayors and Aldermen
of All the Cities of Germany
in Behalf of Christian Schools

Grace and peace from God our Father and the Lord Jesus Christ. Honored and dear Sirs: Having three years ago been put under the ban and outlawed, I should have kept silent, had I regarded the command of men more than that of God. Many persons in Germany both of high and low estate assail my discourses and writings on that account, and shed much blood over them. But God who has opened my mouth and bidden me speak, stands firmly by me, and without any counsel or effort of mine strengthens and extends my cause the more, the more they rage, and seems, as the second Psalm says, to "have them in derision." By this alone any one not blinded by prejudice may see that the work is of God; for it exhibits the divine method, according to which God's cause spreads most rapidly when men exert themselves most to oppose and suppress it. . . .

First of all we see how the schools are deteriorating throughout Germany. The universities are becoming weak, the monasteries are declining, and, as Isaiah says, "The grass withereth, the flower fadeth, because the spirit of the Lord bloweth upon it," through the Gospel. For through the word of God the unchristian and sensual character of these institutions is becoming known. And because selfish parents see that they can no longer place their children upon the bounty of monasteries and cathedrals, they refuse to educate them. "Why should we educate our children," they say, "if they are not to become priests, monks, and nuns, and thus earn a support?"

. . . I beg you all, in the name of God and of our neglected youth, not to think of this subject lightly, as many do who see not what the prince of this world intends. For the right instruction of youth is a matter in which Christ and all the world are concerned. Thereby are we all aided. And consider that great Christian zeal is needed to overcome the silent, secret, and artful machinations of the devil. If we must annually expend large sums on muskets, roads, bridges, dams, and the like, in order that the city may have temporal peace and comfort, why should we not apply as much to our poor, neglected youth, in order that we may have a skillful school-master or two?

There is one consideration that should move every citizen, with devout gratitude to God, to contribute a part of his means to the support of schools—the consideration that if divine grace had not released him from exactions and robbery, he would still have to give large sums of money for indulgences, masses, vigils, endowments, anniversaries, mendicant friars, brotherhoods, and other similar impositions. And let him be sure that where turmoil and strife exist, there the devil is present, who did not writhe and struggle so long as men blindly contributed to convents and masses. For Satan feels that his cause is suffering injury. Let this, then, be the first consideration to move you,—that in this work we are fighting against the devil, the most artful and dangerous enemy of men. . . .

It is indeed a sin and shame that we must be aroused and incited to the duty of educating our children and of considering their highest interests, whereas nature itself should move us thereto, and the example of the heathen affords us varied instruction.

*   *   *

But all that, you say, is addressed to parents; what does it concern the members of the council and the mayors? That is true; but how, if parents neglect it? Who shall attend to it then? Shall we therefore let it alone, and suffer the children to be neglected? How will the mayors and council excuse themselves, and prove that such a duty does not belong to them?

Parents neglect this duty from various causes.

In the first place, there are some who are so lacking in piety and uprightness that they would not do it if they could, but like the ostrich, harden themselves against their own offspring, and do nothing for them. Nevertheless these children must live among us and with us. How then can reason and, above all, Christian charity, suffer them to grow up ill-bred, and to infect other children, till at last the whole city be destroyed, like Sodom, Gomorrah, and some other cities?

In the second place, the great majority of parents are unqualified for it, and do not understand how children should be brought up and taught. For they have learned nothing but to provide for their bodily wants; and in order to teach and train children thoroughly, a separate class is needed.

In the third place, even if parents were qualified and willing to do it themselves, yet on account of other employments and household duties they have no time for it, so that necessity requires us to have teachers for public schools, unless each parent employ a private instructor. But that would be too expensive for persons of ordinary means, and many a bright boy, on account of poverty, would be neglected. Besides, many parents die and leave orphans; and how they are usually cared for by guardians, we might learn, even if observation were not enough, from the sixty-eighth Psalm, where God calls himself the "Father of the fatherless," as of those who are neglected by all others. Also there are some who have no children, and therefore feel no interest in them.

Therefore it will be the duty of the mayors and council to exercise the greatest care over the young. For since the happiness, honor, and life of the city are committed to their hands, they would be held recreant before God and the world, if they did not, day and night, with all their power, seek its welfare and improvement. Now the welfare of a city does not consist alone in great treasures, firm walls, beautiful houses, and munitions of war; indeed, where all these are found, and reckless fools come into power, the city sustains the greater injury. But the highest welfare, safety, and power of a city consists in able, learned, wise, upright, cultivated citizens, who can secure, preserve, and utilize every treasure and advantage. . . .

Since, then, a city must have well-trained people, and since the greatest need, lack, and lament is that such are not to be found, we must not wait till they grow up of themselves; neither can they be hewed out of stones nor cut out of wood; nor will God work miracles, so long as men can attain their object through means within their reach. Therefore we must see to it, and spare no trouble or expense to educate and form them ourselves. For whose fault is it that in all cities there are at present so few skillful people except the rulers, who have allowed the young to grow up like trees in the forest, and have not cared how they were reared and taught? The growth, consequently, has been so irregular that the forest furnishes no timber for building purposes, but like a useless hedge, is good only for fuel.

＊　　＊　　＊

Yet there must be civil government. For us, then, to permit ignoramuses and blockheads to rule when we can prevent it, is irrational and barbarous. Let us rather make rulers out of swine and wolves, and set them over people who are indifferent to the manner in which they are governed. It is barbarous for men to think thus: "We will now rule; and what does it concern us how those fare who shall come after us?" Not over human beings, but over swine and dogs should such people rule, who think only of their own interests and honor in governing. Even if we exercise the greatest care to educate able, learned and skilled rulers, yet much care and effort are necessary in order to secure prosperity. How can a city prosper, when no effort is made?

But, you say again, if we shall and must have schools, what is the use to teach Latin, Greek, Hebrew, and the other liberal arts? Is is not enough to teach the Scriptures, which are necessary to salvation, in the mother tongue? To which I answer: I know, alas! that we Germans must always remain irrational brutes, as we are deservedly called by surrounding nations. But I wonder why we do not also say: of what use to us are silk, wine, spices, and other foreign articles, since we ourselves have an abundance of wine, corn, wool, flax, wood, and stone in the German states, not only for our necessities, but also for embellishment and ornament? The languages and other liberal arts, which are not only harmless, but even a greater ornament, benefit, and honor than these things, both for understanding the Holy Scriptures and carrying on the civil government, we are disposed to despise; and the foreign articles which are neither necessary nor useful, and which besides greatly impoverish us, we are unwilling to dispense with. Are we not rightly called German dunces and brutes?

Indeed, if the languages were of no practical benefit, we ought still to feel an interest in them as a wonderful gift of God, with which he has now blessed Germany almost beyond all other lands. . . .

Therefore, my beloved countrymen, let us open our eyes, thank God for this precious treasure, and take pains to preserve it, and to frustrate the design of Satan. For we cannot deny that, although the Gospel has come and daily comes through the Holy Spirit, it has come by means of other languages, and through them must increase and be preserved. For when God wished through the apostles to spread the

Gospel abroad in all the world, he gave the languages for that purpose; and by means of the Roman empire he made Latin and Greek the language of many lands, that his Gospel might speedily bear fruit far and wide. He has done the same now. For a time no one understood why God had revived the study of the languages; but now we see that it was for the sake of the Gospel, which he wished to bring to light and thereby expose and destroy the reign of Antichrist. For the same reason he gave Greece a prey to the Turks, in order that Greek scholars, driven from home and scattered abroad, might bear the Greek tongue to other countries, and thereby excite an interest in the study of languages.

In the same measure that the Gospel is dear to us, should we zealously cherish the languages. For God had a purpose in giving the Scriptures only in two languages, the Old Testament in the Hebrew, and the New Testament in the Greek. What God did not despise, but chose before all others for His Word, we should likewise esteem above all others. . . .

And let this be kept in mind, that we will not preserve the Gospel without the languages. The languages are the scabbard in which the Word of God is sheathed. They are the casket in which this jewel is enshrined; the cask in which this wine is kept; the chamber in which this food is stored. And, to borrow a figure from the Gospel itself, they are the baskets in which this bread, and fish, and fragments are preserved. If through neglect we lose the languages (which may God forbid), we will not only lose the Gospel, but it will finally come to pass that we will lose also the ability to speak and write either Latin or German. Of this let us take as proof and warning the miserable and shocking example presented in the universities and cloisters, in which not only the Gospel has been perverted, but also the Latin and German languages have been corrupted, so that the wretched inmates have become like brutes, unable to speak and write German or Latin, and have almost lost their natural reason.

The apostles considered it necessary to embody the New Testament in the Greek language, in order, no doubt, that it might be securely preserved unto us as in a sacred shrine. For they foresaw what has since taken place, namely, that when the divine revelation is left to oral tradition, much disorder and confusion arise from conflicting opinions and doctrines. And there would be no way to prevent this evil and to protect the simple-minded, if the New Testament was not definitely recorded in writing. Therefore it is evident that where the languages are not preserved, there the Gospel will become corrupted.

Experience shows this to be true. For immediately after the age of the apostles, when the languages ceased to be cultivated, the Gospel, and the true faith, and Christianity itself, declined more and more, until they were entirely lost under the Pope. And since the time that the languages disappeared, not much that is noteworthy and excellent has been seen in the Church; but through ignorance of the languages very many shocking abominations have arisen. On the other hand, since the revival of learning, such a light has been shed abroad, and such important changes have taken place, that the world is astonished, and must acknowledge that we have the Gospel almost as pure and unadulterated as it was in the times of the apostles, and much purer than it was in the days of St. Jerome and St. Augustine. In a word, since the Holy Ghost, who does nothing foolish or useless, has often bestowed the gift of tongues, it is our evident duty earnestly to cultivate the languages, now that God has restored them to the world through the revival of learning. . . .

So much for the utility and necessity of the languages, and of Christian schools for our spiritual interests and the salvation of the soul. Let us now consider the body and inquire: though there were no soul, nor heaven, nor hell, but only the civil government, would not this require good schools and learned men more than do our spiritual interests?

. . .We know, or ought to know, how necessary and useful a thing it is, and how acceptable to God, when a prince, lord, counsellor, or other ruler, is well-trained and skillful in discharging, in a Christian way, the functions of his office.

Even if there were no soul, (as I have already said,) and men did not need schools and the languages for the sake of Christianity and the Scriptures, still, for the establishment of the best schools everywhere, both for boys and girls, this consideration is of itself sufficient, namely, that society, for the maintenance of civil order and the proper regulation of the household, needs accomplished and well-trained men and women. Now such men are to come from boys, and such women from girls; hence it is necessary that boys and girls be properly taught and brought up. As I have before said, the ordinary man is not qualified for this task, and can not, and will not do it. Princes and lords ought to do it; but they spend their time in pleasure-driving, drinking, and folly, and are burdened with the weighty duties of the cellar, kitchen and bedchamber. And though some would be glad to do it, they must stand in fear of the rest, lest they be taken for fools or heretics. Therefore, honored members of the city councils, this work must remain in your hands; you have more time and better opportunity for it than princes and lords.

But each one, you say, may educate and discipline his own sons and daughters. To which I reply: We see indeed how it goes with this teaching and training. And where it is carried to the highest point, and is attended with success, it results in nothing more than that the learners, in some measure, acquire a forced external propriety of manner; in other respects they remain dunces, knowing nothing, and incapable of giving aid or advice. But were they instructed in schools or elsewhere by thoroughly qualified male or female teachers, who taught the languages, other arts, and history, then the pupils would hear the history and maxims of the world, and see how things went with each city, kingdom, prince, man, and woman; and thus, in a short time, they would be able to comprehend, as in a mirror, the character, life, counsels, undertakings, successes, and failures, of the whole world from the beginning. From this knowledge they could regulate their views, and order their course of life in the fear of God, having become wise in judging what is to be sought and what avoided in this outward life, and capable of advising and directing others. But the training which is given at home is expected to make us wise through our own experience. Before that can take place, we shall die a hundred times, and all through life act injudiciously, for much time is needed to give experience.

Now since the young must leap and jump, or have something to do, because they have a natural desire for it which should not be restrained, (for it is not well to check them in everything,) why should we not provide for them such schools, and lay before them such studies? By the gracious arrangement of God, children take delight in acquiring knowledge, whether languages, mathematics, or history. And our schools are no longer a hell or purgatory, in which children are tortured over cases and tenses, and in which with much flogging, trembling, anguish and wretchedness they learn nothing. If we take so much time and pains to teach our children to play cards, sing, and dance, why should we not take as much time to teach them reading and other branches of knowledge, while they are young and at leisure, are quick at learning, and take delight in it? As for myself, if I had children and were able, I would have them learn not only the languages and history, but also singing, instrumental music, and the whole course of mathematics. For what is all this but mere child's play, in which the Greeks in former ages trained their children, and by this means became wonderfully skillful people, capable for every undertaking? How I regret that I did not read more poetry and history, and that no one taught me in these branches. Instead of these I was obliged with great cost, labor, and injury, to read Satanic filth, the Aristotelian and Scholastic philosophy, so that I have enough to do to get rid of it.

But you say, who can do without his children and bring them up, in this manner, to be young gentlemen? I reply: it is not my idea that we should establish schools as they have been heretofore, where a boy has studied Donatus and Alexander twenty or thirty years, and yet has learned nothing. The world has changed, and things go differently. My idea is that boys should spend an hour or two a day in school, and the rest of the time work at home, learn some trade and do whatever is desired, so that study and work may go on together, while the children are young and can attend to both. They now spend tenfold as much time in shooting with crossbows, playing ball, running, and tumbling about.

In like manner, a girl has time to go to school an hour a day, and yet attend to her work at home; for she sleeps, dances, and plays away more than that. The real difficulty is found alone in the absence of an earnest desire to educate the young, and to aid and benefit mankind with accomplished citizens. The devil much prefers blockheads and drones, that men may have more abundant trials and sorrows in the world.

But the brightest pupils, who give promise of becoming accomplished teachers, preachers, and workers, should be kept longer at school, or set apart wholly for study, as we read of the holy martyrs, who brought up St. Agnes, St. Agatha, St. Lucian, and others. For this purpose also the cloisters and cathedral schools were founded, but they have been perverted into another and accursed use. There is great need for such instruction; for the tonsured crowd is rapidly decreasing, and besides, for the most part, the monks are unskilled to teach and rule, since they know nothing but to care for their stomachs, the only thing they have been taught. Hence we must have persons qualified to dispense the Word of God and the Sacraments, and to be pastors of the people. But where will we obtain them, if schools are not established on a more Christian basis, since those hitherto maintained, even if they do not go down, can produce nothing but depraved and dangerous corrupters of youth?

There is consequently an urgent necessity, not only for the sake of the young, but also for the maintenance of Christianity and of civil government, that this matter be immediately and earnestly taken hold of, lest afterwards, although we would gladly attend to it, we shall find it impossible to do so and be obliged to feel in vain the pangs of remorse forever. . . .

LUTHER ON THE DUTY OF SENDING CHILDREN TO SCHOOL

(1530)   From ''Sermon on the Duty of Sending Children to School,'' as quoted in F.V.N. Painter, ed., *Luther on Education* (Philadelphia, 1899), pp. 215-18, 269-71.

You see plainly how Satan is now attacking us on all sides, both with power and cunning, and brings about every misery, that he may destroy the holy Gospel and the kingdom of God, or, if he can not destroy it, that he may at least hinder it in every way, and prevent its progress and success. Among his various crafty devices, one of the greatest, if not the greatest, is to delude the common people into withholding their children from school and instruction, while he suggests to them such hurtful thoughts as these: "Since there is no hope for the cloisters and priesthood as formerly, we do not need learned men and study, but must consider how we may obtain food and wealth."

That is a master-piece of Satanic art; since he sees that he can not have his way in our times, he thinks to accomplish his purpose with our descendants, whom before our eyes he seeks to withhold from learning and knowledge. And thus, when we are dead, he will have a naked and defenseless people before him, with whom he can do as he pleases. For if the Scriptures and learning perish, what will remain in Germany, but a lawless horde of Tartars or Turks, yea, a multitude of wild beasts? Such results he does not allow to appear at present, and powerfully blinds the people, that when the evil does come, and they are obliged to learn it from experience, he may laugh at their misery and lamentation, which they can no longer do any thing to help. They will then be forced to say, "We have waited too long," and would give a hundred florins for half a scholar, while now they would not give five florins for a thorough one.

And because they are not willing now to support and keep pious, honorable, and skillful school-masters and teachers who at small expense and with great industry and pains would educate their children in the fear of God, in science, doctrine, and honor, it would almost serve them right to have again, as in former times, a set of ignorant and unprincipled pedagogues who at great cost would teach their children nothing but to be blockheads, and who besides would dishonor their wives, daughters, and maid-servants. Such will be the reward of their great, shameful ingratitude, into which the devil so cunningly leads them.

Since now as pastors we are to watch against these and other wicked devices, we must not sleep, but advise, urge, and admonish, with all might, industry, and care, that the common people may not allow themselves to be deceived and led astray by the devil. Therefore let every one take heed to himself and to his office that he may not sleep and thus let the devil become god and lord; for if we are silent and sleep, so that the youth are neglected and our descendants become Tartars or wild beasts, we will have to bear the responsibility and render a heavy account.

Although I know that many of you, without my admonition, attend to this matter faithfully (in reference to which I formerly addressed a special treatise to the Mayors and Aldermen of the German cities), yet, if some perchance forget it, or wish to follow my example in laboring at it more diligently, I send you this sermon, which I have more than once delivered to our people here, that you may see that I strive earnestly with you, and that we thus everywhere do our duty and in our office are justified before God. Much depends truly upon us, since we see that some who are even called ministers, go about the matter as if they wished to let all schools, discipline, and doctrine perish, or even to help to destroy them, since they cannot, as hitherto, lead the wanton life to which Satan impels them. . . .

Inasmuch as I see, dear friends, that the common people are placing themselves in opposition to the schools, and that they wish to bring up their children without other instruction than that pertaining to their bodily wants; and inasmuch also as they do not consider what a fearful and unchristian course they are thus pursuing, and what a great and murderous injury they are inflicting, in the service of Satan, upon society, I have undertaken to address you this admonition, in the hope that perchance there are some who yet in some measure at least believe that there is a God in heaven, and a hell ready for the wicked (for all the world acts as if there were neither a God in heaven nor devils in hell), and in the hope also that there are some who will heed the admonition after contemplating the advantages and disadvantages of education.

✻   ✻   ✻

But I maintain that the civil authorities are under obligation to compel the people to send their children to school, especially such as are promising, as has elsewhere been said. For our rulers are certainly bound to maintain the spiritual and secular offices and callings, so that there may always be preachers, jurists, pastors, scribes, physicians, school-masters, and the like; for these can not be dispensed with. If the government can compel such citizens as are fit for military service to bear spear and rifle, to mount ramparts, and perform other martial duties in time of war; how much more has it a right to compel the people to send their children to school, because in this case we are warring with the devil, whose object it is secretly to exhaust our cities and principalities of their strong men, to destroy the kernel and leave a shell of ignorant and helpless people, whom he can sport and juggle with at pleasure. That is starving out a city or country, destroying it without a struggle, and without its knowledge. The Turk does differently, and takes every third child in his empire to educate for whatever he pleases. How much more should our rulers require children to be sent to school, who, however, are not taken from their parents, but are educated for their own and the general good, in an office where they have an adequate support.

Therefore, let him who can, watch; and wherever the government sees a promising boy, let him be sent to school. If the father is poor, let the child be aided with the property of the Church. The rich should make bequests to such objects, as some have done, who have founded scholarships; that is giving money to the Church in a proper way. You do not thus release the souls of the dead from purgatorial fire, but you help, through the maintenance of divinely appointed offices, to prevent the living from going to purgatory—yea, you secure their deliverance from hell and entrance into heaven, and bestow upon them temporal peace and happiness. That would be a praiseworthy, Christian bequest, in which God would take pleasure, and for which He would honor and bless you, that you might have joy and peace in Him. Now, my dear Germans, I have warned you enough; you have heard your prophet. God grant that we may follow His Word, to the praise and honor of our dear Lord, for His precious blood so graciously shed for us, and preserve us from the horrible sin of ingratitude and forgetfulness of His benefits. Amen.

PHILIP MELANCTHON'S SAXONY SCHOOL PLAN (1528) From Melancthon, *The Book of Visitation,* as quoted in *American Journal of Education,* vol. IV, pp. 749-51.

P reachers also should exhort the people of their charge to send their children to school, so that they may be trained up to teach sound doctrine in the church, and to serve the state in a wise and able manner. Some imagine that it is enough for a teacher to understand German. But this is a misguided fancy. For he, who is to teach others, must have great practice and special aptitude; to gain this, he must have studied much, and from his youth up. For St. Paul tells us, in 1 Tim., 3: 2, that a bishop must be "apt to teach." And herein he would have us infer that bishops must possess this quality in greater measure than laymen. So also he commends Timothy, (1 Tim., 4: 6,) in that he has learned from his youth up, having been "nourished up in the words of faith, and of good doctrine." For this is no small art, namely, to teach and direct others in a clear and correct manner, and it is impossible that unlearned men should attain to it. Nor do we need able and skillful persons for the church alone, but for the government of the world too; and God requires it at our hands. Hence parents should place their children at school, in order there to arm and equip them for God's service, so that God can use them for the good of others.

But in our day there are many abuses in children's schools. And it is that these abuses may be corrected, and that the young may have good instruction, that we have prepared this plan. In the first place, the teachers must be careful to teach the children Latin only, not German, nor Greek, nor Hebrew, as some have heretofore done, burdening the poor children with such a multiplicity of pursuits, that are not only unproductive, but positively injurious. Such schoolmasters, we plainly see, do not think of the improvement of the children at all, but undertake so many languages solely to increase their own reputation. In the second place, teachers should not burden the children with too many books, but should rather avoid a needless variety. Thirdly, it is indispensable that the children be classified into distinct groups.

The First Group

The first group should consist of those children who are learning to read. With these the following method is to be adopted: They are first to be taught the child's-manual, containing the alphabet, the creed, the Lord's prayer, and other prayers. When they have learned this, Donatus and Cato may both be given them; Donatus for a reading-book, and Cato they may explain after the following manner: the schoolmaster must give them the explanation of a verse or two, and then in a few hours call upon them to repeat what he has thus said; and in this way they will learn a great number of Latin words, and lay up a full store of phrases to use in speech. In this they should be exercised until they can read well. Neither do we consider it time lost, if the feebler children, who are not especially quick-witted, should read Cato and Donatus not once only, but a second time. With this they should be taught to write, and be required to shew their writing to the schoolmaster every day. Another mode of enlarging their knowledge of Latin words is to give them every afternoon some words to commit to memory, as has been the custom in schools hitherto. These children must likewise be kept at music, and be made to sing with the others, as we shall show, God willing, further on.

The Second Group

The second group consists of children who have learned to read, and are now ready to go into grammar. With these the following regulations should be observed: The first hour after noon every day all the children, large and small, should be practiced in music. Then the schoolmaster must interpret to the second group the fables of

Aesop. After vespers, he should explain to them the Paedology of Mosellanus; and, when this is finished, he should select from the Colloquies of Erasmus some that may conduce to their improvement and discipline. This should be repeated on the next evening also. When the children are about to go home for the night, some short sentence may be given them, taken perhaps from a poet, which they are to repeat the next morning, such as *"Amicus certus in re incerta cernitur."*—A true friend becomes manifest in adversity. Or *"Fortuna, quem nimium foret, stultum facit,"*—Fortune, if she fondles a man too much, makes him a fool. Or this from Ovid: *"Vulgus amicitias utilitate probat."*—The rabble value friendships by the profit they yield.

In the morning the children are again to explain Aesop's fables. With this the teacher should decline some nouns or verbs, many or few, easy or difficult, according to the progress of the children, and then ask them the rules and the reasons for such inflection. And at the same time when they shall have learned the rules of construction, they should be required to *construe,* (parse,) as it is called; this is a very useful exercise, and yet there are not many who employ it. After the children have thus learned Aesop, Terence is to be given to them; and this they must commit to memory, for they will now be older, and able to work harder. Still the master must be cautious, lest he overtask them. Next after Terence, the children may take hold of such of the comedies of Plautus as are harmless in their tendency, as the *Aulularia,* the *Trinummus,* the *Pseudolus,* etc.

The hour before mid-day must be invariably and exclusively devoted to instruction in grammar: first etymology, then syntax, and lastly prosody. And when the teacher has gone thus far through with the grammar, he should begin it again, and so on continually, that the children may understand it to perfection. For if there is negligence here, there is neither certainty nor stability in whatever is learned beside. And the children should learn by heart and repeat all the rules, so that they may be driven and forced, as it were, to learn the grammar well.

If such labor is irksome to the schoolmaster, as we often see, then we should dismiss him, and get another in his place,—one who will not shrink from the duty of keeping his pupils constantly in the grammar. For no greater injury can befall learning and the arts, than for youth to grow up in ignorance of grammar.

This course should be repeated daily, by the week together; nor should we by any means give children a different book to study each day. However, one day, for instance, Sunday or Wednesday, should be set apart, in which the children may receive Christian instruction. For some are suffered to learn nothing in the Holy Scriptures; and some masters there are who teach children nothing but the Scriptures; both of which extremes must be avoided. For it is essential that children be taught the rudiments of the Christian and divine life. So likewise there are many reasons why, with the Scriptures, other books too should be laid before them, out of which they may learn to read. And in this matter we propose the following method: Let the schoolmaster hear the whole group, making them, one after the other, repeat the Lord's prayer, the creed, and the ten commandments. But if the group is too large, it may be divided, so that one week one part may recite, and the remaining part the next.

After one recitation, the master should explain in a simple and correct manner the Lord's prayer, after the next the creed, and at another time the ten commandments. And he should impress upon the children the essentials, such as the fear of God, faith, and good works. He must not touch upon polemics, nor must he accustom the children to scoff at monks or any other persons, as many unskillful teachers use to do.

With this the schoolmaster may give the boys some plain psalms to commit to memory, which comprehend the sum and substance of the Christian life, which inculcate the fear of the Lord, faith, and good works. As the 112th Psalm, "Blessed is the man that feareth the Lord;" the 34th, "I will bless the Lord at all times;" the 128th, "Blessed is every one that feareth the Lord, that walketh in his ways;" the 125th, "They that trust in the Lord shall be as Mount Zion, which can not be removed, but abideth forever;" the 127th, "Except the Lord build the house, they labor in vain that build it;" the 133d, "Behold how good and how pleasant it is for brethren to dwell together in unity!" or other such plain and intelligible psalms, which likewise should be expounded in the briefest and most correct manner possible, so that the children may know, both the substance of what they have learned and where to find it.

On this day too the teacher should give a grammatical exposition of Matthew; and, when he has gone through with it, he should commence it anew. But, when the boys are somewhat more advanced, he may comment upon the two epistles of Paul to Timothy, or the 1st Epistle of John, or the Proverbs of Solomon. But teachers must not undertake any other books. For it is not profitable to burden the young with deep and difficult books as some do, who, to add to their own reputation, read Isaiah, Paul's Epistle to the Romans, St. John's Gospel, and others of a like nature.

The Third Group

Now when these children have been well trained in grammar, those among them who have made the greatest proficiency should be taken out, and formed into the third group. The hour after mid-day they, together with the rest, are to devote to music. After this the teacher is to give an explanation of Virgil. When he has finished this, he may take up Ovid's Metamorphoses, and in the latter part of the afternoon Cicero's "Offices," or "Letters to Friends." In the morning Virgil may be reviewed, and the teacher, to keep up practice in the grammar, may call for constructions and inflections, and point out the prominent figures of speech.

The hour before mid-day, grammar should still be kept up, that the scholars may be thoroughly versed therein. And when they are perfectly familiar with etymology and syntax, then prosody (*metrica*) should be opened to them, so that they can thereby become accustomed to make verses. For this exercise is a very great help toward understanding the writings of others; and it likewise gives the boys a rich fund of words, and renders them accomplished many ways. In course of time, after they have been sufficiently practiced in the grammar, this same hour is to be given to logic and rhetoric. The boys in the second and third groups are to be required every week to write compositions, either in the form of letters or of verses. They should also be rigidly confined to Latin conversation, and to this end the teachers themselves must, as far as possible, speak nothing but Latin with the boys; thus they will acquire the practice by use, and the more rapidly for the incentives held out to them.

ERASMUS URGES TRANSLATING THE BIBLE INTO THE VERNACULAR

(**1529**)   From Erasmus, *An Exhortation to the Diligent Studye of Scripture* (Hesse, 1529), no pagination.

I t must needs be a high and excellent thing, and no trifle which that heavenly and marvelous master [Christ] came to teach openly. Why do we not go about to know, search and try out with a godly curiosity this fruitful Philosophy? Since that this kind of wisdom, being so profound and inscrutable that utterly it damneth and confoundeth as foolish all the wisdom of this world, may be gathered out of so small books as out of most pure springs. And that with much less labor than the doctrine of Aristotle out of so many brawling and contentious books, or of such infinite commentaries which do so much dissent. . . .

I do greatly dissent from those men which would not that the scripture of Christ should be translated into all tongues that it might be read diligently of the private and secular men and women. As though Christ had taught such dark and insensible things that they could scant be understood of a few divines. Or else as though the pith and substance of the Christian religion consisted chiefly in this, that it be not known. Peradventure it were most expedient that the councils of kings should be kept secret, but Christ would that his councils and mysteries should be spread abroad as much as is possible. I would desire that all women should read the gospel and Paul's epistles, and I would to God they were translated into the tongues of all men. So that they might not only be read and known of the Scots and Irishmen, but also of the Turks and Saracens. Truly it is one degree to good living, yea the first (I had almost said the chief) to have a little sight in the scripture, though it be but a gross knowledge and not yet consummate. Be it in case that some would laugh at it, yea and that some should err and be deceived, I would to God the plowman would sing a text of the scripture at his plowing, and that the weaver at his loom with this would drive away the tediousness of time. I would the wayfaring man with this pastime would assuage the weariness of his journey. And to be short I would that all the communication of the Christian should be of the scripture, for in a manner such are we ourselves as our daily tales are.

JOHN CALVIN ON THE VALUE OF A CHRISTIAN EDUCATION

(**1536**)   From John Calvin, *Institutes of the Christian Religion,* Ford Lewis Brattles, trans. (Philadelphia, 1960), XXI, pp. 16-18.

Book IV, Chapter 1

Education through the church, its value and its obligation

But let us proceed to set forth what pertains to this topic. Paul writes that Christ, "that he might fill all things," appointed some to be "apostles, some prophets, some evangelists, some pastors and teachers, for the equipment of the saints, for the work of the ministry, for the building up of the body of Christ, until we all reach the unity of the faith and of the knowledge of the Son of God, to perfect manhood, to the measure of the fully mature age of Christ." We see how God, who could in a moment perfect his own, nevertheless desires them to grow up into manhood solely under the education of the church. We see the way set for it: the preaching of the heavenly doctrine has been enjoined upon the pastors. We see that all are brought under the same regulation, that with a gentle and teachable spirit they may allow themselves to be governed by teachers appointed to this function. . . . From this it follows that all those who spurn the spiritual food, divinely extended to them through the hand of the church, deserve to perish in famine and hunger. God breathes faith into us only by the instrument of his gospel. . . .

By this plan He willed of old that holy assemblies be held at the sanctuary in order that the doctrine taught by the mouth of the priest might foster agreement in faith. The Temple is called God's "resting place"; the sanctuary, his "dwelling," where he is said to sit among the cherubim. Glorious titles, they are used solely to bring esteem, love, reverence, and dignity to the ministry of the heavenly doctrine. Otherwise, the appearance of a mortal and despised man would much detract from them. To make us aware, then, that an inestimable treasure is given us in earthen vessels, God himself appears in our midst, and, as Author of this order, would have men recognize him as present in his institution.

Accordingly, after he forbade his people to devote themselves to auguries, divinations, magic arts, necromancy, and other superstitions, he added that he would give what ought to suffice for all: that they should never be destitute of prophets. But as he did not entrust the ancient folk to angels but raised up teachers from the earth truly to perform the angelic office, so also today it is his will to teach us through human means. As he was of old not content with the law alone, but added priests as interpreters from whose lips the people might ask its true meaning, so today he not only desires us to be attentive to its reading, but also appoints instructors to help us by their effort. This is doubly useful. On the one hand, he proves our obedience by a very good test when we hear his ministers speaking just as if he himself spoke. On the other, he also provides for our weakness in that he prefers to address us in human fashion through interpreters in order to draw us to himself, rather than to thunder at us and drive us away. Indeed, from the dread with which God's majesty justly overwhelms them, all the pious truly feel how much this familiar sort of teaching is needed.

Those who think the authority of the Word is dragged down by the baseness of the men called to teach it disclose their own ungratefulness. For, among the many excellent gifts with which God has adorned the human race, it is a singular privilege that he deigns to consecrate to himself the mouths and tongues of men in order that his voice may resound in them. Let us accordingly not in turn dislike to embrace obediently the doctrine of salvation put forth by his command and by his own mouth. For, although God's power is not bound to outward means, he has nonetheless bound us to this ordinary manner of teaching. Fanatical men, refusing to hold fast to it, entangle themselves in many deadly snares. Many are led either by pride, dislike, or rivalry to the conviction that they can profit enough from private reading and meditation; hence they despise public assemblies and deem preaching superfluous. But, since they do their utmost to sever or break the sacred bond of unity, no one escapes the just penalty of this unholy separation without bewitching himself with pestilent errors and foulest delusions. In order, then, that pure simplicity of faith may flourish among us, let us not be reluctant to use this exercise of religion which God, by ordaining it, has shown us to be necessary and highly approved. No one—not even a fanatical beast—ever existed who would tell us to close our ears to God. But in every age the prophets and godly teachers have had a difficult struggle with the ungodly, who in their stubbornness can never submit to the yoke of being taught by human word and ministry. This is like blotting out the face of God which shines upon us in teaching. . . .

CALVIN'S CATECHISM FOR CHILDREN (1545)   From J.K.S. Reid, ed. and trans., *Calvin: Theological Treatises* (London, 1954), pp. 88-89, 91-92.

Letter to the Reader

It has always been a practice and diligent care of the Church, that children be rightly brought up in Christian doctrine. To do this more conveniently, not only were schools formerly opened and individuals enjoined to teach their families properly, but also it was accepted public custom and practice to examine children in the Churches concerning the specific points which should be common and familiar to all Christians. That this be done in order, a formula was written out, called Catechism or Institute. After this, the devil, miserably rending the Church of God and bringing upon it his fearful destruction (of which the marks are all too evident in most parts of the world), subverted this sacred policy; nor did he leave surviving anything more than certain trivialities, which give rise only to superstitions, without any edifying fruit. Of this kind is that Confirmation, as they call it, made up of gesticulations which are more than ridiculous and suited rather to monkeys, and rest on no foundation. What we now bring forward, therefore, is nothing else than the use of a practice formerly observed by Christians and the true worshippers of God, and never neglected until the Church was wholly corrupted.

John Calvin to the Faithful Ministers of Christ who Preach the Pure Doctrine of the Gospel in East Friesland

Since it is proper for us by every means to endeavour to make that unity of faith shine forth among us which is so highly commended by Paul, the solemn profession of faith which is joined to our common Baptism ought to be directed chiefly to this end. It might therefore be wished, not only that there exist a perpetual consent by all in pious doctrine, but that there be also a single form of Catechism for all Churches. But since for many reasons it will hardly ever be otherwise than that each Church have its own Catechism, we should not too strenuously resist it; provided, however, that the variety in the kind of teaching be such that we are all directed to the one Christ, by whose truth, if we be united in it, we may grow together into one body and one spirit, and with one mouth also proclaim whatever belongs to the sum of the faith. Catechists who do not pursue this end, besides seriously injuring the Church by the dissemination of material of dissension in religion, introduce also an impious profanation of Baptism. For what further use is Baptism, unless this remain its foundation, that we all agree in one faith? Those who publicly bring out Catechisms ought therefore to be all the more diligently careful, lest by producing something rashly they do grave harm to piety and inflict a deadly wound upon the Church, not only for the present but also in posterity.

*   *   *

Concerning the Faith

Minister: What is the chief end of human life?

Child: That men should know God by whom they were created.

M: What reason have you for saying so?

C: Because he created us for this, and placed us in the world, that he might be glorified in us. And it is certainly proper that our life, of which he is the beginning, be directed to his glory.

M: What then is man's supreme good?

C: The very same.

M: Why do you hold this to be the supreme good?

C: Because without it our condition is more unhappy than that of any of the brutes.

M: So then we clearly perceive that nothing worse can happen to man than not to live to God?

C: It is so.

M: What then is true and right knowledge of God?

C: When he is so known, that his own proper honour is done him.

M: What is the right way of honouring him?

C: To put all our trust in him; to study to serve him all our life, by obeying his will; to call upon him, whenever any need impels us, seeking in him salvation and whatever good things can be desired; and lastly, to acknowledge him with both heart and mouth to be the only author of all good things.

M: Now to consider these things in order and explain them more fully—what is the first head in this division of yours?

C: That we place all our trust in God.

M: How is this done?

C: When we know him to be mighty and perfectly good.

M: Is this enough?

C: Far from it.

M: Why?

C: Because we are unworthy that he should exercise his power to help us, or for our salvation show us how good he is.

M: What then is needed further?

C: Just that each of us should affirm with his mind, that he is loved by him, and that he is willing to be his Father and the Author of his salvation.

M: Where will this be apparent to us?

C: In his Word, where he reveals his mercy to us in Christ, and testifies of his love towards us.

M: Then the foundation and beginning of faith in God is to know him in Christ? (John 17:3).

C: Quite so.

M: Now I would hear from you in a few words what the sum of this knowledge is.

C: It is contained in the confession of faith, or rather in the formula of confession, which all Christians hold in common. It is commonly called the Apostles' Creed, because from the beginning of the Church it was always received among all the pious, and because either it came from the lips of the apostles or was faithfully collected from their writings.

M: Repeat it.

C: I believe in God the Father Almighty, Maker of heaven and earth; and in Jesus Christ his only Son our Lord, who was conceived by the Holy Ghost, born of the Virgin Mary, suffered under Pontius Pilate, was crucified, dead and buried: He descended into hell; the third day he rose again from the dead, he ascended into heaven, and sitteth on the right hand of God the Father Almighty; from thence he shall come to judge the quick and the dead. I believe in the Holy Ghost; the Holy Catholic Church; the communion of saints; the resurrection of the body; and the life everlasting. Amen.

* * *

M: Now explain what you meant by saying that the Lord in this commandment wished to offer relief to servants.

C: That some kind of relaxation might be given to those who are in the power of others. Indeed this also contributes to maintain a common polity. For when one day is assigned for rest, everyone accustoms himself to work the rest of the time.

M: Let us see now how far this command refers to us.

C: As to ceremony, since its reality existed in Christ, I hold it to be abrogated (Col. 2:20).

M: How?

C: Just because our old nature is by virtue of his death crucified, and we are raised up to newness of life.

M: How much of the commandment then remains for us?

C: Not to neglect the sacred ordinances which contribute to the spiritual polity of the Church; especially to attend the sacred assemblies for the hearing of the Word of God, the celebration of the mysteries, and the regular prayers as they will be ordained.

M: But does the symbol lead us no further?

C: Certainly: for it recalls us to the reality behind it, namely, that being grafted into the body of Christ and made members of his, we cease from our own works and so resign ourselves to the government of God.

M: Let us pass to the second table.

C: It begins: Honour thy father and thy mother.

M: What does this word honour mean for you?

C: That children be with modesty and humility compliant and obedient to their parents, that they give them reverence, that they help them in need, and that they devote their labour to them. For in these three branches is contained that honour which is owed to parents.

M: Go on.

C: To the command a promise is added: that thy days may be long upon the land which the Lord thy God giveth thee.

M: What does this mean?

C: That by God's blessing those that offer due honour to their parents will live long.

M: When this life is so full of hardships, why does God promise its long continuance as a blessing?

C: However great the miseries to which it is exposed, yet there is a blessing of God towards believers in his nourishing and preserving them here, if only for this reason, that it is proof of his paternal favour.

JOHN KNOX ON THE NECESSITY OF SCHOOLS (1560) From "The Book of Discipline," in John Knox, *The History of the Reformation of Religion in Scotland*, Cuthbert Lennox, ed. (London, 1905), pp. 382-87.

VII. Of Schools and Universities

As the office and duty of the godly magistrate is not only to purge the Church of God from all superstition, and to set it at liberty from bondage of tyrants, but also to provide, to the uttermost of his power, that it may abide in the same purity to the posterities following, we cannot but freely communicate our judgments to your honours in this behalf.

1. *The Necessity of Schools.*—Seeing that God hath determined that His Church here on earth shall be taught not by angels but by men; and seeing that men are born ignorant of all godliness; and seeing, also, how God ceaseth to illuminate men miraculously, suddenly changing them, as He changed His Apostles and others in the primitive Church: it is necessary that your honours be most careful for the virtuous education and godly upbringing of the youth of this realm, if ye now thirst unfeignedly for the advancement of Christ's glory, or desire the continuance of His benefits to the generation following. For as the youth must succeed to us, so ought we to be careful that they have knowledge and erudition, for the profit and comfort of that which ought to be most dear to us, to wit, the Church and Spouse of the Lord Jesus.

Therefore we judge it necessary that every several church have a schoolmaster appointed, such an one as is able, at least, to teach Grammar and the Latin tongue, if the town be of any reputation. If it be upaland, where the people convene to doctrine but once in the week, then must either the reader or the minister there take care of the children and youth of the parish, instructing them in their first rudiments, and especially in the Catechism, as we have it now translated in the Book of our Common Order, called the Order of Geneva. And, farther, we think it expedient that in every notable town, and especially in the town of the Superintendent, there be erected a college, in which the Arts, at least Logic and Rhetoric, together with the tongues, shall be read by sufficient Masters. For these honest stipends must be appointed; and provision must be made for those that are poor, and are not able by themselves, nor by their friends, to be sustained at letters, especially such as come from landward.

The fruit and commodity hereof shall speedily appear. For, first, the youths and tender children shall be nourished and brought up in virtue, in presence of their friends; by whose good care may be avoided those many inconveniences into which youth commonly falls, either by too much liberty, which they have in strange and unknown places while they cannot rule themselves; or else for lack of good care, and of such necessities as their tender age requireth. Secondarily, the exercise of the children in every church shall be great instruction to the aged.

Lastly, the great schools, called Universities, shall be replenished with those that are apt to learn; for this must be carefully provided, that no father, of what estate or condition that ever he be, use his children at his own fantasy, especially in their youth. All must be compelled to bring up their children in learning and virtue.

The rich and potent may not be permitted to suffer their children to spend their youth in vain idleness, as heretofore they have done. They must be exhorted, and by the censure of the Church compelled to dedicate their sons, by good exercise, to the profit of the Church and to the Commonwealth; and this they must do at their own expense, because they are able. The children of the poor must be supported and sustained as the charge of the Church, until trial be taken whether the spirit of docility be found in them or not. If they be found apt to letters and learning, then may they not (we mean, neither the sons of the rich, nor yet the sons of the poor) be permitted to reject learning. They must be charged to continue their study, so that the Commonwealth may have some comfort by them. For this purpose must discreet, learned, and grave men be appointed to visit all schools for the trial of their exercise, profit, and continuance; to wit, the ministers and elders, with the best learned in every town, shall every quarter take examination how the youth have profited.

A certain time must be appointed to reading, and to learning of the Catechism; a certain time to Grammar, and to the Latin tongue; a certain time to the Arts, Philosophy, and to the other tongues; and a certain time to that study in which they intend chiefly to travail for the profit of the Commonwealth. This time being expired, we mean in every course, the children must either proceed to farther knowledge, or else they must be sent to some handicraft, or to some other profitable exercise. Care must always be taken that first they have the form of knowledge of Christian religion, to wit, the knowledge of God's law and commandments; the use and office of the same; the chief articles of our belief; the right form to pray unto God; the number, use, and effect of the Sacraments; the true knowledge of Christ Jesus, of His office and natures, and such others. Without this knowledge, neither deserveth any man to be named a Christian, nor ought any to be admitted to the participation of the Lord's Table; and, therefore, these principles ought to be taught and must be learned in youth.

2. *The Times appointed to every Course.*—Two years we think more than sufficient to learn to read perfectly, to answer the Catechism, and to have some entrance to the first rudiments of Grammar. For the full accomplishment of the Grammar, we think other three or four years, at most, sufficient. For the Arts, to wit, Logic and Rhetoric, and for the Greek tongue, we allow four years. The rest of youth, until the age of twenty-four years, should be spent in that study wherein the learner would profit the Church or Commonwealth, be it in the Laws or Physic or Divinity. After twenty-four years have been spent in the schools, the learner must be removed to serve the Church or Commonwealth, unless he be found a necessary reader in the same College or University. If God shall move your hearts to establish and execute this order, and put these things into practice, your whole realm, we doubt not, within few years, shall serve itself with true preachers and other officers necessary for your Commonwealth.

3. *The Erection of Universities.*—The Grammar schools and schools of the tongues being erected as we have said, next we think it necessary that there be three

Universities in this whole realm, established in the towns accustomed: the first in St. Andrews, the second in Glasgow, and the third in Aberdeen.

In the first University and principal, which is St. Andrews, there be three Colleges. And in the first College, which is the entrance of the University, there be four classes or sessions: the first, to the new supposts, shall be only Dialectic; the next, only Mathematics; the third, of Physic only; the fourth, of Medicine. And in the second College, two classes or sessions: the first, in Moral Philosophy; the second, in the Laws. And in the third College, two classes or sessions: the first, in the tongues, to wit, Greek and Hebrew; the second, in Divinity.

4. *Of Readers, and of the Degrees, of Time, and Study.*—In the first College, and in the first class, shall be a reader of Dialectic, who shall accomplish his course thereof in one year. In the Mathematic, which is the second class, shall be a reader who shall complete his course of Arithmetic, Geometry, Cosmography, and Astrology in one year. In the third class, shall be a reader of Natural Philosophy, who shall complete his course in a year. And he who, after these three years, by trial and examination, shall be found sufficiently instructed in these aforesaid sciences, shall be laureate and graduate in Philosophy. In the fourth class, shall be a reader of Medicine, who shall complete his course in five years. After the study for this time, he who is by examination found sufficient, shall be graduate in Medicine.

In the second College, in the first class, there shall be one reader only in the Ethics, Economics, and Politics, who shall complete his course in the space of one year. In the second class, shall be two readers in the Municipal and Roman Laws, who shall complete their courses in four years. After this time, those who by examination are found sufficient, shall be graduate in the Laws.

In the third College, in the first class, there shall be a reader of the Hebrew, and another of the Greek tongue, who shall complete the grammars thereof in half a year, and for the remnant of the year, the reader of the Hebrew shall interpret a Book of Moses, the Prophets or the Psalms; so that his course and class shall continue a year. The reader of the Greek shall interpret some book of Plato, together with some place of the New Testament. And in the second class, there shall be two readers in Divinity, one in the New Testament, the other in the Old. These shall complete their course in five years. After this time, those shall be graduate in Divinity who shall be found by examination sufficient.

We think it expedient that no one be admitted unto the first College, and to be suppost of the University, unless he have from the master of the school, and from the minister of the town where he was instructed in the tongues, a testimonial of his learning, docility, age, and parentage. Likewise, trial shall be taken by certain examiners, deputed by the rector and Principals, and if he be found sufficiently instructed in Dialectic, he shall forthwith, that same year, be promoted to the class of Mathematic.

None shall be admitted to the class of Medicine but he that shall have his testimonial of his time well spent in Dialectic, Mathematic, and Physic, and of his docility in the last.

None shall be admitted to the class of the Laws but he that shall have sufficient testimonials of his time well spent in Dialectic, Mathematic, Physic, Ethic, Economics, and Politics, and of his docility in the last.

None shall be admitted unto the class and session of Divinity but he that shall have sufficient testimonials of his time well spent in Dialectic, Mathematic, Physic, Ethic, Economic, Moral Philosophy, and the Hebrew tongue, and of his docility in Moral Philosophy and the Hebrew tongue. But neither shall such as will apply them to hear the Laws be compelled to hear Medicine; nor such as apply them to hear Divinity be compelled to hear either Medicine or the Laws.

In the second University, which is Glasgow, there shall be two Colleges only. In the first shall be a class of Dialectic, another in Mathematic, the third in Physic, ordered in all sorts as St. Andrews. In the second College there shall be four classes: the first in Moral Philosophy, Ethics, Economics, and Politics; the second, of the Municipal and Roman Law; the third, of the Hebrew tongue; the fourth, in Divinity. These shall be ordered in all sorts, as we have written in the order of the University of St. Andrews.

The third University of Aberdeen shall be conform to this University of Glasgow, in all sorts.

We think it needful that there be chosen from the body of the University a Principal for every College—a man of learning, discretion, and diligence. He shall receive the whole rents of the College, and distribute the same according to the erection of the College, and shall daily hearken the diet accounts, adjoining to him weekly one of the readers or regents. In the oversight of the readers and regents he shall watch over their diligence, in their reading, as well as their exercitation of the youth in the matter taught. He shall have charge of the policy and uphold of the place; and for punishment of crimes, shall hold a weekly convention with the whole members of the College. He shall be accountable yearly to the Superintendent, Rector, and rest of the Principals convened, about the first of November. His election shall be in this sort. There shall be three of the most sufficient men of the University, not Principals already, nominated by the members of the College (sworn to follow their consciences) whose Principal is departed, and publicly proponed through the whole University. After eight days the Superintendent, by himself or his special Procurator, with the Rector and rest of the Principals, as a chapter convened, shall confirm that one of the three whom they think most sufficient, being before sworn to do the same with single eye, without respect to fee or favour.

✳   ✳   ✳

The ministers and the poor, together with the schools, when order shall be taken thereanent, must be sustained upon the charges of the Church. Provision must therefore be made, how and from whom the necessary sums must be lifted.

A CHILD'S PRAYER WRITTEN BY JOHN KNOX (c. 1564)   From Frederick Eby, ed., *Early Protestant Educators* (New York, 1931), pp. 295-97.

A Prayer to be Said of the Childe, before He Studie His Lesson

Out of the 119 Psalme.—Wherein shal the Child addresse his way? in guiding himselfe according to thy worde. Open myne eyes, and I shal knowe the merveiles of thy Law. Give me understanding, and I shal kepe thy Law, yea I shal kepe it with mine whole heart.

Lord, which art the fountaine of all wisedome and knowledge, seeing it hath pleased thee to give me the meane to be taught in my youth, for to learne to guide me godly and honestly all the course of my life; it may also please thee to lighten myne understanding (the which of it selfe is blinde), that it may comprehend and receive that doctrine and learning which shalbe taught me: it may please thee to strengthen my memorie to kepe it well; it may please thee also to dispose myne hearte willinglie to receive it with suche desire as apperteineth, so that by myne ingratitude, the occasion which thou givest me, be not lost. That I may thus do, it may please thee to powre upon me thyne Holie Sprit, the Sprit, I say, of all understanding, trueth, judgement, wisdome, and learning, the which may make me able so to profite, that the paines that shalbe taken in teaching me be not in vaine. And to what studie so ever I apply my selfe, make me, O Lord, to addresse it unto the right end: that is, to knowe thee in our Lord Jesus Christ, that I may have ful trust of salvation in thy grace, and to serve thee uprightly according to thy pleasure, so that whatsoever I learne, it may be unto me as an instrument to help me thereunto.

And seing thou dost promise to give wisdome to the lytle and humble ones, and to confounde the proude in the vanitie of their wits, and lykewise to make thy selfe knowen to them that be of an upright heart, and also to blynde the ungodly and wicked; I beseech thee to facion me unto true humilitie, so that I may be taught first to be obedient unto thee, and next unto my superiors, that thou hast appointed over me: further, that it may please thee to dispose mine heart unfeinedly to seke thee, and to forsake all evil and filthie lustes of the flesh: And that in this sorte, I may now prepare my selfe to serve thee once in that estate which it shal please thee to appoint for me, when I shal come to age.

Out of the 25 Psalme.—The Lord reveileth his secrets unto them that feare him, and maketh them to knowe his alliance.

SCOTTISH SCHOOL LAW (1646)   From *Acts of Parliament of Scotland,* vol. VI, p. 216.

The Estates of Parliament now conveened, in the fifth session of this first Triennall Parliament, Considering how prejudiciall the want of Schools in many congregations hath been, and how beneficiall the founding thereof in every congregation will be to this Kirk and Kingdom; Do therefore Statute and Ordain, That there be a Schoole founded, and a Schoole master appointed in every Parish (not already provided) by advice of the Presbyterie: And to this purpose, that the Heritors in every congregation meet among themselves, and provide a commodious house for a Schoole, and modifie a stipend to the Schoole master, which shall not be under Ane hundred Merks, nor above Tua hundred Merks, to be paid yeerly at two Terms: And to this effect that they set down a stent upon every ones rent of stock and teind in the Parish, proportionally to the worth thereof, for maintenance of the Schoole, and payment of the Schoole masters stipend; Which stipend is declared to be due to the Schoole masters by and attour the casualities which formerly belonged to Readers and Clerks of Kirk Sessions. And if the Heritors shall not conveene, or being conveened shall not agree amongst themselves, Then, and in that case the

Presbyterie shall nominate twelve honest men within the bounds of the Presbyterie, who shall have power to establish a Schoole, modifie a stipend for the Schoole master, with the latitude before expressed, and set down a stent for payment thereof upon the Heritors, which shall be as valide and effectuall as if the same had been done by the Heritors themselves.

PLAN FOR CHRISTIAN EDUCATION ADOPTED BY THE SYNOD OF DORT (1618) From *American Journal of Education*, vol. V, pp. 77-78.

In order that the Christian youth may be diligently instructed in the principles of religion, and be trained in piety, three modes of catechising should be employed. I. In the House, by Parents. II. In the Schools, by Schoolmasters. III. In the Churches, by Ministers, Elders, and Catechists, especially appointed for the purpose. That these may diligently employ their trust, the Christian magistrates shall be requested to promote, by their authority, so sacred and necessary a work; and all who have the oversight of churches and schools shall be required to pay special attention to this matter.

I. *Parents.* The office of Parents is diligently to instruct their children and their whole household in the principles of the Christian religion, in a manner adapted to their respective capacities; earnestly and carefully to admonish them to the cultivation of true piety; to engage their punctual attendance on family worship, and take them with them to the hearing of the Word of God. They should require their children to give an account of the sermons they hear, especially those on the Catechism; assign them some chapters of Scripture to read, and certain passages to commit to memory; and then impress and illustrate the truths contained in them in a familiar manner, adapted to the tenderness of youth. Thus they are to prepare them for being catechised in the schools, and by attendance on these to encourage them and promote their edification. Parents are to be exhorted to the faithful discharge of this duty, by the public preaching of the Word; but specially at the ordinary period of family visitation, previous to the administration of the Lord's Supper; and also at other times by the minister, elders, etc. Parents who profess religion, and are negligent in this work, shall be faithfully admonished by the ministers; and, if the case requires it, they shall be censured by the Consistory, that they may be brought to the discharge of their duty.

II. *Schools.* Schools, in which the young shall be properly instructed in the principles of Christian doctrine, shall be instituted, not only in cities but also in towns and country places where heretofore none have existed. The Christian magistracy shall be requested that well-qualified persons may be employed and enabled to devote themselves to the service; and especially that the children of the poor may be gratuitously instructed, and not be excluded from the benefit of the schools. In this office none shall be employed but such as are members of the Reformed Church, having certificates of an upright faith and pious life, and of being well versed in the truths of the Catechism. They are to sign a document, professing their belief in the Confession of Faith and the Heidelberg Catechism, and promising that they will give catechetical instruction to the youth in the principles of Christian truth according to the same. The schoolmasters shall instruct their scholars according to their age and capacity, at least two days in the week, not only causing them to commit to memory, but also by instilling into their minds an acquaintance with the truths of the Catechism. (An elementary small Catechism, the Compendium, and the Heidelberg Catechism, are those specified to be used by the different grades of children and youth.) The schoolmasters shall take care not only that the scholars commit these Catechisms to memory, but that they shall suitably understand the doctrines contained in them. For this purpose, they shall suitably explain to every one, in a manner adapted to his capacity, and frequently inquire if they understand them. The schoolmasters shall bring every one of the pupils committed to their charge to the hearing of the preached Word, and particularly the preaching on the Catechism, and require from them an account of the same.

III. *Ministerial Supervision.* In order that due knowledge may be obtained of the diligence of the schoolmasters, and the improvement of the youth, it shall be the duty of the Masters, with an Elder, and, if necessary, with a magistrate, to visit all the schools, private as well as public, frequently, in order to excite the teachers to earnest diligence, to encourage and counsel them in the duty of catechising, and to furnish an example by questioning them, addressing them in a friendly and affectionate manner, and exciting them to early piety and diligence. If any of the schoolmasters should be found neglectful or perverse, they shall be earnestly admonished by the ministers, and, if necessary, by the Consistory, in relation to their office. The ministers, in the discharge of their public duty in the Church, shall preach on the Catechism. These sermons shall be comparatively short, and accommodated, as far as practicable, to the comprehension of children as well as adults. The labors of those ministers will be praiseworthy who diligently search out country places, and see that catechetical instruction be supplied and faithfully preserved. Experience teaches that the ordinary instruction of the Church, catechetical and other, is not sufficient for many, to instill that knowledge of the Christian religion which should, among the people of God, be well grounded; and also testifies that the living voice has very great influence; that familiar and suitable questions and answers, adapted to the apprehension of each individual, is the best mode of catechising, in order to impress the principles of religion upon the heart. It shall be the duty of a minister to go, with an elder, to all capable of instruction, and collect them in their houses, the Consistory chamber, or some other suitable place, (a number particularly of those more advanced in years,) and explain familiarly to them, the articles of the Christian faith, and catechise them according to the circumstances of their different capacities, progress, and knowledge. They shall question them on the matter of the public sermons on the Catechism. Those who desire to unite with the Church shall, three or four weeks before the administration of the Lord's Supper, be more carefully and frequently instructed, that they may be better qualified, and be more free to give a satisfactory account of their faith. The ministers shall employ diligent care to ascertain those who give any hopeful evidence of serious concern for the salvation of their soul, and invite them to them; assembling those together who have like impressions, and encouraging to friendly intercourse and free conversation with each other. These meetings shall commence with appropriate prayer and exhortation. If all this shall be done by the ministers with that cordiality, faithfulness, zeal, and discretion that become those that must give an account of the flock committed to their charge, it is not to be doubted that in a short time abundant fruit of their labors shall be found in growth in religious knowledge, and holiness of life, to the glory of God, and the prosperity of the Church of Christ.

PREFACE TO THE DOUAY-RHEIMS BIBLE (1609) From Henry Cotton,
Rhemes and Doway (Oxford, 1855), pp. 287-94, 296-97.

At last through Gods goodnes (most dearly beloved) we send you here the greater part of the Old Testament: as long since you received the New; faithfully translated into English. The residue is in had to be finished: and your desire thereof shal not now (God prospering our intention) be long frustrate. As for the impediments, which hitherto have hindered this worke, they al proceded (as manie do know) of one general cause, our poore estate in banishment. Wherin expecting better meanes; greater difficulties rather ensued. Nevertheles you wil hereby the more perceive our fervent good wil, ever to serve you, in that we have brought forth this Tome, in these hardest times, of above fourtie yeares, since this College was most happely begune. Wherfore we nothing doubt, but you our dearest, for whom we have dedicated our lives, wil both pardon the long delay, which we could not wel prevent, and accept now this fruict of our laboures, with like good affection, as we acknowledge them due, and offer the same unto you.

If anie demand, why it is now allowed to have the holie Scriptures in vulgar tongues, which generally is not permitted, but in the three sacred only: for further declaration of this & other like pointes we remite you to the Preface, before the New Testament. Only here, as by an Epitome, we shal repete the summe of al, that is there more largely discussed.

To this first question therfore we answer, that both just reason, & highest authoritie of the Church judge it not absolutely necessarie, nor alwayes convenient, that holie Scriptures should be in vulgar tongues. For being as they are, hard to be understood, even by the lerned, reason doth dictate to reasonable men, that they were not written, nor ordayned to be read indifferently of al men. Experience also teacheth, that through ignorance, ioyned often with pride and presumption, manie reading Scriptures have erred grosly, by misunderstanding God's word.

*   *   *

We had some partes in English translated by Venerable Bede: as Malmesburie witnesseth. And Thomas Arundel Archbishop of Canterburie in a Councel holden at Oxford, straietly ordayned, that no heretical translation set forth by Wicliffe, and his complices, nor anie other vulgar Edition should be suffered, til it were approved by the Ordinarie of the Diocese; alleaging S. Jerom's judgement of the difficultie & danger in translating holie Scriptures out of one tongue into an other. And therfore it must nedes be much more dangerous, when ignorant people read also corrupted translations. Now since Luther and his folowers have pretended, that the Catholique Romane faith and doctrine should be contrarie to Gods written word, & that the Scriptures were not suffered in vulgar languages, lest the people should see the truth, & withal these new maisters corruptly turning the Scriptures into divers tongues, as might best serve their owne opinions: against this false suggestion and practise, Catholique Pastores have, for one especial remedie, set forth true and sincere translations in most languages of the Latin Church. But so, that people must read them with license of their spiritual superior, as in former times they were in like sort limited. Such also of the Laitie, yea and of the meaner lerned Clergie, as were permitted to reade holie Scriptures, did not presume to interprete hard places, nor high Mysteries, much lesse to dispute and contend; but leaving the discussion

THE
EUROPEAN
HERITAGE

therof to the more lerned, searched rather, and noted the godlie and imitable examples of good life, and so lerned more humilitie, obedience, hatred of sinne, feare of God, zele of Religion, and other vertues. And thus holie Scriptures may be rightly used in anie tongue, to teach, to argue, to correcte, to instruct in justice, that the man of God may be perfect, and (as S. Paul addeth) instructed to everie good worke, when men labour rather to be doers of God's wil & word, then readers or hearers only, deceiving themselves.

But here an other question may be proposed: Why we translate the Latin text, rather then the Hebrew, or Greke, which Protestants preferre, as the fountaine tongues wherin holie Scriptures were first written? To this we answer, that if in dede those first pure Editions were now extant, or if such as be extant were more pure then the Latin, we would also preferre such fountaines before the rivers, in whatsoever they should be found to disagree. But the ancient best lerned Fathers & Doctors of the Church do much complaine, and testifie to us that both the Hebrew and Greke Editions are fouly corrupted by Jewes and Heretikes, since the Latin was truly translated out of them whiles they were more pure. And that the same Latin hath bene farre better conserved from corruptions. So that the old Vulgate Latin Edition hath bene preferred, and used for most authentical above a thousand and three hundered yeares. For by this verie terme S. Jerom calleth that Version the vulgate or common, which he conferred with the Hebrew of the Old Testament and with the Greke of the New: which he also purged from faultes committed by writers, rather amending then translating it. . . .

If moreover we consider S. Jerom's lerning, pietie, diligence, and sinceritie, together with the commodities he had of best copies, in al languages then extant, and of other lerned men, with whom he conferred: and if we so compare the same with the best meanes that hath bene since, surely no man of indifferent judgement wil match anie other Edition with S. Jerom's: but easely acknowledge with the whole Church God's particular providence in this great Doctor, as wel for expounding, as most especialy for the true text and Edition of Holie Scriptures. Neither do we flee unto this old Latin text, for more advantage. For besides that it is free from partialitie, as being most ancient of al Latin copies, and long before the particular Controversies of these dayes beganne; the Hebrew also, & the Greke when they are truly translated, yea and Erasmus his Latin, in sundrie places, prove more plainly the Catholique Romaine doctrine, then this which we relie upon. So that Beza and his folowers take also exception against the Greke, when Catholiques allege it against them. Yea the same Beza preferreth the old Latin version before al others, & freely testifieth, that the old Interpreter translated religiously. What then do our countriemen, that refuse this Latin, but deprive themselves of the best, and yet al this while, have set forth none, that is allowed by al Protestantes, for good or sufficient.

How wel this is donne the lerned may judge, when by mature conference, they shal have made trial therof. And if anie thing be mistaken, we wil (as stil we promise) gladly correct it. Those that traslated it about thirtie yeares since, were wel knowen to the world, to have bene excellent in the tongues, sincere men, and great Divines. Only one thing we have done touching the text, wherof we are especially to geve notice. That whereas heretofore in the best Latin Editions, there remained manie places differing in wordes, some also in sense, as in long processe of time, the writers erred in their copies; now lately by the care & diligence of the Church, those divers readings were maturely and juditiously examined and conferred with sundrie the best written and printed bookes, & so resolved upon, that al which before were leift in the margent, are either restored into the text, or els omitted; so that now none such remaine in the margent. For which cause, we have again conferred this English translation, and conformed it to the most perfect Latin Edition. Where yet by the way we must geve the vulgar reader to understand, that very few or none of the former varieties touched Controversies of this time; so that this Recognition is no way suspicious of partialitie, but is merely donne for the more secure conservation of the true text; and more ease, and satisfaction of such, as otherwise should have remained more doubtful.

Now for the strictnes observed in translating some wordes, or rather the not translating of some, which is in more danger to be disliked, we doubt not but the discrete lerned reader deeply weighing and considering the importance of sacred wordes, and how easely the translatour may misse the sense of the Holie Ghost, wil hold that which is here donne for reasonable and necessarie.

We have also the example of the Latin, and Greke, where some wordes are not translated, but left in Hebrew, as they were first spoken & written; which seeing they could not or were not convenient to be translated into Latin or Greke, how much lesse could they, or was it reason to turn them into English? S. Augustin also yeldeth a reason, exemplifying in the words Amen and Alleluia for the more sacred authoritie therof: which doubtles is the cause why some names of solemne Feastes, Sacrifices, & other holie thinges are reserved in sacred tongues, Hebrew, Greke, or Latin.

Againe for necessitie, English not having a name, or sufficient terme, we either kepe the word as we find it, or only turne it to our English termination, because it would otherwise require manie wordes in English, to signifie one word of an other tongue. In which cases, we commonly put the explication in the margent. Briefly, our Apologie is easie against English Protestantes; because they also reserve some wordes in the original tongues, not translated into English; as Sabbath, Ephod, Pentecost, Proselyte, and some others. The sense wherof is in dede as soone lerned, as if they were turned so nere as is possible into English. And why then may we not say Prepuce, Phase or Pasch, Azimes, Breades of Proposition, Holocaust, and the like? rather than as Protestantes translate them, Foreskinne, Passeover, The feast of sweete breades, Shewbreades, Burnt offerings, &c. By which termes, whether they be truly translated into English or no, we wil passe over. Sure it is an Englishman is stil to seke, what they meane, as if they remained in Hebrew or Greke. It more importeth, that nothing be wittingly and falsly translated, for advantage of doctrine in matter of faith. . . .

With this then we wil conclude most deare (we speake to you al, that understand our tongue, whether you be of contrarie opinions in faith, or of mundane feare participate with an other Congregation, or professe with us the same Catholique Religion) to you al we present this worke: dayly beseching God Almightie, the Divine Wisedom, Eternal Goodnes, to create, illuminate, and replenish your spirites, with his Grace, that you may attaine eternal glorie, everie one in his measure, in those manie Mansions, prepared and promised by our Saviour in his Father's house. Not only to those which first received, & folowed his Divine doctrine, but to al that should afterwardes beleve in him, & kepe the same preceptes. For there is one God, one also Mediatour of God and men; Man Christ Jesus. Who gave himself a Redemption for al. Wherby appeareth his wil, that al should be saved. Why then are al not saved? The Apostle addeth, that they must first come to the knowlege of the truth. Because without faith it is impossible to please God.

* * *

To you therfore (dearest frendes mortal) we direct this speach; admonishing ourselves & you, in the Apostles wordes, that for so much as we have not yet resisted tentations to (last) bloud (and death itself) patience is stil necessarie for us, that doing the wil of God, we may receive the promise. So we repine not in tribulation, but ever love them that hate us, pittying their case, and rejoicing in our owne. For neither can we see during this life, how much good they do us; nor know how manie of them shal be (as we hartely desire they al may be) saved: our Lord and Saviour having paide the same price by his death, for them and for us. Love al therfore, pray for al.

* * *

Do not lose your confidence, which hath a greate remuneration. For yet a litle, and a very litle while, he that is to come, wil come, and he wil not slacke. Now the just liveth by faith, beleeving with hart to justice, and confessing with mouth to salvation. But he that withdraweth himself shal not please Christ's soule. Attend to your salvation, dearest countriemen. You that are farre of, draw nere, put on Christ. And you that are within Christ's fold, kepe your standing, persevere in him to the end. His grace dwel and remaine in you, that glorious crownes may be geven you. Amen.

THE EDUCATIONAL THEORY OF THE SOCIETY OF JESUS

(c. 1556)   From "The Constitutions of the Society of Jesus," part IV, as quoted in Edward A. Fitzpatrick, ed., *St. Ignatius and the* Ratio Studiorum (New York, 1933), pp. 49-51, 68-71, 100-01, 106-07.

Concerning the Instruction in Letters of Those
Who Are to Be Kept in the Society and in Other
Things Which Pertain to the Helping of the
Neighbor

Since the direct objective at which the Society aims is to help the souls of its members and of the neighbor to attain to the final end for which they were created, and since in addition to setting a good moral example, learning and methods of presenting it are necessary for the attaining of this end, therefore, after it seems that a fitting foundation for self-denial and for the necessary progress in virtue has been laid for those who have been admitted to probation, the education in letters and of the manner of utilizing them, so that they can aid to a better knowledge and service of God, our Creator and Lord, will be treated (Explanation A).

(Explanation A) Since the aim and end of this Society is by going to various parts of the world in obedience to the Vicar of our Lord Christ or to the Superior of the same Society, to preach the word of God, to hear confessions, and to make use of the other possible means, with the grace of God to help souls, it seemed necessary or at least eminently reasonable that those who enter upon this task should be men of good character, and in their learning suited to such a position. And because there are comparatively few people who are good and at the same time learned; and since of this number the greater part wish to rest from the labors which they have undertaken, we can see that it is going to be extremely difficult for the Society to be increased in numbers by men of this calibre, who are at once good and lettered; partly because of the great labors which our Rule demands, and partly because of the required self-renunciation. Therefore we who are interested in the preservation and increase of the Society to the greater praise and service of God and our Lord, must hold a different course, that of admitting mere youths, who by their native disposition give promise of a good character and intellect, so that they may develop into upright and learned men for the purpose of cultivating the vineyard of Christ our Lord; and of undertaking the college under those conditions which are contained in the Apostolic Letters, in the universities (if they are out of college), whether or not these universities be conducted by the Society. By this reasoning we are convinced in the Lord that it would be for the greater worship of the Divine Majesty, if those who are to devote themselves entirely to this service were increased in number and if they made progress in letters and virtue. There will be treated therefore first what pertains to the colleges and then what pertains to the universities. The matters concerning the colleges include first about the Founders; second about the already founded colleges, their material and temporal welfare; thirdly, about the Scholastics, who devote themselves to study, about their admission, their care, the subjects and methods of helping them as much as possible, and removal from study; and fourthly, about the government of these institutions.

It is for this purpose that the Society embraces college and sometimes even universities or *Studia generalia,* to which they may go who give a good indication of their character in the houses, while they are on probation, and yet are not sufficiently instructed in the doctrine necessary for our Rule, and where they may be instructed in this doctrine and in other things which pertain to the aid of souls. First, therefore, we shall treat of those things which pertain to the college, and then of what belongs to the university with the help which the Divine Wisdom will deign to grant us for His own glory and praise.

✳   ✳   ✳

Concerning the Doctrine Which the Scholastics of the
Society Ought to Study

Since the aim of the doctrine which is studied in this Society is with the aid of Divine grace to further the interests of their own souls and the souls of their neighbors, this, therefore, shall be the measure in general and for particular persons. From this measure therefore let it be decided what studies ours shall devote themselves to and how far they shall go in them. Speaking in general (Explanation A), the humane letters of the different tongues, and logic, natural and moral philosophy, metaphysics, and theology both scholastic and what is called "positive" (Explanation B), and sacred Scripture will conduce toward this end (Explanation C), and those who are sent to the colleges will pursue the studies of these faculties. And they will devote themselves with even greater diligence to those subjects which the supreme moderator of studies, considering times, places, and persons, etc., judges to be more advantageous in the Lord, to this above-mentioned end.

(Explanation A) Under humane letters, rhetoric in addition to grammar is to be understood.

(Explanation B) If in college there is not sufficient time to read the Councils, the Decrees, the Holy Doctors, and the other books on morals, after they have left the colleges each one can in private study and with the approval of his Superiors finish them, especially if he has laid a solid foundation in scholastic philosophy.

(Explanation C) According to the age, measure of the intelligence, disposition of mind, and instruction in letters of each one, or according to the measure of the common good which is hoped for, one should exercise himself in all of these faculties or in as many as possible; he who cannot excel in all ought to take care that he excels in some one of them.

2. In regard to particular persons (Explanation D), what this or that one should study is left to the prudence of the Superiors: but he who is naturally endowed with talent would be able to do more useful work in proportion as he has laid a solid foundation in the before-mentioned faculties.

(Explanation D) Some can be sent to college of whom it is not expected that they will come out learned in the manner spoken of, but rather that they may help others. A priest of this kind can hear confessions, etc. Both these and others in whom there is not much promise, because of advanced age or other causes, that they will make much progress in all of the faculties, it is meet that according to the prescription of the Superior they should devote themselves to those studies to which they can progress and let them take care to progress in the knowledge of languages, and in those subjects useful for the confessional and finally in those subjects which will be more profitable for the common good of souls.

3. Concerning the time to be devoted to any of the sciences, and when any one is to advance to further studies, the Rector after suitable examinations will consider and determine on the basis of suitable examination.

4. Let them follow in each faculty that teaching which is safer and more approved (Explanation E) and the authors who teach it; the responsibility for this will be in the hands of the Rector (who is to follow what shall be determined in the whole Society to be for the greater glory of God).

(Explanation E) No lectures should be given on those parts of books of humane letters which are contrary to virtue. The Society may use the rest as the "spoils of the Egyptians." The works of Christians, even though they may be good, are not to be read if the author is bad, lest some become attached to the author. It is meet, coming down to particulars, to decide just which books in letters and in the other disciplines may be taught and which may not.

By What Method the Scholastics Are to Be Helped to Learn These Studies Well

In order that the Scholastics may advance as much as possible in these subjects, they should strive first of all to guard the purity of their souls and to have a right intention in their study; seeking nothing else in letters but the Divine glory and the good of souls, they should beg frequently in their prayers for grace to make progress in learning toward this end.

2. Besides they should decide to apply their minds to their studies seriously and constantly, and they should persuade themselves that they will do nothing more

pleasing to God in the colleges than, if with the intention mentioned above, they diligently apply themselves to study.

Although it may happen that they may never use what they have learned, they should think that that labor of studying undertaken out of obedience and charity (as is proper) is a work of great merit in the sight of the Divine and Supreme Majesty.

*　　*　　*

Concerning the Sciences Which Are to Be Taught in the Universities of the Society

Since the aim of the Society and of its pursuits is to help the neighbor to a knowledge and love of God and to the salvation of their souls, and since for this end the chief means is the faculty of theology, the universities of the Society will lean most heavily upon this department, and it will treat thoroughly through suitable professors what pertain to scholastic doctrine and to the Sacred Scriptures and even as much of positive theology as is appropriate to our end (not touching, however, on that part of the Canons which gives rise to litigation).

2. And since instruction in theology and the application of it (especially in these times) demands a knowledge of the humane letters (Explanation A) both Latin and Greek and of the Hebrew tongue, suitable professors in these subjects also, and in sufficient numbers, shall be secured. Professors of other languages (Explanation B) may also be secured such as Chaldaic, Arabic, Indian, when these seem necessary or useful for the mentioned end, taking into account difference of country and the reasons which suggest the study of these languages.

(Explanation A) Under humane letters is to be understood besides grammar what pertains to rhetoric, poetry, and history.

(Explanation B) Since in some colleges and universities the object is to prepare men to help the Saracens or the Turks it will be proper to study Arabic and Chaldaic; if among the people of the Indies, then Indian; and so likewise the other languages which can be useful in other countries for similar causes.

3. So, since the arts and natural sciences (Explanation C) dispose the mind for theology, and serve to perfect its knowledge and application and of themselves help toward the same end, let them be treated with whatever diligence is proper and by learned professors, seeking in all things sincerely the honor and glory of God.

(Explanation C) There will be treated logic, physics, metaphysics, moral science, and even mathematics in so far as it helps toward the attaining of our proposed end. To teach others to read and write could also be a work of charity, if the number of persons in the Society were sufficient for us to undertake all things, but on account of the lack of members we do not ordinarily teach them.

4. The study of medicine and law, being more remote from the purpose of our Institute, will not be treated in the universities of the Society or at least the Society itself will not of itself undertake this task.

*　　*　　*

Concerning the Books Which Are to Be Read

In general (as was said in treating of colleges), those books are to form the subject of lectures which are considered in any subject to be of solid and sound doctrine.

Those (Explanation A) are not to be touched whose doctrine or whose authors are suspect. In each university these ought to be listed. In theology the Old and New Testament are to be lectured upon (Explanation B), and the scholastic doctrine of St. Thomas (Explanation C), and in that part of theology which is called "positive" those authors are to be chosen who seem to contribute most to our aim.

(Explanation A) Although a book may be free from all suspicion of evil teaching, it is not well to read it, if the author is suspect. For ordinarily it happens that he who reads a book becomes attached to the author, so that the authority which the author has in what he has said well, may persuade one into believing what he does not say well. For it rarely happens that some poison is not mixed in with that which comes from a heart filled with poison.

(Explanation B) Let the Master of Sentences be lectured upon. But if as time goes on some other author would be more useful to the students, as, for example, if some "summa" or book of scholastic theology is finished which seems better adapted to our times, then with serious consideration, and after diligent examination by men who in the whole Society are thought most able, and with the approbation of the General, it may be lectured upon. In the other sciences too, and in the humane letters, if some books composed in the Society are accepted as being more useful than others which are commonly in use, let this be done, with great carefulness, having always before our eyes our aim, the greater universal good.

(Explanation C) As some part of the Canon Law, or the Councils, etc.

2. In regard to the books in the classical languages of Latin and Greek let the universities as well as the colleges, as far as possible, abstain from reading to youths books in which there is anything that can hurt good morals (Explanation D), unless the objectionable words and subjects are expurgated.

(Explanation D) If some cannot be expurgated at all, as Terence, then they should not be read at all; lest the kind of subjects offend the purity of souls.

3. In logic and natural philosophy, moral philosophy, and metaphysics, the doctrine of Aristotle is to be followed. And in other liberal arts and in the commentaries of both of these authors and the authors of humane letters, let a selection be made, let those be listed whom the pupils ought to know and whom the teachers themselves ought to follow before all others in the teaching which they themselves give. The Rector is to proceed in all the matters which he passes upon in accordance with what is thought in the whole Society to contribute most to the glory of God.

IGNATIUS LOYOLA'S PLAN OF STUDY FOR THE SOCIETY OF JESUS: THE RATIO STUDIORUM (1599)   From Edward A. Fitzpatrick, ed., *St. Ignatius and the Ratio Studiorum* (New York, 1933), pp. 150-55, 230-33.

Common Rules for All Professors of Higher Faculties

Purpose.—The special duty of a teacher shall be to move his hearers, both within class and out, as opportunity offers, to a reverence and love of God and of the virtues which are pleasing in His sight, and to pursue all their studies to that end.

2. *Prayer before Class.*—To keep this in mind, someone shall recite a short prayer adapted to this purpose at the beginning of class, and the teacher and all the pupils shall listen attentively with bared head; or at least the teacher shall sign himself with the sign of the Cross and begin.

3. *Helping Students to Devotion.*—He shall also assist his pupils by frequent prayers to God and by the example of his own religious life. It will be appropriate for him not to neglect exhortations, at least on the days before feast days, and at the beginning of the longer vacations. He shall urge them strongly to pray to God, to examine their consciences at evening, to receive frequently and duly the sacraments of penance and the Eucharist, to attend Mass daily and sermons on all feast days, to avoid bad habits, to detest vice, and to cultivate the virtues worthy of a Christian.

4. *Obedience to the Prefect.*—He shall obey the Prefect of Studies in all matters which pertain to studies and the discipline of the classes; he shall give him for revision all theses before they are presented; he shall not undertake to explain any book or writer not in the usual course, or introduce any new method in teaching or disputation.

5. *Moderation in Refuting.*—In those questions in which he is free to hold either side, he shall defend his view in such a way as to allow moderate and kindly consideration for the opposite view, especially if the previous teacher has held that view. But if writers can be reconciled, he must be careful not to neglect to do so. Finally, he shall conduct himself with moderation in citing and refuting authorities.

6. *Avoiding New Opinions.*—Even in matters where there is no risk to faith and devotion, no one shall introduce new questions in matters of great moment, or any opinion which does not have suitable authority, without first consulting his superiors; he shall not teach anything opposed to the axioms of learned men or the general belief of scholars. Rather, all should follow closely the approved doctors and, as far as local custom permits, the views accepted in Catholic schools.

7. *Brevity in Refuting Others' Views and Proving his Own.*—He shall not bring forward any views which are useless, antiquated, absurd, or patently false; nor shall he use too much time in mentioning and refuting such views. He shall strive to prove his conclusions not by the number of his arguments but by their effectiveness. He shall not digress to extraneous matter, nor shall he treat any part of his subject-matter more extensively than circumstances require, nor in the wrong place. He shall not heap up possible objections, but shall bring forward briefly only the strongest of them, unless their refutation is quite clear from his explanation of the thesis.

8. *Authorities to Be Quoted Infrequently, but Accurately.*—He shall not cite the authorities of learned men too often; but if he has the evidence of outstanding writers to confirm his views, he shall faithfully quote the other's own words, if

possible, but briefly, especially the sacred Scriptures, the Councils, and the holy Fathers. It does not befit the dignity of a teacher to cite any author which he has not himself read.

9. *Dictation.*—If anyone can teach without dictating, yet in such a way that the pupils can easily tell what ought to be written down, it is preferable for him not to dictate. Certainly teachers who dictate should not pause after every word, but speak for a single breath and then, if necessary, repeat the words; they should not dictate the entire thesis and then explain it, but dictate and explain in turn.

10. *Referring Students to Books.*—If the teacher brings forward material from books which are easily available, he shall explain rather than dictate; rather, he shall refer the students to those books which treat the matter in hand accurately and in detail.

11. *Repetitions in Class.*—After the lecture let him remain in the classroom or near the classroom for at least a quarter of an hour so that the students may approach him to ask questions, so that he may sometimes ask an account of the lectures, and so that the lectures may be repeated.

12. *Review at Home.*—Every day except Saturdays, vacations, and feast days, an hour is to be designated at which the members of the Order shall review the matter of their classes and hold disputations, so that in this way talents may be exercised and difficulties which have occurred may be removed. And so one or another should be told beforehand to recite from memory, but no longer than a quarter of an hour; then one or two should raise objections and a like number answer them; then if time remains, doubtful points should be raised; in order that such time may be left, the teacher shall insist strictly on the form of argumentation and, when no new points are raised, bring it to an end.

13. *General Repetitions.*—The repetition of all past lectures at the end of the year is to be so arranged that unless something interferes, a whole month should be left free not only from (regular) repetitions but also from lectures.

14. *Weekly Disputations.*—On Saturday, or some other day of the week, according to the custom of the school, there shall be a disputation in each class, lasting for two hours, or longer when there is a large attendance of externs. If there are two feast days in one week, or if the weekly vacation falls on a feast day, there shall be no disputation on Saturday, but a lecture; but if this shall happen for three successive weeks, one disputation shall be held.

15. *Monthly Disputations.*—Where the accepted custom of the school does not prevent, disputations should be held, in both the forenoon and the afternoon, on a fixed day every month except the last three summer months, or, if the number of pupils is small, every other month; as many pupils as there are teachers shall individually defend the questions of their respective teachers.

16. *Supporting the Objections.*—Some of our other learned men and teachers, although of other branches, shall be present at these disputations; to make the discussion more lively, they shall press the objections which are raised; but shall not undertake the support of any argument in which the original objector is still arguing earnestly and with good effect. Visiting teachers shall also be permitted to do this and so may be invited to bring objections according to custom, unless the usage of the locality does not permit.

17. *Disputation Limited to the More Learned.*—Only the more learned of the pupils shall engage in public disputation; others shall be instructed privately until they are so well trained as not to be considered unworthy of public appearance.

18. *Arrangement for the Disputation.*—The teacher shall consider the day of disputations no less fruitful and worthy of attention than a day of lecture, and

remember that the benefit and spirit of the disputation depend upon him; he shall preside in such a way that he may himself seem to take part on both sides; he shall praise anything good which is said, and call it to the attention of all; if some unusually difficult objection is proposed, he shall make a brief suggestion to support the defender or direct the objector; he shall not keep silent too long, nor yet speak all the time, but let the pupils set forth what they know; he shall himself correct or amplify what is set forth; he shall order the objector to proceed as long as the objection has any force; in fact, he shall add to the difficulty and not pass over it if the one who is bringing objections proceeds too soon to a new objection; he shall not permit an objection which is practically answered to be pressed too far, nor an answer which is unsound to stand too long; after a discussion, he shall briefly define and explain the entire matter. If there is anything else which is customary to make disputations better attended or more spirited, it shall be carefully preserved.

19. *Conference with his Beadle.*—He shall occasionally consult with his helper, or Beadle, appointed by the Rector, and question him about the status of the entire class and the industry and progress of the externs; he shall see to it that the other performs his tasks faithfully and accurately.

20. *Progress of the Students.*—He shall, with the help of Divine grace, be earnest and diligent in all his duties and observant of the progress of his students, both in lectures and in other literary exercises; he shall not appear more friendly to one pupil than another; he shall despise no one; he shall attend to the studies of the poor the same as those of the rich; he shall especially seek the progress of each of his Scholastics.

Rules for the Professor of Sacred Scripture

Special Attention to Literal Meaning.—He shall realize that his duties are to explain sacred literature piously, learnedly, and seriously, according to the true and literal meaning, in order to strengthen true faith in God and the establishment of sound morals.

2. *The Vulgate Edition.*—Among his other duties, it is especially important that he defend the version adopted by the Church.

3. *Observing and Comparing Phrases of Sacred Scripture.*—To learn this true sense he shall carefully observe the expressions and phrases peculiar to sacred Scripture; he shall not only consider the context of the place which he is reading, but also carefully compare other places in which the same phrases have the same or different meanings.

✳   ✳   ✳

Rules of the Professor of Lower Grammar Classes

Grade.—The grade of this school is the perfect knowledge of the rudiments and a beginning knowledge of syntax, if it begins with the declensions up to the construction of the common verbs, and indeed where there will be two divisions of this class. The nouns, verbs, rudiments, and the fourteen rules of construction and the kinds of nouns will be given in the lower division from the first book of grammar; but in the upper division there will be given from the first book the declensions of nouns without the appendices, and the preterits and supines, but from the second book, the introduction, to syntax, without appendices up to impersonal verbs. In Greek, however, the lower division will learn to read and write; the upper division will learn simple nouns, the substantive verb, and the baritone verb. But for prelections nothing except certain very easy letters of Cicero which have been selected for this purpose shall be used, and if possible, they should be printed separately.

2. *Division of Time.*—The division of time will be the following: In the first hour of the morning Cicero and grammar will be recited by heart to the Decurions. The Preceptor will correct the written work collected by the Decurions, assigning in the meanwhile various exercises to the students which will be spoken of below in Rule 4. In the second hour in the morning the last prelection of Cicero will be briefly repeated, and a new one will be explained during half an hour and recited; at the end the theme will be dictated. The last half-hour of the morning in both divisions something from the first book of grammar according to what is assigned for each division will be explained and repeated, either every other day to each of the orders or daily to both. Afterwards, however, all will be recited either to the master or to one another in a concertatio.

But on those days when there is no new precept to be explained in the afternoon (for on most days a precept is to be assigned), then this morning prelection will take the place of the afternoon prelection; but the last half-hour in the morning will be given mostly to a concertatio or exercise.

The first hour in the afternoon both Latin and Greek grammar will be recited, the master inspecting the marks given by the Decurions and correcting the written work during half an hour at most, which was assigned in the morning, or is left over from what was brought from home. At the end the last prelection in grammar will be reviewed. The second hour of the morning in the higher division syntax will be explained, and in the lower division the rudiments, the genders of nouns, and afterwards the fourteen precepts; to Greek, however, a little more than a quarter of an hour shall be given. In the last half-hour there will be a concertatio or an explanation of something dictated from the rules of grammar.

On Saturdays let the prelections of the whole week be publicly recited from memory for the first hour of the morning; let them be reviewed the second hour; during the last half-hour let there be a concertatio or a declamation.

Let the same order be followed after lunch, except that the catechism is recited the first hour, along with grammar. Let the last half-hour be spent in an explanation of the catechism or in a pious exhortation, unless this was held on Friday; but if it was, let the time be occupied by that subject in whose place the catechism had been substituted.

3. *Method of Correcting a Paper.*—In correcting a paper, let him show if it is in contradiction to the precepts of grammar, spelling, or punctuation; if difficulties have been avoided, let him explain everything according to the standards of grammatical precepts; and let him not neglect to repeat the conjugations and declensions as opportunity offers.

4. *Exercises while Written Work Is Being Corrected.*—The exercises of the students while the master corrects the written work will be, for example, to put into Latin what is dictated in the vernacular from some rule of syntax; to translate a lesson in Cicero from Latin into the vernacular, and to transcribe the same in Latin; to pick out questions from the precepts of grammar, especially those recently explained and expressions to be proposed to the rivals; to make concordances and write Greek and other things of this kind.

CURRICULUM FOR THE EDUCATION OF THE JESUITS (1599) From *The Ratio Studiorum* as quoted in Frederick Farrington, *French Secondary Schools* (New York, 1910), pp. 394-95.

CLASS	SUBJECTS OF INSTRUCTION, AND TIME ALLOWANCE		AUTHORS AND REMARKS
	Morning	Afternoon	
Sixth	Recitation on the Latin author, and on Latin and Greek grammar . . . . . ¾ h. Correction of task. . . . ½ h. Latin translation, review and advance . . . . ¾ h. Mother tongue and accessory exercises . . . . . ½ h.	Recitation on the Latin author, and on the grammar . . 1 h. Translation of Latin author. Greek reading, a quarter-hour twice a week. Dictation of the composition work . . . . 1 h. Discussion. Mother tongue and accessory exercises . . . . . ½ h.	Cicero, Extracts; Phaedrus, Fables; Nepos, Lives. Greek, Exercises in reading and writing.
Fifth	Recitation on the Latin author, and on Latin and Greek grammar . . . . . ¾ h. Correction of task. . . . ½ h. Translation, review and advance . . . . ¾ h. Mother tongue and accessory exercises . . . . . ½ h.	Recitation on the Latin author, and on the grammar . . 1 h. Translation of Latin and Greek authors alternately every two days. Dictation of the composition work . . . . . 1 h. Discussion. Mother tongue and accessory exercises . . . . . ½ h.	Cicero, Selected letters; Caesar; Ovid, Selections; AEsop, Fables; Cebes; Lucian, Selected dialogues.
Fourth	Recitation on the Latin and Greek grammar . . . . . ¾ h. Correction of task. . . . ½ h. Translation, review and advance . . . . ¾ h. Mother tongue and accessory exercises . . . . . ½ h.	Recitation on Latin grammar, versification, and the author, on successive days . . . . 1 h. Translation of a Latin poet and a Greek author, alternately every other day. Dictation of the composition work . . . . 1 h. Discussion. Mother tongue and accessory exercises . . . . . ½ h.	Cicero, Letters, De amicitia, De senectute; Easy speeches of Cicero; Sallust; Quintus Curtius; Extracts from Livy, Ovid, Catullus, Tibullus, Propertius, and Virgil: Eclogues; Georgics, 4th bk.; AEneid, 5th and 7th bks. Greek: St. Chrysostom, Xenophon, and other similar authors.

CLASS	SUBJECTS OF INSTRUCTION, AND TIME ALLOWANCE		AUTHORS AND REMARKS
	Morning	Afternoon	
Third	Recitation on the Latin author, and on the grammar. General principles of elocution and style ..... ¾ h. Correction of task .... ½ h. Translation, review and advance .... ¾ h. Mother tongue and accessory exercises ..... ½ h.	Recitation on the Latin author, and on the grammar .. 1 h. Translation, every other day, and a Greek (or interpretation of a French) author. Dictation of the composition work .... 1 h. Discussion and accessory exercises .... ½ h.	Cicero, Speeches; Caesar; Sallust; Livy; Quintus Curtius; AEneid (save the fourth book); Horace, Odes (selected). Greek: Isocrates; St. Chrysostom; St. Basil; Plato; Plutarch; Phocylides; Theognis; St. Gregory of Nazianzus; Synesius.
Second	No special program	No special program	No special program
Rhetoric	Memory work. Translation, review and advance .... 1 h. Reading from an orator, review and advance. Dictation of a text from an oration. Discussion and accessory exercises ... 1 h.	Translation of passages from the rhetoric. Translation of a Greek, or interpretation of a French author .... 1 h. Reading from one of the poets. Correction of the task of the morning. Dictation of the subject of an oration .... 1 h.	For the principles of rhetoric, Cicero and Quintilian. No special directions as to the Latin authors to be translated. Greek: Demosthenes, Plato, Thueydides, Homer, Hesiod, Pindar, St. Gregory of Nazianzus, St. Basil, St. Chrysostom. On holidays one of the historians or some passage of historical significance is explained.

DISCIPLINE AT THE "LITTLE SCHOOLS" OF PORT ROYAL, FRANCE

(c. 1560) From H. C. Barnard, ed. and trans., *The Port Royalists on Education* (Cambridge, Mass., 1918), pp. 114-18.

1. Claude Lancelot

He [M. de Saint-Cyran] did not wish us to have recourse to the cane as a means of punishment except for serious faults and then only after having tried all other methods one after the other. For he wished us first to bear with their faults in order that we might test ourselves in the sight of God and do nothing upon impulse, and also that we might pray to God on their behalf before we reproved them. Next he wished us merely to warn them by certain signs, then by words; and after rebuking them, to use threats, to deprive them for a while of something that they liked—*e.g.* their playtime, their lunch or part of their dinner—and to resort to the cane only in the last extremity and for serious offenses, especially in the case of those who could obviously be won over by kindness and persuasion. At the same time he wished us to employ this method of punishment for such as were naturally frivolous and hot-tempered, who were given to telling falsehoods and bursting into laughter on the most solemn occasions. In short, like S. Benedict, he did not wish that they should be forgiven for faults committed in church.

He used to say that to employ punishments without having first prayed long was to act like a Jew and to fail to recognise that everything depends on the blessing of God and on His grace which we should endeavour to draw down upon our pupils by our forbearance towards them. He added that sometimes we ought even to punish and chastise ourselves on their behalf, not only because we ought always to be afraid of being partly responsible for their faults, either by our hastiness or our negligence, but also because this is a duty incumbent upon all alike who find themselves entrusted with the charge of others. He used to say that we must keep a constant watch to counteract that kept by the devil, who is always seeking an entrance into these tender souls. He therefore used to recommend us by our own prayers to assist the prayers of the children under our care; and thus, since they cannot be expected to be always on their guard, to relieve them of part of this duty. He used to make a point of warning us that in order to train children well we must pray more than scold, and speak more about them to God, than about God to them. For he did not like us to give them long lectures on piety and to weary them with precepts. He wished us to confine such instruction as far as possible to the occasions and opportunities which God brings about, as indicated by the impulse which he gives us and the willingness to hear which He shows us in them; for the impulse to give no less than the gift itself depends on God and what we say under such conditions would have quite a different result from what we could say on our own initiative.

2. Pierre Coustel

When repeated rebukes and warnings have proved fruitless we must at last change our methods and bring to their senses by punishment those whom plain reason has not been sufficient to keep within the limits of their duty; this is particularly necessary when they are untruthful or disobedient, when they are guilty of disgraceful conduct or cheating, and when they refuse to apply themselves to their lessons as they should. . . . Scripture supports what I have just pointed out when it says: "He that spareth the rod hateth his son"; while to adopt the opposite course is but to follow the example of God Himself, for "whom the Lord loveth He chasteneth." Granting then this maxim that children must be punished when they do wrong, we may next ask what course should be adopted in the event of this regrettable necessity.

(1) Recourse should be had to punishment only after the other means which have already been employed have proved useless; in the same way the wise surgeon uses the red-hot iron to cure a wound only when less drastic remedies have failed. We may therefore first of all deprive them of their recreation, keep them in, or make them feel ashamed in front of their schoolfellows or parents.

(2) The cane should be used as seldom as possible for fear lest children should become accustomed and hardened to it.

(3) We should punish them only in a pure spirit of affection and with a sincere desire for their true benefit. A father is always a father; and whatever severity he is at times compelled to use towards his child, he can never rid himself of the love which nature has planted deep in his heart. A master as far as possible should be of the same frame of mind.

(4) We should never administer punishment in a fit of passion or anger. If we feel our temper rising we should try to calm ourselves and, if possible, defer the punishment to some other time, for fear of doing anything unadvisedly. For anger should never outstrip reason which is the mistress, but should merely follow it and carry out its orders.

(5) According to S. Bernard, we should never administer punishment save with fear and trembling. "When a fault is so far beyond excuse," he says, "that one cannot be merciful without weakening justice, one should none the less punish only with trembling and grief, being stirred more by the necessity of carrying out one's duty than by eagerness to punish the culprit. For this reason it should always be manifest that one goes to such lengths against one's will."

(6) When children are so incorrigible and hardened that nothing is to be gained by severity and punishments serve to make them worse rather than better, one is considerably embarrassed. Must they be allowed to do whatever they like and must we give up the medicine because our patients are incurable? Moreover, what is the use of giving oneself considerable trouble to no purpose? In such cases it seems that all we can do is to regard them as severe penances imposed upon us by God, and we must endure them patiently without ever losing hope that, in His goodness and mercy, they may change for the better; since with time and trouble even the most savage animals can be tamed.

*   *   *

Contrive that their studies appear as a kind of pastime or game rather than as a troublesome and tedious employment. This was doubtless why the ancients represented the Muses with a very cheerful and lively air—some touching a guitar or playing a lute, others dancing or singing, and all disporting themselves in different ways. This again is the reason why the school is called *ludus literarius* and the schoolmaster *ludimagister*. We must not then exact from children while they are of a tender age an application and devotion to study equal to that which we have a right to demand from fully formed minds. This would mean giving them a dislike for study, which might have undesirable consequences and which also might possibly persist as they grew older.

The Age of Science

COPERNICUS ON ASTRONOMY (c. 1543)   From *The Commentariolus,* as quoted in Edward Rosen, ed. and trans., *Three Copernican Treatises* (New York, 1939), pp. 57-60.

Our ancestors assumed, I observe, a large number of celestial spheres for this reason especially, to explain the apparent motion of the planets by the principle of regularity. For they thought it altogether absurd that a heavenly body, which is a perfect sphere, should not always move uniformly. They saw that by connecting and combining regular motions in various ways they could make any body appear to move to any position.

Callippus and Eudoxus, who endeavored to solve the problem by the use of concentric spheres, were unable to account for all the planetary movements; they had to explain not merely the apparent revolutions of the planets but also the fact that these bodies appear to us sometimes to mount higher in the heavens, sometimes to descend; and this fact is incompatible with the principle of concentricity. Therefore it seemed better to employ eccentrics and epicycles, a system which most scholars finally accepted.

Yet the planetary theories of Ptolemy and most other astronomers, although consistent with the numerical data, seemed likewise to present no small difficulty. For these theories were not adequate unless certain equants were also conceived; it then appeared that a planet moved with uniform velocity neither on its deferent nor about the center of its epicycle. Hence a system of this sort seemed neither sufficiently absolute nor sufficiently pleasing to the mind.

Having become aware of these defects, I often considered whether there could perhaps be found a more reasonable arrangement of circles, from which every apparent inequality would be derived and in which everything would move uniformly about its proper center, as the rule of absolute motion requires. After I had addressed myself to this very difficult and almost insoluble problem, the suggestion at length came to me how it could be solved with fewer and much simpler constructions than were formerly used, if some assumptions (which are called axioms) were granted me. They follow in this order.

Assumptions

1. There is no one center of all the celestial circles or spheres.

2. The center of the earth is not the center of the universe, but only of gravity and of the lunar sphere.

3. All the spheres revolve about the sun as their mid-point, and therefore the sun is the center of the universe.

4. The ratio of the earth's distance from the sun to the height of the firmament is so much smaller than the ratio of the earth's radius to its distance from the sun that the distance from the earth to the sun is imperceptible in comparison with the height of the firmament.

5. Whatever motion appears in the firmament arises not from any motion of the firmament, but from the earth's motion. The earth together with its circumjacent elements performs a complete rotation on its fixed poles in a daily motion, while the firmament and highest heaven abide unchanged.

6. What appear to us as motions of the sun arise not from its motion but from the motion of the earth and our sphere, with which we revolve about the sun like any other planet. The earth has, then, more than one motion.

7. The apparent retrograde and direct motion of the planets arises not from their motion but from the earth's. The motion of the earth alone, therefore, suffices to explain so many apparent inequalities in the heavens.

Having set forth these assumptions, I shall endeavor briefly to show how uniformity of the motions can be saved in a systematic way. However, I have thought it well, for the sake of brevity, to omit from this sketch mathematical demonstrations, reserving these for my larger work. But in the explanation of the circles I shall set down here the lengths of the radii; and from these the reader who is not unacquainted with mathematics will readily perceive how closely this arrangement of circles agrees with the numerical data and observations.

Accordingly, let no one suppose that I have gratuitously asserted, with the Pythagoreans, the motion of the earth; strong proof will be found in my exposition of the circles. For the principal arguments by which the natural philosophers attempt to establish the immobility of the earth rest for the most part on the appearances; it is particularly such arguments that collapse here, since I treat the earth's immobility as due to an appearance.

The Order of the Spheres

The celestial spheres are arranged in the following order. The highest is the immovable sphere of the fixed stars, which contains and gives position to all things. Beneath it is Saturn, which Jupiter follows, then Mars. Below Mars is the sphere on which we revolve; then Venus; last is Mercury. The lunar sphere revolves about the center of the earth and moves with the earth like an epicycle. In the same order also, one planet surpasses another in speed of revolution, according as they trace greater or smaller circles. Thus Saturn completes its revolution in thirty years, Jupiter in twelve, Mars in two and one-half, and the earth in one year; Venus in nine months, Mercury in three. . . .

GALILEO DEFENDS THE COPERNICAN SYSTEM (1630) From Galileo,
Dialogue Concerning the Two Chief World Systems—Ptolemaic and Copernican, Stillman Drake, trans. (Berkeley, 1953), pp. 5-7.

Several years ago there was published in Rome a salutary edict which, in order to obviate the dangerous tendencies of our present age, imposed a seasonable silence upon the Pythagorean opinion that the earth moves. There were those who impudently asserted that this decree had its origin not in judicious inquiry, but in passion none too well informed. Complaints were to be heard that advisers who were totally unskilled at astronomical observations ought not to clip the wings of reflective intellects by means of rash prohibitions.

Upon hearing such carping insolence, my zeal could not be contained. Being thoroughly informed about that prudent determination, I decided to appear openly in the theater of the world as a witness of the sober truth. I was at that time in Rome; I was not only received by the most eminent prelates of that Court, but had their applause; indeed, this decree was not published without some previous notice of it having been given to me. Therefore I propose in the present work to show to foreign nations that as much is understood of this matter in Italy, and particularly in Rome, as transalpine diligence can ever have imagined. Collecting all the reflections that properly concern the Copernican system, I shall make it known that everything was brought before the attention of the Roman censorship, and that there proceed from this clime not only dogmas for the welfare of the soul, but ingenious discoveries for the delight of the mind as well.

To this end I have taken the Copernican side in the discourse, proceeding as with a pure mathematical hypothesis and striving by every artifice to represent it as superior to supposing the earth motionless—not, indeed, absolutely, but as against the arguments of some professed Peripatetics. These men indeed deserve not even that name, for they do not walk about; they are content to adore the shadows, philosophizing not with due circumspection but merely from having memorized a few ill-understood principles.

Three principal headings are treated. First, I shall try to show that all experiments practicable upon the earth are insufficient measures for proving its mobility, since they are indifferently adaptable to an earth in motion or at rest. I hope in so doing to reveal many observations unknown to the ancients. Secondly, the celestial phenomena will be examined, strengthening the Copernican hypothesis until it might seem that this must triumph absolutely. Here new reflections are adjoined which might be used in order to simplify astronomy, though not because of any necessity imposed by nature. In the third place, I shall propose an ingenious speculation. It happens that long ago I said that the unsolved problem of the ocean tides might receive some light from assuming the motion of the earth. This assertion of mine, passing by word of mouth, found loving fathers who adopted it as a child of their own ingenuity. Now, so that no stranger may ever appear who, arming himself with our weapons, shall charge us with want of attention to such an important matter, I have thought it good to reveal those probabilities which might render this plausible, given that the earth moves.

I hope that from these considerations the world will come to know that if other nations have navigated more, we have not theorized less. It is not from failing to take count of what others have thought that we have yielded to asserting that the earth is motionless, and holding the contrary to be a mere mathematical caprice, but (if for nothing else) for those reasons that are supplied by piety, religion, the knowledge of Divine Omnipotence, and a consciousness of the limitations of the human mind.

I have thought it most appropriate to explain these concepts in the form of dialogues, which, not being restricted to the rigorous observance of mathematical laws, make room also for digressions which are sometimes no less interesting than the principal argument.

Many years ago I was often to be found in the marvelous city of Venice, in discussions with Signore Giovanni Francesco Sagredo, a man of noble extraction and trenchant wit. From Florence came Signore Filippo Salviati, the least of whose glories were the eminence of his blood and the magnificence of his fortune. His was a sublime intellect which fed no more hungrily upon any pleasure than it did upon fine meditations. I often talked with these two of such matters in the presence of a certain Peripatetic philosopher whose greatest obstacle in apprehending the truth seemed to be the reputation he had acquired by his interpretations of Aristotle.

Now, since bitter death has deprived Venice and Florence of those two great luminaries in the very meridian of their years, I have resolved to make their fame live on in these pages, so far as my poor abilities will permit, by introducing them as interlocutors in the present argument. (Nor shall the good Peripatetic lack a place; because of his excessive affection toward the *Commentaries* of Simplicius, I have thought fit to leave him under the name of the author he so much revered, without mentioning his own.) May it please those two great souls, ever venerable to my heart, to accept this public monument of my undying love. And may the memory of their eloquence assist me in delivering to posterity the promised reflections.

DESCARTES' DISCOURSE ON METHOD (1637)   From Descartes, *The Method, Meditations, and Selections from the Principles of Descartes,* John Veitch, trans. (London, 1887), pp. 11-20, 32-35, 37, 40, 60-61, 75-76.

It is true that, while busied only in considering the manners of other men, I found here, too, scarce any ground for settled conviction, and remarked hardly less contradiction among them than in the opinions of the philosophers. So that the greatest advantage I derived from the study consisted in this, that, observing many things which, however extravagant and ridiculous to our apprehension, are yet by common consent received and approved by other great nations, I learned to entertain too decided a belief in regard to nothing of the truth of which I had been persuaded merely by example and custom: and thus I gradually extricated myself from many errors powerful enough to darken our Natural Intelligence, and incapacitate us in great measure from listening to Reason. But after I had been occupied several years in thus studying the book of the world, and in essaying to gather some experience, I at length resolved to make myself an object of study, and to employ all the powers of my mind in choosing the paths I ought to follow; an undertaking which was accompanied with greater success than it would have been had I never quitted my country or my books.

I was then in Germany, attracted thither by the wars in that country, which have not yet been brought to a termination; and as I was returning to the army from the coronation of the Emperor, the setting in of winter arrested me in a locality where, as I found no society to interest me, and was besides fortunately undisturbed by any cares or passions, I remained the whole day in seclusion, with full opportunity to occupy my attention with my own thoughts. Of these one of the very first that occurred to me was, that there is seldom so much perfection in works composed of many separate parts, upon which different hands have been employed, as in those completed by a single master. Thus it is observable that the building, which a single architect has planned and executed, are generally more elegant and commodious than those which several have attempted to improve, by making old walls serve for purposes for which they were not originally built. Thus also, those ancient cities which, from being at first only villages, have become, in course of time, large towns, are usually but ill laid out compared with the regularly constructed towns which a professional architect has freely planned on an open plain; so that although the several buildings of the former may often equal or surpass in beauty those of the latter, yet when one observes their indiscriminate juxtaposition, there a large one and here a small, and the consequent crookedness and irregularity of the streets, one is disposed to allege that chance rather than any human will guided by reason, must have led to such an arrangement. And if we consider that nevertheless there have been at all times certain officers whose duty it was to see that private buildings contributed to public ornament, the difficulty of reaching high perfection with but the materials of others to operate on, will be readily acknowledged. In the same way I fancied that those nations which, starting from a semi-barbarous state and advancing to civilisation by slow degrees, have had their laws successively determined, and, as it were, forced upon them simply by experience of the hurtfulness of particular crimes and disputes, would by this process come to be possessed of less perfect institutions than those which, from the commencement of their association as communities, have followed the appointments of some wise legislator. . . . In the same way I thought that the sciences contained in books, (such of them at least as are made up of probable reasonings, without demonstrations,) composed as they are of the opinions of many different individuals massed together, are farther removed from truth than the simple inference which a man of good sense using his natural and unprejudiced judgment draws respecting the matters of his experience. And because we have all to pass through a state of infancy to manhood, and have been of necessity, for a length of time, governed by our desires and preceptors, (whose dictates were frequently conflicting, while neither perhaps always counselled us for the best,) I farther concluded that it is almost impossible that our judgments can be so correct or solid as they would have been, had our Reason been mature from the moment of our birth, and had we always been guided by it alone.

It is true, however, that it is not customary to pull down all the houses of a town with the single design of rebuilding them differently, and thereby rendering the streets more handsome; but it often happens that a private individual takes down his own with the view of erecting it anew, and that people are even sometimes constrained to this when their houses are in danger of falling from age, or when the foundations are insecure. With this before me by way of example, I was persuaded that it would indeed be preposterous for a private individual to think of reforming a state by fundamentally changing it throughout, and overturning it in order to set it up amended; and the same I thought was true of any similar project for reforming the body of the Sciences, or the order of teaching them established in the Schools: but as for the opinions which up to that time I had embraced, I thought that I could not do better than resolve at once to sweep them wholly away, that I might afterwards be in a position to admit either others more correct, or even perhaps the same when they had undergone the scrutiny of Reason. I firmly believed that in this way I would much better succeed in the conduct of my life, than if I built only upon old foundations, and leant upon principles which, in my youth, I had taken upon trust. For although I recognised various difficulties in this undertaking, these were not, however, without remedy, nor once to be compared with such as attend the slightest reformation in public affairs. Large bodies, if once overthrown, are with great difficulty set up again, or even kept erect when once seriously shaken, and the fall of such is always disastrous. Then if there are any imperfections in the constitutions of states, (and that many such exist the diversity of constitutions is alone sufficient to assure us,) custom has without doubt materially smoothed their inconveniences, and has even managed to steer altogether clear of, or insensibly corrected a number which sagacity could not have provided against with equal effect; and, in fine, the defects are almost always more tolerable than the change necessary for their removal; in the same manner that highways which wind among mountains, by being much frequented, become gradually so smooth and commodious, that it is much better to follow them than to seek a straighter path by climbing over the tops of rocks and descending to the bottoms of precipices.

Hence it is that I cannot in any degree approve of those restless and busy meddlers who, called neither by birth nor fortune to take part in the management of public affairs, are yet always projecting reforms; and if I thought that this Tract contained aught which might justify the suspicion that I was a victim of such folly, I would by no means permit its publication. I have never contemplated anything higher than the reformation of my own opinions, and basing them on a foundation wholly my own.

* * *

. . . I had become aware, even so early as during my college life, that no opinion, however absurd and incredible, can be imagined, which has not been maintained by some one of the philosophers; and afterwards in the course of my travels I remarked that all those whose opinions are decidedly repugnant to ours are not on that account barbarians and savages, but on the contrary that many of these nations make an equally good, if not a better, use of their Reason than we do. I took into account also the very different character which a person brought up from infancy in France or Germany exhibits, from that which, with the same mind originally, this individual would have possessed had he lived always among the Chinese or with savages, and the circumstance that in dress itself the fashion which pleased us ten years ago, and which may again, perhaps, be received into favour before ten years have gone, appears to us at this moment extravagant and ridiculous.

* * *

Among the branches of Philosophy, I had, at an earlier period, given some attention to Logic, and among those of the Mathematics to Geometrical Analysis and Algebra,—three Arts or Sciences which ought, as I conceived, to contribute something to my design. But, on examination, I found that, as for Logic, its syllogisms and the majority of its other precepts are of avail rather in the communication of what we already know, or even as the Art of Lully, in speaking without judgment of things of which we are ignorant, than in the investigation of the unknown; and although this Science contains indeed a number of correct and very excellent precepts, there are, nevertheless, so many others, and these either injurious or superfluous, mingled with the former, that it is almost quite as difficult to effect a severance of the true from the false as it is to extract a Diana or a Minerva from a rough block of marble. . . . By these considerations I was induced to seek some other Method which would comprise the advantages of the three and be exempt from their defects. And as a multitude of laws often only hampers justice, so that a state is best governed when, with few laws, these are rigidly administered; in like manner, instead of the great number of precepts of which Logic is composed, I believed that the four following would prove perfectly sufficient for me, provided I took the firm and unwavering resolution never in a single instance to fail in observing them.

The *first* was never to accept anything for true which I did not clearly know to be such; that is to say, carefully to avoid precipitancy and prejudice, and to comprise nothing more in my judgment than what was presented to my mind so clearly and distinctly as to exclude all ground of doubt.

The *second*, to divide each of the difficulties under examination into as many parts as possible, and as might be necessary for its adequate solution.

The *third*, to conduct my thoughts in such order that, by commencing with objects the simplest and easiest to know, I might ascend by little and little, and, as it were, step by step, to the knowledge of the more complex; assigning in thought a certain order even to those objects which in their own nature do not stand in a relation of antecedence and sequence.

And the *last*, in every case to make enumerations so complete, and reviews so general, that I might be assured that nothing was omitted.

The long chains of simple and easy reasonings by means of which geometers are accustomed to reach the conclusions of their most difficult demonstrations, had led me to imagine that all things, to the knowledge of which man is competent, are mutually connected in the same way, and that there is nothing so far removed from us as to be beyond our reach, or so hidden that we cannot discover it, provided only we abstain from accepting the false for the true, and always preserve in our thoughts the order necessary for the deduction of one truth from another. And I had little difficulty in determining the objects with which it was necessary to commence, for I was already persuaded that it must be with the simplest and easiest to know, and, considering that of all those who have hitherto sought truth in the Sciences, the mathematicians alone have been able to find any demonstrations, that is, any certain and evident reasons, I did not doubt but that such must have been the rule of their investigations. I resolved to commence, therefore, with the examination of the simplest objects, not anticipating, however, from this any other advantage than that to be found in accustoming my mind to the love and nourishment of truth, and to a distaste for all such reasonings as were unsound.

* * *

I am in doubt as to the propriety of making my first meditations in the place above mentioned matter of discourse; for these are so metaphysical, and so uncommon, as not, perhaps, to be acceptable to every one. And yet, that it may be determined whether the foundations that I have laid are sufficiently secure, I find myself in a measure constrained to advert to them. I had long before remarked that, in relation to practice, it is sometimes necessary to adopt, as if above doubt, opinons which we discern to be highly uncertain, as has been already said; but as I then desired to give my attention solely to the search after truth, I thought that a procedure exactly the opposite was called for, and that I ought to reject as absolutely false all opinions in regard to which I could suppose the least ground for doubt, in order to ascertain whether after that there remained aught in my belief that was wholly indubitable. Accordingly, seeing that our senses sometimes deceive us, I was willing to suppose that there existed nothing really such as they presented to us, and because some men err in reasoning, and fall into paralogisms, even on the simplest matters of Geometry, I, convinced that I was as open to error as any other, rejected as false all the reasonings I had hitherto taken for demonstrations; and finally, when I considered that the very same thoughts (presentations) which we experience when awake may also be experienced when we are asleep, while there is at that time not one of them true, I supposed that all the objects (presentations) that had ever entered into my mind when awake, had in them no more truth than the illusions of my dreams. But immediately upon this I observed that, whilst I thus wished to think that all was false, it was absolutely necessary that I, who thus thought, should be somewhat; and as I observed that this truth, *I think, hence I am*, was so certain and of such evidence, that no ground of doubt, however extravagant, could be alleged by the Sceptics capable of shaking it, I concluded that I might, without scruple, accept it as the first principle of the Philosophy of which I was in search.

❋   ❋   ❋

In the next place, from reflecting on the circumstance that I doubted, and that consequently my being was not wholly perfect, (for I clearly saw that it was a greater perfection to know than to doubt,) I was led to inquire whence I had learned to think of something more perfect than myself; and I clearly recognised that I must hold this notion from some Nature which in reality was more perfect. As for the thoughts of many other objects external to me, as of the sky, the earth, light, heat, and a thousand more, I was less at a loss to know whence these came; for since I remarked in them nothing which seemed to render them superior to myself, I could believe that, if these were true, they were dependencies on my own nature, in so far as it possessed a certain perfection, and, if they were false, that I held them from nothing, that is to say, that they were in me because of a certain imperfection of my nature. But this could not be the case with the idea of a Nature more perfect than myself; for to receive it from nothing was a thing manifestly impossible; and, because it is not less repugnant that the more perfect should be an effect of, and dependence on the less perfect, than that something should proceed from nothing, it was equally impossible that I could hold it from myself: accordingly, it but remained that it had been placed in me by a Nature which was in reality more perfect than mine, and which even possessed within itself all the perfections of which I could form any idea; that is to say, in a single word, which was God. . . .

❋   ❋   ❋

For, in fine, whether awake or asleep, we ought never to allow ourselves to be persuaded of the truth of anything unless on the evidence of our Reason. And it must be noted that I say of our *Reason*, and not of our imagination or of our senses: thus, for example, although we very clearly see the sun, we ought not therefore to determine that it is only of the size which our sense of sight presents; and we may very distinctly imagine the head of a lion joined to the body of a goat, without being therefore shut up to the conclusion that a chimaera exists; for it is not a dictate of Reason that what we thus see or imagine is in reality existent; but it plainly tells us that all our ideas or notions contain in them some truth; for otherwise it could not be that God, who is wholly perfect and veracious, should have placed them in us.

*   *   *

And if I write in French, which is the language of my country, in preference to Latin, which is that of my preceptors, it is because I expect that those who make use of their unprejudiced natural Reason will be better judges of my opinions than those who give heed to the writings of the ancients only; and as for those who unite good sense with habits of study, whom alone I desire for judges, they will not, I feel assured, be so partial to Latin as to refuse to listen to my reasonings merely because I expound them in the vulgar Tongue.

The Age of Enlightenment

FENELON ON THE EDUCATION OF GIRLS (1687)   From Francois de Salignac de La Mothe Fenelon, *The Education of Girls*, Kate Lupton, trans. (Boston, 1891), pp. 11-14, 34-37.

Nothing is more neglected than the education of girls. Custom and maternal caprice often decide the matter entirely, and it is taken for granted that little instruction should be given to their sex. The education of boys is regarded as a most important affair with reference to the public welfare; and although almost as many mistakes are made in it as in the education of girls, at least the world is convinced that, there, much wisdom is necessary to success. On that subject, the most competent persons have undertaken to lay down rules. How many teachers and colleges for boys do we see! What vast expenditures in their behalf for editions of books, for scientific researches, for methods of teaching the languages, and for the choice of professors! All these great preparations are often more pretentious than effective, but at least they mark the lofty conception that the world has of the education of boys. As for girls, it is said, they should not be learned; inquisitiveness makes them vain and affected: it is enough for them to know how some day to manage their households and to obey their husbands without argument. Men do not fail to make use of the fact that they have known many women whom learning has made ridiculous, after which they think themselves justified in blindly abandoning their daughters to the guidance of ignorant and indiscreet mothers.

True, we must be on our guard against making them ridiculous blue-stockings. Women, as a rule, have still weaker and more inquisitive minds than men; therefore it is not expedient to engage them in studies that may turn their heads: they are not destined to govern the state, to make war, or to minister in holy things; so they may pass by certain extended fields of knowledge that belong to politics, the art of war, jurisprudence, philosophy, and theology. Most of the mechanic arts, even, are not suited to women, who are fashioned for moderate exertions only. Their bodies as well as their minds are less strong and robust than those of men. As a compensation, nature has given them for their portion neatness, industry, and thrift, in order to keep them quietly occupied in their homes.

But what follows from this natural weakness of women? The weaker they are, the more important it is to strengthen them. Have they not duties to fulfil, and duties, too, that lie at the foundation of all human life? Is it not the women, who ruin or uphold families, who regulate every detail of domestic life, and who consequently decide what touches the whole human race most nearly? In this way they exert a controlling influence on the good or bad morals of nearly all the world.

A discreet, diligent, pious woman is the soul of an entire large household; she provides in it alike for temporal and spiritual welfare. Even men, who have exclusive authority in public, cannot, by their decisions, establish a real prosperity unless women aid them in its achievement.

The world is not an abstraction; it is the aggregate of all its families. And who can regulate these with nicer care than women, who, besides their natural authority and assiduity in their homes, have the additional advantage of being born careful, attentive to details, industrious, winning, and persuasive? Or can men hope for any happiness for themselves if their most intimate companionship—that of marriage— be turned to bitterness? And as to children, who will eventually constitute the entire human race,—what will become of them if their mothers spoil them in their early years?

Such, then, are the occupations of women, which are no less important to the public than those of men, since they involve the tasks of managing a household, making a husband happy, and training children well. Virtue, moreover, is no less incumbent on women than on men; and, not to speak of the good or harm they may do to mankind, women constitute half of the human race redeemed by the blood of Christ and destined to eternal life.

In conclusion, we must consider, besides the good that women do if properly brought up, the evil they may cause in the world when they lack a training that inspires virtue. It is evident that a bad education is productive of more harm in the case of women than in that of men, since the excesses of the latter often proceed both from the bad training received from their mothers and from the passions awakened in them at a later age by other women. What intrigues, what subversions of law and morality, what bloody wars, what innovations against religion, what revolutions in government caused by the profligacy of women, are presented to us in history! Such is the proof of the importance of training girls well: let us inquire into the means of accomplishing this object.

* * *

From these considerations it must be concluded that parents ought always to preserve the authority for correction, for there are some dispositions that must be restrained by fear; but—I repeat it—this motive should be employed only when no other will avail.

Children, who as yet act only as fancy dictates and who confound in their minds things that are presented to them in connection with each other, hate study and virtue because of a preconceived aversion to the individual that speaks to them of these subjects. Hence proceeds that sombre and repellent idea of piety which lasts throughout life: frequently this is all that remains of a severe education. Often you should tolerate things that need correction, and await the moment when the child's mind shall be disposed to profit by the correction. Never reprove a child in its first excitement, nor in yours. If you chide in yours, the child will see that you are actuated by temper and hastiness and not by reason and affection; you will lose your authority irretrievably. If you reprove the child in its first excitement, its mind will not be calm enough to confess its fault, to subdue its passion, and to realize the value of your advice; you will even expose the child to the danger of losing the respect due you. Show always that you are master of yourself; nothing will better prove this than your patience. Watch every moment for several days, if necessary, in order to time a correction well. Do not speak of a defect to a child without adding some method of overcoming it that may encourage the attempt, for the mortification and discouragement the cold correction produces must be avoided. If you find a child somewhat reasonable, I think you should insensibly lead it to ask to be told of its defects: this is the way to point these out without wounding the child. You should never even mention several faults at the same time.

We must take into consideration that children as yet have weak intellects; that their time of life renders them susceptible only to pleasure; and often an exactness and a seriousness are demanded of them of which those who require these would be incapable. A dangerous impression of weariness and gloom is made upon their dispositions by speaking to them constantly of words and things that they do not understand,—no liberty, no enjoyment; always lessons, silence, constrained attitudes, correction, and threats.

The ancients understood the matter far better. It was through the pleasure of poetry and music that the chief branches of knowledge, the maxims of virtue, and refinement of behavior were introduced among the Hebrews, the Egyptians, and the Greeks. Persons that are not well read will find difficulty in believing this, so far remote is it from our custom; yet he who knows anything of history has no room to doubt that such was the common practice for many centuries. Let us, at least, go back in ours to uniting the agreeable with the useful as far as possible.

But, although you cannot expect to dispense wholly with the use of fear for the generality of children, whose natural disposition is unyielding and intractable, it must not be resorted to until all other remedies have been patiently tried. Children should also be made to comprehend clearly the full extent of your requirements, and on what conditions you will be satisfied with them; for cheerfulness and confidence must characterize their habitual frame of mind, or their spirit will be crushed and their courage lessened. If they are quick, they will be irritated; if they are slow, they will be made stupid. Fear is like the violent remedies that are employed in critical maladies; these cleanse the system, but impair the constitution, and wear out the organs: a mind controlled by fear is always weaker on that account.

Besides, although it may not be best to be ever threatening without punishing, for fear of making one's threats contemptible, it is, nevertheless, well to punish even less than you threaten. As to the punishment, the pain should be as light as possible, but accompanied by every circumstance that can provoke the child to shame and remorse. For example, speak of all you have done to avoid this extremity; seem to be distressed thereat, talk with others, before the child, of the misfortune of those that so far lack reason and character as to bring punishment on themselves; withdraw the ordinary tokens of affection until you see that consolation is needed; make the punishment public or private according as you think it will be more useful to the child to cause it great shame, or to show it that you spare it that disgrace: reserve this public shame as a last resort; avail yourself, at times, of some discreet person that may console the child, say to it what at that time you ought not yourself to say, heal its false shame, and give it a disposition to return to you, and to whom the child in its emotion can open its heart more freely than it would dare to do before you. But, above all, never seem to demand any but necessary submissions from a child; try to make such requirements that the child will pass judgment on itself, that it will carry them out with a good grace, and that for you shall remain only the task of softening the pain already accepted. Each one ought to make use of these general rules according to individual needs; human beings, and especially children, are not always consistent: what is wholesome to-day is dangerous to-morrow; a constantly uniform management cannot be advisable.

The fewer formal lessons you can give, the better; an infinite amount of instruction more profitable than lessons proper may be introduced into cheerful conversations. I have known several children that learned to read with the greatest facility: all that is necessary is to tell them pleasing tales taken from books in their presence and to teach them the letters gradually; they will then desire the ability to go themselves to the source from which they derived pleasure.

Two things will spoil everything: these are teaching them to read in Latin first, which takes away all the pleasure of reading, and trying to give them the habit of reading with a forced and ridiculous exaggeration of emphasis; a well-bound book, even gilt-edged, with beautiful pictures and clear print, should be provided. Everything that delights the fancy facilitates study; you must try to select a book full of short and marvellous stories.

After this is done, give yourself no trouble about the child's learning to read; do not even weary it by making it read too carefully; leave it to pronounce naturally, as it talks; other tones are always unpleasant and savor of college declamation. When the tongue becomes loosened, the chest stronger, and the habit of reading greater, the child will read without difficulty, with more grace and more distinctness.

ROUSSEAU ON EDUCATION (1762)   From Jean Jacques Rousseau, *Emile*, Barbara Foxley, trans. (London, 1911), pp. 1-3, 5-7, 11, 18, 30-31, 37, 40, 42-43, 50, 53-54, 56-58, 72-73, 80-81, 90, 128-29, 131, 141-42, 147.

Preface

This collection of scattered thoughts and observations has little order or continuity; it was begun to give pleasure to a good mother who thinks for herself. My first idea was to write a tract a few pages long, but I was carried away by my subject, and before I knew what I was doing my tract had become a kind of book, too large indeed for the matter contained in it, but too small for the subject of which it treats. For a long time I hesitated whether to publish it or not, and I have often felt, when at work upon it, that it is one thing to publish a few pamphlets and another to write a book. After vain attempts to improve it, I have decided that it is my duty to publish it as it stands. I consider that public attention requires to be directed to this subject, and even if my own ideas are mistaken, my time will not have been wasted if I stir up others to form right ideas. A solitary who casts his writings before the public without any one to advertise them, without any party ready to defend them, one who does not even know what is thought and said about those writings, is at least free from one anxiety—if he is mistaken, no one will take his errors for gospel.

I shall say very little about the value of a good education, nor shall I stop to prove that the customary method of education is bad; this has been done again and again, and I do not wish to fill my book with things which everyone knows. I will merely state that, go as far back as you will, you will find a continual outcry against the established method, but no attempt to suggest a better. The literature and science of our day tend rather to destroy than to build up. We find fault after the manner of a master; to suggest, we must adopt another style, a style less in accordance with the pride of the philosopher. In spite of all those books, whose only aim, so they say, is public utility, the most useful of all arts, the art of training men, is still neglected. Even after Locke's book was written the subject remained almost untouched, and I fear that my book will leave it pretty much as it found it.

We know nothing of childhood; and with our mistaken notions the further we advance the further we go astray. The wisest writers devote themselves to what a man ought to know, without asking what a child is capable of learning. They are always looking for the man in the child, without considering what he is before he becomes a man. It is to this study that I have chiefly devoted myself, so that if my method is fanciful and unsound, my observations may still be of service. I may be greatly mistaken as to what ought to be done, but I think I have clearly perceived the material which is to be worked upon. Begin thus by making a more careful study of your scholars, for it is clear that you know nothing about them; yet if you read this book with that end in view, I think you will find that it is not entirely useless.

With regard to what will be called the systematic portion of the book, which is nothing more than the course of nature, it is here that the reader will probably go wrong, and no doubt I shall be attacked on this side, and perhaps my critics may be right. You will tell me, "This is not so much a treatise on education as the visions of a dreamer with regard to education." What can I do? I have not written about other people's ideas of education, but about my own. My thoughts are not those of others; this reproach has been brought against me again and again. But is it within my power to furnish myself with other eyes, or to adopt other ideas? It is within my power to refuse to be wedded to my own opinions and to refuse to think myself wiser than others. I cannot change my mind; I can distrust myself. This is all I can do, and this I have done. If I sometimes adopt a confident tone, it is not to impress the reader, it is to make my meaning plain to him. Why should I profess to suggest as doubtful that which is not a matter of doubt to myself? I say just what I think.

When I freely express my opinion, I have so little idea of claiming authority that I always give my reasons, so that you may weigh and judge them for yourselves; but though I would not obstinately defend my ideas, I think it my duty to put them forward; for the principles with regard to which I differ from other writers are not matters of indifference; we must know whether they are true or false, for on them depends the happiness or the misery of mankind.

People are always telling me to make practical suggestions. You might as well tell me to suggest what people are doing already, or at least to suggest improvements which may be incorporated with the wrong methods at present in use. There are matters with regard to which such a suggestion is far more chimerical than my own, for in such a connection the good is corrupted and the bad is none better for it. I would rather follow exactly the established method than adopt a better method by halves. There would be fewer contradictions in the man; he cannot aim at one and the same time at two different objects. Fathers and mothers, what you desire that you can do. May I count on your goodwill?

There are two things to be considered with regard to any scheme. In the first place, "Is it good in itself?" In the second, "Can it be easily put into practice?"

With regard to the first of these it is enough that the scheme should be intelligible and feasible in itself, that what is good in it should be adapted to the nature of things, in this case, for example, that the proposed method of education should be suitable to man and adapted to the human heart.

The second consideration depends upon certain given conditions in particular cases; these conditions are accidental and therefore variable; they may vary indefinitely. Thus one kind of education would be possible in Switzerland and not in France; another would be adapted to the middle classes but not to the nobility. The scheme can be carried out, with more or less success, according to a multitude of circumstances, and its results can only be determined by its special application to one country or another, to this class or that. Now all these particular applications are not essential to my subject, and they form no part of my scheme. It is enough for me that, wherever men are born into the world, my suggestions with regard to them may be carried out, and when you have made them what I would have them be, you have done what is best for them and best for other people. If I fail to fulfil this promise, no doubt I am to blame; but if I fulfil my promise, it is your own fault if you ask anything more of me, for I have promised you nothing more.

Book I

God makes all things good; man meddles with them and they become evil. He forces one soil to yield the products of another, one tree to bear another's fruit. He confuses and confounds time, place, and natural conditions. He mutilates his dog, his horse, and his slave. He destroys and defaces all things; he loves all that is deformed and monstrous; he will have nothing as nature made it, not even man himself, who must learn his paces like a saddlehorse, and be shaped to his master's taste like the trees in his garden.

Yet things would be worse without this education, and mankind cannot be made by halves. Under existing conditions a man left to himself from birth would be more of a monster than the rest. Prejudice, authority, necessity, example, all the social conditions into which we are plunged, would stifle nature in him and put nothing in her place. She would be like a sapling chance sown in the midst of the highway, bent hither and thither and soon crushed by the passers-by.

Tender, anxious mother, I appeal to you. You can remove this young tree from the highway and shield it from the crushing force of social conventions. Tend and water it ere it dies. One day its fruit will reward your care. From the outset raise a wall round your child's soul; another may sketch the plan, you alone should carry it into execution.

Plants are fashioned by cultivation, man by education. If a man were born tall and strong, his size and strength would be of no good to him till he had learnt to use them; they would even harm him by preventing others from coming to his aid; left to himself he would die of want before he knew his needs. We lament the helplessness of infancy; we fail to perceive that the race would have perished had not man begun by being a child.

We are born weak, we need strength; helpless, we need aid: foolish, we need reason. All that we lack at birth, all that we need when we come to man's estate, is the gift of education.

This education comes to us from nature, from men, or from things. The inner growth of our organs and faculties is the education of nature, the use we learn to make of this growth is the education of men, what we gain by our experience of our surroundings is the education of things.

Thus we are each taught by three masters. If their teaching conflicts, the scholar is ill-educated and will never be at peace with himself; if their teaching agrees, he goes straight to his goal, he lives at peace with himself, he is well-educated.

Now of these three factors in education nature is wholly beyond our control, things are only partly in our power; the education of men is the only one controlled by us; and even here our power is largely illusory, for who can hope to direct every word and deed of all with whom the child has to do.

Viewed as an art, the success of education is almost impossible, since the essential conditions of success are beyond our control. Our efforts may bring us within sight of the goal, but fortune must favour us if we are to reach it.

What is this goal? As we have just shown, it is the goal of nature. Since all three modes of education must work together, the two that we can control must follow the lead of that which is beyond our control. Perhaps this word Nature has too vague a meaning. Let us try to define it.

Nature, we are told, is merely habit. What does that mean? Are there not habits formed under compulsion, habits which never stifle nature? Such, for example, are the habits of plants trained horizontally. The plant keeps its artificial shape, but the sap has not changed its course, and any new growth the plant may make will be vertical. It is the same with a man's disposition; while the conditions remain the same, habits, even the least natural of them, hold good; but change the conditions, habits vanish, nature reasserts herself. Education itself is but habit, for are there not people who forget or lose their education and others who keep it? Whence comes this difference? If the term nature is to be restricted to habits conformable to nature we need say no more.

We are born sensitive and from our birth onwards we are affected in various ways by our environment. As soon as we become conscious of our sensations we tend to seek or shun the things that cause them, at first because they are pleasant or unpleasant, then because they suit us or not, and at last because of judgments formed by means of the ideas of happiness and goodness which reason gives us. These tendencies gain strength and permanence with the growth of reason, but hindered by our habits they are more or less warped by our prejudices. Before this change they are what I call Nature within us.

Everything should therefore be brought into harmony with these natural tendencies, and that might well be if our three modes of education merely differed from one another; but what can be done when they conflict, when instead of training man for himself you try to train him for others? Harmony becomes impossible. Forced to combat either nature or society, you must make your choice between the man and the citizen, you cannot train both.

*   *   *

The new-born child requires to stir and stretch his limbs to free them from the stiffness resulting from being curled up so long. His limbs are stretched indeed, but he is not allowed to move them. Even the head is confined by a cap. One would think they were afraid the child should look as if it were alive.

Thus the internal impulses which should lead to growth find an insurmountable obstacle in the way of the necessary movements. The child exhausts his strength in vain struggles, or he gains strength very slowly. He was freer and less constrained in the womb; he has gained nothing by birth.

The inaction, the constraint to which the child's limbs are subjected can only check the circulation of the blood and humours; it can only hinder the child's growth in size and strength, and injure its constitution. Where these absurd precautions are absent, all the men are tall, strong, and well-made. Where children are swaddled, the country swarms with the hump-backed, the lame, the bow-legged, the rickety, and every kind of deformity. In our fear lest the body should become deformed by free movement, we hasten to deform it by putting it in a press. We make our children helpless lest they should hurt themselves.

Is not such a cruel bondage certain to affect both health and temper? Their first feeling is one of pain and suffering; they find every necessary movement hampered; more miserable than a galley slave, in vain they struggle, they become angry, they cry. Their first words you say are tears. That is so. From birth you are always checking them, your first gifts are fetters, your first treatment, torture. Their voice alone is free; why should they not raise it in complaint? They cry because you are hurting them; if you were swaddled you would cry louder still.

*   *   *

I have therefore decided to take an imaginary pupil, to assume on my own part the age, health, knowledge, and talents required for the work of his education, to guide him from birth to manhood, when he needs no guide but himself. This method seems to me useful for an author who fears lest he may stray from the practical to the visionary; for as soon as he departs from common practice he has only to try his method on his pupil; he will soon know, or the reader will know for him, whether he is following the development of the child and the natural growth of the human heart.

This is what I have tried to do. Lest my book should be unduly bulky, I have been content to state those principles the truth of which is self-evident. But as to the rules which call for proof, I have applied them to Emile or to others, and I have shown, in very great detail, how my theories may be put into practice. Such at least is my plan; the reader must decide whether I have succeeded. At first I have said little about Emile, for my earliest maxims of education, though very different from those generally accepted, are so plain that it is hard for a man of sense to refuse to accept them, but as I advance, my scholar, educated after another fashion than yours, is no longer an ordinary child, he needs a special system. Then he appears upon the scene more frequently, and towards the end I never lose sight of him for a moment, until, whatever he may say, he needs me no longer.

I pass over the qualities required in a good tutor; I take them for granted, and assume that I am endowed with them. As you read this book you will see how generous I have been to myself.

*   *   *

The only habit the child should be allowed to contract is that of having no habits; let him be carried on either arm, let him be accustomed to offer either hand, to use one or other indifferently; let him not want to eat, sleep, or do anything at fixed hours, nor be unable to be left alone by day or night. Prepare the way for his control of his liberty and the use of his strength by leaving his body its natural habit, by making him capable of lasting self-control, of doing all that he wills when his will is formed.

As soon as the child begins to take notice, what is shown him must be carefully chosen. The natural man is interested in all new things. He feels so feeble that he fears the unknown: the habit of seeing fresh things without ill effects destroys this fear. Children brought up in clean houses where there are no spiders are afraid of spiders, and this fear often lasts through life. I never saw peasants, man, woman, or child, afraid of spiders.

Since the mere choice of things shown him may make the child timid or brave, why should not his education begin before he can speak or understand? I would have him accustomed to see fresh things, ugly, repulsive, and strange beasts, but little by little, and far off till he is used to them, and till having seen others handle them he handles them himself. If in childhood he sees toads, snakes, and crayfish, he will not be afraid of any animal when he is grown up. Those who are continually seeing terrible things think nothing of them.

All children are afraid of masks. I begin by showing Emile a mask with a pleasant face, then some one puts this mask before his face; I begin to laugh, they all laugh too, and the child with them. By degrees I accustom him to less pleasing masks, and at last hideous ones. If I have arranged my stages skilfully, far from being afraid of the last mask, he will laugh at it as he did at the first. After that I am not afraid of people frightening him with masks.

When Hector bids farewell to Andromache, the young Astyanax, startled by the nodding plumes on the helmet, does not know his father; he flings himself weeping upon his nurse's bosom and wins from his mother a smile mingled with tears. What must be done to stay this terror? Just what Hector did; put the helmet on the ground and caress the child. In a calmer moment one would do more; one would go up to the helmet, play with the plumes, let the child feel them; at last the nurse would take the helmet and place it laughingly on her own head, if indeed a woman's hand dare touch the armour of Hector.

If Emile must get used to the sound of a gun, I first fire a pistol with a small charge. He is delighted with this sudden flash, this sort of lightning; I repeat the process with more powder; gradually I add a small charge without a wad, then a larger; in the end I accustom him to the sound of a gun, to fireworks, cannon, and the most terrible explosions.

I have observed that children are rarely afraid of thunder unless the peals are really terrible and actually hurt the ear, otherwise this fear only comes to them when they know that thunder sometimes hurts or kills. When reason begins to cause fear, let use reassure them. By slow and careful stages man and child learn to fear nothing.

In the dawn of life, when memory and imagination have not begun to function, the child only attends to what affects its senses. His sense experiences are the raw material of thought; they should, therefore, be presented to him in fitting order, so that memory may at a future time present them in the same order to his understanding; but as he only attends to his sensations it is enough, at first, to show him clearly the connection between these sensations and the things which cause them. He wants to touch and handle everything; do not check these movements which teach him invaluable lessons. Thus he learns to perceive the heat, cold, hardness, softness, weight, or lightness of bodies, to judge their size and shape and all their physical properties, by looking, feeling, listening, and, above all, by comparing sight and touch, by judging with the eye what sensation they would cause to his hand.

It is only by movement that we learn the difference between self and not self; it is only by our own movements that we gain the idea of space. The child has not this idea, so he stretches out his hand to seize the object within his reach or that which is a hundred paces from him. You take this as a sign of tyranny, an attempt to bid the thing draw near, or to bid you bring it. Nothing of the kind, it is merely that the object first seen in his brain, then before his eyes, now seems close to his arms, and he has no idea of space beyond his reach. Be careful, therefore, to take him about, to move him from place to place, and to let him perceive the change in his surroundings, so as to teach him to judge of distances.

*　　*　　*

From the very first children hear spoken language; we speak to them before they can understand or even imitate spoken sounds. The vocal organs are still stiff, and only gradually lend themselves to the reproduction of the sounds heard; it is even doubtful whether these sounds are heard distinctly as we hear them. The nurse may amuse the child with songs and with very merry and varied intonation, but I object to her bewildering the child with a multitude of vain words of which it understands nothing but her tone of voice. I would have the first words he hears few in number, distinctly and often repeated, while the words themselves should be related to things which can first be shown to the child. That fatal facility in the use of words we do not understand begins earlier than we think. In the schoolroom the scholar listens to the verbiage of his master as he listened in the cradle to the babble of his nurse. I think it would be a very useful education to leave him in ignorance of both.

*　　*　　*

It is an intolerable piece of pedantry and most superfluous attention to detail to make a point of correcting all children's little sins against the customary expression, for they always cure themselves with time. Always speak correctly before them, let them never be so happy with any one as with you, and be sure that their speech will be imperceptibly modelled upon yours without any correction on your part.

But a much greater evil, and one far less easy to guard against, is that they are urged to speak too much, as if people were afraid they would not learn to talk of themselves. This indiscreet zeal produces an effect directly opposite to what is meant. They speak later and more confusedly; the extreme attention paid to everything they say makes it unnecessary for them to speak distinctly, . . .

*　　*　　*

Let the child s vocabulary, therefore, be limited; it is very undesirable that he should have more words than ideas, that he should be able to say more than he thinks. One of the reasons why peasants are generally shrewder than townsfolk is, I think, that their vocabulary is smaller. They have few ideas, but those few are thoroughly grasped.

The infant is progressing in several ways at once; he is learning to talk, eat, and walk about the same time. This is really the first phase of his life. Up till now, he was little more than he was before birth; he had neither feeling nor thought, he was barely capable of sensation; he was unconscious of his own existence.

Book II

. . . With our foolish and pedantic methods we are always preventing children from learning what they could learn much better by themselves, while we neglect what we alone can teach them. Can anything be sillier than the pains taken to teach them to walk, as if there were any one who was unable to walk when he grows up through his nurse's neglect? How many we see walking badly all their life because they were ill taught?

Emile shall have no head-pads, no go-carts, no leading-strings; or at least as soon as he can put one foot before another he shall only be supported along pavements, and he shall be taken quickly across them. Instead of keeping him mewed up in a stuffy room, take him out into a meadow every day; let him run about, let him struggle and fall again and again, the oftener the better; he will learn all the sooner to pick himself up. The delights of liberty will make up for the many bruises. My pupil will hurt himself oftener than yours, but he will always be merry; your pupils may receive fewer injuries, but they are always thwarted, constrained, and sad. I doubt whether they are any better off.

As their strength increases, children have also less need for tears. They can do more for themselves, they need the help of others less frequently. With strength comes the sense to use it. It is with this second phase that the real personal life has its beginning; it is then that the child becomes conscious of himself. During every moment of his life memory calls up the feeling of self; he becomes really one person, always the same, and therefore capable of joy or sorrow. Hence we must begin to consider him as a moral being.

Although we know approximately the limits of human life and our chances of attaining those limits, nothing is more uncertain than the length of the life of any one of us. Very few reach old age. The chief risks occur at the beginning of life; the shorter our past life, the less we must hope to live. Of all the children who are born scarcely one half reach adolescence, and it is very likely your pupil will not live to be a man.

What is to be thought, therefore, of that cruel education which sacrifices the present to an uncertain future, that burdens a child with all sorts of restrictions and begins by making him miserable, in order to prepare him for some far-off happiness which he may never enjoy? Even if I considered that education wise in its aims, how could I view without indignation those poor wretches subjected to an intolerable slavery and condemned like galley-slaves to endless toil, with no certainty that they will gain anything by it? The age of harmless mirth is spent in tears, punishments, threats, and slavery. You torment the poor thing for his good; you fail to see that you are calling Death to snatch him from these gloomy surroundings. Who can say how many children fall victims to the excessive care of their fathers and mothers? They are happy to escape from this cruelty; this is all that they gain from the ills they are forced to endure: they die without regretting, having known nothing of life but its sorrows.

Men, be kind to your fellow-men; this is your first duty, kind to every age and station, kind to all that is not foreign to humanity. What wisdom can you find that is greater than kindness? Love childhood, indulge its sports, its pleasures, its delightful instincts. Who has not sometimes regretted that age when laughter was ever on the lips, and when the heart was ever at peace? Why rob these innocents of the joys which pass so quickly, of that precious gift which they cannot abuse? Why fill with bitterness the fleeting days of early childhood, days which will no more return for them than for your? Fathers, can you tell when death will call you children to him? Do not lay up sorrow for yourselves by robbing them of the short span which nature has allotted to them. As soon as they are aware of the joy of life, let them rejoice in it, so that whenever God calls them they may not die without having tasted the joy of life.

*   *   *

Nature provides for the child's growth in her own fashion, and this should never be thwarted. Do not make him sit still when he wants to run about, nor run when he wants to be quiet. If we did not spoil our children's wills by our blunders their desires would be free from caprice. Let them run, jump, and shout to their heart's content. All their own activities are instincts of the body for its growth in strength; but you should regard with suspicion those wishes which they cannot carry out for themselves, those which others must carry out for them. Then you must distinguish carefully between natural and artificial needs, between the needs of budding caprice and the needs which spring from the overflowing life just described.

*   *   *

"Reason with children" was Locke's chief maxim; it is in the height of fashion at present, and I hardly think it is justified by its results; those children who have been constantly reasoned with strike me as exceedingly silly. Of all man's faculties, reason, which is, so to speak, compounded of all the rest, is the last and choicest growth, and it is this you would use for the child's early training. To make a man reasonable is the coping stone of a good education, and yet you profess to train a child through his reason! You begin at the wrong end, you make the end the means. If children understood reason they would not need education, but by talking to them from their earliest age in a language they do not understand you accustom them to be satisfied with words, to question all that is said to them, to think themselves as wise as their teachers; you train them to be argumentative and rebellious; and whatever you think you gain from motives of reason, you really gain from greediness, fear, or vanity with which you are obliged to reinforce your reasoning.

Most of the moral lessons which are and can be given to children may be reduced to this formula:

Master. You must not do that.
Child. Why not?
Master. Because it is wrong.
Child. Wrong! What is wrong?
Master. What is forbidden you.
Child. Why is it wrong to do what is forbidden?
Master. You will be punished for disobedience.
Child. I will do it when no one is looking.
Master. We shall watch you.
Child. I will hide.
Master. We shall ask you what you were doing.
Child. I shall tell a lie.
Master. You must not tell lies.
Child. Why must not I tell lies?
Master. Because it is wrong, etc.

That is the inevitable circle. Go beyond it, and the child will not understand you. What sort of use is there in such teaching? I should greatly like to know what you would substitute for this dialogue. It would have puzzled Locke himself. It is no part of a child's business to know right and wrong, to perceive the reason for a man's duties.

Nature would have them children before they are men. If we try to invert this order we shall produce a forced fruit immature and flavourless, fruit which will be rotten before it is ripe; we shall have young doctors and old children. Childhood has its own ways of seeing, thinking, and feeling; nothing is more foolish than to try and substitute our ways; and I should no more expect judgment in a ten-year-old child than I should expect him to be five feet high. Indeed, what use would reason be to him at that age? It is the curb of strength, and the child does not need the curb.

Give your scholar no verbal lessons; he should be taught by experience alone; never punish him, for he does not know what it is to do wrong; never make him say, "Forgive me," for he does not know how to do you wrong. Wholly unmoral in his actions, he can do nothing morally wrong, and he deserves neither punishment nor reproof.

Already I see the frightened reader comparing this child with those of our time; he is mistaken. The perpetual restraint imposed upon your scholars stimulates their activity; the more subdued they are in your presence, the more boisterous they are as soon as they are out of your sight. They must make amends to themselves in some way or other for the harsh constraint to which you subject them. Two schoolboys from the town will do more damage in the country than all the children of the village. Shut up a young gentleman and a young peasant in a room; the former will have upset and smashed everything before the latter has stirred from his place. Why is that, unless that the one hastens to misuse a moment's licence, while the other, always sure of freedom, does not use it rashly. And yet the village children, often flattered or constrained, are still very far from the state in which I would have them kept.

Let us lay it down as an incontrovertible rule that the first impulses of nature are always right; there is no original sin in the human heart, the how and why of the entrance of every vice can be traced. The only natural passion is self-love or selfishness taken in a wider sense. This selfishness is good in itself and in relation to ourselves; and as the child has no necessary relations to other people he is naturally indifferent to them; his self-love only becomes good or bad by the use made of it and the relations established by its means. Until the time is ripe for the appearance of reason, that guide of selfishness, the main thing is that the child shall do nothing because you are watching him or listening to him; in a word, nothing because of other people, but only what nature asks of him; then he will never do wrong.

I do not mean to say that he will never do any mischief, never hurt himself, never break a costly ornament if you leave it within his reach. He might do much damage without doing wrong, since wrong-doing depends on the harmful intention which will never be his. If once he meant to do harm, his whole education would be ruined; he would be almost hopelessly bad.

Greed considers some things wrong which are not wrong in the eyes of reason. When you leave free scope to a child's heedlessness, you must put anything he could spoil out of his way, and leave nothing fragile or costly within his reach. Let the room be furnished with plain and solid furniture; no mirrors, china, or useless ornaments. My pupil Emile, who is brought up in the country, shall have a room just like a peasant's. Why take such pains to adorn it when he will be so little in it? I am mistaken, however; he will ornament it for himself, and we shall soon see how.

But if, in spite of your precautions, the child contrives to do some damage, if he breaks some useful article, do not punish him for your carelessness, do not even scold him; let him hear no word of reproval, do not even let him see that he has vexed you; behave just as if the thing had come to pieces of itself; you may consider you have done great things if you have managed to hold your tongue.

May I venture at this point to state the greatest, the most important, the most useful rule of education? It is: Do not save time, but lose it. I hope that every-day readers will excuse my paradoxes; you cannot avoid paradox if you think for yourself, and whatever you may say I would rather fall into paradox than into prejudice. The most dangerous period in human life lies between birth and the age of twelve. It is the time when errors and vices spring up, while as yet there is no means to destroy them; when the means of destruction are ready, the roots have gone too deep to be pulled up. If the infant sprang at one bound from its mother's breast to the age of reason, the present type of education would be quite suitable, but its natural growth calls for quite a different training. The mind should be left undisturbed till its faculties have developed; for while it is blind it cannot see the torch you offer it, nor can it follow through the vast expanse of ideas a path so faintly traced by reason that the best eyes can scarcely follow it.

Therefore the education of the earliest years should be merely negative. It consists, not in teaching virtue or truth, but in preserving the heart from vice and from the spirit of error. If only you could let well alone, and get others to follow your example; if you could bring your scholar to the age of twelve strong and healthy, but unable to tell his right hand from his left, the eyes of his understanding would be open to reason as soon as you began to teach him. Free from prejudices and free from habits, there would be nothing in him to counteract the effects of your labours. In your hands he would soon become the wisest of men; by doing nothing to begin with, you would end with a prodigy of education.

Reverse the usual practice and you will almost always do right. Fathers and teachers who want to make the child, not a child but a man of learning, think it never too soon to scold, correct, reprove, threaten, bribe, teach, and reason. Do better than they; be reasonable, and do not reason with your pupil, more especially do not try to make him approve what he dislikes; for if reason is always connected with disagreeable matters, you make it distasteful to him, you discredit it at an early age in a mind not yet ready to understand it. Exercise his body, his limbs, his senses, his strength, but keep his mind idle as long as you can. Distrust all opinions which appear before the judgment to discriminate between them. Restrain and ward off strange impressions; and to prevent the birth of evil do not hasten to do well, for goodness is only possible when enlightened by reason. Regard all delays as so much time gained; you have achieved much, you approach the boundary without loss. Leave childhood to ripen in your children. In a word, beware of giving anything they need to-day if it can be deferred without danger to to-morrow.

There is another point to be considered which confirms the suitability of this method: it is the child's individual bent, which must be thoroughly known before we can choose the fittest moral training. Every mind has its own form, in accordance with which it must be controlled; and the success of the pains taken depends largely on the fact that he is controlled in this way and no other. Oh, wise man, take time to observe nature; watch your scholar well before you say a word to him; first leave the germ of his character free to show itself, do not constrain him in anything, the better to see him as he really is. Do you think this time of liberty is wasted? On the contrary, your scholar will be the better employed, for this is the way you yourself will learn not to lose a single moment when time is of more value.

If, however, you begin to act before you know what to do, you act at random; you may make mistakes, and must retrace your steps; your haste to reach your goal will only take you further from it. Do not imitate the miser who loses much lest he should lose a little. Sacrifice a little time in early childhood, and it will be repaid you with usury when your scholar is older. The wise physician does not hastily give prescriptions at first sight, but he studies the constitution of the sick man before he prescribes anything; the treatment is begun later, but the patient is cured, while the hasty doctor kills him.

*   *   *

I am far from thinking, however, that children have no sort of reason. On the contrary, I think they reason very well with regard to things that affect their actual and sensible well-being. But people are mistaken as to the extent of their information, and they attribute to them knowledge they do not possess, and make them reason about things they cannot understand. Another mistake is to try to turn their attention to matters which do not concern them in the least, such as their future interest, their happiness when they are grown up, the opinion people will have of them when they are men—terms which are absolutely meaningless when addressed to creatures who are entirely without foresight. But all the forced studies of these poor little wretches are directed towards matters utterly remote from their minds. You may judge how much attention they can give to them.

The pedagogues, who make a great display of the teaching they give their pupils, are paid to say just the opposite; yet their actions show that they think just as I do. For what do they teach? Words! words! words! Among the various sciences they boast of teaching their scholars, they take good care never to choose those which might be really useful to them, for then they would be compelled to deal with things and would fail utterly; the sciences they choose are those we seem to know when we know their technical terms—heraldry, geography, chronology, languages, etc., studies so remote from man, and even more remote from the child, that it is a wonder if he can ever make any use of any part of them.

You will be surprised to find that I reckon the study of languages among the useless lumber of education; but you must remember that I am speaking of the studies of the earliest years, and whatever you may say, I do not believe any child under twelve or fifteen ever really acquired two languages.

*   *   *

When I thus get rid of children's lessons, I get rid of the chief cause of their sorrows, namely their books. Reading is the curse of childhood, yet it is almost the only occupation you can find for children. Emile, at twelve years old, will hardly know what a book is. "But," you say, "he must, at least, know how to read." When reading is of use to him, I admit he must learn to read, but till then he will only find it a nuisance.

If children are not to be required to do anything as a matter of obedience, it follows that they will only learn what they perceive to be of real and present value, either for use or enjoyment; what other motive could they have for learning? The art of speaking to our absent friends, of hearing their words; the art of letting them know at first hand our feelings, our desires, and our longings, is an art whose usefulness can be made plain at any age. How is it that this art, so useful and pleasant in itself, has become a terror to children? Because the child is compelled to acquire it against his will, and to use it for purposes beyond his comprehension. A child has no great wish to perfect himself in the use of an instrument of torture, but make it a means to his pleasure, and soon you will not be able to keep him from it.

*   *   *

Present interest, that is the motive power, the only motive power that takes us far and safely. Sometimes Emile receives notes of invitation from his father or mother, his relations or friends; he is invited to a dinner, a walk, a boating expedition, to see some public entertainment. These notes are short, clear, plain, and well written. Some one must read them to him, and he cannot always find anybody when wanted; no more consideration is shown to him than he himself showed to you yesterday. Time passes, the chance is lost. The note is read to him at last, but it is too late. Oh! if only he had known how to read! He receives other notes, so short, so interesting, he would like to try to read them. Sometimes he gets help, sometimes none. He does his best, and at last he makes out half the note; it is something about going to-morrow to drink cream—Where? With whom? He cannot tell—how hard he tries to make out the rest! I do not think Emile will need a "bureau." Shall I proceed to the teaching of writing? No, I am ashamed to toy with these trifles in a treatise on education.

I will just add a few words which contain a principle of great importance. It is this—What we are in no hurry to get is usually obtained with speed and certainty. I am pretty sure Emile will learn to read and write before he is ten, just because I care very little whether he can do so before he is fifteen; . . .

While his delicate and flexible limbs can adjust themselves to the bodies upon which they are intended to act, while his senses are keen and as yet free from illusions, then is the time to exercise both limbs and senses in their proper business. It is the time to learn to perceive the physical relations between ourselves and things. Since everything that comes into the human mind enters through the gates of sense, man's first reason is a reason of sense-experience. It is this that serves as a foundation for the reason of the intelligence; our first teachers in natural philosophy are our feet, hands, and eyes. To substitute books for them does not teach us to reason, it teaches us to use the reason of others rather than our own; it teaches us to believe much and know little.

Before you can practise an art you must first get your tools; and if you are to make good use of those tools, they must be fashioned sufficiently strong to stand use. To learn to think we must therefore exercise our limbs, our senses, and our bodily organs, which are the tools of the intellect; and to get the best use out of these tools, the body which supplies us with them must be strong and healthy. Not only is it quite a mistake that true reason is developed apart from the body, but it is a good bodily constitution which makes the workings of the mind easy and correct.

Book III

The whole course of man's life up to adolescence is a period of weakness; yet there comes a time during these early years when the child's strength overtakes the demands upon it, when the growing creature, though absolutely weak, is relatively strong. His needs are not fully developed and his present strength is more than enough for them. He would be a very feeble man, but he is a strong child.

What is the cause of man's weakness? It is to be found in the disproportion between his strength and his needs. It is our passions that make us weak, for our natural strength is not enough for their satisfaction. To limit our desires comes to the same thing, therefore, as to increase our strength. When we can do more than we want, we have strength enough and to spare, we are really strong. This is the third stage of childhood, the stage with which I am about to deal. I still speak of childhood for want of a better word; for our scholar is approaching adolescence, though he has not yet reached the age of puberty.

About twelve or thirteen the child's strength increases far more rapidly than his needs. The strongest and fiercest of the passions is still unknown, his physical development is still imperfect and seems to await the call of the will. He is scarcely aware of extremes of heat and cold and braves them with impunity. He needs no coat, his blood is warm; no spices, hunger is his sauce, no food comes amiss with this age; if he is sleepy he stretches himself on the ground and goes to sleep; he finds all he needs within his reach; he is not tormented by any imaginary wants; he cares nothing what others think; his desires are not beyond his grasp; not only is he self-sufficing, but for the first and last time in his life he has more strength than he needs.

I know beforehand what you will say. You will not assert that the child has more needs than I attribute to him, but you will deny his strength. You forget that I am speaking of my own pupil, not of those puppets who walk with difficulty from one room to another, who toil indoors and carry bundles of paper. Manly strength, you say, appears only with manhood; the vital spirits, distilled in their proper vessels and spreading through the whole body, can alone make the muscles firm, sensitive, tense, and springy, can alone cause real strength. This is the philosophy of the study; I appeal to that of experience. In the country districts, I see big lads hoeing, digging, guiding the plough, filling the wine-cask, driving the cart, like their fathers; you would take them for grown men if their voices did not betray them. Even in our towns, ironworkers', tool makers', and blacksmiths' lads are almost as strong as their masters and would be scarcely less skilful had their training begun earlier. If there is a difference, and I do not deny that there is, it is, I repeat, much less than the difference between the stormy passions of the man and the few wants of the child. Moreover, it is not merely a question of bodily strength, but more especially of strength of mind, which reinforces and directs the bodily strength.

This interval in which the strength of the individual is in excess of his wants is, as I have said, relatively though not absolutely the time of greatest strength. It is the most precious time in his life; it comes but once; it is very short, all too short, as you will see when you consider the importance of using it aright.

He has, therefore, a surplus of strength and capacity which he will never have again. What use shall he make of it? He will strive to use it in tasks which will help at need. He will, so to speak, cast his present surplus into the storehouse of the future; the vigorous child will make provision for the feeble man; but he will not store his goods where thieves may break in, nor in barns which are not his own. To store them aright, they must be in the hands and the head, they must be stored within himself. This is the time for work, instruction, and inquiry. And note that this is no arbitrary choice of mine, it is the way of nature herself.

Human intelligence is finite, and not only can no man know everything, he cannot even acquire all the scanty knowledge of others. Since the contrary of every false proposition is a truth, there are as many truths as falsehoods. We must, therefore, choose what to teach as well as when to teach it. Some of the information within our reach is false, some is useless, some merely serves to puff up its possessor. The small store which really contributes to our welfare alone deserves the study of a wise man, and therefore of a child whom one would have wise. He must know not merely what is, but what is useful.

From this small stock we must also deduct those truths which require a full grown mind for their understanding, those which suppose a knowledge of man's relations to his fellow-men—a knowledge which no child can acquire; these things, although in themselves true, lead an inexperienced mind into mistakes with regard to other matters.

We are now confined to a circle, small indeed compared with the whole of human thought, but this circle is still a vast sphere when measured by the child's mind. Dark places of the human understanding, what rash hand shall dare to raise your veil? What pitfalls does our so-called science prepare for the miserable child. Would you guide him along this dangerous path and draw the veil from the face of nature? Stay your hand. First make sure that neither he nor you will become dizzy. Beware of the specious charms of error and the intoxicating fumes of pride. Keep this truth ever before you—Ignorance never did any one any harm, error alone is fatal, and we do not lose our way through ignorance but through self-confidence.

* * *

Let us transform our sensations into ideas, but do not let us jump all at once from the objects of sense to objects of thought. The latter are attained by means of the former. Let the senses be the only guide for the first workings of reason. No book but the world, no teaching but that of fact. The child who reads ceases to think, he only reads. He is acquiring words not knowledge.

Teach your scholar to observe the phenomena of nature; you will soon rouse his curiosity, but if you would have it grow, do not be in too great a hurry to satisfy this curiosity. Put the problems before him and let him solve them himself. Let him know nothing because you have told him, but because he has learnt it for himself. Let him not be taught science, let him discover it. If ever you substitute authority for reason he will cease to reason; he will be a mere plaything of other people's thoughts.

You wish to teach this child geography and you provide him with globes, spheres, and maps. What elaborate preparations! What is the use of all these symbols; why not begin by showing him the real thing so that he may at least know what you are talking about?

One fine evening we are walking in a suitable place where the wide horizon gives us a full view of the setting sun, and we note the objects which mark the place where it sets. Next morning we return to the same place for a breath of fresh air before sun-rise. We see the rays of light which announce the sun's approach; the glow increases, the east seems afire, and long before the sun appears the light leads us to expect its return. Every moment you expect to see it. There it is at last! A shining point appears like a flash of lightning and soon fills the whole space; the veil of darkness rolls away, man perceives his dwelling place in fresh beauty. During the night the grass has assumed a fresher green; in the light of early dawn, and gilded by the first rays of the sun, it seems covered with a shining network of dew reflecting the light and colour. The birds raise their chorus of praise to greet the Father of life, not one of them is mute; their gentle warbling is softer than by day, it expresses the langour of a peaceful waking. All these produce an impression of freshness which seems to reach the very soul. It is a brief hour of enchantment which no man can resist; a sight so grand, so fair, so delicious, that none can behold it unmoved.

*   *   *

A man must know many things which seem useless to a child, but need the child learn, or can he indeed learn, all that the man must know? Try to teach the child what is of use to a child and you will find that it takes all his time. Why urge him to the studies of an age he may never reach, to the neglect of those studies which meet his present needs? "But," you ask, "will it not be too late to learn what he ought to know when the time comes to use it?" I cannot tell; but this I do know, it is impossible to teach it sooner, for our real teachers are experience and emotion, and man will never learn what befits a man except under its own conditions. A child knows he must become a man; all the ideas he may have as to man's estate are so many opportunities for his instruction, but he should remain in complete ignorance of those ideas which are beyond his grasp. My whole book is one continued argument in support of this fundamental principle of education.

As soon as we have contrived to give our pupil an idea of the word "Useful," we have got an additional means of controlling him, for this word makes a great impression on him, provided that its meaning for him is a meaning relative to his own age, and provided he clearly sees its relation to his own well-being.

*   *   *

"What is the use of that?" In future this is the sacred formula, the formula by which he and I test every action of our lives. This is the question with which I invariably answer all his questions; it serves to check the stream of foolish and tiresome questions with which children weary those about them. These incessant questions produce no result, and their object is rather to get a hold over you than to gain any real advantage. A pupil, who has been really taught only to want to know what is useful, questions like Socrates; he never asks a question without a reason for it, for he knows he will be required to give his reason before he gets an answer.

*   *   *

I hate books; they only teach us to talk about things we know nothing about. Hermes, they say, engraved the elements of science on pillars lest a deluge should destroy them. Had he imprinted them on men's hearts they would have been preserved by tradition. Well-trained minds are the pillars on which human knowledge is most deeply engraved.

Is there no way of correlating so many lessons scattered through so many books, no way of focussing them on some common object, easy to see, interesting to follow, and stimulating even to a child? Could we but discover a state in which all man's needs appear in such a way as to appeal to the child's mind, a state in which the ways of providing for these needs are as easily developed, the simple and stirring portrayal of this state should form the earliest training of the child's imagination.

Eager philosopher, I see your own imagination at work. Spare yourself the trouble; this state is already known, it is described, with due respect to you, far better than you could describe it, at least with greater truth and simplicity. Since we must have books, there is one book which, to my thinking, supplies the best treatise on an education according to nature. This is the first book Emile will read; for a long time it will form his whole library, and it will always retain an honoured place. It will be the text to which all our talks about natural science are but the commentary. It will serve to test our progress towards a right judgment, and it will always be read with delight, so long as our taste is unspoilt. What is this wonderful book? Is it Aristotle? Pliny? Buffon? No; it is *Robinson Crusoe.*

Robinson Crusoe on his island, deprived of the help of his fellow-men, without the means of carrying on the various arts, yet finding food, preserving his life, and procuring a certain amount of comfort; this is the thing to interest people of all ages, and it can be made attractive to children in all sorts of ways. We shall thus make a reality of that desert island which formerly served as an illustration. The condition, I confess, is not that of a social being, nor is it in all probability Emile's own condition, but he should use it as a standard of comparison for all other conditions. The surest way to raise him above prejudice and to base his judgments on the true relations of things, is to put him in the place of a solitary man, and to judge all things as they would be judged by such a man in relation to their own utility.

La CHALOTAIS' PLAN OF NATIONAL EDUCATION (1763)   From Louis-Rene de Caradeuc la Chalotais, "Essay on National Education or Plan of Studies for Young Persons," as quoted in F. de La Fontainerie, ed. and trans., *French Liberalism and Education in the Eighteenth Century* (New York, 1932), pp. 40-44, 68-69.

Some Preliminary Reflections Concerning the Usefulness of Letters, Bad Means of Teaching Them, and the Qualifications of Teachers

The Sovereign Courts have been occupied for the past year with the means of establishing in our colleges persons capable of teaching the youth of the Nation. It avails little to destroy, if we do not think of rebuilding. We had a system of education which was fit, at the most, to prepare individuals for the study of scholastic philosophy. The public welfare, the honor of the Nation require that we substitute a civil education which will prepare each coming generation to follow successfully the different occupations in the State.

In this memorial, I propose to prove the necessity and indicate the means of doing this. In order to judge adequately, it is perhaps necessary to go further back, and to show the usefulness of the sciences and letters, to what extent a good or a bad education may influence the happiness or the unhappiness of a nation, and to consider at the same time what a nation has the right to exact of its teachers.

Knowledge is necessary to man. If he has duties to fulfil, it is necessary that he should know them: to know them is to possess the most useful of all knowledge; it is to be already well advanced in the course in which useful citizens are trained. Ignorance is good for nothing, and it is harmful to everything. It is impossible for any light to come forth from darkness, and it is not possible to walk in darkness without going astray.

*   *   *

We must apply ourselves in childhood and in youth, otherwise we become incapable of doing so for the rest of our lives. Nature makes a difference between men (no one can doubt this); education makes a greater one perhaps. Talent is a gift of Nature; but there enters into talent well appraised a great deal of what is called acquired art, that is, habit. If it were possible to analyse the talent of a Bossuet, of a Corneille, of a Racine, of a La Fontaine, we should in truth find a richer ground, but perfected by long and continual effort. Cultivation always increases the good quality and the fertility of the soil. Application without talent will make only mediocre men; talent without application will never produce superior men.

To suppose that Nature does everything, that exercise and application add nothing to natural talents is a pernicious maxim which renders good minds listless and increases the discouragement of mediocre ones. We realize from experience that almost all men do not go as far as they could go, if they brought to what they do a greater application. There must be no misapprehension, all who are born to have intelligence do not become men of intelligence. It is to the general advantage that men of all professions should be convinced that it is impossible to know well what has not been learned well. To deny the power of education is to deny in spite of experience the power of habits. What could not an education established by law and guided by examples do! It would change in a few years the customs of an entire nation. Among the Spartans, it conquered Nature itself. There is an art of improving the breed of animals, could not there also be one of perfecting the human race?

*   *   *

If humanity is susceptible of a certain degree of perfection, it is by means of education that it can reach it. The object of the legislator should be to procure for minds the highest possible degree of accuracy and capacity, for characters the highest degree of excellence and of elevation, for bodies the highest degree of strength and health.

We must not hope to attain easily this point of perfection. Too many obstacles oppose themselves especially amongst us; but it must always be our aim. This is the only means of approaching it.

*   *   *

I shall not enter into the details which would be endless, and I exhort teachers to read all the good books on education and on the choice of studies. I shall establish the principles, and present a general formula for a literary education. I shall indicate the principal subjects for study at each age, and note the good elementary books which are lacking. The consequences and the details will present themselves of their own accord.

What is the best plan of studies for the education of youth, and what method should be followed to put this plan into effect?

It may be seen that it is not a question here of a full treatise on education, which would require more extensive views; but simply of a plan of studies that could be substituted for those of the colleges.

I accept throughout this memorial the distinction made by the Abbe Fleury between knowledge which is necessary, useful and agreeable and that which is the most generally useful, according to the needs of different persons.

This distinction is enough, provided we take care to accommodate the studies to the differences in the age of the students, to indicate clearly their aim, not to confuse the means with the end, the words with the things and the instrument with the art itself; provided we indicate exactly in each subject the limits of knowledge beyond which the human mind cannot go: and this seems to me to be the most essential thing in any plan for education.

Principles of a Plan of Studies

A plan is the design of an edifice composed of several parts which should harmonize and form a whole. A plan of studies for young people is the order and the arrangement of teaching according to which the knowledge which precedes should serve for acquiring that which follows, and everything should concur in attaining the end according to the aims which have been proposed.

It seems that this method ought not to be a great mystery. The principles to be observed in teaching children should be the same as those by which Nature itself teaches them. Nature is the best of teachers.

It suffices then to observe how the first knowledge enters the minds of children and how grown men themselves acquire it.

Experience—against which it is vain to philosophize—teaches us that we possess at birth only an empty capacity which gradually fills itself, and that there are no other channels than sensation and reflection by which ideas can enter the mind.

HELVETIUS ON EDUCATION (1772)   From Claude-Adrien Helvetius, *A Treatise on Man*, W. Hooper, trans. (London, 1810), vol. I, pp. 3-6, 8-9, 92-94.

The understanding is nothing more than the assemblage of our ideas. Our ideas, says Locke, come to us by the senses; and from this principle, as from mine, it may be concluded that our understanding is nothing more than an acquisition.

To regard it as a mere gift of nature, or the effect of a particular organization, without being able to name the organ by which it is produced, is to bring back to philosophy the occult qualities; it is to believe without proof, and judge at a venture.

History and experience equally inform us that the understanding is independent of the greater or less acuteness of the senses; that men of different constitutions are susceptible of the same passions and the same ideas.

The principles of Locke, far from contradicting this opinion, confirm it; they prove that education makes us what we are; that men the more resemble each other as their instructions are more similar; and consequently that a German resembles a Frenchman more than an Asiatic; and another German more than a Frenchman; and in short, if the understandings of men be very different, it is because none of them have the same education.

Such are the facts on which I have composed this work; I offer it with more confidence to the public, as the analogy of my principles with those of Locke assure me of their truth. . . .

What is a science? A series of propositions which all relate to one general and original principle. Is morality a science? Yes; if in corporeal sensation I have discovered the sole principle of which all the precepts of morality are the necessary consequences. It is an evident proof of the truth of this principle, that it explains all the modes of being of mankind, that it developes the causes of their understanding, their stupidity, their love, their hatred, their errors and contradictions. This principle ought to be the more easily and universally adopted, as the existence of corporeal sensibility is a fact allowed by all, as the idea of it is clear, the notion distinct, the expression determinate, and, lastly, as no error can mix itself with so simple an axiom.

Corporeal sensibility seems to have been given to men as a tutelar angel, charged to watch incessantly over their preservation. Let men be happy; this perhaps is the sole view of nature, and the sole principle of morality. When the laws are good, private interest will never be destructive of that of the public: every one will be employed in pursuing his felicity; every one will be fortunate and just; because every one will perceive that his happiness depends upon that of his neighbour. . . .

Pleasure and pain are the bonds by which private interest may be always united with that of the nation: they both take their source from corporeal sensibility. The sciences of morality and legislation cannot therefore be any thing else than deductions from this simple principle.

*   *   *

If it be true that the talents and the virtues of a people determine their power and their happiness, no question can be more important than this: are the talents and virtues of each individual, the effect of his organisation, or of the education he receives?

I am of the latter opinion, and propose to prove here what perhaps is only advanced in the Treatise on the Understanding. If I can demonstrate that man is, in fact, nothing more than the product of his education, I shall doubtless reveal an important truth to mankind. They will learn, that they have in their own hands the instrument of their greatness and their felicity, and that to be happy and powerful nothing more is requisite than to perfect the science of education.

CONDORCET'S REPORT ON EDUCATION (1792)

CONDORCET'S REPORT ON EDUCATION (1792) From Marquis de Condorcet, "Report on the General Organization of Public Instruction," as quoted in F. de La Fontainerie, ed. and trans., *French Liberalism and Education in the Eighteenth Century* (New York, 1932), pp. 323-29, 332-33, 374-78.

Report on the General Organization of Public Instruction

PRESENTED TO THE NATIONAL ASSEMBLY ON BEHALF OF THE COMMITTEE ON PUBLIC INSTRUCTION, APRIL 20, and 21, 1792

To offer to all individuals of the human race the means of providing for their needs, of assuring their welfare, of knowing and exercising their rights, of understanding and fulfilling their obligations.

To assure each one the facility of perfecting his skill, of rendering himself capable of the social functions to which he has the right to be called, of developing to the fullest extent those talents with which Nature has endowed him; and thereby to establish among all citizens an actual equality, thus rendering real the political equality recognized by the law.

This should be the first aim of any national education; and, from such a point of view, this education is for the government an obligation of justice.

To direct the teaching in such a manner that the perfecting of the industries shall increase the pleasures of the generality of the citizens and the welfare of those who devote themselves to them, that a greater number of men shall be capable of exercising the functions necessary to society, and that the ever-increasing progress of enlightenment shall provide an inexhaustible source of help in our needs, of remedies for our ills, of means of individual happiness and of general prosperity.

In short, to cultivate in each generation the physical, intellectual and moral faculties, and thereby contribute to the general and gradual improvement of the human race—which should be the final aim of every social institution.

This, likewise, should be the object of education, and it is for the government a duty imposed on it by the common interest of society, by that of all mankind.

But, while considering from these two points of view the immense task which has been entrusted to us, we have felt from the very first that there is one part of the general system of education which it is possible to isolate without hurt to the whole, and that it is even necessary to do this, in order to hasten the creation of the new system: that is the distribution and general organization of establishments for public instruction.

In fact, whatever differences of opinion there may be concerning the exact content of each grade of instruction, concerning the methods of teaching, concerning the greater or less degree of authority accorded to parents or granted to teachers, concerning the assembling of students in boarding schools established by the government, concerning the means by which may be joined to education properly called the development of the physical and moral faculties; nevertheless, the general organization can be the same. Moreover, the necessity of designating the locations for such establishments and of having elementary books prepared long before these institutions can function, obliges us to urge the enactment of a law concerning that part of the work which has been entrusted to us.

We have felt that in this plan for a general organization, our first care should be to make education, on the one hand, as general, on the other, as complete as circumstances will permit. All should receive equally such education as can be given to all, but, at the same time, no group of citizens should be denied a higher grade of instruction than can be given to the mass. In the first case, because it is useful to those who receive it; in the second, because it benefits even those who do not receive it.

As the first requisite of all education is that only the truth be taught, all institutions established by the government should be as free as possible from all political control, and, since this independence cannot be absolute, it results from the same principle that they must depend only on the Assembly of the Representatives of the People. Because, of all political bodies, this is the least subject to corruption, and least likely to be influenced by personal considerations, the most easily guided by the opinions of enlightened men, and, above all, as it is the one from which necessarily all changes emanate, it is the least inimical to the progress of enlightenment, the least opposed to the improvements which this progress should bring to pass.

Finally, it has seemed to us that education should not cease when the individual leaves school. It should be of concern to all ages; for there is no age at which it is not possible and profitable to learn, and this later instruction is even more necessary because the education received in childhood was confined to the narrowest limits. In fact, one of the principal causes of the ignorance in which the poorer classes of society are to-day plunged is that it is easier for them to obtain a primary education than to preserve the advantages derived from it.

We do not wish that henceforth a single man in the realm may be able to say: "The law assures me an entire equality of rights, but I am denied the means of knowing them. I should be subject only to the law, whereas my ignorance makes me subject to everything around me. In my childhood, it is true, I was taught all I needed to know, but, as I was obliged to work to earn my living, I soon lost the little learning that I had, and now nothing is left to me but the sorrow of knowing that my ignorance is not due to a decree of Nature but to the injustice of society."

We believe that the government should say to the poorer citizens: "The poverty of your parents prevented you from obtaining any but the most indispensable knowledge, but you are assured the means of preserving and understanding it. If Nature has given you talents, you can develop them, and they will not be lost, either to you or to your country."

Thus, education should be universal. That is to say, it should be within the reach of all classes of citizens. It should be equally shared, in so far as is compatible with the necessary limitations imposed by the cost, by the distribution of the population, and by the greater or less amount of time that children can devote to it. It should, in the various grades, comprise the entire sum of human knowledge, and should assure to all, of whatever age, the possibility of preserving knowledge already obtained or of acquiring new.

Finally, no branch of the government should have the authority, or even the means, of preventing the teaching of new truths or the development of theories contrary to its special policies or its momentary interests.

These have been the principles which have guided us in our work.

We have distinguished five grades of instruction under the names: (1) primary schools; (2) secondary schools; (3) institutes; (4) lyceums; (5) the National Society of Sciences and Arts.

In the primary schools will be taught all that each individual will need to know for his personal guidance and for the enjoyment of the fullness of his rights. This instruction will also suffice even for those who will profit by the lessons intended to render men capable of fulfilling those simpler duties for which it is desirable that all good citizens be qualified; such as juryman, municipal official, etc.

Every village of at least four hundred inhabitants will have a school and a teacher.

As it would be unjust that in a department where the dwellings are dispersed or in small groups the inhabitants should be deprived of equal advantages, a primary school will be located in every district wherein will be found villages distant more than two thousand yards from another containing four hundred inhabitants. In these schools will be taught reading and writing—which, of necessity, will require some knowledge of grammar. To this will be added the rules of arithmetic; simple methods for measuring a plot of ground, for estimating the height of buildings; an elementary description of the products of the country, of agricultural and industrial procedures; the fundamental moral concepts and the rules of conduct which are derived from them: in short, those principles of social order that can be made comprehensible to children.

This instruction will be divided into four courses, each of which can be completed in one year by a child of normal capacity. Such a period of four years, which permits a convenient division for schools where it will not be possible to have more than one teacher, also coincides nearly enough with the interval, for children of the poorer classes, between the time when they begin to be capable of learning and that when they can be employed in some useful work or can be regularly apprenticed.

Every Sunday, the village schoolmaster will deliver a lecture for citizens of all ages. We have considered these lectures a means of giving the young people the necessary knowledge which it has not been possible to include in their primary education. In these lectures, the principles and rules of ethics will be further expounded, as well as those of the laws of the Nation which every citizen must know, or else he would not know his rights and would, therefore, be unable to exercise them.

Thus, in these schools, the fundamental truths of the social sciences will precede their application. Neither the French Constitution nor the Declaration of the Rights of Man will be presented to any class of citizens as tables handed down from heaven that must be worshipped and believed. Enthusiasm will not be founded on prejudice or on habits acquired in childhood; and it will be possible to say: "This Declaration of the Rights of Man, which teaches you, at the same time, what you owe to society and what you have the right to demand of it; this Constitution, which you should maintain at the risk of your life, are only the development of those simple principles dictated by reason, of which you have learned, in your first years, to recognize the eternal truth." As long as there are men who will not obey reason alone, who will receive their opinions from others, in vain will all chains have been broken. Even though these borrowed opinions be true, the human race would remain no less divided in two classes: those who think and those who believe; that is to say, masters and slaves.

By thus continuing to learn throughout life, it will be possible to prevent knowledge acquired in school from being quickly forgotten, a helpful mental activity will be maintained, and the people will be taught such new laws, such agricultural practices, and such economic methods as they will need know. It will even be possible to teach them how to learn for themselves: how to look for a word in the dictionary; how to use the index of a book; how to follow, on a chart, on a plan, or on a design, narrations or descriptions, notes or extracts. These means of learning, which in a more extensive education are acquired by habit alone, must be taught directly, in an education limited to a shorter time and to a small number of lessons.

*   *   *

The secondary schools are intended for children whose families can do without their work for a longer time, and can devote to their education a greater number of years and even a certain sum of money.

There will be a secondary school in each district, and also in each town of four thousand inhabitants. An arrangement, similar to that of which we have spoken in reference to the primary schools, will prevent any inequality in the distribution of these establishments. The course of study will be the same in all, but each school will have one, two or three teachers, according to the number of children that will be expected to attend.

Some knowledge of mathematics, of natural history, of applied chemistry, a more extensive development of the principles of ethics and of the social sciences, and elementary instruction in commerce will form the main part of the teaching.

The teachers will deliver weekly lectures which will be open to all citizens. Each school will have a small library and a small museum containing a few meteorological instruments, a few models of machines and looms and some natural history specimens. This will provide a new source of information. Without doubt, at first, these collections will be of almost no value, but they will be enlarged in time; they will be increased by gifts and exchanges, and will create a taste for observation and study; which, in turn, will contribute to their progress.

This grade of instruction may, in some respects, be regarded as general, or rather, as necessary to establish in the general instruction a more absolute equality. The rural populations are, it is true, really excluded from it, unless they are of sufficient means to be able to send their children away to school; but in such cases, those who are destined to trades must, of necessity, finish their apprenticeship in the neighboring towns, where they will receive in the secondary schools at least such instruction as they will need the most. On the other hand, farm-workers have in the year periods of rest, of which a part can be devoted to the acquirement of knowledge; whereas artisans are deprived of this leisure. Thus the advantage of private and voluntary study compensates in one case for the advantage of more extensive instruction in the other; and, in this manner, equality is still maintained, rather than destroyed, by the establishment of secondary schools.

Furthermore, as industrial processes are perfected, the work becomes more and more subdivided, and there is an increasing tendency to give each individual a purely mechanical task limited to a small number of simple movements; a task which is better and more easily done, but through habit alone, and in which the mind almost entirely ceases to function. Hence, the perfecting of the industries will become, for a part of the human race, a cause of stupidity, will produce in every nation a class of men incapable of rising above the grossest interests, and thus introduce both a humiliating inequality and the seed of dangerous troubles, unless a more extensive education offers to individuals of this class a resource against the inevitable effects of the monotony of their daily occupations.

So the advantage which the secondary schools seem to give the towns is, in reality, only another means of rendering the equality more complete.

*   *   *

This state of independence of all external authority, in which we have placed public education, need cause no fear; since any abuse would be instantly corrected by the legislative power, which has direct authority over the entire system of education. Does not the existence of independent instruction and of independently established learned societies also oppose to this abuse a force of opinion so much the more important because, under a popular constitution, no institution can exist unless public opinion adds its strength to that of the law? Besides, there is a final authority which, in all things pertaining to the sciences, nothing can resist: the general opinion of enlightened men in all Europe; an opinion which it is impossible to mislead or to corrupt. On it alone depends any brilliant and enduring celebrity; it is its approval that added to local celebrity gives it greater solidity and brilliance. It is, in a word, for scientists, for men of letters, for philosophers, a sort of anticipated posterity whose judgments are as impartial and almost as sure as those of posterity itself, and a supreme power, from whose authority they cannot attempt to escape.

Finally, the independence of instruction is, in a manner, a part of the rights of the human race. Since man has received from Nature a perfectibility whose unknown limits extend—if they even exist—much beyond what we can yet perceive, and the knowledge of new truths is for him the only means of developing this happy faculty—the source of his happiness and of his glory, what power could have the right to say to him: "This is what you need know; this is as far as you may go"? Since truth alone is useful, since every error is an evil, by what right would any power, whatever it be, dare to determine wherein lies truth, wherein lies error?

Besides, any power which would forbid the teaching of an opinion contrary to that which has served as a basis for the established laws, would attack directly the freedom of thought, would frustrate the aim of every social institution: the perfecting of the laws, which is the necessary consequence of the combat of opinions and the progress of knowledge.

*   *   *

The plan which we present to the Assembly has been prepared in conformity with the results of an examination of the present state of knowledge in France and in Europe, together with what we have been able to learn from the observations of several centuries concerning the progress of the human intelligence in the sciences and in the arts, and, finally, with what can be expected and foreseen of its further progress.

We have sought all that could more certainly help to assure it a steadier advance and more rapid progress.

A time will come, without doubt, when learned societies instituted by governmental authority will become superfluous and, thenceforth, dangerous; a time when even any public establishment of instruction will be useless. This will be when there will no longer be any general error to be feared; when all the motives which appeal to interest or to the passions in behalf of prejudices will have lost their influence; when enlightenment will be equally spread both over all parts of a same territory and among all classes of a same society; when all the sciences and all the applications of the sciences will be equally delivered from the yoke of all superstitions and from the poison of false doctrines; when, at last, each man will find in his own knowledge, in the soundness of his mind, arms sufficient to repulse all the ruses of charlatanry. But this time is still distant, and our object should be to prepare for it, to hasten the epoch of its coming. Thus, while working to create these new institutions, we have necessarily been occupied, at the same time, in hastening the coming of the happy moment when they will become useless.

CONDORCET ON THE FUTURE OF MAN (1795)   From Marquis de Condorcet, *Outlines of an Historical View of the Progress of the Human Mind* (London, 1795), pp. 1-5, 14-15, 18-20, 316-19, 333-34.

Man is born with the faculty of receiving sensations. In those which he receives, he is capable of perceiving and of distinguishing the simple sensations of which they are composed. He can retain, recognise, combine them. He can preserve or recal them to his memory; he can compare their different combinations; he can ascertain what they possess in common, and what characterises each; lastly, he can affix signs to all these objects, the better to know them, and the more easily to form from them new combinations.

This faculty is developed in him by the action of external objects, that is, by the presence of certain complex sensations, the constancy of which, whether in their identical whole, or in the laws of their change, is independent of himself. It is also exercised by communication with other similarly organised individuals, and by all the artificial means which from the first developement of this faculty, men have succeeded in inventing.

Sensations are accompanied with pleasure or pain, and man has the further faculty of converting these momentary impressions into durable sentiments of a corresponding nature, and of experiencing these sentiments either at the sight or recollection of the pleasure or pain of beings sensitive like himself. And from this faculty, united with that of forming and combining ideas, arise, between him and his fellow creatures, the ties of interest and duty, to which nature has affixed the most exquisite portion of our felicity, and the most poignant of our sufferings.

Were we to confine our observations to an enquiry into the general facts and unvarying laws which the developement of these faculties presents to us, in what is common to the different individuals of the human species, our enquiry would bear the name of metaphysics.

But if we consider this developement in its results, relative to the mass of individuals co-existing at the same time on a given space, and follow it from generation to generation, it then exhibits a picture of the progress of human intellect. This progress is subject to the same general laws, observable in the individual developement of our faculties; being the result of that very developement considered at once in a great number of individuals united in society. But the result which every instant presents, depends upon that of the preceding instants, and has an influence on the instants which follow.

This picture, therefore, is historical; since, subjected as it will be to perpetual variations, it is formed by the successive observation of human societies at the different eras through which they have passed. It will accordingly exhibit the order in which the changes have taken place, explain the influence of every past period upon that which follows it, and thus show, by the modifications which the human species has experienced, in its incessant renovation through the immensity of ages, the course which it has pursued, and the steps which it has advanced towards knowledge and happiness. From these observations on what man has heretofore been, and what he is at present, we shall be led to the means of securing and of accelerating the still further progress, of which, from his nature, we may indulge the hope.

Such is the object of the work I have undertaken; the result of which will be to show, from reasoning and from facts, that no bounds have been fixed to the improvement of the human faculties; that the perfectibility of man is absolutely indefinite; that the progress of this perfectibility, henceforth above the control of every power that would impede it, has no other limit than the duration of the globe upon which nature has placed us. The course of this progress may doubtless be more or less rapid, but it can never be retrograde; at least while the earth retains its situation in the system of the universe, and the laws of this system shall neither effect upon the globe a general overthrow, nor introduce such changes as would no longer permit the human race to preserve and exercise therein the same faculties, and find the same resources.

* * *

There remains only a third picture to form,—that of our hopes, or the progress reserved for future generations, which the constancy of the laws of nature seems to secure to mankind. And here it will be necessary to shew by what steps this progress, which at present may appear chimerical, is gradually to be rendered possible, and even easy; how truth, in spite of the transient success of prejudices, and the support they receive from the corruption of governments or of the people, must in the end obtain a durable triumph; by what ties nature has indissolubly united the advancement of knowledge with the progress of liberty, virtue, and respect for the natural rights of man; how these blessings, the only real ones, though so frequently seen apart as to be thought incompatible, must necessarily amalgamate and become inseparable, the moment knowledge shall have arrived at a certain pitch in a great number of nations at once, the moment it shall have penetrated the whole mass of a great people, whose language shall have become universal, and whose commercial intercourse shall embrace the whole extent of the globe. This union having once taken place in the whole enlightened class of men, this class will be considered as the friends of human kind, exerting themselves in concert to advance the improvement and happiness of the species.

We shall expose the origin and trace the history of general errors, which have more or less contributed to retard or suspend the advance of reason, and sometimes even, as much as political events, have been the cause of man's taking a retrograde course towards ignorance.

* * *

Are we not arrived at the point when there is no longer any thing to fear, either from new errors, or the return of old ones; when no corrupt institution can be introduced by hypocrisy, and adopted by ignorance or enthusiasm; when no vicious combination can effect the infelicity of a great people? Accordingly would it not be of advantage to know how nations have been deceived, corrupted, and plunged in misery.

Every thing tells us that we are approaching the era of one of the grand revolutions of the human race. What can better enlighten us as to what we may expect, what can be a surer guide to us, amidst its commotions, than the picture of the revolutions that have preceded and prepared the way for it? The present state of knowledge assures us that it will be happy. But it is not upon condition that we know how to assist it with all our strength? And, that the happiness it promises may be less dearly bought, that it may spread with more rapidity over a greater space, that it may be more complete in its effects, is it not requisite to study, in the history of the human mind, what obstacles remain to be feared, and by what means those obstacles are to be surmounted?

*   *   *

If man can predict, almost with certainty, those appearances of which he understands the laws; if, even when the laws are unknown to him, experience of the past enables him to foresee, with considerable probability, future appearances; why should we suppose it a chimerical undertaking to delineate, with some degree of truth, the picture of the future destiny of mankind from the results of its history? The only foundation of faith in the natural sciences is the principle, that the general laws, known or unknown, which regulate the phenomena of the universe, are regular and constant; and why should this principle, applicable to the other operations of nature, be less true when applied to the developement of the intellectual and moral faculties of man? In short, as opinions formed from experience, relative to the same class of objects, are the only rule by which men of soundest understanding are governed in their conduct, why should the philosopher be proscribed from supporting his conjectures upon a similar basis, provided he attribute to them no greater certainty than the number, the consistency, and the accuracy of actual observations shall authorise?

Our hopes, as to the future condition of the human species, may be reduced to three points: the destruction of inequality between different nations; the progress of equality in one and the same nation; and lastly, the real improvement of man.

Will not every nation one day arrive at the state of civilization attained by those people who are most enlightened, most free, most exempt from prejudices, as the French, for instance, and the Anglo-Americans? Will not the slavery of countries subjected to kings, the barbarity of African tribes, and the ignorance of savages gradually vanish? Is there upon the face of the globe a single spot the inhabitants of which are condemned by nature never to enjoy liberty, never to exercise their reason?

Does the difference of knowledge, of means, and of wealth, observable hitherto in all civilized nations, between the classes into which the people constituting those nations are divided; does that inequality, which the earliest progress of society has augmented, or, to speak more properly, produced, belong to civilization itself, or to the imperfections of the social order? Must it not continually weaken, in order to give place to that actual equality, the chief end of the social art, which, diminishing even the effects of the natural difference of the faculties, leaves no other inequality subsisting but what is useful to the interest of all, because it will favour civilization, instruction, and industry, without drawing after it either dependence, humiliation or poverty? In a word, will not men be continually verging towards that state, in which all will possess the requisite knowledge for conducting themselves in the common affairs of life by their own reason, and of maintaining that reason uncontaminated by prejudices; in which they will understand their rights, and exercise them according to their opinion and their conscience; in which all will be able, by the developement of their faculties, to procure the certain means of providing for their wants; lastly, in which folly and wretchedness will be accidents, happening only now and then, and not the habitual lot of a considerable portion of society?

In fine, may it not be expected that the human race will be meliorated by new discoveries in the sciences and the arts, and, as an unavoidable consequence, in the means of individual and general prosperity; by farther progress in the principles of conduct, and in moral practice; and lastly, by the real improvement of our faculties, moral, intellectual and physical, which may be the result either of the improvement of the instruments which increase the power and direct the exercise of those faculties, or of the improvement of our natural organization itself?

*   *   *

The equality of instruction we can hope to attain, and with which we ought to be satisfied, is that which excludes every species of dependence, whether forced or voluntary. We may exhibit, in the actual state of human knowledge, the easy means by which this end may be attained even for those who can devote to study but a few years of infancy, and, in subsequent life, only some occasional hours of leisure. We might shew, that by a happy choice of the subjects to be taught, and of the mode of inculcating them, the entire mass of a people may be instructed in every thing necessary for the purposes of domestic economy; for the transaction of their affairs; for the free developement of their industry and their faculties; for the knowledge, exercise and protection of their rights; for a sense of their duties, and the power of discharging them; for the capacity of judging both their own actions, and the actions of others, by their own understanding; for the acquisition of all the delicate or dignified sentiments that are an honour to humanity; for freeing themselves from a blind confidence in those to whom they may entrust the care of their interests, and the security of their rights; for chusing and watching over them, so as no longer to be the dupes of those popular errors that torment and way-lay the life of man with superstitious fears and chimerical hopes; for defending themselves against prejudices by the sole energy of reason; in fine, for escaping from the delusions of imposture, which would spread snares for their fortune, their health, their freedom of opinion and of conscience, under the pretext of enriching, of healing, and of saving them.

The Reformation — England

THOMAS CRANMER'S PREFACE TO THE "GREAT BIBLE," THE FIRST
AUTHORIZED ENGLISH BIBLE (1540)   From Harold R. Willoughby, ed., *The First
English Bible and the Cranmer Preface* (Chicago, 1942), pp. 38-39, 43-45, 49-50.

A
Prologue or Preface
made by
The Most Reverend Father in God,
Thomas, Archbishop of Canterbury,
Metropolitan and Primate of England.

For two sundry sorts of people, it seemeth much necessary that something
be said in the entry of this book by the way of a preface or prologue; whereby
hereafter it may be both the better accepted of them which hitherto could not well
bear it, and also the better used of them which heretofore have misused it. For truly
some there are that be too slow and need the spur, some other seem too quick and
need more of the bridle; some lose their game by short shooting, some by over
shooting; some walk too much on the left hand, some too much on the right. In the
former sort be all they that refuse to read, or to hear read, the Scripture in their
vulgar tongues; much worse, they that also let [hinder] or discourage the other from
the reading or hearing thereof. In the latter sort be they which by their inordinate
reading, indiscreet speaking, contentious disputing, or otherwise by their licentious
living, slander and hinder the Word of God most of all other, whereof they would
seem to be greatest furtherers. These two sorts, albeit they be most far unlike the
one to the other, yet they both deserve in effect like reproach. Neither can I well
tell whither [which] of them I may judge the more offender; him that doth
obstinately refuse so godly and goodly knowledge, or him that so ungodly and so
ungoodly doth abuse the same.

And as touching the former, I would marvel much that any man should be so
mad as to refuse in darkness, light; in hunger, food; in cold, fire: for the Word of
God is light. . . . I would marvel, I say at this, save that I consider how much
custom and usage may do. So that if there were a people, as some write *(De
Cimmeriis)*, which never saw the sun by reason that they be situated far toward the
north pole, and be enclosed and overshadowed with high mountains; it is credible
and like enough that if, by the power and will of God, the mountains should sink
down and give place that the light of the sun might have entrance to them, at the
first some of them would be offended therewith. And the old proverb affirmeth, that

THE
EUROPEAN
HERITAGE

119

after tillage of corn was first found many delighted more to feed of mast and acorns, wherewith they had been accustomed, than to eat bread made of good corn. Such is the nature of custom, that it causeth us to bear all things well and easily, wherewith we have been accustomed, and to be offended with all things thereunto contrary. And therefore I can well think them worthy pardon, which at the coming abroad of Scripture doubted and drew back. But such as will persist still in their wilfulness, I must needs judge not only foolish, forward, and obstinate, but also peevish, perverse, and indurate.

And yet, if the matter should be tried by custom we might also allege custom for the reading of the Scripture in the vulgar tongue, and prescribe the more ancient custom. For it is not much above one hundred year[s] ago since Scripture hath not been accustomed to be read in the vulgar tongue within this realm; and many hundred years before that it was translated and read in the Saxon's tongue, which at that time was our mother's tongue: whereof there remaineth yet divers copies found lately in old abbeys, of such antique manners of writing and speaking, that few men now been [are] able to read and understand them. And when this language waxed old and out of common usage, because folk should not lack the fruit of reading, it was again translated in the newer language. Whereof yet also many copies remain and be daily found.

But now to let pass custom and to weigh, as wise men ever should, the thing in his own nature: let us here discuss what it availeth Scripture to be had and read of the lay and vulgar people.

✲   ✲   ✲

Hitherto, all that I have said I have taken and gathered out of the foresaid sermon of this holy doctor, St. John Chrysostom. Now if I should in like manner bring forth what the self-same doctor speaketh in other places, and what other doctors and writers say concerning the same purpose, I might seem to you to write another Bible rather than to make a preface to the Bible. Wherefore, in few words to comprehend the largeness and utility of the Scripture, how it containeth fruitful instruction and erudition for every man: if any things be necessary to be learned, of the Holy Scripture we may learn it. If falsehood shall be reproved, thereof we may gather wherewithal. If anything be to be corrected and amended, if there need any exhortation or consolation, of the Scripture we may well learn. In the Scriptures be the fat pastures of the soul; therein is no venomous meat, no unwholesome thing; they be the very dainty and pure feeding. He that is ignorant shall find there what he should learn. He that is a perverse sinner shall there find his damnation to make him to tremble for fear. He that laboureth to serve God shall find there his glory and the promises of eternal life, exhorting him more diligently to labour. Herein may princes learn how to govern their subjects; subjects obedience, love, and dread to their princes: husbands how they should behave them unto their wives, how to educate their children and servants; and contrary, the wives, children, and servants may know their duty to their husbands, parents, and masters. Here may all manner of persons, men, women, young, old, learned, unlearned, rich, poor, priests, laymen, lords, ladies, officers, tenants, and mean men, virgins, wives, widows, lawyers, merchants, artificers, husbandmen, and all manner of persons, of what estate or condition soever they be, may in this book learn all things what they ought to believe, what they ought to do, and what they should not do, as well concerning Almighty God as also concerning themselves and all other[s]. Briefly, to the reading of the Scripture none can be enemy, but that either be so sick that they love not to hear of any medicine, or else that be so ignorant that they know not Scripture to be the most healthful medicine.

Therefore, as touching this former part, I will here conclude, and take it as a conclusion sufficiently determined and approved, that it is convenient and good the Scripture to be read of all sorts and kinds of people, and in the vulgar tongue, without further allegations or probations for the same; which shall not need, since that this one place of John Chrysostom is enough and sufficient to persuade all them that be not forwardly and perversely set in their own willful opinion; specially now that the King's Highness, being supreme head next under Christ of this Church of England, hath approved with his royal assent the setting forth thereof, which only to all true and obedient subjects ought to be a sufficient reason for the allowance of the same, without further delay, reclamation, or resistance, although there were no preface nor other reason herein expressed.

*   *   *

Therefore to conclude this latter part, every man that cometh to the reading of this holy book ought to bring with him first and foremost this fear of Almighty God, and then next a firm and stable purpose to reform his own self according thereunto; and so to continue, proceed, and prosper from time to time, showing himself to be a sober and fruitful hearer and learner; which if he do, he shall prove at the length well able to teach, though not with his mouth, yet with his living and good example, which is sure the most lively and most effectuous form and manner of teaching. He that otherwise intermeddleth with this book, let him be assured that once he shall make account therefore, when he shall have said to him, as it is written in the prophet David, *Peccatori dicit Deus,* etc: "Unto the ungodly, said God, why dost thou preach my laws, and takest my testament in thy mouth, whereas thou hatest to be reformed, and hast cast my words behind thee? When thou sawest a thief, thou consentedest unto him, and hast been partaker with adulterers. Thou hast let thy mouth speak wickedness, and with thy tongue thou hast set forth deceit. Thou sattest and spakest against thy brother, and hast slandered thine own mother's son. These things hast thou done, and I held my tongue, and thou thoughtest (wickedly) that I am even such a one as thyself. But I will reprove thee, and set before thee the things that thou hast done. O consider this, ye that forget God, lest I pluck you away, and there be none to deliver you. Whoso offereth me thanks and praise, he honoureth me; and to him that ordereth his conversation right will I show the salvation of God."

To the Moste Vertvovs and Noble Qvene Elisabet, Quene of England, France, ad Ireland, &c. Your humble Subiects of the English Churche at Geneua, wish grace and peace from God the Father through Christ Iesus our Lord.

*   *   *

How hard a thing it is, and what great impedimentes let, to enterprise any worthie act, not only dailie experience sufficiently sheweth (moste noble and vertuous Quene) but also that notable prouerbe doeth cofirme the fame, which admonisheth vs, that all thigs are hard which are faire and excellet. And what enterprise can there be of greater importance, and more acceptable vnto God, or more worthie of singuler commendation, then the building of the Lords Temple, the house of God, the Church of Christ, whereof the Sonne of God is the head and perfection?

When Zerubbabel went about to builde the material Temple, according to the commandement of the Lord, what difficulties and stayes daily arose to hinder his worthy indeuours, y bookes of Ezra & Esdras playnely witnesse: how that not only he and the people of God were sore molested with foreyn aduersaries, (whereof some maliciously warred against them, and corrupted the Kings officers: and others craftely practised vnder pretence of religion) but also at home with domestical enemies, as false Prophets, craftie worldlings, faint hearted soldiers, and oppressors of their brethren, who aswel by false doctrine and lyes, as by subtil counsel, cowardies, and extortion, discouraged the heartes almoste of all: so that the Lords worke was not only interrupted and left of for a long tyme, but scarcely at the length with great labour and danger after a sort brought to passe.

Which thing when we weigh aright, and consider earnestly how muche greater charge God hath laid vpon you in making you a builder of his spiritual Temple, we cannot but partely feare, knowing the crafte and force of Satan our spiritual enemie, and the weakenes and vnabilitie of this our nature: and partely be feruent in our prayers toward God that he wolde bring to perfection this noble worke which he hath begon by you: and therefore we indeuour our selues by all meanes to ayde, & to bestowe our whole force vnder your graces stadard, whome God hath made as our Zerubbabel for the erecting of this moste excellent Temple, and to plant and maynteyn his holy worde to the aduancement of his glorie, for your owne honour and saluatio of your soule, and for the singuler comfort of that great flocke which Christ Jesus the great shepherd hath boght with his precious blood, and committed vnto your charge to be fed both in body and soule.

Considering therefore how many enemies there are, which by one meanes or other, as the aduersaries of Iudah and Beniamin went about to stay the building of that Temple, so labour to hinder the course of this building (whereof some are Papistes, who vnder pretence of sauoring Gods worde, traiterously seke to erect idolatrie and to destroy your maiestie: some are worldlings, who as Demas haue forsake Christ for the love of this worlde: others are ambicious prelats, who as Amasiah & Diotrephes can abide none but them selues: and as Demetrius many practise sedition to maynteyne their errors) we persuaded our selues that there was no way so expedient and necessarie for the preseruation of the one, and destruction of the other, as to present vnto your Maiestie the holy Scriptures faithfully and playnely translated according to the langages wherein thei were first written by the holy Gost. For the worde of God is an euident token of Gods loue and our assurance of his defence, wheresoeuer it is obediently receyued: it is the trial of the Spirits: and as the Prophet saieth, It is as a fyre and hammer to breake the stonie heartes of them that resist Gods mercies offred by the preaching of the same. Yea it is sharper then any two edged sworde to examine the very thoghtes and to judge the affections of the heart, and to discouer whatsoeuer lyeth hid vnder hypocrisie and wolde be secret from the face of God and his Churche. So that this must be the first fundacion and groundworke, according whereunto the good stones of this building must be framed, and the euil tried out and reiected.

Now as he that goeth about to lay a fundacion surely, first taketh away suche impedimentes, as might iustely ether hurt, let or difforme the worke: so is it necessarie that your graces zeale appeare herein, that nether the craftie persuasion of man, nether worldly policie, or natural feare dissuade you to roote out, cut downe and destroy these wedes and impedimentes which do not only deface your building, but vtterly indeuour, yea & threaten the ruine thereof. For when the noble Iosias entreprised the like kinde of worke, among other notable and many things he destroyed, not only with vtter confusion the idoles with their appertinances, but also burnt (in signe of detestatio) the idolatrous priests bones vpon their altars, and put to death the false prophetes and sorcerers, to performe the wordes of the Lawe of God: and therefore the Lord gaue him good successe & blessed him wonderfully, so long as he made Gods worde his line and rule to followe, and enterprised nothing before he had inquired at the mouth of the Lord.

And if these zealous begynnings seme dangerous and to brede disquietnes in your dominions, yet by the storie of King Asa it is manifest, that the quietnes and peace of kingdomes standeth in the vtter abolishing of idolatrie, and in aduancing of true religion: for in his dayes Iudah lyued in rest and quietnes for the space of fyue and thirtie yere, til at length he began to be colde in the zeale of the Lord, feared the power of man, imprisoned the Prophet of God, and oppressed the people: then the Lord sent him warres, & at length toke him away by death.

Wherefore great wisdome, not worldelie, but heauenly is here required, which your grace must earnestly craue of the Lord, as did Salomon, to whome God gaue an vnderstanding heart to iudge his people aright, and to discerne betwene good and bad. For if God for the furnishing of the olde temple gaue the Spirit of wisdome & vnderstanding to them that shulde be the workemen thereof, as to Bezaleel, Aholiab, and Hiram: how muche more wil he indewe your grace and other godly princes and chefe gouernours with principal Spirit, that you may procure and commande things necessarie for this moste holy Temple, forese and take hede of things that might hinder it, and abolish and destroy whatsoeuer might impare and ouerthrowe the same?

Moreover the maruelous diligence and zeale of Iehoshaphat, Iosiah, and Hezekiah are by the singuler prouidence of God left as an example to all godly rulers to reforme their countreys and to establish the worde of God with all spede, lest the wrath of the Lord fall vpon them for the neglecting thereof. For these excellent Kings did not onely imbrace the worde promptely and ioyfully, but also procured earnestly and commanded the same to be taught, preached and maynteyned through all their countreys and dominions, bynding them and all their subiects bothe great and smale with solemne protestations and couenantes before

God to obey the worde, and to walke after the waies of the Lord. Yea and in the daies of Kyng Asa it was enacted that whosoeuer wolde not seke the Lord God of Israel, shulde be slayne, whether he were smale or great, man or woman. And for the establishing hereof and performance of this solemne othe, aswel Priests as Iudges were appointed and placed through all the cities of Iudah to instruct the people in the true knollage and feare of God, and to minister iustice according to the worde, knowing that, except God by his worde dyd reigne in the heartes and soules, all mans diligence and indeuors were of none effect: for without this worde we cannot discerne betwene iustice, and iniurie, protection and oppression, wisdome and foolishnes, knollage and ignorance, good and euil. Therefore the Lord, who is the chefe gouernour of his Church, willeth that nothing be attempted before we haue inquired thereof at his mouth. For seing he is our God, of duetie we must giue him this preeminence, that of our selues we enterprise nothing, but that which he hath appointed, who only knoweth all things, and gouerneth them, as may best serue to his glorie and our saluation. We oght not therefore to preuent him, or do anything without his worde, but assone as he hath reueiled his wil, immediately to put it in execution.

Now as concerning the maner of this building, it is not according to man, nor after the wisdome of the flesh, but of the Spirit, & according to the worde of God, whose wais are diuers from mans wais. For if it was not lawful for Moses to builde the material Tabernacle after any other sorte then God had shewed him by a patern, nether to prescribe any other ceremonies & lawes then suche as the Lord had expresly commaded: how can it be lawful to procede in this spiritual building any other waies, then Iesus Christ the Sonne of God, who is bothe the fundacion, head and chief corner stone thereof, hath commanded by his worde? And for asmuche as he hath established and left an order in his Churche for the building vp of his body, appointing some to be Apostles, some Prophetes, others Euangelistes, some pastors, and teachers, he signifieth that euery one according as he is placed in this body which is the Church, oght to inquire of his ministres concerning the wil of the Lord, which is reueiled in his worde. For thei are, saieth Ieremiah, as the mouth of the Lord: yea he promiseth to be with their mouth, & that their lippes shal kepe knollage, & that the trueth & the law shal be in their mouth. For it is their office chefely to vnderstand the Scriptures & teache them. For this cause the people of Israel in matters of difficultie vsed to aske the Lord ether by the Prophets, or by the meanes of the hie Priest, who bare Vrim & Thummim, which were tokens of light & knollage, of holines & perfectio which shulde be in the hie Priest. Therefore when Iehoshaphat toke this order in the Church of Israel, he appointed Amariah to be the chief concerning the worde of God, because he was moste expert in the law of the Lord, and colde gyue cousel and gouerne according vnto the same. Els there is no degre or office which may haue that autoritie and priuiledge to decise concerning Gods worde, except with all he hath the Spirit of God, and sufficient knollage and judgement to define according thereunto. And as euery one is indued of God with greater giftes, so oght he to be herein chefely heard, or at least that without the expresse worde none be heard: for he that hathe not the worde, speaketh not by the mouthe of the Lord. Agayne, what danger it is to do any thing, seme it neuer so godly or necessarie, without consulting with Gods mouth, the examples of the Israelites, deceiued hereby through the Gibeonites: and of Saul, whose intention semed good and necessarie: and of Iosiah also, who for great considerations was moued for the defence of true religion & his people, to fight against Pharaoh Necho King of Egypt, may sufficiently admonish vs.

Last of all (moste gracious Quene) for the aduancement of this building and rearing vp of the worke, two things are necessarie, First, that we haue a lyuely & stedfast faith in Christ Iesus, who must dwel in our heartes, as the only meanes and assurance of our saluation: for he is the ladder that reacheth from the earth to heauen: he lifteth vp his Churche and setteth it in the heauenly places, he maketh vs lyuely stones and buildeth vs vpon him selfe: he joyneth vs to him selfe as to mebres and body to the head: yea he maketh him selfe and his Churche one Christ. The next is, that our faith bring forthe good fruites, so that our godly conuersation may serue vs as a witnes to confirme our election, and be an example to all others to walke as apperteyneth to the vocation whereunto thei are called: lest the worde of God be euil spoken of, and this building be stayed to growe vp to a iust height, which ca not be without the great prouocatio of Gods iuste vengeance and discouraging of many thousandes through all the worlde, if thei shulde se that our life were not holy and agreable to our profession. For the eyes of all that feare God in all places beholde your countreyes as an example to all that beleue, and the prayers of all the godly at all tymes are directed to God for the preseruatio of your maiestie. For considering Gods wonderful mercies toward you at all seasons, who hath pulled you out of the mouthe of the lyons, and how that from your youth you haue bene broght vp in the holy Scriptures, the hope of all men is so increased, that thei ca not but looke that God shulde bring to passe some woderful worke by your grace to the vniuersal comfort of his Churche. Therefore euen aboue stregth you must shewe your selfe strong and bolde in Gods matters: and thogh Satan lay all his power and craft together to hurt and hinder the Lordes building: yet be you assured that God wil fight from heauen against this great dragon, the ancient serpent, which is called the deuil and Satan, til he haue accomplished the whole worke and made his Churche glorious to him selfe, without spot or wrincle. For albeit all other kingdomes and monarchies, as the Babylonians, Persians, Grecians & Romains haue fallen & taken end: yet the Churche of Christ euen vnder the Crosse hath from the begynning of the worlde bene victorious, and shal be euerlastingly. Trueth it is, that sometyme it semeth to be shadowed with a cloude, or driue with a stormie persecution, yet suddenly the beames of Christ the sunne of iustice shine and bring it to light and libertie. If for a tyme it lie couered with ashes, yet it is quickely kindeled agayne by the wynde of Gods Spirit: thogh it seme drowned in the sea, or parched and pyned in the wildernes, yet God giueth euer good successe, for he punisheth the enemies, and deliuereth his, nourisheth them and stil preserueth the vnder his wyngs. This Lord of lordes & King of kings who hath euer defended his, strengthe, cofort and preserue your maiestie, that you may be able to build vp the ruines of Gods house to his glorie, the discharge of your conscience, and to the comfort of all them that loue the comming of Christ Iesus our Lord. From Geneua. 10. April. 1560.

A NOTE TO THE READER FROM THE MARIAN EXILES (1560)   From *The Geneva Bible: A Facsimile of the 1560 edition* (Madison, Wis., 1969), no pagination.

B esides the manifolde and continual benefites which almightie God bestoweth vpon vs, bothe corporal and spiritual, we are especially bounde (deare brethren) to giue him thankes without ceasing for his great grace and vnspeakable mercies, in that it hath pleased him to call vs vnto this meruelous light of his Gospel, & mercifully to regarde vs after so horrible backesliding and falling away from Christ to Antichrist, from light to darcknes, from the liuing God to dumme and dead idoles, & that after so cruel murther of Gods Saintes, as alas, hathe bene among vs, we are not altogether cast of, as were the Israelites, and many others for the like, or not so manifest wickednes, but receyued agayne to grace with moste euident signes and tokens of Gods especial loue and fauour. To the intent therefore that we may not be vnmyndeful of these great mercies, but seke by all meanes (according to our duetie) to be thankeful for the same, it behoueth vs so to walke in his feare and loue, that all the daies of our life we may procure the glorie of his holy name. Now forasmuche as this thing chefely is atteyned by the knollage and practising of the worde of God (which is the light to our paths, the keye of the kingdome of heauen, our comfort in affliction, our shielde and sworde against Satan, the schoole of all wisdome, the glasse wherein we beholde Gods face, the testimonie of his fauour, and the only foode and nourishment of our soules) we thoght that we colde bestowe our labours & studie in nothing which colde be more acceptable to God and comfortable to his Churche then in the translating of the holy Scriptures into our natiue tongue: the which thing, albeit that diuers heretofore haue indeuored to atchieue: yet considering the infancie of those tymes and imperfect knollage of the tongues, in respect of this ripe age and cleare light which God hath now reueiled, the translations required greatly to be perused and reformed. Not that we vendicat any thing to our selues aboue the least of our brethren (for God knoweth with what feare and trembling we haue bene now, for the space of two yeres and more day and night occupied herein) but being earnestly desired, and by diuers, whose learning and godlynes we reuerence, exhorted, and also incouraged by the ready willes of suche, whose heartes God likewise touched, not to spare any charges for the fortherance of suche a benefite and fauour of God toward his Churche (thogh the tyme then was moste dangerous and the persecution sharpe and furious) we submitted our selues at length to their godly iudgementes, and seing the great oportunitie and occasions, which God presented vnto vs in this Churche, by reason of so many godly and learned men: and suche diuersities of translations in diuers tongues, we vndertoke this great and wonderful worke (with all reuerence, as in the presence of God, as intreating the worde of God, whereunto we thinke our selues vnsufficient) which now God according to his diuine prouidence and mercie hath directed to a moste prosperous end. And this we may with good conscience protest, that we haue in euery point and worde, according to the measure of that knollage which it pleased al mightie God to giue vs, faithfully rendred the text, and in all hard places moste syncerely expounded the same. For God is our witnes that we haue by all meanes indeuored to set forthe the puritie of the worde and right sense of the holy Gost for the edifying of the brethren in faith and charitie.

Now as we haue chiefely obserued the sense, and laboured alwaies to restore it to all integritie: so haue we moste reuerently kept the proprietie of the wordes, considering that the Apostles who spake and wrote to the Gentiles in the Greke tongue, rather constrayned them to the liuely phrase of the Ebrewe, then entreprised farre by mollifying their langage to speake as the Gentils did. And for this and other causes we haue in many places reserued the Ebrewe phrases, notwithstanding that thei may seme somewhat hard in their eares that are not wel practised and also delite in the swete sounding phrases of the holy Scriptures. Yet lest ether the simple shulde be discouraged, or the malicious haue any occasion of iust cauillation, seing some translations read after one sort, and some after another, whereas all may serue to good purpose and edification, we haue in the margent noted that diuersitie of speache or reading which may also seme agreable to the mynde of the holy Gost and propre for our langage with thismarke.

A gayne where as the Ebrewe speache semed hardly to agre with ours, we haue noted it in the margent after this sort", vsing that which was more intelligible. And albeit that many of the Ebrewe names be altered from the olde text, and restored to the true writing and first original, whereof thei haue their signification, yet in the vsual names litle is changed for feare of troubling the simple readers. Moreouer whereas the necessitie of the sentence required any thing to be added (for suche is the grace and proprietie of the Ebrewe and Greke tongues, that it can not but ether by circumlocution, or by adding the verbe or some worde be vnderstand of them that are not wel practised therein) we haue put it in the text with another kynde of lettre, that it may easely be discerned from the common lettre. As touching the diuision of the verses, we haue followed the Ebrewe examples, which haue so euen from the begynning distinct them. Which thing as it is moste profitable for memorie: so doeth it agre with the best translations, & is moste easie to finde out both by the best Concordances, and also by the cotations which we have dilygently herein perused and set forthe by this starre*. Besides this the principal matters are noted and distincted by this marke . Yea and the argumentes bothe for the booke and for the chapters with the nombre of the verse are added, that by all meanes the reader might be holpen. For the which cause also we haue set ouer the head of euery page some notable worde or sentence which may greatly further aswel for memorie, as for the chief point of the page. And considering how hard a thing it is to vnderstand the holy Scriptures, and what errors, sectes and heresies growe dailie for lacke of the true knollage thereof, and how many are discouraged (as thei pretend) because thei can not atteine to the true and simple meaning of the same, we haue also indeuored bothe by the diligent reading of the best commentaries, and also by the conference with the godly and learned brethren, to gather brief annotations vpon all the hard places, aswel for the vnderstanding of suche wordes as are obscure, and for the declaration of the text, as for the application of the same as may moste apperteine to Gods glorie and the edification of his Churche. Forthermore whereas certeyne places in the bookes of Moses, of the Kings and Ezekiel semed so darke that by no description thei colde be made easie to the simple reader, we haue so set them forthe with figures and notes for the ful declaration thereof, that thei which can not by iudgement being holpen by the annotations noted by the lettres a b c. &c. atteyn thereunto, yet by the perspectiue, and as it were by the eye may sufficiently knowe the true meaning of all suche places. Whereunto also we haue added certeyne mappes of Cosmographie which necessarely serue for the perfect vnderstanding and memorie of diuers places and countreys, partly described, and partly by occasion touched, bothe in the olde and newe Testament. Finally that nothing might lacke which might be boght by labors, for the increase of knowlage and fortherance of Gods glorie, we haue adioyned two moste profitable tables, the one seruing for the interpretation of the Ebrewe names: and the other conteyning all the chefe and principal matters of the whole Bible: so that nothing (as we trust) that any colde iustely desire, is omitted. Therefore, as brethren that are partakers of the same hope and saluation with vs, we beseche you, that this riche perle and inestimable treasure may not be offred in vayne, but as sent from God to the people of God, for the increase of his kingdome, the comfort of his Churche, and discharge of our conscience, whome it hath pleased him to saife vp for this purpose, so you wolde willingly receyue the worde of God, earnestly studie it and in all your life practise it, that you may now appeare in dede to be the people of God, not walking any more according to this worlde, but in the frutes of the Spirit; that

God in vs may be fully glorified through Christ Iesus our Lord, who lyueth and reigneth for euer. Amen.

DEDICATION TO THE KING JAMES BIBLE (1611) From *The Holy Bible* (London, 1833), no pagination.

To the Most High and Mighty Prince
JAMES,
by the Grace of God,
King of Great Britain, France, and Ireland,
Defender of the Faith, &c.
The Translators of the Bible Wish Grace, Mercy, and Peace,
through Jesus Christ our Lord.

Great and manifold were the blessings, most dread Sovereign, which Almighty God, the Father of all mercies, bestowed upon us the people of England, when first he sent Your Majesty's Royal Person to rule and reign over us. For whereas it was the expectation of many, who wished not well unto our Sion, that upon the setting of that bright Occidental Star, Queen Elizabeth of most happy memory, some thick and palpable clouds of darkness would so have overshadowed this Land, that men should have been in doubt which way they were to walk; and that it should hardly be known, who was to direct the unsettled State; the appearance of Your Majesty, as of the Sun in his strength, instantly dispelled those supposed and surmised mists, and gave unto all that were well affected exceeding cause of comfort; especially when we beheld the Government established in Your Highness, and Your hopeful Seed, by an undoubted Title, and this also accompanied with peace and tranquillity at home and abroad.

But among all our joys, there was no one that more filled our hearts, than the blessed continuance of the preaching of God's sacred Word among us; which is that inestimable treasure, which excelleth all the riches of the earth; because the fruit thereof extendeth itself, not only to the time spent in this transitory world, but directeth and disposeth men unto that eternal happiness which is above in heaven.

Then not to suffer this to fall to the ground, but rather to take it up, and to continue it in that state, wherein the famous Predecessor of Your Highness did leave it: nay, to go forward with the confidence and resolution of a Man in maintaining the truth of Christ, and propagating it far and near, is that which hath so bound and firmly knit the hearts of all Your Majesty's loyal and religious people unto You, that Your very name is precious among them: their eye doth behold You with comfort, and they bless You in their hearts, as that sanctified Person, who, under God, is the immediate Author of their true happiness. And this their contentment doth not diminish or decay, but every day increaseth and taketh strength, when they observe, that the zeal of Your Majesty toward the house of God doth not slack or go backward, but is more and more kindled, manifesting itself abroad in the farthest parts of Christendom, by writing in defence of the Truth, (which hath given such a blow unto that man of sin, as will not be healed,) and every day at home, by religious and learned discourse, by frequenting the house of God, by hearing the Word preached, by cherishing the Teachers thereof, by caring for the Church, as a most tender and loving nursing Father.

There are infinite arguments of this right christian and religious affection in Your Majesty; but none is more forcible to declare it to others than the vehement and perpetuated desire of accomplishing and publishing of this work, which now with all humility we present unto Your Majesty. For when Your Highness had once out of deep judgment apprehended how convenient it was, that out of the Original Sacred Tongues, together with comparing of the labours, both in our own, and other foreign Languages, of many worthy men who went before us, there should be one more exact Translation of the holy Scriptures into the English Tongue; Your Majesty did never desist to urge and to excite those to whom it was commended, that the work might be hastened, and that the business might be expedited in so decent a manner, as a matter of such importance might justly require.

And now at last, by the mercy of God, and the continuance of our labours, it being brought unto such a conclusion, as that we have great hopes that the Church of England shall reap good fruit thereby; we hold it our duty to offer it to Your Majesty, not only as to our King and Sovereign, but as to the principal Mover and Author of the work: humbly craving of Your most Sacred Majesty, that since things of this quality have ever been subject to the censures of illmeaning and discontented persons, it may receive approbation and patronage from so learned and judicious a Prince as Your Highness is, whose allowance and acceptance of our labours shall more honour and encourage us, than all the calumniations and hard interpretations of other men shall dismay us. So that if, on the one side, we shall be traduced by Popish Persons at home or abroad, who therefore will malign us, because we are poor instruments to make God's holy Truth to be yet more and more known unto the people, whom they desire still to keep in ignorance and darkness; or if, on the other side, we shall be maligned by selfconceited Brethren, who run their own ways, and give liking unto nothing, but what is framed by themselves, and hammered on their anvil; we may rest secure, supported within by the truth and innocency of a good conscience, having walked the ways of simplicity and integrity, as before the Lord; and sustained without by the powerful protection of Your Majesty's grace and favour, which will ever give countenance to honest and christian endeavours against bitter censures and uncharitable imputations.

The Lord of heaven and earth bless Your Majesty with many and happy days, that, as his heavenly hand hath enriched Your Highness with many singular and extraordinary graces, so You may be the wonder of the world in this latter age for happiness and true felicity, to the honour of that great GOD, and the good of his Church, through Jesus Christ our Lord and only Saviour.

PREFACE TO THE KING JAMES BIBLE (1611) From Edgar J. Goodspeed, ed., *The Translators to the Reader: Preface to the King James Version 1611* (Chicago, 1935), pp. 15, 18-21, 23, 25, 27-28, 33-37.

The Translators to the Reader.

Zeal to promote the common good, whether it be by devising anything ourselves, or revising that which hath been laboured by others, deserveth certainly much respect and esteem, but yet findeth but cold entertainment in the world. It is welcomed with suspicion instead of love, and with emulation instead of thanks: and if there be any hole left for cavil to enter, (and cavil, if it do not find a hole, will make one) it is sure to be misconstrued, and in danger to be condemned. This will easily be granted by as many as know story, or have any experience. For, was there ever anything projected, that savoured any way of newness or renewing, but the same endured many a storm of gainsaying, or opposition? A man would think that Civility, wholesome Laws, learning and eloquence, Synods, and Church-maintenance, (that we speak of no more things of this kind) should be as safe as a Sanctuary, and out of shot, as they say, that no man would lift up the heel, no, nor dog move his tongue against the motioners of them. For by the first, we are distinguished from brute beasts led with sensuality: By the second, we are bridled and restrained from outrageous behaviour, and from doing of injuries, whether by fraud or by violence: By the third, we are enabled to inform and reform others, by the light and feeling that we have attained unto ourselves: Briefly, by the fourth being brought together to a parley face to face, we sooner compose our differences than by writings, which are endless: And lastly, that the Church be sufficiently provided for, is so agreeable to good reason and conscience, that those mothers are holden to be less cruel, that kill their children as soon as they are born, than those nursing fathers and mothers (wheresoever they be) that withdraw from them who hang upon their breasts (and upon whose breasts again themselves do hang to receive the Spiritual and sincere milk of the word) livelihood and support fit for their estates. Thus it is apparent, that these things which we speak of, are of most necessary use, and therefore, that none, either without absurdity can speak against them, or without note of wickedness can spurn against them.

*　　*　　*

But now what piety without truth? what truth (what saving truth) without the word of God? What word of God (whereof we may be sure) without the Scripture? The Scriptures we are commanded to search. John 5:39. Isa. 8:20. They are commended that searched and studied them. Acts 17:11 and 8:28,29. They are reproved that were unskilful in them, or slow to believe them. Matt. 22:29. Luke 24:25. They can make us wise unto salvation. II Tim. 3:15. If we be ignorant, they will instruct us; if out of the way, they will bring us home; if out of order, they will reform us; if in heaviness, comfort us; if dull, quicken us; if cold, inflame us. *Tolle, lege; Tolle, lege,* Take up and read, take up and read the Scriptures, (for unto them was the direction) it was said unto S. Augustine by a supernatural voice.

* * *

The Scriptures then being acknowledged to be so full and so perfect, how can we excuse ourselves of negligence, if we do not study them, of curiosity, if we be not content with them? Men talk much . . . of the Philosopher's stone, that it turned copper into gold; of *Cornu-copia*, that it had all things necessary for food in it, of *Panaces* the herb, that it was good for all diseases, of *Catholican* the drug, that it is instead of all purges; of Vulcan's armor, that it was an armor of proof against all thrusts, and all blows, etc. Well, that which they falsely or vainly attributed to these things for bodily good, we may justly and with full measure ascribe unto the Scripture, for spiritual. It is not only an armor, but also a whole armory of weapons, both offensive and defensive; whereby we may save ourselves and put the enemy to flight. It is not an herb, but a tree, or rather a whole paradise of trees of life, which bring forth fruit every month, and the fruit thereof is for meat, and the leaves for medicine. It is not a pot of *Manna*, or a cruse of oil, which were for memory only, or for a meal's meat or two, but as it were a shower of heavenly bread sufficient for a whole host, be it never so great; and as it were a whole cellar full of oil vessels; whereby all our necessities may be provided for, and our debts discharged. In a word, it is a Panary of wholesome food, against fenowed traditions; a Physician's shop (Saint Basil called it) of preservatives against poisoned heresies; a Pandect of profitable laws, against rebellious spirits; a treasury of most costly jewels, against beggarly rudiments; finally a fountain of most pure water springing up unto everlasting life. And what marvel? The original thereof being from heaven, not from earth; the author being God, not man; the inditer, the holy spirit, not the wit of the Apostles or Prophets; the Penmen such as were sanctified from the womb, and endued with a principal portion of God's spirit; the matter, verity, piety, purity, uprightness; the form, God's word, God's testimony, God's oracles, the word of truth, the word of salvation, etc.; the effects, light of understanding, stableness of persuasion, repentance from dead works, newness of life, holiness, peace, joy in the holy Ghost; lastly, the end and reward of the study thereof, fellowship with the Saints, participation of the heavenly nature, fruition of an inheritance immortal, undefiled, and that never shall fade away: Happy is the man that delighteth in the Scripture, and thrice happy that meditateth in it day and night.

But how shall men meditate in that, which they cannot understand? How shall they understand that which is kept close in an unknown tongue? as it is written, *Except I know the power of the voice, I shall be to him that speaketh, a Barbarian, and he that speaketh, shall be a Barbarian to me.* The Apostle excepteth no tongue; not Hebrew the ancientest, not Greek the most copious, not Latin the finest. Nature taught a natural man to confess, that all of us in those tongues which we do not understand, are plainly deaf; we may turn the deaf ear unto them.

* * *

Therefore as one complaineth, that always in the Senate of Rome, there was one or other that called for an interpreter: so lest the Church be driven to the like exigent, it is necessary to have translations in a readiness. Translation it is that openeth the window, to let in the light; that breaketh the shell, that we may eat the kernel; that putteth aside the curtain, that we may look into the most Holy place; that removeth the cover of the well, that we may come by the water, even as Jacob rolled away the stone from the mouth of the well, by which means the flocks of

Laban were watered. Indeed without translation into the vulgar tongue, the unlearned are but like children at Jacob's well (which was deep) without a bucket or something to draw with: or as that person mentioned by Isaiah, to whom when a sealed book was delivered, with this motion, Read this, I pray thee, he was fain to make this answer, I cannot, for it is sealed.

While God would be known only in Jacob, and have his Name great in Israel, and in none other place, while the dew lay on Gideon's fleece only, and all the earth besides was dry; then for one and the same people, which spake all of them the language of Canaan, that is, Hebrew, one and the same original in Hebrew was sufficient. But when the fulness of time drew near, that the Sun of righteousness, the Son of God should come into the world, whom God ordained to be a reconciliation through faith in his blood, not of the Jew only, but also of the Greek, yea, of all them that were scattered abroad; then lo, it pleased the Lord to stir up the spirit of a Greek Prince (Greek for descent and language) even of Ptolemy Philadelph King of Egypt, to procure the translating of the Book of God out of Hebrew into Greek.

* * *

There were also within a few hundred years after CHRIST, translations many into the Latin tongue: for this tongue also was very fit to convey the Law and the Gospel by, because in those times very many Countries of the West, yea of the South, East and North, spake or understood Latin, being made Provinces to the Romans. But now the Latin Translations were too many to be all good, for they were infinite (*Latini Interpretes nullo modo numerari possunt*, saith S. Augustine.) Again they were not out of the Hebrew fountain (we speak of the Latin Translations of the Old Testament) but out of the Greek stream, therefore the Greek being not altogether clear, the Latin derived from it must needs be muddy. This moved S. Jerome a most learned father, and the best linguist without controversy, of his age, or of any that went before him, to undertake the translating of the Old Testament, out of the very fountains themselves; which he performed with that evidence of great learning, judgment, industry and faithfulness, that he hath forever bound the Church unto him, in a debt of special remembrance and thankfulness.

Now though the Church were thus furnished with Greek and Latin Translations, even before the faith of CHRIST was generally embraced in the Empire: (for the learned know that even in S. Jerome's time, the Consul of Rome and his wife were both Ethnics, and about the same time the greatest part of the Senate also) yet for all that the godly-learned were not content to have the Scriptures in the Language which they themselves understood, Greek and Latin, (as the good Lepers were not content to fare well themselves, but acquainted their neighbors with the store that God had sent, that they also might provide for themselves) but also for the behoof and edifying of the unlearned which hungered and thirsted after righteousness, and had souls to be saved as well as they, they provided Translations into the vulgar for their Countrymen, insomuch that most nations under heaven did shortly after their conversion, hear CHRIST speaking unto them in their mother tongue, not by the voice of their Minister only, but also by the written word translated.

* * *

So that, to have the Scriptures in the mother tongue is not a quaint conceit lately taken up, either by the Lord Cromwell in England, or by the Lord Radevile in

Polony, or by the Lord Ungnadius in the Emperor's dominion, but hath been thought upon, and put in practice of old, even from the first times of the conversion of any Nation; no doubt, because it was esteemed most profitable, to cause faith to grow in men's hearts the sooner, and to make them to be able to say with the words of the Psalm, *As we have heard, so we have seen.*

Now the Church of Rome would seem at the length to bear a motherly affection towards her children, and to allow them the Scriptures in their mother tongue: but indeed it is a gift, not deserving to be called a gift, an unprofitable gift: they must first get a Licence in writing before they may use them, and to get that, they must approve themselves to their Confessor, that is, to be such as are, if not frozen in the dregs, yet soured with the leaven of their superstition. Howbeit, it seemed too much to Clement the Eighth that there should be any Licence granted to have them in the vulgar tongue, and therefore he overruleth and frustrateth the grant of Pius the Fourth. So much are they afraid of the light of the Scripture, (*Lucifugae Scripturarum,* as Tertullian speaketh) that they will not trust the people with it, no not as it is set forth by their own sworn men, no not with the Licence of their own Bishops and Inquisitors. Yea, so unwilling they are to communicate the Scriptures to the people's understanding in any sort, that they are not ashamed to confess, that we forced them to translate it into English against their wills. This seemeth to argue a bad cause, or a bad conscience, or both.

✳   ✳   ✳

How many books of profane learning have been gone over again and again, by the same translators, by others? Of one and the same book of Aristotle's Ethics, there are extant not so few as six or seven several translations. Now if this cost may be bestowed upon the gourd, which affordeth us a little shade, and which today flourisheth, but tomorrow is cut down; what may we bestow, nay what ought we not to bestow upon the Vine, the fruit whereof maketh glad the conscience of man, and the stem whereof abideth forever? And this is the word of God, which we translate. What is the chaff to the wheat, saith the Lord? *Tanti vitreum, quanti verum margaritum* (saith Tertullian,) if a toy of glass be of that reckoning with us, how ought we to value the true pearl? Therefore let no man's eye be evil, because his Majesty's is good; neither let any be grieved, that we have a Prince that seeketh the increase of the spiritual wealth of Israel (let Sanballats and Tobiahs do so, which therefore do bear their just reproof) but let us rather bless God from the ground of our heart, for working this religious care in him, to have the translations of the Bible maturely considered of and examined. For by this means it cometh to pass, that whatsoever is sound already (and all is sound for substance, in one or other of our editions, and the worst of ours far better than their authentic vulgar) the same will shine as gold more brightly, being rubbed and polished; also, if anything be halting, or superfluous, or not so agreeable to the original, the same may be corrected, and the truth set in place. And what can the King command to be done, that will bring him more true honour than this? and wherein could they that have been set a work, approve their duty to the King, yea their obedience to God, and love to his Saints more, than by yielding their service, and all that is within them, for the furnishing of the work? But besides all this, they were the principal motives of it, and therefore ought least to quarrel it: for the very Historical truth is, that upon the importunate petitions of the Puritans, at his Majesty's coming to this Crown, the Conference at Hampton Court having been appointed for hearing their complaints: when by force of reason they were put from all other grounds, they had recourse at the last, to this shift, that they could not with good conscience subscribe to the Communion book, since it maintained the Bible as it was there translated, which was as they said, a most corrupted translation. And although this was judged to be but a very poor and empty shift; yet even hereupon did his Majesty begin to bethink himself of the good that might ensue by a new translation, and presently after gave order for this Translation which is now presented unto thee. Thus much to satisfy our scrupulous Brethren.

Now to the latter we answer; that we do not deny, nay we affirm and avow, that the very meanest translation of the Bible in English, set forth by men of our profession, (for we have seen none of theirs of the whole Bible as yet) containeth the word of God, nay, is the word of God.

But it is high time to leave them, and to show in brief what we proposed to ourselves, and what course we held in this our perusal and survey of the Bible. Truly (good Christian Reader) we never thought from the beginning, that we should need to make a new Translation, nor yet to make of a bad one a good one, (for then the imputation of Sixtus had been true in some sort, that our people had been fed with gall of Dragons instead of wine, with whey instead of milk:) but to make a good one better, or out of many good ones, one principal good one, not justly to be excepted against; that hath been our endeavor, that our mark. To that purpose there were many chosen, that were greater in other men's eyes than in their own, and that sought the truth rather than their own praise. Again, they came or were thought to come to the work, not *exercendi causa* (as one saith) but *exercitati*, that is, learned, not to learn:

*   *   *

Therefore such were thought upon, as could say modestly with Saint Jerome, *Et Hebraeum Sermonem ex parte didicimus, et in Latino pene ab ipsis incunabulis etc. detriti sumus. Both we have learned the Hebrew tongue in part, and in the Latin we have been exercised almost from our very cradle.* S. Jerome maketh no mention of the Greek tongue, wherein yet he did excel, because he translated not the old Testament out of Greek, but out of Hebrew. And in what sort did these assemble? In the trust of their own knowledge, or of their sharpness of wit, or deepness of judgment, as it were in an arm of flesh? At no hand. They trusted in him that hath the key of David, opening and no man shutting; they prayed to the Lord the Father of our Lord, to the effect that S. Augustine did; O let thy Scriptures be my pure delight, let me not be deceived in them, neither let me deceive by them. In this confidence, and with this devotion did they assemble together; not too many, lest one should trouble another; and yet many, lest many things haply might escape them. If you ask what they had before them, truly it was the Hebrew text of the Old Testament, the Greek of the New. These are the two golden pipes, or rather conduits, where-through the olive branches empty themselves into the gold. Saint Augustine calleth them precedent, or original tongues; Saint Jerome, fountains. The same Saint Jerome affirmeth, and Gratian hath not spared to put it into his Decree, That as the credit of the old Books (he meaneth of the Old Testament) is to be tried by the Hebrew Volumes, so of the New by the Greek tongue, he meaneth by the original Greek. If truth be to be tried by these tongues, then whence should a Translation be made, but out of them? These tongues therefore, the Scriptures we say in those tongues, we set before us to translate, being the tongues wherein God was pleased to speak to his Church by his Prophets and Apostles. Neither did we run over the work with that posting haste that the Septuagint did, if that be true which is reported of them, that they finished it in 72 days; neither were we barred or hindered from going over it again, having once done it, like S. Jerome, if that be true which himself reporteth, that he could no sooner write anything, but presently it was caught from him, and published, and he could not have leave to mend it: neither, to be short, were we the first that fell in hand with translating the Scripture into English, and consequently destitute of former helps, as it is written of Origen, that he was the first in a manner, that put his hand to write Commentaries upon the Scriptures, and therefore no marvel, if he overshot himself many times. None of these things: the work hath not been huddled up in 72 days, but hath cost the workmen, as light as it seemeth, the pains of twice seven times seventy two days and more: matters of such weight and consequence are to be speeded with maturity: for in a business of moment a man feareth not the blame of convenient slackness. Neither did we think much to consult the Translators or Commentators, Chaldee, Hebrew, Syrian, Greek, or Latin, no nor the Spanish, French, Italian, or Dutch; neither did we disdain to revise that which we had done, and to bring back to the anvil that which we had hammered: but having and using as great helps as were needful, and fearing no reproach for slowness, nor coveting praise for expedition, we have at the length, through the good hand of the Lord upon us, brought the work to that pass that you see.

Some peradventure would have no variety of senses to be set in the margin, lest the authority of the Scriptures for deciding of controversies by that show of uncertainty, should somewhat be shaken. But we hold their judgment not to be sound in this point. For though, whatsoever things are necessary are manifest, as S. Chrysostom saith, and as S. Augustine, In those things that are plainly set down in the Scriptures, all such matters are found that concern Faith, Hope, and Charity. Yet for all that it cannot be dissembled, that partly to exercise and whet our wits, partly to wean the curious from loathing of them for their every-where plainness, partly also to stir up our devotion to crave the assistance of God's spirit by prayer, and lastly, that we might be forward to seek aid of our brethren by conference, and never scorn those that be not in all respects so complete as they should be, being to seek in many things ourselves, it hath pleased God in his divine providence, here and there to scatter words and sentences of that difficulty and doubtfulness, not in doctrinal points that concern salvation, (for in such it hath been vouched that the Scriptures are plain) but in matters of less moment, that fearfulness would better beseem us than confidence, and if we will resolve, to resolve upon modesty with S. Augustine, (though not in this same case altogether, yet upon the same ground) *Melius est dubitare de occultis, quam litigare de incertis*, it is better to make doubt of those things which are secret, than to strive about those things that are uncertain. There be many words in the Scriptures, which be never found there but once, (having neither brother nor neighbor, as the Hebrews speak) so that we cannot be holpen by conference of places. Again, there be many rare names of certain birds, beasts and precious stones, etc. concerning which the Hebrews themselves are so divided among themselves for judgment, that they may seem to have defined this or that, rather because they would say something, than because they were sure of that which they said, as S. Jerome somewhere saith of the Septuagint. Now in such a case, doth not a margin do well to admonish the Reader to seek further, and not to conclude or dogmatize upon this or that peremptorily? For as it is a fault of incredulity, to doubt of those things that are evident: so to determine of such things as the Spirit of God hath left (even in the judgment of the judicious) questionable, can be no less than presumption. Therefore as S. Augustine saith, that variety of Translations is profitable for the finding out of the sense of the Scriptures: so diversity of signification and sense in the margin, where the text is not so clear, must needs do good, yea, is necessary, as we are persuaded. We know that Sixtus Quintus expressly forbiddeth, that any variety of readings of their vulgar edition, should be put in the margin, (which though it be not altogether the same thing to that we have in hand, yet it looketh that way) but we think he hath not all of his own side his favorers, for this conceit. They that are wise, had rather have their judgments at liberty in differences of readings, than to be captivated to one, when it may be the other. If they were sure that their high Priest had all laws shut up in his breast, as Paul the Second bragged, and that he were as free from error by special privilege, as the Dictators of Rome were made by law inviolable, it were another matter; then his word were an Oracle, his opinion a decision. But the eyes of the world are now open, God be thanked, and have been a great while, they find that he is subject to the same affections and infirmities that others be, that his skin is penetrable, and therefore so much as he proveth, not as much as he claimeth, they grant and embrace.

Another thing we think good to admonish thee of (gentle Reader) that we have not tied ourselves to an uniformity of phrasing, or to an identity of words, as some peradventure would wish that we had done, because they observe, that some learned men somewhere, have been as exact as they could that way. Truly, that we might not vary from the sense of that which we had translated before, if the word signified the same in both places (for there be some words that be not of the same sense everywhere) we were especially careful, and made a conscience, according to our duty. But, that we should express the same notion in the same particular word; as for example, if we translate the Hebrew or Greek word once by *Purpose*, never to call it *Intent*; if one where *Journeying*, never *Traveling*; if one where *Think*, never *Suppose*; if one where *Pain*, never *Ache;* if one where *Joy*, never *Gladness*, etc. Thus to mince the matter, we thought to savour more of curiosity than wisdom, and that rather it would breed scorn in the Atheist, than bring profit to the godly Reader. For is the kingdom of God become words or syllables? why should we be in bondage to them if we may be free, use one precisely when we may use another no less fit, as commodiously?

Many other things we might give thee warning of (gentle Reader) if we had not exceeded the measure of a Preface already. It remaineth, that we commend thee to God, and to the Spirit of his grace, which is able to build further than we can ask or think. He removeth the scales from our eyes, the vail from our hearts, opening our wits that we may understand his word, enlarging our hearts, yea correcting our affections, that we may love it above gold and silver, yea that we may love it to the end. Ye are brought unto fountains of living water which ye digged not; do not cast earth into them with the Philistines, neither prefer broken pits before them with the wicked Jews. Others have laboured, and you may enter into their labours; O receive not so great things in vain, O despise not so great salvation! Be not like swine to tread under foot so precious things, neither yet like dogs to tear and abuse holy things. Say not to our Saviour with the Gergesites, Depart out of our coasts; neither yet with Esau sell your birthright for a mess of pottage. If light be come into the world, love not darkness more than light; if food, if clothing be offered, go not naked, starve not yourselves.

SELECTIONS FROM THE KING JAMES BIBLE (1611) From *The Holy Bible* (London, 1833), pp. 1-4, 82-83, 599-600.

Genesis.

CHAPTER 1.

In the beginning God created the heaven and the earth.

2 And the earth was without form, and void; and darkness was upon the face of the deep. And the Spirit of God moved upon the face of the waters.

3 And God said, Let there be light: and there was light.

4 And God saw the light, that it was good: and God divided the light from the darkness.

5 And God called the light Day, and the darkness he called Night. And the evening and the morning were the first day.

6 And God said, Let there be a firmament in the midst of the waters, and let it divide the waters from the waters.

7 And God made the firmament, and divided the waters which were under the firmament from the waters which were above the firmament: and it was so.

8 And God called the firmament Heaven. And the evening and the morning were the second day.

9 And God said, Let the waters under the heaven be gathered together unto one place, and let the dry land appear: and it was so.

10 And God called the dry land Earth; and the gathering together of the waters called he Seas: and God saw that it was good.

11 And God said, Let the earth bring forth grass, the herb yielding seed, and the fruit tree yielding fruit after his kind, whose seed is in itself, upon the earth: and it was so.

12 And the earth brought forth grass, and herb yielding seed after his kind, and the tree yielding fruit, whose seed was in itself, after his kind: and God saw that it was good.

13 And the evening and the morning were the third day.

14 And God said, Let there be lights in the firmament of the heaven to divide the day from the night; and let them be for signs, and for seasons, and for days, and years:

15 And let them be for lights in the firmament of the heaven to give light upon the earth: and it was so.

16 And God made two great lights; the greater light to rule the day, and the lesser light to rule the night: he made the stars also.

17 And God set them in the firmament of the heaven to give light upon the earth,

18 And to rule over the day and over the night, and to divide the light from the darkness: and God saw that it was good.

19 And the evening and morning were the fourth day.

20 And God said, Let the waters bring forth abundantly the moving creature that hath life, and fowl that may fly above the earth in the open firmament of heaven.

21 And God created great whales, and every living creature that moveth, which

the waters brought forth abundantly, after their kind, and every winged fowl after his kind: and God saw that it was good.

22 And God blessed them, saying, Be fruitful, and multiply, and fill the waters in the seas, and let fowl multiply in the earth.

23 And the evening and the morning were the fifth day.

24 And God said, Let the earth bring forth the living creature after his kind, cattle, and creeping thing, and beast of the earth after his kind: and it was so.

25 And God made the beast of the earth after his kind, and cattle after their kind, and every thing that creepeth upon the earth after his kind: and God saw that it was good.

26 And God said, Let us make man in our image, after our likeness: and let them have dominion over the fish of the sea, and over the fowl of the air, and over the cattle, and over all the earth, and over every creeping thing that creepeth upon the earth.

27 So God created man in his own image, in the image of God created he him; male and female created he them.

28 And God blessed them, and God said unto them, Be fruitful, and multiply, and replenish the earth, and subdue it: and have dominion over the fish of the sea, and over the fowl of the air, and over every living thing that moveth upon the earth.

29 And God said, Behold, I have given you every herb bearing seed, which is upon the face of all the earth, and every tree, in the which is the fruit of a tree yielding seed; to you it shall be for meat.

30 And to every beast of the earth, and to every fowl of the air, and to every thing that creepeth upon the earth, wherein there is life, I have given every green herb for meat: and it was so.

31 And God saw every thing that he had made, and, behold, it was very good. And the evening and the morning were the sixth day.

CHAPTER 2.

Thus the heavens and the earth were finished, and all the host of them.

2 And on the seventh day God ended his work which he had made; and he rested on the seventh day from all his work which he had made.

3 And God blessed the seventh day, and sanctified it: because that in it he had rested from all his work which God created and made.

4 These are the generations of the heavens and of the earth when they were created, in the day that the Lord God made the earth and the heavens,

5 And every plant of the field before it was in the earth, and every herb of the field before it grew: for the Lord God had not caused it to rain upon the earth, and there was not a man to till the ground.

6 But there went up a mist from the earth, and watered the whole face of the ground.

7 And the Lord God formed man of the dust of the ground, and breathed into his nostrils the breath of life; and man became a living soul.

8 And the Lord God planted a garden eastward in Eden; and there he put the man whom he had formed.

9 And out of the ground made the Lord God to grow every tree that is pleasant to the sight, and good for food; the tree of life also in the midst of the garden, and the tree of knowledge of good and evil.

10 And a river went out of Eden to water the garden; and from thence it was parted, and became into four heads.

11 The name of the first is Pison: that is it which compasseth the whole land of Havilah, where there is gold;

12 And the gold of that land is good: there is bdellium and the onyx stone.

13 And the name of the second river is Gihon: the same is it that compasseth the whole land of Ethiopia.

14 And the name of the third river is Hiddekel: that is it which goeth toward the east of Assyria. And the fourth river is Euphrates.

15 And the Lord God took the man, and put him into the garden of Eden to dress it and to keep it.

16 And the Lord God commanded the man, saying, Of every tree of the garden thou mayest freely eat:

17 But of the tre of the knowledge of good and evil, thou shalt not eat of it: for in the day that thou eatest thereof thou shalt surely die.

18 And the Lord God said, It is not good that the man should be alone; I will make him an help meet for him.

19 And out of the ground the Lord God formed every beast of the field, and every fowl of the air; and brought them unto Adam to see what he would call them: and whatsoever Adam called every living creature, that was the name thereof.

20 And Adam gave names to all cattle, and to the fowl of the air, and to every beast of the field; but for Adam there was not found an help meet for him.

21 And the Lord God caused a deep sleep to fall upon Adam, and he slept: and he took one of his ribs, and closed up the flesh instead thereof;

22 And the rib, which the Lord God had taken from man, made he a woman, and brought her unto the man.

23 And Adam said, This is now bone of my bones, and flesh of my flesh: she shall be called Woman, because she was taken out of Man.

24 Therefore shall a man leave his father and his mother, and shall cleave unto his wife: and they shall be one flesh.

25 And they were both naked, the man and his wife, and were not ashamed.

CHAPTER 3.

Now the serpent was more subtil than any beast of the field which the Lord God had made. And he said unto the woman, Yea, hath God said, Ye shall not eat of every tree of the garden?

2 And the woman said unto the serpent, We may eat of the fruit of the trees in the garden:

3 But of the fruit of the tree which is in the midst of the garden, God hath said, Ye shall not eat of it, neither shall ye touch it, lest ye die.

4 And the serpent said unto the woman, Ye shall not surely die:

5 For God doth know that in the day ye eat thereof, then your eyes shall be opened, and ye shall be as gods, knowing good and evil.

6 And when the woman saw that the tree was good for food, and that it was pleasant to the eyes, and a tree to be desired to make one wise, she took of the fruit thereof, and did eat, and gave also unto her husband with her; and he did eat.

7 And the eyes of them both were opened, and they knew that they were naked; and they sewed fig leaves together, and made themselves aprons.

8 And they heard the voice of the Lord God walking in the garden in the cool

of the day: and Adam and his wife hid themselves from the presence of the Lord God amongst the trees of the garden.

9 And the Lord God called unto Adam, and said unto him, Where art thou?

10 And he said, I heard thy voice in the garden, and I was afraid, because I was naked; and I hid myself.

11 And he said, Who told thee that thou wast naked? Hast thou eaten of the tree, whereof I commanded thee that thou shouldest not eat?

12 And the man said, The woman whom thou gavest to be with me, she gave me of the tree, and I did eat.

13 And the Lord God said unto the woman, What is this that thou hast done? And the woman said, The serpent beguiled me, and I did eat.

14 And the Lord God said unto the serpent, Because thou hast done this, thou art cursed above all cattle, and above every beast of the field; upon thy belly shalt thou go, and dust shalt thou eat all the days of thy life:

15 And I will put enmity between thee and the woman, and between thy seed and her seed; it shall bruise thy head, and thou shalt bruise his heel.

16 Unto the woman he said, I will greatly multiply thy sorrow and thy conception; in sorrow thou shalt bring forth children; and thy desire shall be to thy husband, and he shall rule over thee.

17 And unto Adam he said, Because thou hast hearkened unto the voice of thy wife, and hast eaten of the tree, of which I commanded thee, saying, Thou shalt not eat of it: cursed is the ground for thy sake; in sorrow shalt thou eat of it all the days of thy life;

18 Thorns also and thistles shall it bring forth to thee; and thou shalt eat the herb of the field;

19 In the sweat of thy face shalt thou eat bread, till thou return unto the ground; for out of it wast thou taken: for dust thou art, and unto dust shalt thou return.

20 And Adam called his wife's name Eve; because she was the mother of all living.

21 Unto Adam also and to his wife did the Lord God make coats of skins, and clothed them.

22 And the Lord God said, Behold, the man is become as one of us, to know good and evil: and now, lest he put forth his hand, and take also of the tree of life, and eat, and live for ever:

23 Therefore the Lord God sent him forth from the garden of Eden, to till the ground from whence he was taken.

24 So he drove out the man; and he placed at the east of the garden of Eden Cherubims, and a flaming sword which turned every way, to keep the way of the tree of life.

*　　*　　*

Exodus.

CHAPTER 19.

10 And the Lord said unto Moses, Go unto the people, and sanctify them to day and to morrow, and let them wash their clothes,

11 And be ready against the third day: for the third day the Lord will come down in the sight of all the people upon mount Sinai.

12 And thou shalt set bounds unto the people round about, saying, Take heed to yourselves, that ye go not up into the mount, or touch the border of it: whosoever toucheth the mount shall be surely put to death:

13 There shall not an hand touch it, but he shall surely be stoned, or shot through; whether it be beast or man, it shall not live: when the trumpet soundeth long, they shall come up to the mount.

14 And Moses went down from the mount unto the people, and sanctified the people; and they washed their clothes.

15 And he said unto the people, Be ready against the third day: come not at your wives.

16 And it came to pass on the third day in the morning, that there were thunders and lightnings, and a thick cloud upon the mount, and the voice of the trumpet exceeding loud; so that all the people that was in the camp trembled.

17 And Moses brought forth the people out of the camp to meet with God; and they stood at the nether part of the mount.

18 And mount Sinai was altogether on a smoke, because the Lord descended upon it in fire: and the smoke thereof ascended as the smoke of a furnace, and the whole mount quaked greatly.

19 And when the voice of the trumpet sounded long, and waxed louder and louder, Moses spake, and God answered him by a voice.

20 And the Lord came down upon mount Sinai, on the top of the mount: and the Lord called Moses up to the top of the mount; and Moses went up.

21 And the Lord said unto Moses, Go down, charge the people, lest they break through unto the Lord to gaze, and many of them perish.

22 And let the priests also, which come near to the Lord, sanctify themselves, lest the Lord break forth upon them.

23 And Moses said unto the Lord, The people cannot come up to mount Sinai: for thou chargedst us, saying, Set bounds about the mount, and sanctify it.

24 And the Lord said unto him, Away, get thee down, and thou shalt come up, thou, and Aaron with thee: but let not the priests and the people break through to come up unto the Lord, lest he break forth upon them.

25 So Moses went down unto the people, and spake unto them.

CHAPTER 20.

And God spake all these words, saying,

2 I am the Lord thy God, which have brought thee out of the land of Egypt, out of the house of bondage.

3 Thou shalt have no other gods before me.

4 Thou shalt not make unto thee any graven image, or any likeness of any thing that is in heaven above, or that is in the earth beneath, or that is in the water under the earth:

5 Thou shalt not bow down thyself to them, nor serve them: for I the Lord thy God am a jealous God visiting the iniquity of the fathers upon the children unto the third and fourth generation of them that hate me;

6 And shewing mercy unto thousands of them that love me, and keep my commandments.

7 Thou shalt not take the name of the Lord thy God in vain; for the Lord will not hold him guiltless that taketh his name in vain.

8 Remember the sabbath day, to keep it holy.

9 Six days shalt thou labour, and do all thy work:

10 But the seventh day is the sabbath of the Lord thy God: in it thou shalt not do any work, thou, nor thy son, nor thy daughter, thy manservant, nor thy maidservant, nor thy cattle, nor thy stranger that is within thy gates:

11 For in six days the Lord made heaven and earth, the sea, and all that in them is, and rested the seventh day: wherefore the Lord blessed the sabbath day, and hallowed it.

12 Honour thy father and thy mother: that thy days may be long upon the land which the Lord thy God giveth thee.

13 Thou shalt not kill.

14 Thou shalt not commit adultery.

15 Thou shalt not steal.

16 Thou shalt not bear false witness against thy neighbour.

17 Thou shalt not covet thy neighbour's house, thou shalt not covet thy neighbour's wife, nor his manservant, nor his maidservant, nor his ox, nor his ass, nor any thing that is thy neighbour's.

18 And all the people saw the thunderings, and the lightnings, and the noise of the trumpet, and the mountain smoking: and when the people saw it, they removed, and stood afar off.

19 And they said unto Moses, Speak thou with us, and we will hear: but let not God speak with us, lest we die.

20 And Moses said unto the people, Fear not: for God is come to prove you, and that his fear may be before your faces, that ye sin not.

21 And the people stood afar off, and Moses drew near unto the thick darkness where God was.

22 And the Lord said unto Moses, Thus thou shalt say unto the children of Israel, Ye have seen that I have talked with you from heaven.

23 Ye shall not make with me gods of silver, neither shall ye make unto you gods of gold.

24 An altar of earth thou shalt make unto me, and shalt sacrifice thereon thy burnt offerings, and thy peace offerings, thy sheep, and thine oxen: in all places where I record my name I will come unto thee, and I will bless thee.

25 And if thou wilt make me an altar of stone, thou shalt not build it of hewn stone: for if thou lift up thy tool upon it, thou hast polluted it.

26 Neither shalt thou go up by steps unto mine altar, that thy nakedness be not discovered thereon.

   ❋ ❋ ❋

Psalm 23.

The Lord is my shepherd; I shall not want.

2 He maketh me to lie down in green pastures: he leadeth me beside the still waters.

3 He restoreth my soul: he leadeth me in the paths of righteousness for his name's sake.

4 Yea, though I walk through the valley of the shadow of death, I will fear no evil; for thou art with me; thy rod and thy staff they comfort me.

5 Thou preparest a table before me in the presence of mine enemies: thou anointest my head with oil; my cup runneth over.

6 Surely goodness and mercy shall follow me all the days of my life: and I will dwell in the house of the Lord for ever.

Psalm 24.

The earth is the Lord's, and the fulness thereof; the world, and they that dwell therein.

2 For he hath founded it upon the seas, and established it upon the floods.

3 Who shall ascend into the hill of the Lord? or who shall stand in his holy place?

4 He that hath clean hands, and a pure heart; who hath not lifted up his soul unto vanity, nor sworn deceitfully.

5 He shall receive the blessing from the Lord, and righteousness from the God of his salvation.

6 This is the generation of them that seek him, that seek thy face, O Jacob. Selah.

7 Lift up your heads, O ye gates; and be ye lift up, ye everlasting doors; and the King of glory shall come in.

8 Who is this King of glory? The Lord strong and mighty, the Lord mighty in battle.

9 Life up your heads, O ye gates; even lift them up, ye everlasting doors; and the King of glory shall come in.

10 Who is this King of glory? The Lord of hosts, he is the King of glory. Selah.

✳   ✳   ✳

The Gospel According to St. Matthew.

CHAPTER 4.

Then was Jesus led up of the spirit into the wilderness to be tempted of the devil.

2 And when he had fasted forty days and forty nights, he was afterward an hungred.

3 And when the tempter came to him, he said, If thou be the Son of God, command that these stones be made bread.

4 But he answered and said, It is written, Man shall not live by bread alone, but by every word that proceedeth out of the mouth of God.

5 Then the devil taketh him up into the holy city, and setteth him on a pinnacle of the temple,

6 And saith unto him, If thou be the Son of God, cast thyself down: for it is written, He shall give his angels charge concerning thee: and in their hands they shall bear thee up, lest at any time thou dash thy foot against a stone.

7 Jesus said unto him, It is written again, Thou shalt not tempt the Lord thy God.

8 Again, the devil taketh him up into an exceeding high mountain, and sheweth him all the kingdoms of the world, and the glory of them;

9 And saith unto him, All these things will I give thee, if thou wilt fall down and worship me.

10 Then saith Jesus unto him, Get thee hence, Satan: for it is written, Thou shalt worship the Lord thy God, and him only shalt thou serve.

11 Then the devil leaveth him, and, behold, angels came and ministered unto him.

12 Now when Jesus had heard that John was cast into prison, he departed into Galilee;

13 And leaving Nazareth, he came and dwelt in Capernaum, which is upon the sea coast, in the borders of Zabulon and Nephthalim:

14 That it might be fulfilled which was spoken by Esaias the prophet, saying,

15 The land of Zabulon, and the land of Nephthalim, by the way of the sea, beyond Jordan, Galilee of the Gentiles;

16 The people which sat in darkness saw great light; and to them which sat in the region and shadow of death light is sprung up.

17 From that time Jesus began to preach, and to say, Repent: for the kingdom of heaven is at hand.

18 And Jesus, walking by the sea of Galilee, saw two brethren, Simon called Peter, and Andrew his brother, casting a net into the sea: for they were fishers.

19 And he saith unto them, Follow me, and I will make you fishers of men.

20 And they straightway left their nets, and followed him.

21 And going on from thence, he saw other two brethren, James the son of Zebedee, and John his brother, in a ship with Zebedee their father, mending their nets; and he called them.

22 And they immediately left the ship and their father, and followed him.

23 And Jesus went about all Galilee, teaching in their synagogues, and preaching the gospel of the kingdom, and healing all manner of sickness and all manner of disease among the people.

24 And his fame went throughout all Syria: and they brought unto him all sick people that were taken with divers diseases and torments, and those which were possessed with devils, and those which were lunatick, and those that had the palsy; and he healed them.

25 And there followed him great multitudes of people from Galilee, and from Decapolis, and from Jerusalem, and from Judaea, and from beyond Jordan.

CHAPTER 5.

And seeing the multitudes, he went up into a mountain: and when he was set, his disciples came unto him:

2 And he opened his mouth, and taught them, saying,

3 Blessed are the poor in spirit: for their's is the kingdom of heaven.

4 Blessed are they that mourn: for they shall be comforted.

5 Blessed are the meek: for they shall inherit the earth.

6 Blessed are they which do hunger and thirst after righteousness: for they shall be filled.

7 Blessed are the merciful: for they shall obtain mercy.

8 Blessed are the pure in heart: for they shall see God.

9 Blessed are the peacemakers: for they shall be called the children of God.

10 Blessed are they which are persecuted for righteousness' sake: for their's is the kingdom of heaven.

11 Blessed are ye, when men shall revile you, and persecute you, and shall say all manner of evil against you falsely, for my sake.

12 Rejoice, and be exceeding glad: for great is your reward in heaven: for so persecuted they the prophets which were before you.

13 Ye are the salt of the earth: but if the salt have lost his savour, wherewith

shall it be salted? it is thenceforth good for nothing, but to be cast out, and to be trodden under foot of men.

14 Ye are the light of the world. A city that is set on an hill cannot be hid.

15 Neither do men light a candle, and put it under a bushel, but on a candlestick; and it giveth light unto all that are in the house.

16 Let your light so shine before men, that they may see your good works, and glorify your Father which is in heaven.

17 Think not that I am come to destroy the law, or the prophets: I am not come to destroy, but to fulfil.

18 For verily I say unto you, Till heaven and earth pass, one jot or one tittle shall in no wise pass from the law, till all be fulfilled.

19 Whosoever therefore shall break one of these least commandments, and shall teach men so, he shall be called the least in the kingdom of heaven: but whosoever shall do and teach them, the same shall be called great in the kingdom of heaven.

20 For I say unto you, That except your righteousness shall exceed the righteousness of the scribes and Pharisees, ye shall in no case enter into the kingdom of heaven.

21 Ye have heard that it was said by them of old time, Thou shalt not kill; and whosoever shall kill shall be in danger of the judgment:

22 But I say unto you, That whosoever is angry with his brother without a cause shall be in danger of the judgment: and whosoever shall say to his brother, Raca, shall be in danger of the council: but whosoever shall say, Thou fool, shall be in danger of hell fire.

23 Therefore if thou bring thy gift to the altar, and there rememberest that thy brother hath ought against thee;

24 Leave there thy gift before the altar, and go thy way; first be reconciled to thy brother, and then come and offer thy gift.

25 Agree with thine adversary quickly, whiles thou art in the way with him; lest at any time the adversary deliver thee to the judge, and the judge deliver thee to the officer, and thou be cast into prison.

26 Verily I say unto thee, Thou shalt by no means come out thence, till thou hast paid the uttermost farthing.

27 Ye have heard that it was said by them of old time, Thou shalt not commit adultery:

28 But I say unto you, That whosoever looketh on a woman to lust after her hath committed adultery with her already in his heart.

29 And if thy right eye offend thee, pluck it out, and cast it from thee: for it is profitable for thee that one of thy members should perish, and not that thy whole body should be cast into hell.

30 And if thy right hand offend thee, cut it off, and cast it from thee: for it is profitable for thee that one of thy members should perish, and not that thy whole body should be cast into hell.

31 It hath been said, Whosoever shall put away his wife, let him give her a writing of divorcement:

32 But I say unto you, That whosoever shall put away his wife, saving for the cause of fornication, causeth her to commit adultery: and whosoever shall marry her that is divorced committeth adultery.

33 Again, ye have heard that it hath been said by them of old time, Thou shalt not forswear thyself, but shalt perform unto the Lord thine oaths:

34 But I say unto you, Swear not at all; neither by heaven; for it is God's throne:

35 Nor by the earth; for it is his footstool: neither by Jerusalem; for it is the city of the great King.

36 Neither shalt thou swear by thy head, because thou canst not make one hair white or black.

37 But let your communication be, Yea, yea; Nay, nay: for whatsoever is more than these cometh of evil.

38 Ye have heard that it hath been said, An eye for an eye, and a tooth for a tooth:

39 But I say unto you, That ye resist not evil: but whosoever shall smite thee on thy right cheek, turn to him the other also.

40 And if any man will sue thee at the law, and take away thy coat, let him have thy cloke also.

41 And whosoever shall compel thee to go a mile, go with him twain.

42 Give to him that asketh thee, and from him that would borrow of thee turn not thou away.

43 Ye have heard that it hath been said, Thou shalt love thy neighbour, and hate thine enemy.

44 But I say unto you, Love your enemies, bless them that curse you, do good to them that hate you, and pray for them which despitefully use you, and persecute you;

45 That ye may be the children of your Father which is in heaven: for he maketh his sun to rise on the evil and on the good, and sendeth rain on the just and on the unjust.

46 For if ye love them which love you, what reward have ye? do not even the publicans the same?

47 And if ye salute your brethren only, what do ye more than others? do not even the publicans so?

48 Be ye therefore perfect, even as your Father which is in heaven is perfect.

CHAPTER 6.

Take heed that ye do not your alms before men, to be seen of them: otherwise ye have no reward of your Father which is in heaven.

2 Therefore when thou doest thine alms, do not sound a trumpet before thee, as the hypocrites do in the synagogues and in the streets, that they may have glory of men. Verily I say unto you, They have their reward.

3 But when thou doest alms, let not thy left hand know what thy right hand doeth:

4 That thine alms may be in secret: and thy Father which seeth in secret himself shall reward thee openly.

5 And when thou prayest, thou shalt not be as the hypocrites are: for they love to pray standing in the synagogues and in the corners of the streets, that they may be seen of men. Verily I say unto you, They have their reward.

6 But thou, when thou prayest, enter into thy closet, and when thou hast shut thy door, pray to thy Father which is in secret; and thy Father which seeth in secret shall reward thee openly.

7 But when ye pray, use not vain repetitions, as the heathen do: for they think that they shall be heard for their much speaking.

8 Be not ye therefore like unto them: for your Father knoweth what things ye have need of, before ye ask him.

9 After this manner therefore pray ye: Our Father which art in heaven, Hallowed be thy name.

10 Thy kingdom come. Thy will be done in earth, as it is in heaven.

11 Give us this day our daily bread.

12 And forgive us our debts, as we forgive our debtors.

13 And lead us not into temptation, but deliver us from evil: For thine is the kingdom, and the power, and the glory, for ever. Amen.

14 For if ye forgive men their trespasses, your heavenly Father will also forgive you:

15 But if ye forgive not men their trespasses, neither will your Father forgive your trespasses.

16 Moreover when ye fast, be not, as the hypocrites, of a sad countenance: for they disfigure their faces, that they may appear unto men to fast. Verily I say unto you, They have their reward.

17 But thou, when thou fastest, anoint thine head, and wash thy face;

18 That thou appear not unto men to fast, but unto thy Father which is in secret: and thy Father, which seeth in secret, shall reward thee openly.

19 Lay not up for yourselves treasures upon earth, where moth and rust doth corrupt, and where thieves break through and steal:

20 But lay up for yourselves treasures in heaven, where neither moth nor rust doth corrupt, and where thieves do not break through nor steal:

21 For where your treasure is, there will your heart be also.

22 The light of the body is the eye: if therefore thine eye be single, thy whole body shall be full of light.

23 But if thine eye be evil, thy whole body shall be full of darkness. If therefore the light that is in thee be darkness, how great is that darkness!

24 No man can serve two masters: for either he will hate the one, and love the other; or else he will hold to the one, and despise the other. Ye cannot serve God and mammon.

25 Therefore I say unto you, Take no thought for your life, what ye shall eat, or what ye shall drink; nor yet for your body, what ye shall put on. Is not the life more than meat, and the body than raiment?

26 Behold the fowls of the air: for they sow not, neither do they reap, nor gather into barns; yet your heavenly Father feedeth them. Are ye not much better than they?

27 Which of you by taking thought can add one cubit unto his stature?

28 And why take ye thought for raiment? Consider the lilies of the field, how they grow; they toil not, neither do they spin:

29 And yet I say unto you, That even Solomon in all his glory was not arrayed like one of these.

30 Wherefore, if God so clothe the grass of the field, which to day is, and to morrow is cast into the oven, shall he not much more clothe you, O ye of little faith?

31 Therefore take no thought, saying, What shall we eat? or, What shall we drink? or, Wherewithal shall we be clothed?

32 (For after all these things do the Gentiles seek:) for your heavenly Father knoweth that ye have need of all these things.

33 But seek ye first the kingdom of God, and his righteousness; and all these things shall be added unto you.

34 Take therefore no thought for the morrow: for the morrow shall take thought for the things of itself. Sufficient unto the day is the evil thereof. . . .

✳   ✳   ✳

The Gospel According to St. John.

CHAPTER 1.

In the beginning was the Word, and the Word was with God, and the Word was God.

2 The same was in the beginning with God.

3 All things were made by him; and without him was not any thing made that was made.

4 In him was life; and the life was the light of men.

5 And the light shineth in darkness; and the darkness comprehended it not.

6 There was a man sent from God, whose name was John.

7 The same came for a witness, to bear witness of the Light, that all men through him might believe.

8 He was not that Light, but was sent to bear witness of that Light.

9 That was the true Light, which lighteth every man that cometh into the world.

10 He was in the world, and the world was made by him, and the world knew him not.

11 He came unto his own, and his own received him not.

12 But as many as received him, to them gave he power to become the sons of God, even to them that believe on his name:

13 Which were born, not of blood, nor of the will of the flesh, nor of the will of man, but of God.

14 And the Word was made flesh, and dwelt among us, (and we beheld his glory, the glory as of the only begotten of the Father,) full of grace and truth.

15 John bare witness of him, and cried, saying, This was he of whom I spake, He that cometh after me is preferred before me: for he was before me.

16 And of his fulness have all we received, and grace for grace.

17 For the law was given by Moses, but grace and truth came by Jesus Christ.

18 No man hath seen God at any time; the only begotten Son, which is in the bosom of the Father, he hath declared him.

19 And this is the record of John, when the Jews sent priests and Levites from Jerusalem to ask him, Who art thou?

20 And he confessed, and denied not; but confessed, I am not the Christ.

21 And they asked him, What then? Art thou Elias? And he saith, I am not. Art thou that prophet? And he answered, No.

22 Then said they unto him, Who art thou? that we may give an answer to them that sent us. What sayest thou of thyself?

23 He said, I am the voice of one crying in the wilderness, Make straight the way of the Lord, as said the prophet Esaias.

24 And they which were sent were of the Pharisees.

25 And they asked him, and said unto him, Why baptizest thou then, if thou be not that Christ, nor Elias, neither that prophet?

26 John answered them, saying, I baptize with water: but there standeth one among you, whom ye know not;

27 He it is, who coming after me is preferred before me, whose shoe's latchet I am not worthy to unloose.

28 These things were done in Bethabara beyond Jordan, where John was baptizing.

29 The next day John seeth Jesus coming unto him, and saith, Behold the Lamb of God, which taketh away the sin of the world.

30 This is he of whom I said, After me cometh a man which is preferred before me: for he was before me.

31 And I knew him not: but that he should be made manifest to Israel, therefore am I come baptizing with water.

32 And John bare record, saying, I saw the Spirit descending from heaven like a dove, and it abode upon him.

33 And I knew him not: but he that sent me to baptize with water, the same said unto me, Upon whom thou shalt see the Spirit descending, and remaining on him, the same is he which baptizeth with the Holy Ghost.

34 And I saw, and bare record that this is the Son of God.

35 Again the next day after John stood, and two of his disciples;

36 And looking upon Jesus as he walked, he saith, Behold the Lamb of God!

37 And the two disciples heard him speak, and they followed Jesus.

38 Then Jesus turned, and saw them following, and saith unto them, What seek ye? They said unto him, Rabbi, (which is to say, being interpreted, Master,) where dwellest thou?

39 He saith unto them, Come and see. They came and saw where he dwelt, and abode with him that day: for it was about the tenth hour.

40 One of the two which heard John speak, and followed him, was Andrew, Simon Peter's brother.

41 He first findeth his own brother Simon, and saith unto him, We have found the Messias, which is, being interpreted, the Christ.

42 And he brought him to Jesus. And when Jesus beheld him, he said, Thou art Simon the son of Jona: thou shalt be called Cephas, which is by interpretation, A stone.

43 The day following Jesus would go forth into Galilee, and findeth Philip, and saith unto him, Follow me.

44 Now Philip was of Bethsaida, the city of Andrew and Peter.

45 Philip findeth Nathanael, and saith unto him, We have found him, of whom Moses in the law, and the prophets, did write, Jesus of Nazareth, the son of Joseph.

46 And Nathanael said unto him, Can there any good thing come out of Nazareth? Philip saith unto him, Come and see.

47 Jesus saw Nathanael coming to him, and saith of him, Behold an Israelite indeed, in whom is no guile!

48 Nathanael saith unto him, Whence knowest thou me? Jesus answered and said unto him, Before that Philip called thee, when thou wast under the fig tree, I saw thee.

49 Nathanael answered and saith unto him, Rabbi, thou art the Son of God; thou art the King of Israel.

50 Jesus answered and said unto him, Because I said unto thee, I saw thee under the fig tree, believest thou? thou shalt see greater things than these.

51 And he saith unto him, Verily, verily, I say unto you, Hereafter ye shall see heaven open, and the angels of God ascending and descending upon the Son of man.

THE
EUROPEAN
HERITAGE

The Renaissance — England

THOMAS MORE ON LEARNING GREEK (1516) From Sir Thomas More, *Utopia*, J. Rawson Lumby, ed. (Cambridge, 1940), Raphe Robyson, trans., pp. 117-20.

The people be gentle, merie, quicke, and fyne witted, delitinge in quietnes, and when nede requireth, hable to abide and suffer much bodelie laboure. Els they be not greatly desirous and fond of it; but in the exercise and studie of the mind they be never wery. When they had herd me speak of the Greke literature or lerning (for in Latin there was nothing that I thought they would greatly alow, besides historiens and poetes) they made wonderfull earneste and importunate sute unto me that I would teach and instructe them in that tonge and learninge. I beganne therfore to reade unto them, at the first truelie more bicause I would not seme to refuse the laboure, then that I hooped that they would any thing profite therein. But when I had gone forward a litle, I perceaved incontinente by their diligence, that my laboure should not be bestowed in vaine. For they began so easelie to fashion their letters, so plainlie to pronounce the woordes, so quickelie to learne by hearte, and so suerlie to rehearse the same, that I marvailed at it, savinge that the most parte of them were fine and chosen wittes and of ripe age, piked oute of the companie of the learned men, whiche not onelie of their owne free and voluntarie will, but also by the commaundemente of the counsell, undertoke to learne this langage. Therefore in lesse then thre yeres space there was nothing in the Greke tonge that they lacked. They were hable to rede good authors withoute anie staye, if the booke were not false. This kynde of learninge, as I suppose, they toke so muche the sooner, bycause, it is sumwhat allyaunte to them. For I thinke that this nation tooke their beginninge of the Grekes, bycause their speche, which in al other poyntes is not much unlyke the Persian tonge, kepeth dyvers signes and tokens of the Greke langage in the names of their cityes and of theire magistrates. They have of me (for when I was determyned to entre into my iiii. voyage, I caste into the shippe in the steade of marchandise a prety fardel of bookes, bycause I intended to come againe rather never, than shortly) they have, I saye, of me the moste parte of Platoes workes, more of Aristotles, also Theophrastus of plantes, but in divers places (which I am sorye for) unperfecte. For whiles we were a shipborde, a marmoset chaunced upon the booke, as it was negligentlye layde by, which wantonlye playinge therewyth plucked oute certeyne leaves, and toore them in pieces. Of them that have wrytten the grammer, they have onelye Lascaris. For Theodorus I caried not wyth me, nor never a dictionayre but Hesichius, and Dioscorides. They sett great stoore by Plutarches bookes. And they be delyted wyth Lucianes mery conceytes and jestes. Of the poetes they have Aristophanes, Homer,

Euripides, and Sophocles in Aldus small prynte. Of the historians they have Thucidides, Herodotus, and Herodian. Also my companion, Tricius Apinatus, caried with him phisick bokes, certein smal woorkes of Hippocrates and Galenes Microtechne. The whyche boke they have in greate estimation. For thoughe there be almost no nation under heaven that hath lesse nede of phisicke then they, yet this notwithstandyng, phisicke is no where in greater honour. Bycause they counte the knowledge of it among the goodlyeste and most profytable partes of philosophie. For whyles they by the helpe of this philosophie searche oute the secrete mysteryes of nature, they thinke themselfes to receave therby not onlye wonderfull greate pleasure, but also to obteine great thankes and favour of the autour and maker therof. Whome they thinke, according to the fassion of other artificers, to have set furth the marvelous and gorgious frame of the world for man with great affeccion intentively to beholde. Whom only he hath made of witte and capacitie to considre and understand the excellencie of so great a woorke. And therefore he beareth (say they) more goodwil and love to the curious and diligent beholder and vewer of his woork and marvelour at the same, then he doth to him, which like a very brute beaste without witte and reason, or as one without sense or moving, hathe no regarde to soo greate and soo wonderfull a spectacle. The wittes therefore of the Utopians, inurede and exercised in learnynge, be marveilous quycke in the invention of feates helpinge annye thinge to the advantage and wealthe of lyffe. Howbeit ii. feates theye maye thanke us for. That is, the scyence of imprinting, and the crafte of makinge paper. And yet not onelye us but chiefelye and principallye themselfes.

For when we shewede to them Aldus his print in bookes of paper, and told them of the stuffe wherof paper is made, and of the feate of graving letters, speaking sumwhat more, then we colde plainlye declare (for there was none of us, the knewe perfectlye either the one or the other) they furthwith very wittely conjectured the thinge. And where as before they wrote onely in skinnes, in barkes of tryes, and in rides, nowe they have attempted to make paper, and to imprint letters. And thoughe at the first yt proved not all of the beste, yet by often assayinge the same they shortelye got the feate of bothe. And have so broughte the matter aboute, that yf they had copyes of Greeke authores, they coulde lack no bookes.

COLET'S STATUTES OF ST. PAUL'S SCHOOL (c. 1518)   From Samuel Knight, *The Life of Dr. John Colet* (Oxford, 1823), pp. 302-03, 305-10, 312-13.

John Colett the sonne of Henrye Colett dean of Paules desiring nothyng more thanne education and bringing uppe children in good maners, and literature, in the yere of our Lorde A M fyve hundreth and twelfe bylded a schole in the estende of Paulis churche of CLIII to be taught fre in the same. And ordeyned there a maister, and a surmaister, and a chappelyn, with sufficiente and perpetuale stipendes ever to endure, and sett patrones and defenders governours and rulers of that same schoole the most honest and faithful fellowshipe of the mercers of London. And for because nothing can continue longe and endure in good ordre without lawes and statutes, I the said John have expressed and shewed my minde what I wolde shoulde be truly and diligentlye observed and kepte of the sayde maister and surmaister, and chapelyn, and of the mercers governours of the schole that in this boke may appere to what intent I founde this schole.

Capitulum Primum de Magistro Primario

In the grammar scole founded in the churche yard of Paules at the estende in the yeare of our Lorde 1518 by John Colet deane of the same churche in the honour of Christe Jesu *in pueritia* and of his blessid modir Marie. In that scole shall be firste an hyghe maister. This hyghe maister in doctrine learnyng and teachinge shall directe all the scole, this maister shall be chosen by the wardens and assistance of the mercery; a man hoole in body honest and vertuous and lerned in good and cleane Latin literature, and also in Greke, yf such may be gotten a wedded man, a single man, or a preste that hath no benefice with cure, nor service that may lett the due besinesse in the scole.

The mercers shall assemble togither in the scole house with such advise and counsell of well literatur and learned men as they can gett, they shall chose this maister and give unto him his charge saying unto him on this wyse.

Sir, we have chosen you to be maister and teacher of this scole to teache the children of the same not allonly good literature, but allso good maners certifieing you that this is no rome of continuance and perpetuitie, but upon your dewtie in the scole. And every yere at Candlemasse when the mercers be assembled in the scole-house ye shall submit you to our examination, and found doinge your duetie according ye shall continue, otherwise reasonable warned, ye shall contente you to departe, and you of your partie not warned of us, but of your mynde in any season willing to departe ye shall give us warning XII monthes before, without we can be shortlyer well provided of another.

Also being maister ye shall not absente you, but upon license of the surveyors for the tyme being.

✣   ✣   ✣

The Surmaister

There shall be also a surmaister, some manne vertuouse in levinge, and well lettered that shall teache under the maister as the hygh maister shall appoynt hym, some single man, or wedded, or a preste that hath no benefice with cure, nor service that may let his due diligence in the scole.

This surmaister the hyghe maister shall chose as often as the rome shall be voide, A man hoole in body and when the high maister hath appointed him upon one he shall call to the scole the surveyors of the scole, and before them he shall say to the surmaister on this wise; Sir, before these my maisters here the surveyors of this scole; I shew unto you that I have chosen you to be under maister of this scole, and to teache alway from tyme to tyme as I shall appoynte you, and supply my rome in my absence when it shall be graunted me by my maisters the mercers, wardens, and surveyors, And for such more labor in my absence I shall somewhat se to you as my maisters here shall thinke best, thanne the surveyors shall exorte the surmaister diligently to do his dewtie. And shall saye unto hym on this wyse. Your rome is no perpetuite but according to your labor and diligence ye shall continue, otherwise found not according and reasonable warned of us ye shall departe. Yf it shall be so that at any tyme ye will departe of your owne mynde ye shall geve us a half years warninge.

Yf any controversy be betwixt you and the highe maister ye shall stande at our discretion in every thinge. . . .

Lett the highe maister se the scole to be kept cleane by the poor childe, and be swepte every Satorday, and also the leades, and from tyme to tyme to call upon the mercers for necessary reparations.

The Chapelyn

There shall be also in the scole a preste, that dayly as he can be disposed shall singe masse in the chapell of the scole, and pray for the children to prosper in good life and in good literature, to the honor of God and our Lord Christ Jesu. At his masse when the bell in the scole shall knyll to sacringe, then all the children in the scole knelynge in their seats shall with lift upp handes pray in the time of sacringe. After the sacringe when the bell knylleth agayne, they shall sitt downe agayne to theire bokes learninge. This preste some good honest and vertuouse man shall be chosen from tyme to tyme by the wardens and assistance of the mercery, he shall also learne, or yf he be lerned helpe to teache in the scole, if it shall seme convenient to the highe maister or else not. He shall have no benefice with cure nor service nor no other office, nor occupation, but attende allonly uppon the scole, he shall teache the children the Catechyzon and instruction of the Articles of the Faythe and the X Commandments in Inglishe.

His wagis shall be viiil. by the yere, and a lyvery gowne of xxvis. viiid. delivered in clothe.

His chamber and lodginge shall be in the newe house in the olde Chayn, or in the maisters lodging as shall be thought beste.

He shall not have his rome by writinge, or seale, but at libertie according to his deserving.

His absence may be once in the yere, yf it nede be, as yt shall seme best to the surveyors of the scole for that yere. And than with license askyd and obteyned of the said surveyors.

In sekenesse he shall be nothing abridged of his wages. But let it be sene that he be hoole in body when he is chosen.

Yf he fall to unthriftiness and misbehaviour after lefull warning, let him be repellid and another chosen within viii dayes or assone after as can be.

The Children

There shall be taught in the scole children of all nations and contres indifferently to the number of . . . according to the number of the seates in the scole. The maister shall admit these children as they be offirid from tyme to tyme, but first se that they canne saye the Catechyzon and also that he can rede, and write competently else let him not be admitted in no wise.

A childe at the first admission once for ever shall paye . . . for wrytinge of his name, this money of the admissions shall the poor scoler have that swepeth the scole and kepeth the seats cleane.

* * *

In every forme one principall childe shal be placid in the chayre, president of that forme.

The children shall come unto the scole in the mornynge at vii of the clocke bothe winter and somer, and tarye there untyll a xi, and returne againe at one of the clocke and departe at v and thrise in the daye prostrate they shall say the prayers with due tract and pawsing as they be conteyned in a table in the scole, that is to say in the mornynge, and at none, and at eveninge.

In the scole in no tyme in the yere, they shall use talough candell in no wise, but alonly waxe candell, at the costes of theyr frendes.

Also I will they bring no meate nor drinke, nor bottel nor use in the school no breakefasts, nor drinkings, in the tyme of learnynge in no wise, yf they nede drincke let them be provided in some other place.

I will they use no cockfightinge, nor rydinge about of victorye, nor disputing at saint Bartilimewe, which is but foolish babling, and losse of time. I will also that they shall have no remedyes [play-dayes]. Yf the maister grantith any remedyes he shall forfeit xls. *totiens quotiens* excepte the kyng, or an archbisshopp, or a bishop present in his own person in the scole desire it.

All these children shall every Childermas daye come to Paulis churche and hear the childe bishop sermon; and after be at the hygh masse, and each of them offer a *id.* to the childe bysshop and with them the maisters and surveyors of the scole.

In general processions when they be warnid they shall go twayne and twayne together soberlye, and not singe out, but say devoutlye tweyne and tweyne vii psalmes with the letanye.

To theyr vrine they shall go thereby to a place appointed, and a poore childe of the scole shall se it conveyed awaye fro tyme to tyme, and have the avayle of the vrine, for other causes yf nede be they shall go to the watersyde.

Yf any childe after he is receyved, and admitted into the scole go to any other scole, to learne there after the maner of that scole, than I will that suche childe for no mans suite shall be hereafter received into our scole, but go where him lyste, where his frendes shall thincke shall be better learninge. And this I will be shewed unto his frendes or other that offer him at his first presenting in to the scole.

What Shall Be Taught

As touching in this scole what shall be taught of the maisters and learned of the scolers, it passeth my witte to devyse, and determyne in particular, but in general to speake and sume what to saye my mynde, I would they were taught always in good literature bothe Laten and Greke, and good autors such as have the verrye Romayne eloquence joyned with wisdom, specially Cristen autors, that wrote theire wisdome with clean and chaste Laten, other in verse or in prose, for my intent is by this scole specially to encrease knowlege and worshippinge of God and our Lord Christ Jesu, and good Cristen life and maners in the children. And for that entent I will the children learne first above all the catechizon in Englishe and after the accidens, that I made, or some other, yf any be better to the purpose, to induce children more spedely to Laten speeche. And then *Institutum Christiani Hominis*, which that learned Erasmus made at my requeste, and the boke called *Copia* of the same Erasmus. And then other authors Christian, as Lactantius, Prudentius, and Proba and Sedulius, and Juvencus and Baptista Mantuanus, and suche other as shall be thought convenient and most to purpose unto the true Laten speeche, all barbary, all corruption, all Laten adulterate which ignorant blinde foles brought into this worlde and with the same hath dystained and poysonyd the olde Laten speche and the veraye Romayne tongue whiche in the tyme of Tully and Salust, and Virgill, and Terence, was usid, whiche also sainte Jerome and sainte Ambrose and saint Austen and many holy doctors lernid in theyre tymes. I saye that fylthines and all suche abusion whiche the later blynde worlde brought in whiche more rather may be called blotterature then litterature, I utterly abannyshe and exclude out of this scole, and charge the maisters that they teache alwaye that is beste, and instruct the children in Greke and redynge Laten in redynge unto them suche autors that hathe with wisdome joyned the pure chaste eloquence.

*   *   *

Libertye to Declare the Statutes

And notwithstanding these statutes and ordinances before written in which I have declared my mynde and will. Yet because in tyme to come many thyngs may and shall survyve and growe by many occasions and causes whiche at the making of this booke was not possible to come to mynde. In consideration of the assured truthe and circumspect wisedome and faithfull goodnes of the most honest and substantial felowshype of the mercery of London to whome I have commytted all the care of the schole, and trustyng in theyre fidelite and love that they have to God and man and to the scole, and also belevyng verely, that they shall allwaye drede the great wrath of God. Both all this that is sayde, and all that is not sayde whiche hereafter shall come unto my mynde whyle I live to be sayde, I leve it hoolely to theyre discretion and charite: I mean of the wardens and assistances of the felowshype with suche other counsell as they shall call unto them good lettered and learned men, they to adde and diminishe of this boke, and to supply in it every defaulte. And also to declare in it every obscurite and darknes as tyme and place and just occasion shall require; calling the dredefull God to loke uppon them in all suche besynes and exorting them to feare the terrible judgment of God whiche seeth in derkness, and shall render to everye man accordynge to his workes. And finally prayinge the great Lorde of mercye for theyre faythfull dealing in this matters now and alweye to send unto them in this worlde muche wealthe and prosperyte, and after this lyfe muche joye and glorye.

COLET'S ARTICLES OF ADMISSION TO ST. PAUL'S SCHOOL
(c. 1518) From J. H. Lupton, *Life of Dean Colet* (Hamden, Conn., 1961), pp. 285-86.

The mayster shal reherse these artycles to them that offer theyr chyldren, on this wyse here folowynge.

If your chylde can rede & wryte latyn & englisshe sufficiently, soo that he be able to rede & wryte his owne lessons, than he shal be admytted into the schole for a scholer.

If your childe after reasonable season proued be founde here vnapte & vnable to lernynge, than ye warned therof shal take hym awaye, that he occupye not here rowme in vayne.

If he be apte to lerne, he shal be content that he contynue here tyl he haue some competent literature.

If he be absent vi dayes & in that mean season ye shewe not cause reasonable (reasonable cause is al onely sekenes) than his rowme to be voyde, without he be admytted agayne & paye iiij.d.

Also after cause shewed yf he contynue so absent tyl the weke of admyssyon in the nexte quarter, & than ye shewe not the contynuaunce of his sekenes, than his rowme to be voyde and he none of the schole, tyl he be admytted agayne & paie iiii.d. for wrytinge of his name.

Also yf he fall thryse in to absence, he shall be admytted no more.

Your chylde shal on childermasse daie wayte upon the bysshop at Poules and offer there.

Also ye shal fynde hym waxe in wynter.

Also ye shal fynde hym convenient bokes to his lernynge.

If the offerer be content with these artycles, than let his chylde be admytted.

THOMAS ELYOT ON THE EDUCATION OF A GENTLEMAN (1531) From Sir Thomas Elyot, *The Boke Named the Governour*, Foster Watson, ed. (London, 1907), pp. 18-25, 34-37, 41-44, 47-49.

The Education or Fourme of Bringing Up
of the Childe of a Gentilman, Which Is to Haue
Authoritie in a Publike Weale

For as moche as all noble authors do conclude, and also commune experience proueth, that where the gouernours of realmes and cities be founden adourned with vertues, and do employ theyr study and mynde to the publike weale, as well to the augmentation therof as to the establysshynge and longe continuaunce of the same: there a publike weale must nedes be both honorable and welthy. To the entent that I wyll declare howe suche personages may be prepared, I will use the policie of a wyse and counnynge gardener: who purposynge to haue in his gardeine a fyne and preciouse herbe, that shulde be to hym and all other repairynge therto, excellently comodiouse or pleasant, he will first serche throughout his gardeyne where he can finde the most melowe and fertile erth: and therein wil he put the sede of the herbe to growe and be norisshed: and in most diligent wise attende that no weede be suffred to growe or aproche nyghe unto it: and to the entent it may thrive the faster, as soone as the fourme of an herbe ones appereth, he will set a vessell of water by hit, in suche wyse that it may continually distille on the rote swete droppes; and as it spryngeth in stalke, under sette it with some thyng that it breake nat, and alway kepe it cleane from weedes. Semblable ordre will I ensue in the fourmynge the gentill wittes of noble mennes children, who, from the wombes of their mother, shal be made propise or apte to the gouernaunce of a publike weale.

Fyrste, they, unto whom the bringing up of suche children apperteineth, oughte, againe the time that their mother shall be of them deliuered, to be sure of a nourise whiche shulde be of no seruile condition or vice notable. For, as some auncient writers do suppose, often times the childe soukethe the vice of his nouryse with the milke of her pappe. And also obserue that she be of mature or ripe age, nat under XX yeres, or aboue XXX, her body also beinge clene from all sikenes or deformite, and hauing her complection most of the right and pure sanguine. For as moche as the milke therof comminge excelleth all other bothe in swetenes and substance. More ouer to the nourise shulde be appointed an other woman of approued vertue, discretion, and grauitie, who shall nat suffre, in the childes presence, to be shewed any acte or tache dishonest, or any wanton or unclene worde to be spoken: and for that cause al men, except physitions only, shulde be excluded and kepte out of the norisery. Perchance some wyll scorne me for that I am so serious, sainge that ther is no suche damage to be fered in an infant, who for tendernes of yeres hath nat the understanding to decerne good from iuell. And yet no man wyll denie, but in that innocency he wyll decerne milke from butter, and breadde from pappe, and er he can speake he wyll with his hande or countenaunce signifie whiche he desireth. And I verily do suppose that in the braynes and hertes of children, whiche be membres spirituall, whiles they be tender, and the litle slippes of reason begynne in them to burgine, ther may happe by iuel custome some pestiferous dewe of vice to perse the sayde membres, and infecte and corrupt the softe and tender buddes, wherby the frute may growe wylde, and some tyme conteine in it feruent and mortal poyson, to the utter destruction of a realme.

And we haue in daily experience that litle infantes assayeth to folowe, nat onely the wordes, but also the faictes and gesture, of them that be prouecte in yeres. For we daylye here, to our great heuines, children swere great othes and speake lasciuious and unclene wordes, by the example of other whom they heare, wherat the leude parentes do reioyce, sone after, or in this worlde, or els where, to theyr great payne and tourment. Contrary wise we beholde some chyldren, knelynge in theyr game before images, and holdyng up theyr lytell whyte handes, do moue theyr praty mouthes, as they were prayeng: other goynge and syngynge as hit were in procession: wherby they do expresse theyr disposition to the imitation of those thynges, be they good or iuell, whiche they usually do se or here. Wherfore nat only princis, but also all other children, from their norises pappes, are to be kepte diligently from the herynge or seynge of any vice or euyl tache. And incontinent as sone as they can speake, it behoueth, with most pleasaunt allurynges, to instill in them swete maners and vertuouse custome. Also to prouide for them suche companions and playfelowes, whiche shal nat do in his presence any reprocheable acte, or speake any uncleane worde or othe, ne to aduaunt hym with flatery, remembrynge his nobilitie, or any other like thyng wherin he mought glory: onlas it be to persuade hym to vertue, or to withdrawe him from vice, in the remembryng to hym the daunger of his euill example. For noble men more greuously offende by theyr example than by their dede. Yet often remembrance to them of their astate may happen to radycate in theyr hartes intollerable pride, the moost daungerous poyson to noblenes: wherfore there is required to be therin moche cautele and sobrenesse.

The Ordre of Lernynge That a Noble Man Shulde
Be Trayned in Before He Come to Thaige of Seuen Yeres

Some olde autours holde oppinion that, before the age of seuen yeres, a chylde shulde nat be instructed in letters; but those writers were either grekes or latines, amonge whom all doctrine and sciences were in their maternall tonges; by reason wherof they saued all that longe tyme whiche at this dayes is spente in understand-yng perfectly the greke or latyne. Wherfore it requireth nowe a longer tyme to the understandynge of bothe. Therfore that infelicitie of our tyme and countray compelleth us to encroche some what upon the yeres of children, and specially of noble men, that they may sooner attayne to wisedome and grauitie than priuate persones, consideryng, as I haue saide, their charge and example, whiche, aboue all thynges, is most to be estemed. Nat withstandyng, I wolde nat haue them inforced by violence to lerne, but accordynge to the counsaile of Quintilian, to be swetely allured therto with praises and suche praty gyftes as children delite in. And their fyrst letters to be paynted or lymned in a pleasaunt maner: where in children of gentyl courage haue moche delectation. And also there is no better allectyue to noble wyttes than to induce them in to a contention with their inferiour companions: they somtyme purposely suffring the more noble children to vainquys-she, and, as it were, gyuying to them place and soueraintie, thoughe in dede the inferiour chyldren haue more lernyng. But there can be nothyng more conuenient than by litle and litle to trayne and exercise them in spekyng of latyne infourmyng them to knowe first the names in latine of all thynges that cometh in syghte, and to name all the partes of theyr bodies: and gyuynge them some what that they couete or desyre, in most gentyl maner to teache them to aske it agayne in latine. And if by this meanes they may be induced to understande and speke latine: it shall afterwards be lasse grefe to them, in a maner, to lerne any thing, where they understande the langage wherein it is writen. And, as touchynge grammere, there is at this day better introductions, and more facile, than euer before were made, concernyng as wel greke as latine, if they be wisely chosen. And hit shal be no reproche to a noble man to instruct his owne children, or at the leest wayes to examine them, by the way of daliaunce or solace, considerynge that the emperour Octauius Augustus disdayned nat to rede the warkes of Cicero and Virgile to his children and neuewes. And why shulde nat noble men rather so do, than teache their children howe at dyse and cardes, they may counnyngly lese and consume theyr owne treasure and substaunce? Moreouer teachynge representeth the auctoritie of a prince: wherfore Dionyse, kynge of Sicile, whan he was for tyranny expelled by his people, he came in to Italy, and there in a commune schole taught grammer, where with, whan he was of his enemies embraided, and called a schole maister, he answered them, that al though Sicilians had exiled hym, yet in despite of them all he reigned, notynge therby the authorite that he had ouer his scholers. Also whan hit was of hym demanded what auailed hym Plato or philosophy, wherin he had ben studious: he aunswered that they caused hym to sustayne aduersitie paciently, and made his exile to be to hym more facile and easy: whiche courage and wysedome consydered of his people, they eftsones restored him unto his realme and astate roiall, where, if he had procured agayne them hostilite or warres, or had returned in to Sicile with any violence, I suppose the people wolde haue alway resysted hym, and haue kepte hym in perpetuall exile: as the romaynes dyd the proude kynge Tarquine, whose sonne rauysshed Lucrece. But to retourne to my purpose, hit shall be expedient that a noble mannes sonne, in his infancie, haue with hym continually onely suche as may accustome hym by litle and litle to speake pure and elegant latin. Semblably the nourises and other women aboute hym, if it be possible, to do the same: or, at the leste way, that they speke none englisshe but that which is cleane, polite, perfectly and articulately pronounced, omittinge no lettre or sillable, as folisshe women often times do of a wantonnesse, wherby diuers noble men and gentilmennes chyldren, (as I do at this daye knowe), haue attained corrupte and foule pronuntiation.

This industry used in fourminge litel infantes, who shall dought, but that they, (not lackyng naturall witte,) shall be apt to receyue lerninge, whan they come to mo yeres? And in this wise maye they be instructed, without any violence or inforsinge: using the more parte of the time, until they come to the age of vii yeres, in suche disportis, as do appertaine to children, wherin is no resemblance or similitude of vice.

At What Age a Tutour Shulde Be Prouided, and What
Shall Appertaine to His Office To Do

After that a childe is come to seuen yeres of age, I holde it expedient that he be taken from the company of women: sauynge that he may haue, one yere, or two at the most, an auncient and sad matrone, attendynge on hym in his chambre, whiche shall nat haue any yonge woman in her company: for though there be no perille of offence in that tender and innocent age, yet, in some children, nature is more prone to vice than to vertue, and in the tender wittes be sparkes of voluptuositie: whiche, norished by any occasion or obiecte, encrease often tymes in to so terrible a fire, that therwith all vertue and reason is consumed. Wherfore, to eschewe that daunger, the most sure counsaile is, to withdrawe him from all company of women, and to assigne unto hym a tutor, whiche shulde be an auncient and worshipfull man, in whom is aproued to be moche gentilnes, mixte with grauitie, and, as nighe as can be, suche one as the childe by imitation folowynge may growe to be excellent. And if he be also lerned, he is the more commendable.

The office of a tutor is firste to knowe the nature of his pupil, that is to say, wherto he is mooste inclined or disposed, and in what thyng he setteth his most delectation or appetite. If he be of nature curtaise, piteouse, and of a free and liberall harte, it is a principall token of grace, (as hit is by all scripture determined.) Than shall a wyse tutor purposely commende those vertues, extolling also his pupill for hauyng of them; and therwith he shall declare them to be of all men mooste fortunate, whiche shall happen to haue suche a maister. And moreouer shall declare to hym what honour, what loue, what commodite shall happen to him by these vertues. And, if any haue ben of disposition contrary, than to expresse the enormities of theyr vice, with as moche detestation as may be. And if any daunger haue therby ensued, misfortune, or punisshement, to agreue it in suche wyse, with so vehement wordes, as the childe may abhorre it, and feare the semblable aduenture.

In What Wise Musike May Be to a Noble Man Necessarie:
And What Modestie Ought to Be Therin

The discretion of a tutor consisteth in temperance: that is to saye, that he suffre nat the childe to be fatigate with continuall studie or lernyng, wherwith the delicate and tender witte may be dulled or oppressed: but that there may be there with entrelased and mixte some pleasaunt lernynge and exercise, as playenge on instruments of musike, whiche moderately used and without diminution of honour, that is to say, without wanton countenance and dissolute gesture, is nat to be contemned. For the noble kynge and prophete Dauid, kyng of Israell (whom almighty god said that he had chosen as a man accordinge to his harte or desire) duringe his lyfe, delited in musike: and with the swete harmony that he made on his harpe, he constrayned the iuell spirite that vexed kynge Saul to forsake hym, continuynge the tyme that he harped.

* * *

What Ordre Shulde Be in Lernynge and Whiche Autours
Shulde Be Fyrst Redde

Nowe lette us retourne to the ordre of lernyng apt for a gentyll man. Wherein I am of the opinion of Quintilian that I wolde haue hym lerne greke and latine autors both at one time: orels to begyn with greke, for as moche as that it is hardest to come by: by reason of the diuersite of tonges, which be fyue in nombre: and all must be knowen, or elles uneth any poet can be well understande. And if a childe do begyn therin at seuen yeres of age, he may continually lerne greke autours thre yeres, and in the meane tyme use the latin tonge as a familiar langage: whiche in a noble mannes sonne may well come to passe, hauynge none other persons to serue him or kepyng hym company, but suche as can speake latine elegantly. And what doubt is there but so may he as sone speake good latin, as he maye do pure frenche, whiche nowe is broughte in to as many rules and figures, and as longe a grammer as is latine or greke. I wyll nat contende who, amonge them that do write grammers of greke, (whiche nowe all most be innumerable,) is the beste: but that I referre to the discretion of a wyse mayster. Alway I wolde aduyse hym nat to detayne the childe to longe in that tedious labours, eyther in the greke or latyne grammer. For a gentyll wytte is there with sone fatigate.

Grammer beinge but an introduction to the understanding of autors, if it be made to longe or exquisite to the lerner, hit in a maner mortifieth his corage: And by that time he cometh to the most swete and pleasant redinge of olde autours, the sparkes of feruent desire of lernynge is extincte with the burdone of grammer, lyke as a lyttel fyre is sone quenched with a great heape of small stickes: so that it can neuer come to the principall logges where it shuld longe bourne in a great pleasaunt fire.

Nowe to folowe my purpose: after a fewe and quicke rules of grammer, immediately, or interlasynge hit therwith, wolde be redde to the childe Esopes fables in greke: in whiche argument children moche do delite. And surely it is a moche pleasant lesson and also profitable, as well for that it is elegant and brefe, (and nat withstanding it hath moche varietie in wordes, and therwith moche helpeth to the understandinge of greke) as also in those fables is included moche morall and politike wisedome. Wherfore, in the teaching of them, the maister diligently must gader to gyther those fables, whiche may be most accommodate to the ad-uauncement of some vertue, wherto he perceiueth the childe inclined: or to the rebuke of some vice, wherto he findeth his nature disposed. And therin the master ought to exercise his witte, as wel to make the childe plainly to understande the fable, as also declarynge the signification therof compendiously and to the purpose, fore sene alwaye, that, as well this lesson, as all other autours whiche the childe shall lerne, either greke or latine, verse or prose, be perfectly had without the boke: wherby he shall nat only attaine plentie of the tonges called Copie, but also encrease and nourisshe remembrance wonderfully.

The nexte lesson wolde be some quicke and mery dialoges, elect out of Luciane, which be without ribawdry, or to moche skorning, for either of them is exactly to be eschewed, specially for a noble man, the one anoyeng the soule, the other his estimation concerning his grauitie. The comedies of Aristophanes may be in the place of Luciane, and by reason that they be in metre they be the sooner lerned by harte. I dare make none other comparison betwene them for offendinge the frendes of them both: but thus moche dare I say, that it were better that a childe shuld neuer rede any parte of Luciane than all Luciane.

I coulde reherce diuers other poetis whiche for mater and eloquence be very necessary, but I feare me to be to longe from noble Homere: from whom as from a fountaine proceded all eloquence and lernyng. For in his bokes be contained, and moste perfectly expressed, nat only the documentes marciall and discipline of armes, but also incomparable wisedomes, and instructions for politike gouernaunce of people: with the worthy commendation and laude of noble princis: where with the reders shall be so all inflamed, that they most feruently shall desire and coueite, by the imitation of their vertues, to acquire semblable glorie. For the whiche occasion, Aristotel, moost sharpest witted and excellent lerned Philosopher, as sone as he had receiued Alexander from kynge Philip his father, he before any other thynge taught hym the moost noble warkes of Homere: wherin Alexander founde suche swetenes and frute, that euer after he had Homere nat onely with hym in all his iournayes, but also laide hym under his pillowe whan he went to reste: and often tymes wolde purposely wake some houres of the nyght, to take as it were his passe tyme with that mooste noble poete.

For by the redinge of his warke called *Iliados*, where the assembly of the most noble grekes agayne Troy is recited with theyr affaires, he gathered courage and strength agayne his ennemies, wysdome, and eloquence, for consultations, and persuations to his people and army. And by the other warke called *Odissea*, whiche recounteth the sondry aduentures of the wise Ulisses, he, by the example of Ulisses, apprehended many noble vertues, and also lerned to eskape the fraude and deceitfull imaginations of sondry and subtile crafty wittes. Also there shall he lerne to enserche and perceiue the maners and conditions of them that be his familiars, siftinge out (as I mought say) the best from the warst, wherby he may surely committe his affaires, and truste to euery persone after his vertues. Therfore I nowe conclude that there is no lesson for a yonge gentil man to be compared with Homere, if he be playnly and substancially expouned and declared by the mayster.

Nat withstandinge, for as moche as the saide warkes be very longe, and do require therfore a great time to be all lerned and kanned, some latine autour wolde be therwith myxte, and specially Virgile; whiche, in his warke called *Eneidos*, is most lyke to Homere, and all moste the same Homere in latine. Also, by the ioynynge to gether of those autours, the one shall be the better understande by the other. And verily (as I before saide) none one autour serueth to so diuers witts as doth Virgile.

*   *   *

The Moste Commodious and Necessary Studies
Succedyng Ordinatly the Lesson of Poetes

After that xiv. yeres be passed of a childes age, his maister if he can, or some other, studiouslye exercised in the arte of an oratour, shall firste rede to hym some what of that parte of logike that is called *Topica*, eyther of Cicero, or els of that noble clerke of Almaine, which late floured, called Agricola: whose warke prepareth inuention, tellynge the places from whens an argument for the profe of any mater may be taken with litle studie: and that lesson, with moche and diligent lernyng, hauyng mixte there with none other exercise, will in the space of halfe a yere be perfectly kanned. Immediately after that, the arte of Rhetorike wolde be semblably taught, either in greke, out of Hermogines, or of Quintilian in latine, begynnyng at the thirde boke, and instructyng diligently the childe in that parte of rhethorike, principally, whiche concerneth persuation: for as moche as it is moste apte for consultations. There can be no shorter instruction of Rhetorike than the treatise that Tulli wrate unto his sonne, which boke is named the partition of rhetorike. And in good faythe, to speake boldly that I thinke: for him that nedeth nat, or doth nat desire, to be an exquisite oratour, the litle boke made by the famous Erasmus, (whom all gentill wittis are bounden to thanke and supporte), whiche he calleth *Copiam Verborum et Rerum*, that is to say, plentie of wordes and maters, shall be sufficient.

*   *   *

Cosmographie beinge substancially perceiued, it is than tyme to induce a childe to the redinge of histories: but fyrst to set hym in a feruent courage, the mayster in the moost pleasant and elegant wise expressinge what incomparable delectation, utilitie, and commodite, shal happen to emperours, kinges, princis, and all other gentil men by reding of histories: shewinge to hym that Demetrius Phalareus, a man of excellent wisdome and lerninge, and whiche in Athenes had ben longe exercised in the publick weale, exhorted Ptholomee, kyng of Egipt, chiefly aboue all other studyes, to haunte and embrace histories, and suche other bokes, wherin were contayned preceptes made to kynges and princes: sayng that in them he shulde rede those thinges whiche no man durst reporte unto his persone. Also Cicero, father of the latin eloquence, calleth an historie the witnesse of tymes, maistres of life, the lyfe of remembrance, of trouthe the lyght, and messager of antiquite.

*   *   *

By the time that the childe do com to xvii yeres of age, to the intent his courage be bridled with reason, hit were nedefull to rede unto hym some warkes of philosophie; specially that parte that may enforme him unto vertuous maners, whiche parte of philosophie is called morall. Wherfore there wolde be radde to hym, for an introduction, two the fyrste bokes of the warke of Aristotell called *Ethicae*, wherin is contained the definitions and propre significations of euery vertue; and that to be lerned in greke; for the translations that we yet haue be but a rude and grosse shadowe of the eloquence and wisedome of Aristotell. Forthe with wolde folowe the warke of Cicero, called in Latin *De officiis,* wherunto yet is no propre englisshe worde to be gyuen; but to prouide for it some maner of exposition, it may be sayde in this fourme: 'Of the dueties and maners appertaynynge to men.' But aboue all other, the warkes of Plato wolde be most studiously radde whan the iugement of a man is come to perfection, and by the other studies is instructed in the fourme of speakynge that philosophers used. Lorde god, what incomparable swetnesse of wordes and mater shall he finde in the saide warkes of Plato and Cicero; wherin is ioyned grauitie with dilectation, excellent wysedome with diuine eloquence, absolute vertue with pleasure incredible, and euery place is so infarced with profitable counsaile, ioyned with honestie, that those thre bokes be almoste sufficient to make a perfecte and excellent gouernour. The prouerbes of Salomon with the bokes of Ecclesiastes and Ecclesiasticus be very good lessons. All the historiall partes of the bible be righte necessarye for to be radde of a noble man, after that he is mature in yeres. And the residue (with the newe testament) is to be reuerently touched, as a celestiall iewell or relike, hauynge the chiefe interpretour of those bokes trewe and constant faithe, and dredefully to sette handes theron, remembrynge that Oza, for puttyng his hande to the holy shryne that was called *Archa federis,* whan it was broughte by kyng Dauid from the citie of Gaba, though it were wauerynge and in daunger to fall, yet was he stryken of god, and fell deed immediately. It wolde nat be forgoten that the lytell boke of the most excellent doctour Erasmus Roterodamus, (whiche he wrate to Charles, nowe beynge emperour and than prince of Castile) whiche booke is intituled the Institution of a christen prince, wolde be as familyare alwaye with gentilmen, at all tymes, and in euery age, as was Homere with the great king Alexander, or Xenophon with Scipio; for as all men may iuge that haue radde that warke of Erasmus, that there was neuer boke written in latine that, in so lytle a portion, contayned of sentence, eloquence, and vertuous exhortation, a more compendious abundaunce. And here I make an ende of the lernynge and studie wherby noble men may attayne to be worthy to haue autorite in a publike weale. Alway I shall exhorte tutours and gouernours of noble chyldren, that they suffre them nat to use ingourgitations of meate or drinke, ne to slepe moche, that is to saye, aboue viii houres at the moste. For undoubtedly bothe repletion and superfluous slepe be capitall enemies to studie, as they be semblably to helth of body and soule. Aulus Gellius sayth that children, if they use of meate and slepe ouer moche, be made therwith dull to lerne, and we se that therof slownesse is taken, and the children's personages do waxe uncomely, and lasse growe in stature. Galen wyll nat permitte that pure wyne, without alay of water, shulde in any wyse be gyuen to children, for as moche as it humecteth the body, or maketh it moyster and hotter than is conuenient, also it fylleth the heed with fume, in them specially, whiche be lyke as children of hote and moiste temperature. These be well nighe the wordes of the noble Galen.

THE RE-FOUNDATION OF CANTERBURY CATHEDRAL AND GRAMMAR
SCHOOL (1541)   From Arthur Leach, ed., *Educational Charters and Documents, 598–1909* (Cambridge, 1911), p. 453.

The Incorporation, Statutes and Injunctions of the
Cathedral Church of Canterbury

Henry VIII by the grace of God, king of England, France and Ireland, Defender of the Faith, and on earth supreme head of the Church of England and Ireland, to all the sons of holy mother church to whose notice this present writing shall come, greeting.

Whereas it seemed good to us and the great men of our realm and to all the senate whom we call Parliament, God thereunto as we believe moving us, to suppress and abolish and to convert to far better uses, for the true worship of Almighty God and the far greater benefit of the Commonwealth, the monasteries which existed everywhere in our realm, both because the sincere and most ancient religion, the most admired uprightness of life, and the most profound knowledge of languages and learning, the praise of which virtues it appears flourished in the earliest monasteries, now in the progress of time have become corrupt and deficient, and changed to the foulest superstition and the most disgraceful idleness and lust and the grossest ignorance of Holy Scripture, and because of their grave and manifold enormities, as for other just and reasonable causes; Wherefore we, thinking it more in conformity with the divine will and a more Christian thing that where ignorance and superstition reigned there the true worship of God should flourish and the holy gospel of Christ be assiduously and in purity preached; and further that for the increase of Christian faith and piety the youth of my realm may be instructed in good literature and the poor for ever maintained, we have in place of the same monasteries erected and established churches, some of which we will shall be called cathedrals and others collegiate churches.

CURRICULUM AT ETON COLLEGE (1560)   From Sir Henry Churchill Maxwell-Ltle, *A History of Eton College* (London, 1899), p. 150.

In the First Form, Cato, and Vives, viz. the *Disticha de Moribus* of Dionysius Cato, and the *Exercitatio Linguae Latinae* of John Lewis Vives.

In the Second, Terence, Lucian's *Dialogues* (in Latin), and Aesop's *Fables* (in Latin).

In the Third, Terence, Aesop's *Fables* (in Latin), and selections by Sturmius from Cicero's *Epistles*.

In the Fourth, Terence, Ovid's *Tristia*, and the *Epigrams* of Martial, Catullus, and Sir Thomas More.

In the Fifth, Ovid's *Metamorphoses*, Horace, Cicero's *Epistles*, Valerius Maximus, Lucius Florus, Justin, and the *Epitome Troporum* of Susenbrotus.

In the Sixth and Seventh, Caesar's *Commentaries*, Cicero *de Officiis*, and *de Amicitia*, Virgil, Lucan and the *Greek Grammar*.

STATUTES OF THE WESTMINSTER SCHOOL (1560)   From Arthur Leach, ed., *Educational Charters and Documents, 598–1909* (Cambridge, 1911), pp. 497-525.

Elizabeth, by the grace of God of England, France, and Ireland queen, defender of the faith, etc. to our beloved in Christ the Dean and Chapter of our collegiate church of the Blessed Peter of Westminster, Health in Jesu the Saviour.

The rate or distribution of the college of the Blessed Peter at Westminster, founded by the most illustrious Queen Elizabeth:

There shall be a Dean of the college, who shall be a priest and a preacher.

12 Prebendaries. They shall be priests and preachers.

A Reader of Theology.

There shall be 29 for the daily performance piously and holily of the holy worship of God in the said collegiate church, of whom

6 shall be priests, and one of them Precentor.

12 Clerks.

1 Teacher of the choristers.

10 Singing boys or choristers.

2 Masters to educate the youth.

40 Grammar scholars.

12 Poor men.

Chapter 4. The Two Masters of the Boys and Their Duty

There shall be two masters, one of whom shall be called Head Master. The one shall be a master of grammar or of arts, the other a bachelor of arts at least, if this can conveniently be done. All the scholars shall be under their government, both of them shall be religious, learned, honourable and painstaking, so that they may make their pupils pious, learned, gentlemanly and industrious. The Dean of Christ Church, Oxford, and the Master of Trinity College, Cambridge, shall in turn elect these masters, with the consent of the Dean of Westminster. Their duty shall be not only to teach Latin, Greek and Hebrew Grammar, and the humanities, poets and orators, and diligently to examine in them, but also to build up and correct the boys' conduct, to see that they behave themselves properly in church, school, hall and chamber, as well as in all walks and games, that their faces and hands are washed, their heads combed, their hair and nails cut, their clothes both linen and woollen, gowns, stockings and shoes kept clean, neat, and like a gentleman's, and so that lice or other dirt may not infect or offend themselves or their companions, and that they never go out of the college precincts without leave. They shall further appoint various monitors from the gravest scholars to oversee and note the behaviour of the rest everywhere and prevent anything improper or dirty being done. If any monitor commits an offence or neglects to perform his duty he shall be severely flogged as an example to others.

Chapter 5. *The Twofold Election of Scholars*

The scholars being 40 in number, we will that in their election regard shall chiefly be had to their teachableness, the goodness of their disposition, their learning, good behaviour and poverty; and the more any of the candidates excels the rest in these respects, the more, as is right, he shall be preferred; and the choristers of the college and the sons of tenants of the college property, if they answer to the other requirements, shall always have the preference.

✳   ✳   ✳

Chapter 9. *Divine Worship*

THE CHORISTERS AND THE CHORISTERS' MASTER

We decree and ordain that there shall be in our church aforesaid 10 choristers, boys of tender age with clear voices, able to sing and learn the art of music and to play on musical instruments, who shall serve the choir, minister and sing. For their good instruction one shall be elected of good reputation, upright life, sincere religion, learned in music and skilled in singing and playing on musical instruments, and he shall diligently devote his time to teaching the boys the aforesaid sciences and exercises and in the performance of the other duties in choir. We will that he shall be called master of the choristers. We think that for this office doctors and bachelors of music should be preferred to others.

We will that whenever he shall be absent from our church he shall substitute another, to be approved by the Dean, or in his absence the Sub-dean. He shall also look after the boys' health, and we commit to his trust and care their education and liberal instruction in grammar (until they shall be thought fit to be admitted to our school) and in modesty of behaviour and manners. If he is negligent or idle in teaching or not prudent and careful of the boys' health or their right education, and therefore found intolerable, he shall, if after three warnings he does not amend, be put out from his office. The Choristers' Master shall be bound by oath faithfully to perform his duty in person. The choristers, after they have learnt the eight parts of speech by heart and know how to write fairly well, shall come to our school every week-day so as to become more proficient in grammar, and shall stay there for two hours at least and be instructed by the masters.

THE GRAMMAR BOYS

The grammar boys shall daily at 5 a.m., before they leave their chamber, and at 8 p.m. before they go to bed, kneeling in their chamber, clearly and devoutly say in turns morning and evening prayers.

✳   ✳   ✳

Chapter 10. The Teaching and Ordering of the Scholars

All the scholars shall spend the night in one or two chambers, two in a bed.

At 5 o'clock that one of the Monitors of Chamber (who shall be four in number) who shall be in course for that week, shall intone 'Get up.' They shall immediately all get up and, kneeling down, say Morning Prayers, which each shall begin in turn, and all the rest follow, in alternate verses, saying, 'O Lord, holy father, almighty, everlasting God,' as in Chapter 10 On Divine worship.

Prayers finished they shall make their beds. Then each shall take any dust or dirt there may be under his bed into the middle of the chamber, which, after being placed in various parts of the chamber, shall then be swept up into a heap by four boys, appointed by the Monitor, and carried out.

Then two and two in a long line they shall all go down to wash their hands; when they come back from washing they shall go into school and each take his place.

PRAYERS TO BE SAID IN SCHOOL

At 6 o'clock the Master shall come in and, kneeling at the top of the school, begin the following prayers, the boys following in alternate verses. [Ps. 67 and responses after.]

Prayers finished, the Master shall go down to the First or lowest class and hear a part of speech and of a verb in its turn. He shall pass on from the First class to the Second, from the Second to the Third, from the Third, if he thinks fit, to the Fourth, which sits in his part of the school till 7 o'clock, to examine if any obscurity arises.

Meanwhile one of the Prefects of School goes to the head of each form in the Head Master's as well as in the Usher's part, and gets from them in writing the names of those absent from morning prayers and hands them to the Usher. Another Prefect (who always performs this duty by himself) carefully inspects each boy's hands and face, to see if they have come with unwashed hands to school, and when the Head Master comes in immediately presents them to him. This order shall be kept every day.

At 7 o'clock the Fourth Form shall transfer itself from the Usher's part to the Head Master's. He shall come into school, and all the heads of each form shall after 7 o'clock hand him the names of their absents. And one of the Prefects of School shall hand the names of those who were absent from school after 6 and 7 o'clock in the evening on the day before to the Head Master and Usher respectively. Then all the classes shall say by heart what has been read to them in this order; viz. the Custos shall always begin and shall carefully observe the rest saying it afterwards.

At 8 o'clock the Head Master shall set some sentence to the Fourth Class to translate to the Fifth to vary, and to the Sixth and Seventh to turn into verse. The Custos shall take it from his lips and translate it first. The Usher too shall set some sentence to the Third and Second Form to translate, and to the First also, but for them it shall be very short.

The vulguses shown up by each shall be written on the same morning, and next day they shall say it in order by heart, before or about 9 o'clock. The Custos of each of the upper forms shall first say by heart the lesson of the form next to him and explain it. Then the Head Master shall read the same lesson to his boys as the Usher to his.

On Mondays and Wednesdays the four highest forms shall write a prose on a theme set them; in the Second, Third, and First Form each shall set himself a sentence and translate it into Latin.

On Tuesdays and Thursdays the higher forms shall round off the themes set them in verse, the other two shall write them in prose.

On Mondays and Tuesdays the Schoolmaster shall read

To Form
{ Fourth, Terence, Sallust, and Greek Grammar.
Fifth, Justin, Cicero on Friendship, and Isocrates.
Sixth and Seventh, Caesar's Commentaries, Livy,
    Demosthenes and Homer.

On those days the Usher shall read

To Form
{ Third, Terence, Sallust.
Second, Terence or Aesop's Fables.
First, Ludovico Vives or Cato.

On Wednesdays and Thursdays the Schoolmaster shall read to the

Fourth, Ovid's Tristia, Cicero on Duty, and Lucian's Dialogues in Greek.

Fifth, Ovid's Metamorphoses, or Plutarch in Greek.

Sixth and Seventh, Virgil and Homer.

On those days the Usher shall read to the

Third, Sturmius' Select Epistles of Cicero.

Second, Sacred Dialogues, Erasmus' Conversations.

First, Ludovico Vives, Corderius' Dialogues, or Boys' Talks.

From these lessons the boys shall gather the flowers, phrases or idioms, also antitheses, epithets, synonyms, proverbs, similes, comparisons, stories, descriptions of seasons, places, persons, fables, sayings, figures of speech, apophthegms.

At 9, when they have read the lesson to their forms, an interval should be given to the pupils to think over the lessons. Then they, standing upright in either part of the school, shall follow one who leads, appointed at the discretion of the Monitor. The prayers to be said in school before dinner, supper and play. . . .

Then two and two in a long line they shall go quietly to Hall and stand on either side of Hall till grace before meat is said.

Three or more of the scholars appointed by the Schoolmaster shall stand before the table in the middle of Hall, one of whom, at the selection of the Dean or Sub-dean or his vicegerent, or the Schoolmaster, shall begin to say grace and consecrate the table, and all the rest then present shall say the responses together as above in Chapter 10 Of Divine worship.

Dinner done and grace said as above-written the scholars shall return to school in the same way as they left it. And the same order shall be observed wherever they go.

At 1 o'clock the Usher shall come in, and shall ask the Fourth Form, who are there until one, sitting in his part, what the Master read before dinner, and discuss each part of speech with them; the heads of the first four classes shall, when he comes in, show him the names of those absent.

At 2 o'clock the Fourth Form shall go to their own seats, and, the Master now coming in, the heads of each class shall hand him the names of those absent. The Head Master shall spend the time between 2 and 4 o'clock in examining the Fifth, Sixth and Seventh Forms, and shall make some vulguses out of the lesson set to exercise them in Latin, so however that half an hour before four the heads of the three upper forms shall bring up their own and the other boys' themes, which he shall examine carefully.

As a knowledge of singing is found to be of the greatest use for a clear and distinct elocution, we will that all the pupils in the Grammar School shall spend two hours each week, viz. from 2 to 3 p.m. on Wednesdays and Fridays, in the art of music, and for their better instruction in that art we will that the choristers' master shall carefully teach the pupils of the Grammar School, and the same master shall receive from each of them (except those who have been choristers) 6d. for each term from their tutors.

At 4 o'clock the Head Master may, if he wishes, go out of school, returning before 5 o'clock.

At 5 or before, when the Head Master comes into school, the Usher may go out for half an hour.

During this time they shall say out of these authors as much as the Master has set them, one of the Monitors of School asking for it;

Form Fourth: from figures of speech and the method of verse-making.

Form Fifth: Valerius Maximus, Flowers of Lucian, Cicero's Epistles, Susenbrotus.

Form Sixth, Greek; Seventh, Hebrew Grammar, with a lesson in the Psalms in both languages, viz. Greek and Hebrew.

To the Usher the absences of his forms shall be shown; the themes of the Third Form; and the Sentences of the Second Form which each has set himself and turned into Latin.

Then every boy shall say by heart such part of the rules as has been prescribed for him, then too vulguses shall be made by the boys so that they may better understand the rules of grammar, and so the Latin language become familiar in every way.

At 6 o'clock they shall go out and return in the same order as before dinner and observe the same order in Hall.

At 7 o'clock two of the highest form who have been appointed by the Schoolmaster to teach the rest of the forms shall get their subjects together and practise those committed to their charge for half-an-hour in explaining what has been read to them and in turning sentences from English into Latin. Also they shall read aloud and put in order what has been dictated that day by the Usher. The heads of each class shall perform this duty, but the Monitors of the School shall pay attention to all so as to render them perfect in learning and behaviour.

Then when prayers are over they shall be dismissed to Hall to drink.

At 8 o'clock they shall always go to bed, after they have said prayers.

Evening Prayers to be said in chamber before going to bed.

[Prayers set out.]

PUNISHMENTS ON FRIDAY

... On Fridays, after saying the lesson which they had set the day before, those who have committed any grave crime are accused; for it is right that they should pay the penalties of evil-doers. Then everyone is to repeat with the greatest diligence the lessons which have been read to them that week, partly before dinner up to 11, partly from 1 to 2, leaving out nothing of what they have read in the morning during the whole week.

After 3 they shall say to their teachers whatever they have learnt during the same week, between 4 and 5.

Before 5 the master shall read to the

Fourth, Apophthegms, Epigrams of Martial, Catullus or others.

Fifth, Horace.

Sixth and Seventh, Lucan, Silius Italicus.

For 7 o'clock next day the Master shall set a theme for the Sixth and Seventh Form on which to do varyings in verse, for the Fifth in prose: and for 1 p.m. the same day to be explained again by them more at length, and to the Fourth in prose.

Before 5 the Usher shall read

To the Third and Second, Aesop's Fables, and to the First Cato.

SATURDAY

At 7 all the Forms shall say what had been read to them the day before. Varyings shall be given up to the Schoolmaster. The Usher shall examine in all he read the day before.

At 1 they shall hear the boys say the dictation of the week.

At 2 on the 7th day, two or three appointed by the Schoolmaster, shall declaim on a set theme, publicly in Hall before the whole College, a bell being rung beforehand when the Master orders it.

THINGS TO BE OBSERVED EVERY DAY

Before 7 no leave out of school shall be given except as nature may require, and not even in that case to more than three at a time, and then it is allowed to go out with the club, which they use for the purpose.

That boy shall be made custos in each class who has spoken in English, or who cannot repeat one of the rules he has learnt without making more than three mistakes, or through neglect of writing perfectly has made three mistakes in spelling in his notes.

SAINTS' DAYS

Before midday, at least one hour shall be spent, sometimes in learning the catechism, sometimes in learning Scripture; in the afternoon the three highest forms shall show up to the Head Master in verse, the Fourth and Third in Latin prose, and the Second and First in English, a summary of the sermon preached the same day in the morning in the collegiate church.

Monitors of the boys: Four of School, one of Hall, two of church, four of chamber, four of playing field, two of town boys. One of the unclean and dirty boys, who do not wash their hands and faces, and make themselves too dirty; and he shall also be the censor of manners.

STATUTE AS TO LEAVE TO PLAY

The boys shall never play without the leave of the Dean, or in his absence of his vicegerent and the Schoolmaster, and then only in the afternoon, and not oftener than once a week for any reason, and in a week in which a Saint's day falls, no leave to play shall be given.

That the youth may spend Christmas-tide with better result, and better become accustomed to proper action and pronunciation, we decree, that every year, within 12 days after Christmas day, or afterwards with the leave of the Dean, the Master and Usher together shall cause their pupils and the choristers to act, in private or public, a Latin comedy or tragedy in Hall, and the Choristers' Master an English one. And if they do not each do their part, the defaulter shall be fined 10 shillings.

✳   ✳   ✳

Chapter 13. Going Outside the College Precinct

The masters shall never, not even for a day, be away from home except for the most urgent cause, to be approved by the Dean or in his absence the Sub-dean and prebendaries at home, and then no longer than has been directed by the same.

The boys shall never leave the company of their fellows on pain of the rod, and shall never go outside the College gate without leave from the Sub-dean and Schoolmaster, and then not without a companion of good character; and if they do they shall be severely beaten with the rod. But if parents or friends have summoned their boys from our school for one day or more for what shall appear to the Dean or Sub-dean and Schoolmaster reasonable excuse, the boys shall write their names in their own hands in the Register, and if they stay away more than 20 days in a year shall wholly lose their place in college.

Chapter 14. Avoiding the Contagion of Air

The time for going away from the college to avoid contagion of the plague or of the air shall be settled by the Dean and prebendaries in residence. The masters and boys shall meet at the house belonging to the church built at Chiswick when and as often as the Dean shall see fit. There they shall have their prayers, lessons, and the rest of the usual school exercises and advantages, and shall live altogether under the same rules as if they were staying in our college of Westminster. . . .

[A clause follows absolutely prohibiting alienation of Chiswick manor.]

One of the officers, to be named by the Sub-dean, shall go into the country with them as governor of all, and one of the chaplains, and one butler, one cook and a scullion shall serve them.

HUMPHREY GILBERT'S PLAN FOR QUEEN ELIZABETH'S ACADEMY

(c. 1570)   From F. J. Furnival, ed., *Queen Elizabethes Academy by Sir Humphrey Gilbert* (London, 1896), pp. 1-12.

Forasmuch as (most excellent sovereign) the most part of noble men and gentlemen that happen to be your Majesty's Wards, the Custody of their bodies being of bounty granted to some, in reward of service or otherwise, not without your honorable Confidence of their good education, yet, nevertheless, most commonly by such to whom they are committed, or by those to whom such Committees have sold them, being either of evil, . . . or insufficient qualities, are, through the defaults of their guardians, for the most part brought up, to no small grief of their friends, in Idleness and lascivious pastimes, estranged from all serviceable virtues to their prince and Country, obscurely drowned in education for sparing Charges, of purpose to abase their minds, lest, being better qualified, they should disdain to stoop to the marriage of such purchasers' daughters; . . . It were good (as I think, under Your Highness' most gracious Correction,) that, for their better educations, there should be an Academy erected in sort as follows:—

First, there shall be one schoolmaster, who shall teach Grammar, both Greek and Latin . . .

Also there shall be one who shall read and teach the Hebrew tongue, . . .

Also there shall be one who shall read and teach both Logic and Rhetoric, and shall weekly, on certain days therefore appointed, see his scholars dispute and exercize the same, . . .[1]

My Reason. This kind of education is fittest for them, because they are wards to the prince, by reason of knights service. And also, by this exercize, art shall be practiced, reason sharpened, and all the noble exploits that ever were or are to be done, together with the occasions of their victories or overthrows, shall continually be kept in fresh memory; Whereby wise counsel in doubtful matters of war and state shall not be to seek among this trained Company when need shall require. . . .

Also there shall be one Reader of moral Philosophie, who shall only read the politic part thereof, . . .[2]

Also there shall be one Reader of natural philosophy, . . .

Also there shall be placed two Mathematicians, And the one of them shall one day read Arithmetic, and the other day Geometry, which shall be only employed to Embattlings, fortifications, and matters of war, with the practice of Artillery, and use of all manner of Instruments belonging to the same. And shall once every month practice Cannonry with all sorts of encampings and Embattlings, . . .

Also there shall be entertained into the said Academy one good horseman, to teach noble men and gentlemen to ride, make, and handle, a ready horse, exercizing them to run at Ring, Tilt, Tourney, and course of the field, if they shall be armed. And also to skirmish on horseback with pistols, . . .

Also there shall be entertained one perfect trained Soldier, who shall teach them to handle the Harquebus, and to practice in the said Academy all kinds of Skirmishings, Embattlings, and sundry kinds of marchings, . . .

[1]When the Orator shall practice his scholars in the exercize thereof, he shall chiefly do it in Orations made in English, both politic and military, taking occasions out of Discourses of histories, approving or reproving the matter, not only by reason, but also with the examples and stratagems both antique and modern. For of what Commodity such use of art will be in our tongue may partly be seen by the scholastical rawness of some newly come from the universities: besides, in what language soever learning is attained, the appliance to use is principally in the vulgar speech, as in preaching, in parliament, in Counsel, in Commission, and other offices of Common Wealth. I omit to show what ornament will thereby grow to our tongue, and how able it will appear for strength and plenty when, by such exercizes, learning shall have brought unto it the Choice of words, the building of sentences, the garnishment of figures, and other beauties of Oratory, . . .

[2]This philosopher shall distinctly divide his Readings by the day into two sorts,—The one concerning Civil policy, The other concerning Martial policy.

Of Peace. In the discourses touching Peace, he shall allege particularly the estates of all monarchies and best known Common wealths or principates that both have been and are, Together with the distinct manner of their governments touching Civil policy, And the principal Cause concerning Justice, or their Revenues, whereby they [be] any way increased or diminished. And the same to be done, as near as Conveniently may be, with special appliance of our own histories, to the present estate and government of this Realm. By which means Children shall learn more at home of the civil policies of all foreign Countries, and our own, than most old men do which have travelled farthest abroad.

Of Wars. And touching wars, he shall also particularly declare what manner of forces they had and have, and what were and are the distinct disciplines and kinds of arming, training, and maintaining, of their soldiers in every particular kind of service.

My Reason. By directing the lectures to the ends aforesaid, men shall be taught more wit and policy than School learnings can deliver. And therefore meetest for the best sort, to whom it chiefly appertains to have the managing of matters of estate and policy. For the greatest School clerks are not always the wisest men. Whereupon Lycurgus, among other laws, ordained that Schools should be for children, and not for philosophy. For such as govern Common wealths, ought rather to bend themselves to the practices thereof, than to be tied to the bookish Circumstances of the same.

The other Mathematician shall read one day Cosmography and Astronomy, and the other day tend the practices thereof, . . . with the knowledge of necessary stars, making use of instruments appertaining to the same; . . .

Also there shall be one who shall teach to draw Maps, Sea Charts, etc.

Also there shall be entertained one Doctor of physic, who shall one day read physic, and another day Chirurgery [surgery] in the English tongue, . . .[3]

Also there shall be one Lawyer, who shall read the grounds of the common laws, and shall draw the same, as near as may be, into Maxims, as is done in the book of the civil laws entitled *de Regulis Iuris*, for the more facile teachings of his Auditory. And also shall set down and teach exquisitely the office of a Justice of peace and Sheriff, not meddling with pleas or cunning points of the law; . . .[4]

Also there shall be one Teacher of the French tongue, . . .

Also there shall be one Teacher of the Italian tongue, . . .

Also there shall be one Teacher of the Spanish tongue, . . .

Also there shall be one Teacher of the high Dutch tongue, . . .

Also there shall be one Master of defense, who shall be principally expert in the Rapier and dagger, the Sword and target, the grip of the dagger, the battle axe and

---

[3] This physician shall continually practice together with the natural philosopher, by the fire and otherwise, to search and try out the secrets of nature, as many ways as they possibly may. And shall be sworn once every year to deliver into the Treasurer's office, fair and plain written in Parchment, without Equivocations or Enigmatical phrases, under their hands, all those their proofs and trials made within the forepassed year, Together with the true event of things, and all other necessary accidents growing thereby, To the end that their Successors may know both the way of their working, and the event thereof, the better to follow the good, and avoid the evil, which in time must of force bring great things to light, if in Alchemistry there be any such things hidden. . . .

[4] *My Reason.* It is necessary that noble men and gentlement should learn to be able to put their own Case in law, and to have some Judgment in the office of a Justice of peace and Sheriff; for through the want thereof the best are oftentimes subject to the direction of far their Inferiors. . . .

the pike, and shall there publicly teach, who shall also have a dispensation against the Statute of Rogues, . . .

Also there shall be one who shall keep a dancing and vaulting school; . . .

Also there shall be one Teacher of Music, and to play on the Lute, the Bandora, and Cytterne, &c; . . .

Also there shall be one keeper of the Library of the Academy, . . .[5]

Certain Orders to Be Observed

All the aforesaid public Readers of art and the common laws shall once within every six years set forth some new books in print, according to their several professions.

Also every one of those which shall publicly teach any of the languages as aforesaid, shall once every three years publish in print some Translation into the English tongue of some good work, as near as may be for the advancing of those things which shall be practiced in the said Academy.

All which books shall for ever be entitled as set forth by the gentlemen of Queen Elizabeth's Academy, whereby all the nations of the world shall, once every six years at the furthest, receive great benefit, to your highness' immortal fame.

*   *   *

There are divers necessary things to be further Considered of, all which I omit until your Majesty be resolved what to do herein.

The Commodities Which Will Ensue by Erecting This Academy

At this present, the estate of gentlemen cannot well train up their children within this Realm but either in Oxford or Cambridge, whereof this ensueth:

First, being there, they utterly lose their times if they do not follow learning only. For there is no other gentlemanlike quality to be attained.

Also, by the evil example of such, those which would apply their studies are drawn to licentiousness and Idleness; and, therefore, it were every way that they were in any other place than there.

And whereas in the universities men study only school learnings, in this Academy they shall study matters of action meet for present practice, both of peace and war. And if they will not dispose themselves to letters, yet they may learn languages, or martial activities for the service of their country. If neither the one nor the other, Then may they exercise themselves in qualities meet for a gentleman. And also the other universities shall then better suffice to relieve poor scholars, where now the youth of nobility and gentlemen, taking up their scholarships and fellowships, do disappoint the poor of their livings and advancements.

Also all those gentlemen of the Inns of court which shall not apply themselves to the study of the laws, may then exercise themselves in this Academy in other qualities meet for a gentleman. The Courtiers and other gentlemen about London,

[5] All Printers in England shall for ever be Charged to deliver into the Library of the Academy, at their own Charges, one Copy, well bound, of every book, proclamation, or pamphlet, that they shall print. . . .

having good opportunity, may likewise do the same. All which do now for the most part lose their times.

Further, whereas by wardship the most part of noble men and gentlemen within this Realm have been brought up ignorantly and void of good educations, your Majesty may by order appoint them to be brought up during their minorities in this Academy, . . .

*　*　*

It being also no small Commodity that the nobility of England shall be thereby in their youths brought up in amity and acquaintance. And above all other, this chiefly is to be accounted of, that, by these means, all the best sort shall be trained up in the knowledge of God's word (which is the only foundation of true obedience to the prince), who otherwise, through evil teachers, might be corrupted with papistry.

O noble prince that God shall bless so far as to be the only means of bringing this sealed, frozen, Island into such everlasting honor that all nations of the World shall know and say, when the face of an English gentleman appeareth, that he is either a Soldier, a philosopher, or a gallant Courtier; whereby in glory your Majesty shall make yourself second to no prince living.

*　*　*

To conclude, by erecting this Academy, there shall be hereafter, in effect, no gentleman within this Realm but good for some what, Whereas now the most part of them are good for nothing. And yet thereby the Court shall not only be greatly increased with gallant gentlemen, but also with men of virtue, whereby your Majesty's and Successors' courts shall be for ever, instead of a Nursery of Idleness, become a most noble Academy of Chivalric policy and philosophy, to your great fame. And better it is to have Renown among the good sort, than to be lord over the whole world. For so shall your Majesty make yourself to live among men for ever (whereas all flesh hath but small continuance), and therewithal bring yourself into God's favor, so far as the benefits of good works may prevail.

ACT OF PARLIAMENT INCORPORATING THE UNIVERSITIES OF
OXFORD AND CAMBRIDGE (1571)　From James Heywood and Thomas Wright,
eds., *Cambridge Transactions during the Puritan Controversies of the Sixteenth and Seventeenth Centuries* (London, 1854), pp. 50-55.

For the greate love and favor that the queenes most excellent majestie beareth towardes her highnes Universities of Oxford and Cambridge, and for the greate zeale and care that the lords and commons of this present parliament have for the mayntenaunce of good and godly literature and the vertuouse education of youth within either of the same Universities, here before graunted, ratified, and confirmed by the queenes highnes and her most noble progenitors, may be had in greater estymation, and be of greater force and strengthe, for the better increase of larning, and the further suppressing of vice: Be it therefore enacted by the aucthoritye of this present parlyament, that the right honorable Robert erle of Leicester, nowe chauncellor of the said Universitie of Oxford, and his successors for ever, and the masters and schollers of the same Universitie of Oxford for the tyme being, shalbe incorporated and have a perpetuall succession in facte, dede, and name, by the name of the chauncellor, masters, and schollers of the Universitie of Oxford, and that the same chauncellor, maisters, and schollers of the same Universitie of Oxford for the tyme being, from henceforth by the name of chauncellor, maisters, and schollers of the Universitie of Oxford, and by none other name or names, shalbe called and named for evermore; and that they shall have a common seale to serve for their necessarie causes touching and concerning the sayd chauncellor, maysters, and schollers of the said Universitie of Oxford and their successors: And likewyse that the right honorable Sir William Cicill, knight, baron of Burghley, nowe chauncellor of the said Universitie of Cambridg, and his successors for ever, and the masters and schollers of the same Universitie of Cambridg for the tyme being, shalbe incorporated, and have a perpetual succession in fact, deede, and name, by the name of the chauncellor, maisters, and schollers of the Universitie of Cambridge, and that the same chauncellor, masters, and schollers of the said Universitie of Cambridg for the tyme being, from henceforth by the name of chauncellor, maisters, and schollers of the Unyversitie of Cambridg, and by none other name or names, shalbe called and named for evermore; and that they shall have a comon seale to serve for their necessarye causes touching and concerning the said chauncellor, maisters, and schollers of the said Universitie of Cambridg and their successors: And further, that aswell the chauncellor, maiesters, and schollers of the said Universitie of Oxford, and their successors, by the name of chauncellor, masters, and schollers of the Universitie of Oxford, as the chauncellor, maisters, and schollers of the sayd Universitie of Cambridge, and theire successors, by the name of chauncellor, maisters, and schollers of the Universitie of Cambridg, may severally impleade and be ympleaded, and sue or be sued, for all manner of causes, quarels, actions, realles, personall, and mixt, of whatsoever kynde, qualitie, or nature they be, and shall and maye challeng and demaunde all manner of liberties and fraunchises, and also aunswere and defend themselves, under and by the name aforesaid, in the same causes, quarels, and actions, for every thinge and thinges whatsoever, for the proffit and right of either of the foresaid Universities to be don, before any manner of judge either spirituall or temporall, in any courtes and places within the queenes highnes domynions, whatsoever they be.

And be it further enacted by the aucthoritie aforesaid, That the letters patents of the queenes highness most noble father, kinge Henry theight, made and graunted to the chauncellor and schollers of the Universitie of Oxford, bearing date the first daye of Aprill in the foureteine yere of his raigne, and the lettres patentes of the queenes majestie that nowe is, made and graunted unto the chauncellor, maisters, and schollers of the Universitie of Cambridge, bearing date the sixe and twentie daye of Aprill in the third yeare of her highnes most gratious raigne, and also all other lettres patentes by any of the progenitors or predecessors of our said soveraigne ladye made to either of the said corporated bodies severally, or to anye of their predecessors of either of the said Universities, by whatsoever name or names the said chauncellor, masters, and schollers of either of the said Universities in anye of the said lettres patentes have ben heretofore named, shall from

henceforth be good, effectuall, and avaylable in the lawe, to all intentes, constructions, and purposes, to the foresaid nowe chauncellor, maisters, and schollers of
either of the said Universities, and to their successors for evermore, after and
according to the fourme, wordes, sentences, and true meaning of every of the same
lettres patentes, as amply, fullye, and largely, as yf the same lettres patentes were
recited verbatim in this present acte of parlyament; any thing to the contrary in any
wyse notwithstandinge.

And furthermore be yt enacted by thaucthoritye aforesaid, That the chauncellor,
masters, and schollers of either of the said Universities severally, and their
successors for ever, by the same name of chauncellor, maisters, and schollors of
either of the said Universities of Oxforde and Cambridge, shall and may severally
have, holde, possesse, enjoye, and use, to them and to their successors for ever more,
all manner of mannors, lorshippes, rectories, parsonages, lands, tenementes, rents,
services, annuyties, advousons of churches, possessions, pencions, portions, and
hereditamentes, and all manner of liberties, fraunchises, immunytes, quietances, and
pryvileges, view of frankpledge, lawedaies, and other thinges whatsoever they be,
the which either of the said corporated bodies of either of the said Universities had
held, occupied, or enjoyed, or of right ought to have had, used, occupied, and
enjoyed, at any tyme or tymes before the making of this acte of parlyament;
according to the true intent and meaninge aswell of the said lettres patentes made
by the said noble prynce kyng Henrye theight, made and graunted to the
chauncellor and schollers of the Unyversitie of Oxford, bearing date as is aforesaid,
as of the lettres patentes of the queenes majestie, made and graunted unto the
chauncellor, masters, and schollers of the Universitie of Cambridge, bearing date as
aforesaid, and as accordinge to the true intent and meaninge of all other the
foresaid lettres patentes whatsover; any statute or other thinge or thinges
whatsoever heretofore made or don to the contrary in anye manner of wyse
notwithstandinge.

And be it further enacted by thaucthority aforesaid, That all manner of
instrumentes, indentures, obligations, writinges obligatory, and recognisaunces,
made or knowledged by any person or persons, or body corporate, to either of the
said corporated bodies of either of the said Universities, by what name or names
soever the said chauncellor, maisters, and schollers of either of the said Universities
have ben heretofore called in any of the said instrumentes, indentures, obligations,
writings obligatori, or recognizaunces, shalbe from henceforth avaylable, stand, and
contynue of good, perfect, and full force and strength, to the nowe chauncellor,
maisters, and schollers of either of the said Universities, and to their successors, to
all intentes, constructions, and purposes, althoughe they or their predecessors, or
any of them, in any of the said instruments, indentures, obligations, writings
obligatory, or recognyzaunzes, be named by any name contrary or dyverse to the
name of the nowe chauncellor, maisters, and schollers of either of the said
Universities.

And bee it also enacted by thaucthoritie aforesaid, That aswell the said lettres
patentes of the quenes highnes said father kinge Henry theight, bearing date as is
before expressed, made and graunted to the said corporate bodye of the said
Universitie of Oxon, as the lettres patentes of the queenes majestie aforesaid,
graunted to the chauncellor, maister, and schollers of the Universitie of Cambridg,
bearing date as aforesaid, and all other lettres patentes by any of the progenitors or
predecessors of her highnes, and all manner of liberties, fraunchises, immunyties,
quietances, and privilidges, letes, lawedayes, and other thinges whatsoever, therein
expressed, geven, or graunted to the said chauncellor, maisters, or schollers of either

of the said Universities, or to anye of their predecessors of either of the said Universities, by whatsoever name the said chauncellor, maisters, and schollers of either of the said Universities in any of the said lettres patentes be named, in and by vertue of this present acte shalbe from henceforth ratyfied, stablished, and confirmed unto the said chauncellor, maisters, and schollers of either of the said Universities, and to their successors for ever; any statute, lawe, usage, custom, construction, or other thing to the contrary in any wyse notwithstanding.

Savinge to all and every person and persons, and bodies politike and incorporate, the heyres and successors, and the heirs and successors of every of them, other then to the quenes majestie, her heires and successors, all such rightes, titles, interestes, entrees, leases, conditions, charges, and demaundes, which they and every of them had, might, or should have had, of, in, or to any the mannors, lordshippes, rectories, parsonages, landes, tenementes, rentes, services, annuyties, advousons of churches, pencions, porcions, hereditamentes, and all other thinges in the said lettres patentes, or in any of them, mencioned or comprysed, by reason of any right, title, charge, interest, or condicion, to them or any of them, or to the auncestors or predecessors of them or any of them, devolute or growne, before the several dates of the same lettres patentes, or by reason of any gyfte, graunte, demyse, or other acte or actes, at any tyme made or don betwene the said chauncelor, maisters, and schollers of either of the said Universities of Cambridge and Oxford, or any of them or others, by what name or names soever the same were made or don, in like manner and fourme as they and every of them had or might have had the same before the making of this acte; any thinge, &c.

Provyded alwaies and be it enacted by thaucthoritie aforesaid, That this acte or anye thinge therein contayned shall not extend to the prejudice or hurt of the liberties and privileges of right belonging to the maior, bayliffes, and burgeses of the towne of Cambridge and cittie of Oxford; but that they the said maiors, bayliffes, and burgeses, and every of them and their successors, shalbe and contyneu fre, in such sort and degree, and enjoye such liberties, fredomes, and ymmunyties, as they or any of them lawfully may or might have don before the making of this presente acte; any thing contayned in this present acte to the contrary notwithstandinge.

HENRY PEACHAM ON THE EDUCATION OF GENTLEMEN (1622) From G. S. Gordon, ed., *Peacham's Compleat Gentleman* (London, 1906), pp. 18-21, 38-42, 213.

Of the Dignitie and Necessitie of Learning
in Princes and Nobilitie

Since Learning then is an essentiall part of Nobilitie, as unto which wee are beholden, for whatsoever dependeth on the culture of the minde; it followeth, that who is nobly borne, and a Scholler withall, deserveth double Honour, being both $\epsilon \upsilon \gamma \epsilon \nu \eta \varsigma$ and $\pi o \lambda \upsilon \mu \alpha \theta \eta \varsigma$: for heereby as an Ensigne of the fairest colours, he is afarre off discerned, and winneth to himselfe both love and admiration, heighthing with skill his Image to the life, making it precious, and lasting to posteritie.

It was the reply of that learned King of Arragon to a Courtier of his, who affirmed, that Learning was not requisite in Princes and Nobilitie, *Questa e voce d'un bue, non d'un Huomo*. For if a Prince bee the Image of God, governing and adorning all things, and the end of all gouernment the observation of Lawes; That thereby might appeare the goodnesse of God, in protecting the good, and punishing the bad, that the people might be fashioned in their lives and manners, and come neere in the light of knowledge unto him, who must protect and defend them, by establishing Religion, ordaining Lawes; by so much (as the Sunne from his Orbe of Empire) ought he to out-runne the rest in a vertuous race, and out-shine them in knowledge, by how much he is mounted neerer to heaven, and so in view of all, that his least eclipse is taken to a minute.

What (tell me) can be more glorious, or worthy the Scepter, than to know God aright; the Mysteries of our salvation in Jesus Christ, to converse with God in soule, and oftner than the meere naturall man, to advance him in his Creatures? to bee able with Salomon to dispute from the loftiest Cedar on Libanus, to the lowest Hisop upon the wall; to be the Conduit Pipe and instrument, whereby (as in a goodly Garden) the sweet streames of heavens blessings are conveyed in piety, peace and plenty, to the nourishing of thousands, and the flourishing of the most ingenious Arts and Sciences.

Wherefore, saith the Kingly Prophet, *Erudimini Reges*, &c. as if he should say: how can you Kings and Judges of the earth understand the grounds of your Religion, the foundation and beginnings of your Lawes, the ends of your duties and callings: much lesse determine of such controversies, as daily arise within your Realmes and circuits, define in matters of Faith, publique Justice, your private and Occonomicke affaires: if from your cradles yee have beene nursed (as Salomons foole) with ignorance, brutish Ignorance, mother of all misery, that infecteth your best actions with folly, rancketh you next to the beast, maketh your talke and discourse loathsome and heavy to the hearer, as a burthen vpon the way, your selves to be abused by your vassals, as blind men by their Boyes, and to bee led up and downe at the will and pleasure of them, whose eyes and eares you borrow.

Hence the royall Salomon, above all riches of God, desired wisedome and vnderstanding, that he might governe, and goe before so mighty a people. And the ancient Romanes, when their voyces were demanded at the Election of their Emperor, cryed with one consent, *Quis melior quam literatus?* Hence the Persians would elect none for their King, except he were a great Philosopher: and great Alexander acknowledged his, εὐ εἰναι, from his Master Aristotle.

Rome saw her best dayes under her most learned Kings and Emperours: as Numa, Augustus, Titus, Antoninus, Constantine, Theodosius, and some others. Plutarch giveth the reason: Learning (saith hee) reformeth the life and manners, and affoordeth the wholesomest advice for the government of a Common-wealth. I am not ignorant, but that (as all goodnesse else) shee hath met with her mortall enemies, the Champions of Ignorance, as Licinius gave for his Mot or Poesie: *Pestes Reipublicae literae* ; and Lewis the eleventh, king of France, would ever charge his sonne to learne no more Latine than this, *Qui nescit dissimulare, nescit regnare* ; but these are the fancies of a few, and those of ignorant and corrupted iudgements.

Since learning then joyned with the feare of God, is so faithfull a guide, that without it Princes undergoe but lamely (as Chrysostome saith) their greatest affaires; they are blind in discretion, ignorant in knowledge, rude and barbarous in manners and living: the necessity of it in Princes and Nobility, may easily be gathered, who howsoever they flatter themselves, with the fauourable Sunshine of their great estates and Fortunes, are indeed of no other account and reckoning with men of wisedome and understanding, than Glowormes, that onely shine in the darke of Ignorance, and are admired of Idiots and the vulgar for the out-side; Statues or Huge Colossos full of Lead and rubbish within; or the AEgyptian Asse, that thought himselfe worshipfull for bearing golden Isis upon his backe.

Sigismund King of the Romanes, and sonne to Charles the fourth Emperour, greatly complained at the Councell of Constance, of his Princes and Nobility, whereof there was no one that could answer an Embassador, who made a speech in Latine; whereat Lodouicke, the Elector Palatine, tooke such a deepe disdaine in himselfe, that with teares ashamed, he much lamented his want of learning; and presently hereupon returning home, began (albeit hee was very old) to learne his Latine tongue. Eberhard also, the first Duke of Wirtenberg, at an assembly of many Princes in Italy (who discoursed excellently in Latine, while he stood still and could say nothing) in a rage strooke his Tutor or Governor there present, for not applying him to his Booke when he was young. I gladly alleadge these examples, as by a publike Councell to condemne opinion of Heresie, beleeving to teach, and teaching to beleeve, the unnecessity of learning in Nobility; an errour as prejudiciall to our Land, as sometime was that rotten Chest to AEthiopia, whose corrupted ayre vented after many hundreds of yeeres, brought a plague not onely upon that Country, but over the whole world.

I cease to vrge further, the necessity and dignity of learning, having (as Octavius said to Decius, a Captaine of Anthonies,) to the understanding spoken sufficient: but to the ignorant too much, had I said lesse.

✻   ✻   ✻

Of a Gentlemans Carriage in the Vniversitie

Having hitherto spoken of the dignitie of learning in generall, the dutie and qualitie of the Master, of ready Method for understanding the Grammar, of the Parent, of the child: I turne the head of my Discourse, with my Schollers Horse, (whom me thinkes I see stand ready brideled) for the Vniversitie. And now M. William Howard, give mee leave (having passed that, I imagine, *Limbus puerorum*, and those perillous pikes of the Grammar rules) as a well-willer unto you and your studies, to beare you company part of the way, and to direct henceforth my Discourse wholly to your selfe.

Since the Vniversitie, whereinto you are embodied, is not untruly called the Light and Eye of the Land, in regard from hence, as from the Center of the Sunne, the glorious beames of Knowledge disperse themselves over all, without which a Chaos of blindnesse would repossesse us againe: thinke now that you are in publike view, and *nucibus relictis*, with your gowne you have put on the man, that from hence the reputation of your whole life taketh her first growth and beginning. For as no glory crowneth with more abundant praise, than that which is here wonne by diligence and wit: so there is no infamie abaseth the value and esteeme of a Gentleman all his life after, more than that procured by Sloath and Error in the Vniversities; yea, though in those yeeres whose innocencie have ever pleaded their pardon; whereat I have not a little mervailed, considering the freedome and priviledge of greater places.

But as in a delicate Garden kept by a cunning hand, and overlooked with a curious eye, the least disorder or ranknesse of any one flower, putteth a beautifull bed or well contrived knot out of square, when rudenesse and deformity is borne withall, in rough and undressed places: so beleeve it, in this Paradise of the Muses, the least neglect and impression of Errors foot, is so much the more apparrant and censured, by how much the sacred Arts have greater interest in the culture of the mind, and correction of manners.

Wherefore, your first care, even with pulling off your Boots, let be the choice of your acquaintance and company. For as infection in Cities in a time of sicknesse is taken by concourse, and negligent running abroad, when those that keepe within, and are wary of themselves, escape with more safety; so it falleth out here in the Vniversity, for this Eye hath also her diseases as well as any other part of the body, (I will not say with the Physitians more) with those, whose private houses and studies being not able to containe them, are so cheape of themselves, and so plyable to good fellowship abroad: that in mind and manners (the tokens plainely appearing) they are past recovery ere any friend could heare they were sicke.

Entertaine therefore the acquaintance of men of the soundest reputation for Religion, Life, and Learning, whose conference and company may bee unto you μουσειον εμψυχον και περιπατουν, a living and a moving Library. For conference and converse was the first Mother of all Arts and Science, as being the greatest discovery of our ignorance and increaser of knowledge, teaching, and making us wise by the iudgements and examples of many: and you must learne herein of Plato, φιλομαθη, φιληκοον, και ζητητικον ειναι, that is, To be a lover of knowledge; desirous to heare much: and lastly, to enquire and aske often.

For the companions of your recreation, consort your selfe with Gentlemen of your owne ranke and quality; for that friendship is best contenting and lasting. To be over free and familiar with inferiors, argues a basenesse of Spirit, and begetteth contempt: for as one shall here at the first prize himself, so let him looke at the same rate for ever after to be valued of others.

Carry your selfe even and fairely, *Tanquam in statera*, with that moderation in your speech and action, (that you seeme with Vlysses, to have Minerva alwayes at your elbow:) which should they be weighed by Envy her selfe, she might passe them for currant; that you be thought rather leaving the Vniversity, than lately come thither. But heereto the regard of your worth, the dignity of the place, and aboundance of so many faire presidents, will be sufficient Motives to stirre you up.

Husband your time to the best, for, The greedy desire of gaining Time, is a covetousnesse onely honest. And if you follow the advice of Erasmus, and the practice of Plinius Secundus, *Diem in operas partiri*, to divide the day into severall taskes of study, you shall find a great ease and furtherance hereby: remembring ever to referre your most serious and important studies unto the morning. Which finisheth alone (say the learned) three parts of the worke. Iulius Caesar having spent the whole day in the field about his military affaires, divided the night also, for three severall vses: one part for his sleepe: a second, for the Common-wealth and publike businesse; the third, for his booke and studies. So carefull and thrifty were they then of this precious treasure which we as prodigally lavish out, either vainely or viciously, by whole months and yeeres, untill we be called to an account by our great Creditor, who will not abate vs the vaine expence of a minute.

But forasmuch: as the knowledge of God, is the true end of all knowledge, wherein as in the boundlesse and immense Ocean, all our studies and endeuours ought to embosome themselves: remember to lay the foundation of your studies, The feare and service of God, by oft frequenting Prayer and Sermons, reading the Scriptures, and other Tractates of Piety and Devotion: which howsoever prophane and irreligious Spirits condemne and contemne, as Politian a Canon of Florence, being upon occasion asked if hee ever read the Bible over: Yes once (quoth he) I read it quite thorow, but never bestowed my time worse in all my life. Beleeve you with Chrysostome that the ignorance of the Scriptures, is the beginning and fountaine of all evill: That the Word of God is (as our Saviour calleth it) the key of knowledge; which given by inspiration of God, is profitable to teach, to convince, to correct and to instruct in righteousnesse.

*   *   *

Of Exercise of the Body

I now from your private study and contemplation, bring you abroad into the open fields, for exercise of your Body, by some honest recreation, since Aristotle requireth the same in the Education of Nobility and all youth, since the mind from the Ability of the Body gathereth her strength and vigor. Anciently by the Civill Law these kinds of Exercises were onely allowed of, that is $\pi\upsilon\gamma\mu\alpha\chi\iota\alpha$, $\delta\iota\sigma\kappa\sigma\varsigma$, $\delta\rho\sigma\mu\sigma\varsigma$, $\delta\iota\alpha\lambda\mu\alpha$, $\pi\alpha\lambda\eta$, and which are the exercise of Armes by single combate, as running at Tilt-barriers, &c. Coiting, throwing the hammer, sledge, and such like, Running, jumping, leaping, and lastly wrestling: for the first, it is the most Noble, those Epithites of $\iota\pi\pi\sigma\chi\alpha\rho\mu\eta\varsigma$ and $\iota\pi\pi\sigma\delta\alpha\mu\sigma\varsigma$, have beene the attributes of Kings and Princes, whose delight in ancient times was to ride and mannage great horses. Hereby you are ennabled for command, and the service of your Countrey. And what, saith Tully, can be more glorious, then to bee able to preserue and succour our Country, when shee hath neede of our helpe?

JOHN MILTON DESCRIBES A COMPLETE EDUCATION (1644)   From Oscar Browning, ed., *Milton's Tractate on Education* (Cambridge, 1897), pp. 1-6, 8-12, 14-17, 22-23.

I am long since perswaded, that to say, or do ought worth memory and imitation, no purpose or respect should sooner move us, then simply the love of God, and of mankind. Nevertheless to write now the reforming of Education, though it be one of the greatest and noblest designs that can be thought on, and for the want whereof this Nation perishes, I had not yet at this time been induc't, but by your earnest entreaties, and serious conjurements; as having my mind for the present half diverted in the pursuance of some other assertions, the knowledge and the use of which, cannot but be a great furtherance both to the enlargement of truth, and honest living, with much more peace. Nor should the laws of any private friendship have prevail'd with me to divide thus, or transpose my former thoughts, but that I see those aims, those actions which have won you with me the esteem of a person sent hither by some good providence from a far country to be the occasion and the incitement of great good to this Island. And, as I hear, you have obtain'd the same repute with men of most approved wisdom, and some of highest authority among us. Not to mention the learned correspondence which you hold in forreign parts, and the extraordinary pains and diligence which you have us'd in this matter both here, and beyond the Seas; either by the definite will of God so ruling, or the peculiar sway of nature, which also is Gods working. Neither can I think that so reputed, and so valu'd as you are, you would to the forfeit of your own discerning ability, impose upon me an unfit and overponderous argument, but that the satisfaction which you profess to have receiv'd from those incidental Discourses which we have wander'd into, hath prest and almost constrain'd you into a perswasion, that what you require from me in this point, I neither ought, nor can in conscience deferre beyond this time both of so much need at once, and so much opportunity to try what God hath determin'd. I will not resist therefore, whatever it is either of divine, or humane obligement that you lay upon me; but will forthwith set down in writing, as you request me, that voluntary Idea, which hath long in silence presented it self to me, of a better Education, in extent and comprehension far more large, and yet of time far shorter, and of attainment far more certain, then hath been yet in practice. Brief I shall endeavour to be; for that which I have to say, assuredly this Nation hath extream need should be done sooner then spoken. To tell you therefore what I have benefited herein among old renowned Authors, I shall spare; and to search what many modern Januas and Didactics more than ever I shall read, have projected, my inclination leads me not. But if you can accept of these few observations which have flowr'd off, and are, as it were, the burnishing of many studious and contemplative years altogether spent in the search of religious and civil knowledge, and such as pleas'd you so well in the relating, I here give you them to dispose of.

The end then of Learning is to repair the ruines of our first Parents by regaining to know God aright, and out of that knowledge to love him, to imitate him, to be like him, as we may the neerest by possessing our souls of true vertue, which being united to the heavenly grace of faith makes up the highest perfection. But because our understanding cannot in this body found it self but on sensible things, nor arrive so clearly to the knowledge of God and things invisible, as by orderly conning over the visible and inferior creature, the same method is necessarily to be follow'd in all discreet teaching. And seeing every Nation affords not experience and tradition enough for all kind of Learning, therefore we are chiefly taught the Languages of those people who have at any time been most industrious after Wisdom; so that Language is but the Instrument conveying to us things usefull to be known. And though a Linguist should pride himself to have all the Tongues that Babel cleft the world into, yet, if he have not studied the solid things in them as well as the Words & Lexicons, he were nothing so much to be esteem'd a learned man, as any Yeoman or Tradesman competently wise in his Mother Dialect only. Hence appear the many mistakes which have made Learning generally so unpleasing and so unsuccessful; first we do amiss to spend seven or eight years meerly in scraping together so much miserable Latine and Greek, as might be learnt otherwise easily and delightfully in one year. And that which casts our proficiency therein so much behind, is our time lost partly in too oft idle vacancies given both to Schools and Universities, partly in a preposterous exaction, forcing the empty wits of Children to compose Theams, Verses and Orations, which are the acts of ripest judgment and the final work of a head fill'd by long reading and observing, with elegant maxims, and copious invention. These are not matters to be wrung from poor striplings, like blood out of the Nose, or the plucking of untimely fruit: besides the ill habit which they get of wretched barbarizing against the Latin and Greek idiom, with their untutor'd Anglicisms, odious to be read, yet not to be avoided without a well continu'd and judicious conversing among pure Authors digested, which they scarce taste, whereas, if after some preparatory grounds of speech by their certain forms got into memory, they were led to the praxis thereof in some chosen short book lesson'd thoroughly to them, they might then forthwith proceed to learn the substance of good things, and Arts in due order, which would bring the whole language quickly into their power. This I take to be the most rational and most profitable way of learning Languages, and whereby we may best hope to give account to God of our youth spent herein: And for the usual method of teaching Arts, I deem it to be an old errour of Universities not yet well recover'd from the Scholastick grossness of barbarous ages, that in stead of beginning with Arts most easie, and those be such as are most obvious to the sence, they present their young unmatriculated Novices at first comming with the most intellective abstractions of Logick and Metaphysicks; So that they having but newly left those Grammatick flats and shallows where they stuck unreasonably to learn a few words with lamentable construction, and now on the sudden transported under another climate to be tost and turmoil'd with their unballasted wits in fadomless and unquiet deeps of controversie, do for the most part grow into hatred and contempt of Learning, mockt and deluded all this while with ragged Notions and Babblements, while they expected worthy and delightful knowledge;

       ✻   ✻   ✻

I call therefore a compleat and generous Education that which fits a man to perform justly, skilfully and magnanimously all the offices both private and publick of Peace and War. And how all this may be done between twelve, and one and twenty, less time then is now bestow'd in pure trifling at Grammar and Sophistry, is to be thus order'd.

       ✻   ✻   ✻

First to find out a spatious house and ground about it fit for an Academy, and big enough to lodge a hundred and fifty persons, whereof twenty or thereabout may be attendants, all under the government of one, who shall be thought of desert sufficient, and ability either to do all, or wisely to direct, and oversee it done. This place should be at once both School and University, not heeding a remove to any other house of Schollership, except it be some peculiar Colledge of Law, or Physick, where they mean to be practitioners; but as for those general studies which take up all our time from Lilly to the commencing, as they term it, Master of Art, it should be absolute. After this pattern, as may Edifices may be converted to this use, as shall be needful in every City throughout this Land, which would tend much to the encrease of Learning and Civility every where. This number, less or more thus collected, to the convenience of a foot Company, or interchangeably two Troops of Cavalry, should divide their daies work into three parts, as it lies orderly. Their Studies, their Exercise, and their Diet.

For their Studies, First they should begin with the chief and necessary rules of some good Grammar, either that now us'd, or may better: and while this is doing, their speech is to be fashion'd to a distinct and clear pronuntiation, as near as may be to the Italian, especially in the Vowels. For we Englishmen being far Northerly, do not open our mouths in the cold air, wide enough to grace a Southern Tongue; but are observ'd by all other Nations to speak exceeding close and inward: So that to smatter Latine with an English mouth, is as ill a hearing as Law-French. Next to make them expert in the usefullest points of Grammar, and withall to season them, and win them early to the love of vertue and true labour, ere any flattering seducement, or vain principle seise them wandering, some easie and delightful Book of Education would be read to them; whereof the Greeks have store, as Cebes, Plutarch, and other Socratic discourses. But in Latin we have none of classic authority extant, except the two or three first Books of Quintilian, and some select pieces elsewhere. But here the main skill and groundwork will be, to temper them such Lectures and Explanations upon every opportunity, as may lead and draw them in willing obedience, enflam'd with the study of Learning, and the admiration of Vertue; stirr'd up with high hopes of living to be brave men, and worthy Patriots, dear to God, and famous to all ages. That they may despise and scorn all their childish, and ill-taught qualities, to delight in manly, and liberal Exercises: which he who hath the Art, and proper Eloquence to catch them with, what with mild and effectual perswasions, and what with the intimation of some fear, if need be, but chiefly by his own example, might in a short space gain them to an incredible diligence and courage: infusing into their young brests such an ingenuous and noble ardor, as would not fail to make many of them renowned and matchless men. At the same time, some other hour of the day, might be taught them the rules of Arithmetick, and soon after the Elements of Geometry even playing, as the old manner was. After evening repast, till bedtime their thoughts will be best taken up in the easie grounds of Religion, and the story of Scripture. The next step would be to the Authors of Agriculture, Cato, Varro, and Columella, for the matter is most easie, and if the language be difficult, so much the better, it is not a difficulty above their years. And here will be an occasion of inciting and inabling them hereafter to improve the tillage of their Country, to recover the bad Soil, and to remedy the waste that is made of good: for this was one of Hercules praises. Ere half of these Authors be read (which will soon be with plying hard, and daily) they cannot chuse but be masters of any ordinary prose. So that it will be then seasonable for them to learn in any modern Author, the use of the Globes, and all the Maps; first with the old names, and then with the new: or they might be then capable to read any compendious method of natural Philosophy. And at the same time might be entering into the Greek tongue, after the same manner as was before prescrib'd in the Latin; whereby the difficulties of Grammar being soon overcome, all the Historical Physiology of Aristotle and Theophrastus are open before them, and as I may say, under contribution. The like access will be to Vitruvius, to Seneca's natural questions, to Mela, Celsus, Pliny, or Solinus. And having thus past the principles of Arithmetick, Geometry, Astronomy, and Geography with a general compact of Physicks, they may descend in Mathematicks to the instrumental science of Trigonometry, and from thence to Fortification, Architecture, Enginry, or Navigation. And in natural Philosophy they may proceed leisurely from the History of Meteors, Minerals, plants and living Creatures as far as Anatomy. Then also in course might be read to them out of some not tedious Writer the Institution of Physick; that they may know the tempers, the humours, the seasons, and how to manage a crudity: which he who can wisely and timely do, is not only a great Physitian to himself, and to his friends, but also may at some time or other, save an Army by this frugal and expenseless means only; they may then begin the study of Economics. And either now, or before this, they may have easily learnt at any odd hour the Italian Tongue. And soon after, but with wariness and good antidote, it would be wholesome enough to let them taste some choice Comedies, Greek, Latin, or Italian: Those Tragedies also that treat of Household matters, as *Trachiniae,*

Alcestis, and the like. The next remove must be to the study of Politicks; to know the beginning, end, and reasons of Political Societies; that they may not in a dangerous fit of the Common-wealth be such poor, shaken, uncertain Reeds, of such a tottering Conscience, as many of our great Counsellers have lately shewn themselves, but stedfast pillars of the State. After this they are to dive into the grounds of Law, and legal Justice; deliver'd first, and with best warrant by Moses; and as far as humane prudence can be trusted, in those extoll'd remains of Grecian Lawgivers, Licurgus, Solon, Zaleucus, Charondas, and thence to all the Roman Edicts and Tables with their Justinian; and so down to the Saxon and common Laws of England, and the Statutes. Sundayes also and every evening may be now understandingly spent in the highest matters of Theology, and Church History ancient and modern: and ere this time the Hebrew Tongue at a set hour might have been gain'd, that the Scriptures may be now read in their own original; whereto it would be no impossibility to add the Chaldey, and the Syrian Dialect. When all these employments are well conquer'd, then will the choice Histories, Heroic Poems, and Attic Tragedies of stateliest and most regal argument, with all the famous Political Orations offer themselves; which if they were not only read; but some of them got by memory, and solemnly pronounc't with right accent, and grace, as might be taught, would endue them even with the spirit and vigor of Demosthenes or Cicero, Euripides, or Sophocles. And now lastly will be the time to read with them those organic arts which inable men to discourse and write perspicuously, elegantly, and according to the fitted stile of lofty, mean, or lowly. Logic therefore so much as is useful, is to be referr'd to this due place with all her well couch't Heads and Topics, untill it be time to open her contracted palm into a gracefull and ornate Rhetorick taught out of the rule of Plato, Aristotle, Phalereus, Cicero, Hermogenes, Longinus. To which Poetry would be made subsequent, or indeed rather precedent, as being less suttle and fine, but more simple, sensuous and passionate. . . . These are the Studies wherein our noble and our gentle Youth ought to bestow their time in a disciplinary way from twelve to one and twenty; unless they rely more upon their ancestors dead, then upon themselves living. In which methodical course it is so suppos'd they must proceed by the steddy pace of learning onward, as at convenient times for memories sake to retire back into the middle ward, and sometimes into the rear of what they have been taught, untill they have confirm'd, and solidly united the whole body of their perfeted knowledge, like the last embattelling of a Roman Legion. Now will be worth the seeing what Exercises and Recreations may best agree, and become these Studies.

*　　*　　*

Now lastly for their Diet there cannot be much to say, save only that it would be best in the same House; for much time else would be lost abroad, and many ill habits got; and that it should be plain, healthful, and moderate I suppose is out of controversie. Thus Mr. Hartlib, you have a general view in writing, as your desire was, of that which at several times I had discourst with you concerning the best and Noblest way of Education; not beginning as some have done from the Cradle, which yet might be worth many considerations, if brevity had not been my scope, many other circumstances also I could have mention'd, but this to such as have the worth in them to make trial, for light and direction may be enough. Only I believe that this is not a Bow for every man to shoot in that counts himself a Teacher; but will require sinews almost equal to those which Homer gave Ulysses, yet I am withall perswaded that it may prove much more easie in the assay, then it now seems at distance, and much more illustrious: howbeit not more difficult then I imagine, and that imagination presents me with nothing but very happy and very possible according to best wishes; if God have so decreed, and this age have spirit and capacity enough to apprehend.

GUIDANCE FOR A STUDENT AT ST. JOHN'S COLLEGE, CAMBRIDGE (c. **1640**)   From Richard Holdsworth, "Directions for a Student in the Universitie," as quoted in Harris Fletcher, *The Intellectual Development of John Milton* (Urbana, Ill., 1961), pp. 624, 634-41, 650-55.

That such Directions are requisite ~. That the want of such Directions is not the least impedim^t to the o proficiencie of young students will appeare many ways o Some who perhaps have, or at the least once had real desires to be Scholars fall in to idlnes & duncery o because they know not how to set themselves on worke. Others grow remisse & Carelesse in theyr studies, o following them as if were but the half part because they are ignorant how great a taske they have, how o many leavs & volumes to be turned over, before they can justly deserve the name of a Scholar or a degree in the Universitie. Those linger & loiter like—o wanderers in a mistie wildernes, that know they have somewhither to goe but neither know whether nor how far, nor to what purpose. Others agin intend well but misimploy their time in books w:^ch might without prejudice be omitted; neglecting in the mean time ~ such as are more necessary for the attaimm^t of true Scholarship. Others are of a dispairing humour, & thinke they can never have studied enough bec: they looke upon Learning as a taske without End or Limits and though they study night & day yet they suppose they know not half of that they ought to know to make them ordinary scholars. Besides though a Student know by name all the books he ought to read, yet if he know not how to read them to the best advantage, it will be a great prejudice to his studies, & though he did know how to read them, yet if he know not of what bulk, & biggnes each of them is, & so have to allot to each a due proportion of time, he shall probablie stay so long upon some, that he shall be forced to neglect the rest. Lastly no Tutor, especialie in diversity & variety of Pupils can be so punctual as in due time to prescribe to each in all particulars what they ought to study & how the day ought to be spent: and though he should doe so, yet perhaps his Pupils could not so well aprehend & remember it.

For all those several inconviences these Directions are intended as a remedy. They will shew you what you ought to doe, what books to read, & how, & when, & what time may be allowd to each breifly, how every month in the whole 4 years before you come to be Batchelour is to be imploied.

Wherin I shall first give you a short Synopsis of all the books with the yeare & month they ought to be read in. Then I shall come to speake more in particular of each, how, in what manner, & to what end they are to be read. & lastly I shall give y^o some other general directions, about the right ordering of y time & studys, & Carriage in other things.

Let not these Directions be thrown asyde after once writig or reading over but have them allwaies at hand that by frequent writing, reading & looking over them upon each occasion you may be stirred up to the observation thereof.

*   *   *

Anni Prim Antemerid
Systema Logicum brevius & majus
Februar: Mart:

This will give you the grounds of Logick, & therfore as a groundworke must be gott very perfectly, & exactly as The Accidence, or Grammer in Latine. It is a great disgrace & a signe of an idle student to stick at any question w: may be answerd out of it; & a neglect in this will be a hinderance to all his following studies in the same faculty. This is to be understood likewise of the first Systeme in every Science.

Systema] Συστημαι. απο το Componi constitui, compingi compositionem, collectionem seu compagem significat. That is a frame or collection of the precepts and rules of an Art or Science.

This first Systeme may either be a printed one the shortest and exactest one that can be gott or else a written one of your Tutors own collecting: & for some reasons I should rather preferre the latter. First because those that are printed are most of them rather fitted to riper judgments, then for the capacitie & convenience of young beginners containing many things either too difficult, or lesse necessary for such an one. An other reason is because it is found by experience, that a teacher is more carefull & earnest to inculcate his own notions tha an others, as best understanding why, & to what end every thing there is sayd & bec: there every thing fully agrees with his own judgment wch will scarce happen in an other's works. A third reason may be this, that a Scholar by writing it over shall have gott some knowledge of it, before his Tutor come to read, and explain it to him, w:^{ch} will make him understand it a great deale better, than if he had not looked over it at all. After you have gone once over this Systeme, it will be good to repeat it over agin to y^r Tutor before you leave it for the better impression of it in y^r mem'ry

When y^o come from lectures with y^r Tutor spend some time in recollecting what he hath explaind; & the rest of ye morn: in such studies as I shall direct you for the after noone of w:^{ch} hereafter.

Systema majus (Martio.)

After y^o have gone thus twice through ye 1st Syst: or grounds of Log: w:^{ch} will be done in less than 2 months y^o are to spend ye rest of this quarter in going through another w:^{ch} shall be fuller & larger partly to give y^o a fuller & larger understanding of w:^{t} y^o Learn'd in the former w:^{ch} is better done by several bookes, then one, & ye same; & partly to supply w^t was defective in ye former by reason of brevity[.] There are many printed ones of this nature; but I shall chiefly comend Burgerdicius; it is comonly approv'd & recd: and contains a more perfect, & usefull Log: than most doe: it aqu^{ts} y^o with Aristotles termes. . . .

EDUCATION
IN THE
UNITED STATES

188

This your Tutor shall not need to explaine to you as he did the former, but you are to be left to y^r self to read, & understand it alone; w:^{ch} you will easily doe if you have not bin negligent in the study of the other; & besides you will finde more, content, & better retain that w:^{ch} you get out of y own industrie, than w^t you receave from y Tutor. Only as you read it you must gather some short notes out of it, for reasons w:^{ch} I shall give you hereafter, when I shall speake of gathering notes in general. Cap. 4.

Particularly for those w:^{ch} you gather out of Burgerdicius observe this order, let them be as short as may be, & therfore note nothing w:^{ch} you learnt in y former Systeme, & know already, & if it be such a thing as you thinke you can rememb^r write only as much as will serve to put you in minde of it. (if you will) by way of question. if it seem something difficult to retaine, note it down so much y larger. That you may the better understand my meaning take this example, for the beginning of Burgerdicius

Ex Burgerdicij Logica

Unde dicitur Logica? Pag. 1.
λογος ενδιαθετος et προφορικος.
2 Logica alio nomine Dialectica. Unde dicta?
Dialectica universaliter, & particulariter. Logica naturalis. habitualis systematica.
3 Qomodo probatur Logicam esse artem, & non scientiam? Quid est Ars?

Anni Primi Ante merid:

4. ποιειν non semper significat actionem ex palpabali materia vel opus manens.
Logica finis duplex.
Logica docens & utendis. Quid sunt. Quaenam sunt.
5 objecta primaria, & secundaria utriusque officia docentis? utentis?
6 Pars Logica Thematica. Organica. &c:

Such notes as these are sufficient to call to your minde, by looking over your Paper booke what you have read there, & by them either your Tutor, or y^r self may examine y^r studies. You see I set the page of Burgerdicius, out of w:^{ch} the notes are taken in the margine, that when ever y^r memory failes, y^o may have a ready recourse to the Author himselfe

Controversiae Logicae
April Maij—

After thus having got the grounds of positive Logic you are to come to Controversies, & acquaint your self with the several questions that are usualy disputed, as, Utrum Logica sit Ars? Utrum quinque sunt Predicabilia? &c. . . .

Anni Primi Antemerid:

Finde out your question, & read it in each of them with what ever you finde thereabout belonging to the explication of the same, by w^ch: means you will come to a full understanding of the Controversie, for one will supply where the other is defective, & this will help out where that is obscure.

This being done gather the sum, & substance of it in to your Paper-book, as short, & cleare as you can, which you may doe most easily, & readily, in this method. First set down the state of ye Question. Then give a reason or 2 why it is held so, & Lastly choos 2 or 3 of the principal Arguments, from the rest of their answers. Should y^r notes be larger it would be both tedious, & take up too much of y^r time. This will be enough to make you able to give an acct of it upon any occasion, & with a little warning dispute on it. And indeed this is as much as one can well carry away in a Controversy, & as much as most doe. He that striveth to remember evry Nicety & petty objection, or disjunction, shall perhaps in a short time forgett all.

If in y^r Authors you meet with diversity of Oppinions, follow that w:^ch is most generaly recd in the Schooles.

All this while I would have you medle with ye most usual, & easiest questions, w^ch: y^r Tutor, or some Freind will collect to you.

Anni primi Ante merid.—
Mense June
Systema aliud Logicum

This month I would have you to bestow in reading one Systeme more of Logick; if you may still be more exactly confirmd in the grounds of it. By this time you will come to read Logick with more ease, & delite, you will see everything clearer, & plainer, then you did formerly, and observe many things you then neglected. Read it with notes after the same manner you did Burgerdicius: only y^r notes may be fewer, bec: you shall meet with fewer things w:^ch you know not already. Here I commend Crackinthorp Kekerman, Molineus, Saunderson, or some of the like nature.

Controversiae Logicae.
& Disput. Jul. Aug. Sep.

After that Systeme you are to return to y^r Controversies, & continue your study in them, after the manner allready prescribed all this quarter. And must take to task not only the easiest, but all you meet with[.] At the begining of this quarter allso you are to begine to dispute by course in your Tutors Chambers, & so continue that exercise through all your studies, & in every faculty according as y^o come to it as long as y^r Tutor shall thinke it necessarie.

Systema Ethicum brevius
Mense Octobris

Anni Primi Antemerid:

This is to give you the true grounds of your faculty, or Science w:^ch you are to study. If you have not a write one, take Burgerdicius Idea, Stierius Golius, or ye like. Your Tutor will read it to you, & dispatch it in a 14^nt, or 3 weeks time.

Systema Ethicum majus
Novemb[r] Decemb[r] —

This is for Confirmation, & perfection of the other. Eustachius is very good, & may be read in a short time Read it as Burgerdicius. I allow a quarter of a year to these two though much less would serve, bec: I would have you set now, and the a week, or 2, or 4 days apart for looking over your Logicke notes, & recolecting these studys by them.

   Your disputing in y Tutors Chamber by course as I said before is to be Continued both in this & the following years, as long as is requisite.

Studia Pomeridiana

Thus far of the Morning studies, for the first yeare. I come now to those of the afternoon for y same. Which are to be the Greek & Latine toungs History Oratory, & Poetry. Studies not less necessary than the first, if not more usefull, especialy Latine, & Oratory, without w: all the other Learning though never so eminent, is in a manner voide & useless, without those you will be bafeld in your disputes, disgraced, & vilified in Publicke examinations, laught at in speeches, & Declamations. You will never dare to appear in any act of credit in y[e] University, nor must you look for Preferment by your Learning only. The necessity of this studie above the rest is the cause that it is to be continued through all the four yeares in the after noons, . . wheras other studies have but each a parcel of y[r] time alotted to them.

These Directions
Januarij—

After you have written out your first Logicke Systeme, w[ch] till you have done is to be your imploym[t] both in the forenoon, & afternoon, you are to spend so much time in the afternoones, as will serve to write out these Directions, that you may see before you the rest of y[r] studies.

Goodwines Romane Antiquitys
Jan: Febr:

This book is to be read before you come to other Latine authors, as being very usefull in the understanding of them. it acquaints you with ye maners & Customes of the Romanes, & so gives life to many Latine phrases, . . .

Anni primi Antemerid:

Gather short notes after the same manner as is prescribed in Burgerdicius his Logicke. This book would be dispatchd in lesse then a month, though you should read but 5 leaves a day.

Justini Historia
Febr: Mart:

This book will acquaint you in some manner with the general historie of the whole world. all other are either too long, too short, too particular, or too difficult for a beginner. Gather short notes as is allready prescribed, but lett them be only in questions in such things as seem easy to remember, or else like the contents of a chapter in the bible, observe also as you goe along all the useful phrases, & idiotismes, & give them some little mark in the the [sic] margine, that so easily you may looke them agin when you have done the contents, & write them down with the english signification at the end of each particular book, unless you had rather write them downe in a book by themselves, wherin shall be nothing else but phrases out of that, & other bookes. Sentences & remarkable passages you are to write in an other book as I shall direct hereafter. See chap: 5.

Ciceron: Epistol: Erasm: Coll:
Terent: April: Maij Jun:

This quarter I would have wholy imploied in these bookes towards the gaining of the purity of the Latine style wch in some measure you may doe in that space.

Allow to each of these a month. I doe not expect y^o shall read them through in that time, but only as much as you can doe with ordinary assiduity in each.

Let this be your manner in reading of them; Gather out in to a paperbook all the phrases, & idiotismes w:^{ch} you know not allready, whether they be such as consist in single words or sentences, with the English signification and use as you goe along. This studie you may thinke teadious, but the benefit will be a sufficient requital[.] Spend every other afternoon, or at least two in a weeke in making latine exercises in a plain stile, for reading only without practise, will never make you a Latinist. Those may either be translations out of some plain English bookes, as Historie Dialogues Relations, or some stories, & passages w:^{ch} you know & have lately heard & desire to retaine, or if you will, Dialogues Epistles & Stories of y own inventing wherin you may bring in most of the usefull idiotismes w: you gatherd: And so whilest you read Tully, Epistoles; Stories when you read Erasmus; Dialogues when Terence. Only the first houre in every after noon must be set a part for getting without booke some Epistles in Tully, some Coll: in Erasmus, or some Comedys in Terence.

There are two ways to get without book, either conning it as boys doe, or frequent reading over the same thing for certain days together, w:^{ch} is easier, & will be as effectual to all ends, & purposes, as the former; though perhaps you shall not be able to repeat much without book to geather, yet evry particular sentence will be as ready to you, & that readinesse as usefull, as if you had con'd it, & indeed that plodding way of conning doth tire and lode the memory rather then begett a readines. There is no such effectuall means for the attaining of a language as this getting without book, & therfore however it may seeme tedious, & unpleasing it must not be neglected because of this tediousnes. I allot the first hour of the afternoon when you are fresh, after w:^{ch} the tediousnes of that hour will make you come with more delight to y other studies[.] One of those hours for getting without book in each book may be imployd in repeating, that is in reading over what you have formerly so gott.

Before you read Ovids' Metamorphosis it will be requisite to run over some book of Mythology. Natalis Comes is somewhat too large, & tedious Sr Francis Bacon too short I direct you to this as most convenient, you may read it with short memorial notes like the contents of a Chapter.

Also before you read Ovid it will be very good to gett two Maps one of Old Greece the other of the Romane Empire & spend one afternoon or two in acquainting you self with them, by the assistance either of your Tutor, or some frend[.] These will help you very much, not only to understand and remember all Ovids fabulous Histories but allso all other Greek or Latine Historians w: y° shall read hereafter.

[Always search] in the Map the places you read of. The end of reading Ovids' Metamorphosis is to acquaint you with all the fables, & mythologie of Poets, which afford invention for theams verses & orations: and besides this will adde much to gaining the Latine. For though it be a Poetick style yet it is not so figurative & lofty as other Poets are but keeps nerer to the true Idiome & propriety of words it will allso help to perfect you in y^r quantity of silables without wch you will never pronounce latine right, and lastly it will initiate you in a Poetick style. Read it if you will with Farnabie's notes, and keep short contents of each fable. but howsoever gather all sayings sentences & remarkable passages w:^{ch} you think you can any ways make use of into your Paper book w:^{ch} you purposly have for such things.

Testament Graecum
Septemb:

Spend this last Month of this quarter as much as you can in reading in your Greek Testament, that you may not only retaine, but make some progres in that Language. read it with your Lexicon, & pass by no word without full understanding of it giving a mark with your Pen at such words as you doubt you cannot remember, or writing them down in some paper, that so you may the more easily remember them.

Anni primi Pomerid:
Terent: Ciceron: Epist: Erasm: Coll:
Octob Novemb:

Amongst your other exercises of the second quarter, I will suppose that besides what you noted in Terence, you got one Comedy without book, at least after the same manner there prescribed. the first busines of this quarter shall be to read y^r rest of him w:^{ch} remaines unnoted or ungott without booke, & this without any notes, w:^{ch} will not be above a weeks worke this partly for variety of studys, and exercise in the style for thus you will meet with many Idiotismes againe and againe, & so remember them without noting, for the same reason you may spend the rest of the first month in reading Tullis Epistles, & Erasmus Colloquies—But the second month I would have you spend in them, or in any two of them w: you most affect, after the same maer you did before in the second quarter, & with the same exercises, which if you did doe you shall not doubt by this time to be a Latinist, at least in such a manner as the following studies will easily perfect.

Theognis. Decemb

Read this booke with your Lexicon only as you did the Greek Testament gathering out some of the most usefull sentences into your paperbooke for that purpose.

Thus much for the first yeare; before I come to the second I shall speake a word or two of such books as you are to use on evenings Lordsdays, & othertimes set apart for devotion; y^t
That you may encrease in Piety, & saving knowledge as well as in humane learning w:^{ch} if not seasond with that is vain, & useless.

De Religione

For the right spending therfor of the time aforesayd besure never to be without some of the most Pious, & most approved works of those Authours, or the like, according as your Tutor or a Freind will direct you. B. Hall, Sibs. Preston Bolton. Davnant, Perkins, Drexelius, &c.

Besides w:^{ch} books of Devotion I will suppose that you neglect not reading of the Holy Scriptures. He that reads 3 Chapters a day will read the Bible through once in a yeare if only when he comes at the Psalmes he reades of them for one Chapter, so dispatching them in sixten days[.] This reading of the Scriptures may be used without preiudice to your other studies, if you begin the morning with one Chapter, the afternoon with another, & read a third after supper or when you goe to bed.

Anni Secunda Antemerid:
Systema Phis: brevius Systema majus
Mensibus. Jun: Feb: Mart:

The former part of this quarter is to be spent in reading of a short Physick System with y^r Tutor, & the latter part in reading some other allone as Magirus, Eustachius or the like with notes as in Burgerdicius.

Controversiae, Logic: Ethic: Phis.
Mens: April: Maio, Jun:

Read these, & study them with Collections, after the same manner w:^{ch} I prescribed in the last yeare for your Logick controversies. Get these or the like, for your study of Controversies. In Ethicks Morisanus Eustachius Burgerdicius, &c: In Phisicks Coll: Conimbrecence Coll: Compliot: Tolet: Aegidius Pererius Zaberella Picolomeneus Wendlin.

Systema Metaphisic: Brevius, Majus,
Mensib: Jul: Aug: Septemb:

This third quarter is to be spent in Metaphisicks after the same manner as the first was in Phisicks.

Controvers: omne genus.
Mensib: Octob: Nov: Decemb:

Observe the same method still for Controversies & for those in Metaphisicks gett Scheibler. Fonesca. Eustachius Suares. or the like.

Studia Pomeridiana
Gramat: Lat: Valla de Elegant:
Gramat: Graec: Vigerij, Idiot:
Mens: Jan: Feb: Mart:

Gramers must not be forgotten: it is now a yeare agoe or more since you came from schoole & unless you look over them now & then, you shall perceave them to slip out of your memry & now reading them over with a riper judgment, you shall see as it were with clearer eyes then before, & observe many things w:^{ch} you formerly pas'd over unregarded. After the Latine Gramer, read Valla, gather the summe of each Chapt: in to a paper booke setting downe the use & most proper signification of the Elegancie there treated of in English—The use of this booke is to acquaint you with the choicest elegancies & Idiotismes of the Latine toung, & to put you in a way to observe them as you read Authors w:^{ch} otherwise y^{o} would scarce doe. Danes his Scholion to his Latine Gramer is allso a book of good use in this kinde.

You may allow half the quarter to those two, & the other half to the Greek Grammer, & Vigerius. . . .

✻   ✻   ✻

Of Gathering Notes. c. 4

Young Students many times neglect gathering of Notes out of bookes they read, either because their memorie is good enough to retain them without noting, or else bec: they are sloathfull, & will take no pains.

Let such as trust too much to theyr memories know that however for the present the things seem so fresh in their memories that they think they can not forgett them, yet they will finde ye process of time and other studies will so wipe them out that they shall remember very little in a whole book, unless they have memorial notes to run over now and then.

And besides though this noting were of no use to the memorie, yet it hath another advantage which allone would make it worthy in the mean while & that is it helps you to the fuller, & clearer understanding of what you read, while you endeavour to abreviate and contract the sence, & makes you take notice of many things w: otherwise you would have passed over.

They that neglect it out of Idelnes should consider that one booke read with Notes for the reasons aledgd brings a better stock of Learning, when if in the same time they should have read three without, becauʒe either you will not read them so exactly or not remember them long: whereas by Noting you make it intirely your own for ever after.

Again this Gathering of Notes will keep y^{o} from growing dull & listless in y^{r} studies, as one often shall that only reads.

And lastly it is necessary for Tutors sattisfaction of your Studies.

What kind of notes ought to be gatherd out of each book, I have all ready spoake in particular.

Besides I would have you keep a Note or Catalogue of all that you meet with in your studies, which you understand not; w:^{ch} at any time either your Tutor or some Freind may sattisfie you in. Write them in some paper book rather than in a loos paper, and leave space for the resolution after every one; It will be a content to you after some years to find them there, & to be able to say such, & such a thing I scrupled at and had this answer.

Of a Common place book

I have observ'd in many Students a commendable endeavour to make Common place books, in w:^{ch} they might recorde the best of theyr studies to certain heads of future use and memorie. But few of them either continue constant in it, or bring it to any perfection.

Neither doe I much wonder at it, when I consid: the toyle & the interuption it must needs creat to theyr studies, to rise evry foot to a great Folio book, & toss it and turn it for evry little passage y^t is to be writt downe.

I was told of one, who to prevent this toyle, caused a box to be made with as many partitions as he could have had heads in his booke, so that writing his Collection in any bit of paper, he might without more trouble throwe it in to its Topick, & look over each divisio on occasion.

But perhaps you like this no better than I however I shall councell you rather then to trouble your self with any Voluminous Common place booke especially in these your rawer studies, to follow this order in your Collection.

Get some handsome paper bookes of a portable size in Octavo, & rule them so with Inke or black lead that there may be space left on the side for a margin & at the top for a title: Into them collect all the remarkable things wch you meet with in your Hystorians, Oratours, & Poets.

Ever as you find them promiscuously, especialy if out of the same book, in the title space set downe the name of the Authour with the book, or Cap: & after every Collection, the number of the page, or Section whence it is taken, that so you may speedily recourse to the Authour him self upon occasion.

These Collections you shall render so ready and familiar to you by frequent reading them over on evenings, or times set a part for that purpose, that they will offer themselves to your memory on any occasion, which if you could doe would be far above the use of any Common place book, but if you finde by experience that your memorie is not either faithfull, or quick to doe this, you may at any time with a little pains reduce such bookes of Collection to a Commonplace book w:^{ch} shall be only a kind of large Index to them setting downe with every reference, a word or two of each Collection to put you in minde of the rest; w:^{ch} reference that you may the better marke y^o you must page all your fore-sayd bookes of Collections (if you will continue the number from one to another or else at the least distinguish them one from another either by different names or the order of the Alphabet.

A Common place booke ought to be fitted to that profession you follow, whether of Law, Divinity, Phisick or the like, w:^{ch} probably you cannot resolve upo when you begin first your studies, & therfore now Collect many things uselesse, heterogenus raw, Common, and Childish, w:^{ch} in a riper Judgment you would be ashamed vexed to have your Common places filled with, wheras in such an one as is here described when you are come to maturitie of Judgement, and have pitched upon your Profession, you may avoyd this inconvenience referring to your Commonplace booke only what you like in your former Collections, & Omitting all the rest.

Of Hearing Acts Sermons
Speeches &c.

Endeavour to remember something at least, and if y° can the most remarkable things, in every dispute, Lecture Sermon, Speech, or Discourse, w:^{ch} you shall heare & when you come into your studie write them downe in one of these paper bookes w:^{ch} you have for Collections, and after the same manner, that so if need be y°: may referre any of them allso, to y^r Common place booke hereafter.

Here Names of Com'nPl: Book Autho^{es}
[in a different hand but perhaps only the rougher hand of the same person]

General Directions
Of Idlenes, & Neglect of Studies

It's strange methinks that any whome either his own or his friends intentions have designed for a Scholar, should by a Carelesse neglect of studies, prove a Dunce in Learning. For besides that he must never expect content or credit in the world, it's the greatest reproche, & disgrace that may be, even among the Vulgare, & illiterate, to goe for a Dunce: and among Scholars he shall never dare to speake, or entertain any discourse but must sit by with a dejected nose, & a downe Countenance, in a continual fear least he be engaged to betray his ignorance, & many times is fain to take patiently the taunts, and reproches of such as discover him. Whence it most Commonlie comes to passe, that such an one finding no content, either in his studies, or in Scholars companie, begins to hate both and turning Sott & Clown, is company for every Coblar, in a blinde Alehouse, or at least is drawn in by some half witted fellow like himself to some new ridiculous oppinions, & turns Tubpreacher, & Sectary. It is a wonder I say that so many young Students doe Concider of this no better than they doe. And the reason is this neglect, and carelesnes steales upon them insensiblie, & by degrees, till at length it begrown to an habit, & getts such a sway & Command over them that they can not till it be too late recover themselves out of it, w:^{ch} at the first might easily have bin prevented.

You shall often find a listlessnesse upon your selfe not to leave your Pastime, & companie, & goe to your studie at due houres, & be prone to thinke to stay but half an houre, or an houre longer, for once, & use it not, can be no great harme. This listlesse humour must not be yeilded to, leaste it growe upon you, as it will in a short time. have but so much command over your self as to step into your studie, & get your book in your hand and it is allready gone. the same may be sayd of sleeping in the mornings, and the consequence is as dangerous: You shall often repent you lye still, but shall never repent you are Risen, or desire to be in bed agin. Step but out of bed & the danger is over.

Many loose or great deale of time in visiting, w:^{ch} must be avoyded as much as may be. A little acquaintance in the University is enough; & if you will not be interupted by frequent visits. the only way is to be sparing in them your self to others.

Take heed of loosing your time at your first coming to the University as many doe, for he that's once cast be hind hand with those of his own standing, is soon disheartend in his progresse, & so put out of conceit with his studies, that he seldome proves a Scholar.

Young Scholars lately come from the Grammar schoole & finding themselves now at more liberty than formerly have seldome discretion to use it a right, till it be too late, wheras they are to task, & limit themselves to theyr studies & resolve to use all possible means & endeavours to be the best scholars, though they had neither Tutor, nor Governor to look over them, and they y^t will not doe this are but

Children yett, & fitter to be under the lash & ferula then in an University, where he that will studie no more then what he is constrained to doe is sure to prove a Dunce.

Take heed of neglecting any kinde of studie because they seem more difficult then the rest; as making exercises & getting them without booke, for most commonly, as the pains to the benefit in such kind of studies is greater; & besides they bring this advantage over & above, that by reason of those, your Other studies will seem more easy; & delitefull, & y° will goe to them with more readynes then you would otherwise have done.

Be over carefull to performe your Acts well, that you may be encouraged by the applause, & not put out of conceit with your studies by discredit and reproche, for that causes many to throwe their studies quicke asyde, & seek for content in other things.

Of Debauch'd Carriage, &
Ill Company

Young Students that are well inclined, will think perhaps they stand not in need of any caution against ill companie, or debauch'd carriage, seeing in their present thought they abhorre nothing more, but these as they are to be commended for theyr good resolutions so they are to be admonishd not to be too confident of themselves, for many intending nothing less, have often by the trecherie of their own nature bin corrupted & changed before they were a ware. And indeed none can be so far blind, & mad, whiles they are yet sober and unbesotted with debaucherie, as to intend or desire to turne Rakells w:^{ch} were nothing else but willfullie to cast themselves into contempt & beggery for all theire life after. for that wee see is the certaine fate of Scholars, that either are or have bin such; their best preferment must be some mean place, w:^{ch} will scarce find them threadbare cloaths, & Tabacco, lett their parts and Learning be never so good, want of goverment, & sober carriage will keep them as much from preferment as ignorance and duncery. It is a known, & an ordinarie observation that very few or none that have bin cried up for the greatest wits & parts in the University, have ever come to any conciderable preferment, or credible way of living if they were addicted to drinking & Ill companie.

Nay a bad Scholar of sober carriage & behaviour, shall sooner be preferr'd then a Rakell with the greatest parts. such an one while he is young may make a shift to borrow money to warme his brain in the Alehouse, & be cried up by the Tapster & his Comrades to be a noble Gent: a Witt a Scholar. But if scape the Feavour, the Dropsie, the Pox, & live a little longer, his end must be either a sorry Pedant, or some sottish Sr John in a Country village the scorne, & contempt of the parish

And though he be one that hath means enough otherwise, & doth not depend for a livelyhood upon his Learning, or Behaviour, yet must he not thinke this wise without inconveniences: He that will sitt tipling in a Tavern, & be drunk, shall never finde that respect & authoritie amongst those where he lives, w:^{ch} men of sober carriage doe. And it's usualy observed that men addicted to this vice, though otherwise of good parts, are more shallow, & inconciderate in their Councils, & more uneffectual, & unsuccessfull in Busynes.

I speake nothing of the Sorrowe, & tears of carefull Parents who expected comfort: & the disrespect of friends who are ashamed to owne you: the joy of Enemies to see you such an one as they would have you to be: and w:^{ch} is most of all to be concidered, the inevitable danger, unless God in his Mercie reclaime you of Eternal Damnation of Hell fire.

The evils of this unfortunate course of life are so evident that any one would wonder he should so far forgett himself, as either to fall into it, or being in it, not immediatlie to hast out of it againe. But the Nature of it is such, that it changes their very minde & Judgment so that wheras before they approved a stayd carriage tooke delight in their studies, and Instructors, now they find no content or delight in them; thinke no life happie or amiable but that of Good Fellows in a Tavern and deride all as simple and dull people that seek to reclaime them by good councel.

Before they are thus besotted and bewitch'd with it were the time to prevent it; but then allso it steales upon them by insensible steps and engageth them before they are aware; & therfore I say the safest way is not for any one to be too confident of their own strength and resolutions against it so as to be carelesse & secure in this particular, least they stumble where so many have faln.

These are the signes of one that is warping this way. He begins to be out of conceit with a sober, retired way of life and thinks he ought to indulge with Mirth, Pastime, & Libertie. He counts constant hard students a kinde of simple flat heads, and fears least he should prove such an one himself. He begins to have a favourable oppinion of Rakells and doth not love to have them calld so.

He hath now perhaps bin at the Tavern once or twice and thinks there is no great Harme in it, & that he may Lawfully doe it now and then with Moderation.

He thinks he gains much by Discourse and that this will quicken his Wit, & Parts, & make him compay for men of Quality; when as otherwise he should be but a Sheep a Meer Scholar.

These Falacies have made many Rakels, and he that findes in himself any of those signes is in a suspicious way to be one, if he doe not forth with fall close agin to his studies & sobernes of disposition and carriage. And the worst signe of all is, if he will not Beleive me when I tell him so; The misery of it is indeed that none knows or will be persuaded that he is growing a Rakell while he is growing, and when he is come to be one, he thinks it better to be so than otherwise.

PROPOSED LIBRARY FOR YOUNG STUDENTS (c. 1655) From "A Library for Young Schollers Compiled by an English Scholar-Priest about 1655," as quoted in Alma Dejordy and Harris Fletcher, eds., *Illinois Studies in Language and Literature* (Urbana, Ill., 1961), vol. XLVIII, pp. 1-11.

$\mathbf{F}$or the furnishing your Library (for younger Schollers) with Bookes of Historie, Chronologie &C. with Authors in all the Arts, & Liberall Sciences, with Criticks, & Antiquaries &C. I suppose it is not your Designe, or intention, to buy all of each kinde; & that you have neither a minde, nor mony, for such a vast Collection. And therfore I shall onely name you some Authors, which to mee (& possibly may to others) seeme of more necessary use. As for Example.

1. In Logique.
    1. Phillippus de Trier his Manductio ad Logicam. Herbipoli. 1641. that's the Last Edition (for it hath been often printed) 'tis a short, & a rationall Systeme of Logicke.
    2. Martinus Smiglecius.
    3. Ruvio.
    4. Ant: Rubij Logica Mexicana.
    5. Tolletus.
    6. Zabarell.
    7. Hurtado.
    8. Collegium Conimbricensis, Complutensis.
    9. D. Masius.
    10. Paulus Vallius's Societ: Jesu. fol. Lugd. 1622.
    Note. 1. That I conceave Masius & Vallius, have the most, & easiest arguments, & soe, (by reason of their perspicuitie) best, for Beginners.
    2. That Smiglecius, Ruvio, Rubius, Tolet, Zabarell, are more exact, & rationall, & therfore fittest for persons of little more maturitie.
    3. That Hurtado hath more difficultie, & subtiltie then the rest, and th[e]rfore will require a Reader of more standing, & vnderstanding, then other Authors; with him I reckon Scotus in vniversam Logicam, his Quaest: in Porphyrium, Quaestiones in Lib. prior & Posteriorum. &C.
    4. That there are many particular Tracts, not in vniversam Logicam, but writ of purpose in some particular head. As
        1. Scheiblers Topicks.
        2. Flavells Demonstrations.
        3. Griffin Powells Analyticorum Posteriorum Analysis, or, his Demonstrations.
        4. Eiusdem liber de sophisticis Elenchis.
        5. Elenchj Sophisticj, by Fausto Socinus, acutely done, good for any, best for a Divine, because hee gives Examples, & Instances in Divinitie.
        6. Promptuarium argumentorum by Pet. de Alliaco.
        7. Alexand. Aphrodissaej Topica, analytica. Elenchj, Graeco-Lat:
    5. That the best Arguments, & Discourses of many parts of Logick (as the Praedicables, Praedicaments &C. are in Suarez, & others

that write Metaphysicks.

6. Because the most of these Books of Logique wee vse, were written by Popish Authors, who that they may defend their wild, & senselesse position of Transubstantiation in Divinitie, are necessitated to mainteine many irrationall, & inconsistent Assertions in Logick, especially about the nature of Proprium, & Accidens, & of Quantitie; It will concerne the Younger Students to consider before they consent to what they say in those particulars.

2. In Ethicks, or Morall Philosophy.

    1. Pavonius, it is an ingenious summe of Ethicks.
       Crellij Ethices elementa Racoviae. 1635.
       Prodijt non adeo pridem, Cerellij
    2. Case. vid. Joh. Ethica, se moralis doctrina in. 4to.
       opus doctum & perspicuum.
    3. Buridan.
    4. Suarez.
    5. Piccolominaeus.
    6. Hen. Velstonij [sic for Velstenij] Centuria Quaest: Ethic. Witteberg. 4to. 1611. & postea Giessae, 8vo. 1620.
    7. Conimbrisensis Collegij Disputationes. 4to.
    8. Adoardj Gualandj Methodus Moralis Philosophiae absolutissima. fol. Venet: 1604.
    9. Jacob Martinj Disputationes Ethicae. 8vo. Witteberg. 1624.
   10. Aristotelis Ethica per Magirum, aut Riccobonum.

Note. 1. That for the Speculative & Disputeing part of Ethicks, the best Arguments, & Discourses are not to bee found in these Books, nor in any such, but in the Schoolemen, such as

    1. Aquinas in. 22ae. of his Summes.
    2. In his Commentators, such as
        1. Gabriel Vasquez.
        2. Greg. de Valentia.
        3. Joh. Malderus.
        4. Didacus Alvarez.
        5. Fran: Cumet.
        6. Greg. Martinez, &C. In which Authors all Morall quaestions are fully, & acutely discusd.

2. That for the Positive part of Moralitie; there are many excellent Authors, not Christians onely, but Pagans too, very well worth the haveing, & perusall, such as

    1. Plutarchs Moralls.
    2. Plato.
    3. Seneca the Philosopher
    4. All Tullyes Tracts, as de Officijs &C.
    5. Epictetus with Simplicius, & Arrianus, put out by Salmasius.
    6. Hierocles in $\chi \rho \upsilon \sigma \epsilon \alpha$ $\epsilon \pi \eta$ Pythagorae.
    7. Maximus Tyrius.
    8. Vita Antoninj Imperatoris per seipsum, &C.
    9. Stobaeus, an excellent, & Classicall Author, of his you have
        1. Loci Communes. Graeco-Lat: Fr. 1581.
        2. Eclogae Graeco-Lat: 1575.
        3. Sententiae Graeco-Lat: 1608.

10. Andronicij Rhodij libellusπερι παθων editus vna cum Anonymo, de virtutib. & Vitijs: August. Vindelicorum apud Nich: Mangerum.

11. Videsis etiam, Sapientiae Moralis praecepta, & paraenesis a Veterib. Sapientib. tradita, & in vnum volumen ex M.Stis. Codicib. collecta, atque edita cum notis Melch. Goldastj. in. 4to. Hannoviae. 1612.

12. Vide etiam Ethicorum Aristotelis ad Nicomachum paraphrasin, Gr. & Lat: editam per D. Herensium in. 4to. Lugd. Batav. 1607.

13. Salustinj Philosophus de Dijs, & Mundo. Grae. Lat: per Leonem Allatium, vna cum Demophilj, Democratis, & Secundj, veterum Philosophorum Sententijs Moralib. Lugd. Bat. 1639. in 12mo. Aureus Libellus.

3. For Physicks, or Naturall Philosophy (after Aristotle) such as these.

1. Ruvio.   ⎫   Inter Antiquos videris Alexand. Aphrodisaeum de
2. Tollet.   ⎬   Mixtione, de Meteoris, de Anima, & Fato, de sensu
3. Pererius   ⎭   & sensibilj. &C. extant Graece, & Latine omnia.

4. Jac. Carpentarij descriptionis vniversae naturae pars prior, & pars posterior, de Plantis, & Animalib. in 4to. vtraque pars Parisijs prodijt, haec, Anno. 1565. illa An. 1560.

5. Aegidij Romanj Commentationes in Libros Physicorum, de Generatione & Corrupt. Meteororum, de Anima, Parva Naturalia &C. Anno. 1604. Vrsellis.

6. Joh. Duns Scotj in. 8. libros Physicorum Aristotelis in. 4to. Colon. 1518. [sic for 1618].

7. Jac. Martinj Theorematum Phisicorum generalium, recitationes decem. Witteberg. 1604. in 4to.

8. Theodorj Merochitae Philosophj in vniversam Aristotelis naturalem Philosophiam, Commentaria vere aurea Grae: Lat: per Gentianum Heruetum. in 4to. Lugd. 1625.

9. Bannes de Generatione & Corrupt.

10. Fromundj Meteora; the best of that subiect extant.

11. Joh. Chrysostomj Magnenj, Democritus reviviscens, seu vita, & Philosophia Democritj. Lugd. Bat. 1648. You may adde to these, Gassendus, Des-Cartes, Digby, White, Bacons Naturall History, or Centuries of Experiments.

4. For Metaphysicks, I say

1. That Aristotles Metaphysicks is the most impertinent Booke (sit venia) in all his works; indeed, a rapsodie of Logicall scraps.

2. Soncinas.

3. Petrus Fonseca.

4. Scheiblerus.

5. Jacob. Martinj partitiones, & quaestiones Metaphysicae. Witteberg. 1615.

6. Corn: Martinj Metaphysica. Jenae. 1623.

8. [sic] Dominicj a Flandria quaestiones in. 12. lib. Metaphysicae Aristotelis.

9. Fran. Suarez.

5. For Mathematicks, I referre you to the Professers of those Sciences, who, as their knowledge is more, soe (I am confident) their Charitie

will not bee lesse, in communicateing their Directions in this particular.

6. For Chronologie, there are infinite Authors, you may consult these & such like, (who wrote de *parte technica Cronologiae.*

1. Paulj Crusij liber de Epochis, seu Annis Temporum, & Imperiorum. Basil. 8vo. 1578.
2. Scaliger de Emendatione Temporum.
3. Thomas Lydyat his Tractatus de varijs Annorum formis, Wherein hee meets with, & manifests the mistakes, of Scaliger, and Clavius. 8vo. Lond. 1605.
4. Dionysij Petavij opus de doctrina Temporum. in. 2. vol. Paris. 1627. a large, & very learned worke, wherein hee takes Jos. Scaliger to taske (as Lydyat did) & discovers his oversight, only his Inke hath too much gall in it.
5. Dionysij Petavij rationarium Temporum. 2. vol. in. 8vo. Paris, 1636.
6. Alphonsus a Caranza scripsit contra Petavium, & suum Temporis rationarium.
7. Lilius Giraldus de Annis, & mensib.
8. vid. Christoph. Clavium, & Michael Maestlonum in scriptis adversarijs de Calendario Romano. Clavius his Computus Ecclesiasticus, is a very ingenious & vseful Tract, 'tis sometimes by it selfe, sometimes at the end of his Apologia pro Calendario Romano. Rom: 1588. 'tis also translated into English, but rarely to bee found.
9. Jos. Zerlinus [*sic*, usually Zarlinus] de vera Annj forma, seu de certa eius emendatione. 4to. Venet.
10. Phil. Melanchthon de mensib. Graecorum.
11. Theod. Gaza de mensib. Atticis, Latio donatus Johanne Perello interpret. quj nonnulla adiunxit de Epactis, de Anno Intercalarj Attico. &C.
12. There be many others have writ of the Technicall part of Chronologie, & well worth the haveing, when they may conveniently bee got, as for Example. Hadrianus Junius de Anno Mensib. et Fastis. &C. Joseph Lartinus de vera Annj forma. Bernard Hederus de Anno, eiusque partib. & accidentib. David Origanus in the begining of his Ephemerides, Conradus Pawell his Concilium Chronologicum. 4to. Basil. 1627. &C. Besides these Technicall writers it will be convenient that you get some of those Practicall Authors, who write Chronology either $\kappa\alpha\theta$' $\dot{o}\mu\acute{a}\delta\alpha$ or $\kappa\alpha\tau\grave{a}$ $\pi\lambda\alpha\tau o\varsigma$ (as the Greeks call it) such as these.

1. Helvicus, Editionis vltimae, a Book of perpetuall, & necessarie vse.
2. Sethus Calvisius.
3. Funcius.
4. Jas. Vsserius Armachanus.
5. Ed. Simpson his Chronicon Catholicum nuperrime editum, opus sane doctum, & posteris profuturum. &C.

7. For Historians, they will bee of infinite vse for your Library, & Learneing, such as. 1. Herodòtus. 2. Thucidides. 3. Xenophon. 4. Polybius.

5. Diodorus Siculus. 6. D. Cassius. 7. Dion: Halicarnassaeus. 8. Plutarch. And amongst the Latines such as Livy, Tacitus, Suetonius, Ammianus Marcellinus, Sulpitius Severus, Herodianus, All the Scriptores Historiae Augustae. &C. But for Histories.

1. I shall referre you to Mr. Deg. Wheares Methodus Historiae, where you have an exact enumeration both of Greeke, & Latine Historians. (Gerardj Johannis Vossij opus de Historicis Latinis. 4to. Et de Historicis Graecis. 1. 4. Lugd. Bat: 1650. are incomparably the best, most learned, and most vsefull for this purpose) & Latine Historians, his Censure vpon them, & the methode, & order of Reading of them.

2. I shall advise you (when you buy) to buy the best Editions, for you will finde infinite benefitt by that, both by the goodnesse of the Print, the incorruptnesse of the Text, & the advantage of the Notes. As for instance.

   1. Tacitus of Lipsius his Edition, & with his Notes; or, ex recognitione Janj Gruterj, cum Notis Alciatj, Ferrettj, Vrsinj, Mercerj, Collerj, Rhenanj, Vertranij, Donatj, & Pichevae [sic for Pichenae]. Fr. 1607.
   2. Scriptores Historiae Augustae of Causabons [sic for Casaubons] Edition at Paris, 1603.
   3. Sulpitius Severus of Georg. Horius [sic for Hornius] his Edition. Lugd. Bat. 1647. Soe of the rest.

3. In reading of Historie (besides Chronologie, of which before) there will bee a necessitie of Geography, that you mistake not by reason of the many different names of Places, & Countryes, of Cittyes, Rivers, Mountaines &C. you have many Authors of good note, which will bee very helpful to you in this particular. For Example.

   1. Abr. Ortelij thesaurus Geographicus, an excellent worke, instar ominum.
   2. Stephanus Byzantinus de Vrbib.
   3. Aethicj Geographia antiqua. Paris. 1577.1.
   4. Ptolomaej Geographia Grae-Lat: per G. Mercatorem & P. Montanum.
   5. Strabo cum notis Casaubonj, & tabula totius orbis. An. 1587.
   6. Antoninj Augustj itinerarium, cum Comment: Hieron: Saritae [sic for Suritae]. Col. 1600.
   7. Jos. Scaligerj Nomenclator Geographicus ad calcem Commentariorum Caesaris.
   8. Theatrum vrbium per Adrianum Romanum.
   9. Phil. Ferrarij Lexicon Geographicum. 4to. Mediolanj. 1627.
   10. Onomasticon Geographicum per Gul. Xilandrum.
   11. Georgraphia Nubiensis per Gab. Sionitam. Paris. 1619.
   12. Itinerarium totius orbis cum Auctario Nic: Reusnerj. Basil. 1502. [sic for 1592].
   13. Vide Geographica. 1. Marcianj Heracleotae. 2. Sculacis Caryandensis. 3. Artemedorj Ephesij. 4. Dicaearchj Messaenij. 5. Isiodorj Characaenj. per Dav: Hoeschaelium. August. Vindelicorum. 1600. in 8vo.

8. For Oratores such as these will well become your Library.

1. Demosthenes Graeco-Lat; cum Comm: Vlpianj, & Annotat: Hier. Wolphij. Bas. (1527) 1572.
2. Isocrates Gr. Lat: cum Annot: Hieron; Wolphij. Bas. 1576.
3. Themistius Gr: Lat: ex Editione. D. Petavij. Paris. 1618.
4. Julianus Imperator. cum Notis D. Petavij. Paris. 1630.
5. Libanij Sophistae Declamationes Grae: Lat: Paris. 1601.
6. Oratorum praestantissimorum Graeciae, Antiphontis, Andocidis, & Isaej orationes. xxx. Item, Orationes politicas Dinarchj, Lesbonactis, Lycurgi, Herodis, Dematis, vno vol. Graece & Lat: edidit Alphonsus Miniatus. Hannoviae. 1629.
7. Orationes Aelij Aristidis, gr: & Lat: tribus tomis edidit Gulielmus Canterus. An. 1604.
8. Orationes Aeschinis cum alijs. 12. Rhetorum orationib. extant in fol. Venet. apud Aldum.
9. Lysiae Atheniensis (vnius ex. 10. Graeciae oratorib.) orationes. 34. (tot solum de. 300. supersunt) de Graecis Latine reddita, & notis illustratae a Jodoco Vander Heidio. in. 8vo. Hannoviae. 1615.
10. Ciceronis, Quintilianj, Livij &C. orationes. There bee infinite more of this kind, by Authors both antient, & moderne, of whom you may finde a long Catalogue in Bibliotheca Classica Georgij Draudij. tom. 2. verbo. Orationes. pagin: 1440. 1441.
    You may adde to these such Authors as write of the art, & nature of of [sic] Oratory, such as, D.
    1. Longinus περι υψους Edit: vlt. gr. lat. cum notis G. Langbanij.
    2. Hermogines his τεχνη ρητορικη τελιοταιτη cum versione Latina,
       & Comment: Gasp. Laurentij. Col. Alobrogum. An. 1614.
    3. Claudij Galenj Pergamenj de optimo dicendj liber contra Academicos & Pyrrhonios. fol. Antw. Plant.
    4. Dionys. Halicarnassaeus, de Charecterib. antiquorum Orator. de Compositione Orationis, & Elocutione, Praecepta de oratione Panygyrica, Nuptialj, Natalitia, & Epithalamijs, per M. Antonium Antimachum. Bas. 1639.

9. For Poets.
   1. You have an exact collection of all the Graeke Poets in. 2. folioe's, with all the Fragments of them extant, in Gr. & Lat: Printed at Geneva. An. 1614. a Booke fitt for a Studie, or Librarye, as conteineing many particulars noe where else to bee gott.
   2. You have Corpus omnium Veterum Poetarum Latinorum, secundum seriem temporum, in quinque Libris distinctum. in. 4to. Genevae. 1611.
   3. If you had these in your Library, yet it would bee of singular vse & advantage, to have the severall Poets, both of Gr. & Latine of the best Editions, with the Scholia, & Annotations. For Example, such as these.
      1. Homer, with Eustathius his παρεκβολαι. Edit: Romae. enough of it selfe to make a man a Graecian, not only for the words, but for the Mores Graeciae, Civiles, & Sacrj, their τελαται μοστικαι, their ritus solennes, indeed, the whole

antiquitie of Greece; besides, it hath a most compleat, &
excellent Index, made by Debares, which is an absolute
Lexicon Homericum, & directs you to every word, &
the vse of it both in Homer himselfe, & Eustathius his
παρεκβολαι.

2. Hesiod, Lycophron &C. with the scholia of Isaac Tzetzes;
   soe Euripides, Sophocles, Pindar &C. with their Scholia; soe
   Nicander, with the Annotations of Joh. Gorraeus in Latine;
   & the Greeke scholia incertj Authoris; soe Virgill with Servius
   (his best Scholiast) & those others printed with him; soe
   Plautus (with the large, & good Notes) of Dionys. Lambinus
   his Edition, Genev. 1622. & soe for the rest.

3. You have an excellent Collection of the Greek Epigrammatists
   in. 7. Bookes, Greeke & Latine, cum Annotationib. Joh.
   Brodaej, Vincentij Opsopaej, Hen: Stephanj, in fol. Franc.
   An. 1600.

4. All those Poets put out by Farnaby (as Virgill, Seneca, Martiall
   &C are for the text, beyond any Edition, & for the
   Notes, though short, yet hardly any better.1.

5. And to this head concerneing Poets, I shall referre two peices
   of Hugo Grotius, Librj quantivis redimendj.
   1. Dicta Poetarum quae apud Stobaeum extant, emendata,
      & Latino carmine reddita ab Hug: Grotio; quib. accesserunt
      Plutarch, & Basilij Magnj de vsu Graecorum Poetarum
      Libellj. Paris. 1623.
   2. Excepta ex Tragoedijs, & Comoedijs Graecis tum quae
      extant, tum quae perierunt; emendata, & Latinis versib.
      reddita ab Hugone Grotio; The Authors out of which
      those Excepta are taken, are above. 100. most of which,
      had aeternally perished. Nisi tantillas tot Scriptorum
      Relliquias alias immature intermorituras, vrnis &
      funerj superstites, in Grotius manu vindice posteritatj
      commendasset. Hee hath Notes, & exact Indices to each
      worke, & hee hath rendred them in a stile soe high, &
      excellent, that (had hee not told vs in his Title page) it
      is hard to tell which is the Translation. This last, was
      printed in. 4to. at Paris. 1626.

These I conceave the most convenient Authors, for this purpose, there
are infinite more, which (if you have a mind & mony,) may bee gott
for your Library. You may find a Catalogue of them in Georg:
Draudius his Bibliotheca Classica, parte. 2, verbo Poesis, & Poeta pag.
1577. 1578. 1579.

10. For Epistles (& there are many Collections of them worthy a Library,
    & the study, & industry of Yonger Students) these, & such like are
    considerable,
    1. Epistolae Hippocratis, Democratj, Heraclitj, Diogenis, &
       Crateris, Gr: Lat: in 8vo. Heidelbergae. 1600.
    2. Aristaenetj Epistolae Grae: Lat: cum notis. 8vo. Paris. 1601.
    3. Isocratis Epistolae aliquot in. 4to. Argent: 1568.
    4. Julianj Apostatae Epistolae Gr: Lat. Paris. in. 8vo. 1565.
    5. Philostratj Lemnij Epist: in 8vo. Lugd Bat: 1616.

6. Platonis Epist: Gr: Lat: cum eruditissimis Notis, Logicis, Opticis, Politicis. Colon. 1600. in 8vo.

7. Apollonij Thyanaej, Anacharsidis, Euripedis, Theanus Epist: a Jac: Lectio editae in. 8vo. 1601.

8. Marcj Brutj Phalaridis, & Mithridatis Epist: Gr. Lat: in 8vo. apud Hier. Commelinum. 1597.

9. Photij Patriarchae Constantinorum *(sic)* Epistolae, Latine redittae, et notis illustratae per R. Monntacutium Episcopum olim Norvicensem in fol. Lond. 1651. quem consule Epistola. 207. pa. 305. vbj (inter praecipuas) laudat Phalaridis, & M. Brutj Epistolas et tum postea, Libanij, Julianj &C. Epistolas.

10. Epistolae Graecanicae mutuae antiquorum Rhetorum, Philosophor. Oratorum, Regum, Imperatorum &C Latio donatae a Jac: Cuiacio. fol. Aureliae Allobrogum. 1606. quo volumine Authorum. 140. Epistolae continentur opus eximium, & quantivis redimendum.

11. M. T. Ciceronis Epistolae Familiares ad Atticum, & Q. Fratrem, quarum infinitae pene Editiones, quas vide apud Georg. Draudium Bibliothecae Classicae Vol. 2. verbo. Epistolae, pag. 1362. 1363. &C.

12. C. Plinij Secundj Epistolae, cum Annotationib. Joh: Mariae Catanej in. 4to. Gen:

13. Eiusdem & Traianj Imperatoris Epist: Amaeboae, item eiusdem Plinij & Pacatj, Mamertinj, Nazarij Panegyricj. &C. cum Notis Isaacj Casaubonj. 4to. Genev: 1599.

14. Plinij Junioris Epistolae cum Commentarijs. fol. Basil.

15. Lucij Annaej Senecae Epistolae. 123. cum Notis Muretj, & Gruterj 8vo. Genev: 1594. Eiusdem ad Lucilium Epistolarum liber, cum Notis Muretj, Pintianj, Erasmj, Opsopaej, Gruterj, & Juretj, in. 8vo. 1604.

16. Aurelij Symmachj Epistolarum ad diversos, librj. 10. cum notis Jac: Lectij. JC. in 8vo. Genev: 1587.

17. Epistolae Regum, Principum, Rerumpub. & Sapientum virorum. 8vo. Argent: 1592.

18. Selectiores Epae. clarorum virorum. P. Bembj, Jac: Saboletj, [sic] Christ: Longolij, Paul Manutij &C. in. 3. libros digestae &C. in. 8vo. Antuer. 1574.

19. Illustrium virorum Epistolae selectiores, superiorj seculo scriptae, vel a Belgis, vel ad Belgas. Lugd. Bat: in. 8vo. 1617.

20. Melch. Goldastj Philologicarum Epist: Cent: vna, cum Epistola Bessarionis, Petrarch: [sic for Patriarch:] Constantinopol. ad Senatum Venetum. in. 8vo. An: 1610.

21. Epist: Erasmj, Melanchthonis, T. Morj, Ludovici Vivis, editae a Cor. Bec. [sic for Bee], duob. vol. fol. Lond. An. 1642. opus eximium et posteris profuturum.

22. Hugonis Grotij (του πανν κι μακαριτου) Epistolae ad Gallos Lugd. Bat: 1648. Alij prostant infinitj pene Epistolarum Libellulj, Lipsij sc: Scaligerj, Puteanj, Woverij, Gilb: Cognatj, Paraej & quos nec numerare licet, nedum perlegere.

11. Among other Books of Humane Learneing (for this Paper meddles not with Divinity, the great Mistress (cuj omnes Literae humaniores

ex officio famulantur) Your Library must not want Grammarians, and Criticks, those Authors which explaine antient wordes, & things; such as explaine Insolentes dicendj formulas, Ritus gentium solenness, & grandaevas rerum origines a seculo nostro longe remotas. And in this kind there are infinite Authors, & collections of Antiquityes, which may bee of excellent vse to those, who have a mind to read, & mony to buy the Bookes, some (of more convenient note) I shall commend vnto you, as

1. Janus Gruterus his thesaurus Criticus, or Lampas Artium Liberalium. Fr: 1602.
2. Eiusdem Inscriptiones antiquae, cum notis Tyronis, ac Senecae in Bibl. Bodliana. G. 5. 10.
3. Guidonis Pancirollj rerum Memorabilium seu de perditarum, tom: 2. cum Comment: Hen: Salmuth. Fr. 1629.
4. Notitia Dignitatum vtriusque Imperij, Orientis sc: & Occidentis, vltra Arcadij, Honorijque tempora, cum Guidonis Pancerollj Commentarijs. fol. Gen. 1623.
5. Ludov: Coelij Rhodiginj Lectionum Antiquar. lib. 30. fol. Francof: 1599.
6. Janj Gulielmj Laurembergij Antiquarius, in quo praeter antiqua, & obsoleta verba, ac voces minus vsetatas, dicendj formulae insolentes, ritus plurimj Populo Romano, & Graecis peculiares docte exponuntur. Francof: 1623.
7. Hen: Canisij Antiquae Lectiones, Ingolstadij. 1604.
8. Ludovicj Carrionis Antiquarum Lectionum Commentarij. 3s. 8vo. Antwerp. 1576. Marculfus de Formulis, & Bar. Brissonius de Formulis, And Auctores Linguae Latinae in vnum Corpus redactj, cum Notis Dio: Gothofredj, An. 1633. in. 4to. may bee added to these, as Bookes of excellent, & dayly vse.
9. Eilhardj Lubinj Antiquarius, seu priscorum, & invsitatorum vocabulorum interpretatio, ordine Alphabetico. France: 1625.
10. Justj Lipsij antiquarum Lectionum Commentarius, quo varia scriptorum loca, praesertim Plautj, illustrantur. Antwerp. 8vo. 1572.

*   *   *

The Age of Science — England

FRANCIS BACON DESCRIBES THE NEW LEARNING (1605)   From Francis Bacon, *The Advancement of Learning,* as quoted in Joseph Devey, ed., *The Physical and Metaphysical Works of Lord Bacon* (London, 1872), pp. 71-77.

To the King

It is befitting, excellent King, that those who are blessed with a numerous offspring, and who have a pledge in their descendants that their name will be carried down to posterity, should be keenly alive to the welfare of future times, in which their children are to perpetuate their power and empire. Queen Elizabeth, with respect to her celibacy, was rather a sojourner than an inhabitant of the present world, yet she was an ornament to her age and prosperous in many of her undertakings. But to your Majesty, whom God has blessed with so much royal issue, worthy to immortalize your name, it particularly appertains to extend your cares beyond the present age, which is already illuminated with your wisdom, and extend your thoughts to those works which will interest remotest posterity. Of such designs, if affection do not deceive me, there is none more worthy and noble than the endowment of the world with sound and fruitful knowledge. For why should a few favourite authors stand up like Hercules' Columns, to bar further sailing and discovery, especially since we have so bright and benign a star in your Majesty to guide and conduct us?

It remains, therefore, that we consider the labours which princes and others have undertaken for the advancement of learning, and this markedly and pointedly, without digression or amplification. Let it then be granted, that to the completion of any work munificent patronage is as essential as soundness of direction and conjunction of labours. The first multiplies energy, the second prevents error, and the third compensates for human weakness. But the principal of these is direction, or the pointing out and the delineation of the direct way to the completion of the object in view. For "claudus in via antevertit cursorem extra viam;" and Solomon appositely says, "If the iron is not pointed, greater strength is to be used;"—so what really prevaileth over everything is wisdom, by which he insinuates that a wise selection of means leads us more directly to our object than a straining or accumulation of strength. Without wishing to derogate from the merit of those who in any way have advanced learning, this much I have been led to say, from perceiving that their works and acts have tended rather to the glory of their name than the progression or proficiency of the sciences,—to augment the man of learning in the minds of philosophers, rather than reform or elevate the sciences themselves.

The institutions which relate to the extension of letters are threefold, viz., schools and universities, books, and professors. For as water, whether of the dew of heaven or spring of the earth, would speedily lose itself in the ground unless collected into conduits and cisterns, so it seemeth this excellent liquor of knowledge, whether it descend from Divine inspiration or spring from human sense, would soon hide itself in oblivion, unless collected in books, traditions, academies, and schools, it might find a permanent seat, and a fructifying union of strength.

The works which concern the seats of learning are four,—buildings, endowments, privileges, and charters, which all promote quietness and seclusion, freedom from cares and anxieties. Such stations resemble those which Virgil prescribes for beehiving:—

> Principio sedes apibus, statioque petenda
> Quo neque sit ventis aditus.

The works which relate to books are two,—first, libraries, which are as the shrines where the bones of old saints full of virtue lie buried; secondly, new editions of writers, with correcter impressions, more faultless versions, more useful commentaries, and more learned annotations.

Finally, the works which pertain to the persons of the learned are, besides the general patronage which ought to be extended to them, twofold. The foundation of professorships in sciences already extant, and in those not yet begun or imperfectly elaborated.

These are, in short, the institutions on which princes and other illustrious men have displayed their zeal for letters. To me, dwelling upon each patron of letters, that notion of Cicero occurs, which urged him upon his return not to particularize, but to give general thanks,—"Difficile non aliquem, in gratum quenquam, praeterire." Rather should we, conformably to Scripture, look forward to the course we have yet to run, than regard the ground already behind us.

First, therefore, I express my surprise, that among so many illustrious colleges in Europe, all the foundations are engrossed by the professions, none being left for the free cultivation of the arts and sciences. Though men judge well who assert that learning should be referred to action, yet by reposing too confidently in this opinion, they are apt to fall into the error of the ancient fable, which represented the members of the body at war with the stomach, because it alone, of all the parts of the frame, seemed to rest, and absorb all the nourishment. For if any man esteem philosophy and every study of a general character to be idle, he plainly forgets that on their proficiency the state of every other learning depends, and that they supply strength and force to its various branches. I mainly attribute the lame progress of knowledge hitherto to the neglect or the incidental study of the general sciences. For if you want a tree to produce more than its usual burden of fruit, it is not anything you can do to the branches that will effect this object, but the excitation of the earth about its roots and increasing the fertility of the soil; nor must it be overlooked that this restriction of foundations and endowments to professional learning has not only dwarfed the growth of the sciences, but been prejudicial to states and governments themselves. For since there is no collegiate course so free as to allow those who are inclined to devote themselves to history, modern languages, civil policy, and general literature; princes find a dearth of able men to manage their affairs and efficiently conduct the business of the commonwealth.

Since the founders of colleges plant, and those who endow them water, we are naturally led to speak in this place of the mean salaries apportioned to public lectureships, whether in the sciences or the arts. For such offices being instituted not for an ephemeral purpose, but for the constant transmission and extension of learning, it is of the utmost importance that the men selected to fill them be learned and gifted. But it is idle to expect that the ablest scholars will employ their whole energy and time in such functions unless the reward be answerable to that competency which may be expected from the practice of a profession. The sciences will only flourish on the condition of David's military law,—that those who remain with the baggage shall have equal part with those who descend to the fight, otherwise the baggage will be neglected. Lecturers being in like manner guardians of the literary stores whence those who are engaged in active service draw, it is but just that their labours should be equally recompensed, otherwise the reward of the fathers of the sciences not being sufficiently ample, the verse will be realized,—

Et patrum invalidi referent jejunia nati.

The next deficiency we shall notice is, the want of philosophical instruments, in crying up which we are aided by the alchemists, who call upon men to sell their books, and to build furnaces, rejecting Minerva and the Muses as barren virgins, and relying upon Vulcan. To study natural philosophy, physic, and many other sciences to advantage, books are not the only essentials,—other instruments are required; nor has the munificence of men been altogether wanting in the provisions. For spheres, globes, astrolabes, maps, and the like, have been provided for the elucidation of astronomy and cosmography; and many schools of medicine are provided with gardens for the growth of simples, and supplied with dead bodies for dissection. But these concern only a few things. In general, however, there will be no inroad made into the secrets of nature unless experiments, be they of Vulcan or Daedalus, furnace, engine, or any other kind, are allowed for; and therefore as the secretaries and spies of princes and states bring in bills for intelligence, so you must allow the spies and intelligences of nature to bring in their bills, or else you will be ignorant of many things worthy to be known. And if Alexander placed so large a treasure at Aristotle's command, for the support of hunters, fowlers, fishers, and the like, in much more need do they stand of this beneficence who unfold the labyrinths of nature.

Another defect I discover is the neglect in vice-chancellors, heads of houses, princes, inspectors, and others, of proper supervision or diligent inquiry into the course of studies, with a view to a thorough reformation of such parts as are ill suited to the age, or of unwise institution. For it is one of your Majesty's sage maxims, that as respects customs and precedents, we must consider the times in which they took their rise, since much is detracted from their authority, if such are found feeble and ignorant. It is, therefore, all the more requisite, since the university statues were framed in very obscure times, to institute an inquiry into their origin. Of errors of this nature I will give an example or two from such objects as are most obvious and familiar. The one is, that scholars are inducted too early into logic and rhetoric,—arts which, being the cream of all others, are fitter for graduates than children and novices. Now, being the gravest of the sciences, these arts are composed of rules and directions, for setting forth and methodizing the matter of the rest, and, therefore, for rude and blank minds, who have not yet gathered that which Cicero styles *sylva* and *supellex* matter, and fecundity, to begin with those arts is as if one were to paint or measure the wind, and has no other effect than to degrade the universal wisdom of these arts into childish sophistry and contemptible affectation. This error has had the inevitable result of rendering the treatises on those sciences superficial, and dwarfing them to the capacities of children. Another error to be noticed in the present academical system is the separation between invention and memory, their exercises either being nothing but a set form of words, where no play is given to the understanding, or extemporaneous, in the delivery of which no room is left to the memory. In practical life, however, a blending of the powers of judgment and memory is alone put into requisition, so that these practices, not being adapted to the life of action, rather pervert than discipline the mind. This defect is sooner discovered by scholars than by others, when they come to the practice of the civil professions. . . .

The next want I discover is the little sympathy and correspondence which exists between colleges and universities, as well throughout Europe as in the same state and kingdom. In this we have an example in many orders and sodalities, which, though scattered over several sovereignties and territories, yet enter into a kind of contract, fraternity, and correspondence with one another, and are associated under common provincials and generals. And, surely, as nature creates brotherhood in families, and trades contract brotherhood in communities, and the anointment of God establishes a brotherhood in kings and bishops, in like manner there should spring up a fraternity in learning and illumination, relating to that paternity which is attributed to God, who is called the Father of lights.

Lastly, I may lament that no fit men have been engaged to forward those sciences which yet remain in an unfinished state. To supply this want it may be of service to perform, as it were, a lustrum of the sciences, and take account of what have been prosecuted and what omitted. For the idea of abundance is one of the causes of dearth; and the multitude of books produces a deceitful impression of superfluity. This, however, is not to be remedied by destroying the books already written, but by making more good ones, which, like the serpent of Moses, may devour the serpents of the enchanters. The removal of the defects I have enumerated, except the last, are indeed opera basilica, towards which the endeavours of one man can be but as an image on a cross road, which points out the way, but cannot tread it. But as the survey of the sciences which we have proposed lies within the power of a private individual, it is my intention to make the circuit of knowledge, noticing what parts lie waste and uncultivated and abandoned by the industry of man, with a view to engage, by a faithful mapping out of the deserted tracks, the energies of public and private persons in their improvement. My attention, however, is alone confined to the discovery, not to the correction of errors. For it is one thing to point out what land lies uncultivated, and another thing to improve imperfect husbandry.

In completing this design, I am ignorant neither of the greatness of the work nor my own incapacity. My hope, however, is, that, if the extreme love of my subject carry me too far, I may at least obtain the excuse of affection. It is not granted to man to love and be wise: "amare et sapere." On such topics opinion is free, and that liberty of judgment which I exercise myself lies equally at the disposition of all. And I for my part shall be as glad to receive correction from others as I am ready to point out defects myself. It is the common duty of humanity: "nam qui erranti comiter monstrat viam." I, indeed, foresee that many of the defects and omissions I shall point out will be much censured, some as being already completed, and others as too difficult to be effected. For the first objection I must refer to the details of my subject; with regard to the last, I take it for granted that those works are possible which may be accomplished by some person, though not by every one; which may be done by many, though not by one; which may be completed in the succession of ages, though not within the hour-glass of one man's life; and which may be reached by public effort, though not by private endeavour. Nevertheless, if any man prefer the sentence of Solomon—"Dicit piger, Leo est in via;" to that of Virgil, "possunt, quia posse videntur"—I shall be content to have my labours received but as the better kind of wishes. For as it requires some knowledge to ask an apposite question, he also cannot be deemed foolish who entertains sensible desires.

APHORISMS OF FRANCIS BACON (1620) From Francis Bacon, *Novum Organum,* as quoted in Joseph Devey, ed., *The Physical and Metaphysical Works of Lord Bacon* (London, 1872), pp. 383, 386-87, 389-91.

On the Interpretation of Nature and the Empire of Man

Man, as the minister and interpreter of nature, does and understands as much as his observations on the order of nature, either with regard to things or the mind, permit him, and neither knows nor is capable of more.

II. The unassisted hand and the understanding left to itself possess but little power. Effects are produced by the means of instruments and helps, which the understanding requires no less than the hand; and as instruments either promote or regulate the motion of the hand, so those that are applied to the mind prompt or protect the understanding.

III. Knowledge and human power are synonymous, since the ignorance of the cause frustrates the effect; for nature is only subdued by submission, and that which in contemplative philosophy corresponds with the cause in practical science becomes the rule.

IV. Man whilst operating can only apply or withdraw natural bodies, nature internally performs the rest.

V. Those who become practically versed in nature are, the mechanic, the mathematician, the physician, the alchemist, and the magician, but all (as matters now stand) with faint efforts and meagre success.

*   *   *

XIV. The syllogism consists of propositions, propositions of words, words are the signs of notions. If, therefore, the notions (which form the basis of the whole) be confused and carelessly abstracted from things, there is no solidity in the superstructure. Our only hope, then, is in genuine induction.

XV. We have no sound notions either in logic or physics; substance, quality, action, passion, and existence are not clear notions; much less weight, levity, density, tenuity, moisture, dryness, generation, corruption, attraction, repulsion, element, matter, form, and the like. They are all fantastical and ill-defined.

XVI. The notions of less abstract natures, as man, dog, dove, and the immediate perceptions of sense, as heat, cold, white, black, do not deceive us materially, yet even these are sometimes confused by the mutability of matter and the intermixture of things. All the rest which men have hitherto employed are errors, and improperly abstracted and deduced from things.

XVII. There is the same degree of licentiousness and error in forming axioms as in abstracting notions, and that in the first principles, which depend on common induction; still more is this the case in axioms and inferior propositions derived from syllogisms.

XVIII. The present discoveries in science are such as lie immediately beneath the surface of common notions. It is necessary, however, to penetrate the more secret and remote parts of nature, in order to abstract both notions and axioms from things by a more certain and guarded method.

XIX. There are and can exist but two ways of investigating and discovering truth. The one hurries on rapidly from the senses and particulars to the most general axioms, and from them, as principles and their supposed indisputable truth, derives and discovers the intermediate axioms. This is the way now in use. The other constructs its axioms from the senses and particulars, by ascending continually and gradually, till it finally arrives at the most general axioms, which is the true but unattempted way.

XX. The understanding when left to itself proceeds by the same way as that which it would have adopted under the guidance of logic, namely, the first; for the mind is fond of starting off to generalities, that it may avoid labour, and after dwelling a little on a subject is fatigued by experiment. But those evils are augmented by logic, for the sake of the ostentation of dispute.

XXI. The understanding, when left to itself in a man of a steady, patient, and reflecting disposition (especially when unimpeded by received doctrines), makes some attempt in the right way, but with little effect, since the understanding, undirected and unassisted, is unequal to and unfit for the task of vanquishing the obscurity of things.

XXII. Each of these two ways begins from the senses and particulars, and ends in the greatest generalities. But they are immeasurably different; for the one merely touches cursorily the limits of experiment and particulars, whilst the other runs duly and regularly through them,—the one from the very outset lays down some abstract and useless generalities, the other gradually rises to those principles which are really the most common in nature.

XXIII. There is no small difference between the idols of the human mind and the ideas of the Divine mind,—that is to say, between certain idle dogmas and the real stamp and impression of created objects, as they are found in nature.

XXIV. Axioms determined upon in argument can never assist in the discovery of new effects; for the subtilty of nature is vastly superior to that of argument. But axioms properly and regularly abstracted from particulars easily point out and define new particulars, and therefore impart activity to the sciences.

XXV. The axioms now in use are derived from a scanty handful, as it were, of experience, and a few particulars of frequent occurrence, whence they are of much the same dimensions or extent as their origin. And if any neglected or unknown instance occurs, the axiom is saved by some frivolous distinction, when it would be more consistent with truth to amend it.

XXVI. We are wont, for the sake of distinction, to call that human reasoning which we apply to nature the anticipation of nature (as being rash and premature), and that which is properly deduced from things the interpretation of nature.

*   *   *

XXXVI. We have but one simple method of delivering our sentiments, namely, we must bring men to particulars and their regular series and order, and they must for a while renounce their notions, and begin to form an acquaintance with things.

XXXVII. Our method and that of the sceptics agree in some respects at first setting out, but differ most widely, and are completely opposed to each other in their conclusion; for they roundly assert that nothing can be known; we, that but a small part of nature can be known, by the present method; their next step, however, is to destroy the authority of the senses and understanding, whilst we invent and supply them with assistance.

XXXVIII. The idols and false notions which have already preoccupied the human understanding, and are deeply rooted in it, not only so beset men's minds that they become difficult of access, but even when access is obtained will again meet and trouble us in the instauration of the sciences, unless mankind when forewarned guard themselves with all possible care against them.

XXXIX. Four species of idols beset the human mind, to which (for distinction's sake) we have assigned names, calling the first Idols of the Tribe, the second Idols of the Den, the third Idols of the Market, the fourth Idols of the Theatre.

XL. The formation of notions and axioms on the foundation of true induction is the only fitting remedy by which we can ward off and expel these idols. It is, however, of great service to point them out; for the doctrine of idols bears the same relation to the interpretation of nature as that of the confutation of sophisms does to common logic.

XLI. The idols of the tribe are inherent in human nature and the very tribe or race of man; for man's sense is falsely asserted to be the standard of things; on the contrary, all the perceptions both of the senses and the mind bear reference to man and not to the universe, and the human mind resembles those uneven mirrors which impart their own properties to different objects, from which rays are emitted and distort and disfigure them.

XLII. The idols of the den are those of each individual; for everybody (in addition to the errors common to the race of man) has his own individual den or cavern, which intercepts and corrupts the light of nature, either from his own peculiar and singular disposition, or from his education and intercourse with others, or from his reading, and the authority acquired by those whom he reverences and admires, or from the different impressions produced on the mind, as it happens to be preoccupied and predisposed, or equable and tranquil, and the like; so that the spirit of man (according to its several dispositions), is variable, confused, and as it were actuated by chance; and Heraclitus said well that men search for knowledge in lesser worlds, and not in the greater or common world.

XLIII. There are also idols formed by the reciprocal intercourse and society of man with man, which we call idols of the market, from the commerce and association of men with each other; for men converse by means of language, but words are formed at the will of the generality, and there arises from a bad and unapt formation of words a wonderful obstruction to the mind. Nor can the definitions and explanations with which learned men are wont to guard and protect themselves in some instances afford a complete remedy,—words still manifestly force the understanding, throw everything into confusion, and lead mankind into vain and innumerable controversies and fallacies.

XLIV. Lastly, there are idols which have crept into men's minds from the various dogmas of peculiar systems of philosophy, and also from the perverted rules of demonstration, and these we denominate idols of the theatre: for we regard all the systems of philosophy hitherto received or imagined, as so many plays brought out and performed, creating fictitious and theatrical worlds. Nor do we speak only of the present systems, or of the philosophy and sects of the ancients, since numerous other plays of a similar nature can be still composed and made to agree with each other, the causes of the most opposite errors being generally the same. Nor, again, do we allude merely to general systems, but also to many elements and axioms of sciences which have become inveterate by tradition, implicit credence, and neglect. We must, however, discuss each species of idols more fully and distinctly in order to guard the human understanding against them.

THE ROYAL SOCIETY OF LONDON (1662) From Thomas Sprat, *The History of the Royal Society of London for the Improving of Natural Knowledge* (London, 1734), pp. 1-3, 58-61, 64-67, 149-50.

I shall here present to the World, an Account of the first Institution of the Royal Society; and of the Progress, which they have already made: In hope, that this learned and inquisitive Age, will either think their Indeavours worthy of its Assistance; or else will be thereby provok'd, to attempt some greater Enterprize (if any such can be found out) for the Benefit of human Life, by the Advancement of Real Knowledge.

Perhaps this Task, which I have propos'd to my self, will incur the Censure of many judicious Men, who may think it an over-hasty and presumptuous Attempt; and may object to me, that the History of an Assembly which begins with so great Expectations, ought not to have been made publick so soon; till we could have produced very many considerable Experiments, which they had try'd, and so have given undeniable Proofs of the Usefulness of their Undertaking.

In answer to this, I can plead for my self, that what I am here to say, will be far from preventing the Labours of others in adorning so worthy a Subject; and is premis'd upon no other account, than as the noblest Buildings are first wont to be represented in a few Shadows or small Models; which are not intended to be equal to the chief Structure it self, but only to shew in little, by what Materials, with what Charge, and by how many Hands, that is afterwards to be rais'd. Although, therefore, I come to the Performance of this Work, with much less Deliberation, and Ability, than the Weightiness of it requires; yet I trust, that the Greatness of the Design it self, on which I am to speak, and the Zeal which I have for the Honour of our Nation, which have been the chief Reasons that have mov'd me to this Confidence of Writing, will serve to make something for my Excuse. For what greater matter can any Man desire, about which to employ his Thoughts, than the Beginnings of an Illustrious Company, which has already laid such excellent Foundations of so much Good to Mankind? Or, what can be more delightful for an English Man to consider, than that notwithstanding all the late Miseries of his Country, it has been able in a short Time so well to recover it self, as not only to attain to the Perfection of its former Civility, and Learning, but also to set on foot a new Way of Improvement of Arts, as great and as beneficial (to say no more) as any the wittiest or the happiest Age has ever invented?

But besides this, I can also add, in my Defence, that though the Society, of which I am to write, is not yet four Years old, and has been of necessity hitherto chiefly taken up, about preparatory Affairs; yet even in this Time, they have not wholly neglected their principal End, but have had Success, in the Trial of many remarkable Things; of which I doubt not, but I shall be able, as I pass along, to give Instances enough to satisfy the Curiosity of all sober Inquirers into Truth. And in short, if for no other End, yet certainly for this, a Relation of their first Original ought to be expos'd to the View of Men: That by laying down, on what course of Discovery they intend to proceed, the Gentlemen of the Society may be more solemnly engag'd, to prosecute the same. For now they will not be able, handsomely to draw back, and to forsake such honourable Intentions; when the World shall have taken notice, that so many prudent Men have gone so far, in a Business of this universal Importance, and have given such undoubted Pledges of many admirable Inventions to follow.

✻   ✻   ✻

It shall suffice my purpose, that Philosophy had its Share in the Benefits of that glorious Action: For the Royal Society had its beginning in the wonderful pacifick Year, 1660. So that if any Conjectures of good Fortune, from extraordinary Nativities, hold true, we may presage all Happiness to this Undertaking. And I shall here join my solemn Wishes, that as it began in that Time, when our Country was freed from Confusion and Slavery; so it may, in its Progress, redeem the Minds of Men from Obscurity, Uncertainty, and Bondage.

These Gentlemen therefore finding the Hearts of their Countrymen inlarg'd by their Joys, and fitted for any noble Proposition; and meeting with the Concurrence of many worthy Men, who, to their immortal Honour, had follow'd the King in his Banishment, Mr. Erskin, Sir Robert Moray, Sir Gilbert Talbot, &c. began now to imagine some greater Thing, and to bring out experimental Knowledge from the Retreats, in which it had long hid itself, to take its Part in the Triumphs of that universal Jubilee. And indeed Philosophy did very well deserve that Reward, having been always Loyal in the worst of Times: For though the King's Enemies had gain'd all other Advantages; though they had all the Garrisons, and Fleets, and Ammunitions, and Treasures, and Armies on their side; yet they could never, by all their Victories, bring over the Reason of Men to their Party.

While they were thus ordering their Platform, there came forth a Treatise, which very much hasten'd its Contrivance; and that was a Proposal by Master Cowley, of erecting a Philosophical College. The Intent of it was, that in some places near London, there should liberal Salaries be bestowed on a competent Number of Learned Men, to whom should be committed the Operations of Natural Experiments. This Model was every way practicable; unless perhaps, in two Things, he did more consult the Generosity of his own Mind, than of other Men's: the one was the Largeness of the Revenue, with which he would have his College at first indowed; the other, that he imposed on his Operators a second Task of great Pains, the Education of Youth.

The last of these is indeed a matter of great Weight; the Reformation of which ought to be seriously examined by prudent Men. For it is an undeniable Truth, which is commonly said, that there would be Need of fewer Laws, and less Force to govern Men, if their Minds were rightly inform'd, and set strait, while they were young, and pliable. But perhaps this Labour is not so proper for Experimenters to undergo; for it would not only devour too much of their Time, but it would go near to make them a little more magisterial in Philosophy, than became them; by being long accustomed to command the Opinions, and direct the Manners, of their Scholars. And as to the other Particular, the large Estate which he required to the Maintenance of his College; it is evident, that it is so difficult a Thing to draw Men in to be willing to divert an ancient Revenue, which has long run in another Stream, or to contribute out of their own Purses, to the supporting of any new Design, while it shews nothing but Promises, and Hopes; that, in such cases, it were (it may be) more adviseable to begin upon a small Stock, and so to rise by degrees, than to profess great Things at first, and to exact too much Benevolence all in one Lump together. However, it was not the excellent Author's Fault, that he thought better of the Age than it did deserve. His Purpose in it was like himself, full of Honour and Goodness: Most of the other Particulars of his Draught the Royal Society is now putting in Practice.

* * *

I will here, in the first place, contract into few Words, the whole Sum of their Resolutions; which I shall often have occasion to touch upon in Parcels. Their Purpose is, in short, to make faithful Records of all the Works of Nature, or Art, which can come within their Reach; that so the present Age, and Posterity, may be able to put a Mark on the Errors, which have been strengthned by long Prescription; to restore the Truths, that have lain neglected; to push on those, which are already known, to more various Uses; and to make the way more passable, to what remains unrevealed. This is the Compass of their Design.

* * *

By their naturalizing Men of all Countries, they have laid the Beginnings of many great Advantages for the future. For by this Means, they will be able, to settle a constant Intelligence, throughout all civil Nations, and make the Royal Society the general Bank and Free-port of the World: A Policy, which whether it would hold good in the Trade of England, I know not; but sure it will in the Philosophy. We are to overcome the Mysteries of all the Works of Nature; and not only to prosecute such as are confin'd to one Kingdom, or beat upon one Shore: We should then refuse to list all the Aids, that will come in, how remote soever. If I could fetch my Materials whence I pleas'd, to fashion the Idea of a perfect Philosopher; he should not be all of one Clime, but have the different Excellencies of several Countries. First, he should have the Industry, Activity, and inquisitive Humor of the Dutch, French, Scotch, and English, in laying the ground Work, the Heap of Experiments: And then he should have added the cold, and circumspect, and wary Disposition of the Italians and Spaniards, in meditating upon them, before he fully brings them into Speculation. All this is scarce ever to be found in one single Man; seldom in the same Countrymen: It must then be supplied, as well as it may, by a publick Council, wherein the various Dispositions of all these Nations may be blended together. To this purpose, the Royal Society has made no Scruple to receive all inquisitive Strangers of all Countries into its Number. And this they have constantly done, with such peculiar Respect, that they have not oblig'd them to the Charge of Contributions; they have always taken Care, that some of their Members should assist them in interpreting all that pass'd, in their publick Assemblies; and they have freely open'd their Registers to them; thereby inviting them to communicate foreign Rarities, by imparting their own Discoveries. This has been often acknowledg'd by many learned Men, who have travel'd hither; who have been introduc'd to their Meetings, and have admir'd the Decency, the Gravity, the Plainness, and the Calmness of their Debates. This they have publish'd to the World; and this has rous'd all our Neighbours to fix their Eyes upon England. From hence they expect the great Improvements of Knowledge will flow; and though, perhaps, they send their Youth into other Parts to learn Fashion, and Breeding; yet their Men come hither for nobler Ends, to be instructed in the Masculine, and the solid Arts of Life; which is a Matter of as much greater Reputation, as it is more honourable to teach Philosophers, than Children.

By their Admission of Men of all Professions, these two Benefits arise: The one, that every Art, and every Way of Life already establish'd, may be secure of receiving no Damage by their Counsels. A Thing which all new Inventions ought carefully to consult. It is in vain to declare against the Profit of the most, in any Change that we would make. We must not always deal with the violent Current of popular Passions, as they do with the furious Eager in the Severn; where the safest Way is to set the Head of the Boat directly against its Force. But here Men must follow the Shore; wind about leisurably; and insinuate their useful Alterations by soft and unperceivable Degrees. From the Neglect of this Prudence, we often see Men of great Wit, to have been overborn by the Multitude of their Opposers; and to have found all their subtile Projects too weak for Custom and Interest: While being a little too much heated with a Love of their own Fancies, they have raised to themselves more Enemies than they needed to have done, by defying at once too many Things in Use. But here this Danger is very well prevented. For what Suspicion can Divinity, Law, or Physick, or any other Course of Life have, that they shall be impair'd by these Men's Labours; when they themselves are as capable of sitting amongst them as any others? Have they not the same Security that the whole Nation has for its Lives and Fortunes? Of which this is esteemed the Establishment, that Men of all Sorts and Qualities, give their Voice in every Law that is made in Parliament. But the other Benefit is, that by this equal Balance of all Professions, there will no one Particular of them overweigh the other, or make the Oracle only speak their private Sense; which else it were impossible to avoid. It is natural to all Ranks of Men, to have some one Darling, upon which their Care is chiefly fixed. If Mechanicks alone were to make a Philosophy, they would bring it all into their Shops, and force it wholly to consist of Springs, and Wheels, and Weights; if Physicians, they would not depart far from their Art; scarce any Thing would be considered, besides the Body of Man, the Causes, Signs, and Cures of Diseases. So much is to be found in Men of all Conditions, of that which is called Pedantry in Scholars; which is nothing else but an obstinate Addiction to the Forms of some private Life, and not regarding general Things enough. This Freedom therefore, which they use, in Embracing all Assistance, is most advantageous to them; which is the more remarkable, in that they diligently search out and join to them, all extraordinary Men, though but of ordinary Trades. And that they are likely to continue this comprehensive Temper hereafter, I will shew by one instance; and it is the Recommendation which the King himself was pleased to make, of the judicious Author of the Observations on the Bills of Mortality: In whose Election, it was so far from being a Prejudice, that he was a Shop-keeper of London; that his Majesty gave this particular Charge to his Society, that if they found any more such Tradesmen, they should be sure to admit them all, without any more ado. From hence it may be concluded, what is their Inclination towards the manual Arts; by the careful Regard which their Founder and Patron, has engag'd them to have for all Sorts of Mechanick Artists.

But, though the Society entertains very many Men of particular Professions, yet the far greater Number are Gentlemen, free and unconfin'd. By the Help of this there was hopeful Provision made against two Corruptions of Learning, which have been long complain'd of, but never remov'd: The one, that Knowledge still degenerates to consult present Profit too soon; the other, that Philosophers have been always Masters and Scholars; some imposing, and all the other submitting; and not as equal Observers without Dependence.

*   *   *

When these Statutes were presented to his Majesty, he was pleas'd to superscribe himself their Founder and Patron; his Royal Highness, and his Highness Prince Rupert, at the same time, declaring themselves Fellows.

Nor has the King only incourag'd them, by Kindness and Words, and by Acts of State; but he has also provok'd them to unwearied Activity in their Experiments, by the most effectual Means of his Royal Example. There is scarce any one sort of Work, whose Advancement they regard; but from his Majesty's own Labours they have receiv'd a Pattern for their Indeavours about it. They design the multiplying and beautifying of Mechanick Arts: And the Noise of Mechanick Instruments is heard in Whitehall itself. They intend the Perfection of Graving, Statuary, Limning, Coining, and all the Works of Smiths, in Iron, or Steel, or Silver: And the most excellent Artists of these kinds have Provision made for their Practice, even in the Chambers and Galleries of his Court. They purpose the Trial of all manner of Operations by Fire; And the King has under his own Roof found place for Chymical Operators. They resolve to restore, to enlarge, to examine Physick; and the King has indow'd the College of London with new Privileges, and has planted a Physick Garden under his own Eye. They have bestow'd much Consideration on the propagating of Fruits and Trees: And the King has made Plantations enough, even almost to repair the Ruins of a Civil War. They have begun an exact Survey of the Heavens; and St. James's Park may witness, that Ptolomy and Alphonso were not the only Monarchs, who observ'd the Motions and Appearances of the Stars. They have studied the promoting of Architecture in our Island; and the Beauty of our late Buildings, and the Reformation of his own Houses, do sufficiently manifest his Skill and Inclination to that Art: of which Magnificence, we had seen more Effects e'er this, if they had not been call'd off by this War, from Houses of Convenience, to those of Strength. They have principally consulted the Advancement of Navigation; and the King has been most ready to reward those, that shall discover the Meridian. They have employ'd much Time in examining the Fabrick of Ships, the Forms of their Sails, the Shapes of their Keels, the Sorts of Timber, the planting of Fir, the bettering of Pitch, and Tar, and Tackling. And in all maritime Affairs of this Nature, his Majesty is acknowledg'd to be the best Judge amongst Seamen and Shipwrights, as well as the most powerful amongst Princes.

By these and many other Instances it appears, that the King has not only given Succour to the Royal Society, in the prosecution of their Labours; but has also led them on their Way, and trac'd out to them the Paths, in which they ought to tread. And with this propitious Inclination of his Majesty, and the highest Degrees of Men, the Genius of the Nation itself irresistibly conspires.

NEWTON DESCRIBES A NEW WAY OF REASONING (1686)   From Isaac
Newton, *The Mathematical Principles of Natural Philosophy*, Andrew Motte, trans. (London,
1729); as revised by Florian Cajori (Berkeley, 1934), pp. 398-400.

Rule I—We Are to Admit No More Causes of Natural Things Than Such as Are Both True
and Sufficient to Explain Their Appearances

To this purpose the philosophers say that Nature does nothing in vain,
and more is in vain when less will serve; for Nature is pleased with simplicity, and
affects not the pomp of superfluous causes.

Rule II—Therefore to the Same Natural Effects We Must, as Far as Possible, Assign the
Same Causes

As to respiration in a man and in a beast; the descent of stones in Europe and in
America; the light of our culinary fire and of the sun; the reflection of light in the
earth, and in the planets.

Rule III—The Qualities of Bodies, Which Admit Neither Intensification nor Remission
of Degrees, and Which Are Found to Belong to All Bodies Within the Reach of
Our Experiments, Are to Be Esteemed the Universal Qualities of All Bodies Whatsoever

For since the qualities of bodies are only known to us by experiments, we are to
hold for universal all such as universally agree with experiments; and such as are not
liable to diminution can never be quite taken away. We are certainly not to
relinquish the evidence of experiments for the sake of dreams and vain fictions of
our own devising; nor are we to recede from the analogy of Nature, which is wont
to be simple, and always consonant to itself. We no other way know the extension
of bodies than by our senses, nor do these reach it in all bodies; but because we
perceive extension in all that are sensible, therefore we ascribe it universally to all
others also. That abundance of bodies are hard, we learn by experience; and because
the hardness of the whole arises from the hardness of the parts, we therefore justly
infer the hardness of the undivided particles not only of the bodies we feel but of all
others. That all bodies are impenetrable, we gather not from reason, but from
sensation. The bodies which we handle we find impenetrable, and thence conclude
impenetrability to be an universal property of all bodies whatsoever. That all bodies
are movable, and endowed with certain powers (which we call the inertia) of
persevering in their motion, or in their rest, we only infer from the like properties
observed in the bodies which we have seen. The extension, hardness, impenetrability, mobility, and inertia of the whole, result from the extension, hardness,
impenetrability, mobility, and inertia of the parts; and hence we conclude the least
particles of all bodies to be also all extended, and hard and impenetrable, and
movable, and endowed with their proper inertia. And this is the foundation of all
philosophy. Moreover, that the divided but contiguous particles of bodies may be

separated from one another, is matter of observation; and, in the particles that remain undivided, our minds are able to distinguish yet lesser parts, as is mathematically demonstrated. But whether the parts so distinguished, and not yet divided, may, by the powers of Nature, be actually divided and separated from one another, we cannot certainly determine. Yet, had we the proof of but one experiment that any undivided particle, in breaking a hard and solid body, suffered a division, we might by virtue of this rule conclude that the undivided as well as the divided particles may be divided and actually separated to infinity.

Lastly, if it universally appears, by experiments and astronomical observations, that all bodies about the earth gravitate towards the earth, and that in proportion to the quantity of matter which they severally contain; that the moon likewise, according to the quantity of its matter, gravitates towards the earth; that, on the other hand, our sea gravitates towards the moon; and all the planets one towards another; and the comets in like manner towards the sun; we must, in consequence of this rule, universally allow that all bodies whatsoever are endowed with a principle of mutual gravitation. For the argument from the appearances concludes with more force for the universal gravitation of all bodies than for their impenetrability; of which, among those in the celestial regions, we have no experiments, nor any manner of observation. Not that I affirm gravity to be essential to bodies: by their *vis insita* I mean nothing but their inertia. This is immutable. Their gravity is diminished as they recede from the earth.

Rule IV—In Experimental Philosophy We Are to Look Upon Propositions Inferred
by
General Induction From Phenomena as Accurately or Very Nearly True,
Notwithstanding
Any Contrary Hypotheses That May Be Imagined, Till Such Time
As Other Phenomena Occur, By Which They May Either Be Made More
Accurate,
Or Liable to Exceptions

This rule we must follow, that the argument of induction may not be evaded by hypotheses.

ON THE NEWTONIAN SYSTEM AND NATURAL PHILOSOPHY

(1729)   From Roger Cotes' Preface to Isaac Newton, *The Mathematical Principles of Natural Philosophy,* Andrew Motte, trans. (London, 1729), as revised by Florian Cajori (Berkeley, 1934), pp. xx-xxvii, xxxii.

222

We hereby present to the benevolent reader the long-awaited new edition of Newton's *Philosophy,* now greatly amended and increased. The principal contents of this celebrated work may be gathered from the adjoining Table. What has been added or modified is indicated in the author's Preface. There remains for us to add something relating to the method of this philosophy.

Those who have treated of natural philosophy may be reduced to about three classes. Of these some have attributed to the several species of things, specific and occult qualities, according to which the phenomena of particular bodies are supposed to proceed in some unknown manner. The sum of the doctrine of the Schools derived from Aristotle and the Peripatetics is founded on this principle. They affirm that the several effects of bodies arise from the particular natures of those bodies. But whence it is that bodies derive those natures they don't tell us; and therefore they tell us nothing. And being entirely employed in giving names to things, and not in searching into things themselves, they have invented, we may say, a philosophical way of speaking, but they have not made known to us true philosophy.

Others have endeavored to apply their labors to greater advantage by rejecting that useless medley of words. They assume that all matter is homogeneous, and that the variety of forms which is seen in bodies arises from some very plain and simple relations of the component particles. And by going on from simple things to those which are more compounded they certainly proceed right, if they attribute to those primary relations no other relations than those which Nature has given. But when they take a liberty of imagining at pleasure unknown figures and magnitudes, and uncertain situations and motions of the parts, and moreover of supposing occult fluids, freely pervading the pores of bodies, endued with an all-performing subtilty, and agitated with occult motions, they run out into dreams and chimeras, and neglect the true constitution of things, which certainly is not to be derived from fallacious conjectures, when we can scarce reach it by the most certain observations. Those who assume hypotheses as first principles of their speculations, although they afterwards proceed with the greatest accuracy from those principles, may indeed form an ingenious romance, but a romance it will still be.

There is left then the third class, which possess experimental philosophy. These indeed derive the causes of all things from the most simple principles possible; but then they assume nothing as a principle, that is not proved by phenomena. They frame no hypotheses, nor receive them into philosophy otherwise than as questions whose truth may be disputed. They proceed therefore in a twofold method, synthetical and analytical. From some select phenomena they deduce by analysis the forces of Nature and the more simple laws of forces; and from thence by synthesis show the constitution of the rest. This is that incomparably best way of philosophizing, which our renowned author most justly embraced in preference to the rest, and thought alone worthy to be cultivated and adorned by his excellent labors. Of this he has given us a most illustrious example, by the explication of the System of the World, most happily deduced from the Theory of Gravity. That the attribute of gravity was found in all bodies, others suspected, or imagined before him, but he was the only and the first philosopher that could demonstrate it from appearances, and make it a solid foundation to the most noble speculations.

I know indeed that some persons, and those of great name, too much prepossessed with certain prejudices, are unwilling to assent to this new principle, and are ready to prefer uncertain notions to certain. It is not my intention to detract from the reputation of these eminent men; I shall only lay before the reader such considerations as will enable him to pass an equitable judgment in this dispute.

Therefore, that we may begin our reasoning from what is most simple and nearest to us, let us consider a little what is the nature of gravity in earthly bodies, that we may proceed the more safely when we come to consider it in the heavenly bodies that lie at the remotest distance from us. It is now agreed by all philosophers that all circumterrestrial bodies gravitate towards the earth. That no bodies having no weight are to be found, is now confirmed by manifold experience. That which is relative levity is not true levity, but apparent only, and arises from the preponderating gravity of the contiguous bodies.

Moreover, as all bodies gravitate towards the earth, so does the earth gravitate again towards all bodies. That the action of gravity is mutual and equal on both sides, is thus proved. Let the mass of the earth be divided into any two parts whatever, either equal or unequal; now if the weights of the parts towards each other were not mutually equal, the lesser weight would give way to the greater, and the two parts would move on together indefinitely in a right line towards that point to which the greater weight tends, which is altogether contrary to experience. Therefore we must say that the weights with which the parts tend to each other are equal; that is, that the action of gravity is mutual and equal in contrary directions.

The weights of bodies at equal distances from the centre of the earth are as the quantities of matter in the bodies. This is inferred from the equal acceleration of all bodies that fall from a state of rest by their weights; for the forces by which unequal bodies are equally accelerated must be proportional to the quantities of the matter to be moved. Now, that all falling bodies are equally accelerated, appears from this, that when the resistance of the air is taken away, as it is under an exhausted receiver of Mr. Boyle, they describe equal spaces in equal times; but this is yet more accurately proved by the experiments with pendulums.

The attractive forces of bodies at equal distances are as the quantities of matter in the bodies. For since bodies gravitate towards the earth, and the earth again towards bodies with equal moments, the weight of the earth towards each body, or the force with which the body attracts the earth, will be equal to the weight of the same body towards the earth. But this weight was shown to be as the quantity of matter in the body; and therefore the force with which each body attracts the earth, or the absolute force of the body, will be as the same quantity of matter.

Therefore the attractive force of the entire bodies arises from and is composed of the attractive forces of the parts, because, as was just shown, if the bulk of the matter be augmented or diminished, its power is proportionately augmented or diminished. We must therefore conclude that the action of the earth is composed of the united actions of its parts, and therefore that all terrestrial bodies must attract one another mutually, with absolute forces that are as the matter attracting. This is the nature of gravity upon earth; let us now see what it is in the heavens.

That every body continues in its state either of rest or of moving uniformly in a right line, unless so far as it is compelled to change that state by external force, is a law of Nature universally received by all philosophers. But it follows from this that bodies which move in curved lines, and are therefore continually bent from the right lines that are tangents to their orbits, are retained in their curvilinear paths by some force continually acting. Since, then, the planets move in curvilinear orbits, there must be some force operating, by the incessant actions of which they are continually made to deflect from the tangents.

Now it is evident from mathematical reasoning, and rigorously demonstrated, that all bodies that move in any curved line described in a plane, and which, by a radius drawn to any point, whether at rest or moved in any manner, describe areas about that point proportional to the times, are urged by forces directed towards that point. This must therefore be granted. Since, then, all astronomers agree that the primary planets describe about the sun, and the secondary about the primary, areas proportional to the times, it follows that the forces by which they are continually turned aside from the rectilinear tangents, and made to revolve in curvilinear orbits, are directed towards the bodies that are placed in the centres of the orbits. This force may therefore not improperly be called centripetal in respect of the revolving body, and in respect of the central body attractive, from whatever cause it may be imagined to arise.

Moreover, it must be granted, as being mathematically demonstrated, that, if several bodies revolve with an equable motion in concentric circles, and the squares of the periodic times are as the cubes of the distances from the common centre, the centripetal forces will be inversely as the squares of the distances. Or, if bodies revolve in orbits that are very nearly circular and the apsides of the orbits are at rest, the centripetal forces of the revolving bodies will be inversely as the squares of the distances. That both these facts hold for all the planets, all astronomers agree. Therefore the centripetal forces of all the planets are inversely as the squares of the distances from the centres of their orbits. If any should object, that the apsides of the planets, and especially of the moon, are not perfectly at rest, but are carried progressively with a slow kind of motion, one may give this answer, that, though we should grant that this very slow motion arises from a slight deviation of the centripetal force from the law of the square of the distance, yet we are able to compute mathematically the quantity of that aberration, and find it perfectly insensible. For even the ratio of the lunar centripetal force itself, which is the most irregular of them all, will vary inversely as a power a little greater than the square of the distance, but will be well-nigh sixty times nearer to the square than to the cube of the distance. But we may give a truer answer, by saying that this progression of the apsides arises not from a deviation from the law of inverse squares of the distance, but from a quite different cause, as is most admirably shown in this work. It is certain then that the centripetal forces with which the primary planets tend to the sun, and the secondary planets to their primary, are accurately as the inverse squares of the distances.

From what has been hitherto said, it is plain that the planets are retained in their orbits by some force continually acting upon them; it is plain that this force is always directed towards the centres of their orbits; it is plain that its intensity is increased in its approach and is decreased in its recession from the centre, and that it is increased in the same ratio in which the square of the distance is diminished, and decreased in the same ratio in which the square of the distance is augmented. Let us now see whether, by making a comparison between the centripetal forces of the planets and the force of gravity, we may not by chance find them to be of the same kind. Now, they will be of the same kind if we find on both sides the same laws and the same attributes. Let us then first consider the centripetal force of the moon, which is nearest to us.

The rectilinear spaces which bodies let fall from rest describe in a given time at the very beginning of the motion, when the bodies are urged by any forces whatsoever, are proportional to the forces. This appears from mathematical reasoning. Therefore the centripetal force of the moon revolving in its orbit is to the force of gravity at the surface of the earth, as the space which in a very small interval of time the moon, deprived of all its circular force and descending by its centripetal force towards the earth, would describe, is to the space which a heavy body would describe, when falling by the force of its gravity near to the earth, in the same small interval of time. The first of these spaces is equal to the versed sine of the arc described by the moon in the same time, because that versed sine measures the translation of the moon from the tangent, produced by the centripetal force, and therefore may be computed, if the periodic time of the moon and its distance from the centre of the earth are given. The last space is found by experiments with pendulums, as Mr. Huygens has shown. Therefore by making a calculation we shall find that the first space is to the latter, or the centripetal force of the moon revolving in its orbit will be to the force of gravity at the surface of the earth, as the square of the semidiameter of the earth to the square of the semidiameter of the orbit. But by what was shown before, the very same ratio holds between the centripetal force of the moon revolving in its orbit, and the centripetal force of the moon near the surface of the earth. Therefore the centripetal force near the surface of the earth is equal to the force of gravity. Therefore these are not two different forces, but one and the same; for if they were different, these forces united would cause bodies to descend to the earth with twice the velocity they would fall with by the force of gravity alone. Therefore it is plain that the centripetal force, by which the moon is continually either impelled or attracted out of the tangent and retained in its orbit, is the very force of terrestrial gravity reaching up to the moon. And it is very reasonable to believe that this force should extend itself to vast distances, since upon the tops of the highest mountains we find no sensible diminution of it. Therefore the moon gravitates towards the earth; but on the other hand, the earth by a mutual action equally gravitates towards the moon, which is also abundantly confirmed in this philosophy, where the tides in the sea and the precession of the equinoxes are treated of, which arise from the action both of the moon and of the sun upon the earth. Hence lastly, we discover by what law the force of gravity decreases at great distances from the earth. For since gravity is noways different from the moon's centripetal force, and this is inversely proportional to the square of the distance, it follows that it is in that very ratio that the force of gravity decreases.

Let us now go on to the other planets. Because the revolutions of the primary planets about the sun and of the secondary about Jupiter and Saturn are phenomena of the same kind with the revolution of the moon about the earth, and because it has been moreover demonstrated that the centripetal forces of the primary planets are directed towards the centre of the sun and those of the secondary towards the centres of Jupiter and Saturn, in the same manner as the centripetal force of the moon is directed towards the centre of the earth, and since, besides, all these forces are inversely as the squares of the distances from the centres, in the same manner as the centripetal force of the moon is as the square of the distance from the earth, we must of course conclude that the nature of all is the same. Therefore as the moon gravitates towards the earth and the earth again towards the moon, so also all the secondary planets will gravitate towards their primary, and the primary planets again towards their secondary, and so all the primary towards the sun, and the sun again towards the primary.

Therefore the sun gravitates towards all the planets, and all the planets towards the sun. For the secondary planets, while they accompany the primary, revolve the meanwhile with the primary about the sun. Therefore, by the same argument, the planets of both kinds gravitate towards the sun and the sun towards them. That the secondary planets gravitate towards the sun is moreover abundantly clear from the inequalities of the moon, a most accurate theory of which, laid open with a most admirable sagacity, we find explained in the third Book of this work.

That the attractive force of the sun is propagated on all sides to prodigious distances and is diffused to every part of the wide space that surrounds it, is most evidently shown by the motion of the comets, which, coming from places immensely distant from the sun, approach very near to it, and sometimes so near that in their perihelia they almost touch its body. The theory of these bodies was altogether unknown to astronomers till in our own times our excellent author most happily discovered it and demonstrated the truth of it by most certain observations. So that it is now apparent that the comets move in conic sections having their foci in the sun's centre, and by radii drawn to the sun describe areas proportional to the times. But from these phenomena it is manifest and mathematically demonstrated, that those forces by which the comets are retained in their orbits are directed towards the sun and are inversely proportional to the squares of the distances from its centre. Therefore the comets gravitate towards the sun, and therefore the attractive force of the sun not only acts on the bodies of the planets, placed at given distances and very nearly in the same plane, but reaches also the comets in the most different parts of the heavens, and at the most different distances. This therefore is the nature of gravitating bodies, to exert their force at all distances to all other gravitating bodies. But from thence it follows that all the planets and comets attract one another mutually, and gravitate towards one another, which is also confirmed by the perturbation of Jupiter and Saturn, observed by astronomers, and arising from the mutual actions of these two planets upon each other, as also from that very slow motion of the apsides, above taken notice of, which arises from a like cause.

We have now proceeded so far, that it must be acknowledged that the sun, and the earth, and all the heavenly bodies attending the sun, attract one another mutually. Therefore all the least particles of matter in every one must have their several attractive forces proportional to their quantities of matter, as was shown above of the terrestrial bodies. At different distances these forces will be also inversely as the squares of their distances; for it is mathematically demonstrated, that globes attracting according to this law are composed of particles attracting according to the same law.

The foregoing conclusions are grounded on this axiom which is received by all philosophers, namely, that effects of the same kind, whose known properties are the same, take their rise from the same causes and have the same unknown properties also. For if gravity be the cause of the descent of a stone in Europe, who doubts that it is also the cause of the same descent in America? If there is a mutual gravitation between a stone and the earth in Europe, who will deny the same to be mutual in America? If in Europe the attractive force of a stone and the earth is composed of the attractive forces of the parts, who will deny the like composition in America? If in Europe the attraction of the earth be propagated to all kinds of bodies and to all distances, why may we not say that it is propagated in like manner in America? All philosophy is founded on this rule; for if that be taken away, we can affirm nothing as a general truth. The constitution of particular things is known by observations and experiments; and when that is done, no general conclusion of the nature of things can thence be drawn, except by this rule.

Since, then, all bodies, whether upon earth or in the heavens, are heavy, so far as we can make any experiments or observations concerning them, we must certainly allow that gravity is found in all bodies universally. And in like manner as we ought not to suppose that any bodies can be otherwise than extended, movable, or impenetrable, so we ought not to conceive that any bodies can be otherwise than heavy. The extension, mobility, and impenetrability of bodies become known to us only by experiments; and in the very same manner their gravity becomes known to us. All bodies upon which we can make any observations, are extended, movable, and impenetrable; and thence we conclude all bodies, and those concerning which we have no observations, are extended and movable and impenetrable. So all bodies on which we can make observations, we find to be heavy; and thence we conclude all bodies, and those we have no observations of, to be heavy also. If anyone should say that the bodies of the fixed stars are not heavy because their gravity is not yet observed, they may say for the same reason that they are neither extended nor movable nor impenetrable, because these properties of the fixed stars are not yet observed. In short, either gravity must have a place among the primary qualities of all bodies, or extension, mobility, and impenetrability must not. And if the nature of things is not rightly explained by the gravity of bodies, it will not be rightly explained by their extension, mobility, and impenetrability.

Some I know disapprove this conclusion, and mutter something about occult qualities. They continually are cavilling with us, that gravity is an occult property, and occult causes are to be quite banished from philosophy. But to this the answer is easy: that those are indeed occult causes whose existence is occult, and imagined but not proved; but not those whose real existence is clearly demonstrated by observations. Therefore gravity can by no means be called an occult cause of the celestial motions, because it is plain from the phenomena that such a power does really exist. Those rather have recourse to occult causes, who set imaginary vortices of a matter entirely fictitious and imperceptible by our senses, to direct those motions.

But shall gravity be therefore called an occult cause, and thrown out of philosophy, because the cause of gravity is occult and not yet discovered? Those who affirm this, should be careful not to fall into an absurdity that may overturn the foundations of all philosophy. For causes usually proceed in a continued chain from those that are more compounded to those that are more simple; when we are arrived at the most simple cause we can go no farther. Therefore no mechanical account or explanation of the most simple cause is to be expected or given; for if it could be given, the cause were not the most simple. These most simple causes will you then call occult, and reject them? Then you must reject those that immediately depend upon them, and those which depend upon these last, till philosophy is quite cleared and disencumbered of all causes.

Some there are who say that gravity is preternatural, and call it a perpetual miracle. Therefore they would have it rejected, because preternatural causes have no place in physics. It is hardly worth while to spend time in answering this ridiculous objection which overturns all philosophy. For either they will deny gravity to be in bodies, which cannot be said, or else, they will therefore call it preternatural because it is not produced by the other properties of bodies, and therefore not by mechanical causes. But certainly there are primary properties of bodies; and these, because they are primary, have no dependence on the others. Let them consider whether all these are not in like manner preternatural, and in like manner to be rejected; and then what kind of philosophy we are like to have.

Some there are who dislike this celestial physics because it contradicts the opinions of Descartes, and seems hardly to be reconciled with them. Let these enjoy their own opinion, but let them act fairly, and not deny the same liberty to us which they demand for themselves. Since the Newtonian Philosophy appears true to us, let us have the liberty to embrace and retain it, and to follow causes proved by phenomena, rather than causes only imagined and not yet proved. The business of true philosophy is to derive the natures of things from causes truly existent, and to inquire after those laws on which the Great Creator actually chose to found this most beautiful Frame of the World, not those by which he might have done the same, had he so pleased. It is reasonable enough to suppose that from several causes, somewhat differing from one another, the same effect may arise; but the true cause will be that from which it truly and actually does arise; the others have no place in true philosophy. The same motion of the hour-hand in a clock may be occasioned either by a weight hung, or a spring shut up within. But if a certain clock should be really moved with a weight, we should laugh at a man that would suppose it moved by a spring, and from that principle, suddenly taken up without further examination, should go about to explain the motion of the index; for certainly the way he ought to have taken would have been actually to look into the inward parts of the machine, that he might find the true principle of the proposed motion. The like judgment ought to be made of those philosophers who will have the heavens to be filled with a most subtile matter which is continually carried round in vortices. For if they could explain the phenomena ever so accurately by their hypotheses, we could not yet say that they have discovered true philosophy and the true causes of the celestial motions, unless they could either demonstrate that those causes do actually exist, or at least that no others do exist. Therefore if it be made clear that the attraction of all bodies is a property actually existing in *rerum natura,* and if it be also shown how the motions of the celestial bodies may be solved by that property, it would be very impertinent for anyone to object that these motions ought to be accounted for by vortices; even though we should allow such an explication of those motions to be possible. But we allow no such thing; for the phenomena can by no means be accounted for by vortices, as our author has abundantly proved from the clearest reasons. So that men must be strangely fond of chimeras, who can spend their time so idly as in patching up a ridiculous figment and setting it off with new comments of their own.

*   *   *

From this fountain it is that those laws, which we call the laws of Nature, have flowed, in which there appear many traces indeed of the most wise contrivance, but not the least shadow of necessity. These therefore we must not seek from uncertain conjectures, but learn them from observations and experiments. He who is presumptuous enough to think that he can find the true principles of physics and the laws of natural things by the force alone of his own mind, and the internal light of his reason, must either suppose that the world exists by necessity, and by the same necessity follows the laws proposed; or if the order of Nature was established by the will of God, that himself, a miserable reptile, can tell what was fittest to be done. All sound and true philosophy is founded on the appearances of things; and if these phenomena inevitably draw us, against our wills, to such principles as most clearly manifest to us the most excellent counsel and supreme dominion of the All-wise and Almighty Being, they are not therefore to be laid aside because some men may perhaps dislike them. These men may call them miracles or occult qualities, but names maliciously given ought not to be a disadvantage to the things themselves, unless these men will say at last that all philosophy ought to be founded in atheism. Philosophy must not be corrupted in compliance with these men, for the order of things will not be changed.

Fair and equal judges will therefore give sentence in favor of this most excellent method of philosophy, which is founded on experiments and observations. And it can hardly be said or imagined, what light, what splendor, hath accrued to that method from this admirable work of our illustrious author, whose happy and sublime genius, resolving the most difficult problems, and reaching to discoveries of which the mind of man was thought incapable before, is deservedly admired by all those who are somewhat more than superficially versed in these matters. The gates are now set open, and by the passage he has revealed we may freely enter into the knowledge of the hidden secrets and wonders of natural things. He has so clearly laid open and set before our eyes the most beautiful frame of the System of the

World, that if King Alphonso were now alive, he would not complain for want of the graces either of simplicity or of harmony in it. Therefore we may now more nearly behold the beauties of Nature, and entertain ourselves with the delightful contemplation; and, which is the best and most valuable fruit of philosophy, be thence incited the more profoundly to reverence and adore the great Maker and Lord of all. He must be blind who from the most wise and excellent contrivances of things cannot see the infinite Wisdom and Goodness of their Almighty Creator, and he must be mad and senseless who refuses to acknowledge them.

LOCKE ON THE NATURE OF THE MIND (**1690**)   From John Locke, "An Essay Concerning Human Understanding," as quoted in *The Works of John Locke* (London, 1824), vol. I, pp. 13, 54-55, 77-80.

It is an established opinion amongst some men, that there are in the understanding certain innate principles; some primary notions, characters, as it were, stamped upon the mind of man, which the soul receives in its very first being; and brings into the world with it. It would be sufficient to convince unprejudiced readers of the falseness of this supposition, if I should only shew (as I hope I shall in the following parts of this discourse) how men, barely by the use of their natural faculties, may attain to all the knowledge they have, without the help of any innate impressions; and may arrive at certainty, without any such original notions or principles. For I imagine any one will easily grant, that it would be impertinent to suppose, the ideas of colours innate in a creature, to whom God hath given sight, and a power to receive them by the eyes, from external objects: and no less unreasonable would it be to attribute several truths to the impressions of nature, and innate characters, when we may observe in ourselves faculties, fit to attain as easy and certain knowledge of them, as if they were originally imprinted on the mind.

But because a man is not permitted without censure to follow his own thoughts in the search of truth, when they lead him ever so little out of the common road; I shall set down the reasons that made me doubt of the truth of that opinion, as an excuse for my mistake, if I be in one; which I leave to be considered by those, who, with me, dispose themselves to embrace truth, wherever they find it.

* * *

2. If we will attentively consider newborn children, we shall have little reason to think, that they bring many ideas into the world with them. For bating perhaps some faint ideas of hunger and thirst, and warmth, and some pains which they may have felt in the womb, there is not the least appearance of any settled ideas at all in them; especially of ideas, answering the terms which make up those universal propositions, that are esteemed innate principles. One may perceive how, by degrees, afterwards, ideas come into their minds; and that they get no more, nor no other, than what experience, and the observations of things, that come in their way, furnish them with: which might be enough to satisfy us, that they are not original characters stamped on the mind.

＊　　＊　　＊

Of Ideas in General, and Their Original

1. Every man being conscious to himself that he thinks, and that which his mind is applied about, whilst thinking, being the ideas that are there, it is past doubt, that men have in their minds several ideas, such as are those expressed by the words, Whiteness, Hardness, Sweetness, Thinking, Motion, Man, Elephant, Army, Drunkenness, and others. It is in the first place then to be inquired, how he comes by them. I know it is a received doctrine, that men have native ideas, and original characters, stamped upon their minds, in their very first being. This opinion I have, at large, examined already; and, I suppose, what I have said, in the foregoing book, will be much more easily admitted, when I have shewn, whence the understanding may get all the ideas it has, and by what ways and degrees they may come into the mind; for which I shall appeal to every one's own observation and experience.

2. Let us then suppose the mind to be, as we say, white paper, void of all characters, without any ideas; how comes it to be furnished? Whence comes it by that vast store which the busy and boundless fancy of man has painted on it, with an almost endless variety? Whence has it all the materials of reason and knowledge? To this I answer, in one word, from experience; in all that our knowledge is founded, and from that it ultimately derives itself. Our observation employed either about external sensible objects, or about the internal operations of our minds, perceived and reflected on by ourselves, is that which supplies our understandings with all the materials of thinking. These two are the fountains of knowledge, from whence all the ideas we have, or can naturally have, do spring.

3. First, Our senses, conversant about particular sensible objects, do convey into the mind several distinct perceptions of things, according to those various ways wherein those objects do affect them: and thus we come by those ideas we have, of Yellow, White, Heat, Cold, Soft, Hard, Bitter, Sweet, and all those which we call sensible qualities; which when I say the senses convey into the mind, I mean, they from external objects convey into the mind what produces there those perceptions. This great source of most of the ideas we have, depending wholly upon our senses, and derived by them to the understanding, I call sensation.

4. Secondly, The other fountain, from which experience furnisheth the understanding with ideas, is the perception of the operations of our own mind within us, as it is employed about the ideas it has got; which operations, when the soul comes to reflect on and consider, do furnish the understanding with another set of ideas, which could not be had from things without; and such are Perception, Thinking, Doubting, Believing, Reasoning, Knowing, Willing, and all the different actings of our own minds; which we being conscious of and observing in ourselves, do from these receive into our understandings as distinct ideas, as we do from bodies affecting our senses. This source of ideas every man has wholly in himself; and though it be not sense, as having nothing to do with external objects, yet it is very like it, and might properly enough be called internal sense. But as I call the other sensation, so I call this reflection, the ideas it affords being such only as the mind gets by reflecting on its own operations within itself. By reflection then, in the following part of this discourse, I would be understood to mean that notice which the mind takes of its own operations, and the manner of them; by reason whereof there come to be ideas of these operations in the understanding. These two, I say, viz. external material things, as the objects of sensation; and the operations of our

own minds within, as the objects of reflection; are to me the only originals from whence all our ideas take their beginnings. The term operations here I use in a large sense, as comprehending not barely the actions of the mind about its ideas, but some sort of passions arising sometimes from them, such as is the satisfaction or uneasiness arising from any thought.

5. The understanding seems to me not to have the least glimmering of any ideas, which it doth not receive from one of these two. External objects furnish the mind with the ideas of sensible qualities, which are all those different perceptions they produce in us: and the mind furnishes the understanding with ideas of its own operations.

These, when we have taken a full survey of them and their several modes, combinations, and relations, we shall find to contain all our whole stock of ideas; and that we have nothing in our minds which did not come in one of these two ways. Let any one examine his own thoughts, and thoroughly search into his understanding; and then let him tell me, whether all the original ideas he has there, are any other than of the objects of his senses, or of the operations of his mind, considered as objects of his reflection; and how great a mass of knowledge soever he imagines to be lodged there, he will, upon taking a strict view, see that he has not any idea in his mind, but what one of these two have imprinted; though perhaps, with infinite variety compounded and enlarged by the understanding, as we shall see hereafter.

6. He that attentively considers the state of a child, at his first coming into the world, will have little reason to think him stored with plenty of ideas, that are to be the matter of his future knowledge: It is by degrees he comes to be furnished with them. And though the ideas of obvious and familiar qualities imprint themselves before the memory begins to keep a register of time or order, yet it is often so late before some unusual qualities come in the way, that there are few men that cannot recollect the beginning of their acquaintance with them: and if it were worth while, no doubt a child might be so ordered as to have but a very few even of the ordinary ideas, till he were grown up to a man. But all that are born into the world being surrounded with bodies that perpetually and diversly affect them; variety of ideas, whether care be taken of it or no, are imprinted on the minds of children. Light and colours are busy at hand every-where, when the eye is but open; sounds and some tangible qualities fail not to solicit their proper senses, and force an entrance to the mind: but yet, I think, it will be granted easily, that if a child were kept in a place where he never saw any other but black and white till he were a man, he would have no more ideas of scarlet or green, than he that from his childhood never tasted an oyster or a pineapple has of those particular relishes.

7. Men then come to be furnished with fewer or more simple ideas from without, according as the objects they converse with afford greater or less variety; and from the operations of their minds within, according as they more or less reflect on them. For though he that contemplates the operations of his mind cannot but have plain and clear ideas of them; yet unless he turns his thoughts that way, and considers them attentively, he will no more have clear and distinct ideas of all the operations of his mind, and all that may be observed therein, than he will have all the particular ideas of any landscape, or of the parts and motions of a clock, who will not turn his eyes to it, and with attention heed all the parts of it. The picture or clock may be so placed, that they may come in his way every day; but yet he will have but a confused idea of all the parts they are made up of, till he applies himself with attention to consider them each in particular.

LOCKE ON EDUCATION (1693) From John Locke, "Some Thoughts Concerning Education," as quoted in John W. Adamson, ed., *The Educational Writings of John Locke* (Cambridge, 1922), pp. 25-26, 28, 46, 71, 74, 76, 93, 104-05, 116-17, 121, 123, 125, 146, 178-79.

A sound mind in a sound body, is a short but full description of a happy state in this world: he that has these two, has little more to wish for; and he that wants either of them, will be but little the better for any thing else. Men's happiness or misery is most part of their own making. He whose mind directs not wisely, will never take the right way; and he whose body is crazy and feeble, will never be able to advance in it. I confess there are some men's constitutions of body and mind so vigorous and well framed by nature, that they need not much assistance from others, but by the strength of their natural genius, they are from their cradles carried towards what is excellent; and, by the privilege of their happy constitutions are able to do wonders. But examples of these are but few; and I think I may say that, of all the men we meet with, nine parts of ten are what they are, good or evil, useful or not, by their education. 'Tis that which makes the great difference in mankind. The little, and almost insensible impressions on our tender infancies, have very important and lasting consequences; and there 'tis, as in the fountains of some rivers, where a gentle application of the hand turns the flexible waters into channels, that make them take quite contrary courses; and by this little direction, given them at first in the source, they receive different tendencies, and arrive at last at very remote and distant places.

2. *Health.*—I imagine the minds of children, as easily turned, this or that way, as water itself; and though this be the principal part, and our main care should be about the inside, yet the clay cottage is not to be neglected. I shall therefore begin with the case, and consider first the health of the body, as that which perhaps you may rather expect, from that study I have been thought more peculiarly to have applied myself to; and that also, which will be soonest dispatched, as lying, if I guess not amiss, in a very little compass.

❋   ❋   ❋

30. And thus I have done with what concerns the body and health, which reduces itself to these few and easily observable rules. Plenty of open air, exercise, and sleep; plain diet, no wine or strong drink, and very little or no physic; not too warm and strait clothing; especially the head and feet kept cold, and the feet often used to cold water and exposed to wet.

31. *Mind.*—Due care being had to keep the body in strength and vigour, so that it may be able to obey and execute the orders of the mind: the next and principal business is, to set the mind right, that on all occasions it may be disposed to do nothing but what may be suitable to the dignity and excellency of a rational creature.

32. If what I have said in the beginning of this discourse be true, as I do not doubt but it is, viz. that the difference to be found in the manners and abilities of men, is owing more to their education than to any thing else; we have reason to conclude, that great care is to be had of the forming children's minds, and giving them that seasoning early, which shall influence their lives always after. For when they do well or ill, the praise or blame will be laid there: and when any thing is

done untowardly, the common saying will pass upon them, that it is suitable to their breeding.

33. As the strength of the body lies chiefly in being able to endure hardships, so also does that of the mind. And the great principle and foundation of all virtue and worth is placed in this, that a man is able to deny himself his own desires, cross his own inclinations, and purely follow what reason directs as best, though the appetite lean the other way.

34. *Early.*—The great mistake I have observed in people's breeding their children has been, that this has not been taken care enough of in its due season; that the mind has not been made obedient to rules, and pliant to reason, when at first it was most tender, most easy to be bowed.

*   *   *

I shall name one more that comes now in my way. By this method we shall see, whether what is required of him be adapted to his capacity, and any way suited to the child's natural genius and constitution: for that too must be considered in a right education. We must not hope wholly to change their original tempers, nor make the gay pensive and grave; nor the melancholy sportive, without spoiling them. God has stamped certain characters upon men's minds, which, like their shapes, may perhaps be a little mended; but can hardly be totally altered and transformed into the contrary.

He, therefore, that is about children, should well study their natures and aptitudes, and see, by often trials, what turn they easily take, and what becomes them; observe what their native stock is, how it may be improved, and what it is fit for: he should consider what they want, whether they be capable of having it wrought into them by industry, and incorporated there by practice; and whether it be worth while to endeavour it. For, in many cases, all that we can do, or should aim at, is, to make the best of what nature has given, to prevent the vices and faults to which such a constitution is most inclined, and give it all the advantages it is capable of. Every one's natural genius should be carried as far as it could; but to attempt the putting another upon him, will be but labour in vain; and what is so plastered on, will at best sit but untowardly, and have always hanging to it the ungracefulness of constraint and affectation.

67. *Manners.*—Manners, as they call it, about which children are so often perplexed, and have so many goodly exhortations made them, by their wise maids and governesses, I think, are rather to be learnt by example than rules:

*   *   *

90. *Governor.*—In all the whole business of education, there is nothing like to be less hearkened to, or harder to be well observed, than what I am now going to say; and that is, That I would, from their first beginning to talk, have some discreet, sober, nay wise person about children, whose care it should be to fashion them aright, and keep them from all ill, especially the infection of bad company. I think this province requires great sobriety, temperance, tenderness, diligence, and discretion, qualities hardly to be found united in persons that are to be had for ordinary salaries, nor easily to be found any where. As to the charge of it, I think it will be the money best laid out that can be about our children; and therefore, though it may be expensive more than is ordinary, yet it cannot be thought dear. He

that at any rate procures his child a good mind, well-principled, tempered to virtue and usefulness, and adorned with civility and good breeding, makes a better purchase for him, than if he laid out the money for an addition of more earth to his former acres. Spare it in toys and play-games, in silk and ribbons, laces and other useless expenses, as much as you please; but be not sparing in so necessary a part as this. 'Tis not good husbandry to make his fortune rich, and his mind poor. I have often, with great admiration, seen people lavish it profusely in tricking up their children in fine clothes, lodging and feeding them sumptuously, allowing them more than enough of useless servants, and yet at the same time starve their minds, and not take sufficient care to cover that, which is the most shameful nakedness, viz., their natural wrong inclinations and ignorance. This I can look on as no other than a sacrificing to their own vanity; it showing more their pride, than true care of the good of their children. Whatsoever you employ to the advantage of your son's mind, will show your true kindness, though it be to the lessening of his estate.

*　　*　　*

The great work of a governor is to fashion the carriage, and form the mind; to settle in his pupil good habits, and the principles of virtue and wisdom; to give him, by little and little, a view of mankind; and work him into a love and imitation of what is excellent and praiseworthy; and in the prosecution of it, to give him vigour, activity, and industry. The studies which he sets him upon, are but, as it were, the exercises of his faculties, and employment of his time, to keep him from sauntering and idleness, to teach him application, and accustom him to take pains, and to give him some little taste of what his own industry must perfect. For who expects, that under a tutor a young gentleman should be an accomplished critic, orator, or logician; go to the bottom of metaphysics, natural philosophy, or mathematics; or be a master in history or chronology? Though something of each of these is to be taught him: but it is only to open the door, that he may look in, and, as it were, begin an acquaintance, but not to dwell there: and a governor would be much blamed, that should keep his pupil too long, and lead him too far in most of them. But of good breeding, knowledge of the world, virtue, industry, and a love of reputation, he cannot have too much: and if he have these, he will not long want what he needs or desires of the other.

And since it cannot be hoped, he should have time and strength to learn all things, most pains should be taken about that which is most necessary; and that principally looked after, which will be of most and frequentest use to him in the world.

*　　*　　*

134. That which every gentleman (that takes any care of his education) desires for his son, besides the estate he leaves him, is contained I suppose in these four things, Virtue, Wisdom, Breeding, and Learning. I will not trouble myself whether these names do not some of them sometimes stand for the same thing, or really include one another. It serves my turn here to follow the popular use of these words, which, I presume, is clear enough to make me be understood, and I hope there will be no difficulty to comprehend my meaning.

135. *Virtue.*—I place Virtue as the first and most necessary of those endowments that belong to a man or a gentleman, as absolutely requisite to make him valued

and beloved by others, acceptable or tolerable to himself; without that, I think, he will be happy neither in this nor the other world.

136. *God.*—As the foundation of this, there ought very early to be imprinted on his mind a true notion of God, as of the independent Supreme Being, Author and Maker of all things, from whom we receive all our good, who loves us, and gives us all things; and, consequent to it, a love and reverence of this Supreme Being.

* * *

140. *Wisdom.*—Wisdom I take, in the popular acceptation, for a man's managing his business ably and with foresight in this world. This is the product of a good natural temper, application of mind and experience together, . . .

* * *

141. *Breeding.*—The next good quality belonging to a gentleman is good breeding. There are two sorts of ill breeding; the one, a sheepish bashfulness; and the other, a misbecoming negligence and disrespect in our carriage; both which are avoided by duly observing this one rule, Not to think meanly of ourselves, and not to think meanly of others.

* * *

147. *Learning.*—You will wonder, perhaps, that I put learning last, especially if I tell you I think it the least part. This will seem strange in the mouth of a bookish man: and this making usually the chief, if not only bustle and stir about children, this being almost that alone, which is thought on, when people talk of education, makes it the greater paradox. When I consider what a-do is made about a little Latin and Greek, how many years are spent in it, and what a noise and business it makes to no purpose, I can hardly forbear thinking that the parents of children still live in fear of the school-master's rod, which they look on as the only instrument of education; as a language or two to be its whole business. How else is it possible, that a child should be chained to the oar seven, eight, or ten of the best years of his life, to get a language or two, which I think might be had at a great deal cheaper rate of pains and time, and be learned almost in playing?

* * *

178. At the same time that he is learning French and Latin, a child, as has been said, may also be entered in arithmetic, geography, chronology, history, and geometry, too. For if these be taught him in French or Latin, when he begins once to understand either of these tongues, he will get a knowledge in these sciences, and the language to boot.

* * *

195. *Greek.*—This is, in short, what I have thought concerning a young gentleman's studies; wherein it will possibly be wondered that I should omit Greek, since amongst the Grecians is to be found the original, as it were, and foundation of

all that learning which we have in this part of the world. I grant it so; and will add, that no man can pass for a scholar, that is ignorant of the Greek tongue. But I am not here considering of the education of a professed scholar, but of a gentleman, to whom Latin and French, as the world now goes, is by every one acknowledged to be necessary. When he comes to be a man, if he has a mind to carry his studies farther, and look into the Greek learning, he will then easily get that tongue himself; and if he has not that inclination, his learning of it under a tutor will be but lost labour, and much of his time and pains spent in that which will be neglected and thrown away as soon as he is at liberty. For how many are there of a hundred, even amongst scholars themselves, who retain the Greek they carried from school; or ever improve it to a familiar reading, and perfect understanding of Greek authors?

✳   ✳   ✳

201. *Trade.*—I have one more thing to add, which as soon as I mention I shall run the danger to be suspected to have forgot what I am about, and what I have above written concerning education, which has all tended towards a gentleman's calling, with which a trade seems wholly to be inconsistent. And yet, I cannot forbear to say, I would have him learn a trade, a manual trade; nay, two or three, but one more particularly.

✳   ✳   ✳

212. *Travel.*—The last part usually in education is travel, which is commonly thought to finish the work, and complete the gentleman. I confess, travel into foreign countries has great advantages; but the time usually chosen to send young men abroad, is, I think, of all other, that which renders them least capable of reaping those advantages. Those which are proposed, as to the main of them, may be reduced to these two; first, language; secondly, an improvement in wisdom and prudence by seeing men, and conversing with people of tempers, customs, and ways of living, different from one another, and especially from those of his parish and neighbourhood. But from sixteen to one and twenty, which is the ordinary time of travel, men are, of all their lives, the least suited to these improvements.

✳   ✳   ✳

216. Though I am now come to a conclusion of what obvious remarks have suggested to me concerning education, I would not have it thought that I look on it as a just treatise on this subject. There are a thousand other things that may need consideration; especially if one should take in the various tempers, different inclinations, and particular defaults, that are to be found in children; and prescribe proper remedies. The variety is so great, that it would require a volume; nor would that reach it. Each man's mind has some peculiarity, as well as his face, that distinguishes him from all others; and there are possibly scarce two children who can be conducted by exactly the same method. Besides that, I think a prince, a nobleman, and an ordinary gentleman's son, should have different ways of breeding. But having had here only some general views, in reference to the main end and aims in education, and those designed for a gentleman's son, who[m] being then very little, I considered only as white paper, or wax, to be moulded and fashioned as one

pleases, I have touched little more than those heads, which I judged necessary for the breeding of a young gentleman of his condition in general; and have now published these my occasional thoughts, with this hope, that, though this be far from being a complete treatise on this subject, or such as that every one may find what will just fit his child in it; yet it may give some small light to those, whose concern for their dear little ones makes them so irregularly bold, that they dare venture to consult their own reason, in the education of their children, rather than wholly to rely upon old custom.

LOCKE ON IMPROVING THE MIND (1697)   From John Locke, "Of the Conduct of the Understanding," as quoted in John W. Adamson, ed., *The Educational Writings of John Locke* (Cambridge, 1922), pp. 183, 190-91, 195-96, 198, 216-18.

There is, it is visible, great variety in men's understandings, and their natural constitutions put so wide a difference between some men in this respect, that art and industry would never be able to master, and their very natures seem to want a foundation to raise on it that which other men easily attain unto. Amongst men of equal education there is great inequality of parts. And the woods of America, as well as the schools of Athens, produce men of several abilities in the same kind. Though this be so, yet I imagine most men come very short of what they might attain unto, in their several degrees, by a neglect of their understandings. A few rules of logic are thought sufficient in this case for those who pretend to the highest improvement, whereas I think there are a great many natural defects in the understanding capable of amendment, which are overlooked and wholly neglected. And it is easy to perceive that men are guilty of a great many faults in the exercise and improvement of this faculty of the mind, which hinder them in their progress, and keep them in ignorance and error all their lives. Some of them I shall take notice of, and endeavour to point out proper remedies for, in the following discourse.

*   *   *

4. *Of Practice and Habits.*—We are born with faculties and powers capable almost of anything, such at least as would carry us farther than can easily be imagined: but it is only the exercise of those powers which gives us ability and skill in anything, and leads us towards perfection.

A middle-aged ploughman will scarce ever be brought to the carriage and language of a gentleman, though his body be as well-proportioned, and his joints as supple, and his natural parts not any way inferior. The legs of a dancing-master and the fingers of a musician fall as it were naturally, without thought or pains, into regular and admirable motions. Bid them change their parts, and they will in vain endeavour to produce like motions in the members not used to them, and it will require length of time and long practice to attain but some degrees of a like ability. What incredible and astonishing actions do we find rope-dancers and tumblers bring their bodies to! Not but that sundry in almost all manual arts are as wonderful; but

I name those which the world takes notice of for such, because on that very account they give money to see them. All these admired motions, beyond the reach and almost conception of unpractised spectators, are nothing but the mere effects of use and industry in men whose bodies have nothing peculiar in them from those of the amazed lookers-on.

As it is in the body, so it is in the mind: practice makes it what it is; and most even of those excellencies which are looked on as natural endowments, will be found, when examined into more narrowly, to be the product of exercise, and to be raised to that pitch only by repeated actions. Some men are remarked for pleasantness in raillery; others for apologues and apposite diverting stories. This is apt to be taken for the effect of pure nature, and that the rather because it is not got by rules, and those who excel in either of them never purposely set themselves to the study of it as an art to be learnt.

To what purpose all this but to show that the difference so observable in men's understandings and parts does not arise so much from their natural faculties as acquired habits. He would be laughed at that should go about to make a fine dancer out of a country hedger at past fifty. And he will not have much better success who shall endeavour at that age to make a man reason well, or speak handsomely, who has never been used to it, though you should lay before him a collection of all the best precepts of logic or oratory. Nobody is made anything by hearing of rules or laying them up in his memory; practice must settle the habit of doing, without reflecting on the rule; and you may as well hope to make a good painter or musician extempore, by a lecture and instruction in the arts of music and painting, as a coherent thinker or a strict reasoner by a set of rules showing him wherein right reasoning consists.

*   *   *

What then should be done in the case? I answer, we should always remember what I said above, that the faculties of our souls are improved and made useful to us just after the same manner as our bodies are. Would you have a man write or paint, dance or fence well, or perform any other manual operation dexterously and with ease; let him have ever so much vigour and activity, suppleness and address naturally, yet nobody expects this from him unless he has been used to it, and has employed time and pains in fashioning and forming his hand or outward parts to these motions. Just so it is in the mind; would you have a man reason well, you must use him to it betimes, exercise his mind in observing the connexion of ideas and following them in train. Nothing does this better than mathematics, which therefore I think should be taught all those who have the time and opportunity, not so much to make them mathematicians as to make them reasonable creatures; for though we all call ourselves so because we are born to it if we please, yet we may truly say, nature gives us but the seeds of it; we are born to be, if we please, rational creatures, but it is use and exercise only that makes us so, and we are indeed so no farther than industry and application has carried us. And therefore, in ways of reasoning which men have not been used to, he that will observe the conclusions they take up must be satisfied they are not all rational.

*   *   *

7. *Mathematics.*—I have mentioned mathematics as a way to settle in the mind an habit of reasoning closely and in train; not that I think it necessary that all men should be deep mathematicians, but that, having got the way of reasoning, which that study necessarily brings the mind to, they might be able to transfer it to other parts of knowledge as they shall have occasion. For in all sorts of reasoning every single argument should be managed as a mathematical demonstration; the connexion and dependence of ideas should be followed, till the mind is brought to the source on which it bottoms, and observes the coherence all along, . . .

*   *   *

20. *Reading.*—This is that which I think great readers are apt to be mistaken in. Those who have read of every thing are thought to understand every thing too; but it is not always so. Reading furnishes the mind only with materials of knowledge, it is thinking makes what we read ours. We are of the ruminating kind, and it is not enough to cram our selves with a great load of collections; unless we chew them over again they will not give us strength and nourishment.

JONATHAN SWIFT DESCRIBES THE WAR BETWEEN THE ANCIENT AND MODERN AUTHORS (1697)   From Jonathan Swift, "The Battle of the Books," as quoted in John Nichols, ed., *The Works of the Rev. Jonathan Swift* (London, 1808), vol. II, pp. 386-393.

Now, whoever will please to take this scheme, and either reduce or adapt it to an intellectual state, or commonwealth of learning, will soon discover the first ground of disagreement, between the two great parties at this time in arms; and may form just conclusions, upon the merits of either cause. But the issue or events of this war, are not so easy to conjecture at: for, the present quarrel is so inflamed by the warm heads of either faction, and the pretensions somewhere or other so exorbitant, as not to admit the least overtures of accommodation. This quarrel first began, as I have heard it affirmed by an old dweller in the neighbourhood, about a small spot of ground, lying and being upon one of the two tops of the hill Parnassus; the highest and largest of which, had, it seems, been, time out of mind, in quiet possession of certain tenants, called the ancients; and the other was held by the moderns. But these, disliking their present station, sent certain ambassadors to the ancients, complaining of a great nuisance; how the height of that part of Parnassus, quite spoiled the prospect of theirs, especially towards the East; and therefore, to avoid a war, offered them the choice of this alternative; either that the ancients, would please to remove themselves and their effects, down to the lower summit, which the moderns would graciously surrender to them, and advance in their place: or else the said ancients, will give leave to the moderns, to come with shovels and mattocks, and level the said hill, as low as they shall think it convenient. To which the ancients made answer; how little they expected such a message as this, from a colony, whom they had admitted, out of their own free grace, to so near a neighbourhood. That, as to their own seat, they were aborigines of it, and therefore to talk with them of a removal or surrender, was a language they did not understand. That, if the height of the hill on their side, shortened the prospect of the moderns, it was a disadvantage they could not help; but desired them to consider, whether that injury (if it be any) were not largely recompensed, by the shade and shelter it afforded them. That, as to the levelling or digging down, it was either folly or ignorance to propose it, if they did, or did not know, how that side of the hill was an entire rock, which would break their tools and hearts, without any damage to itself. That they would therefore advise the moderns, rather to raise their own side of the hill, than dream of pulling down that of the ancients: to the former of which, they would not only give license, but also largely contribute. All this was rejected by the moderns, with much indignation, who still insisted upon one of the two expedients; and so this difference broke out into a long and obstinate war, maintained on the one part, by resolution, and by the courage of certain leaders and allies; but on the other, by the greatness of their number, upon all defeats affording continual recruits. In this quarrel, whole rivulets of ink have been exhausted, and the virulence of both parties, enormously augmented. Now, it must be here understood, that ink is the great missive weapon in all battles of the learned, which conveyed through a sort of engine, called a quill, infinite numbers of these are darted at the enemy, by the valiant on each side, with equal skill and violence, as if it were an engagement of porcupines. This malignant liquor, was compounded by the engineer who invented it, of two ingredients, which are, gall and copperas; by its bitterness and venom to suit in some degree; as well as to foment, the genius of the combatants. And as the Grecians after an engagement, when they could not agree about the victory, were wont to set up trophies on both sides, the beaten party being content to be at the same expense, to keep itself in countenance (a laudable and ancient custom, happily revived of late, in the art of war); so the learned, after a sharp and bloody dispute, do on both sides hang out their trophies too, whichever comes by the worst. These trophies have largely inscribed on them the merits of the cause: a full impartial account of such a battle, and how the victory fell clearly to the party that set them up. They are known to the world under several names; as, disputes, arguments, rejoinders, brief considerations, answers, replies, remarks, reflections, objections, confutations. For a very few days they are fixed up in all publick places, either by themselves or their representatives for passengers to gaze at; whence the chiefest and largest are removed to certain magazines, they call libraries, there to remain in a quarter purposely assigned them, and thenceforth begin to be called books of controversy.

In these books, is wonderfully instilled and preserved, the spirit of each warrior, while he is alive; and after his death, his soul transmigrates there, to inform them. This, at least, is the more common opinion; but I believe, it is with libraries, as with other cemeteries; where some philosophers affirm, that a certain spirit, which they call *brutum hominis,* hovers over the monument, till the body is corrupted, and turns to dust, or to worms, but then vanishes or dissolves; so we may say, a restless spirit haunts over every book, till dust or worms have seized upon it; which to some may happen in a few days, but to others later: and therefore books of controversy, being, of all others, haunted by the most disorderly spirits, having always been confined in a separate lodge from the rest; and for fear of a mutual violence against each other, it was thought prudent by our ancestors, to bind them to the peace, with strong iron chains. Of which invention the original occasion was this. When the works of Scotus first came out, they were carried to a certain library, and had lodgings appointed them; but this author was no sooner settled, than he went to visit his master Aristotle; and there both concerted together to seize Plato by main force, and turn him out from his ancient station among the divines, where he had peaceably dwelt near eight hundred years. The attempt succeeded, and the two usurpers have reigned ever since in his stead: but to maintain quiet for the future, it was decreed that all polemicks of the larger size, should be held fast with a chain.

By this expedient, the publick peace of libraries might certainly have been preserved, if a new species of controversial books had not arose of late years, instinct with a more malignant spirit, from the war above-mentioned between the learned, about the higher summit of Parnassus.

When these books were first admitted into the publick libraries, I remember to have said, upon occasion, to several persons concerned, how I was sure they would create broils wherever they came, unless a world of care were taken: and therefore I advised, that the champions of each side should be coupled together, or otherwise mixed, that, like the blending of contrary poisons, their malignity might be employed among themselves. And it seems, I was neither an ill prophet, nor an ill counsellor; for it was nothing else but the neglect of this caution, which gave occasion to the terrible fight, that happened on Friday last, between the ancient and modern books, in the King's Library. Now, because the talk of this battle is so fresh in every body's mouth, and the expectation of the town so great to be informed in the particulars; I, being possessed of all qualifications requisite in an historian, and retained by neither party, have resolved to comply with the urgent importunity of my friends, by writing down a full impartial account hereof.

The guardian of the Regal Library, a person of great valour, but chiefly renowned for his humanity, had been a fierce champion for the moderns; and, in an engagement upon Parnassus, had vowed, with his own hands, to knock down two of the ancient chiefs, who guarded a small pass on the superiour rock: but, endeavouring to climb up, was cruelly obstructed by his own unhappy weight, and tendency towards his centre; a quality, to which those of the modern party are extreme subject; for being light-headed, they have, in speculation, a wonderful agility, and conceive nothing too high for them to mount; but, in reducing to practice, discover a mighty pressure about their posteriors, and their heels. Having thus failed in his design, the disappointed champion bore a cruel rancour to the ancients; which he resolved to gratify, by showing all marks of his favour to the books of their adversaries, and lodging them in the fairest apartments; when at the same time, whatever book had the boldness to own itself for an advocate of the ancients, was buried alive in some obscure corner, and threatened, upon the least displeasure, to be turned out of doors. Besides, it so happened, that about this time there was a strange confusion of place, among all the books in the library; for which, several reasons were assigned. Some imputed it to a great heap of learned dust, which a perverse wind blew off from a shelf of moderns, into the keeper's eyes. Others affirmed, he had a humour to pick the worms out of the schoolmen, and swallow them fresh and fasting; whereof some fell upon his spleen, and some climbed up into his head, to the great perturbation of both. And lastly, others maintained, that by walking much in the dark about the library, he had quite lost the situation of it out of his head; and therefore, in replacing his books, he was apt to mistake, and clap Des Cartes next to Aristotle; poor Plato had got between Hobbes and the Seven wise masters, and Virgil was hemmed in with Dryden on one side, and Withers on the other.

Mean while those books, that were advocates for the moderns, chose out one from among them, to make a progress through the whole library, examine the number and strength of their party, and concert their affairs. This messenger performed all things very industriously, and brought back with him a list of their forces in all fifty thousand, consisting chiefly of light-horse, heavy-armed foot, and mercenaries: whereof the foot, were in general but sorrily armed, and worse clad: their horses large, but extremely out of case and heart; however some few, by trading among the ancients, had furnished themselves tolerably enough.

While things were in this ferment, discord grew extremely high; hot words passed on both sides, and ill blood was plentifully bred. Here a solitary ancient, squeezed up among a whole shelf of moderns, offered fairly to dispute the case, and to prove by manifest reason, that the priority was due to them, from long possession; and in regard of their prudence, antiquity, and above all, their great merits toward the moderns. But these denied the premises, and seemed very much to wonder, how the ancients could pretend to insist upon their antiquity, when it was so plain (if they went to that) that the moderns, were much the more ancient of the two. . . .

ADOLPHUS SPEED'S PROPOSAL FOR AN ACADEMY FOR YOUNG GENTLEMEN (c. 1640)
From G. H. Turnbull, ed., *Hartlib, Dury and Comenius: Gleanings from Hartlib's Papers* (London, 1947), pp. 117-18.

Adolphus Speed to Samuel Hartlib

A very choice place for conveniencie of Aire, House-roome, Gardens, and walks most compleat, pleasant, and healthfull, severall Masters in the house, being absolute, compleat Gentlemen and excellent Scholars; These to teach them Hebrew, Greek, Latin, and French, by incomparably more methodicall, compendious and facile waies then formerly by any: by lessening there former tedium by more than halfe. But above all they are to be taught the explanation of the Scriptures, and the principles of Religion by a devout, a most Religious and a piously learned Minister in the House with them; And shall be taught to write by sufficient Pen-men, and the best and most perfect way of shortwriting, to take out Sermons, and to be able to convert them into Hebrew, Greeke, Latine and French, as some of very tender yeares have lately done; They shall likewise be fully instructed in Heraldry by a deserving Antiquary of very great knowledge therein; And shall have a skilfull and well experienced Picture drawn to perfect them in that Art, if they shall delight therein; Masters of Musick, and Dancing—Masters constantly to attend them, skilfull Fencers in a gentle and a moderate way to ins+ruct and exercise them (for their Recreation) in that Science, Horsmasters with speciall care and diligence to teach them all manner of Horsemanship, and severall easie and well guided Horses kept for them to those purposes, with all necessarie Rings, and Riding-places provided for them: A Gentleman skilfull in all military affaires to train them up (for their delight) in the exercise of Armes.

They shall further (if their Parents be so pleased) be taught the true experimentall naturall Phylosophy and what is most necessary of the Mathematicks, to wit, Arithmetick, Geometry, Geography, Cosmography, perspective and Architecture, and also whatsoever is most excellent of the practicall Mathematicks, whatsoever belongeth to Fortification, besieging, defending of places, fire-works, ordering of Battalies and marches of Armes etc. A discreet care to be taken for such wholesome diet, as shall be most convenient for them at all seasons, with a direction of a Doctor of Physick very famous and of exceeding great judgement, constantly in the House to overlook them, and to advise with their Parents and friends for the timely prevention of any infirmity they shall be inclinable unto, or shall happen unto them.

MRS. DURY ON THE EDUCATION OF GIRLS (c. 1640)   From Dorothy Dury, "Of the Education of Girls," as quoted in G. H. Turnbull, ed., *Hartlib, Dury and Comenius: Gleanings from Hartlib's Papers* (London, 1947), pp. 120-21.

Madame,

From you as the instrument of others, I received a call, to consider the manner of the education of the youth of our sexe, which according to my measure I have done, and therefore present you heerewith briefe heads of such an undertaking, that if the Lord approve it, you may be instrumentall to communicate it, as you find it may be profitable to this generation. I have not much hope that this Draught will be either received or approved; but I expect rather that it shall meet with disdain and contempt. However I am not ashamed of laying downe this meane and simple way to breed youth in; because it is (according to my light) agreeing with the simplicitie of the Gospell, which was, is, and must be despised by the world: but we must not so walke (for I hope we have not so learned Christ) as to conforme or comply with the world, what ever good might seem plausibly to arise out of such a conformity or compliance; and therefore I have chosen to make Christ our example, which teacheth us to deny all worldly lusts, and to live soberly, counting it our spirituall meat and drinke to doe the will of the Father; and therfore ought we to shun all things, which we dare not owne to him, as part of that. Upon this ground I have in this little draught, left out the teaching of youth dauncing and curious workes; both which serve onely, to fill the fancy with unnecessary, unprofitable and proud imaginations. My experience as well as my reason tells me this; for my owne education was to learne both, and all I got by them was a great trouble to forget both, that so I might stand lesse in opposition to the simplicity of the Gospell in my affections and practise; and though this was difficult at first yet I found afterwards a great benefit; in being willing to be despised for my homely and meane walking, endeavouring to cast off those high lookes and mincing gate, which is gotten by dauncing; both which are condemned by the prophet Esay expressly (Esai. 3. 16.17. etc.): and since I have been encouraged to this, by finding that no people governed but by reason it selfe, can shew any reall good arising to humane society from those practises which all of mankind should aime at, that will live reasonably and not fantastically.

As for curious workes I see them, some of the inventions found out by man, and condemned by God; as being only for shew, and to foment the working of fancy, and not able to bring the least helpe to the well-being of man; but on the other hand they take up thoughts, and fill the mind with those toyes, which hinder more serious, profitable, and comfortable imployments.

I could never see a ground to pray for a blessing upon either of these; which plainly shewed me as a good Christian, I could not practise either; for certainly upon all that we doe, even all naturall actions, we may seeke a blessing, if that we have an eye to God's glory in them; for God in Nature teacheth us them, and in them a necessary good to humane Societie or to our selves, neither of which can I yet find to be in these two imployments; I have yet one reason more against dauncing and unnecessary workes, namely, that I am sure time spent, in that which is necessary to humane society is without dispute best: and seeing our time is short here, and that we should be as pilgrims and strangers in this world; I would always chuse to live in the practise of those things, which are undoubtedly the best, and not take up that which I must defend by doubtful arguments. Much more I could say upon these subjects, but now I will only tell you, that as I will not censure those who educate youth in them; so I will take my owne liberty not to practise with them; knowing I must walke by my light, they by theirs.

As for that part of their practise common in schooles to teach them dressing, curling, and such like, I must also disclaime it upon the same grounds that I reject the two former practises, namely, because it brings no good to the soule or body of mankind: neither from Religion or Reason hath it a ground, no more than those above named: besides we may see what great inconveniences daily come from that custome in this nation, so as I am not willing to name them; but (to speake modestly) we see they become such admirers of themselves, as the dotage upon their owne persons makes them useless to all others, both in regard of their purses and bodily assistance; for all they get is too little to lay out in fine cloaths, so as charitie is quite lost, whereof the usefullnes, excellency, and necessity is expressed *Rom. 13. ch.* and *I Cor. 13 chap.* And as for doing the offices of love, which as Christians we owe one to another; cloaths are so made in observance unto fashion, that they cannot stirre in them without pain to the wearers, so that for want of exercise they become even unhealthy themselves, and are unable to helpe others.

Again, it fills their mind with so much pride, as they despise all, not set out as they are: and for that the Lord gives them up to their hearts lusts, which betrayes them to all that their sinfull nature can desire: so as we see generally our sexe in this Kingdome minds nothing but idlenes and pleasure, and live as not using reason, nor knowing God who hath declared that we must account for every idle word and thought.

Thus (Madame) I have briefly shewed you, why I dissent from the ordinary way of educating youth, in which I have my owne satisfaction: if God shall make my reasons satisfactory to others, as they may be profited, I shall rejoyce; and if not, I hope, I shall neither refuse the contempt which may light upon me for following the Lord Christ in the way I have learnt him: nor refuse to take up that part of his crosse, which brings with it the hatred of the world. But indeed I do not only expect contempt from them that know not God, but also from those that pretend, and it may be really in a measure do know him: yet I say again, I must not walke by their light, nor take the ease of the broad way, but I must strive to goe in at the narrow and straight gate, that so I may tread in the steps of the Lord Christ. My owne breeding and practise hath been too dangerously ill for me, to returne to those things either in my selfe, or to teach others. It may be said to me, what fruit have you of those things, wherof now you are ashamed: therfore I must renounce them, and desire the Lord that he will manifest to others his will in this, that all may see the excellencie of the simplicitie of the Gospell declared in the life and doctrine of Christ, to whose free grace she earnestly commends you, who is (or desires to be) found in him.

WILLIAM PETTY ON EDUCATION (1648)   From *W.* [*illiam*] *P.* [*etty's*] *Advice to Mr. Samuel Hartlib for the Advancement of Some Particular Parts of Learning* (London, 1648), pp. 1-9, 17-18, 22-23.

The Advice for Advancement of Some
Particular Parts of Learning

To give an exact Definition or nice Division of Learning, or of the Advancement thereof, we shall not undertake (it being already so accurately done by the great Lord Verulam) Intending onely to shew where our owne shoe pincheth us, or to point at some pieces of Knowledge, the improvement wherof (as we at least conceive) would make much to the generall good and comfort of all mankind and withall to deliver our own opinion by what meanes they may be raised some one degree neerer to perfection.

*   *   *

And now we shall think of whetting our tooles and preparing sharp Instruments for this hard work, by delivering our thoughts concerning Education, which are,

1. That there be instituted *Ergastula Literaria*, Literary-workhouses, where Children may be taught as well to doe something towards their living, as to Read and Write.

That the businesse of Education be not (as now) committed to the worst and unworthiest of men, but that it be seriously studied and practised by the best and abler persons.

That all Children of above seven yeares old may be presented to this kind of Education, none being to be excluded by reason of the poverty and unability of their Parents, for hereby it hath come to passe, that many are now holding the Plough, which might have beene made fit to steere the State. Wherefore let such poor children be imployed on works wherby they may earne their living, equall to their strength and understanding, and such as they may performe as well as elder and abler persons, viz. attending Engines, &c. And if they cannot get their whole living, and their Parents can contribute nothing at all to make it up, let them stay somewhat the longer in the Work-house.

That since few children have need of reading before they know, or can be acquainted with the Things they read of, or of writing, before their thoughts are worth the recording, or they are able to put them into any forme, (which we call inditing) much lesse of learning languages, when there bee Books enough for their present use in their owne mother Tongue; our opinion is, that those Things being withall somewhat above their capacity, (as being to be attained by Judgement, which is weakest in children) be deferred awhile, and others more needfull for them, such as are in the order of Nature before those afore mentioned, and are attainable by the help of Memory, which is either most strong or unpreoccupied in children, be studied before them. We wish therefore that the Educands be taught to observe and remember all sensible Objects and Actions, whether they be Naturall or Artificiall, which the Educators must upon all occasions expound unto them.

That they use such Exercises whether in work, or for recreation, as tend to the health, agility and strength of their bodies.

That they be taught to Read by much more compendious meanes then are in common use, which is a thing certainly very easie and feasible.

That they be not onely taught to Write according to our Common Way, but also to Write Swiftly and in Reall Characters, as likewise the dextrous use of the Instruments for Writing many Copies of the same thing at once.

That the Artificiall Memory be thought upon, and if the precepts thereof be not too farre above Childrens Capacities, We conceive it not improper for them to learn that also.

That in no case the Art of Drawing and designing be omitted, to what course of Life soever those children are to be applied, since the use thereof for expressing the conceptions of the mind, seemes (at least to us) to be little inferiour to that of Writing, and in many cases performeth what by words is impossible.

That the Elements of Arithmetick and Geometry be by all studied, being not onely of great and frequent use in all humane Affaires but also sure guides and helps to Reason, and especiall Remedies for a volatile and unstedy mind.

That effectuall Courses be taken to try the Abilities of the Bodies and Minds of Children, the strength of their Memory, inclination of their Affections either to Vice or Vertue, and to which of them in particular, and withall to alter what is bad in them, and increase and improve what is good, applying all, whether good or bad, to the least Inconveniencie and most Advantage.

That such as shall have need to learne Forraine Languages (the use whereof would be much lessened, were the Reall and Common Characters brought into practise) may be taught them by incomparably more easie wayes then are now usuall.

That no ignoble, unnecessary, or condemned Part of Learning be taught in those houses of Education, so that if any man shall vainely fall upon them, he himselfe onely may be blamed.

That such as have any naturall ability and fitnesse to Musick be Encouraged and Instructed therein.

That all Children, though of the highest ranke, be taught some gentile Manufacture in their minority, such as are

Turning of curious Figures.

Making Mathematicall Instruments, Dialls, and how to use them in Astronomicall Observations.

Making Watches and other Trochilick motions.

Limning and Painting on Glasse or in Oyle Colours.

Graving, Etching, Carving, Embossing and Molding in sundry matters.

The Lapidaries Art of knowing, cutting and setting Iewells.

Grinding of Glasses Dioptricall and Catoptricall.

Botanicks and Gardening.

Making Musicall Instruments.

Navarchy and making Modells for buildings and rigging of Ships.

Architecture and making Modells for houses.

The Confectioners, Perfumers or Diers Arts.

Chymistry, refining Metalls and Counterfeiting Iewells.

Anatomy making Sceletons and excarnating bowells.

Making Mariners Compasses, Globes, and other Magnetick Devices.

And all, for these Reasons.

1. They shall be lesse subject to be cousened by Artificers.

2. They will become more industrious in generall.

3. They will certainly bring to passe most excellent Works, being as Gentlemen, ambitious to excell ordinarie Work-men.

4. They being able to make Experiments themselves, may doe it with lesse charge, and more care then others will doe it for them.

5. The *Resp. Artium* will be much advanced, when such as are rich and able, are also willing to make Luciferous Experiments.

6. It may engage them to be Mecaenates and Patrons of Arts.

7. It will keepe them from worse occasions of spending their time and estates.

8. As it will be a great Ornament in prosperity, so it wil be a great Refuge and stay in adversity and common calamity.

As for what remaines of Education, we cannot but hope that those, whom we have desired should make it their trade, will Supply it, and render the Idea therof much more perfect.

We have already recommended the studie of the Elements of Arithmetick and Geometry to all Men in generall, but they being the best grounded parts of Speculative knowledge, and of so Vast use in all Practicall Arts. We cannot but commend deeper enquiries into them. And although the way of advancing them in particular, may be drawne from what we have already delivered, concerning the Advancement of learning in generall, yet for the more explicit understanding of our meaning herein, we referre to Master Pells most excellent Idea thereof, written to Master Hartlib.

In the next place for the Advancement of all Mechanicall Arts and Manufactures, we wish that there were erected a Gymnasium Mechanicum or a Colledge of Trades-men (or for more expedition untill such a place could be built, that the most convenient houses for such a purpose may be either bought or hired) wherein we would that one at least of every Trade (but the Prime most Ingenious Work-man, the most desirous to improve his Art,) might be allowed therein, a handsom dwelling Rent free, which with the Credit of being admitted into this Society, and the quick sale which certainly they would have of their Commodities, when all men would repaire thither, as to a Market of rare and exquisite pieces of Workmanship, would be a sufficient Motive to attract the very ablest Mechanicks, and such as we have described, to desire a fellowship in this Colledge.

From this Institution we may clearly hope when the excellent in all Arts are not onely Neighbours, but intimate Friends and Brethren, united in a Common desire and zeal to promote them, that all Trades will miraculously prosper, and new Inventions would be more frequent, then new fashions of Clothes and household-stuffe. Here would be the best and most effectuall opportunities and meanes, for writing a History of Trades in perfection and exactnesse, and what Experiments and stuffe would all those Shops and Operations afford to Active and Philosophicall heads, out of which, to extract that Interpretation of Nature, whereof there is so little, and that so bad as yet extant in the world?

Within the walls of this Gymnasium or College, should be a Nosecomium Academicum according to the most exact and perfect Idea thereof a compleate *Theatrum Botanicum,* stalls and Cages for all strange Beastes and Birds, with Ponds and Conservatories for all exotick Fishes, here all Animalls capable thereof should be made fit for some kind of labour and imployment, that they may as well be of use living as dead; here should be a Repositorie of all kind of Rarities Naturall and Artificiall pieces of Antiquity, Modells of all great and noble Engines, with Designes and Platformes of Gardens and Buildings. The most Artificiall Fountaines and Water-works, a Library of Select Bookes, an Astronomicall Observatory for celestiall Bodies and Meteor, large pieces of Ground for severall Experiments of Agriculture, Galleries of the rarest Paintings and Statues, with the fairest Globes, and Geographcall Maps of the best descriptions, and so farre as it possible, we would have this place to be the Epitome or Abstract of the whole world. So that a man conversant within those walls, would certainly prove a greater Schollar, then the Walking Libraries so called, although he could neither write nor read. But if a Child, before he learned to read or write, were made acquainted with all Things, and Actions (as he might be in this Colledge) how easily would he understand all good Bookes afterwards, and smell out the fopperies of bad ones. As for the Situation, Modell, Policy Oeconomy, with the Number of Officers and Retainers to this Colledge, and the Priviledges thereof, it is as yet time enough to delineate. Only we wish that a Society of Men might be instituted as carefull to advance Arts as the Iesuites are to Propagate their Religion for the government and mannaging of it.

But what relish will there be in all those dainties whereof we have spoken, if we want a palate to tast them, which certainly is Health, the most desirable of all earthly blessings, and how can we in any reason expect Health, when there are so many great difficulties in the curing of diseases and no proportionable Course taken to remove them? we shall therefore pursue the Meanes of acquiring the Publicke Good and comfort of Mankind a little further, and vent our conceits concerning a Nosocomium Academicum or an Hospitall to cure the Infirmities both of Physician and Patient.

We intended to have given the most perfect Idea of this Nosocomium Academicum, and consequently to have treated of the Situation and Fabrick of the House, Garden, Library, Chymicall Laboratorie, Anatomicall Theater, Apotheca, with all the Instruments and Furniture belonging to each of them, as also of the whole Policy and Oeconomy thereof. But since such a work could not be brought to passe without much charge (the very naming wherof doth deter men even from the most noble and necessary Attempts) we are contented to pourtray only such a Nosocomium, as may be made out of one of our old Hospitals, without any new donations or creeping to Benefactors, onely with a little paines taken by the Reforming hand of Authority.

JOHN DURY ON EDUCATION (c. 1650) From John Dury, *The Reformed School*, H. M. Knox, ed. (Liverpool, 1958), pp. 28-33, 36-37, 39-41.

The Rules of Education

The chief rule of the whole work is that nothing may be made tedious and grievous to the children, but all the toilsomeness of their business the governor and ushers are to take upon themselves; that by diligence and industry all things may be so prepared, methodized and ordered for their apprehension that their work may unto them be as a delightful recreation by the variety and easiness thereof.

The things to be looked unto in the care of their education are (1) Their advancement in piety; (2) The preservation of their health; (3) The forming of their manners; (4) Their proficiency in learning.

That they may be advanced in piety, they shall be exercised every day (1) in prayers, (2) in reading the Scriptures, (3) in catechetical conferences, (4) and on the Lord's day in the duties of solemn worship.

Their daily prayers, reading of Scriptures, and conferences shall go together in this order.

In the evening when the time of retiring is come, every usher shall see his scholars in their chamber (for if they could be all that belong to each usher made to sleep in one large chamber like a gallery, two and two in a bed, the way of overseeing and uniting them in their exercises would be most commodious); and when they are going to unclothe themselves, one of their number shall be taken in his turn according to a list to go before the rest in a short prayer, or the usher himself shall do it before they begin to put off their clothes, each of them kneeling at the bedside where he is to sleep; and the prayer being ended, he whose turn it is shall read unto them some part of the Holy Scriptures while they unclothe themselves, and pray in two or three words for a blessing upon their rest. He whose turn it is to do this duty shall sleep that night with the usher to whose care he is committed, and in the morning shall rise with him half an hour before the rest to waken his fellow-scholars (at the hour appointed), to cause them rise; which whiles they are a-doing and putting on their clothes and combing their heads, he shall again, with a previous short ejaculation, read some part of the Scripture unto them, and with a short prayer (every one of the rest kneeling or standing by the bed where he slept) thank God for his preservation over them in the night past, and crave his direction, blessing and protection for the day following. This is to be done within the space of half an hour, to be measured by a sand-glass; after which time every one shall go abroad for the space of another half-hour to stretch, wash, and cleanse himself till, by the ringing of a bell, the whole family be called together. At this meeting the women and girls shall be in one room by themselves and the men and boys in another, so that they shall not see one another and yet both be able to hear him who shall be appointed to go before them all in the family-duty. He shall be some man of the Association in his daily or weekly turn, as they shall appoint it, who shall with a short prayer crave a blessing upon their meeting, and read a parcel of the Holy Scriptures, and conclude the reading with a short prayer; all which shall not exceed the space of half an hour, and the next half-hour following shall be spent in catechetical exercises and conferences according to the order which the governor shall settle in that matter differently towards the different ages and degrees of proficiency in the younger and more aged scholars. As for the members of the Association, their conferences shall not be stinted within such a time, but may be extended at pleasure; only the way how they ought to be ordered, that all may profit thereby and confusion may be avoided, is to be determined by the governor, with their approbation.

At dinner and supper-time (which shall not exceed half an hour) one of the children shall in his turn daily crave a blessing, in the name of all, upon their food, and read a part of the Scripture unto them while they are at table; and when they have done, they shall jointly sing a stave or two of a Psalm of thanksgiving.

After supper, before they go to their chambers, they shall meet all again in their several rooms each sex by themselves, to join in prayer and in reading the word, as in the morning they did, for the space of half an hour; and another half-hour afterward shall be spent in conferences, wherein the children shall be encouraged and accustomed to propose questions to their teachers, or to one another, concerning matters of doubt which may have been incident unto their thoughts, either from the reading of Scripture or some other thing observed in the day-time; which being done, they shall all retire unto their several quarters and prepare to go to bed.

This course of daily exercise in piety is to be continued without interruption; nobody is to be exempted from it but only in case of sickness.

On the Lord's day, over and above this daily sacrifice within doors to be observed, the children shall be brought forth unto the public meetings to join with the congregation of others in the worship of God; and at the intervals of times between the public meetings and the last sermon and supper-time, conferences shall be entertained with them concerning the things which they have heard.

And if those of the Association should entertain any prophetical exercises amongst themselves, or with others from without, then some of the most advanced scholars should be admitted to be present with them.

This care of advancing piety and keeping the Lord's day is to be made the chief of all things belonging to their education.

Concerning the Preservation of their Health

The next principal care is concerning the preservation of their health, wherein all things belonging (1) to their diet, (2) their sleeping, (3) to their bodily exercises, (4) and to their cleanliness are to be rightly ordered and overseen; that the orders may be observed.

CONCERNING THEIR DIET

Their diet shall be appointed for every day of the week what it shall be, and when it shall be given them.

Their breakfast, at 8 of the clock in the morning, of bread and butter or some other thing, they may be at it for the space of half an hour.

Their dinner of good healthful plain food, a competency is to be upon the table for them precisely at 12 of the clock.

Their supper of some food of light and easy digestion is to be upon the table precisely at half an hour past six of the clock, and before seven taken away.

Bread and beer of good quality shall not be refused to any that shall desire it, in case of not being satisfied with the ordinary allowance.

In case of sickness there should be a peculiar room appointed for them and some to attend them with such a diet as shall be prescribed, and to entertain them with such thoughts and conversation as shall be fitting for their disposition of mind.

CONCERNING THEIR SLEEP AND REST

In winter the aged scholars shall be wakened at five, in summer at four of the clock in the morning; the younger, in summer at five, in winter at six in the morning; and they shall all be in bed before, or at nine of the clock at night. The governors, ushers and steward, if they be in health, should not go to bed till ten.

THE
EUROPEAN
HERITAGE

251

They shall exercise and stir their bodies in the morning-season before dinner from 11 till 12 o'clock; and before supper they shall again exercise themselves, in summer from half an hour past five till half an hour past six, and in winter from five till six; and from half an hour past twelve after dinner till half an hour past one, it shall be free for them to do private businesses, in their chambers or elsewhere.

The particular ways of exercising their bodies shall not be left at random, but ordered to some advantage of the Association of their own experience in matters of husbandry, or manufactures, or of military employments.

CONCERNING THEIR CLEANLINESS

They must be taught cleanliness without curiosity and made in love with it, as it is useful for health; in which respect the care of it must be recommended to them and observed in them, (1) in their feeding, that through greediness they eat or drink nothing that is nasty; (2) in their body, head, hands, feet and clothing, that they keep themselves from filthiness of sweat, from vermin and other uncleanness; (3) in their chamber, that they defile it not with stench, or suffer it to be unswept, but that they keep it clean and sweet with refreshment of air.

Concerning the Forming of their Manners

Godliness and bodily health are absolutely necessary, the one for spiritual and the other for their temporal felicity. Next unto these two, to make up and perfect the state of their happiness, care must be taken of their manners, by which word I understand their outward life, as well in respect of the action which they do as in respect of their carriage and behaviour in performing the same; that those may be just and honest, this civil and unblamable. For good manners, in this sense, are far to be preferred unto all human learning of what kind soever; because without moral honesty all the perfection of learning is nothing else but an instrument of wickedness to increase and aggravate the miseries of mankind, whereas without learning this alone with bodily health is a sufficient ground to partake of temporal felicity.

And because in the ordinary schools this care is wholly neglected and the youth is left to habituate itself to its corrupt inclinations, while their wits are sharpened and exercised in all the subtilties of human arts and sciences, therefore Satan doth fortify his strongholds by these within them, to make them impregnable; and their spirits (as we find by doleful experience in these times) are heightened to that degree of unconscionableness in deceit, mischief and malice that nothing in former ages can be compared thereunto; which should make us so much the more careful to rectify this evil in our scholars, by how much it is neglected by others and destructive to all.

The way, then, to reform our scholars in this matter and the care to be taken of them should have two parts. The one should relate unto the inward principles of morality, to work the true impressions thereof upon their spirits. The other should relate unto their outward behaviour and carriage towards their neighbour, to make it decent and without offence. And the first of these cannot be rightly taken up without the last, because without the observation of their unseemly behaviour and offensive carriages, a discovery cannot be made of the diseases of their souls, that the remedies of wholesome instructions, admonitions and corrections may be applied thereunto. This, then, is the masterpiece of the whole art of education, to watch over the children's behaviour in their actions of all sorts, so as their true inclinations may be discovered; that the inward causes of their vicious disposition and distempers being found out, the true and proper remedies thereof may be applied unto them. And this is to be the subject whereof the governor and ushers are to have daily conference every night; that upon the particular discoveries of the several inclinations of their scholars by the qualities of their unruliness, they may judiciously determine what to do with them, and how to proceed towards them to reform that which is amiss. . . .

*　　*　　*

Concerning their Proficiency in Learning

The last and least part of true education is only minded in the ordinary schools, and that in a very superficial and preposterous way; for children are taught to read authors and learn words and sentences before they can have any notion of the things signified by those words and sentences, or of the author's strain and wit in setting them together, and they are made to learn by heart the general rules, sentences, and precepts of arts before they are furnished with any matter whereunto to apply those rules and precepts. And when they are taught these things wherein reason is to be employed, they are led into a maze of subtile and unprofitable notions, whereby their minds are puffed up with a windy conceit of knowledge, their affections taken off from the plainness of useful truths, their natural corrupt inclinations to pride, vain-glory, and contentiousness not reformed but rather strengthened in perversity; so that they become both unwilling to seek and incapable to receive any truth either divine or human in its simplicity, for their heads are filled with certain terms and empty shows of learning which neither contain any substance or solidity of matter or give them any address by way of method to make use of that which they know for the benefit of mankind.

Now, to rectify this cause of our ignorance and disorderliness which hath taken possession of all schools and universities and hath spread itself over all matters of human learning, we shall endeavour to seek out the true method of teaching sciences by the grounds and rules which, we hope, none that is rational and free from prejudice will contradict.

Concerning the Grounds and Rules of Teaching Sciences

We take this to be the fundamental and undeniable maxim of all order to be kept in teaching of sciences and educating of youth unto any part of learning: viz., that the whole way of his undertaking must be made answerable unto the nature of the end, and proportionate unto the property of the means and parts of learning; and whatsoever is not subordinate unto that and proportionate unto these, is done irrationally and unprofitably towards the advancement of learning. The grounds, therefore, from whence we shall gather all our rules to direct us in the true method of profiting, are three: the first, concerning the end; the second, concerning the means; the third, concerning the parts of learning.

The true end of all human learning is to supply in ourselves and others the defects which proceed from our ignorance of the nature and use of the creatures and the disorderliness of our natural faculties in using them and reflecting upon them.

*   *   *

CONCERNING THE MEANS OF LEARNING

The true means by which all human sciences are attainable are three, and no more: the first is sense; the second, tradition; and the third, reason.

Sense is the first, because it conveys unto our imagination the shapes and images of all things which memory doth keep in store, that reason may make use thereof; nor can any tradition be entertained with profit but that whereof the imagination hath received from sense the original representations.

Tradition is the second, because it is nothing else but a communication of those observations which others have made of the creatures whereby our want of knowledge of them is supplied. For we ought *to enquire of the former age, and be willing to make search of their fathers: because we are but of yesterday and know nothing, and our days upon earth are a shadow* (Job. 8. 8, 9).

Reason is the third and last means of human learning, because it makes use of all the reports of our senses and of other men's tradition; and without these it can make no inferences to enlarge knowledge or teach us the right use of creatures for necessary occasions.

From the subordination of these means to one another and their properties to advance us unto learning, we shall gather these following rules of teaching arts and sciences.

1. The arts or sciences which may be received by mere sense should not be taught any other way, for it is no wisdom to make work to ourselves: 'Frustra fit per plura quod fieri potest per paucioia'.

2. Whatsoever in any art or science can be made obvious unto sense is first to be made use of, as a precognition unto that which is to be delivered by way of traditional or rational precept.

3. As in Nature sense is the servant of imagination, imagination of memory, memory of reason, so in teaching arts and sciences we must set these faculties awork in this order towards their proper objects in everything which is to be taught: whence this will follow, that as the faculties of man's soul naturally perfect each other by their natural subordination, so the arts which perfect those faculties should be gradually suggested, and the objects wherewith the faculties are to be conversant according to the rules of art should be offered in that order which is answerable to their proper ends and uses and not otherwise: for the proportion of everything to its own end doth determine the order and place wherein we are to make use of it; for nothing is truly useful but as it is in its natural place.

4. As children faculties break forth in them by degrees to be vigorous with their years and the growth of their bodies, so they are to be filled with objects whereof they are capable, and plied with arts: whence followeth that while children are not capable of the acts of reasoning, the method of filling their senses and imaginations with outward objects should be plied; nor is their memory at this time to be charged further with any objects than their imagination rightly ordered and fixed doth of itself impress the same upon them. Moreover hence followeth that no

general rules are to be given unto any, concerning anything either to be known or practised according to the rule of any art or science, till sense, imagination and memory have received their impressions concerning that whereunto the rule is to be applied; and so far as those faculties are stored with matters of observation, so far rules may be given to direct the mind in the use of the same and no further. Lastly hence followeth that the arts or sciences which flow not immediately from particular and sensual objects but tend immediately to direct the universal acts of reasoning, must be taught after all the rest, because their use is to regulate that which is to make use of all the rest, viz., the rational faculty; therefore, it is a very absurd and preposterous course to teach logic and metaphysics before or with other human sciences which depend more upon sense and imagination than reasoning.

COMENIUS ON THE CLAIMS OF CHILDHOOD AND THE OBLIGATIONS OF PARENTS (c. 1630) From Will S. Monroe, ed., *Comenius' School of Infancy* (Boston, 1896), pp. 1-2, 4, 8-11.

Claims of Childhood

That children are an inestimable treasure the Spirit of God, by the lips of David, testifies, saying: "Lo, the children are the heritages of the Lord; the fruit of the womb His reward; as arrows in the hand, so are children. Blessed is the man who has filled his quiver with them; he shall not be confounded." David declares those to be happy on whom God confers children.

2. The same is also evident from this, that God, purposing to testify His love towards us, calls us children, as if there were no more excellent name by which to commend us.

3. Moreover, He is very greatly incensed against those who deliver their children to Moloch. It is also worthy our most serious consideration that God, in respect of the children of even idolatrous parents, calls them children born to Him; thus indicating that they are born, nor for ourselves, but for God, and, as God's offspring, they claim our most profound respect.

4. Hence, in Malachi, children are called the seed of God, whence arises the offspring of God.

5. For this reason the eternal Son of God, when manifested in the flesh, not only willed to become the participator of the nature of children, but likewise deemed children a pleasure and a delight. Taking them in His arms, as little brothers and sisters, He carried them about, and kissed them and blessed them.

6. Not only this, He likewise uttered a severe threat against any one who should offend them, even in the least degree, commanding them to be respected as Himself, and condemning, with severe penalties, any who offended even the smallest of them.

7. Should any one wish to inquire why He so delighted with little children, and so strictly enjoined upon us such respectful attention to them, many reasons may be ascertained. And first, if at present the little ones seem unimportant to you, regard them not as they now are, but as, in accordance with the intention of God, they may

and ought to be. You will see them, not only as the future inhabitants of the world and possessors of the earth, and God's vicars amongst His creatures when we depart from this life, but also equally participators with us in the heritage of Christ, a royal priesthood, a chosen people, associates of angels, judges of devils, the delight of heaven, the terror of hell—heirs of the most excellent dignities throughout all the ages of eternity. What can be imagined more excellent than this?

*   *   *

10. Secondly, they are the pure and dearly purchased possession of Christ; since Christ, who came to seek the lost, is said to be the Savior of all, except those who by incredulity and impenitence shut themselves out from being participators in His merits. These are the purchased from among men, that they may be the first-fruits unto God and the Lamb; having not yet defiled themselves with the allurements of sin; but they follow the Lamb whithersoever he goeth. And that they may continue so to follow, they ought to be led, as it were, with the hand by a pious education.

11. Finally, God so embraces children with abounding love that they are a peculiar instrument of divine glory, as the Scriptures testify, "From the lips of infants and sucklings thou hast perfected praise, because of thine enemies; that thou mayest destroy the enemy and avenger." How it comes to pass that God's glory should receive increase from children, is certainly not at once obvious to our understanding; but God, the discerner of all things, knows and understands, and declares it to be so.

*   *   *

Obligations of Parents

1. Should it enter the mind of any one to inquire why it pleased the Divine Majesty to produce these celestial gems not at once in the full number which He purposed to have for eternity, as He did the angels, such inquirer will discover no other reason than that, in doing so, he honors human kind by making them as it were his coadjutors in multiplying creatures. Not, however, that from that source alone they draw pleasure, but that they may exercise their zeal in rightly educating and training them for eternity.

2. Man accustoms the ox for plowing, the hound for hunting, the horse for riding and driving, because for these uses they were created, and they cannot be applied to other purposes; man, however, being more noble than all those creatures, ought to be educated for the highest objects, so that as far as possible he may correspond in excellences to God, whose image he bears. The body, no doubt, being taken from the earth, is earthy, is conversant with the earth, and must again be turned into earth; whereas the soul, being inspired by God, is from God, and ought to remain in God and elevate itself to God.

3. Parents, therefore, will not fully perform their duty, if they merely teach their offspring to eat, to drink, to walk about, to talk, and to be adorned with clothing; for these things are merely subservient to the body, which is not the man, but his tabernacle only; the guest (the rational soul) dwells within, and rightly claims greater care than its outward tenement. Plutarch has rightly derided such parents as desire beauty, riches, and honors for their children, and endeavor to promote them

in these respects, regarding very little the adornment of the soul with piety and virtue, saying: "That those persons valued the shoe more than the foot." And Crates the Theban, a Gentile philosopher, vehemently complaining of the madness of such parents, declared, as the poet relates:—

"Were I permitted to proclaim aloud everywhere,
I should denounce all those infatuated and shamefully wicked,
Whom destructive money agitates with excessive zeal.
Ye gather riches for your children, and neither nourish them with doctrine,
Nor cherish within them intellectual capability."

4. The first care, therefore, ought to be of the soul, which is the principal part of the man, so that it may become, in the highest degree possible, beautifully adorned. The next care is for the body, that it may be made a habitation fit and worthy of an immortal soul. Regard the mind as rightly instructed which is truly illuminated from the effulgence of the wisdom of God, so that man, contemplating the presence of the Divine Image in himself, may diligently observe and guard that excellence.

5. Now there are two departments of true celestial wisdom which man ought to seek, and into which he ought to be instructed. The one, a clear and true knowledge of God and all of his wonderful works; the other, prudence,—carefully and wisely to regulate self and all external and internal actions appertaining to the present and future life.

6. Primarily as to the future life, because properly speaking that is life, from which both death and mortality pass into exile, since the present is not so much life as the way to life; consequently, whosoever has attained so much in this life as to prepare himself by faith and piety for a future life, must be judged to have fully performed his duty here.

7. Yet, notwithstanding this, inasmuch as God, by bestowing longevity upon many, assigns them certain duties, places in the course of their life various occurrences, supplying occasions for acting prudently. Parents must by all means provide for the training of their children in the duties of faith and piety; so must they also provide for the more polite culture in the moral sciences, in the liberal arts, and in other necessary things; to the end that when grown up they may become truly men, prudently managing their own affairs, and be admitted to the various functions of life, which, whether ecclesiastical or political, civil or social, God has willed them to fulfill, and thus, having righteously and prudently passed through the present life, they may, with the greater joy, migrate to the heavens.

8. In a word, the purpose for which youth ought to be educated is threefold: (1) Faith and Piety; (2) Uprightness in respect of morals; (3) Knowledge of languages and arts. These, however, in the precise order in which they are here propounded, and not inversely. In the first place, youth must be exercised in piety, then in the morals or virtues, finally in the more advanced literature. The greater the proficiency the youth makes in the latter, the better.

9. Whosoever has within his house youth exercising themselves in these three departments, possesses a garden in which celestial plantlets are sown, watered, bloom, and flourish; a studio, as it were, of the Holy Spirit, in which He elaborates and polishes those vessels of mercy, those instruments of glory, so that in them, as lively images of God, the rays of His eternal and infinite power, wisdom, and bounty, may shine more and more. How inexpressibly blessed are parents in such a paradise!

The Great Didactic

Setting forth
The whole Art of Teaching
all Things to all Men
or
A certain Inducement to found such Schools in all
the Parishes, Towns, and Villages of every
Christian Kingdom, that the entire
Youth of both Sexes, none
being excepted, shall

Quickly, Pleasantly, & Thoroughly

Become learned in the Sciences, pure in Morals,
trained to Piety, and in this manner
instructed in all things necessary
for the present and for
the future life,

in which, with respect to everything that is suggested,

ITS FUNDAMENTAL PRINCIPLES are set forth from the essential
nature of the matter,
ITS TRUTH is proved by examples from the several
mechanical arts,
ITS ORDER is clearly set forth in years, months, days, and
hours, and, finally,
AN EASY AND SURE METHOD is shown, by which it can
be pleasantly brought into existence.

COMENIUS CALLS FOR NEW METHODS OF TEACHING (c. 1657)   From
The Great Didactic of John Amos Comenius, M. W. Keatinge. ed. and trans. (London,
1896). pp. 222-27, 279, 294-95, 328-32.

We have already shown that every one ought to receive a universal
education, and this at school. But do not, therefore, imagine that we demand from
all men a knowledge (that is to say, an exact or deep knowledge) of all the arts and
sciences. This would neither be useful of itself, nor, on account of the shortness of
life, can it be attained by any man. For we see that each science is so vast and so
complicated (as are physics, arithmetic, geometry, astronomy, or even agriculture
and arboriculture) that it would occupy the lifetime of even the strongest intellects
if they wished to master it thoroughly by investigation and experiment. Thus did
Pythagoras devote himself to arithmetic, Archimedes to mechanics, Agricola to
metallurgy, and Longolius (who spent his whole life in endeavouring to acquire a
perfect Ciceronian style) to rhetoric. It is the principles, the causes, and the uses of
all the most important things in existence that we wish all men to learn; all, that is
to say, who are sent into the world to be actors as well as speculators. For we must
take strong and vigorous measures that no man, in his journey through life, may
encounter anything so unknown to him that he cannot pass sound judgment upon it
and turn it to its proper use without serious error.

2. We must, therefore, concentrate our energies on obtaining that, throughout
our whole lives, in schools and by the aid of schools: (i) our talents may be
cultivated by study of the sciences and of the arts; (ii) languages may be learned; (iii)
honest morals may be formed; (iv) God may be sincerely worshipped.

3. He spoke wisely who said that schools were the workshops of humanity, since
it is undoubtedly through their agency that man really becomes man, that is to say,
(to refer to our previous analysis): (i) a rational creature; (ii) a creature which is lord
over all creatures and also over. himself; (iii) a creature which is the delight of his
Creator. This will be the case if schools are able to produce men who are wise in
mind, prudent in action, and pious in spirit.

*   *   *

The Principles of Facility in Teaching and in Learning

1. We have already considered the means by which the educationist may attain
his goal with certainty, we will now proceed to see how these means can be suited
to the minds of the pupils, so that their use may be easy and pleasant.

2. Following in the footsteps of nature we find that the process of education
will be easy.

(i)   If it begin early, before the mind is corrupted.
(ii)   If the mind be duly prepared to receive it.
(iii)   If it proceed from the general to the particular.
(iv)   And from what is easy to what is more difficult.
(v)   If the pupil be not overburdened by too many subjects.
(vi)   And if progress be slow in every case.

(vii) If the intellect be forced to nothing to which its natural bent does not incline it, in accordance with its age and with the right method.

(viii) If everything be taught through the medium of the senses.

(ix) And if the use of everything taught be continually kept in view.

(x) If everything be taught according to one and the same method.

These, I say, are the principles to be adopted if education is to be easy and pleasant.

The Principles of Thoroughness in Teaching and in Learning

1. It is a common complaint that there are few who leave school with a thorough education, and that most men retain nothing but a veneer, a mere shadow of true knowledge. This complaint is corroborated by facts.

2. The cause of this phenomenon appears on investigation to be twofold: either that the schools occupy themselves with insignificant and unimportant studies, to the neglect of those that are more weighty, or that the pupils forget what they have learned, since most of it merely goes through their heads and does not stick fast there. This last fault is so common that there are few who do not lament it. For if everything that we have ever read, heard, and mentally appreciated were always ready to hand in our memories, how learned we should appear! We do, it is true, make practical use of much that we have learned, but the amount that we recollect is unsatisfactory, and the fact remains that we are continually trying to pour water into a sieve.

3. But can no cure be found for this? Certainly there can, if once more we go to the school of nature, and investigate the methods that she adopts to give endurance to the beings which she has created.

I maintain that a method can be found by means of which each person will be enabled to bring into his mental consciousness not only what he has learned, but more as well; since he will recall with ease all that he has learned from teachers or from books, and, at the same time, will be able to pass sound judgment on the objective facts to which his information refers.

4. This will be possible:

(i) If only those subjects that are of real use be taken in hand.

(ii) If these be taught without digression or interruption.

(iii) If a thorough grounding precede instruction in detail.

(iv) If this grounding be carefully given.

(v) If all that follows be based on this grounding, and on nothing else.

(vi) If, in every subject that consists of several parts, these parts be linked together as much as possible.

(vii) If all that comes later be based on what has gone before.

(viii) If great stress be laid on the points of resemblance between cognate subjects.

(ix) If all studies be arranged with reference to the intelligence and memory of the pupils, and the nature of language.

(x) If knowledge be fixed in the memory by constant practice.

✳   ✳   ✳

41. The example of nature shows that several things can be done at one time and by means of the same operation. It is an undoubted fact that a tree grows above the ground and beneath it at the same time, and that its wood, its bark, its leaves, and its fruit, all develope simultaneously. The same observation applies to animals, whose limbs all develope and grow stronger at the same time. Further, each limb performs several operations. The feet, for instance, not only support a man but also move him forwards and backwards in various ways. The mouth is not only the entrance to the body, but also serves as a masticator and as a trumpet that sounds whenever called upon to do so. With a single inspiration the lungs cool the heart, purify the brain, and assist in voice-production.

42. We find the same thing in the arts: (1) In the sun-dial, the single shadow cast by the gnomon points out the hour of the day, the sign of the zodiac in which the sun is moving, the length of the day and of the night, the day of the month, and several other things. (2) One pole serves to direct, to turn, and to hold back a carriage. (3) A good orator or writer instructs, excites, and pleases at the same time, even though his subject may make it difficult to combine these three elements.

43. The instruction of the young should be similarly organised, so that every activity may produce several results. It may be laid down as a general rule that each subject should be taught in combination with those which are correlative to it; that is to say, words should be studied in combination with the things to which they refer; while reading and writing, exercises in style and in logical thought, teaching and learning, amusement and serious study, should be continually joined together.

44. Words, therefore, should always be taught and learned in combination with things, just as wine is bought and sold together with the cask that contains it, a dagger with its sheath, a tree with its bark, and fruit with its skin. For what are words but the husks and coverings of things? Therefore, when instruction is given in any language, even in the mother-tongue itself, the words must be explained by reference to the objects that they denote; and contrariwise, the scholars must be taught to express in language whatever they see, hear, handle, or taste, so that their command of language, as it progresses, may ever run parallel to the growth of the understanding.

The rule shall therefore run as follows:

The scholar should be trained to express everything that he sees in words, and should be taught the meaning of all the words that he uses. No one should be allowed to talk about anything that he does not understand, or to understand anything without at the same time being able to express his knowledge in words. For he who cannot express the thoughts of his mind resembles a statue, and he who chatters, without understanding what he says, resembles a parrot.

But we wish to train up *men*, and to do so as quickly as possible, and this end can only be attained when instruction in language goes hand in hand with instruction in facts.

45. From this it follows that we ought to exclude from our schools all books that merely teach words and do not at the same time lead to a knowledge of useful objects. We must bestow our labour on that which is of real importance, and, therefore (as Seneca says in his 9th Letter), must devote ourselves to the improvement of our understanding rather than to the enlargement of our vocabulary. Any reading that is necessary can be got through quickly out of school-hours without tedious explanations or attempts at imitation; since the time thus spent could be better employed in the study of nature.

THE
EUROPEAN
HERITAGE

261

46. Exercises in reading and writing should always be combined. Even when scholars are learning their alphabet, they should be made to master the letters by writing them; since it is impossible to find a more agreeable method or one that will give them a greater incentive to work. For, since all children have a natural desire to draw, this exercise will give them pleasure, and the imagination will be excited by the twofold action of the senses. Later on, when they can read with ease, they should be made to exercise their powers on subject-matter that would in any case have to be learned, that is to say, something calculated to give them practical information or to instil morality or piety. The same plan may be adopted when they learn to read Latin, Greek, or Hebrew. It will be of great advantage to read and copy the declensions and conjugations over and over again, until, by this means, reading, writing, the meaning of the words, and the formation of the case-endings, have been thoroughly learned. In this case we have a fourfold result from a single exercise. A system of concentration that is of such vital importance should be applied to all branches of study, in order that, as Seneca says, what is learned by reading may be given form by writing, or that, as St. Augustine says of himself, we may write while we make progress and make progress while we write.

47. As a rule, no care is shown in the choice of the subjects that are given as exercises in style, and there is no connection between the successive subjects. The result is that they are exercises in style and nothing else, and have very little influence on the reasoning powers; indeed it frequently happens that, after much time and study have been devoted to them, they prove absolutely worthless and of no use for the business of life. Literary taste should therefore be taught by means of the subject-matter of the science or art on which the reasoning powers of the class are being exercised. The teacher should tell his pupils stories about the originators of the subject and the times in which they lived, or should give them exercises in imitation based on the subject matter, so that, by a single effort, notions of style may be imbibed, the reasoning powers may be improved, and, since either the teacher or the pupils are continually talking, the faculty of speech also may be exercised.

48. Towards the end of the 18th chapter I have shown that it is possible for the scholars to give instruction in the subject that they have just learned, and, since this process not only makes them thorough but also enables them to make progress more rapidly, it should not be overlooked in this connection.

49. Finally, it will be of immense use, if the amusements that are provided to relax the strain on the minds of the scholars be of such a kind as to lay stress on the more serious side of life, in order that a definite impression may be made on them even in their hours of recreation. For instance, they may be given tools, and allowed to imitate the different handicrafts, by playing at farming, at politics, at being soldiers or architects, etc. In spring they may be taken into the garden or into the country, and may be taught the various species of plants, vying with one another to see who can recognise the greater number. In this way they will be introduced to the rudiments of medicine, and not only will it be evident which of them has a natural bent towards that science, but in many the inclination will be created. Further, in order to encourage them, the mock titles of doctor, licentiate, or student of medicine may be given to those who make the greatest progress. The same plan may be adopted in other kinds of recreation. In the game of war the scholars may become field-marshals, generals, captains, or standard-bearers. In that of politics they may be kings, ministers, chancellors, secretaries, ambassadors, etc., and, on the same principle, consuls, senators, lawyers, or officials; since such pleasantries often lead to serious things. Thus would be fulfilled Luther's wish that the studies of the

young at school could be so organised that the scholars might take as much pleasure in them as in playing at ball all day, and thus for the first time would schools be a real prelude to practical life.

COMENIUS DESCRIBES A VERNACULAR SCHOOL (1657)   From M. W. Keatinge, ed., *Comenius* (New York, 1931), pp. 211-17.

In chap. ix. I demonstrated that all the young of both sexes should be sent to the public schools, I now add that they should first be sent to the Vernacular-School. Some writers hold the contrary opinion. . . . Alsted. . . would persuade us that only those boys and girls who are destined for manual labour should be sent to the Vernacular-School, while boys whose parents wish them to receive a higher education should be sent straight to the Latin-School. Moreover, he adds: "Some will doubtless disagree with me, but the system that I propose is the one which I would wish adopted by those whose educational interests I have most at heart." From this view my whole didactic system forces me to dissent.

2. (i.) The education that I propose includes all that is proper for a man, and is one in which all men who are born into this world should share. All therefore, as far as is possible, should be educated together, that they may stimulate and urge on one another.

(ii.) We wish all men to be trained in all the virtues, especially in modesty, sociability, and politeness, and it is therefore undesirable to create class distinctions at such an early age, or to give some children the opportunity of considering their own lot with satisfaction and that of others with scorn.

(iii.) When boys are only six years old, it is too early to determine their vocation in life, or whether they are more suited for learning or for manual labour. At this age, neither the mind nor the inclinations are sufficiently developed, while, later on, it will be easy to form a sound opinion on both. In the same way, while plants are quite small, a gardener cannot tell which to hoe up and which to leave, but has to wait until they are more advanced. Nor should admission to the Latin-School be reserved for the sons of rich men, nobles, and magistrates, as if these were the only boys who would ever be able to fill similar positions. . . .

3. (iv.) The next reason is that my universal method has not as its sole object the Latin language, that nymph on whom such unbounded admiration is generally wasted, but seeks a way by which each modern language may be taught as well (that every spirit may praise the Lord more and more). This design should not be frustrated by the complete and arbitrary omission of the Vernacular-School.

4. (v.) To attempt to teach a foreign language before the mother-tongue has been learned is as irrational as to teach a boy to ride before he can walk. To proceed step by step is of great importance, as we have seen in chap. xvi. Principle 4. Cicero declared that he could not teach elocution to those who were unable to speak, and, in the same way, my method confesses its inability to teach Latin to those who are ignorant of their mother-tongue, since the one paves the way for the other.

5. (vi.) Finally, what I have in view is an education in the objects that

surround us, and a brief survey of this education can be best obtained from books written in the mother-tongue, which embody a list of the things that exist in the external world. This preliminary survey will render the acquisition of Latin far easier, for it will only be necessary to adapt a new nomenclature to objects that are already known; while to the knowledge of actual facts may be added by degrees that of the causes which underlie those facts.

6. Proceeding, therefore, on the basis of my fourfold division of schools, we may define the Vernacular-School as follows. The aim and object of the Vernacular-School should be to teach to all the young, between the ages of six and twelve, such things as will be of use to them throughout their whole lives. That is to say:

(i.) To read with ease both print and writing in their mother-tongue.

(ii.) To write, first with accuracy, then with speed, and finally with confidence, in accordance with the grammatical rules of the mother-tongue. These rules should be written in a popular form, and the boys should be exercised in them.

(iii.) To count, with ciphers and with counters, as far as is necessary for practical purposes.

(iv.) To measure spaces, such as length, breadth, and distance, with skill.

(v.) To sing well-known melodies, and, in the case of those who display especial aptitude, to learn the elements of advanced music.

(vi.) To learn by heart the greater number of the psalms and hymns that are used in the country. For, if brought up in the praise of God, they will be able (as the Apostle says) to exhort one another with psalms and hymns and spiritual songs, singing to God from their hearts.

(vii.) Besides the Catechism they should know the most important stories and verses in the Bible, and should be able to repeat them word for word.

(viii.) They should learn the principles of morality, which should be drawn up in the shape of rules and accompanied by illustrations suitable to the age and understanding of the pupils. They should also begin to put these principles into practice.

(ix.) They should learn as much economics and politics as is necessary to enable them to understand what they see daily at home and in the state.

(x.) They should also learn the general history of the world; its creation, its fall, its redemption, and its preservation by God up to the present day.

(xi.) In addition, they should learn the most important facts of cosmography, such as the spherical shape of the heavens, the globular shape of the earth suspended in their midst, the tides of the ocean, the shapes of seas, the courses of rivers, the principal divisions of the earth, and the chief kingdoms of Europe; but, in particular, the cities, mountains, rivers, and other remarkable features of their own country.

(xii.) Finally, they should learn the most important principles of the mechanical arts, both that they may not be too ignorant of what goes on in the world around them, and that any special inclination towards things of this kind may assert itself with greater ease later on.

7. If all these subjects have been skilfully handled in the Vernacular-School, the result will be that those youths who begin the study of Latin or who enter on agriculture, trade, or professional life will encounter nothing which is absolutely new to them; while the details of their trades, the words that they hear in church, and the information that they acquire from books, will be to them nothing but the more detailed exposition or the more particular application of facts with which they are already acquainted. They will thus find themselves all the fitter to use their understanding, their powers of action, and their judgment.

8. To attain this result we employ the following means:—

(i.) All the children in the Vernacular-School, who are destined to spend six years there, should be divided into six classes, each of which, if possible, should have a classroom to itself, that it may not hinder the others.

(ii.) Specially prepared books should be supplied to each class, and these should contain the whole subject-matter of the literary, moral, and religious instruction prescribed for the class. Within these limits no other books should be needed, and, by their aid, the desired result should infallibly be obtained. They should embody a complete grammar of the mother-tongue, in which should be comprised the names of all the objects that children of this age can understand, as well as a selection of the most common phrases in use.

9. These class-books should be six in number, corresponding to the number of classes, and should differ, not in their subject-matter, but in their way of presenting it. Each should embrace all the above-mentioned subjects; but the earlier ones should treat of them in a general manner, choosing their better known and easier features; while those which come later should draw attention to the less known and more complex details, or should point out some fresh way of treating the subject, and thus excite interest and attention. The truth of this will soon be evident.

10. Care must be taken to suit all these books to the children for whom they are intended; for children like whimsicality and humour, and detest pedantry and severity. Instruction, therefore, should ever be combined with amusement, that they may take pleasure in learning serious things which will be of genuine use to them later on, and that their dispositions may be, as it were, perpetually enticed to develope in the manner desired.

11. The titles of these books should be of such a kind as to please and attract the young, and should at the same time express the nature of their contents. Suitable names might be borrowed from the nomenclature of a garden, that sweetest possession of youth. Thus, if the whole school be compared to a garden, the book of the lowest class might be called the violet-bed, that of the second class the rose-bed, that of the third the grass-plot, and so on.

12. Of the matter and form of these books I will speak in greater detail elsewhere. I will only add that, as they are written in the mother-tongue, the technical terms of the arts should also be expressed in the vernacular, and not in Latin or Greek. For we wish the young to make progress with as little delay as possible.

THE
EUROPEAN
HERITAGE

265

School-Teaching, Schools, Manuals and Books—England

OATH OF A GRAMMAR SCHOOL MASTER (1566)   From Nicholas Carlisle, *A Concise Description of the Endowed Grammar Schools In England And Wales* (London, 1818), vol. II, p. 714.

I do swear by the contents of this book, that I will freely without exacting any money, diligently instruct and teach the children of this parish, and all others that shall resort to me, in Grammar and other humane doctrine, according to the statutes thereof made,—and I shall not read to them any corrupt or reprobate books or works set forth at any time contrary to the determination of the universal catholique church, whereby they may be infected in their youth in any kind of heresie or corrupt doctrine, or else to be indured to insolent manner of living: And further shall observe all the statutes and ordinances of this schoole now made, or hereafter to be made which concern me, and shall doe nothing in the prejudice thereof, but help to maintain the same from time to time during my aboad herein to the best of my power—so help me God, ant the contents of this book.

ROGER ASCHAM ON PROGRESSIVE TEACHING METHODS (1570)   From Roger Ascham, "The Scholemaster," as quoted in William A. Wright, ed., *Roger Ascham, English Works* (Cambridge, Mass., 1904), pp. 175-85.

A Preface to the Reader

When the great plage was at London, the yeare 1563, the Quenes Maiestie Queene Elizabeth, lay at her Castle of Windsore: Where, vpon the 10. day of December, it fortuned, that in Sir William Cicells chamber, hir Highnesse Principall Secretarie, there dined togither these personages, M. Secretarie him selfe, Syr William Peter, Syr J. Mason, D. Wotton, Syr Richard Sackuille Treasurer of the Exchecker, Syr Walter Mildmaye Chauncellor of the Exchecker, M. Haddon Master of Requestes, M. John Astely Master of the Iewell house, M. Bernard Hampton, M.

Nicasius, and J. Of which number, the most part were of hir Maiesties most honourable priuie Counsell, and the reast seruing hir in verie good place. I was glad than, and do reioice yet to remember, that my chance was so happie, to be there that day, in the companie of so manie wise & good men togither, as hardly than could haue beene piked out againe, out of all England beside.

M. Secretarie hath this accustomed maner, though his head be neuer so full of most weightie affaires of the Realme, yet, at diner time he doth seeme to lay them alwaies aside: and findeth euer fitte occasion to taulke pleasantlie of other matters, but most gladlie of some matter of learning: wherein, he will curteslie heare the minde of the meanest at his Table.

Not long after our sitting doune, I haue strange newes brought me, sayth M. Secretarie, this morning, that diuerse Scholers of Eaton, be runne awaie from the Schole, for feare of beating. Whereupon, M. Secretarie tooke occasion, to wishe, that some more discretion were in many Scholemasters, in vsing correction, than commonlie there is. Who many times, punishe rather, the weakenes of nature, than the fault of the Scholer. Whereby, many Scholers, that might else proue well, be driuen to hate learning, before they knowe, what learning meaneth: and so, are made willing to forsake their booke, and be glad to be put to any other kinde of liuing.

M. Peter, as one somewhat seuere of nature, said plainlie, that the Rodde onelie, was the sworde, that must keepe, the Schole in obedience, and the Scholer in good order. M. Wotton, a man milde of nature, with soft voice, and fewe wordes, inclined to M. Secretaries judgement, and said, in mine opinion, the Scholehouse should be in deede, as it is called by name, the house of playe and pleasure, and not of feare and bondage: and as I do remember, so saith Socrates in one place of Plato. And therefore, if a Rodde carie the feare of a Sworde, it is no maruell, if those that be fearefull of nature, chose rather to forsake the Plaie, than to stand alwaies within the feare of a Sworde in a fonde mans handling. M. Mason, after his maner, was verie merie with both parties, pleasantlie playing, both, with the shrewde touches of many courste boyes, and with the small discretion of many leude Scholemasters. M. Haddon was fullie of M. Peters opinion, and said, that the best Scholemaster of our time, was the greatest beater, and named the Person. Though, quoth I, it was his good fortune, to send from his Schole, vnto the Vniuersitie, one of the best Scholers in deede of all our time, yet wise men do thinke, that that came so to passe, rather, by the great towardnes of the Scholer, than by the great beating of the Master: and whether this be true or no, you your selfe are best witnes. I said somewhat farder in the matter, how, and whie, yong children, were soner allured by loue, than driuen by beating, to atteyne good learning: wherein I was the bolder to say my minde, bicause M. Secretarie curteslie prouoked me thereunto: or else, in such a companie, and namelie in his praesence, my wonte is, to be more willing, to vse mine eares, than to occupie my tonge.

Syr Walter Mildmaye, M. Astley, and the rest, said verie litle: onelie Syr Rich. Sackuill, said nothing at all. After dinner I went vp to read with the Queenes Maiestie. We red than togither in the Greke tongue, as I well remember, that noble Oration of Demosthenes against AEschines, for his false dealing in his Ambassage to king Philip of Macedonie. Syr Rich. Sackuile came vp sone after: and finding me in hir Maiesties priuie chamber, he tooke me by the hand, & carying me to a windoe, said, M. Ascham, I would not for a good deale of monie, haue bene, this daie, absent from diner. Where, though I said nothing, yet I gaue as good eare, and do consider as well the taulke, that passed, as any one did there. M. Secretarie said very wisely, and most truely, that many yong wittes be driuen to hate learninge, before they know what learninge is. I can be good witnes to this my selfe: For a fond Scholemaster, before I was fullie fourtene yeare olde, draue me so, with feare of beating, from all loue of learninge, as nowe, when I know, what difference it is, to haue learninge, and to haue litle, or none at all, I feele it my greatest greife, and finde it my greatest hurte, that euer came to me, that it was my so ill chance, to light vpon so lewde a Scholemaster. But seing it is but in vain, to lament thinges paste, and also wisdome to looke at thinges to cum, surely, God willinge, if God lend me life, I will make this my mishap, some occasion of good hap, to litle Robert Sackuile my sonnes sonne. For whose bringinge vp, I would gladlie, if it so please you, vse speciallie your good aduice. I heare saie, you haue a sonne, moch of his age: we wil deale thus togither. Point you out a Scholemaster, who by your order, shall teache my sonne and yours, and for all the rest, I will prouide, yea though they three do cost me a couple of hundred poundes by yeare: and beside, you shall finde me as fast a Frend to you and yours, as perchance any you haue. Which promise, the worthie Ientleman surelie kept with me vntill his dying daye.

We had than farther taulke togither, of bringing vp of children: of the nature, of quicke, and hard wittes: of the right choice of a good witte: of Feare, and loue in teachinge children. We passed from children and came to yonge men, namely, Ientlemen: we taulked of their to moch libertie, to liue as they lust: of their letting louse to sone, to ouer moch experience of ill, contrarie to the good order of many good olde common welthes of the Persians and Grekes: of witte gathered, and good fortune gotten, by some, onely by experience, without learning. And lastlie, he required of me verie earnestlie, to shewe, what I thought of the common goinge of Englishe men into Italie. But, sayth he, bicause this place, and this tyme, will not suffer so long taulke, as these good matters require, therefore I pray you, at my request, and at your leysure, put in some order of writing, the cheife pointes of this our taulke, concerning the right order of teachinge, and honestie of liuing, for the good bringing vp of children & yong men. And surelie, beside contentinge me, you shall both please and profit verie many others. I made some excuse by lacke of habilitie, and weakenes of bodie: well, sayth he, I am not now to learne, what you can do. Our deare frende, good M. Goodricke, whose iudgement I could well beleue, did once for all, satisfye me fullie therein. Againe, I heard you say, not long agoe, that you may thanke Syr John Cheke, for all the learninge you haue: And I know verie well my selfe, that you did teach the Quene. And therefore seing God did so blesse you, to make you the Scholer of the best Master, and also the Scholemaster of the best Scholer, that euer were in our tyme, surelie, you should please God, benefite your countrie, & honest your owne name, if you would take the paines, to impart to others, what you learned of soch a Master, and how ye taught such a scholer. And, in vttering the stuffe ye receiued of the one, in declaring the order ye tooke with the other, ye shall neuer lacke, neither matter, nor maner, what to write, nor how to write in this kinde of Argument.

I beginning some farther excuse, sodeinlie was called to cum to the Queene. The night following, I slept litle, my head was so full of this our former taulke, and I so mindefull, somewhat to satisfie the honest request of so deare a frend, I thought to praepare some litle treatise for a New yeares gift that Christmas. But, as it chanceth to busie builders, so, in building thys my poore Scholehouse (the rather bicause the forme of it is somewhat new, and differing from others) the worke rose dailie higher and wider, than I thought it would at the beginninge.

And though it appeare now, and be in verie deede, but a small cotage, poore for the stuffe, and rude for the workemanship, yet in going forward, I found the site so good, as I was lothe to giue it ouer, but the making so costlie, outreaching my habilitie, as many tymes I wished, that some one of those three, my deare frendes, with full pursses, Syr Tho. Smithe, M. Haddon, or M. Watson, had had the doing of it. Yet, neuerthelesse, I my selfe, spending gladlie that litle, that I gatte at home by good Syr John Cheke, and that that I borrowed abroad of my frend Sturmius, beside somewhat that was left me in Reuersion by my olde Masters, Plato, Aristotle, and Cicero, I haue at last patched it vp, as I could, and as you see. If the matter be meane, and meanly handled, I pray you beare, both with me, and it: for neuer worke went vp in worse wether, with mo lettes and stoppes, than this poore Scholehouse of mine. Westminster Hall can beare some witnesse, beside moch weakenes of bodie, but more trouble of minde, by some such sores, as greue me to toche them my selfe, and therefore I purpose not to open them to others. And, in middes of outward iniuries, and inward cares, to encrease them withall, good Syr Rich. Sackuile dieth, that worthie Ientleman: That earnest fauorer and furtherer of Gods true Religion: That faithfull Seruitor to his Prince and Countrie: a louer of learning, & all learned men: Wise in all doinges: Curtesse to all persons: shewing spite to none: doing good to many: and as I well found, to me so fast a frend, as I neuer lost the like before. Whan he was gone, my hart was dead. There was not one, that woare a blacke gowne for him, who caried a heuier hart for him, than I. Whan he was gone, I cast this booke awaie: I could not looke vpon it, but with weping eyes, in remembring him, who was the onelie setter on, to do it, and would haue bene, not onelie a glad commender of it, but also a sure and certaine comfort, to me and mine, for it. Almost two yeares togither, this booke lay scattered, and neglected, and had bene quite giuen ouer of me, if the goodnesse of one had not giuen me some life and spirite againe. God, the mouer of goodnesse, prosper alwaies him & his, as he hath many times comforted me and mine, and, I trust to God, shall comfort more and more.

*   *   *

Thys hope hath helped me to end this booke: which, if he allowe, I shall thinke my labours well imployed, and shall not moch aesteme the misliking of any others. And I trust, he shall thinke the better of it, bicause he shall finde the best part thereof, to cum out of his Schole, whom he, of all men loued and liked best.

Yet some men, frendly enough of nature, but of small iudgement in learninge, do thinke, I take to moch paines, and spend to moch time, in settinge forth these childrens affaires. But those good men were neuer brought vp in Socrates Schole, who saith plainlie, that no man goeth about a more godlie purpose, than he that is mindfull of the good bringing vp, both of hys owne, and other mens children.

Therfore, I trust, good and wise men, will thinke well of this my doing. And of other, that thinke otherwise, I will thinke my selfe, they are but men, to be pardoned for their follie, and pitied for their ignoraunce.

In writing this booke, I haue had earnest respecte to three speciall pointes, trothe of Religion, honestie in liuing, right order in learning. In which three waies, I praie God, my poore children may diligently waulke: for whose sake, as nature moued, and reason required, and necessitie also somewhat compelled, I was the willinger to take these paines.

For, seing at my death, I am not like to leaue them any great store of liuing, therefore in my life time, I thought good to bequeath vnto the, in this litle booke, as in my Will and Testament, the right waie to good learning: which if they followe, with the feare of God, they shall verie well cum to sufficiencie of liuinge.

I wishe also, with all my hart, that yong M. Rob. Sackuille, may take that fructe of this labor, that his worthie Grauntfather purposed he should haue done: And if any other do take, either proffet, or pleasure hereby, they haue cause to thanke M. Robert Sackuille, for whom speciallie this my Scholemaster was prouided.

And one thing I would haue the Reader consider in readinge this booke, that bicause, no Scholemaster hath charge of any childe, before he enter into hys Schole, therefore I leauing all former care, of their good bringing vp, to wise and good Parentes, as a matter not belonging to the Scholemaster, I do appoynt thys my Scholemaster, than, and there to begin, where his office and charge beginneth. Which charge lasteth not long, but vntill the Scholer be made hable to go to the Vniuersitie, to procede in Logike, Rhetoricke, and other kindes of learning.

Yet if my Scholemaster, for loue he beareth to hys Scholer, shall teach hym somewhat for hys furtherance, and better iudgement in learning, that may serue him seuen yeare after in the Vniuersitie, he doth hys Scholer no more wrong, nor deserueth no worse name therby, than he doth in London, who sellinge silke or cloth vnto his frend, doth giue hym better measure, than either hys promise or bargaine was.

The First Booke for the Youth

After the childe hath learned perfitlie the eight partes of speach, let him then learne the right ioyning togither of substantiues with adiectiues, the nowne with the verbe, the relatiue with the antecedent. And in learninge farther hys Syntaxis, by mine aduice, he shall not vse the common order in common scholes, for making of latines: wherby, the childe commonlie learneth, first, an euill choice of wordes, (and right choice of wordes, saith Caesar, is the foundation of eloquence) than, a wrong placing of wordes: and lastlie, an ill framing of the sentence, with a peruerse iudgement, both of wordes and sentences. These faultes, taking once roote in yougthe, be neuer, or hardlie, pluckt away in age. Moreouer, there is no one thing, that hath more, either dulled the wittes, or taken awaye the will of children from learning, then the care they haue, to satisfie their masters, in making of latines.

For, the scholer, is commonlie beat for the making, whe the master were more worthie to be beat for the mending, or rather, marring of the same: The master many times, being as ignorant as the childe, what to saie properlie and fitlie to the matter.

Two scholemasters haue set forth in print, either of them a booke, of soch kinde of latines, Horman and Whittington.

A childe shall learne of the better of them, that, which an other daie, if he be wise, and cum to iudgement, he must be faine to vnlearne againe.

There is a waie, touched in the first booke of Cicero *De Oratore*, which, wiselie brought into scholes, truely taught, and costantly vsed, would not onely take wholly away this butcherlie feare in making of latines, but would also, with ease and pleasure, and in short time, as I know by good experience, worke a true choice and placing of wordes, a right ordering of sentences, an easie vnderstandyng of the tonge, a readines to speake, a facultie to write, a true iudgement, both of his owne, and other mens doinges, what tonge so euer he doth vse.

The waie is this. After the three Concordances learned, as I touched before, let the master read vnto hym the Epistles of Cicero, gathered togither and chosen out by Sturmius, for the capacitie of children.

First, let him teach the childe, cherefullie and plainlie, the cause, and matter of the letter: then, let him construe it into Englishe, so oft, as the childe may easilie carie awaie the vnderstanding of it: Lastlie, parse it ouer perfitlie. This done thus, let the childe, by and by, both construe and parse it ouer againe: so, that it may appeare, that the childe douteth in nothing, that his master taught him before. After this, the childe must take a paper booke, and sitting in some place, where no man shall prompe him, by him self, let him translate into Englishe his former lesson. Then shewing it to his master, let the master take from him his latin booke, and pausing an houre, at the least, than let the childe translate his owne Englishe into latin againe, in an other paper booke. When the childe bringeth it, turned into latin, the master must compare it with Tullies booke, and laie them both togither: and where the childe doth well, either in chosing, or true placing of Tullies wordes, let the master praise him, and saie here ye do well. For I assure you, there is no such whetstone, to sharpen a good witte and encourage a will to learninge, as is praise.

But if the childe misse, either in forgetting a worde, or in chaunging a good with a worse, or misordering the sentence I would not haue the master, either froune, or chide with him, if the childe haue done his diligence, and vsed no trewandship therein. For I know by good experience, that a childe shall take more profit of two fautes, ientlie warned of, then of foure thinges, rightly hitt. For than, the master shall haue good occasion to saie vnto him. N. Tullie would haue vsed such a worde, not this: Tullie would haue placed this word here, not there: would haue vsed this case, this number, this person, this degree, this gender: he would haue vsed this moode, this tens, this simple, rather than this compound: this aduerbe here, not there: he would haue ended the sentence with this verbe, not with that nowne or participle. etc.

In these fewe lines, I haue wrapped vp, the most tedious part of Grammer: and also the ground of almost all the Rewles, that are so busilie taught by the Master, and so hardlie learned by the Scholer, in all common Scholes: which after this sort, the master shall teach without all error, and the scholer shall learne without great paine: the master being led by so sure a guide, and the scholer being brought into so plaine and easie a waie. And therefore, we do not contemne Rewles, but we gladlie teach Rewles: and teach them, more plainlie, sensiblie, and orderlie, than they be commonlie taught in common Scholes. For whan the Master shall compare Tullies booke with his Scholers translation, let the Master, at the first, lead and teach his Scholer, to ioyne the Rewles of his Grammer booke, with the examples of his present lesson, vntill the Scholer, by him selfe, be hable to fetch out of his Grammer, euerie Rewle, for euerie Example: So, as the Grammer booke be euer in the Scholers hand, and also vsed of him, as a Dictionarie, for euerie present vse. This is a liuely and perfite waie of teaching of Rewles: where the common waie, vsed in common Scholes, to read the Grammer alone by it selfe, is tedious for the Master, hard for the Scholer, colde and vncumfortable for them bothe.

Let your Scholer be neuer afraide, to aske you any dout, but vse discretlie the best allurements ye can, to encorage him to the same: lest, his ouermoch fearinge of you, driue him to seeke some misorderlie shifte: as, to seeke to be helped by some other booke, or to be prompted by some other Scholer, and so goe aboute to begile you moch, and him selfe more.

With this waie, of good vnderstanding the mater, plaine construinge, diligent parsinge, dailie translatinge, cherefull admonishinge, and heedefull amendinge of faultes: neuer leauinge behinde iuste praise for well doinge, I would haue the Scholer brought vp withall, till he had red, & translated ouer ye first booke of Epistles chosen out by Sturmius, with a good peece of a Comedie of Terence also.

All this while, by mine aduise, the childe shall vse to speake no latine: For, as

Cicero saith in like mater, with like wordes, *loquendo, male loqui discunt.* And, that excellent learned man, G. Budaeus, in his Greeke Commentaries, sore complaineth, that whan he began to learne the latin tonge, vse of speaking latin at the table, and elsewhere, vnaduisedlie, did bring him to soch an euill choice of wordes, to soch a crooked framing of sentences, that no one thing did hurt or hinder him more, all the daies of his life afterward, both for redinesse in speaking, and also good iudgement in writinge.

In very deede, if childre were brought vp, in soch a house, or soch a Schole, where the latin tonge were properlie and perfitlie spoken, as Tib. and Ca. Gracci were brought vp, in their mother Cornelias' house, surelie, than the dailie vse of speaking, were the best and readiest waie, to learne the latin tong. But, now, commonlie, in the best Scholes in England, for wordes, right choice is smallie regarded, true proprietie whollie neglected, confusion is brought in, barbariousnesse is bred vp so in yong wittes, as afterward they be, not onelie marde for speaking, but also corrupted in iudgement: as with moch adoe, or neuer at all, they be brought to right frame againe.

Yet all men couet to haue their children speake latin: and so do I verie earnestlie too. We bothe, haue one purpose: we agree in desire, we wish one end: but we differ somewhat in order and waie, that leadeth rightlie to that end. Other would haue them speake at all aduentures: and, so they be speakinge, to speake, the Master careth not, the Scholer knoweth not, what. This is, to seeme, and not to bee: except it be, to be bolde without shame, rashe without skill, full of wordes without witte. I wish to haue them speake so, as it may well appeare, that the braine doth gouerne the tonge, and that reason leadeth forth the taulke.

RICHARD MULCASTER DESCRIBES THE EDUCATION OF CHILDREN

(**1581**)   From Richard Mulcaster, *Positions Concerning the Training Up of Children* (London, 1887), pp. xi-xvi, 1-5.

The Argvmemtes Handled in Every Particvlar Title

1

The entrie to the Positions, conteining the occasion of this present discourse, and the causes why it was penned in English.

2

Wherfore these Positions serue, what they be, and how necessarie it was to begin at them.

3

Of what force circunstance is in matters of action, and how warily authorities be to be vsed, where the contemplatiue reason receiues the check of the actiue circunstance, if they be not well applyed. Of the alledging of authours.

Of laughing, and weeping. And whether children be to be forced toward vertue and learning.

Of holding the breath.

Of daunsing, why it is blamed, and how deliuered from blame.

Of wrastling.

Of fensing, or the vse of the weapon.

Of the Top, and scourge.

Of walking.

Of running.

Of leaping.

Of swimming.

Of riding.

Of hunting.

Of shooting.

Of the ball.

Of the circumstances, which are to be considered in exercise.

The nature and qualitie of the exercise.

Of the bodies which are to be exercised.

Of the exercising places.

Of the exercising time.

Of the quantitie that is to be kept in exercise.

Of the manner of exercising.

An aduertisement to the training master. Why both the teaching of the minde and the training of the bodie be assigned to the same master. The inconueniences which ensue, where the bodie and the soule be made particular subiectes to seuerall professions. That who so will execute any thing well, must of force be fully resolued, in the excellencie of his owne subiect. Out of what kinde of writers the exercising maister maie store himselfe with cunning. That the first groundes would be laide by the cunningest workeman. That priuate discretion in any executour is of more efficacie, then his skill.

36

That both yong boyes, and youg maidens are to be put to learne. Whether all boyes be to be set to schoole. That to many learned be burdenous: to few to bare: wittes well sorted ciuill: missorted seditious. That all may learne to write and reade without daunger. The good of choice, the ill of confusion. The children which are set to learne hauing either rich or poore freindes, what order and choice is to be vsed in admitting either of them to learne. Of the time to chuse.

37

The meanes to restraine the ouerflowing multitude of scholers. The cause why euery one desireth, to haue his childe learned, and yet must yeilde ouer his owne desire to the disposition of his countrie. That necessitie and choice be the best restrainers. That necessitie restraineth by lacke and law. Why it may be admitted that all may learne to writ and reade that can, but no further. What is to be thought of the speaking and vnderstanding of latine, and in what degree of learning that is. That considering our time, and the state of religion in our time law must needes helpe this restraint, with the aunswere to such obiections as are made to the contrarie. That in choice of wittes, which must deale with learning, that wit is fittest for our state which aunswereth best the monarchie, and how such a wit is to be knowne. That choice is to helpe in schooling, in admission into colledges, in proceding to degrees, in preferring to liuings, where the right and wrong of all the foure pointes be handled at full.

That yong maindens are to be set to learning, which is proued by the custome of our countrie, by our duetie towardes them, by their naturall abilitie, and by the worthie effectes of such, as haue bene well trained. The ende whereunto their education serueth, which is the cause why and how much they learne. Which of them are to learne. When they are to beginne to learne: What and how much they may learne. Of whom and where they ought to be taught.

Of the training vp of yong gentlemen. Of priuate and publike education, with their generall goodes and illes. That there is no better way for gentlemen to be trained by in any respect, then the common is, being well appointed. Of rich mens children, which be no gentlemen. Of nobilitie in generall. Of gentlemanly exercises. What it is to be a nobleman or a gentleman. That infirmities in noble houses be not to be triumphed ouer. The causes and groundes of nobilitie. Why so many desire to be gentlemen. That gentlemen ought to professe learning, and liberall sciences for many good and honorable effectes. Of trauelin into forraine contries, with all the braunches, allowance and disallowance thereof: and that it were to be wished that gentlemen would professe, to make sciences liberall in vse, which are liberall in name. Of the training vp of a yong prince.

40

Of the generall place and time of education. Publike places elementarie, grammaticall, collegiat. Of bourding of children abroad from their parentes howses: and whether that be the best. The vse and commoditie of a large and well situate training place. Obseruations to be kept in the generall time.

41

Of teachers and trainers in generall: and that they be either Elementarie, Grammatticall, or Academicall. Of the elementarie teachers abilitie and enter-tainement: of the grammer maisters abilitie and his entertainement. A meane to haue both excellent teachers and cunning professours in all kindes of learning: by the diuision of colledges according to professions: by sorting like yeares into the same rowmes: by bettering the studentes allowance and liuing: by prouiding and maintaining notable well learned readers. That for bringing learning forward in her right and best course, there would be seuen ordinarie ascending colledges for tounges, for mathematikes, for philosophie, for teachers, for physicians, for lawyers, for diuines. And that the generall studie of law, would be but one studie. Euery of these pointes with his particular proufes sufficient for a position. Of the admission of teachers.

42

How long the childe is to continew in the elementarie, eare he passe to the toungues and grammer. The incurable infirmities which posting haste maketh in the whole course of studie. How necessarie a thing sufficient time is for a scholer.

43

How to cut of most inconueniences wherewith schooles and scholers, masters and parentes be in our schooling now most troubled: whereof there be too meanes, vniformitie in teaching and publishing of schoole orders. That vniformitie in teaching hath for companions dispatch in learning and sparing of expenses. Of the abbridging of the number of bookes. Of curtesie and correction. Of schoole faultes. Of friendlines betwene parentes and maisters.

44

That conference betwene those which haue interest in children: Certaintie of direction in places where children vse most: and Constancie in well keeping that, which is certainely appointed, be the most profitable circunstances both for vertuous mannering and cunning schooling.

The peroration, wherein the summe of the whole booke is recapitulated and proofes vsed, that this enterprise was first to be begon by Positions, and that these be the most proper to this purpose. A request concerning the well taking of that which is so well meant.

First Chapter
The Entrie to the Positions
Conteining the Occasion of This Present Discourse, and
the Causes Why It Was Penned in English

✻   ✻   ✻

I do write in my naturall English toungue, bycause though I make the learned my iudges, which vnderstand Latin, yet I meane good to the vnlearned, which vnderstand but English. And better it is for the learned to forbeare Latin, which they neede not then for the vnlearned to haue it, which they know not. By the English both shall see, what I say, by Latin but the one, which were some wrong, where both haue great interest, and the vnlearned the greater bycause the vnlearned haue not any but only such English helpes, the learned can fetch theirs from the same fountaines, whence I fetch mine. My meaning is principally to helpe mine owne countrie, whose language will helpe me, to be vnderstood of them, whom I would perswade: to get some thankes of them, for my good will to do well: to purchace pardon of them, if my good will do not well. The parentes and friendes with whom I haue to deale, be mostwhat no latinistes: and if they were, yet we vnderstand that tongue best, whervnto we are first borne, as our first impression is alwaie in English, before we do deliuer it in Latin. And in perswading a knowen good by an vnknowen waie, are we not to cal vnto vs, all the helpes that we can, to be thoroughly vnderstood? He that vnderstands no Latin can vnderstand English, and he that vnderstands Latin very well, can vnderstand English farre better, if he will confesse the trueth, though he thinke he haue the habite and can Latin it exceading well. When mine argument shall require Latin, as it will eare long, I will not then spare it, in the degree, that I haue it, but till it do, I will serue my countrie that waie, which I do surely thinke will proue most intelligible vnto her. For though the argument, which is dedicate to learning, and must therfore of force vse the termes of learning: which be mysteries to the multitude, maie seeme to offer some darkness and difficultie in that point: yet it is to be construed, that the thing it selfe must be presented in her owne colours, which the learned can discry, at the first blush, as of their acquaintance, who must be spoken to in their owne kinde: as the vnlearned must be content to enquire, bycause we straine our termes to haue them intitled. And yet, in all my drift, for all my faire promise, I dare warrant my countrie no more, then probabilitie doth me, which if it deceiue me, yet I haue it to leane vnto, and perhaps of such pith, as might easely haue beguiled a wiser man then me. But till I proue beguiled, I will dwell in hope, that I am not, to deliuer my minde with the better courage, and therby to shew that I thinke my selfe right. For the greatest enemy, that can be to any wel meaning conceit is, to mistrust his own power, and to dispaire of his good speede where happy fortune makes euident shew.

THE
EUROPEAN
HERITAGE

Chapter 2
Wherfore These Positions Serve, What They Be, and How
Necessarie It Was to Begin at Them

My purpose is to helpe the hole trade of teaching, euen from the very first foundation: that is, not only the Grammarian, and what shall follow afterward, but also the Elementarie, which is the verie infantes train, from his first entrie, vntill he be thought fit to passe thence to the Grammar schoole. My labour then beginning so low, am I not to follow the president of such writers, as in the like argumentes, haue vsed the like methode? The maner of proceding which the best learned authors do vse, in those argumentes, which both for the matter be of most credit, and for the maner of best accompt, kepeth alwaie such a currant, as they at the first laie downe certaine groundes, wherin both they and their readers, whether scholers onely, or iudges alone, do resolutely agree. Which consent enureth to this effect, that they maie therby either directly passe thorough to their ende without empeachment: or else if any difficulty do arise in the way, they may easely compound it, by retiring themselues to those primitiue groundes. The Mathematicall, which is counted the best maister of sound methode, of whome all other sciences do borrow their order, and way in teaching well, eare he passe to any either probleme or theoreme, setts downe certaine definitions, certaine demaundes, certaine naturall and necessarie confessions, which being agreed on, betwen him and his learner, he proceedeth on to the greatest conclusions in his hole profession, as those which be acquainted with Euclide and his friendes, do verie wel know. Wil the naturall philosopher medle with his maine subject, before he haue handled his first principles, matter, forme, priuation, motion, time, place, infinitie, vacuitie, and such other, whervnto Aristotle hath dedicated eight whole bookes? What shall I neede to take more paines in rehersall of any other writer, whether Lawyer, Physician, or any else, which entreateth of his peculiar argument learnedly, to prooue that I am first to plant by positions, seeing the verie diuine himself, marcheth on of this foote and groundeth his religion vpon principles of beleefe? I professe my selfe to be a scholer, wherby I do know this methode, which the learned do kepe, and I deale with an argument, which must needes at the first be verie nicely entertained, till proofe giue it credit, what countenaunce soeuer hope maie seeme to lend it, in the meane while. I maie therefore seeme to deale against mine owne knowledge, if I do not fortifie myselfe with such helpes, as vpon probable reason, maie first purchace their owne standing, and being themselues staid in place of liking maie helpe vp all the reste.

I am specially to further two degrees in learning, first the Elementarie which stretcheth from the time that the child is to be set to do any thing, till he be remoued to his Grammar: then the Grammarian, while the child doth continew, in the schoole of language, and learned tounges, till he be remoued for his ripenes, to some Vniuersitie: which two pointes be both of great moment.

For the Elementarie: Bycause sufficiency in the child, before he passe thence, helpes the hole course of the after studie, and insufficiencie skipping from thence to soone, makes a very weake sequele. For as sufficient time there, without to much hast, to post from thence to timely, draweth on the residew of the schoole degrees, in their best beseeming time, and in the ende sendeth abroad sufficient men for the seruice of their countrie: so to hedlong hast scouring thence to swiftly at the first, (for all that it seemeth so petie a thing,) in perpetuall infirmity of matter, procureth also to much childishnes in yeares to be then in place, when iudgement with skill, and ripenes with grayhaires should carie the contenaunce. And is not this pointe then to be well proyned, where hast is such a foe, and ripenes such a freind? Where pushing forward at the first before maturitie bid on, will still force that, which followeth till at the last it marre all?

For the Grammarian: As it is a thing not vnseemely for me to deale in, being my selfe a teacher, so is it verie profitable for my countrie to heare of, which in great varietie of teaching doth seeme to call for some vniforme waie. And to haue her youth well directed in the tounges, which are the waies to wisdome, the lodges of learning, the harbours of humanitie, the deliuerers of diuinitie, the treasuries of all store, to furnish out all knowledge in the cunning, and all iudgement in the wise, can it be but well taken, if it be well perfourmed?

EDMOND COOTE PROMISES TO TEACH ENGLISH (1596)   From the Frontispiece of Edmond Coote, *The English School-Maister: A Facsimile Reprint of the First Edition* (Menston, Yorkshire, England, 1968).

The English Schoole Maister

Teaching all his Scholers, of what age soever, the most easie, short, and perfect order of distinct reading, and true writing our English tongue that hath ever yet been knowne and published by any.

And further also teacheth a direct course, how any unskilfull person may easily both understand any hard english words, which they shall in the Scriptures, Sermons, or elsewhere heare or reade: and also bee made able to use the same aptly themselves. And generally whatsoever is necessary to be knowne for English speech: so that he which hath this booke only, needeth buy no other to make him fit, from his letters, unto the Grammar schoole, for an apprentice, or any other his owne private use, so farre as concerneth English. And therefore is made not onely for children, (though the first booke be meere childish for them) but also for all other especially that are ignorant in the Latine tongue.

In the next page the Schoole-maister hangeth forth his table, to the view of all beholders, setting forth some of the choice commodities of his profession.

Devised for thy sake that wanteth any part of this skill, by Edmund Coote Maister of the Free-schoole in Bury S. Edmond, Perused and approved by publike authorities.

EDMOND COOTE ON EDUCATION (1596)   From the Foreword and Preface of
Edmond Coote, *The English School-Maister: A Facsimile Reprint of the First Edition*
(Menston, Yorkshire, England, 1968).

I professe to teach thee, that art vtterly ignorant, to reade perfectly, to
write truly, and with iudgement to vnderstand the reason of our English tongue
with great expedition, ease, and pleasure.

I will teach thee that art vnperfect in either of them, to perfect thy skill in few
dayes with great ease.

I vndertake to teach all my scholers, that shall be trayned vp for any grammar
schoole, that they shall neuer erre in writing the true orthography of any word truly
pronounced: which what ease and benefite it will bring vnto Scholemaisters, they
best know: and the same profit doe I offer vnto all other both men & women, that
now for want hereof are ashamed to write vnto their best friends: for which I haue
heard many gentlewomen offer much.

I assure all Schoolemaisters of the English tongue, that they shall not onely
teach their scholers with greater perfection: but also they shal with more ease and
profit, and in shorter time teach a hundreth scholers, then before they could teach
fortx.

I hope by this plaine and short kinde of teaching to encourage many to read,
that neuer otherwise would haue learned. And so more knowledge will be brought
into this Land, and moe bookes bought, then otherwise would haue been.

I shall ease the poorer sort, of much charge that they haue been at in
maintayning their children long at Schoole and in buying many Bookes.

Strangers that now blame our tongue of difficultie and vncertaintie, shall by me
plainly see and vnderstand those thinges which they haue thought hard.

I doe teach thee, the first part of Arithmeticke, to know or write any nomber.

By the practise thereunto adioyned all learners shall so frame & tune their voyce,
as that they shall truely and naturally pronounce any kind of stile eyther in prose or
verse.

By the same practise Children shall learne in a Catechisme the knowledge of the
principles of true Religion, with precepts of vertue and ciuill behauiour.

I haue made a part of a briefe Chronologie for practise of reading hardwords,
wherin also thou shalt be much helped for the vnderstanding of the Bible, and other
histories: and a grammar Scholer learne to knowe when his authors both Greeke
and Latine liued, and when the principall Histories in them were done.

I haue set downe a Table conteining and teaching the true writing and
vnderstanding of any hard english word, borrowed from the Greeke, Latine, or
French, and how to know the one from the other, with the interpretation thereof by
a plaine English word: whereby Children shall be prepared for the vnderstanding of
thousands of Latine words before they enter the gramar Schole, which also will
bring much delight and iudgement to others. Therefore if thou vnderstandest not
any word in this Booke, not before expounded, seeke the Table.

If I may be generally receyued, I shall cause one vniforme maner of teaching: a
thing which as it hath brought much profite vnto the Latine Tongue, so would it
doe to all other languages, if the like were practised.

Finally, I haue giuen thee such examples for fayre writing, wherby in euery
schoole all bad hands may bee abandoned, that if thou shouldest buy the like of any

other (which thou shall seldome find in England) they alone would cost thee much more money then I aske thee for my whole profession.

If thou desirest to bee further satisfied, for the performance of these things; reade the preface where thou shalt also see the reason of somethings in the first booke, which thou mightest otherwise dislike.

The Preface for Direction to
the Reader

Other men in their writings (gentle Reader) may iustly vse such stile, as may declare learning or eloquence fit for a scholer: but I am enforced of necessitie to affect that plaine rudenes, which may best fit the capacitie of those persons, with whom I haue to deale. The learneder sort are able to vnderstand my purpose, and to teach this treatise without further direction, I am now therefore to direct my speech vnto the vnskilfull, which desire to make vse of it for their owne priuate benefit: And vnto such men and women of trades (as Taylors, Weauers, Shop-keepers, Seamsters, and such other) as haue vndertaken the charge of teaching others. Giue me leaue therefore (I beseech thee) to speake plainly and familiarly vnto thee, yea let me intreate thee to giue diligent regard to those things which I shall deliuer vnto thee, I seeke nothing by thee, but thine owne pleasure, ease and profit, and the good of thy scholers. If peraduenture for two or three dayes at the first, it may seeme somewhat hard or strange vnto thee, yet be not discouraged, neither cast it from thee: for if thou take diligent paines in it but foure dayes, thou shalt learne many very profitable things that thou neuer knewest, yea thou shalt know more for the English tongue, then any man of thy calling (not being a Grammarian in England knoweth: thou shalt teach thy scholers with better commendation and profit then any other, not following this order, teacheth: And thou maiest sit on thy shop-bord, at thy loomes, or at thy needle, and neuer hinder thy worke, to heare thy scholers, after thou hast once made this little booke familiar vnto thee. The practise and order of studie I know is a stranger vnto thee: yet must thou now bee sure that thou passe not ouer any one word, before thou well vnderstandest it. If thou canst not finde out the meaning and true vse of any rule or word, and hauing none present to helpe thee, make a marke thereat with a pen or pin, vntill thou meetest with your Minister, or other learned scholer of who thou maist enquire: and do not think it any discredite to declare thy want, being in a matter pertayning to Grammar, or other such things, as those of thy condition, are vsually vnacquainted with: rather assure thy selfe, that al wise men will commend thee, that desirest knowledge, which many reiect: and they which refuse to be directed, I know are such as delight in their sottish ignorance, like Scoggens priest, who because he had vsed his old assumptions for these dozen yeres, would not forsake it, for the others new assumptions, though it were neuer so good. Two things generally you must marke for the vse of this booke: first, the true vnderstanding of it for the matter: secondly, the manner of learning it, if thou be onely a scholer, then the order of teaching it, if thou bee also a teacher. And for the first, where I professe to teach with farre more ease and pleasure to the learner, and therfore with greater speede then other: vnderstand the reason. Thou hast but two principall things to learne, to spell truly any word of one syllable, and to diuide truly any word of many. For the first I haue disposed syllables so in the first booke (howsoeuer at the first sight they may seeme common) as that thou canst meete none but either thou hast it there set downe, or at least so many like both for beginning or end, as that none can be propounded vnto thee, which thou shalt not be skilful in. And I haue so begun with the easiest, proceeding by degrees vnto harder, that the first learned, all the other will follow with very little labour. These syllables knowne, because al words be they neuer so long or hard be made of them, thou hast nothing to learne but to diuide them: for which I haue layd downe so easie & certaine rules, (beleeue me that haue tried) as that thou shalt neuer erre in any hard word: I doubt not, but thine owne experience shal find this true, and so my promise in that point performed to the full. Maruaile not why in this first book I haue differed in writing many syllables from the vsuall manner, yea from my selfe in the rest of the worke: as *templ* without (*e*), *sun* with one (*n*) and *plums*, not *plummes*, &c. my reason is, I haue there put no moe letters then are of absolute necessitie, when in the rest I haue followed custome: yea, often I write the same word diuersly (if it be vsed indifferently) the better to acquaint thee with any kinde of writing. Touching the speeches at the end of the 1.2.4.7. and 8. chapters, regard not the matter (being vaine) but my purpose, which is to bring thee to present vse of reading words of one syllable, which thou hast learned to spell, and so thou maiest haue nothing in the second booke to learne, but only diuision of words, and other harder obseruations. The titles of the chapters and notes in the margent (which I would alwayes haue thee diligently read and marke) will make these things more plaine vnto thee.

Also, where I vndertake to make thee to write the true Orthographie of any word truly pronounced, I must meane it of those words, whose writing is determined: for there are many wherein the best English men in this land are not agreed. As some write *malicious*, deriuing it from *malice*. Other write *malitious*, as from the Latine *malitiosus*. So some write *German* from the Latine, some *Germain* from the French. Neither do I deale with proper names, strange words of arte in seuerall sciences, nor the vnknowne termes of peculiar countries, (if they differ from ordinary rules) vnles sometime vpon some speciall occasion. I know ere this, thou thirstest that art a teacher, to heare how thou maiest with more ease and profit teach a hundreth scholers then before fortie: follow mine aduise, and I warrant the successe. Let euery one of thy scholers (for the best thou hast shall learne that here which he neuer knew, neither needeth he any other for English) prouide and use this booke: then diuide thy scholers into 2.3 or 4 sorts, as thy number is (for moe thou needest not, although thou hast a hundreth scholers) and place so many of them as are neerest of like forwardnes, in one lesson or forme, as in Grammar schooles, and so go through thy whole number, not making aboue foure companies at the most: so that thou shalt haue but foure lectures to heare, though thou hast an hundreth scholers, whereas before thou haddest fortie lectures, though but fortie scholers. Then when thou wouldest heare any forme, call them forth all, bee they ten, twentie, or moe together: heare two or three that thou most suspectest to be most negligent, or of dullest conceit, and let all the other attend: or let one read one line, sentence or part, another the next, and so through: so that all do somewhat, and none know, when or what shall be required of him, encourage the most diligent and tenderest natures. And thus doubt not but thou shalt doe more good vnto twentie in one houre, then before vnto foure in seuerall lessons: for the apposing each other, as I haue directed in the end of the second booke, emulation, and feare of discredite, will make them enuie who shall excell. By this meanes also euery one in a higher forme shall be well able to helpe those vnder him, and that without losse of time, seeing thereby he repeateth that which he lately learned. Now touching the framing and sweete tuning of thy voyce, I haue giuen thee this helpe, I haue added for prose al sorts of stile both dialogue and other: and for verse, Psalmes and other verses of all the seuerall sorts vsuall, which being well taught, wil frame thee to the naturall reading of any English. But here I must make earnest request vnto all carefull Ministers, that as they tender the good education of the youth in their parishes, they would sometimes repayre vnto the schooles of such teachers as are not Grammarians, to heare their children pronounce, and to helpe such with their direction, that desire to vse this booke in their schooles: for it is lamentable to see into what ignorant handling sillie little children chaunce, which should at the first bee most skilfully grounded, which is the only cause of such wofull ignorance in so many men and women, that cannot write without great error one sentence of true English: therefore let parents now bee wise vnto whom they commit their children.

But to returne vnto my teaching trades-man, if thou desirest to be enformed how to teach this treatise, marke diligently the directions giuen in all places of the booke: and as thy scholer is in saying his lesson, marke what words he misseth, and them note with a penne or pinne, and let him repeate them at the next lecture, and so vntil he bee perfect, not regarding those where he is skilfull. And let his fellowes also remember them to appose him in them in their appositions. But me thought I heard thee say that my reasons haue perswaded thee to be willing to teach this: but thou canst not moue all their parents to bee willing to bestow so much money on a booke at the first: Tell them from me that they need buy no moe, and then they shall saue much by the bargaine. Buy they will reply, that his little yong child will haue torne it before it be halfe learned. Then answer him, that a remedie is prouided for that also, which is this: first, the Printer vpon the sight hereof, hath framed his horne bookes, according to the order of this booke, making the most part of my second page the matter thereof: which in mine opinion he did with good reason: for a child may by this treatise almost learne to spell perfectly in as little time, as learne well the other horne-booke. But this latter being first learned, being the ground-worke of spelling, all the rest of this worke will be gotten with small labour. Secondly, I haue so disposed the placing of my first booke, that if the child should teare out euery leafe as fast as he learneth it, yet it shall not bee greatly hurtfull, for euery new following chapter repeateth and teacheth againe all that went before. I hope if he bee a reasonable man that this answer will suffice. Touching my Chronologie and table, I haue before the entrance into them prefixed the manner how to vnderstand the vse of them, whereunto I referre thee, hauing been alreadie ouer tedious. For the particular ordinary sounding of the letters, I wholly omit, leauing it to the ordering of the teacher, especially it being before sufficiently and learnedly handled by another. Thus haue I so plainly pratled and lisped vnto thee, as that I hope thou vnderstandest my purpose, and single heart for thy good: which if I find thou acceptest, I may peraduenture hereafter proceede in my course for the easie and speedie attayning the learned languages, an argument which as it is more pertinent to my profession, so might it rather be expected from me then this poore pamphlet.

But in the meane time, if in this thou finde my words true, accept my good will, and giue glorie to God.

JOHN BRINSLEY ON THE PURPOSE OF GRAMMAR SCHOOL

(1627)   From John Brinsley, *Ludus Literarius or The Grammar Schoole*, E. T. Campagnac, ed. (London, 1917), pp. xiii - xix.

The Contents in Generall of
the Chiefe Points Aymed at, and Hoped to Be
Effected by This Worke

To teach Schollers how to bee able to reade well, and write true Orthography, in a short space.

2. To make them ready in all points of Accedence and Grammar, to answere any necessary question therein.

3. To say without booke all the usuall and necessary rules to construe the Grammar rules, to give the meaning, use, and order of the Rules; to shew the examples, and to apply them: which being well performed, will make all other learning easie and pleasant.

4. In the severall fourmes and Authors to construe truely, and in propriety of words and sence, to parse of themselves, and to give a right reason of every word why it must bee so, and not otherwise; and to reade the English of the Lectures perfectly out of the Latine.

5. Out of an English Grammaticall translation of their Authors, to make and to construe any part of the Latine, which they have learned to prove that it must be so: and so to reade the Latine out of the English, first, in the plaine Grammaticall order; after, as the wordes are placed in the Author, or in other good composition. Also to parse in Latine, looking onely upon the Translation.

6. To take their lectures for themselves, except in the very lowest formes, and first enterers into construction; or to doe it with very Little helpe, in some more difficult things.

7. To enter surely in making Latine, without danger of making false Latine, or using any barbarous phrase.

8. To make true Latine, and pure Tullies phrase, and to prove it to be true and pure. To doe this in ordinary morall matters, by that time that they have bin but two yeeres in construction.

9. To make Epistles imitating Tully, short and pithy, in Tullies Latine, and familiar.

10. To translate into English, according to propriety both of words and sense: and out of the English to reade the Latine againe, to prove it, and give a reason of every thing.

11. To take a piece of Tully, or of any other familiar easie Author, Grammatically translated, and in propriety of words, and to turne the same out of the translation into good Latine, and very neere unto the words of the Authour; so as in most you shall hardly discerne, whether it be the Authour's Latine, or the scholler's.

12. To correct their faults of themselves, when they are but noted out unto them, or a question is asked of them.

13. To be able in each fourme (at any time whensoever they shall be apposed of a sudden, in any part of their Authors, which they have learned) to construe, parse, reade into English, and forth of the translation to construe and to reade into the Latine of their Authors; first, into the naturall order, then into the order of the Author, or neere unto it.

14. In Virgill or Horace to resolve any piece, for all these points of learning, and to doe it in good Latine;

Construing to give propriety of words and sense.
Scanning the verses, and giving a reason in thereof.
Shewing the difficulties of Grammar.
Observing the elegacies in tropes & figures.
Noting phrases and Epithetes.

15. So to reade over most of the chiefe Latine Poets, as Virgill, Horace, Persius, &c. by that time that by reason of their yeeres, they be in any measure thought fit for their discretion, to goe unto the University: yea to goe thorow the rest of themselves, by ordinary helpes.

16. In the Greeke Testament to construe perfectly, and parse as in the Latine, to reade the Greeke backe again out of a translation Latine or English: also to construe, parse, and to prove it out of the same. To do the like in Isocrates, or any familiar pure Greeke Author; as also in Theognis, Hesiod, or Homer, and to resolve as in Virgill or Horace.

17. In the Hebrew to construe perfectly, and to resolve as in the Greeke Testament; and to reade the Hebrew also out of the translation. Which practice of dayly reading somewhat out of the translations into the Originals, must needes make them both very cunning in the tongues, and also perfect in the texts of the Originals themselves, if it be observed constantly; like as it is in dayly reading Latine out of the Translation.

18. To answer most of the difficulties in all Classicall Schoole-Authors; as in Terence, Virgil, Horace, Persius, &c.

19. To oppose schollerlike in Latine, of any Grammar question necessary, in a good forme of words; both what may bee objected against Lillies rules, and how to defend them.

20. To write Theames full of good matter, in pure Latine, and with judgement.

21. To enter to make a verse with delight, without any bodging at all; and to furnish with copie of Poeticall phrase, out of Ovid, Virgil, and other the best Poets.

22. So to imitate and expresse Ovid or Virgil, as you shall hardly discerne, unlesse you know the places, whether the verses be the Authour's or the scholler's: and to write verses *ex tempore* of any ordinary Theames.

23. To pronounce naturally and sweetely, without vain affectation; and to begin to doe it from the lowest fourmes.

24. To make right use of the matter of their Authours, besides the Latine; even from the first beginners: as of Sententiae and Confabulatiunculae Pueriles, Cato, Esop's fables, Tullies Epistles, Tullies Offices, Ovid's Metamorphosis, and so on to the highest. To helpe to furnish them, with variety of the best morall matter, and with understanding, wisedome and precepts of vertue, as they grow; and withall to imprint the Latine so in their minds thereby, as hardly to be forgotten.

25. To answer concerning the matter contained in their Lectures, in the Latine of their Authors, from the lowest fourmes, and so upward.

26. To construe any ordinary Author *ex tempore*.

27. To come to that facility and ripenesse, as not onely to translate leasurely, & with some meditation, both into English and Latine, as before in the Sect. or Article 10. and 11. but more also, to read any easie Author forth of Latine into English, and out of a translation of the same Grammatically translated, to read it into Latine againe. As Corderius, Terence, Tullies Offices, Tullie *de natura Deorum*,

Apthonius. To doe this in Authors and places which they are not acquainted with, and almost as fast as they are able to reade the Author alone.

28. To write fayre in Secretary, Romane, Greeke, Hebrue; as they grow in knowledge of the tongues.

29. To know all the principall and necessarie Radices, Greeke and Hebrue; and to be able to proceede in all the learned tongues of themselves, through ordinary helpes, and much more by the worthy helpes & meanes, to be had in the Universities.

30. To be acquainted with the grounds of Religion, and the chiefe Histories of the Bible. To take all the substance of the Sermons, for Doctrines, proofes, uses, if they be plainely and orderly delivered: and to set them downe afterwards in a good Latine stile, or to reade them *ex tempore* in Latine, out of English: To conceive and answer the severall points of the Sermons, and to make a briefe repetition of the whole Sermon without booke.

31. To be set in the high way, and to have the rules and grounds, how to attaine to the puritie and perfection of the Latine tongue, by their further labour and practice in the University.

32. To grow in our English tongue, according to their ages and growthes in other learning: To utter their minds in the same both in proprietie and purity; and so to be fitted for Divinitie, Law, or what other calling or faculty soever they shall be after imployed in.

33. Finally, thus to proceed together with the tongues in the understanding and knowledge of the learning, or matter contained in the same. To become alike expert, in all good learning meete for their yeeres and studies; that so proceeding still, after they are gone from the Grammar schooles, they may become most exquisite in all kinds of good learning to which they shall be applied.

These things may be effected in good sort, through God's blessing, in the severall fourms, as the schollers proceed, by so many in each fourme as are apt and industrious, only by the directions following, if they be constantly observed; If the Masters being of any competent sufficiencie, will take meet paines; and if the schollers being set to schoole so soone as they shall bee meete, may be kept to learning ordinarily, having bookes and other necessary helpe & encouragements. That so all schollers of any towardlinesse and diligence may be made absolute Grammarians, and every way fit for the Universitie, by fifteene yeeres of age; or by that time that they shall bee meete by discretion and government. And all this to bee done with delight and certaintie, both to master and schollers, with strift and contention amongst the schollers themselves, without that usuall terrour and cruelty, which hath beene practised in many places, and without so much as severitie amongst good natures.

How greatly all this would tend to the furtherance of the publike good, every one may judge; which yet it will doe so much the more, as the Lord shall vouchsafe a further supply, to the several meanes and courses that are thus begun, by adjoyning daily the helpes and experiments of many mo learned men, of whom we conceive good hope, that they will be ready to lend their helping hands, to the perfiting of so good a Worke.

JOHN BRINSLEY ON THE TEACHING OF ENGLISH (1627) From John Brinsley, *Ludus Literarius or The Grammar School,* E. T. Campagnac, ed. (London, 1917), pp. 12-16.

Spoud: Before wee enter into this question, let me put you in minde of one thing, which doth much trouble mee concerning this very matter. That it seemeth to mee an unreasonable thing, that the Grammar Schooles should bee troubled with teaching A.B.C. seeing it is so great a hinderance to those paines which wee should take with our Grammar Schollers, for whom wee are appointed: Because it doth take up almost one halfe of our time, and thereby doth deprive us of a chiefe part of the fruit of our labours; especially when our mindes are so distracted, and our thoughts carried so many wayes, to doe good to all. The very little ones in a towne, in most countrey townes which are of any bignesse, would require a whole man, of themselves, to bee alwaies hearing, poasing & following them, so as they ought to be applyed: for continuall applying in a right course, is in this and all other parts of learning, above all other meanes. And young ones, by a little slaking our hands, run faster backe, then ever they went forward; as boates going up the streame.

Besides, it is an extreme vexation, that we must be toiled amongst such little petties, and in teaching such matters, whereof wee can get no profit, nor take any delight in our labours.

Phil: I am well inured with this grievance, which you speake of, and doe know by long experience your complaint to bee too just in this behalfe. I myselfe have complained of it many a time. For it were much to be wished, that none might bee admitted to the Grammar schooles, untill they were able to reade English: as namely, that they could reade the New Testament perfectly, and that they were in their Accidences, or meet to enter into them. There might bee some other schoole in the towne, for these little ones to enter them. It would helpe some poore man or woman, who knew not how to live otherwise, and who might doe that well, if they were rightly directed. Also it would be such an ease to all Grammar Schoolemasters, as they might doe much more good in their places. Wherefore, all such Schoolemasters who are incumbred with this inconvenience, are not onely to wish, but also to labour to have it reformed in their severall schooles. Yet notwithstanding, where it cannot be redressed, it must be borne with wisdome and patience as an heavy burden. Patience shall make it much more light. And therefore every one is to doe his best indeavour, to know how to make it most easie, if it doe lie upon him. Moreover, seeing we purpose, God willing, to goe thorow all the whole course of learning, and also sith our labour is to finde out the meanes, whereby to make the way plaine, to traine up every childe from the very first entrance into learning, (as was said) untill wee have brought him into the Universitie, we cannot omit any point, which may tend unto the fame, much lesse the first steppe of all. For, a child well entred is halfe made: according to that Proverbe, *Principium, dimidium totius.* The foundation well layd, the building must needs goe forward much more happily. This is specially true in learning; wherein children feeling a sweetnesse in the beginning, are very much incouraged, as daily experience will manifest to every one.

Spoud: I see well the necessitie of undergoing this burden, in those places where remedy cannot be had, without greater inconveniences. And therefore, sith that necessitie hath no law, nor for myselfe I know no meanes how to bee freed from it;

THE
EUROPEAN
HERITAGE

I pray you let us returne againe unto the point, and let mee still intreat of you your best direction, to make this burden so light as may bee. This is a thing worth the diligence of all, who must be imployed amongst little ones: to wit, to teach children how to read well, and to pronounce their letters truly; as also to spell right, and to know how to write true Orthography in a short space. For (that I may acknowledge the truth, and which hath bin no small discredit unto mee in this behalfe) I have had some who have beene with me, two or three yeeres, before they could reade well. And that which hath yet been much more grievous to mee. I have sometimes beene so abashed and ashamed, that I have not knowne what to say, when some being a little discontented, or taking occasion to quarrell about paying my stipend, have cast this in my teeth, that their children have been under me six or seven yeeres, and yet have not learned to reade English well. I myselfe have also knowne, that their complaints have been true in part; though I have taken all the paines with them that ever I could devise. Therefore good Sir, set downe as plainely and shortly as you can, how this may be helped. Both myselfe and many others shal be much beholden for your direction in this first entrance. For my maner of entring them, it is that which I take to be everywhere: to teach & heare them so oft over untill they can say a lesson, and so to a new.

Phil: I likewise have been well acquainted with this your trouble: and therefore I will indevour, to afford you so much as I have yet learned, how to avoid these clamours; and how any poore man who will imploy his paines, may learn to teach children to read well in a short time, though this may seem unbefitting our profession.

First the childe is to be taught, how to call every letter, pronouncing each of them plainely, fully and distinctly; I meane, in a distinct and differing sound, each from others, and also naturally, from the very first entrance to learning. More specially to bee carefull, for the right pronouncing the five vowels, in the first place, as *a, e, i, o, u.* Because these are first and most naturall, and doe make a perfect sound, so that they may bee pronounced fully of themselves; and they being rightly uttered, all the rest are more plaine. After these vowels, to teach them to pronounce every other letter: which are therefore called Consonants, because they cannot make a perfect sound of themselves, without a Vowell.

This may be done, and also the teaching of children to spell any syllable, before the child do know any letter on the booke; and that, some wise and experienced doe hold the surest and best course. But they are, at least, to be taught to pronounce their letters thus, as they doe learne them; to prevent the griefe and wearisomnesse of teaching them to forget evil customes in pronouncing, which they tooke up in their first ill learning. And so ever in teaching to read, the teachers are to continue the like care of sweet and naturall pronunciation.

Secondly, for the knowing of the letters (besides that common manner practised in Schooles, which is by oft reading over all the letters forwards and backwards untill they can say them) they may be much furthered thus; That is, by causing the childe to find out, and to shew you which is *a,* which *b,* which *c,* which *f,* and so any other letter. First to finde them in the Alphabet, then in any other place. Or if you will let them learne but one letter at once, untill they can readily know or finde out that letter in any place, and after that another in the same manner: This is holden the surer and more easie way: But this at your owne judgement.

3. You may helpe them to spell thus, besides that course which is usuall. Let so many as are beginners, or who cannot reade perfectly, stand together, and then poase them without booke, one by one. First, in syllables of two letters, as they are set downe in their A.B.C. and where one misseth, let his next fellow tell: if he

cannot, then, let some other. Then examine them in syllables of three letters, after in moe. And ever what syllable they misse, marke it with a dent with the nayle, or a pricke with a pen, or the like: and when you have marked out those wherein they so misse, poase them oft over, not forgetting due praise to them who doe best. One halfe houre would be spent daily in this kind of examining, untill they be perfect in any syllable, or word. To make children to take a delight in spelling, let them spell many syllables together, which differ but only in one letter, as hand, band, land, sand, &c. These syllables and words following, I have observed, to bee of the hardest for children to spell: I will set you them downe together in this short briefe. They may serve for spelling, reading, or writing, and may soone be gotten by being often poased, read or written over.

CHARLES HOOLE ON THE CURRICULUM AND TEACHING METHODS OF ROTHERHAM GRAMMAR SCHOOL (1660)   From Charles Hoole, *A New Discovery of the Old Art of Teaching Schoole, in Four Small Treatises,* E. T. Campagnac, ed. (London, 1913), pp. 129-39, 233-37.

How to Make the Scholars of the Fourth Form Very Perfect in the Art of Grammar, and Elements of Rhetorick; & How to Enter Them upon Greek in an Easy Way. How to Practise Them (as They Read Terence, and Ovid de Tristibus, *and His* Metamorphosis, *and* Janua Latinae Linguae, *and Sturmius, and Textor's* Epistles) *in Getting Copy of Words, and Learning Their Derivations and Differences, and in Varying Phrases. How to Shew Them the Right Way of Double translating, and Writing a Most Pure Latine Style. How to Acquaint Them with All Sorts of English and Latine Verses, and to Enable Them to Write Familiar and Elegant Epistles either in English or Latine, upon All Occasions*

The Usher having throughly performed his Duty, so as to lay a sure foundation by teaching Grammar, and lower Authours, and using other helps formentioned, to acquaint his Scholars with the words, and order of the Latine tongue, as well for speaking, as writing it: The Master may more cheerfully proceed to build further, and in so doing, he should be as carefull to keep what is well gotten, as diligent to adde thereunto. I would advise therefore, that the Scholars of this fourth form may,

1. Every morning read six or ten verses (as formerly) out of the Latine Testament into English, that thus they may be become well acquainted with the matter, and words of that most holy Book; and after they are acquainted with the Greek Testament, they may proceed with it in like manner.

2. Every Thursday morning repeat a part out of the Latine Grammar, according as it is last divided, that by that meanes they may constantly say it over once every quarter. And because their wits are now ripe for understanding Grammar notions, where ever they meet with them, I would have them every one to provide a Paper-book of two quires in Quarto, in the beginning whereof, they should write the Heads of Grammar by way of common place, as they see it in my Latine Grammar,

and having noted the pages, they should again write over the same Heads, (leaving a larger or lesse distance betwixt them, as they conceive they may finde more or lesse matter to fill them withall) in the leaves of their Book, and insert all niceties of Grammar that they finde, either in their daily lessons, or in perusing other Books at spare houres, especially such as either methodically, or critically treat of Grammar; amongst which I commend Mr. Brinsley's posing of the Accidents. The Animadversions upon Lilies Grammar, Stockwoods disputations, Mr. Pooles English Accidents, Hermes Anglo-Latinus, Phalerii Supplementa ad Grammaticam, Mr. Birds, Mr. Shirleyes, Mr. Burleyes, Mr. Hawkins, Mr. Gregories, Mr. Haynes, Mr. Danes, Mr. Farnabies, and other late printed new Grammars, (which they may read in private one after another) will afford them several observations. As for Authores Grammaticae Antiqui, which are commonly printed together; Dispauterius, Linacer, Melancthon, Valerius, Alvarez, Rhemus, Sulpitius, Vossius, and the like, either ancient or modern, they may take the opportunity to read them, after they come to higher Forms, and pick out of them such pretty notes, as they have not formerly met withall, and write them in their Common place-booke. And because it may seem a needlesse labour for every Scholar to be thus imployed, and it is (almost) impossible for one alone to procure so many Grammars, it were to be wished, that in every Schoole of note, there might be a Library, wherein all the best Grammars that can be gotten, might be kept, and lent to those boyes, that are more industriously addicted to Grammar Art, and which intend to be Scholars, that they may read them over, and refer what they like in them to its proper Head. And to encourage them in so doing, the Master may do well at the first to direct them, and afterwards at leisure times to cast an eye upon their Books, and see what they have collected of themselves. But be sure that they keep their Paper-book fair, and that they write constantly in it, with a legible and even hand.

3. Thus they may have liberty to learn Rhetorick on Mondayes, Tuesdayes, and Wednesdayes, for morning Parts. And to enter them in that Art of fine speaking, they may make use of *Elementa Rhetorices*, lately printed by Mr. Dugard, and out of it learn the Tropes and Figures, according to the definitions given by Talaeus, and afterwards more illustrated by Mr. Butler. Out of either of which books, they may be helped with store of examples, to explain the Definitions, so as they may know any Trope or Figure that they meet with in their own Authours. When they have throughly learnt that little book, they may make a Synopsis of it, whereby to see its order, and how every thing hangs together, and then write the Common place heads in a Paper-book (as I have mentioned before touching Grammar) unto which they may referre; whatever they like in the late *English Rhetorick*, Mr. Farnabies *Index Rhetoricus*, Susenbrotus, Mr. Hornes *Compendium Rhetorices*, or the like, till they be better able to peruse other Authours, that more fully treat of the Art; as, Vossius's *Partitiones Oratoriae, Orator extemporaneus*, Tesmari *exercitationes Rhetoricae*, Nic. Caussinus. Paiot *de elequentia*, and many others; with which a School-Library should be very well furnished for the Scholars to make use on, accordingly as they increase in ability of learning.

These *Elementa Rhetorices* in their first going over, should be explained by the Master, and construed by the Scholars, and every example compared with its Definition. And the Scholars should now be diligent of themselves to observe every Trop and Figure, that occurre in their present Authours, and when they say, to render it with its full definition, and if any be more eminent and worthy observation then others, to write it down in their Common-place-book, and by this means they will come to the perfect understanding of them in a quarter of a yeares time, and with more ease commit it all to memory by constant parts, saying a whole Chapter together at once; which afterwards they may keep by constant Repetitions, as they do their Grammar.

4. When they have passed their Rhetorick, you may let them bestow those hours, which they spent about it, in getting the Greek Grammar for morning parts. And because in learning this Language, as well as the Latine, we are to proceed by one Rule, which is most common and certain; I preferre Camdens Greek Grammar before any that I have yet seen, (though perhaps it be not so facill, or so compleat as some latelier printed, especially those that are set out by my worthy friends, Mr. Busbie of Westminster, and Mr. Dugard of Merchant Taylors Schoole) in the first going over of which, I would have them to repeat onely the Greek letters, and their divisions, the Accents, and eight Parts of Speech, the Articles, Declensions, and Conjugations, the Adverbs, Conjunctions, and Prepositions by several parts, as they are best able to get them, and to write down so much as they say at once in a fair Paper-book, very exactly observing and marking every Accent, and note of distinction. And this will quickly enable them to write or read Greek very truly, especially if they minde the abbreviated characters, which are now lately printed at the end of most of these Grammars. This work will take up about a quarter of a years time.

In the next half year, they may get over the whole Grammar in that order, as it is printed. And in the interim thereof, they may make use of their Greek Testament every morning after prayers, in like manner as they formerly used their Latine one. They may begin with the Gospel of S. John, which at the first you may help them to construe and parse verbatim, but after a while when they have gathered strength to do somewhat of themselves, you may let them make use of Pasors Lexicon, which they will better do, by help of the Themes, which I caused to be printed in the Margent of the Greek Testament, which will lead them to Pasor, to see the Analysis of any word in the Testament. Mr. Dugard hath lately compleated his *Lexicon Graeci Testamenti Alphabeticum, una cum explicatione Grammatica vocum singularum, in usum Tironum; nec non concordantia singulis vocibus apposita, in usum Theologiae canditatorum*; which were it once committed to the presse, as it now lyeth ready in his hand, would be a most excellent help to young Scholars, to proceed in the Greek Testament of themselves, in an understanding and Grammatical way. And I hope it will not be long ere he publish it for common use. When they have gone over the Declensions and Conjugations, and are able to write Greek in a very fair and legible character, let them write out the Paradigmes of every Declension and Conjugation, and divide the moveable part of the words, from the Terminations, as you may see it done in Mr. Dugards *Rudimenta Grammaticae Graecae.* After they are thus acquainted with every particular example, they may write out all the Declensions one by another, and the three voyces of the Verbs throughout all moods and tenses in all Conjugations, that so they may more readily compare them one by another, and see what Tenses are alike, or which are wanting in every voyce. If these things were drawn into Tables, to be hanged up in the Schoole, they would help the weaker boyes.

And to supply them with store of Nouns & Verbs, you may let them repeat as many nouns as they can wel get at once, out of Mr. *Gregories Nomenclatura*; and afterwards as many Sentences as they can wel say at once, out of Seidelius, or the latter end of Clavis *Graecae linguae*, by the repeating, construing and parsing, whereof they will learn all the Primitive words of the Greek Tongue, and be able to decline them. And thus they will be very well fitted to fall upon any approved Greek Authour, when they come into the next Form. But if you would have them learne to speak Greeke, let them make use of Posselius's *Dialogues*, or Mr. Shirleyes

Introductorium, in English, Latine, and Greek. I commonly appointed Tuesdayes and Thursdayes afternoones for this employment, before or after my Scholars had performed their other Tasks.

* * *

1. Let them write out every Lesson very fair and exactly, as they see it printed before them both in English and Latine. And this will be a means to perfect them in Orthography, and to imprint what they learn in that Authour in their mindes. They should have a Quarto Paper-book for this purpose, wherein nothing else should be written.

2. Let them translate about four or six lines Grammatically in a loose paper, that by this means they may better take notice of the way of construing.

3. Let them construe the whole Lesson both Grammatically, and according to the phrase, and this will acquaint them with the proprieties of both Tongues.

4. Let them parse it according to the Grammatical order, examining every word to the utmost of what Grammar teacheth concerning it, and this will make them thorowly to understand Lilie, and sometimes to consult other Grammars, where he comes short in a Rule.

5. Let them cull out the most significant words, and phrases, and write them in a Pocket-book, with figures referring where to finde them in their Authour; and let them ever and anon be conning these by heart, because these (of all others) will stand them in most stead for speaking Latine, or writing Colloquies and Epistles.

* * *

How the Master Should Maintain
His Authority Amongst His Scholars

Authority is the true mother of all due order, which the Master must be careful in every thing to maintain, otherwise he may command what he pleaseth, but withall, he must give the Scholars liberty to do what they list. Which what an horrible confusion in their places, what insufferable neglect of their tasks, what unrulinesse in point of behaviour, what perpetual torment to the painful Master, and his Ushers, and what unavoydable disgrace it bringeth upon a Schoole, let them that are Actors, or Spectators thereof, give testimony. 1. That therefore the Master may have all his lawful commands put in execution with due alacrity, and his decent orders diligently observed, I conceive it requisite, that,

1. He be sure in all things to behave as a Master over himself, not only by refraining those enormities and grosser faults, which may render him scandalous to every one, but checking his own Passions, especially that of Anger; and if at any time he seem to have cause to be provoked to it, and feel it to come too violently upon him, let him rather walk aside awhile out of the Schoole to divert it, then express it openly amongst his Scholars by unseemly words or gestures. He should indeed endeavour to behave himself unblameably in all Christian-like conversation before all men, but so amongst his Scholars, that they may have much wherein to imitate him, but nothing whereby to disgrace him. And towards his neighbours, his affability should be such, as to win their love and respects, so that they may be

ready at all times to countenance the Masters well-doing, and to vindicate the credit of him and his Schoole, when they hear it unjustly traduced.

2. When he commands, or forbids any thing to be done, he should acquaint his Scholars with the end intended, and the benefits or inconveniences which attend such, or such a course. For children have so much use of reason as to delight to heare perswasive arguments of reason, though the declivity of corrupt nature makes, that they do not much minde them, where there is no feare of a rod for doing amisse. Yet sometimes it may be best to say onely, Do this, or do it not, where you think it of no concernment to them to know the reason, and would make trial of their readinesse to obey, without asking why or wherefore.

3. One main way to bring Scholars to a loving and awfull respect of their Master, is for him to shew himselfe at all times pleasing and chearful towards them, and unwilling to punish them for every error; but withall to carry so close an eye upon all their behaviour, that he can tell them privately, betwixt himself and them alone, of many faults they commit, . . .

4. But nothing works more upon good natured children, then frequent encouragements and commendations for well-doing; and therefore, when any taske is performed, or order observed according to his minde, the Master should commend all his Scholars, but especially the most observant, and encourage the weak, and timerous, and admonish the perversest amongst them to go on in imitating their example, in hopes of finding as much favour at his hands, as they see them to have.

5. In some places a Master is apt to be molested with the reproachfull clamours of the meaner sort of people, that cannot (for the most part) endure to have their children corrected, be the fault never so heinous, but presently they must come to the Schoole to brave it out with him; which if they do, the Master should there in a calme manner admonish them before all his Scholars, to cease their clamour, and to consider how rash they are to interrupt his businesse, and to blame him for doing that duty to which he is entrusted by themselves, and others, their betters: But if they go about to raise scandalous reports upon him, he may do well to get two or three judicious neighbours to examine the matter, and to rebuke the parties for making so much adoe upon little or no occasion.

CHARLES HOOLE DESCRIBES A "PETTY-SCHOOL" (1660) From Charles Hoole, *A New Discovery of the Old Art of Teaching Schoole, in Four Small Treatises,* E. T. Campagnac, ed. (London, 1913), pp. 1-11, 20-23

How a Childe May Be Helped in the First
Pronounciation of His Letters

My aim being to discover the old Art of teaching Schoole, and how it may be improved in every part suteable to the years and capacities of such children as are now commonly taught; I shall first begin my discourse concerning a petty-Schoole, & here or else where I shall not busie my self or Reader about what a childe of an extraordinary towardliness, and having a teacher at home, may attain unto, and in how short a space, but onely shew how a multitude of various wits may be taught all together with abundance of profit and delight to every one, wch is the proper and main work of our ordinary Schooles.

Whereas then, it is usual in Cities and greater Towns to put children to Schoole about four or five years of age, and in Country villages, because of further distance, not till about six or seven; I conceive, The sooner a child is put to School, the better it is, both to prevent ill habits, which are got by play and idleness, and to enure him betimes to affect learning and well doing. Not to say, how the great uncertainty of parents lives, should make them careful of their Childrens early education, which is like to be the best part of their patrimony, what ever good thing else they may leave them in this World.

I observe that betwixt three and four years of age a childe hath great propensity to peep into a book, and then is the most seasonable time (if conveniences may be had otherwise) for him to begin to learn; and though perhaps then he cannot speak so very distinctly, yet the often pronounciation of his letters, will be a means to help his speech, especially if one take notice in what organ or instrument he is most defective, and exercise him chiefly in those letters which belong unto it.

Now there are five organs or instruments of speech, in the right hitting of which, as the breath moveth from within, through the mouth, a true pronunciation of every letter is made, viz. the lips, the teeth, the tongue, the roof of the mouth, and the throat; According to which if one rank the twenty four letters of our English Alphabet, he shall find that A, E, I, O, U, proceed by degrees from the throat, along betwixt the tongue and the roof of the mouth to the lips contracted, and that Y is somewhat like I, being pronounced with other letters, but if it be named by it self, it requireth some motion of the lips. B, F, M, P, W, and V consonant, belong to the lips. C, S, X, Z, to the teeth. D, L, N, T, R, to the tongue. B, H, K, Q, to the roof of the mouth. But the sweet and natural pronunciation of them is gotten rather by imitation then precept, and therefore the teacher must be careful to give every letter its distinct and clear sound, that the childe may get it from his voice, and be sure to make the child open his mouth well as he uttereth a letter, lest otherwise he drown or hinder the sound of it. For I have heard some foreiners to blame us English-men for neglecting this mean to a plain and audible speaking, saying, that the cause, why we generally do not speak so fully as they, proceeded from an ill habit of mumbling, which children got at their first learning to read; which it was their care; therfore to prevent or remedy betimes, and so it should be ours, seeing Pronounciation is that that sets out a man, and is sufficient of it self to make one an Oratour.

How a Childe May Be Taught with Delight to Know All His Letters in a Very Little Time

The usual way to begin with a child, when he is first brought to Schoole, is to teach him to know his letters in the Horn-book, where he is made to run over all the letters in the Alphabet or Christ-cross-row both forwards and backwards, until he can tel any one of them, which is pointed at, and that in the English character.

This course we see hath been very effectual in a short time, with some more ripe witted children, but othres of a slower apprehension (as the most and best commonly are) have been thus learning a whole year together, (and though they have been much chid and beaten too for want of heed) could scarce tell six of their letters at twelve moneths end, who, if they had been taught in a way more agreeable to their meane apprehensions (wch might have wrought more readily upon the senses, and affected their mindes with what they did) would doubtlesse have learned as cheerfully, if not as fast as the quickest.

I shall therefore mention sundry ways that have been taken to make a childe know his letters readily, out of which the discreet Teacher may chuse what is most likely to suit with his Learner.

I have known some that (according to Mr. Brinsley's direction) have taught little ones to pronounce all the letters, and to spell pretty well, before they knew one letter in a book; and this they did, by making the childe to sound the five vowels *a, e, i, o, u*, like so many bells upon his fingers ends, and to say which finger was such or such a vowel, by changes. 2 Then putting single consonants before the vowels, [leaving the hardest of them till the last] and teaching him how to utter them both at once, as *va, ve, vi, vo, vu, da, de, di, do, du*. 3. and again, by putting the vowels before a consonant to make him say, *as, es, is, os, us, ad, ed, id, od, ud*. Thus; they have proceeded from syllables of two or three, or more letters, till a child hath been pretty nimble in the most. But this is rather to be done in a private house, then a publick Schoole; how ever this manner of exercise now and then amongst little Scholars will make their lessons more familiar to them.

The greatest trouble at the first entrance of children is to teach them how to know their letters one from another, when they see them in the book altogether; for the greatnesse of their number and variety of shape do puzle young wits to difference them, and the sence can but be intent upon one single object at once, so as to take its impression, and commit it to the imagination and memory. Some have therefore begun but with one single letter, and after they have shewed it to the childe in the Alphabet, have made him to finde the same any where else in the book, till he knew that perfectly; and then they have proceeded to another in like manner, and so gone through the rest.

Some have contrived a piece of ivory with twenty four flats or squares, in every one of which was engraven a several letter, and by playing with a childe in throwing this upon a table, and shewing him the letter onely which lay uppermost, have in few dayes taught him the whole Alphabet.

Some have got twenty four pieces of ivory cut in the shape of dice, with a letter engraven upon each of them, and with these they have played at vacant hours with a childe, till he hath known them all distinctly. They begin first with one, then with two, afterwards with more letters at once, as the childe got knowledge of them. To teach him likewise to spell, they would place consonants before or after a vowel, and then joyn more letters together so as to make a word, and sometimes divide it into syllables, to be parted or put together; now this kind of letter sport may be profitably permitted among you beginers in a School & in stead of ivory, they may have white bits of wood, or small shreads of paper or past-board, or parchment with a letter writ upon each to play withall amongst themselves.

Some have made pictures in a little book or upon a scroll of paper wrapt upon two sticks within a box of iceing-glass, and by each picture have made three sorts of that letter, with which its name beginneth; but those being too many at once for a childe to take notice on, have proved not so useful as was intended. Some likewise have had pictures and letters printed in this manner on the back side of a pack of cards, to entice children, that naturally love that sport, to the love of learning their books.

Some have writ a letter in a great character upon a card, or chalked it out upon a trencher, and by telling a child what it was, and letting him strive to make the like, have imprinted it quickly in his memory, and so the rest one after another.

One having a Son of two years and a half old, that could but even go about the house, and utter some few gibberish words in a broken manner; observing him one day above the rest to be busied about shells, and sticks, and such like toys, which himself had laid together in a chair, and to misse any one that was taken from him, he saw not how, and to seek for it about the house; became very desireous to make experiment what that childe might presently attain to in point of learning; Thereupon he devised a little wheel, with all the Capital Romane letters made upon a paper to wrap round about it, and fitted it to turn in a little round box, which had a hole so made in the side of it, that onely one letter might be seen to peep out at once; This he brought to the childe, & showed him onely the letter *O*, and told him what it was; The childe being overjoyed with his new gamball, catcheth the box out of his Fathers hand, and run's with it to his playfellow a year younger then himself, and in his broken language tell's him there was an *O*, an *O*; And when the other asked him where, he said, in a hole, in a hole, and shewed it him; which the lesser childe then took such notice of, as to know it againe ever after from all the other letters. And thus by playing with the box, and enquiring concerning any letter that appeared strange to him, what it was, the childe learnt all the letters of the Alphabet in eleven dayes, being in this Character *A B C*, and would take pleasure to shew them in any book to any of his acquaintance that came next. By this instance you may see what a propensity there is in nature betimes to learning, could but the Teachers apply themselves to their young Scholars tenuity; and how by proceeding in a cleare & facil method, that all may apprehend, every one may benefit more or less by degrees. According to these contrivances to forward children, I have published *a New Primar*; in the first leafe, whereof I have set the Roman Capitalls (because that Character is now most in use, & those letters the most easie to be learn't) and have joyned therewith the pictures or images of some things whose names begins with that letter, by which a childs memory may be helped to remember how to call his letters; as *A*, for an Ape, *B*. for a Bear, &c. This Hieroglyphicall devise doth so affect Children (who are generally forward to communicate what they know) that I have observed them to teach others, that could not so readily learn, to know all the letters in a few houres space, by asking them, what stands A. for? and so concerning other letters backwards and forwards, or as they best liked.

Thus when a childe hath got the names of his letters, & their several shapes withall in a playing manner, he may be easily taught to distinguish them in the following leaf, which containeth first the greater, and then the smaller Roman Characters, to be learned by five at once or more, as the childe is able to remember them; other Characters I would have forborn, till one be well acquainted with these, because so much variety at the first doth but amaze young wits, and our English characters, (for the most part) are very obscure, & more hard to be imprinted in the memory. And thus much for the learning to know letters; we shall next (and according to Order in Teaching) proceed to an easie way of distinct spelling.

*　　*　　*

How a Child May Be Taught to Read
Any English Book Perfectly

The ordinary way to teach children to read is, after they have got some knowledge of their letters, & a smattering of some syllables and words in the horn-book, to turn them into the *A B C.* or Primar, and therein to make them name the letters, and spell the words, till by often use they can pronounce (at least) the shortest words at the first sight. This method take's with those of prompter wits, but many of more slow capacities, not finding any thing to affect them, and so make them heed what they learne, go on remissely from lesson to lesson, and are not much more able to read, when they have ended their book, then when they begun it. Besides, the *A B C.* being now (I may say) generally thrown aside, and the ordinary Primar not printed, and the very fundamentalls of christian Religion (which were wont to be contained in those books, and were commonly taught children at home by heart before they went to Schoole) with sundry people (almost in all places) slighted, the matter which is taught in most books now in use, is not so familiar to them, and therefore not so easie for Children to learn.

But to hold still to the sure foundation, I have caused the Lords Prayer (Sect. 20.) the Creed (Sect. 21.) and the ten Commandements (Sect. 23.) to be printed in the Roman character, that a childe having learned already to know his letters and how to spell, may also be initiated to read by them, which he will do the more cheerfully, if he be also instructed at home to say them by heart.

As he read's these, I would have a childe name what words he can at the first sight, and what he cannot, to spell them, and to take notice what pauses and numbers are in his lesson. And to go them often over, till he can tell any tittle in them, either in or without the book.

When he is thus well entered in the Roman character, I would have him made acquainted with the rest of the characters now in use (Sect. 23.) which will be easily done, by comparing one with another, and reading over those Sentences, Psalms, Thanksgivings, and Prayers (which are printed in greater and lesse characters of sundry sorts) till he have them pretty well by heart.

Thus having all things which concerne reading English made familiar to him, he may attaine to a perfect habit of it. 1. By reading the single Psalter. 2. The Psalms in meeter. 3. The Schoole of good manners, or such like easie books, which may both profit and delight him. All which I would wish he may read over at lest thrice, to make the matter, as well as the words, leave an impression upon his mind. If any where he stick at any word (as seeming too hard) let him marke it with a pin, or the dint of his nayle, and by looking upon it againe, he will remember it.

When he can read any whit readily, let him begin the Bible, and read over the book of Genesis, (and other remarkable Histories in other places of Scripture, which are most likely to delight him) by a chapter at a time; But acquaint him a little with the matter beforehand, for that will intice him to read it, and make him more observant of what he read's. After he hath read, ask him such generall Questions out of the Story, as are most easie for him to answer, and he will the better remember it. I have known some, that by hiring a child to read two or three chapters a day, and to get so many verses of it by heart, have made them admirable proficients, and that betimes, in the Scriptures; which was Timothies excellency, and his Grandmothers great commendation. Let him now take liberty to exercise himself in any English book (so the matter of it be but honest) till he can perfectly read in any place of a book that is offered him; and when he can do this, I adjudge him fit to enter into a Grammar Schoole, but not before.

For thus learning to read English perfectly, I allow two or three years time, so that at seven or eight years of age, a child may begin Latine.

OATH REQUIRED OF TEACHERS IN ENGLAND (1714) From *The Statutes at Large From the Twelfth Year of Queene Anne, to the Fifth Year of King George I*, vol. XII, pp. 187, 189.

I do sincerely promise and swear, That I will be faithful, and bear true allegiance to his majesty King George. So help me God.

* * *

I do swear, that I do from my heart abhor, detest and abjure, as impious and heretical, that damnable doctrine and position, That princes excommunicated or deprived by the Pope, or any authority by the see of Rome, may be deposed or murthered by their subjects, or any other whatsoever. And I do declare, that no foreign prince, person, prelate, state or potentate, hath or ought to have any jurisdiction, power, superiority, pre-eminence or authority, ecclesiastical or spiritual, within this realm. So help me God.

AESOP'S FABLES (c. 600 B.C.) From Aesop's *Fables*, V. S. Vernon Jones, trans. (London, 1912), pp. 66-67.

The Walnut Tree

A walnut tree, which grew by the roadside, bore every year a plentiful crop of nuts. Every one who passed by pelted its branches with sticks and stones, in order to bring down the fruit, and the tree suffered severely. "It is hard," it cried, "that the very persons who enjoy my fruit should thus reward me with insults and blows."

The Man and the Lion

A man and a lion were companions on a journey, and in the course of conversation they began to boast about their prowess, and each claimed to be superior to the other in strength and courage. They were still arguing with some heat when they came to a cross-road where there was a statue of a Man strangling a Lion. "There!" said the Man triumphantly, "look at that! Doesn't that prove to you that we are stronger than you?" "Not so fast, my friend," said the Lion: "this is only your view of the case. If we Lions could make statues, you may be sure that in most of them you would see the Man underneath."

There are two sides to every question.

The Tortoise and the Eagle

A tortoise, discontented with his lowly life, and envious of the birds he saw disporting themselves in the air, begged an Eagle to teach him to fly. The Eagle protested that it was idle for him to try, as nature had not provided him with wings; but the Tortoise pressed him with entreaties and promises of treasure, insisting that it could only be a question of learning the craft of the air. So at length the Eagle consented to do the best he could for him, and picked him up in his talons. Soaring with him to a great height in the sky he then let him go, and the wretched Tortoise fell headlong and was dashed to pieces on a rock.

The Kid on the Housetop

A kid climbed up on to the roof of an outhouse, attracted by the grass and other things that grew in the thatch; and as he stood there browsing away, he caught sight of a Wolf passing below, and jeered at him because he couldn't reach him. The Wolf only looked up and said, "I hear you, my young friend; but it is not you who mock me, but the roof on which you are standing."

THE GOOD WIFE TEACHES HER DAUGHTER (c. 1430)   From Edith Rickert, ed., *The Babees Book*, as quoted in the texts of F. J. Furnivall (London, 1923), pp. 31-32, 132-133.

How the Good Wife Taught Her Daughter

The good wife taught her daughter,
    Full many a time and oft,
    A full good woman to be;
For said she: "Daughter to me dear,
Something good now must thou hear,
    If thou wilt prosper thee.

Daughter, if thou wilt be a wife,
    Look wisely that thou work;
Look lovely and in good life,
    Love God and Holy Kirk.
Go to church whene'er thou may,
    Look thou spare for no rain,

For best thou farest on that day;
  To commune with God be fain.
  He must needs well thrive,
  That liveth well all his life,
    My lief[1] child.

Gladly give thy tithes and thy offerings both,
To the poor and the bed-rid—look thou be not loth.
Give of thine own goods and be not too hard,
For seldom is the house poor where God is steward.
    Well is he proved
    Who the poor hath loved,
      My lief child.

When thou sittest in the church, o'er thy beads bend;
Make thou no jangling with gossip or with friend.
Laugh thou to scorn neither old body nor young,
But be of fair bearing and of good tongue.
    Through thy fair bearing
    Thy worship hath increasing,
      My lief child.

And when thou art set, and table served thee before,
Pare not your nails, 'file[2] not your cloth—learn ye that lore.

An thy master speak to thee, take thy cap in hand,
If thou sit at meat, when he talketh [to thee] see thou stand.

Lean not to the one side when thou speakest, for nothing,
Hold still both hand and foot, and beware of trifling.

Stand sadly[3] in telling thy tale whenas thou talkest;
Trifle with nothing, and stand upright when thou speakest.

Thwart[4] not thou with thy fellow, nor speak with high voice;
Point not thy tale with thy fingers, use not such toys.[5]

Have audience when thou speakest, speak with authority,
Else if thou speak wisdom, little will it avail thee.

Pronounce thy speech with a pause, mark well thy word;
It is good hearing a child; beware with whom ye bourd.[6]

Talk not to thy sovereign, no time when he doth drink;
When he speaketh, give him audience—that is good, I think.

Before that you sit, see that your knife be bright,
Your hands clean, your nails pared is a good sight.

---

[1] Dear.
[2] Defile.
[3] Soberly.
[4] Don't cross thy fellow.
[5] Tricks.
[6] Jest.

When thou shalt speak, roll not too fast thine eye;
Gaze not to and fro, as one that were void of courtesy.

For a man's countenance often times declareth his thought;
His look with his speech will judge him, good or naught.

And see your knife be sharp to cut your meat withal;
So the more cleanlier cut your meat you shall.

Ere thou put much bread in thy pottage, look thou it assay;
Fill not thy spoon too full, lest thou lose somewhat by the way.

JOHN RUSSELL'S BOOK OF NURTURE (c. 1460) From Edith Rickert, ed., *The Babees Book,* from the texts of F. J. Furnivall (London, 1923), pp. 56-58.

"**I** will that ye eschew forever the 'simple conditions' of a person that is not taught.

"Do not claw your head or your back as if you were after a flea, or stroke your hair as if you sought a louse.

"Be not glum, nor twinkle with your eyes, nor be heavy of cheer; and keep your eyes free from winking and watering.

"Do not pick your nose or let it drop clear pearls, or sniff, or blow it too loud, lest your lord hear.

"Twist not your neck askew like a jackdaw; wring not your hands with picking or trifling or shrugging, as if ye would saw [wood]; nor puff up your chest, nor pick your ears, nor be slow of hearing.

"Retch not, nor spit too far, nor laugh or speak too loud. Beware of making faces and scorning; and be no liar with your mouth. Nor yet lick your lips or drivel.

"Do not have the habit of squirting or spouting with your mouth, or gape, or yawn, or pout. And do not lick a dish with your tongue to get out dust.

"Be not rash or reckless—that is not worth a clout.

"Do not sigh with your breast, or cough, or breathe hard in the presence of your sovereign, or hiccough, or belch, or groan never the more. Do not trample with your feet, or straddle your legs, or scratch your body—there is no sense in showing off. Good son, do not pick your teeth, or grind, or gnash them, or with puffing and blowing cast foul breath upon your lord. . . . These gallants in their short coats—that is ungoodly guise. Other faults on this matter, I spare not to disapprove in my opinion, when [a servant] is waiting on his master at table. Every sober sovereign must despise all such things.

"A man might find many more conditions than are named here; but let every honest servant avoid them for his own credit.

"Panter, yeoman of the cellar, butler and ewerer, I will that ye obey the marshal, sewer and carver."

"Good sir, I pray you teach me the skill of carving, and the fair handling of a knife, and all the ways that I shall break open, unlace and penetrate all manner of fowl, flesh and fish—how I shall demean me with each."

THE YOUNG CHILDREN'S BOOK (c. 1500) From Edith Rickert, ed., *The Babees Book,* from the texts of F. J. Furnivall (London, 1923), pp. 21-25.

Whoso will thrive must be courteous, and learn the virtues in his youth, or in his age he is outcast among men. Clerks who know the Seven Sciences say that Courtesy came from heaven when Gabriel greeted our Lady and Elizabeth met with her; and in it are included all virtues, as all vices in rudeness.

Arise betimes from your bed, cross your breast and your forehead, wash your hands and face, comb your hair, and ask the grace of God to speed you in all your works; then go to Mass and ask mercy for all your trespasses. Say "Good morning" courteously to whomsoever you meet by the way.

When ye have done, break your fast with good meat and drink, but before eating cross your mouth, your diet will be the better for it. Then say your grace—it occupies but little time—and thank the Lord Jesus for your food and drink. Say also a *Pater Noster* and an *Ave Maria* for the souls that lie in pain, and then go labour as you are bound to do. Be not idle, for Holy Scripture says to you of Christian faith that if you work, you must eat what you get with your hands. A man's arms are for working as a bird's wings for flying.

Look you be true in word and deed, the better shall you prosper; for truth never works a man shame, but rather keeps him out of sin. The ways to Heaven are twain, mercy and truth, say clerks; and he who will come to the life of bliss, must not fail to walk therein.

Make no promise save it be good, and then keep it with all your might, for every promise is a debt that must not be remitted through falsehood.

Love God and your neighbour, and thus may ye say without fear or dread that you keep all the law.

Uncalled go to no council, scorn not the poor, nor hurt any man, learn of him that can teach you, be no flatterer or scoff, oppress not your servants, be not proud, but meek and gentle, and always walk behind your betters.

When your better shows his will, be silent; and in speaking to any man keep your hands and feet quiet, and look up into his face, and be always courteous.

Point not with your finger at anything, nor be lief to tell tidings. If any man speak well of you or of your friends, he must be thanked. Have a few words and wisely placed, for so may you win a good name.

Use no swearing or falsehood in buying or selling, else shall you be shamed at the last. Get your money honestly, and keep out of debt and sin. Be eager to please, and so live in peace and quiet.

Advise you well of whom you speak, and when and where and to whom.

Whenever you come unto a door, say, "God be here," ere you go further, and speak courteously, wherever you are, to sire or dame or their household.

Stand, and sit not down to meat until you are told by him that rules the hall; and do not change your seat, but sit upright and mannerly where he bids, and eat and drink and be fellowly, and share with him that sits by you—thus teaches Dame Courtesy.

Take your salt with a clean knife.

Be cool of speech and quarrel not, nor backbite a man who is away, but be glad to speak well of all. Hear and see and say nothing, then shall ye not be put to proof.

Hold you pleased with the meat and drink set before you, nor ask for better.

Wipe your mouth before you drink lest it foul the edge of the cup; and keep your fingers, your lips and your chin clean, if you would win a good name. When your meat is in your mouth, do not drink or speak or laugh—Dame Courtesy forbids. Praise your fare, wheresoever you be, for whether it be good or bad it must be taken in good part.

Whether you spit near or far, hold your hand before your mouth to hide it.

Keep your knife clean and sharp, and cleanse it on some cut bread, not on the cloth, I bid you; a courteous man is careful of the cloth. Do not put your spoon in the dish or on the edge of it, as the untaught do, or make a noise when you sup as do boys. Do not put the meat off your trencher into the dish, but get a voider and empty it into that.

When your better hands you a cup, take it with both hands lest it fall, and drink yourself and set it by; and if he speaks to you, doff your cap and bow your knee.

Do not scratch yourself at the table so that men call you a daw, nor wipe your nose or nostrils, else men will say you are come of churls. Make neither the cat nor the dog your fellow at the table. And do not play with the spoon, or your trencher, or your knife; but lead your life in cleanliness and honest manners.

This book is made for young children that bide not long at the school. It may soon be conned and learned, and will make them good if they be bad. God give them grace to be virtuous, for so may they thrive.

HUGH RHODE'S BOOK OF NURTURE (c. 1550)   From Edith Rickert, ed., *The Babees Book*, from the texts of F. J. Furnivall (London, 1923), pp. 129-31.

Use early rising in the morning, for it hath
    properties three;
Holy, healthy, wealthy—in my youth thus my father
    taught me.

At six of the clock at farthest, accustom thee to rise;
Look thou forget not to bless thee once or twice.

In the morning use some devotion, and let for no need;
Then all the day afterward the better shalt thou speed.

Sponge and brush thy clothes clean that thou shalt on
    wear;
Cast up your bed, and take heed ye lose none of your
    gear.

Make clean thy shoes, comb thy head, mannerly thee
    brace;
See thou forget not to wash both thy hands and face.

Put on thy clothing for thy degree,[1] honestly do it
    make.

Bid your fellow good morrow, ere ye your way forth
  take.

To your friends and to father and mother look ye take
  heed;
For any haste do them reverence, the better shalt
  thou speed.
Dread the cursing of father and mother, for it is a
  heavy thing;
Do thy duty to them, the contrary will be to thy
  dispraising.
When thy father and mother come in sight, do them
  reverence,
And ask them blessing if they have been long out of
  presence.
Cleanly appoint you your array, beware then of disdain;
Then be gentle of speech and mannerly you retain.
And as ye pass the town or street, sadly² go forth your
  way,
[Nor] gaze nor scoff, nor scold, with man nor child
  make no fray.
Fair speech doth great pleasure; it seemeth of gentle
  blood;
Gentle is to use fair speech; it requireth nothing
  but good.

And when thou comest into the church thy prayers
  for to say,
Kneel, sit, stand or walk, devoutly look thou pray.
Cast not your eye to and fro, all things for to see;
Then shalt thou be judged plainly a wanton for to be.
When thou art in the church, [see thou] do churchly
  works;
Communication use thou not to women, priests nor
  clerks.
When your devotion is done and time is toward dinner;
Draw home to your master's presence, there do your
  [en]deavour.
An ye be desired to serve, or sit, or eat meat at the table,
Incline to good manners, and to nurture yourself enable.
If your sovereign call you with him to dine or sup,
Give him reverence to begin, both of meat and cup.
And beware for anything, press not thyself too
  high;
To sit in the place appointed thee—that is courtesy.

¹ According to thy station.
² Soberly.

LILY'S LATIN GRAMMAR (c. 1522)   From the Preface and Foreword of William Lily, *A Short Introduction of Grammar* (London, 1733).

The Preface

Although the very great importance of having the first Rudiments of Grammar well laid, in order to all future progress in Learning, is a thing manifest in it self, and acknowledged by all sober men; (those Empiricks who have pretended to a compendious art of teaching, without Rule or Method, having been abundantly confuted by their shameful misadventures) yet the particular Conduct of Grammatical Institution has in all times been variously discoursed, and no less diversly pursued. In the Reign of King HENRY the Eight, when Philology had in a manner the whole vogue of Reputation, a publick uniform way of Institution was upon great advice by Authority prescribed. But since then, the Art of Grammar having received large Advantages by the Labours of Learned Men in the foregoing and present Age; it has come to pass, that the Methods which were generally received, have upon that account, and perhaps the not so laudable inducements of Singularity and Innovation, with the profitable Harvest to be reaped from thence, fallen into Contempt; and private Schemes have been taken up, not only against the plain command of Authority, but the general interest of Learners, who, seldom growing up under the Care of one Master, were in this case upon every change constrained to begin afresh, to their great discouragement, and manifest loss of time. Now on the other part, it would be very unfortunate, if because one general Method is by Law imposed, and for the common benefit to be admitted, we should therefore be obliged for ever, to forfeit the advantage to be reaped from the improvements of succeeding times.

To obviate this, seems to be no ill expedient, that the known forms of institution being retained, the additional observations of late Writers by way of Comment be taken in; and such entire heads of discourse as were before omitted, be placed distinctly and apart, so as without any search or trouble to fall under the notice of the common Reader. Whereby those who have been bred up to the received Grammar, (which most have been) may readily know where to help themselves, upon any emergent difficulty; and also escape the charge of buying, and the labour of turning over those large and expensive Books, wherein the knowledge of the Grammar, as an Art, is exactly taught.

So that here nothing is pretended to be beyond the toil of diligence of analyzing the several Grammarians that have written; and referring their Rules and Observations to our own received Method; which work, being not invidious by the ambition of an assuming undertaking, will we hope be entertained with favour and acceptance: for men do not usually grudge to any rival the honour of taking pains. Withal this kind of work being very liable to mistake, confusion, and other misadventures, it is desired that those errours may not be severely charged, which are acknowledged before hand. Yet farther, to avert a rigid censure, it is declared, that what is now done appears only as an Essay, that if the thing proposed be found reasonable, it may upon a review receive farther degrees of perfection, and be made to serve the uses of the publick; to which both this, and all the other labours of our Press entirely dedicate themselves.

Having thus accounted for the present undertaking, with the learned Reader; it may be seasonable to recommend it also to the learner: by saying that Grammar is the Sacrist, that bears the Key of Knowledge, by whom alone admittance can be had into the Temple of the Muses and treasures of Arts; even whatever can enrich the Mind, and raise it from the level of a Barbarian and Idiot to the dignity of an Intelligence. But this Sacrist is a severe Mistress, who being once contemned, will certainly revenge the Injury: it being evident that no Person ever yet despised Grammar, who had not this fault returned upon him; and was not in very remarkable instances exposed thereby, and rendered despicable, It is true, Grammar only deals in Words; which are of much less intrinsic value than things; but since we can only form and express our notions of things, by the intervention of Speech, we cannot take benefit from one without the assistance of the other. Indeed words are as mony, which, though it neither feeds, nor clothes, nor cures, or does any thing else that conduces to human life, yet virtually performs all this; but does it under this remarkable difference, that Princes have power over the rate of Coin, but the Grammarian only over Words. It would be observed farther, that Grammar, as she is a severe Mistress, is also a coy one; and hardly admits any courtship, but of the youthful votary. There are indeed many who by great industry, have redeemed the want of early Institution; but in the performances of such, there still appears somewhat of stiffness and force; and what has more in it of Art than Nature: when on the other side he that begins an early Court, has greater assurances of favour; with little difficulty becomes a Denison of Rome and Athens, in whatsoever Climate he happens to be born; and makes their Languages his mother tongue: thereby obtaining a free address to all the wisdom of precedent ages, and the friendship of the Heroes of them; to treat familiarly with Xenophon and Caesar, Demosthenes and Cicero, Thucydides and Livy, or whomsoever else he chuses for an acquaintance. He first will read; then equal their Atchievements; and having filled his head with their arts and knowledge, will crown it also with their Lawrels.

Whom these temptations cannot move to study, let him throw away his book, and like an illiterate criminal perish for not reading in it: let him live a fool, and dye a brute.

To the Reader

To exhort every man to the learning of Grammar that intendeth to attain to the understanding of the tongues (wherein is contained a great treasure of wisdom and knowledge) it would seem much vain and little needful; for so much as it is to be known, that nothing can surely be ended, whose beginning is either feeble or faulty; and no building be perfect, when as the foundation and ground-work is ready to fall, and unable to uphold the burden of the frame. Wherefore it were better for the thing it self, and more profitable for the learner, to understand how he may best come to that which he ought most necessarily to have, and to learn the plainest way of obtaining that which must be his best and certainest guide both of reading and speaking, than to fall in doubt of the goodness and necessity thereof: which I doubt, whether he shall more lament that he lacketh, or esteem that he hath it: and whether he shall oftner stumble at trifles, and be deceived in light matters, when he hath it not, or judge truly and faithfully of divers weighty things, when he hath it.

The which hath seemed to many very hard to compass aforetime, because that they who profess this art of teaching Grammar, did teach divers Grammars, and not one: and if by chance they taught one Grammar, yet they did it diversly, and so could not do it all best; because there is but one bestness, not only in every thing, but also in the manner of every thing.

As for the diversity of Grammars, it is well and profitably taken away by the King's Majesty's wisdom, who foreseeing the inconvenience, and favourably providing the remedy, caused one kind of Grammar by sundry learned men to be diligently drawn, and so to be set out only; every where to be taught for the use of learners, and for avoiding the hurt in changing of School-masters.

The variety of teaching is diverse yet, and always will be; for that every School-master liketh that he knoweth, and seeth not the use of that he knoweth not, and therefore judgeth that the most sufficient way, which he seeth to be the readiest mean, and perfectest kind, to bring a learner to have a through knowledge therein.

Wherefore it is not amiss, if one seeing by tryal an easier and readier way than the common sort of teachers do, would say what he hath proved, and for the commodity allowed; that others not knowing the same, might by experience prove the like, and then by proof reasonably judge the like: not hereby excluding the better way when it is found; but in the mean season forbidding the worse.

The first and chiefest point is, that the diligent Master make not the Scholar hast too much; but that he in continuance and diligence of teaching, make him to rehearse so, that until he hath perfectly that which is behind, he suffer him not to go forward: for this posting hast overthroweth and hurteth a great sort of wits, and casteth them into amazedness, when they know not how they shall either go forward or backward; but stick fast as one plunged, that cannot tell what to do, or which way to turn him: and then the Master thinketh the Scholar to be a dullard, and the Scholar thinketh the thing to be uneasy, and too hard for his wit: and the one hath an evil opinion of the other, when oftentimes it is neither, but in the kind of teaching. Wherefore the best and chiefest point throughly to be kept is, that the Scholar have in mind so perfectly that which he hath learned, and understand it so, that not only it be not a stop for him, but also a light and help to the residue that followeth. This shall be the Master's ease, and the Child's incouraging, when the one shall see his labour take good effect, and thereby in teaching be less tormented; and the other shall think the thing easier, and so with more gladness be ready to go about the same.

In going forward, let him have of every declension of Nouns, and conjugations of Verbs, so many several examples as they pass them; that it may seem to the School-master, no word in the Latin tongue to be so hard for that part, as the Scholar shall not be able praisably to enter into the forming thereof. And surely the multitude of examples (if the easiest and commonest be taken first, and so come to the stranger and harder) must needs bring this profit withal, that the Scholar shall best understand, and soonest conceive the reason of the rules, and best be acquainted with the fashion of the tongue. Wherein it is profitable, not only that he can orderly decline his Noun, and his Verb; but every way, forward, backward, by cases, by persons: that neither case of Noun, nor person of Verb can be required, that he cannot without stop or study tell. And until this time I count not the Scholar perfect, nor ready to go any farther till he hath this already learned.

This when he can perfectly do, and hath learned every part, not by rote, but by reason; and is more cunning in the understanding of the thing, than in rehearsing of the words (which is not past a quarter of a years diligence, or very little more, to a painful and diligent man, if the Scholar hath mean wit) then let him pass to the Concords, to know the agreement of parts among themselves, with like way and diligence as is afore described.

Wherein plain and sundry examples, and continual rehearsal of things learned, and specially the daily declining of a Verb, and turning of it into all fashions, shall make the great and heavy labour so easy and so pleasant for the framing of sentences, that it will be rather a delight unto them, that they be able to do well; than pain in searching of an unusual and unacquainted thing.

When these Concords be well known unto them, (an easy and pleasant pain, if the fore grounds be well and throughly beaten in) let them not continue in learning of their rules orderly, as they lie in their *Syntax*, but rather learn some pretty book, wherein is contain'd not only the eloquence of the tongue, but also a good plain lesson of honesty and godliness, and thereof take some little sentence as it lieth, and learn to make the same first out of English into Latin, not seeing the book, or construing it thereupon. And if there fall any necessary rule of the *Syntax* to be known, then to learn it, as the occasion of the sentence giveth cause that day: which sentence once made well, and as nigh as may be with the words of the book, then to take the book and construe it, and so shall he be less troubled with the parsing of it, and easiliest carry his lesson in mind.

And although it was said before, that the Scholars should learn but a little at once, it is not meant that when the Master hath heard them a while he should let them alone (for that were negligence for both parts) but I would, all their time they be at School, they should never be idle, but always occupied in a continual rehearsing and looking back again to those things they have learned, and be more bound to keep well their old, than to take forth any new.

Thus if the Master occupy them, he shall see a little lesson take a great deal of time, and diligently enquiring and examining of the parts and the rules, not to be done so quickly and speedily as it might be thought to be. Within a while by this use, the Scholar shall be brought to a good kind of readiness of making Latin, to the which if there be adjoyned some use of speaking (which must necessarily be had) he shall be brought past the wearisome bitterness of his learning.

A great help to further this readiness of making and speaking shall be, if the Master give him an English book, and cause him ordinarily to turn every day some part into Latin. This exercise cannot be done without his rules, and therefore doth establish them, and ground them surely in his mind for readiness, and maketh him more able to speak suddenly, whensoever any present occasion is offered for the same. And it doth help his learning more a great deal, to turn out of English into Latin, than on the contrary.

Furthermore, we see many can understand Latin, that cannot speak it; and when they read the Latin word in the book, can tell you the English thereof at any time: but when they have laid away their book, they cannot contrariwise tell you for the English the Latin again whensoever you will ask them. And therefore this exercise helpeth this sore well, and maketh those words which they understand, to be readier by use unto them, and so perfecteth them in the tongue handsomely.

These precepts, well kept, will bring a man clean past his Grammar-book, and make him as ready as his book, and so meet to farther things, whereof it were out of season to give precepts here. And therefore this may be for this purpose enough, which to good School-masters and skilful is not so needful, to other meaner and less practised it may be not only worth the labour of reading, but also of the using.

COMENIUS' ILLUSTRATED TEXTBOOK (c. 1633) From *The Orbis Pictus of John Amos Comenius*, Charles Hoole, trans. (Syracuse, 1887), pp. 1-3, 52-53.

The Master and the Boy.

Master. Come, Boy, learn to be wise.

Pupil. What doth this mean, *to be wise?*

Master. To understand rightly to do rightly, and to speak out rightly all that are necessary.

Pupil. Who will teach me this?

Master. I, by God's help.

Pupil. How?

Master. I will guide thee thorow all.

I will shew thee all.

I will name thee all.

Pupil. See, here I am; lead me in the name of God.

Magister & Puer.

Master. Veni, Puer, disce sapere.

Pupil. Quid hoc est, *Sapere?*

Master. Intelligere recte, agere recte, et eloqui recte omnia necessaria.

Pupil. Quis docebit me hoc?

Master. Ego, cum DEO.

Pupil. Quomodo?

Master. Ducam te per omnia.

Ostendam tibi omnia.

Nominabo tibi omnia.

Pupil. En, adsum; duc me in nomine DEI.

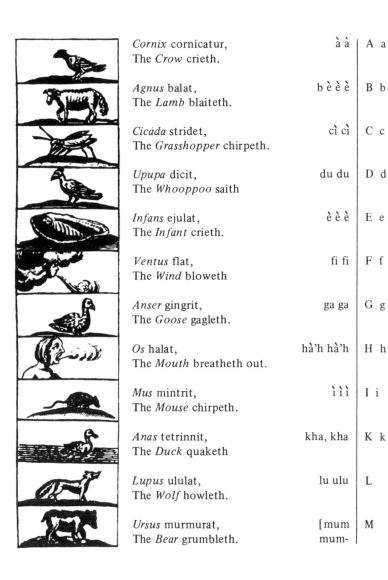

Cornix cornicatur, The *Crow* crieth.	à à	A a
Agnus balat, The *Lamb* blaiteth.	b è è è	B b
Cicăda stridet, The *Grasshopper* chirpeth.	cì cì	C c
Upupa dicit, The *Whooppoo* saith	du du	D d
Infans ejulat, The *Infant* crieth.	è è è	E e
Ventus flat, The *Wind* bloweth	fi fi	F f
Anser gingrit, The *Goose* gagleth.	ga ga	G g
Os halat, The *Mouth* breatheth out.	hà'h hà'h	H h
Mus mintrit, The *Mouse* chirpeth.	ì ì ì	I i
Anas tetrinnit, The *Duck* quaketh	kha, kha	K k
Lupus ululat, The *Wolf* howleth.	lu ulu	L
Ursus murmurat, The *Bear* grumbleth.	[mum mum-	M

There are five outward Senses;

The *Eye*, 1. seeth Colours, what is white or black, green or blew, red or yellow.

The *Ear*, 2. heareth *Sounds,* both natural, Voices and Words; and artificial,
Musical Tunes.

The *Nose*, 3. scenteth smells and stinks.

The *Tongue*, 4. with the roof of the Mouth tastes *Savours,* what is sweet or bitter, keen or biting, sower or harsh.

The *Hand*, 5. by touching discerneth the quantity and quality of things;
the hot and cold,
the moist and dry,
the hard and soft,
the smooth and rough,
the heavy and light.

The inward *Senses* are three.

The *Common Sense,* 7. under the *forepart of the head,* apprehendeth things taken from the outward Senses.

The *Phantasie*, 6. under the *crown of the head* judgeth of those things, thinketh and dreameth,

The *Memory*, 8. under the *hinder part of the head*, layeth up every thing and fetcheth them out: it loseth some, and this is *forgetfulness.*

Sleep, is the rest of the Senses.

Sunt quinque externi *Sensus;*

Oculus, 1. videt *Colores,* quid album vel atrum, viride vel coeruleum, rubrum aut luteum, sit.

Auris, 2. audit *Sonos,* tum naturales, Voces & Verba; tum artificiales,
Tonos Musicos.

Nasus, 3, olfacit odores & foetores.

Lingua, 4. cum Palato gustat *Sapores,* quid dulce aut amarum, acre aut acidum, acerbum aut austerum.

Manus, 5. tangendo dignoscit quantitatem, & qualitatem rerum;
calidum & frigidum,
humidum & siccum,
durum & molle,
laeve & asperum,
grave & leve.

Sensus interni sunt tres.

Sensus Communis, 7. sub *sincipite* apprehendit res perceptas a Sensi bus externis.

Phantasia, 6. sub *vertice,* dijudicat res istas, cogitat, somniat.

Memoria, 8. sub *occipitio,* recondit singula & depromit: deperdit quaedam, & hoc est *oblivio.*

Somnus, est requies Sensuum.

BUNYAN'S PILGRIM'S PROGRESS (1678)   From John Bunyan, *The Pilgrim's Progress* (London, 1895), pp. 1-7.

As I walk'd through the wilderness of this world, I lighted on a certain place, where was a Denn; And I laid me down in that place to sleep: And as I slept I dreamed a Dream. I dreamed, and behold I saw a Man cloathed with Raggs, standing in a certain place, with his face from his own House, a Book in his hand, and a great burden upon his back. I looked, and saw him open the Book, and Read therein; and as he Read, he wept and trembled: and not being able longer to contain, he brake out with a lamentable cry: saying, what shall I do?

I saw also that he looked this way, and that way, as if he would run; yet he stood still, because as I perceived, he could not tell which way to go. I looked then, and saw a Man named Evangelist coming to him, and asked, Wherefore dost thou cry? He answered, Sir, I perceive, by the Book in my hand, that I am Condemned to die, and after that to come to Judgement; and I find that I am not willing to do the first, nor able to do the second.

Then said Evangelist, Why not willing to die? since this life is attended with so many evils? The Man answered, Because I fear that this burden that is upon my back, will sinck me lower then the Grave; and I shall fall into Tophet. And Sir, if I be not fit to go to Prison, I am not fit (I am sure) to go to Judgement, and from thence to Execution; And the thoughts of these things make me cry.

Then said Evangelist, If this be thy condition, why standest thou still? He answered, Because I know not whither to go. Then he gave him a Parchment-Roll, and there was written within, Fly from the wrath to come.

The Man therefore Read it, and looking upon Evangelist very carefully; said, Whither must I fly? Then said Evangelist, pointing with his finger over a very wide Field, Do you see yonder Wicket-gate? The Man said, No. Then said the other, Do you see yonder shining light? He said, I think I do. Then said Evangelist, Keep that light in your eye, and go up directly thereto, so shalt thou see the Gate; at which when thou knockest, it shall be told thee what thou shalt do.

So I saw in my Dream, that the Man began to run; Now he had not run far from his own door, but his Wife and Children perceiving it, began to cry after him to return: but the Man put his fingers in his Ears, and ran on crying, Life, Life, Eternal Life: so he looked not behind him, but fled towards the middle of the Plain.

The Neighbours also came out to see him run, and as he ran, some mocked, others threatned; and some cried after him to return: Now among those that did so, there were two that were resolved to fetch him back by force: The name of the one was Obstinate, and the name of the other Pliable. Now by this time the Man was got a good distance from them; But however they were resolved to pursue him; which they did, and in little time they over-took him. Then said the Man, Neighbours, Wherefore are you come? They said, To perswade you to go back with us; but he said, That can by no means be: You dwell, said he, in the City of Destruction (the place also where I was born,) I see it to be so; and dying there, sooner or later, you will sink lower then the Grave, into a place that burns with Fire and Brimstone; Be content good Neighbours, and go along with me.

What! said Obstinate, and leave our Friends, and our comforts behind us!

Yes, said Christian, (for that was his name) because that all is not worthy to be compared with a little of that that I am seeking to enjoy, and if you will go along with me, you shall fare as I my self; for there where I go, is enough, and to spare; Come away, and prove my words.

Obst. What are the things you seek, since you leave all the World to find them?

Chr. I seek an Inheritance, incorruptible, undefiled, and that fadeth not away; and it is laid up in Heaven, and fast there, to be bestowed at the time appointed, on them that diligently seek it.

Ob. Tush, said Obstinate, away with your Book; will you go back with us, or no?

Ch. No, not I, said the other; because I have laid my hand to the Plow.

Ob. Come then, Neighbour Pliable, let us turn again, and go home without him; There is a Company of these Craz'd-headed Coxcombs, that when they take a fancy by the end, are wiser in their own eyes then seven men that can render a Reason.

Pli. Then said Pliable, Don't revile; if what the good Christian says is true, the things he looks after, are better then ours: my heart inclines to go with my Neighbour.

Obst. What! more Fools still? be ruled by me and go back; who knows whither such a brain-sick fellow will lead you? Go back, go back, and be wise.

Ch. Come with me Neighbour Pliable; there are such things to be had which I spoke of, and many more Glories besides. If you believe not me, read here in this Book; and for the truth of what is exprest therein, behold all is confirmed by the blood of him that made it.

Pli. Well Neighbour Obstinate (said Pliable) I begin to come to a point; I intend to go along with this good man, and to cast in my lot with him: But my good Companion, do you know the way to this desired place?

Ch. I am directed by a man whose name is Evangelist, to speed me to a little Gate that is before us, where we shall receive instruction about the way.

Pli. Come then good Neighbour, let us be going.

Then they went both together.

Obst. And I will go back to my place, said Obstinate. I will be no Companion of such miss-led fantastical Fellows.

Now I saw in my Dream, that when Obstinate was gon back, Christian and Pliable went talking over the Plain; and thus they began their discourse,

Christ. Come Neighbour Pliable, how do you do? I am glad you are perswaded to go along with me; and had even Obstinate himself, but felt what I have felt of the Powers and Terrours of what is yet unseen, he would not thus lightly have given us the back.

Pliable. Come Neighbour Christian, since there is none but us two here, tell me now further, what the things are, and how to be enjoyed, whither we are going?

Ch. I can better conceive of them with my Mind, then speak of them with my Tongue: But yet since you are desirous to know, I will read of them in my Book.

Pli. And do you think that the words of your Book are certainly true?

Ch. Yes verily, for it was made by him that cannot lye.

THE ADVENTURES OF ROBINSON CRUSOE (1719)   From Daniel Defoe, *The Life And Strange Surprising Adventures of Robinson Crusoe*, George A. Aitken, ed. (London, 1895), pp. 108-09, 118-19, 132-33, 170.

I had been now in this unhappy island above ten months; all possibility of deliverance from this condition seemed to be entirely taken from me; and I firmly believed that no human shape had ever set foot upon that place. Having now secured my habitation, as I thought, fully to my mind, I has a great desire to make a more prefect discovery of the island, and to see what other productions I might find, which I yet knew nothing of.

It was the 15th of July that I began to take a more particular survey of the island itself. I went up the creek first, where, as I hinted, I brought my rafts on shore. I found, after I came about two miles up, that the tide did not flow any higher, and that it was no more than a little brook of running water, and very fresh and good; but this being the dry season, there was hardly any water in some parts of it, at least, not enough to run in any stream, so as it could be perceived.

On the bank of this brook I found many pleasant savannas or meadows, plain, smooth, and covered with grass; and on the rising parts of them, next to the higher grounds, where the water, as might be supposed, never overflowed, I found a great deal of tobacco, green, and growing to a great and very strong stalk. There were divers other plants, which I had no notion of, or understanding about, and might perhaps have virtues of their own, which I could not find out.

I searched for the cassava root, which the Indians, in all that climate, make their bread of, but I could find none. I saw large plants of aloes, but did not then understand them. I saw several sugar-canes, but wild, and, for want of cultivation, imperfect. I contented myself with these discoveries for this time, and came back, musing with myself what course I might take to know the virtue and goodness of any of the fruits or plants which I should discover; but could bring it to no conclusion; for, in short, I had made so little observation while I was in the Brazils, that I knew little of the plants in the field, at least very little that might serve me to any purpose now in my distress.

The next day, the 16th, I went up the same way again; and after going something farther than I had gone the day before, I found the brook and the savannas began to cease, and the country become more woody than before. In this part I found different fruits, and particularly I found melons upon the ground in great abundance, and grapes upon the trees. The vines had spread indeed over the trees, and the clusters of grapes were just now in their prime, very ripe and rich. This was a surprising discovery, and I was exceeding glad of them; but I was warned by my experience to eat sparingly of them, remembering that when I was ashore in Barbary the eating of grapes killed several of our Englishmen, who were slaves there, by throwing them into fluxes and fevers. But I found an excellent use for these grapes; and that was, to cure or dry them in the sun, and keep them as dried grapes or raisins are kept, which I thought would be, as indeed they were, as wholesome as agreeable to eat, when no grapes might be to be had.

*   *   *

In this time I found much employment, and very suitable also to the time, for I found great occasion of many things which I had no way to furnish myself with but by hard labour and constant application; particularly, I tried many ways to make myself a basket; but all the twigs I could get for the purpose proved so brittle, that they would do nothing. It proved of excellent advantage to me now, that when I was a boy I used to take great delight in standing at a basket-maker's in the town where my father lived, to see them make their wicker-ware; and being, as boys usually are, very officious to help, and a great observer of the manner how they worked those things, and sometimes lending a hand, I had by this means full knowledge of the methods of it, that I wanted nothing but the materials; when it came into my mind that the twigs of that tree from whence I cut my stakes that grew might possibly be as tough as the sallows, and willows, and osiers in England, and I resolved to try.

Accordingly, the next day, I went to my country house, as I called it; and cutting some of the smaller twigs, I found them to my purpose as much as I could desire; whereupon I came the next time prepared with a hatchet to cut down a quantity, which I soon found, for there was great plenty of them. These I set up to dry within my circle or hedge, and when they were fit for use, I carried them to my cave; and here during the next season I employed myself in making, as well as I could, a great many baskets, both to carry earth, or to carry or lay up anything as I had occasion. And though I did not finish them very handsomely, yet I made them sufficiently serviceable for my purpose. And thus, afterwards, I took care never to be without them; and as my wicker-ware decayed, I made more, especially I made strong deep baskets to place my corn in, instead of sacks, when I should come to have any quantity of it.

Having mastered this difficulty, and employed a world of time about it, I bestirred myself to see, if possible, how to supply two wants. I had no vessels to hold anything that was liquid, except two runlets, which were almost full of rum, and some glass bottles, some of the common size, and others which were case-bottles square, for the holding of waters, spirits, &c. I had not so much as a pot to boil anything, except a great kettle, which I saved out of the ship, and which was too big for such use as I desired it, viz., to make broth, and stew a bit of meat by itself. The second thing I would fain have had was a tobacco-pipe; but it was impossible to me to make one. However, I found a contrivance for that, too, at last.

I employed myself in planting my second rows of stakes or piles and in this wicker-working all the summer or dry season, when another business took me up more time than it could be imagined I could spare.

I mentioned before that I had a great mind to see the whole island, and that I had travelled up the brook, and so on to where I built my bower, and where I had an opening quite to the sea, on the other side of the island. I now resolved to travel quite across to the seashore on that side; so taking my gun, a hatchet, and my dog, and a larger quantity of powder and shot than usual, with two biscuit-cakes and a great bunch of raisins in my pouch for my store, I began my journey.

✳   ✳   ✳

Within doors, that is, when it rained, and I could not go out, I found employment on the following occasions; always observing, that all the while I was at work, I diverted myself with talking to my parrot, and teaching him to speak, and I quickly learned him to know his own name, and at last to speak it out pretty loud,

"Poll," which was the first word I ever heard spoken in the island by any mouth but my own. This, therefore, was not my work, but an assistant to my work; for now, as I said, I had a great employment upon my hands, as follows, viz., I had long studied, by some means or other, to make myself some earthen vessels, which indeed I wanted sorely, but knew not where to come at them. However, considering the heat of the climate, I did not doubt but if I could find out any such clay, I might botch up some such pot as might, being dried in the sun, be hard enough and strong enough to bear handling, and to hold anything that was dry, and required to be kept so; and as this was necessary in the preparing corn, meal, &c., which was the thing I was upon, I resolved to make some as large as I could, and fit only to stand like jars, to hold what should be put into them.

It would make the reader pity me, or rather laugh at me, to tell how many awkward ways I took to raise this paste; what odd, misshapen, ugly things I made; how many of them fell in, and how many fell out, the clay not being stiff enough to bear its own weight; how many cracked by the over-violent heat of the sun, being set out too hastily; and how many fell in pieces with only removing, as well before as after they were dried; and, in a word, how, after having laboured hard to find the clay, to dig it, to temper it, to bring it home, and work it, I could not make above two large earthen ugly things (I cannot call them jars) in about two months' labour.

However, as the sun baked these two very dry and hard, I lifted them very gently up, and set them down again in two great wicker baskets, which I had made on purpose for them, that they might not break; and as between the pot and the basket there was a little room to spare, I stuffed it full of the rice and barley straw, and these two pots being to stand always dry, I thought would hold my dry corn, and perhaps the meal, when the corn was bruised.

Though I miscarried so much in my design for large pots, yet I made several smaller things with better success; such as little round pots, flat dishes, pitchers, and pipkins, and any things my hand turned to; and the heat of the sun baked them strangely hard. But all this would not answer my end, which was to get an earthen pot to hold what was liquid, and bear the fire, which none of these could do. It happened after some time, making a pretty large fire for cooking my meat, when I went to put it out after I had done with it, I found a broken piece of one of my earthenware vessels in the fire, burnt as hard as a stone, and red as a tile. I was agreeably surprised to see it, and said to myself, that certainly they might be made to burn whole, if they would burn broken.

This set me to studying how to order my fire, so as to make it burn me some pots. I had no notion of a kiln, such as the potters burn in, or of glazing them with lead, though I had some lead to do it with; but I placed three large pipkins, and two or three pots in a pile, one upon another, and placed my firewood all round it, with a great heap of embers under them. I plied the fire with fresh fuel round the outside,

*　　*　　*

In this place also I had my grapes growing, which I principally depended on for my winter store of raisins, and which I never failed to preserve very carefully, as the best and most agreeable dainty of my whole diet. And indeed they were not agreeable only, but physical, wholesome, nourishing, and refreshing to the last degree.

As this was also about half-way between my other habitation and the place where I had laid up my boat, I generally stayed and lay here in my way thither; for I used frequently to visit my boat, and I kept all things about, or belonging to her, in very good order. Sometimes I went out in her to divert myself, but no more hazardous voyages would I go, nor scarce ever above a stone's cast or two from the shore, I was so apprehensive of being hurried out of my knowledge again by the currents or winds, or any other accident. But now I come to a new scene of my life.

It happened one day, about noon, going towards my boat, I was exceedingly surprised with the print of a man's naked foot on the shore, which was very plain to be seen in the sand. I stood like one thunder-struck, or as if I had seen an apparition. I listened, I looked round me, I could hear nothing, nor see anything. I went up to a rising ground, to look farther. I went up the shore, and down the shore, but it was all one; I could see no other impression but that one. I went to it again to see if there were any more, and to observe if it might not be my fancy; but there was no room for that, for there was exactly the very print of a foot—toes, heel, and every part of a foot. How it came thither I knew not, nor could in the least imagine. But after innumerable fluttering thoughts, like a man perfectly confused and out of myself, I came home to my fortification, not feeling, as we say, the ground I went on, but terrified. . . .

Apprenticeship and Relief
of the Poor—England

AN APPRENTICESHIP LAW (1563)   From *An Act Containing Divers Orders for Artificers, Labourers, Servants of Husbandry and Apprentices*, 5 Eliz. I c.4 (1563).

Although there remain and stand in Force presently a great Number of Acts and Statutes concerning the Retaining, Departing, Wages and Orders of Apprentices, Servants and Labourers, as well in Husbandry as in divers other Arts, Mysteries and Occupations; yet . . . for that the Wages and Allowances limited and rated in many of the said Statutes, are in divers Places too small and not answerable to this Time, respecting the Advancement of Prices of all Things belonging to the said Servants and Labourers; the said Laws cannot conveniently, without the great Grief and Burden of the poor Labourer and hired Man, be put in good and due Execution: . . . So if the Substance of as many of the said Laws as are meet to be continued, shall be digested and reduced into one sole Law and Statute, and in the same an uniform Order prescribed and limited concerning the Wages and other Orders for Apprentices, Servants and Labourers, there is good Hope that it will come to pass, that the same Law (being duly executed) should banish Idleness, advance Husbandry, and yield unto the hired Person, both in the Time of Scarcity and in the Time of Plenty, a convenient Proportion of Wages.

Be it therefore enacted by the Authority of this present Parliament, . . .

*   *   *

III. . . .That no Manner of Person or Persons, . . . shall retain, hire or take into Service, . . . [any person] to work for any less Time or Term than for one whole Year, in any of the Sciences, Crafts, Mysteries or Arts of Clothiers, Woolen Cloth Weavers, Tuckers, Fullers, Clothworkers, Sheremen, Dyers, Hosiers, Taylors, Shoemakers, Tanners, Pewterers, Bakers, Brewers, Glovers, Cutlers, Smiths, Farriers, Curriers, Sadlers, Spurriers, Turners, Cappers, Hatmakers or Feltmakers, Bowyers, Fletchers, Arrow-head-makers, Butchers, Cooks or Millers.

IV. And be it further enacted, That every Person being unmarried; (2) and every other Person being under the Age of thirty Years, that after the Feast of Easter next shall marry, (3) and having been brought up in any of the said Arts, Crafts or Sciences; (4) or that hath used or exercised any of them by the Space of three Years or more; (5) and not having Lands, Tenement Rents or Hereditament, Copyhold or Freehold, . . . of the clear yearly Value of forty Shillings; (6) nor being worth of his own Goods the clear Value of ten Pound; . . . (9) nor being retained with any Person in Husbandry, or in any of the aforesaid Arts and Sciences, according to this Statute; (10) nor lawfully retained in any other Art or Science; (11) nor being lawfully retained in Houshold, or in any Office, with any Nobleman, Gentleman or others, according to the Laws of this Realm; (12) nor have a convenient Farm, or other Holding in Tillage, whereupon he may employ his Labour; (13) Shall, during the Time that he or they shall be so unmarried, or under the said Age of thirty Years, upon Request made by any Person using the Art of Mystery wherein the said Person so required hath been exercised (as is aforesaid) be retained; (14) and shall not refuse to serve according to the Tenor of this Statute, upon the Pain and Penalty hereafter mentioned.

V. And be it further enacted, That no Person which shall retain any Servant, shall put away his or her said Servant, (2) and that no Person retained according to this Statute, shall depart from his Master, Mistress or Dame, before the end of his or her term;

✻   ✻   ✻

XV. And for the Declaration and Limitation what Wages Servants, Labourers and Artificers, either by the Year or Day or otherwise, shall have and receive, Be it enacted by the Authority of this present Parliament, That the Justices of Peace of every Shire, . . . and the Sheriff of that County if he conveniently may, and every Mayor, Bailiff or other Head Officer with any City or Town Corporate wherein is any Justice of Peace, . . . calling unto them such discreet and grave Persons of the said County or of the said City or Town Corporate as they shall think meet, and conferring together, respecting the Plenty or Scarcity of the Time and other Circumstances necessarily to be considered, shall have Authority by Virtue thereof, within the Limits and Precincts of their several Commissions, to limit, rate and appoint the Wages, . . .

✻   ✻   ✻

XVIII. And be it further enacted by the Authority aforesaid, That if any Person . . . shall by any secret Ways or Means, directly or indirectly retain or keep any Servant, Workman or Labourer, or shall give any more or greater Wages or other Commodity, contrary to the Rates or Wages that shall be assessed or appointed . . . that then every Person that shall so offend, and be thereof lawfully convicted . . . shall suffer Imprisonment by the Space of ten Days without Bail or Mainprise, and shall lose and forfeit five Pounds of lawful Money of England.

XIX. And that every Person that shall be so retained and take Wages contrary to this Estatute . . . shall suffer Imprisonment by the Space of one and twenty Days, without Bail or Mainprise.

✻   ✻   ✻

XXV. And for the better Advancement of Husbandry and Tillage, and to the Intent that such as are fit to be made Apprentices to Husbandry, may be bounden thereunto, (2) Be it enacted by the Authority of this present Parliament, That every Person being an Housholder, and having and using Half a Plough-land at the least in Tillage, may have and receive as an Apprentice any Person above the Age of ten

Years, and under the Age of eighteen Years, to serve in Husbandry, until the Age of twenty-four Years, as the Parties can agree, and the said Retainer and Taking of an Apprentice, to be made and done by Indenture.

XXVI. And be it further enacted, That every Person being an Housholder, and twenty-four Years old at the least, dwelling or inhabiting, or which shall dwell and inhabit in any City or Town Corporate, and using and exercising any Art, Mystery or Manual Occupation there, shall and may, . . . have and retain the Son of any Freeman, not occupying Husbandry, nor being a Labourer, and inhabiting in the same, or in any other City or Town that now is or hereafter shall be and continue incorporate, to serve and be bound as an Apprentice . . . for seven Years at the least, so as the Term and Years of such Apprentice do not expire or determine afore such Apprentice shall be of the Age of twenty-four Years at the least.

XXVII. Provided always, and be it enacted, That it shall not be lawful to any Person dwelling in any City or Town Corporate, using or exercising any of the Mysteries or Crafts of a Merchant trafficking by Traffick or Trade into any of the Parts beyond the Sea, Mercer, Draper, Goldsmith, Ironmonger, Imbroiderer or Clothier, that doth or shall put Cloth to making and Sale, to take any Apprentice or Servant to be instructed or taught in any of the Arts, Occupations, Crafts or Mysteries which they or any of them do use or exercise; except such Servant or Apprentice be his Son; (2) or else that the Father and Mother of such Apprentice or Servant shall have, at the Time of Taking such Apprentice or Servant, Lands, Tenements or other Hereditaments, of the clear yearly Value of forty Shillings of one Estate of Inheritance or Freehold at the least, . . .

XXVIII. And be it further enacted, That . . . it shall be lawful to every Person being an Housholder, and four and twenty Years old at the least, and not occupying Husbandry, nor being a Labourer, dwelling or inhabiting, or that shall hereafter dwell or inhabit in any Town not being incorporate, that now is or hereafter shall be a Market-town, so long as the same shall be weekly used and kept as a Market-Town, and using or exercising any Art, Mystery or Manual Occupation, . . . to have in like Manner to Apprentice or Apprentices, the Child or Children of any other Artificer or Artificers, not occupying Husbandry, nor being a Labourer, which now do or hereafter shall inhabit or dwell in the same, or in any other such Market-Town within the same Shire, to serve as Apprentice or Apprentices, . . .

XXIX. Provided always, and be it enacted, That it shall not be lawful to any Person, dwelling or inhabiting in any such Market-Town, using or exercising the Feat, Mystery or Art of a Merchant, trafficking or trading into the Parts beyond the Seas, Mercer, Draper, Goldsmith, Ironmonger, Imbroiderer or Clothier, that doth or shall put Cloth to Making and Sale, to take any Apprentice, or in any wise to teach or instruct any Person in the Arts, Sciences or Mysteries last before recited, . . . except such Servant or Apprentice shall be his Son; or else that the Father or Mother of such Apprentice shall have Lands, Tenements or other Hereditaments, at the Time of taking such Apprentice, of the clear yearly Value of three Pounds, . . .

XXX. And be it further enacted, that it shall be lawful to any Person using or exercising the Art or Occupation of a Smith, Wheel-wright, Plough-wright, Mill-wright, Carpenter, Rough Mason, Plasterer, Sawyer, Lime-burner, Brick-maker, Bricklayer, Tyler, Slater, Helier, Tyle-maker, Linnen-weaver, Turner, Cowper, Millers, Earthen Potters, Woolen Weaver weaving Housewives or Houshold Cloth only and none other Cloth, Fuller, otherwise called Tucker or Walker, Burner of Oare and Wood-Ashes, Thatcher or Shingler, wheresoever, he or they shall dwell or inhabit, to have or receive the Son of any Person as Apprentice in Manner and Form aforesaid, to be taught and instructed in these Occupations only, and in none other, albeith the Father or Mother of any such Apprentice have not any Lands, Tenements or Hereditaments.

XXXI. And be it further enacted by the Authority aforesaid, That . . . it shall not be lawful to any Person or Persons, other than such as do now lawfully use or exercise any Art, Mystery or Manual Occupation, (2) to set up, occupy, use or exercise any Craft, Mystery or Occupation, now used or occupied within the Realm of England or Wales; [3] except he shall have been brought up therein seven Years at the Least as an Apprentice, in Manner and Form abovesaid; (4) nor to set any Person on work in such Mystery, Art or Occupation, being not a Workman at this Day; (5) except he shall have been Apprentice as is aforesaid; (6) or else having served as an Apprentice as is aforesaid, shall or will become a Journeyman, or be hired by the Year; (7) upon Pain that every Person willingly offending or doing the contrary, shall forfeit and lose for every Default forty Shillings for every Month.

THE POOR-RELIEF AND APPRENTICESHIP LAW (1601)   From *An Act for the Relief of the Poor,* 43 Eliz. I c.2 (1601).

Be it enacted by the Authority of this present Parliament, That the Churchwardens of every Parish, and Four, Three or Two substantial Householders there, as shall be thought meet, having respect to the Proportion and Greatness of the same Parish and Parishes, to be nominated yearly in the Easter Week, or within One Month after Easter, under the Hand and Seal of Two or more Justices of the Peace in the same County, whereof one to be of the Quorum, dwelling in or near the same Parish or Division where the same Parish doth lie, shall be called Overseers of the Poor of the same Parish; And they, or the greater Part of them, shall take Order from Time to Time, by and with the Consent of Two or more such Justices of Peace as is aforesaid, for setting to work the Children of all such whose Parents shall not by the said Churchwardens and Overseers, or the greater Part of them, be thought able to keep and maintain their Children; and also for setting to work all such Persons, married or unmarried, having no Means to maintain them, and use no ordinary and daily Trade of Life to get their Living by: And also to raise weekly or otherwise (by Taxation of every Inhabitant, Parson, Vicar and other, and of every Occupier of Lands, Houses, Tithes impropriate, Propriations of Tithes, Coal Mines or salable Underwoods in the said Parish, in such competent Sum and Sums of Money, as they shall think fit) a convenient Stock of Flax, Hemp, Wool, Thread, Iron and other necessary Ware and Stuff, to set the Poor on work, and also competent Sums of Money for and towards the necessary Relief of the Lame, Impotent, Old, Blind, and such other among them, being poor and not able to work, and also for the putting out of such Children to be Apprentices, to be gathered out of the same Parish, according to the Ability of the same Parish, and to do and execute all other Things, as well for the disposing of the said Stock as otherwise concerning the premises, as to them shall seem convenient.

II. Which said Churchwardens and Overseers so to be nominated, or such of them as shall not be let by Sickness or other just Excuse, to be allowed by Two such justices of Peace or more as is aforesaid, shall meet together at the least once every

Month in the Church of the said Parish, upon the Sunday in the Afternoon after Divine Service, there to consider of some good Course to be taken, and of some meet Order to be set down in the Premises; and shall within Four Days after the End of their Year, and after other Overseers nominated as aforesaid, make and yield up to such Two Justices of Peace as is aforesaid, a true and perfect Account of all Sums of Money by them received, or rated and sessed and not received, and also of such Stock as shall be in their Hands, or in the Hands of any of the Poor to work, and of all other Things concerning their said Office; and such Sum or Sums of Money as shall be in their Hands shall pay and deliver over to the said Churchwardens and Overseers newly nominated and appointed as aforesaid; upon Pain that every one of them absenting themselves, without lawful Cause as aforesaid, from such Monthly Meeting for the Purpose aforesaid, or being negligent in their Office, or in the Execution of the Orders aforesaid, being made by and with the Assent of the said Justices of Peace, or any Two of them before mentioned, to forfeit for every such Default or Absence or Negligence Twenty Shillings.

III. And be it also enacted, That if the said Justices of Peace do perceive that the Inhabitants of any Parish are not able to levy among themselves sufficient Sums of Money for the Purposes aforesaid, that then the said Two Justices shall and may tax, rate and assess as aforesaid any other of other Parishes, or out of any Parish, within the Hundred where the said Parish is, to pay such Sum or Sums of Money to the Churchwardens and Overseers of the said poor Parish for the said purposes, as the said Justices shall think fit, according to the Intent of this Law: And if the said Hundred shall not be thought to the said Justices able and fit to relieve the said several Parishes not able to provide for themselves as aforesaid, then the Justices of Peace at their General Quarter-Sessions, or the greater Number of them, shall rate and assess as aforesaid, any other of other Parishes, or out of any Parish, within the said County, for the Purposes aforesaid, as in their Discretion shall seem fit.

IV. And that it shall be lawful, as well for the present as subsequent Churchwardens and Overseers, or any of them, by Warrant from any Two such Justices of Peace, as is aforesaid, to levy as well the said Sums of Money, and all Arrearages, of every one that shall refuse to contribute according as they shall be assessed, by Distress and Sale of the Offender's Goods, as the Sums of Money or Stock which shall be behind upon any Account to be made as aforesaid, rendering to the Parties the Overplus; and in Defect of such Distress, it shall be lawful for any such Two Justices of the Peace to commit him or them to the Common Gaol of the County, there to remain without Bail or Mainprize until Payment of the said Sum, Arrearages and Stock; and the said Justices of Peace, or any one of them, to send to the House of Correction or Common Gaol such as shall not employ themselves to Work, being appointed thereunto as aforesaid; and also any such Two Justices of Peace to commit to the said Prison every one of the said Churchwardens and Overseers which shall refuse to account, there to remain, without Bail or Mainprize, until he have made a true account, and satisfied and paid so much as upon the said Account shall be remaining in his Hands.

V. And be it further enacted, That it shall be lawful for the said Churchwardens and Overseers, or the greater Part of them, by the Assent of any Two Justices of the Peace aforesaid, to bind any such Children, as aforesaid, to be Apprentices, where they shall see convenient, till such Man Child shall come to the Age of Four and twenty Years, and such Woman Child to the Age of One and twenty Years, or the time of her Marriage; the same to be as effectual to all purposes, as if such Child were of full Age, and by Indenture of Covenant bound him or herself. And to the Intent that necessary Places of Habitation may more conveniently be provided for such poor-impotent People; Be it enacted by the Authority aforesaid, That it shall and may be lawful for the said Churchwardens and Overseers, or the greater Part of them, by the Leave of the Lord or Lords of the Manor, whereof any Waste or Common within their Parish is or shall be parcel, and upon Agreement before with him or them made in Writing, under the Hands and Seals of the said Lord or Lords, or otherwise, according to any Order to be set down by the Justices of Peace of the said County at their General Quarter-Sessions, or the greater Part of them, by like leave and Agreement of the said Lord or Lords in Writing under his or their Hands and Seals, to erect, build and set up in fit and convenient Places of Habitation in such Waste or Common, at the general Charges of the Parish, or otherwise of the Hundred or County, as aforesaid, to be taxed, rated and gathered in manner before expressed, convenient Houses of Dwelling for the said impotent Poor; and also to place Inmates, or more Families than one in one Cottage or House; one Act made in the one and thirtieth of her Majesty's Reign, intituled, *An Act against the erecting and maintaining of Cottages,* or any Thing therein contained to the contrary notwithstanding: Which Cottages and Places for Inmates shall not at any Time after be used or employed to or for any other Habitation, but only for Impotent and Poor of the same Parish, that shall be there placed from Time to Time by the Churchwardens and Overseers of the Poor of the same Parish, or the most Part of them, upon the Pains and Forfeitures contained in the said former Act made in the said One and thirtieth Year of her Majesty's Reign.

VI. Provided always, That if any Person or Persons shall find themselves grieved with any Sess or Tax, or other Act done by the said Churchwardens and other Persons, or by the said Justices of Peace, that then it shall be lawful for the Justices of Peace, at their General Quarter-Sessions, or the greater Number of them, to take such Order therein, as to them shall be thought convenient; and the same to conclude and bind all the said Parties.

SUBSCRIPTION FORM FOR A CHARITY SCHOOL (c. 1700) From Arthur Leach, ed., *Educational Charters and Documents, 598 - 1909* (Cambridge, 1911), pp. 539-41.

Whereas Prophaness and Debauchery are greatly owing to a gross Ignorance of the Christian Religion, especially among the poorer sort; And whereas nothing is more likely to promote the practice of Christianity and Virtue, than an early and pious Education of Youth; And whereas many Poor People are desirous of having their Children Taught, but are not able to afford them a Christian and Useful Education; We whose Names are underwritten, do agree to pay Yearly, at Four equal Payments, (during Pleasure) the several and respective Sums of Money over against our Names respectively subscribed, for the setting up of a Charity-School in the Parish of _____ in the City of _____ or in the County of _____ for Teaching [Poor Boys, or Poor Girls, or] Poor children to Read and Instructing them in the Knowledge and Practice of the Christian Religion, as profess'd and taught in the Church of England; and for Learning them such other Things as are suitable to their Condition and Capacity. That is to say

A. B. do subscribe

In many Schools the Orders are to the effects following:

I. The master to be elected for this School, shall be,

1. A member of the Church of England of a sober life and conversation, not under the Age of 25 years.

2. One that frequents the Holy Communion.

3. One that hath a good Government of himself and his Passions.

4. One of a Meek Temper and Humble Behaviour.

5. One of a good Genius for Teaching.

6. One who understands well the Grounds and Principles of the Christian Religion and is able to give a good account thereof to the Minister of the Parish or Ordinary on Examination.

7. One who can Write a good Hand, and who understands the Grounds of Arithmetick.

8. One who keeps good order in his Family.

9. One who is approved by the Minister of the Parish (being a Subscriber) before he is presented to be Licensed by the Ordinary.

II. The following Orders shall be observed by the Master and Scholars.

1. The Master shall constantly attend his proper Business in the School during the Hours appointed for Teaching viz. from 7 to 11 in the Morning and from 1 to 5 in the Evening the Summer half year: And from 8 to 11 in the Morning and from 1 to 4 in the Evening the Winter half year; that he may improve the Children in good Learning to the utmost of his Power and prevent the Disorders that frequently happen for want of the Master's Presence and Care.

2. To the End the chief design of this School, which is for the Education of Poor Children in the Rules and Principles of the Christian Religion as professed and taught in the Church of England, may be the better promoted; The Master shall make it his chief Business to instruct the Children in the Principles thereof, as they are laid down in the Church catechism; which he shall first teach them to pronounce distinctly, and plainly; and then, in order to practice, shall explain it to the meanest capacity, by the help of *The whole Duty of Man,* or some good Exposition approved of by the Minister.

And this shall be done constantly twice a week; that everything in the Catechism may be the more perfectly repeated and understood. And the Master shall take particular care of the Manners and Behaviour of the Poor Children.

And by all proper methods shall discourage and correct the beginnings of Vice, and particularly, Lying, Swearing, Cursing, taking God's name in vain, and the Prophanation of the Lord's Day etc. . . .

3. The Master shall teach them the true spelling of Words, and Distinction of Syllables, with the Points and Stops, which is necessary to true and good Reading, and serves to make the Children more mindful of what they Read.

4. As soon as the Boys can read competently well, the Master shall teach them to write a fair legible Hand, with the Grounds of Arithmetick, to fit them for Services or Apprentices.

NOTE. The Girls learn to read etc. and generally to knit their Stockings and Gloves, to Mark, Sew, make and mend their Cloaths, several learn to write, and some to spin their Cloaths.

[5, 6. To provide for Church going on Sundays and Saints' days and twice daily Prayers in School from the Prayer-Book.]

7. [Names-calling at beginning of School] . . . Great Faults as Swearing, Stealing etc. shall be noted down in monthly or weekly bills to be laid before the

Subscribers or Trustees every time they meet, in order to their correction or expulsion.

8. [Holidays.]

9. [Provides that the School is to be free, no charge whatever being made.]

10. [The children are to be sent to school clean.]

11. The Children shall wear their Caps, Bands, Cloaths, and other marks of Distinction every Day, whereby their Trustees and Benefactors may know them, and see what their Behaviour is abroad.

The ordinary charge of a School in London for Fifty Boys Cloath's comes to about £75 per annum, for which a School-Room, Books and Firing is provided, a Master paid, and to each Boy is given yearly Three Bands, one Cap, one Coat, one Pair of Stockings, and one Pair of Shoes.

[The cost for a school of 50 Girls is put at £60 a year to include]

Two Coifs, Two Bands, One Gown and Petticoat, one pair of knit Gloves, One Pair of Stockings, and Two Pair of Shoes.

BOOKS TO BE USED IN THE SCHOOLS OF THE SOCIETY FOR PROMOTING CHRISTIAN KNOWLEDGE (c. 1700)   From W. O. B. Allen and Edmund McClure, *Two Hundred Years: The History of the Society for Promoting Christian Knowledge, 1698 - 1898* (London, 1898), p. 187.

A Bible, Testament, and Common-Prayer Book.

The Church-Catechism.

The Church-Catechism broke into short Questions.

Lewis's Exposition of the Church-Catechism.

Worthington's Scripture-Catechism.

The first Principles of practical Christianity.

Dr. Woodward's Short Catechism, with an Explanation of divers hard Words.

New Method of Catechizing.

Prayers for the Charity-Schools.

The Christian Scholar.

An Exercise for Charity-Schools upon Confirmation.

Pastoral Advice before, and after Confirmation.

The Whole Duty of Man by Way of Question and Answer.

Abridgement of the History of the Bible, which may be well bound up at the Beginning of the Bible, or at the End.

The Anatomy of Orthography: Or, a practical Introduction to the Art of Spelling and Reading English.

The Duty of Public Worship proved, &c.

Lessons for Children, Historical and Practical, &c.

Hymns for the Charity-Schools.

CHARTER OF THE SOCIETY FOR THE PROPAGATION OF THE GOSPEL IN FOREIGN PARTS (1701)

From Charles Pascoe, comp., *Classified Digest of the Records for the Society for the Propagation of the Gospel in Foreign Parts, 1701–1900* (London, 1901), vol. II, pp. 932–35.

William the Third, By the Grace of God, of England, Scotland, France, and Ireland, King, Defender of the Faith. To all Christian People, to whom these Presents shall come, Greeting

Whereas Wee are credibly informed that in many of our Plantacons, Colonies, and Factories beyond the Seas, belonging to Our Kingdome of England, the Provision for Ministers is very mean. And many others of Our said Plantacons, Colonies, and Factories are wholy destitute, and unprovided of a Mainteynance for Ministers, and the Publick Worshipp of God; and for Lack of Support and Mainteynance for such, many of our Loveing Subjects doe want the Administration of God's Word and Sacraments, and seem to be abandoned to Atheism and Infidelity and alsoe for Want of Learned and Orthodox Ministers to instruct Our said Loveing Subjects in the Principles of true Religion, divers Romish Preists and Jesuits are the more encouraged to pervert and draw over Our said Loving Subjects to Popish Superstition and Idolatry

And whereas Wee think it Our Duty as much as in Us lyes, to promote the Glory of God, by the Instruccon of Our People in the Christian Religion And that it will be highly conducive for accomplishing those Ends, that a sufficient Mainteynance be provided for an Orthodox Clergy to live amongst them, and that such other Provision be made, as may be necessary for the Propagation of the Gospell in those Parts:

And whereas Wee have been well assured, That if Wee would be gratiously pleased to erect and settle a Corporacon for the receiving, manageing, and disposeing of the Charity of Our Loveing Subjects, divers Persons would be induced to extend their Charity to the Uses and Purposes aforesaid

*   *   *

Be, and shall for ever hereafter be, and by Vertue of these Presents shall be one Body Politick and Corporate, in Deed and in Name, by the Name of, The Society for the Propogation of the Gospell in Forreigne Parts: And them and their Successors, by the same Name, Wee doe by these Presents, for Us, Our Heires, and Successors, really and fully Make, Ordaine, Constitute, and Declare One Body Politick and Corporate, in Deed and in Name.

And that by the same Name, they and their Successors shall and may have perpetuall Succession.

*   *   *

And lastly Our Pleasure is, That these Our Letters Patents, or the Inrollment thereof, shall be good, firme, valid, and effectuall in the Law, according to Our Royall Intentions herein before declared In Witnes whereof, Wee have caused these Our Letters to be made Patents Witnes Ourselfe at Westminster the Sixteenth Day of June, in the Thirteenth Yeare of our Reigne.

INSTRUCTIONS FOR SCHOOLMASTERS EMPLOYED BY THE SOCIETY FOR THE PROPAGATION OF THE GOSPEL IN FOREIGN PARTS

(**1706**)   From Charles Pascoe, comp., *Classified Digest of the Records for the Society for the Propagation of the Gospel in Foreign Parts, 1701–1900* (London, 1901), vol. I, pp. 844-45.

That they well consider the End for which they are employed by the Society, viz. The instructing and disposing Children to believe and live as Christians.

II. In order to this End, that they teach them to read truly and distinctly, that they may be capable of reading the Holy Scriptures, and other pious and useful Books, for informing their Understandings, and regulating their Manners.

III. That they instruct them thoroughly in the Church-Catechism; teach them first to read it distinctly and exactly, then to learn it perfectly by Heart; endeavouring to make them understand the Sense and Meaning of it, by the help of such Expositions as the Society shall send over.

IV. That they teach them to write a plain and legible Hand, in order to the fitting them for useful Employment; with as much Arithmetick as shall be necessary to the same Purpose.

V. That they be industrious, and give constant Attendance at proper School-Hours.

VI. That they daily use, Morning and Evening, the Prayers composed for their Use in this Collection, with their Scholars in the School, and teach them the Prayers and Graces composed for their Use at Home.

VII. That they oblige their Scholars to be constant at Church on the Lord's Day, Morning and Afternoon, and at all other Times of Publick Worship; that they cause them to carry their Bibles and Prayer Books with them, instructing them how to use them there, and how to demean themselves in the several Parts of Worship; that they be there present with them, taking Care of their reverent and decent Behaviour, and examine them afterwards, as to what they have heard and learned.

VIII. That when any of their Scholars are fit for it, they recommend them to the Minister of the Parish, to be publickly Catechized in the Church.

IX. That they take especial Care of their Manners, both in their Schools and out of them; warning them seriously of those Vices to which Children are most liable; teaching them to abhor Lying and Falsehood, and to avoid all sorts of Evil-speaking; to love Truth and Honesty; to be modest, gentle, well-behaved, just and affable, and courteous to all their Companions; respectful to their Superiors, particularly towards all that minister in holy Things, and especially to the Minister of their Parish; and all this from a Sense and Fear of Almighty God; endeavouring to bring them in their tender Years to that Sense of Religion, which may render it the constant Principle of their Lives and Actions.

X. That they use all kind and gentle Methods in the Government of their Scholars, that they may be loved as well as feared by them; and that when Correction is necessary, they make the Children to understand, that it is given them out of kindness, for their Good, bringing them to a Sense of their Fault, as well as of their Punishment.

XI. That they frequently consult with the Minister of the Parish, in which they dwell, about the Methods of managing their Schools, and be ready to be advised by him.

XII. That they do in their whole Conversation shew themselves Examples of Piety and Virtue to their Scholars, and to all with whom they shall converse.

XIII. That they be ready, as they have Opportunity, to teach and instruct the Indians and Negroes and their Children.

A TYPICAL ENGLISH INDENTURE (1708)   From O. Jocelyn Dunlop, *English Apprenticeship and Child Labour: A History* (London, 1912), pp. 352-53.

This Indenture made the sixteenth day of January in the Seaventh yeare of the Reigne of our Sovraigne Lady Anne of Greate Brittaine ffrance and Ireland Queene Defender of the ffaith ex Anno q° Dom 1708 Betweene William Selman of the pish of Corsham in the County of Wiltes Husbandman And Richard Selman son of the sd William Selman of the one pte And Thomas Stokes holder of the pish of Corsham aforesaid Broadweaver of the other pte Witnesseth that the said Richard Selman of his owne voluntarie will and with the consent of his sd ffather William Selman Hath put himselfe an Apprntice unto the said Thomas Stokes and with him hath convenanted to dwell as his Appntice from the day of the date hereof untill the full end and terme of Seaven Yeares fully to be compleate and ended during all which tyme the said Richard Selman shall well and faithfully serve him the said Thomas Stokes his master his secrets lawfully to be kept shall keep his Commandm^ts lawfull and honest shall doe and execute hurt unto his said Master hee shall not doe nor consent to be done Tavernes or Alehouses hee shall not haunt Dice Cardes or any other unlawfull games hee shall not use ffornication with any woman hee shall not committ during such tyme as he shall stay in his Masters service Matrymony with any woman hee shall not Contract or espouse himselfe during the said Terme of Seven yeares The goods of his said Masters inordinately hee shall not wast nor to any man lend without his Masters Lycence from his Masters house or business hee shall not absent himselfe or plong himselfe by Night or by day without his Masters leave, but as a true and faithfull servant shall honestly behave himselfe towards his sd Master and all his both in words and deedes And the said Thomas Stokes doth for himselfe his Executors and Administrators promise and Covenant to and with the sd William Selman and Richard Selman his Appntice to teach or cause the said Richard Selman to be taught and instructed in the trade Art science or occupacon of a Broadweaver after the best manner that he can or may with moderate Correction finding and allowing unto his sd Servant meate drinke Apparrell Washing Lodging and all other things whatsoev fitting for an appntice of that trade during the said term of Seaven yeares And to give unto his sd Appntice at the end of the sd terme double Apparell (to witt) one suite for holy dayes and one for worken dayes, In witness whereof the said pties to these psent Indentures interchangeably have sett their hands and seales the day and yeare first above written Sealed and Delived in the psence of

Thomas Stokes

COLONIALS

The Southern Colonies

RICHARD HAKLUYT THE ELDER ON REASONS FOR COLONIZING
VIRGINIA (1585) From "Pamphlet for the Virginia Enterprise," as quoted in Eva G. R.
Taylor, ed., *The Original Writings and Correspondence of the Two Richard Hakluyts* (London,
1935), vol. II, pp. 327–32.

Inducements to the Liking of the Voyage
Intended Towards Virginia in 40. and 42. Degrees of Latitude,
Written 1585. by M. Richard Hakluyt the Elder,
Sometime Student of the Middle Temple

The glory of God by planting of religion among those infidels.

2. The increase of the force of the Christians.

3. The possibilitie of the inlarging of the dominions of the Queenes most excellent Maiestie, and consequently of her honour, revenues, and of her power by this enterprise.

4. An ample vent in time to come of the Woollen clothes of England, especially those of the coursest sorts, to the maintenance of our poore, that els sterve or become burdensome to the realme: and vent also of sundry our commodities upon the tract of that firme land, and possibly in other regions from the Northerne side of that maine.

5. A great possibilitie of further discoveries of other regions from the North part of the same land by sea, and of unspeakable honor and benefit that may rise upon the same, by the trades to ensue in Iapan, China, and Cathay, &c.

6. By returne thence, this realme shall receive (by reason of the situation of the climate, and by reason of the excellent soile) Oade, Oile, Wines, Hops, Salt, and most or all the commodities that we receive from the best parts of Europe, and we shall receive the same better cheape, than now we receive them, as we may use the matter.

7. Receiving the same thence, the navie, the humane strength of this realme, our merchants and their goods shal not be subiect to arrest of ancient enemies & doubtfull friends, as of late yeeres they have beene.

8. If our nation do not make any conquest there, but only use trafficke and change of commodities, yet by meane the countrey is not very mightie, but divided into pety kingdoms, they shall not dare to offer us any great annoy, but such as we may easily revenge with sufficient chastisement to the unarmed people there.

9. Whatsoever commodities we receive by the Steelyard merchants, or by our

owne merchants from Eastland, be it Flaxe, Hempe, Pitch, Tarre, Masts, Clap-boord, Wainscot, or such like; the like good may we receive from the North and Northeast part of that countrey neere unto Cape Briton, in returne for our course Woollen clothes, Flanels and Rugges fit for those colder regions.

10. The passage to and fro, is thorow the maine Ocean sea, so as we are not in danger of any enemies coast.

11. In the voyage, we are not to crosse the burnt Zone, nor to passe thorow frozen seas encombred with ice and fogs, but in temperate climate at all times of the yeere: and it requireth not, as the East Indie voiage doth, the taking in of water in divers places, by reason that it is to be sailed in five or six weeks: and by the shortnesse, the merchant may yeerely make two returnes (a factory once being erected there) a matter in trade of great moment.

12. In this trade by the way in our passe to and fro, we have in tempests and other haps, all the ports of Ireland to our aid, and no neere coast of any enemy.

13. By this ordinary trade we may annoy the enemies to Ireland, and succour the Queenes Maiesties friends there, and in time we may from Virginia yeeld them whatsoever commoditie they now receive from the Spaniard; and so the Spaniards shall want the ordinary victual that heertofore they received yeerely from thence, and so they shall not continue trade, nor fall so aptly in practise against this government, as now by their trade thither they may.

14. We shall, as it is thought, enioy in this voyage, either some small Islands to settle on, or some one place or other on the firme land to fortifie for the saftie of our ships, our men, and our goods, the like whereof we have not in any forren place of our trafficke, in which respect we may be in degree of more safetie, and more quiet.

15. The great plentie of Buffe hides, and of many other sundry kinds of hides there now presently to be had, the trade of Whale and Seale fishing, and of divers other fishings in the great rivers, great bayes, and seas there, shall presently defray the charge in good part or in all of the first enterprise, and so we shall be in better case than our men were in Russia, where many yeeres were spent, and great summes of money consumed, before gaine was found.

16. The great broad rivers of that maine that we are to enter into so many leagues navigable or portable into the maine land, lying so long a tract with so excellent and so fertile a soile on both sides, doe seeme to promise all things that the life of man doth require, and whatsoever men may wish, that are to plant upon the same, or to trafficke in the same.

17. And whatsoever notable commoditie the soile within or without doth yeeld in so long a tract that is to be carried out from thence to England, the same rivers so great and deepe, do yeeld no small benefit for the sure, safe, easie and cheape cariage of the same to shipboord, be it of great bulke or of great weight.

18. And in like sort whatsoever commoditie of England the Inland people there shall need, the same rivers doe worke the like effect in benefit for the incariage of the same, aptly, easily, and cheaply.

19. If we finde the countrey populous, and desirous to expel us, and iniuriously to offend us, that seeke but iust and lawfull trafficke, then by reason that we are lords of navigation, and they not so, we are the better able to defend our selves by reason of those great rivers, & to annoy them in many places.

20. Where there be many petie kings or lords planted on the rivers sides, and by all likelihood mainteine the frontiers of their severall territories by warres, we may by the aide of this river ioine with this king heere, or with that king there, at our pleasure, and may so with a few men be revenged of any wrong offered by any of

them; or may, if we will proceed with extremitie, conquer, fortifie, and plant in soiles most sweet, most pleasant, most strong, and most fertile, and in the end bring them all in subiection and to civilitie.

21. The knowen abundance of Fresh fish in the rivers, and the knowen plentie of Fish on the sea coast there, may assure us of sufficient victuall in spight of the people, if we will use salt and industrie.

22. The knowen plentie and varietie of Flesh, of divers kinds of beasts at land there, may seeme to say to us, that we may cheaply victuall our navies to England for our returnes, which benefit every where is not found of merchants.

23. The practise of the people of the East Indies, when the Portugals came thither first, was to cut from the Portugals their lading of Spice: and heereby they thought to overthrow their purposed trade. If these people shall practise the like, by not suffering us to have any commoditie of theirs without conquest, (which requireth some time) yet may we mainteine our first voyage thither, till our purpose come to effect, by the sea-fishing on the coasts there, and by dragging for pearles, which are said to be on those parts; and by returne of those commodities, the charges in part shall be defraied: which is a matter of consideration in enterprises of charge.

24. If this realme shall abound too too much with youth, in the mines there of Golde, (as that of Chisca and Saguenay) of Silver, Copper, Yron, &c. may be an imployment to the benefit of this realme; in tilling of the rich soile there for graine, and in planting of Vines there for Wine; or dressing of those Vines which grow there naturally in great abundance, Olives for Oile; Orenge trees, Limons, Figs and Almonds for fruit; Oad, Saffron, and Madder for Diers; Hoppes for Brewers; Hempe, Flaxe; and in many such other things, by imploiment of the soile, our people void of sufficient trades, may be honestly imploied, that els may become hurtfull at home.

25. The navigating of the seas in the voyage, and of the great rivers there, will breed many Mariners for service, and mainteine much navigation.

26. The number of raw Hides there of divers kindes of beasts, if we shall possesse some Island there, or settle on the firme, may presently imploy many of our idle people in divers severall dressings of the same, and so we may returne them to the people that can not dresse them so well; or into this realm, where the same are good merchandize; or to Flanders, &c. which present gaine at the first, raiseth great incouragement presently to the enterprise.

27. Since great waste Woods be there, of Oake, Cedar, Pine, Wall-nuts, and sundry other sorts, many of our waste people may be imployed in making of Ships, Hoies, Busses and Boats; and in making of Rozen, Pitch and Tarre, the trees naturall for the same, being certeinly knowen to be neere Cape Briton and the Bay of Menan, and in many other places there about.

28. If mines of white or gray marble, Jet, or other rich stone be found there, our idle people may be imployed in the mines of the same, and in preparing the same to shape, and so shaped, they may be caried into this realme as good balast for our ships, and after serve for noble buildings.

29. Sugar-canes may be planted aswell as they are now in the South of Spaine, and besides the imploiment of our idle people, we may receive the commodity cheaper, and not inrich infidels or our doubtful friends, of whom now we receive that commoditie.

30. The daily great increase of Woolles in Spaine, and the like in the West Indies, and the great imploiment of the same into Cloth in both places, may moove us to endevour, for vent of our Cloth, new discoveries of peopled regions, where

hope of sale may arise; otherwise in short time many inconveniences may possibly ensue.

31. This land that we purpose to direct our course to, lying in part in the 40 degree of latitude, being in like heat as Lisbone in Portugall doth, and in the more Southerly part as the most Southerly coast of Spaine doth, may by our diligence yeeld unto us besides Wines and Oiles and Sugars, Orenges, Limons, Figs, Resings, Almonds, Pomegranates, Rice, Raw-silks such as come from Granada, and divers commodities for Diers, as Anile and Cochenillio, and sundry other colours and materials. Moreover, we shall not onely receive many precious commodities besides from thence, but also shal in time finde ample vent of the labour of our poore people at home, by sale of Hats, Bonets, Knives, Fish-hooks, Copper kettles, Beads, Looking-glasses, Bugles, & a thousand kinds of other wrought wares, that in short time may be brought in use among the people of that countrey, to the great reliefe of the multitude of our poore people, and to the woonderfull enriching of this realme. And in time, such league & entercourse may arise betweene our Stapling seats there, and other ports of our Northern America, and of the Islands of the same, that incredible things, and by few as yet dreamed of, may speedily follow, tending to the impeachment of our mightie enemies, and to the common good of this noble government.

| The ends of this voyage are these: | { | 1. To plant Christian religion.
2. To trafficke.
3. To conquer. | } | Or, to doe all three. |

To plant Christian religion without conquest, will bee hard. Trafficke easily followeth conquest: conquest is not easie. Trafficke without conquest seemeth possible, and not uneasie. What is to be done, is the question.

THE CHARTER OF VIRGINIA (1606)   From Alexander Brown, ed., *The Genesis of the United States* (Boston, 1890), vol. I, pp. 53-54.

We greatly commending, and graciously accepting of, their [members of the Virginia Company of London] desires for the furtherance of so noble a work, which may, by the providence of Almighty God, hereafter tend to the glory of his divine Majesty, in propagating of Christian religion to such people, as yet live in darkness and miserable ignorance of the true knowledge and worship of God, and may in time bring the infidels and savages, living in those parts, to human civility and to settled and quiet government; Do by these our letters pattents, graciously accept of, and agree to, their humble and well intended desires.

REQUEST OF JAMES I THAT HIS ARCHBISHOPS PROPAGATE THE GOSPEL AMONG THE HEATHENS IN VIRGINIA (1617)   From Edward Neill, *Virginia Vetusta During the Reign of James the First* (New York, 1885), pp. 167-68.

You haue heard ere this time of ye attempt of diuerse Worthie men, our Subjects to plant in Virginia (under ye warrant of our L'res patents) People of this Kingdom, as well as for ye enlarging of our Dominions, as for propagation of ye Gospell amongst Infidells: wherein there is good progresse made, and hope of further increase; so as the undertakers of that Plantation are now in hand wth the erecting of some Churches and Schooles for ye education of ye children of those Barbarians w'ch cannot but be to them a very great charge, . . . In wch wee doubt not but that you and all others who wish well to the encrease of Christian Religion will be willing to give all assistance and furtherance you may, and therein to make experience of the zeal of deuotion of our well minded Subjects, especially those of ye Clergie. Where fore Wee doe require you and hereby authorize you to write yor Letters to ye seuerall Bishops of ye Diocese in yor Province, that they doe giue order to the Ministers and other zealous men of their Dioceses, both by their owne example in contribution, and by exhortation to others, to move our people within their seuerall charges to contribute to so good a Worke in as liberall a manner as they may for the better aduancing whereof our pleasure is that those Collections be made in the particular parishes four seuerall tymes within these two years next coming: and that the seuerall accounts of each parish together wth the moneys collected, be retourned from time to time to ye Bishop of ye Dioceses and by them be transmitted half yearly to you: and so to be deliuered to the Treasurer of that Plantation to be employed for the Godly purposes intended and no other.

INSTRUCTIONS TO GOVERNOR-ELECT GEORGE YEARDLEY TO BUILD A COLLEGE AT HENRICO, VIRGINIA (1618)   From Susan M. Kingsbury, ed., *The Records of the Virginia Company of London* (Washington, 1906–1935), vol. III, p. 102.

And Whereas by a special Grant and licence from his Majesty a general Contribution over this Realm hath been made for the building and planting of a college for the training up of the Children of those Infidels in true Religion moral virtue and Civility and for other godly uses We do therefore according to a former Grant and order hereby ratifie confirm and ordain that a convenient place be chosen and set out for the planting of a University at the said Henrico in time to come and that in the mean time preparation be there made for the building of the said College for the Children of the Infidels according to such Instructions as we shall deliver And we will and ordain that ten thousand acres partly of the Lands they impaled and partly of other Land within the territory of the said Henrico be alotted and set out for the endowing of the said University and College with convenient possessions.

FUNDS FOR A COLLEGE AT HENRICO, VIRGINIA (1619)

From Susan M. Kingsbury, ed., *The Records of the Virginia Company of London* (Washington, 1906–1935), vol. I, p. 220.

It was also by mr Trer propounded to the Cort as a thing most worthy to be taken into consideracon both for the glory of God, and honor of the Company, that forasmuch as the King in his most gracious fauor hath graunted his Lres to the seuerall Bishops of this Kingdome for the collecting of monies to erect and build a Colledge in Virginia for the trayning and bringing vp of Infidells children to the true knowledge of God & vnderstanding of righteousnes. And considering what publique notice may be taken in foreslowing to sett forward the accon, especially of all those Wch hath contributed to the same, that therefore to begin that pious worke, there is allready towards it—1500li,—or thereabouts, whereof remayning in cash 800li, the rest is to be answered out of the Stock of the Generall Company for so much Wch they borrowed, besides the likelihood of more to come in; ffor mr Treasuror hauing some conference Wth the Bishop of Lichfield, he hath not heard of any Colleccon that hath beene for that busines in his Diocese; but promiseth when he hath a warrt therevnto he will Wthall dilligence further the enterprize; Wherevpon he conceaued it the fittest; that as yet they should not build the Colledge, but rather forebeare a while; and begin first with the meanes they haue to provide and settle an Annuall revennue, and out of that to begin the ereccon of the said Colledge: And for the performance hereof also moued, that a certaine peece of Land be Laid out at Henrico being the place formerly resolued of Wch should be called the Colledge Land, and for the planting of the same send presently ffifty good persons to be seated thereon and to occupy the same according to order, and to haue halfe the benefitt of their Labor and the other halfe to goe in setting forward the worke, and for mayntenance of the Tutors & Schollers.

LIST OF GIFTS FOR THE COLLEGE IN VIRGINIA (1619-1621)

From Susan M. Kingsbury, ed., *The Records of the Virginia Company of London* (Wash. D.C., 1906–1935) vol. III, p. 575.

A person vnknowne gaue for the vse of the Colledge, a Communion-cup with a Couer, and a Plate for the bread, a Siluer guilt: a crimson veluet Carpet with gold lace and fringe, and a linnen damaske Tablecloath: all valued at

l. s. d.

30. 0. 0.

A person vnknowne sent a Letter, the Copy whereof is registred; directed thus, To *Sir Edwin Sandys, the faithfull Treasurer of* VIRGINIA: and subscribed, *Dust and Ashes:* And afterwards by an vnknowne person sent a box to the house of *Sir Edwin Sandys* with the same direction: which being opened in Court, therein was found in gold 550. pounds, to be disposed of for the education of children of the Infidels, in Christian religion and ciuility. } 550. 0. 0.

Master *Nicholas Farrar* of London, deceased, hath by his Will giuen, 300 li. to the Colledge in VIRGINIA, to bee paid when there shall be ten of the Infidels children placed in it; and in meane time 24. pounds by the yeare to bee disbursed vnto three discreete and godly men in the Colonie, which shall honestly bring three of the Infidels children in Christian Religion, and some good course to liue by. } 300. 0. 0.

A person refusing to be named, hath giuen to the benefit of the Plantation } 10. 0. 0.

The Gentlemen and Mariners that came in the *Royall-Iames* from the *East Indies*, being at *Cape Bona-Speranza*, homeward bound, gaue towards the building of the Free Schoole in VIRGINIA, to be called the *East Indie Schoole*, } 70. 8. 6.

Towards the furtherance of the *East Indie Schoole*, an vnknowne person hath added the summe of } 30. 0. 0.

A person refusing to be named, hath giuen the summe of 40. shillings *per annum* for euer, for a Sermon, to be preached before the VIRGINIA Company. } 40s. *per an.*

At the Quarter Court held the 30. of *Ianuary* 1621. by a person not wiling as yet to be knowne, was sent in gold 25 li. to helpe forward the *East Indie Schoole.* } 25. 0. 0.

At the same Quarter Court a small Bible with a Couer richly wrought, a great Church-Bible, the Booke of Common Prayer, and other bookes were presented to be sent to *Virginia*, in the name of a person who had the yeare before sent for the vse of the Colledge at *Henrico; S. Augustine De ciuitate Dei*, Master *Perkins* his workes, and an exact Map of *America*: the giuer is not known, but the books are valued at } 10. 0. 0.

Giuen by Master *Thomas Bargraue*, a Minister in VIRGINIA deceased, for the vse of the College, a Library valued at } 100. *marks*

There is a Contribution made by the Inhabitants in VIRGINIA for the building of a house of entertainment for new commers, at *Iames-Citie*: amounting to the value of } 1500. 0. 0.

The Gentlemen and Mariners that came lately home from the *East Indies*, in the two Ships called the *Hart* and *Roe-Bucke*, being at the Cape of *Bona Speranza*, homeward bound, gaue towards the building of the aforesaid Free-Schoole in VIRGINIA the summe of } 66. 13. 4.

INDIUN MASSACRE DESTROYS THE PROSPECTS OF THE COLLEGE IN VIRGINIA (1622)

INDIAN MASSACRE DESTROYS THE PROSPECTS OF THE COLLEGE IN VIRGINIA (1622) From "Letter from Edward Waterhouse," as quoted in Susan M. Kingsbury, ed., *The Records of the Virginia Company of London* (Washington, 1906–1935), vol. III, pp. 550-51.

The country being in this estate, an occasion was ministered of sending to Opachankano the King of these Sauages, about the middle of March last, what time the Messenger returned backe with these words from him, That he held the peace concluded so firme, as the Skie should sooner fall then it dissolue; yea, such was the treacherous dissimulation of that people who then had contriued our destruction, that euen two dayes before the Massacre, some of our men were guided thorow the woods by them in safety: and one Browne, who then to learne the language liued among the Warrascoyacks (a Prouince of that King) was in friendly manner sent backe by them to Captaine Hamor his Master, and many the like passages, rather increasing our former confidence, then any wise in the world ministering the least suspition of the breach of the peace, or of what instantly ensued; yea, they borrowed our owne Boates to conuey themselues crosse the Riuer (on the bankes of both sides whereof all our Plantations were) to consult of the diuellish murder that ensued, and of our vtter extirpation, which God of his mercy (by the meanes of some of themselues conuerted to Christianitie) preuented; and as well on the Friday morning (the fatal day) the 22 of March, as also in the euening, as in other dayes before, they came vnarmed into our houses, without Bowes or arrowes, or other weapons, with Deere, Turkies, Fish, Furres, and other prouisions, to sell, and trucke with vs, for glasse, beades, and other trifles: yea in some places, sate downe at Breakfast with our people at their tables, whom immediately with their owne tooles and weapons, eyther laid downe, or standing in their houses, they basely and barbarously murthered, not sparing eyther age or sexe, man, woman or childe; so sodaine in their cruell execution, that few or none discerned the weapon or blow that brought them to destruction. In which manner they also slew many of our people then at their seuerall workes and husbandries in the fields, and without their houses, some in planting Corne and Tobacco, some in gardening, some in making Bricke, building, sawing, and other kindes of husbandry, they well knowing in what places and quarters each of our men were, in regard of their daily familiarity, and resort to vs for trading and other negotiations, which the more willingly was by vs continued and cherished for the desire we had of effecting that great master-peece of workes, their conuersion. And by this means that fatall Friday morning, there fell vnder the bloudy and barbarous hands of that perfidious and inhumane people, contrary to all lawes of God and men, of Nature & Nations, three hundred forty seuen men, women, and children, most by their owne weapons; and not being content with taking away life alone, they fell after againe vpon the dead, making as well as they could, a fresh murder, defacing, dragging, and mangling the dead carkasses into many pieces, and carrying some parts away in derision, with base and brutish triumph. . . .

INSTRUCTIONS TO MINISTERS AND PARENTS FOR INSTILLING PIETY
IN VIRGINIA HOUSEHOLDS (1632, 1645)   From William W. Hening, ed.,
Statutes at Large of Virginia, 1619–1782 (Richmond, 1809–1823), vol. I, pp. 157, 311–
12.

It is also thought fit, That upon every Sunday the minister shall half an hour or more before evening prayer examine, catechise, and instruct the youth and ignorant persons of his parish, in the ten commandments, the articles of the belief and in the Lord's prayer; and shall diligently hear, instruct and teach them the catechism, set forth in the book of common prayer[:] And all fathers, mothers, masters and mistresses shall cause their children, servants or apprentices which have not learned the catechism to come to the church at the time appointed, obediently to hear, and to be ordered by the minister until they have learned the same: And if any of the said fathers, mothers, masters and mistresses, children, servants or apprentices, shall neglect their duties as the one sort in not causing them to come and the other in refusing to learn as aforesaid, they shall be censured by the courts in those places holden. And this act to take beginning at Easter next.

*   *   *

Whereas it was enacted the 12th of June, 1641, and continued by an act 17th of February, 1644, That all ministers should preach in the forenoon and catechise in the afternoon of every Sunday, And in case they should fail to do so, that then they forfeit 500 lb. of tobacco to be disposed of by the vestry for the use of the parish lb: Be it now further enacted, That all masters of families upon warning given by the ministers in the several places where they shall officiate, do cause their children and servants to repair to the places appointed to be instructed and catechised as aforesaid upon the like penalty that is imposed on the minister, in case of his default, to be disposed as aforesaid, unless sufficient cause be shown to the contrary.

THE WILL OF BENJAMIN SYMS (1634)   From Edgar W. Knight, ed.,
Documentary History of Education in the South Before 1860 (Chapel Hill, N. C., 1949–
1953), vol. I, pp. 203-05.

In the name of God Amen this Twelfth day of Febry Anno Domini one thousand Six hundred and thirty four I Benjamin Syms being of perfect health, & memory praised be God make & ordain this my last Will and testament, in manner & forme following Viz

    I commend my soul into the hands of God my Creator and
    Redeemer and my body to the Earth from whence it came to have
    Christian burial whereas there is due to me two hundred acres of

land lying in the old Poquoson River and Eight Milch cows — I bequeath it as followth Viz The use of the said land with the milk and Increase Male of the said cattle to be for the mantayance of an honest & learned man to keep upon the said Ground a free School to Educate & teach the Children of the adjoining Parishes of Elizb City & Poquoton from Mary's Mount downwards to the Poquoson River.

Item My Will and desire is that the Worshipful the Commander and ye rest of the Commissioners of this liberty with the ministers and Church Wardens of the said Parish where the said School is founded to see it from time to time justly & truly performed.

Item My Will and Desire is that when it please God there is sufficient Increase of the said cattle yt some part of them be saved for the erecting a very sufficient School house and the Rest of the Increase that are left to be disposed of before nominated and in Repairing the said School.

Item My Will is that the Increase of the said Cattle after the said School Master is sufficiently stocked for his maintaynance shall be spent according to the directions of the said Commander & Commitions with the rest of them to manteyne poor children, or decayed or maimed persons of the said parish.

Item I give and bequeath unto George Thompson the Soun of Roger Thompson, late of Barstable in the County of Duenshire decd one thousand, pos weight of Tobacco in leafe.

Item Whereas there is due unto me one bond of one hundred pounds from Thomas Worth in the County of Cornewall, which said bond is now in the hands of Wassell Webbing of Baching in the County of Essen I Doe also give & bequeath to the said George Thompson.

Item My Will and desire is that if the said George Thompson or Angell Thompson should decease that then whatever I have bequeath In this my Will & testament to Remaine to the surviver.

Item I Doe further will and desire that if should please God to take away both the Said George & Angell Thompson that then whatever I have bequeath them in this my will to Return to the use and benifit of the said School for want of Heirs of Either of their bodys lawfully begotten.

Item I give and bequeath unto Angell Thompson son of the said Roger Thompson decd three thousand pounds of Tobacco in leaf with twelve young Cattle with all the Increase of those cattle which belongs unto me unto this my Will be with all such goods, hoggs Poultry and household stuffe as are or shall be found belonging unto me with twelve barrels of corn.

Item I give and bequeath unto the said Angle Thompson two hundred and fifty acres of land which is due unto me for transportations, of five Servants in the Peter & John of London in the year our Lord one thousand Six hundred twenty Six Capt. John being the commander of the said ship.

Item I give and bequeath five hundr Pounds of Toba to be imployed to the use of the Church of the old Poquoson.

Item I give and bequeath to the minister of the said Parish which shall beat the time when this my will shall be two hundd pounds of Tobacco.

Item I request my well beloved friends Mr. Thomas Oldis and John Snode to be Overseers to see those legacies Performed according, to the full Intent and meaning of my last will and Testament. To whom I give as a rememberance of my love three hundd Pounds of Toba and one Ewe goate being at the house of John Branch at Back River.

In witness whereof I have hereunto set my hand and seal the day and year first above written

---

THE WILL OF THOMAS EATON (1659) From Edgar W. Knight, ed., *Documentary History of Education in the South Before 1860* (Chapel Hill, N.C., 1949– 1953), vol. I. pp. 205-06.

To all Christian people to whom these presents shall come, I, Thos. Eaton of Black River, in the County of Elizabeth City (hereby) send Greeting in our Lord God everlasting. Know ye that I the said Thomas Eaton, being at present weake in body but whole & (perfect) in memory, praised be God, out of my own free will (and the love) that I beare towards the Inhabitants of the County of Elizabeth City, I have for the maintenance of an able school master (to) educate and teach the children borne within said County of Elizabeth City—

Given, granted, assigned, set over and confirmed and doo by these presents give, grant, assign, set over and confirm after the time of my decease for the use aforesaid, Five hundred acres of land whereon the (sd) Free school shall bee kept being a part of a dividend of six hundred and (f   ) acres graunted unto me by pattent bearing date the fifth day of June Anno 1638, Beginning from the beaver damm   westerly towards the head of the Back River & Southerly Woods, with all houses, edifices, orchards and Rights to belonging to it. Two negroes called by the names of Twelve Cows and two bulls, twenty hogs, young and old, one bedstead, a table, a cheese press, twelve milk trays, an Iron kettle, contayning about twelve gallons, pot rack and pot hooks, Milk Pailes, water tubs and powdering tubbs, to have and to hould the said land with all other the premises before mentioned for the use afores'd, with all ye male increase thereof, for ye maintenance of said schoolmaster such one as by the Commissioners, Mynister & churchwardens whom I doo nominate and appoint as trustees in trust for the ordering and settling thereof from time to time shall be thought fit, and I, the said Thomas Eaton do further order & appoint that no free education bee allowed but to such children as shalbe borne within the said county. And that when there shall be found to bee sufficient maintenance for the sd. schoolmaster that ye overplus thereof shalbe imployed for the maintenance of poor impotent persons Widowes and Orphans, inhabitants in the said county as by my said Trustees shalbe thought fit. All wch the premises before mentioned to be enjoyed for the use aforesaid, without anie manner of claime or demand, disturbance, incumbrance or hindrance of anie person or persons, clayming by from or under mee forever by these presents, and further know ye, that I, ye said Thomas Eaton have delivered at the time of the ensealing and delivery hereof, part of the sd. land in name of all the rest of the premises before mentioned.

In witness whereof I have hereunto set my hand & seal this nineteenth day of September, Anno Dni. 1659.

VIRGINIA APPRENTICESHIP LAW (1643)   From William W. Hening, ed.,
Statutes at Large of Virginia, 1619–1782 (Richmond, 1809–1823), vol. I, pp. 260–61.

Whereas there hath been the general suffering of the colony, that the orphans of divers deceased persons have been very much abused and prejudiced in their estates by the negligence of overseers and guardians of such orphans, Be it therefore enacted and confirmed, that the guardians and overseers of all orphans shall carefully keep and preserve such estates as shall be committed to their trust either by order of court or otherwise. And shall likewise deliver an exact account once every year to the commissioners of the several county courts respectively of the said estates and of the increase and improvement, who are hereby required to keep an exact register thereof, And all overseers and guardians of such orphans are enjoined by the authority aforesaid to educate and instruct them according to their best endeavours in Christian religion and in rudiments of learning and to provide for them necessaries according to the competence of their estates, And where any shall be found delinquent in the premises the commissioners of the said county courts are required to take the care of the said orphans and their estates into due consideration and to see them provided for according to their estates and qualities.

WORKHOUSE LAW FOR POOR CHILDREN IN VIRGINIA (1646)   From
William W. Hening, ed., *Statutes at Large of Virginia, 1619–1782* (Richmond, 1809–
1823), vol. I, pp. 336–37.

Whereas sundry laws and statutes by act of parliament established, have with great wisdom ordained, for the better educating of youth in honest and profitable trades and manufactures, as also to avoid sloth and idleness wherewith such young children are easily corrupted, as also for relief of such parents whose poverty extends not to give them breeding, That the justices of the peace should at their discretion, bind out children to tradesmen or husbandmen to be brought up in some good and lawful calling, And whereas God Almighty, among many his other blessings, hath vouchsafed increase of children to this colony, who now are multiplied to a considerable number, who if instructed in good and lawful trades may much improve the honor and reputation of the country, and no less their own good and their parents' comfort: But for as much as for the most part the parents, either through fond indulgence or perverse obstinancy, are most averse and unwilling to part with their children, Be it therefore enacted by authority of this Grand Assembly, according to the aforesaid laudable custom in the kingdom of England, That the commissioners of the several counties respectively do, at their discretion, make choice of two children in each county at the age of eight or seven years at the least, either male or female, which are to be sent up to James City between this and June next to be employed in the public flax houses under such master and mistress as shall be there appointed, In carding, knitting and spinning, etc. And that the said children be furnished from the said county with six barrels of corn, two coverlets, or one rug and one blanket: One bed, one wooden bowl or tray, two pewter spoons, a sow shoat of six months old, two laying hens, with convenient apparel both linen and woolen, with hose and shoes, And for the better provision of housing for the said children, It is enacted, That there be two houses built by the first of April next of forty foot long apiece with good and substantial timber, The houses to be twenty foot broad apiece, eight foot high in the pitch and a stack of brick chimneys standing in the midst of each house, and that they be lofted with sawn boards and made with convenient partitions, And it is further thought fit that the commissioners have caution not to take up any children but from such parents who by reason of their poverty are disabled to maintain and educate them, Be it likewise agreed, That the Governor hath agreed with the Assembly for the sum of 10000 lb. of tobacco to be paid him the next crop, to build and finish the said houses in manner and form before expressed.

APPRENTICESHIP INDENTURES IN VIRGINIA IN THE SEVENTEENTH CENTURY   From *William and Mary College Quarterly Historical Magazine*, vol. V, pp. 221-23.

Y ork Court, 20 Oct., 1646.—It is ordered, with the consent of Mr. Edmund Chisman, father-in-law to John Lilly, orphant; William Barber, father-in-law to the orphans of John Dennett, vizt.: Thomas Dennett, Margaret Dennett, and Sarah Dennett; & Daniel ffoxe, father-in-law to the orphants of Clark & Munday, that the estates belonging to the sd sevrall orphants, wch this day they have filed an accot of to this cort, shall henceforward with all there increase freely come & belong unto the said orphans wth out any charges for the future subsistance or education of the sd orphans, or for there care, paines, or charge in prserving & looking to ye sd sevrall orphants estates, as long as they or any of them shall remaine under the tuition of ye above sd Edmund Chisman, William Barber, & Daniel ffoxe, &c.

York County.—Orphants Cort held August 24th, 1648.
Present: Capt Nicholas Martin, Capt John Chisman, Mr Hugh Gwyn, Mr ffrancis Willis, Mr ffrancis Morgan.
Whereas John foster, orphant to John foster, late of Hampton pish, deceased, whoe is left without any mentaynance or estate whatsoever, and Stephen Gill, godfather to ye sd foster, haveing made humble suite to this court that the sd John foster, whoe hath by him beene already provided for and kept about a yeare, that he may have the tuition and bringing upp of ye sd John foster, and that he may be put wth him for some certayne tyme by this cort. It is therefore ordered that the sd John foster shall live & remaine under tuition & bringing upp of ye sd Stephen Gill, for ye space of nine yeares from ye date hereof. Dureing which tyme ye sd Gill is hereby injoined to p'vide sufficiently for ye sd foster, & to take care that he bee brought upp in ye feare of God and taught to Reade.

Lancaster County, Jan'y 6, 1655.—The court hath ordered Jno, ye base child of Thomas Mannan, borne of Eliza: Tomlin, shall, according to ye will of ye mother, bee kept by Roger Harris & his wife until he arrive at ye Age of 18 years, he, ye sd Harris providing yt ye sd child be taught to write & reade. And yt ye sd Harris have all of ye tobacco due from Jno Robinson pd him at ye crop on ye 10th of November next, the same being 600 & caske.

Surry County, June 15, 1681.—Wm. Rogers bound apprentice to Thomas Bage to serve till 21—his master to teach him his trade of blacksmith, and to read & wright, &c.

* * *

May 4, 1697. Ordered that unless Jno Clements do put John High to school to learne to reade & write, he do appeare at the next court, and bring ye said John with him, that the court may then do therein as shall be found fitt.

Elizabeth City County, July 18, 1698.—Ann Chandler, orphan of Daniel Chandler, bound apprentice to Phyllemon Miller till 18 or day of marriage, to be taught to read a chapter in the Bible, ye Lord's prayer, and ten commandments, and sempstress work.

Isle of Wight County.—At an Orphan's Court held on the 1st May, Anno 1694.
Prsent: Col. Arthur Smith, Capt. Henry Applewhait, Mr. Hen. Baker, Mr. Thos. Giles, Mr. Antho. Holladay, justices.
Charles Edwards having exhibited a peticon to this Court for Grace Griswood, an Orphan Girl, that she might live with him, ye sd Charles, till eighteen years old or marryed. It is thereupon ordered yt the sd Orphan doe live & abide with the sd Edwards till age or marryage as aforesaid, & ye sd Charles doth hereby oblige himselfe to mainteyn her decently & see yt she be taught to read, sew, spinn & knitt, & at the expiration of the tyme to have sufficient cloathing as shall be thought well by the court.

York Court, May ye 26th 1690.—Whereas Thomas Thorpe and Ellinor his wife sued Robt Green to this court, and in their peticon declare that they did binde Richard Gilbert there son An Apprentice to ye Defent for the space of nine yeares by one Indenture under hand and seale to bee Instructed and taught in ye Arts and Mistery of a taylor and to teach or cause him to be taught to reade & to write a Leagable hand, and not to Imploye him to Labour in the Grownd, Excepting in helping to make corne for the Defendts ffamely, but ye defendt without regard to ye said Indenture Dayley keeps the said Apprentice to Labour in the Ground from year to year and omitts giveing him Learning or teach him his trade which is to ye said Apprentice utter Rewing and undoing. Therefore itt is ordered that ye said Robt Green doe at ye next court Enter into a Bond of 4000 lb tobacco & cash, with good and sufficient security for the true pformance of ye said Indenture and to fulfill every clause and Artickle therein expressed, according to ye true Interest and meaning ye same.

LAW TO EMPOWER VIRGINIA COUNTY COURTS TO BUILD WORK HOUSES (1668)
From William W. Hening, ed., *Statutes at Large of Virginia, 1619–1782* (Richmond, 1809–1823), vol. II, pp. 266-67.

Whereas the prudence of all states ought as much as in them lies endeavor the propagation and increase of all manufactures conducing to the necessities of their subsistence, and God having blessed this country with a soil capable of producing most things necessary for the use of man if industriously improved, It is enacted by this Grand Assembly and the authority thereof that for the better converting wool, flax, hemp, and other commodities into manufactures, and for the increase of artificers in the country, that the commissioners of each county court, with the assistance of the respective vestries of the parishes in their counties, shall be and hereby are empowered to build houses for the educating and instructing poor children in the knowledge of spinning, weaving, and other useful occupations and trades, and power granted to take poor children from indigent parents to place them to work in those houses.

REPORT OF GOVERNOR BERKELEY ON VIRGINIA SCHOOLS (1671)
From William W. Hening, ed., *Statutes at Large of Virginia, 1619–1782* (Richmond, 1809–1823), vol. II, p. 517.

What course is taken about the instructing the people within your government in the christian religion; and what provision is there made for the paying of your ministry?

Answer: The same course that is taken in England out of towns; every man according to his ability instructing his children. We have forty-eight parishes, and our ministers are well paid, and by my consent should be better if they would pray oftener and preach less. But of all other commodities, so of this, the worst are sent us, and we had few that we could boast of, since the persecution in Cromwell's tyranny drove divers worthy men hither. But, I thank God, there are no free schools nor printing, and I hope we shall not have these hundred years; for learning has brought disobedience, and heresy, and sects into the world, and printing has divulged them, and libels against the best government. God keep us from both!

Parson

ON THE EDUCATION OF ORPHANS AND THE POOR IN NORTH CAROLINA (1695, 1703, 1716) From *Colonial Records of North Carolina*, vol. I, pp. 448, 577; vol. II, p. 266.

Upon ye Peticon of Honell Thomas Harvey esqr Ordered yt Wm ye son of Timothy Pead late of the County of Albemarle Decd being left destitute be bound unto ye sd Thomas Harvey esqr and Sarah his wife untill he be at ye age of twenty one years and the said Thomas Harvey to teach him to read. (February, 1695.)

(2) Upon a petition of Gabriell Newby for two orphants left him by Mary Hancock the late wife of Thoms Hancocke and proveing the same by the oathes of Eliz. Steward and her daughter the Court doe agree to bind them unto him he Ingagen & promising before the Court to doe his endeavours to learne the boy the trade of a wheelwright and likewise give him at the expiration of his time one year old heifer and to ye girle at her freedome one Cow and Calfe besides the Custome of the Country and has promised to ye next orphans Court to Sign Indentures for that effect. (March, 1703.)

(3) Upon the Peticon of John Swain praying that Elizabeth Swain his sister an Orphane Girle bound by the Precinct Court of Chowan to John Worley Esqr May in time of her service be taught to read by her said Master Ordered, that she be taught to read. (November, 1716.)

LEGISLATION ON ORPHANS IN NORTH CAROLINA (1715) From Walter Clark, ed., *The State Records of North Carolina* (Goldsboro, N.C., 1886–1907), vol. XXIII, p. 70.

And Be It Further Enacted by the Authority afors'd that all Orphans shall be Educated & provided for according to their Rank & degree out of the Income or Interest of their Estate & Stock if the same will be sufficient Otherwise such Orphan shall be bound Apprentice to some Handycraft Trade (the Master or Mistress of such Orphan not being of the Profession of the People called Quakers) till they shall come of Age unless some of kin to such Orphan will undertake to maintain & Educate him or them for the interest or income of his or her Estate without Diminution of the Principal whether the same be great or small shall be always delivered to the Orphan when at Age.

Quaker

THE DIARY OF A VIRGINIA GENTLEMAN (1711-1712) From ''The Secret
Diary of William Byrd of Westover,'' 1709-1712, as quoted in Roy Pearce, ed., *Colonial
American Writing* (New York, 1950), pp. 436-46.

D*ecember 23, 1711.* I rose about 7 o'clock and read a chapter in Hebrew
and some Greek in Homer. I said my prayers and ate boiled milk for breakfast. I
wrote out a chronology of the Bible which the Governor lent me and did not go to
church, God forgive me. About 12 o'clock Dr. Cocke came to me in order to go to
Queen's Creek and we got on horseback about one and rode there and [found] them
pretty well. The weather was cold and had hindered them from going to church
likewise. We waited till 3 o'clock for dinner and then I ate some turkey and chine
and after dinner we sat by a fire and chatted and were merry, without much scandal
to our [talk]. The Doctor was very pleasant company, as he commonly is. We had
some roast apples and wine, with which we diverted ourselves till about 10 o'clock
and then we retired to our lodgings where I said my prayers and had good health,
good thoughts, and good humor, thank God Almighty.

24. I rose about 7 o'clock but read nothing because all the company was up.
However, I said my prayers and ate boiled milk for breakfast. It was very cold and
had frozen very hard. However, about 10 we took leave and rode to Williamsburg.
Mr. Bland came to my lodging and told me he had bought Mr. Brodnax's land for
me that lay near the Falls and was to give him 165 pounds for it. Then I went to the
coffeehouse, where I met all my brothers of the Council that were in town. About
12 o'clock Colonel Ludwell and I went to the Governor's to learn from himself how
long he intended to keep us and to persuade him to give leave to the House of
Burgesses to adjourn for a month without their asking, which he at last consented
to. He asked us to dine but we [. . .] to the rest of the Council and dined with them
at the coffeehouse and I ate some beef for dinner. I paid all my debts and about 3
o'clock we went to the capitol to expect the coming of the Governor, who
adjourned the assembly till the 24th of January and then we all took leave and went
away and I went to Queen's Creek and surprised a good company there. I ate some
toast and cider and roast apples and sat and chatted till 10 o'clock and then I
recommended the company to the divine protection and said a short prayer and had
good thoughts and good health and good humor, thank God Almighty.

25. I rose about 7 o'clock and read nothing because I prepared for my journey
to Colonel Duke's. However I said my prayers and ate boiled milk for breakfast.
The weather threatened snow but it did not frighten me from taking my leave about
11 o'clock, but before that I wrote a letter to Mr. C-s and enclosed to Mr. Graeme
who was to go soon in the man-of-war. About 2 o'clock I got to Colonel Duke's and
found both him and his old woman in good health, only the last was grown very
deaf. We sat and talked till about 4 and then we went to dinner and I ate some wild
duck. In the meantime the Colonel sent a negro man to see whether the river was
open at my brother Duke's and he brought word it was, and therefore I took leave
of the Colonel and his old countess and rode away to the river and with some
difficulty got over as soon as it was dark. I found all well there and we drank a
bottle of wine. About 9 o'clock I went to bed. I said my prayers and had good
health, good thoughts, and good humor, thank God Almighty.

26. I rose about 7 o'clock and read nothing because I prepared for my journey.
However I said my prayers and ate boiled milk for breakfast. It was cold and

threatened rain or snow. About 9 I took leave and rode towards home and between Captain Stith's and home I met my wife and Mrs. Dunn going to Williamsburg to see what was become of me, but they turned back with me home where I found all well, thank God Almighty, except old Jane who was very ill of a fever. About 3 o'clock we went to dinner and I ate some wild goose. In the afternoon I looked about and found all things in good order. . . .

*　　*　　*

29. I rose about 7 o'clock and read two chapters in Hebrew and some Greek in Lucian. I said my prayers and ate boiled milk for breakfast. I had abundance of talk with Mr. G-r-l about the affairs of Falling Creek and he told me some of his wants and so did George Smith, which I endeavored to supply as well as I could. I gave John G-r-l leave to go visit his mother. Poor old Jane died this morning about 9 o'clock and I caused her to be buried as soon as possible because she stank very much. It was not very cold today. I danced my dance. Mr. G-r-l and George Smith went away about 12 o'clock. I ate some broiled goose for dinner. In the afternoon I set my razor, and then went out to shoot with bow and arrow till the evening and then I ran to breathe myself and looked over everything. At night I read some Latin in Terence till about 10 o'clock. I said my prayers and had good health, good thoughts, and good humor, thank God Almighty.

30. I rose about 7 o'clock and read a chapter in Hebrew and three chapters in the Greek Testament. I said my prayers very devoutly and ate boiled milk for breakfast. The weather was very clear and warm so that my wife walked out with Mrs. Dunn and forgot dinner, for which I had a little quarrel with her and another afterwards because I was not willing to let her have a book out of the library. About 12 o'clock came Mr. Bland from Williamsburg but brought no news. He stayed to dinner and I ate some roast beef. In the afternoon we sat and talked till about 4 o'clock and then I caused my people to set him over the river and then I walked with the women about the plantation till they were very weary. At night we ate some eggs and drank some Virginia beer and talked very gravely without reading anything. However I said my prayers and spoke with all my people. I had good health, good thoughts, and good humor, thank God Almighty. I danced my dance in the morning.

31. I rose about 7 o'clock and read a chapter in Hebrew and six leaves in Lucian. I said my prayers and ate boiled milk for breakfast. The weather continued warm and clear. . . .

January, 1712. 4. I rose about 7 o'clock and read two chapters in Hebrew and some Greek in Homer. I said my prayers and ate boiled milk for breakfast. I danced my dance and then settled several accounts. The weather was clear and warm. My wife was indisposed with the colic but recovered pretty soon again, thank God, by the help of good drams of caraway water. I took a walk in the garden till dinner. I ate no meat this day but only fruit. In the afternoon I weighed some money and then went into the new orchard to trim some trees and stayed there till it was dark almost and then took a little walk about the plantation. In the evening Tom Turpin brought 30 hogs from the Falls and told me all was well, thank God. At night I read some Latin in Terence and said my prayers and had good health, good thoughts, and good humor, thank God Almighty. I ate some broiled turkey for supper.

5. I rose about 7 o'clock and read nothing because Tom Turpin was here. He

came with 30 hogs from the Falls. He told me all was well above. I said my prayers and ate boiled milk for breakfast. I danced my dance. About 9 o'clock came Major Harrison and the captain of the "Pelican". I gave them a bottle of sack. Then we played at billiards and I won 7 shillings, and sixpence. About one o'clock we went to dinner and I ate some boiled beef. In the afternoon we were merry and made the Quaker captain drink the Queen's health on his knees. About 2 o'clock came my brother and sister Custis and sat down to dinner. They brought no news. My sister was much tired. In the evening the captain and Major Harrison went away to Mrs. Harrison's where I understood that Mr. Clayton was come. We drank a bottle of wine at night. This day a negro of mine at Falling Creek had a tree fall on his head and had his brains beat out. I neglected to say my prayers and had good health, good thoughts, and good humor, thank God Almighty. . . .

7. I rose about 7 o'clock and read nothing because we prepared to go to Colonel Hill's. I ate chocolate for breakfast. I said a short prayer. About 10 o'clock our ladies made a shift to get dressed, when we got on horseback and my horse was very frolicsome. The weather was cold and very clear. We called at Captain Llewellyn's and took Lew Eppes and his wife with us to Colonel Hill's, where we found all well. . . . About 2 o'clock we went to dinner and I ate some boiled pork for dinner. In the afternoon we went to see the ship and found them far advanced. Then we returned and saw my sloop bringing to at the Hundred, where my people left behind 50 bushels of wheat from G-r-l. In the evening we were very merry and the women offered violence to me because I would not dance and my wife quarrelled with her sister because she would not dance. About 10 o'clock we went to bed. I recommended myself and my family to the protection of Almighty God, and had good health, good thoughts, and good humor, thank God Almighty.

8. I rose about 7 o'clock and read a little in Horace. I neglected to say my prayers because the women came in with a dram of strong water of which I drank two drams. Then I left the women and went to the men and talked with them. About 9 o'clock came Colonel Frank Eppes to discourse with me concerning the rangers in the upper county and he told me nobody would accept of that place because the pay was too little. I ate some roast beef for breakfast contrary to my custom. About 10 o'clock we went away home and found all well, thank God. We expected Mr. Clayton and Major Harrison from Prince George court and therefore we ordered dinner late. About 3 o'clock came Dr. Cocke and brought me some English letters, by which I learned there were plenipotentiaries appointed to agree about a peace, which God prosper. About 5 o'clock came Mr. Clayton, Major Harrison, and his brother Harry. We went to supper and I ate some boiled beef. We were very merry and I gave them some of my best wine. We played at cards and I won 15 shillings. I neglected to say my prayers because the company kept me up late but I had good health, good thoughts, and good humor, thank God Almighty. Parson Finney dined with us also and stayed all night.

9. I rose about 7 o'clock and found the weather exceedingly cold. I neglected to say my prayers because of the company. However I drank chocolate for breakfast and ate some cake. After breakfast we went to play and I won 10 pounds at cards. About 10 o'clock Major Harrison and his brother Harry went away but the rest of the company was persuaded to stay a day longer, only Parson Finney, who went away likewise. Mr. Clayton and I took a walk till dinner and then I ate some roast mutton which was very good. My sloop went away this morning to Falling Creek. In the afternoon we were merry without drinking but did not venture out because of the [. . .] cold weather. In the evening Peter came from the Falls and told me all was well, thank God. We drank some of my best wine and were merry but would

not let the women part from us. About 10 we ate some bread and cheese and drank a bottle on it, and about 11 we went to bed. My wife had got some cold and was disordered in her hip. I neglected to say my prayers but had good health, good thoughts, and good humor, thank God Almighty, only I was a little displeased at a story somebody had told the Governor that I had said that no Governor ought to be trusted with 20,000 pounds. Little Peter brought a wild goose with him and two ducks.

10. I rose about 7 o'clock and found it terribly cold. My wife was a little better. I neglected my prayers and ate boiled milk for breakfast but the company ate some chicken pie. About 11 o'clock my company took leave and went away and then I could do everything which too much company had hindered me from. I read this day no Hebrew nor Greek in Lucian but read my English letters and settled some accounts. Mr. Chamberlayne came from Appomattox and told me all was well there, thank God. He would dine with me whether I asked him or not and I ate roast beef. In the afternoon I weighed some money and settled some accounts till the evening and then took a walk about the plantation. Redskin Peter pretended he fell and hurt himself but it was dissimulation. I had a cow die this day. At night I read some Latin in Terence. Then I said my prayers and had good health, good thoughts, and good humor, thank God Almighty.

11. I rose about 7 o'clock and read two chapters in Hebrew and some Greek in Lucian. I said my prayers and ate boiled milk for breakfast. I danced my dance. It was not so cold as it has been because the wind came to south. My wife was a little indisposed with a cold. I settled several accounts and put many things in order till dinner. I ate some raspberries for dinner. In the afternoon I set my razor and then went into the new orchard and trimmed the trees till the evening and then I took a walk about the plantation. Redskin Peter was very well again after he had worn the bit 24 hours and went to work very actively. Before I came in I took a run for my health. At night I read some Latin in Terence. I said my prayers and had thoughts, good health, and good humor, thank God Almighty.

12. I rose about 8 o'clock and read two chapters in Hebrew and some Greek in Lucian. I said my prayers devoutly and ate boiled milk for breakfast. I danced my dance. Jacky's arm was almost well, thank God. The weather was warm but the wind was northeast. My wife was well again, thank God, and went about again as usual. I read some Latin in Terence till dinner and then I ate some roast pork. In the afternoon I went into the orchard and trimmed the young trees till I was called away by one of the girls who told me that Mr. Peter Butts would speak with me. His business was to desire me to get a sheriff's place for his brother and in order to persuade me to it told me several things of Ned and how he had once hindered my man Tony from paying 30 pounds for lying with an Indian wife. A man came from New Kent concerning a protested bill and he stayed here all night. In the evening I took a walk and at night read some Latin in Terence. I said my prayers and had good health, good thoughts, and good humor, thank God Almighty.

CURRICULUM OF A SOUTH CAROLINA SCHOOLMASTER (1728) From
Helen E. Livingston, "Thomas Morritt, Schoolmaster at the Charleston Free School, 1723–
1728," *Historical Magazine of the Protestant Episcopal Church,* vol. XIV, pp. 158-59.

The Latin tongue is the Intent of my Mission and for that Method I shall observe no other than what is usualy practis'd in other Gramer Schools in Engl^d. I shall chiefly use Lilly for the rudimental part & then I shall proceed to Sententia puerites, Corderii Colloquies, Latin Test., Erasmus, Ovid's Metamorphoses, Virgil, Horace, Lucius, Justine. Tacitus or Suetonius or Valerius Maximus & Claudian and as for the Greek Authors I shall teach such parts of Isocrates & Lucian's Dialog: as are usually published for the use of Schools, the Minor Poets with Hesiod's Greek Test. Homer & Euripides & in order to give the Boys a tast of Class Geography I shall cause to be read Dionysious Periegetis and Cluver Geographia and these I shall be somew^t particular upon to Compare them wth the modern Geography . . . Justin & others I shall cause to be frequently read & perused to give the boys a Tast of Cronology . . . Kennet's Goodwin and Potter's Antiquity shall be also read in order to be acquainted with the rights Customs & Ceremonies of the Antients these at Spare times or at home I shall endeavor to oblige the boys to read over together with the History of the Heathen Gods, Pantheon &c. but as for those boys wch I shall have constantly in the House wth me & such as are boarders I do intend besides these Books already menconed to make them read 3 times a week at least if not every night Classick History especialy such historians as we have Translated into our Language. those books I will cause to be read an hour at nights between 8 & 9 & I shall not omit at that time to instruct them in Cronology & Geography & teach them the use of the Globes. . . .

My method is to keep the boys in Corderii Colloq: & Bezas Test: so long till the same become familiar on openg to any part of before I put any other Books into their hands by wch means I find they are easily brot to be Capable of understanding Erasmus or Lucius. I have 10 Boys sent me out of the Country beside one that came from Philad^a & another that came from the Bahaman Islands which are Boarders & 10 Charity Boys recommended by the Com^{rs} two of wch are Mulatos in all 52 of wch I daily expect an Augmentation rather than a decrease.

The Middle Atlantic Colonies

INSTRUCTION FROM THE CLASSIS OF AMSTERDAM TO SCHOOLMASTERS IN THE DUTCH POSSESSIONS (1636)   From Thomas E. Finegan, ed., *Free Schools: A Documentary History of the Free School Movement in New York State* (New York, 1921), p. 16.

He is to instruct the youth both on shipboard and on land, in reading, writing, ciphering, and arithmetic, with all zeal and diligence; he is also to implant the fundamental principles of true Christian religion and salvation, by means of catechizing; he is to teach them the customary forms of prayers and also to accustom them to pray; he is to give heed to their manners, and bring these as far as possible to modesty and propriety, and to this end he is to maintain good discipline and order, and further to do all that is required of a good, diligent and faithful schoolmaster.

THE HIRING OF A TEACHER IN NEW NETHERLANDS (1637)   From Hugh Hastings, ed., *Ecclesiastical Records of the State of New York* (Albany, 1853–87), vol. I, p. 122.

Adam Rolands, having requested to go to New Netherland as a schoolmaster, reader (voorlezer), and precentor (voorsanger), was accepted, as recommended, upon his good testimonials and the trial of his gifts, on August 4, 1637; and was sent thither.

REQUEST OF THE RESIDENTS OF NEW NETHERLANDS FOR A
SCHOOL (1650)   From J. Franklin Jamson, ed., *Narratives of New Netherlands, 1609–1664* (New York, 1909), p. 353.

There should be a public school, provided with at least two good masters, so that first of all in so wild a country, where there are many loose people, the youth be well taught and brought up, not only in reading and writing, but also in the knowledge and fear of the Lord. As it is now, the school is kept very irregularly, one and another keeping it according to his pleasure and as long as he thinks proper. There ought also to be an almshouse and an orphan asylum, and other similar institutions.

THE LICENSING OF A TEACHER IN ALBANY (1665)   From Daniel Pratt, ed., *Annals of Public Education in the State of New York from 1626 to 1746* (Albany, 1872), p. 57.

Whereas, the teaching of the English tongue is necessary in this government; I have, therefore, thought fitt to give license to John Shutte to be the English Schoolmaster at Albany; And, upon condition that the said John Shutte shall not demand any more wages from each Schollar than is given by the Dutch to their Dutch Schoolmasters, I have further granted to the said John Shutte that hee shall bee the onely English Schoolmaster at Albany.

Given under my hand, at Fort James in New York, the 12th day of October, 1665.

       Rich'rd Nicolls.

PETITION BY JEWS FOR BURGHER RIGHT IN AMSTERDAM
(1657)   From American Jewish Historical Society, *Publications*, vol. XVIII, p. 36.

To the Noble Worships, the Director General
and Council of New Netherland

We, the undersigned, of the Jewish Nation here, make known, with due reverence, how that one of our Nation repaired to the City Hall of this City and requested of the Noble Burgomasters that he might obtain his Burgher certificate, like other Burghers, which to our great surprise was declined and refused by the Noble Burgomasters, and whereas the Worshipful Lords consented under date of

February 15, 1655, at the request of our Nation, that we should enjoy here the same freedom as other inhabitants of New Netherland enjoy, as appears from the petition here annexed; further that our Nation enjoys in the City of Amsterdam in Holland the Burgher right, and he who asks therefor receives a Burgher certificate there, as appears by the Burgher certificate hereto annexed; also that our Nation, as long as they have been here, have, with others, borne and paid, and still bear, all Burgher burdens: We, therefore, reverently request your Noble Worships to please not exclude nor shut us out from the Burgher right, but to notify the Noble Burgomasters that they should permit us, like other Burghers, to enjoy the Burgher right, and for this purpose to give us the customary Burgher certificate, in conformity with the order of the Worshipful Lords Directors above mentioned. Upon which, awaiting your Noble Worships' gracious and favorable apostille, we shall remain, as heretofore,

Below stood: Your Noble Worships' Humble Servants,
Salvador Dandrada, Jacob Cohen Henricques,
Abraham deLucena, Joseph d'Acosta.

On the above petition is apostilled:

The Burgomasters of this City are hereby authorized and at the same time charged to admit the petitioners herein and their Nation to the Burghership, in due form. Dated as above.
P. Stuyvesant, Nicasius deSille, Pieter Tonneman.

PETITION OF AMSTERDAM JEWS TO THE WEST INDIA COMPANY
(1655)   From American Jewish Historical Society, *Publications*, vol. XVIII, pp. 8-11.

The merchants of the Portuguese Nation residing in this City respectfully remonstrate to your Honors that it has come to their knowledge that your Honors raise obstacles to the giving of permits or passports to the Portuguese Jews to travel and to go to reside in New Netherland, which if persisted in will result to the great disadvantage of the Jewish nation. It also can be of no advantage to the general Company but rather damaging.

There are many of the nation who have lost their possessions at Pernambuco and have arrived from there in great poverty, and part of them have been dispersed here and there. So that your petitioners had to expend large sums of money for their necessaries of life, and through lack of opportunity all cannot remain here to live. And as they cannot go to Spain or Portugal because of the Inquisition, a great part of the aforesaid people must in time be obliged to depart for other territories of their High Mightinesses the States-General and their Companies, in order there, through their labor and efforts, to be able to exist under the protection of the administrators of your Honorable Directors, observing and obeying your Honors' orders and commands.

It is well known to your Honors that the Jewish nation in Brazil have at all times been faithful and have striven to guard and maintain that place, risking for that purpose their possessions and their blood.

Yonder land is extensive and spacious. The more of loyal people that go to live there, the better it is in regard to the population of the country as in regard to the payment of various excises and taxes which may be imposed there, and in regard to the increase of trade, and also to the importation of all the necessaries that may be sent there.

Your Honors should also consider that the Honorable Lords, the Burgomasters of the City and the Honorable High Illustrious Mighty Lords, the States-General, have in political matters always protected and considered the Jewish nation as upon the same footing as all the inhabitants and burghers. Also it is conditioned in the treaty of perpetual peace with the King of Spain that the Jewish nation shall also enjoy the same liberty as all other inhabitants of these lands.

Your Honors should also please consider that many of the Jewish nation are principal shareholders in the Company. They having always striven their best for the Company, and many of their nation have lost immense and great capital in its shares and obligations.

The Company has by a general resolution consented that those who wish to populate the Colony shall enjoy certain districts of land gratis. Why should now certain subjects of this State not be allowed to travel thither and live there? The French consent that the Portuguese Jews may traffic and live in Martinique, Christopher and others of their territories, whither also some have gone from here, as your Honors know. The English also consent at the present time that the Portuguese and Jewish nation may go from London and settle at Barbados, whither also some have gone.

As foreign nations consent that the Jewish nation may go to live and trade in their territories, how can your Honors forbid the same and refuse transportation to this Portuguese nation who reside here and have been settled here well on to sixty years, many also being born here and confirmed burghers, and this to a land that needs people for its increase?

Therefore the petitioners request, for the reasons given above (as also others which they omit to avoid prolixity), that your Honors be pleased not to exclude but to grant the Jewish nation passage to and residence in that country; otherwise this would result in a great prejudice to their reputation. Also that by an Apostille and Act the Jewish nation be permitted, together with other inhabitants, to travel, live and traffic there, and with them enjoy liberty on condition of contributing like others, &c. Which doing, &c.

The Petition Is Granted [April 26, 1655]

Therefore after many deliberations we have finally decided and resolved to apostille upon a certain petition presented by said Portuguese Jews that these people may travel and trade to and in New Netherland and live and remain there, provided the poor among them shall not become a burden to the company or to the community, but be supported by their own nation. You will now govern yourself accordingly.

NEW YORK'S GRANT OF RELIGIOUS TOLERATION (1683)
From Hugh Hastings, ed., *Ecclesiastical Records of the State of New York* (Albany, 1901), vol. II, pp. 864-65.

That no person or persons, which profess faith in God by Jesus Christ, shall at any time, be any ways molested, punished, disquieted, or called in question for any difference in opinion or matter of religious concernment, who do not actually disturb the civill peace of the Province, but that all and every such person or persons may, from time to time, and at all times freely have and fully enjoy his or their judgements or consciences in matters of religion throughout all the Province, they behaving themselves peaceably and quietly and not using this liberty to Licentiousnesse nor to the civill injury or outward disturbance of others. . . .

And whereas all the respective Christian Churches now in practice within the City of New York, and the other places of this Province, do appear to be privileged [sic] Churches, and have been soe established and confirmed by the former authority of this Government; Bee it hereby enacted by this present Generall Assembly, and by the Authority thereof, That all the said respective Christian Churches be hereby confirmed therein, and thatt they and every of them shall from henceforth, forever, be held and reputed as privileged Churches, and enjoy all their former freedoms of their religion in Divine Worship and Church Discipline; and thatt all former contracts made and agreed on for the maintenences of the several ministers of the said Churches, shall stand and continue in full force and vertue, and thatt all Contracts for the future to be made, shall be of the same power; and all persons that are unwilling to perform their part of the said contract shall be constrained thereunto by a warrant from any Justice of the Peace; Provided it be under forty shillings, or otherwise, as the law directs; Provided also That all other Christian Churches that shall hereafter come and settle within this Province, shall have the same privileges.

TOLERATION OF RELIGION ACT IN MARYLAND (1649)
From W. H. Browne, ed., *The Archives of Maryland* (Baltimore, 1883–   ), vol. I, pp. 244-47.

And whereas the inforceing of the conscience in matters of Religion hath frequently fallen out to be of dangerous Consequence in those commonwealthes where it hath been practiced, And for the more quiett and peaceable governement of this Province, and the better to preserve mutuall Love and amity amongst the Inhabitants thereof. Be it Therefore . . . enacted (except as in this present Act is before Declared and sett forth) that noe person or persons whatsoever within this Province, or the Islands, Ports, Harbors, Creekes, or havens thereunto belonging professing to believe in Jesus Christ, shall from henceforth bee any waies troubled, Molested or discountenanced for or in respect of his or her religion nor in the free exercise thereof within this Province or the Islands thereunto belonging nor any way compelled to the beleife or exercise of any other Religion against his or her consent, soe as they be not unfaithful to the Lord Proprietary, or molest or conspire against the civil Government established or to bee established in this Province under him or his heires. And that all & every person and persons that shall presume Contrary to this Act and the true intent and meaning thereof directly or indirectly either in person or estate willfully to wronge disturbe trouble or molest any person whatsoever within this Province professing to believe in Jesus Christ for or in respect of his or her religion or the free exercise thereof within this Province other than is provided for in this Act that such person or persons soe offending, shalbe compelled to pay trebble damages to the party soe wronged or molested, and for every such offence shall also forfeit 20^s sterling in money or the value thereof . . . , Or if the parties soe offending as aforesaid shall refuse or bee unable to recompense the party soe wronged, or to satisfy such ffyne or forfeiture, then such offender shalbe severely punished by publick whipping & imprisonment during the pleasure of the Lord proprietary, or his Leiuetenant or cheife Governor of this Province for the tyme being without baile or maineprise.

A WILL AND TESTAMENT ON BEHALF OF CATHOLIC EDUCATION IN MARYLAND (1653)   From J. A. Burns, *The Catholic School System in the United States* (New York, 1908), pp. 96-97.

The Last Will and Testament of Edward Cotton made the 4th of April 1653 he having perfect sense and memory as followeth. First, I give and bequeath my soul to God my Maker and Redeemer to the fellowship of all the holy Angells and Saints and my body to the earth from whence it came to be decently buried with all Christian Rites and Ceremonies according to my quality. . . .   Thirdly, I doe appoint my Loving friends Thomas Mathews and Ralph Crouch my Executors Equally to have Power to take and Dispose of all my whole Estate whatsoever in manner and form as followeth, not to be accountable unto any person or persons whatsoever. First, to pay all my Debts whatsoever in the first Place. Secondly, to sett my man David Thomas free at the time of my Death, provided that he do discharge my Executors from a bill of Fifteen hundred weight of Tobacco which I am bound for unto Walter Beane. Thirdly, to give unto Mr. Starkey [the parish priest at Newtown] my old Chestnut Colloured Mare and my horse now 3 years old, this Spring . . . Ninthly, I doe give all my female Cattle and their Increase for Ever to be disposed of by my aforesaid Executors as they shall think fitt unto charitable uses which may be most to God's honor, the Stock to be preserved and the Profitt to be made use of to the use of a schooll, if they shall think convenient, and for the Male Cattle that are or that hereafter shall encrease I doe give to the aforesaid use reserving to my aforesaid Executors the privilege to Kill for their own use some of the Male Cattle, the better to Enable them to do Charitable offices presuming that they will make no Waste contrary to this my Will and all the rest of my estate to be disposed of as aforesaid to good uses as they shall think fitt. . . . Eleventhly, I doe give them power to appoint at their death some other faithful person in their stead whom they shall think fitt with the same power as they or he hath. Twelfthly, my desire is if they shall think Convenient that the Schooll be kept at Newtowne, and that the Cattle may be in the Care of John Warren upon such agreement as my Executors shall make Provided that this my desire do not hinder them from doing a greater good to the honour of God otherwise which I do leave absolute in their power and to their Discretion. . . .

In Witness whereof I have hereunto sett my hand.

EDWARD COTTON.

A NEW JERSEY APPRENTICE CONTRACT (1680) From New Jersey Historical Society, *Proceedings*, New Series, vol. XV, pp. 269-70.

This indenture made the first day of May in the year of our Lord 1680. Between Nathaniel Bunn of the town of Woodbridge, in the province of New Jersey, by and with the consent of his mother Hester Bunn, widow, the one party, and Bernerd Filder of the abovesaid town and province, potter, the other party, witnesseth that the above-named Nathaniel Bunn, by and with the consent of his mother abovesaid, doth by these presents covenant, agree and bind himself an apprentice unto the above-named Bernerd Filder until the abovesaid Nathaniel be of the age of one and twenty years, which will be the five and twentieth day of March, one thousand six hundred eighty and six, during which time of five years, ten months and upwards, the abovesaid Nathaniel doth by these presents engage to be true and faithful in his said master's service, and mistress's during her widowhood and not longer; his master and mistress's secrets to keep and not purloin or embezzle any of his master's estate, nor consent to the purloining or embezzlement of any part thereof by any person or persons whatsoever, his said master's lawful commands obey and not absent himself from his master's service, neither by day nor night, without his said master's leave, but in all things behave himself as a faithful apprentice ought to do during the full time and term abovesaid.

In consideration whereof the above-named Bernerd Filder doth by these presents covenant, promise, and engage to find and allow the above-named Nathaniel Bunn, during the time and term abovesaid, sufficient meat, drink, washing, and lodging, and at the expiration of the term abovesaid to allow him two suits of apparel, one of good cloth or stuff fit for holy days, and to pay or cause to be paid unto him, the abovesaid Nathaniel, the full and just sum of five pounds sterling, in good pay of this country, and the abovesaid Bernerd doth by these presents engage not to sell the said Nathaniel to any man whatsoever, nor to carry him out of this government of New Jersey, except into the government of New York, or some part of New England, and the abovesaid Bernerd doth by these presents engage to learn, teach, and instruct the abovesaid Nathaniel the art, trade, and mystery of a potter and of tile making, if he goes upon that, and also to teach him to write and cipher, and if the said Bernerd should marry and decease within the time abovesaid, then the abovesaid Nathaniel to serve his mistress during the time of her widowhood and no longer. In witness whereof the parties to these presents have interchangeably set, too, their hands and seal the day and year above-written and the said Bernerd is to let the abovesaid Nathaniel, at his going away from him, have his military arms that the said Nathaniel trains with whilst an apprentice and furnish him with a new Bible.

A PENNSYLVANIA EDUCATION LAW (1683)   From J. P. Wickersham, *History of Education in Pennsylvania* (Lancaster, Pa., 1886), p. 39.

And to the end that poor as well as rich may be instructed in good and commendable learning, which is to be preferred before wealth, *Be it enacted, etc.*, That all persons in this Province and Territories thereof, having children, and all guardians and trustees of orphans, shall cause such to be instructed in reading and writing, so that they may be able to read the Scriptures and to write by the time they attain to twelve years of age; and that then they be taught some useful trade or skill, that the poor may work to live, and the rich if they become poor may not want: of which every County Court shall take care. And in case such parents, guardians, or overseers shall be found deficient in this respect, every such parent, guardian, or overseer shall pay for every such child, five pounds, except there should appear an incapacity in body or understanding to hinder it.

ESTABLISHMENT OF THE FIRST SCHOOL IN PHILADELPHIA
(1683)   From "Minutes of the Pennsylvania Colonial Council," as quoted in J. P. Wickersham, *History of Education in Pennsylvania* (Lancaster, Pa., 1886), p. 41.

At a Council held at Philadelphia, ye 26th of ye 10th month, 1683. Present: Wm. Penn, Propor & Govr., Theo. Holmes, Wm. Haigue, Lasse Cock, Wm. Clayton.

The Govr and Provll Councill having taken into their Serious Consideration the great Necessity there is of a School Master for ye instruction & Sober Education of youth in the towne of Philadelphia, Sent for Enock flower, an Inhabitant of the Said Towne, who for twenty Year past hath been exercised in that care and imployment in England, to whom haveing Communicated their Minds, he Embraced it upon the following Terms: to Learne to read English 4s by the Quarter, to Learne to read and write 6s by ye Quarter, to learne to read, Write and Cast accot 8s by ye Quarter; for Boarding a Scholler, that is to say, dyet, Washing, Lodging, & Scooling, Tenn pounds for one whole year.

THOMAS BUDD RECOMMENDS A SYSTEM OF PUBLIC SCHOOLS TO TEACH ACADEMIC SUBJECTS AND TRADES IN PENNSYLVANIA

(**1685**)   From Thomas Budd, *Good Order Established in Pennsylvania and New Jersey,* Frederick J. Shepard, ed. (Cleveland, 1902), pp. 43-49.

Now it might be well if a Law were made by the Governours and general Assemblies of Pennsilvania and New-Jersey, that all Persons inhabiting in the said Provinces, do put their Children seven years to the publick School, or longer, if the Parents please.

2. That Schools be provided in all Towns and Cities, and persons of known honesty, skill and understanding be yearly chosen by the Governour and General Assembly, to teach and instruct Boys and Girls in all the most useful Arts and Sciences that they in their youthful capacities may be capable to understand, as the learning to Read and Write true English, Latine, and other useful Speeches and Languages, and fair Writing, Arithmatick and Book-keeping; and the Boys to be taught and instructed in some Mystery or Trade, as the making of Mathematical Instruments, Joynery, Turnery, the making of Clocks and Watches, Weaving, Shoe-making, or any other useful Trade or Mystery that the School is capable of teaching; and the Girls to be taught and instructed in Spinning of Flax and Wool, and Knitting of Gloves and Stockings, Sewing, and making of all sorts of useful Needle-Work, and the making of Straw-Work, as Hats, Baskets, &c. or any other useful Art or Mystery that the School is capable of teaching.

3. That the Scholars be kept in the Morning two hours at Reading, Writing, Book-keeping, &c. and other two hours at work in that Art, Mystery or Trade that he or she most delighteth in, and then let them have two hours to dine, and for Recreation; and in the afternoon two hours at Reading, Writing, &c. and the other two hours at work at their several Imployments.

4. The seventh day of the Week the Scholars may come to school only in the fore-noon, and at a certain hour in the afternoon let a Meeting be kept by the School-masters and their Scholars, where after good instruction and admonition is given by the Masters, to the Scholars and thanks returned to the Lord for his Mercies and Blessings that are daily received from him, then let a strict examination be made by the Masters, of the Conversation of the Scholars in the week past, and let reproof, admonition and correction be given to the Offendors, according to the quantity and quality of their faults.

5. Let the like Meetings be kept by the School-Mistresses, and the Girls apart from the Boys. By strictly observing this good order, our Children will be hindred of running into that Excess of Riot and Wickedness that youth is incident to, and they will be a comfort to their tender Parents.

6. Let one thousand Acres of Land be given and laid out in a good place, to every publick School that shall be set up, and the Rent or incom of it to go towards the defraying of the charge of the School.

7. And to the end that the Children of poor People, and the Children of Indians may have the like good Learning with the Children of Rich People, let them be maintained free of charge to their Parents, out of the Profits of the school, arising by the Work of the Scholars, by which the Poor and the Indians, as well as the Rich, will have their Children taught, and the Remainder of the Profits, if any be, to be

disposed of in the building of School-houses, and Improvements on the thousand Acres of Land, which belongs to the School.

WILLIAM PENN ON EDUCATION (1693) From William Penn, *Some Fruits of Solitude in Reflections and Maxims,* Edmund Gosse, ed. (London, 1901), pp. 1-6.

Ignorance

It is admirable to consider how many Millions of People come into, and go out of the World, Ignorant of themselves, and of the World they have lived in.

2. If one went to see Windsor-Castle, or Hampton-Court, it would be strange not to observe and remember the Situation, the Building, the Gardens, Fountains, &c. that make up the Beauty and Pleasure of such a Seat? And yet few People know themselves; No, not their own Bodies, the Houses of their Minds, the most curious Structure of the World; a living walking Tabernacle: Nor the World of which it was made, and out of which it is fed; which would be so much our Benefit, as well as our Pleasure, to know. We cannot doubt of this when we are told that the Invisible Things of God are brought to light by the Things that are seen; and consequently we read our Duty in them as often as we look upon them, to him that is the Great and Wise Author of them, if we look as we should do.

3. The World is certainly a great and stately Volume of natural Things; and may be not improperly styled the Hieroglyphicks of a better: But, alas! how very few Leaves of it do we seriously turn over! This ought to be the Subject of the Education of our Youth, who, at Twenty, when they should be fit for business, know little or nothing of it.

Education

4. We are in Pain to make them Scholars, but not Men! To talk, rather than to know, which is true Canting.

5. The first Thing obvious to Children is what is Sensible; and that we make no Part of their Rudiments.

6. We press their Memory too soon, and puzzle, strain and load them with Words and Rules; to know Grammer and Rhetorick, and a strange Tongue or two, that it is ten to one may never be useful to them; Leaving their natural Genius to Mechanical and Physical, or natural Knowledge uncultivated and neglected; which would be of exceeding Use and Pleasure to them through the whole Course of their Life.

7. To be sure, Languages are not to be despised or neglected. But Things are still to be preferred.

8. Children had rather be making of Tools and Instruments of Play; Shaping, Drawing, Framing, and Building, &c. than getting some Rules of Propriety of Speech by Heart: And those also would follow with more Judgment, and less Trouble and Time.

9. It were Happy if we studied Nature more in natural Things; and acted according to Nature; whose Rules are few, plain and most reasonable.

10. Let us begin where she begins, go her Pace, and close always where she ends, and we cannot miss of being good Naturalists.

11. The Creation would not be longer a Riddle to us: The Heavens, Earth, and Waters, with their respective, various and numerous Inhabitants: Their Productions, Natures, Seasons, Sympathies and Antipathies; their Use, Benefit and Pleasure, would be better understood by us: And an eternal Wisdom, Power, Majesty and Goodness, very conspicuous to us, thro' those sensible and passing Forms: The World wearing the Mark of its Maker, whose Stamp is everywhere visible, and the Characters very legible to the Children of Wisdom.

12. And it would go a great way to caution and direct People in their Use of the World, that they were better studied and known in the Creation of it.

13. For how could Man find the Confidence to abuse it, while they should see the Great Creator stare them in the Face, in all and every Part thereof?

14. Their Ignorance makes them insensible, and that Insensibility hardly in misusing this noble Creation, that has the Stamp and Voice of a Deity every where, and in every Thing to the Observing.

15. It is pity therefore that Books have not been composed for Youth, by some curious and careful Naturalists, and also Mechanicks, in the Latin Tongue, to be used in Schools, that they might learn Things with Words: Things obvious and familiar to them, and which would make the Tongue easier to be obtained by them.

16. Many able Gardiners and Husbandmen are yet Ignorant of the Reason of their Calling; as most Artificers are of the Reason of their own Rules that govern their excellent Workmanship. But a Naturalist and Mechanick of this sort, is Master of the Reason of both, and might be of the Practice too, if his Industry kept pace with his Speculation; which were very commendable; and without which he cannot be said to be a complete Naturalist or Mechanick.

17. Finally, if Man be the Index or Epitomy of the World, as Philosophers tell us, we have only to read our selves to be learned in it. But because there is nothing we less regard than the Characters of the Power that made us, which are so clearly written upon us and the World he has given us, and can best tell us what we are and should be, we are even Strangers to our own Genius: The Glass in which we should see that true instructing and agreeable Variety, which is to be observed in Nature, to the Admiration of that Wisdom and Adoration of that Power which made us all.

The New England Colonies

THE ACT AGAINST PURITANS (1593) From 35 Elizabeth, Cap. I, as quoted in Henry Gee and W. J. Hardy, eds., *Documents Illustrative of English Church History* (London, 1921), pp. 492-95.

For the preventing and avoiding of such great inconveniencies and perils as might happen and grow by the wicked and dangerous practices of seditious sectaries and disloyal persons; be it enacted by the Queen's most excellent majesty, and by the Lords spiritual and temporal, and the Commons, in this present Parliament assembled, and by the authority of the same, that if any person or persons above the age of sixteen years, which shall obstinately refuse to repair to some church, chapel, or usual place of common prayer, to hear divine service established by her majesty's laws and statutes in that behalf made, and shall forbear to do the same by the space of a month next after, without lawful cause, shall at any time after forty days next after the end of this session of Parliament, by printing, writing, or express words or speeches, advisedly and purposely practise or go about to move or persuade any of her majesty's subjects, or any other within her highness's realms or dominions, to deny, withstand, and impugn her majesty's power and authority in causes ecclesiastical, united, and annexed to the imperial crown of this realm; or to that end or purpose shall advisedly and maliciously move or persuade any other person whatsoever to forbear or abstain from coming to church to hear divine service, or to receive the communion according to her majesty's laws and statutes aforesaid, or to come to or be present at any unlawful assemblies, conventicles, or meetings, under colour or pretence of any exercise of religion, contrary to her majesty's said laws and statutes; or if any person or persons which shall obstinately refuse to repair to some church, chapel, or usual place of common prayer, and shall forbear by the space of a month to hear divine service, as is aforesaid, shall after the said forty days, either of him or themselves, or by the motion, persuasion, enticement, or allurement of any other, willingly join, or be present at, any such assemblies, conventicles, or meetings, under colour or pretence of any such exercise of religion, contrary to the laws and statutes of this realm, as is aforesaid; that then every such person so offending as aforesaid, and being thereof lawfully convicted, shall be committed to prison, there to remain without bail or mainprise, until they shall conform and yield themselves to come to some church, chapel, or usual place of common prayer, and hear divine service, according to her majesty's laws and statutes aforesaid, and to make such open submission and declaration of their said conformity, as hereafter in this Act is declared and appointed.

COLONIALS

363

Provided always, and be it further enacted by the authority aforesaid, that if any such person or persons, which shall offend against this Act as aforesaid, shall not within three months next after they shall be convicted of their said offence, conform themselves to the obedience of the laws and statutes of this realm, in coming to the church to hear divine service, and in making such public confession and submission, as hereafter in this Act is appointed and expressed, being thereunto required by the bishop of the diocese, or any justice of the peace of the county where the same person shall happen to be, or by the minister or curate of the parish; that in every such case every such offender, being thereunto warned or required by any justice of the peace of the same county where such offender shall then be, shall upon his and their corporal oath before the justices of the peace in the open quarter sessions of the same county, or at the assizes and gaol-delivery of the same county, before the justices of the same assizes and gaol-delivery, abjure this realm of England, and all other the queen's majesty's dominions for ever, unless her majesty shall license the party to return, and thereupon shall depart out of this realm at such haven or port, and within such time, as shall in that behalf be assigned and appointed by the said justices before whom such abjuration shall be made, unless the same offender be letted or stayed by such lawful and reasonable means or causes, as by the common laws of this realm are permitted and allowed in cases of abjuration for felony; and in such cases of let or stay, then within such reasonable and convenient time after, as the common law requires in case of abjuration for felony, as is aforesaid; and that the justices of peace before whom any such abjuration shall happen to be made, as is aforesaid, shall cause the same presently to be entered of record before them, and shall certify the same to the justices of assizes and gaol-delivery of the said county, at the next assizes or gaol-delivery to be holden in the same county.

And if any such offender, which by the tenor and intent of this Act is to be abjured as is aforesaid, shall refuse to make such abjuration as is aforesaid, or after such abjuration made, shall not go to such haven, and within such time as is before appointed, and from thence depart out of this realm, according to this present Act, or after such his departure shall return or come again into any her majesty's realms or dominions, without her majesty's special licence in that behalf first had and obtained; that then, in every such case, the person so offending shall be adjudged a felon, and shall suffer as in case of felony, without benefit of clergy.

And furthermore be it enacted by the authority of this present Parliament, that if any person or persons that shall at any time hereafter offend against this Act, shall before he or they be so warned or required to make abjuration according to the tenor of this Act, repair to some parish church on some Sunday or other festival day, and then and there hear divine service, and at service-time, before the sermon, or reading of the gospel, make public and open submission and declaration of his and their conformity to her majesty's laws and statutes, as hereafter in this Act is declared and appointed; that then the same offender shall thereupon be clearly discharged of and from all and every the penalties and punishments inflicted or imposed by this Act for any of the offences aforesaid.

JOHN WINTHROP ON THE PURITAN MISSION (1630) From "A Modell of Christian Charity," as quoted in *The Winthrop Papers* (Boston, 1929), vol. II, pp. 282-84, 292-95.

A Modell of Christian Charity

WRITTEN
ON BOARDE THE ARRABELLA,
ON THE ATTLANTICK OCEAN.

By the Honorable John Winthrop Esquire.

In His passage, (with the great Company of Religious people, of which Christian Tribes he was the Brave Leader and famous Governor;) from the Island of Great Britaine, to New-England in the North America.

Anno 1630.

Christian Charitie

A MODELL HEREOF.

God Almightie in his most holy and wise providence hath soe disposed of the Condicion of mankinde, as in all times some must be rich some poore, some highe and eminent in power and dignitie; others meane and in subieccion.

❊   ❊   ❊

This Lawe of the Gospell propoundes likewise a difference of seasons and occasions there is a time when a christian must sell all and giue to the poore as they did in the Apostles times. There is a tyme allsoe when a christian (though they giue not all yet) must giue beyond theire abillity, as they of Macedonia. Cor: 2. 6. likewise community of perills calls for extraordinary liberallity and soe doth Community in some speciall seruice for the Churche. Lastly, when there is noe other meanes whereby our Christian brother may be releiued in this distresse, wee must help him beyond our ability, rather then tempt God, in putting him vpon help by miraculous or extraordinary meanes.

❊   ❊   ❊

It rests now to make some applicacion of this discourse by the present designe which gaue the occasion of writeing of it. Herein are 4 things to be propounded: first the persons, 2ly, the worke, 3ly, the end, 4ly the meanes.

1. For the persons, wee are a Company professing our selues fellow members of Christ, In which respect onely though wee were absent from eache other many miles, and had our imploymentes as farre distant, yet wee ought to account our selues knitt together by this bond of loue, and liue in the exercise of it, if wee would haue comforte of our being in Christ, this was notorious in the practise of the Christians in former times, as is testified of the Waldenses from the mouth of one of the adversaries Aeneas Syluius, mutuo [solent amare] pene antequam norint, they vse to loue any of theire owne religion even before they were acquainted with them.

2ly. for the worke wee haue in hand, it is by a mutuall consent through a speciall overruleing providence, and a more then an ordinary approbation of the Churches of Christ to seeke out a place of Cohabitation and Consorteshipp vnder a due forme of Government both ciuill and ecclesiasticall. In such cases as this the care of the publique must oversway all private respects, by which not onely conscience, but meare Ciuill policy doth binde vs; for it is a true rule that perticuler estates cannott subsist in the ruine of the publique.

3ly. The end is to improue our liues to doe more seruice to the Lord the comforte and encrease of the body of christe whereof wee are members that our selues and posterity may be the better preserued from the Common corrupcions of this euill world to serue the Lord and worke out our Salvacion vnder the power and purity of his holy Ordinances.

4ly for the meanes whereby this must bee effected, they are 2fold, a Conformity with the worke and end wee aime at, these wee see are extraordinary, therefore wee must not content our selues with vsuall ordinary meanes whatsoever wee did or ought to haue done when wee liued in England, the same must wee doe and more allsoe where wee goe: That which the most in theire Churches maineteine as a truthe in profession onely, wee must bring into familiar and constant practise, as in this duty of loue wee must loue brotherly without dissimulation, wee must loue one another with a pure hearte feruently wee must beare one anothers burthens, wee must not looke onely on our owne things, but allsoe on the things of our brethren, neither must wee think that the lord will beare with such faileings at our hands as hee dothe from those among whome wee haue lived. . . . Thus stands the cause betweene God and vs, wee are entered into Covenant with him for this worke, wee haue taken out a Commission, the Lord hath giuen vs leaue to drawe our owne Articles wee haue professed to enterprise these Accions vpon these and these ends, wee haue herevpon besought him of favour and blessing: Now if the Lord shall please to heare vs, and bring vs in peace to the place wee desire, then hath hee ratified this Covenant and sealed our Commission, [and] will expect a strickt performance of the Articles contained in it, but if wee shall neglect the observacion of these Articles which are the ends wee haue propounded, and dissembling with our God, shall fall to embrace this present world and prosecute our carnall intencions, seekeing great things for our selues and our posterity, the Lord will surely breake out in wrathe against vs be revenged of such a periured people and make vs knowe the price of the breache of such a Covenant.

Now the onely way to avoyde this shipwracke and to provide for our posterity is to followe the Counsell of Micah, to doe Justly, to loue mercy, to walke humbly with our God, for this end, wee must be knitt together in this worke as one man, wee must entertaine each other in brotherly Afeccion, wee must be willing to abridge our selues of our superfluities, for the supply of others necessities, wee must vphold a familiar Commerce together in all meekenes, gentlenes, patience and liberallity, wee must delight in eache other, make others Condicions our owne reioyce together, mourne together, labour, and suffer together, allwayes haueing before our eyes our Commission and Community in the worke, our Community as members of the same body, soe shall wee keepe the vnitie of the spirit in the bond of peace, the Lord will be our God and delight to dwell among vs, as his owne people and will commaund a blessing vpon vs in all our wayes, soe that wee shall see much more of his wisdome power goodnes and truthe then formerly wee haue beene acquainted with, wee shall finde that the God of Israell is among vs, when tenn of vs shall be able to resist a thousand of our enemies, when hee shall make vs a prayse and glory, that men shall say of succeeding plantacions: the lord make it like that of New England: for wee must Consider that wee shall be as a Citty vpon a Hill, the eies of all people are vppon vs; soe that if wee shall deale falsely with our god in this worke wee haue vndertaken and soe cause him to withdrawe his present help from vs, wee shall be made a story and a by-word through the world, wee shall open the mouthes of enemies to speake euill of the wayes of god and all professours for Gods sake; wee shall shame the faces of many of gods worthy seruants, and cause theire prayers to be turned in Cursses vpon vs till wee be consumed out of the good land whether wee are goeing: And to shutt vpp this discourse with that exhortacion of Moses that faithfull seruant of the Lord in his last farewell to Israell Deut. 30. Beloued there is now sett before vs life, and good, deathe and euill in that wee are Commaunded this day to loue the Lord our God, and to loue one another to walke in his wayes and to keepe his Commaundements and his Ordinance, and his lawes, and the Articles of our Covenant with him that wee may liue and be multiplyed, and that the Lord our God may blesse vs in the land whether wee goe to possesse it: But if our heartes shall turne away soe that wee will not obey, but shall be seduced and worshipp [serue cancelled] other Gods our pleasures, and proffitts, and serue them; it is propounded vnto vs this day, wee shall surely perishe out of the good Land whether wee passe over this vast Sea to possesse it;

Therefore lett vs choose life,
that wee, and our Seede,
may liue; by obeyeing his
voyce, and cleaueing to him,
for hee is our life, and
our prosperity.

AN ANTI-CATHOLIC LAW OF MASSACHUSETTS BAY (1647)   From Nathaniel B. Shurtleff, ed., *Records of the Governor and Company of Massachusetts Bay, 1628–1686*, (Boston, 1853–1854), vol. III, p. 112.

This Court, taking into consideration the great warrs & combustions which are this day in Europe, & that the same are obserued to be cheifly raysed & fomented by the secrit practises of those of the Jesuiticall order, for the prevention of like euills amongst o^{r}selues, its ordred, by the authorities of this Court, that no Jesuit or ecclesiasticall pson ordayned by ye authoritie of the pope shall henceforth come wthin o^r jurisdiction; & if any pson shall give any cause of suspision that he is one of such societie, he shalbe brought before some of the magists, & if he cannot free himselfe of such suspitio, he shalbe comitted or bound on to the next Court of Assistants, to be tried & proceeded with by banish^{nt} or otherwise, as the Court shall see cause, & if any such pson so banished shalbe taken the 2d time wthin this jurisdiction, he shall vppon lawfull triall & conviction, be put to death; pvided this law shall not extend to any such Jesuit as shalbe cast vppon o^r shores by shippwrack or other accydent, so as he contynew no longer then he may haue opptunitie of passage for his departure, nor to any such as shall come in company wth any messenger sent hither vppon publick occasions, or any marchant or master of any shipp belonging to any place not in enmitie wth the state of England or o^rselves, so as they depart agayne wth the same messenger, marchant, or m^r, & behaue themselues inoffenciuely duringe their abode here.

LETTER ON TOLERANCE FROM ROGER WILLIAMS TO THE TOWN OF PROVIDENCE (1655)   From *Publications of the Narragansett Club,* vol. VI, pp. 278-79.

That ever I should speak or write a tittle, that tends to such an infinite liberty of conscience, is a mistake, and which I have ever disclaimed and abhorred. To prevent such mistakes, I shall at present only propose this case: There goes many a ship to sea, with many hundred souls in one ship, whose weal or woe is common, and is a true picture of a commonwealth, or a human combination or society. It hath fallen out sometimes, that both papists and protestants, Jews and Turks, may be embarked in one ship; upon which suppose I affirm, that all the liberty of conscience, that ever I pleaded for, turns upon these two hinges—that none of the papists, protestants, Jews, or Turks, be forced to come to the ship's prayers or worship, nor compelled from their own particular prayers or worship, if they practice any. I further add, that I never denied, that notwithstanding this liberty, the commander of this ship ought to command the ship's course, yea, and also command that justice, peace and sobriety, be kept and practiced, both among the seamen and all the passengers. If any of the seamen refuse to perform their services, or passengers to pay their freight; if any refuse to help, in person or purse, towards the common charges or defence; if any refuse to obey the common laws and orders of the ship, concerning their common peace or preservation; if any shall mutiny and rise up against their commanders and officers; if any should preach or write that there ought to be no commanders or officers, because all are equal in Christ, therefore no masters nor officers, no laws nor orders, nor corrections nor punishments;—I say, I never denied, but in such cases, whatever is pretended, the commander or commanders may judge, resist, compel and punish such transgressors, according to their deserts and merits. This if seriously and honestly minded, may, if it so please the Father of lights, let in some light to such as willingly shut not their eyes.

I remain studious of your common peace and liberty.

ROGER WILLIAMS ON TRUTH AND CONSCIENCE (c. 1665)   From
Publications of the Narragansett Club, vol. III, pp. 216-17.

The Bloudy Tenent of Persecution
To Every Courteous Reader

While I plead the Cause of Truth and Innocencie against the bloody Doctrine of Persecution for cause of conscience, I judge it not unfit to give alarme to my selfe, and all men to prepare to be persecuted or hunted for cause of conscience.

Whether thou standest charged with 10 or but 2 Talents, if thou huntest any for cause of conscience, how canst thou say thou followest the Lambe of God who so abhorr'd that practice? . . .

Who can now but expect that after so many scores of yeares preaching and professing of more Truth, and amongst so many great contentions amongst the very best of Protestants, a fierie furnace should be heat, and who sees not now the fires kindling?

I confesse I have little hopes till those flames are over, that this Discourse against the doctrine of persecution for cause of conscience should passe currant (I say not amongst the Wolves and Lions, but even amongst the Sheep of Christ themselves) yet *liberavi animam meam,* I have not hid within my breast my souls belief: And although sleeping on the bed either of the pleasures or profits of sinne thou thinkest thy conscience bound to smite at him that dares to waken thee? Yet in the middest of all these civill and spirituall Wars (I hope we shall agree in these particulars.)

First, how ever the proud (upon the advantage of an higher earth or ground) or'elooke the poore and cry out Schismatickes, Hereticks, &c. shall blasphemers and seducers scape unpunished? &c. Yet there is a sorer punishment in the Gospel for despising of Christ then Moses, even when the despiser of Moses was put to death without mercie, Heb. 10.28,29. He that beleeveth not shall bee damned, Marke 16.16.

Secondly, what ever Worship, Ministry, Ministration, the best and purest are practised without faith and true perswasion that they are the true institutions of God, they are sin, sinfull worships, Ministries, &c. And however in Civill things we may be servants unto men, yet in Divine and Spirituall things the poorest pesant must disdaine the service of the highest Prince: Be ye not the servants of men, I Cor. 14.

Thirdly, without search and triall no man attaines this faith and right perswasion, I Thes. 5. Try all things.

In vaine have English Parliaments permitted English Bibles in the poorest English houses, and the simplest man or woman to search the Scriptures, if yet against their soules perswasion from the Scripture, they should be forced (as if they lived in Spaine or Rome it selfe without the sight of a Bible) to beleeve as the Church beleeves.

Fourthly, having tried, we must hold fast, I Thessal. 5. upon the losse of a Crowne, Revel. 13. we must not let goe for all the flea bitings of the present afflictions, &c. having bought Truth deare, we must not sell it cheape, not the least graine of it for the whole World, no not for the saving of Soules, though our owne most precious; least of all for the bitter sweetning of a little vanishing pleasure.

COLONIALS

For a little puffe of credit and reputation from the changeable breath of uncertaine sons of men.

For the broken bagges of Riches on Eagles wings: For a dreame of these, any or all of these which on our death-bed vanish and leave tormenting stings behinde them: Oh how much better is it from the love of Truth, from the love of the Father of lights, from whence it comes, from the love of the Sonne of God, who is the way and the Truth, to say as he, John 18. 37. For this end was I borne, and for this end came I into the World that I might beare witnesse to the Truth.

INSTRUCTIONS FOR THE PUNISHMENT OF INCORRIGIBLE CHILDREN IN CONNECTICUT (1642)   From J. Hammond Trumbull, ed., *Public Records of the Colony of Connecticut* (Hartford, 1850), vol. I, p. 78.

Forasmuch as incorrigeableness is also adjudged to be a sin of death, but no law yet amongst us [has been] established for the execution thereof: For the preventing [of] that great evil it is ordered, that whatsoever child or servant within these liberties shall be convicted of any stubborn or rebellious carriage against their parents or governors, which is a forerunner of the forementioned evil, the Governor or any two Magistrates have liberty and power from this Court to commit such person or persons to the house of correction, and there to remain under hard labor and severe punishment so long as the Court or the major part of the Magistrates shall judge meet.

INSTRUCTIONS FOR THE PUNISHMENT OF INCORRIGIBLE CHILDREN IN MASSACHUSETTS (1646)   From Nathaniel B. Shurtleff, ed., *Records of the Governor and Company of Massachusetts Bay, 1628–1686* (Boston, 1853–1854), vol. III, p. 101.

If any child[ren] above sixteen years old and of sufficient understanding shall curse or smite their natural father or mother, they shall be put to death, unless it can be sufficiently testified that the parents have been very unchristianly negligent in the education of such children, or so provoked them by extreme and cruel correction that they have been forced thereunto to preserve themselves from death or maiming. . . .

If a man have a stubborn or rebellious son of sufficient years of understanding, viz. sixteen, which will not obey the voice of his father or the voice of his mother, and that when they have chastened him will not harken unto them, then shall his father and mother, being his natural parents, lay hold on him and bring him to the magistrates assembled in Court, and testify to them by sufficient evidence that this their son is stubborn and rebellious and will not obey their voice and chastisement, but lives in sundry notorious crimes. Such a son shall be put to death.

MICHAEL WIGGLESWORTH, "THE DAY OF DOOM" (1662)   From the *Proceedings of the Massachusetts Historical Society*, vol. XII, pp. 83-93.

---

*   *   *

Then were brought near with trembling fear,
a number numberless,
Of Blind Heathen, and brutish men
that did God's Law transgress;

CLVII

Whose wicked ways Christ open lays,
and makes their sins appear,
They making pleas their case to ease,
if not themselves to clear.
"Thy Written Word," say they, "good Lord,
we never did enjoy;
We ne'er refus'd, nor it abus'd;
Oh, do not us destroy!"

*   *   *

CLXVI

Then to the Bar all they drew near
Who died in infancy,
And never had or good or bad
effected pers'nally;
But from the womb unto the tomb
were straightway carried,
(Or at the least ere they transgress'd)
Who thus began to plead:

CLXVII

"If for our own transgressi-on,
or disobedience,
We here did stand at thy left hand,
just were the Recompense;

But Adam's guilt our souls hath spilt,
his fault is charg'd upon us;
And that alone hath overthrown
and utterly undone us.

CLXVIII

"Not we, but he ate of the Tree,
Whose fruit was interdicted;
Yet on us all of his sad Fall
the punishment's inflicted.
How could we sin that had not been,
or how is his sin our,
Without consent, which to prevent
we never had the pow'r?

CLXIX

"O great Creator why was our Nature
depraved and forlorn?
Why so defil'd, and made so vil'd,
whilst we were yet unborn?
If it be just, and needs we must
transgressors reckon'd be,
Thy Mercy, Lord, to us afford,
which sinners hath set free.

CLXX

"Behold we see Adam set free,
and sav'd from his trespass,
Whose sinful Fall hath split us all,
and brought us to this pass.
Canst thou deny us once to try,
or Grace to us to tender,
When he finds grace before thy face,
who was the chief offender?"

CLXXI

Then answered the Judge most dread:
"God doth such doom forbid,
That men should die eternally
for what they never did.
But what you call old Adam's Fall,
and only his Trespass,

You call amiss to call it his,
both his and yours it was.

"He was design'd of all Mankind
to be a public Head;
A common Root, whence all should shoot,
and stood in all their stead.
He stood and fell, did ill or well,
not for himself alone,
But for you all, who now his Fall
and trespass would disown.

"If he had stood, then all his brood
had been established
In God's true love never to move,
nor once awry to tread;
Then all his Race my Father's Grace
should have enjoy'd for ever,
And wicked Sprites by subtile sleights
could them have harmed never.

"Would you have griev'd to have receiv'd
through Adam so much good,
As had been your for evermore,
if he at first had stood?
Would you have said, 'We ne'er obey'd
nor did thy laws regard;
It ill befits with benefits,
us, Lord, to so reward?'

"Since then to share in his welfare,
You could have been content,
You may with reason share in his treason,
and in the punishment.
Hence you were born in state forlorn,
with Natures so depraved;
Death was your due because that you
had thus yourselves behaved.

"You think 'If we had been as he,
whom God did so betrust,
We to our cost would ne'er have lost
all for a paltry lust.'
Had you been made in Adam's stead,
you would like things have wrought,
And so into the self-same woe,
yourselves and yours have brought.

"I may deny you once to try,
or Grace to you to tender,
Though he finds Grace before my face
who was the chief offender;
Else should my Grace cease to be Grace,
for it would not be free,
If to release whom I should please
I have no liberty.

"If upon one what's due to none
I frankly shall bestow,
And on the rest shall not think best
compassion's skirt to throw,
Whom injure I? will you envy
and grudge at others' weal?
Or me accuse, who do refuse
yourselves to help and heal?

"Am I alone of what's my own,
no Master or no Lord?
And if I am, how can you claim
what I to some afford?
Will you demand Grace at my hand,
and challenge what is mine?
Will you teach me whom to set free,
and thus my Grace confine?

"You sinners are, and such a share
as sinners, may expect;
Such you shall have, for I do save
none but mine own Elect.
Yet to compare your sin with their
who liv'd a longer time,
I do confess yours is much less,
though every sin's a crime.

"A crime it is, therefore in bliss
you may not hope to dwell;
But unto you I shall allow
the easiest room in Hell."
The glorious King thus answering,
they cease, and plead no longer;
Their Consciences must needs confess
his Reasons are the stronger.

*   *   *

Oh piercing words, more sharp than swords!
What! to depart from Thee,
Whose face before for evermore
the best of Pleasures be!
What! to depart (unto our smart),
from thee *Eternally!*
To be for aye banish'd away
with Devil's company!

What! to be sent to Punishment,
and flames of burning Fire!
To be surrounded, and eke confounded
with God's revengeful Ire!
What! to abide, not for a tide,
these Torments, but for Ever!
To be releas'd, or to be eas'd,
not after years, but Never!

COLONIALS

Oh fearful Doom! now there's no room
for hope or help at all;
Sentence is past which aye shall last;
Christ will not it recall.
Then might you hear them rend and tear
the Air with their out-cries;
The hideous noise of their sad voice
ascendeth to the Skies.

CCV

They wring their hands, their caitiff-hands,
and gnash their teeth for terror;
They cry, they roar for anguish sore,
and gnaw their tongues for horror.
But get away without delay,
Christ pities not your cry;
Depart to Hell, there may you yell,
and roar Eternally.

INSTRUCTIONS FOR PUNISHING DISORDERLINESS AND RUDENESS IN MASSACHUSETTS YOUTH (1675) From Nathaniel B. Shurtleff, ed., *Records of the Governor and Company of Massachusetts Bay, 1628–1686* (Boston, 1853–1854), vol. V, pp. 60-61.

Whereas there is manifest pride openly appearing amongst us in that long hair, like women's hair, is worn by some men, either their own or others hair made into periwigs, and by some women wearing borders of hair, and their cutting, curling, and immodest laying out their hair, which practise doth prevail and increase, especially among the younger sort:

This Court doth declare against this ill custom as offensive to them, and divers sober Christians among us, and therefore do hereby exhort and advise all persons to use moderation in this respect; and further, do empower all grand juries to present to the County Court such persons, whether male or female, whom they shall judge to exceed in the premises; and the County Courts are hereby authorized to proceed against such delinquents either by admonition, fine, or correction, according to their good discretion. . . .

Whereas there is much disorder and rudeness in youth in many congregations in time of the worship of God, whereby sin and profaneness is greatly increased, for reformation whereof:

It is ordered by this Court, that the selectmen do appoint such place or places in the meeting house for children or youth to sit in where they may be most together and in public view, and that the officers of the churches, or selectmen, do appoint some grave and sober person or persons to take a particular care of and inspection over them, who are hereby required to present a list of the names of such who, by their own observance or the information of others, shall be found delinquent, to the next magistrate or Court, who are empowered for the first offense to admonish them, for the second offense to impose a fine of five shillings on their parents or governors, or order the children to be whipped, and if incorrigible, to be whipped with ten stripes or sent to the house of correction for three days.

PURITAN CHILDREN REMINDED OF THEIR DUTIES (1682)   From Samuel Willard, *Covenant-Keeping the Way to Blessedness* (Boston, 1682), pp. 117-18.

The main errand which brought your fathers into this Wilderness was not only that they might themselves enjoy, but that they might settle for their children, and leave them in full possession of the free, pure, and uncorrupted liberties of the Covenant of Grace. They have made this profession openly to the world. Yea, let reason speak and say what else was there which could have tempted them to come into a land which was not sown, leaving the pleasant enjoyments of a good land, and of which many of them had a good share, running through so many hazards, wrestling with so many hardships, not expecting (and it would have seemed vain and presumptuous to have expected) any worldly advantage, or likelihood of any other compensation for such expenses as they were at, and difficulties they broke through, but only this? And if this were the portion they thought worth so much that they might have it to leave them, it concerns you to mind and regard it. It was their love to your souls that embarked them in this design, and it will be horrible ingratitude in you to slight it. You cannot neglect God's Covenant, but you do withal cast reflections upon, and greatly undervalue, yea, and despise that work, which will be New England's glory, and was so signally owned and abetted by God's providence in the day of it; and will be unworthy heirs of your father's estates, if you do not prosecute their begun designs.

INCREASE MATHER OPPOSES DANCING (1684)   From Increase Mather, *An Arrow Against Profane and Promiscuous Dancing Drawn Out of a Quiver of the Scriptures* (Boston, 1684), pp. 1-3, 27-30.

Concerning the controversy about Dancing, the Question is not, whether all Dancing be in it self sinful. It is granted, that Pyrrhical or Polemical Saltation: i.e. when men vault in their Armour, to shew their strength and activity, may be of use. Nor is the question, whether a sober and grave Dancing of Men with Men, or of Women with Women, be not allowable; we make no doubt of that, where it may be done without offence, in due season, and with moderation. The Prince of Philosophers has observed truly, that Dancing or Leaping, is a natural expression of joy: So that there is no more Sin in it, than in laughter, or any outward expression of inward Rejoycing.

But our question is concerning Gynecandrical Dancing, or that which is commonly called Mixt or Promiscuous Dancing, viz. of Men and Women (be they elder or younger persons) together: Now this we affirm to be utterly unlawful, and that it cannot be tollerated in such a place as New-England, without great Sin. And that it may appear, that we are not transported by Affection without Judgment, let the following Arguments be weighed in the Ballance of the Sanctuary.

Arg. I. That which the Scripture condemns is sinful. None but Atheists will deny this Proposition: But the Scripture condemns Promiscuous Dancing. This Assumption is proved, I. From the Seventh Commandment. It is an Eternal Truth to be observed in expounding the Commandments, that whenever any sin is forbidden, not only the highest acts of that sin, but all degrees thereof, and all occasions leading thereto are prohibited. Now we cannot find one Orthodox and Judicious Divine, that writeth on the Commandments, but mentions Promiscuous Dancing, as a breach of the seventh Commandment, as being an occasion, and an incentive to that which is evil in the sight of God. Yea, this is so manifest as that the Assembly in the larger Catechism, do expresly take notice of Dancings, as a violation of the Commandments. It is sad, that when in times of Reformation, Children have been taught in their C[a]techism, that such Dancing is against the Commandment of God, that now in New-England they should practically be learned the contrary. The unchast Touches and Gesticulations used by Dancers, have a palpable tendency to that which is evil. Whereas some object, that they are not sensible of any ill motions occasioned in them, by being Spectators or Actors in such Saltations; we are not bound to believe all which some pretend concerning their own Mortification. . . .

Now they that frequent Promiscuous Dancings, or that send their Children thereunto, walk disorderly, and contrary to the Apostles Doctrine. It has been proved that such a practice is a Scandalous Immorality, and therefore to be removed out of Churches by Discipline, which is the Broom of Christ, whereby he keeps his Churches clean. . . .

And shall Churches in N E who have had a Name to be stricter and purer than other Churches, suffer such a scandalous evil amongst them? if all that are under Discipline be made sensible of this matter, we shall not be much or long infested with a Choreutical Demon. . . .

The Catechism which Wicked men teach their Children is to Dance and to Sing. Not that Dancing, or Musick, or Singing are in themselves sinful: but if the Dancing Master be wicked they are commonly abused to lasciviousness, and that makes them to become abominable. But will you that are Professors of Religion have your Children to be thus taught? the Lord expects that you should give the Children who are Baptized into his Name another kind of Education, that you should bring them up in the nurture and admonition of the Lord: And do you not hear the Lord Expostulating the case with you, and saying, you have taken my Children, the Children that were given unto me; the Children that were solemnly engaged to renounce the Pomps of Satan; but is this a light matter that you have taken these my Children, and initiated them in the Pomps and Vanities of the Wicked one, contrary to your Covenant? What will you say in the day of the Lords pleading with you? we have that charity for you as to believe that you have erred through

Ignorance, and not wickedly: and we have therefore accounted it our Duty to inform you in the Truth. If you resolve not on Reformation, you will be left inexcusable. However it shall be, we have now given our Testimony and delivered our own Souls. Consider what we say, and the Lord give you understanding in all things.

"CONCERNING LIGHTNING AND THUNDER" FROM THE ALMANAC FOR 1648 As quoted in Perry Miller and Thomas H. Johnson, eds., *The Puritans,* (New York, 1938), p. 745.

Lightning is an exhalation hot and dry, as also hot and moist; which being Elevated by the Sun to the middle Region of the Air, is there included or shut up within a cloud and cannot ascend; but by an Antiperistasis grows hotter and is enkindled, attenuated, and so seeks for more room, which it not finding in the cloud, violently rends the same, breaks out of it, and continues burning so long that it comes to the very ground.—By its rending of the cloud, there is caused a most dreadful noise or rumbling, and this we call Thunder: So that Thunder is improperly reckoned among the kinds or *species* of *Meteors.*

Of Lightning, [*fulmen*] there are three sorts, *viz.* piercing, [*Terebrans*], dashing in pieces [*disentiens*] and burning [*urens*]. Piercing Lightning, (which is also called white Lightning,) does consist of a most Subtile and thin exhalation and is very penetrating.

Observ. By reason of its subtile nature, many strange effects are produced thereby; A sword blade will be melted in its scabbard, and the scabbard not hurt at all: The pores in the scabbard are so great, that this Lightning passeth through them without any hurt, but coming to a more solid body (as the sword blade is) it meets with opposition there, and so through its heat melts it.

The *Second* sort of Lightning, is such as consists of a more fat and thick exhalation, which meeting with things, burnes not to ashes, but blasts and scorcheth them.

Observ. With this Lightning, there happens to be (yet seldome) a Stone, that is called a Thunderbolt, which breaketh forth with the exhalation, (as a bullet out of a gun) and breaks into pieces whatever it meets. When it strikes the earth it is reported to go not above five foot deep.

The *Third* sort of Lightning is fulmen urens [*burning Lightning*] and is more fiery then flamy; of a more grosse and earthy substance then the preceding sorts.

Observ. If Lightning kill one in his sleep, he dyes with his eyes opened, the Reason is because it just wakes him and kills him before he can shut his eyes again: If it kills one waking his eyes will be found to be shut, because it so amaseth him, that he winketh and dyes before he can open his eyes again.

Caution. It is not good to stand looking on the lightning at any time, for if it hurts no otherway, yet it may dry up or so waste the Chrystalline Humour of the eyes that it may cause the sight to perish, or it may swell the face, making it to break out with scabs, caused by a kind of poyson in the exhalation which the pores of the face and eyes do admit.

SAMUEL DANFORTH DESCRIBES A COMET (1665)   From "An Astronomical Description of the Late Comet or Blazing Star. . ." As Quoted in Perry Miller and Thomas H. Johnson, eds., *The Puritans,* (New York, 1938), pp. 738-39.

An Astronomical Description

I. *This Comet is no sublunary Meteor or sulphureous Exhalation, but a Celestial Luminary, moving in the starry Heavens.*

The Truth hereof may be demonstrated, 1. *By the vast Dimensions of it's body.* Some Comets have been observed by Astronomers to be halfe as big as the *Moon,* some bigger than the *Moon,* yea some bigger then the *Earth.* The exact Dimensions of this Comet, I may not presume to determine, but it seemeth not to be of the smallest size. Now 'tis not easy to imagine how the *Earth* should afford matter for a *Meteor* of such a huge magnitude, except we grant the greater part of the lower World, to be turned into an exhalation. 2. *By the smalness of it's Parallax.* The Parallax is the Distance between the *true* place of a *Planet* and the *apparent.* The lower and neerer any *Planet* is to the Earth, it hath the greater *Parallax.* . . .

IV. *This Comet is not a new fixed Star, but a Planetick or Erratick Body, wandring up & down in the etherial firmament under the fixed stars.*

Some learned Astronomers distinguish these more noble and celestial *Phaenomena or Appearances* into *Fixed* and *Erratick.* Several new Stars have appeared which are fixed, i.e. they keep the same place in the *Heavens,* and the same distance from the *fixed Stars.* One in *Cassiopeia* Anno 1572. which continued a year and four months. . . .

July 20 1663. That bright and radiant Star, a Star of the first magnitude, *Mr. Samuel Stone,* the strength and glory of *Connecticut,* rested from his labours and sorrows, and fell a sleep sweetly and placidly in the Lord. A little before Him, Mr *Iohn Miller* and Mr. *Samuel Newman,* faithful, painful and affectionate Preachers of the Gospel, were also taken from us by death. Thus our Pillars are cut down, our strongest Stakes pluck't up, and our breaches not repaired. Is it a small thing in our eyes, our principal Congregations & Head-townes, should be so badly bereaved, as they are at this day?

3. The sad *Mildew* and *Blasting,* whereby we have been greatly afflicted the last Summer, and some of us the Summer before: our principal grain being turned into an husk & rotteness.

4. Severe *Drought* this last Summer, which burnt up the Pastures and the latter growth.

5. Early *Frosts,* which smote our *Indian Corn,* and greatly impoverished our latter Harvest.

Unto these and some other no less threatning Visitations, is superadded this strange and fearful Appearance in the Heavens, which is now seconded by a new Appearance this Spring, concomitant to the translation of our Honoured and Aged Governour, Mr. *John Endicot,* from hence to a better World: By all which doubtless the Lord calls upon *New-England* to awake and to repent.

TO THIS END CONSIDER.

I. What a jealous eye the Lord hath upon us, observing how we carry and behave our selves at such a time as this.

LETTERS OF THE WINTHROPS (1629-1630)   From Perry Miller and Thomas H. Johnson, eds., *The Puritans*, (New York, 1938), pp. 465-469.

John Winthrop to His Wife

The Largnesse and trueth of my loue to thee makes me allwayes mindfull of thy wellfare, and settes me on to worke to beginne to write, before I heare from thee: the verye thought of thee affordes me many a kynde refreshinge, what will then the enioyinge of thy sweet societye, which I prize aboue all worldly comfortes?

Yet such is the folye and miserye of man, as he is easylye brought to contemne the true good he enioyes, and to neglect the best thinges which he holdes onely in hope, and bothe vpon and vngrounded desire of some seeminge good which he promiseth to himselfe: and if it be thus with vs, that are Christians, who haue a sure worde to directe vs, and the holy Faith to liue by, what is the madnesse and bondage of those who are out of Christ? O: the riches of Christ! O: the sweetnesse of the worde of Grace! it rauisheth my soule in the thought heerof, so as when I apprehende but a glimpse of the dignitye and felicitye of a Christian, I can hardly perswade my heart, to hope for so great happynesse: let men talke what they will of riches, honors pleasures etc.; let vs haue Christ crucified, and let them take all besides: for indeed, he who hath Christ hath all thinges with him, for he enioyeth an allsufficiencie which makes him abundantly riche in pouertye, honorable in the lowest abasementes, full of ioye and consolation in the sharpest Afflictions, liuinge in death, and possessinge aeternitye in this vale of miserye: therefore blesse we God, for his free and infinite mercye, in bestowinge Christ vpon vs: let vs entertaine and loue him with our whole heartes: let vs trust in him, and cleaue to him, with denyall of our selues, and all thinges besides, and account our portion the best in the world: that so beinge strengthned and comforted in his loue, we may putt forth our selues, to improue our life and meanes, to doe him seruice: there are very fewe howers lefte of this daye of our labour, then comes the night, when we shall take our rest, in the morninge we shall awake vnto glorye and immortalitye, when we shall haue no more worke to doe, no more paines or griefe to endure, no more care, feare, want, reproach, or infirmitye; no more sinne, corruption or temptation.

I am forced to patch vp my lettres, heer a peece and there another. I haue now receiued thine, the kyndly fruites of thy most sweet Affection. Blessed be the Lorde for the wellfare of thy selfe and all our familye. I receiued lettres from my 2: sonnes with thee, remember my loue and blessinge to them, and to my daughter Winth[rop] for whose safetye I giue the Lord thankes: I haue so many lettres to write as I cannot write to them now: our freindes heer are in reasonable health, and desire to be kindly remembered to you all. Commende me to all my good friends, my louinge neighbours goodman Cole and his wife, to whom we are allwayes much behouldinge. I will remember M[ary] her gowne and petticoate, and the childrens girdles. So with my most affectionate desires of thy wellfare, and my blessinge to all our children, I kisse my sweet wife, and comende thee and all ours to the gratious protection of our heauenly father, and rest Thy faithfull husbande still present with thee in his most vnkinde absence

Jo: Winthrop.

May 8 1629.

I am sorye for my neighbour Bluetes horse, but he shall loose nothinge by him. tell my sonne Hen: I will pay the mony he writes of.

Margaret Winthrop to Her Husband

To my very loueinge Husband John Winthrope Esquire theese dd.

Most louinge and good Husband, I haue receued your letters. the true tokens of your loue and care of my good, now in your abcence as well as when you are present, it makes me thinke that sayinge falce out of sight out of minde. I am sure my hart and thoughts are all wayes neere you to doe you good and not euill all the dayse of my life.

I hope through gods blessinge your paynes will not be all together lost which you bestow vpon me in rightinge those serious thoughts of your owne which you sent me did make a very good supply in stead of a sarmon. I shall often reade them and desyre to be of gods famyle to home so many blessings be-longe and pray that I may not be one separated from god whose concience is always accusinge them. I shall not neede to right to you of any thing this weke my sonne and brother Goslinge can tell you how we are. and I shall thinke longe for your cominge home. and thus with my best loue to you I beseech the lord to send vs a comfortable meetinge in his good time I commit you to the Lord. Your louinge and obedient wife

Margaret Winthrope.

[*Ca.* May 18, 1629.]

Margaret Winthrop to Her Husband

To hir very louinge and deare Husban John Winthrope Esquire at mr. Downings house in fleet strete neere thee Condite these dd.

My deare Husband, I knowe thou art desyrus to heere often from vs which makes me take plesure in rightinge to thee, and in relatinge my true affections to thee and desyers of your wished welfayer. the good lord be euer with thee and prosper all thy affayres [in] this great and waytty busines which is now in hand, that it may be for the glory of his most holy name and furtherance of his gospell, but I must part with my most deare Husban, which is a uery hard tryall for me to vndergoe, if the lord doe not supporte and healpe me in it, I shalbe vnable to beare it. I haue now receiued thy kinde letter which I cannot reade without sheding a great many teares, but I will resine thee and giue thee into the hands of the almyti god who is all soficient for thee, whome I trust will keepe thee and prosper thee in the way thou art to goe, if thou walke before him in truth and vprightnesse of hart, he will neuer fayle of his promise to thee. therefore my good Husban chere vp thy hart in god and in the expectation of his fauors and blessings in this thy change, with asurance of his loue in Christ Jesus our lord for our change heare after when we shall liue with him in glory for euer. as for me his most vnworthy seruant I will cleaue to my Husban Crist as neere as I can though my infirmytes be great he is able to heale them and wil not forsake me in the time of neede. I know I shall haue thy prayers to god for me that what is wanting in thy presence may be supplyed by the comfort of gods spirit. I am now full of passion haueinge nuly receiued thy letter and not able to right much. my sonne F[orth] will right about other busines. I begine to feare I shall see thee no more before thou goest which I should be very sory for and earnestly intreat thee that thou wilt com once more downe if it be possible. and thus with my due respect to thy selfe brother and sister D. thankes for my leamers to my sister, my loue to my sonnes, I commit thee to god and rest Your faythfull and obedient wife

Margaret Winthrope.

My good sister F. remembers hir loue.
[Groton, February 2, 1630.]

JOHN WINTHROP OF MASSACHUSETTS ON THE EDUCATION OF WOMEN (1645) From John Winthrop, *The History of New England from 1630–1649,* James Savage, ed. (Boston, 1826), vol. II, pp. 216-17.

Mr. Hopkins, the governour of Hartford upon Connecticut, came to Boston, and brought his wife with him, (a godly young woman, and of special parts,) who was fallen into a sad infirmity, the loss of her understanding and reason, which had been growing upon her divers years, by occasion of her giving herself wholly to reading and writing, and had written many books. Her husband, being very loving and tender of her, was loath to grieve her; but he saw his errour, when it was too late. For if she had attended her household affairs, and such things as belong to women, and not gone out of her way and calling to meddle in such things as are proper for men, whose minds are stronger &c. she had kept her wits, and might have improved them usefully and honourably in the place God had set her. He brought her to Boston, and left her with her brother, one Mr. Yale, a merchant, to try what means might be had here for her. But no help could be had.

"BEFORE THE BIRTH OF ONE OF HER CHILDREN," BY ANNE BRADSTREET (1678)

From John Ellis, ed., *The Works of Anne Bradstreet in Prose and Verse* (Charlestown, Mass., 1867), pp. 269-70.

All things within this fading world have end.
Adversity doth still our joys attend;
No ties so strong, no friends so dear and sweet,
But with death's parting blow are sure to meet.
The sentence passed is most irrevocable,
A common thing, yet, oh, inevitable.
How soon, my dear, death may my steps attend,
How soon it may be thy lot to lose thy friend,
We both are ignorant; yet love bids me
These farewell lines to recommend to thee,
That when that knot's untied that made us one
I may seem thine who in effect am none.
And if I see not half my days that are due,
What nature would God grant to yours and you.
The many faults that well you know I have
Let be interred in my oblivion's grave;
If any worth or virtue were in me,
Let that live freshly in thy memory,
And when thou feelest no grief, as I no harms,
Yet love thy dead, who long lay in thine arms;
And when thy loss shall be repaid with gains
Look to my little babes, my dear remains,
And if thou love thyself, or lovedst me,
These oh protect from stepdam's injury.
And if chance to thine eyes shall bring this verse,
With some sad sighs honor my absent hearse;
And kiss this paper for thy love's dear sake,
Who with salt tears this last farewell did take.

"TO MY DEAR AND LOVING HUSBAND" BY ANNE BRADSTREET (1678)

From John Ellis, ed., *The Works of Anne Bradstreet in Prose And Verse* (Charlestown, Mass., 1867), p. 232.

If ever two were one, then surely we;
If ever man were loved by wife, then thee;
If ever wife was happy in a man,
Compare with me, ye women, if you can.

I prize thy love more than whole mines of gold,
Or all the riches that the East doth hold.

My love is such that rivers cannot quench,
Nor aught but love from thee give recompense.
Thy love is such I can no way repay:
The heavens reward thee manifold, I pray.
Then while we live in love let's so persevere
That when we live no more we may live ever.

THE JOURNEY OF SARAH KEMBLE KNIGHT (1704) From *The Journal of Madam Knight*, as Quoted in Perry Miller and Thomas H. Johnson, eds., *The Puritans* (New York, 1938) pp. 425-27.

Monday, Octb'r. ye second, 1704.—About three o'clock afternoon, I begun my Journey from Boston to New-Haven; being about two Hundred Mile. My Kinsman, Capt. Robert Luist, waited on me as farr as Dedham, where I was to meet ye Western post.

I vissitted the Reverd. Mr. Belcher, ye Minister of ye town, and tarried there till evening, in hopes ye post would come along. But he not coming, I resolved to go to Billingses where he used to lodg, being 12 miles further. But being ignorant of the way, Mad^m Billings, seing no persuasions of her good spouses or hers could prevail with me to Lodg there that night, Very kindly went wyth me to ye Tavern, where I hoped to get my guide, And desired the Hostess to inquire of her guests whether any of them would go with mee. But they being tyed by the Lipps to a pewter engine, scarcely allowed themselves time to say what clownish

[Here half a page of the MS. is gone.]

Peices of eight, I told her no, I would not be accessary to such extortion.

Then John shan't go, sais shee. No, indeed, shan't hee; And held forth at that rate a long time, that I began to fear I was got among the Quaking tribe, beleeving not a Limbertong'd sister among them could out do Madm. Hostes.

Upon this, to my no small surprise, son John arrose, and gravely demanded what I would give him to go with me? Give you, sais I, are you John? Yes, says he, for want of a Better; And behold! this John look't as old as my Host, and perhaps had bin a man in the last Century. Well, Mr. John, sais I, make your demands. Why, half a pss. of eight and a dram, sais John. I agreed, and gave him a Dram (now) in hand to bind the bargain.

My hostess catechis'd John for going so cheep, saying his poor wife would break her heart

[Here another half page of the MS is gone.]

His shade on his Hors resembled a Globe on a Gate post. His habitt, Hors and furniture, its looks and goings Incomparably answered the rest.

Thus Jogging on with an easy pace, my Guide telling mee it was dangero's to Ride hard in the Night, (wh^{ch} his horse had the sence to avoid,) Hee entertained me with the Adventurs he had passed by late Rideing, and eminent Dangers he had escaped, so that, Remembring the Hero's in Parismus and the Knight of the Oracle, I didn't know but I had mett wth a Prince disguis'd.

When we had Ridd about an how'r, wee come into a thick swamp, wch. by Reason of a great fogg, very much startled mee, it being now very Dark. But nothing dismay'd John: Hee had encountered a thousand and a thousand such Swamps, having a Universall Knowledge in the woods; and readily Answered all my inquiries wch. were not a few.

In about an how'r, or something more, after we left the Swamp, we come to Billinges, where I was to Lodg. My Guide dismounted and very Complasantly help't me down and shewd the door, signing to me wth his hand to Go in; wch I Gladly did—But had not gone many steps into the Room, ere I was Interogated by a young Lady I understood afterwards was the Eldest daughter of the family, with these, or words to this purpose, (viz.) Law for mee—what in the world brings You here at this time a night?—I never see a woman on the Rode so Dreadfull late, in all the days of my versall life. Who are You? Where are You going? I'me scar'd out of my witts—with much now of the same Kind. I stood aghast, Prepareing to reply, when in comes my Guide—to him Madam turn'd, Roreing out: Lawfull heart, John, is that You?—how de do! Where in the world are you going with this woman? Who is she? John made no Ansr. but sat down in the corner, fumbled out his black Junk, and saluted that instead of Debb; she then turned agen to mee and fell anew into her silly questions, without asking me to sitt down.

I told her shee treated me very Rudely, and I did not think it my duty to answer her unmannerly Questions. But to get ridd of them, I told her I come there to have the post's company with me to-morrow on my Journey, &c. Miss star'd awhile, drew a chair, bid me sitt, And then run up stairs and putts on two or three Rings, (or else I had not seen them before,) and returning, sett herself just before me, showing the way to Reding, that I might see her Ornaments, perhaps to gain the more respect. But her Granam's new Rung sow, had it appeared, would affected me as much. I paid honest John wth money and dram according to contract, and Dismist him, and pray'd Miss to shew me where I must Lodg. Shee conducted me to a parlour in a little back Lento, wch was almost fill'd wth the bedsted, wch was so high that I was forced to climb on a chair to gitt up to ye wretched bed that lay on it; on wch having Stretcht my tired Limbs, and lay'd my head on a Sad-colourd pillow, I began to think on the transactions of ye past day.

Tuesday, October ye third, about 8 in the morning, I with the Post proceeded forward without observing anything remarkable; And about two, afternoon, Arrived at the Post's second stage, where the western Post mett him and exchanged Letters. Here, having called for something to eat, ye woman bro't in a Twisted thing like a cable, but something whiter; and laying it on the bord, tugg'd for life to bring it into a capacity to spread; wch having wth great pains accomplished, shee serv'd in a dish of Pork and Cabage, I suppose the remains of Dinner. The sause was of a deep Purple, wch I tho't was boil'd in her dye Kettle; the bread was Indian, and every thing on the Table service Agreeable to these. I, being hungry, gott a little down, but my stomach was soon cloy'd, and what cabbage I swallowed serv'd me for a Cudd the whole day after.

*   *   *

MEMORIES OF A LEARNED WOMAN (1735) From Ebenezer Turell, *Memoirs of the Life and Death of the Pious and Ingenious Mrs. Jane Turell* (Boston, 1735), pp. 60-61, 78-79, 116-19.

Her Father the Reverend Dr. Benjamin Colman (thro' the gracious Favour of God) is still living among us, one universally acknowleg'd to be even from his younger Times (at Home and Abroad) a bright Ornament and Honour to his Country, and an Instrument in God's Hand of bringing much Good to it.

Her Mother Mrs. Jane Colman was a truly gracious Woman, Daughter of Mr. Thomas Clark Gentleman.

Mrs. Turell was their third Child, graciously given them after they had mourn'd the Loss of the two former; and for seven Years their only one. Her Constitution from her early Infancy was wonderful weak and tender, yet the Organs of her Body so form'd as not to obstruct the free Operations of the active and capacious Spirit within. The Buddings of Reason and Religion appear'd on her sooner than usual.— Before her second Year was compleated she could speak distinctly, knew her Letters, and could relate many Stories out of the Scriptures to the Satisfaction and Pleasure of the most Judicious. I have heard that Governour Dudley, with other Wise and Polite Gentlemen, have plac'd her on a Table and setting round it own'd themselves diverted with her Stories.— Before she was four Years old (so strong and tenacious was her Memory) she could say the greater Part of the Assembly's Catechism, many of the Psalms, some hundred Lines of the best Poetry, read distinctly, and make pertinent Remarks on many things she read.—

She grew in Knowlege (the most useful) day by day, and had the Fear of God before her Eyes.

She pray'd to God sometimes by excellent Forms (recommended to her by her Father and suited to her Age & Circumstances) and at other times *ex corde*, the Spirit of God helping her Infirmities. When her Father upon a Time enquir'd of her what Words she used in Prayer to God, she answer'd him,—"That when she was upon her Knees God gave her Expressions.

Even at the Age of four, five, & six she ask'd many astonishing Questions about divine Mysteries, and carefully laid up and hid the Answers she received to them, in her Heart. . . .

Before She had seen Eighteen, she had read, and (in some measure) digested all the English Poetry, and polite Pieces in Prose, printed and Manuscripts in her Father's well furnish'd Library, and much she borrow'd of her Friends and Acquaintance. She had indeed such a Thirst after Knowledge that the Leisure of the Day did not suffice, but she spent whole Nights in reading.

I find she was sometimes fir'd with a laudable Ambition of raising the honour of her Sex, who are therefore under Obligations to her; and all will be ready to own she had a fine Genius, and is to be placed among those who have excell'd.

When I was first inclin'd (by the Motions of God's Providence and Spirit) to seek her Acquaintance (which was about the Time she entred her nineteenth Year) I was surpriz'd and charm'd to find her so accomplish'd. I found her in a good measure Mistress of the politest Writers and their Works; could point out the Beauties in them, and had made many of their best Tho'ts her own: And as she went into more free Conversation, she discours'd how admirably on many Subjects!

I grew by Degrees into such an Opinion of her good Taste, that when she put

COLONIALS

me upon translating a Psalm or two, I was ready to excuse my Self, and if I had not fear'd to displease her should have deny'd her Request.

After her Marriage which was on August 11th. 1726, her Custom was once in a Month or two, to make some new Essay in Verse or Prose, and to read from Day to Day as much as a faithful Discharge of the Duties of her new Condition gave Leisure for: and I think I may with Truth say, that she made the writing of Poetry a Recreation and not a Business.

What greatly contributed to increase her Knowlege in Divinity, History, Physick, Controversy, as well as Poetry, was her attentive hearing most that I read upon those Heads thro' the long Evenings of the Winters as we sat together. . . .

Having related these Things, you will not wonder if I now declare my self a Witness of her daily close Walk with God during her married State, and of her Retirements for Reading, Self-Examination and Devotion.

It was her Practice to read the Bible out in Course, once in a Year, the Book of Psalms much oftner, besides many Chapters and a Multitude of Verses which she kept turn'd down in a Bible, which she had been the Owner and Reader of more than twenty Years. If I should only present my Readers with a Catalogue of these Texts, I doubt not but that they would admire the Collection, be gratified with the Entertainment; and easily conjecture many of her holy Frames and Tempers from them.—I must own, considering her tender Make and often Infirmities she exceeded in Devotion. And I have tho't my self oblig'd sometimes (in Compassion to her) to call her off, and put her in mind of God's delighting in Mercy more than in Sacrifice.

How often has she lain whole Nights by me mourning for Sin, calling upon God, and praising him, or discoursing of Christ and Heaven? And when under Doubts intreating me to help her (as far as I could) to a full Assurance of God's Love. Sometimes she would say, "Well, I am content if you will shew me that I have the Truth of Grace." And I often satisfy'd her with one of Mr. Baxter's Marks of Love to Christ, namely, Lamenting & panting after him; for this kind of Love she was sure she exercis'd in the most cloudy Hours of her Life.

I may not forget to mention the strong and constant Guard she plac'd at the Door of her Lips. Who ever heard her call an ill Name? or detract from any Body? When she apprehended she receiv'd Injuries, Silence and Tears were her highest Resentments. But I have often heard her reprove others for rash and angry Speeches.

In every Relation she sustain'd she was truly Exemplary, sensible how much of the Life and Power of Religion consists in the conscientious Practice and Performance of Relative Duties.

No Child had a greater Love to and Reverence for her Parents, she even exceeded in Fear and Reverence of her Father, notwithstanding all his Condescentions to her, and vast Freedoms with her.

As a Wife she was dutiful, prudent and diligent, not only content but joyful in her Circumstances. She submitted as is fit in the Lord, look'd well to the Ways of her Houshold, and her own Works praise her in the Gates.

Her very Apparel discover'd Modesty and Chastity: She lov'd to appear neat and clean, but never gay and fine.

To her Servants she was good and kind, and took care of them, especially of the Soul of a Slave who dy'd (in the House) about a Month before her.

She respected all her Friends and Relatives, and spake of them with Honour, and never forgot either their Counsels or their Kindnesses.

She often spake of her Obligations to her Aunt Staniford, which were great living and dying.

She honour'd all Men, and lov'd every Body. Love and Goodness was natural to her, as her Father expresses it in a Letter Years ago.

Her tender Love to her only Sister, has been already seen; and was on all Occasions manifested, and grew exceedingly to her Death. A few Days before it, I heard her speak to her particularly of preparing for another World. "Improve (said she) the Time of Health, 'tis the only Time for doing the great Work in."

And in Return for her Love and amiable Carriage, She had the Love and Esteem of all that knew her. Those that knew her best lov'd her best, and praise her most.

Her Humility was so great, that she could well bear (without being elated) such Praises as are often found in her Father's Letters to us. viz. "I greatly esteem as well as highly love you: The best of Children deserves all that a Child can of a Father: My Soul rejoyces in you: My Joy, my Crown. I give Thanks to God for you daily. I am honour'd in being the Father of such a Daughter."

Her Husband also, and he praiseth her as a Meet Help both in Spirituals and Temporals.

Her Relations and Acquaintance ever manifested the highest Value for her.

The People, among whom she liv'd the last eight Years of her Life, both Old and Young had a Love and Veneration for her; as a Person of the strictest Virtue and undefil'd Religion. Her Innocence, Modesty, Ingenuity, & Devotion charm'd all into an Admiration of her. And I question whether there has been more Grief and Sorrow shown at the Death of any private Person, by People of all Ranks, to whom her Virtues were known; Mourning, for the Loss sustain'd by our selves, not for her, nor as others who have no Hope. For it is beyond Doubt that she died in the Lord, and is Blessed.

A BOSTON REGULATION ON THE TERM OF APPRENTICESHIP

(**1660**)   From Robert F. Seybolt, *Apprenticeship and Apprenticeship Education in Colonial New England and New York* (New York, 1917), pp. 37-38.

Att a Towne's meeting . . . Whereas itt is found by sad experience that youthes of this town, beinge put forth Apprentices to severall manufactures and sciences, but for 3 or 4 yeares time, contrary to the Customes of all well governed places, whence they are uncapable of being Artists in their trades, beside their unmeetness att the expiration of their Apprenticeship to take charge of others for government and manuall instruction in their occupations which, if not timely amended, threatens the welfare of this Town.

It is therefore ordered that no person shall henceforth open a shop in this Town, nor occupy any manufacture or science, till hee hath completed 21 years of age, nor except hee hath served seven yeares Apprenticeship, by testimony under the hands of sufficient witnesses. And that all Indentures made between any master and servant shall bee brought in and enrolled in the Towne's Records within one month after the contract made, on penalty of ten shillings be paid by the master att the time of the Apprentices being made free.

AN EXAMPLE OF A MAINE INDENTURE OF APPRENTICESHIP

(**1674**)   From Richard B. Morris, *Government and Labor in Early America* (New York, 1946), p. 366.

This Indenture witnesseth that I John Maisters of Wells, In the County of York, [Maine] with the Consent of my father Nathall Masters doe bind my selfe an apprentice to William Partridg of Wells Carpenter, in the same County, to continew with, abide and faithfully serve him my master as a faithfull apprentice out to doe, the full and Just tearme of four years, to bee fully ended from the date thereof; The sayd apprentice his sd Maister faithfully to serue, his lawfull secrets keepe, hee shall not play at unlawfull games, nor unseasonably absent him selfe from his sayd Maisters busines, hee shall not frequent Tavernes, nor lend, nor spend the goods or victualls of his sd Maister, without his leaue, hee shall not Contract Matrimony, or Committ fornication, but truely and trustily obserue his sd Maisters lawful Comands as a faithfull servant out to due. The sd Maister his sd apprentice shall teach, and Instruct in the Trade of a Carpenter, to the best of his skill, according to what his sayd apprentice is Capable of, and alsoe doe promiss to teach him to write and siffer, If hee bee Capable, and to giue him a set of Tools at the end of his tyme, and to prouide him dureing the sd apprentishipe, Convenjent Meate drinke, lodging and washing, and seauen pounds per Ann: for to bind him aparell, and provided his Maister shall goe out of the County, hee shall not haue him his sayd servant to goe along with him, without his sd apprentice Consent. In witness wr of [whereof] Wee haue here unto set our hands and seales inter-Changeably this sixteenth day of Septembr, one thousand six hundred seaventy foure:

John Maisters his marke   [his seale]

William Partridg   [his seale]

EXAMPLES OF INDENTURES OF APPRENTICESHIP IN NEW ENGLAND IN THE SEVENTEENTH CENTURY   From Marcus W. Jernegan, *Laboring and Dependent Classes in Colonial America* (Chicago, 1931), pp. 119-23.

These are to show, that Elizabeth Brailbrook widow of Watertown, hath put her daughter (with the consent of the selectmen) into the hands of Simont Tomson & his wife of Ipswich ropemaker to be as an apprentice, until she comes to the age of eighteen years, in which time the said Sarah is to serve them in all lawful Comands, and the said Simont is to teach her to reade the English Tongue, and to instruct her in the knowledge of God and his Ways. (1656)

It is agreed between the Selectmen and br. Tolman that hee shall take Henry lakes child to keepe it untill it com to 21 years of age etc. and therefore to haue 26 pounds and to give security to the towne and to teach it to reade and wright and when it is capable if he lives the said br Tolman to teach it his trade. (1651)

At a generall towne meeteing Nov. 7, 1670. Ordered that John Edy seit shall goe to John Fisk his house and to George Lorance and Willyam preist houseis to inquir a bought their Children wither they be Lerned to read the english tong and in case they be defective to warne in the said John George and Willyam to the next meeting of the selectmen. (1670)

Willyam priest John Fisk and George Lorance being warned to a meeting of the select men at John Bigulah his house they makeing their a peerance: and being found defecttive weer admonished for not Learning their Children to read the english toung; weer convinced did acknowledg their neglect and did promise a mendment. (1670)

Nathan fisk John whitney and Isaak mickstur meaking return of their inquiry aftur childrens edduccation finde that John fisks children ear naythur taught o read nor yet thear caticise. (1672)

Charlestowne Selectmen being presented for not observing the Law conc'ning the Katechiseing of Children, and Keeping them to imployment. The Court comended it to ye selectmen, that they attend their duty there in as the law directed, and make returne thereof to the next Court, and to pay costs—2s.6d. (c. 1675)

A MASSACHUSETTS APPRENTICE CONTRACT (1713)   From *Historical Collection of the Essex Institute* (Salem, Mass., 1859), vol. I, pp. 14-15.

This indenture, made the first day of September, RRae, Anno Nunc Magna Brittania Duodecimo annoq Dom., 1713, witnesseth that Nicholas Bourguess, a youth of Guernsey, of his own free and voluntary will, and by and with the consent of his present master, Captain John Hardy of Guernsey, aforesaid mariner, has put himself a servant unto Mr. William English, of Salem, in the county of Essex, within the province of the Massachusetts Bay in New England, mariner, for the space of four years from the day of the date hereof until the aforesaid term of four years be fully complete and ended; during all which time the said servant, his said master, his heirs, executors, administrators, or assignees dwelling within the province aforesaid, shall well and faithfully serve, their lawful commands obey. He shall not absent himself from his or their service without leave or licence first had from him or them; his master's money, goods, or other estate he shall not purloin, embezzle, or waste; at unlawful games he shall not play; taverns or alehouses he shall not frequent; fornication he shall not commit, nor matrimony contract; but in all things shall demean himself as a faithful servant during the term aforesaid, and the aforesaid master on his part, doth for himself, his heirs, and assignees, covenant, promise, and agree to and with the said servant: that he or they shall and will provide and find him with sufficient meat, drink, clothing, washing, and lodging, and in case of sickness, with physic and attendance during the term aforesaid, and to learn him to read a chapter well in the Bible, if he may be capable of learning it, and to dismiss him with two suits of apparel for all parts of his body—the one for

Lord's Days, the other for working days. In testimony and for confirmation whereof the parties aforenamed have interchangeably set their hands and seals the day and year first above written.

Nicholas Bourguess, John Hardy.

Signed, sealed and delivered in presence of us
Margaret Sewall, Jr.
Susannah Sewall.
Stephen Sewall, Notary Public and Justice Peace.

A CONNECTICUT INDENTURE OF APPRENTICESHIP (1727)   From H. R. Stiles, *The History of Ancient Windsor, Connecticut* (New York, 1859), vol. I, p. 442.

This Indenture witnesseth that Jonathan Stoughton, son of Thomas Stoughton of Windsor in the county of hartford and Coloney of Connecticut in new england, with his father's consent hath put him selfe an apprentice to Nathan day of the aboue sd windsor county and coloney: blacksmith and white smith to Learn his art, trade or mystery after the manner of an Apprentice to serue him until the sd Jonathan Stoughton attaines the age of twenty-one years, during all which time the sd apprentice his master faithfully shall serue, his secrets keep, his Lawfull commands gladly obaye he shall not do any damage to his sd master nor see it don by others without giveing notice thereof to his sd master, he shall not waste his sd master's goods or Lend them unLawfully to aney, he shall not commit fornication nor contract matrimony within the sd terme. at cards, dice or any other unlawfull game he shall not play whereby his sd master may suffer damage. he shall not absent himself day nor night from his master's service without his leave, nor haunt ale houses, Taverns or playhouses butt in all things behave himselfe as a faithfull apprentice ought to do during ye sd terme, and the sd master shall do his utmost to teach and Instruct ye sd apprentice In the boue mentioned blacksmith and white smiths trade and mistery and to teach or caus the sd apprentice to be Taught the art of Arithmatick to such a degree that he may be able to keep a book well, and provide for him meat, drink, apparel, washing and lodging and phisick in sickness and health suitable for such an apprentice during the sd terme, and att the end of sd terme the sd master shall furnish the sd apprentice with two good new suits of apparel boath wooling and lining for all parts of his body suitable for such an apprentice besids that apparel he carrieth with him and for the performance of all and every the sd covenants and agreement either of the sd parties bind themselves unto the other by these presents in witness whereof they have interchangeably put their hands and seals this first day of September in the year of our Lord god, 1727.

MASSACHUSETTS SCHOOL LAW OF 1642 From Nathaniel B. Shurtleff, ed., *Records of the Governor and Company of Massachusetts Bay in New England* (Boston, 1853–1854), vol. II, pp. 6-7.

This court, taking into consideration the great neglect of many parents and masters in training up their children in learning, and labor, and other implyments which may be proffitable to the common wealth, do hereupon order and decree, that in euery towne the chosen men appointed for managing the prudentiall affajres of the same shall henceforth stand charged with the care of the redresse of this evill, so as they shalbee sufficiently punished by fines for the neglect thereof, upon presentment of the grand iury, or other information or complaint in any Court within this jurisdiction; and for this end they, or the greater number of them, shall have power to take account from time to time of all parents and masters, and of their children, concerning their calling and implyment of their children, especially of their ability to read and understand the principles of religion and the capitall lawes of this country, and to impose fines upon such as shall refuse to render such accounts to them when they shall be required; and they shall have power, with consent of any Court or the magistrate, to put forth apprentices the children of such as they shall [find] not to be able and fitt to imploy and bring up . . . and they are to take care of such as are sett to keep cattle be set to some other imployment withall; as spinning upon the rock, knitting, weaving tape, etc. and that boyes and girles be not sufferd to converse together, so as may occasion any wanton, dishonest, or immodest behavior; and for their better performance of this trust committed to them, they may divide the towne amongst them, appointing to every of the said townesmen a certaine number of families to have special oversight of. They are also to provide that a sufficient quantity of materialls, as hemp, flaxe, etc., may be raised in their severall townes, and tooles and implements provided for working out the same; and for their assistance in this so needful and beneficiall imployment, if they meete with any difficulty or opposition which they cannot well master by their own power, they may have recourse to some of the magistrates, who shall take such course for their help and incuragment as the occasion shall require according to iustice; and the said townsmen, at the next Court in those limits, after the end of their year, shall give a breife account in writing of their proceedings herein, provided that they have bene so required by some Court or magistrate a month at least before; and this order to continew for two yeares, and till the Court shall take further order.

MASSACHUSETTS SCHOOL LAW OF 1645 From Nathaniel B. Shurtleff, ed., *Records of the Governor and Company of Massachusetts Bay in New England* (Boston, 1853–1854), vol. II, p. 99.

Whereas it is conceived that the training of youth to the art and practice of arms will be of great use in the country in divers respects, and among the rest that the use of bows and arrows may be of good concernment, in defect of powder, upon any occasion, it is therefore ordered, that all youth within this jurisdiction, from ten years old to the age of sixteen years, shall be instructed, by some one of the officers of the band, or some other experienced soldier whom the chief officer shall appoint, upon the usual training days, in the exercise of arms, as small guns, half pikes, bows and arrows, etc., according to the discretion of the said officer or soldier, provided that no child shall be taken to this exercise against their parents minds; this order to be of force within one month after the publication thereof.

MASSACHUSETTS SCHOOL LAW OF 1647   From Nathaniel B. Shurtleff, ed., *Records of the Governor and Company of Massachusetts Bay in New England* (Boston, 1853–1854), vol. II, p. 203.

It being one chiefe project of that ould deluder, Satan, to keepe men from the knowledge of the Scriptures, as in former times by keeping them in an unknowne tongue, so in these latter times by perswading from the used of tongues, that so at least the true sence and meaning of the originall might be clouded by false glosses of saint seeming deceivers, that learning may not be buried in the grave of our fathers in the church and commonwealth, the Lord assisting our endeavors,—

It is therefore ordered, that every towneship in this iurisdiction, after the Lord hath increased them to the number of 50 housholders, shall then forthwith appoint one within their towne to teach all such children as shall resort to him to write and reade, whose wages shall be paid either by the parents or masters of such children, or by the inhabitants in generall, by way of supply, as the maior part of those that order the prudentials of the towne shall appoint; provided, those that send their children be not oppressed by paying much more than they can have them taught for in other townes; and it is further ordered, that where any towne shall increase to the number of 100 families or householders, they shall set up a grammer schoole, the master thereof being able to instruct youth so farr as they may be fited for the university, provided, that if any towne neglect the performance hereof above one yeare, that every such towne shall pay £5 to the next schoole till they shall performe this order.

MASSACHUSETTS SCHOOL LAW OF 1648   From Marcus W. Jernegan, "Compulsory Education in the American Colonies," as quoted in *School Review*, vol. XXVI, pp. 740-41.

Forasmuch as the good education of children is of singular behoof and benefit to any Common-wealth; and whereas many parents and masters are too indulgent and negligent of their duty in that kinde. It is therefore ordered that the Select men of everie town, in the severall precincts and quarters where they dwell, shall have a vigilant eye over their brethren and neighbours, to see, first that none of them shall suffer so much barbarism in any of their families as not to indeavour to teach by themselves or others, their children and apprentices so much learning as may inable them perfectly to read the english tongue, and knowledge of the Capital lawes; upon penaltie of twentie shillings for each neglect therin. Also that all masters of families doe once a week (at the least) catechize their children and servants in the grounds and principles of Religion, and if any be unable to doe so much: that then at least they procure such children or apprentices to learn some short orthodox catechism without book, that they may be able to answer unto the questions that shall be propounded to them out of such catechism by their parents or masters or any of the Select men when they shall call them to a tryall of what they have learned in this kinde. And further that all parents and masters do breed and bring up their children and apprentices in some honest lawfull calling, labour or imployment, either in husbandry, or some other trade profitable for themselves, and the Common-wealth if they will not or can not train them up in learning to fit them for higher imployments. And if any of the Select men after admonition by them given to such masters of families shal finde them still negligent of their dutie in the particulars aforementioned, wherby children and servants become rude, stubborn and unruly; the said Select men with the help of two Magistrates, or the next County court for the Shire, shall take such children or apprentices from them and place them with some masters for years (boyes till they come to twenty one, and girls eighteen years of age compleat) which will more strictly look into and force them to submit unto government according to the rules of this order, if by fair means and former instructions they will not be drawn unto it.

VIOLATION BY THE TOWN OF TOPSFIELD OF THE MASSACHUSETTS SCHOOL LAW OF 1642 (1668) From *Records and Files of the Quarterly Courts of Essex County, Massachusetts, 1636–1671* (Salem, Mass., 1911–1914), vol. IV, p. 212.

W arrant to the constable of Topsfield, dated Mar. 2, 1668: "Whereas the law published by the Honered Generall Court lib. I, pag 76, doe require all Townes from time to time to dispose of all single persons and inmates within their Towns to service or otherwise and in pag. 16, tit. children & youth, It is required of the selectmen that they see that all youth under family Government be taught to read perfectly the english tongue, have knowledge in the capital laws, and be taught some orthodox catechism, and that they be brought up to some honest employment, profitable to themselves and to the commonwealth, and in case of neglect, on the part of famaly Governours, after admonition given them, the sayd selectmen are required, with the helpe of two magistrates, or next court of that shire, to take such children or apprentices from them, and place them forth with such as will looke more straitly to them. The neglect wherof, as by sad experience from court to court abundantly appears, doth occasion much sin and prophanes to increase among us, to the dishonor of God, and the ensueing of many children and servants, by the dissolute lives and practices of such as doe live from under family Government and is a great discouragement to most family governours, who conscientiy indeavour to bring up their youth in all christian nurture, as the laws of God and this commonwealth doth require;" said constable was ordered to acquaint the selectmen of the town that "the court doth expect and will require that the sayd laws be accordingly attended, the prevalency of the former neglect notwithstanding, and you are also required to take a list of the names of those young persons within the bounds of your Town, and all adjacent farmes, though out of all Towne bounds, who do live from under family government viz. doe not serve their parents or masters, as children apprentices, hired servants, or journeymen ought to do, and usually did in our native country, being subject to there commands & discipline and the same you are to returne to the next court to be held at Ipswich the 30 day of this month, etc.; signed by Robert Lord, cleric; and served by Thomas Dorman, constable of Topsfield, who returned that he had made the selectmen acquainted with Mathew Hooker, who was all that he found in the town."

FOUNDING OF THE FREE SCHOOL OF DEDHAM, MASSACHUSETTS

(**1645**)   From *Dedham Town Records*, vol. III, p. 108.

January 1, 1645--The sd Inhabitants takeing into Consideration the great necesitie of prouiding some means for the Education of the youth in or sd Town did with vnanimous consent declare by voate their willingness to promote that worke promising to put their hands to prouide maintenance for a Free Schoole in our said Towne.

And farther did risolue & consent testefying it by voate to rayse the some of Twenty pounds p annu: towards the maintaining of a Schoole mr to keep a free Schoole in our sd Towne

And also did resolue & consent to betrust the sd 20£ p. annu: & certaine lands in or Towne formerly set a part for publique vse: into the hand of Foefees to be presently Chosen by themselues to imploy the sd 20£ and the land aforesd to be improued for the vse of the said Schoole: that as the profits shall arise from ye sd land euery man may be proportionably abated of his some of sd 20£ aforesaid freely to be giuen to ye vse aforesaid, And yt ye said Foefees shall haue power to make a Rate for the necesary charg of improuing the sd land: they giueing account thereof to the Towne or to those whome they shall depute.

4 Jan., 1645—Granted to the Foesees for ye free Schoole in Dedham for the vse of the sd Schoole a percell of the Training ground so much as shalbe set out to them by the Towne which said pcell is granted from this present day vnto the last day of the Eight month which shalbe in ye year 1650.

Hen: Chickeringe Eli Lusher & Hen Phillips deputed to set out the sd parcell of land aboue said.

FOUNDING OF THE FREE SCHOOL OF ROXBURIE, MASSACHUSETTS

(**1645**)   From C. K. Dillaway, *A History of the Grammar School in Roxburie* (Roxbury, 1860), pp. 7-8.

Whereas, the Inhabitantes of Roxburie, in consideration of their relligeous care of posteritie, have taken into consideration how necessarie the education of theire children in Literature will be to fitt them for public service, both in Churche and Commonwealthe, in succeeding ages. They therefore unanimously have consented and agreed to erect a free schoole in the said Towne of Roxburie, and to allow Twenty pounds per annum to the Schoolemaster, to bee raised out of the Messuages and part of the Lands of the severall donors (Inhabitantes of the said Towne) in severall proportions as hereafter followeth under their handes. And for the well ordering thereof they have chosen and elected some Feoffees who shall have power to putt in or remove the Schoolemaster, to see to the well ordering of the schoole and schoolars, to receive and pay the said twenty pounds per annum to the Schoolemaster, and to dispose of any other gifte or giftes which hereafter may or shall be given for the advancement of learning and education of children. . . .

In consideration of the premises, the Donors hereafter expressed for the severall proportions or annuities by them voluntarily undertaken and underwritten, Have given and granted and by these presents doe for themselves their heires and Asignees respectively hereby give and grant unto the present Feoffees . . . the severall rents and summes hereafter expressed under their handes . . . To have and to hould receive and enjoy the said annual rents or summes to the only use of the Free Schoole in Roxburie.

REGULATIONS ADOPTED BY DORCHESTER, MASSACHUSETTS FOR THE TOWN GRAMMAR SCHOOL (**1645**)   From *Fourth Report of the Boston Record Commissioners* (Boston, 1880), pp. 54-57.

Upon a general and lawful warning of all the inhabitants, the 14th of the 1st month 1645, these rules and orders presented to the town concerning the school of Dorchester are confirmed by the major part of the inhabitants then present.

First . . . three able and sufficient men of the plantation shall be chosen to be wardens or overseers of the school abovementioned, who shall have the charge, oversight, and ordering thereof and of all things concerning the same . . . and shall continue in their office and place for term of their lives respectively, unless by reason of any of them removing his habitation out of the town, or for any other weighty reason, the inhabitants shall see cause to elect or choose others in their room.

COLONIALS

*   *   *

Secondly, the said wardens shall have full power to dispose of the school stock, whether the same be in land or otherwise, both such as is already in being and such as may by any good means hereafter be added, and shall collect and receive the rents, issues, and profits arising and growing of and from the said stock . . .

Thirdly, the said wardens shall take care, and do their utmost, and best endeavor, that the said school may from time to time be supplied with an able and sufficient schoolmaster, who nevertheless is not to be admitted into the place of schoolmaster without the general consent of the inhabitants or the major part of them.

Fourthly, so often as the said school shall be supplied with a schoolmaster . . . the wardens shall from time to time pay or cause to be paid unto the said schoolmaster such wages . . . as shall of right come due to be paid.

Fifthly, the said wardens shall from time to time see that the schoolhouse be kept in good and sufficient repair . . .

Sixthly, the said wardens shall take care that every year, at or before the end of [December], there be brought to the schoolhouse twelve sufficient cart- or wainloads of wood for fuel, to be for the use of the schoolmaster and the scholars in winter . . .

Lastly, the said wardens shall take care that the schoolmaster for the time being do faithfully perform his duty in his place, as schoolmasters ought to do, as well as in other things as in these which are hereafter expressed, viz.:

First, that the schoolmaster shall diligently attend his school and do his utmost endeavor for benefiting his scholars according to his best discretion without unnecessarily absenting himself to the prejudice of his scholars and hindering their learning.

Secondly, that from the beginning of [March], until the end of [September], he shall every day begin to teach at seven of the clock in the morning and dismiss his scholars at five in the afternoon. And for the other five months, that is from the beginning of [October], until the end of [February], it shall every day begin at eight of the clock in the morning and end at four in the afternoon.

Thirdly, every day in the year the usual time of dismissing at noon shall be at eleven, and to begin again at one, except that

Fourthly, every second day in the week he shall call his scholars together between twelve and one of the clock to examine them what they have learned on the Sabbath day preceding, at which time also he shall take notice of any misdemeanor or disorder that any of his scholars shall have committed on the Sabbath, to the end that at some convenient time due admonition and correction may be administered by him according as the nature and quality of the offense shall require; at which said examination any of the elders or other inhabitants that please may be present to behold his religious care herein and to give their countenance and approbation of the same.

Fifthly, he shall equally and impartially receive and instruct such as shall be sent and committed to him for that end, whether their parents be poor or rich, not refusing any who have right and interest in the school.

Sixthly, such as shall be committed to him he shall diligently instruct as they shall be able to learn, both in humane learning and good literature, and likewise in point of good manners and dutiful behavior towards all, especially their superiors, as they shall have occasion to be in their presence whether by meeting them in the street or otherwise.

Seventhly, every sixth day of the week at two of the clock in the afternoon he shall catechize his scholars in the principles of Christian religion, either in some catechism which the wardens shall provide and present, or in defect thereof, in some other.

Eighthly, and because all man's endeavors without the blessing of God must needs be fruitless and unsuccessful, therefore, it is to be a chief part of the schoolmaster's religious care to commend his scholars and his labors amongst them unto God by prayer, morning and evening, taking care that his scholars do reverently attend during the same.

Ninthly, and because the rod of correction is an ordinance of God necessary sometimes to be dispensed unto children, but such as may easily be abused by overmuch severity and rigor on the one hand, or by overmuch indulgence and lenity on the other, it is therefore ordered and agreed that the schoolmaster, for the time being, shall have full power to minister correction to all or any of his scholars without respect of persons, according as the nature and quality of the offense shall require whereto. All his scholars must be duly subject and no parent or other of the inhabitants shall hinder or go about to hinder the master therein. Nevertheless, if any parent or others shall think there is a just cause of complaint against the master for too much severity, such shall have liberty, friendlily and lovingly, to expostulate with the master about the same; and if they shall not attain to satisfaction, the matter is then to be referred to the wardens who shall inpartially judge betwixt the master and such complainants . . .

And because it is difficult, if not impossible, to give particular rules that shall reach all cases which may fall out, therefore, for a conclusion, it is ordered and agreed in general, that where particular rules are wanting, there it shall be a part of the office and duty of the wardens to order and dispose of all things that concern the school, in such sort as in their wisdom and discretion they shall judge most conducible for the glory of God and the training up of the children of the town in religion, learning, and civility . . . .

*   *   *

RULES OF THE HOPKINS GRAMMAR SCHOOL OF NEW HAVEN
(**1648**)   As quoted in *American Journal of Education,* vol. IV, p. 710.

The Erection of the said Schoole being principally for the Institucion of hopeful youth in the Latin tongue, and other learned Languages soe far as to prepare such youths for the Colledge and publique service of the Country in Church, & Commonwealth. The Chiefe work of the Schoole Master is to Instruct all such youth as are or may be by theire parents or Friends sent, or Committed unto him to that end with all diligence faithfulness and Constancy out of any of the townes of this County of New haven upon his sallary accompt only, otherwise Gratis. And if any Boyes are sent to the Master of the said Schoole from any other part of the Colony, or Country, Each such boy or youth to pay ten shillings to the Master at or upon his entrance into the said Schoole.

2. That noe Boyes be admitted into the said Schoole for the learning of English

Books, but such as have been before taught to spell the letters well & begin to Read, thereby to perfect theire right Spelling, & Reading, or to learne to write, & Cypher for numeracion, & addicion, & noe further, & that all others either too young & not instructed in letters & spelling, & all Girles be excluded as Improper & inconsistent with such a Grammar Schoole as the law injoines, as is the Designe of this Settlement, And that noe Boyes be admitted from other townes for the learning of English, without liberty & specially licence from the Comitte.

3. That the Master & Schollars duly attend the Schoole Houres viz. from 6 in the morning to 11 o Clock in the forenoone, And from 1 a Clock in the afternone to 5 a Clock in the afternoone in Summer and 4 in Winter.

4. That the Master shall make a list or Catalogue of his Schollars names And appoint a Monitor in his turne fore one week or longer tyme as the Master shall see Cause, who shall every morning & noone at least once a day at the set tyme Call over the names of the Schollars and Note down the Late Commers, or Absent, And in fit season Call such to an accompt That the faulty, & truants may be Corrected or reproved, as their fault shall desearve.

5. That the Schollars being called together the Master shall every morning begin his work with a short Prayer for a blessing on his Laboures & theire Learning.

6. That the prayer being ended the Master shall Assigne to every of his Schollars theire places of Sitting according to theire degrees of learning. And that (having theire Parts, or Lessons appointed them) they keep theire Seates, & stir not out of Doors, with [out] Leave of the Master, and not above two at one tyme, & soe successively: unless in Cases of necessity.

7. That the Schollars behave themselves at all tymes, especially in Schoole tyme with due Reverence to their Master, & with Sobriety & quietnes among themselves, without fighting, Quarrelling or calling one anothr or any others, bad names, or useing bad words in Cursing, taking the name of God in vaine, or other prophane, obscene, or Corrupt speeches which if any doe, That the Master Forthwith give them due Correcion. And if any prove incorrigible in such bad manners & wicked Corrupting language & speeches, notwithstanding formr warnings, admonishions & Correcion that such be expelled the Schoole as pernicious & dangerous examples to the Rest.

8. That if any of the Schoole Boyes be observed to play, sleep, or behave themselves rudely, or irreverently, or be any way disorderly at meeting on the Saboath Days or any other tyme of the Publique worships of God that upon informacion or Complaint thereof to the due Conviccion of the offender or offenders, The Master shall give them due Correccions to the degree of the Offence. And that All Correccions be with Moderacion.

9. That noe Lattine Boyes be allowed upon any pretence (sickness, and disability excepted) to withdraw, or absent themselves from the Schoole, without liberty graunted by the Master, and that noe such liberty be granted but upon ticket from the Parents or frends, & on grounds sufficient as in Cases extraordinary or absolute necessity.

10. That all the Lattin Schollars, & all other of the Boyes of Competent age and Capacity give the Master an accompt of one passage or sentence at least of the sermons the foregoing Saboth on the 2d day morning. And that from 1 to 3 in the afternoone of every last day of the week be Improved by the Master in Catechizing of his Schollars that are Capeable.

ESTABLISHMENT OF A FREE SCHOOL IN HAMPTON, NEW HAMPSHIRE (1649) From Elsie W. C. Parsons, *Educational Legislation and Administration of the Colonial Governments* (New York, 1899), p. 164.

The selectmen of this town of Hampton have agreed with John Legat for this present year ensuing, to teach and instruct all the children of or belonging to our town, both male and female (which are capable of learning) to write and read and cast accounts (if it be desired), as diligently and carefully as he is able to teach and instruct them. And so diligently to follow the said employment at all such time and times this year ensuing, as the weather shall be fitting for the youth to come together to one place to be instructed. And also to teach and instruct them once in a week, or more, in some orthodox catechism provided for them by their parents or masters.

And in consideration hereof we have agreed to pay, or cause to be paid, unto the said John Legat the sum of £20, in corn and cattle and butter, at price current, as payments are made of such goods in this town, and this to be paid by us quarterly. . . . John Legat entered upon schooling the 21 day of the 3 month, 1649.

PLYMOUTH COLONY SCHOOL LAW OF 1677 From *Plymouth Colony Records*, vol. IX, Laws, pp. 246-47.

This Court doth therfore order; That in whatsoeuer Townshipp in this Gourment consisting of fifty familier or vpwards; any meet man shalbe obtained to teach a Gramer scoole such townshipp shall allow att least twelue pounds in currant marchantable pay to be raised by rat on all the Inhabitants of such Towne and those that haue the more emediate benifitt therof by theire childrens going to scoole with what others may voulentarily giue to promote soe good a work and generall good, shall make vp the resedue Nessesarie to maintaine the same and that the proffitts ariseing of the Cape ffishing; heertofore ordered to maintaine a Gramer scoole in this Collonie, be distributed to such Townes as haue such Gramer scholes for the maintainance therof; not exceeding fiue pounds p annum to any such Towne vnlesse the Court Treasurer or other appointed to manage that affaire see good cause to adde thervnto to any respectiue Towne not exceeding fiue pounds more p annum; and further this Court orders that euery such Towne as consists of seauenty families or vpwards and hath not a Gramer scoole therin shall allow and pay vnto the next Towne which hath such Gramer scoole kept vp amongst them, the sume of fiue pounds p annum in currant Marchantable pay, to be leuied on the Inhabitants of such defectiue Townes by rate and gathered and deliuered by the Constables of such Townes as by warrant from any Majestrate of this Jurisdiction shalbe required.

CONNECTICUT SCHOOL LAW OF 1650   As quoted in *American Journal of Education*, vol. IV, p. 660.

$\mathbf{F}$orasmuch as the good Education of Children is of singular behoofe and benefitt to any Commonwealth; and whereas many parents and masters are too indulgent and negligent of theire duty in that kind;

It is therefore ordered by this Courte and Authority thereof, that the Select men of euery Towne in the several precincts and quarters where they dwell, shall have a vigilant eye over their brethern and neighbors, to see, first, that none of them shall suffer so much barbarism in any of their families, as not to endeavor to teach by themselves or others, their children and apprentices so much learning as may enable them perfectly to read the English tongue, and knowledge of the capital laws, upon penalty of twenty shillings for each neglect therein; also, that all masters of families, do, once a week, at least catechise their children and servants, in the grounds and principles of religion; and if any be unable to do so much, that then, at the least, they procure such children or apprentices to learn some short orthodox catechism, without book, that they may be able to answer to the questions that shall be propounded to them out of such catechisms by their parents or masters, or any selectmen, when they shall call them to a trial of what they have learned in this kind; and further, that all parents and masters do breed and bring up their children and apprentices in some honest lawful [calling,] labor, or employment, either in husbandry or some other trade profitable for themselves and the commonwealth, if they will not nor can not train them up in learning, to fit them for higher employments, and if any of the selectmen, after admonition by them given to such masters of families, shall find them still negligent of their duty, in the particulars aforementioned, whereby children and servants become rude, stubborn and unruly, the said selectmen, with the help of two magistrates, shall take such children or apprentices from them, and place them with some masters for years, boys until they come to twenty-one, and girls to eighteen years of age complete, which will more strictly look unto and force them to submit unto government, according to the rules of this order, if by fair means and former instructions they will not be drawn unto it.

CONNECTICUT SCHOOL LAW OF 1690   From *Public Records of the Colony of Connecticut*, vol. IV, pp. 30-31.

$\mathbf{T}$his Court, observing that notwithstanding the former orders made for the education of children and servants, there are many persons unable to read the English tongue, and thereby incapable to read the holy word of God, or the good laws of the colony, which evil, that it grow no farther upon their Majesties' subjects here, it is hereby ordered that all parents and masters shall cause their respective children and servants, as they are capable, to be taught to read distinctly the English tongue, and that the grand jury men in each town do once in the year at least visit each family they suspect to neglect this order, and satisfy themselves whether all children under age and servants in such suspect families can read well the English tongue, or be in a good procedure to learn the same or not; and if they find any such children and servants not taught as their years are capable of, they shall return the names of the parents or masters of the said children so untaught to the next county court, where the said parents or masters shall be fined twenty shillings for each child or servant whose teaching is or shall be neglected, contrary to this order, unless it shall appear to the satisfaction of the court that the said neglect is not voluntary but necessitated by the incapacity of the parents or masters, or their neighbours, to cause them to be taught as aforesaid, or the incapacity of the said children or servants to learn.

This Court considering the necessity and great advantage of good literature, do order and appoint that there shall be two free schools kept and maintained in this colony, for the teaching of all such children as shall come there, after they can first read the psalter, to teach such reading, writing, arithmetic, the Latin and Greek tongues; the one at Hartford, the other at New Haven, the masters whereof shall be chosen by the magistrates and ministers of the said county, and shall be inspected and again displaced by them if they see cause, and that each of the said masters shall have annually for the same the sum of sixty pounds in country pay, thirty pounds of it to be paid out [of the] country treasury, the other thirty to be paid in the school revenue given by particular persons, or to be given to that use, so far as it will extend, and the rest to be paid by the respective towns of Hartford and New Haven.

This Court considering the necessity many parents or masters may be under to improve their children and servants in labour for a great part of the year, do order that if the town schools in the several towns, as distinct from the free school, be, according to law already established, kept up six months in each year to teach to read and write the English tongue, the said towns so keeping their respective schools six months in every year shall not be presentable or fineable by law for not having a school according to law, notwithstanding any former law or order to the contrary.

BROOKLINE'S FREE SCHOOL FOR POOR CHILDREN (1687) From Robert F. Seybolt, *Apprenticeship and Apprenticeship Education in Colonial New England and New York* (New York, 1917), p. 42.

Brookline. "Voted that for the Annual maintenance of the Schoolmaster twelve pounds per annum in or as money be Raised equally by a Rate accordinge to the usual manner of Raising publick charges by the three men And that the Remainder necessary to support the charge of the Master be laid equally on the scholars heads *save any persons that are poor to be abated wholly or in part.*"

BOSTON SCHOOL TAXES (1699) From Robert F. Seybolt, *Apprenticeship and Apprenticeship Education in Colonial New England and New York* (New York, 1917), p. 22.

Action of a Town Meeting, September 18, 1699

"It was then voted that the Selectmen should raise a Tax on the inhabitants of s^d. town to the value of 800 pounds for the relief of the poor, for the payment of Schoolmasters & payment for repairing the Town house and all other necessary Charges arising wth in s^d. town."

FINES USED FOR THE SUPPORT OF THE BOSTON FREE SCHOOL (1700) From Robert F. Seybolt, *Apprenticeship and Apprenticeship Education in Colonial New England and New York* (New York, 1917), p. 21.

A law, passed June 29, 1700, required that all who sold "wine, brandy, rhum, or other distilled liquors, beer, ale, perry, or cyder, by retail, without having licence . . . shall forfeit and pay the sum of four pounds, one-half thereof to the informer, and the other half to and for the use and support of a free grammar- or writing school or schools in the town where the offence shall be committed." Those who failed "to give a true list of their estate and polls" were subject to a fine of forty shillings, one "half to be paid for and towards the support of the schoolmaster in said town."

REQUIREMENT THAT NON-RESIDENTS OF BOSTON MUST PAY FOR THE INSTRUCTION OF THEIR CHILDREN (1711) From Robert F. Seybolt, *The Public Schools of Colonial Boston* (Cambridge, Mass., 1935), p. 40.

Whereas the Support of the Free Schools of this Town hath been, and still is, at ye Cost & charge of the Inhabitants of ye Said Town and the Select men being informed of Several Instances, of Children Sent to ye Sd Schools, whose parents, or others who of Right ought to defray the Charge of their Education, do belong to other Townes or Precincts.

Where fore they ye Sd Select men do direct the Sd School masters to demand & receive of the persons Sending any Such children the accustomed recompence for their Schooling, and to Return unto ye Select men a List of their names, once (at ye Least) every year.

PETITION FROM NORTH BOSTON FOR A FREE GRAMMAR SCHOOL

(1712)   From Robert F. Seybolt, *The Public Schools of Colonial Boston* (Cambridge, Mass., 1935), p. 22.

It Cannot but be Thot Strange that One Grammer School Should be Thot sufficient for a Town of above Two Thousand Families when the Law of the Provinces Imposes one upon Every Town that hath above One Hundred.

Education is as great and Good an Interest as can be prossecuted by any People, and the more Liberally it is Prossecuted the more is done for the honour and Welfare of such a People.

The Gramer School in this Town is as full of Scholars as can well Consist with a faithful Discharge of Duty to them.

The North Part of this Town bares no Inconsiderable Share in the Publick Expences and we hope are not altogether unworthy of the Publick benefitts.

It is known that when an hundred and odd Children have been found in the Publick Gramer School not one of that Hundred nor any but the few odd Ones have been Sent from that Part of the Town.

The Distance hath hindred many Parents from Exposing their Tender Children to the Travells of the Winter and the Sumer thither.

Some that Can't be satisfy'd without bestowing a good Cultivation on their Children are at the Charge of a Private Gramer School in the Neighbourhood. Others do Send their Children abroad in the Country.

When the People of that Neighbourhood were Prevail'd withall to Come into the Vote for Additional Incouragements unto the Present Gramer School, they were made to hope that they should ere long be favoured with another Nearer unto themselves.

If the Town will Smile on this just and fair Proposal, it is Probable their will Appear some particular Gentleman whose desire to Serve the Publick will Exert itself on this Occasion and make liberal advances towards the Providing of such Necessary Preliminaries.

These Considerations are humbly offer'd to the Inhabitants of Boston to be Laid in the Ballances of Equity in the Next General Meeting.

On the following day, the town thanked Thomas Hutchinson for offering to build a schoolhouse "at his own Charge," and voted "That there be a Free Grammer School at the North end of this Town." The building, erected on Bennet St. late in 1712, was opened April 20, 1713.

CURRICULUM OF THE BOSTON LATIN GRAMMAR SCHOOL
(1712)   From ''Letter from Nathaniel Williams to Nehemiah Hobart,'' in Robert F. Seybolt,
The Public Schools of Colonial Boston (Cambridge, Mass., 1935), pp. 69-71.

The three first years are spent first in Learning by heart & then acc: to their capacities understanding the Accidence and Nomenclator, in construing & parsing acc: to the English rules of Syntax Sententiae Pueriles Cato & Corderius & Aesops Fables.

The 4th year, or sooner if their capacities allow it, they are entred upon Erasmus to which they are allou'd no English, but are taught to translate it by the help of the Dictionary and Accidence, which English translatio of theirs is written down fair by each of them, after the recital of the lesson, and then brought to the Master for his observation and correction both as to the Translatio & orthography: This when corrected is carefully reserved till fryday, and then render'd into the Latin of the Author exactly instead of the old way of Repitition, and in the afternoon of that day it is (a part of it) varied for them as to mood tense number &c and given them to translate into Latin, still keeping to the words of the Author. an Example of which you have in the paper marked on the backside A. These continue to read Aesops Fables with ye English translation, the better to help them in the afores^d translat^g. They are also now initiated in the Latin grammar, and begin to give the latin rules in Propr: As in pres: & Syntax in their parsing; and at the latter end of the year enter upon Ovid de Tristibus (which is recited by heart on the usual time of fryday afternoon) & upon translating English into Latin, out of m^r Garretson's Exercises.

The fifth year they are entred upon Tullies Epistles (Still continuing the use of Erasmus in the morning & Ovid de Trist: afternoon) the Elegancies of which are remarkd and improv'd in the afternoon of the day they learn it, by translating an English which contains the phrase somthing altered, and besides recited by heart on the repetition day. Ov: Metam: is learn'd by these at the latter end of the year, so also Prosodia Scanning & turning & making of verses, & 2 days in the week they continue to turn Mr Gar: Engl: Ex: into Latin, w the afternoons exerc: is ended, and turn a fable into verse a distich in a day.

The sixth year they are entred upon Tullies Offices & Luc: Flor: for the forenoon, continuing the use of Ovid's Metam: in the afternoon, & at the end of the Year they read Virgil: The Elegancies of Tull: Off: are improved in the afternoon as is afores^d of Tull: Epist^l. & withal given the master in writing when the lesson is recited, & so are the phrases they can discover in Luc: Fl: All which that have been mett with in that week are comprehended in a Dialogue on Fryday forenoon, and after noon they turn a Fable into Lat: Verse. Every week these make a Latin Epistle, the last quarter of the Year, when also they begin to learn Greek, & Rhetorick.

The seventh Year they read Tullie's Orations & Justin for the Latin & Greek Testam^t Isocrates Orat: Homer & Hesiod for the Greek in the forenoons & Virgil Horace Juvenal & Persius afternoons, as to their Exercises after the afternoon lessons are ended they translate Mundays & Tuesdays an Eng: Dialogue containing a Praxis upon the Phrases out of Godwin's Roman Antiquities. Wensdays they compose a Praxis on the Elegancies & Pithy sentences in their lesson in Horace in Lat: verse. On Repition days, bec: that work is easy, their time is improved in ye Forenoon in makeing Dialogues containing a Praxis upon a Particle out of M^r

Walker, in the afternoon in Turning a Psalm or something Divine into Latin verse. Every fortnight they compose a theme, & now & then turn a Theme into a Declamation, the last quarter of the year.

INSPECTION OF THE SCHOOLS BY THE BOSTON SCHOOL BOARD

(1738)   From Robert F. Seybolt, *The Public Schools of Colonial Boston* (Cambridge, Mass., 1935), pp. 61-62.

The Report of the Select Men of the Visitation of the Public Schools, being Presented, was Read, as follows. Vis^t.

To the Inhabitants of Boston, Town Meeting assembled,
Mar. 12, 1738

Pursuant to a Vote of the Town of Boston at their annual meeting the 13th. of March, 1737. Desiring Us the Select Men to Visit the several Public Schools in the Town, &c.—

We accordingly Attended that Service on the 26th. of June last past, Accompanied by the following Gentlemen, Viz^t.

The Hon. Thomas Hutchinson Esqr.
The Hon. Adam Winthrop Esqr.
The Hon. Ezekiel Lewis Esqr.
The Hon. Anthony Stoddard Esqr.
The Hon. Jacob Wendell Esqr.
The Rev. Mr. William Hooper
The Rev. Mr. Samuel Mather.

And now Report, as follows.

That the Number of Scholars instructed in the Public Schools is as follows, Viz^t.

In the South Grammar School, about One Hundred and Twenty.
In the North Grammar School, about Sixty.
In the North Writing School, about Two Hundred & Eighty.
In the Writing School in Queen Street, about Seventy three.
In the South Writing School, about Sixty two.—

That We heard the Performances of the Lattin Scholars at each Grammar School, And inspected the Performances of the Scholars in the other Schools, both in Writing and Arithmetick, And heard the younger Scholars read—And that in general they perform'd to the great satisfaction of the Visitors—And We have grounds to hope that the Masters in the said several Schools do faithfully Dischardge the Trust reposed in them.

And We look upon it as a point of Justice due to the Master of the South Writing School, to Report, that the Writing both of the Master and Scholars has been of late much improved.—

John Jeffries.
Jon^a. Armitage.
David Collson.   }
Alex^a. Forsyth.   Select Men.
Caleb Lyman.

Jonas Clarke.

Thos. Hutchinson Junr.

Voted, That the Report of the Select Men, of the Visitation of the Schools, now Read, be Accepted—

Voted, That the Select Men be, and hereby are Desired to Visit the Public Schools within the Town, the year ensuing, Desiring such Gentlemen to accompany them therein, as they shall think proper.

COTTON MATHER "ON THE EDUCATION OF CHILDREN" (1706) From Washington Ford, ed., *The Diary of Cotton Mather* (Boston, 1911), pp. 534-37.

I pour out continual Prayers and Cries to the God of all Grace for them, that He will be a Father to my Children, and bestow His Christ and His Grace upon them, and guide them with His Councils, and bring them to His Glory.

And in this Action, I mention them distinctly, every one by Name unto the Lord.

II. I begin betimes to entertain them with delightful Stories, especially scriptural ones. And still conclude with some Lesson of Piety; bidding them to learn that Lesson from the Story.

And thus, every Day at the Table, I have used myself to tell a Story before I rise; and make the Story useful to the Olive Plants about the Table.

III. When the Children at any time accidentally come in my way, it is my custome to lett fall some Sentence or other, that may be monitory and profitable to them.

This Matter proves to me, a Matter of some Study, and Labour, and Contrivance. But who can tell, what may be the Effect of a continual Dropping?

IV. I essay betimes, to engage the Children, in Exercises of Piety; and especially secret Prayer, for which I give them very plain and brief Directions, and suggest unto them the Petitions, which I would have them to make before the Lord, and which I therefore explain to their Apprehension and Capacity. And I often call upon them; Child, Don't you forgett every Day, to go alone, and pray as I have directed you!

V. Betimes I try to form in the Children a Temper of Benignity. I putt them upon doing of Services and Kindnesses for one another, and for other Children. I applaud them, when I see them Delight in it. I upbraid all Aversion to it. I caution them exquisitely against all Revenges of Injuries. I instruct them, to return good Offices for evil Ones. I show them, how they will by this Goodness become like to the Good God, and His Glorious Christ. I lett them discern, that I am not satisfied, except when they have a Sweetness of Temper shining in them.

VI. As soon as tis possible, I make the Children learn to write. And when they can write, I employ them in Writing out the most agreeable and profitable Things, that I can invent for them. In this way, I propose to fraight their minds with excellent Things, and have a deep Impression made upon their Minds by such Things.

VII. I mightily endeavour it, that the Children may betimes, be acted by Principles of Reason and Honour.

I first begett in them an high Opinion of their Father's Love to them and of his being best able to judge, what shall be good for them.

Then I make them sensible, tis a Folly for them to pretend unto any Witt and Will of their own; they must resign all to me, who will be sure to do what is best; my word must be their Law.

I cause them to understand, that it is an hurtful and a shameful thing to do amiss. I aggravate this, on all Occasions; and lett them see how amiable they will render themselves by well doing.

The first Chastisement, which I inflict for an ordinary Fault, is, to lett the Child see and hear me in an Astonishment, and hardly able to beleeve that the Child could do so base a Thing, but beleeving that they will never do it again.

I would never come, to give a child a Blow; except in Case of Obstinacy: or some gross Enormity.

To be chased for a while out of my Presence, I would make to be look'd upon, as the sorest Punishment in the Family.

I would by all possible insinuations gain this Point upon them, that for them to learn all the brave Things in the world, is the bravest Thing in the world. I am not fond of proposing Play to them, as a Reward of any diligent Application to learn what is good; lest they should think Diversion to be a better and a nobler Thing than Diligence.

I would have them come to propound and expect, at this rate, I have done well, and now I will go to my Father; He will teach me some curious Thing for it. I must have them count it a Priviledge, to be taught; and I sometimes manage the Matter so, that my Refusing to teach them Something, is their Punishment.

The slavish way of Education, carried on with raving and kicking and scourging (in Schools as well as Families,) tis abominable; and a dreadful Judgment of God upon the World.

VIII. Tho' I find it a marvellous Advantage to have the Children strongly biased by Principles of Reason and Honour, (which, I find, Children will feel sooner than is commonly thought for:) yett I would neglect no Endeavours, to have higher Principles infused into them.

I therefore betimes awe them with the Eye of God upon them.

I show them, how they must love Jesus Christ; and show it, by doing what their Parents require of them.

I often tell them of the good Angels, who love them, and help them, and guard them; and who take Notice of them: and therefore must not be disobliged.

Heaven and Hell, I sett before them, as the Consequences of their Behaviour here.

IX. When the Children are capable of it, I take them alone, one by one; and after my Charges unto them, to fear God, and serve Christ, and shun Sin, I pray with them in my Study and make them the Witnesses of the Agonies, with which I address the Throne of Grace on their behalf.

X. I find much Benefit, by a particular Method, as of Catechising the Children, so of carrying the Repetition of the public Sermons unto them.

The Answers of the Catechism I still explain with abundance of brief Quaestions, which make them to take in the Meaning of it, and I see, that they do so.

And when the Sermons are to be Repeated, I chuse to putt every Truth, into a Quaestion, to be answered still, with, Yes, or, No. In this way I awaken their Attention, as well as enlighten their Understanding. And in this way I have an Opportunity, to ask, Do you desire such, or such a Grace of God? and the like. Yea, I have an Opportunity to demand, and perhaps, to obtain their Consent unto the glorious Articles of the New Covenant. The Spirit of Grace may fall upon them in this Action; and they may be siez'd by Him, and Held as His Temples, thro' eternal Ages.

COTTON MATHER'S ADVICE TO PARENTS (1710) From Cotton Mather, *Bonifacius: An Essay upon the Good, that is be Devised and Designed, by those Who Desire to Answer the Great End of Life and to Do Good While they Live* (Boston, 1710), pp. 52-70, 106-12, 147-48.

Parents, Oh! How much ought you to be continually Devising, and even Travailing, for the Good of your Children. Often Devise; How to make them Wise Children; How to carry on a Desireable Education for them; an Education that shall render them Desireable; How to render them Lovely, and Polite Creatures, and Serviceable in their Generation. Often Devise, how to Enrich their Minds with valuable Knowledge; How to Instil Generous, and Gracious and Heavenly Principles into their Minds; How to Restrain and Rescue them from the Pathes of the Destroyer, and fortify them against their Special Temptations. There is a World of Good, that you have to Do for them. You are without Bowels, Oh! be not such Monsters! if you are not in a continual Agony to do for them all the Good that ever you can. . . .

I will Prosecute this Matter by Transcribing a Copy of PARENTAL RES-OLUTIONS, which I have some-where met withal.

* * *

'I would betimes entertain the Children with Delightful Stories out of the Bible. In the Talk, of the Table, I would go thro' the Bible, when the Olive Plants about my table are capable of being so Watered. But I would always conclude the Stories with some Lessons of Piety, to be inferred from them.

'I would single out Some Scriptural Sentences, of the greatest Importance; and some also that have Special Antidotes in them against the Common Errors and Vices of Children. They shall quickly get those Golden Sayings by heart, and be rewarded with Silver or Gold, or Some Good Thing, when they do it. . . .

'I would betimes cause my Children to Learn the Catechism. In Catechising of them, I would break the Answer into many lesser and Proper Questions; and by their Answer to them Observe and Quicken their Understandings. I would bring every truth, into some Duty and Practice, and Expect them to Confess it, and Consent unto it, and Resolve upon it. As we go on in our Catechising, they shall, when they are able, Turn to the Proofs, and Read them, and say to me, What they prove, and How. Then I will take my times to put nicer and harder Questions to them; and improve the Times of Conversation with my Family, which every man ordinarily has or may have, conferences on matters of Religion.

'Restless would I be, till I may be able to Say of my Children, Behold They Pray! I would therefore Teach them to Pray. But after they have Learnt a Form of Prayer, I will press them, to proceed unto Points which are not in their Form. I will show them the State of their own Souls; and on every Stroke Enquire of them, What they think ought now to be their Prayer. I will direct them, that every Morning they shall take one Text or Two out of the Sacred Scripture, and Shape it into a Desire, which they shall add unto their Usual Prayer. When they have heard a Sermon, I will mention to them over again the main Subject of it, and ask them thereupon, What they have now to Pray for. I will charge them, with all possible cogency, to Pray in Secret; And often call upon them, Child, I hope, you don't forget my charge to you, about Secret Prayer; Your crime is very great, if you do!

'I would betimes do what I can, to beget a Temper of Benignity in my Children, both towards one another and towards all other people. I will instruct them how Ready they should be to Communicate unto others, a part of what they have; and they shall see, my Encouragements, when they discover a Loving, a Courteous, an Helpful Disposition. I will give them now and then a piece of Money for them with their own Little Hands to dispense unto the Poor. Yea, if any one has hurt them, or vex'd them, I will not only forbid them all Revenge, but also oblige them to do a Kindness as soon as may be to the Vexatious Person. All Courseness of Language or Carriage in them, I will discountenance it.

'I would be Sollicitous to have my Children Expert, not only at Reading handsomely, but also at Writing a fair Hand. I will then assign them such Books to Read, as I may judge most agreeable and profitable; obliging them to give me some Account of what they Read; but keep a Strict Eye upon them, that they don't Stumble on the Devils Library, and poison themselves with foolish Romances, or Novels, or Playes, or Songs, or Jests that are not convenient. I will set them also, to Write out such things as may be of the greatest Benefit unto them; and they shall have their Blank Books, neatly kept on purpose, to Enter such Passages as I advise them to. I will particularly require them now and then, to Write a Prayer of their own Composing, and bring it unto me; that so I may discern, what sense they have of their own Everlasting Interests.

'I Wish that my Children may as soon as may be, feel the Principles of Reason and Honor, working in them, and that I may carry on their Education, very much upon those Principles. Therefore, first, I will wholly avoid, that harsh, fierce, crabbed usage of the Children that would make them Tremble, and Abhor to come into my Presence. I will so use them, that they shall fear to offend me, and yet mightily Love to see me, and be glad of my coming home, if I have been abroad. . . . I would raise in them, an High Opinion of their Fathers Love to them, and of his being better able to Judge What is Good for them, than they are for themselves. I would bring them to Believe, Tis best for them to be and do as I would have them. . . . I will never dispence a Blow, except it be for an atrocius Crime, or for a lesser Fault Obstinately persisted in; either for an Enormity, or for an Obstinacy. I would ever Proportion chastisements unto Miscarriages; not smite bitterly for a very small piece of Childishness, and only frown a little for some real Wickedness. Nor shall my Chastisements ever be dispensed in a Passion, and a Fury; but with them, I will first show them the Command of GOD, by Transgressing whereof they have displeased me. The Slavish Raving, Fighting Way of Education too Commonly used, I look upon it as a considerable Article in the Wrath and Curse of God, upon a miserable World.

'As soon as we can, weel get up to yet Higher Principles. I will often tell the Children, What cause they have to Love a Glorious Christ, who has Dy'd for them. And, How much He will be Well-pleased with their Well-Doing. And what a Noble Thing, tis to follow His Example; which Example I will describe unto them. I will often tell them, That the Eye of God is upon them; the Great GOD knows all they do and Hears all they Speak. I will often tell them, That there will be a Time, when they must appear before the Judgment-Seat of the Holy LORD; and they must Now do nothing, that may Then be a Grief and Shame unto them. I will Set before them, the Delights of that Heaven that is prepar'd for Pious Children; and the Torments of that Hell that is prepared of old, for naughty ones. I will inform them of the Good Offices which the Good Angels do for Little Ones, that have the Fear of God and are afraid of Sin. . . .

'I would be very watchful and Cautious, about the Companions of my Children. I will be very Inquisitive, what Company they keep; If they are in hazard of being Ensnared by any Vicious Company, I will earnestly pull them out of it, as Brands out of the Burning. I will find out, and procure Laudable Companions for them. . . .

'I incline, that among all the Points of a Polite Education which I would endeavour for my Children, they may each of them, the Daughters as well as the Sons, have so much Insight into some Skill, which lies in the way of Gain, (the Limners, or the Scriveners, or the Apothecaries, or Some other Mystery, to which their own Inclination may most carry them,) that they may be able to Subsist themselves, and get something of a Livelihood, in case the Providence of God should bring them into Necessities. . . .

'As soon as ever I can, I would make my Children apprehensive of the main END, for which they are to Live; that so they may as soon as may be, begin to Live, and their Youth no be nothing but Vanity. I would show them, that their main END must be To Acknowledge the Great GOD, and His Glorious CHRIST; and bring Others to Acknowledge Him: And that they are never Wise nor Well, but when they are doing so. I would show them, what the Acknowledgments are, and how they are to be made. I would make them able to Answer the Grand Question, Why they Live; and what is the End of the Actions that they fill their Lives? Teach them, How their Creator and Redeemer is to be Obey'd in every thing; and how everything is to be done in Obedience to Him; Teach them, How even their Diversions, and their Ornaments, and the Tasks of their Education, must all be to fit them for the further Service of Him to whom I have devoted them. . . . '

✳   ✳   ✳

The School-Master has manifold Opportunities to Do Good. God made him sensible of his Obligations! We read, The Little Ones hath their Angels. It is an Hard work to keep a School. But it is a Good work; and it may be so done, as to be in some Sort like the Work of Angels. The Tutors of the Children may be like their Tutelar Angels. . . .

Tutors, will you not look upon the Children under your Wing as committed unto you, by the Glorious LORD, with a charge of this importance; Take them, and bring them up for me, and I will pay you your Wages! . . .

Sirs, Let it be a Great Intention with you, To instil Documents of Piety into the Children. Esteem it, Your and Their Great Interest, That they would So Know the Holy Scriptures as to be made Rise unto Salvation; and Know the Saviour, whom to know is Life Eternal, Oh! Take all occasions to Drop Some Honey out of the Rock upon them! Happy the Children, and as Happy the Master there they who made the Relation of their Conversion to Serious Piety, may say, There was a School-Master that brought us to CHRIST! You have been told; 'Certainly, Tis a Nobler work, to make the Little Ones Know their Saviour, than to know their Letters. The Lessons of Jesus are Nobler Things than the Lessons of Cato. A Sanctifying Transformation of their Souls, were a Nobler Thing, than meerly to construe Ovids Metamorphosis. He was a Good School-Master, of whom there was this Testimony given. . . .'

CATECHISING; That should be a frequent and at least, a Weekly, Exercise of the School. And in the most Edifying, and Aplicatory, and Admonatory manner carried on. . . .

Dr. Reynolds, in a Funeral Sermon on an Eminent School-Master has a passage worthy to be written in Letters of Gold. 'If Grammar Schools have Holy and Learned men for over them, not only the Brains, but also the Souls of the Children might be there enriched, and the work of Learning and of Grace too, be Betimes wrought in them.' In order to this, tis to be proposed That you would not only Pray with your Scholars every day, but also take occasion from the Publick Sermons, and from Remarkable Occurences of Providence in your Neighbourhood, often to inculcate the Lessons of Piety upon the Children.

Tutors in the College, may do well Successively to treat each of their Pupils alone, with all possible Solemnity and Affection, about their interior state; show them how to Repent of Sin, and Believe on Christ; and bring them to Express Resolutions of Serious Piety. Sirs, you may do a thousand Things, to render your Pupils Orthodox in their Principles, Regular in their Practices, Qualified for Services!

I have read this Experiment of One who had pupils under his charge; He made it his Custom, that in every Recitation, he would, from something or other occurring in it, make an occasion, to let fall some Sentence, which had a Tendency to promote the Fear of God in their Hearts; which thing Sometimes did indeed put him to more than a little Study; but the Good Effect Sufficiently Recompenced it!

If I should Press for certain Authors to be made Classical in the Grammar-Schools which are not commonly used there; Such as Castalio for the Latin Tongue, and Posselius for the Greek; or, if I should beg, with certain Modern Writers, That there may be a Northwest Passage found, for the Attaining of the Latin Tongue, that instead of, a Journey which may be dispatched in a Few Days, they may not wander, like the Children of Israel, many years in the Wilderness: Or, if I should recite Austins complaints, of Little Boys Learning the filthy Actions of the Pagan Gods in the Schools, . . . and Luthers, 'That our Schools are more Pagan than Christian;' And the Reports and Wishes of a late Writer, who sayes; 'I knew an aged and famous School-Master, that after he had kept School about Fifty years, said with a Sad Countenance, That it was a great Trouble unto him that he spent so much Time in Reading Pagan authors to his Scholars, and wished it were customary to Read such a Book as Duports Verses upon Job, rather than Homer, and such Books. I pray God, put it in the Hearts of a Wise Parliament, to Purge our Schools; that instead of Learning Vain Fictions, and Filthy Stories they may be acquainted with Books containing Grave Sayings, and things that may make them truely Wise and Useful in the World:' I suppose, there will be little Notice taken of such Proposals: I had as good never mention them; Tis with Dispair that I make mention of them.

Among the Occasions to be taken for Instilling of Piety into the Scholars, there is One peculiarly at the Writing-Schools. An inveterate Sinner I have read of, Converted into Serious Piety, by accidentally seeing that Sentence of Austin written in a Window; He that hath Promised Pardon to the Penitent Sinner, has not Promised Repentance to the Presumptious One. Who can tell what Good may be done to the Young Scholar, by a Sentence in a Copybook? Let their Copies be of

Sentences worthy to be had in Everlasting Remembrance; of Sentences, that shall have the brightest Maxims of Wisdom in them. . . .

At the Grammar School also, the Scholars may be ordered for their Exercises to turn such things into Latin, as may be likewise for their Instruction and Establishment, in the Principles of Christianity. . . . Their Epistles, why may they not be on such Subjects as may most befriend Vertue in them!

I will add this; To carry on the Discipline of the School, with Rewards, as well as Punishments, is most certainly very Adviseable, very Preferrible. There may be Invented many ways of Rewarding, the Diligent and the Laudable; . . . a Child of any Ingenuity, under the Expectations and Encouragements of being Rewarded, will do the uttermost. . . . If a Fault must be Punished, Let Instruction, both unto the Delinquent and unto the Spectator, accompany the Correction. Let the Odious Nature of the Sin, that has Enforced the Correction, be declared; and let nothing be done in a Passion; all be done with all the Evidence of compassion that may be.

COTTON MATHER ON POETRY AND STYLE (1726) From Perry Miller and Thomas H. Johnson, eds., *The Puritans* (New York, 1938), pp. 684-86

Poetry, whereof we have now even an Antediluvian piece in our hands, has from the beginning been in such request, that I must needs recommend unto you some acquaintance with it. Though some have had a soul so unmusical, that they have decried all verse as being but a meer playing and fiddling upon words; all versifying, as if it were more unnatural than if we should chuse dancing instead of walking; and rhyme, as if it were but a sort of morisce-dancing with bells: yet I cannot wish you a soul that shall be wholly unpoetical. An old Horace has left us an art of poetry, which you may do well to bestow a perusal on. And besides your lyric hours, I wish you may so far understand an epic poem, that the beauties of an Homer and a Virgil may be discerned with you. As to the moral part of Homer, it is true, and let me not be counted a Zoilus for saying so, that by first exhibiting their gods as no better than rogues, he set open the flood-gates for a prodigious inundation of wickedness to break in upon the nations, and was one of the greatest apostles the devil ever had in the world. Among the rest that felt the ill impressions of this universal corrupter, (as men of the best sentiments have called him,) one was that overgrown robber, of execrable memory, whom we celebrate under the name of Alexander the Great; who by his continual admiring and studying of his Iliad, and by following that false model of heroic virtue set before him in his Achilles, became one of the worst of men, and at length inflated with the ridiculous pride of being himself a deity, exposed himself to all the scorn that could belong to a lunatic. And hence, notwithstanding the veneration which this idol has had, yet Plato banishes him out of a common-wealth, the welfare whereof he was concerned for. Nevertheless, custom or conscience obliges him to bear testimonies unto many points of morality. And it is especially observable, that he commonly propounds prayer to heaven as a most necessary preface unto all important enterprizes; and when the action comes on too suddenly for a more extended supplication, he yet will not let it come on without an ejaculation; and he never speaks of any supplication but he brings in a gracious answer to it. I have seen a travesteering high-flier, not much to our dishonour, scoff at Homer for this; as making his actors to be like those whom the English call dissenters. . . .

. . . Nevertheless, it is observed, that the Pagans had no rules of manners that were more laudable and regular than what are to be found in him. And some have said, it is hardly possible seriously to read his works without being more disposed unto goodness, as well as being greatly entertained. To be sure, had Virgil writ before Plato, his works had not been any of the books prohibited. But then, this poet also has abundance of rare antiquities for us: and such things, as others besides a Servius, have imagined that they have instructed and obliged mankind, by employing all their days upon. Wherefore if his Aeneid, (which though it were once near twenty times as big as he has left it, yet he has left it unfinished,) may not appear so valuable to you, that you may think twenty-seven verses of the part that is the most finished in it, worth one and twenty hundred pounds and odd money, yet his Georgics, which he put his last hand to, will furnish you with many things far from despicable. But after all, when I said, I was willing that the beauties of these poets might become visible to your visive faculty in poetry, I did not mean that you should judge nothing to be admittable into an epic poem, which is not authorized by their example; but I perfectly concur with one who is inexpressibly more capable to be a judge of such a matter than I can be; that it is a false critic who, with a petulant air, will insult reason itself, if it presumes to oppose such authority.

I proceed now to say, that if (under the guidance of a Vida) you try your young wings now and then to see what flights you can make, at least for an epigram, it may a little sharpen your sense, and polish your style for more important performances; for this purpose you are now even overstocked with patterns, and— *Poemata passim,* you may, like Nazianzen, all your days make a little recreation of poetry in the midst of your painful studies. Nevertheless, I cannot but advise you. Withhold thy throat from thirst. Be not so set upon poetry, as to be always poring on the passionate and measured pages. Let not what should be sauce, rather than food for you, engross all your application. Beware of a boundless and sickly appetite for the reading of the poems which now the rickety nation swarms withal; and let not the Circaean cup intoxicate you. But especially preserve the chastity of your soul from the dangers you may incur, by a conversation with muses that are no better than harlots: among which are others besides Ovid's Epistles, which for their tendency to excite and foment impure flames, and cast coals into your bosom, deserve rather to be thrown into the fire, than to be laid before the eye which a covenant should be made withal. Indeed, not merely for the impurities which they convey but also on some other accounts; the powers of darkness have a library among us, whereof the poets have been the most numerous as well as the most venemous authors. Most of the modern plays, as well as the romances, and novels and fictions, which are a sort of poems, do belong to the catalogue of this cursed library. The plays, I say, in which there are so many passages that have a tendency to overthrow all piety, that one, whose name is Bedford, has extracted near seven thousand instances of them, from the plays chiefly of but five years preceding; and says awfully upon them, They are national sins, and therefore call for national plagues; and if God should enter into judgment, all the blood in the nation would not be able to atone for them.

THE EDUCATION OF THE REVEREND JOHN BARNARD (1766) From
"Autobiography of the Reverend John Barnard," as quoted in *Massachusetts Historical Society Collections*, 3rd. ser., vol. V, pp. 178-87.

I, John Barnard was born at Boston, 6th Nov. 1681; descended from reputable parents, viz. John and Esther Barnard, remarkable for their piety and benevolence, who devoted me to the service of God, in the work of the ministry, from my very conception and birth; and accordingly took special care to instruct me themselves in the principles of the Christian religion, and kept me close at school to furnish my young mind with the knowledge of letters. By that time I had a little passed my sixth year, I had left my reading school, in the latter part of which my mistress made me a sort of usher, appointing me to teach some children that were older than myself, as well as smaller ones; and in which time I had read my Bible through thrice. My parents thought me to be weakly, because of my thin habit and countenance, and therefore sent me into the country, where I spent my seventh summer, and by the change of air and diet and exercise I grew more fleshy and hardy; and that I might not lose my reading, was put to a school-mistress, and returned home in the fall.

In the spring of my eighth year I was sent to the grammar school, under the tuition of the aged, venerable, and justly famous Mr. Ezekiel Cheever. But after a few weeks, an odd accident drove me from the school. There was an older lad entered the school the same week with me; we strove who should outdo; and he beat me by the help of a brother in the upper class, who stood behind master with the accidence open for him to read out off; by which means he could recite his . . . three and four times in a forenoon, and the same in the afternoon; but I who had no such help, and was obliged to committ all to memory, could not keep pace with him; so that he would be always one lesson before me. My ambition could not bear to be outdone, and in such a fraudulent manner, and therefore I left the school. About this time arrived a dissenting minister from England, who opened a private school for reading, writing, and Latin. My good father put me under his tuition, with whom I spent a year and a half. The gentleman receiving but little encouragement, threw up his school, and returned me to my father, and again I was sent to my aged Mr. Cheever, who placed me in the lowest class; . . .

In the time of my absence from Mr. Cheever, it pleased God to take to himself my dear mother, who was not only a very virtuous, but a very intelligent woman. She was exceeding fond of my learning, and taught me to pray. My good father also instructed me, and made a little closet for me to retire to for my morning and evening devotion. But, alas! how childish and hypocritical were all my pretensions to piety, there being little or no serious thoughts of God and religion in me. . . .

Though my master advanced me, as above, yet I was a very naughty boy, much given to play, insomuch that he at length openly declared, "You Barnard, I know you can do well enough if you will; but you are so full of play that you hinder your classmates from getting their lessons; and therefore, if any of them cannot perform their duty, I shall correct you for it." One unlucky day, one of my classmates did not look into his book, and therefore could not say his lesson, though I called upon him once and again to mind his book; upon which our master beat me. I told master the reason why he could not say his lesson was, his declaring he would beat me if any of the class were wanting in their duty; since which this boy would not look into his book, though I called upon him to mind his book, as the class could witness. The boy was pleased with my being corrected, and persisted in his neglect, for which I was still corrected, and that for several days. I thought, in justice, I ought to correct the boy, and compel him to a better temper; and therefore, after school was done, I went up to him, and told him I had been beaten several times for his neglect; and since master would not correct him I would, and I should do so often as I was corrected for him; and then drubbed him heartily. The boy never came to school any more, and so that unhappy affair ended.

Though I was often beaten for my play, and my little roguish tricks, yet I don't remember that I was ever beaten for my book more than once or twice. One of these was upon this occasion. Master put our class upon turning Aesop's Fables into Latin verse. Some dull fellows made a shift to perform this to acceptance; but I was so much duller at this exercise, that I could make nothing of it; for which master corrected me, and this he did two or three days going. I had honestly tried my possibles to perform the task; but having no poetical fancy, nor then a capacity opened of expressing the same idea by a variation of phrases, though I was perfectly acquainted with prosody, I found I could do nothing; and therefore plainly told my master, that I had diligently labored all I could to perform what he required, and perceiving I had not genius for it, I thought it was in vain to strive against nature any longer; and he never more required it of me. Nor had I any thing of a poetical genius till after I had been at College some time, when upon reading some of Mr. Cowley's works, I was highly pleased, and a new scene opened before me.

From the grammar school I was admitted into the college in Cambridge, in New England, in July, 1696, under the Presidentship of the very revered and excellent Dr. Increase Mather, (who gave me for a thesis, *Habenti dabitur,*) and the tutorage of those two great men, Mr. John Leverett, (afterwards President) and Mr. William Brattle (afterwards the worthy minister of Cambridge.) Mr. Leverett became my special tutor for about a year and a half, to whom succeeded Mr. Jabez Fitch, (afterwards the minister of Ipswich with Mr. John Rogers, who at the invitation of the church in Portsmouth, New Hampshire, removed to them.) Upon my entereing into college, I became chamber-mate, the first year, to a senior and junior sophister; which might have been greatly to my advantage, had they been of a studious disposition, and made any considerable progress in literature. But, alas! they were an idle pack, who knew but little, and took no pains to increase their knowledge. When therefore, according to my disposition, which was ambitious to excel, I applied myself close to books, and began to look forward into the next year's exercises, this unhappy pair greatly discouraged me, and beat me off from my studies, so that by their persuasions I foolishly threw by my books, and soon became as idle as they were. Oh! how baneful is it to be linked with bad company! and what a vile heart had I to hearken to their wretched persuasions! I never, after this, recovered a good studious disposition, while I was at college. Having a ready, quick memory, which rendered the common exercises of the college easy to me, and being an active youth, I was hurried almost continually into one diversion or another, and gave myself to no particular studies, and therefore made no great proficiency in any part of solid learning. . . .

In the last year of my being at college, it pleased God, in righteous judgment, so far to deliver me up to the corrupt workings of my own heart, that I fell into a scandalous sin, in which some of my classmates were concerned. This roused me more seriously to bethink myself of the wickedness of my heart and life; and though I had kept up some little show of religion, yet now I saw what a terrible punishment it was to be left of God, and exposed to his wrath and vengeance, and set myself upon seeking an interest in the favor of God, through the blessed Mediator; and resolved, through the grace of God assisting of me, to lead a sober, a righteous, and a godly life, and improve my time and talents in the service of my Maker and Redeemer, and applied myself more closely to my studies: but I found I could not recover what I had lost by my negligence.

In July, 1700, I took my first degree, Dr. Increase Mather being President; after which I returned to my honoured father's house, where I betook myself to close studying, and humbling myself before God with fasting and prayer, imploring the pardon of all my sins, through the mediation of Christ; begging the divine Spirit to sanctify me throughout, in spirit, soul, and body, and fit me for, and use me in the service of the sanctuary, and direct and bless all my studies to that end. I joined to the North Church in Boston, under the pastoral care of the two Mathers. . . .

While I continued at my good father's I prosecuted my studies; and looked something into the mathematics, though I gained but little; our advantages therefor being noways equal to what they have, who now have the great Sir Isaac Newton, and Dr. Halley, and some other mathematicians, for their guides. About this time I made a visit to the college, as I generally did once or twice a year, where I remember the conversation turning upon the mathematics, one of the company, who was a considerable proficient in them, observing my ignorance, said to me he would give me a question, which if I answered in a month's close application, he should account me an apt scholar. He gave me the question. I, who was ashamed of the reproach cast upon me, set myself hard to work, and in a fortnight's time returned him a solution to the question, both by trigonometry and geometry, with a canon by which to resolve all questions of the like nature. When I showed it to him, he was surprised, said it was right, and owned he knew no way of resolving it but by algebra, which I was an utter stranger to. I also gave myself to the study of the Biblical Hebrew, turned the Lord's prayer, the creed, and part of the Assembly's Catechism into Hebrew, (for which I had Dr. Cotton Mather for my corrector,) and entered on the task of finding the radix of every Hebrew word in the Bible, with design to form a Hebrew Concordance; but when I proceeded through a few chapters in Genesis, I found the work was done to my hand by one of the Buxtorfs. So I laid it by.

The pulpit being my great design, and divinity my chief study, I read all sorts of authors, and as I read, compared their sentiments with the sacred writings, and formed my judgment of the doctrines of Christianity by that only and infallible standard of truth; which led me insensibly into what is called the Calvinistical scheme, (though I never to this day have read Calvin's Works, and cannot call him master,) which sentiments, by the most plausible arguments to the contrary, that have fallen in my way, (and I have read the most of them,) I have never yet seen cause to depart from.

Through the importunity of my friends, I preached my first sermon, . . . to a society of young men, meeting on Lord's day evening for the exercises of religion, (to which I belonged) in the August twelvemonth after I took my first degree; and some months after preached publicly at Gloucester. By August, 1702, I became almost a constant preacher, both on week days, and on the Lord's day. . . . This constant preaching took me off from all other studies. About two months before I took my second degree, the reverend and deservedly famous Mr. Samuel Willard, then Vice-President, called upon me, (though I lived in Boston), to give a common-place in the college hall; which I did, endeavoring to prove the divine inspiration and authority of the holy Scriptures. When I had concluded, the President was so good as to say openly in the hall, *"Bene fecisti, Barnarde, et gratias ago tibi."*

PROVINCIALS

The Great Awakening

JONATHAN EDWARDS DESCRIBES A MODEL CHILD (1736)   From
Jonathan Edwards, *A Narrative of Many Surprising Conversions in Northampton and Vicinity, 1736* (Worcester, Mass., 1832), pp. 66-69.

I now proceed to the other instance that I would give an account of, which is of the little child forementioned. Her name is Phebe Bartlet, daughter of William Bartlet. I shall give the account as I took it from the mouths of her parents, whose veracity, none that know them doubt.

She was born in March, in the year 1731. About the latter end of April, or beginning of May, 1735, she was greatly affected by the talk of her brother, who had been hopefully converted a little before, at about eleven years of age, and then seriously talked to her about the great things of religion. Her parents did not know of it at that time, and were not wont, in the counsels they gave to their children, particularly to direct themselves to her, by reason of her being so young, and, as they supposed not capable of understanding; but after her brother had talked to her, they observed her very earnestly to listen to the advice they gave to the other children, and she was observed very constantly to retire, several times in a day, as was concluded, for secret prayer, and grew more and more engaged in religion, and was more frequent in her closet, till at last she was wont to visit it five or six times in a day, and was so engaged in it, that nothing would at any time divert her from her stated closet exercises. Her mother often observed and watched her, when such things occurred, as she thought most likely to divert her, either by putting it out of her thoughts, or otherwise engaging her inclinations, but never could observe her to fail. She mentioned some very remarkable instances.

She once, of her own accord, spake of her unsuccessfulness, in that she could not find God, or to that purpose. But on Thursday, the last day of July, about the middle of the day, the child being in the closet, where it used to retire, its mother heard it speaking aloud, which was unusual, and never had been observed before; and her voice seemed to be as of one exceeding importunate and engaged, but her mother could distinctly hear only these words (spoken in her childish manner, but seemed to be spoken with extraordinary earnestness, and out of distress of soul), Pray BLESSED LORD give me salvation! I PRAY, BEG pardon all my sins! When the child had done prayer, she came out of the closet, and came and sat down by her mother, and cried out aloud. Her mother very earnestly asked her several times, what the matter was, before she would make any answer, but she continued exceedingly crying, and wreathing her body to and fro, like one in anguish of spirit. Her mother then asked her whether she was afraid that God would not give her salvation. She then answered yes, I am afraid I shall go to hell! Her mother then endeavored to quiet her at all—but she continued thus earnestly crying and taking on for some time, till at length she suddenly ceased crying and began to smile, and presently said with a smiling countenance, Mother, the kingdom of heaven is come to me! Her mother was surprised at the sudden alteration, and at the speech, and knew not what to make of it, but at first said nothing to her. The child presently spake again, and said, there is another come to me, and there is another, there is three; and being asked what she meant, she answered, One is thy will be done; and there is another, enjoy him forever; by which it seems that when the child said there is three come to me, she meant three passages of its catechism that came to her mind.

After the child had said this, she retired again into her closet; and her mother went over to her brother's, who was next neighbor; and when she came back, the child being come out of the closet, meets her mother with this cheering speech; I can find God now! Referring to what she had before complained of, that she could not find God. Then the child spoke again, and said, I love God! Her mother asked her how well she loved God, whether she loved God better than her father and mother; she said, yes. Then she asked her whether she loved God better than her little sister Rachel, she answered yes, better than any thing!

JONATHAN EDWARDS ON THE NECESSITY OF RELIGIOUS EDUCATION (c. 1737)   From Tyron Edwards, ed., *Works of Jonathan Edwards* (New York, 1842), vol. I, pp. 132-37.

JOHN 18:37.—TO THIS END WAS I BORN,
AND FOR THIS CAUSE CAME I INTO THE WORLD,
THAT I SHOULD BEAR WITNESS UNTO THE TRUTH.

These are the words of our blessed Savior. In them he informs us, that one end of his incarnation and ministry was, that by bearing witness to the truth, he might communicate the knowledge of it. The same is doubtless the end of the ordinary ministry of the gospel, and should be the object aimed at by every minister. From our text therefore I deduce this doctrine:

The great duty of the ministers of the gospel is, to preach the truth.

Under this doctrine I purpose,

I. To show what truth ministers of the gospel ought to preach.

II. To mention some reasons in confirmation of the doctrine.

I. I am to show what truth a minister of the gospel ought to preach.

Truth is very extensive and of various kinds. There is truth in every science, in mathematics, philosophy, history, etc. It will not be pretended, that mathematical and philosophical truth is the proper subject of the evangelical ministry. Nor is historical truth, any further than it illustrates the gospel, by exhibiting the facts of it, or other important facts relating to the works and the character of God.

The truth then intended in the doctrine is primarily evangelical truth, and secondarily all other truth which relates to the gospel and tends to illustrate it; as all truth relating to God and His character, especially His moral perfections; all truth relating to His supreme, universal and sovereign government; all truth relating to His law, its requirements and threatenings; relating to sin, its nature and evil; relating to ourselves our present fallen state, and the ruin consequent of the fall.

. . . For a minister to neglect the study of those truths from indolence, is still worse; it is inexcusable. Ministers are bound to be at least as industrious as other men, and many arguments might be mentioned why they should, if their health admit, be still more industrious.

But it is to be feared, that some neglect study on a still different principle. They are afraid, that if they study thoroughly and attend to what has been or may be said on certain important subjects, they shall be convinced, that those doctrines are true, which in some places are extremely unpopular. Therefore they do not wish to be convinced of their truth, and will not attend to them, lest they should be convinced; or lest they should be under a necessity of giving their opinion concerning them, and thus expose themselves to the censure of one party or the other, either the advocates or the opposers of those doctrines. For this reason they will not read those books, in which those doctrines are contained, nor converse much with those persons, who hold them. And if they be asked their opinion, they make this apology for not giving it, that they have not read the books, nor examined the arguments relating to those doctrines; and of set purpose they avoid to do either.

Now can this be justified? What is this but shutting their eyes against the light? And how can this be done with a good conscience? Are we not commanded to "prove all things, and to hold fast that which is good?" Besides; this conduct argues a want of liberality of sentiment, and a contractedness, which it is presumed, they who act in this manner, would not wish to have imputed to them. A man of true liberality of sentiment and feeling, is willing to hear both sides of every important question, and is not afraid that he shall receive too much light.

Hence we learn, that it is the duty of ministers of the gospel, to preach the truth plainly and in a manner that is intelligible to their people in general. I have endeavored to show, that it is their principal duty to preach the truth; but to preach it in obscure and unintelligible terms is not very different from not preaching it at all. The words of the apostle Paul are worthy of notice in this case. 1 Cor. 14:19, "In the church I had rather speak five words with my understanding, that with my voice I might teach others also, than ten thousand words in an unknown tongue."

*　　*　　*

We infer that ministers are not bound to preach *plain* things only. This is the idea of some; and that ministers ought never to meddle with things which are not plain. But unless this be so explained, as to be nothing but what all will grant, it can never be supported. If by plain things, be meant things which are already plain and well known to the hearers, then a minister is never to teach his people anything; and he is bound to preach so to them, that they shall not, under his preaching, make the least improvement in christian knowledge; which is absurd and what no man will undertake to support. But if by *plain things* he meant, things which are capable of being made plain to the hearers, or which, if they will be attentive and candid, may, by the evidence of reason or revelation, be made to appear to be credible and manifest truths; it is granted that in this sense a minister must preach plain things only. But the proposition thus explained, comes to nothing.

Also hence we see the absurdity of parents refusing to teach their children any particular sentiments in religion, even those which they themselves believe; and leaving them to judge for themselves, without any such instruction. This is advocated and practised by some, on the pretences, that their children have a right of private judgment in religion and a liberty of conscience; that teaching them any particular religious sentiments would curtail this liberty, would shackle their judgment and their genius, and would prevent improvement. But these reasons, if they prove anything prove too much, and so confute themselves. Children grown to a proper age have a right to judge for themselves in politics, as well as religion. They have a right to judge, whether monarchy or democracy, whether a free or a despotic government be the best. Also they have a right to judge for themselves in morals, whether it be best and obligatory on them, to be temperate and prudent, and to observe truth and justice in their intercourse with their fellow-men. Yet no man will be thought to curtail his son's right of private judgment or his liberty of conscience, by teaching him the principles of true civil liberty, or the moral duties of temperance, prudence, and justice. Nay, our children at a proper age, have a right to judge for themselves what business to follow in life and in what manner to carry it on. Yet no man scruples to bring up his son to some particular business. Nor does any man imagine, that he curtails the liberty of his son, by educating him for a scholar, a husbandman or a mechanic. Nor is it ever thought that if parents educate their children to some particular business, they cramp their genius or prevent improvement. On the principle which I am considering, a parent must never teach his son anything. Though he wish to have him a husbandman, he must never teach him the use of the plough or scythe; though he wish to have him a carpenter, he must never teach the use of the saw or chisel; though he wish to have him a scholar, he must never teach him to read or write; for the son has the same right of private judgment concerning the best mode of reading and writing, and of using any kind of utensils, which he has to judge in matters of religion; and teaching him any of the things just mentioned would be as likely to prevent improvement by cramping his genius, as teaching him the principles of christianity.

As these ideas of the education of children are contrary to reason, they are equally contrary to scripture. That commands us to "train up a child in the way he should go," with encouragement that "when he is old, he shall not depart from it," and to "bring up our children in the nurture and admonition of the Lord."

Some allow indeed, that children are to be taught that the scriptures are the word of God; but are not to be taught the particular doctrines contained in the scriptures; that as to the meaning and contents of the scriptures, they are to judge entirely for themselves. But why are they not to be taught, as well that the scriptures contain such and such particular doctrines, as that the scriptures themselves are the word of God? They have the same right of private judgment in the one of these cases as the other. To teach our children, that the scriptures are the word of God, and not to teach them any of the particular doctrines of scripture, is like carefully teaching them that a certain volume contains the laws of our country; but at the same time cautiously avoiding to teach them any of the laws which are contained in that volume; or teaching them, that husbandry is the best business of life; yet not teaching them anything in particular concerning husbandry.

JONATHAN EDWARDS ON THE WORK OF GOD IN NORTHAMPTON

(1737)   From "A Faithful Narrative of the Surprising Work of God in the Conversion of Many Hundred Souls in Northampton. . ." (1737), as quoted in *The Works of President Edwards* (New York, 1844), vol. III, pp. 233-37.

At the latter end of the year 1733, there appeared a very unusual flexibleness, and yielding to advice, in our young people. It had been too long their manner to make the evening after the Sabbath, and after our public lecture, to be especially the times of their mirth, and company keeping. But a sermon was now preached on the Sabbath before the lecture, to show the evil tendency of the practice, and to persuade them to reform it; and it was urged on heads of families, that it should be a thing agreed upon among them, to govern their families, and keep their children at home, at these times. . . . It was more privately moved, that they should meet together the next day, in their several neighborhoods, to know each other's minds. Which was accordingly done, and the motion complied with throughout the town. But parents found little or no occasion for the exercise of government in the case; the young people declared themselves convinced by what they had heard from the pulpit, and were willing of themselves to comply with the counsel that had been given. And it was immediately, and, I suppose, almost universally complied with, and there was a thorough reformation of these disorders thenceforward, which has continued ever since.

Presently after this, there began to appear a remarkable religious concern at a little village belonging to the congregation, called Pascommuck, where a few families were settled, at about three miles distance from the main body of the town. At this place a number of persons seemed to be savingly wrought upon. In the April following, anno 1734, there happened a very sudden and awful death of a young man in the bloom of his youth; who being violently seized with a pleurisy, and taken immediately very delirious, died in about two days; which (together with what was preached publicly on that occasion) much affected many young people. This was followed with another death of a young married woman, who had been considerably exercised in mind, about the salvation of her soul, before she was ill, and was in great distress, in the beginning of her illness, but seemed to have satisfying evidences of God's saving mercy to her, before her death, so that she died very full of comfort, in a most earnest and moving manner, warning and counselling others. This seemed much to contribute to the solemnizing of the spirits of many young persons, and there began evidently to appear more of a religious concern on people's minds.

In the fall of the year, I proposed it to the young people, that they should agree among themselves to spend the evenings after lectures, in social religion, and to that end divide themselves into several companies to meet in various parts of the town; which was accordingly done, and those meetings have been since continued, and the example imitated by elder people. This was followed with the death of an elderly person, which was attended with many unusual circumstances, by which many were much moved and affected.

About this time began the great noise that was in this part of the country, about Arminianism, which seemed to appear with a very threatening aspect upon the interest of religion here. The friends of vital piety trembled for fear of the issue. But it seemed, contrary to their fear, strongly to be overruled for the promoting of religion. Many who looked on themselves as in a Christless condition seemed to be awakened by it, with fear that God was about to withdraw from the land, and that we should be given up to heterodoxy, and corrupt principles, and that then their opportunity for obtaining salvation would be past. And many who were brought a little to doubt about the truth of the doctrines they had hitherto been taught, seemed to have a kind of trembling fear with their doubts, lest they should be led into by-paths, to their eternal undoing. And they seemed with much concern and engagedness of mind to inquire what was indeed the way in which they must come to be accepted with God. There were some things said publicly on that occasion, concerning justification by faith alone.

Although great fault was found with meddling with the controversy in the pulpit, by such a person, and at that time, and though it was ridiculed by many elsewhere, yet it proved a word spoken in season here, and was most evidently attended with a very remarkable blessing of heaven to the souls of the people in this town. They received thence a general satisfaction, with respect to the main thing in question, which they had in trembling doubts and concern about, and their minds were engaged the more earnestly to seek that they might come to be accepted of God, and saved in the way of the gospel, which had been made evident to them to be the true and only way. And then it was, in the latter part of December, that the Spirit of God began extraordinarily to set in, and wonderfully to work amongst us. And there were, very suddenly, one after another, five or six persons, who were, to all appearance, savingly converted, and some of them wrought upon in a very remarkable manner.

Particularly, I was surprised with the relation of a young woman, who had been one of the greatest company keepers in the whole town. When she came to me, I had never heard that she was become in any wise serious, but by the conversation I then had with her, it appeared to me, that what she gave an account of, was a glorious work of God's infinite power and sovereign grace, and that God had given her a new heart, truly broken and sanctified. I could not then doubt of it, and have seen much in my acquaintance with her since to confirm it.

Though the work was glorious, yet I was filled with concern about the effect it might have upon others. I was ready to conclude (though too rashly) that some would be hardened by it, in carelessness and looseness of life, and would take occasion from it to open their mouths in reproaches of religion. But the event was the reverse, to a wonderful degree. God made it, I suppose, the greatest occasion of awakening to others, of any thing that ever came to pass in the town. I have had abundant opportunity to know the effect it had, by my private conversation with many. The news of it seemed to be almost like a flash of lightning, upon the hearts of young people, all over the town, and upon many others. Those persons amongst us, who used to be farthest from seriousness, and that I most feared would make an ill improvement of it, seemed greatly to be awakened with it. Many went to talk with her, concerning what she had met with, and what appeared in her seemed to be to the satisfaction of all that did so.

Presently upon this, a great and earnest concern about the great things of religion, and the eternal world, became universal in all parts of the town, and among persons of all degrees, and all ages. The noise amongst the dry bones waxed louder and louder. All other talk but about spiritual and eternal things was soon thrown by. All the conversation in all companies, and upon all occasions, was upon these things only, unless so much as was necessary for people carrying on their ordinary secular business. Other discourse than of the things of religion, would scarcely be tolerated in any company. The minds of people were wonderfully taken off from the world; it was treated amongst us as a thing of very little consequence. They seemed to follow their worldly business, more as a part of their duty, than from any disposition they had to it. The temptation now seemed to lie on that hand, to neglect worldly affairs too much, and to spend too much time in the immediate exercise of religion. Which thing was exceedingly misrepresented by reports that were spread in distant parts of the land, as though the people here had wholly thrown by all worldly business, and betook themselves entirely to reading and praying, and such like religious exercises.

But though the people did not ordinarily neglect their worldly business . . . religion was with all sorts the great concern, and the world was a thing only by the by. The only thing in their view was to get the kingdom of heaven, and every one appeared pressing into it. The engagedness of their hearts in this great concern could not be hid. It appeared in their very countenances. It then was a dreadful thing amongst us to lie out of Christ, in danger every day of dropping into hell, and what persons minds were intent upon was to escape for their lives, and to *fly from the wrath to come.* All would eagerly lay hold of opportunities for their souls, and were wont very often to meet together in private houses, for religious purposes. And such meetings, when appointed, were wont greatly to be thronged.

There was scarcely a single person in the town, either old or young, that was left unconcerned about the great things of the eternal world. Those that were wont to be the vainest, and loosest, and those that had been most disposed to think and speak slightly of vital and experimental religion; were now generally subject to great awakenings. And the work of conversion was carried on in a most astonishing manner, and increased more and more. Souls did, as it were, come by flocks to Jesus Christ. From day to day, for many months together, might be seen evident instances of sinners brought *out of darkness into marvellous light,* and delivered *out of an horrible pit, and from the miry clay, and set upon a rock* with *a new song of praise to God in their mouths.*

This work of God, as it was carried on, and the number of true saints multiplied, soon made a glorious alteration in the town; so that in the spring and summer following, anno 1735, the town seemed to be full of the presence of God. It never was so full of love, nor so full of joy, and yet so full of distress as it was then. There were remarkable tokens of God's presence in almost every house. It was a time of joy in families on the account of salvation's being brought unto them; parents rejoicing over their children as new born, and husbands over their wives, and wives over their husbands. *The goings of God were then seen in his sanctuary, God's day was a delight, and his tabernacles were amiable.* Our public assemblies were then beautiful. The congregation was alive in God's service, every one earnestly intent on the public worship, every hearer eager to drink in the words of the minister as they came from his mouth. The assembly in general were, from time to time, in tears while the word was preached, some weeping with sorrow and distress, others with joy and love, others with pity and concern for the souls of their neighbors.

JONATHAN EDWARDS DESCRIBES THE "CHILDREN OF WRATH"

(1740) From "Thoughts on the Revival of Religion in New England," as quoted in *The Works of President Edwards* (New York, 1856), vol. III, pp. 202-03.

What has more especially given offence to many, and raised a loud cry against some preachers, as though their conduct were intolerable, is their frightening poor innocent children, with talk of hell fire, and eternal damnation. But if those that complain so loudly of this, really believe, what is the general profession of the country, viz. That all are by nature the children of wrath, and heirs of hell; and that every one that has not been born again, whether he be young or old, is exposed, every moment, to eternal destruction, under the wrath of Almighty God; I say, if they really believe this, then such a complaint and cry as this, betrays a great deal of weakness and inconsideration. As innocent as children seem to be to us, yet, if they are out of Christ, they are not so in God's sight, but are young vipers, and are infinitely more hateful than vipers, and are in a most miserable condition, as well as grown persons; and they are naturally very senseless and stupid, being born as the wild asses colt, and need much to awaken them. Why should we conceal the truth from them? Will those children that have been dealt tenderly with, in this respect, and lived and died insensible of their misery, until they come to feel it in hell, ever thank parents, and others, for their tenderness, in not letting them know what they were in danger of. If parents' love towards their children was not blind, it would affect them much more to see their children every day exposed to eternal burnings, and yet senseless, than to see them suffer the distress of that awakening, that is necessary in order to their escape from them, and that tends to their being eternally happy, as the children of God. A child that has a dangerous wound, may need the painful lance, as well as grown persons; and that would be a foolish pity, in such a case, that should hold back the lance, and throw away the life. I have seen the happy effects of dealing plainly, and thoroughly with children, in the concerns of their souls, without sparing them at all, in many instances; and never knew any ill consequences of it in any one instance.

SERMON BY JONATHAN EDWARDS **(1741)** From "Sinners in the Hands of an Angry God," as quoted in H. Norman Gardiner, ed., *Selected Sermons of Jonathan Edwards* (New York, 1904), pp. 88-89, 96-97.

The God that holds you over the pit of hell, much as one holds a spider or some loathsome insect over the fire, abhors you, and is dreadfully provoked; his wrath towards you burns like fire; he looks upon you as worthy of nothing else, but to be cast into the fire; he is of purer eyes than to bear to have you in his sight; you are ten thousand times so abominable in his eyes, as the most hateful and venomous serpent is in ours. You have offended him infinitely more than ever a stubborn rebel did his prince: and yet it is nothing but his hand that holds you from falling into the fire every moment. 'Tis ascribed to nothing else, that you did not go to hell the last night; that you were suffered to awake again in this world after you closed your eyes to sleep; and there is no other reason to be given why you have not dropped into hell since you arose in the morning, but that God's hand held you up. There is no other reason to be given why you han't gone to hell since you have sat here in the house of God, provoking his pure eyes by your sinful wicked manner of attending his solemn worship. Yea, there is nothing else that is to be given as a reason why you don't this very moment drop down into hell.

O sinner! consider the fearful danger you are in. 'Tis a great furnace of wrath, a wide and bottomless pit, full of the fire of wrath, that you are held over in the hand of that God whose wrath is provoked and incensed as much against you as against many of the damned in hell. You hang by a slender thread, with the flames of divine wrath flashing about it, and ready every moment to singe it and burn it asunder; and you have no interest in any Mediator, and nothing to lay hold of to save yourself, nothing to keep off the flames of wrath, nothing of your own, nothing that you ever have done, nothing that you can do, to induce God to spare you one moment.

＊　　＊　　＊

And you that are young men and young women, will you neglect this precious season that you now enjoy, when so many others of your age are renouncing all youthful vanities and flocking to Christ? You especially have now an extraordinary opportunity; but if you neglect it, it will soon be with you as it is with those persons that spent away all the precious days of youth in sin and are now come to such a dreadful pass in blindness and hardness.

And you children that are unconverted, don't you know that you are going down to hell to bear the dreadful wrath of that God that is now angry with you every day and every night? Will you be content to be the children of the devil, when so many other children in the land are converted and are become the holy and happy children of the King of kings?

And let every one that is yet out of Christ and hanging over the pit of hell, whether they be old men and women or middleaged or young people or little children, now hearken to the loud calls of God's word and providence. This acceptable year of the Lord that is a day of such great favor to some will doubtless be a day of as remarkable vengeance to others. Men's hearts harden and their guilt increases apace at such a day as this, if they neglect their souls. And never was there so great danger of such persons being given up to hardness of heart and blindness of mind. God seems now to be hastily gathering in his elect in all parts of the land; and probably the bigger part of adult persons that ever shall be saved will be brought in now in a little time, and that it will be as it was on that great outpouring of the Spirit upon the Jews in the Apostles' days, the election will obtain and the rest will be blinded. If this, should be the case with you, you will eternally curse this day, and will curse the day that ever you was born to see such a season of the pouring out of God's Spirit, and will wish that you had died and gone to hell before you had seen it. Now undoubtedly it is as it was in the days of John the Baptist, the axe is in an extraordinary manner laid at the root of the trees, that every tree that bringeth not forth good fruit may be hewn down and cast into the fire.

Therefore let every one that is out of Christ now awake and fly from the wrath to come. The wrath of Almighty God is now undoubtedly hanging over great part of this congregation. Let every one fly out of Sodom. *"Haste and escape for your lives, look not behind you, escape to the mountain, lest ye be consumed."*

SERMON BY EVANGELIST GILBERT TENNENT (1735) From *Solemn Warning to the Secure World from the God of Terrible Majesty . . .* (Boston, 1735). pp. vii-ix.

Beloved Brethren, You have often heard your Danger describ'd, you have had many a Call, by the *Word*, and *Providence of God*, as well as by your own *Consciences*, and are you not awaken'd yet? O strange! O mournful! Others have been (through Grace) *convinc'd* and *chang'd* effectually by the Means you enjoy, and won't these be a Witness against you at the *Tribunal* of *Christ?* What will you be able to say in your own Vindication? Then won't *Blushing* and *Confusion* cover you, and *guilty Silence* be your Answer? What, does the Word prove a Savour of Life unto Life to others, and of Death unto Death to you? O dreadful! What do you intend to do *dear Brethren?* Will you sleep for ever? Will you sleep till *Death* and *Hell awake you?* Or do you think that you may go to *Heaven* in this *Slumber* of carnal *Security?* If you do you shall find your selves miserably mistaken! as is fully prov'd in the following Tract. Be not deceiv'd Brethren, *The Kingdom of Heaven suffers Violence, and the violent* (and they only) *take it by Force,* Matth. 11. 12. Let me address you as the *Prophet Elijah* did the People of *Israel*, 1 Kings 18. 21. *How long halt ye between two Opinions? If the Lord be God follow him: but if Baal then follow him.* Or as the *Shipmaster* to *Jonah,* who was fast asleep in the midst of a great Tempest, Jonah 1. 5. *What meanest thou, O Sleeper? Arise, call upon thy God, if so be he will think upon us that we perish not,* Verse 6. [———] just and pertinent Note of Mr. *Henry,* upon this Passage of Scripture, *"That those who sleep in a Storm may well be ask'd what they mean?"* Brethren, You sleep in a greater *Storm* than *Jonah* did; that only concern'd the *Body,* but this the precious *Soul;* that a *temporal,* but this an *eternal Death.* You are (whether you know it or not sensibly) every Moment ready to be *swallow'd* up by the *boisterous Billows* of *God's* justly *incensed Ire,* and the *Vessel* of your *Souls* like to be *broken* by a dreadful *Inundation* of his vindictive *Fury* and *Revenge:* Deut. 32. 41, 35. *Rom.* 12. 19. *"And yet will you sleep, what Metal are you made of? What God do you fear? Or are you deaf to all the Menaces of Heaven?"* Will not the *Terrors* of an *eternal God,* and an *eternal Hell* make you *afraid?* What mean you? Are you yet wholly lost to *Sense,* to *Reason,* and to *Conscience?* Are you *degenerated* into *Beasts?* Or *petrified* into *Stones?* Are you cover'd with the *Leviathan's Scales* that no *Arrow* from the *Bow* of *God* will *pierce* you! Mayn't the Example of *Jonas's* Fellow Mariners make you asham'd? Jonah 1. 5. *Then the Mariners were afraid, and cry'd every Man to his God, and cast forth the Wares that were in the Ship, into the Sea, to lighten it of them. But perhaps you mock at Fear, and are not affrighted, though the Heavens* look *black,* and *God's Lightnings* and *Thunders,* from *blazing, trembling Sinai, flash* and *groan,* and *rore hideously!* Tho' *God's Law* condemn you, and your own *Consciences tell* you, that you shall surely perish, if ye die in the same State you are now in, yet you boldly, or rather shall I say impudently, or stupidly brave it out in the Face of an *angry Heaven!* And run upon the thick *Bosses* of *God's Bucklers,* and are not afraid when *God's* great *Ordnance* is *level'd* at your *naked Bosom.* You won't be perswaded by any *Importunity* to cast these *Goods* out of the Ship, (as the Mariners did) which will if retain'd sink it in *Death*. I mean your *darling Lusts* which you must *forsake* or *perish*. Mat. 5. 29. Again, the affrighted Mariners *cry'd every one to his God*, Ver. 5. Why don't you awake poor Souls, and cry every one of you to *God*, with the utmost Vehemence, as the *Disciples of Christ* did in a *Storm*, when the Waves were like to overwhelm the Vessel, *Lord, save us we perish!* Mat. 8. 25. Or as *Peter's* Hearers, Acts 2. 37. *Men and Brethren, What shall we do to be saved?* Sirs, Suffer me to acost you in the Language of *Paul* to the *Ephesians*, Chap. 5. 14. *Awake thou that sleepest, and arise from the Dead, and Christ shall give thee Light; for the Time past of our Life may suffice us, to have wrought the Will of the Gentiles.* 1 Pet. 4. 3. *Awake to Righteousness and sin not: for some have not the Knowledge of God: I speak this to your Shame.* I Cor. 15. 34. *And especially knowing the Time, that now it is high Time to awake out of Sleep.* But I can't in Regard of you add the Apostle's Reason, Rom. 13. 11. *For now is your Salvation nearer than when ye believed.* No Brethren! I am oblig'd in *Faithfulness* to *God*, and *Love* to you, to tell that inasmuch as you did not, and now do not *believe*, that your *Damnation* is nearer than when ye first *heard* the *Gospel* of *Christ*, and *Salvation* by his *Blood;* because of your *unbelieving Obstinacy* and *presumptuous Security.*

Awake, Awake Sinners, stand up and look where you are hastning, least *you drink of the Hand of the Lord, the Dregs of the Cup of his Fury; the Cup of trembling, and wring them out,* Isai. 51. 17. *Awake ye Drunkards,* and *weep and howl,* Joel 1. 5. For what can ye expect (so continuing) but to drink of that *Cup of Trembling* I but now mention'd.

Awake ye prophane Swearers, and remember ye will not get a *drop of Water* to cool your cursing cursed Tongues in Hell, when they and you shall *flame* in the *broad burning Lake,* Luke 16. 24. *God has said he will not hold you Guiltless, that take his Name in vain,* Exod 20. 7.

Awake ye unclean Adulterers, and *Whoremongers,* and remember that without a speedy Repentance, your dismal abode shall be ever with *unclean Devils, the Soul of a God* shall be *aveng'd* upon you, Jer. 5. 8, 29.

Awake ye Sabbath-Breakers, and *reform;* or *God* will *break* you upon the *Wheels* of his *Vengeance,* and *torture* you eternally upon the *Rack* of his *Justice,* Neham. 13. 16, 17, 18.

And let all other sorts of *prophane Sinners* be entreated to *awake* out of *Sleep* and consider their *Danger.*

GILBERT TENNENT ON THE "UNSEARCHABLE RICHES OF CHRIST"

(1737)   From Gilbert Tennent. "The Unsearchable Riches of Christ Considered in Two Sermons on Ephes. iii. 8. Prech'd at New Brunswick in August. 1737." in *Sermons on Sacramental Occasions by Divers Ministers* (Boston. 1739). pp. i-v.

The Desire of Happiness is co-natural to the human Soul, and yet remains with it, notwithstanding the Ruins of its Apostacy from the blessed GOD.

But alass, such brutal Blindness infatuates the Understandings, and such sensual

Pravity byasses the Wills of the most; that they pursue wrong Measures to attain the Happiness they desire.

Some of a lofty Genius, with unwearied Assiduity, labour to secure Honours, thinking therein to obtain Happiness; and to that End they climb the aspiring Top of *Parnassus*, emaciate their Bodies, and waste their animal Spirits in long and deep Studies, thinking by their labour'd and learn'd Lucubrations, to spread and eternize their Fame. Others for the same Purpose, boldly tread the Crimson Fields of War, fearlessly open their senseless Bosoms to all the numerous Engines and sudden Avenues of pregnant Dangers, and of cruel Deaths, thinking themselves great Gainers, if through the Loss of their Lives, they can secure martial Honours and perpetuate Renown for their heroick Bravery, in the Records of Fame. But alass! how much is the unhappy Simplicity of those gallant Souls to be pity'd! for what Good can martial Glory do to the dead?

Others by deeper but securer Policies, & more ungenerous Methods, seek to mount the Wings of Honour, and reach the highest Pinacle of Fame, by labouring to enhance great Places in the Church and State, through the softest Flatteries and most subtil Stratagems; Methods to be abhorr'd by every honest and ingenious Mind. But when Men have obtain'd Honour, what is it? It is neither a substantial, nor a durable Good; it cannot make us good or happy; it may indeed *corrupt* us, by elating our Pride; but it can never *content* us: We may as easily grasp an Arm full of our own Shadow, as content our Minds with Fame; and as it is a meer empty Bubble in its Nature, and often corrupting in its Effects; so it is various and vanishing in its Continuance, as fickle as the Wind.

Some on the contrary of a baser Temper, and meaner Mould, being void of every Thing sublime or noble, dreaming that Happiness is to be had in terrene Pleasures, plunge themselves in a Pool of lawless Sensuality; so that in order to be happy, they make themselves Beasts, nay worse than they; living in Defiance to all the Dictates of Reason, and of GOD; purchasing at the Price of their eternal Salvation, these poor Pleasures, which being of a gross Nature, limited Degree, and contracted Duration, debase the Dignity of the Soul, and defile its Honours; but can neither suit its noble Nature, and perpetual Existence, nor satisfy its sublime and intense Desires.

But there is yet another Generation, of as mean and sordid Wretches, in whose grovling Bosoms, beats nothing that is great or generous; who imagine Happiness is to be had in temporal Wealth and Riches. *This,* these *Moles* are in the continual and eager Chase of; to *this Mark* all the Lines of their busy Thoughts, anxious Cares, subtle Projects, humerous Speeches, strong Desires, and unwearied Labours bend and terminate. But poor Creatures, if ye did obtain that Measure of Riches ye seek after, do ye think it would better your State, bound your Wishes, or secure your Happiness? No! no! don't ye see the contrary with your Eyes, that the most grow in Wickedness, in Proportion to the Increase of their Wealth, and that instead of satiating, it does but whet their Appetite for more; and ye should remember that the *Redemption of the Soul is precious, and that it ceaseth for ever.* As to these Things, a high Mountain afar off seems to touch the Clouds, but when we come near, the Distance seems as great as before. Not to add, that temporal Enjoyments are of very uncertain Continuance. *Why then do ye spend your Money for that which is not Bread, and your Labours for that which satisfies not?* . . . O! that I could persuade you, dears Sirs, to seek with restless and persevering Importunity, an Interest in those unsearchable Riches; without them ye cannot be rich, in any valuable Respect, and with them ye cannot be poor.

I wou'd direct my Exhortation to graceless Persons, in various Conditions of Life.

Are ye poor in Temporals, and do ye find but little Rest and Comfort in this World? Oh! then will ye be persuaded to accept of the most durable and noble *Riches, Riches* most dearly purchased, by no less a Price than the Blood of GOD; *Riches* most freely, frequently, and condescendingly offered, by the Love of GOD in the Ministry of his Servants, upon the most easy and most honourable Terms, that the Majesty and Purity of the divine Nature, and the Dignity and Felicity of the human Nature could admit. Poor Sinners, you are under peculiar Obligations to seek for and accept of the Riches of Grace and Glory, least ye be miserable in both Worlds. It is a most dreadful and shocking Consideration, to think that ye should make a hard Shift, to rub through the many Difficulties, Labours, and Sorrows of this present World, to enter into ten thousand Times worse in the next. Where there will be no *Hope,* no *Ease,* no *Interruption,* no *End.* Alas, my Brethren! It had been better for you ye had never been born, than that this should be your *dismal, dismal* Lot. Others have some sorry sensual Comfort in this Life, but ye have none, or next to none. Oh! it is most terrible to think, to be without Comfort and Quiet in both Worlds! Dear Sirs! If ye had but the Riches of a SAVIOUR'S Love, it wou'd sweeten your present Difficulties, conform you to the suffering REDEEMER, support your sorrowful Souls, with the certain Prospect of perfect Felicity, and distinguished Glory, in the next State. For as the Apostle observes, with a noble Emphasis, 2 Cor. iv. 17. *Our light Affliction, which is but for a Moment, worketh for us a far more exceeding; and eternal Weight of Glory.*

O unhappy Sinners! It would not be hard to persuade you, I suppose, to accept of worldly Riches, and why then will ye not be induc'd to accept of Riches worth Millions of Worlds? Sirs, here, in the blessed Gospel, is the glorious *Pearl* of Price, the inestimable *Jewels* of the Covenant, try'd *Gold,* more pure and noble than that of *Ophir, Peru,* and *Mexico;* and white *Raiment,* to enrich and adorn you; and will ye not accept them, on the reasonable Terms they are offered? O cruel Murder! O vile Ingratitude! O detestable Madness! Be astonished and horribly afraid ye Heavens and Earth at this! Ah ye blessed Angels; ye cannot but wonder to see this terrible Tragedy acted! O ye Saints of GOD! look how the adorable dying SAVIOUR, and the rich Purchase of his Blood, is slighted by indigent, ungrateful, and degenerous Rebels! Oh! Can ye keep your Hearts from Mourning on this Account? See what huge Numbers of Mankind are lying in their Blood and Gore, and yet wont accept of Help and Healing, when it is freely offered. If ye can keep your Hearts from Bleeding upon this Occasion, they are very hard indeed! Ah! It pierces my very Soul, to see my Lord and the Riches of his bleeding Love, treated with such Indifference; while on the contrary, Things of an infinitely meaner Nature, and shorter Duration, are courted and labour'd for with the greatest Vehemence. Truly, Brethren, I know not how to express my Sorrows on this Account; if I could bewail it in Tears of Blood, I would.

Are ye in Bondage and Servitude? here is a spiritual, noble, and everlasting Liberty offered to you, in the Riches of Christ! Oh! if the Son of the Father's Love do but make you free, ye will be free indeed.

Are ye rich in worldly Goods? then I beseech you seriously and speedily to consider, that awful Parable of *Dives* and *Lazarus,* and especially the 23, 24, and 25 Verses of it. *And in Hell he lift up his Eyes being in Torments, and seeth* Abraham *afar off, and* Lazarus *in his Bosom. And he cryed, and said. Father* Abraham *have Mercy on me, and send* Lazarus *that he may dip the Tip of his Finger in Water, and cool my Tongue; for I am tormented in this Flame. But* Abraham *said, Son,* remember that thou in thy Life-time receivedst thy good Things, and likewise Lazarus *evil* Things: But now he is comforted, and thou art tormented. O poor unhappy Sinners! see what a dreadful Change there will be in your Condition in a little Time. Remember ye that now wallow in generous Wines, ye will quickly (except ye repent) want Water to cool your flaming Tongues, but shall not obtain a single Drop; ye will be obliged to make your humble Court to these pious Poor, you now contemn as the Dirt under your Feet.

BENJAMIN FRANKLIN DESCRIBES GEORGE WHITEFIELD'S VISIT TO PHILADELPHIA (1739) From *The Autobiography of Benjamin Franklin,* Leonard W. Labaree et al., eds., (New Haven, 1964), pp. 175-78.

In 1739 arriv'd among us from England the Rev. Mr. Whitefiel, who had made himself remarkable there as an itinerant Preacher. He was at first permitted to preach in some of our Churches; but the Clergy taking a Dislike to him, soon refus'd him their Pulpits and he was oblig'd to preach in the Fields. The Multitudes of all Sects and Denominations that attended his Sermons were enormous, and it was matter of Speculation to me who was one of the Number, to observe the extraordinary Influence of his Oratory on his Hearers, and how much they admir'd and respected him, notwithstanding his common Abuse of them, by assuring them they were naturally *half Beasts and half Devils.* It was wonderful to see the Change soon made in the Manners of our Inhabitants; from being thoughtless or indifferent about Religion, it seem'd as if all the World were growing Religious; so that one could not walk thro' the Town in an Evening without Hearing Psalms sung in different Families of every Street. And it being found inconvenient to assemble in the open Air, subject to its Inclemencies, the Building of a House to meet in was no sooner propose'd and Persons appointed to receive Contributions, but sufficient Sums were soon receiv'd to procure the Ground and erect the Building which was 100 feet long and 70 broad, about the Size of Westminster-hall; and the Work was carried on with such Spirit as to be finished in a much shorter time than could have been expected. Both House and Ground were vested in Trustees, expressly for the Use of any Preacher of any religious Persuasion who might desire to say something to the People of Philadelphia, the Design in building not being to accommodate any particular Sect, but the Inhabitants in general, so that even if the Mufti of Constantinople were to send a Missionary to preach Mahometanism to us, he would find a Pulpit at his Service. (The Contributions being made by People of different Sects promiscuously, Care was taken in the Nomination of Trustees to avoid giving a Predominancy to any Sect, so that one of each was appointed, viz. one Church of England-man, one Presbyterian, one Baptist, one Moravian, &c.).

Mr. Whitfield, in leaving us, went preaching all the Way thro' the Colonies to Georgia. The Settlement of that Province had lately been begun; but instead of being made with hardy industrious Husbandmen accustomed to Labour, the only People fit for such an Enterprise, it was with Families of broken Shopkeepers and other insolvent Debtors, many of indolent and idle habits, taken out of the Gaols, who being set down in the Woods, unqualified for clearing Land, and unable to endure the Hardships of a new Settlement, perished in Numbers, leaving many helpless Children unprovided for. The Sight of their miserable Situation inspired the benevolent Heart of Mr. Whitefield with the Idea of building an Orphan House there, in which they might be supported and educated. Returning northward he preach'd up this Charity, and made large Collections; for his Eloquence had a wonderful Power over the Hearts and Purses of his Hearers, of which I myself was an Instance. I did not disapprove of the Design, but as Georgia was then destitute of Materials and Workmen, and it was propos'd to send them from Philadelphia at a great Expence, I though it would have been better to have built the House here and brought the Children to it. This I advis'd, but he was resolute in his first Project, and rejected my Counsel, and I thereupon refus'd to contribute. I happened soon after to attend one of his Sermons, in the Course of which I perceived he intended to finish with a Collection, and I silently resolved he should get nothing from me. I had in my Pocket a Handful of Copper Money, three or four silver Dollars, and five Pistoles in Gold. As he proceeded I began to soften, and concluded to give the Coppers. Another Stroke of his Oratory made me asham'd of that, and determin'd me to give the Silver; and he finish'd so admirably, that I empty'd my Pocket wholly into the Collector's Dish, Gold and all.

AN ACCOUNT OF GEORGE WHITEFIELD IN MIDDLETOWN, CONNECTICUT (1740)   From George Leon Walker, *Some Aspects of the Religious Life of New England, with Special Reference to Congregationalists* (Boston, 1897), pp. 89-92.

Now it pleased God to send Mr. Whitfeld into this land, and my hearing of his preaching at Philadelphia like one of the old aposels, and [of] many thousands flocking after him to hear the gospel, and great numbers . . . converted to Christ, I felt the spirit of God drawing me by conviction. I longed to see and hear him and wished he would come this way. And I soon heard he was come to New York and the Jerseys, and [of] great multitudes flocking after him under great concern for their Soule, and many converted, wich brought on my concern more and more, hoping soon to see him. But next I herd he was on Long Iland, and next at Boston, and next at Northampton. And then one morning, all on a Suding about 8 or 9 o Clock, there came a messenger and said Mr. Whitfeld preached at Hartford and Weathersfield yesterday and is to preach at Middeltown this morning at 10 o clock. I was in my field at work [and] I dropt my tool that I had in my hand and run home and run thru my house and bade my wife get ready quick to goo and hear Mr. Whitfeld preach at Middeltown. And [I] run to my pasture for my hors with all my might, fearing I should be too late to hear him. I brought my hors home and soon mounted and took my wife up and went forward as fast as I thought the hors could bear, and when my hors began to be out of breath I would get down and put my wife on the Saddel, and bit her ride as fast as she could, and not Stop or Slak for except I bade her. And so I would run untill I was almost out of breth, and then mount my hors again, and so I did severel times to favour my hors. We improved every moment to get along as if we was fleeing for our lives, all this while fearing we should be too late to hear the Sarmon, for we had twelve miles to ride double in littel more than an hour.

And we went round by the upper housen parish, and when we came within about half a mile of the road that comes down from Hartford, Weathersfield and Stepney to Middeltown, on high land, I saw before me a Cloud or fog, rising—I first thought—off from the great river. But as I came nearer the road I heard a noise, something like a low rumbling thunder, and I presently found it was the rumbling of horses feet coming down the road and this Cloud was a Cloud of dust made by the running of horses feet. It arose some rods into the air over the tops of the hills and trees. And when I came within about twenty rods of the road, I could see men and horses Slipping along in the Cloud like shadows. And when I came nearer it was like a stedy streem of horses and their riders, scarcely a horse more then his length behind another, all of a lather and fome with swet, ther breth rooling out of their noistrels. . . . Every hors semed to go with all his might to carry his rider to hear the news from heaven for the saving of their Souls. It made me trembel to see the Sight—how the world was in a strugle!

I found a vacance between two horses to slip in my hors, and my wife said, "Law, our cloaths will be all spoiled. See how they look?" for they was so covered with dust that they looked almost all of a color, coats and hats and shirts and horses.

We went down in the Streeme. I herd no man speak a word all the way, three mile, but evry one presing forward in great haste. And when we gat down to the old meating house, thare was a great multitude. It was said to be 3 or 4000 of people assembled together.

We gat of from our horses and shook off the dust, and the ministers was then coming to the meating house. I turned and looked toward the great river and saw the fery boats running swift forward and backward, bringing over loads of people. The ores rowed nimble and quick. Everything—men, horses and boats—all seamed to be struglin for life. The land and the banks over the river looked black with people and horses all along the 12 miles. I see no man at work in his field, but all seamed to be gone.

When I see Mr. Whitfeld come upon the Scaffold, he looked almost angellical— a young, slim, slender youth before some thousands of people, and with a bold, undaunted countenance. And my hearing how God was with him everywhere as he came along, it solomnized my mind, and put me in a trembling fear before he began to preach, for he looked as if he was Cloathed with authority from the great God. And a sweet, solomn Solemnity sat upon his brow, and my hearing him preach gave me a heart wound, by god's blessing. My old foundation was broken up and I saw that my righteousness would not save me. Then I was convinced of the doctrine of Election, and went right to quareling with God about it, because all that I could do would not save me, and he had decreed from Eternity who should be saved and who not. I began to think I was not Elected, and that God made some for heaven and me for hell. And I thought God was not Just in so doing. I thought I did not stand on even Ground with others if, as I thought, I was made to be damned. My heart then rose against God exceedingly for his making me for hell. [And] this distress lasted almost two years.

AN ACCOUNT OF RELIGIOUS CONDITIONS IN PENNSYLVANIA

(c. 1750) From Gottlieb Mittleberger, *Journey to Pennsylvania in 1750 and Return to Germany in 1754*, C. T. Elan, trans. (Philadelphia, 1898), pp. 54-55, 61-63.

Coming to speak of Pennsylvania again, that colony possesses great liberties above all other English colonies, inasmuch as all religious sects are tolerated there. We find there Lutherans, Reformed, Catholics, Quakers, Mennonists or Anabaptists, Herrnhuters or Moravian Brethren, Pietists, Seventh Day Baptists, Dunkers, Presbyterians, Newborn, Freemasons, Separatists, Freethinkers, Jews, Mohammedans, Pagans, Negroes, and Indians. The Evangelicals and Reformed, however, are in the majority. But there are many hundred unbaptized souls there that do not even wish to be baptized. Many pray neither in the morning nor in the evening, neither before nor after meals. No devotional book, not to speak of a Bible, will be found with such people. In one house and one family, four, five, and even six sects may be found. . . .

The preachers in Pennsylvania receive no salaries or tithes, except what they annually get from their church members, which varies very much; for many a father of a family gives according to his means and of his own free will, 2, 3, 4, 5, or 6 florins a year, but many others give very little. For baptizing children, for funeral sermons and marriage ceremonies they generally receive a dollar. The preachers have no free dwellings or other *beneficia.* But they receive many presents from their parishioners. The same is true of the schoolmasters. But since 1754 England and Holland give annually a large sum of money for the general benefit of the many poor in Pennsylvania, and for the support of six Reformed English churches and as many Reformed English free schools. Nevertheless, many hundred children cannot attend these schools, on account of their great distance and the many forests. Many planters lead, therefore, a very wild and heathenish life; for as it is with the schools, so it is also with the churches in the rural districts, because churches and school-houses are usually built around at such places only where most neighbours and church members live.

The preachers throughout Pennsylvania have no power to punish anyone, or to compel anyone to go to church; nor has anyone a right to dictate to the other, because they are not supported by any *Consistorio.* Most preachers are hired by the year like the cowherds in Germany; and if one does not preach to their liking, he must expect to be served with a notice that his services will no longer be required. It is, therefore, very difficult to be a conscientious preacher, especially as they have to hear and suffer much from so many hostile and often wicked sects. The most exemplary preachers are often reviled, insulted, and scoffed at like the Jews, by the young and old, especially in the country. I would, therefore, rather perform the meanest herdsman's duties in Germany than be a preacher in Pennsylvania. Such unheard of rudeness and wickedness spring from the excessive liberties of the land, and from the blind zeal of the many sects. To many a one's soul and body, liberty in Pennsylvania is more hurtful than useful. There is a saying in that country: Pennsylvania is the heaven of the farmers, the paradise of the mechanics, and the hell of the officials and preachers.

"English" Schools, Private Schoolmasters and Tutors

PRIVATE SCHOOL ADVERTISEMENTS IN BOSTON (Eighteenth Century) From Robert F. Seybolt, ed., *The Private Schools of Colonial Boston* (Cambridge, Mass., 1935), pp. 11, 13, 15-16, 19, 81-82.

1706

Mistris Mary Turfrey at the South End of Boston, Intends to board Young Gentlewomen; If any Gentlemen desires their Daughters should be under her Education: They may please to agree with her on Terms.[1]

1709

Opposite to the Mitre Tavern in Fish-street near to Scarlets-Wharff, Boston, are Taught Writing, Arithmetick in all its parts; And also Geometry, Trigonometry, Plain and Sphaerical, Surveying, Dialling, Gauging, Navigation, Astronomy; The Projection of the Sphaere, and the use of Mathematical Instruments: By Owen Harris.

Who Teaches at as easie Rates, and as speedy as may be.[2]

1714

At the house of Mr James Ivers, formerly call'd the Bowling Green House in Cambridge-Street Boston, is now set up a Boarding School, where will be carefully Taught, Flourishing, Embroidery, and all Sorts of Needle-Work, also Filigrew, Painting upon Glass, Writing, Arithmetick, and Singing Psalm Tunes.[3]

[1] *Boston News-Letter*, Sept. 2–9, 16–23, Sept. 30–Oct. 7, 1706.

[2] *Boston News-Letter*, March 14–21, 1708/9.

[3] *Boston News-Letter*, Apr. 12–19, 1714.

1716

This is to give Notice, That at the House of Mr. George Brownell, late School Master in Hanover Street Boston, are all sorts of Millinary Works done; making up Dresses, and flowering of Muslin, making of furbelow'd Scarffs, and Quilting, and cutting of Gentlewomens Hair in the newest Fashion; and also young Gentlewomen and Children taught all sorts of fine Works, as Feather-Work, Filegre and Painting on Glass, Embroidering a new way, Turkey-Work for Handkerchiefs, two ways, fine new Fashion Purses, flourishing and plain Work, and Dancing cheaper than ever was taught in Boston, Brocaded-Work for Handkerchiefs and short Aprons upon Muslin, artificial Flowers work'd with a Needle.[4]

1720

At the house formerly Sir Charles Hobby's are taught Grammar, Writing after a free and easy manner, in all the hands usually practiced, Arithmetick Vulgar and Decimal in a concise and practical Method, Merchants Accompts, Geometry, Algebra, Mensuration, Geography, Trigonometry, Astronomy, Navigation and other parts of the Mathematicks, with the use of the Globes and other Mathematical Instruments, by Samuel Grainger.

They whose Business won't permit 'em to attend the usual School Hours, shall be carefully attended and instructed in the Evenings.[5]

1720

This is to acquaint all Gentlemen and others, that Edward Enstone, Dancing Master is removed to a Large House in King Street Boston, where young Ladies may be Accomodated with Boarding, and taught all sorts of Needle-work with Musick and Dancing, &c.

N.B. Dancing Days are Monday, Thursday and Saturday in the afternoons. Thursdays being Publick for all Gentlemen and Ladies that please to come and see the Performance.[6]

1728

Caleb Philipps Teacher of the New Method of Short Hand, is remov'd opposite to the north door of the Town House in King-street. As this way of Joyning 3, 4, 5 &c. words in one in every Sentence by the Moods, Tenses, Persons, and Verb, do's not in the least spoil the Long Hand, so it is not anything like the Marks for Sentences in the Printed Character Books being all wrote according to the Letter, and a few Plain and Easy Rules.

N.B. Any Persons in the Country desirous to Learn this Art, may by having the several Lessons sent Weekly to them, be as perfectly instructed as those that live in Boston.[7]

[4]*Boston News-Letter*, Aug. 20–27, 1716.
[5]*Boston Gazette*, Mar. 21–22, 1719/20.
[6]*Boston Gazette*, Sept. 12–19, 19–26, Sept. 26–Oct. 3, 1720.
[7]*Boston Gazette*, Mar. 18–25, March 25–April 1, 1728.

Young ladies, or young Gentlemen, who have a mind to be acquainted with the French Language; to be perfected in reading, speaking or writing the English;—to be introduced to, or compleated in their Improvements, in Arithmetic, Penmanship, or Epistolary Writing, may be properly assisted in pursuing either of these Attainments, from 5 to 7 o'Clock in the Morning, at the School on Court Square, opposite the East Door of the State House; where constant Attendance will be given, and the most useful Branches of common Education taught in the best approved Manner.

"On Morning Wings, how active springs the Mind!"[8]

ADVERTISEMENTS FOR EVENING SCHOOLS (Eighteenth Century) From Robert F. Seybolt, ed., *The Evening School in Colonial America* (Urbana, Ill., 1925), pp. 60-63.

Philadelphia, 1743. To be TAUGHT by CHARLES FORTESQUE, late Free-School-Master of Chester, at his House, in the Alley commonly called Mr. Taylors

The Latin Tongue, English in a Grammatical Manner, Navigation, Surveying, Mensuration, Dialling, Geography, Use of the Globes, the Gentleman's Astronomy, Chronology, Arithmetic, Merchants Accompts, &c. The above to be taught at Night School as well as Day—He likewise intends for the future to instruct his Latin Scholars in Writing himself.

NOTE, He hath private Lodgings for single Persons.[1]

Boston, 1748

Mr. Pelham's Writing and Arithmetick School, near the Town House (during the Winter Season) will be open from Candle-Light 'till Nine in the Evening as usual, for the Benefit of those employ'd in Business all the Day; and at his Dwelling House near the Quaker's Meeting in Lindell's Row, All Persons may be supply'd with the best Virginia Tobacco cut, spun into the very best Pigtail, and all other Sorts; also Snuff, at the cheapest Rates.[2]

[8] *New England Chronicle*, July 4, 11, 18, 1776.

[1] *Pennsylvania Gazette*, Nov. 24, Dec. 1, 6, 15, 20, 1743.

[2] *Boston Evening Post*, Sept 12, 19, 26, 1748.

New York City, 1753

John Lewis, Schoolmaster, in Broad-Street, has begun Night School, and teaches Reading, Writing, Arithmetic, Navigation, Surveying, &c.[3]

New York City, 1755. NOTICE is hereby GIVEN that JOHN SEARSON

Who teaches School at the House of Mrs. Coon opposite to the Post Office, proposes (God Willing) to open an Evening School, on Thursday the 25th of this Instant September; where may be learn'd Writing, Arithmetic Vulgar and Decimal, Merchants Accounts, Mensuration, Geometry, Trigonometry, Surveying, Dialling, and Navigation in a short, plain, and methodical Manner, and at very reasonable Rates. Said Searson having a large and commodious Room, together with his own diligent Attendance, the Scholars will have it in their Power to make a good Progress in a short Time.[4]

Philadelphia, 1760

NOTICE is hereby given, that on Monday, the 6th of October, at Mr. William's School-house, in Videll's Alley, Second-street, will be opened a Night School, and there taught as follows, viz. READING, WRITING, and ARITHMETIC, VULGAR and DECIMAL; BOOK-KEEPING METHODIZED; the ELEMENTS of GEOMETRY and TRIGONOMETRY, with their Application to NAVIGATION, SURVEYING, DIALLING &c. ALGEBRA, with the Application of it to a Variety of PROBLEMS in ARITHMETIC, GEOMETRY, TRIGONOMETRY, CONIC SECTIONS, and STEREOMETRY. With the several methods of solving and constructing EQUATIONS of the higher kind. By ROBERT KENNEDY, JOHN MAXFIELD, and DAVID KENNEDY.
N. B. The Latin and Greek will be also taught.[5]

New York City, 1765

Taught by Thomas Carroll, At his Mathematical School, in Broad-street, in the City of New York.
Writing, Vulgar and Decimal Arithmetic; the Extraction of the Roots; Simple and Compound Interest; how to purchase or sell Annuities, Leases for Lives, or in Reversion, Freehold Estates, &c. at Simple and Compound Interest; the Italian Method of Bookkeeping; Euclid's Elements of Geometry; Algebra and Conic Sections; Mensuration of Superficies and Solids, Surveying in Theory, and all its different Modes in Practice, with two universal Methods to determine the Areas of right lined Figures, and some useful Observations on the whole; Also Gauging, Dialling, Plain and Spheric Trigonometry, Navigation; the Construction and Use of the Charts, and Instruments necessary for keeping a Sea-Journal (with a Method to keep the same, were the Navigator deprived of his Instruments and Books &c. by

[3]N. Y. Gazette or Weekly Post Boy, Oct. 8, 15, Nov. 26, Dec. 3, 1753.
[4]N. Y. Gazette or Weekly Post Boy, Sept. 15, 19, 29, Oct. 6, 13, 1755.
[5]Pennsylvania Gazette, Sept. 18, 25, Oct. 2, 1760.

any Accident) the Projection of the Sphere, according to the Orthographic and Stereographic Principles; Fortification, Gunnery, and Astronomy; Sir Isaac Newton's Laws of Motion; the Mechanical Powers viz. The Balance, Lever, Wedge, Screw and Axes in Peritrochio explained, Being not only an Introduction necessary to the more abstruse Parts of Natural and Experimental Philosophy, but also to every Gentleman in Business.

He will lecture to his Scholars, every Saturday, on the different Branches then taught in his School, the Advantage of which may in a little Time, make them rather Masters (of what they are then learning) than Scholars. He invites Gentlemen to visit his School, and be Judges of the progress his Pupils will make, and the Benefit they must receive from him.

He will attend a Morning School in Summer from 6 to nine for young Ladies only, from Nine to Twelve and from Two P.M. to Five for all others who choose to attend; and a Night School from Six to Nine for young Gentlemen; or he will divide the Time in any other Way, if thought more agreeable. Young Ladies and Gentlemen may be instructed in the more easy and entertaining Parts of Geography with the true Method of drawing the Plan of any Country &c. without which they cannot properly be said to understand that useful Branch of Knowledge; during this Course, Care will be taken to explain the true Copernican or Solar System, the Laws of Attraction, Gravitation, Cohesion &c. in an easy and familiar manner, and if he is encouraged to purchase proper Apparatus, he will exhibit a regular Course of experimental Philosophy. He will not accept any but decent Scholars, nor crowd his School with more than he can teach at a Time. On this plan, if the Gentlemen of this City are convinced of the vast Utility it must be to the Youth here, and are of the Opinion that he may be a useful Member amongst them, and encourage him as such, he will do all in his Power to merit their Approbation, and give general Satisfaction; but if otherwise, he will accept of any Employment in the writing way, settling Merchants' Accounts, drawing Plans, & or of a decent Place in the Country till the Return of the Vessels from Ireland, to which he has warm Invitations. He must observe that he was not under the Necessity of coming here to teach, he had Views of living more happy, but some unforseen and unexpected Events have happened since his Arrival here, which is the Reason of his applying thus to the Publick.

N. B. Mrs. Carroll proposes teaching young Ladies plain work, Samples, French Quilting, Knotting for Bed Quilts, or Toilets, Dresden, flowering on Cat Gut, Shading (with Silk, or Worsted) on Cambrick, Lawn, and Holland.[6]

Philadelphia, 1771

An Evening School, by Maguire and Power, will be opened on Monday, the eighth of October next, at the School-room of said Maguire, in Second-street, near Lodge-alley; where will be taught with the greatest care and diligence, reading, writing, and arithmetic; the most useful branches of the mathematics, book-keeping, geography; the use of globes and maps; and how to make maps.[7]

[6] *N. Y. Mercury*, May 6, 13, 20, Sept. 30, Oct. 7, 1765.
[7] *Pennsylvania Gazette*, Sept. 12, 1771.

Newark, Del., 1772. To the Public JOHN WILSON At the Academy in Newark, New-Castle County; has opened A NIGHT-SCHOOL

Where can be taught English reading and writing, with propriety and elegance, geography, chronology, arithmetic, book-keeping, geometry, and the construction of logarithms, plain and spherical trigonometry, mensuration of superficies and solids, gauging, dialling, fortification, architecture, navigation, surveying, the projection of the sphere, the use of the globes, conic sections, gunnery, algebra, the theory of the pendulums, fluxions, &c. &c. by

JOHN WILSON.[8]

FRENCH AND SPANISH LESSONS IN NEW YORK (1735)   From Robert F. Seybolt, ed., *Source Studies in American Colonial Education: The Private School* (Urbana, Ill., 1925), p. 39.

This is to give Notice that over against the Sign of the black Horse in Smith-street, near the old Dutch Church, is carefully taught the French and Spanish Languages, after the best Method that is now practised in Great Britain which for the encouragement of those who intend to learn the same is taught for 20s per Quarter.

Note, that the said Person teaches Reading, Writing and Arithmetick, at very reasonable Terms, which is per Quarter for Readers 5s. for Writers 8s, for Cypherers 1s.[1]

[8] *Pennsylvania Gazette*, Dec. 9, 1772.
[1] *New York Gazette*, July 14–21, 21–28, July 28–Aug. 4, 4–11, 1735.

DESCRIPTION OF A COMMERCIAL SCHOOL IN PHILADELPHIA

(1751) From Robert F. Seybolt, ed., *Source Studies in American Colonial Education: The Private School* (Urbana, Ill., 1925), pp. 39-40.

Andrew Lamb

Is removed to Mr. Abraham Taylor's Alley, near Second-street, which was formerly a school with good conveniences, and continues to qualify youth for business, &c. viz.

Writing, arithmetick, vulgar and decimal, merchants accompts, the Italian method, by double entry, Dr. and Cr. the only true way that is now used; Navigation in all its parts, both theory and practice, viz. Geometry, Trigonometry, and Plain-sailing; Traverse, Mercator, and Parallel Sailing; Coasting, Bearing and Distance of Land, and Current Sailing. All these are geometrically, logarithmetrically, and instrumentally performed. Next the practice, which is the main thing intended; and here I shall give you a complete journal from the Lizard to the Rock of Lisbon, with leeway and variation allowed each course, and rules to apply them, and an amplitude at sun rising and setting, and applied to the east and west variation; this is one of the journals that I kept to Lisbon, and is therefore recommended to all ingenious artists, as a pattern for any other voyage; and I can shew several journals of my own works to the American plantations, and one from England to Cape Henlopen, in 20 days, 1748. And to make mercator charts, a new and easy method, and to work any journal in them, which makes a traverse in the mercator charts, and is proved so exact as the proportions in mercator's sailing, by the latitudes and longitudes every day at noon; and sheweth the plain tract which the ship made the whole voyage, and a true method to correct all journals, and to bring the ship safe to the desired port, which is the only thing intended by a good journal. Also Surveying, Gauging, Dailling, and Spherical Geometry, Trigonometry in all its various cases, and Great-Circle Sailing, applied in several problems, which proves the meridional parts in mercators sailing to a fair demonstration; and the application of all the most useful and necessary problems in great variety of astronomy. All these are carefully taught and diligently attended, by

ANDREW LAMB

N.B. I teach in their own houses at certain hours, when desired, with due attendance and diligence. I have above 30 years experience in teaching both the theory and practice of navigation.

Sailors, take a friend's advice, be not cheated by land-men that pretend to navigation, for they know nothing of a sea journal, which is the principal thing you want to know, and the use of sea-charts: My Scholars are qualified to go mates the first voyage, and bring me a good account of their journals.[1]

[1] *Pennsylvania Gazette,* February 19, March 19, April 4 and 18, June 20, 1751.

ANNOUNCEMENT OF THE OPENING OF AN EVENING SCHOOL FOR YOUNG LADIES (1753)
From Robert F. Seybolt, ed., *The Evening School in Colonial America* (Urbana, Ill., 1925), p. 60.

On Monday, the ninth of April instant (by permission of Providence) will be opened,

A School to teach writing in all the hands of use; arithmetic, vulgar and decimal; merchants accounts; psalmody, by a proper and regular method; for the amusement of such young ladies as are pleased to employ the summer evenings in those useful and necessary exercises, from the hour of 5 to 8; carefully taught, in Third-street, near the New Presbyterian Church, by

WILLIAM DAWSON.

ADVERTISEMENT FOR A DAY SCHOOL FOR YOUNG LADIES (1770)
From Robert F. Seybolt, ed., *Source Studies in American Colonial Education: The Private School* (Urbana, Ill., 1925), p. 71.

As I have discovered sundry inconveniences to result from teaching YOUTH of both sexes, and having been frequently solicited by several respectable families in this city, to establish a school, for the instruction of YOUNG LADIES only, in READING, WRITING, ARITHMETIC, and ACCOMPTS; I have opened a school for said purpose in LAETITIA-COURT; contiguous to Front, Second and Market-streets. As the utility of such an undertaking (properly conducted) is undeniably evident, I hope for the encouragement of the public, which I shall endeavour to deserve, by a constant assiduity to promote the improvement of my pupils in the aforesaid branches, as also in having the strictest regard to their morals—Such misses as are obliged to attend other schools, I shall take for half days.

MATTHEW MAGUIRE

N. B. As I have already engaged a considerable number of young ladies, those who intend to apply are requested to be speedy, as I am determined to take no more than such a number as I shall be able to give proper attendance to. A night school is opened at the above place for young men.

TEACHERS' ADVERTISEMENTS IN THE SOUTH (18th Century)   From
Edgar W. Knight, ed., *A Documentary History of Education in the South Before 1860*
(Chapel Hill, N.C., 1949), vol. II, pp. 652–56.

At the house of Mrs. Delaweare on Broad Street is taught these sciences.

Arithmetic	Surveying	Astronomy
Algebra	Dialling	Gauging
Geometry	Navigation	Fortification
Trigonometry		

The STEREOGRAPHIC or ORTHOGRAPHIC Projection of the Sphere. The use of the Globe and the Italian method of Bookkeeping by

John Miller.
—*The South Carolina Gazette,* May 12, 1733.

Reading, writing and arithmetick to be taught by EDWARD CLARK at the House of one Mrs. LYDIA VIART's near the new intended Market.
—*The South-Carolina Gazette,* December 13 to December 20, 1735.

Reading, Writing, Arithmetick vulgar and decimal, Geometry, Trigonometry plain and spherical, Mensuration of solid and superficial Bodies, Navigation, Surveying, Gaging, and many other useful Branches of the Mathematicks, Euclid's Elements, Italian, bookkeeping, and Grammar, &c: explain'd and taught in the clearest manner by ARCHIBALD HAMILTON, who may be heard of at MR. COON's Taylor in Church-street. N.B. He attends at any time and Place requir'd to teach, or to keep Books; and is willing upon a reasonable and speedy Encouragement to undertake a School in Town or Country for teaching all or any Part of what is above specified, otherwise to go off the country.
—*The South-Carolina Gazette,* February 12 to February 19, 1737. Also
February 19 to 26 and February 26 to March 5, 1737.

This is to give Notice, That the Subscriber having resigned teaching the Free School in the Parish of St. Thomas, intends (in the middle of March next) to remove to his plantation at Cainhoy situate bluff on Wando River, Twelve Miles from Charles-Town, being a very pleasant healthful Situation, where I intend to continue to keep a boarding School, having built a convenient Mansion house, school-house &c. for that Purpose. And whereas it may be objected that I keep a Store and Ferry at the said Plantation, and therefore I give this further Notice, that I have other Persons employed to do those Businesses, and that I intend to do not Manner of Business in School hours; but constantly and diligently to attend the school and doubt not but that I shall (as I have for these 18 years past) give a general satisfaction.

Robert How.
—*The South-Carolina Gazette,* Feb. 6, 1744.

On Monday, being the 25th Instant June, the Subscriber intends (God willing) to open School in the Parish of St. Thomas, at the Place where Mr. Robert How formerly taught, being about Half a Mile from the Brick Church and Twelve from Charles-Town. The House erected for that Purpose is a fine spacious Building, wherein an Hundred Children may be genteely accommodated: Those inclinable for boarding their Children with me, may depend on the utmost Care and Diligence, by teaching them exactly and expeditiously Reading; Writing in all the usual Hands; Arithmetick, in all its Parts; Merchant's Accompts, or, the Italian Method of Book-keeping, &c.

Stephen Hartley.
—*The South-Carolina Gazette*, June 4, 1744.

White Point

Reading, Writing in all the Hands us'd in Great Briatain, Arithmetick in whole Numbers, and Fractions vulgar and decimal, Merchants Accompts, in the true Italian Method of double Entry, by Debtor and Creditor, and Dancing are taught at the House of Mrs. Fisher on White Point, by

George Brownell and John Pratt
—*The South-Carolina Gazette*, Sept. 3, 10, 17, 1744.

Nathanial and Mary Gittens have open'd a School in King street, where will be taught reading, writing, arithmetic, and several sorts of Needle work. They likewise intend to commence an Evening School the 10th of September for writing, arithmetick, and young Ladies to draw. Great care will be taken in teaching, and good Attendance by Nath & Mary Gittens.

—*The South-Carolina Gazette*, Sept. 17, 1744.

This is to give Notice, to all young Gentlemen and Ladies inclinable to be taught the Art of Drawing, That an Evening School for that Purpose will be open'd on the first of November next, at my House in Friend street, where every Branch of that Art will be taught with the greatest Exactness by

Jeremiah Theus
—*The South-Carolina Gazette*, Nov. 5, 1744.

ANY sober diligent Person that is duly qualified to keep a Country School, is desired to apply to Mr. Thomas Brewer, of Nansemond County; where he will meet with Encouragement; he promising to assure such Master Twenty Four Scholars.— *The Virginia Gazette* February 9, 1738, p. [4]; February 16, 1738, p. [4], February 23, 1738, p. [4].

A SOBER, diligent Person, of a good Character, that is qualified to teach Children to write and cypher, and read good English, and is willing to agree for 3, 5 or 7 Years, by applying to the Subscriber, living in Prince-George County, may meet with an Employer, who will give as an Encouragement to such Person 20 1. per Annum.

Theophilus Field
—*The Virginia Gazette*, December 12, 1745, p. [4]; December 19, 1745, p. [4].

A SOBER Person, of good Morals, capable of teaching Children to Read ENGLISH well, and to Write and Cypher, by applying to the Subscriber, living in the lower Part of PRINCE GEORGE County, and the Neighbours adjacent, may depend on meeting with good Encouragement, as a School-Master.

Thomas Hall

—*The Virginia Gazette*, March 21, 1750/1, p. [4]; March 28, 1751, p. [4]; April 4, 1751, p. [4]; July 11, 1951, p. [4]; July 18, 1751, p. [4]; July 25, 1751, p. [4].

Williamsburg, June 13, 1751.

A SOBER Person, of good Morals, capable of teaching Children to Read ENGLISH well, and to Write and Cypher, by applying to the Subscriber, at the Capitol Landing of this City, may depend on meeting with good Encouragement, as a School-Master.

Matthew Moody

—*The Virginia Gazette*, June 13, 1751, p. [4]; June 20, 1751, p. [4]; June 27, 1751, p. [4].

ANY single Man, capable of teaching GREEK, LATIN, and the Mathematicks, who can be well recommended, may meet with good Encouragement, by applying to the Subscriber, in PRINCE-GEORGE County.

Theophilus Field

—*The Virginia Gazette*, March 27, 1752, p. [3]; April 3, 1752, p. [3]; April 10, 1752, p. [4].

Williamsburg, June 12, 1752.

MR. SINGLETON takes this Opportunity of informing Gentlemen and Others, That he proposes to Teach the VIOLIN in this City, and Places adjacent, at a Pistole each per Month, and a Pistole Entrance, provided a sufficient Number of Scholars can be engaged, (not less than Six in any one Place:) He will give Attendance at YORK, HAMPTON, and NORFOLK, on the aforesaid Terms.

—*The Virginia Gazette*, June 12, 1752, p. [2].

JOHN WALKER,

LATELY arriv'd in Williamsburg from London, and who for ten Years past has been engag'd in the Education of Youth, undertakes to instruct young Gentlemen in Reading, Writing, Arithmetick, the most material Branches of Classical Learning, and ancient and modern Geography and History; but, as the noblest End of Erudition and Human Attainments, he will exert his principal Endeavours to improve their Morals, in Proportion to their Progress in Learning, that no Parent may repent his Choice in trusting him with the Education of his Children.

MRS. WALKER, likewise, teaches young Ladies all Kinds of Needle Work; makes Capuchins, Shades, Hats, and Bonnets; and will endeavour to give Satisfaction to those who shall honour her with their Custom.

The above-mentioned JOHN WALKER, and his Wife, live at MR. COBB's new House, next to MR. COKE's, near the Road going down to the Capitol Landing; where there is also to be sold, Mens Shoes and Pumps, Turkey Coffee, Edging and Lace for Ladies Caps, and some Gold Rings.—*The Virginia Gazette*, November 17, 1752, p. [2]; also November 24, 1752, p. [3]; December 1, 1752, p. [3].

A PERSON who understands teaching of Reading, Writing and Arithmetic, and comes well recommended, may meet with good Encouragement, by applying to the Subscriber in PRINCE-GEORGE County.

Theodorick Bland
—*The Virginia Gazette*, August 27, 1756, p. [4].

Corotoman, May 20, 1766.
A Person well recommended for his sobriety and good behaviour, and is capable of teaching children to read and write, will meet with employment by applying to

Charles Carter
—*The Virginia Gazette*, May 23, 1766, p. [3]; May 30, 1766, p. [3]; June 6
1766, p. [4].

Williamsburg, September 4, 1766.
THE Trustees for Mrs. WHALEY'S charity to MATTEY'S School (the Minister and Church-Wardens of BRUTON parish) give this notice that in the forenoon of Monday the 22d instant they will meet in the Church of WILLIAMBSBURG, to choose a master for that school. They hope they have it in their power to make such proposals as shall encourage a diligent and useful person to accept of the office.—
The Virginia Gazette, September 5, 1766. Supplement, p. [3]; also September 12, 1766, p. [3]; September 19, 1766, p. [3].

Norfolk county, March 23, 1767.
IF WILLIAM JONES, teacher of Latin, &c. and was tutor to my children last summer, is now unengaged, and will return to me, he shall meet with encouragement from

John Brickell
—*The Virginia Gazette*, April 2, 1767, p. [3]; also April 9, 1767, p. [3].

INDENTURE OF APPRENTICESHIP OF SALOMON MORACHE TO ISAAC HAYS (1749)

From Morris U. Schappes, ed., *A Documentary History of the Jews in the United States, 1654-1875* (New York, 1950), pp. 31-32.

This indenture Witnesseth, That Salomon Morache, Son of Estter-Morache, Widow, of the City of New-York . . . Hath put himself and by these Presents, with the Advice and Consent, of his said Mother . . . doth voluntarily, and of his own free Will and Accord, put himself Apprentice to Isaac Hays of the said City of New-York, Merchant, . . . to learn the Art, Trade and Mystery of a Merchant . . . and after the Manner of an Apprentice, to serve from the Day of the Date hereof, for, and during, and until the full End and Term of Five years . . . next ensuing, during all which Time, the said Apprentice his said Master faithfully shall serve, his Secrets keep, his lawful Commands every where readily obey. He shall do no Damage to his said Master, nor see it to be done by others without letting or giving

Notice thereof to his said Master. He shall not waste his said Master's Goods, nor lend them unlawfully to any. He shall not commit Fornication, nor contract Matrimony within the said Term. At Cards, Dice, or any other unlawful Game, he shall not play, whereby his said Master may have Damage. With his own Goods, nor the Goods of others, without Licence from his said Master, he shall neither buy nor sell without the consent of his mast^r. He shall not absent himself Day nor Night from his said Master's Service, without his Leave: Nor haunt Ale-houses, Taverns, or Play-houses; but in all Things behave himself as a faithful Apprentice ought to do, during the said Term. And the said Master shall use the utmost of his Endeavour to teach, or cause to be taught or instructed, the said Apprentice in the Trade of Mystery of a Merchant . . . and procure and provide for him sufficient Meat, Drink, Apparel,—Lodging and Washing, fitting for an Apprentice, during the said Term of Five years, and shall give him Evening Schooling every Winter during the said Term: He shall also allow him Three Pounds, New-York Money, in the Second-year of the said Term:—Five Pounds in the third year; Seven Pounds in the Fourth: year, and Twelve Pounds in the last year; and at the Expiration thereof, if the said Apprentice goes to any of the West-India Islands, his said Master shall consign Ten Tons of Provisions to him, on his, the said Master's own Account,—

And for the true Performance of all and singular the Covenants and Agreements aforesaid, the said Parties bind themselves each unto the other firmly by these Presents. IN WITNESS thereof, the said Parties have interchangeably set their Hands and Seals hereunto. Dated the Fifteenth Day of May—in the Twenty-Second. Year of the Reign of our Sovereign Lord George the Second—King of GREAT BRITAIN, &c. ANNOQUE DOMINI One Thousand Seven Hundred and Forty-Nine—

Isaac Hays

Sealed and Delivered in the Presence of
    her
Estter X Marache
    mark
Dan Gomez
Ash^r Myers

REQUEST OF CONGREGATION SHEARITH ISRAEL FOR A SCHOOLMASTER (1760)   From American Jewish Historical Society, *Publications*. vol. XXVII, pp. 17-18.

M^r. Benj Pereira   *New York*, Decr. 16 1760
S^r. After our compliments to you and your family wee take this opper^y to acquaint you that at a meeting of the Elders of this K. K. it was agreed that wee should apply to you and that you will be good enough to Engage a Suitable Master Capable to Teach our Children ye Hebrew Language; English & Spanish he ought to know; but he will not Suit unless he understands Hebrew and English at Least: this must Require your particular care: A Single: modest: Sober: person will be most

agreeable however on your good Judgement wee shall depend as you Very well know our minds and Tempers. and can make Choice of Such as will be Suitable and Capable of ye undertaken: he must oblige himself to keep a publick School at the usual Hours of the forenoons on every Customary Day at our Jesiba. Children whos parents are in needy Circumstances he must Teach Gratis: his Salary shall be first at Forty pounds New york money pr year and shall Commence from the Day of his Arrival here, and all other Children he Teaches must and will pay him as has been done heretofore. wee flatter ourselfs you will Excuse the Trouble wee give you as it will Very much oblige our whole Congregation and in a more particular manner the Parnassim who are

S^r your most ob^t Humble [Servt.]

THE HIRING OF A SCHOOLMASTER BY CONGREGATION SHEARITH ISRAEL (1762)   From American Jewish Historical Society, *Publications, vol. XXIX, pp. 85-86.*

Iyar 2nd 5522 [April 25, 1762] The Parnassim, and Assistants; agreed with Mr Abraham Is. Abrahams to keep a publick school in the Hebra, to teach the Hebrew Language, and translate the same into English, also to teach English Reading Writing & Cyphering.

The Congregation to allow him Twenty Pounds per Annum with liberty of having offerings made him in Synagogue. He is to teach all such Children gratis, that can not afford to pay. all others are to be paid for Quarterly, as he may agree with those who send them to school;

In case the Hazan should be absent or indisposed, Said Abrahams is to perform in that function, and if the foremention'd allowances should happen to fall short of Expectation or his deserts, upon application to the Parnassim and Assistants They are to take it into Consideration.

Sivan 3 5522 [May 25, 1762] At a meeting of the Parnassim and Assistants Mr Abram. Is: Abrahams Declared he could not undertake keeping school for the sum above mention'd. The Majority therefore resolved to allow said Abrahams Forty Pounds per annum out of the Sedaka

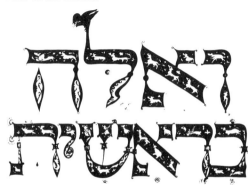

ADVERTISEMENT OF A JEWISH PRIVATE SCHOOLMASTER (1790) From *The Pennsylvania Packet,* and the *Daily Advertiser,* March 1, 4, 6, 9, 11, 1790.

Hebrew taught by Abraham Cohen, Son to the Rev'd JACOB COHEN— For Particulars enquire at the above Rev'd JACOB COHEN'S, Cherry Alley, between Third and Fourth Streets.

N. B. Spanish also taught as above.

THOMAS JEFFERSON ON HIS OWN EDUCATION (c. 1760) From Albert E. Bergh, ed., *The Writings of Thomas Jefferson* (Washington, 1905), vol. I, pp. 2-4.

My father's education had been quite neglected; but being of a strong mind, sound judgment, and eager after information, he read much and improved himself, insomuch that he was chosen, with Joshua Fry, Professor of Mathematics in William and Mary College, to continue the boundary line between Virginia and North Carolina, which had been begun by Colonel Byrd; and was afterwards employed with the same Mr. Fry, to make the first map of Virginia which had ever been made, that of Captain Smith being merely a conjectural sketch. They possessed excellent materials for so much of the country as is below the blue ridge; little being then known beyond that ridge. He was the third or fourth settler, about the year 1737, of the part of the country in which I live. He died, August 17th, 1757, leaving my mother a widow, who lived till 1776, with six daughters and two sons, myself the elder. To my younger brother he left his estate on James River, called Snowden, after the supposed birthplace of the family: to myself, the lands on which I was born and live.

He placed me at the English school at five years of age; and at the Latin at nine, where I continued until his death. My teacher, Mr. Douglas, a clergyman from Scotland, with the rudiments of the Latin and Greek languages, taught me the French; and on the death of my father, I went to the Reverend Mr. Maury, a correct classical scholar, with whom I continued two years; and then, to wit, in the spring of 1760, went to William and Mary college, where I continued two year. It was my great good fortune, and what probably fixed the destinies of my life, that Dr. William Small of Scotland, was then professor of Mathematics, a man profound in most of the useful branches of science, with a happy talent of communication, correct and gentlemanly manners, and an enlarged and liberal mind. He, most happily for me, became soon attached to me, and made me his daily companion when not engaged in the school; and from his conversation I got my first views of the expansion of science, and of the system of things in which we are placed. Fortunately, the philosophical chair became vacant soon after my arrival at college, and he was appointed to fill it *per interim:* and he was the first who ever gave, in that college, regular lectures in Ethics, Rhetoric and Belles Lettres. He returned to Europe in 1762, having previously filled up the measure of his goodness to me, by procuring for me, from his most intimate friend, George Wythe, a reception as a student of law, under his direction, and introduced me to the acquaintance and familiar table of Governor Fauquier, the ablest man who had ever filled that office. With him, and at his table, Dr. Small and Mr. Wythe, his *amici omnium horarum*, and myself, formed a *partie quarree*, and to the habitual conversations on these occasions I owed much instruction. Mr. Wythe continued to be my faithful and beloved mentor in youth, and my most affectionate friend through life. In 1767, he led me into the practice of the law at the bar of the General court, at which I continued until the Revolution shut up the courts of justice.

JAMES MAURY ON THE EDUCATION APPROPRIATE FOR A VIRGINIA GENTLEMAN (1762)

From Helen Bulloc, ed., "A Dissertation on Education in the Form of a Letter from James Maury to Robert Jackson, July 17, 1762," as quoted in *Papers of the Albermarle County Historical Society*, vol. II, pp. 39-60.

An Acquaintance with the Languages, antiently spoken in Greece & Italy, is necessary, absolutely necesary, for those, who wish to make any reputable Figure in Divinity, Medicine or Law.

It is also delightful, ornamental & useful, nay even necessary to such, as, in some other Parts of the World, turn in the more exalted Spheres of Life.

For Instance, it is so to the English Gentleman of the upper Class, whose Opulence places him far above the perplexing Pursuits and sordid Cares, in which Persons of inferior Fortunes are usually engaged.

It is likewise most eminently to the British Nobleman, whose vast annual Revenues rank him with, nay set him above, many, who, in other Countries, claim the royal Stile & Title; & warrant his indulging himself in the Enjoyment of that calm Retreat from the Bustle of the World, of that studious Leisure and Philosophic Repose, which furnish him with the happiest Opportunities, not barely of making transient Visits to, but even fixing his Residence within, those sacred Recesses, sequestered Seats & classic Grounds, which are the Muses' favourite Haunts; a Repose, a Leisure, a Retreat, which nought, but his Countries pressing Calls, on some great Emergencies, has a Right to break in upon or interrupt.

To such as are included in the two last Instances, Studies of this Sort, besides being useful Embellishments, which indeed they are to all who are at Liberty to pursue them, are also, in the highest Degree, necessary. For, Sir, so active a Principle is the human Mind, that tho' Fortune exempt a Man from the Necessity of what we call Business, yet it can by no Means be reconciled to a torpid & dronish State of Inaction. Now a Taste & Relish for the liberal Sciences and politer Arts, by furnishing the Mind with Materials to work upon, rescue such from Pursuits, which are either trivial or unworthy of Man, especially Men of this elevated Rank, or else criminal, destructive & flagitious. . . .

It long has been, & still is, Matter of Doubt with me whether the Study of the Grecian & Roman Tongues be (I do not say necessary, for it seems quite obvious it is not, but even) proper for all our Youth, who are sent to a Grammar-school, who have Genius equal to the Task, & the Circumstances of whose Parents bid fair for placing them above manual Labor & servile Employments, after their Attainment to Manhood. In the Instances above-mentioned, indeed, the Propriety, & even Necessity, of these Studies, are undeniable: but in this Case, which involves almost all our Youth above the lower Ranks in this Quarter of the World, I am far from convinced, that they are necessary or proper.

In Education it can be no irrational Maxim, that the Part, which either the Circumstances, the natural Turn, the inclination, or the Talents of the Learner may either require or incline or capacitate him to act in the World, be ever in his Teacher's View; & that even his puerile Studies & earlier Exercises always converge & centre in that one Point.

What his future Circumstances may be in Reference to Fortune, may with Probability be conjectured from those of his Parents; which, if they be but a Remove or two from the Vulgar, are generally nearly guessed at in this country.

Whether he may have a natural Turn or Genius for either of the learned Professions, is what cannot usually be discovered very early in Life. However, as I cannot at present recollect that the Son of any one Parent of a larger Fortune has, of late Years, been brought up to either of the three; since the Profits of neither are adequate to the Expence of a proper Education for, or to the Fatigue of a diligent Discharge of, the Duties of either of them; a Tutor, methinks, may hence conclude, that such Parents will not judge it eligible to train up their Sons for either of them.

✳   ✳   ✳

Things standing thus among us, few Men of Fortune will expend on their Son's Education the Sums requisite to carry them thro' a regular Course of Studies, proper to qualify them for shining in either of these Professions. If therefore the Parents possess considerable Estates, a Preceptor may well in general conclude, their Sons are not destined for either of these.

It is then to be considered, what Kind of Education may be most suited for such, who, when they shall settle in the World, are to be masters of competent Fortunes, which they are to improve, either by the Culture of our Staple, by Merchandise, or by some other Method, than either of the Learned Professions. And such are most of those among us, who class with the Gentry.

Now, Sir, the Business, which these are usually obliged to pursue;—the variety of Cares, insep[ar]able from their Situation & Way of Life; render it quite obvious, they can have but little Opportunity or Leisure, after they launch out into the busy World, to apply to the Study of the Languages.—Moreover, a few, very few of them prosecute their Studies, either in private or public Schools, so long as their twentieth Year. Besides, they commonly marry very Young, & are thence in the early Stages of Life encumbered with Families. And, tho' you suppose them born to the greatest Fortunes, yet the prudent Management of a large Virginia Estate requires so frequent & close an Inspection, in Order, not only to improve, but preserve it, that the Possessor, when once he comes to be charged with the Care of it, can expect but little of that Leisure & Repose, which are requisite for a pleasurable or successful Engagement in such Parts of Literature, as the Languages, Criticism, & curious & deep Researches into Antiquity.

And yet, Sir, Parts of Literature there evidently are, with which even a Virginia Gentleman ought to have some Acquaintance; destitute of which, he must inevitably make but a ridiculous & awkward Figure in Life. And the Rudiments of these must be acquired in Childhood & Youth, or not at all.

For, if he have not some general Acquaintance with History, he can give or receive but very little Satisfaction or Benefit in private Conversation; nor can acquit himself with any tolerable Measure of Honor & Dexterity in any of those public Stations, which are generally filled by Persons of his Rank. Some of his Time then must be spent this Way.

Again, without a Smattering at least in Geography & Chronology, his Progress in historical Knowledge will be extremely slow; & a Study, which, with those Helps, would have been pleasant & delightful, as well as instructive, without them, will be fruitless & distasteful. These then also come in for Part of his Attention.

But further, if he have not, at least a general knowledge of the Laws, Constitution, Interests & religion of his Country; when called by Authority to the Distribution of Justice, or by his Country to bear a Part in the weighty Business of Legislation, he must ever be at a Loss how to Act. He may as often both act & judge wrong, as right; & so will but illy answer the just Expectations, either of him, who nominates to the one, or of those, who elect to the other of those momentous Trusts. These Branches of [sic] together with the customary Vacations & the needless Interruptions, which are here given to the Studies of Youth thro' the indiscreet Fondness of Parents, will allow but a small Pittance of Time for gaining an Insight into these most useful Departments of Literature. So that to me it seems quite plain, one or other must be neglected. In which Case, I deem it no Matter of intricate Discussion to determine where the Preference is due.

For, Sir, tho' the Knowledge of these ancient Tongues be valuable; may it not yet be bought too dear? And, if the Acquisition of it, or rather laying a Foundation for acquiring it (more than which is not usually done at School) be a Business, which our Gentlemen cannot afterwards take Time to Pursue; & if the Pursuit of it, while at School, must divert them from that of those other Studies just now mentioned, which are to be of daily Use to them as long as they live; surely, the Time, devoted to the Study of these Languages, is, in this Case, but illy spent. For, in the first Place, it is a Study, which they cannot master, while at School, nor, in the next, perfect themselves in afterwards. . . .

But, Sir, let us change the Prospect. From viewing a Virginia Gentleman, born to an affluent Fortune, of which we have but very few (if no Fortunes are properly affluent, but such, as leave the Possessors an Overplus of Income, after all their Wants, whether real or imaginary, have been supplied) let us contemplate another, who will be obliged to call in the Assistance of some lucrative Business to help out his little Patrimony to support himself & his family, when he shall have one, in such Manner, as to prevent his mingling with & being lost among the vulgar Herd. And here, I trust, the Reasonableness of what has been said, will be still more evident & conspicuous.

Here then is a Person, to be educated, who, when come to a state of Manhood, besides the necessary Cares of Economy & good Husbandry, must recur to some profitable Vocation to preserve & improve his patrimonial Estate.

It will not, I believe, be denyed, that about his 14 or 15th Year he should be put under some Person, eminent in the Business he chooses, in Order to gain an Insight into all its Modes, Forms & Mysteries, without which it is not to be carried on with Reputation or Success. The earlier then he lays a Foundation for the general Knowledge, mentioned above, as necessary for every Gentleman, the sooner he will be at Liberty to engage in Exercises, peculiarly adapted to qualify him for the Part he is to act. And the sooner this can be done, so much the better.

Gentlemen of this Sort are frequently called to the highest Posts of Honor and Trust in this Country. It is therefore reasonable to crowd as much of this most useful Knowledge as possible into that short Parenthesis of Time (if the Expression may be allowed) which stands between these two Periods, his beginning to learn the first Elements, & his quitting his scholastic Studies, to apply himself principally to acquire a Skill in the destined Business, whatever it be. But, if that short Space be filled with Latin & Greek; I doubt, his Pains & Time cannot justly be said to have been laid out to Advantage. For it is not possible for him to acquire a tolerable Stock of classical Knowledge, at the same Time have Leisure for such useful & necessary Studies, as English Grammar, reading, writing, arithmetic, History, Geography, Chronology, the more practical Parts of the Mathematics, Rhetoric, Eloquence & other Species of polite & useful Learning; nor for gaining an Acquaintance with, & taste for, some of the most instructive, entertaining & finished Productions of Genius in his own Language. And yet as much general Knowledge of these Kinds ought to be acquired while under a Tutor, as possible; since afterwards but little can be done that Way. For his Application to the Business he makes Choice of, after he is removed from School, which is usually early in Life, both during his Apprenticeship, and when he shall be at Liberty to act for himself, will find him so much Employment, in the first Period to qualify himself for it, & in the next to prosecute it with Advantage, as will soon convince him, that the Study of those Languages, which were once the great Object of his Attention, must now be either wholly laid aside, or else resumed only by way of Amusement, in some of those vacant Intervals, which, I believe, you, Sir, have been taught by Experience, Gentlemen of Business, incumbered also with the Cares of an Estate, in such a Country as ours, but rarely enjoy.

But if our Gentleman of Business proposes to conduct it with Prudence, Dexterity & Success; if he proposes to give or receive Pleasure & Delight in any of those short Snatches of Leisure, which his Affairs may allow him for social Enjoyment; if he would not lose his Share in Conversation, that turns upon Topics of higher Import, than the Chances of a Card or a Dye, the Pedigree & Virtues of some renowned Stud, or the important & manly Science of breeding, keeping & fighting Cocks; if he aspires to store his Mind with such Knowledge & Wisdom, as may render him a Comfort to himself, & useful, if not ornamental, to Society; if he wish to be Master of the Art of communicating what he knows, either by writing, or orally, amidst a Groupe of Friends of Taste, or in public Assemblies, with a tolerable Degree of Propriety, Energy and Elegance:—if, I say, he would reap such an Harvest as this, the Seeds must be sown in the proper Season. . . .

The Truth of it is, where there is a Strong Presumption, that a Youth, when he shall have attained unto Manhood, will become a Man of Business; it is but reasonable he should, while under his Tutor, be chiefly employed in Studies, that will be useful to him in the approaching active Scenes of Life. Others, however valuable, curious, or entertaining in themselves, yet, if they tend not this Way, are not to him worth the Time & Paines, that must be bestowed on them. Such a Pupil, it is evident, & such are most of our Gentlemen's Sons in this Country, ought to be instructed as soon as possible in the most necessar[y] Branches of useful, practical Knowledge. And, if, at the same Time, he be regularly conducted thro' a Course of English Grammar, if due care be taken to acquaint him with his Mother Tongue by reading such Authors, as have written in it, & as, if a judicious Choice be made, will refine his Taste, strengthen his Judgment, enrich & entertain his Fancy, augment his Knowledge, better his Heart & raise his Piety, & so be of Service to him thro' every Period of his Existence; depend upon it, he will be extremely well equipped for acting his Part with signal Credit & Applause. Nay, without the Aid of foreign Languages, I can almost venture to affirm, he will be able to convey what he knows or thinks on any Subject, either on Paper or viva voce, in a neater, more elegant & better adjusted Dress, than the Thoughts & Sentiments of most of those amongst our Gentry, who have spent many Years in the Study of those Languages, are generally observed to come abroad in.

And this will answer all the Ends, which a Person, who is to fill such a Station in Life, can expect or wish from this part of Education. To which, I believe, we may further add, that this is much more than can (I do not say be expected, because Men's Expectations may be too sanguine, but than can) be, or than is usually effected by the present Mode of educating our Youth: of which, perhaps, no favourable Opinion will be formed, if we are to judge from the Proficiency in Literature, that has been made by the Generality, either of those, who have received their Education here, or of others, who have been sent to Great Britain for that Purpose. As to the former, the Causes of their Miscarriage are too obvious to escape our Notice. And, as to the Plan, on which the latter have been educated, it would be surprising indeed, were the success of it generally such, as to prove it proper for our Youth.—For our Youth, I repeat it again; because the Genius of our People, their Way of Life, their Circumstances in Point of Fortune, the Customs & Manners & Humors of the Country, difference us in so many important Respects from Europeans, that a Plan of Education, however judiciously adapted to these last, would no more fit us, than an Almanac, calculated for the Latitude of London, would that of Williamsburg.

PHILIP FITHIAN ON HIS TEACHING EXPERIENCES IN VIRGINIA (1773-1774)   From Hunter Farish, ed., *Journal and Letters of Philip Vickers Fithian, 1773–1774: A Plantation Tutor of the Old Dominion* (Williamsburg, Va., 1943), pp. 25-26, 34-35, 66-67, 72, 208.

Monday Novemr 1st We began School—The School consists of eight—Two of Mr Carters Sons—One Nephew—And five Daughters—The eldest Son is reading Salust; Gramatical Exercises, and latin Grammer—The second Son is reading english Grammar Reading English: Writing, and Cyphering in Subtraction—The Nephew is Reading and Writing as above; and Cyphering in Reduction—The eldest daughter is Reading the Spectator; Writing; and beginning to Cypher—The second is reading next out of the Spelling-Book, and beginning to write—The next is reading in the Spelling-Book—The fourth is Spelling in the beginning of the Spelling-Book—And the last is beginning her letters—

Tuesday 2. Busy in School—begun to read Pictete—

Letter of Philip V. Fithian to the Reverend Enoch Green

Revd Sir.   —Westmoreland. Novr 2d 1773.

According as I appointed I take this early oppertunity of acquainting you that I am arrived safe; and I am to assure you that I find the place fully equal to my highest expectations—I am situated in the Northern-Neck, in a most delightful Country; in a civil, polite neighbourhood; and in a family remarkable for regularity, and economy, tho' confessedly of the highest quality and greatest worth of any in Virginia. I teach only Mr Carters children, and only one of them is to learn Languages, and he is reading Salust and the Greek grammer, is seventeen years old, and seems to be a Boy of Genius—the other two learn writing and Arithmetic—But he has four Daughters, young Misses that are at times to be taught writing and English—I have the terms as I expected, and find the place wholly agreeable—and am strongly solicited to stay many years—But money nor conveniency shall detain me long from my most important connections at home—You may expect me in may at the Synod. Please to have my compliments to Mrs Green, to Miss Betsy if at Deerfield, and to my acquaintances that shall enquire and accept to yourself the

Respect of your humble Servt

Letter of Philip V. Fithian
to the Reverend Enoch Green

Revd Sir.   Decemr 1st 1773.

As you desired I may not omit to inform you, so far as I can by a letter, of the business in which I am now engaged, it would indeed be vastly agreeable to me if it was in my power to give you particular intelligence concerning the state and plan of my employment here.

I set out from home the 20th of Octr and arrived at the Hon: Robert Carters, of Nominy, in Westmorland County, the 28th I began to teach his children the first of November. He has two sons, and one Nephew; the oldest Son is turned of seventeen, and is reading Salust and the greek grammer; the others are about fourteen, and in english grammer, and Arithmetic. He has besides five daughters which I am to teach english, the eldest is turned of fifteen, and is reading the spectator; she is employed two days in every week in learning to play the Forte-Piana, and Harpsicord—The others are smaller, and learning to read and spell. Mr Carter is one of the Councellors in the general court at Williamsburg, and possest of as great, perhaps the clearest fortune according to the estimation of people here, of any man in Virginia: He seems to be a good scholar, even in classical learning, and is remarkable one in english grammar; and notwithstanding his rank, which in general seems to countenance indulgence to children, both himself and Mrs Carter have a manner of instructing and dealing with children far superior, I may say it with confidence, to any I have every seen, in any place, or in any family. They keep them in perfect subjection to themselves, and never pass over an occasion of reproof; and I blush for many of my acquaintances when I say that the children are more kind and complaisant to the servants who constantly attend them than we are to our superiors in age and condition. Mr Carter has an overgrown library of Books of which he allows me the free use. It consists of a general collection of law books, all the Latin and Greek Classicks, vast number of Books on Divinity chiefly by writers who are of the established Religion; he has the works of almost all the late famous writers, as Locke, Addison, Young, Pope, Swift, Dryden, etc. in Short, Sir, to speak moderately, he has more than eight times your number—His eldest Son, who seems to be a Boy of genius and application is to be sent to Cambridge University, but I believe will go through a course either in Philadelphia or Princeton College first. As to what is commonly said concerning Virginia that it is difficult to avoide being corrupted with the manners of the people, I believe it is founded wholly in a mistaken notion that persons must, when here frequent all promiscuous assemblies; but this is so far from truth that any one who does practise it, tho' he is accused of no crime, loses at once his character; so that either the manners have been lately changed or the report is false, for he seems now to be best esteemed and most applauded who attends to his business, whatever it be, with the greatest diligence. I believe the virginians have of late altered their manner very much, for they begin to find that their estates by even small extravagance, decline, and grow involved with debt, this seems to be the spring which induces the People of fortune who are the pattern of all behaviour here, to be frugal, and moderate. You may expect me at home by the permission of Providence the latter end of april next, or the beginning of May; and as I proposed I shall present my exercises for the examination of the Presbytery; and if they think proper I shall gladly accept of a licence in the fall: I must beg your favour to mention me to such of my acquaintants in Deerfield as you think proper, but especially to Mrs Green, Miss Betsy, your family, and Mrs Pecks—I must also beg you to transmit so much of this intelligence to Mr Hunter as that my relations in Greenwich may know that I am through the mercy of heaven in good health. I beg, Sir, you will not fail to write, and let it be known to Mr Hunter, that a letter will come as secure by the Post as from Cohansie to Philadelphia; the Letters are to be directed to me thus, To Mr Philip V. Fithian at Mr Carters of Nominy, to be left at Hobes Hole

I am, Sir, yours
Philip V. Fithian

Monday 13 Mr Carter is preparing for a Voyage in his Schooner, the Hariot, to the Eastern Shore in Maryland, for Oysters: there are of the party, Mr Carter, Captain Walker Colonel Richd Lee, and Mr Lancelot Lee. With Sailors to work the vessel—I observe it is a general custom on Sundays here, with Gentlemen to invite one another home to dine, after Church; and to consult about, determine their common business, either before or after Service—It is not the Custom for Gentlemen to go into Church til Service is beginning, when they enter in a Body, in the same manner as they come out; I have known the Clerk to come out and call them in to prayers.—They stay also after the Service is over, usually as long, sometimes longer, than the Parson was preaching—Almost every Lady wears a red Cloak; and when they ride out they tye a white handkerchief over their Head and face, so that when I first came into Virginia. I was distress'd whenever I saw a Lady, for I thought She had the tooth-Ach!—The People are extremely hospitable, and very polite both of which are most certainly universal Characteristics of the Gentlemen in Virginia—some swear bitterly, but the practise seems to be generally disapproved—I have heard that this Country is notorious for Gaming, however this be, I have not seen a Pack of Cards, nor a Die, since I left home, nor gaming nor Betting of any kind except at the Richmond-Race. Almost every Gentleman of Condition, keeps a Chariot and Four; many drive with six Horses—I observe that all the Merchants and shopkeepers in the Sphere of my acquaintance and I am told it is the Case through the Province, are young Scotch-Men; several of whom I know, as Cunningham, Jennings, Hamilton, Blain;—And it has been the custom heretofore to have all their Tutors, and Schoolmasters from Scotland, tho' they begin to be willing to employ their own Countrymen—Evening Ben Carter and myself had a long dispute on the practice of fighting—He thinks it best for two persons who have any dispute to go out in good-humour and fight manfully, and says they will be sooner and longer friends than to brood and harbour malice—Mr Carter is practising this Evening on the Guittar He begins with the Trumpet Minuet. He has a good Ear for Music; a vastly delicate Taste: and keeps good Instruments, he has here at Home a Harpsichord, Forte-Piano, Harmonica, Guittar, Violin, and German Flutes, and at Williamsburg, has a good Organ, he himself also is indefatigable in the Practice.

Wednesday 15. Busy in School—To day Dined with us Mrs Turburville, and her Daughter Miss Letty Miss Jenny Corbin, and Mr Blain. We dined at three. The manner here is different from our way of living in Cohansie—In the morning so soon as it is light a Boy knocks at my Door to make a fire; after the Fire is kindled, I rise which now in the winter is commonly by Seven, or a little after, By the time I am drest the Children commonly enter the School-Room, which is under the Room I sleep in; I hear them round one lesson, when the Bell rings for eight o-Clock (for Mr Carter has a large good Bell of upwards of 60 Lb. which may be heard some miles, and this is always rung at meal Times;) the Children then go out; and at half after eight the Bell rings for Breakfast, we then repair to the Dining-Room; after Breakfast, which is generally about half after nine, we go into School, and sit til twelve, when the Bell rings, and they go out for noon; the dinner-Bell rings commonly about half after two, often at three, but never before two.—After dinner is over, which in common, when we have no Company, is about half after three we go into School, and sit till the Bell rings at five, when they separate til the next morning; I have to myself in the Evening, a neat Chamber, a large Fire, Books, and Candle and my Liberty, either to continue in the school room, in my own Room or to sit over at the great House with Mr and Mrs Carter—We go into Supper commonly about half after eight or at nine and I usually go to Bed between ten and Eleven. Altho the family in which I live, is certainly under as good political Regulations, and every way as suitable and agreeable as I can expect, or even could desire; and though the Neighbourhood is polite, and the Country pleasant, yet I cannot help reflecting on my situation last winter, which was near the lovely Laura for whom I cannot but have the truest, and the warmest Esteem! possibly, If Heaven shall preserve my life, in some future time, I may again enjoy her good society.

Mr Carter heard this Evening that Captain Walker cannot go to Maryland, he is thus stop'd.

Sunday 2. The weather warm and Damp—The Family rode to Church to-day and are to dine out. Mr Carter at my request, gave me the Keys of his Book-Cases and allowed me to spend the Day alone in his Library.

The place seems suitable for Study, and the Day ought to be spent in serious contemplation; therefore, as I proposed Yesterday, I shall collect together and write down what I have been doing in the last Year. But will my Life bear the review? Can I look upon my Actions and not Blush! And shall I be no less careful, or have no better Success, in the prosecution of my Duty the Year to come, if I shall be kept alive to the Close of it?— In the Beginning of the last year I was in Deerfield, in Cumberland County New-Jersey, with the Rev'd Mr Green; Under him I studied the Hebrew-Language and Divinity. I left the college the last of September 1772. After having setled my business at Home, I entered upon the Study of Divinity with the Rev'd Andrew Hunter; I was with him about a Month, and on the first of December I went to Mr Green with a design to acquaint myself with the Hebrew Tongue; he put me to the Grammar, which I learn'd through, and read some Chapters in the Psalter in the Course of the Winter: In Divinity, he advised me to read Ridgeleys body of Divinity for a System: And he gave me several separate treatisses on Repentance, Regeneration, Faith, etc., and towards spring gave me subjects to consider in the Sermon-Way. Yet how barren am I still? It is an arduous task to bring the Mind to close application; and still greater to lay up and retain useful Knowledge. I continued with Mr Green and pursued my studies, I hope with some Success till August 1773, when I was solicited by Dr Witherspoon to go into Virginia and teach in a Gentlemans Family—The Offer seem'd profitable; I was encouraged by the Dr and was to have his Recommendation—I had likewise myself a strong inclination to go—Yet I was in great Doubt, and Wholly undetermined for some Weeks, because many of my friends, and some of my near Relations opposed my leaving Home, and all seem'd utterly unwilling to advise to go—It is time, according to the Course of my Life they said that I was settling to some constant Employment, and they told me I ought especially to enter with as great speed as convenient into that plan of Life for which I have in particular had my Education— That Virginia is sickly—That the People there are profane, and exceeding wicked— That I shall read there no Calvinistic Books, nor hear any Presbyterian Sermons— That I must keep much Company, and therefore spend as much, very probably much more Money than my Salary—These considerations unsettled for a while my mind—On the other hand I proposed to myself the following advantages by going— A longer opportunity for Study than my friends would willingly allow me If I should remain at home—A more general acquaintance with the manners of Mankind; and a better Knowledge of the Soil and Commerce of these neighbouring Provinces—And a more perfect acquaintance with the Doctrines, and method of Worship in the established Church in these Colonies, and especially with the Conduct of the Clergy of which there have been so many bad reports—All these however, when I had laid them together, seem'd to overbear the others, so that I determined at last to break through and go!—Here now I am in a strange Province; But I am under no more nor stronger temptations to any kind of vice, perhaps not so great as at Cohansie,— unless sometimes when I am solicited to dance I am forc'd to blush, for my Inability—I have the opportunity of living with Credit perfectly retired—in a well regulated family—With a man of Sense—May God help me to walk in his fear and Gloryfy his Name!

Monday 10th. The Morning very cold—Dined with us to-day Mr Sanford a Captain of a Sloop which trades out of Potowmack to Norfolk—I wrote out some Exercises for Bob and Harry—In the Evening the Colonel began with a small Still to disttill some Brandy from a Liquor made of Pisimmonds. I set Ben this Evening to writing. I likewise gave Catalines Speech in Salust to commit to memory in Latin, which he is to pronounce Extempore. In the Evening I borrowed of Ben Carter 15s.—I have plenty of Money with me, but it is in Bills of Philadelphia currency and will not pass at all here.

Tuesday 11. The morning very cold—As cold I think, and the Frost seems to be as intense and powerful as I have ever known it either at Cohansie or at Princeton. This morning I put Ben to construe some Greek, he has yet no Testament, I gave him therefore Esops Fables in Greek, and Latin. I also took out of the Library, and gave him to read Gordon, upon Geography. Ben seem'd scared with his Greek Lesson, he swore, and wished for Homer that he might kick Him, as he had been told Homer invented Greek.

PHILIP FITHIAN ADVISES HOW TO ACT AS A TUTOR (1774) From Hunter Farish, ed., *Journal and Letters of Philip Vickers Fithian, 1773–1774: A Plantation Tutor of the Old Dominion* (Williamsburg, Va., 1943), pp. 208-22.

Sir:

I never reflect, but with secret, and peculiar pleasure, on the time when I studied in Deerfield with you, & several other pleasant Companions, under our common, & much respected instructor, Mr Green. And I acknowledge now, with a thankful heart, the many favours, which I received from your family while I was a member of it. This sense of obligation to your Family, And personal friendship for you, have excited me, when it was in my power, to introduce you to the business which I now occupy; into a family, where, if you be prudent and industrious, I am confident you will speedily acquire to yourself both Honour & Profit—But inasmuch as you are wholly a stranger to this Province; & have had little or no Experience in the business which you ar shortly to enter upon; & lest, from common Fame, which is often erroneous, you shall have entertained other notions of the manners of the People here, & of your business as a Tutor, than you will find, when you come, to be actually true; I hope you will not think it vain or untimely, if I venture to lay before you some Rules for your direction which I have collected from a year's observation. I shall class what I have to say in the following order. First. I shall attempt to give you some direction for the plan of your Conduct among your neighbours, & the People in General here, so long as you sustain the character of a Tutor. Then I shall advise you concerning the rules which I think will be most profitable & convenient in the management of your little lovely charge, the School. Last of all. I shall mention several Rules for your personal conduct. I choose to proceed in the order I have laid down, as well that you may more fully & speedily recieve my mind, as that you may also the more readily select out and apply what you shall find to be most necessary.

1. When you have thought of removinging, for a Time, out of the Colony in which you was born, & in which you have hitherto constantly resided, I make no doubt but you have at the same time expected to find a very considerable alteration of manners, among your new acquaintances, & some peculiarities toto Caelo different, from any you have before been accustomed to. Such a thought is natural; And you will if you come into Virginia, in much shorter time than a year, be convinced that it is just.

* * *

. . . you will find the tables turned the moment you enter this Colony. The very Slaves, in some families here, could not be bought under 30,000 pounds. Such amazing property, no matter how deep it is involved, blows up the owners to an imagination, which is visible in all, but in various degrees according to their respective virtue, that they are exalted as much above other Men in worth & precedency, as blind stupid fortune has made a difference in their property; excepting always the value they put upon posts of honour, & mental acquirements— For example, if you should travel through this Colony, with a well-confirmed testimonial of your having finished with Credit a Course of studies at Nassau-Hall; you would be rated, without any more questions asked, either about your family, your Estate, your business, or your intention, at 10,000 pounds; and you might come, & go, & converse, & keep company, according to this value; & you would be dispised & slighted if yo[u] rated yourself a farthing cheaper. But when I am giving directions to you, from an expectation that you will be shortly a resident here, altho you have gone through a College Course, & for any thing I know, have never written a Libel, nor stolen a Turkey, yet I think myself in duty bound to advise you, lest some powdered Coxcomb should reproach your education, to cheapen your price about 5000 pounds; because any young Gentleman travelling through the Colony, as I said before, is presum'd to be acquainted with Dancing, Boxing, playing the Fiddle, & Small-Sword, & Cards. Several of which you was only entering upon, when I left New-Jersey; towards the Close of last year; and if you stay here any time your Barrenness in these must be detected. I will however allow, that in the Family where you act as tutor you place yourself, according to your most accute Calculation, at a perfect equidistance between the father & the eldest Son. Or let the same distance be observed in every article of behaviour between you & the eldest Son, as there ought to be, by the latest & most approved precepts of Moral-Philosophy, between the eldest Son, & his next youngest Brother. But whenever you go from Home, where you are to act on your own footing, either to a Ball; or to a Horse-Race, or to a Cock-Fight, or to a Fish-Feast, I advise that you rate yourself very low, & if you bett at all, remember that 10,000 pounds in Reputation & learning does not amount to a handful of Shillings in ready Cash!--One considerable advantage which you promise yourself by coming to this Colony is to extend the Limits of your acquaintance; this is laudable, & if you have enough of prudence & firmness, it will be of singular advantage—Yet attempt slowly & with the most Jealous Circumspection—If you fix your familiarity wrong in a single instance, you are in danger of total, if not immediate ruin—You come here, it is true, with an intention to teach, but you ought likewise to have an inclination to learn. At any rate I solemnly injoin it upon you, that you never suffer the spirit of a Pedagogue to attend you without the walls of your little Seminary.

* * *

In all promiscuous Company be as silent & attentive as Decency will allow you, for you have nothing to communicate, which such company, will hear with pleasure, but you may learn many things which, in after life, will do you singular service.—In regard to Company in general, if you think it worth the while to attend to my example, I can easily instruct you in the manner of my Conduct in this respect. I commonly attend Church; and often, at the request of Gentlemen, after Service according to the custom, dine abroad on Sunday—I seldom fail, when invited by Mr or Mrs Carter, of going out with them; but I make it a point, however strongly solicited to the contrary, to return home with them too—Except in one of these cases, I seldom go out, but with a valuable variety of books I live according to Horace's direction, & love "Secretum Iter et fallentis Semita Vitae." Close retirement and a life by Stealth. The last direction I shall venture to mention on this head, is, that you abstain totally from Women. What I would have you understand from this, is that by a train of faultless conduct in the whole course of your tutorship, you make every Lady within the Sphere of your acquaintance, who is between twelve & forty years of age, so much pleased with your person, & so fully satisfied as to your abilities in the capacity of—a Teacher; & in short, fully convinced, that, from a principle of Duty, you have, both by night & by day endeavoured to acquit yourself honourably, in the Character of a Tutor; & that, on this account, you have their free & hearty consent, without making any manner of demand upon you, either to stay longer in the County with them, which they would choose, or whenever your business calls you away, that they may not have it in their Power either by charms or Justice to detain you, & when you must leave them, have their sincere wishes & constant prayrs for Length of days & much prosperity, I therefore beg that you will attend litterally to this advice, & abstain totally from Women.

But this last precaution, which I have been at some pains to dress in the plainest language, I am much inclined to think, will be wholly useless in regard to you, notwithstanding it is founded in that Honour and Equity which is on all hands allow'd to be due from one Sex to the other, & to many of your age, & Standing no doubt would be entirely salutary. Because the necessary connections which you have had with the Fair, from your Puberty upwards have been so unfavourable & illfated, that instead of apprehending any danger on the score of over fondness, I am fearful your rancour has grown so inveterate at length, as, not only to preserve you, in thought & practice, pure of every Fleshly foible, but has carried you so far towards the other extream, as that you will need many persuasions, when your circumstances shall seem to require it, to bring you back to a rational & manly habit of thinking & acting with respect to the Sex; which yet, after all (& eternally will continue to be, tho it is so much courted & whined after) if considered in the fullest manner, & set forth to the best advantage, never rises above its divine definition Viz "The weaker Vessel." But without detaining you any longer with a matter merely depending on accident or Circumstance I pass on to the second General Head; in which "Ludis atque Jocis amotis" I shall offer to your consideration & recommend for your practice several Rules concerning the management of the School.

2. You will act wisely, if, from the beginning, you convince all your Scholars which you may easily do, of your abilities in the several branches, which you shall profess to teach; you are not to tell them, totidem Verbis, "that you understand, perhaps as well as any man on the Continent both the Latin & Greek Classicks"; "& have gone through the usual Course in the noted College of New-Jersey, under Dr Witherspoon, so universally known & admired, where you have studied Criticism, Oratory, History, not to mention Mathematical & philosophical Studies, & dipt a good way into the French-Language, & that you have learn'd a smattering of Dancing, Cards &c. &c. &c." For Dun-p or Hack-n or the most profound dunce in your College or School would have too much sense to pass such impudence by, & not despise and reproach it; but you may speedily & certainly make them think you a "Clever Fellow" (which is a phrase in use here for a good Scholar) if you never mention any thing before them, only what you seem to be wholly master of—This will teach them never to dispute your determination, & always to rely upon your Judgment; two things which are most essential for your peace, & their advantage. That you may avoid yourself of this with certainty I shall recommend for your practice the following method, as useful at least, if not intirely necessary. Read over carefully, the lessons in Latin & Greek, in your leisure hours, that the story & Language be fresh in your memory, when you are hearing the respective lessons; for your memory is treacherous, & I am pretty certain it would confound you if you should be accosted by a pert School-Boy, in the midst of a blunder, with "Physician heal thyself"!—You ought likewise to do this with those who are working Figures; probably you may think that because the highest Cypherer is only in decimal arithmetic, it is not there fore worth your critical attention to be looking previously into the several Sums. But you are to consider that a sum in the Square-Root, or

even in the Single Rule of three direct, is to your Pupils of as great importance, as the most abstruse problem in the Mathematicks to an able artist; & you may lay this down for a Maxim, that they will reckon upon your abilities, according as they find you acquainted & expert in what they themselves are studying. If therefore you have resolution (as I do not question your ability) to carry this plan which I have laid down into execution; you will thereby convince them of the propriety of their Subordination to you, & obedience to your instructions, so that you may lead them, without any resistance, and fix them to the Study of whatever Science you think proper, in which they will rise according to their respective Capacities.

I have said that you ought to strive "from the beginning" in fixing this very material article in the minds of your Scholars, Viz a Sense of your authority; for one error of Judgment, or false determination will diminish your Ability with them more than doing forty things with truth would increase your authority—They act in this case as you would do in the company of a number of Strangers—A whole evenings conversation, if it was tolerable good Sense, would perhaps make little or no impression on you; But if through hast in speaking, or inattention, any one should let fall a sentence either remarkably foolish, or grossly wicked, it would be difficult if not impossible to persuade you presently that the author was not either a thick-Scull, or a Villain!—The education of children requires constant unremitting attention. The meanest qualification you can mention in a useful teacher is diligence And without diligence no possible abilities or qualifications can bring children on either with speed or profit. There must be a Combination of qualifications which must all operate strongly & uniformly. In short, give this said Pedagogizing the softest name you will, it is still a "difficult Task." You will meet with numberless difficulties, in your new imployment, which you never dreamt had yet existence. All these you must endeavour to resist & Subdue. This I have seen compared to a Man swimming against a current of Water. But I am mistaken if you will agree, after having six months practice, that the comparison be strong as the truth: You will add to the figure, I am certain, & throw into the Current sharp fragments of Ice, & Blocks, which would make swimming not only difficult but dangerous! I am not urging these things to discourage you; they are hints for your direction, which, if you will attend to, tho' at first the practice seem rough & unpleasant, shall yet make the remainder of your task pleasing, & the whole of it useful, I will mention several of these Obstacles that you may the more easily guard against them. You will, in the first place, be often solicited, probably oftner than you would wish, to ride abroad; this, however, if you do it moderately, & in seasonable time, & go to proper company, I recommend as conducive to health to one in your sedentary manner of living. But if you go much into company, you will find it extremely difficulty to break away with any manner of credit till very late at night or in most cases for several days, & if you are wanting to your School, you do manifest injury to your Imployer. In this case, I advise you to copy Mr Carter. Whenever he invites you, ride. You may stay, and talk, & drink, & ride to as great excess as he; & may with safety associate yourself with those whom you find to be his intimates. In all other Cases, except when you ride to Church, at least till you are very intimate in the Colony, you had better ride to a certain Stump, or to some noted plantation, or pretty landscape; you will have in this every advantage of exercise, the additional advantage of undisturbed Meditation, & you will be under no Jealous apprehension in point of behaviour, nor any restraint as to the time of your return.

Another current difficulty will be petitions for holidays. You must have good deal of steadiness if you are able to evade cleverly this practice which has grown so habitual to your little charge from a false method in their early education that they absolutely claim it as a necessary right. You must never suffer your fondness for one Scholar to grow so manifest, as that all your School shall see you look over a fault in him or her which same fault, if committed by another, you severely chastise. This will certainly produce in the others hatred & contempt. A fourth difficulty, and the last I shall mention, consists in knowing when, & in what measure to give the Boys Liberty to go from Home. The two younger Boys are wholly under your inspection; so that not only the progress they make in learning, but their moral Conduct (for both of these are critically observed & examined) either justifies or condemns your management to the World. If you keep them much at home, & close to business, they themselves will call you unfeeling and cruel; & refuse to be industrious; if you suffer them to go much abroad they are certainly out of the way of improvement by Study, probably, by discovering their gross Ignorance, they will expose to ridicule both themselves & all their former instructors, & possibly they may commit actual Crimes so as very much to injure themselves; & scandalize their family; but in each of these you will have a large share of blame, perhaps more than the parents, or even the Boys themselves—It will be said that the parents gave them no licence relying wholly on your Judgment & prudence, this will in good measure Justify them to the world. And as to the Boys they are full of youthful impetuosity & vigour, & these compel them, when they are free of restraint, to commit actions which with proper management they had surely avoided. I say, when you lay these things together, & view them on every side you will find so many perplexities arising in your mind, from a sense of ignorance of your duty, that you will proceed with caution & moderation, & will be carefull to examine with some precision into the circumstances of time, company, & Business when you license them to go out entirely at the risk of your Reputation—But the practice of three or four Weeks will give you a more full notion of these & many other incidents than I am able now either to recollect or express; I shall have gained my End if these hints prevent you from setting off wrong, & doing inadvertantly at first what your Scholars will assert to be precedents for your after conduct. I go on, therefore, in the third place as I proposed,

3. To mention several Rules for your personal conduct. The happy Education which you have had in point of religion, you ought to consider as an important and distinguishing Blessing of Heaven. That train of useful Instruction, Advice & Example to which you have been accustomed from your infancy is a more perfect, & will be a safer guide in your future walk, than any directions I am able to give you. You have taken notice of a method for Assistance in Composition, which Longinus recommends.

Place, says he, in imagination, several eminent ancient Authors before your Eyes, & suppose that they inspect your Work, a Sense of inferiority would make you diligent, & your composition accurate. Perhaps the same advice when transferr'd to Morality, would be equally salutary. Unless it be objected that a Belief of Gods presence at all times in every place is the strongest possible restraint against commiting Sin. This I constantly admit; but when I consider how easily our minds are put in motion, & how strongly they are sometimes agitated merely by the senses, & that the senses are affected most by things which fall under their immediate notice, I am fully convinced that if some such plan as I have just mentioned should be fallen upon, & practised, it would make a visible and useful change in our behaviour--In this place I think it needful to caution you against hasty & ill founded prejudices. When you enter among a people, & find that their manner of living, their Eating, Drinking, Diversions, Exercise &c, are in many respects different from any thing you have been accustomed to, you will be apt to fix your opinion in an instant, & (as some divines deal with poor Sinners) you will condemn all before you without any meaning or distinction what seems in your Judgment disagreeable at first view, when you are smitten with the novelty. You will be making ten thousand Comparisons. The face of the Country, The Soil, the Buildings, the Slaves, the Tobacco, the method of spending Sunday among Christians; Ditto among the Negroes; the three grand divisions of time at the Church on Sundays, Viz. before Service giving & receiving letters of business, reading Advertisements, consulting about the price of Tobacco, Grain &c, & settling either the lineage, Age, or qualities of favourite Horses 2. In the Church at Service, prayrs read over in haste, a Sermon seldom under & never over twenty minutes, but always made up of sound morality, or deep studied Metaphysicks. 3. After Service is over three quarters of an hour spent in strolling round the Church among the Crowd, in which time you will be invited by several different Gentlemen home with them to dinner. The Balls, the Fish-Feasts, the Dancing-Schools, the Christnings the Cock fights, the Horse-Races, the Chariots, the Ladies Masked, for it is a custom among the Westmorland Ladies whenever they go from home, to muffle up their heads, & Necks, leaving only a narrow passage for the Eyes, in Cotton or silk handkerchiefs; I was in distress for them when I first came into the Colony, for every Woman that I saw abroad, I looked upon as ill either with the Mumps or Tooth-Ach!—I say, you will be often observing & comparing these things which I have enumerated, & many more that now escape me, with the manner of spending Money time & credit at Cohansie: You are young, &, (you will allow me the Expression) in the morning of Life. But I hope you have plann'd off, and entered upon the work which is necessary to be performed in the course of your Day; if not, I think it my duty to acquaint you, that a combination of the amusements which I have just now mentioned, being always before your Eyes, & inviting your Compliance will have a strong tendency to keep you doubtful & unsetled, in your notions of Morality & Religion, or else will fix you in a false & dangerous habit of thinking & acting, which must terminate at length in Sorrow & despair.

You are therefore, if you count any thing upon the value of my advice, to fix the plan in which you would spend your life; let this be done with deliberation, Candour, & precission, looking to him for direction, by fervent Prayr, who is the "Wonderful Counsellor"; & when you have done this, let no importunity of whatever kind prevail over you, & cause you to transgress your own Limitations. I have already exceeded the usual bounds of an Epistle. But you will easily pardon a little prolixity, when I assure you it flows from a heart deeply impressed with a sense of the many difficulties which you must encounter, & the dangers which will surround you when you come first out from the peaceful recess of Contemplation, & enter, young and unexperienced, into the tumultuous undiscerning World. I submit these hints to your consideration, & have nothing more than sincere & ardent wishes for your present & perpetual Felicity.

DIARY OF JOHN HARROWER (1774-1776)   From "Diary of John Harrower 1773-1776," *American Historical Review*, vol. VI, pp. 72, 77, 78-81, 88, 96, 107.

Jan. 1774

Wednesday, *26th.* This day I being reduced to the last shilling I had was obliged to engage to go to Virginia for four years as a schoolmaster for Bedd, Board, washing and five pound during the whole time. I have also wrote my wife this day a particular Accot. of every thing that has happned to me since I left her untill this date; At 3 pm this day I went on board the Snow Planter Capt. Bowers Comt. for Virginia now lying at Ratliff Cross, and imediatly as I came Onbd. I rec. my Hammock and Bedding. at 4 pm came Alexr. Steuart onbd. the same Ship. he was Simbisters Servt. and had only left Zetland about three weeks before me. we were a good deall surprised to meet wt. on another in this place.

Thursday, 27th. This day ranie weather. the ships crew imployed in rigging the ship under the Direction of the mate and I was imployed in getting my Hammock slung. at 2 pm came onbd. Alexr. Burnet nephew to Mr. Francis Farquharson writter in Edinburgh and one Samuel Mitchell a Cooper from Yorkshire and both entred into the berth and Mace with Stewart and me.

Saturday, 29th. This day came on bd. Alex. Kennedy a young man from Edinbf. who hade been a Master Cooper there and a Glasgow Man by trade a Barber both which we took into our Mace, which compleated it being five Scotsmen and one Yorkshireman, and was always called the Scots mace, And the Capt. told me he was from the Toun of Aberbothick in Scotland, but tht he [had] not been there since he was fifteen years of age but hade been always in the Virginia trade which I was verry glad to hear.

Munday, 31st. This day I went ashore and bought a penknife, a paper Book, and some paper and pens and came on board to Dinner. It is surprising to see the No. of good tradesmen of all kinds, tht. come onbd. every day.

*   *   *

May, 1774

Tuesday, 17th. This day Mr. Anderson the Merch. sent for me into the [cabin] and verry genteely told me that on my recomendations he would do his outmost to get me settled as a Clerk or bookeeper if not as a schoolmaster which last he told me he thought wou'd turn out more to my advantage upon being settled in a good famely.

The ships crew and servants employed in getting ashore all the cask out of the hould, no sales th day.

Wednesday, 18th. This day the ships crew and servants imployed in getting out the ballast and unrigging the ship. One Cooper, one Blacksmith and one Shoemaker were settled with Masters this day.

Thursday, 19th. One Farmer's time sold and one Cabinet Maker on tryall.

Satu:day, 21st. This day one Mr. Cowly a man 'twixt fifty and sixty years of age, a servt., also three sons of his their ages from eight to fourteen were all settled with one McDonald a Scotchman.

Munday, 23d. This morning a great number of Gentlemen and Ladies driving into Town it being an annuall Fair day and tomorrow the day of the Horse races. at 11 AM Mr. Anderson begged to settle as a schoolmaster with a friend of his one Colonel Daingerfield and told me he was to be in Town tomorrow, or perhaps tonight, and how soon he came he shou'd aquant me. at same time all the rest of the servants were ordred ashore to a tent at Fredericksb^g. and severall of their Indentures were then sold. about 4 pm I was brought to Colonel Daingerfield, when we imediatly agreed and my Indenture for four years was then delivered him and he was to send for me the next day. at same time ordred to get all my dirty Cloaths of every kind washed at his expense in Toun; at night he sent me five shillings onb^d. by Capt. Bowers to keep my pocket.

Tuesday, 24th. This morning I left the Ship at 6 AM having been sixteen weeks and six days on board her. I hade for Breackfast after I came ashore one Chappin sweet milk for which I paid 3 1/2 Cur^y. at 11 AM went to see a horse race about a mille from Toun, where there was a number of Genteel Company as well as others. here I met with the Colonel again and after some talk with him he gave me cash to pay for washing all my Cloaths and something over. The reace was gain'd by a Bay Mare, a white boy ridder. There was a gray Mare started with the Bay a black boy ridder but was far distant the last heat.

Wednesday, 25th. I Lodged in a Tavern last night and paid 7 1/2 for my Bedd and 7 1/2 for my breackfast. this morning a verry heavy rain untill 11 AM. Then I rec^d. my Linens &c. all clean washed and packing every thing up I went onboard the ship and Bought this Book for which I paid 18d. St^r. I also bought a small Divinity book called the Christian Monitor and spelling book, both at 7 1/2 and an Arithmetick at 1/6d. all for my Acco^t.

Thursday, 26th. This day at noon the Colonel sent a Black with a cuple of Horses for me and soon after I set out on Horseback and aravied at his seat of Belvidera about 3 pm and after I hade dined the Colonel took me to a neat little house at the upper end of an Avenue of planting at 500 yd^s. from the Main house, where I was to keep the school, and Lodge myself in it.

This place is verry pleasantly situated on the Banks of the River Rappahannock about seven miles below the Toun of Fredericksburgh and the school's right above the Warff so that I can stand in the door and pitch a stone onboard of any ship or Boat going up or coming doun the river.

Freiday, 27th. This morning about 8 AM the Colonel delivered his three sons to my Charge to teach them to read write and figure. his oldest son Edwin 10 years of age, intred into two syllables in the spelling book, Bathourest [Bathurst] his second son six years of age in the Alphabete and William his third son 4 years of age does not know the letters.

Sunday, 29th. There is no church nearer Belvidera than Fredericksburgh, and for want of a sadle I was obligded to stay at home all day and when I was alone in the school I thought on the following verses.

1st

In Virginia now I am, at Belvidera settled,
but may they ever mercy find, who hade the cause
that I am from my sweet wife seperated
And Obligded to leave my Infant Children Fatherless.

As a schoolmaster, I am here;
And must for four years, remain so;
May I indeavour the Lord to fear,
And always his commands do.

3^{d}

For in Gods strength I do rely,
that he at his appointed time,
Will bring me back my family,
if I his precepts do but mind.

4th

O May my God provide for them,
Who unto me are near and dear;
tho they afar off me are from
O Jesus keep them in thy fear.

5th

Do thou enable me to labour,
and my fortune do thou mind;
that what I get by thy favour,
I to my family may send.

6th

O Lord my God do thou them save
from dangers and from death
And may they food and rayment have
and for the same may thankfull be
while they have breath.

7th

And may we all ever gloryfie thy name
and loud thy praises sing
and unto all make known the fame
of Jehova our almighty king.

8th

O ever blessed be the Lord,
the King of all the earth is he,
let us exalt his name with one Accord
and thankfull unto him be ye.
          Finis.

EDUCATION
IN THE
UNITED STATES

470

＊　　＊　　＊

June, 1774

Munday, 20th. This morning entred to school Philip and Dorothea Edge's Children of M[r]. Benjaman Edge Planter. Same day Colonel Dangerfield began to cut down his wheat, which they do with a syth.

Tuesday, 21st. This day M[r]. Samuel Edge Planter came to me and begged me to take a son of his to school who was both deaf and dum, and I consented to try what I cou'd do with him.

To Mrs. John Harrower
December, 1774

My dearest life,

Since my aravil here I wrote you 14th June and 7th Augt. last to both which I shall partly refer you. I now rite you with a shaking hand and a feeling heart to enqair of your and my Dr. Infants welfare, this being the return of the day of the year on which I was obliged to leave you and my Dr. Infants early in the morning which day will be ever remembred by me with tears untill it shall please God to grant us all a happy meeting again. I trust in the mercies of a good God this will find you and my Dr. Infants in perfect health as I am and have been ever since I came here, for neither the heat in summer nor what I have as yet felt of the cold in winter gives me the least uneasiness I thank God for it. About 20 days ago I only laid aside my summer dress, and put on a suit of new Claret Coulerd Duffle neatly mounted but no lyning in the Coat only faced in the breasts. I wrote you in my first letter, that I was designed Please God to prepare a way for you and my Infants in this Country; and I begg youll give me your thoughts fully upon it, in your first letter after receipt of this with respect to your moving here. If you do your method must be thus; Take your Passage to Leith, from thence go to Glasgow and from that to Greenock where you will ship for this country. But this you are not to attemp untill I have your thoughts upon it and I send you a recomendation to a Mercht. in Glasgow and cash to bear your expences. I have as yet only ten scollars One of which is both Deaff and Dumb and his Father pays me ten shilling per Quarter for him he has been now five Mos. with [me] and I have brought him tolerably well and understands it so far, that he can write mostly for anything he wants and understands the value of every figure and can work single addition a little. he is about fourteen years of age. Another of them is a young man a house Carpenter who attends me every night with candle light and every Sunday that I don't go to Church for which he pays me fourty shillings a year. He is Carpenter for a gentleman who lives two miles from me and has Thirty pound a year, free bedd and board.

The Cols. Children comes on pretty well. the Eldest is now reading verry distinctly in the Psalter according to the Church of England and the other two boys ready to enter into it; the Col. and his Lady being extreamly well satisfied wt. my Conduct in every respect; On 31st Jully last M[rs]. Daingerfield was delivd. of a fourth son who is now my nameson. I am now verry impatient to hear from you and I [beg] of you not to slip a Packqut without writting me, Accord to the directions I formerly sent you which I shall again repeat in this for fear of my former letters being miscarried which I hope not; The next time [I] write you I hope to be able to make you a small remittance.

*   *   *

July, 1775

Wednesday, 19th. This day I was Informed that M^rs. Daingerfield hade made a Complaint upon me to the Col. for not waiting after Breackfast and dinner (sometimes) in order to take the Children along with me to scholl; I imagine she has a grudge against me since the middle of Feby last the reason was, that one night in the Nursery I wheep'd Billie for crying for nothing and she came in and carried him out from me. Some nights after he got into the same humour and his Papa The Col. hearing him call'd me and Asked why I cou'd hear him do so and not correct him for it; Upon that I told him how M^rs. Daingerfield had behaved when I did correct him. At that he was angry w^t her.

*   *   *

June, 1776

Saturday, 8th. At noon I went to M^rs. Bataile's and entred two of her Daughters to writting, Viz. Miss Sallie and Miss Betty and continoued teaching them until night, when I agreed to attend them every Saturday afternoon and every other Sunday from this date until 8th. June 1777 (If it please God to spare me) for four pound Virginia currancy.

Sunday, 9th. After breakfast I rode to M^r. McAlleys and teach'd his son to write untill 4 pm and then came home in the evening.

Freiday, 14th. At noon Went to Jno. McDearmons and had 6 Yds. stript Cotton warped for 2 Veastcoats and two handkerchiefs all prepared at my own expence.

Wednesday, 19th. At noon went to snow creek and the boys and dined at the spring on Barbaque and fish. At 5 pm I went to M^rs. Battaile and teac'd until 1/2 an hour past 7.

Wednesday 26th. At 5 pm I went to M^r. Becks and had a short Coat cut out of cotton cloth wove Jeans. I bought the cotton and paid for spinning it at the rate of 2/6 per lb. and one shilling per Yd. for weaving.

Sunday, July 7th. This morning I rode to Mansfield and breackfast with M^r. Reid and stayed and dined with him and in the afternoon he and I rode to see the Rowgallies that was building where we met with M^r. Anderson and Jacob Whitely and went to Town with them to Whitelys where we Joyned in Compy. with M^r. Wright and one M^r. Bruce from King George. about 11 pm we brock up and every one went to his own home as I did.

Wednesday, 10th. At 6 pm went to M^rs. Battaile's and teach'd untill sunset and then return'd home and soon after hea[r]d a great many guns fired toward Toun. about 12 pm the Colo. Despatched Anthy. Frazer there to see what was the cause of [it] who returned, and informed him that there was great rejoicings in Toun on Accot. of the Congress having declared the 13 United Colonys of North America Independent of the Crown of great Britain.

Thursday, 25th. I imployed this morng. and forenoon getting Lead off Snowcreek house.

ADVERTISEMENT FOR AN ACADEMY IN YORK COUNTY, ENGLAND
(1769)   From *The* (Williamsburg) *Virginia Gazette,* November 27, 1769, p. 5.

At the Academy in Leeds, which is pleasantly situated in the county of York, in England, Young Gentlemen are genteely boarded, and diligently instructed in English, the Classicks, Modern Languages, Penmanship, Arithmetick, Merchants Accounts, Mathematicks, Modern Geography, Experimental Philosophy, and Astronomy, for twenty guineas per annum, if under twelve years of age, by Mr. Aaron Grimshaw, and able masters. Drawing, Musick, and Dancing, are extra charges. Due regard is paid to the young Gentlemens health, morals, and behaviour.

ADVERTISEMENT FOR REVEREND B. BOOTH'S ACADEMY AT
LIVERPOOL, ENGLAND **(1776)**   From *The* (Williamsburg) *Virginia Gazette,*
November 27, 1776, p. 2.

At the Rev. B. Booth's Academy, the Seat of the Late Lady Mollineaux's at
Woolton, Five Miles from Liverpool, Young Gentlemen Are Educated on the
Following Terms:

	£	s.	d.
For Board, and learning English, Latin, Greek, Writing, Arithmetick, Merchants Accounts, Geography, Navigation, Astronomy, Surveying, Mathematicks in general, Drawing and Perspective,	21	0	0
		per Ann.	
Entrance for do	1	1	0
Musick, per quarter,	1	1	0
Entrance for do	0	10	6
Dancing, per quarter,	0	15	0
Entrance for do	0	5	0
Fencing, per quarter,	1	1	0
Entrance for do	0	10	6
Fire, per annum,	0	5	0

Washing, according to their age, from 7 s. 6 d.
  to 10 s. per quarter.

Particulars relating to those who do not board in the Academy, may be   had from the master.

DESCRIPTION OF A SCHOOL FOR POOR CHILDREN ORGANIZED BY THE SOCIETY FOR THE PROPAGATION OF THE GOSPEL IN FOREIGN PARTS (1772)

From Edgar W. Knight, ed., *A Documentary History of Education In the South Before 1860*, (Chapel Hill, N.C., 1949-1953), vol. II, pp. 95-97.

James Reed on the School at Newbern, February 15, 1772

My last was on the 2d of July 1771, since which, there has been great Contention about our little Academy. I should have sent you a more early account of it cou'd I have done it with any satisfaction; but I found it difficult to find out the whole truth & the real causes of Discontent. The most material Intelligence I have been able to receive, even after the most diligent search, has been only from Mr. Tomlinson himself, Mr. Parrot, Mr. Tomlinson's late assistant, & one dissenting Trustee. The rest of the Trustees whether from a Consciousness of having acted wrong, or some worse motive entirely declined all conversation with me about it.

When Mr. Tomlinson opened his School, he was apprized of the excessive Indulgence of American Parents, and the great difficulty of keeping up a proper discipline, more especially as his school consisted of numbers of both Sexes. He was therefore very cautious, and used every little artifice to avoid severity as much as possible. But when the children grew excessive headstrong, stubborn and unruly, & likely to endanger the welfare of his School, he used to correct and turn them out of School, & make some little difficulties about their Readmission. Unfortunately for Mr. Tomlinson, this piece of policy gave very great umbrage to two of the trustees, who ever since their children were corrected and turned out of School, have been his most implacable Enemies. One of them has acquired a very considerable fortune by trade, & has four or five of the trustees entirely at his Devotion. The Circumstances & Influence of the others are inconsiderable.

You may see by the Act of Assembly for establishing the School, which I sent you the 23rd of January 1767, that one penny per Gallon, for a limited time, is laid upon all spiritous Liquors imported into Neuse River, for the Benefit of the School; out of which Twenty pounds per ann: is to be paid to the Schoolmaster, to enable him to keep an assistant & the rest is to be applied to the education of poor children, not exceeding Ten. Mr. Tomlinson presuming that this duty upon Spiritous Liquors wou'd be honestly applied by the Encouragement of the trustees, wrote to his correspondent in London, who procured him an assistant, Mr. Parrot, properly qualified in every respect, & entered into bond with him for a term of years in behalf of Mr. Tomlinson. About twelve months after the arrival of Mr. Parrot, great umbrage was given to the potent trustee, by Mr. Tomlinson correcting and turning one of his children out of school for very disobedient & stubborn Behavior; and a dissenting Minister, about the same time opened a School at Wilmington, which is near one hundred miles distant, when Six Boys, which Mr. Tomlinson had under his Care from that place, were taken away, for the Conveniency of being nearer home, which reduced his scholars to about forty four. The trustees had never sent more than five poor children to School, And as Mr. Tomlinson found his School reduced, he petitioned the trustees to send him five more, the better to enable him to continue Mr. Parrot. But behold the consequence! a meeting of the trustees was appointed (not a general one, for I had no notice of it, but such as could be depended upon to answer particular purposes) & an order made, the original inclosed, that he should dismiss the five poor Children which were then at school, under a pretext of want of money to repair the Schoolhouse. I call it a Pretext, because their own Accounts will shew, that they had money enough then due & in their treasurer's hands, not only to have made all necessary repairs, & continued the five poor children, but likewise to have educated five more according to Mr. Tomlinson's Request. And tho' some repairs were really wanting, yet they have not laid out a single shilling in any Repairs from that day to this. And the dissenting trustee, who was at that Meeting, lately informed me, that the five poor children were taken away, not for want of Money, but with a design to distress Mr. Tomlinson.

When Mr. Tomlinson found his School still more reduced by the dismission of the five poor children, he represented to Mr. Parrot the hardship of continuing him as assistant, who generously consented to cancel the Bonds & provide for himself. The greatest difficulty seemed then to be removed. Mr. Tomlinson had sufficient Employment for himself in the School, & Mr. Parrot who is a good Mathematician & Penman supported himself by Hackney writing.

But tho' Mr. Tomlinson was now perfectly easy, yet resentment could not sleep. The Correcting and turning the children of two of the trustees out of the School, was, like the Sin against the Holy Ghost, never to be forgiven. Mr. Tomlinson's Destruction was determined upon, but how to accomplish it was the difficulty. Mr. Parrot was therefore tampered with to open a School in opposition to him. But Mr. Parrot saw thro' their design to making a tool of him; and tho' he detested their proposal yet he gave soft answers, implying, that if the School should be at any time vacant, he would accept it, provided he had no better employment. Mr. Tomlinson was therefore to be turned out to make room for him; but Governor Tryon was in the way, who had been an Eye Witness of Mr. Tomlinson's conduct, and had a particular value and esteem for him. But at length Governor Tryon was removed to New York, and a new Governor succeeded him, who was a Stranger to Mr. Tomlinson, and then was the time to strike the fatal Blow. Accordingly on the 14th of last September, there was a meeting of the trustees (not a general one, for tho' a Trustee, I had no notice of it, not being a proper person for such business as they were then about) when they did their utmost to turn Mr. Tomlinson out of the School. A copy of their proceedings on that day, you have enclosed, & upon which I would beg leave to remark; That when they took the poor children away, there was no Complaint of neglect, but only of want of money. But now Mr. Tomlinson is accused of neglecting his School by the Trustees, & what is very surprising by no body else. They were the only accusers & the only Judges.

Mr. Tomlinson has taught School here upwards of Eight years, and I never heard him accused of neglecting his School till after the 14th of September 1771, & since that time, only by one Person, who is greatly in his Debt, besides the trustees that endeavoured to displace him. And I verily believe, they might with as much Justice have accused him of Robbery or Wilful Murder.

Benjamin Franklin and
the New Education

BENJAMIN FRANKLIN'S SELF-EDUCATION   From Benjamin Franklin,
Autobiography (New York, 1909), vol. I, pp. 10-11, 14-19, 56-59, 80-86, 117-19.

$\mathbf{M}$y elder brothers were all put apprentices to different trades. I was put to the grammar-school at eight years of age, my father intending to devote me, as the tithe of his sons, to the service of the Church. My early readiness in learning to read (which must have been very early, as I do not remember when I could not read), and the opinion of all his friends, that I should certainly make a good scholar, encouraged him in this purpose of his. My uncle Benjamin, too, approved of it, and proposed to give me all his short-hand volumes of sermons, I suppose as a stock to set up with, if I would learn his character. I continued, however, at the grammar-school not quite one year, though in that time I had risen gradually from the middle of the class of that year to be the head of it, and farther was removed into the next class above it, in order to go with that into the third at the end of the year. But my father, in the meantime, from a view of the expense of a college education, which having so large a family he could not well afford, and the mean living many so educated were afterwards able to obtain—reasons that he gave to his friends in my hearing—altered his first intention, took me from the grammar-school, and sent me to a school for writing and arithmetic, kept by a then famous man, Mr. George Brownell, very successful in his profession generally, and that by mild, encouraging methods. Under him I acquired fair writing pretty soon, but I failed in the arithmetic, and made no progress in it. At ten years old I was taken home to assist my father in his business, which was that of a tallow-chandler and sope-boiler; a business he was not bred to, but had assumed on his arrival in New England, and on finding his dying trade would not maintain his family, being in little request. Accordingly, I was employed in cutting wick for the candles, filling the dipping mold and the molds for cast candles, attending the shop, going of errands, etc.

I disliked the trade, and had a strong inclination for the sea, but my father declared against it; however, living near the water, I was much in and about it, learnt early to swim well, and to manage boats; and when in a boat or canoe with other boys, I was commonly allowed to govern, especially in any case of difficulty; and upon other occasions I was generally a leader among the boys, and sometimes led them into scrapes, of which I will mention one instance, as it shows an early projecting public spirit, tho' not then justly conducted.

There was a salt-marsh that bounded part of the mill-pond, on the edge of which, at high water, we used to stand to fish for minnows. By much trampling, we had made it a mere quagmire. My proposal was to build a wharff there fit for us to stand upon, and I showed my comrades a large heap of stones, which were intended for a new house near the marsh, and which would very well suit our purpose. Accordingly, in the evening, when the workmen were gone, I assembled a number of my play-fellows, and working with them diligently like so many emmets, sometimes two or three to a stone, we brought them all away and built our little wharff. The next morning the workmen were surprised at missing the stones, which were found in our wharff. Inquiry was made after the removers; we were discovered and complained of; several of us were corrected by our fathers; and though I pleaded the usefulness of the work, mine convinced me that nothing was useful which was not honest. . . .

From a child I was fond of reading, and all the little money that came into my hands was ever laid out in books. Pleased with the Pilgrim's Progress, my first collection was of John Bunyan's works in separate little volumes. I afterward sold them to enable me to boy R. Burton's Historical Collections; they were small chapmen's books, and cheap, 40 or 50 in all. My father's little library consisted chiefly of books in polemic divinity, most of which I read, and have since often regretted that, at a time when I had such a thirst for knowledge, more proper books had not fallen in my way, since it was now resolved I should not be a clergyman. Plutarch's Lives there was in which I read abundantly, and I still think that time spent to great advantage. There was also a book of De Foe's, called an Essay on Projects, and another of Dr. Mather's, called Essays to do Good, which perhaps gave me a turn of thinking that had an influence on some of the principal future events of my life.

This bookish inclination at length determined my father to make me a printer, though he had already one son (James) of that profession. In 1717 my brother James returned from England with a press and letters to set up his business in Boston. I liked it much better than that of my father, but still had a hankering for the sea. To prevent the apprehended effect of such an inclination, my father was impatient to have me bound to my brother. I stood out some time, but at last was persuaded, and signed the indentures when I was yet but twelve years old. I was to serve as an apprentice till I was twenty-one years of age, only I was to be allowed journeyman's wages during the last year. In a little time I made great proficiency in the business, and became a useful hand to my brother. I now had access to better books. An acquaintance with the apprentices of booksellers enabled me sometimes to borrow a small one, which I was careful to return soon and clean. Often I sat up in my room reading the greatest part of the night, when the book was borrowed in the evening and to be returned early in the morning, lest it should be missed or wanted.

And after some time an ingenious tradesman, Mr. Matthew Adams, who had a pretty collection of books, and who frequented our printing-house, took notice of me, invited me to his library, and very kindly lent me such books as I chose to read. I now took a fancy to poetry, and made some little pieces, my brother, thinking it might turn to account, encouraged me, and put me on composing occasional ballads. One was called *The Lighthouse Tragedy,* and contained an account of the drowning of Captain Worthilake, with his two daughters: the other was a sailor's song, on the taking of *Teach* (or Blackbeard) the pirate. They were wretched stuff, in the Grub-street-ballad style; and when they were printed he sent me about the town to sell them. The first sold wonderfully, the event being recent, having made a great noise. This flattered my vanity; but my father discouraged me by ridiculing my performances, and telling me verse-makers were generally beggars. So I escaped being a poet, most probably a very bad one; but as prose writing had been of great use to me in the course of my life, and was a principal means of my advancement, I shall tell you how, in such a situation, I acquired what little ability I have in that way.

There was another bookish lad in the town, John Collins by name, with whom I was intimately acquainted. We sometimes disputed, and very fond we were of argument, and very desirous of confuting one another, which disputatious turn, by the way, is apt to become a very bad habit, making people often extremely disagreeable in company by the contradiction that is necessary to bring it into practice; and thence, besides souring and spoiling the conversation, is productive of disgusts and, perhaps enmities where you may have occasion for friendship. I had caught it by reading my father's books of dispute about religion. Persons of good sense, I have since observed, seldom fall into it, except lawyers, university men, and men of all sorts that have been bred at Edinborough.

A question was once, somehow or other, started between Collins and me, of the propriety of educating the female sex in learning, and their abilities for study. He was of opinion that it was improper, and that they were naturally unequal to it. I took the contrary side, perhaps a little for dispute's sake. He was naturally more eloquent, had a ready plenty of words; and sometimes, as I thought, bore me down more by his fluency than by the strength of his reasons. As we parted without settling the point, and were not to see one another again for some time, I sat down to put my arguments in writing, which I copied fair and sent to him. He answered, and I replied. Three or four letters of a side had passed, when my father happened to find my papers and read them. Without entering into the discussion, he took occasion to talk to me about the manner of my writing; observed that, though I had the advantage of my antagonist in correct spelling and pointing (which I ow'd to the printing-house), I fell far short in elegance of expression, in method and in perspicuity, of which he convinced me by several instances. I saw the justice of his remark, and thence grew more attentive to the manner in writing, and determined to endeavor at improvement.

About this time I met with an odd volume of the *Spectator*. It was the third. I had never before seen any of them. I bought it, read it over and over, and was much delighted with it. I thought the writing excellent, and wished, if possible, to imitate it. With this view I took some of the papers, and, making short hints of the sentiment in each sentence, laid them by a few days, and then, without looking at the book, try'd to compleat the papers again, by expressing each hinted sentiment at length, and as fully as it had been expressed before, in any suitable words that should come to hand. Then I compared my *Spectator* with the original, discovered some of my faults, and corrected them. But I found I wanted a stock of words, or a readiness in recollecting and using them, which I thought I should have acquired before that time if I had gone on making verses; since the continual occasion for words of the same import, but of different length, to suit the measure, or of different sound for the rhyme, would have laid me under a constant necessity of searching for variety, and also have tended to fix that variety in my mind, and make me master of it. Therefore I took some of the tales and turned them into verse; and, after a time, when I had pretty well forgotten the prose, turned them back again. I also sometimes jumbled my collections of hints into confusion, and after some weeks endeavored to reduce them into the best order, before I began to form the full sentences and compleat the paper. This was to teach me method in the arrangement of thoughts. By comparing my work afterwards with the original, I discovered many faults and amended them; but I sometimes had the pleasure of fancying that, in certain particulars of small import, I had been lucky enough to improve the method or the language, and this encouraged me to think I might possibly in time come to be a tolerable English writer, of which I was extremely ambitious. My time for these exercises and for reading was at night, after work or before it began in the morning, or on Sundays, when I contrived to be in the printing-house alone, evading as much as I could the common attendance on public worship which my father used to exact on me when I was under his care, and which indeed I still thought a duty, though I could not, as it seemed to me, afford time to practise it.

When about 16 years of age I happened to meet with a book, written by one Tryon, recommending a vegetable diet. I determined to go into it. My brother, being yet unmarried, did not keep house, but boarded himself and his apprentices in another family. My refusing to eat flesh occasioned an inconveniency, and I was frequently chid for my singularity. I made myself acquainted with Tryon's manner of preparing some of his dishes, such as boiling potatoes or rice, making hasty pudding, and a few others, and then proposed to my brother, that if he would give me, weekly, half the money he paid for the board, I would board myself. He instantly agreed to it, and I presently found that I could save half what he paid me. This was an additional fund for buying books. But I had another advantage in it. My brother and the rest going from the printing-house to their meals, I remained there alone, and, despatching presently my light repast, which often was no more than a bisket or a slice of bread, a handful of raisins or a tart from the pastrycook's, and a glass of water, had the rest of the time till their return for study, in which I made the greater progress, from that greater clearness of head and quicker apprehension which usually attend temperance in eating and drinking.

And now it was that, being on some occasion made asham'd of my ignorance in figures, which I had twice failed in learning when at school, I took Cocker's book of Arithmetick, and went through the whole by myself with great ease. I also read Seller's and Shermy's books of Navigation, and became acquainted with the little geometry they contain; but never proceeded far in that science. And I read about this time Locke *On Human Understanding*, and the *Art of Thinking*, by Messrs. du Port Royal.

While I was intent on improving my language, I met with an English grammar (I think it was Greenwood's), at the end of which there were two little sketches of the arts of rhetoric and logic, the latter finishing with a specimen of a dispute in the Socratic method; and soon after I procur'd Xenophon's Memorable Things of Socrates, wherein there are many instances of the same method. I was charm'd with it, adopted it, dropt my abrupt contradiction and positive argumentation, and put on the humble inquirer and doubter. And being then, from reading Shaftesbury and Collins, become a real doubter in many points of our religious doctrine, I found this method safest for myself and very embarrassing to those against whom I used it; therefore I took a delight in it, practis'd it continually, and grew very artful and expert in drawing people, even of superior knowledge, into concessions, the consequences of which they did not foresee, entangling them in difficulties out of which they could not extricate themselves, and so obtaining victories that neither myself nor my cause always deserved. I continu'd this method some few years, but gradually left it, retaining only the habit of expressing myself in terms of modest diffidence; never using, when I advanced any thing that may possibly be disputed, the words *certainly, undoubtedly,* or any others that give the air of positiveness to an opinion; but rather say, I conceive or apprehend a thing to be so and so; it appears to me, or *I should think it so or so*, for such and such reasons; or *I imagine it to be so;* or *it is so, if I am not mistaken.* This habit, I believe, has been of great advantage to me when I have had occasion to inculcate my opinions, and persuade men into measures that I have been from time to time engag'd in promoting;

*　　*　　*

I should have mentioned before, that, in the autumn of the preceding year, I had form'd most of my ingenious acquaintance into a club of mutual improvement, which we called the JUNTO; we met on Friday evenings. The rules that I drew up required that every member, in his turn, should produce one or more queries on any point of Morals, Politics, or Natural Philosophy, to be discuss'd by the company; and once in three months produce and read an essay of his own writing, on any subject he pleased. Our debates were to be under the direction of a president, and to be conducted in the sincere spirit of inquiry after truth, without fondness for dispute, or desire of victory; and, to prevent warmth, all expressions of positiveness in opinions, or direct contradiction, were after some time made contraband, and prohibited under small pecuniary penalties.

. . . the club was the best school of philosophy, morality, and politics that then existed in the province; for our queries, which were read the week preceding their discussion, put us upon reading with attention upon the several subjects, that we might speak more to the purpose; and here, too, we acquired better habits of conversation, every thing being studied in our rules which might prevent our disgusting each other. From hence the long continuance of the club, which I shall have frequent occasion to speak further of hereafter.

ISSUES DISCUSSED AT MEETINGS OF THE JUNTO (1732)   From Leonard W. Labaree, ed., *The Papers of Benjamin Franklin* (New Haven, 1959–   ), vol. I, pp. 256–59.

Previous question, to be answer'd at every meeting.

Have you read over these queries this morning, in order to consider what you might have to offer the Junto [touching] any one of them? viz.

1. Have you met with any thing in the author you last read, remarkable, or suitable to be communicated to the Junto? particularly in history, morality, poetry, physic, travels, mechanic arts, or other parts of knowledge.

2. What new story have you lately heard agreeable for telling in conversation?

3. Hath any citizen in your knowledge failed in his business lately, and what have you heard of the cause?

4. Have you lately heard of any citizen's thriving well, and by what means?

5. Have you lately heard how any present rich man, here or elsewhere, got his estate?

6. Do you know of any fellow citizen, who has lately done a worthy action, deserving praise and imitation? or who has committed an error proper for us to be warned against and avoid?

7. What unhappy effects of intemperance have you lately observed or heard? of imprudence? of passion? or of any other vice or folly?

8. What happy effects of temperance? of prudence? of moderation? or of any other virtue?

9. Have you or any of your acquaintance been lately sick or wounded? If so, what remedies were used, and what were their effects?

10. Who do you know that are shortly going voyages or journies, if one should have occasion to send by them?

11. Do you think of any thing at present, in which the Junto may be serviceable to *mankind?* to their country, to their friends, or to themselves?

12. Hath any deserving stranger arrived in town since last meeting, that you heard of? and what have you heard or observed of his character or merits? and whether think you, it lies in the power of the Junto to oblige him, or encourage him as he deserves?

13. Do you know of any deserving young beginner lately set up, whom it lies in the power of the Junto any way to encourage?

14. Have you lately observed any defect in the laws of your *country,* [of] which it would be proper to move the legislature for an amendment? Or do you know of any beneficial law that is wanting?

15. Have you lately observed any encroachment on the just liberties of the people?

16. Hath any body attacked your reputation lately? and what can the Junto do towards securing it?

17. Is there any man whose friendship you want, and which the Junto or any of them, can procure for you?

18. Have you lately heard any member's character attacked, and how have you defended it?

19. Hath any man injured you, from whom it is in the power of the Junto to procure redress?

20. In what manner can the Junto, or any of them, assist you in any of your honourable designs?

21. Have you any weighty affair in hand, in which you think the advice of the Junto may be of service?

22. What benefits have you lately received from any man not present?

23. Is there any difficulty in matters of opinion, of justice, and injustice, which you would gladly have discussed at this time?

24. Do you see any thing amiss in the present customs or proceedings of the Junto, which might be amended?

Any person to be qualified, to stand up, and lay his hand on his breast, and be asked these questions; viz.

1. Have you any particular disrespect to any present members? *Answer.* I have not.

2. Do you sincerely declare that you love mankind in general; of what profession or religion soever? *Answ.* I do.

3. Do you think any person ought to be harmed in his body, name or goods, for mere speculative opinions, or his external way of worship? *Ans.* No.

4. Do you love truth for truth's sake, and will you endeavour impartially to find and receive it yourself and communicate it to others? *Answ.* Yes.

BENJAMIN FRANKLIN ON THE SMALL WORTH OF A COLLEGE

EDUCATION (1722) From "Silence Dogood, No. 4," as quoted in Leonard W. Labaree, ed., *The Papers of Benjamin Franklin* (New Haven, 1959–   ), vol. I, pp. 14-18.

To the Author of the N-England Courant.

Sir,   May 14, 1722

Discoursing the other Day at Dinner with my Reverend Boarder, formerly mention'd, (whom for Distinction sake we will call by the Name of Clericus,) concerning the Education of Children, I ask'd his Advice about my young Son William, whether or no I had best bestow upon him Academical Learning, or (as our Phrase is) *bring him up at our College:* He perswaded me to do it by all Means, using many weighty Arguments with me, and answering all the Objections that I could form against it; telling me withal, that he did not doubt but that the Lad would take his Learning very well, and not idle away his Time as too many there now-a-days do. These Words of Clericus gave me a Curiosity to inquire a little more strictly into the present Circumstances of that famous Seminary of Learning; but the Information which he gave me, was neither pleasant, nor such as I expected.

As soon as Dinner was over, I took a solitary Walk into my Orchard, still ruminating on Clericus's Discourse with much Consideration, until I came to my usual Place of Retirement under the *Great Apple-Tree;* where having seated my self, and carelessly laid my Head on a verdant Bank, I fell by Degrees into a soft and undisturbed Slumber. My waking Thoughts remained with me in my Sleep, and before I awak'd again, I dreamt the following Dream.

I fancy'd I was travelling over pleasant and delightful Fields and Meadows, and thro' many small Country Towns and Villages; and as I pass'd along, all Places resounded with the Fame of the Temple of Learning: Every Peasant, who had wherewithal, was preparing to send one of his Children at least to this famous Place; and in this Case most of them consulted their own Purses instead of their Childrens Capacities: So that I observed, a great many, yea, the most part of those who were travelling thither, were little better than Dunces and Blockheads. Alas! alas!

At length I entred upon a spacious Plain, in the Midst of which was erected a large and stately Edifice: It was to this that a great Company of Youths from all Parts of the Country were going; so stepping in among the Crowd, I passed on with them, and presently arrived at the Gate.

The Passage was kept by two sturdy Porters named *Riches* and *Poverty*, and the latter obstinately refused to give Entrance to any who had not first gain'd the Favour of the former; so that I observed, many who came even to the very Gate, were obliged to travel back again as ignorant as they came, for want of this necessary Qualification. However, as a Spectator I gain'd Admittance, and with the rest entred directly into the Temple.

In the Middle of the great Hall stood a stately and magnificent Throne, which was ascended to by two high and difficult Steps. On the Top of it sat Learning in awful State; she was apparelled wholly in Black, and surrounded almost on every Side with innumerable Volumes in all Languages. She seem'd very busily employ'd in writing something on half a Sheet of Paper, and upon Enquiry, I understood she was preparing a Paper, call'd, *The New-England Courant.* On her Right Hand sat

English, with a pleasant smiling Countenance, and handsomely attir'd; and on her left were seated several *Antique Figures* with their Faces vail'd. I was considerably puzzl'd to guess who they were, until one informed me, (who stood beside me,) that those Figures on her left Hand were *Latin, Greek, Hebrew,* &c. and that they were very much reserv'd, and seldom or never unvail'd their Faces here, and then to few or none, tho' most of those who have in this Place acquir'd so much Learning as to distinguish them from *English*, pretended to an intimate Acquaintance with them. I then enquir'd of him, what could be the Reason why they continued vail'd, in this Place especially: He pointed to the Foot of the Throne, where I saw *Idleness*, attended with *Ignorance*, and these (he informed me) were they, who first vail'd them, and still kept them so.

Now I observed, that the whole Tribe who entred into the Temple with me, began to climb the Throne; but the Work proving troublesome and difficult to most of them, they withdrew their Hands from the Plow, and contented themselves to sit at the Foot, with Madam *Idleness* and her Maid *Ignorance*, until those who were assisted by Diligence and a docible Temper, had well nigh got up the first Step: But the Time drawing nigh in which they could no way avoid ascending, they were fain to crave the Assistance of those who had got up before them, and who, for the Reward perhaps of a *Pint of Milk*, or a *Piece of Plumb-Cake*, lent the Lubbers a helping Hand, and sat them in the Eye of the World, upon a Level with themselves.

The other Step being in the same Manner ascended, and the usual Ceremonies at an End, every Beetle-Scull seem'd well satisfy'd with his own Portion of Learning, tho' perhaps he was *e'en just* as ignorant as ever. And now the Time of their Departure being come, they march'd out of Doors to make Room for another Company, who waited for Entrance: And I, having seen all that was to be seen, quitted the Hall likewise, and went to make my Observations on those who were just gone out before me.

Some I perceiv'd took to Merchandizing, others to Travelling, some to one Thing, some to another, and some to Nothing; and many of them from henceforth, for want of Patrimony, liv'd as poor as Church Mice, being unable to dig, and asham'd to beg, and to live by their Wits it was impossible. But the most Part of the Crowd went along a large beaten Path, which led to a Temple at the further End of the Plain, call'd, *The Temple of Theology.* The Business of those who were employ'd in this Temple being laborious and painful, I wonder'd exceedingly to see so many go towards it; but while I was pondering this Matter in my Mind, I spy'd *Pecunia* behind a Curtain, beckoning to them with her Hand, which Sight immediately satisfy'd me for whose Sake it was, that a great Part of them (I will not say all) travel'd that Road. In this Temple I saw nothing worth mentioning, except the ambitious and fraudulent Contrivances of Plagius, who (notwithstanding he had been severely reprehended for such Practices before) was diligently transcribing some eloquent Paragraphs out of Tillotson's *Works*, &c., to embellish his own.

Now I bethought my self in my Sleep, that it was Time to be at Home, and as I fancy'd I was travelling back thither, I reflected in my Mind on the extream Folly of those Parents, who, blind to their Childrens Dulness, and insensible of the Solidity of their Skulls, because they think their Purses can afford it, will needs send them to the Temple of Learning, where, for want of a suitable Genius, they learn little more than how to carry themselves handsomely, and enter a Room genteely, (which might as well be acquir'd at a Dancing-School,) and from whence they return, after Abundance of Trouble and Charge, as great Blockheads as ever, only more proud and self-conceited.

While I was in the midst of these unpleasant Reflections, Clericus (who with a

Book in his Hand was walking under the Trees) accidentally awak'd me; to him I related my Dream with all its Particulars, and he, without much Study, presently interpreted it, assuring me, *That it was a lively Representation of* Harvard College, *Etcetera.* I remain, Sir, Your Humble Servant,

SILENCE DOGOOD

BENJAMIN FRANKLIN'S ARTICLES OF BELIEF AND LITURGY

(**1728**) From ''Articles of Belief and Acts of Religion,'' as quoted in Albert H. Smyth, ed., *The Writings of Benjamin Franklin* (New York, 1905), vol. II, pp. 91-100.

First Principles

I believe there is one supreme, most perfect Being, Author and Father of the Gods themselves. For I believe that Man is not the most perfect Being but one, rather that as there are many Degrees of Beings his Inferiors, so there are many Degrees of Beings superior to him.

Also, when I stretch my Imagination thro' and beyond our System of Planets, beyond the visible fix'd Stars themselves, into that Space that is every Way infinite, and conceive it fill'd with Suns like ours, each with a Chorus of Worlds forever moving round him, then this little Ball on which we move, seems, even in my narrow Imagination, to be almost Nothing, and myself less than nothing, and of no sort of Consequence.

When I think thus, I imagine it great Vanity in me to suppose, that the Supremely Perfect does in the least regard such an inconsiderable Nothing as Man. More especially, since it is impossible for me to have any positive clear idea of that which is infinite and incomprehensible, I cannot conceive otherwise than that he the Infinite Father expects or requires no Worship or Praise from us, but that he is even infinitely above it.

But, since there is in all Men something like a natural principle, which inclines them to DEVOTION, or the Worship of some unseen Power;

And since Men are endued with Reason superior to all other Animals, that we are in our World acquainted with;

Therefore I think it seems required of me, and my Duty as a Man, to pay Divine Regards to SOMETHING.

I conceive then, that the INFINITE has created many beings or Gods, vastly superior to Man, who can better conceive his Perfections than we, and return him a more rational and glorious Praise.

As, among Men, the Praise of the Ignorant or of Children is not regarded by the ingenious Painter or Architect, who is rather honour'd and pleas'd with the approbation of Wise Men & Artists.

It may be that these created Gods are immortal; or it may be that after many Ages, they are changed, and others Supply their Places.

Howbeit, I conceive that each of these is exceeding wise and good, and very powerful; and that Each has made for himself one glorious Sun, attended with a beautiful and admirable System of Planets.

It is that particular Wise and good God, who is the author and owner of our System, that I propose for the object of my praise and adoration.

For I conceive that he has in himself some of those Passions he has planted in us, and that, since he has given us Reason whereby we are capable of observing his Wisdom in the Creation, he is not above caring for us, being pleas'd with our Praise, and offended when we slight Him, or neglect his Glory.

I conceive for many Reasons, that he is a good Being; and as I should be happy to have so wise, good, and powerful a Being my Friend, let me consider in what manner I shall make myself most acceptable to him.

Next to the Praise resulting from and due to his Wisdom, I believe he is pleas'd and delights in the Happiness of those he has created; and since without Virtue Man can have no Happiness in this World, I firmly believe he delights to see me Virtuous, because he is pleased when he sees Me Happy.

And since he has created many Things, which seem purely design'd for the Delight of Man, I believe he is not offended, when he sees his Children solace themselves in any manner of pleasant exercises and Innocent Delights; and I think no Pleasure innocent, that is to Man hurtful.

I love him therefore for his Goodness, and I adore him for his Wisdom.

Let me then not fail to praise my God continually, for it is his Due, and it is all I can return for his many Favours and great Goodness to me; and let me resolve to be virtuous, that I may be happy, that I may please Him, who is delighted to see me happy. Amen!

Adoration

PREL. Being mindful that before I address the Deity, my soul ought to be calm and serene, free from Passion and Perturbation, or otherwise elevated with Rational Joy and Pleasure, I ought to use a Countenance that expresses a filial Respect, mixed with a kind of Smiling, that Signifies inward Joy, and Satisfaction, and Admiration.

O wise God, my good Father!

Thou beholdest the sincerity of my Heart and of my Devotion; Grant me a Continuance of thy Favour!

1. O Creator, O Father! I believe that thou art Good, and that thou art pleas'd with the pleasure of thy children. —Praised be thy name for Ever!

2. By thy Power hast thou made the glorious Sun, with his attending Worlds; from the energy of thy mighty Will, they first received [their prodigious] motion, and by thy Wisdom hast thou prescribed the wondrous Laws, by which they move. —Praised be thy name for Ever!

3. By thy Wisdom hast thou formed all Things. Thou hast created Man, bestowing Life and Reason, and placed him in Dignity superior to thy other earthly Creatures. —Praised be thy name for Ever!

4. Thy Wisdom, thy Power, and thy Goodness are everywhere clearly seen; in the air and in the water, in the Heaven and on the Earth; Thou providest for the various winged Fowl, and the innumerable Inhabitants of the Water; thou givest Cold and Heat, Rain and Sunshine, in their Season, & to the Fruits of the Earth Increase. —Praised be thy name for Ever!

5. Thou abhorrest in thy Creatures Treachery and Deceit, Malice, Revenge, [intemperance,] and every other hurtful Vice; but Thou art a Lover of Justice and Sincerity, of Friendship and Benevolence, and every Virtue. Thou art my Friend, my Father, and my Benefactor. —Praised be thy name, O God, for Ever! Amen!

[After this, it will not be improper to read part of some such Book as Ray's *Wisdom of God in the Creation*, or *Blackmore on the Creation*, or the Archbishop of Cambray's *Demonstration of the Being of a God*, &c., or else spend some Minutes in a serious Silence, contemplating on those Subjects.]

Then sing MILTON'S HYMN TO THE CREATOR. . . .

[Here follows the Reading of some Book, or part of a Book, Discoursing on and exciting to Moral Virtue.]

Petition

Inasmuch as by Reason of our Ignorance We cannot be certain that many Things, which we often hear mentioned in the Petitions of Men to the Deity, would prove real Goods, if they were in our Possession, and as I have reason to hope and believe that the Goodness of my Heavenly Father will not withold from me a suitable share of Temporal Blessings, if by a Virtuous and holy Life I conciliate his Favour and Kindness, Therefore I presume not to ask such things, but rather humbly and with a Sincere Heart, express my earnest desires that he would graciously assist my Continual Endeavours and Resolutions of eschewing Vice and embracing Virtue; which Kind of Supplications will at least be thus far beneficial, as they remind me in a solemn manner of my Extensive duty.

That I may be preserved from Atheism & Infidelity, Impiety, and Profaneness, and, in my Addresses to Thee, carefully avoid Irreverence and ostentation, Formality and odious Hypocrisy, —Help me, O Father!

That I may be loyal to my Prince, and faithful to my country, careful for its good, valiant in its defence, and obedient to its Laws, abhorring Treason as much as Tyranny, —Help me, O Father!

That I may to those above me be dutiful, humble, and submissive; avoiding Pride, Disrespect, and Contumacy, —Help me, O Father!

That I may to those below me be gracious, condescending, and Forgiving, using Clemency, protecting innocent Distress, avoiding Cruelty, Harshness, and oppression, Insolence, and unreasonable Severity, —Help me, O Father!

That I may refrain from Censure, Calumny and Detraction; that I may avoid and abhor Deceit and Envy, Fraud, Flattery, and Hatred, Malice, Lying, and Ingratitude, —Help me, O Father!

That I may be sincere in Friendship, faithful in trust, and Impartial in Judgment, watchful against Pride, and against Anger (that momentary Madness), —Help me, O Father!

That I may be just in all my Dealings, temperate in my pleasures, full of Candour and Ingenuity, Humanity and Benevolence, —Help me, O Father!

That I may be grateful to my Benefactors, and generous to my Friends, exercising Charity and Liberality to the Poor, and Pity to the Miserable, —Help me, O Father!

That I may avoid Avarice and Ambition, Jealousie, and Intemperance, Falsehood, Luxury, and Lasciviousness, —Help me, O Father!

That I may possess Integrity and Evenness of Mind, Resolution in Difficulties, and Fortitude under Affliction; that I may be punctual in performing my promises, Peaceable and prudent in my Behaviour, —Help me, O Father!

That I may have Tenderness for the Weak, and reverent Respect for the

Ancient; that I may be Kind to my Neighbours, good-natured to my Companions, and hospitable to Strangers, —Help me, O Father!

That I may be averse to Talebearing, Backbiting, Detraction, Slander, & Craft, and overreaching, abhor Extortion, Perjury, and every Kind of wickedness, —Help me, O Father!

That I may be honest and open-hearted, gentle, merciful, and good, cheerful in spirit, rejoicing in the Good of others, —Help me, O Father!

That I may have a constant Regard to Honour and Probity, that I may possess a perfect innocence and a good Conscience, and at length become truly Virtuous and Magnanimous, —Help me, good God; help me, O Father!

BENJAMIN FRANKLIN'S PLAN FOR ARRIVING AT MORAL PERFECTION
(c. 1749)   From Benjamin Franklin, *Autobiography* (New York, 1909), vol. I, pp. 117-19.

I had been religiously educated as a Presbyterian; and tho' some of the dogmas of that persuasion, such as *the eternal decrees of God, election, reprobation, etc.,* appeared to me unintelligible, others doubtful, and I early absented myself from the public assemblies of the sect, Sunday being my studying day, I never was without some religious principles. I never doubted, for instance, the existence of the Deity; that he made the world, and govern'd it by his Providence; that the most acceptable service of God was the doing good to man; that our souls are immortal; and that all crime will be punished, and virtue rewarded, either here or hereafter. These I esteem'd the essentials of every religion; and, being to be found in all the religions we had in our country, I respected them all, tho' with different degrees of respect, as I found them more or less mix'd with other articles, which, without any tendency to inspire, promote, or confirm morality, serv'd principally to divide us, and make us unfriendly to one another. This respect to all, with an opinion that the worst had some good effects, induc'd me to avoid all discourse that might tend to lessen the good opinion another might have of his own religion; and as our province increas'd in people, and new places of worship were continually wanted, and generally erected by voluntary contributions, my mite for such purpose, whatever might be the sect, was never refused.

✳   ✳   ✳

It was about this time I conceiv'd the bold and arduous project of arriving at moral perfection. I wish'd to live without committing any fault at any time; I would conquer all that either natural inclination, custom, or company might lead me into. As I knew, or thought I knew, what was right and wrong, I did not see why I might not always do the one and avoid the other. But I soon found I had undertaken a task of more difficulty than I had imagined. While my care was employ'd in guarding against one fault, I was often surprised by another; habit took the advantage of inattention; inclination was sometimes too strong for reason. I concluded, at length, that the mere speculative conviction that it was our interest to be completely virtuous, was not sufficient to prevent our slipping; and that the contrary habits must be broken, and good ones acquired and established, before we can have any dependence on a steady, uniform rectitude of conduct. For this purpose I therefore contrived the following method.

In the various enumerations of the moral virtues I had met with in my reading, I found the catalogue more or less numerous, as different writers included more or fewer ideas under the same name. Temperance, for example, was by some confined to eating and drinking, while by others it was extended to mean the moderating every other pleasure, appetite, inclination, or passion, bodily or mental, even to our avarice and ambition. I propos'd to myself, for the sake of clearness, to use rather more names, with fewer ideas annex'd to each, than a few names with more ideas; and I included under thirteen names of virtues all that at that time occurr'd to me as necessary or desirable, and annexed to each a short precept, which fully express'd the extent I gave to its meaning.

These names of virtues, with their precepts, were:

1. Temperance

Eat not to dullness; drink not to elevation.

2. Silence

Speak not but what may benefit others or yourself; avoid trifling conversation.

3. Order

Let all your things have their places; let each part of your business have its time.

4. Resolution

Resolve to perform what you ought; perform without fail what you resolve.

5. Frugality

Make no expense but to do good to others or yourself, i.e., waste nothing.

6. Industry

Lose no time; be always employ'd in something useful; cut off all unnecessary actions.

7. Sincerity

Use no hurtful deceit; think innocently and justly, and, if you speak, speak accordingly.

8. *Justice*

Wrong none by doing injuries, or omitting the benefits that are your duty.

9. *Moderation*

Avoid extreams; forbear resenting injuries so much as you think they deserve.

10. *Cleanliness*

Tolerate no uncleanliness in body, cloaths, or habitation.

11. *Tranquillity*

Be not disturbed at trifles, or at accidents common or unavoidable.

12. *Chastity*

Rarely use venery but for health or offspring, never to dulness, weakness, or the injury of your own or another's peace or reputation.

13. *Humility*

Imitate Jesus and Socrates.

My intention being to acquire the *habitude* of all these virtues, I judg'd it would be well not to distract my attention by attempting the whole at once, but to fix it on one of them at a time; and, when I should have gone of that, then to proceed to another, and so on, till I should have gone thro' the thirteen; and, as the previous acquisition of some might facilitate the acquisition of certain others, I arrang'd them with that view, as they stand above. Temperance first, as it tends to procure that coolness and clearness of head, which is so necessary where constant vigilance was to be kept up, and guard maintained against the unremitting attraction of ancient habits, and the force of perpetual temptations. This being acquir'd and establish'd, Silence would be more easy; and my desire being to gain knowledge at the same time that I improv'd in virtue, and considering that in conversation it was obtain'd rather by the use of the ears than of the tongue, and therefore wishing to break a habit I was getting into of prattling, punning, and joking, which only made me acceptable to trifling company, I gave *Silence* the second place. This and the next, *Order*, I expected would allow me more time for attending to my project and my studies. *Resolution*, once become habitual, would keep me firm in my endeavors to obtain all the subsequent virtues; *Frugality* and Industry freeing me from my remaining debt, and producing affluence and independence, would make more easy the practice of Sincerity and Justice, etc., etc. Conceiving then, that, agreeably to the advice of Pythagoras in his Golden Verses, daily examination would be necessary, I contrived the following method for conducting that examination.

I made a little book, in which I allotted a page for each of the virtues. I rul'd each page with red ink, so as to have seven columns, one for each day of the week, marking each column with a letter for the day. I cross'd these columns with thirteen red lines, marking the beginning of each line with the first letter of one of the virtues, on which line, and in its proper column, I might mark, by a little black spot, every fault I found upon examination to have been committed respecting that virtue upon that day. I determined to give a week's strict attention to each of the virtues successively. Thus, in the first week, my great guard was to avoid every the least offence against *Temperance,* leaving the other virtues to their ordinary chance, only marking every evening the faults of the day. Thus, if in the first week I could keep my first line, marked T, clear of spots, I suppos'd the habit of that virtue so much strengthen'd, and its opposite weaken'd, that I might venture extending my attention to include the next, and for the following week keep both lines clear of spots. Proceeding thus to the last, I could go thro' a course compleat in thirteen weeks, and four courses in a year. And like him who, having a garden to weed, does not attempt to eradicate all the bad herbs at once, which would exceed his reach and his strength, but works on one of the beds at a time, and, having accomplish'd the first, proceeds to a second, so I should have, I hoped, the encouraging pleasure of seeing on my pages the progress I made in virtue, by clearing successively my lines of their spots, till in the end, by a number of courses, I should be happy in viewing a clean book, after a thirteen weeks' daily examination. . . .

Form of the pages.

	S.	M.	T.	W.	T.	F.	S.
TEMPERANCE.							
EAT NOT TO DULNESS; **DRINK NOT TO ELEVATION.**							
T.							
S.	*	*		*		*	
O.	* *	*	*		*	*	*
R.			*			*	
F.		*			*		
I.			*				
S.							
J.							
M.							
C.							
T.							
C.							
H.							

BENJAMIN FRANKLIN'S ADVICE TO A YOUNG MAN (1748)   From "Advice to a Young Tradesman, Written by an Old One" (July 21, 1748), as quoted in Leonard W. Labaree, ed., *The Papers of Benjamin Franklin* (New Haven, 1959–   ), vol. III, pp. 306-8.

To my Friend A. B.

As you have desired it of me, I write the following Hints, which have been of Service to me, and may, if observed, be so to you

Remember that TIME is Money. He that can earn Ten Shillings a Day by his Labour, and goes abroad, or sits idle one half of that Day, tho' he spends but Sixpence during his Diversion or Idleness, ought not to reckon That the only Expence; he has really spent or rather thrown away Five Shillings besides.

Remember that CREDIT is Money. If a Man lets his Money lie in my Hands after it is due, he gives me the Interest, or so much as I can make of it during that Time. This amounts to a considerable Sum where a Man has good and large Credit, and makes good Use of it.

Remember that Money is of a prolific generating Nature. Money can beget Money, and its Offspring can beget more, and so on. Five Shillings turn'd, is *Six:* Turn'd again, 'tis Seven and Three Pence; and so on 'til it becomes an Hundred Pound. The more there is of it, the more it produces every Turning, so that the Profits rise quicker and quicker. He that kills a breeding Sow, destroys all her Offspring to the thousandth Generation. He that murders a Crown, destroys all it might have produc'd, even Scores of Pounds.

Remember that Six Pounds a Year is but a Groat a Day. For this little Sum (which may be daily wasted either in Time or Expence unperceiv'd) a Man of Credit may on his own Security have the constant Possession and Use of an Hundred Pounds. So much in Stock briskly turn'd by an industrious Man, produces great Advantage.

Remember this Saying, *That the good Paymaster is Lord of another Man's Purse.* He that is known to pay punctually and exactly to the Time he promises, may at any Time, and on any Occasion, raise all the Money his Friends can spare. This is sometimes of great Use: Therefore never keep borrow'd Money an Hour beyond the Time you promis'd, lest a Disappointment shuts up your Friends Purse forever.

The most trifling Actions that affect a Man's Credit, are to be regarded. The Sound of your Hammer at Five in the Morning or Nine at Night, heard by a Creditor, makes him easy Six Months longer. But if he sees you at a Billiard Table, or hears your Voice in a Tavern, when you should be at Work, he sends for his Money the next Day. Finer Cloaths than he or his Wife wears, or greater Expence in any particular than he affords himself, shocks his Pride, and he duns you to humble you. Creditors are a kind of People, that have the sharpest Eyes and Ears, as well as the best Memories of any in the World.

Good-natur'd Creditors (and such one would always chuse to deal with if one could) feel Pain when they are oblig'd to ask for Money. Spare 'em that Pain, and they will love you. When you receive a Sum of Money, divide it among 'em in Proportion to your Debts. Don't be asham'd of paying a small Sum because you owe a greater. Money, more or less, is always welcome; and your Creditor had rather be at the Trouble of receiving Ten Pounds voluntarily brought him, tho' at

PROVINCIALS

ten different Times or Payments, than be oblig'd to go ten Times to demand it before he can receive it in a Lump. It shews, besides, that you are mindful of what you owe; it makes you appear a careful as well as an honest Man; and that still encreases your Credit.

Beware of thinking all your own that you possess, and of living accordingly. 'Tis a Mistake that many People who have Credit fall into. To prevent this, keep an exact Account for some Time of both your Expences and your Incomes. If you take the Pains at first to mention Particulars, it will have this good Effect; you will discover how wonderfully small trifling Expences mount up to large Sums, and will discern what might have been, and may for the future be saved, without occasioning any great Inconvenience.

In short, the Way to Wealth, if you desire it, is as plain as the Way to Market. It depends chiefly on two Words, INDUSTRY and FRUGALITY; i.e. Waste neither Time nor Money, but make the best Use of both. He that gets all he can honestly, and saves all he gets (necessary Expences excepted) will certainly become RICH; If that Being who governs the World, to whom all should look for a Blessing on their honest Endeavours, doth not in his wise Providence otherwise determine.

BENJAMIN FRANKLIN'S WAY TO WEALTH (1757)   From Preface to *Poor Richard Improved . . . .*, as quoted in Leonard W. Labaree, ed., *The Papers of Benjamin Franklin* (New Haven, 1959–   ), vol. VII, pp. 340-50.

Courteous Reader,

I have heard that nothing gives an Author so great Pleasure, as to find his Works respectfully quoted by other learned Authors. This Pleasure I have seldom enjoyed; for tho' I have been, if I may say it without Vanity, an *eminent Author* of Almanacks annually now a full Quarter of a Century, my Brother Authors in the same Way, for what Reason I know not, have ever been very sparing in their Applauses; and no other Author has taken the least Notice of me, so that did not my Writings produce me some solid *Pudding,* the great Deficiency of *Praise* would have quite discouraged me.

I concluded at length, that the People were the best Judges of my Merit; for they buy my Works; and besides, in my Rambles, where I am not personally known, I have frequently heard one or other of my Adages repeated, with, *as Poor Richard says,* at the End on't; this gave me some Satisfaction, as it showed not only that my Instructions were regarded, but discovered likewise some Respect for my Authority; and I own, that to encourage the Practice of remembering and repeating those wise Sentences, I have sometimes *quoted myself* with great Gravity.

Judge then how much I must have been gratified by an Incident I am going to relate to you. I stopt my Horse lately where a great Number of People were collected at a Vendue of Merchant Goods. The Hour of Sale not being come, they were conversing on the Badness of the Times, and one of the Company call'd to a plain clean old Man, with white Locks, *Pray, Father Abraham, what think you of the Times? Won't these heavy Taxes quite ruin the Country? How shall we be ever able to pay them? What would you advise us to?*—Father Abraham stood up, and reply'd, If you'd have my Advice, I'll give it you in short, for a *Word to the Wise is enough*, and *many Words won't fill a Bushel*, as *Poor Richard says*. They join'd in desiring him to speak his Mind, and gathering round him, he proceeded as follows;

Friends, says he, and Neighbours, the Taxes are indeed very heavy, and if those laid on by the Government were the only Ones we had to pay, we might more easily discharge them; but we have many others, and much more grievous to some of us. We are taxed twice as much by our *Idleness*, three times as much by our *Pride*, and four times as much by our *Folly*, and from these Taxes the Commissioners cannot ease or deliver us by allowing an Abatement. However let us hearken to good Advice, and something may be done for us; *God helps them that help themselves*, as Poor Richard says, in his Almanack of 1733.

It would be thought a hard Government that should tax its People one tenth Part of their *Time*, to be employed in its Service. But *Idleness* taxes many of us much more, if we reckon all that is spent in absolute *Sloth*, or doing of nothing, with that which is spent in idle Employments or Amusements, that amount to nothing. *Sloth*, by bringing on Diseases, absolutely shortens Life. *Sloth, like Rust, consumes faster than Labour wears, while the used Key is always bright*, as Poor Richard says. But *dost thou love Life, then do not squander Time, for that's the Stuff Life is made of*, as Poor Richard says. How much more than is necessary do we spend in Sleep! forgetting that *The sleeping Fox catches no Poultry*, and that *there will be sleeping enough in the Grave*, as Poor Richard says. If Time be of all Things the most precious, *wasting Time* must be, as Poor Richard says, *the greatest Prodigality*, since, as he elsewhere tells us, *Lost Time is never found again;* and what we call *Time-enough, always proves little enough:* Let us then be up and be doing, and doing to the Purpose; so by Diligence shall we do more with less Perplexity. *Sloth makes all Things difficult, but Industry all easy*, as Poor Richard says; and *He that riseth late, must trot all Day, and shall scarce overtake his Business at Night*. While *Laziness travels so slowly, that Poverty soon overtakes him*, as we read in Poor Richard, who adds, *Drive thy Business, let not that drive thee;* and *Early to Bed, and early to rise, makes a Man healthy, wealthy and wise*. . . .

Methinks I hear some of you say, *Must a Man afford himself no Leisure?* I will tell thee, my Friend, what Poor Richard says, *Employ thy Time well if thou meanest to gain Leisure;* and, *since thou art not sure of a Minute, throw not away an Hour*. Leisure, is Time for doing something useful; this Leisure the diligent Man will obtain, but the lazy Man never; so that, as Poor Richard says, a *Life of Leisure and a Life of Laziness are two Things*. Do you imagine that Sloth will afford you more Comfort than Labour? No, for as Poor Richard says, *Trouble springs from Idleness, and grievous Toil from needless Ease. Many without Labour, would live by their* WITS *only, but they break for want of Stock*. Whereas Industry gives Comfort, and Plenty, and Respect: *Fly Pleasures, and they'll follow you. The diligent Spinner has a large Shift;* and *now I have a Sheep and a Cow, every Body bids me Good morrow;* all which is well said by Poor Richard.

But with our Industry, we must likewise be *steady, settled* and *careful*, and oversee our own Affairs *with our own Eyes*, and not trust too much to others; for, as Poor Richard says,

> I never saw an oft removed Tree,
> Nor yet an oft removed Family,
> That throve so well as those that settled be.

And again, *Three Removes is as bad as a Fire;* and again, *Keep thy Shop, and thy Shop will keep thee;* and again, *If you would have your Business done, go; If not, send.* And again,

> He that by the Plough would thrive,
> Himself must either hold or drive.

. . . So much for Industry, my Friends, and Attention to one's own Business; but to these we must add *Frugality,* if we would make our *Industry* more certainly successful. A Man may, if he knows not how to save as he gets, *keep his Nose all his Life to the Grindstone,* and die not worth a *Groat* at last. *A fat Kitchen makes a lean Will,* as Poor Richard says; and,

> Many Estates are spent in the Getting,
> Since Women for Tea forsook Spinning and Knitting,
> And Men for Punch forsook Hewing and Splitting.

If you would be wealthy, says he, in another Almanack, *think of Saving as well as of Getting: The Indies have not made Spain rich, because her* Outgoes *are greater than her* Incomes. Away then with your expensive Follies, and you will not have so much Cause to complain of hard Times, heavy Taxes, and chargeable Families; for, as Poor Dick says,

> Women and Wine, Game and Deceit,
> Make the Wealth small, and the Wants great.

And farther, *What maintains one Vice, would bring up two Children.* You may think perhaps, That a *little* Tea, or a *little* Punch now and then, Diet a *little* more costly, Clothes a *little* finer, and a *little* Entertainment now and then, can be no *great* Matter; but remember what Poor Richard says, *Many* a Little *makes a Mickle;* and farther, *Beware of* little *Expences; a small Leak will sink a great Ship;* and again, *Who Dainties love, shall Beggars prove;* and moreover, *Fools make Feasts, and wise Men eat them.*

. . . Be *industrious* and *free;* be *frugal* and *free.* At present, perhaps, you may think yourself in thriving Circumstances, and that you can bear a little Extravagance without Injury; but,

> For Age and Want, save while you may;
> No Morning Sun lasts a whole Day,

as Poor Richard says. Gain may be temporary and uncertain, but ever while you live, Expence is constant and certain; and *'tis easier to build two Chimnies than to keep one in Fuel,* as Poor Richard says. So *rather go to Bed supperless than rise in Debt.*

> Get what you can, and what you get hold;
> 'Tis the Stone that will turn all your Lead into Gold,

as Poor Richard says. And when you have got the Philosopher's Stone, sure you will no longer complain of bad Times, or the Difficulty of paying Taxes.

This Doctrine, my Friends, is *Reason* and *Wisdom;* but after all, do not depend too much upon your own *Industry,* and *Frugality,* and *Prudence,* though excellent Things, for they may all be blasted without the Blessing of Heaven; and therefore ask that Blessing humbly, and be not uncharitable to those that at present seem to want it, but comfort and help them. Remember Job suffered, and was afterwards prosperous.

And now to conclude, *Experience keeps a dear School, but Fools will learn in no other, and scarce in that;* for it is true, *we may give Advice, but we cannot give Conduct,* as Poor Richard says: However, remember this, *They that won't be counselled, can't be helped,* as Poor Richard says: And farther, That *if you will not hear Reason, she'll surely rap your Knuckles.*

Thus the old Gentleman ended his Harangue. The People heard it, and approved the Doctrine, and immediately practised the contrary, just as if it had been a common Sermon; for the Vendue opened, and they began to buy extravagantly, not withstanding all his Cautions, and their own Fear of Taxes. I found the good Man had thoroughly studied my Almanacks, and digested all I had dropt on those Topicks during the Course of Five-and-twenty Years. The frequent Mention he made of me must have tired any one else, but my Vanity was wonderfully delighted with it, though I was conscious that not a tenth Part of the Wisdom was my own which he ascribed to me, but rather the *Gleanings* I had made of the Sense of all Ages and Nations. However, I resolved to be the better for the Echo of it; and though I had at first determined to buy Stuff for a new Coat, I went away resolved to wear my old One a little longer. *Reader,* if thou wilt do the same, thy Profit will be as great as mine. I am, as ever, Thine to serve thee,

RICHARD SAUNDERS. July 7, 1757.

BENJAMIN FRANKLIN PLANS AN ACADEMY (1749) From "Proposals Relating to the Education of Youth in Pennsylvania" (1749), as quoted in Leonard W. Larabee, ed., *The Papers of Benjamin Franklin* (New Haven, 1959–), vol. III.

Advertisement to the Reader

It has long been regretted as a Misfortune to the Youth of this Province, that we have no ACADEMY, in which they might receive the Accomplishments of a regular Education.

The following Paper of *Hints* towards forming a Plan for that Purpose, is so far approv'd by some publick-spirited Gentlemen, to whom it has been privately communicated, that they have directed a Number of Copies to be made by the Press, and properly distributed, in order to obtain the Sentiments and Advice of Men of Learning, Understanding, and Experience in these Matters; and have determin'd to use their Interest and best Endeavours, to have the Scheme, when compleated, carried gradually into Execution; in which they have Reason to believe they shall have the hearty Concurrence and Assistance of many who are Wellwishers to their Country.

Those who incline to favour the Design with their Advice, either as to the Parts of Learning to be taught, the Order of Study, the Method of Teaching, the Oeconomy of the School, or any other Matter of Importance to the Success of the

Undertaking, are desired to communicate their Sentiments as soon as may be, by Letter directed to B. Franklin, Printer, in Philadelphia.

Authors Quoted in This Paper

1. The famous Milton, whose Learning and Abilities are well known and who had practised some Time the Education of Youth, so could speak from Experience.

2. The great Mr. Locke, who wrote a Treatise on Education, well known, and much esteemed, being translated into most of the modern Languages of Europe.

3. *Dialogues on Education*, 2 Vols. Octavo, that are much esteem'd, having had two Editions in 3 Years. Suppos'd to be wrote by the ingenious Mr. Hutcheson (Author of *A Treatise on the Passions*, and another on the *Ideas of Beauty and Virtue*) who has had much Experience in Educating of Youth, being a Professor in the College at Glasgow, &c.

4. The learned Mr. Obadiah Walker, who had been many Years a Tutor to young Noblemen, and wrote a Treatise *on the Education of a young Gentleman;* of which the Fifth Edition was printed 1687.

5. The much admired Mons. Rollin, whose whole Life was spent in a College; and wrote 4 Vols. on Education, under the Title of, *The Method of Teaching and Studying the Belles Lettres;* which are translated into English, Italian, and most of the modern Languages.

6. The learned and ingenious Dr. George Turnbull, Chaplain to the present Prince of Wales; who has had much Experience in the Educating of Youth, and publish'd a Book, Octavo, intituled, *Observations on Liberal Education, in all its Branches,* 1742.

With some others.

The good Education of Youth has been esteemed by wise Men in all Ages, as the surest Foundation of the Happiness both of private Families and of Commonwealths. Almost all Governments have therefore made it a principal Object of their Attention, to establish and endow with proper Revenues, such Seminaries of Learning, as might supply the succeeding Age with Men qualified to serve the Publick with Honour to themselves, and to their Country.

Many of the first Settlers of these Provinces, were Men who had received a good Education in Europe, and to their Wisdom and good Management we owe much of our present Prosperity. But their Hands were full, and they could not do all Things. The present Race are not thought to be generally of equal Ability: For though the American Youth are allow'd not to want Capacity; yet the best Capacities require Cultivation, it being truly with them, as with the best Ground, which unless well tilled and sowed with profitable Seed, produces only ranker Weeds.

That we may obtain the Advantages arising from an Increase of Knowledge, and prevent as much as may be the mischievous Consequences that would attend a general Ignorance among us, the following *Hints* are offered towards forming a Plan for the Education of the Youth of Pennsylvania, viz.

It is propos'd,

That some Persons of Leisure and publick Spirit, apply for a CHARTER, by which they may be incorporated, with Power to erect an ACADEMY for the Education of Youth, to govern the same, provide Masters, make Rules, receive Donations, purchase Lands, &c. and to add to their Number, from Time to Time such other Persons as they shall judge suitable.

That the Members of the Corporation make it their Pleasure, and in some

Degree their Business, to visit the Academy often, encourage and countenance the Youth, countenance and assist the Masters, and by all Means in their Power advance the Usefulness and Reputation of the Design; that they look on the Students as in some Sort their Children, treat them with Familiarity and Affection, and when they have behav'd well, and gone through their Studies, and are to enter the World, zealously unite, and make all the Interest that can be made to establish them, whether in Business, Offices, Marriages, or any other Thing for their Advantage, preferably to all other Persons whatsoever even of equal Merit.

*　　*　　*

That a House be provided for the ACADEMY, if not in the Town, not many Miles from it; the Situation high and dry, and if it may be, not far from a River, having a Garden, Orchard, Meadow, and a Field or two.

That the House be furnished with a Library (if in the Country, if in the Town, the Town Libraries may serve) with Maps of all Countries, Globes, some mathematical Instruments, an Apparatus for Experiments in Natural Philosophy, and for Mechanics; Prints, of all Kinds, Prospects, Buildings, Machines, &c.

That the RECTOR be a Man of good Understanding, good Morals, diligent and patient, learn'd in the Languages and Sciences, and a correct pure Speaker and Writer of the English Tongue; to have such Tutors under him as shall be necessary.

That the boarding Scholars diet together, plainly, temperately, and frugally.

That to keep them in Health, and to strengthen and render active their Bodies, they be frequently exercis'd in Running, Leaping, Wrestling, and Swimming, &c.

That they have peculiar Habits to distinguish them from other Youth, if the Academy be in or near the Town; for this, among other Reasons, that their Behaviour may be the better observed.

As to their STUDIES, it would be well if they could be taught *every Thing* that is useful, and *every Thing* that is ornamental: But Art is long, and their Time is short. It is therefore propos'd that they learn those Things that are likely to be *most useful* and *most ornamental*, Regard being had to the several Professions for which they are intended.

All should be taught to write a *fair Hand*, and swift, as that is useful to All. And with it may be learnt something of *Drawing*, by Imitation of Prints, and some of the first Principles of Perspective.

Arithmetick, Accounts, and some of the first Principles of *Geometry* and *Astronomy.*

The English Language might be taught by Grammar; in which some of our best Writers, as Tillotson, Addison, Pope, Algernon Sidney, Cato's Letters, &c. should be Classicks: The *Stiles* principally to be cultivated, being the *clear* and the *concise.* Reading should also be taught, and pronouncing, properly, distinctly, emphatically; not with an even Tone, which *under-does,* nor a theatrical, which *over-does* Nature.

To form their Stile, they should be put on Writing Letters to each other, making Abstracts of what they read; or writing the same Things in their own Words; telling or writing Stories lately read, in their own Expressions. All to be revis'd and corrected by the Tutor, who should give his Reasons, explain the Force and Import of Words, &c.

To form their Pronunciation, they may be put on making Declamations, repeating Speeches, delivering Orations, &c. The Tutor assisting at the Rehearsals, teaching, advising, correcting their Accent, &c.

But if HISTORY be made a constant Part of their Reading, such as the Translations of the Greek and Roman Historians, and the modern Histories of antient Greece and Rome, &c. may not almost all Kinds of useful Knowledge be that Way introduc'd to Advantage, and with Pleasure to the Student? As

GEOGRAPHY, by reading with Maps, and being required to point out the Places *where* the greatest Actions were done, to give their old and new Names, with the Bounds, Situation, Extent of the Countries concern'd &c.

CHRONOLOGY, by the Help of Helvicus or some other Writer of the Kind, who will enable them to tell *when* those Events happened; what Princes were Cotemporaries, what States or famous Men flourish'd about that Time, &c. The several principal Epochas to be first well fix'd in their Memories.

ANTIENT CUSTOMS, religious and civil, being frequently mentioned in History, will give Occasion for explaining them; in which the Prints of Medals, Basso Relievo's, and antient Monuments will greatly assist.

MORALITY, by descanting and making continual Observations on the Causes of the Rise or Fall of any Man's Character, Fortune, Power, &c. mention'd in History; the Advantages of Temperance, Order, Frugality, Industry, Perseverance, &c. &c. Indeed the general natural Tendency of Reading good History, must be, to fix in the Minds of Youth deep Impressions of the Beauty and Usefulness of Virtue of all Kinds, Publick Spirit, Fortitude, &c.

History will show the wonderful Effects of ORATORY, in governing, turning and leading great Bodies of Mankind, Armies, Cities, Nations. When the Minds of Youth are struck with Admiration at this, then is the Time to give them the Principles of that Art, which they will study with Taste and Application. Then they may be made acquainted with the best Models among the Antients, their Beauties being particularly pointed out to them. Modern Political Oratory being chiefly performed by the Pen and Press, its Advantages over the Antient in some Respects are to be shown; as that its Effects are more extensive, more lasting, &c.

History will also afford frequent Opportunities of showing the Necessity of a *Publick Religion*, from its Usefulness to the Publick; the Advantage of a Religious Character among private Persons; the Mischiefs of Superstition, &c. and the Excellency of the CHRISTIAN RELIGION above all others antient or modern.

History will also give Occasion to expatiate on the Advantage of Civil Orders and Constitutions, how Men and their Properties are protected by joining in Societies and establishing Government; their Industry encouraged and rewarded, Arts invented, and Life made more comfortable: The Advantages of *Liberty*, Mischiefs of *Licentiousness*, Benefits arising from good Laws and a due Execution of Justice, &c. Thus may the first Principles of sound *Politicks* be fix'd in the Minds of Youth.

On *Historical* Occasions, Questions of Right and Wrong, Justice and Injustice, will naturally arise, and may be put to Youth, which they may debate in Conversation and in Writing. When they ardently desire Victory, for the Sake of the Praise attending it, they will begin to feel the Want, and be sensible of the Use of *Logic*, or the Art of Reasoning to *discover* Truth, and of Arguing to *defend* it, and *convince* Adversaries. This would be the Time to acquaint them with the Principles of that Art. Grotius, Puffendorff, and some other Writers of the same Kind, may be used on these Occasions to decide their Disputes. Publick Disputes warm the Imagination, whet the Industry, and strengthen the natural Abilities.

When Youth are told, that the Great Men whose Lives and Actions they read in History, spoke two of the best Languages that ever were, the most expressive, copious, beautiful; and that the finest Writings, the most correct Compositions, the most perfect Productions of human Wit and Wisdom, are in those Languages, which have endured Ages, and will endure while there are Men; that no Translation can do them Justice, or give the Pleasure found in Reading the Originals; that those Languages contain all Science; that one of them is become almost universal, being the Language of Learned Men in all Countries; that to understand them is a distinguishing Ornament, &c. they may be thereby made desirous of learning those Languages, and their Industry sharpen'd in the Acquisition of them. All intended for Divinity should be taught the Latin and Greek; for Physick, the Latin, Greek and French; for Law, the Latin and French; Merchants, the French, German, and Spanish: And though all should not be compell'd to learn Latin, Greek, or the modern foreign Languages; yet none that have an ardent Desire to learn them should be refused; their English, Arithmetick, and other Studies absolutely necessary, being at the same Time not neglected.

If the new *Universal History* were also read, it would give a *connected* Idea of human Affairs, so far as it goes, which should be follow'd by the best modern Histories, particularly of our Mother Country; then of these Colonies; which should be accompanied with Observations on their Rise, Encrease, Use to Great-Britain, Encouragements, Discouragements, &c. the Means to make them flourish, secure their Liberties, &c.

With the History of Men, Times and Nations, should be read at proper Hours or Days, some of the best *Histories of Nature*, which would not only be delightful to Youth, and furnish them with Matter for their Letters, &c. as well as other History; but afterwards of great Use to them, whether they are Merchants, Handicrafts, or Divines; enabling the first the better to understand many Commodities, Drugs, &c. the second to improve his Trade or Handicraft by new Mixtures, Materials, &c. and the last to adorn his Discourses by beautiful Comparisons, and strengthen them by new Proofs of Divine Providence. The Conversation of all will be improved by it, as Occasions frequently occur of making Natural Observations, which are instructive, agreeable, and entertaining in almost all Companies. *Natural History* will also afford Opportunities of introducing many Observations, relating to the Preservation of Health, which may be afterwards of great Use. Arbuthnot on Air and Aliment, Sanctorius on Perspiration, Lemery on Foods, and some others, may now be read, and a very little Explanation will make them sufficiently intelligible to Youth.

While they are reading Natural History, might not a little *Gardening, Planting, Grafting, Inoculating,* &c. be taught and practised; and now and then Excursions made to the neighbouring Plantations of the best Farmers, their Methods observ'd and reason'd upon for the Information of Youth. The Improvement of Agriculture being useful to all, and Skill in it no Disparagement to any.

The History of *Commerce,* of the Invention of Arts, Rise of Manufactures, Progress of Trade, Change of its Seats, with the Reasons, Causes, &c. may also be made entertaining to Youth, and will be useful to all. And this, with the Accounts in other History of the prodigious Force and Effect of Engines and Machines used in War, will naturally introduce a Desire to be instructed in *Mechanicks,* and to be inform'd of the Principles of that Art by which weak Men perform such Wonders, Labour is sav'd, Manufactures expedited, &c. &c. This will be the Time to show them Prints of antient and modern Machines, to explain them, to let them be copied, and to give Lectures in Mechanical Philosophy.

With the whole should be constantly inculcated and cultivated, that *Benignity of Mind,* which shows itself in *searching for* and *seizing* every Opportunity *to serve* and *to oblige;* and is the Foundation of what is called GOOD BREEDING; highly useful to the Possessor, and most agreeable to all.

The Idea of what is *true Merit*, should also be often presented to Youth, explain'd and impress'd on their Minds, as consisting in an *Inclination* join'd with an *Ability* to serve Mankind, one's Country, Friends and Family; which *Ability* is (with the Blessing of God) to be acquir'd or greatly encreas'd by *true Learning;* and should indeed be the great *Aim* and *End* of all Learning.

BENJAMIN FRANKLIN'S IDEA OF AN ENGLISH SCHOOL (1751)   From "Idea of the English School, Sketch'd Out for the Consideration of the Trustees of the Philadelphia Academy," as quoted in Leonard W. Labaree, ed., *The Papers of Benjamin Franklin* (New Haven, 1959–   ), vol. IV, pp. 102-8.

It is expected that every Scholar to be admitted into this School, be at least able to pronounce and divide the Syllables in Reading, and to write a legible Hand. None to be receiv'd that are under [   ] Years of Age. [Left blank in the original]

First or Lowest Class

Let the first Class learn the *English Grammar* Rules, and at the same time let particular Care be taken to improve them in *Orthography.* Perhaps the latter is best done by *Pairing* the Scholars, two of those nearest equal in their Spelling to be put together; let these strive for Victory, each propounding Ten Words every Day to the other to be spelt. He that spells truly most of the other's Words, is Victor for that Day; he that is Victor most Days in a Month, to obtain a Prize, a pretty neat Book of some Kind useful in their future Studies. This Method fixes the Attention to Children extreamly to the Orthography of Words, and makes them good Spellers very early. 'Tis a Shame for a Man to be so ignorant of this little Art, in his own Language, as to be perpetually confounding Words of like Sound and Different Significations; the Consciousness of which Defect, makes some Men, otherwise of good Learning and Understanding, averse to Writing even a common Letter.

Let the Pieces read by the Scholars in this Class be short, such as Croxall's Fables, and little Stories. In giving the Lesson, let it be read to them; let the Meaning of the difficult Words in it be explained to them, and let them con it over by themselves before they are called to read to the Master, or Usher; who is to take particular Care that they do not read too fast, and that they duly observe the Stops and Pauses. A Vocabulary of the most usual difficult Words might be formed for their Use, with Explanations; and they might daily get a few of those Words and Explanations by Heart, which would a little exercise their Memories; or at least they might write a Number of them in a small Book for the Purpose, which would help to fix the Meaning of those Words in their Minds, and at the same Time furnish every one with a little Dictionary for his future Use.

The Second Class to Be Taught

Reading with Attention, and with proper Modulations of the Voice according to the Sentiments and Subject.

Some short Pieces, not exceeding the Length of a *Spectator*, to be given this Class as Lessons (and some of the easier *Spectators* would be very suitable for the Purpose.) These Lessons might be given over Night as Tasks, the Scholars to study them against the Morning. Let it then be required of them to give an Account, first of the Parts of Speech, and Construction of one or two Sentences; this will oblige them to recur frequently to their Grammar, and fix its principal Rules in their Memory. Next of the *Intention* of the Writer, or the *Scope* of the Piece; the Meaning of each Sentence, and of every uncommon Word. This would early acquaint them with the Meaning and Force of Words, and give them that most necessary Habit, of Reading with Attention.

The Master then to read the Piece with the proper Modulations of Voice, due Emphasis, and suitable Action, where Action is required; and put the Youth on imitating his Manner.

Where the Author has us'd an Expression not the best, let it be pointed out; and let his Beauties be particularly remarked to the Youth.

Let the Lessons for Reading be varied, that the Youth may be made acquainted with good Stiles of all Kinds in Prose and Verse, and the proper Manner of reading each Kind. Sometimes a well-told Story, a Piece of a Sermon, a General's Speech to his Soldiers, a Speech in a Tragedy, some Part of a Comedy, an Ode, a Satyr, a Letter, Blank Verse, Hudibrastick, Heroic, &c. But let such Lessons for Reading be chosen, as contain some useful Instruction, whereby the Understandings or Morals of the Youth, may at the same Time be improv'd.

It is requir'd that they should first study and understand the Lessons, before they are put upon reading them properly, to which End each Boy should have an English Dictionary to help him over Difficulties. When our Boys read English to us, we are apt to imagine *they* understand what *they* read because *we* do, and because 'tis their Mother Tongue. But they often read as Parrots speak, knowing little or nothing of the Meaning. And it is impossible a Reader should give the due Modulation to his Voice, and pronounce properly, unless his Understanding goes before his Tongue, and makes him Master of the Sentiment. Accustoming Boys to read aloud what they do not first understand, is the Cause of those even set Tones so common among Readers, which when they have once got a Habit of using, they find so difficult to correct: By which Means, among Fifty Readers we scarcely find a good One. For want of good Reading, Pieces publish'd with a View to influence the Minds of Men for their own or the publick Benefit, lose Half their Force. Were there but one good Reader in a Neighbourhood, a publick Orator might be heard throughout a Nation with the same Advantages, and have the same Effect on his Audience, as if they stood within the Reach of his Voice.

The Third Class to Be Taught

Speaking properly and gracefully, which is near of Kin to good Reading, and naturally follows it in the Studies of Youth. Let the Scholars of this Class begin with learning the Elements of Rhetoric from some short System, so as to be able to give an Account of the most usual Tropes and Figures. Let all their bad Habits of Speaking, all Offences against good Grammar, all corrupt or foreign Accents, and all improper Phrases, be pointed out to them. Short Speeches from the Roman or other History, or from our *Parliamentary Debates*, might be got by heart, and deliver'd with the proper Action, &c. Speeches and Scenes in our best Tragedies and Comedies (avoiding every Thing that could injure the Morals of Youth) might likewise be got by Rote, and the Boys exercis'd in delivering or acting them; great Care being taken to form their Manner after the truest Models.

For their farther Improvement, and a little to vary their Studies, let them now begin to read *History*, after having got by Heart a short Table of the principal Epochas in Chronology. They may begin with Rollin's *Antient and Roman Histories*, and proceed at proper Hours as they go thro' the subsequent Classes, with the best Histories of our own Nation and Colonies. Let Emulation be excited among the Boys by giving, Weekly, little Prizes, or other small Encouragements to those who are able to give the best Account of what they have read, as to Times, Places, Names of Persons, &c. This will make them read with Attention, and imprint the History well in their Memories. In remarking on the History, the Master will have fine Opportunities of instilling Instruction of various Kinds, and improving the Morals as well as the Understandings of Youth.

The Natural and Mechanic History contain'd in *Spectacle de la Nature*, might also be begun in this Class, and continued thro' the subsequent Classes by other Books of the same Kind: For next to the Knowledge of *Duty*, this Kind of Knowledge is certainly the most useful, as well as the most entertaining. The Merchant may thereby be enabled better to understand many Commodities in Trade; the Handicraftsman to improve his Business by new Instruments, Mixtures and Materials; and frequently Hints are given of new Manufactures, or new Methods of improving Land, that may be set on foot greatly to the Advantage of a Country.

The Fourth Class to Be Taught

Composition. Writing one's own Language well, is the next necessary Accomplishment after good Speaking. 'Tis the Writing-Master's Business to take Care that the Boys make fair Characters, and place them straight and even in the Lines: But to *form their Stile*, and even to take Care that the Stops and Capitals are properly disposed, is the Part of the English Master. The Boys should be put on Writing Letters to each other on any common Occurrences, and on various Subjects, imaginary Business, &c. containing little Stories, Accounts of their late Reading, what Parts of Authors please them, and why. Letters of Congratulation, of Compliment, of Request, of Thanks, of Recommendation, of Admonition, of Consolation, of Expostulation, Excuse, &c. In these they should be taught to express themselves clearly, concisely, and naturally, without affected Words, or high-flown Phrases. All their Letters to pass through the Master's Hand, who is to point out the Faults, advise the Corrections, and commend what he finds right. Some of the best Letters published in our own Language, as Sir William Temple's, those of Pope, and his Friends, and some others, might be set before the Youth as Models, their Beauties pointed out and explained by the Master, the Letters themselves transcrib'd by the Scholar.

Dr. Johnson's *Ethices Elementa*, or first Principles of Morality, may now be read by the Scholars, and explain'd by the Master, to lay a solid Foundation of Virtue and Piety in their Minds. And as this Class continues the Reading of History, let them now at proper Hours receive some farther Instructions in Chronology, and in that Part of Geography (from the Mathematical Master) which is necessary to understand the Maps and Globes. They should also be acquainted with the modern Names of the Places they find mention'd in antient Writers. The Exercises of good Reading and proper Speaking still continued at suitable Times.

Fifth Class

To improve the Youth in *Composition,* they may now, besides continuing to write Letters, begin to write little Essays in Prose; and sometimes in Verse, not to make them Poets, but for this Reason, that nothing acquaints a Lad so speedily with Variety of Expression, as the Necessity of finding such Words and Phrases as will suit with the Measure, Sound and Rhime of Verse, and at the same Time well express the Sentiment. These Essays should all pass under the Master's Eye, who will point out their Faults, and put the Writer on correcting them. Where the Judgment is not ripe enough for forming new Essays, let the Sentiments of a *Spectator* be given, and requir'd to be cloath'd in a Scholar's own Words; or the Circumstances of some good Story, the Scholar to find Expression. Let them be put sometimes on abridging a Paragraph of a diffuse Author, sometimes on dilating or amplifying what is wrote more closely. And now let Dr. Johnson's *Noetica,* or first Principles of human Knowledge, containing a Logic, or Art of Reasoning, &c. be read by the Youth, and the Difficulties that may occur to them be explained by the Master. The Reading of History, and the Exercises of good Reading and just Speaking still continued.

Sixth Class

In this Class, besides continuing the Studies of the preceding, in History, Rhetoric, Logic, Moral and Natural Philosophy, the best English Authors may be read and explain'd; as Tillotson, Milton, Locke, Addison, Pope, Swift, the higher Papers in the *Spectator* and *Guardian,* the best Translations of Homer, Virgil and Horace, of *Telemachus, Travels of Cyrus,* &c.

Once a Year, let there be publick Exercises in the Hall, the Trustees and Citizens present. Then let fine gilt Books be given as Prizes to such Boys as distinguish themselves, and excel the others in any Branch of Learning; making three Degrees of Comparison; giving the best Prize to him that performs best; a less valuable One to him that comes up next to the best; and another to the third. Commendations, Encouragement and Advice to the rest; keeping up their Hopes that by Industry they may excel another Time. The Names of those that obtain the Prizes, to be yearly printed in a List.

The Hours of each Day are to be divided and dispos'd in such a Manner, as that some Classes may be with the Writing-Master, improving their Hands, others with the Mathematical Master, learning Arithmetick, Accompts, Geography, Use of the Globes, Drawing, Mechanicks, &c. while the rest are in the English School, under the English Master's Care.

Thus instructed, Youth will come out of this School fitted for learning any Business, Calling or Profession, except such wherein Languages are required; and tho' unacquainted with any antient or foreign Tongue, they will be Masters of their own, which is of more immediate and general Use; and withal will have attain'd many other valuable Accomplishments; the Time usually spent in acquiring those Languages, often without Success, being here employ'd in laying such a Foundation of Knowledge and Ability, as, properly improv'd, may qualify them to pass thro' and execute the several Offices of civil Life, with Advantage and Reputation to themselves and Country.

BENJAMIN FRANKLIN ON EDUCATIONAL CONSERVATISM IN PHILADELPHIA (1789)   From "Observations Relative to the Intentions of the Original Founders of the Academy in Philadelphia," as quoted in Albert H. Smyth, ed., *The Writings of Benjamin Franklin* (New York, 1907), vol. X, pp. 9-16, 24-25, 28-31.

As the English School in the Academy has been, and still continues to be, a Subject of Dispute and Discussion among the Trustees since the Restitution of the Charter, and it has been propos'd that we should have some Regard to the original Intention of the Founders in establishing that School, I beg leave for your Information, to lay before you what I know of that Matter originally; and what I find on the Minutes relating to it, by which it will appear how far the Design of that School has been adher'd to or neglected.

Having acquir'd some little Reputation among my Fellow-Citizens, by projecting the Public Library in 1732, and obtaining the Subscriptions by which it was establish'd, and by proposing and promoting with Success sundry other Schemes of Utility, in 1749 I was encouraged to hazard another Project, that of a Public Education for our Youth. As in the Scheme of the Library I had provided only for English Books, so in this new Scheme my Ideas went no farther than to procure the Means of a good English Education. A Number of my Friends, to whom I communicated the Proposal, concurr'd with me in these Ideas; but Mr. Allen, Mr. Francis, Mr. Peters, and some other Persons of Wealth and Learning, whose Subscriptions and Countenance we should need, being of Opinion that it ought to include the learned Languages, I submitted my Judgment to theirs, retaining however a strong Prepossession in favour of my first Plan, and resolving to preserve as much of it as I could, and to nourish the English School by every Means in my Power.

Before I went about to procure Subscriptions, I thought it proper to prepare the Minds of the People by a Pamphlet, which I wrote, and printed, and distributed with my Newspapers, gratis: The Title was, *Proposals relating to the Education of Youth in Pennsylvania.* I happen to have preserv'd one of them; and by reading a few Passages it will appear how much the English Learning was insisted upon in it; and I had good reason to know that this was a prevailing Part of the Motives for Subscribing with most of the original Benefactors. I met with but few Refusals in soliciting the Subscriptions; and the Sum was the more considerable, as I had put the Contribution on this footing that it was not to be immediate and the whole paid at once, but in Parts, a Fifth annually during Five Years. To put the Machine in Motion, Twenty-four of the principal Subscribers agreed to take themselves the Trust; and a Set of Constitutions for their Government, and for the Regulation of the Schools were drawn up by Mr. Francis and myself, which were sign'd by us all, and printed, that the Publick might know what was to be expected. I wrote also a Paper, entitled, *Idea of an English School,* which was printed, and afterwards annex'd to Mr. Peters' Sermon, preach'd at the opening of the Academy. This Paper was said to be *for the Consideration of the Trustees;* and the Expectation of the Publick, that the Idea might in good Part be carried into Execution, contributed to render the Subscriptions more liberal as well as more general. I mention my Concern in these Transactions, to show the Opportunity I had of being well inform'd in the Points I am relating.

The Constitutions are upon Record in your Minutes; and, altho' the Latin and Greek is by them to be taught, the original Idea of a complete English Education was not forgotten, as will appear by the following Extracts.

Page 1. "The English Tongue is to be taught grammatically, and as a Language."

Page 4. In reciting the Qualification of the Person to be appointed Rector, it is said, "that *great Regard* is to be had to his *polite Speaking, Writing, and Understanding the English Tongue.*"

The Rector was to have Two Hundred Pounds a Year, for wch he was to be obliged to "teach 20 Boys, without any Assistance, and 25 more for every Usher provided for him, the Latin and Greek Languages; and at the same time instruct them in History, Geography, Chronology, Logic, Rhetoric, and *the English Tongue.*"

The Rector was also, "on all Occasions consistent with his Duty in the Latin School, to *assist the English Master in improving the Youth under his Care.*"

Page 5. "The Trustees shall with all convenient Speed, contract with any Person that offers who they shall judge most capable of *teaching the English Tongue grammatically and as a Language,* History, Georgraphy, Chronology, Logic, and Oratory; which Person shall be stiled *the English Master.*"

The English Master was to have "One Hundred Pounds a Year, for which he was to teach, without any Assistance, 40 Scholars *the English Tongue grammatically* and at the same time instruct them in History, Geography, Chronology, Logic, and Oratory; and Sixty Scholars more for every Usher provided for him."

It is to be observed in this Place, that here are two distinct Courses in the same Study, that is, of the same Branches of Science, viz. History, Geography, Chronology, Logic, and Oratory, to be carried on at the same time, but not by the same Tutor or Master. The English Master is to teach his Scholars all those Branches of Science, and also the English Tongue grammatically, as a Language. The Latin Master is to teach the same Sciences to his Boys, besides the Greek and Latin. He was also to assist the English Master occasionally without which and his general Care in the Government of the Schools, the giving him double Salary seems not well accounted for. But here is plainly two distinct Schools or Courses of Education provided for. The Latin Master was not to teach the English Scholars Logic, Rhetoric, &c.; that was the Duty of the English Master; but he was to teach those Sciences to the Latin Scholars. We shall see hereafter how easily this original Plan was defeated and departed from.

When the Constitutions were first drawn Blanks were left for the Salaries, and for the Number of Boys the Latin Master was to teach. The first Instance of Partiality in fav^r of the Latin Part of the Institution, was in giving the Title of Rector to the Latin Master, and no Title to the English one. But the most striking Instance was when we met to sign, and the Blanks were first to be fill'd up, the Votes of a Majority carry'd it, to give twice as much Salary to the Latin Master as to the English, and yet require twice as much Duty from the English Master as from the Latin, viz. 200*l.* to the Latin Master to teach 20 Boys; 100*l.* to the English Master to teach 40! However, the Trustees who voted these Salaries being themselves by far the greatest Subscribers, tho' not the most numerous, it was thought they had a kind of Right to predominate in Money Matters; and those who had wish'd an equal Regard might have been shown to both Schools, submitted, tho' not without Regret, and at times some little Complaining; which, with their not being able in nine Months to find a proper Person for *English Master*, who would undertake the Office for so low a Salary, induc'd the Trustees at length, viz. in July 1750, to offer 50*l*. more.

Another Instance of the Partiality above mentioned was in the March preceding, when 100*l*. Sterling was voted to buy *Latin* and *Greek* Books, Maps, Drafts, and Instruments for the Use of the Academy, and nothing for *English Books*.

The great Part of the Subscribers, who had the English Education chiefly in view, were however sooth'd into a Submission to these Partialities, chiefly by the Expectation given them by the Constitution, viz. that the Trustees would make it their Pleasure, and in some degree their Business, to visit the Academy often, to encourage and countenance the Youth, look on the Students as in some Measure their own Children, treat them with Familiarity and Affection; and when they have behaved well, gone thro' their Studies, and are to enter the World, the Trustees shall zealously unite, and make all the Interest that can be made, to promote and establish them, whether in Business, Offices, Marriages, or any other thing for their Advantage, preferable to all other Persons whatsoever, even of equal Merit.

These splendid Promises dazzled the Eyes of the Publick. The Trustees were most of them the principal Gentlemen of the Province. Children taught in other Schools had no reason to expect such powerful Patronage, the Subscribers had plac'd such entire Confidence in them as to leave themselves no Power of changing them if their Conduct of the Plan should be disapprov'd; and so, in hopes of the best, all these Partialities were submitted to.

Near a Year past before a proper Person was found to take Charge of the English School. At length Mr. Dove, who had been many years Master of a School in England, and had come hither with an Apparatus for giving Lectures in Experimental Philosophy, was prevail'd with by me, after his Lectures were finished, to accept that Employment for the Salary offered, tho' he thought it too scanty. He had a good Voice, read perfectly well, with proper Accent and just Pronunciation, and his Method of communicating Habits of the same kind to his Pupils was this. When he gave a Lesson to one of them, he always first read it to him aloud, with all the different Modulations of Voice that the Subject and Sense required. These the scholars, in studying and repeating the Lesson, naturally endeavor'd to imitate; and it was really surprizing to see how soon they caught his Manner, which convinc'd me and others who frequently attended his School, that tho' bad Tones and manners in reading are when once acquir'd rarely, with Difficulty, if ever cur'd, yet, when none have been already form'd, good ones are as easily learn'd as bad. In a few Weeks after opening his School, the Trustees were invited to hear the Scholars read and recite. The Parents and Relations of the Boys also attended. The Performances were surprizingly good, and of course were admired and applauded; and the English School thereby acquired such Reputation, that the Number of Mr. Dove's Scholars soon amounted to upwards of Ninety, which Number did not diminish as long as he continued Master, viz. upwards of two Years: But he finding the Salary insufficient, and having set up a School for Girls in his own House to supply the Deficiency, and quitting the Boys' School somewhat before the Hour to attend the Girls, the Trustees disapprov'd of his so doing, and he quitted their Employment, continu'd his Girls' School, and open'd one for Boys on his own Account. The Trustees provided another English Master; but tho' a good Man, yet not possessing the Talents of an English Schoolmaster in the same Perfection with Mr. Dove, the School diminish'd daily, and soon was found to have but about forty Scholars left. The Performances of the Boys, in Reading and Speaking, were no longer so brilliant; the Trustees of course had not the same Pleasure in hearing them, and the Monthly Visitations, which had so long afforded a delightful Entertainment to large Audiences were gradually badly attended, and at length discontinued; and the English School has never since recovered its original Reputation.

Thus by our injudiciously starving the English Part of our Scheme of Education, we only sav'd Fifty Pounds a Year, which was required as an additional Salary to an acknowledg'd excellent English master, which would have equaled his Encouragement to that of the Latin Master; I say by saving the Fifty Pounds we lost Fifty Scholars, which would have been 200*l.* a Year, and defeated besides one great End of the Institution.

In the mean time our Favours were shower'd upon the Latin Part; the Number of Teachers was encreas'd, and their Salaries from time to time augmented, till if I mistake not, they amounted in the whole to more than 600*l.* a Year, tho' the Scholars hardly ever exceeded 60; so that each Scholar Cost the Funds 10*l.* per annum, while he paid but 4*l.*, which was a Loss of 6*l.* by every one of them.

   * * *

. . . we may observe; 1. That the English School having been long neglected, the Scholars were so diminish'd in Number as to be far from defraying the Expence in supporting it. 2. That the Instruction they receiv'd there, instead of a compleat English Education, which had been promised to the Subscribers by the original Constitutions, were only such as might easily be procured at other Schools in this City. 3. That this unprofitableness of the English School, owing to Neglect of Duty in the Trustees, was now offered as a Reason for demolishing it altogether. For it was easy to see, that, after depriving the Master of his Salary, he could not long afford to continue it. 4. That if the Insufficiency of the Tuition-Money in the English School to pay the Expence, and the Ease with which the Scholars might obtain equal Instruction in other Schools, were good Reasons for depriving the Master of his Salary and destroying that School, they were equally good for dismissing the Latin Masters, and sending their Scholars to other Schools; since it is notorious that the Tuition-Money of the Latin School did not pay much above a fourth Part of the Salaries of the Masters. For such Reasons the Trustees might equally well have got rid of all the Scholars and all the Masters, and remain'd in full Possession of all the College Property, without any future Expence. 5. That by thus refusing any longer to support, instead of Reforming, as they ought to have done, the English School, they shamefully broke through and set at nought the original Constitutions, for the due Execution of which the Faith of the original Trustees had been solemnly pledged to the Publick and diverted the Revenues, proceeding from much of the first Subscriptions, to other Purposes than those which had been promised.

   * * *

I flatter myself, Gentlemen, that it appears by this time pretty clearly from our own Minutes, that the original Plan of the English school has been departed from; that the Subscribers to it have been disappointed and deceived, and the Faith of the Trustees not kept with them; that the Publick have been frequently dissatisfied with the Conduct of the Trustees, and complained of it; that, by the niggardly Treatment of Good Masters, they have been driven out of the School, and the Scholars have followed, while a great Loss of Revenue has been suffered by the Academy; for that the numerous Schools now in the City owe their Rise to our Mismanagement, and that we might as well have had the best Part of the Tuition-Money paid into our Treasury, that now goes into private Pockets; that there has been a constant Disposition to depress the English School in favour of the Latin; and that every Means to procure a more equitable Treatment has been rendered ineffectual; so that no more Hope remains while they continue to have any Connection. It is, therefore, that, wishing as much good to the Latinists as their System can honestly procure for them, we now demand a Separation, and without desiring to injure them; but claiming an equitable Partition of our joint Stock, we wish to execute the Plan they have so long defeated, and afford the Publick the Means of a compleat English Education.

*   *   *

The Origin of Latin and Greek Schools among the different Nations of Europe is known to have been this, that until between 3 and 400 Years past there were no Books in any other Language; all the Knowledge then contain'd in Books, viz. the Theology, the Jurisprudence, the Physic, the Art-military, the Politicks, the Mathematics and Mechanics, the Natural and moral Philosophy, the Logic and Rhetoric, the Chemistry, the Pharmacy, the Architecture, and every other Branch of Science, being in those Languages, it was of course necessary to learn them, as the Gates through which Men must pass to get at that Knowledge.

The Books then existing were manuscript, and these consequently so dear, that only the few Wealthy enclin'd to Learning could afford to purchase them. The common People were not even at the Pains of learning to read, because, after taking that Pains, they would have nothing to read that they could understand without learning the ancient Languages, nor then without Money to purchase the Manuscripts. And so few were the learned Readers 60 Years after the Invention of Printing, that it appears by Letters still extant between the Printers in 1499, that they could not throughout Europe find Purchasers for more than 300 Copies of any ancient Authors. But Printing beginning now to make Books cheap, the Readers increas'd so much as to make it worth while to write and print Books in the Vulgar Tongues. At first these were chiefly Books of Devotion and little Histories; gradually several Branches of Science began to appear in the common Languages, and at this Day the whole Body of Science, consisting not only of Translations, from all the valuable ancients, but of all the new modern Discoveries, is to be met with in those Languages, so that learning the ancient for the purpose of acquiring Knowledge is become absolutely unnecessary.

But there is in Mankind an unaccountable Prejudice in favour of ancient Customs and Habitudes, which inclines to a Continuance of them after the Circumstances, which formerly made them useful, cease to exist. A Multitude of Instances might be given, but it may suffice to mention one. Hats were once thought an useful Part of Dress; it was said they kept the Head warm and screen'd it from the violent Impression of the sun's Rays, and from the Rain, Snow, Hail, &c. Tho' by the Way, this was not the more ancient Opinion or Practice; for among all the Remains of Antiquity, the Bustos, Statues, Coins, medals, &c., which are infinite, there is no Representation of a human Figure with a Cap or Hat on, nor any Covering for the Head, unless it be the Head of a Soldier, who has a Helmet; but that is evidently not a Part of Dress for Health, but as a Protection from the Strokes of a Weapon.

At what Time Hats were first introduced we know not, but in the last Century they were universally worn thro'out Europe. Gradually, however, as the Wearing of Wigs, and Hair nicely dress'd prevailed, the putting on of Hats was disused by genteel People, lest the curious Arrangements of the Curls and Powdering should be disordered; and Umbrellas began to supply their Place; yet still our Considering the Hats as a part of Dress continues so far to prevail, that a Man of fashion is not thought dress'd without having one, or something like one, about him, which he carries under his Arm. So that there are a multitude of the politer people in all the courts and capital cities of Europe, who have never, nor their fathers before them, worn a hat otherwise than as a *chapeau bras*, through the utility of such a mode of wearing it is by no means apparent, and it is attended not only with some expense, but with a degree of constant trouble.

The still prevailing custom of having schools for teaching generally our children, in these days, the Latin and Greek languages, I consider therefore, in no other light than as the *Chapeau bras* of modern Literature.

Thus the Time spent in that Study might, it seems, be much better employ'd in the Education for such a Country as ours; and this was indeed the Opinion of most of the original Trustees.

The Academy Movement

ADVERTISEMENT FOR BENJAMIN FRANKLIN'S PHILADELPHIA ACADEMY (1750) From Robert F. Seybolt, ed., *Source Studies in American Colonial Education: The Private School* (Urbana, Ill., 1925), pp. 98-99.

Notice is hereby given, That the Trustees of the ACADEMY of Philadelphia, intend (God willing) to open the same on the first Monday of January next; wherein Youth will be taught the Latin, Greek, English, French, and German Languages, together with History, Geography, Chronology, Logic, and Rhetoric; also Writing, Arithmetic, Merchants Accounts, Geometry, Algebra, Surveying, Gauging, Navigation, Astronomy, Drawing in Perspective, and other mathematical Sciences; with natural and mechanical Philosophy, &c. agreeable to the Constitutions heretofore published, at the Rate of Four Pounds per annum, and Twenty Shillings entrance.

REMINISCENCES OF THE PHILADELPHIA ACADEMY (c. 1760) From Alexander Graydon, *Memoirs of a Life Chiefly Passed in Pennsylvania . . .* (Harrisburg, Pa., 1811), pp. 16-17, 25-27, 32.

Being now, probably, about eight years of age, it was deemed expedient to enter me at the academy, then, as it now continues to be, under the name of a university, the principal seminary in Pennsylvania; and I was accordingly introduced by my father to Mr Kinnersley, the teacher of English and professor of oratory. He was an Anabaptist clergyman, a large venerable looking man, of no great general erudition, though a considerable proficient in electricity; and who, whether truly or not, has been said to have had a share in certain discoveries in that science, of which Dr Franklin received the whole credit. The task of the younger boys, at least, consisted in learning to read and to write their mother tongue grammatically; and one day in the week (I think Friday) was set apart for the recitation of select passages in poetry and prose. For this purpose, each scholar, in his turn, ascended the stage, and said his speech, as the phrase was. This speech was carefully taught him by his master, both with respect to its pronunciation, and the action deemed suitable to its several parts. Two of these specimens of infantile oratory, to the disturbance of any repose, I had been qualified to exhibit: Family partiality, no doubt, overrated their merit; and hence, my declaiming powers were in a state of such constant requisition, that my oration, like worn-out ditties, became vapid and fatiguing to me, and consequently, impaired my relish for that kind of acquirement. More profit attended my reading. After AEsop's Fables, and an abridgment of the Roman History, Telemachus was put into our hands; and if it be admitted that the human heart may be bettered by instruction, mine, I may aver, was benefited by this work of the virtuous Fenelon. While the mild wisdom of Mentor called forth my veneration, the noble ardour of the youthful hero excited my sympathy and emulation. I took part, like a second friend, in the vicissitudes of his fortune,—I participated in his toils,—I warmed with his exploits,—I wept where he wept, and exulted where he triumphed.

As my lot has been cast in a turbulent period, in a season of civil war and revolution, succeeded by scenes of domestic discord and fury, in all of which I have been compelled to take a part, I deem it of consequence to myself to bespeak toleration for the detail of a schoolboy incident, that may in some degree serve to develope my character. It may equally tend to throw some light on the little world upon whose stage I had now entered. A few days after I had been put under the care of Mr Kinnersley, I was told by my class-mates that it was necessary for me to fight a battle with some one, in order to establish my claim to the honour of being an academy boy; that this could not be dispensed with, and that they would select for me a suitable antagonist, *one of my match*, whom after school I must fight, or be looked upon as a coward. I must confess that I did not at all relish the proposal. Though possessing a sufficient degree of spirit, or at least irascibility, to defend myself when assulted, I had never been a boxer. Being of a light and slender make, I was not calculated for the business.

✻   ✻   ✻

I have said that I was about to enter the Latin school. The person whose pupil I was consequently to become was Mr John Beveridge, a native of Scotland, who retained the smack of his vernacular tongue in its primitive purity. His acquaintance with the language he taught was, I believe, justly deemed to be very accurate and profound. But as to his other acquirements, after excepting the game of backgammon, in which he was said to excel, truth will not warrant me in saying a great deal. He was, however, diligent and laborious in his attention to his school; and had he possessed the faculty of making himself beloved by the scholars, and of exciting their emulation and exertion, nothing would have been wanting in him to an entire qualification for his office. But, unfortunately, he had no dignity of character, and was no less destitute of the art of making himself respected than beloved. Though not, perhaps, to be complained of as intolerably severe, he yet made a pretty free use of the ratan and the ferule, but to very little purpose. He was, in short, no disciplinarian, and, consequently, very unequal to the management of seventy or eighty boys, many of whom were superlatively pickle and unruly. He was assisted, indeed, by two ushers, who eased him in the burden of teaching, but who, in matters of discipline, seemed disinclined to interfere, and disposed to consider themselves rather as subjects than rulers. I have seen them slily slip out of the way when the principal was entering upon the job of capitally punishing a boy, who, from his size, would be likely to make resistance. For this had become nearly a matter of course; and poor Beveridge, who was diminutive in his stature, and neither young nor vigorous, after exhausting himself in the vain attempt to denude the delinquent, was generally glad to compound for a few strokes over his clothes, on any part that was accessible. He had, indeed, so frequently been foiled, that his birch at length was rarely brought forth, and might truly be said to have lost its terrors—it was *tanquam gladium in vagina repositum.* He indemnified himself, however, by a redoubled use of his ratan.

So entire was the want of respect towards him, and so liable was he to be imposed upon, that one of the larger boys, for a wager, once pulled off his wig, which he effected by suddenly twitching it from his head, under pretence of brushing from it a spider; and the unequivocal insult was only resented by the peevish exclamation of *Hoot, mon!*

Various were the rogueries that were played upon him; but the most audacious of all was the following. At the hour of convening in the afternoon, that being found the most convenient, from the circumstance of Mr Beveridge being usually a little beyond the time; the bell having rung, the ushers being at their posts, and the scholars arranged in their classes, three or four of the conspirators conceal themselves without, for the purpose of observing the motions of their victim. He arrives, enters the school, and is permitted to proceed until he is supposed to have nearly reached his chair at the upper end of the room, when instantly the door and every window-shutter is closed. Now, shrouded in utter darkness, the most hideous yells that can be conceived are sent forth from at least threescore of throats; and Ovids, and Virgils, and Horaces, together with the more heavy metal of dictionaries, whether of Cole, of Young, or of Ainsworth, are hurled without remorse at the head of the astonished preceptor, who, on his side, groping and crawling under cover of the forms, makes the best of his way to the door. When attained, and light restored, a death-like silence ensues. Every boy is at his lesson: no one has had a hand or a voice in the recent atrocity: what, then, is to be done, and who shall be chastised?

*   *   *

This most intolerable outrage, from its succeeding beyond expectation, and being entirely to the taste of the school, had a run of several days; and was only then put a stop to by the interference of the *faculty,* who decreed the most exemplary punishment on those who should be found offending in the premises, and by taking measures to prevent a further repetition of the enormity.

*   *   *

We were all, therefore, to be merchants, as to be mechanics was too humiliating; and, accordingly, when the question was proposed, which of us would enter upon the study of Greek, the grammar of which tongue was about to be put into our hands, there were but two or three who declared for it. As to myself, it was my mother's desire, from her knowing it to have been my father's intention to give me the best education the country afforded, that I should go on, and acquire every language and science that was taught in the institution; but, as my evil star would have it, I was thoroughly tired of books and confinement, and her advice, and even entreaties, were overruled by my extreme repugnance to a longer continuance in the college, which, to my lasting regret, I bid adieu to when a little turned of fourteen, at the very season when the minds of the studious begin to profit by instruction. We were at this time reading Horace and Cicero, having passed through Ovid, Virgil, Caesar, and Sallust. From my own experience on this occasion, I am inclined to think it of much consequence that a boy, designed to complete his college studies, should be classed with those of a similar destination.

DESCRIPTION OF THE OPENING OF NEWARK ACADEMY IN NEW JERSEY (1775)   From *Rivington's New York Gazetteer,* March 23, 1775, as quoted in Edgar W. Knight and Clifton L. Hall, eds., *Readings in American Educational History* (New York, 1951), pp. 181-82.

The Academy lately erected in a healthy part of the pleasant town of Newark in New Jersey, about eight miles from the city of New York, will on the third day of April next, be fit for the reception of the masters proper for the instruction of youth, and such children as can with conveniency lodge and board therein. They will be taught the learned languages and several branches of Mathemathicks. There will also be an English School for the teaching of Reading, Writing, Arithmetick, and Bookkeeping in the usual and Italian methods. Different rooms will be made use of for each branch of instruction; and such as choose may have their children taught the English tongue grammatically. The boys are separated from the girls in the English School. Those who can't board in the Academy, may have good lodging near the same in private families. The regulation and general direction of the instruction of the scholars will be under the auspices of the Governors of the Academy, who will from time to time inspect the conduct of the several masters, and examine the improvement of their pupils in learning.

Mr. William Haddon, one long experienced by several of the governors to be well qualified to teach the learned Languages and the Mathematicks, will have the superintendency of the youth to be taught in those branches of learning, and Robert Allan and Son to have the care and keeping of the schools for the instruction of Reading, Writing, Arithmetick, and Bookkeeping, who have discharged their trusts to the great satisfaction of their employers. As the intention of the benefactors and builders of this stately edifice, is for preparing youth to be useful members of the community, the greatest care will be taken to have them not only instructed in the branches of learning which their parents respectively order, but also in the paths of virtue and morality. Care also will be taken that they attend public worship at the usual times of holding the same at the churches to which they belong, there being in the said town two churches, one of the Church of England, and the other the Presbyterian; the ministers of which, for the time being, are always to be of the number of said Governors, and it is hoped that they, with the other Governors, will give that attendance to the trust they have undertaken, as will answer the laudable end proposed, and give ample satisfaction to the parents and the guardians of the children sent to the said Academy.

NEWARK 10th March, 1775

PROVINCIALS

CHARTER OF LIBERTY HALL ACADEMY IN NORTH CAROLINA

(**1777**)   From Walter Clark, ed., *The State Records of North Carolina* (Goldsboro, N.C., 1886-1907), vol. I, pp. 30-32.

I. Whereas the proper Education of Youth in this infant Country is highly necessary, and would answer the most valuable and beneficial Purposes to this State, and the good People thereof; and whereas a very promising Experiment hath been made at a Seminary in the County of Mecklenburg, and a Number of Youths there taught have made great Advancements in the Knowledge of Learned Languages, and in the Rudiments of the Arts and Sciences, in the Course of a regular and finished Education, which they have since compleated at various Colleges in distant Parts of America; and whereas the Seminary aforesaid, and the several Teachers who have successively taught and presided therein, have hitherto been almost wholly supported by private Subscriptions: In order therefore that the said Subscriptions and other Gratuities may be legally possessed and duly applied, and the said Seminary, by the Name of Liberty Hall, may become more extensively and generally useful, for the Encouragement of liberal Knowledge in Languages, Arts and Sciences, and for diffusing the great Advantages of Education upon more liberal, easy, and generous Terms:

II. Be it Enacted, by the General Assembly of the State of North Carolina, and by the Authority of the same, That the said Seminary shall be, and it is hereby declared to be an Academy, by the Name of Liberty Hall.

*   *   *

III. And be it Enacted, by the Authority aforesaid, That the said President and Trustees, and their Successors, or a Majority of them, by the Name aforesaid, shall be able and capable in Law to bargain, sell, grant, demise, alien or dispose of, and convey and assure to the Purchasers, any such Lands, Rents, Tenements or Hereditaments aforesaid, when the Condition of the Grant to them, or the Will of the Devisor, does not forbid it. And further, that the said President and Trustees, and their Successors, for ever, or a Majority of them, shall be able and capable in Law, by the Name aforesaid, to sue and implead, be sued and impleaded, answer and be answered, in all Courts of Record whatsoever.

IV. And be it further Enacted, by the Authority aforesaid, That the said President and Trustees be, and they are hereby impowered, authorized and required, to convene at the Town of Charlotte on the Third Tuesday of October next after passing this Act, and then and there elect and constitute, by Commission in Writing under their Hands, and sealed with the common Seal of the Corporation, such and so many Professors or Tutors as they may think expedient; and then and there, and at all other Times for ever hereafter, when the said President and Trustees, their Successors, or a Majority of them, shall be convened and met together in the said County of Mecklenburg, they shall have full Power and lawful Authority to elect and constitute one or more Professors or Tutors; and also to make and ordain such Laws, Rules and Ordinances, not repugnant to the Laws of this State, for the well ordering and governing the Students, their Morals Studies, and Academical Exercises, as to them shall seem meet; and to give Certificates to such Students as shall leave the said Academy, certifying their literary Merit, and the Progress they shall have made in useful Knowledge, whether it be in learned Languages, Arts or Sciences, or all of them.

VI. Be it further Enacted, by the Authority aforesaid, That the said President and Tutors, before they enter upon the Execution of the Trust reposed in them by this Act, shall take the Oath appointed for Public Officers, and also the following Oath, viz:

I, A. B., do swear, that I will duly and faithfully, to the best of my Skill and Ability, execute and discharge the several Trusts, Powers and Authorities, wherewith I am invested by an Act of the General Assembly, intituled, An Act for incorporating the President and Trustees of Liberty Hall, in the County of Mecklenburg; and that I will endeavour that all Monies, Goods, Chattels, and the Profits of Lands, belonging to this Corporation, shall be duly applied to the Use of the Academy, for the Advancement of Learning, and as near as may be agreeable to the Will of the Donor. SO HELP ME GOD.

And if any President or Trustee of said Academy shall enter upon the Execution of the Trust reposed in him by this Act before taking the said Oaths as above required, he shall forfeit and pay the Sum of Twenty Pounds. Proclamation Money: to be recovered by Action of Debt, in the Name of the Governor of the State for the Time being, and applied to purchase Books for the Use of the said Academy.

✳   ✳   ✳

VIII. And whereas it is necessary to make Provision for the Appointment of succeeding Presidents and succeeding Trustees, in order to keep up a perpetual Succession; Be it therefore Enacted, by the Authority aforesaid, That on the Death, Refusal to qualify, Resignation, or Removal out of the State, of the President or any of the Trustees for the Time being, it shall be lawful for the remaining Trustees, in the Room and Stead of such President, Trustee, or Trustees, or a Majority of them, and they are hereby authorized and required, to convene and meet together in the said County of Mecklenburg, and there elect and appoint another President, or one or more Trustees, dead, refusing to qualify, resigned, or removed out of the State; which President and Trustees so elected and appointed, shall be vested with the same Trusts, Powers and Authorities, as other Fellows and Trustees are invested with by Virtue of this Act, he or they having first taken the Oaths by this Act required.

IX. And be it further Enacted, by the Authority aforesaid, That the said Trustees and their Successors, or a Majority of them, at their Meeting in October annually, and at any other Meeting called for that Purpose (after due Notice given to at least Nine of the Trustees, signifying the Occasion of such Meeting) shall have full Power and Authority to hear any Complaint against the President, or any Professor or Tutor, and for Misbehaviour or Neglect to suspend, or wholly remove him or them from Office, and appoint others to fill the same Office or Offices respectively; and any President so removed from Office, shall from thenceforth cease to be a Member of the Corporation, and the President appointed in his Room and Stead shall be vested with all the Authority and Privileges with which the President by this Act appointed is invested.

X. Provided nevertheless, and be it further Enacted, That this Act, or any Thing therein contained, shall not extend, or be understood to make this Academy one of those Seminaries, mentioned in the Constitution, to oblige this State to support any President, Professor or Tutor, of said Academy, or other Charge or Expence thereof whatsoever; this Act of Incorporation having been obtained at the earnest Prayer and Intreaty of the said Trustees and others, who were desirous to contribute towards the Support thereof.

Read three Times and Ratified in General Assembly, the Ninth Day of May, Anno Dom. 1777.

CHARTER OF PHILLIPS ANDOVER ACADEMY IN MASSACHUSETTS

(**1780**)   From *Acts And Resolves of The General Court of Massachusetts* (Boston, 1780), p. 327.

Whereas, the education of youth has ever been considered by the wise and good, as an object of the highest consequence to the safety and happiness of a people; as at that period the mind easily receives and retains impressions, is formed with peculiar advantage to piety and virtue, and directed to the pursuit of the most useful knowledge; and, whereas the Honorable Samuel Phillips of Andover, in the County of Essex, Esq., and the Honorable John Phillips of Exeter, in the County of Rockingham, and State of New Hampshire, Esq., on the first day of April, in the year of our Lord one thousand seven hundred and seventy eight, by a legal instrument of that date, gave, granted, and assigned to the Honorable William Phillips, Esquire, and others, therein named, and to their heirs, divers lots and parcels of land, in said Instrument described, as well as certain other estate, to the use and upon the trust following, namely, that the rents, profits, and interest thereof, be forever laid out and expended by the Trustees in the said Instrument named, for the support of a Public Free School or Academy, in the town of Andover:—and, whereas the execution of the generous and important design of the grantors aforesaid will be attended with very great embarrassments, unless, by an act of incorporation, the Trustees, mentioned in the said Instrument, and their successors, shall be authorized to commence and prosecute actions at law, and transact such other matters in their corporate capacity, as the interest of the said Academy shall require.

Academy Established

1. Be it therefore enacted by the Council and the House of Representatives in General Court assembled, and by the authorship of the same; that there be and hereby is established in the Town of Andover, and County of Essex, an Academy, by the name of *Phillips Academy*, for the purpose of promoting piety and virtue, and for the education of youth, in the English, Latin and Greek languages, together with Writing, Arithmetic, Music, and the Art of Speaking; also practical Geometry, Logic and Geography, and such other of the liberal Arts and Sciences, or Languages, as opportunity may hereafter permit, and as the Trustees, herein after provided, shall direct.

ACCOUNT OF SCHOOL LIFE AT PHILLIPS ANDOVER ACADEMY, MASSACHUSETTS (1780)
Eliphalet Pearson to the Trustees (1780), as quoted in M. E. Brown and H. G. Brown, *The Story of John Adams, a New England Schoolmaster* (New York, 1900), pp. 47-48.

School begins at eight o'clock with devotional exercises; a psalm is read and sung. Then a class consisting of four scholars repeat memoriter two pages in Greek Grammar, after which a class of thirty persons repeats a page and a half of Latin Grammar; then follows the "Accidence tribe," who repeat two, three, four, five and ten pages each. To this may be added three who are studying arithmetic; one is in the Rule of Three, another in Fellowship, and the third is in Practice. School is closed at night by reading Dr. Doddridge's Family Expositor, accompanied by rehearsals, questions, remarks and reflections, and by the singing of a hymn and a prayer. On Monday the scholars recite what they can remember of the sermons heard on the Lord's Day previous; on Saturday the bills are presented and punishments administered.

CHARTER OF PHILLIPS EXETER ACADEMY IN NEW HAMPSHIRE (1781)
From Frank H. Cunningham, *Familiar Sketches of the Phillips Exeter Academy* (Boston, 1883), pp. 325, 329.

State of New Hampshire

IN THE YEAR OF OUR LORD ONE THOUSAND SEVEN HUNDRED AND EIGHTY-ONE. AN ACT TO INCORPORATE AN ACADEMY IN THE TOWN OF EXETER BY THE NAME OF THE PHILLIPS EXETER ACADEMY

Whereas the education of youth has ever been considered by the wise and good as an object of the highest consequence to the safety and happiness of a people, as at an early period in life the mind easily receives and retains impressions and is most susceptible of the rudiments of useful knowledge, and whereas the Honorable John Phillips, of Exeter, in the county of Rockingham, Esquire, is desirous of giving to Trustees hereinafter to be appointed certain lands and personal estate to be by said Trustees forever appropriated and expended for the support of a public free school or Academy in the town of Exeter, and whereas the execution of such an important design will be attended with very great embarrassments unless by an act of incorporation said Trustees and their successors shall be authorized to commence and prosecute actions at law, and transact such other matters in a corporate capacity as the interests of said Academy shall require,—Be it therefore enacted by the Council and House of Representatives in General Assembly convened and by the authority of the same, that there be and hereby is established, in the town of Exeter and county of Rockingham, an Academy by the name of the Phillips Exeter Academy, for the purpose of promoting piety and virtue, and for the education of youth in the English, Latin, and Greek languages, in writing, arithmetic, music, and the art of speaking, practical geometry, logic, and geography, and such other of the liberal arts and sciences or languages as opportunity may hereafter permit, and as the Trustees hereinafter provided shall direct.

*　　*　　*

And whereas the said institution may be of very great and general advantage to this State, and deserves every encouragement, Be it therefore enacted by the authority aforesaid, that all the lands, tenements, and personal estate that shall be given to said Trustees for the use of the said Academy shall be, and hereby are, forever exampted from all taxes whatsoever.

State of New Hampshire in the House of Representatives, March 30, 1781. The foregoing bill having been read a third time,
Voted, that it pass to be enacted. Sent up for concurrence.

JOHN LANGDON, *Speaker.*

In Council, the 3d of April, 1781. This Bill having been read the third time,
Voted, the same be enacted.

W. WEARE, *President.*
SAM. BROOKS, *Recorder.*

Copy examined by JOSEPH PEARSON, *D. Sec'y.*
Received and recorded 11th March, 1782.

THE CONSTITUTION OF THE PHILLIPS EXETER ACADEMY (1782)　From Frank H. Cunningham, *Familiar Sketches of the Phillips Exeter Academy* (Boston, 1883), pp. 330-32, 334-39.

Constitution

When we reflect upon the grand design of the great Parent of the universe in the creation of mankind; and the improvements of which the mind is capable, both in knowledge and virtue; as well as upon the prevalence of ignorance and vice, disorder and wickedness, and upon the direct tendency and certain issue of such a course of things, such reflection must occasion in thoughtful minds an earnest solicitude to find the source of these evils and their remedy. And small acquaintance with the qualities of young minds, how susceptible and tenacious they are of impressions, evidences that the time of youth is the important period, on the improvement or neglect of which depends the most weighty consequences to individuals themselves, and the community.

A serious consideration of these things, and an observation of the growing neglect of youth, must excite a painful anxiety for the event; and may well determine those whom their Heavenly Benefactor hath blessed with an ability therefore to promote and encourage public free schools or Academies for the purpose of instructing youth not only in the English and Latin grammar, writing, arithmetic, and those sciences wherein they are commonly taught, but more especially to learn them the great end and real business of living. Earnestly wishing that such institutions may grow and flourish, that the advantages of them may be extensive and lasting, that their usefulness may be so manifest as to lead the way to other establishments on the same principles, and that they may finally prove eminent means of advancing the interest of the Great Redeemer. To His patronage and blessing may all friends to learning and religion most humbly commit them.

TO ALL PEOPLE to whom these presents shall come, Greeting: Whereas the General Assembly of the State of New Hampshire did by their Act, on the third day of April, Anno Domini 1781, Incorporate an Academy in the town of Exeter and county of Rockingham, by the name of the Phillips Exeter Academy, for the purposes of promoting piety and virtue, and for the education of youth as is in said Act directed. And whereas by said Act all the lands, tenements, and personal estate that shall be given to Trustees for the use of said Academy are and shall be forever exempted from all taxes whatsoever,—

Therefore, in consideration of the great importance of the design mentioned, and of the powers, privileges, and immunities in and by said Act granted, and for the sole purposes of promoting piety, virtue, and useful literature, I, John Phillips, of Exeter aforesaid, Esquire, have granted, and with most humble thanks to the Lord and Giver of all things for the opportunity, ability, and disposition by Him given, do by these presents most cheerfully grant to the Trustees of the said Phillips Exeter Academy nominated and appointed by said Act, and to their successors in that Trust, all my right, title, and interest in and unto the real estate described as followeth:—

*   *   *

The first Instructor shall be nominated and appointed by the Founder. The Trustees, or a major part of them, shall meet once a year at the Phillips Exeter Academy; their first meeting shall be on the 18th day of December, A. D. 1781, when they shall determine on the time for holding the annual meeting, which may be altered as they shall hereafter find most convenient.

A President, Clerk, and Treasurer shall be annually chosen, who shall officiate till their places are supplied by a new election, and no member shall sustain the office of Clerk and Treasurer at the same time. An Instructor shall not be chosen President, and upon the decease of a President, Clerk, or Treasurer, another shall be chosen in his room at the next annual meeting.

*   *   *

No person shall be chosen as a principal instructor unless he be a member of a church of Christ, in complete standing, whose sentiments are similar to those hereinafter expressed, and will lead him to inculcate the doctrines and perform the duties required in this Constitution; also of exemplary manners, of good natural abilities and literary acquirements, of a natural aptitude for instruction and government; a good acquaintance with human nature is also much to be desired, and in the appointment of any instructor regard shall be had to qualifications only, without preference of friend or kindred, place or birth, education or residence. The Trustees shall make a contract with instructors as to salary, before their entrance upon office; and when the number of scholars shall require more instructors than the Principal, it will be expected that persons of ability who reap some advantage by this institution will cheerfully assist in supporting the additional, so that poor children of promising genius may be introduced, and members who may need some special aid may have it afforded them. It shall be the duty of the Trustees to inquire into the conduct of the instructors, and if they or either of them be found justly chargeable with such misconduct, neglect of duty, or incapacity as the said Trustees shall judge renders them or either of them unfit to continue in office, they shall remove them or either of them so chargeable.

As the welfare of the Academy will be greatly promoted by the students being conversant with persons of good character only, no scholar may enjoy the privileges of this Institution who shall board in any family which is not licensed by the Trustees. And applications will be in vain where the daily worship of God and good government is not said to be maintained. And in order to preserve this Seminary from the baneful influence of the incorrigibly vicious, the Trustees shall determine for what reasons a scholar shall be expelled, and the manner in which the sentence shall be administered.

The Trustees at their annual meetings shall visit the Seminary and examine into the proficiencies of the scholars, examine and adjust all accounts relative to the Seminary, and make any further rules and orders which they find necessary and conformable to this Constitution. The principal instructor may not sit in determining matter wherein he is particularly interested. Extravagant entertainments shall be discountenanced and economy recommended by Trustees and instructors. Applications for admission of scholars are to be made to the principal instructor, and the rules and orders the instructors may make for the good government of the scholars shall be subject to the examination, amendment, or discontinuance of the Trustees.

It shall ever be considered as a principal duty of the instructors to regulate the temper, to enlarge the minds and form the morals of the youth committed to their care. They are to give special attention to the health of the scholars, and ever to urge the importance of an habit of industry. For these purposes they may encourage the scholars to perform some manual labor, such as gardening, or the like, so far as is consistent with cleanliness and the inclinations of their parents; and the fruit of their labor shall be applied, at the discretion of the Trustees, for procuring a Library, or in some other way increasing the usefulness of this Seminary. But above all it is expected that the attention of instructors to the disposition of the minds and morals of the youth under their charge will exceed every other care, well considering that though goodness without knowledge as it respects others is weak and feeble, yet knowledge without goodness is dangerous, and that both united form the noblest character and lay the surest foundation of usefulness to mankind. It is therefore required that they most attentively and vigorously guard against the earliest irregularities; that they frequently delineate in their natural colors the deformity and odiousness of vice, and the beauty and amiableness of virtue; that they spare no pains to convince them of the numberless and indispensable obligations to abhor and avoid the former, and to love and practise the latter; of the several great duties they owe to God, their country, their parents, their neighbors, and themselves; that they critically and constantly observe the variety of their natural tempers, and solicitously endeavor to bring them under such discipline as may tend most effectually to promote their own satisfaction and the happiness of others; that they early inure them to contemplate the several connections and various scenes incident to human life, furnishing such general maxims of conduct as may best enable them to pass through all with care, reputation, and comfort. And whereas many of the students of this Academy may be devoted to the sacred work of the Gospel ministry, therefore that the true and fundamental principles of the Christian religion may be cultivated, established, and perpetuated in the Christian Church, so far as this instition may have influence, it shall be the duty of the instructors, as the age and capacity of the scholars will admit, to teach them the principles of natural religion, as the being of a God, and his perfections, his universal providence and perfect government, of the natural and moral world, and obligations to duty resulting from them. Also to teach them doctrines of revealed religion as they are contained in the sacred scriptures of divine authority, being given by inspiration of God, the doctrine of the Father, the Word, and the Holy Ghost, particularly the doctrine of Christ as true God, the only begotten of the Father, with all the truths they declare relative to his office of Mediator and work of redemption and salvation from the state of sin, guilt, and depravity of nature man has fallen into; the necessity of atonement by the blood of Jesus Christ, and of regeneration by the spirit of God; the doctrine of repentance towards God and of faith in our Lord Jesus Christ considered as duties and gifts of God's grace; and the doctrine of justification by the free grace of God, through the redemption that is in Jesus Christ, whose righteousness in his obedience unto death is the only ground and reason of the sinner's pardon and acceptance as righteous in the sight of God. The doctrine also of the Christian progressive sanctification in dying unto sin and living unto God, in new obedience to all the commandments of Christ proceeding from Gospel motives and views supremely to the glory of God; and the doctrines of the resurrection from the dead and of the great and final judgment, with its consequences of happiness to the righteous and misery to the wicked.

These, and all the doctrines and duties of our holy Christian religion, nothing founded on human authority, will be proved by Scripture testimony. And whereas the most wholesome precepts without frequent repetitions may prove ineffectual, it is further required of the instructors that they not only urge and re-urge, but continue from day to day to impress these instructions; and let them ever remember that the design of this institution can never be answered without their persevering, incessant attention to this duty. Protestants only shall ever be concerned in the Trust or Instruction of this Seminary; and they, having severally approved the Constitution, their government and instructions conformably thereto must appear steady, cordial, and vigorous.

The election of the officers of this Academy shall be by ballot only; and it shall ever be equally open to youth of requisite qualifications from every quarter, provided that none be admitted till, in common parlance, they can read English well, excepting such particular members as the Trustees may hereafter license. And in order to prevent a perversion of the true intent of this foundation, it is again declared that the first and principal design of this institution is the promoting virtue and true piety; useful knowledge in the order before referred to (in the Act of Incorporation) being subservient thereto. And I hereby reserve to myself, during any part of my natural life, the full right to make any special rules for the perpetual government of this Academy which shall be equally binding on those whom they may concern with any clause in these regulations, provided no such rule shall be subversive of the true intent of this foundation. I also reserve a right to appoint one person to succeed me in the Trust after my decease or resignation, to whom shall be transferred the same right of appointment, and to his successors in the said Trust forever. The foregoing regulations, forming the Constitution of the Phillips Exeter Academy, shall ever be read by the President for the time being at the annual meetings of the Trustees of said Academy, that they and their successors may be fully acquainted with, and in all future time be reminded of their duty.

And considering them as true to their Trust, I, the said John Phillips, for myself and my heirs, executors, and administrators, do hereby covenant, grant, and agree to and with the said Trustees and their successors, that I will warrant and defend the before granted premises to them forever against the lawful claims and demands of any person or persons whomsoever holding from, by, or under me. Likewise Elizabeth, my wife, doth hereby freely and voluntarily relinquish all right of dower and power of thirds in the premises. In witness whereof, we have hereunto set our hands and seals, the seventeenth day of May, Anno Domini one thousand seven hundred and eighty-one.

<table>
<tr><td>Signed, sealed, and delivered in presence of</td><td></td><td></td></tr>
<tr><td>P. WHITE.</td><td>JOHN PHILLIPS.</td><td>[SEAL.]</td></tr>
<tr><td>JACOB ABBOT.</td><td>ELIZABETH PHILLIPS.</td><td>[SEAL.]</td></tr>
</table>

ROCKINGHAM SS., January 9, 1782.

John Phillips, Esquire, and Elizabeth, his wife, owned this instrument to be their free act and deed.

      Before me,   PHILLIPS WHITE, *J. Peace.*

Received and recorded, 11th March, 1782.

                                      SAML. BROOKS, *Rdr.*

GRADUATION CERTIFICATES FROM PHILLIPS EXETER ACADEMY

(1790, 1799)   From Laurence M. Crosbie, *The Phillips Exeter Academy: A History* (Exeter, N.H., 1924).

Theo. Mansfield

The bearer of this, Theo. Mansfield, has been a student at the Phillips Exeter Academy. He has read those Classic Authors, a knowledge of which is considered as necessary for an Introduction into one of the Universities. He has likewise read a part of Horace's Odes, & paid some attention to Geography, Mathematicks and English Grammar. His conduct has been uniformly pleasing to his instructors, & he is now regularly dismissed from that Institution,

                         by Benj^m. Abbot, Inst^r. of s^d. Academy.

Exeter Decr. 27th. 1790

The Trustees of Phillips Exeter Academy, with a view to encourage Industry, Science and Morality, have determined that certificates may be granted to students in certain cases. Be it therefore known that Lewis Cass has been a member of the said Academy seven years, and appears on examination to have acquired the principles of the English, French, Latin and Greek languages, Geography, Arithmetic and practical Geometry; that he has made very valuable progress in the study of Rhetoric, History, Natural and Moral Philosophy, Logic, Astronomy and Natural Law; and that he has sustained a good moral character during said term.

In testimony whereof we hereunto set our hands, and affix the seal of said Academy, this second day of October, one thousand seven hundred and ninety-nine.

> John T. Gilman,
> Benjamin Abbot.

CHARTER OF GERMANTOWN ACADEMY, PHILADELPHIA (1782) From
Statutes At Large of Pennsylvania, 1782, Chapter 1109.

An Act to Establish and Incorporate a Public School at Germantown, in the County of Philadelphia

Whereas divers well disposed persons in and about the neighborhood of Germantown in the county of Philadelphia, impressed with the advantages that would result to the rising generation by establishing seminaries for the propagation of useful learning and rendering the attainment thereof cheap, easy and convenient, did many years past by subscription raise a sum of money wherewith they purchased a convenient lot of ground and thereon erected a large and commodious school-house, and for a considerable time have maintained a school therein; but their funds have not been sufficient to extend the utility thereof so far as their wishes and expectations had pointed out, the reason whereof they apprehend to be that they have not been incorporated and thereby enabled to take, receive and collect the donations and subscriptions of persons who have contributed and would have contributed to the same:

And whereas, by the forty-fourth section of the frame of government of this commonwealth it is ordained "That a school or schools shall be established in each county by the legislature for the convenient instruction of youth with such salaries to the masters paid by the public as shall enable them to instruct youth at low prices."

And whereas divers of the inhabitants of Germantown have by petition to this house represented that the situation of the place, the large and commodious buildings already erected and divers other circumstances render it a proper place to establish a school agreeable to the said provision in the frame of government, and have prayed that such a school may be established there and such assistance granted to it as to the wisdom of this House shall seem meet:

And whereas the finances of this state so soon after a long and expensive war, are not in a condition (without an increase of taxes already heavy) to carry into erection immediately the design of the said section by establishing schools at the public expense in all the counties of this state, but it is nevertheless highly proper to promote the laudable attempt of the petitioners by every reasonable encouragement until something further can be done by the legislature in a more extensive way.

Be it therefore enacted and it is hereby enacted by the Representatives of the Freemen of the Commonwealth of Pennsylvania in General Assembly met and by the authority of the same, That there be erected and hereby is erected and established at Germantown in the county of Philadelphia, a public school for the instruction of youth in the learned and foreign languages, reading and writing English, the mathematics, and other useful branches of literature, the name, style and title whereof and the constitution thereof shall be as they are hereinafter mentioned and defined, That is to say,

I. The said school shall forever hereafter be called and known by the name of "The Public School of Germantown in the county of Philadelphia," and shall be under the management, direction and government of a number of trustees not exceeding twenty-one or a quorum or board thereof as herein after mentioned.

II. That the first trustees of the said school shall consist of the following persons, viz.: Henry Hill, Samuel Ashmead and Jacob Rust, Esquires, the Reverend Albert Helfenstein and Frederick Smith, John Vanderen, John Bringhurst, Joseph Ferree, Christian Snider, James Haslet, Samuel Mechlin, Noah Townsend, Samuel Bringhurst, George Bringhurst, Justus Fox, William Ashmead, David Deshler, Doctor Jacob Frelich, Paul Engle, John Fry and Abraham Rittenhouse, which said trustees and their successors to be elected as herein after mentioned shall forever hereafter be, and they are hereby erected, established and declared to be one body politic in deed and in law to all intents and purposes with perpetual succession by the name and title of "The Trustees of the Public School of Germantown, in the county of Philadelphia," by which name and title they and their successors shall be competent and capable at law and in equity to take and hold to themselves and their successors for the use of the said school, any estate in any messuages, lands, tenements, rents, hereditaments, goods, chattels, moneys or other personal state, by the gift, grant, bargain, sale, conveyance, assurance, will, devise or bequest of any persons or body politic whatsoever, Provided the same do not exceed in the whole the yearly value of one thousand pounds, and the same to grant, bargain, sell, convey, assure, demise and to farm, let, place out at interest or otherwise dispose of, for the use of the said school, in such manner as to them or at least seven of them shall seem most beneficial to the institution, and to receive the rents, issues, profits, income and interest of the same, and to apply the same to the proper use and support of the said school, and by the same name to sue, commence, prosecute, defend, implead and be impleaded in any courts of law or equity and in all manner of suits and actions whatsoever; and to make, devise, have and use one common seal to authenticate all the acts and deeds of the corporation, and the same to break, alter and renew at their pleasure, and generally by and in the same name to do and transact all and every the business touching and concerning the premises, or which shall be incidentally necessary thereto, as fully and effectually as any natural person or body politic or corporate within this commonwealth have power to manage their own concerns.

III. The said trustees or a quorum or board of them shall meet at the school-house in Germantown on the first Monday in November next, to enter upon their business and at least once in every year afterwards, at such times as the said trustees shall appoint, of which notice shall be given after the first meeting by public advertisement in two of the public newspapers of the city or county of Philadelphia, at least two weeks before the time of such intended meeting, and if at such or any future meeting seven of the said trustees shall not be present, those of them who shall be present shall have power to adjourn to any future day, whereof notice shall be given as aforesaid: but if at such or any future meeting by adjournment or otherwise, whereof notice shall have been given as aforesaid, seven of the said trustees shall be met, then such seven of them shall be a board or quorum, and a majority of their votes shall be sufficient and capable of doing and transacting all the business and concerns of the said corporation; and particularly of making and enacting ordinances and by-laws for the government of the said school, of electing trustees in the place of those who shall resign their offices or die, of choosing and employing the masters and tutors of the school, of agreeing with them for their salaries and stipends, and removing them for misconduct of breach of the laws of the institution, of appointing committees of their own body to carry into execution all and every the resolutions of their board; of appointing a treasurer, secretary, stewards, managers, and other necessary officers, for the taking care of the estate and managing the concerns of the corporation, and generally of determining all matters and things (although the same be not herein particularly mentioned) which shall occasionally arise and be incidentally necessary to be determined and transacted by the said trustees; Provided always that no ordinances or by-laws shall be of force which shall be repugnant to the laws of this state.

IV. Persons of every religious denomination among Christians shall be capable of being elected trustees, nor shall any person either as master, tutor, officer or pupil be refused admittance for his conscientious persuasion in matters of religion, provided he shall demean himself in a sober, orderly manner, and conform to the rules and regulations of the school.

V. No misnomer of the said corporation shall defeat or annul any gift, grant, devise of bequest to or from the said corporation, provided the intent of the parties shall sufficiently appear upon the face of the gift, grant, will or other writing whereby any estate or interest was intended to pass to or from the said corporation; nor shall any disuser or nonuser of the rights, liberties and privileges, jurisdictions and authorities hereby granted to the said corporation or any of them, create or cause a forfeiture thereof, nor shall the constitution of the said school hereby established be ever altered or alterable by any by-law or ordinance of the said trustees or in any other manner than by an act of the legislature of this state; but the same constitution shall always be construed most beneficially for the said corporation.

And it is further enacted by the authority aforesaid, That all and singular the estate real and personal whatsoever now belonging to and held by any person or persons whatsoever for the use of the said school of Germantown shall be and the same is by force of this act transferred to and vested in the trustees of the public school of Germantown in the county of Philadelphia, and their successors forever, for the use of the last mentioned school, and that it shall and may be lawful for the said trustees to enter into and take possession thereof, and to sue, commence and prosecute all such suits and actions at law for the recovery of all debts and sums of money due, owing and payable to the former trustees of the Germantown school for the use of the said school whether the same be due on bonds, notes or other securities, or by the gift, donation, bequest or promissory subscription of any person or persons whatsoever.

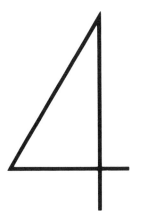

SCHOOLBOOKS
AND
SCHOOLTEACHERS

Schoolbooks

A HORNBOOK OF THE EIGHTEENTH CENTURY   From Plimpton Collection,
Columbia University Library, p. 15.

JOHN COTTON'S CATECHISM (1646)   From John Cotton, *Spiritual Milk for Boston Babes in either England. Drawn out of the Breasts of both Testaments for their Souls Nourishment* (Cambridge, Mass., 1656), p. 4.

Question. What is the fifth commandment?
Answer. Honor thy father and thy mother, that thy days may be long in the land
which the Lord thy God giveth thee.
Question. Who are here meant by father and mother?
Answer. All our superiors, whether in family, school, church, and commonwealth.
Question. What is the honor due to them?
Answer. Reverence, obedience, and (when I am able) recompence. . . .

SELECTIONS FROM THE EARLIEST EXTANT COPY OF THE NEW ENGLAND PRIMER (1727)   From Paul Leicester Ford, ed., *The New England Primer,* . . . (New York, 1897), no pagination.

A   In *Adam's* Fall
We Sinned all.

B   Thy Life to Mend
This *Book* Attend.

C   The *Cat* doth play
And after flay.

D   A *Dog* will bite
A Thief at night.

E   An *Eagles* flight
Is out of fight.

F   The Idle *Fool*
Is whipt at School.

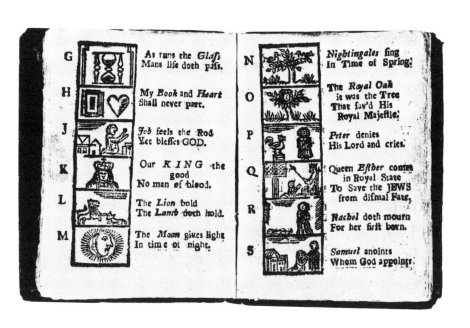

G As runs the *Glass*
   Mans life doth pass.

H My *Book* and *Heart*
   Shall never part.

J *Job* feels the Rod
   Yet blesses GOD.

K Our *KING* the
      good
   No man of blood.

L The *Lion* bold
   The *Lamb* doth hold.

M The *Moon* gives light
   In time of night.

N *Nightingales* sing
   In Time of Spring.

O The *Royal Oak*
   it was the Tree
   That sav'd His
   Royal Majeftie.

P *Peter* denies
   His Lord and cries.

Q Queen *Esther* comes
   in Royal State
   To Save the JEWS
   from difmal Fate.

R *Rachel* doth mourn
   For her firft born.

S *Samuel* anoints
   Whom God appoints.

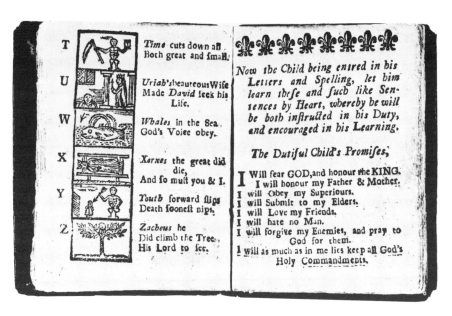

T *Time* cuts down all
   Both great and fmall.

U *Uriah*'s beauteous Wife
   Made *David* feek his
      Life.

W *Whales* in the Sea.
   God's Voice obey.

X *Xerxes* the great did
      die,
   And fo muft you & I.

Y *Youth* forward flips
   Death foonest nips.

Z *Zacheus* he
   Did climb the Tree
   His Lord to fee.

Now the *Child being entred in his
Letters and Spelling, let him
learn thefe and fuch like Sentences by Heart, whereby he will
be both inftructed in his Duty,
and encouraged in his Learning.*

The Dutiful Child's Promifes.

I Will fear GOD, and honour the KING.
  I will honour my Father & Mother.
I will Obey my Superiours.
I will Submit to my Elders.
I will Love my Friends.
I will hate no Man.
I will forgive my Enemies, and pray to
      God for them.
I will as much as in me lies keep all God's
      Holy Commandments.

I will learn my Catechifm.
I will keep the Lord's Day Holy,
I will Reverence God's Sanctuary,
For our GOD is a confuming Fire.

An Alphabet of Leffons for Youth.

A Wife Son makes a glad Father, but a foolifh Son is the heavinefs of his Mother.

B Etter is a little with the fear of the Lord, than great treafure and trouble therewith.

C Ome unto CHRIST all ye that labour and are heavy laden, and He will give you reft.

D O not the abominable thing which I hate, faith the Lord.

E Xcept a Man be born again, he cannot fee the Kingdom of God.

F Oolifhnefs is bound up in the heart of a Child, but the rod of Correction fhall drive it far from him.

G Rieve not the Holy Spirit.

H Olinefs becomes God's Houfe for ever.

I T is good for me to draw near unto God.

K Eep thy Heart with all Diligence, for out of it are the iffues of Life.

L Iars fhall have their part in the lake which burns with fire and brimftone.

M Any are the Afflictions of the Righteous, but the Lord delivers them out of them all.

N OW is the accepted time, now is the day of falvation.

O Ut of the abundance of the heart the mouth fpeaketh.

P Ray to thy Father which is in fecret, and thy Father which fees in fecret, fhall reward thee openly.

Q Uit you like Men, be ftrong, ftand faft in the Faith.

R Emember thy Creator in the days of thy Youth.

S Alvation belongeth to the Lord.

B   Truft

T Ruft in God at all times ye peopl, pour out your hearts before him.

U Pon the wicked God fhall rain an horrible Tempeft.

W O to the wicked, it fhall be ill with him, for the reward of his hands fhall be given him.

X Hort one another daily while is is called to day, left any of you be hardened through the deceitfulnefs of Sin.

Y Oung Men ye have overcome the wicked one.

Z Eal hath confumed me, becaufe thy enemies have forgotten the words of God. *Choice Sentences.*

1. Praying will make thee leave finning, or finning will make thee leave praying.

2. Our Weaknefs and Inabilities break not the bond of our Duties.

3. What we are afraid to fpeak before Men, we fhould be afraid to think before God.

The

Good Children muft,

Fear God all Day,	*Love Chrift alway,*
Parents obey,	*In Secret Pray,*
No falfe thing fay,	*Mind little Play,*
By no Sin ftray,	*Make no delay,*
	In doing Good.

Awake, arife, behold thou haft
Thy Life a Leaf, thy Breath a Blaft;
At Night lye down prepar'd to have
Thy fleep, thy death, thy bed, thy grave.

Learn thefe four Lines by Heart—

Have Communion with few.
Be Intimate with ONE.
Deal juftly with all.
Speak Evil of none.

The Names and Order of the Books
of the Old and New-Teftament.

G Enefis   *Levitieus*
Exodus — *Numbers*

The SHORTER

CATECHISM

Agreed upon by the Reverend

Aſſembly of Divines *at Weſtminſter*

Queſt. WHat is *the chief End of Man* ?

Anſw. Man's chief End is to Glorify God, and to Enjoy Him for ever.

Q. *What Rule hath God given to direct us how we may glorify and enjoy Him* ?

A. The Word of God which is contained in the Scriptures of the
Old

Old and New Teſtament, is th only Rule to direct us how we may glorify and enjoy him.

Q. *What do the Scriptures principally teach* ?

A. The Scriptures principally teach, what Man is to believe concerning God, and what duty God requireth of Man.

Q. *What is God* ?

A. God is a Spirit, Infinite, Eternal, and Unchangeable, in His Being, Wiſdom, Power, Holineſs, Juſtice, Goodneſs and Truth.

Q. *Are there more Gods than One* ?

A. There is but ONE only, the living and true God.

Q. *How many Perſons are there in the God-head* ?

`A.` There are Three Perſons in

THE
SCHOOL
OF
MANNERS.
OR

RULES for Childrens Behaviour:

At Church, at Home, at Table, in Company, in Difcourfe, at School, abroad, and among Boys. With fome other fhort and mixt Precepts.

By the Author of the *Englifh Exercifes*.

The Fourth Edition.

LONDON.

Printed for *Tho. Cockerill*, at the Three Legs and Bible againft Grocers-Hall in the *Poultrey*, 1701.

MANNERS FOR CHILDREN (1701)   From Alice M. Earle, *Child Life in Colonial Days* (New York, 1899), p. 218.

(9)

17. Bite not thy bread, but break it, but not with slovenly Fingers, nor with the same wherewith thou takest up thy meat,

18 Dip not thy Meat in the Sawce.

19. Take not salt with a greazy Knife.

20 Spit not, cough not, nor blow thy Note at Table if it may be avoided ; but if there be necessity, do it aside, and without much noise.

21. Lean not thy Elbow on the Table, or on the back of thy Chair.

22. Stuff not thy mouth so as to fill thy Cheeks ; be content with smaller Mouthfuls.

23. Blow not thy Meat, but with Patience wait till it be cool.

24. Sup not Broth at the Table, but eat it with a Spoon.

SCHOOLBOOKS, AND
SCHOOLTEACHERS

ELEAZER MOODY'S INSTRUCTIONS IN GOOD MANNERS (1754) From
Eleazer Moody, *The School of Good Manners. Composed for the Help of Parents in Teaching their Children How to Carry It in Their Places During Their Minority* (Boston, 1772), pp. 17-19.

When at Home

1. Make a bow always when you come home, and be immediately uncovered.
2. Be never covered at home, especially before thy parents or strangers.
3. Never sit in the presence of thy parents without bidding, tho' no stranger be present.
4. If thou passest by thy parents, and any place where thou seest them, when either by themselves or with company, bow towards them.
5. If thou art going to speak to thy parents, and see them engaged in discourse with company, draw back and leave thy business until afterwards; but if thou must speak, be sure to whisper.
6. Never speak to thy parents without some title of respect, viz., Sir, Madam, &c.
7. Approach near thy parents at no time without a bow.
8. Dispute not, nor delay to obey thy parents commands.
9. Go not out of doors without thy parents leave, and return within the time by them limited.
10. Come not into the room where thy parents are with strangers, unless thou art called, and then decently; and at bidding go out; or if strangers come in while thou art with them, it is manners, with a bow to withdraw.
11. Use respectful and courteous but not insulting or domineering carriage or language toward the servants.
12. Quarrel not nor contend with thy brethren or sisters, but live in love, peace, and unity.
13. Grumble not nor be discontented at anything thy parents appoint, speak, or do.
14. Bear with meekness and patience, and without murmuring or sullenness, thy parents reproofs or corrections: Nay, tho' it should so happen that they be causeless or undeserved.

In Their Discourse

1. Among superiors speak not till thou art spoken to, and bid to speak.
2. Hold not thine hand, nor any thing else, before thy mouth when thou speakest.
3. Come not over-near to the person thou speakest to.
4. If thy superior speak to thee while thou sittest, stand up before thou givest any answer.
5. Sit not down till thy superior bid thee.
6. Speak neither very loud, nor too low.
7. Speak clear, not stammering, stumbling nor drawling.
8. Answer not one that is speaking to thee until he hath done.
9. Loll not when thou art speaking to a superior or spoken to by him.
10. Speak not without, Sir, or some other title of respect.

11. Strive not with superiors in argument or discourse; but easily submit thine opinion to their assertions.
12. If thy superior speak any thing wherein thou knowest he is mistaken, correct not nor contradict him, nor grin at the hearing of it; but pass over the error without notice or interruption.
13. Mention not frivolous or little things among grave persons or superiors.
14. If thy superior drawl or hesitate in his words, pretend not to help him out, or to prompt him.
15. Come not too near two that are whispering or speaking in secret, much less may'st thou ask about what they confer.
16. When thy parent or master speak to any person, speak not thou, nor hearken to them.
17. If thy superior be relating a story, say not, "I have heard it before," but attend to it as though it were altogether new. Seem not to question the truth of it. If he tell it not right, snigger not, nor endeavor to help him out, or add to his relation.
18. If any immodest or obscene thing be spoken in thy hearing, smile not, but settle thy countenance as though thou did'st not hear it.
19. Boast not in discourse of thine own wit or doings.
20. Beware thou utter not any thing hard to be believed.
21. Interrupt not any one that speaks, though thou be his familiar.
22. Coming into company, whilst any topic is discoursed on, ask not what was the preceding talk but hearken to the remainder.
23. Speaking of any distant person, it is rude and unmannerly to point at him.
24. Laugh not in, or at thy own story, wit or jest.
25. Use not any contemptuous or reproachful language to any person, though very mean or inferior.
26. Be not over earnest in talking to justify and avouch thy own sayings.
27. Let thy words be modest about those things which only concern thee.
28. Repeat not over again the words of a superior that asketh thee a question or talketh to thee.

דִּקְדּוּק

עִבְרִית   לְשׁוֹן

DICKDOOK LESHON GNEBREET.

A

G R A M M A R

OF THE

𝕳𝖊𝖇𝖗𝖊𝖜 𝕮𝖔𝖓𝖌𝖚𝖊,

BEING

An E S S A Y

To bring the 𝕳𝖊𝖇𝖗𝖊𝖜 𝕲𝖗𝖆𝖒𝖒𝖆𝖗 into 𝕰𝖓𝖌𝖑𝖎𝖋𝖍,

to Facilitate the

I N S T R U C T I O N

Of all thofe who are defirous of acquiring a clear Idea of this

Primitive Tongue

by their own Studies ;

In order to their more diftinct Acquaintance with the SACRED ORACLES of the Old Teftament, according to the Original.   And

Publifhed more efpecially for the Ufe of the STUDENTS of *HARVARD-COLLEGE* at *Cambridge*, in NEW-ENGLAND.

נֶחְבַּר וְהוּגַת בְּעִיוּן נִמְרָץ עַל יְדֵי

יְהוּדָה מוֹנִישׁ

Compofed and accurately Corrected,

By J U D A H   M O N I S, *M. A.*

B O S T O N, N. E.

Printed by JONAS GREEN, and are to be Sold by the AUTHOR at his Houfe in *Cambridge*.   MDCCXXXV.

DILWORTH'S "NEW GUIDE TO THE ENGLISH TONGUE" (1747 Edition)   From Elwood P. Cubberley, ed., *Readings in Public Education in the United States* (Boston, 1934), p. 52.

A

New GUIDE

TO THE

English Tongue:

In Five PARTS.

CONTAINING,

I. Words, both *common* and *proper*, from *one* to *six Syllables*: The several sorts of *Monosyllables* in the common Words being distinguished by Tables, into Words of *two*, *three*, and *four* Letters, &c. with six short Lessons at the End of each Table, not exceeding the order of Syllables in the foregoing Tables. The several sorts of *Polysyllables* also, being ranged in proper Tables, have their Syllables divided, and Directions placed at the Head of each Table for the *Accent*, to prevent *false Pronunciation*; together with the like Number of Lessons on the foregoing Tables, placed at the End of each Table, as far as to Words of *four* Syllables, for the easier and more speedy Way of teaching Children to Read.

II. A large and useful Table of Words, that are the same in *Sound*, but different in *Signification*; very nececessary to prevent the Writing one word for another of the same *Sound*.

III. A short, but comprehensive *Grammar* of the *English* Tongue, delivered in the most familiar and instructive Method of *Question* and *Answer*; necessary for all such Persons as have the Advantage only of an *English* Education.

IV. An useful Collection of *Sentences* in *Prose* and *Verse*, *Divine*, *Moral*, and *Historical*; together with a select Number of *Fables*, adorn'd with proper Sculptures, for the better Improvement of the Young Beginner. And

V. *Forms* of *Prayer* for Children on several Occasions.

The *Whole*, being recommended by several *Clergymen* and eminent *Schoolmasters*, as the most useful *Performance* for the Instruction of *Youth*, is designed for the Use of SCHOOLS in *Great Britain* and *Ireland*.

The EIGHTH EDITION.

By THOMAS DILWORTH,

AUTHOR of the

SCOOLMASTERS ASSISTANT; and *Schoolmaster in Wappin*.

PHILADELPHIA:

Printed and Sold by B. FRANKLIN, MDCCXLVII.

The Italian Hand

A B C D E F G H I K L M
N O P Q R S T U W X Y Z

a b c d e f g h i k l m n o p q
r s s t u v w x y z &c

Art is gain'd by great Labour & Industry

Secretary Hand

A B C D E F G H I K L M N
O P P Q Q R S T U W X Y Z Z

A a b c d e f g h i j k l m
n o p q r s s t u w x y z z

Fear God and Honour the King

An easy Copy for Round Hand

A B C D E F G H I K L M N
O P Q R S T U W X Y Z

a b c d e f g h i k l m n o p q r s
s t u v w x y z &c 1 2 3 4 5 6 7 8 9 10

Take great Care and you'll Write fair

THE

Schoolmasters Assistant.

BEING A

Compendium of ARITHMETIC,

BOTH

Practical and Theoretical.

In Five PARTS.

CONTAINING

I. Arithmetic in whole Numbers, wherein all the common Rules, having each of them a sufficient Number of Questions, with their Answers, are methodically and briefly handled.

II. Vulgar Fractions, wherein several Things, not commonly met with, are there distinctly treated of, and laid down in the most plain and easy Manner.

III. Decimals, in which, among other Things, are considered the Extraction of Roots; Interest, both Simple and Compound; Annuities; Rebate, and Equation of Payments.

IV. A large Collection of Questions with their Answers, serving to exercise the foregoing Rules, together with a few others, both pleasant and diverting.

V. Duodecimals, commonly called Cross Multiplication; wherein that Sort of Arithmetic is thoroughly considered, and rendered very plain and easy; together with the Method of proving all the foregoing Operations at once by Division of several Denominations, without reducing them into the lowest Terms mentioned.

The Whole being delivered in the most familiar Way of *Question* and *Answer* is recommended by several eminent *Mathematicians, Accomptants*, and *Schoolmasters*, is necessary to be used in *Schools* by all Teachers, who would have their *Scholars* thoroughly understand, and make a quick Progress in ARITHMETIC.

To which is prefixt, An Essay on the *Education* of YOUTH; humbly offer'd to the Consideration of PARENTS.

The Nineteenth Edition.

By THOMAS DILWORTH,

Author of the *New Guide* to the *English* Tongue; *Young Book-keeper's Assistant*, &c. &c. and *Schoolmaster* in *Wapping*.

All Things, which from the very first Original Being of Things, have been framed and made, do appear to be framed by the Reason of Number : *for this was the principal Example or Pattern in the Mind of the* CREATOR.
Anitius Boetius.

Thou [O LORD] *hast ordered all Things in Measure,* Number, *and* Weight.
Wisdom xi. 20.

LONDON:

Printed and Sold by RICHARD and HENRY CAUSTON (Successors to the late Mr. HENRY KENT) at the Printing-Office, No. 21, in *Finch-Lane*, near the *Royal Exchange.* M DCC LXXVI.

SCHOOLBOOKS. AND
SCHOOLTEACHERS

EZEKIEL CHEEVER'S INTRODUCTION TO LATIN (1785 Edition)   From
Elwood P. Cubberley, ed., *Readings in Public Education in the United States* (Boston,
1934), p. 62.

A SHORT

INTRODUCTION

TO THE

LATIN TONGUE:

FOR THE USE OF THE

LOWER FORMS in the LATIN SCHOOL.

BEING THE

ACCIDENCE,

Abridged and compiled in that most easy and accurate Method, wherein the famous Mr. EZEKIEL
CHEEVER taught, and which he found the most
advantageous by Seventy Years Experience.

To which is added,

A CATALOGUE of Irregular NOUNS
and VERBS, difposed alphabetically,

The EIGHTEENTH EDITION.

B O S T O N:
Printed by T. and J. FLEET, in Cornhill.
MDCCLXXXV.

Schoolteachers

LETTER FROM A NEW ENGLAND SCHOOLBOY (1719)   From Alice M. Earle, *Child Life in Colonial Days* (New York, 1899), p. 88.

"HONOUR'D SIR: "BOSTON, NEW ENGLAND, JULY 1, 1719.

"I would have wrote now but to tell ye Truth I do not know what to write for I have not had a letter from you since Capt. Beale, and I am very sorry I can't write to you but I thought it my Duty to write these few lines to you to acquaint you of my welfare, and what proficiency I have made in Learning since my Last to you. My Master is very kind to me. I am now in the Second Form, am Learning Castalio and Ovid's Metamorphosis & I hope I shall be fit to go to College in two Years time which I am resolved to do, God willing and by your leave, I shant detain you any longer but only to give my Duty to your good self & Mother & love to my Brothers & Sisters. Please to give my Duty to my God father and to my Uncle & Aunt Adamson & love to Cozen Henry,

                    "Your dutifull Son,
                        "RICHARD HALL."

LETTERS FROM SCHOOL CHILDREN (1739, 1752)   From Alice M. Earle, *Child Life in Colonial Days* (New York, 1899), pp. 16, 80-81.

Letter from a School Girl

"HONOUR'D SIR: "PHILADELPHIA, March 30, 1739.

"Since my coming up I have entered with Mr. Hackett to improve my Dancing, and hope to make such Progress therein as may answer to the Expense, and enable me to appear well in any Public Company. The great Desire I have of pleasing you will make me the more Assiduous in my undertaking, and I arrive at any degree of Perfection it must be Attributed to the Liberal Education you bestow on me.

"I am with greatest Respect, Dear Pappa,
                    "Yr dutiful Daughter,
                        "MARY GRAFTON.
"RCHD GRAFTON, ESQ.,
New Castle, Delaware."

Letter from a School Boy

"TO MR. CORNELIUS TEN BROECK
        att Albany.
"Stamford, the 13th Day of October, 1752.
    "HONORED FETHAR,
    "These fiew lines comes to let you know that I am in a good State of Health and
I hope this may find you also. I have found all the things in my trunk but I must
have a pare of Schuse. And mama please to send me some Ches Nutts and some
Wall Nutts; you please to send me a Slate, and som pensals, and please to send me
some smok befe, and for bringing my trunk 3/9, and for a pare of Schuse 9 shillings.
You please to send me a pare of indin's Schuse. You please to send me some dride
corn. My Duty to Father and Mother and Sister and to all frinds.
                    "I am your Dutyfull Son,
                        "JOHN TEN BROECK.
"Father forgot to send me my Schuse."

RULES REGULATING A SCHOOLMASTER IN NEW AMSTERDAM

(1661) From Thomas Finegan, ed., *Free Schools: A Documentary History of the Free School Movement in New York State* (Albany, 1921), pp. 16-17.

Instructions and Rules for Schoolmaster Evert Pietersen drawn up by the Burgomasters of this city with advice of the Director General and Council

1. He shall take good care, that the children, coming to his school, do so at the usual hour, namely at eight in the morning and one in the afternoon.

2. He must keep good discipline among his pupils.

3. He shall teach the children and pupils the Christian Prayers, commandments, baptism, Lord's supper, and the questions with answers of the catechism, which are taught here every Sunday afternoon in the church.

4. Before school closes he shall let the pupils sing some verses and a psalm.

5. Besides his yearly salary he shall be allowed to demand and receive from every pupil quarterly as follows: For each child, whom he teaches the a b c, spelling and reading, 30 st.; for teaching to read and write, 50 st.; for teaching to read, write, and cipher, 60 st.; from those who come in the evening and between times pro rata a fair sum. The poor and needy, who ask to be taught for God's sake he shall teach for nothing.

6. He shall be allowed to demand and receive from everybody, who makes arrangements to come to his school and comes before the first half of the quarter

preceding the first of December next, the school dues for the quarter, but nothing from those, who come after the first half of the quarter.

7. He shall not take from anybody, more than is herein stated. Thus done and decided by the Burgomasters of the City of Amsterdam in N.N., November 4, 1661.

CONTRACT WITH A DUTCH SCHOOLMASTER IN FLATBUSH, NEW YORK (1682) From Daniel Pratt, ed., *Annals of Public Education in the State of New York, 1626-1746* (Albany, 1872), pp. 65-67.

School Service

I. The School shall begin at eight o'clock, and go out at eleven; and in the afternoon shall begin at one o'clock and end at four. The bell shall be rung when the school commences.

II. When the school begins, one of the children shall read the morning prayer, as it stands in the catechism, and close with the prayer before dinner; in the afternoon it shall begin with the prayer after dinner, and end with the evening prayer. The evening school shall begin with the Lord's prayer, and close by singing a psalm.

III. He shall instruct the children on every Wednesday and Saturday, in the common prayers, and the questions and answers in the catechism, to enable them to repeat them the better on Sunday before the afternoon service, or on Monday, when they shall be catechised before the congregation. Upon all such occasions, the schoolmaster shall be present, and shall require the children to be friendly in their appearance and encourage them to answer freely and distinctly.

IV. He shall be required to keep his school nine months in succession, from September to June, in each year, in case it should be concluded upon to retain his services for a year or more, or without limitation; and he shall then be required to be regulated by these articles, and to perform the same duties which his predecessor, Jan Thibaud, above named, was required to perform. In every particular therefore, he shall be required to keep school, according to this seven months agreement, and shall always be present himself.

Church Service

I. He shall keep the church clean, and ring the bell three times before the people assemble to attend the preaching and catechism. Also before the sermon is commenced, he shall read a chapter out of the Holy Scriptures, and that, between the second and third ringing of the bell. After the third ringing he shall read the ten commandments, and the twelve articles of our faith, and then take the lead in singing. In the afternoon after the third ringing of the bell, he shall read a short chapter, or one of the Psalms of David, as the congregation are assembling; and before divine service commences, shall introduce it, by the singing of a Psalm or Hymn.

II. When the minister shall preach at Brooklyn, or New-Utrecht, he shall be required to read twice before the congregation, from the book commonly used for that purpose. In the afternoon he shall also read a sermon on the explanation of the catechism, according to the usage and practice approved of by the minister. The children as usual, shall recite their questions and answers out of the catechism, on Sunday, and he shall instruct them therein. He, as chorister, shall not be required to perform these duties, whenever divine service shall be performed in Flatlands, as it would be unsuitable, and prevent many from attending there.

III. For the administration of Holy Baptism, he shall provide a basin with water, for which he shall be entitled to receive from the parents, or witnesses, twelve styvers. He shall, at the expense of the church, provide bread and wine, for the celebration of the Holy Supper; He shall be in duty bound promptly to furnish the minister with the name of the child to be baptized, and with the names of the parents and witnesses. And he shall also serve as minister for the consistory.

IV. He shall give the funeral invitations, dig the grave, and toll the bell, for which service he shall receive for a person of fifteen years and upwards, twelve guilders, and for one under that age, eight guilders. If he should be required to give invitations beyond the limits of the town, he shall be entitled to three additional guilders, for the invitation of every other town, and if he should be required to cross the river, and go to New York, he shall receive four guilders.

School Money

He shall receive from those who attend the day school, for a speller or reader, three guilders a quarter, and for a writer four guilders. From those who attend evening school, for a speller or reader, four guilders, and for a writer, six guilders shall be given.

Salary

In addition to the above, his salary shall consist of four hundred guilders, in grain, valued in Seewant, to be delivered at Brooklyn Ferry, and for his services from October to May, as above stated, a sum of two hundred and thirty-four guilders, in the same kind, with the dwellinghouse, barn, pasture lot and meadows, to the school appertaining. The same to take effect from the first day of October, instant.

Done and agreed upon in Consistory, under the inspection of the Honorable Constable and Overseers, the 8th, of October, 1682.

Constable and Overseers	*The Consistory*
CORNELIUS BARRIAN,	CASPARUS VAN ZUREN, *Minister,*
RYNIER AERTSEN,	ADRIAEN REYERSE,
JAN REMSEN,	CORNELIUS BARENT VANDWYCK.

I agree to the above articles, and promise to perform them according to the best of my ability.

Johannes van Eckkelen

REQUEST OF VIRGINIA ASSEMBLY FOR CHANGE IN LICENSING
SCHOOLMASTERS (1686) From H. R. McIlwaine, ed., *Journals of the House of Burgesses of Virginia, 1659/60-1693* (Richmond, 1931), pp. 270, 274.

To His Excellencie Ffrancis Lord Howard Baron of Effingham His Majesties Lt & Governor Genl of Virginia

The house of Burgesses now assembled, humbly present.

That whereas your Excellencie has been pleased by your late precept to command that all Schoolmasters should make their personall appearance at *James City* there to receive your Excellencies License & approbation to teach & that none Shall be admitted to that Office before they haue there taken out such a qualification and whereas this house doe too Sencibly vnderstand from their Respective Counties, that severall knowing skilfull Schoolmasters leave of their imploy because they are vnable out of such small allowance as they yearly have to endure the charge they are now necessarily exposed to, for the procuring of their Licenses to teach. This house doe therefore in the Name of themselves and all the inhabitants of this Countrey, humbly pray that for the greater ease of such as are willing to employ themselves in so necessary an vndertakeing, your Excellencie would please to appoint in every Countie, some One of such person or persons as to your Excellencie shall seem most fit, for the due examination of them, & that such persons vpon their well approueing their Capacities, may likewise haue power from your Excellency to grant them a license for so moderate & reasonable a fee, as in the like cases is vsuall & Customary to be paid in *England*.

* * *

Mr Speaker and Gentlemen.

I haue recd from you an Address relateing to Schoolmasters in that as in all other matters, I shall give you all reasonable satisfaction and therefore am to tell you, that what Comands to me I have giuen therein are pursueant to his Majesties Speciall Comands to me, as by the Instruction herewith sent vnto you, you may observe, in which not being so forward, as it was expected I should haue been, my memory was therein refreshed by the Lord Bishop of *London*, and as I am Comanded to haue it performed, so I am desireous to have it done with as much ease & encouragement to the inhabitants, as possible may be and as testimonies thereof I will direct, that Examination shall be taken of the fitness & abilities of persons presented for Schoolmasters by the next of his Majesties Councell of this Colonie, & vpon his approueing of the persons they shall be accordingly lycenced for Schoolmasters, with whom I shall cause to be left blanke lycenses vnder my hand & seale to be filled up with the name & names of such person & persons approued of, for which shall be required no more than a Small fee to my Clerke for the writeing the same. Signed

By his Excellencies Comand.
E. Chilton C Genl Assembly

SCHOOLMASTER EZEKIEL CHEEVER PETITIONS TO KEEP HIS POSITION (c. 1687) From H. F. Jenk, ed., *Catalogue of the Boston Public Latin School* (Boston, 1886), p. 268.

To his Excellency Sr. Edmund Andros Knight, Governour & Capt. Generall of his Majesties Territories & Dominions in New England.

The humble peticon of Ezekiel Cheever of Boston Schoolmr. Sheweth, that your poor peticoner hath neer fifty yeares been employed in ye work & office of a publick Grammar-Schoolmr. in severall places in this Countrey, With wt. acceptance & success I submit to the judgment of those, that are able to testify. Now seeing God is pleased mercifully yet to continue my wonted abilities in mind, health of body, vivacity of spirit, delight in my work, which alone I am in anyway fit for, & capable of, & whereby I have my outward subsistence. I almost humly entreat your Excellency, yt according to your former kindness often manifested, I may by your Excellencies favour, allowance, & encouragement still be continued in my present place. And whereas there is due to me about fifty five pounds for my labours past & ye former way of that part of my maintenance usually raised by a rate is thought good to be altered. I with all submission beseech your Excellency, that you would be pleased to give order for my due satisfaction, ye want of which would fall heavy upon me in my old age, & my children also who are otherwise poor enough.

And you poor peticonr. shall ever pray &c.

Your Excellencies most humble servt.
EZEKIEL CHEEVER

COTTON MATHER'S "AN ELEGY ON EZEKIEL CHEEVER" (1708) From Elizabeth Porter Gould, *Ezekiel Cheever, Schoolmaster* (Boston, 1904), pp. 78-84.

Augusto perstringere Carmine Laudes. Quas nulla Eloquij vis Celebrare queat

You that are men & thoughts of manhood know,
Be Just now to the Man that made you so.
Martyr'd by Scholars the stabb'd Cassian dies,
And falls to cursed Lads a Sacrifice.
Not so my Cheever; Not by Scholars slain,
But Prais'd and Lov'd, and wish'd to Life again.
A mighty Tribe of Well-instructed Youth
Tell what they owe to him, and Tell the Truth.
All the Eight parts of Speech he taught to them
They now Employ to Trumpet his Esteem,
They fill Fames Trumpet, and they spread a Fame
To last till the Last Trumpet drown the same.

Magister pleased them well, because 'twas he;

They saw that Bonus did with it agree.
While they said Amo, they the Hint improve
Him for to make the Object of their Love.
No Concord so Inviolate they knew
As to pay Honours to their Master due.
With Interjections they break off at last,
But, Ah, is all they use, Wo, and Alas!
We Learnt Prosodia, but with that Design
Our Master's Name should in our Verses shine.
Our Weeping Ovid but instructed us
To write upon his Death, De Tristibus.
Tully we read, but still with this Intent,
That in his praise we might be Eloquent,
Our Stately Virgil made us but Contrive
As our Anchises to keep him Alive.
When Phoenix, to Achilles was assign'd
A Master, then we thought not Homer blind:
A Phoenix, which Oh! might his Ashes shew!
So rare a Thing we thought our master too.
And if we made a Theme, 'twas with Regret
We might not on his Worth show all our Wit.

Go on, ye Grateful Scholars to proclame
To late Posterity your Master's Name.
Let it as many Languages declare
As on Loretto-Table do appear.

Too much to be by any one exprest:
I'll tell my share, and you shall tell the rest.
Ink is too vile a Liquor; Liquid Gold
Should fill the Pen, by which such things are told.
The Book should Amyanthus-Paper be
All writ with Gold, from all corruption free.

A Learned Master of the Languages
Which to Rich Stores of Learning are the Keyes;
He taught us first Good Sense to understand
And put the Golden Keys into our hand.
We but for him had been for Learning Dumb,
And had a sort of Turkish Mutes become.
Were Grammar quite Extinct, yet at his Brain
The Candle might have well been lit again.
If Rhet'rick had been stript of all her Pride
She from his Wardrobe might have been supply'd.
Do but Name Cheever, and the Echo straight
Upon that name, Good Latin, will Repeat.
A Christian Terence, master of the File
That arms the Curious to Reform their Style.
Now Rome and Athens from their Ashes rise;
See their Platonick Year with vast surprize:

And in our School a Miracle is wrought;
For the Dead Languages to Life are brought.

His Work he Lov'd: Oh! had we done the same!
Our Play-dayes still to him ungrateful came.
And yet so well our Work adjusted Lay,
We came to Work, as if we came to Play.
Our Lads had been, but for his wondrous Cares,
Boyes of my Lady Mores unquiet Pray'rs.
Sure were it not for such informing Schools,
Our Lat'ran too would soon be fill'd with Owles.
'Tis Corlet's pains, and Cheever's we must own,
That thou, New England, art not Scythia grown.
The Isles of Silly had o'er-run this Day
The Continent of our America.
Grammar he taught, which 'twas his work to do;
But he would Hagar have her place to know.

The Bible is the sacred Grammar, where
The Rules of speaking well, contained are.
He taught us Lilly, and he Gospel taught;
And us poor Children to our Saviour brought.
Master of Sentences, he gave us more
Than we in our Sententiae had before.
We Learn't Good Things in Tullies Offices;
But we from him Learn't Better things than these.
With Cato's he to us the Higher gave.
Lessons of Jesus, that our Souls do save.
We Constru'd Ovid's Metamorphosis,
But on ourselves charg'd, not a change to miss.
Young Austin wept, when he saw Dido dead,
Tho' not a Tear for a Lost Soul he had;
Our Master would not let us be so vain,
But us from Virgil did to David train,
Textors Epistles would not Cloathe our Souls;
Pauls too we heard; we went to School at Pauls.

Syrs, Do you not Remember well the Times,
When us he warn'd against our Youthful Crimes;
What Honey dropt from our old Nestors mouth
When with his counsels he Reform'd our Youth;
How much he did to make us Wise and Good;
And with what Prayers, his work he did conclude.
Concern'd that when from him we Learning had,
It might not Armed Wickedness be made!
The Sun shall first the Zodiac forsake,
And Stones unto the Stars their Flight shall make;
First shall the Summer bring large drifts of Snow,
And beauteous Cherries in December grow;
Ere of those Charges we Forgetful are
Which we, O man of God, from thee did hear.

Such Tutors to the Little Ones would be.
Such that in Flesh we should their Angels see;
Ezekiel should not be the Name of such;
We'd Agathangelus not think too much.

Who Serv'd the School, the Church did not forget;
But Thought, and Pray'd, and often wept for it.

Mighty in Prayer: How did he wield thee, Pray'r!
Thou Reverst Thunder: Christ's-Sides-piercing spear?
Soaring we saw the Bird of Paradise:
So Wing'd by Thee, for Flights beyond the Skies.
How oft we saw him tread the Milky Way,
Which to the Glorious Throne of Mercy lay!

Come from the Mount, he shone with ancient Grace,
Awful the Splendor of his Aged Face.
Cloath'd in the Good Old Way, his Garb did wage
A War with the Vain Fashions of the Age,
Fearful of nothing more than hateful Sin;
'Twas that from which he laboured all to win,
Zealous; And in Truths Cause ne'r known to trim;
No Neuter Gender there allow'd by him.
Stars but a Thousand did the Ancients know;
On later Globes they Nineteen hundred grow;
Now such a Cheever added to the Sphere
Makes an Addition to the Lustre there.
Meantime America a Wonder saw;
A Youth in Age, forbid by Nature's Law.

You that in t'other Hemisphere do dwell,
Do of Old Age your dismal Stories tell.
You tell of Snowy Heads and Rheumy Eyes
And things that make a man himself despise,
You say a frozen Liquor chills the Veins,
And scarce the Shadow of a man remains,
Winter of Life, that Sapless Age you call,
And of all Maladies the Hospital;
The Second Nonage of the Soul; the Brain
Cover'd with Cloud; the Body all in pain,
To weak Old Age, you say, there must belong,
Trembling Palsey both of Limb and Tongue;
Dayes all Decrepit; and a Bending Back,
Propt by a Staff, in Hands that ever shake.

Nay, Syrs, our Cheever shall confute you all.
On whom there did none of these Mischefs fall,
He Liv'd and to vast Age no Illness knew;
Till Times Scythe waiting for him Rusty grew.
He Liv'd and Wrought; his Labours were immense;
But ne'er Declined to Praeter perfect Tense.

A Blooming Youth in him at Ninety-Four
We saw; But Oh! when such a sight before!
At Wondrous Age he did his Youth resume,
As when the Eagle mews his Aged plume.
With Faculties of Reason still so bright,
And at Good Services so Exquisite;
Sure our sound Chiliast, we wondering thought,
To the First Resurrection is not brought!
No, He for That was waiting at the Gate,
In the Pure Things that fit a Candidate.
He in Good Actions did his Life Employ,
And to make others Good, he made his Joy,
Thus well-appris'd now of the Life to Come,
To Live here was to him a Martyrdom,
Our brave Macrobius Long'd to see the Day
Which others dread, of being Call'd away,
So, Ripe with Age, he does invite the Hook,
Which watchful does for its large Harvest look;
Death gently cut the Stalk, and kindly laid
Him, where our God His Granary has made.

Who at New-Haven first began to Teach,
Dying Unshipwreck'd, does White-Haven reach.
At that Fair-Haven they all Storms forget;
He there his Davenport with Love does meet.
The Luminous Robe, the Loss whereof with Shame
Our Parents wept, when Naked they became;
Those Lovely Spirits wear it, and therein
Serve God with Priestly Glory, free from Sin.

But in his Paradisian Rest above
To Us does the Blest Shade retain his Love.

With Rip'ned Thoughts Above concern'd for Us,
We can't but hear him dart his Wishes, thus.
'Tutors, Be Strict; But yet be Gentle too,
'Don't by fierce Cruelties fair Hopes undo,
'Dream not, that they who are to Learning slow,
'Will mend by Arguments in Ferio,
'Who keeps the Golden Fleece, Oh, let him not
'A Dragon be, tho' he Three Tongues have got.
'Why can you not to Learning find the way,
'But thro' the Province of Severia?
''Twas Moderatus, who taught Origen;
'A Youth which prov'd one of the Best of men.
'The Lads with Honour first and Reason Rule;
'Blowes are but for the Refractory Fool.
'But, Oh! First Teach them their Great God to fear;
'That you like me, with joy may meet them here.'

H' has said!—

Adieu a little while, Dear Saint, Adieu;
Your Scholar won't be long, Sir, after you.
In the mean time, with Gratitude I must
Engrave an Epitaph upon your Dust.
'Tis true, Excessive Merits rarely safe;
Such an Excess forfeits an Epitaph;
But if Base men the Rules of Justice break,
The Stories (at least upon the Tombs) will speak.

TEACHERS' SALARIES IN BOSTON (1747)   From Robert F. Seybolt, *The Public Schools of Colonial Boston, 1635-1775* (Cambridge, Mass., 1935), p. 29.

Town meeting minutes of May 12, 1747

The Petition of M^r. Zachariah Hicks master of the North Writing School setting forth that four Years ago he had Two hundred & Eighty Pounds old tenor Bills granted him by the Town for his Support which at that time was to his full content and Satisfaction, but within that course of Years the currency of the province has sunk in its Value to that Degree that the aforesaid Sum is become very far Short of Answering the purpose for which it was designed, and he is thereby Exposed to such Difficulties as are too great an Incumbrance to him in the faithful Discharge of his Trust, Praying the Town to Grant him such further allowance as they shall think proper, was now read & after some Debate thereon.—

Voted that the Sum of one hundred Pounds old tenor Bills be Added to M^r. Hicks's Sallary for the Year ensuing, the same to be paid him Quarterly, and to Commence the 22^d. of March last.

TEACHERS' SALARIES IN BOSTON (1762)   From Robert F. Seybolt, *The Public Schools of Colonial Boston, 1635-1775* (Cambridge, Mass., 1935), p. 41.

Meeting of the Freeholders and other inhabitants, May 11, 1762

The Petition of a number of the Masters of the Town Schools, setting forth, that they meet with great difficultys in obtaining payment of the several Salaries which the Town has been pleased to assign them—that notwithstanding a Vote formerly passed for their payment Quarterly, they having been to their great distress kept out of their pay from Year to Year, and for what they do receive at any time are obliged to the friendship of particular Gentlemen, who by the kind permission of the Collectors, are willing to pay their Taxes into their hands, that your Petitioners have some of them nine some twelve and some eighteen Months Salary due to them—that they are informed that the greatest part of the Taxes belonging to the Town is already paid in, or engaged to others, so that they have no prospect of any further payment till the new Taxes are issued, which tis probable will not be done till some time in the next Winter—that this delay of payment obliges them to purchase the necessarys of life at a disadvantage Upon long Credit, or to become troublesome to their friends by borrowing Money for their Supplys, not to mention the continual sollicitude and anxiety which such dependant circumstances necessarily create.—The same being read, and duly considered, it appear'd to the Town that the most likely method to answer the end proposed by the Petitioners must be the raising or borrowing a sum of Money sufficient to defray the common and extraordinary charges of the Year; it was therefore

Voted that the sum of Eight Thousand Pounds be raised by a Tax upon the Polls and Estates within this Town for relief of the Poor, and defreying other necessary Charges, arising within the Town the ensuing Year—

*　　*　　*

Voted, that M^r. David Jeffries Treasurer of the Town be an hereby is directed and fully Impower'd to borrow upon Interest of any Person or Persons, a Sum not exceeding Fifteen hundred Pounds lawful Mony, for the Payment of the School-Masters Salarys now due; the wages of the Watch, as also what may be owing to the Master of the Alms House; the Money so borrowed to be repaid in twelve Months out of the £8000—now Voted to be raised by a Tax.

RELIGIOUS REQUIREMENT FOR THE MASTER OF A SCHOOL IN CHARLESTON, SOUTH CAROLINA (1712)   From Thomas Cooper and David J. McCord, eds., *The Statutes at Large of South Carolina* (Columbia, S.C., 1836-41), vol. II, p. 393.

That the person to be master of the said school shall be of the religion of the Church of *England,* and conform to the same, and shall be capable to teach the learned languages, that is to say, Latin and Greek tongues, and to catechise and instruct the youth in the principles of the Christian religion, as professed in the Church of England.

RELIGIOUS REQUIREMENT FOR THE MASTER OF A SCHOOL IN NEWBURN, NORTH CAROLINA (1773) From *Complete Revisal of All the Acts of the Assembly, of the Province of North Carolina, 1773*, p. 359.

No Person shall be admitted to be Master of the said School, but who is of the established Church of *England;* and who, at the Recommendation of the Trustees or Directors, or the Majority of them, shall be duly licensed by the Governor, or Commander in Chief for the Time being.

INDENTURE OF JOHN CAMPBELL TO A NEW YORK SCHOOLMASTER (1722) From Robert F. Seybolt, ed., *Source Studies in American Colonial Education: The Private School* (Urbana, Ill., 1925), pp. 85-86.

This Indenture Wittnesseth that John Campbel Son of Robert Campbell of the City of New York with the Consent of his father and mother hath put himself and by these presents doth Voluntarily put and bind himself Apprentice to George Brownell of the Same City Schoolmaster to learn the Art Trade or Mystery and with the Said George Brownell to Serve from the twenty ninth day of May one thousand seven hundred and twenty one for and during the Term of ten years and three Months to be Compleat and Ended During all which term the said Apprentice his said Master and Mistress faithfully Shall Serve their Secrets keep and Lawfull Commands gladly everywhere obey he Shall do no damage to his said Master or Mistress nor suffer it to be done by others without Letting or Giving Notice thereof to his said Master or Mistress he shall not Waste his said Master or Mistress Goods or Lend them Unlawfully to any he shall not Committ fornication nor Contract Matrimony within the Said Term at Cards Dice or any other unlawfull Game he shall not Play: he Shall not absent himself by Day or by Night from his Said Master or Mistress Service without their Leave; nor haunt Alehouses Taverns or Playhouses but in all things behave himself as a faithfull Apprentice ought to Do towards his said Master or Mistress during the Said Term. And the said George Brownell Doth hereby Covenant and Promise to teach and Instruct or Cause the said Apprentice to be taught and Instructed in the Art Trade or Calling of a Schoolmaster by the best way or means he or his wife may or can if the Said Apprentice be Capable to Learn and to find and Provide unto the Said Apprentice sufficient meat Drink Apparel Lodging and washing fitting for an Apprentice during the Said Term: and at the Expiration thereof to give unto the Said Apprentice one Suit of Cloth new Consisting of a coatvest coat and Breeches also one New hatt Six New Shirts Three pair of Stockings one pair of New Shoes Suitable for his said Apprentice.

In Testimony Whereof the Parties to these Presents have hereunto Interchangeably Sett their hands and Seals the third day of August in the Eighth year of the Reign of our Sovereign Lord George King of Great Brittain &c. Anno Domini One thousand seven hundred and Twenty One. John Campbel. Signed Sealed and Delivered in the presence of Mary Smith Cornelius Kiersted Memorandum

SCHOOLBOOKS. AND SCHOOLTEACHERS

Appeared before me John Cruger Esq. Alderman and One of his Majesties Justices of the Peace for this City and County. John Campbell and Acknowledged the within Indenture to be his Voluntary Act and Deed New York the 9th Aprill 1722.

EIGHTEENTH CENTURY ADVERTISEMENTS FOR RUNAWAY SCHOOLMASTERS
From Ellwood P. Cubberley, ed., *Readings in Public Education in the United States* (Boston, 1934), pp. 70-71.

Pennsylvania Gazette, June 6, 1751.

Run away on the 28th of last month, from his bail, Samuel Jaques, and James Marshall, of Elizabeth town, Essex county, in East New-Jersey, one Edward Kite, an English man, about 30 years of age, of middle stature, brown complexion, has a fresh colour, black eyes, and has a bold look: Had on when he went away, an old green jacket, an old bob wig, and a speckled shirt, He had some time ago broke one of his Legs, which by observing, will be found to be a little crooked, and is somewhat thicker than the other. He is a cooper by trade, but has lately taught school, and writes a good round hand. Whoever takes up and secures said Edward Kite, so as his bail may have him again, shall have Four Pounds reward, and reasonable Charges, paid by

Samuel Jaques, and James Marshall

N. B. All masters of vessels, and others, are forbid to harbour or carry him off, at their peril.

New York Gazette or Weekly Post-Boy, January 14, 1754.

Run away on the 25th of December last, from John Scott, of Hanover Township, Morris County, and Province of New-Jersey, a Servant Man named James Murphy, about Five Feet, 8 Inches high, much pitted with the Small-Pox, long yellow hair tyed behind: he has been a Soldier in the French Service, talks good French. Served with said Scott, as a School-Master; had on when he went away a new Bearskine Coat with broad Hair Buttons, a light colour'd Rateen Jacket, check Shirt, and Leather Breeches; new Worsted Stockings, and new Pumps. Who ever secures said Servant, so as his Master may have him again, shall have Forty Shillings Reward and reasonable Charges paid by me

John Scott

N. B. All masters of Vessels are discharged on their peril, from carrying him off.

Pennsylvania Gazette, November 25, 1756.

Broke out of Chester gaol, last night, one James Rockett, a very short well set fellow, pretends to be a schoolmaster, of a fair complexion, and smooth fac'd; Had on when he went away, a light coloured camblet coat, a blue cloth jacket, without sleeves, a check shirt, a pair of old dy'd leather breeches, grey worsted stockings, a pair of half worn pumps, and an almost new beaver hat; his hair is cut off, and wears a cap; he is a great taker of snuff, and very apt to get drunk; he has with him two certificatès, one from some inhabitants in Burlington county, Jersey, which he will no doubt produce as a pass. Who ever takes up and secures said Rockett in any gaol, shall have two Pistoles reward, paid by October 27, 1756.

Samuel Smith, Gaoler

Pennsylvania Gazette, December 16, 1756.
Went away from Depford township, Gloucester county, in west-Jersey, a schoolmaster, named Samuel Willis, of little stature, thin face, and pale complexion. Who ever will give information to said Arrell where said Willis is, shall have Twenty Shillings reward.

RICHARD ARRELL

New York Gazette or Weekly Post-Boy, May 1, 1766.
Run away from his Employers, the 12th Insant, one William Serols, of a small Stature, black curl'd Hair; had on when he went away, a blue Broad Cloth Coat, has been newly turned; a blue spotted Swanskin Jacket and blue Breeches: He has taken off Things that were not his own. He has taught a School, and has formerly been in His Majesty's Service. Who ever takes up said Serles, so that he may be brought to Justice, shall have FORTY SCHILLINGS Reward, and all reasonable Charges, paid by us,

William Sparling
David Williamson

New-Brunswick, Middlesex County, New Jersey, April 12, 1766.

TEACHER QUALIFICATIONS IN NEW JERSEY (1760)   From Willard Elsbree, *The American Teacher* (New York, 1939), p. 42.

New York, November 5.
On the 21st Instant, his Excellency Thomas Boone, Esq., Governor of New Jersey, issued a proclamation setting forth, that whereas the Education of Youth is a Matter of great Consequence, and ought not to be trusted but to Persons of good Character, and loyal Principles, and professed Protestants; therefore he requires all Magistrates to inform themselves sufficiently of the Character of the School-Masters in the Province; to administer the Oaths to them, and give them, under the Hands of two, a Certificate of Approbation, by which they may obtain a License; and forbidding all Persons, after the 31st of December, to execute the Office of a Schoolmaster without such License first obtain'd.

ADVERTISEMENT FOR A SERVANT SCHOOLMASTER IN PENNSYLVANIA (1735)   From Ellwood P. Cubberley, ed., *Readings in Public Education in the United States* (Boston, 1934), p. 69.

Pennsylvania Gazette, February 4, 1735.

Any Person who has a Servant to dispose of that is a Scholar, and can teach Children Reading, Writing, and Arithmetick, may hear of a Purchaser by enquiry of the Printer hereof.

ADVERTISEMENT FOR A SERVANT SCHOOLMASTER IN MARYLAND (1786)   From Robert F. Seybolt, ed., *Source Studies in American Colonial Education: The Private School* (Urbana, Ill., 1925), p. 84.

Men and Women Servants
JUST ARRIVED

In the Ship Paca, Robert Caulfield, Master, in five Weeks from Belfast and Cork, a number of healthy Men and Women SERVANTS.

Among them are several valuable tradesmen, viz.

Carpenters, Shoemakers, Coopers, Blacksmiths, Staymakers, Bookbinders, Clothiers, Diers, Butchers, Schoolmasters, Millwrights, and Labourers.

Their indentures are to be disposed of by the Subscribers,

Brown, and Maris,

Baltimore, May 29, 1786.   William Wilson

A PENNSYLVANIA SCHOOLMASTER'S TEACHING METHODS (1730)   From J. P. Wickersham, ed., *A History of Education in Pennsylvania* (Lancaster, Pa., 1886), p. 214.

SIR, you required an account of my method of instruction in school. I endeavor, for beginners, to get Primers with syllables, viz., from one to 2, 3, 4, 5, 6, 7 or 8. I take them several times over them till they are perfect, by way of repeating according as I find occasion, and then to some place forward according to their capacity and commonly every two or three leaves. I make them repeat perhaps two or three times over, and when they get the Primer pretty well I serve them so in the Psalter, and we have some Psalters with the proverbs at the latter end. I give them that to learn, the which I take to be very agreeable, and still follow repetitions till I find they are masters of such places. Then I move them into such places as I judge they are fit for, either in the New or Old Testament, and as I find they advance I move them not regarding the beginning nor ending of the Bible, but moving them where I think they may have benefit by. So making of them perfect in the vowels, consonants and dipthongs, and when they go on in their reading clean without any noising, singing or stumbling, with deliberate way, then I set them to begin the Bible in order to go throughout. And when I begin writing I follow them in the letters till they come to cut pretty clean letters and then one syllable and so to 2, 3, 4, and to the longest words, and when they join handsomely I give them some sweet pleasing verses, some perhaps on their business, some on behaviour, and some on their duty to parents, etc., of such I seldom want them to command, and when they come to manage double copies readily I give them some delightful sentences or Proverbs or some places in the Psalms or any part of the Bible as they are of forwardness and also to other fancies that may be for their benefit. And when I set them cyphering I keep them to my old fancy of repeating and shall go over every rule till they are in a case to move forward and so on. And I find no way that goes beyond that of repeating both in spelling, reading, writing and cyphering, and several gentlemen, viz., Ministers and others have commended it and some schoolmasters take to it, and though I speak it I have met with no children of the standing or time of mine, could come up with them on all accounts or hardly upon any; I also give them tasks, when able, to learn out of books according to their ability, but one girl exceeded all. She had a great many parts in the Bible by heart and had the whole book of St. John and hardly would miss a word. I put them to spell twice a week and likewise to Catechism, and likewise I catechise every Saturday and often on Thursdays. Sometimes I set them to sing Psalms.

AGREEMENT BETWEEN THE CONGREGATION OF THE REFORMED CHURCH, LANCASTER, PENNSYLVANIA, AND A TEACHER (1747) From J. P. Wickersham, ed., *A History of Education in Pennsylvania* (Lancaster, Pa., 1886), p. 140.

On this day, May 4th, 1747, I, the undersigned, John Hoffman, parochial teacher of the church at Lancaster, have promised in the presence of the congregation to serve as chorister, and as long as we have no pastor, to read sermons on Sunday. In summer, I promise to hold catechetical instruction with the young, as becomes a faithful teacher, and also to lead them in singing; and to attend to the clock. On the other hand, the congregation promises me an annual salary consisting of voluntary offerings from all the members of the church, to be written in a special register and arranged according to the amounts contributed, so that the teacher may be adequately compensated for his labor.

Furthermore, I have firmly and irrevocably agreed with the congregation on the aforesaid date that I will keep school on every working day during the entire year, as is the usual custom, and in such a manner as becomes a faithful teacher. In consideration thereof they promise me a free dwelling and four cords of wood, and have granted me the privilege of charging for each child that may come to school the sum of five shillings (I say 5 sh.) for three months, and for the whole year one pound (I write £1). I promise to enter upon my duties without fail, if alive and well, on the 24th of November, 1747.

CHRISTOPHER DOCK ON EDUCATION (1770) From *The Schulordnung* as quoted in Martin Brumbaugh, ed., *The Life and Works of Christopher Dock* (Philadelphia, 1908), pp. 104-14, 118-28.

Concerning Friend Saur's first question, how I receive the children at school, I proceed as follows: the child is first given a welcome by the other children, who extend their hands to him. Then I ask him if he will be diligent and obedient. If he promises this, he is told how to behave; and when he can say his A B C's and point out each letter with his index finger, he is put into the Ab. When he reaches this class his father owes him a penny, and his mother must fry him two eggs for his diligence, and the same reward is due him with each advance; for instance, when he enters the word class. But when he enters the reading class, I owe him a present, if he reaches the class in the required time and has been diligent, and the first day this child comes to school he receives a note stating: "Diligent. One pence." This means he has been admitted to the school; but it is also explained to him that if he is lazy or disobedient his note is taken from him. Continued disinclination to learn and stubbornness causes the pupil to be proclaimed lazy and inefficient before the whole class, and he is told that he belongs in a school for incorrigibles. Then I ask the child again if he will be obedient and diligent. Answering yes, he is shown his place. If it is a boy, I ask the other boys, if a girl, I ask the girls, who among them will take care of this new child and teach it. According to the extent to which the child is known, or its pleasant or unpleasant appearance, more or less children express their willingness. If none apply, I ask who will teach this child for a certain time for a bird or a writing-copy. Then it is seldom difficult to get a response. This is a description of my way of receiving the child into school.

Further Report Concerning the
Assembling of the Children at School:

The children arrive as they do because some have a great distance to school, others a short distance, so that the children cannot assemble as punctually as they can in a city. Therefore, when a few children are present, those who can read their Testament sit together on one bench; but the boys and girls occupy separate benches. They are given a chapter which they read at sight consecutively. Meanwhile I write copies for them. Those who have read their passage of Scripture without error take their places at the table and write. Those who fail have to sit at the end of the bench, and each new arrival the same; as each one is thus released in order he takes up his slate. This process continues until they have all assembled. The last one left on the bench is a "lazy pupil."

When all are together, and examined, whether they are washed and combed, they sing a psalm or a morning hymn, and I sing and pray with them. As much as they can understand of the Lord's Prayer and the ten commandments (according to the gift God has given them), I exhort and admonish them accordingly. This much concerning the assembling of pupils. But regarding prayer I will add this additional explanation. Children say the prayers taught them at home half articulately, and too fast, especially the "Our Father" which the Lord Himself taught His disciples and which contains all that we need. I therefore make a practice of saying it for them kneeling, and they kneeling repeat it after me. After these devotional exercises those who can write resume their work. Those who cannot read the Testament have had time during the assemblage to study their lesson. These are heard recite immediately after prayer. Those who know their lesson receive an O on the hand, traced with crayon. This is a mark of excellence. Those who fail more than three times are sent back to study their lesson again. When all the little ones have recited, these are asked again, and any one having failed in more than three trials a second time is called "Lazy" by the entire class and his name is written down. Whether such a child fear the rod or not, I know from experience that this denunciation of the children hurts more than if I were constantly to wield and flourish the rod. If then such a child has friends in school who are able to instruct him and desire to do so, he will visit more frequently than before. For this reason: if the pupil's name has not been erased before dismissal the pupils are at liberty to write down the names of those who have been lazy, and take them along home. But if the child learns his lesson well in the future, his name is again presented to the other pupils, and they are told that he knew his lesson well and failed in no respect. Then all the pupils call "Diligent" to him. When this has taken place his name is erased from the slate of lazy pupils, and the former transgression is forgiven.

The children who are in the spelling class are daily examined in pronunciation. In spelling, when a word has more than one syllable, they must repeat the whole word, but some, while they can say the letters, cannot pronounce the word, and so cannot be put to reading. For improvement a child must repeat the lesson, and in this way: The child gives me the book, I spell the word and he pronounces it. If he is slow, another pupil pronounces it for him, and in this way he hears how it should be done, and knows that he must follow the letters and not his own fancy.

Concerning A B C pupils, it would be best, having but one child, to let it learn one row of letters at a time, to say forward and backward. But with many, I let them learn the alphabet first, and then ask a child to point out a letter that I name. If a child is backward or ignorant, I ask another, or the whole class, and the first one that points to the right letter, I grasp his finger and hold it until I have put a mark opposite his name. I then ask for another letter, &c. Whichever child has during the day received the greatest number of marks, has pointed out the greatest number of letters. To him I owe something—a flower drawn on paper or a bird. But if several have the same number, we draw lots; this causes less annoyance. In this way not only are the very timid cured of their shyness (which is a great hindrance in learning), but a fondness for school is increased. Thus much in answer to his question, how I take the children into school, how school proceeds before and after prayers, and how the inattentive and careless are made attentive and careful, and how the timid are assisted.

Further I will state that when the little ones have recited for the first time, I give the Testament pupils a verse to learn. Those reading newspapers and letters sit separately, and those doing sums sit separately. But when I find that the little ones are good enough at their reading to be fit to read the Testament, I offer them to good Testament readers for instruction. The willing teacher takes the pupil by the hand and leads him to his seat. I give them two verses to try upon. But if I find that another exercise is necessary after this (such as finding a passage in Scripture, or learning a passage, in which case each reads a verse), I give only one verse, which is not too hard for those trying to read in the Testament. If pupils are diligent and able, they are given a week's trial, in which time they must learn their lesson in the speller with the small pupils and also their lesson with the Testament pupil. If they stand the test they are advanced the next week from the spelling to the Testament class, and they are also allowed to write. But those who fail in the Testament remain a stated time in the A B C class before they are tested again. After the Testament pupils have recited, the little ones are taken again. This done they are reminded of the chapter read them, and asked to consider the teaching therein. As it is the case that this thought is also expressed in other passages of Holy Writ, these are found and read, and then a hymn is given containing the same teaching. If time remains, all are given a short passage of Scripture to learn. This done, they must show their writing exercises. These are examined and numbered, and then the first in turn is given a hard word to spell. If he fails the next must spell it and so on. The one to spell correctly receives his exercise. Then the first is given another hard word, and so each receives his exercise by spelling a word correctly.

As the children carry their dinner, an hour's liberty is given them after dinner. But as they are usually inclined to misapply their time if one is not constantly with them, one or two of them must read a story of the Old Testament (either from Moses and the Prophets, or from Solomon's or Sirach's Proverbs), while I write copies for them. This exercise continues during the noon hour.

It is also to be noted that children find it necessary to ask to leave the room, and one must permit them to do this, not wishing the uncleanness and odor in the school. But the clamor to go out would continue all day, and sometimes without need, so that occasionally two or three are out at the same time, playing. To prevent this I have driven a nail in the door-post, on which hangs a wooden tag. Any one needing to leave the room looks for the tag. If it is on the nail, this is his permit to go out without asking. He takes the tag out with him. If another wishes to leave, he does not ask either, but stands by the door until the first returns, from whom he takes the tag and goes. If the tag is out too long, the one wishing to go inquires who was out last, and from it can be ascertained to whom he gave the tag, so that none can remain out too long.

To teach the uninitiated numbers and figures, I write on the blackboard (which hangs where all can see) these figures

1   2   3   4   5   6   7   8   9   0

far apart, that other figures can be put before and behind them. Then I put an 0 before the 1 and explain that this does not increase the number. Then I erase the 0 and put it after the 1, so that it makes 10. If two ciphers follow it makes 100, if three follow, 1000, &c. This I show them through all the digits. This done I affix to the 1 another 1, making 11. But if an 0 is put between it makes 101, but if it be placed after, it makes 110. In a similar manner I go through all the digits. When this is done I give them something to find in the Testament or hymnal. Those who are quickest have something to claim for their diligence, from me or at home.

As it is desirable for intelligent reading to take note of commas, but as the inexperienced find this difficult, I have this rule: If one of the Testament pupils does not read on, but stops before he reaches a comma or period, this counts one-fourth failure. Similarly if one reads over a comma, it is one-fourth failure. Repeating a word counts one-half. Then all failures are noted, and especially where each one has failed. When all have read, all those who have failed must step forward and according to the number of errors stand in a row. Those who have not failed move up, and the others take the lowest positions.

Regarding the correspondence, I may say that for twelve years I kept two schools, as already said, and for four summers (during the three months that I had free owing to the harvest) I taught school at Germantown. Then the pupils in Skippack, when I went to Sollford, gave me letters, and when I returned, the Sollford pupils did likewise. It was so arranged that Pupils of equal ability corresponded. When one became his correspondent's superior, he wrote to another whose equal he tried to be.

The superscription was only this: My friendly greeting to N. N. The contents of the letter consisted of a short rhyme, or a passage from Scripture, and they told something of their school exercises (their motto for the week and where it is described, &c.). Sometimes one would give the other a question to be answered by a passage of Scripture. I doubt not, if two schoolmasters (dwelling in one place or not) loving one another and desiring their pupils to love one another, were to do this in the love of God, it would bear fruit.

This is a piecemeal description of how children are taught letters, and how their steps are led from one degree to the next, before they can be brought to the aim that we have in view to the glory of God and for their own salvation, and which will be last discussed.

Now regarding his second question: How different children need different treatment, and how according to the greatness of the offense punishment must be increased or lessened.

I should gladly tell my friend all of this truly, but as the subject is such a broad one, I really do not know where to begin or end. This is because the wickedness of youth exhibits itself in so many ways, and the offenses which are taught them by those older than themselves are so various.

*   *   *

Because, as has been said, it would take too long to enumerate all cases, I shall give my friend only a few, together with the means that I have sought to apply. But these means cannot cure the damage. The Lord of Lords, who holds all in His hand, and for whose help we need much to pray in such cases, deserves all the praise if we see improvement.

First, among many children swearing or cursing is so common, expressing itself variously in so many wicked words. If this evil is not warded off, such sour "leaven leavens the whole lump," therefore such children are carefully examined, whether they understand what they are saying. As it is frequently very evident that they do not, they are asked whether they have thought of the words themselves or have heard them; they usually reply that they have heard them from So and So. If asked why they say it also, the answer is usually again, because So and So said it. Thus often ignorance is shown. They do not know why they are saying it. To such it must be explained that they must guard against such words; that they are against God's will and command. If they hear So and So use them, they should tell that person that he or she is doubly sinning, for they got into trouble in school by repeating the words. If such children then promise not to use the words again, they go free the first time. But if after being warned they persist in the bad habit, after being certain that the accusation is true, they are put upon the punishment seat, with the yoke on their neck, as a sign of punishment. On promising to be good in the future they escape with a few slaps. If they again offend, the punishment is increased, and they must furnish surety. The oftener the offense, the more bondsmen. These bondsmen's business is to warn and remind the offender and prevent repetition. This is the rein and the bit to be put into their mouths for such offense, but the change of heart must come from a higher hand, and must be sought with diligent prayer.

*   *   *

I am further asked how I teach the children to refrain from talking, and train them to silence. To this I reply, that it is the hardest lesson for children to learn, and they would hardly do it of their own free will. It takes them long to learn to speak, and having learned they are loath to give up the privilege. But nothing more edifying can be taught children than that there is a time to speak and a time to keep silent, and none more difficult to instil. Indeed, it would seem that we grown ones have not learned this lesson too well ourselves, for we should often be more careful when to speak and when to keep silence. And the little organ, the tongue, is not easily tamed, nor can one punish it with the rod, as other organs. And the mischief done by words is done through the tongue, according to the constitution of the heart (Matth. xii, 25). Although often the talking done among children is not due to evil intention, nothing can be accomplished unless talking and silence each have their time. I have devised several means, all of which worked for a time, but not permanently, so that something new had to be tried. My method is as follows:

First, when the lesson is assigned, they learn it, after the custom of this country and England, by repeating aloud. To keep them all at work I move among them until I think they have had time enough to learn the lesson. Then I rap with the rod on the blackboard and there is silence. I now ask the first to recite; meanwhile a monitor, who has been detailed to this duty, stands on a bench or other high place where he can see all and reports the Christian and surname of each one who talks, studies aloud or does anything else that is forbidden. He also writes the name down. As some use partiality in this work, those who have been proven to be untruthful are discharged from the work unless they apply, and promise to be honest. Also those who have been on the punishment seat for lying are not allowed to be monitors, unless they prove truthful through a period of time. Thus provided with a monitor, one can hear the lesson or go on with something else that is instructive, without interruption. When the work is over this may be forgotten. But if it is noticed that the talkers take advantage of being forgotten, those noted by the monitor must come forward and sit on the punishment bench, one by one. They are given their choice between wearing the yoke or a rap on the hand. Most of them extend their hand for the rod.

This is the information asked for regarding the way I keep the children quiet, but it is by no means my intention to force this method upon any one else. Each must arrange his affairs in the best way that he can. But if my management written here by request and not from choice, should be in any way objected to, because it differs from that of Germany and other places, I will say in defense, that conditions here are different. Among the free inhabitants of Pennsylvania schools are differently constituted from those in Germany. For a schoolmaster there is definitely installed by the government, and the common man cannot readily remove him, hence he is in no great danger if he is too hard with children. Although I freely confess, even if I were thus installed by high authorities, I should still feel that the power to be hard with children was given me for their good. Now experience teaches that a timid child is harmed rather than benefited by harsh words or much application of the rod, and to improve it, other means must be employed. Likewise a stupid child is only harmed. A child that is treated to too much flogging at home is not benefited by it at school, but it is made still worse. If such children are to be helped, it must happen through other means. . . .

*   *   *

Regarding my friend's question, how I treat the children with love that they both love and fear me, I will say that in this respect I cannot take the least credit upon myself, if I am at all successful with children, either in teaching or in performing religious duties. First I owe God particular thanks, because besides calling me to this profession He has given me an extreme love of children. For if it were not for love it would be an unbearable burden to live among children. But love bears and never tires. If a natural mother did not love her children all the little incidents in the education of a child would be unbearably wearisome, but her love makes this burden light. . . .

I have told the friend in answer to his question regarding my treatment of the children with love, that I can take no credit for it. Love is a gift of God. According as one desires it, it is given and according as one guards and uses it, so it can be increased or diminished. But perhaps it can be stated by what qualities one can help or hinder love, profit or lose by it. The divine footprints that we follow in seeking righteous love show us that it is universal and extends to all creatures. "He letteth his sun shine on the wicked and the good, and sendeth rain to the just and the unjust." To partake of the love of God man must follow these footprints. They will guide him in love, from one love to another by a consideration of creatures and protecting them.

The great work of the redemption of the human race was also universal, and if we had accepted it universally, believed, and followed in love the footsteps of Christ we would be firmly grounded in it. We would understand with the Saints the length and breadth, the depth and height of such endless love, and would know and realize that the love of Christ is better than all knowledge. All Christians are called upon to follow in Christ's footsteps, and to do this in love He has left us an example.

ANTHONY BENEZET CRITICIZES THE EDUCATION OF YOUTH IN PENNSYLVANIA (1769) From Anthony Benezet, *Some Serious and Awful Considerations, Recommending to All, Particularly the Youth* . . . (Philadelphia, 1769), pp. 2-3.

All that has been said by the greatest saints and dying men, when the fullest of light and divine knowledge, of the necessity of piety, of the excellency of virtue, of our duty to God, of the vanity of worldly enjoyments; and all the maxims of the wisest philosophers, when in their highest state of wisdom, are proper objects of meditation for the serious minded, and ought, particularly, to constitute the daily lessons of youthful minds. Such was the education of the youth who attended Plato and Socrates; their every day's instruction were so many lectures upon the nature of man, his true end, and the right use of his faculties. Now as Christianity has set every thing that is reasonable, wise, holy and desirable, in its true point of light, so it might well be expected, that the education of the youth should be as much bettered and amended by Christianity, as the faith and doctrines of religion are. But, alas, our modern education is not of this kind, whatever way of life we intend the youth for, we apply to the fire of their minds, and exhort them to improvement from corrupt motives. We generally stir them to action from principles of covetousness, or a desire of distinction, that they may accumulate wealth, excel others, and shine in the eyes of the world. We repeat and inculcate these motives upon them, till they think it a part of their duty to make gain and worldly distinction the chief object of their desire. That this is generally the nature of the education of our sons, is too plain to need any proof. And it is much to be lamented that our daughters, whose right education is of the utmost importance to human life, should not only be brought up in pride, but in the lowest and most contemptible part of it; such as a fondness for their persons, a desire of beauty, and a love of dress; and indeed almost every thing they meet with seems to conspire to make them think of little else. And after all this we complain of the pernicious effects that pride and covetousness have in the world; we wonder to see grown persons actuated and govern'd by these pernicious principles, not considering that they were all the time of their youth called upon to form their actions and industry upon the same principles. An education under Plato and Socrates had no other end, but to teach youth to think, judge, act and follow such rules of life as Plato and Socrates used, and is it not our indispensable duty to use our best endeavour that the end of a Christian education, may be to teach our youth how to think and judge, and act, and live agreeable to the precepts and practice of our blessed Lord and Saviour Jesus Christ.

QUAKERS CALL FOR ESTABLISHMENT OF A SCHOOL OF PIETY AND VIRTUE AND USEFUL LEARNING (1778) From Anthony Benezet and Isaac Zane, "Some Observations Relating to the Establishment of Schools," as quoted in George S. Brookes, *Friend Anthony Benezet* (Philadelphia, 1937), pp. 492-95.

It is the opinion of the Committee, that Friends having united with others, in employing such persons for Masters, who have not submitted to the operation of truth, hath had a tendency to strengthen a disposition in our youth to avoid the Cross, and unite with the spirit of the world; whereby many hurtful and Corrupt things have gained ground amongst us. On reviewing the Minutes of the Yearly Meeting, we find, that at several Meetings, particularly at and since the year 1750, the consideration of the importance of training up our Youth in useful Learning, under the tuition of religious, prudent persons, suitably qualified for that service, came weightily before the Meeting, when it was recommended, that Friends should exert themselves therein as fully as their circumstances would permit, and that the likeliest means to induce persons, properly qualified, to undertake the business, would be to have some certain income fixed, in consideration of which, the Master should be obliged to teach so many children, on behalf of each Monthly, or particular Meeting, as the said Meeting shall judge adequate to the Salary; and that no Master should be employed, but with the approbation of a Committee of the Monthly Meeting, appointed for that and other services, relating to such Schools: But we find, that notwithstanding those pressing recommendations, very little has been effectually done therein. We, therefore, think it necessary, that it be recommended to the Quarterly and from thence to the Monthly and Preparative Meetings, that the former advice of collecting a fund, for the establishment and support of schools, under the care of a standing Committee appointed by the several Monthly or Particular Meetings, should generally take place, and that it be recommended by the Yearly Meeting, to Friends of each quarter, to send up the next year an account of what they have done therein. And we also think it necessary, that this weighty concern should in future become the continued care of the Yearly Meeting, by an annual Query; that so that matter may rest on a solid foundation, and every possible encouragement and assistance may be afforded to Friends in the Settlement of schools, procuring Master &c. thro' the whole extent of the Yearly Meeting. And notwithstanding some difficulties may appear in the raising of a sufficiency, fully to answer the end proposed, yet as improvements of this kind have often arisen from small beginnings, it is desired, that Friends be not discouraged, by their inability, but having faith in the Divine Blessing, being conferred on their benevolent intentions, would begin, by making some provision, agreeable to the circumstances of their respective Meetings. That within the compass of each Meeting, where the settlement of a school is necessary, a lot of ground be provided, sufficient for a garden, orchard, grass for a cow, &c. and that a suitable house, a stable &c. be erected thereon. There are but few meetings but which may, in labour, in materials or money, raise so much as would answer this charge. Such a provision would be an encouragement for a staid person, with a family who will likely to remain a considerable time, perhaps his whole life, in the service, to engage therein. This will obviate the necessity Friends often think themselves under, of hiring no other but a single person, for a Master, on account of boarding him, from one house to another, amongst themselves; hence they are induced to bargain with transient persons, often of doubtful characters; some of whom have proved to be men of corrupt minds, and even their conduct immoral, yet they are seldom likely to remain in the service any longer than some employ more agreeable to support themselves offers: Whereby the Teachers miss the opportunity of improvement, which nothing will give, equal to that experience gained by long practice, in the education of the Youth. A service, which, however it may be slighted by many, if duly performed is as arduous to the teacher, as it is of advantage to the Youth: And which if it was sometimes undertaken by pious minded Persons, more from an inclination of benefiting the Youth, than from a desire of gain, would afford a satisfaction far exceeding that of spending their time either in supineness and ease, delighting themselves in the enjoyment of their wealth, or in the pleasure of amassing more. For indeed as the Apostle observes I Cor. 6, 20; 2 Cor. 5, 15, "Ye are not your own, for ye are bought with a price—that they which live should not henceforth live unto themselves but unto him which died for them." And here a sorrowful consideration occurs, which we desire to mention with caution & tenderness that is the backwardness so apparent amongst us to contribute that part of our substance, which the circumstance of things and the necessities of the people, have on different occasions made necessary; if this had not been the case, a matter of so great importance, as the virtuous education of our Youth, would not have lain neglected, for so long a course of years; after such pressing advices had been so expressly, handed down from the Yearly Meeting: Hence arises a Query, how far our neglect of applying to the necessary service of our fellowmen, such part of the goods many have laid up in store, is one of the causes of the deep affliction which now so feelingly attends, and how small a part of what has been forcibly taken from many, if it had been seasonably, and cheerfully contributed, would have answered the several good purposes, which have either been refused or neglected by us.

The giving proper encouragement to such teachers as are capable by example and precept, to promote the growth of piety and virtue; as well as due instruction in our youth, and are likely to continue in the service, would be attended with farther advantages as well from the experience the teachers would necessarily gain, who in other respects may be incapable of supporting themselves by labour, to be educated and qualified to serve as School-Masters; a consideration well worth our particular care, as well from duty, as interest. The benefit of the youth and the means of a comfortable living for the Master, may be encreased by the conveniency which might be made, for boarding some children, under his care, whose distant situation might otherwise impede their instruction.

And if to what has been proposed, Friends were willing to add the promoting a subscription, towards a fund, the increase of which might be employed in paying the Master's Salary, if necessary, and promoting the Education of the poorer Friend's children; such a fund tho' it might be but small in the beginning being a fixed object, would draw the attention of Friends to contribute, whereas so long as there is no beginning made, this weighty service is neglected, by many who would be glad of giving encouragement to so necessary and good a work. And altho' many may not be able to give much, yet as they are willing to contribute, in proportion to their abilities, it will, like the widow's mite, entitle them to the blessing: People frequently appear to think it is at their option to do what they will with their substance, which they call their own, to give or to withhold, at their pleasure, forgetting that they are but as stewards; accountable to him who has entrusted them: Others think they are justifiable, tho' in the neglect of this plain duty, in order to heap up the more riches for their offspring, contrary to our blessed Saviour's express Command, "Lay not up for yourselves treasures on the earth," and notwithstanding the multiplied experience, daily before our eyes that riches, generally prove as wings to raise their children above truth; or as thick clay to bind them to the earth; but neither of these conclusions will stand the test of that Gospel Injunction, "Thou shalt love thy neighbour as thyself;" nor enable them to give a satisfactory account when that alarming proclamation will be made, "Steward give an account of thy stewardship, for thou mayest be no longer steward."

NEGROES,
INDIANS,
AND
GERMAN IMMIGRANTS

The Negro

VIRGINIA STATUTE ON BAPTISM AND BONDAGE (1667)   From William W. Hening, ed., *Statutes at Large of Virginia, 1619-1782* (Richmond, 1809-23), vol. II, p. 170.

Whereas some doubts have risen whether children that are slaves by birth, and by the charity and piety of their owners made partakers of the blessed sacrament of baptism, should be virtue of their baptism be made free, *it is enacted and declared by this Grand Assembly, and the authority thereof,* that the conferring of baptism does not alter the condition of the person as to his bondage or freedom; that diverse masters, freed from this doubt may more carefully endeavor the propagation of Christianity by permitting children, though slaves, or those of greater growth if capable, to be admitted to that sacrament.

SOUTH CAROLINA STATUTE ON CHRISTIANITY AND SLAVERY (1711)   From J. Brevard, ed., *Digest of the Public Statute Law of South Carolina* (Charleston, 1814), vol. II, p. 229.

Since charity and the Christian religion which we profess obliges us to wish well to the souls of all men, and that religion may not be made a pretence to alter any man's property and right, and that no persons may neglect to baptize their Negroes or slaves, or suffer them to be baptized for fear that thereby they should be manumitted and set free: *Be it therefore enacted,* that it shall be, and is hereby declared, lawful for any Negro or Indian slave, or any other slave or slaves whatsoever, to receive and profess the Christian faith, and be thereunto baptized. But that notwithstanding such slave or slaves shall receive and profess the Christian religion, and be baptized, he or they shall not thereby be manumitted or set free, or his or their owner, master, or mistress lose his or their civil right, property, and authority over such slave or slaves, but that the slave or slaves, with respect to his or their servitude, shall remain and continue in the same state and condition that he or they was in before the making of this act.

AN ACT FOR THE GOVERNING OF NEGROES AND SLAVES IN SOUTH CAROLINA (1712)

From Thomas Cooper and David McCord, eds., *The Statutes at Large of South Carolina* (Columbia, S.C., 1836-41), vol. VII, pp. 352-57.

Whereas, the plantations and estates of this Province cannot be well and sufficiently managed and brought into use, without the labor and service of negroes and other slaves; and forasmuch as the said negroes and other slaves brought unto the people of this Province for that purpose, are of barbarous, wild, savage natures, and such as renders them wholly unqualified to be governed by the laws, customs, and practices of this Province; but that it is absolutely necessary, that such other constitutions, laws and orders, should in this Province be made and enacted, for the good regulating and ordering of them, as may restrain the disorders, rapines and inhumanity, to which they are naturally prone and inclined, and may also tend to the safety and security of the people of this Province and their estates; to which purpose,

I. *Be it therefore enacted,* by his Excellency, William, Lord Craven, Palatine, and the rest of the true and absolute Lords and Proprietors of this Province, by and with the advice and consent of the rest of the members of the General Assembly, now met at Charlestown, for the South-west part of this Province, and by the authority of the same, That all negroes, mulatoes, mustizoes or Indians, which at any time heretofore have been sold, or now are held or taken to be, or hereafter shall be bought and sold for slaves, are hereby declared slaves; and they, and their children, are hereby made and declared slaves, to all intents and purposes; excepting all such negroes, mulatoes, mustizoes or Indians, which heretofore have been, or hereafter shall be, for some particular merit, made and declared free, either by the Governor and council of this Province, pursuant to any Act or law of this Province, or by their respective owners or masters; and also, excepting all such negroes, mulatoes, mustizoes or Indians, as can prove they ought not to be sold for slaves. And in case any negro, mulatoe, mustizoe or Indian, doth lay claim to his or her freedom, upon all or any of the said accounts, the same shall be finally heard and determined by the Governor and council of this Province.

II. And for the better ordering and governing of negroes and all other slaves in this Province, *Be it enacted* by the authority aforesaid, That no master, mistress, overseer, or other person whatsoever, that hath the care and charge of any negro or slave, shall give their negroes and other slaves leave, on Sundays, hollidays, or any other time, to go out of their plantations, except such negro or other slave as usually wait upon them at home or abroad, or wearing a livery; and every other negro or slave that shall be taken hereafter out of his master's plantation, without a ticket, or leave in writing, from his master or mistress, or some other person by his or her appointment, or some white person in the company of such slave, to give an account of his business, shall be whipped; and every person who shall not (when in his power,) apprehend every negro or other slave which he shall see out of his master's plantation, without leave as aforesaid, and after apprehended, shall neglect to punish him by moderate whipping, shall forfeit twenty shillings, the one half to the poor, to be paid to the church wardens of the Parish where such forfeiture shall become due, and the other half to him that will inform for the same, within one week after such neglect; and that no slave may make further or other use of any one ticket than was intended by him that granted the same, every ticket shall particularly mention the name of every slave employed in the particular business, and to what place they are sent, and what time they return; and if any person shall presume to give any negro or slave a ticket in the name of his master or mistress, without his or her consent, such person so doing shall forfeit the sum of twenty shillings; one half to the poor, to be disposed of as aforesaid, the other half to the person injured, that will complain against the person offending, within one week after the offence committed. And for the better security of all such persons that shall endeavor to take any runaway, or shall examine any slave for his ticket, passing to and from his master's plantation, it is hereby declared lawful for any white person to beat, maim or assult, and if such negro or slave cannot otherwise be taken, to kill him, who shall refuse to shew his ticket, or, by running away or resistance, shall endeavor to avoid being apprehended or taken.

*   *   *

XI. *And be it further enacted* by the authority aforesaid, That if any person shall send his negro out of this Province, that hath killed another negro or slave, such person shall pay unto the master or owner of such negro, the full value of such negro so killed as aforesaid; and in case any person shall send, or cause to be sent, his negro out of this Province, that hath killed any white person, knowing the negro to be guilty of such crime, he shall forfeit the sum of five hundred pounds, to the executors of the person killed; to be recovered by action of debt in the court of common pleas in this Province, the action to be brought at any time within one year after the fact committed.

XII. *And it is further enacted* by the authority aforesaid, That if any negroes or other slaves shall make mutiny or insurrection, or rise in rebellion against the authority and government of this Province, or shall make preparation of arms, powder, bullets or offensive weapons, in order to carry on such mutiny or insurrection, or shall hold any counsel or conspiracy for raising such mutiny, insurrection or rebellion, the offenders shall be tried by two justices of the peace and three freeholders, associated together as before expressed in case of murder, burglary, *etc.*, who are hereby empowered and required to try the said slaves so offending, and inflict death, or any other punishment, upon the offenders, and forthwith by their warrant cause execution to be done, by the common or any other executioner, in such manner as they shall think fitting; and if any person shall make away or conceal any negro or negroes, or other slave or slaves, suspected to be guilty of the beforementioned crimes, and not upon demand bring forth the suspected offender or offenders, such person shall forfeit for every negro or slave so concealed or made away, the sum of fifty pounds; *Provided, nevertheless,* that when and as often as any of the beforementioned crimes shall be committed by more than one negro, that shall deserve death, that then and in all such cases, if the Governor and council of this Province shall think fitting, and accordingly shall order, that only one or more of the said criminals should suffer death as exemplary, and the rest to be returned to the owners, that then, the owners of the negroes so offending, shall bear proportionably the loss of the said negro or negroes so put to death, as shall be allotted them by the said justices and freeholders; and if any person shall refuse his part so allotted him, that then, and in all such cases, the said justices and freeholders are hereby required to issue out their warrant of distress upon the goods and chattels of the person so refusing, and shall cause the same to be sold by public outcry, to satisfy the said money so allotted him to pay, and to return the overplus, if any be, to the owner; *Provided, nevertheless,* that the part allotted for any person to pay for his part or proportion of the negro or negroes so put to death, shall not exceed one sixth part of his negro or negroes so excused and pardoned; and in case that shall not be sufficient to satisfy for the negro or negroes that shall be put to death, that the remaining sum shall be paid out of the public treasury of this Province.

AN ACT PROHIBITING TEACHING SLAVES TO WRITE IN SOUTH CAROLINA (1740)   From Thomas Cooper and David McCord, eds., *The Statutes at Large of South Carolina* (Columbia, S.C., 1836-41), vol. VII, p. 413.

And *whereas,* the having of slaves taught to write, or suffering them to be employed in writing, may be attended with great inconveniences; *Be it therefore enacted* by the authority aforesaid, That all and every person or persons whatsoever, who shall hereafter teach, or cause any slave or slaves to be taught, to write, or shall use or employ any slave as a scribe in any manner of writing whatsoever, hereafter taught to write, every such person and persons, shall, for every such offence, forfeit the sum of one hundred pounds current money.

REVEREND PETER FONTAINE'S DEFENSE OF SLAVERY IN VIRGINIA (1757)   From Ann Maury, ed., *Memoirs of a Huguenot Family* (New York, 1853), pp. 351-53.

As to your second query, if enslaving our fellow creatures be a practice agreeable to Christianity, it is answered in a great measure in many treatises at home, to which I refer you. I shall only mention something of our present state here.

Like Adam, we are all apt to shift off the blame from ourselves and lay it upon others, how justly in our case you may judge. The Negroes are enslaved by the Negroes themselves before they are purchased by the masters of the ships who bring them here. It is, to be sure, at our choice whether we buy them or not, so this then is our crime, folly, or whatever you will please to call it.

But our Assembly, foreseeing the ill consequences of importing such numbers among us, has often attempted to lay a duty upon them which would amount to a prohibition, such as £10 or £20 a head; but no governor dare pass such a law, having instructions to the contrary from the Board of Trade at home. By this means they are forced upon us, whether we will or will not. This plainly shows the African Company has the advantage of the colonies, and may do as it pleases with the Ministry.

Indeed, since we have been exhausted of our little stock of cash by the war, the importation has stopped; our poverty then is our best security. There is no more picking for their ravenous jaws upon bare bones; but should we begin to thrive, they will be at the same again. All our taxes are now laid upon slaves and on shippers of tobacco, which they wink at while we are in danger of being torn from them, but we dare not do it in time of peace, it being looked upon as the highest presumption to lay any burden upon trade. This is our part of the grievance, but to live in Virginia without slaves is morally impossible.

Before our troubles, you could not hire a servant or slave for love or money, so that, unless robust enough to cut wood, to go to mill, to work at the hoe, etc., you must starve or board in some family where they both fleece and half starve you. There is no set price upon corn, wheat, and provisions; so they take advantage of the necessities of strangers, who are thus obliged to purchase some slaves and land. This, of course, draws us all into the original sin and curse of the country of purchasing slaves, and this is the reason we have no merchants, traders, or artificers of any sort but what become planters in a short time.

A common laborer, white or black, if you can be so much favored as to hire one, is 1s. sterling or 15d. currency per day; a bungling carpenter, 2s. or 2s. 6d. per day; besides diet and lodging. That is, for a lazy fellow to get wood and water, £19 16s. 3d. current per annum; add to this £7 or £8 more and you have a slave for life.

A MISSIONARY'S REPORT ON THE RISK OF TEACHING NEGROES

(1710)   From Reverend Francis Le Jau to the London Office of the Society for the Propagation of the Gospel in Foreign Parts, February 1, 1710, as quoted in Edgar W. Knight, ed., *A Documentary History of Education in the South Before 1860* (Chapel Hill, N.C., 1949), vol. I, p. 107.

I should say something of propagating the Christian knowledge. We want a schoolmaster in [the] parish for our white people's children, but as for the Negroes or Indians, with all submission, I would desire that such a thing should be taken into consideration as the importance of the matter and the consequences which may follow do deserve. The best scholar of all the Negroes in my parish, and a very sober and honest liver, through his learning was like to create some confusion among all the Negroes in this country. He had a book wherein he read some description of the several judgments that chastise men because of their sins in these latter days; that description made an impression upon his spirit and he told his masters abruptly there would be a dismal time and the moon would be turned into blood and there would be dearth of darkness and went away. When I heard of that I sent for the Negro who ingeniously told me he had read so in a book. I advised him and charged him not to put his own constructions upon his reading after that manner, and to be cautious not to speak so, which he promised to me, but yet would never show me the book. But when he spoke those few words to his master some Negro overheard a part, and it was publicly blazed abroad that an angel came and spake to the man; he had seen a hand that gave him a book, he had heard voices, seen fires, etc. As I had opportunities, I took care to undeceive those who asked me about it. Now it is over. I fear that those men have not judgment enough to make a good use of their learning; and I have thought most convenient not to urge too far that Indians and Negroes should be indifferently admitted to learn to read, but I leave it to the discretion of their masters whom I exhort to examine well their inclinations. I have often observed and lately hear that it had been better if persons of melancholy constitution or those that run into the search after curious matter had never seen a book.

A NORTH CAROLINA TEACHER'S REPORT TO THE SOCIETY FOR THE PROPAGATION OF THE GOSPEL IN FOREIGN PARTS ON TEACHING THE CATECHISM TO SLAVES (1719) From Edgar W. Knight, ed., *A Documentary History of Education in the South Before 1860* (Chapel Hill, N.C., 1949), vol. I, pp. 87-88

In this year I caused a pretty many of the children to learn our catechism, and catechis'd them, in public, in this year I Baptized one Adult White Young Woman, and Thirty White Children, and one Adult Negro Young Woman, and one Mustee Young Woman and three Mustee Young Children, in all 36. I hope I took a method with the Negro Young Man, and with the Mustee Young Woman, whom I baptized, which will please the Society, which was this, I made them get our Church Catechism perfectly without Book, and then I took some pains with them to make them understand it, and especially the Baptismal Covenant, and to persuade them, faithfully and constantly to perform the great things they were to promise at their Baptism, and ever after to perform to God: and then I caused them to say the catechise, one Lords Day, and the other another Lord's Day before a large congregation, without Book which they did both distinctly, and so perfectly, that all that heard them admired their saying it so well, and with great satisfaction to myself, I baptized these two persons   , I had for some time great hopes of being the Minister that should convert and Baptize the rest of the Esqr Duckenfield Slaves, which I was very desirous and ambitious to be, and I would have begrudged no pains, but would most freely and with the greatest pleasure have done all I could to promote and accomplish this so great, and so good work. And in order thereunto I was preparing 4 more of them for Baptism, and had taught one of those 4 their Catechism very perfectly, and the other 3 a good part of it, and now as I was about this good work, the enemies to the conversion and baptism of slaves, industriously and very busily buzzed into the Peoples Ears, that all slaves that were baptized were to be set free, and this silly Buckbear so greatly scared Esqu^r Duckenfield that he told me plainly I should Baptize no more of his slaves 'till the Society had got a Law made in England that no Baptized Slave, should be set free because he is Baptized and send it here, and many more are of the same mind, and so this good work was knocked in the head which is a great trouble to me, because so many slaves are so very desirous to become Christians without any expectation of being set free when they are Baptized—I fear this good work will not be revived and prosper here till such a Law is enacted by the Parliament of Great Britain and this people are acquainted with it, for I perceive nothing else will satisfy them . . .

THE BISHOP OF LONDON CALLS FOR THE CONVERSION OF THE
NEGRO (1727) From David Humphreys, *An Historical Account of the Incorporated Society for the Propagation of the Gospel In Foreign Parts* (London, 1730), pp. 257-71.

To the Masters and Mistresses of Families in the English Plantations abroad; Exhorting them to Encourage and Promote the Instruction of their Negroes in the Christian Faith.

The Care of the Plantations abroad being committed to the Bishop of London as to Religious Affairs; I have thought it my Duty to make particular Enquiries into the State of Religion in those Parts, and to learn, among other Things, what Numbers of Slaves are employ'd within the several Governments, and what Means are used for their Instruction in the Christian Faith. I find the Numbers are prodigiously great; and am not a little troubled, to observe how small a Progress has been made in a Christian Country, towards the delivering those poor Creatures from the Pagan Darkness and Superstition in which they were bred, and the making them Partakers of the Light of the Gospel, and of the Blessings and Benefits belonging to it. And, which is yet more to be lamented, I find there has not only been very little Progress made in the Work, but that all *Attempts* towards it have been by too many industriously discouraged and hindred; partly, by magnifying the *Difficulties* of the Work beyond what they really are; and partly, by mistaken Suggestions of the Change which *Baptism* would make in the Condition of the *Negroes*, to the Loss and Disadvantage of their Masters.

I. As to the Difficulties; it may be pleaded, That the Negroes are *grown Persons* when they come over, and that having been accustomed to the Pagan Rites and Idolatries of their own Country, they are prejudiced against all other Religions, and more particularly against the Christian, as forbidding all that Licentiousness which is usually practiced among Heathens. But if this were a good Argument against attempting the Conversion of Negroes, it would follow, that the Gospel is never to be further propagated than it is at present, and that no Endeavours are to be used for the Conversion of Heathens, at any Time, or in any Country whatsoever; because all Heathens have been accustomed to Pagan Rites and Idolatries, and to such vicious and licentious Living as the Christian Religion forbids. But yet, God be thank'd, Heathens have been converted, and Christianity propagated, in all Ages, and almost all Countries, through the Zeal and Diligence of pious and good Men; and this, without the Help of Miracles. And if the present Age be as zealous and diligent in pursuing the proper *Means* of Conversion, we have no Reason to doubt, but that the Divine Assistance is, and will be, the same in all Ages.

But a farther Difficulty is, that they are utter Strangers to our Language, and we to theirs; and the Gift of Tongues being now ceased, there is no Means left of instructing them in the Doctrines of the Christian Religion. And this, I own, is a real Difficulty, as long as it continues, and as far as it reaches. But, if I am rightly informed, many of the Negroes, who are grown Persons when they come over, do of themselves attain so much of our Language, as enables them to understand, and to be understood, in Things which concern the ordinary Business of Life; and they who can go so far of their own accord, might doubtless be carried much farther, if proper Methods and Endeavours were to bring them to a competent Knowledge of our Language, with a pious View to the instructing them in the Doctrines of our

Religion. At least, some of them, who are more capable and more serious than the rest, might be easily instructed both in our Language and Religion, and then be made use of to convey Instruction to the rest in their own Language. And this, one would hope, may be done with great Ease, wherever there is a hearty and sincere Zeal for the Work.

But whatever Difficulties there may be in instructing those who are *grown-up* before they are brought over; there are not the like Difficulties in the Case of their Children, who are born and bred in our Plantations, who have never been accustomed to Pagan Rites and Superstitions, and who may easily be train'd up, like all other Children, to any Language whatsoever, and particularly to our own; if the making them good Christians be sincerely the Desire and Intention of those, who have the Property in them, and the Government over them.

*   *   *

II. But it is further pleaded, That the Instruction of Heathens in the Christian Faith, is in order to their Baptism; and that not only the *Time* to be allowed for Instructing them, would be an Abatement from the Profits of their Labour, but also that the *Baptizing* them when instructed, would destroy both the Property which the Masters have in them as Slaves bought with their Money, and the Right of selling them again at Pleasure; and that the making them Christians, only makes them less diligent, and more ungovernable.

To which it may be very truly reply'd, That Christianity, and the embracing of the Gospel, does not make the least Alteration in Civil Property, or in any of the Duties which belong to Civil Relations; but in all these Respects, it continues Persons just in the same State as it found them. The Freedom which Christianity gives, is a Freedom from the Bondage of Sin and Satan, and from the Dominion of Mens Lusts and Passions and inordinate Desires; but as to their *outward* Condition, whatever that was before, whether bond or free, their being baptized, and becoming Christians, makes no manner of Change in it: As St. *Paul* has expressly told us, 1 *Cor.* vii. 20. where he is speaking directly to this very Point, *Let every Man abide in the same Calling wherein he was called;* and at the 24th Verse, *Let every Man wherein he is called, therein abide with God.* And so far is Christianity from discharging Men from the Duties of the Station and Condition in which it found them, that it lays them under stronger Obligations to perform those Duties with the greatest Diligence and Fidelity, not only from the Fear of Men, but from a Sense of Duty to God, and the Belief and Expectation of a future Account. So that to say, that Christianity tends to make Men less observant of their Duty in any Respect, is a Reproach that it is very far from deserving; and a Reproach, that is confuted by the whole Tenor of the Gospel Precepts, which inculcate upon all, and particularly upon Servants (many of whom were then in the Condition of Slaves) a faithful and diligent Discharge of the Duties belonging to their several Stations, out of Conscience towards God: And it is also confuted by our own Reason, which tells us how much more forcible and constant the Restraint of *Conscience* is, than the Restraint of *Fear*; and last of all, it is confuted by Experience, which teaches us the great *Value* of those Servants who are truly Religious, compared with those who have no Sense of Religion.

As to their being more ungovernable after Baptism, than before; it is certain that the Gospel every where enjoins, not only Diligence and Fidelity, but also *Obedience*, for Conscience Sake; and does not deprive Masters of any proper

Methods of *enforcing* Obedience, where they appear to be necessary. Humanity forbids all cruel and barbarous Treatment of our Fellow-Creatures, and will not suffer us to consider a Being that is endow'd with Reason, upon a Level with Brutes; and Christianity takes not out of the Hands of Superiors any Degrees of Strictness and Severity, that fairly appear to be necessary for the preserving Subjection and Government. The general Law, both of Humanity and of Christianity, is Kindness, Gentleness, and Compassion, towards all Mankind, of what Nation or Condition soever they be; and therefore we are to make the Exercise of those amiable Virtues, our *Choice* and *Desire*, and to have Recourse to severe and rigorous Methods unwillingly, and only out of Necessity. Of this *Necessity*, you your selves remain the Judges, as much *after* they receive Baptism, as *before;* so that *You* can be in no Danger of suffering by the Change; and as to *Them*, the greatest Hardships that the most severe Master can inflict upon them, is not to be compared to the Cruelty of keeping them in the State of Heathenism, and depriving them of the Means of Salvation, as reached forth to *all Mankind*, in the Gospel of Christ. And, in Truth, one great Reason why Severity is at all necessary to maintain Government, is the *Want* of Religion in those who are to be governed, and who therefore are not to be kept to their Duty by any Thing but *Fear* and *Terror;* than which there cannot be a more uneasie State, either to those who govern, or those who are governed.

III. That these Things may make the greater Impression upon you, let me beseech you to consider your selves not only as Masters, but as *Christian* Masters, who stand oblig'd by your Profession to do all that your Station and Condition enable you to do, towards breaking the Power of Satan, and enlarging the Kingdom of Christ; and as having a great Opportunity put into your Hands, of helping-on this Work, by the Influence which God has given you over such a Number of Heathen Idolaters, who still continue under the Dominion of Satan. In the next Place, let me beseech you to consider *Them*, not barely as Slaves, and upon the same Level with labouring Beasts, but as *Men*-Slaves and *Women*-Slaves, who have the same Frame and Faculties with your selves, and have Souls capable of being made eternally happy, and Reason and Understanding to receive Instruction in order to it. If they came from abroad, let it not be said, that they are as far from the Knowledge of Christ in a Christian Country, as when they dwelt among Pagan Idolaters. If they have been born among you, and have never breathed any Air but that of a Christian Country, let them not be as much Strangers to Christ, as if they had been transplanted, as soon as born, into a Country of Pagan Idolaters.

Hoping that these and the like Considerations will move you to lay this Matter seriously to Heart, and excite you to use the best Means in your Power towards so good and pious a Work; I cannot omit to suggest to you one of the best Motives that can be us'd, for disposing the Heathens to embrace Christianity; and that is, *the good Lives of Christians*. Let them see, in you and your Families, Examples of Sobriety, Temperance and Chastity, and of all the other Virtues and Graces of the Christian Life. Let them observe how strictly you oblige your selves, and all that belong to you, to abstain from Cursing and Swearing, and to keep the Lord's-Day holy, and to attend the publick Worship of God, and the Ordinances which Christ hath appointed in his Gospel. Make them sensible, by the general Tenour of your Behavior and Conversation, that your inward Temper and Disposition is such as the Gospel requires, that is to say, mild, gentle, and merciful; and that as oft as you exercise Rigour and Severity, it is wholly owing to their Idleness or Obstinacy. By these Means, you will open their Hearts to Instruction, and *prepare* them to receive the Truths of the Gospel; to which if you add a pious *Endeavour* and *Concern* to see them duly instructed, you may become the Instrument of saving many Souls, and will not only secure a Blessing from God upon all your Undertakings in this World, but entitle your selves to that distinguishing Reward in the next, which will be given to all those who have been zealous in their Endeavours to promote the Salvation of Men, and enlarge the Kingdom of Christ. And that you may be found in that Number at the Great Day of Accounts, is the sincere Desire and earnest Prayer of

Your faithful Friend,

May 19. 1727.   Edm'. London'.

A CONTEMPORARY ACCOUNT OF THE SOCIETY FOR THE PROPAGATION OF THE GOSPEL'S WORK AMONG THE NEGROES

(**1730**)   From David Humphreys, *An Historical Account of the Incorporated Society for the Propagation of the Gospel in Foreign Parts* (London, 1730), pp. 232-43, 248-49.

The *Negroe* Slaves even in those Colonies, where the Society send Missionaries, amount to many Thousands of Persons, of both Sexes, and all Ages, and most of them are very capable of receiving Instruction. Even the grown Persons brought from *Guinea*, quickly learn *English* enough to be understood in ordinary Matters; but the Children born of *Negroe* Parents in the Colonies, are bred up entirely in the *English* Language.

⁂   ⁂   ⁂

The Society looked upon the Instruction and Conversion of the *Negroes,* as a principal Branch of their Care; esteeming it a great Reproach to the Christian Name, that so many Thousands of Persons should continue in the same State of *Pagan* Darkness, under a Christian Government, and living in Christian Families; as they lay before under, in their own Heathen Countries. The Society, immediately from their first Institution, strove to promote their Conversion; and inasmuch as their Income, would not enable them to send Numbers of Catechists, sufficient to instruct the *Negroes;* yet they resolved to do their utmost, and at least, to give this Work the Mark of their highest Approbation.

They wrote therefore to all their Missionaries, that they should use their best Endeavours, at proper Times, to instruct the *Negroes;* and should especially take Occasion, to recommend it zealously to the Masters, to order their Slaves, at convenient Times, to come to them, that they might be instructed. These Directions had a good Effect, and some Hundreds of *Negroes* have been instructed, received Baptism, and been admitted to the Communion, and lived very orderly Lives. The Reader may remember, there is frequently Mention made above, in the Account of the Labours of the Missionaries, of many *Negroes* at different Times instructed and baptized; to relate the Particulars here, would be too circumstantial, and altogether useless.

It is Matter of Commendation to the Clergy, that they have done thus much in so great and difficult a Work. But alas! what is the Instruction of a few Hundreds, in several Years, with respect to the many Thousands uninstructed, unconverted, living, dying, utter *Pagans*. It must.be confessed, what hath been done is as nothing, with Regard to what a true Christian would hope to see effected. But the Difficulties the Clergy meet with in this good Work are exceeding great. The first is, the *Negroes* want Time to receive Instruction. Several Masters allow their *Negroes* Sundays only, for Rest; and then the Minister of a Parish is fully employed in other Duties, and cannot attend them: Many Planters, in order to free themselves from the Trouble and Charge of Feeding and Cloathing their Slaves, allow them one Day in a Week, to clear Ground and plant it, to subsist themselves and Families. Some allow all Saturday, some half Saturday and Sunday; others allow, only Sunday. How can the *Negroe* attend for Instruction, who on half Saturday and Sunday is to provide Food the Rayment for himself and Family for the Week following? The *Negroe* will urge in his own Excuse, that the Support of himself, and all that is dear to him, doth absolutely depend upon this, his necessary Labour, on Saturday and Sunday. If this be not strictly justifiable, yet it is sure, the miserable Man's Plea, will engage the Reader's Compassion.

This is the Case in some Colonies, in others it differs: In some Places, the Slaves do the whole Labour of the Country, in the Field; in others, they are used only as House Servants. Another Difficulty arises from the Habitations and Settlements of the Masters, being at great Distances from each other in most Places in the Colonies; for which reason, neither can a Minister go to many Families, if the *Negroes* were allowed Time to attend him; nor can a proper Number of them assemble together at one Place, without considerable Loss of Time to their Masters. But the greatest Obstruction is, the Masters themselves do not consider enough, the Obligation which lies upon them, to have their Slaves instructed. Some have been so weak as to argue, the *Negroes* had no Souls; others, that they grew worse by being taught, and made Christians: I would not mention these, if they were not popular Arguments now, *because they have no Foundation in Reason or Truth.*

✽   ✽   ✽

After the Society had given the general Order mentioned before, to all their Missionaries, for the Instruction of the Slaves, they agreed to use another Method, which they believed would more successfully promote this Work. They opened a Catechising School for the Slaves at *New-York*, in the Year 1704, in which City there were computed to be about 1500 *Negroe* and *Indian* Slaves, and many of their Masters well disposed to have them made Christians. The Society hoped this Example set, might kindle a Zeal in some other good People, to carry on this Work, which they were unable to effect; and to erect Schools for the Instruction of the *Negroes,* and employ Catechists to teach them at appointed Times; and that the Legislature in the Colonies, would, by a Law, oblige all Slaves to attend for their instruction. The Society found soon, it was not easie to procure a Person proper to be a Catechist. Mr. *Elias Neau* a Layman, then living in *New-York* City, as a Trader, was represented to be the properest Person for that Office. He was by Nation a *Frenchman,* had made a Confession of the *Protestant* Religion in *France,* for which he had been confined several Years in Prison, and seven Years in the Gallies. When he got released, he went to *New-York,* and traded there, and had the Character, from People of all Persuasions, of a Man of Piety, of sober Deportment, and serious Life.

He accepted of the Offer of being Catechist; and his former Sufferings on the Account of his Religion, did, with great Advantage, recommend him to be a

Teacher of the Christian Faith; and his Humility enabled him to bear with the many Inconveniencies in teaching those poor People. He entred upon his Office, in the Year 1704, with great Diligence. At first he was obliged to go from House to House, to instruct the *Negroes*, this was out of Measure laborious; afterwards he got Leave, that they should come to his House; this was a considerable Relief. There were two Obstructions still; the Time was much too short, and the Place was inconvenient, for teaching the great Number of *Negroes*. A little Time in the Dusk of the Evening, after hard Labour all Day, was the whole Time allowed them for Learning, and for Relaxation, and to visit their Wives and Children; which were generally in other Families, not in their Masters. At this Time their Bodies were so fatigued, that their Attention could not be great. They were dull and sleepy, and remembered they must rise early the next Day, to their Labour. The Place also was incommodious, being the uppermost Floor in Mr. *Neau's* House, which, tho' very large for a private House, yet was not able to hold conveniently, a small Part of the Slaves which might resort thither.

Besides, the *Negroes* were much discouraged from embracing the Christian Religion, upon Account of the very little Regard shewed them in any religious Respect. Their Marriages were performed by mutual Consent only, without the Blessing of the Church; they were buried by those of their own Country or Complexion, in the common Field, without any Christian Office; perhaps some ridiculous Heathen Rites were performed at the Grave, by some of their own People. No Notice was given of their being sick, that they might be visited; on the contrary, frequent Discourses were made in Conversation, that they had no Souls, and perished as the Beasts.

Mr. *Neau* contended with these Difficulties, and notwithstanding all, proved an Instrument of bringing many to a Knowledge of the Christian Faith. He took great Pains in reading to them, in making short Collections out of Books on the Catechism, and in making an Abstract of the Historical Part of the Scriptures; so that many, who could not read, could yet by Memory repeat the History of the Creation of the World, the Flood, the giving of the Law, the Birth, Miracles, and Crucifixion of our Lord, and the chief Articles and Doctrines of Christianity.

This was a Work of great Pains and Humility; Mr. *Neau* performed it diligently; discoursing familiarly with those poor People, and labouring earnestly to accommodate his Discourse to their Capacities. His Labours were very successful; a considerable Number of the Slaves, could give a sufficient Account of the Grounds of their Faith; as several of the Clergy who examined them publickly, before they gave them Baptism, have acquainted the Society.

*   *   *

In the mean Time, while the Society were thinking of farther Ways to advance this Work, a Calamity happened which mightily discouraged this Country from promoting the Instruction of their Slaves. In the Year 1712, a considerable Number of *Negroes* of the *Carmantee* and *Pappa* Nations, formed a Plot to destroy all the *English*, in order to obtain their Liberty; and kept their Conspiracy so secret, that there was no Suspicion of it, till it came to the very Execution. However, the Plot was, by God's Providence, happily defeated. The Plot was this: The *Negroes* sat Fire to a House in *York* City, on a Sunday Night, in *April*, about the going down of the Moon. The Fire alarmed the Town, who from all Parts ran to it; the Conspirators planted themselves in several Streets and Lanes leading to the Fire, and shot or stabbed the People as they were running to it. Some of the Wounded escaped, and acquainted the Government, and presently, by the Signal of firing a great Gun from the Fort, the Inhabitants were called under Arms, and prevented from running to the Fire. A Body of Men was soon raised, which easily scattered the *Negroes;* they had killed about eight Persons, and wounded 12 more. In their Flight some of them short themselves, others their Wives, and then themselves; some absconded a few Days, and then killed themselves for Fear of being taken; but a great many were taken, and 18 of them suffered Death. This wicked Conspiracy was at first apprehended to be general among all the *Negroes,* and opened the Mouths of many, to speak against giving the *Negroes* Instruction. Mr. *Neau* durst hardly appear abroad for some Days, his School was blamed as the main Occasion of this barbarous Plot. But upon the Tryal of these Wretches, there were but two, of all his School, so much as charged with the Plot; and only one, was a baptized Man, and in the Peoples Heat, upon slender Evidence, perhaps too hastily condemned; for soon after he was acknowledged to be innocent by the common Voice. The other was not baptized; it appeared plain that he was in the Conspiracy, but guiltless of his Master's Murder, Mr. *Hooghlands,* an eminent Merchant. Upon full Tryal, the guilty *Negroes,* were found to be such as never came to Mr. *Neau's* School; and what is very observable, the Persons, whose *Negroes* were found to be most guilty, were such as were the declared Opposers of making them Christians.

However, a great Jealousie was now raised, and the common Cry was very loud, against instructing the *Negroes.* The Common Council of *New-York* City made an Order, forbidding the *Negroes* to go about the Streets after Sun-set, without Lanthorns and Candles; this was in Effect, forbidding them to go to Mr. *Neau's* School, for none of them could get Lanthorns, or come to him before Sunset. But some Time after, the more serious and moderate People, abated of this Violence. It appeared to be a Plot of a few only, not a general one of all the *Negroes,* no Consequence attended the Action, and People grew more composed. *Robert Hunter* Esq; then Governor of the Province, observed their Fears were ill-grounded, and that Mr. *Neau's* Scholars were not the guilty *Negroes,* and therefore, in order to support the Design of instructing them, he was pleased to visit the School, attended by the Society's Missionaries, and several Persons of Note, and publickly declared his Approbation of the Design; and afterwards in a Proclamation put out against Immorality and Vice, he recommended it to the Clergy of the Country, to exhort their Congregations from the Pulpit, to promote the Instruction of the *Negroes.*

*   *   *

The Society have been always sensible, the most effectual Way to convert the *Negroes,* was by engaging their Masters, to countenance and promote their Conversion. The late Bishop of St. *Asaph,* Dr. *Fleetwood,* preached a Sermon before this Society in the Year 1711, setting forth the Duty of instructing the *Negroes* in the Christian Religion. The Society thought this, so useful a Discourse, that they printed and dispersed abroad in the Plantations, great Numbers of that Sermon in the same Year; and lately in the Year 1725, reprinted the same, and dispersed again large Numbers. The present Bishop of *London* (Dr. *Gibson*) became a second Advocate for the Conversion of the *Negroes;* and wrote two Letters on this Subject: The first, Addressed *to the Masters and Mistresses of Families in the* English *Plantations abroad, exhorting them to encourage and promote the Instruction of their* Negroes *in the Christian Faith.* The Second, to *the Missionaries there;*

directing them to distribute the said Letter, and exhorting them to give their Assistance, towards the Instruction of the Negroes *within their several Parishes.*

The Society were persuaded, this was the true Method to remove the great Obstruction of their Conversion, and hoping so particular an Application to the Masters and Mistresses, from the See of *London*, would have the strongest Influence; they printed ten Thousand Copies of the Letter to the *Masters* and *Mistresses*, which have been sent to all the Colonies on the Continent, and to all our Islands in the *West-Indies*, to be distributed among the Masters of Families, and other Inhabitants. The Society have received Accounts, that these Letters have influenced many Masters of Families to have their *Negroes* instructed; and hope they will have at length, the desired Effect.

A MISSIONARY'S ACCOUNT OF SOME PROBLEMS IN THE EDUCATION OF NEGRO CHILDREN (1761)   From Edgar W. Knight, ed., *A Documentary History of Education in the South Before 1860* (Chapel Hill, N.C., 1949), vol. I, p. 148.

Copy of Letter from Revd Mr Dan Earl, N. Carolina Edentown, Oct-[17]61

Sir

Mr. Hazlewood a merchant in this Town Showed me a Letter from you, wherein you signifyed to him that a Society called Dr Brays Associates were desirous that a School may be opened here for the Education of Negroe Children under the Care of him Mr Child and myself. But as Mr Child, some time ago moved from hence into Virginia, neither Mr Hazlewood nor myself cou'd learn the Societys Plan till very lately when I waited on him myself for that Purpose. Since which Time I have used my utmost Endeavours to recommend this beneficient and charitable Design to the Inhabitants of this Town, & to represent it in the Light it ought to appear in to all who profess our holy Religion: But am sorry to acquaint you, that my Exhortations and Remonstrances have not as yet had the desired effect, but hope they will consider better of it and not suffer so fair an opportunity of having their young slaves instructed in the Principles of Religion fall to the ground.

They all allow of the great Expediency of the Design but say, that as their Circumstances are low and distressed (which is generally the Case) They cannot spare their Negroes from Service at the age that they are susceptible of Condition, and those that are in affluent Circumstances are so very few that the number of Children sent by them wou'd be so inconsiderable as not to be worth any persons acceptance, as the Teaching of Negroes precludes the taking of White Children, the Parents not allowing their Children to be educated among such. If it shou'd be proposed by your worthy Society to allow any Salary for the Education of white Children, it w^d be readily embraced, & wou'd be productive of great Utility to the poor and ignorant Colony as the great part of them are brought up in profound Ignorance of every kind of Literature, occasioned chiefly by the Poverty and Indigence of the Inhabitants.

I sometime ago signifyed to the Incorporated Society for propagating the gospel in foreign Parts the Want of Education in this Province, as I have the Honour of being in their Service, but have not as yet received any answer.—The Society may rest assured that as I have hitherto, so I shall hereafter incessantly endeavour that their munificent and laudable & charitable Design may answer all the good purposes thereby intended.

A MISSIONARY'S ACCOUNT OF THE PLANTERS' ATTITUDE TOWARD NEGRO EDUCATION IN VIRGINIA (1762)   From Edgar W. Knight, ed., *A Documentary History of Education in the South Before 1860* (Chapel Hill, N.C., 1949), vol I, p. 150.

[Dr. Brays] Associates Office Jany 6th 1763

Read a Letter dated at Williamsburgh Virginia 30th Sept. 1762 from the Revd. Mr. Yates and Robt. Nicholas Esq: wherein They say They have sent a List of the Black Children at present in the School, but can give no Satisfactory Account of those who have left the School the Mistress having kept no regular account. That at a late Visitation of the School they were pretty much pleased with the Scholars performances as they rather exceeded their Expectation, that They believe all the Children have been baptized and that it is general Practice in the Province for Negroe Parents to have their Children baptized that the many Difficulties They have to Struggle with in the Prosecution of the good Work made them Apprehensive that the Success might not answer the Expectation of the Associates but they shall think themselves Fortunate if any Endeavours of Theirs can contribute to the Spiritual Welfare and Happiness of the poor Negroes. They hope, notwithstanding the several obstacles to the Instruction and Reformation of the Negroes (which they enumerate) that this Scheme of Negro Schools properly conducted many have a good Effect. They say the People of that City were very willing to send their Young Negroes to School, and believe that double the present Number of Scholars might easily be procured, wou'd the Fund admit of it; but are fearful Many People do not send them upon right Motives, because They do not suffer them to continue at School long enough to be properly instructed, but keep them at Home as soon as they can be of the least Service in the Family. They add, that the Planters urge it a sin and politick to enlarge the understanding of their Slaves, which will render them more impatient of Slavery. They are apprehensive that the good Impressions made on the Childrens Mind whilst at School will afterwards be too easily effaced by the Examples of other Slaves, especially of their Parents: howevery They are resolved not to be discouraged, but hope by the Blessing of God the undertaking will prosper—They think that Designs of this Nature cannot properly be conducted without certain Uniform Regulations, by which all parties concerned may know how to conduct themselves, and have therefore drawn up a Set of Rules for this Purpose a Copy of which They sent to be submitted to the Judgement of the Associates. They shall soon have Occasion for a few Testaments, Psalters Spelling Books for the use of the School and a Number of Baccu's Sermons to be dispersed among the Planters and conclude with wishing Success to the Associates in all their Designs.

Agreed that the Sincere and hearty Thanks of the Associates be returned to the Revd. Mr. Yates and Mr. Nicholas for their full and very Satisfactory Account of the present State of the Negroe School, and for their generous assurances that notwithstanding the manifold Difficulties and Discouragements they have to contend with, They are resolved to persevere in the Prosecution of this pious and charitable Undertaking.

Agreed that hearty Thanks be returned also for their Care in drawing up Rules and Regulations for the Better Government of the School and that They be made acquainted that the Associates do entirely approve thereof as Judiciously calculated to answer the good End proposed

Agreed that 25 Spelling Books 25 Psalters 20 Testaments and 25 Baccus Sermons be sent for the Use of the Negroe Schools at Williamsburgh.

A DUTCH MINISTER'S SERMON ON CONVERSION OF THE NEGROES

(**1664**)   From Reverend Henricus Selyns to the Classis of Amsterdam, June 9, 1664, as quoted in J. Franklin Jameson, ed., *Narratives of the New Netherland, 1609-1664* (New York, 1909), pp. 408-09.

Very Reverend, Pious and Learned Brethren in Christ:

With Christian salutations of grace and peace, this is to inform you, that with proper submission, we take the liberty of reporting to the Very Rev. Classis the condition and welfare of the Church of Jesus Christ, to which your Reverences called me, as well as my request and friendly prayer for an honorable dismission.

❊   ❊   ❊

As to baptisms, the negroes occasionally request that we should baptize their children, but we have refused to do so, partly on account of their lack of knowledge and of faith, and partly because of the worldly and perverse aims on the part of said negroes. They wanted nothing else than to deliver their children from bodily slavery, without striving for piety and Christian virtues. Nevertheless when it was seemly to do so, we have, to the best of our ability, taken much trouble in private and public catechizing. This has borne but little fruit among the elder people who have no faculty of comprehension; but there is some hope for the youth who have improved reasonably well. Not to administer baptism among them for the reasons given, is also the custom among our colleagues. But the most important thing is, that the Father of Grace and God of Peace has blessed our two congregations with quietness and harmony, out of the treasury of his graciousness; so that we have had no reason to complain to the Rev. Classis, which takes such things, however, in good part; or to trouble you, as we might have anticipated.

PROTEST OF THE GERMANTOWN, PENNSYLVANIA, QUAKERS
AGAINST SLAVERY (1688)   From *Pennsylvania Magazine of History and Biography,*
vol. IV, pp. 28-30.

This is to the monthly meeting held at Richard Worrell's:

These are the reasons why we are against the traffic of mens-body, as follows: Is there any that would be done or handled at this manner? viz., to be sold or made a slave for all the time of his life? How fearful and faint-hearted are many on sea, when they see a strange vessel, being afraid it should be a Turk and they should be taken and sold for slaves in Turkey. Now what is *this* better done than Turks do? Yea, rather it is worse for them which say they are Christians; for we hear that the most part of such Negroes are brought hither against their will and consent, and that many of them are stolen. Now, though they are black, we cannot conceive there is more liberty to have them slaves as it is to have other white ones. There is a saying that we shall do to all men like as we will be done ourselves; making no difference of what generation, descent or colour they are. And those who steal or rob men, and those who buy or purchase them, are they not all alike? Here is liberty of conscience, which is right and reasonable; here ought to be likewise liberty of the body, except of evil-doers, which is another case. But to bring men hither, or to rob and sell them against their will, we stand against. In Europe there are many oppressed for conscience sake; and here there are those oppressed which are of a black colour. And we who know that men must not commit adultery—some do commit adultery *in* others, separating wives from their husbands and giving them to others: and some sell the children of those poor creatures to other men. Oh! do consider well this thing, you who do it, if you would be done at this manner—and if it is done according to Christianity! You surpass Holland and Germany in this thing. This makes an ill report in all those countries of Europe, where they hear of [it], that the Quakers do here handle men like they handle there the cattle. And for that reason some have no mind or inclination to come hither. And who shall maintain this your cause, or plead for it? Truly, we cannot do so except you shall inform us better hereof, viz.: that Christians have liberty to practise these things. Pray, what thing in the world can be done worse towards us than if men should rob or steal us away and sell us for slaves to strange countries; separating husbands from their wives and children. Being now this is not done at that manner we will be done at; therefore, we contradict, and are against this traffic of mens-body. And we who profess that it is not lawful to steal, must, likewise, avoid to purchase such things as are stolen, but rather help to stop this robbing and stealing, if possible. And such men ought to be delivered out of the hands of the robbers and set free as well as in Europe. Then is Pennsylvania to have a good report; instead, it has now a bad one for this sake in other countries; especially whereas the Europeans are desirous to know in what manner *the Quakers* do rule in *their* province; and most of them do look upon us with an envious eye. But if this is done well, what shall we say is done evil?

If once these slaves (which they say are so wicked and stubborn men), should join themselves—fight for their freedom, and handle their masters and mistresses as they did handle them before; will these masters and mistresses take the sword at hand and war against these poor slaves, like we are able to believe, some will not refuse to do? Or, have these Negroes not as much right to fight for their freedom as you have to keep them slaves?

Now, consider well this thing, if it is good or bad. And in case you find it to be good to handle these blacks in that manner, we desire and require you hereby lovingly that you may inform us herein, which at this time never was done, viz., that Christians have liberty to do so. To the end we shall be satisfied on this point, and satisfy likewise our good friends and acquaintances in our native country, to whom it is a terror or fearful thing, that men should be handled so in Pennsylvania.

This is from our meeting at Germantown, held the 18 of the 2 month, 1688, to be delivered to the monthly meeting at Richard Worrell's.

Gerret Hendericks   Francis Daniel Pastorius

Derick op de Graeff   Abraham op den Graeff

AN ACT TO ENCOURAGE THE BAPTIZING OF NEGRO, INDIAN, AND MULATTO SLAVES IN NEW YORK (1706) From Hugh Hastings, ed., *Ecclesiastical Records of the State of New York* (Albany, 1902), vol. III, p. 1673.

Whereas divers of her Majesty's good Subjects, Inhabitants of this Colony now are and have been willing that such Negro, Indian and Mulatto Slaves who belong to them and desire the same, should be Baptized, but are deterr'd and hindered therefrom by reason of a Groundless opinion that hath spread itself in this Colony, that by the Baptizing of such Negro, Indian or Mulatto slave they would become free and ought to be sett at Liberty. In order therefore to put an end to all such Doubts and Scruples as have or hereafter at any time may arise about the same. Be it Enacted by the Governour Councill and Assembly and it is hereby Enacted by the authority of the same, That the Baptizing of any Negro, Indian or Mulatto Slave shall not be any Cause or reason for the setting them or any of them at Liberty.

And be it declared and Enacted by the Governour Councill & Assembly and by the Authority of the same, That all and every Negro, Indian, Mulatto and Mestee and Bastard Child & Children who is, are, and shall be born of any Negro, Indian, Mulatto or Mestee, shall follow ye State and Condition of the Mother & be esteemed reputed taken & adjudged a Slave & Slaves to all intents & purposes whatsoever.

Provided, always & be it declared & Enacted by ye said Authority That no slave whatsoever in this Colony shall Att any time be admitted as a witness for, or against, any Freeman, in any Case matter or Cause, Civill or Criminal whatsoever.

ANNOUNCEMENT OF THE OPENING OF A FREE SCHOOL FOR NEGRO CHILDREN IN NEW YORK (1760)   From *The New-York Mercury*, September 15, 1760, as quoted in Morgan Dix, *A History of the Parish of Trinity Church in the City of New York* (New York, 1898), pp. 294-95.

This is to inform the Public, that a Free School is opened near the New-Dutch-Church, for the instruction of 30 Negro Children, from 5 years old and upwards, in Reading, and in the Principles of Christianity, and likewise sewing and knitting; which School is entirely under the Inspection and Care of the Clergy of the Church of England in this City: Those Persons therefore that have the present Usefulness, and future Welfare of their young Slaves at Heart (especially those born in their Houses), are desired to apply to any one of the Clergy, who will immediately send them to the aforesaid School, and see that they be faithfully instructed.

N.B. All that is required of their Masters and Mistresses, is that they find them in Wood for the Winter. Proper Books will be provided for them gratis.

A MEMORIAL AGAINST SLAVERY BY SAMUEL SEWALL (1700)   From George Moore, *Notes on the History of Slavery in Massachusetts* (Boston, 1866), pp. 83-87.

FORASMUCH *as* LIBERTY *is in real value next unto Life; None ought to part with themselves, or deprive others of it, but upon most mature consideration.*

The Numerousness of Slaves at this Day in the Province, and the Uneasiness of them under their Slavery, hath put many upon thinking whether the Foundation of it be firmly and well laid; so as to sustain the Vast Weight that is built upon it. It is most certain that all Men, as they are the Sons of *Adam*, are Co-heirs, and have equal Right unto Liberty, and all other outward Comforts of Life. GOD *hath given the Earth (with all its commodities) unto the Sons of Adam, Psal.,* 115, 16. *And hath made of one Blood all Nations of Men, for to dwell on all the face of the Earth, and hath determined the Times before appointed, and the bounds of their Habitation: That they should seek the Lord. Forasmuch then as we are the Offspring of* GOD, *etc. Acts* 17. 26, 27, 29. Now, although the Title given by the last ADAM doth infinitely better Men's Estates, respecting GOD and themselves; and grants them a most beneficial and inviolable Lease under the Broad Seal of Heaven, who were before only Tenants at Will; yet through the Indulgence of GOD to our First Parents after the Fall, the outward Estate of all and every of their Children, remains the same as to one another. So that Originally, and Naturally, there is no such thing as Slavery. *Joseph* was rightfully no more a Slave to his Brethren, than they were to him; and they had no more Authority to *Sell* him, than they had to *Slay* him. And if *they* had nothing to do to sell him; the *Ishmaelites* bargaining with them, and paying down Twenty pieces of Silver, could not make a Title. Neither

NEGROES, INDIAN AND GERMAN IMMIGRANTS

589

could *Potiphar* have any better Interest in him than the *Ishmaelites* had. *Gen.* 37, 20, 27, 28. For he that shall in this case plead *Alteration of Property,* seems to have forfeited a great part of his own claim to Humanity. There is no proportion between Twenty Pieces of Silver and LIBERTY. The Commodity itself is the Claimer. If *Arabian* Gold be imported in any quantities, most are afraid to meddle with it, though they might have it at easy rates; lest it should have been wrongfully taken from the Owners, it should kindle a fire to the Consumption of their whole Estate. 'Tis pity there should be more Caution used in buying a Horse, or a little lifeless dust, than there is in purchasing Men and Women: Whereas they are the Offspring of GOD.

Caveat Emptor!

And all things considered, it would conduce more to the Welfare of the Province, to have White Servants for a Term of Years, than to have Slaves for Life. Few can endure to hear of a Negro's being made free; and indeed they can seldom use their Freedom well; yet their continual aspiring after their forbidden Liberty, renders them Unwilling Servants. And there is such a disparity in their Conditions, Colour, and Hair, that they can never embody with us, & grow up in orderly Families, to the Peopling of the Land; but still remain in our Body Politick as a kind of extravasat Blood. As many Negro Men as there are among us, so many empty Places are there in our Train Bands, and the places taken up of Men that might make Husbands for our Daughters. And the Sons and Daughters of *New England* would become more like *Jacob* and *Rachel,* if this Slavery were thrust quite out of Doors. Moreover it is too well known what Temptations Masters are under, to connive at the Fornication of their Slaves; lest they should be obliged to find them Wives, or pay their Fines. It seems to be practically pleaded that they might be lawless; 'tis thought much of, that the Law should have satisfaction for their Thefts, and other Immoralities, by which means, *Holiness to the Lord* is more rarely engraven upon this sort of Servitude. It is likewise most lamentable to think, how in taking Negroes out of *Africa,* and selling of them here, That which GOD has joined together, Men do boldly rend asunder; Men from their Country, Husbands from their Wives, Parents from their Children. How horrible is the Uncleanness, Mortality, if not Murder, that the Ships are guilty of that bring great Crouds of these Miserable Men and Women. Methinks when we are bemoaning the barbarous Usage of our Friends and Kinsfolk in *Africa,* it might not be unreasonable to enquire whether we are not culpable in forcing the *Africans* to become Slaves amongst ourselves. And it may be a question whether all the Benefit received by *Negro* Slaves will balance the Accompt of Cash laid out upon them; and for the Redemption of our own enslaved Friends out of *Africa.* Besides all the Persons and Estates that have perished there.

 Obj. 1. *These Blackamores are of the Posterity of Cham, and therefore are under the Curse of Slavery.* Gen. 9, 25, 26, 27.
 Ans. Of all Offices, one would not beg this; viz. Uncall'd for, to be an Executioner of the Vindictive Wrath of God; the extent and duration of which is to us uncertain. If this ever was a Commission; How do we know but that it is long since out of Date? Many have found it to their Cost, that a Prophetical Denunciation of Judgment against a Person or People, would not warrant them to inflict that evil.

Obj. 2. *The* Nigers *are brought out of a Pagan Country, into places where the Gospel is preached.*

Ans. Evil must not be done, that good may come of it. The extraordinary and comprehensive Benefit accruing to the Church of GOD, and to *Joseph* personally, did not rectify his Brethren's Sale of him.

Obj. 3. *The Africans have Wars one with another: Our Ships bring lawful Captives taken in those wars.*

Ans. For aught is known, their Wars are much such as were between *Jacob's* Sons and their Brother *Joseph.* If they be between Town and Town; Provincial or National: Every War is upon one side Unjust. An Unlawful War can't make lawful Captives. And by receiving, we are in danger to promote, and partake in their Barbarous Cruelties. I am sure, if some Gentlemen should go down to the *Brewsters* to take the Air, and Fish: And a stronger Party from *Hull* should surprise them, and sell them for Slaves to a Ship outward bound; they would think themselves unjustly dealt with; both by Sellers and Buyers. And yet 'tis to be feared, we have no other Kind of Title to our *Nigers. Therefore all things whatsoever ye would that men should do to you, do you even so to them: for this is the Law and the Prophets.* Matt. 7, 12.

Obj. 4. Abraham *had Servants bought with his Money and born in his House.*

Ans. Until the Circumstances of *Abraham's* purchase be recorded, no Argument can be drawn from it. In the mean time, Charity obliges us to conclude, that He knew it was lawful and good.

It is Observable that the *Israelites* were strictly forbidden the buying or selling one another for Slaves. *Levit.* 25. 39. 46. *Jer.* 34.8-22. And GOD gaged His Blessing in lieu of any loss they might conceit they suffered thereby, *Deut.* 15. 18. And since the partition Wall is broken down, inordinate Self-love should likewise be demolished. GOD expects that Christians should be of a more Ingenuous and benign frame of Spirit. Christians should carry it to all the World, as the *Israelites* were to carry it one towards another. And for Men obstinately to persist in holding their Neighbours and Brethren under the Rigor of perpetual Bondage, seems to be no proper way of gaining Assurance that GOD has given them Spiritual Freedom. Our Blessed Saviour has altered the Measures of the ancient Love Song, and set it to a most Excellent New Tune, which all ought to be ambitious of Learning. *Matt.* 5. 43. 44. *John* 13. 34. These *Ethiopians*, as black as they are, seeing they are the Sons and Daughters of the First *Adam,* the Brethren and Sisters of the Last ADAM, and the Offspring of GOD; They ought to be treated with a Respect agreeable.

ANNOUNCEMENT OF THE OPENING OF A SCHOOL FOR NEGRO SERVANTS IN BOSTON (1728)   From *New England Weekly Journal,* April 8, 1728.

Mr. Nath Pigott intends to open a School on Monday, next, for the Instruction of Negro's in Reading, Catechizing & Writing if required, if any are so well inclined as to send their Servants to said school near Mr. Checkley's Meeting House care will be taken for their Instruction as aforesaid.

EZRA STILES' DESCRIPTION OF NEGRO RELIGIOUS INSTRUCTION

(1772)   From Frank Dexter, ed., *The Literary Diary of Ezra Stiles* (New York, 1901), vol. I, p. 248.

[*Feb.*] *24.* Compiling History. In the Evening a very full and serious Meeting of Negroes at my House, perhaps 80 or 90: I discoursed to them on Luke xiv, 16, 17, 18. "A certain man made—Excuse." They sang well. They appeared attentive and much affected; and after I had done, many of them came up to me and thanked me, as they said, for taking so much Care of their souls, and hoped they should remember my Counsels. There are six or seven Negroe Communicants in the Baptist Churches in Town, 4 or 5 in the Church of England, seven in my Church and six or seven in Mr. Hopkins' Church: perhaps 26, and not above 30 professors out of Twelve hundred Negroes in Town.

[*July*] *10.* Reading Origen contra Celsum. I have Eighty Communicants in my Church, of which seven are Negroes. I directed the Negroes to come to me this Evening; when three Negro Brethren and three Negro Sisters met in my Study. I discoursed with them on the great Things of the divine Life and eternal Salvation—counselling and encouraging and earnestly pressing upon them to make their Calling and Election sure, and to walk worthy of their holy profession, and especially to maintain a daily Intercourse with heaven in holy duties and divine Contemplation on the Love of Christ. Then we all fell upon our Knees together, and I poured out fervent Supplications at the Throne of Grace imploring the divine Blessing upon us, and commending ourselves to the holy Keeping of the Most High. We seemed to have the delightful presence of Jesus.

PETITION FOR FREEDOM BY MASSACHUSETTS NEGROES (1773)

From Massachusetts Historical Society, *Collections,* Fifth Series (Boston, 1877), vol. III, pp. 432-33.

To His Excellency Thomas Hutch[inson Gov]ernor of said Province, to The Honorable His Majestys Council, [and to The] Honourable House of Representatives in General Court assembled June 1773

The Petition of us the subscribers in behalf of all thous who by divine Permission are held in a state of slavery, within the bowels of a free Country, Humbly sheweth.—

That your Petitioners apprehend they have in comon with other men a naturel right to be free and without molestation to injoy such Property as thay may acquire by their industry, or by any other means not detrimetal to their fellow men, and that no person can have any just claim to their services unless

To his Excellency Thomas Gage Esq Captain General and Governor in Chief in and over this Province. To the Honourable his Majestys Council and the Honourable House of Representatives in General Court assembled may 25 1774

The Petition of a Grate Number of Blackes of this Province who by divine permission are held in a state of Slavery within the bowels of a free and christian Country
    Humbly Shewing
That your Petitioners apprehind we have in common with all other men a naturel right to our freedoms without Being depriv'd of them by our fellow men as we are a freeborn Pepel and have never forfeited this Blessing by aney compact or agreement whatever. But we were unjustly dragged by the cruel hand of power from our dearest frinds and sum of us stolen from the bosoms of our tender Parents and from a Populous Pleasant and plentiful country and Brought hither to be made slaves for Life in a Christian land. Thus are we deprived of every thing that hath a tendency to make life even tolerable, the endearing ties of husband and wife we are strangers to for we are no longer man and wife then our masters or mestreses thinkes proper marred or onmarred. Our children are also taken from us by force and sent maney miles from us wear we seldom or ever see them again there to be made slaves of for Life which sumtimes is vere short by Reson of Being dragged from their mothers Breest Thus our Lives are imbittered to us on these accounts By our deplorable situation we are rendered incapable of shewing our obedience to Almighty God how can a slave perform the duties of a husband to a wife or parent to his child How can a husband leave master and work and cleave to his wife How can the wife submit themselves to their husbands in all things. How can the child obey thear parents in all things. There is a grat number of us sencear . . . members of the Church of Christ how can the master and the slave be said to fulfil that command Live in love let Brotherly Love contuner and abound Beare yea onenothers Bordenes How can the master be said to Beare my Borden when he Beares me down whith the Have chanes of slavery and operson against my will and how can we fulfill our parte of duty to him whilst in this condition and as we cannot searve our God as we ought whilst in this situation Nither can we reap an equal benefet from the laws of the Land which doth not justifi but condemns slavery or if there had bin aney Law to hold us in Bondege we are Humbely of the Opinon ther never was aney to inslave our children for life when Born in a free Countrey. We therfor urge your Excellency and Honours will give this its deu weight and consideration and that you will accordingly cause an act of the legislative to be pessed that we may obtain our Natural right our freedoms and our children be set at lebety at the yeare of Twenty one for whoues sekes more petequeley your petitioners is in Duty ever to Pray.

PHILLIS WHEATLEY ON SLAVERY (1773)   From Phillis Wheatley, *Poems on Various Subjects, Religious and Moral* (Boston, 1773), pp. 18, 74.

On Being Brought from Africa to America

'Twas mercy brought me from my Pagan land,
Taught my benighted soul to understand
That there's a God, and there's a Saviour too:
Once I redemption neither sought nor knew.
Some view our sable race with scornful eye,
"Their colour is a diabolic die."
Remember, Christians, Negroes, black as Cain,
May be refin'd, and join th' angelic train.

*   *   *

To the Right Honorable William, Earl of Dartmouth, His Majesty's Secretary of State for North America, etc.

Should you, my lord, while you peruse my song,
Wonder from whence my love of Freedom sprung,
Whence flow these wishes for the common good,
By feeling hearts alone best understood,
I, young in life, by seeming cruel fate
Was snatch'd from Afric's fancy'd happy seat:
What pangs excruciating must molest,
What sorrows labour in my parent's breast?
Steel'd was the soul and by no misery mov'd
That from a father seiz'd his babe belov'd:
Such, such my case. And can I then but pray
Others may never feel tyrannic sway?

QUAKER JOHN WOOLMAN ARGUES AGAINST SLAVERY (1754)   From John Woolman, *Some Considerations On The Keeping of Negroes* (Philadelphia, 1754), pp. 1-3, 6-7.

EDUCATION
IN THE
UNITED STATES

594

As Many Times there are different Motives to the same Actions; and one does that from a generous Heart, which another does for selfish Ends:——The like may be said in this Case.

There are various Circumstances amongst them that keep *Negroes*, and different Ways by which they fall under their Care; and, I doubt not, there are many well disposed Persons amongst them who desire rather to manage wisely and justly in this difficult Matter, than to make Gain of it.

But the general Disadvantage which these poor *Africans* lie under in an enlight'ned Christian Country, having often fill'd me with real Sadness, and been like undigested Matter on my Mind, I now think it my Duty, through Divine Aid, to offer some Thoughts thereon to the Consideration of others.

When we remember that all Nations are of one Blood, *Gen.* iii. 20. that in this World we are but Sojourners, that we are subject to the like Afflictions and Infirmities of Body, the like Disorders and Frailties in Mind, the like Temptations, the same Death, and the same Judgment, and, that the Alwise Being is Judge and Lord over us all, it seems to raise an Idea of a general Brotherhood, and a Disposition easy to be touched with a Feeling of each others Afflictions: But when we forget those Things, and look chiefly at our outward Circumstances, in this and some Ages past, constantly retaining in our Minds the Distinction betwixt us and them, with respect to our Knowledge and Improvement in Things divine, natural and artificial, our Breasts being apt to be filled with fond Notions of Superiority, there is Danger of erring in our Conduct toward them.

We allow them to be of the same Species with ourselves, the Odds is, we are in a higher Station, and enjoy greater Favours than they: And when it is thus, that our heavenly Father endoweth some of his Children with distinguished Gifts, they are intended for good Ends; but if those thus gifted are thereby lifted up above their Brethren, not considering themselves as Debtors to the Weak, nor behaving themselves as faithful Stewards, none who judge impartially can suppose them free from Ingratitude.

*   *   *

To consider Mankind otherwise than Brethren, to think Favours are peculiar to one Nation, and exclude others, plainly supposes a Darkness in the Understanding: For as God's Love is universal, so where the Mind is sufficiently influenced by it, it begets a Likeness of itself, and the Heart is enlarged towards all Men. Again, to conclude a People froward, perverse, and worse by Nature than others (who ungratefully receive Favours, and apply them to bad Ends) this will excite a Behaviour toward them unbecoming the Excellence of true Religion.

To prevent such Error, let us calmly consider their Circumstance; and, the better to do it, make their Case ours. Suppose, then, that our Ancestors and we had been exposed to constant Servitude in the more servile and inferior Employments of Life; that we had been destitute of the Help of Reading and good Company; that amongst ourselves we had had few wise and pious Instructors; that the Religious amongst our Superiors seldom took Notice of us; that while others, in Ease, have plentifully heap'd up the Fruit of our Labour, we had receiv'd barely enough to relieve Nature, and being wholly at the Command of others, had generally been treated as a contemptible, ignorant Part of Mankind: Should we, in that Case, be less abject than they now are? Again, If Oppression be so hard to bear, that a wise Man is made mad by it, *Eccl.* vii. 7. then a Series of those Things altering the Behaviour and Manners of a People, is what may reasonably be expected.

When our property is taken contrary to our Mind, by Means appearing to us unjust, it is only through divine Influence, and the Enlargement of Heart from thence proceeding, that we can love our reputed Oppressors: If the Negroes fall short in this, an uneasy, if not a disconsolate Disposition, will be awak'ned, and remain like Seeds in their Minds, producing Sloth and many other Habits appearing odious to us, with which being free Men, they, perhaps, had not been chargeable. (1754)

THOMAS JEFFERSON'S OBJECTIONS TO SLAVERY (1782) From *Notes on Virginia* (1782), as quoted in Paul Leicester Ford, ed., *The Writings of Thomas Jefferson* (New York, 1894), vol. I, pp. 266-67.

Query XVIII

The Particular Customs and Manners that May Happen to Be Received in that State?

It is difficult to determine on the standard by which the manners of a nation may be tried, whether *catholic* or *particular*. It is more difficult for a native to bring to that standard the manners of his own nation, familiarized to him by habit. There must doubtless be an unhappy influence on the manners of our people produced by the existence of slavery among us. The whole commerce between master and slave is a perpetual exercise of the most boisterous passions, the most unremitting despotism on the one part, and degrading submissions on the other. Our children see this, and learn to imitate it; for man is an imitative animal. This quality is the germ of all education in him. From his cradle to his grave he is learning to do what he sees others do. If a parent could find no motive either in his philanthropy or his self-love, for restraining the intemperance of passion towards his slave, it should always be a sufficient one that his child is present. But generally it is not sufficient. The parent storms, the child looks on, catches the lineaments of wrath, puts on the same airs in the circle of smaller slaves, gives a loose to the worst of passions, and thus nursed, educated, and daily exercised in tyranny, cannot but be stamped by it with odious peculiarities. The man must be a prodigy who can retain his manners and morals undepraved by such circumstances. And with what execrations should the statesman be loaded, who permitting one half the citizens thus to trample on the rights of the other, transforms those into despots, and these into enemies, destroys the morals of the one part, and the amor patraiae of the other. For if a slave can have a country in this world, it must be any other in preference to that in which he is born to live and labour for another: in which he must lock up the faculties of his nature, contribute as far as depends on his individual endeavours to the evanishment of a human race, or entail his own miserable condition on the endless generations proceeding from him. With the morals of the people, their industry also is destroyed. For in a warm climate, no man will labour for himself who can make another labour for him. This is so true, that of the proprietors of slaves a very small proportion indeed are ever seen to labour. And can the liberties of a nation be thought secure when we have removed their only firm basis, a conviction in the minds of the people that these liberties are of the gift of God? That they are not to be violated but with his wrath? Indeed I tremble for my country when I reflect that God is just: that his justice cannot sleep forever: that considering numbers, nature and natural means only, a revolution of the wheel of fortune, an exchange of situation, is among possible events: that it may become probable by supernatural interference! The Almighty has no attribute which can take side with us in such a contest.—But it is impossible to be temperate and to pursue this subject through the various considerations of policy, of morals, of history natural and civil. We must be contented to hope they will force their way into every one's mind. I think a change already perceptible, since the origin of the present revolution. The spirit of the master is abating, that of the slave rising from the dust, his condition mollifying, the way I hope preparing, under the auspices of heaven for a total emancipation, and that this is disposed, in the order of events to be with the consent of the masters, rather than by their extirpation.

A PUBLIC LETTER FROM BENJAMIN FRANKLIN ON THE SLAVE TRADE (1790)

From Albert H. Smyth, ed., *The Writings of Benjamin Franklin* (New York, 1907), vol. X, pp. 87-91.

To the Editor of the Federal Gazette

March 23d, 1790.

SIR,

Reading last night in your excellent Paper the speech of Mr. Jackson in Congress against their meddling with the Affair of Slavery, or attempting to mend the Condition of the Slaves, it put me in mind of a similar One made about 100 Years since by Sidi Mehemet Ibrahim, a member of the Divan of Algiers, which may be seen in Martin's Account of his Consulship, anno 1687. It was against granting the Petition of the Sect called *Erika*, or Purists, who pray'd for the Abolition of Piracy and Slavery as being unjust. Mr. Jackson does not quote it; perhaps he has not seen it. If, therefore, some of its Reasonings are to be found in his eloquent Speech, it may only show that men's Interests and Intellects operate and are operated on with surprising similarity in all Countries and Climates, when under similar Circumstances. The African's Speech, as translated, is as follows.

"Allah Bismillah, &c. God is great, and Mahomet is his Prophet.

"Have these *Erika* considered the Consequences of granting their Petition? If we cease our Cruises against the Christians, how shall we be furnished with the Commodities their Countries produce, and which are so necessary for us? If we forbear to make Slaves of their People, who in this hot Climate are to cultivate our Lands? Who are to perform the common Labours of our City, and in our Families? Must we not then be our own Slaves? And is there not more Compassion and more Favour due to us as Mussulmen, than to these Christian Dogs? We have now above 50,000 Slaves in and near Algiers. This Number, if not kept up by fresh Supplies, will soon diminish, and be gradually annihilated. If we then cease taking and

NEGROES, INDIANS, AND GERMAN IMMIGRANTS

plundering the Infidel Ships, and making Slaves of the Seamen and Passengers, our Lands will become of no Value for want of Cultivation; the Rents of Houses in the City will sink one half; and the Revenues of Government arising from its Share of Prizes be totally destroy'd! And for what? To gratify the whims of a whimsical Sect, who would have us, not only forbear making more Slaves, but even to manumit those we have.

"But who is to indemnify their Masters for the Loss? Will the State do it? Is our Treasury sufficient? Will the *Erika* do it? Can they do it? Or would they, to do what they think Justice to the Slaves, do a greater Injustice to the Owners? And if we set our Slaves free, what is to be done with them? Few of them will return to their Countries; they know too well the greater Hardships they must there be subject to; they will not embrace our holy Religion; they will not adopt our Manners; our People will not pollute themselves by intermarrying with them. Must we maintain them as Beggars in our Streets, or suffer our Properties to be the Prey of their Pillage? For Men long accustom'd to Slavery will not work for a Livelihood when not compell'd. And what is there so pitiable in their present Condition? Were they not Slaves in their own Countries?

"Are not Spain, Portugal, France, and the Italian states govern'd by Despots, who hold all their Subjects in Slavery, without Exception? Even England treats its Sailors as Slaves; for they are, whenever the Government pleases, seiz'd, and confin'd in Ships of War, condemn'd not only to work, but to fight, for small Wages, or a mere Subsistence, not better than our Slaves are allow'd by us. Is their Condition then made worse by their falling into our Hands? No; they have only exchanged one Slavery for another, and I may say a better; for here they are brought into a Land where the Sun of Islamism gives forth its Light, and shines in full Splendor, and they have an Opportunity of making themselves acquainted with the true Doctrine, and thereby saving their immortal Souls. Those who remain at home have not that Happiness. Sending the Slaves home then would be sending them out of Light into Darkness.

"I repeat the Question, What is to be done with them? I have heard it suggested, that they may be planted in the Wilderness, where there is plenty of Land for them to subsist on, and where they may flourish as a free State; but they are, I doubt, too little dispos'd to labour without Compulsion, as well as too ignorant to establish a good government, and the wild Arabs would soon molest and destroy or again enslave them. While serving us, we take care to provide them with every thing, and they are treated with Humanity. The Labourers in their own Country are, as I am well informed, worse fed, lodged, and cloathed. The Condition of most of them is therefore already mended, and requires no further Improvement. Here their Lives are in Safety. They are not liable to be impress'd for Soldiers, and forc'd to cut one another's Christian Throats, as in the Wars of their own Countries. If some of the religious mad Bigots, who now teaze us with their silly Petitions, have in a Fit of blind Zeal freed their Slaves, it was not Generosity, it was not Humanity, that mov'd them to the Action; it was from the conscious Burthen of a Load of Sins, and Hope, from the supposed Merits of so good a Work, to be excus'd Damnation.

"How grossly are they mistaken in imagining Slavery to be disallow'd by the Alcoran! Are not the two Precepts, to quote no more, '*Masters, treat your Slaves with kindness; Slaves, serve your Masters with Cheerfulness and Fidelity,*' clear Proofs to the contrary? Nor can the Plundering of Infidels be in that sacred Book forbidden, since it is well known from it, that God has given the World, and all that it contains, to his faithful Mussulmen, who are to enjoy it of Right as fast as they conquer it. Let us then hear no more of this detestable Proposition, the Manumission of Christian Slaves, the Adoption of which would, by depreciating our Lands and Houses, and thereby depriving so many good Citizens of their Properties, create universal Discontent, and provoke Insurrections, to the endangering of Government and producing general Confusion. I have therefore no doubt, but this wise Council will prefer the Comfort and Happiness of a whole Nation of true Believers to the Whim of a few *Erika*, and dismiss their Petition."

The Result was, as Martin tells us, that the Divan came to this Resolution; "The Doctrine, that Plundering and Enslaving the Christians is unjust, is at best *problematical;* but that it is the Interest of this State to continue the Practice, is clear; therefore let the Petition be rejected."

And it was rejected accordingly.

And since like Motives are apt to produce in the Minds of Men like Opinions and Resolutions, may we not, Mr. Brown, venture to predict, from this Account, that the Petitions to the Parliament of England for abolishing the Slave-Trade, to say nothing of other Legislatures, and the Debates upon them, will have a similar Conclusion? I am, Sir, your constant Reader and humble Servant,

Historicus

PRAISE FOR BENJAMIN BANNEKER, A SELF-EDUCATED NEGRO

(1791)   From *Benjamin Banneker's Pennsylvania, Delaware, Maryland, and Virginia Almanack and Ephemeries, for the Year of Our Lord, 1792* (Baltimore, 1791), pp. 2-4.

The Editors of the PENNSYLVANIA, DELAWARE, MARYLAND, *and* VIRGINIA ALMANACK, *feel themselves gratified in the Opportunity of presenting to the Public, through the Medium of their Press, what must be considered an extraordinary Effort of Genius—a COMPLETE and ACCURATE EPHEMERIS for the Year 1792, calculated by a sable Descendant of* Africa, *who, by this Specimen of Ingenuity, evinces, to Demonstration, that mental Powers and Endowments are not the exclusive Excellence of white People, but that the Rays of Science may alike illumine the Minds of Men of every Clime, (however they may differ in the Colour of their Skin) particularly those whom Tyrant-Custom hath too long taught us to depreciate as a Race inferior in intellectual Capacity.—They flatter themselves that a philanthropic Public, in this enlightened Era, will be induced to give their Patronage and Support to this Work, not only on Account of its intrinsic Merit, (it having met the Approbation of several of the most distinguished Astronomers in America, particularly the celebrated Mr. Rittenhouse) but from similar Motives to those which induced the Editors to give this Calculation the Preference, the ardent Desire of drawing modest Merit from Obscurity, and controverting the long-established illiberal Prejudice against the Blacks.*

Though it becomes the Editors to speak with less Confidence of the miscellaneous Part of this Work, they yet flatter themselves, from their Attention to the variegated Selections in Prose and Verse, that their Readers will find it both USEFUL and ENTERTAINING, and not undeserving of that Approbation which they have had the Happiness of experiencing for a Series of Years—an Approbation they are

NEGROES. INDIANS. AND GERMAN IMMIGRANTS

599

most ambitious of meriting, and which, they hope, will crown their present *Wishes* and *Labours* with *Success*.

The Editors have taken the Liberty to annex a Letter from Mr. McHenry, containing Particulars respecting Benjamin, which, it is presumed, will prove more acceptable to the Reader, than anything further in the prefatory Way.

"Baltimore, August 20, 1791.

"Messrs. CODDARD and ANGELL,

"BENJAMIN BANNEKER, a free Negro, has calculated an ALMANACK, for the ensuing year, 1792, which being desirous to dispose of, to the best advantage, he has requested me to aid his application to you for that purpose. Having fully satisfied myself, with respect to his title to this kind of authorship, if you can agree with him for the price of his work, I may venture to assure you it will do you credit, as Editors, while it will afford you the opportunity to encourage talents that have thus far surmounted the most discouraging circumstances and prejudices.

"This Man is about fifty-nine years of age; he was born in *Baltimore County;* his father was an *African*, and his mother the offspring of *African* parents.—His father and mother having obtained their freedom, were enabled to send him to an obscure school, where he learned, when a boy, reading, writing, and arithmetic as far as double position; and to leave him, at their deaths, a few acres of land, upon which he has supported himself ever since by means of economy and constant labour, and preserved a fair reputation. To struggle incessantly against want is no ways favourable to improvement: What he had learned, however, he did not forget; for as some hours of leisure will occur in the most toilsome life, he availed himself of these, not to read and acquire knowledge from writings of genius and discovery, for of such he had none, but to digest and apply, as occasions presented, the few principles of the few rules of arithmetic he had been taught at school. This kind of mental exercise formed his chief amusement, and soon gave him a facility in calculation that was often serviceable to his neighbours, and at length attracted the attention of the Messrs. *Ellicotts*, a family remarkable for their ingenuity and turn to the useful mechanics. It is about three years since Mr. *George Ellicott* lent him *Mayer's* Tables, *Fergusen's* Astronomy, *Leadbeater's* Lunar Tables, and some astronomic instruments, but without accompanying them with either hint or instruction, that might further his studies, or lead him to apply them to any useful result. These books and instruments, the first of the kind he had ever seen, opened a new world to *Benjamin*, and from thenceforward he employed his leisure in astronomical researches. He now took up the idea of the calculations for an ALMANACK, and actually completed an entire set for the last year, upon his original stock of arithmetic. Encouraged by this first attempt, he entered upon his calculation for 1792, which, as well as the former, he began and finished without the least information, or assistance, from any person, or other books than those I have mentioned; so that, whatever merit is attached to his present performance, is exclusively and peculiarly his own.

"I have been the more careful to investigate those particulars, and to ascertain their reality, as they form an interesting fact in the History of Man; and as you may want them to gratify curiosity, I have no objection to your selecting them for your account of *Benjamin.*

"I consider this Negro as a fresh proof that the powers of the mind are disconnected with the colour of the skin, or, in other words, a striking contradiction to Mr. *Hume's* doctrine, that "the Negroes are naturally inferior to the whites, and unsusceptible of attainments in arts and sciences." In every civilized country we shall find thousands of whites, liberally educated, and who have enjoyed greater opportunities of instruction than this Negro, his inferiors in those intellectual acquirements and capacities that form the most characteristic feature in the human race. But the system that would assign to these degraded blacks an origin different from the whites, if it is not ready to be deserted by the philosophers, must be relinquished as similar instances multiply; and that such must frequently happen cannot well be doubted, should no check impede the progress of humanity, which, meliorating the condition of slavery, necessarily leads to its final extinction.—Let, however, the issue be what it will, I cannot but wish, on this occasion, to see the Public patronage keep pace with my black friend's merit.

"I am, Gentlemen, your most obedient servant,

JAMES M'HENRY."

The Indian

SPEECH BY WAHUNSONACOCK (POWHATAN) TO JOHN SMITH AT
WEROWOCOMOCO, VIRGINIA (1609)   From Samuel Griswold Goodrich, *Lives of Celebrated American Indians* (Boston, 1843), pp. 179-80.

I have seen two generations of my people die. Not a man of the two generations is alive now but myself. I know the difference between peace and war better than any man in my country. I am now grown old, and must die soon; my authority must descend to my brothers, Opitchapan, Opechancanough and Catatough;—then to my two sisters, and then to my two daughters. I wish them to know as much as I do, and that your love to them may be like mine to you. Why will you take by force what you may have quietly by love? Why will you destroy us who supply you with food? What can you get by war? We can hide our provisions and run into the woods; then you will starve for wronging your friends. Why are you jealous of us? We are unarmed, and willing to give you what you ask, if you come in a friendly manner, and not with swords and guns, as if to make war upon an enemy. I am not so simple as not to know that it is much better to eat good meat, sleep comfortably, live quietly with my wives and children, laugh and be merry with the English, and trade for their copper and hatchets, than to run away from them, and to lie cold in the woods, feed on acorns, roots and such trash, and be so hunted that I can neither eat nor sleep. In these wars, my men must sit up watching, and if a twig break, they all cry out, "Here comes Captain Smith!" So I must end my miserable life. Take away your guns and swords, the cause of all our jealousy, or you may all die in the same manner.

EDWARD WATERHOUSE ON THE POTENTIAL BENEFITS TO VIRGINIA FROM THE INDIAN MASSACRE (1622)

From Susan M. Kingsbury, ed., *The Records of the Virginia Company of London* (Washington, D.C., 1933), vol. III, pp. 541, 556-59.

To the Honorable Companie of Virginia

Right Honorable and Worthy:

The fame of our late vnhappy accident in *Virginia*, hath spread it selfe, I doubt not, into all parts abroad . . .

Thus haue you seene the particulars of this massacre, out of Letters from thence written, wherein treachery and cruelty haue done their worst to vs, or rather to themselues; for whose vnderstanding is so shallow, as not to perceiue that this must needs bee for the good of the Plantation after, and the losse of this blood to make the body more healthfull, as by these reasons may be manifest.

First, Because betraying of innocency neuer rests vnpunished: And therefore *Agesilaus*, when his enemies (vpon whose oath of being faithfull hee rested) had deceiued him, he sent them thankes, for that by their periury, they had made God his friend, and their enemy.

Secondly, Because our hands which before were tied with gentlenesse and faire vsage, are now set at liberty by the treacherous violence of the Sausages, not vntying the Knot, but cutting it: So that we, who hitherto haue had possession of no more ground then their waste, and our purchase at a valuable consideration to their owne contentment, gained; may now by right of Warre, and law of Nations, inuade the Country, and destroy them who sought to destroy vs: whereby wee shall enjoy their cultiuated places, turning the laborious Mattocke into the victorious Sword (wherein there is more both ease, benefit, and glory) and possessing the fruits of others labours. Now their cleared grounds in all their villages (which are situate in the fruitfullest places of the land) shall be inhabited by vs, whereas heretofore the grubbing of woods was the greatest labour.

Thirdly, Because those commodities which the Indians enjoyed as much or rather more than we, shall now also be entirely possessed by vs. The Deere and other beasts will be in safety, and infinitly increase, which heretofore not onely in the generall huntings of the King (whereat foure or fiue hundred Deere were vsually slaine) but by each particular Indian were destroied at all times of the yeare, without any difference of Male, Damme, or Young. The like may be said of our owne Swine and Goats, whereof they haue vsed to kill eight in tenne more than the English haue done. There will be also a great increase of wild Turkies, and other waighty Fowle, for the Indians neuer put difference of destroying the Hen, but kill them whether in season or not, whether in breeding time, or sitting on their egges, or hauing new hatched, it is all one to them: whereby, as also by the orderly vsing of their fishing Weares, no knowne Country in the world will so plentifully abound in victuall.

Fourthly, Because the way of conquering them is much more easie then of ciuilizing them by faire meanes, for they are a rude, barbarous, and naked people, scattered in small companies, which are helps to Victorie, but hinderances to Ciuilitie: Besides that, a conquest may be of many, and at once; but ciuility is in particular, and slow, the effect of long time, and great industry. Moreouer, victorie of them may bee gained many waies; by force, by surprize, by famine in burning their Corne, by destroying and burning their Boats, Canoes, and Houses, by breaking their fishing Weares, by assailing them in their huntings, whereby they get the greatest part of their sustenance in Winter, by pursuing and chasing them with our horses, and blood-Hounds to draw after them, and Mastiues to teare them, which take this naked, tanned, deformed Sauages, for no other then wild beasts, and are so fierce and fell vpon them, that they feare them worse than their old Deuill which they worship, supposing them to be a new and worse kinde of Deuils then their owne. By these and sundry other wayes, as by driuing them (when they flye) vpon their enemies, who are round about them, and by animating and abetting their enemies against them, may their ruine or subjection be soone effected.

So the Spaniard made great vse for his owne turne of the quarrels and enmities that were amongst the Indians, as throughly vnderstanding and following that Maxime of the Politician, *Diude & impera*, Make diuisions and take Kingdomes: For thus he got two of the greatest Kingdomes of the West Indies, *Peru* and *Mexico*, by the Princes diuisions, and the peoples differences. After the death of *Guainacapa* king of *Peru*, his sonnes *Attabalippa* and *Gascar* falling to war about the kingdom, & each of the striuing to make the *Spaniard* to his friend, *Francis Pizzarro* managing those their diuisions onely to his owne ends, easily stripped them both of that rich Kingdome, and became Master of *Peru*. And so likewise *Ferdinando Cortez* vanquished King *Motezuma*, and gained the Kingdome of *Mexico* from him, by the aid and furtherance of the neighboring people of the Prouince of *Tascala*, being deadly enemies of the *Mexicans;* for which seruice they of *Tascala* are freed by the *Spaniards* from all Tributes to this time. In VIRGINIA the many diuers Princes and people there are at this day opposite in infinite factions one vnto another, and many of them beare a mortall hatred to these our barbarous Sauages, that haue beene likely as false and perfidious heretofore to them, as vnto vs of late. So as the quarrels, and the causes of them, and the different humours of these people being well vnderstood, it will be an easie matter to ouerthrow those that now are, or may bee our enemies hereafter, by ayding and setting on their enemies against them. And by these factions and differences of petty Princes, the *Romans* tooke their greatest aduantage to ouercome this Iland of *Great Britayne*, of which *Tacitus* sayes, *Ita dum singuli pugnant vniuersi vincuntur*. And *Iustin* hath the like saying of the cause of vanquishing the *Grecian* Cities.

Fifthly, Because the *Indians*, who before were vsed as friends, may now most iustly be compelled to seruitude and drudgery, and supply the roome of men that labour, whereby euen the meanest of the Plantation may imploy themselues more entirely in their Arts and Occupations, which are more generous, whilest Sauages performe their inferiour workes of digging in mynes, and the like, of whom also some may be sent for the seruice of the *Sommer Ilands*.

Sixtly, This will for euer hereafter make vs more cautelous and circumspect, as neuer to bee deceiued more by any other treacheries, but will serue for a great instruction to all posteritie there, to teach them that *Trust is the mother of Deceipt*, and to learne them that of the *Italian, Chi non fida, non s'ingamuu*, Hee that trusts not is not deceiued: and make them know that kindnesses are misspent vpon rude natures, so long as they continue rude; as also, that Sauages and Pagans are aboue all other for matter of Iustice euer to be suspected. Thus vpon this Anvile shall wee now beate out to oui selues an armour of proofe, which shall for euer after defend vs from barbarous Incursions, and from greater dangers that otherwise might happen. And so we may truly say according to the *French* Prouerb, *Aquelq̃ chose malheur est bon*, Ill lucke is good for something.

Lastly, We haue this benefit more to our comfort, because all good men doe now take much more care of vs then before, since the fault is on their sides, not on ours, who haue vsed so fayre a cariage, euen to our owne destruction. Especially his *Maiesties* most gratious, tender and paternall care is manifest herein, who by his Royall bounty and goodnesse, hath continued his many fauors vnto vs, with a new, large, & Princely supply of Munition and Armes, out of his Maiesties owne store in the Tower, being gratiously bestowed for the safety and aduancement of the Plantation. As also his Royall fauor is amply extended in a large supply of men and other necessaries throughout the whole Kingdome, which are very shortly to bee sent to VIRGINIA.

A VIRGINIAN'S COMPLAINTS OVER THE FAILURE OF THE ENGLISH AND INDIANS TO INTERMARRY (1705) Robert Beverley, as quoted in Louis Wright, ed., *The History and Present State of Virginia* (Chapel Hill, N.C., 1947), pp. 37-39.

A*nno* 1612, Two Ships more arriv'd with Supplies: and Capt. *Argall*, who commanded one of them, being sent in her to *Patowmeck* to buy Corn, he there met with *Pocahontas*, the Excellent Daughter of *Powhatan;* and having prevail'd with her to come Aboard to a Treat, he detain'd her Prisoner, and carried her to *James-Town*, designing to make Peace with her Father by her Release; But on the Contrary, that Prince resented the Affront very highly; and although he loved his Daughter with all imaginable Tenderness, yet he would not be brought to Terms by that unhandsome Treachery; till about Two Years after a Marriage being proposed between Mr. *John Rolfe*, an *English* Gentleman, and this Lady; which *Powhatan* taking to be a sincere Token of Friendship, he vouchsafed to consent to it, and to conclude a Peace.

Intermarriage has been indeed the Method proposed very often by the *Indians* in the Beginning, urging it frequently as a certain Rule, that the *English* were not their Friends, if they refused it. And I can't but think it wou'd have been happy for that Country, had they embraced this Proposal: For, the Jealousie of the *Indians*, which I take to be the Cause of most of the Rapines and Murders they committed, wou'd by this Means have been altogether prevented, and consequently the Abundance of Blood that was shed on both sides wou'd have been saved; the great Extremities they were so often reduced to, by which so many died, wou'd not have happen'd; the Colony, instead of all these Losses of Men on both Sides, wou'd have been encreasing in Children to its Advantage; the Country wou'd have escaped the *Odium* with undeservedly fell upon it, by the Errors and Convulsions in the first Management; and, in all Likelihood, many, if not most, of the *Indians* would have been converted to Christianity by this kind Method; the Country would have been full of People, by the Preservation of the many *Christians* and *Indians* that fell in the Wars between them. Besides, there would have been a Continuance of all those Nations of *Indians* that are now dwindled away to nothing by their frequent Removals, or are fled to other Parts; not to mention the Invitation that so much Success and Prosperity would have been for others to have gone over and settled

NEGROES, INDIANS, AND GERMAN IMMIGRANTS

there, instead of the Frights and Terrors that were produced by all those Misfortunes that happen'd.

A MINISTER FOR THE SOCIETY FOR THE PROPAGATION OF THE GOSPEL IN FOREIGN PARTS DESCRIBES INDIAN SCHOOLING IN VIRGINIA (1712) From Edgar W. Knight, ed., *A Documentary History of Education in the South Before 1860* (Chapel Hill, N.C., 1949), vol. I, p. 83.

I had several conferences with one Thomas Hoyle King of the Chowan Indians who seem very inclinable to embrace Christianity and proposes to send his son to school in Sarum to have him taught to read and write by way of foundation in order to further proficiency for the reception of Christianity I readily offered my service to instruct him myself and having the opportunity of sending him to Mr. Garratts where I lodge being but three miles distance from his Town. But he modestly declined it for the present till a general peace was concluded between the Indians and Christians I found he had some notions of Noahs flood which he came to the knowledge of and exprest himselfe after this manner—My father told me I tell my Son But I hope in a little time to give the Society a better account of him as well as of those peaceable Indians under his Command Theres one M^r. Mashburn who keeps a school at Sarum on the frontiers of Virginia between the two Governments and neighbouring upon 2 Indian Towns who I find by him highly deserve encouragement and could heartily wish the Society would take it into consideration and be pleased to allow him a Salary for the good services he has done and may do for the future. What children he has under his care can both write and read very distinctly and gave before me such an account of the grounds and principles of the Christian religion that strangely surprised me to hear it. The man upon a small income would teach the Indian Children gratis (whose parents are willing to send them could they but pay for their schooling) as he would those of our English families had he but a fixed dependency for so doing and what advantage would this be to private families in particular and whole Colony in general is easy to determine . . .

DESCRIPTION OF AN INDIAN SCHOOL IN GEORGIA (1736) From Allen Candler, comp., *The Colonial Records of the State of Georgia, 1732-1782* (Atlanta, 1904-16), vol. XXI, pp. 221-23.

Notwithstanding all the Opposition of Men & Devils, I Trust there is A Door now Opening for the Conversion of the Indians. There is already A School almost built amongst them. The House 60 Foot long & 15 Wide. it will be divided into 3 Rooms, One at Each End, consisting of 15 Foot Square, & the School Room in the Middle as large as both the Other. Under one of the End Rooms they have dug A Cellar. The Foreside of the House faces the rising Sun, And the two Ends are due North & South. It Stands on A little Hill which we call Irene, by a Brook Side, about half a Quarter of a A Mile above Tomo-chachees Town, where the River Savannah divides it Self into 3 Streams. This Hill has been made Some Hundred Years ago, for what Reason I can't tell; Perhaps to perpetuate the Memory of Some Illustrious Hero or famous Action. In digging the Cellar, they found Abundance of Oister Shells, and some Bones and Buck Horns. When I fixed upon this Place, the Indians ask'd me if I was not afraid to live upon A Hill, I Answer'd no. They said, the Indians were, because they believed that Fairies haunted Hills. The Moravian Brethren out of their Zeal for the Work, Undertook the Building at a low Price; As soon as it's finish'd, which will be within A few Dayes, One of them with his Wife is to live there with me. I believe in A little Time we Shall have a good Number of Scollars. The Indians, tho' at first they would hardly be persuaded to let one child learn, yet now they are very willing to have them taught, and even Some of the Men Seem to have a desire to learn . . .

Tomochachee is lately recovered from A dangerous Sickness, wherein their own Doctors gave him up, but it pleas'd God to restore him by the Care of Mr Oglethorpe, thro' the Prayers of several Christians for him, I hope he will live to hear the Glad Tidings of the Glorious Gospel, he has been very earnest to promote the School. I don't despair of acquireing their Language, I begin to understand a little of it. And I hope thro' the Prayers of my good Friends in England, I shall be enabled to make a daily Progress in it. I have three Boys that I think will be able to read their Language as Soon as I shall be able to Speak it.

WILLIAM PENN DESCRIBES THE INDIANS (1683)   From A. C. Myers, ed., *Narratives of Early Pennsylvania, West New Jersey and Delaware, 1630-1707* (New York, 1912), pp. 25-29.

XI. The *Natives* I shall consider in their Persons, Language, Manners, Religion and Government, with my sence of their Original. For their Persons, they are generally tall, straight, well-built, and of singular Proportion; they tread strong and clever, and mostly walk with a lofty Chin: Of Complexion, Black, but by design, as the Gypsies in England: They grease themselves with Bears-fat clarified, and using no defence against Sun or Weather, their skins must needs be swarthy; Their Eye is little and black, not unlike a straight-look't Jew: The thick Lip and flat Nose, so frequent with the East-Indians and Blacks, are not common to them; for I have seen as comely European-like faces among them of both, as on your side the Sea: and truly an Italian Complexion hath not much more of the White, and the Noses of several of them have as much of the Roman.

XII. Their Language is lofty, yet narrow, but like the Hebrew: in Signification full, like Short-hand in writing: one word serveth in the place of three, and the rest are supplied by the Understanding of the Hearer: Imperfect in their Tenses, wanting in their Moods, Participles, Adverbs, Conjunctions, Interjections; I have made it my business to understand it, that I might not want an Interpreter on any occasion: And I must say, that I know not a Language spoken in Europe, that hath words of more sweetness or greatness, in Accent and Emphasis, than theirs: for Instance, *Octorockon, Rancocas, Oziction, Shakamacon, Poquerim,* all of which are names of Places, and have Grandeur in them: Of words of Sweetness, *Anna,* is Mother, *Issimus,* a Brother, *Netap,* Friend, *usque ozet,* very good: *pone,* Bread, *metse,* eat, *matta,* no, *hatta,* to have, *payo,* to come: *Sepassen, Passijon,* the Names of Places; *Tamane, Secane, Menanse, Secatereus,* are the names of Persons. If one ask them for anything they have not, they will answer, *matta ne hatta,* which to translate is, not I have, instead of I have not.

XIII. Of their Customs and Manners there is much to be said; I will begin with Children. So soon as they are born, they wash them in Water, and while very young, and in cold Weather to chuse, they Plunge them in the Rivers to harden and embolden them. Having wrapt them in a Clout, they lay them on a straight thin Board, a little more than the length and breadth of the Child, and swadle it fast upon the Board to make it straight; wherefore all Indians have flat Heads; and thus they carry them at their Backs. The Children will go very young, at nine Moneths commonly; they wear only a small Clout round their Waste, till they are big; if Boys, they go a Fishing till ripe for the Woods, which is about Fifteen; then they Hunt, and after having given some Proofs of thier Manhood, by a good return of Skins, they may Marry, else it is a shame to think of a Wife. The Girls stay with their Mothers, and help to hoe the Ground, plant Corn and carry Burthens; and they do well to use them to that Young, they must do when they are Old; for the Wives are the true Servants of their Husbands: otherwise the Men are very affectionate to them.

XVI. When the Young Women are fit for Marriage, they wear something upon their Heads for an Advertisement, but so as their Faces are hardly to be seen, but when they please: The Age they Marry at, if Women, is about thirteen and fourteen; if Men, seventeen and eighteen; they are rarely elder.

XV. Their Houses are Mats, or Barks of Trees set on Poles, in the fashion of an English Barn, but out of the power of the Winds, for they are hardly higher than a Man; they lie on Reeds or Grass. In Travel they lodge in the Woods about a great Fire, with the Mantle of Duffills they wear by day, wrapt about them, and a few Boughs stuck round them.

XVI. Their Diet is Maze, or Indian Corn, divers ways prepared: sometimes Roasted in the Ashes, sometimes beaten and Boyled with Water, which they call *Homine;* they also make Cakes, not unpleasant to eat: They have likewise several sorts of Beans and Pease that are good Nourishment; and the Woods and Rivers are their Larder.

XVII. If an European comes to see them, or calls for Lodging at their House or *Wigwam* they give him the best place and first cut. If they come to visit us, they salute us with an *Itah* which is as much as to say, Good be to you, and set them down, which is mostly on the Ground close to their Heels, their Legs upright; may be they speak not a word more, but observe all Passages: If you give them any thing to eat or drink, well, for they will not ask; and be it little or much, if it be with Kindness, they are well pleased, else they go away sullen, but say nothing.

XVIII. They are great Concealers of their own Resentments, brought to it, I believe, by the Revenge that hath been practised among them; in either of these, they are not exceeded by the Italians. A Tragical Instance fell out since I came into the Country; A King's Daughter thinking her self slighted by her Husband, in suffering another Woman to lie down between them, rose up, went out, pluck't a

Root out of the Ground, and ate it, upon which she immediately dyed; and for which, last Week he made an Offering to her Kindred for Attonement and liberty of Marriage; as two others did to the Kindred of their Wives, that dyed a natural Death: For till Widdowers have done so, they must not marry again. Some of the young Women are said to take undue liberty before Marriage for a Portion; but when marryed, chaste; when with Child, they know their Husbands no more, till delivered; and during their Moneth, they touch no Meat, they eat, but with a Stick, least they should defile it; nor do their Husbands frequent them, till that time be expired.

XIX. But in Liberality they excell, nothing is too good for their friend; give them a fine Gun, Coat, or other thing, it may pass twenty hands, before it sticks; light of Heart, strong Affections, but soon spent; the most merry Creatures that live, Feast and Dance perpetually; they never have much, nor want much: Wealth circulateth like the Blood, all parts partake; and though none shall want what another hath, yet exact Observers of Property. Some Kings have sold, others presented me with several parcels of Land; the Pay or Presents I made them, were not hoarded by the particular Owners, but the neighbouring Kings and their Clans being present when the Goods were brought out, the Parties chiefly concerned consulted, what and to whom they should give them? To every King then, by the hands of a Person for that work appointed, is a proportion sent, so sorted and folded, and with that Gravity, that is admirable. Then that King subdivideth it in like manner among his Dependents, they hardly leaving themselves an Equal share with one of their Subjects: and be it on such occasions, at Festivals, or at their common Meals, the Kings distribute, and to themselves last. They care for little, because they want but little; and the Reason is, a little contents them: In this they are sufficiently revenged on us; if they are ignorant of our Pleasures, they are also free from our Pains. They are not disquieted with Bills of Lading and Exchange, nor perplexed with Chancery-Suits and Exchequer-Reckonings. We sweat and toil to live; their pleasure feeds them, I mean, their Hunting, Fishing and Fowling, and this Table is spread every where; they eat twice a day, Morning and Evening; their Seats and Table are the Ground. Since the European came into these parts, they are grown great lovers of strong Liquors, Rum especially, and for it exchange the richest of their Skins and Furs: If they are heated with Liquors, they are restless till they have enough to sleep; that is their cry, Some more, and I will go to sleep; but when Drunk, one of the most wretchedst Spectacles in the world.

XX. In sickness impatient to be cured, and for it give any thing, especially for their Children, to whom they are extreamly natural; they drink at those times a *Teran* or Decoction of some Roots in spring Water; and if they eat any flesh, it must be of the Female of any Creature; If they dye they bury them with their Apparel, be they Men or Women, and the nearest of Kin fling in something precious with them, as a token of their Love: Their Mourning is blacking of their faces, which they continue for a year; They are choice of the Graves of their Dead; for least they should be lost by time, and fall to common use, they pick off the Grass that grows upon them, and heap up the fallen Earth with great care and exactness.

XXI. These poor People are under a dark Night in things relating to Religion, to be sure, the Tradition of it; yet they believe a God and Immortality, without the help of the Metaphysicks; for they say, There is a great King that made them, who dwells in a glorious Country to the Southward of them, and that the Souls of the good shall go thither, where they shall live again. Their Worship consists of two parts, Sacrifice and *Cantico*. Their Sacrifice is their first Fruits; the first and fattest Buck they kill, goeth to the fire, where is all burnt with a Mournful Ditty of him that performeth the Ceremony, but with such marvellous Fervency and Labour of Body, that he will even sweat to a foam. The other part is their *Cantico*, performed by round-Dances, sometimes Words, sometimes Songs, then Shouts, two being in the middle that begin, and by Singing and Drumming on a Board direct the Chorus: Their Postures in the Dance are very Antick and differing, but all keep measure. This is done with equal Earnestness and Labour, but great appearance of Joy. In the Fall, when the Corn cometh in, they begin to feast one another; there have been two great Festivals already, to which all come that will: I was at one my self; their Entertainment was a green Seat by a Spring, under some shady Trees, and twenty Bucks, with hot Cakes of new Corn, both Wheat and Beans, which they make up in a square form, in the leaves of the Stem, and bake them in the Ashes: And after that they fell to Dance, But they that go, must carry a small Present in their Money, it may be six Pence, which is made of the Bone of a Fish; the black is with them as Gold, the white, Silver; they call it all *Wampum*.

XXII. Their Government is by Kings, which they call *Sachema*, and those by Succession, but always of the Mothers side; for Instance, the Children of him that is now King, will not succeed, but his Brother by the Mother, or the Children of his Sister, whose Sons (and after them the Children of her Daughters) will reign; for no Woman inherits; the Reason they render for this way of Descent, is, that their Issue may not be spurious.

XXIII. Every King hath his Council, and that consists of all the Old and Wise men of his Nation, which perhaps is two hundred People: nothing of Moment is undertaken, be it War, Peace, Selling of Land or Traffick, without advising with them; and which is more, with the Young Men too. 'Tis admirable to consider, how Powerful the Kings are, and yet how they move by the Breath of their People. I have had occasion to be in Council with them upon Treaties for Land, and to adjust the terms of Trade; their Order is thus: The King sits in the middle of an half Moon, and hath his Council, the Old and Wise on each hand; behind them, or at a little distance, sit the younger Fry, in the same figure. Having consulted and resolved their business, the King ordered one of them to speak to me; he stood up, came to me, and in the Name of his King saluted me, then took me by the hand, and told me, That he was ordered by his King to speak to me, and that now it was not he, but the King that spoke, because what he should say, was the King's mind. He first pray'd me, To excuse them that they had not complyed with me the last time; he feared, there might be some fault in the Interpreter, being neither Indian nor English; besides, it was the Indian Custom to deliberate, and take up much time in Council, before they resolve; and that if the Young People and Owners of the Land had been as ready as he, I had not met with so much delay. Having thus introduced his matter, he fell to the Bounds of the Land they had agreed to dispose of, and the Price, (which now is little and dear, that which would have bought twenty Miles, not buying now two). During the time that this Person spoke, not a man of them was observed to whisper or smile; the Old, Grave, the Young, Reverend in their Deportment; they do speak little, but fervently, and with Elegancy: I have never seen more natural Sagacity, considering them without the help, (I was agoing to say, the spoil) of Tradition; and he will deserve the Name of Wise, that Outwits them in any Treaty about a thing they understand. When the Purchase was agreed, great Promises past between us of Kindness and good Neighbourhood, and that the Indians and English must live in Love, as long as the Sun gave light. Which done, another made a Speech to the Indians, in the Name of all the *Sachamakers* or Kings, first to sell them what was done; next, to charge and command them, To Love the Christians, and particularly live in Peace with me, and the People under my Government: That many Governours had been in the River, but that no Governour had come himself to live and stay here before; and having now such a one that had treated them well, they should never do him or his any wrong. At every sentence of which they shouted, and said, Amen, in their way.

XXIV. The Justice they have is Pecuniary: In case of any Wrong or evil Fact, be it Murther it self, they Attone by Feasts and Presents of their *Wampon*, which is proportioned to the quality of the Offence or Person injured, or of the Sex they are of: for in case they kill a Woman, they pay double, and the Reason they render, is, That she breedeth Children, which Men cannot do. 'Tis rare that they fall out, if Sober; and if Drunk, they forgive it, saying, It was the Drink, and not the Man, that abused them.

XXV. We have agreed, that in all Differences between us, Six of each side shall end the matter: Don't abuse them, but let them have justice, and you win them . . .

COURT ORDER FOR THE CONVERSION OF MASSACHUSETTS INDIANS

(1644) From Nathaniel B. Shurtleff, ed., *The Records of the Governor and Company of the Massachusetts Bay in New England* (Boston, 1854), pp. 6-7.

It is ordred, that noe Indian shall come att any towne or howse of the English (without leave) uppon the Lords day, except to attend the publike meeteings; neither shall they come att any English howse uppon any other day in the weeke, but first shall knocke att the dore, and after leave given, to come in, (and not otherwise;) and if any (hereafter) offend contrary to this order, the constable, uppon notice given him, shall bringe him or them Indians, soe offendinge, to a magestrate to bee punisht according to his offence.

Whereas it is the earnest desire of this Courte, that these natives (amongst whome wee live, and whoe have submitted themselves to this governmente) should come to the good knowledge of God, and bee brought on to subject to the scepter of the Lord Jesus, it is therefore ordred, that all such of the Indians as have subjected themselves to our governmente bee henceforward enjoyned (and that they fayle not) to meete att such severall places of appoyntmente as shalbee most convenient on the Lords day, where they may attend such instruction as shalbee given them by those whose harts God shall stirr upp to that worke; and it is hereby further declared (as the desire of this Courte) that those townes that lye most convenient to such places of meetinge of the Indians would make choyce of some of theire brethren (whom God hath best quallified for that worke) to goe to them, (beeinge soe mett,) and instruct them, (by the best interpriter they can gett,) that if possible God may have the glory of the conversion (at least) of some of them in the use of such meanes God gives us to afoard them.

JOHN ELIOT'S ACCOUNT OF TEACHING INDIAN CHILDREN

(1646) From John Eliot, *The Day-Breaking if Not the Sun-Rising of the Gospel with the Indians in New-England* (New York, 1865), pp. 9-10.

Upon November 11, 1646, we came the second time unto the same wigwam of Wabon. We found many more Indians met together than the first time we came to them; and having seats provided for us by themselves, and being sat down a while, we began again with prayer in the English tongue. Our beginning this time was with the younger sort of Indian children in catechizing of them, which being the first time of instructing them, we thought meet to ask them but only three questions in their own language, that we might not clog their minds or memories with too much at first. The questions (asked and answered in the Indian tongue) were these three:

1. Question: Who made you and all the world?
   Answer: God.
2. Question: Who do you look should save you and redeem you from sin and hell?
   Answer: Jesus Christ.
3. Question: How many commandments hath God given you to keep?
   Answer: Ten.

These questions being propounded to the children severally, and one by one, and the answers being short and easy, hence it came to pass that before we went through all, those who were last catechized had more readily learned to answer to them, by hearing the same question so often propounded and answered before their fellows. And the other Indians who were grown up to more years had perfectly learned them, whom we therefore desired to teach their children again when we were absent, that so when we came again we might see their profiting, the better to encourage them hereunto, we therefore gave something to every child.

JOHN ELIOT DESCRIBES A TOWN OF "PRAYING INDIANS" (1647)

From John Eliot, *The Day-Breaking if Not the Sun-Rising of the Gospell with the Indians in New-England* (New York, 1865), pp. 27-32.

Wee have cause to be very thankfull to God who hath moved the hearts of the generall court to purchase so much land for them to make their towne in which the *Indians* are much taken with,[1] and it is somewhat observable that while the Court were considering where to lay out their towne, the *Indians* (not knowing of any thing) were about that time consulting about Lawes for themselves, and there company who sit downe with Waaubon; there were ten of them, two of them are forgotten.

[1]The towne the Indians did desire to know what name it should have, and it was told them it should bee called Noonatomen, which signifies in English rejoycing, because they hearing the word, and seeking to know God, the English did rejoyce at it, and God did rejoyce at it, which pleased them much, & therefore that is to be the name of their town. [Eliot's note.]

Their Lawes were these

1. That if any man be idle a weeke, at most a fortnight, hee shall pay five shillings.

2. If any unmarried man shall lie with a young woman unmarried, he shall pay twenty shillings.

3. If any man shall beat his wife, his hands shall bee tied behind him and carried to the place of justice to bee severely punished.

4. Every young man if not anothers servant, and if unmarried, hee shall be compelled to set up a Wigwam and plant for himselfe, and not live shifting up and downe to other Wigwams.

5. If any woman shall not have her haire tied up but hang loose or be cut as mens haire, she shall pay five shillings.

6. If any woman shall goe with naked breasts they shall pay two shillings sixpence.

7. All those men that weare long locks shall pay five shillings.

8. If any shall kill their lice betweene their teeth, they shall pay five shillings. This Law though ridiculous to English eares yet tends to preserve cleanliness among Indians.

Tis wonderfull in our eyes to understand by these two honest Indians, what Prayers Waaubon and the rest of them use to make, for hee that preacheth to them professeth hee never yet used any of their words in his prayers, from whom otherwise it might bee thought that they had learnt them by rote, one is this.

> Amanaomen Jehovah tahassen metagh.
> Take away Lord my Stony heart.
> Another
> Cheehesom Jehovah kekowhogkew,
> Wash   Lord   my soule.
> Another
> Lord lead me when I die to heaven.

These are but a taste, they have many more, and these more enlarged then thus expressed, yet what are these but the sprinklings of the spirit and blood of Christ Jesus in their hearts? and 'tis no small matter that such dry barren and long-accursed ground should yeeld such kind of increase in so small a time, I would not readily commend a faire day before night, nor promise much of such kind of beginnings, in all persons, nor yet in all of these, for wee know the profession of very many is but a meere paint, and their best graces nothing but meere flashes and pangs, which are suddainly kindled and as soon go out and are extinct againe, yet God doth not usually send his Plough & Seedsman to a place but there is at least some little peece of good ground, although three to one bee naught: and mee thinkes the Lord Jesus would never have made so fit a key for their locks, unlesse hee had intended to open some of their doores, and so to make way for his comming in. Hee that God hath raised up and enabled to preach unto them, is a man (you know) of a most sweet, humble, loving, gratious and enlarged spirit, whom God hath blest, and surely will still delight in & do good by. I did thinke never to have opened my mouth to any, to desire those in England to further any good worke here, but now I see so many things inviting to speake in this businesse, that it were well if you did lay before those that are prudent and able these considerations.

1 That it is prettie heavy and chargeable to educate and traine up those children which are already offered us, in schooling, cloathing, diet, and attendance, which they must have.

2 That in all probabilities many Indians in other places, expecially under our jurisdiction, will bee provoked by this example in these, both to desire preaching, and also to send their children to us, when they see that some of their fellows fare so well among the English, and the civil authoritie here so much favouring and countenancing of these, and if many come in, it will bee more heavy to such as onely are fit to keepe them, and yet have their hands and knees infeebled so many wayes besides.

3 That if any shall doe any thing to encourage this worke, that it may be given to the Colledge for such an end and use, that so from the Colledge may arise the yeerly revenue for their yeerly maintenance. I would not have it placed in any particular mans hands for feare cousenage or misplacing or carelesse keeping and improving; but at the Colledge it's under many hands and eyes the chief and best of the country who have ben & will be exactly carefull of the right and comely disposing of such things; and therefore, if any thing bee given, let it be put in such hands as may immediately direct it to the President of the Colledge, who you know will soone acquaint the rest with it; and for this end if any in England have thus given any thing for this end, I would have them speake to those who have received it to send it this way, which if it bee withheld I thinke 'tis no lesse than sacrilege: but if God moves no hearts to such a work, I doubt not then but that more weake meanes shall have the honour of it in the day of Christ.

A fourth Meeting with the Indians

This day being *Decemb*, 9. the children being catechised, and that place of *Ezekiel* touching the dry bones being opened, and applyed to their condition; the *Indians* offered all their children to us to bee educated amongst us, and instructed by us, complaining to us that they were not able to give any thing to the English for their education: for this reason there are therefore preparations made towards the schooling of them, and setting up a Schoole among them or very neare unto them. Sundry questions also were propounded by them to us, and of us to them; one of them being askt what is sinne? hee answered a noughty heart. Another old man complained to us of his feares, *viz*, that hee was fully purposed to keepe the Sabbath, but still he was in feare whether he should go to hell or heaven; and thereupon the justification of a sinner by faith in Christ was opened unto him as the remedy against all feares of hell. Another complayned of other *Indians* that did revile them, and call them Rogues and such like speeches for cutting off their Locks, and for cutting their Haire in a modest manner as the New-English generally doe; for since the word hath begun to worke upon their hearts, they have discerned the vanitie and pride which they placed in their haire, and have therefore of their owne accord (none speaking to them that wee know of) cut it modestly; there were therefore encouraged by some there present of chiefe place and account with us, not to feare the reproaches of wicked *Indians*, nor their witchcraft and *Pawwaws* and poysonings, but let them know that if they did not dissemble but would seeke God unfaignedly, that they would stand by them, and that God also would be with them. They told us also of divers *Indians* who would come and stay with them three or foure dayes, and one Sabbath, and then they would goe from them, but as for themselves, they told us they were fully purposed to keepe the Sabbath, to which wee incouraged them, and night drawing on were forced to leave them, for this time.

JOHN ELIOT'S DESCRIPTION OF A MEETING WITH THE INDIANS

(**1648**) From William B. Cairns, ed., *Early American Writers* (New York, 1920), pp. 126-28.

As soone as ever fiercenesse of the winter was past, March 3. 1647. I went out to *Noonanetum* to the *Indian* Lecture, where Mr. *Wilson*, Mr. *Allen*, of *Dedham*, Mr. *Dunster*, beside many other Christians were present; on which day perceiving divers of the *Indian* women well affected, and considering that their soules might stand in need of answer to their scruples as well as the mens & yet because we knew how unfit it was for women so much as to aske questions publiquely immediately by themselves; wee did therefore desire them to propound any questions they would be resolved about by first acquainting either their Husbands, or the Interpreter privately therewith: whereupon we heard two questions thus orderly propounded; which because they are the first that ever were propounded by *Indian* women in such an ordinance that ever wee heard of, and because they may bee otherwise usefull, I shall therefore set them downe.

The first question was propounded by the wife of one *Wampooas* a well affected *Indian*, *viz.* "Whether (said she) do I pray when my husband prayes if I speak nothing as he doth, yet if I like what he saith, and my heart goes with it?" (for the *Indians* will many times pray with their wives, and with their children also sometime in the fields) shee therefore fearing lest prayer should onely be an externall action of the lips, enquired if it might not be also an inward action of the heart, if she liked of what he said.

The second question was propounded by the Wife of one *Totherswampe*, her meaning in her question (as wee all perceived) was this *viz.* "Whether a husband should do well to pray with his wife, and yet continue in his passions, & be angry with his wife?" But the modesty and wisdome of the woman directed her to doe three things in one, for thus shee spake to us, *viz.* "Before my husband did pray hee was much angry and froward, but since hee hath begun to pray hee was not angry so much, but little angry": wherein first shee gave an honorable testimony of her husband and commended him for the abatement of his passion; secondly, shee gave implicitly a secret reproofe for what was past, and for somewhat at present that was amisse; and thirdly, it was intended by her as a question whether her husband should pray to God, and yet continue in some unruly passions; but she wisely avoyded that, lest it might reflect too much upon him, although wee desired her to expresse if that was not her meaning.

At this time (beside these questions) there were sundry others propounded of very good use, in all which we saw the Lord Jesus leading them to make narrow inquiries into the things of God, that so they might see the reality of them. I have heard few Christians when they began to looke toward God, make more searching questions that they might see things really, and not onely have a notion of them: I forbeare to mention any of them, because I forget the chiefe of them; onely this wee tooke notice of at this dayes meeting, that there was an aged *Indian* who proposed his complaint in propounding his question concerning an unruly disobedient son, and "what one should do with him in case of obstinacy and disobedience, and that will not heare Gods Word, though his Father command him, nor will not forsake his drunkennesse, though his father forbid him?" Unto which there were many answers to set forth the sinne of disobedience to parents; which were the more quickned and sharpned because wee knew that this rebellious sonne whom the old man meant, was by Gods providence present at this Lecture: Mr *Wilson* was much inlarged, and spake so terribly, yet so graciously as might have affected a heart not quite shut up, which this young *desperado* hearing (who well understood the *English* tongue) instead of humbling himself before the Lords Word, which touched his conscience and condition so neare, hee was filled with a spirit of Satan, and as soone as ever Mr. *Wilsons* speech was ended hee brake out into a loud contemptuous expression; *So*, saith he: which we passed by without speaking againe, leaving the Word with him, which we knew would one day take its effect one way or other upon him.

DIALOGUE BETWEEN INDIAN AND PURITAN (1707-08) From Josiah Cotton, *Vocabulary of the Massachusetts (or Natick) Indian Language* (Cambridge, Mass., 1829), pp. 94-99.

How does your wife, or husband do?

Toh unnuppomântam kummittumwus asuh kãsuk.

What is the matter that Indians very often no speak true?

Toh waj unnak Indiansog moocheke nompe matta sampwe unnoowoōōog.

Have you bin at Squantam lately?

Sun Squantam kuppeyômus paswe.

Do the souldiers go to Canada? No.

Sun aiyeuehteaenūog aūog Canada; matteag.

Then they will do no good, but a great deal of hurt.

Neit nag pish matta toh unne wunnesēog, qut moocheke woskeussēog.

Yes they will put the country to a great deal of charge.

Nux, nag pish mishe ōadtehkontamwog wuttohkeōngash.

Is not the fleet come ashore yet?

Sun chuppoonâog asq koppaemūnnoo.

Do you think they will ever come?

Sun kuttenântam nash pish peyômôōash.

It may be not.

Ammiate matteag.

Very likely not.

Ahche ogqueneunkquat matteag.

I believe they are gone to Spain.

Nuttinantam nag monchuk en Spain.

Why do you remove from Natick?

Tohwaj ontootaãn wutche Natick.

You will get more money there than at Sandwich.

Woh kummoochke wuttehtĩnum teagwas nâut onk Moskeehtŭkqut.

My family is sickly there.

Nutteashinnĭnnēonk wuttit moh-chinnonāop.

And were they healthy at Sandwich? Yes.

Kah sun nag wunne pomantam-wushanneg ut Moskeehtŭk-qut. Nux.

Dont you owe a great deal of money there?

Sunnummatta kummishontuk-quahwhuttĕoh na utt.

Yes, but I hope to clear it quickly.

Nux, qut nuttannoos nuttapoad-tehkónat pāswēse.

What if they would put you in prison?

Toh woh unni kuppŭshagkinuk-quēan.

Then they will hurt themselves and me too.

Neit nag woh woskehheaog wuh-hogkāuh kah nen wonk.

It is very cold to day.

Moochĕke tohkoi yeu kesukod.

Almost I freeze my ears and fingers.

Nāhen togquttïnash nuhtauōg-wash kah nuppoohkuhquānit-chēgat.

Why dont you get a thick cap?

Tohwaj matta ahchuehteoōōou kohpögkag kah onkquontŭ-pape.

Because I have no money.

Newutche matta nuttohtooo teagwash.

And why dont you work hard?

Kah tohwaj mat menukanâkaus-ēan.

So I would with all my heart, but I am sickly.

Ne woh nuttussen nashpe man-ŭsse nuttah, qut nummōmoh-tehŭnam.

But it may be work will cure you, if you would leave off drinking too.

Qut ammiate woh anakausuonk kukketeŏhhuk, tohneit wonk ohksippamwēan.

I think you give good advice, but let me work for you.

Nuttinântam kuttinunūmah wunne kogkahquttüonk ko-owehquttumauish unnanumeh kutanakausuehtauununat.

How many years old are you?

Noh kutteăshe kodtum wōhkom.

Eighteen; and how old is that boy, or girl.

Piog nishwosuk; kah toh unnuk-koohquiyeu noh nonkomp kah nonksq.

Why do boys of that age run about, and do nothing.

Tohwaj nonkompaog ne anooh-quiitcheg pumomashaōg, kah matteag usseog.

You had better let me have him, and I will learn him to write, and read.

An wunnegik kuttinninumiin kah pish nunnehtühpeh wussuk-qŭohamünat kah ogketamün-at.

He shall want for nothing, neither meat, drink, cloathing, or drubbing.

Noh matteag pish quenauehhik-koo asuh metsuonk wuttat-tamooonk ogkooonk asuh sasamitahwhuttuonk.

Idleness is the root of much evil.

Nanompanissūonk wutchappehk moocheke machuk.

Do you come, or else send him tomorrow early.

Pasoo asuh nekonchhuash saup nompoāe.

Dont forget your promise.

Wanantōhkon koonoowaonk.

SOLOMON STODDARD ON BUYING INDIAN LAND (1722) From "An Answer to Some Cases of Conscience Respecting the Country," as quoted in Perry Miller and Thomas H. Johnson, eds., *The Puritans* (New York, 1938), p. 454.

Q. VIII. Did We Any Wrong to the Indians in Buying Their Land at a Small Price?

A. 1. There was some part of the Land that was not purchased, neither was there need that it should; it was *vacuum domicilium;* and so might be possessed by vertue of God's grant to Mankind, Gen. 1. 28. *And God blessed them, and God said unto them, Be fruitful and multiply and replenish the earth, and subdue it: and have dominion over the fish of the sea, and over the fowl of the air, and over every thing that moveth upon the earth.* The *Indians* made no use of it, but for Hunting. By God's first Grant Men were to subdue the Earth. When *Abraham* came into the Land of *Canaan*, he made use of the vacant Land as he pleased: so did *Isaac* and *Jacob.*

2. The Indians were well contented that we should sit down by them. And it would have been for great Advantage, both for this World, and the Other; if they had been wise enough to make use of their Opportunities. It has been common with many People, in planing this World since the Flood, to admit Neighbours, to sit down by them.

3. Tho' we gave but a small Price for what we bought; we gave them their demands, we came to their Market, and gave them their price; and indeed, it was worth but little: And had it continued in their hands, it would have been of little value. It is our dwelling on it, and our Improvements, that have made it to be of Worth.

A CONNECTICUT LAW CALLING FOR THE CONVERSION OF THE INDIAN (1727) From Elsie W. C. Parsons, *Educational Legislation and Administration of the Colonial Governments* (New York, 1899), pp. 112-13.

Whereas this Assembly is informed that many of the Indians in this government put out their children to the English, to be brought up by them, and yet sundry of the persons having such children, do neglect to learn them to read and to instruct them in the principles of the Christian faith, so that such children are still in danger to continue heathens: Which to prevent,

Be it enacted by the Governor, Council and Representatives, in General Court assembled, and by the authority of the same, that every person in this colony that hath taken, or shall take, any of the Indian children of this or the neighboring governments into the care of their families, are hereby ordered to use their utmost endeavor to teach them to read English, and also to instruct them in the principles of the Christian faith by catechising of them, together with other proper methods.

And the selectmen and grand-jurors in the respective towns shall make diligent inquiry, whether the Indian children that are or may be put out as above, are by their masters or mistresses that have the care of them, instructed and taught as abovesaid. And if upon inquiry the said officers shall find that any such master or mistress hath neglected their duty herein, after due warning given, then said officers, or any two of them, shall inform the next assistant or justice of the peace, upon which the said authority shall summon such master or mistress so informed against, to appear before them; and if upon examination it appear that said master or mistress hath neglected to instruct any Indian child or children put to them as aforesaid, they shall be fined at the discretion of said assistant or justice, not exceeding the sum of forty shillings, to be to the use of the school in the town where the master or mistress lives.

DESCRIPTION OF ELEAZER WHEELOCK'S INDIAN SCHOOL IN LEBANON, CONNECTICUT (1762)

From Eleazer Wheelock, "Of the Original Design, Rise, Progress and Present State of the Indian Charity-School in Lebanon, Connecticut" (1762), as quoted in *Old South Leaflets*, First Series (Boston, n.d.), no. 22.

Understanding there are numbers of religious and charitably disposed persons, who only wait to know where their charities may be bestowed in the best manner for the advancement of the kingdom of the great Redeemer; and supposing there may also be in some, evil surmisings about, and a disposition to discredit a cause which they don't love, and have no disposition to promote; I have, to gratify the one, and prevent the mischiefs of the other, thought it my duty to give the publick a short, plain, and faithful narrative of the original design, rise, progress, and present state of the Charity-School here, called Moor's Indian-Charity School, etc. And I hope there is need of little or nothing more than a plain and faithful relation of facts, with the grounds and reasons of them, to justify the undertaking, and all the pains and expence there has been, in the prosecution thereof. And to convince all persons of ability, that this school is a proper object of their charity; and that whatever they shall contribute for the furtherance of it, will be an offering acceptable to God, and properly bestowed for the promoting a design which the heart of the great Redeemer is infinitely set upon.

The considerations first moving me to enter upon the design of educating the children of our heathen natives were such as these; viz.

The great obligations lying upon us, as God's covenant-people, who have all we have better than they in a covenant way, and consequently are under covenant-bonds to improve it in the best manner for the honour and glory of our liberal Benefactor. And can such want of charity to those poor creatures, as our neglect has shewn; and our neglect of that which God has so plainly made to be the matter of our care and duty; and that which the heart of the great Redeemer is so set upon, as they he never desired any other compensation for all the travail of his soul, can it, I say, be without great guilt on our part?

It has seem'd to me, he must be stupidly indifferent to the Redeemer's cause and interest in the world; and criminally deaf and blind to the intimations of the favour and displeasure of God in the dispensations of his providence, who could not perceive plain intimations of God's displeasure against us for this neglect, inscribed in capitals, on the very front of divine dispensations, from year to year, in permitting the savages to be such a sore scourge to our land, and make such depredations on our frontiers, inhumanly butchering and captivating our people: not only in time of war, but when we had good reason to think (if ever we had) that we dwelt safely by them.

And there is good reason to think, that if one half which has been, for so many years past expended in building forts, manning and supporting them, had been prudently laid out in supporting faithful missionaries, and school-masters among them, the instructed and civilized party would have been a far better defence than all our expensive fortresses, and prevented the laying waste so many towns and villages: Witness the consequence of sending Mr. Sergeant to Stockbridge, which was in the very road by which they most usually came upon our people, and by which there has never been one attack made upon us since his going there; and this notwithstanding there has been, by all accounts, less appearance of the saving effects of the gospel there than in any other place, where so much has been expended for many years past.

And not only our covenant bonds, by which we owe our all to God, and our divine Redeemer—our pity to their bodies in their miserable, needy state—our charity to their perishing souls—and our own peace, and safety by them, should constrain us to it; but also gratitude, duty, and loyalty to our rightful sovereign. How great the benefit which would hereby accrue to the Crown of Great Britain, and how much the interests of His Majesty's dominions, especially in America, would be promoted hereby, we can hardly conceive.

And the Christianizing the natives of this land is expressly mentioned in the royal charter granted to this colony, as a motive inducing His Majesty to grant that royal favour to our fathers. And since we are risen up in their stead, and enjoy the inestimable favour granted to them, on this consideration; What can excuse our not performing to our utmost, that which was engaged by, and reasonably expected from, them? But that which is of greatest weight, and should powerfully excite and perswade us hereto, are the many commands, strong motives, precious promises, and tremendous threatenings, which fill so great a part of the sacred pages and are so perfectly calculated to awaken all our powers; to spread the knowledge of the only true God, and Saviour, and make it as extensive and common as possible. It is a work, in which every one in his place, and according to his ability, is under sacred bonds to use his utmost endeavours. But for brevity sake, I omit a particular mention of them, supposing none have read their Bibles attentively, who do not know, that this is a darling subject of them; and that enough is there spoken by the mouth of God himself, to obviate and silence all the objections which sloth, covetousness, or love of the world can suggest against it.

These were some of the considerations which, I think, had some influence to my making an attempt in this affair; though I did not then much think of any thing more than only to clear myself, and family, or partaking in the public guilt of our land and nation in such a neglect of them.

And as there were few or none who seemed so much to lay the necessity and importance of the case to heart, as to exert themselves in earnest, and lead the way therein, I was naturally put upon consideration and enquiry what methods might have the greatest probability of success; and upon the whole was fully perswaded that this, which I have been pursuing, had by far the greatest probability of any that had been proposed, viz. by the mission of their own sons in conjunction with the

English; and that a number of girls should also be instructed in whatever should be necessary to render them fit to perform the female part, as house-wives, school-mistresses, tayloresses, etc. and to go and be with these youth, when they shall be hundreds of miles distant from the English on the business of their mission. And prevent a necessity of their turning savage in their manner of living, for want of those who may do those offices for them, and by this means support the reputation of their mission, and also recommend to the savages a more rational and decent manner of living, than that which they are in and thereby, in time, remedy and remove that great, and hitherto insuperable difficulty, so constantly complained of by all our missionaries among them, as the great impediment in the way to the success of their mission, viz. their continual rambling about; which they can't avoid so long as they depend so much upon fishing, fowling, and hunting for their support. And I am more and more perswaded, that I have sufficient and unanswerable reasons to justify this plan.

As,

1. The deep rooted prejudices they have so generally imbibed against the English, that they are selfish, and have secret designs to incroach upon their lands, or otherwise wrong them in their interests. This jealousy seems to have been occasioned, nourished, and confirmed by some of their neighbours, who have got large tracts of their lands for a very inconsiderable part of their true value, and, it is commonly said, by taking the advantage of them when they were intoxicated with liquor. And also, by unrighteous dealers, who have taken such advantage to buy their skins and furrs at less than half price, etc. And perhaps these jealousies may be, not a little, increased by a conciousness of their own perfidy and inhumanity towards the English. And it seems there is no way to avoid the bad influence and effects of these prejudices, at present, unless it be by the mission of their own sons. And it is reasonable to suppose their jealousies are not less, since the late conquest in this land, by which they are put into our power, than they were before.

2. An Indian missionary may be supported with less than half the expence, that will be necessary to support an Englishman, who can't conform to their manner of living, and who will have no dependence upon them for any part of it. And an Indian who speaks their language, it may reasonably be supposed, will be at least four times as serviceable among them, supposing he be otherwise equally qualified as one who can communicate to or receive nothing from them, but by an interpreter: He may improve all opportunities not only in public, but, "when he sits in the house, walks by the way, when he lies down, and when he rises up:" And speak with as much life and spirit as the nature and importance of the matter require, which is very much lost when communicated by an interpreter.

3. Indian missionaries may be supposed better to understand the tempers and customs of Indians, and more readily to conform to them in a thousand things than the English can; and in things wherein the nonconformity of the English may cause disgust, and be construed as the fruit of pride, and an evidence and expression of their scorn and disrespect.

4. The influence of their own sons among them will likely be much greater than of any Englishman whatsoever. They will look upon such an one as one of them, his interest the same with theirs; and will naturally esteem him as an honour to their nation, and be more likely to submit patiently to his instructions and reproofs than to any English missionary. . . .

5. The acquaintance and friendship which Indian boys from different and distant tribes and places, will contract and cultivate, while together at school, may, and if they are zealously affected will, be improved much for the advantage and

furtherance of the design of their mission; while they send to, hear from, or visit one another, confirming the things which have been spoken. And this without so much ceremony to introduce one another, as will be necessary in the case of English missionaries; and without the cumber and expence of interpreters.

6. Indian missionaries will not disdain to own English ones, who shall be associated with them, (where the English can be introduced) as elder brethren; nor scorn to be advised or reproved, counselled or conducted by them; especially so long as they shall be so much dependent upon the English for their support; which will likely be till God has made them his people; and then, likely, they will not stand in such need of English guides and counsellors. And they will mutually help one another, to recommend the design to the favourable reception and good liking of the pagans, remove their prejudices, conciliate their friendship, and induce them to repose due confidence in the English.

7. In this school, children of different nations may, and easily will learn one another's language, and English youth may learn of them; and so save the vast expence and trouble of interpreters; and their ministry be much more acceptable and edifying to the Indians.

✻   ✻   ✻

When, as soon as the method proposed by the Rev'd. Mess. Sergeant and Brainerd, can be put into execution, viz. to have land appropriated to the use of Indian schools, and prudent skilful farmers, or tradesmen, to lead and instruct the boys, and mistresses to instruct the girls in such manufactures as are proper for them, at certain hours, as a diversion from their school exercises, and the children taken quite away from their parents, and the pernicious influence of Indian examples, there my be some good prospect of great advantage of schools among them.

And must it be esteemed a wild imagination, if it be supposed that well-instructed, sober, religious Indians, may with special advantage be employed as masters and mistresses in such schools; and that the design will be much recommended to the Indians thereby; and that there may be special advantage by such, serving as occasional interpreters for visitors from different nations from time to time; and they hereby receive the fullest conviction of the sincerity of our intentions and be confirmed and established in friendly sentiments of us, and encouraged to send their children, etc.?

I am fully perswaded from the acquaintance I have had with them, it will be found, whenever the trial shall be made, to be very difficult if not impossible, unless the arm of the Lord should be revealed in an eminent manner, to cure them of such savage and sordid practices, as they have been inured to from their mother's virtue, decency and humanity, while they are daily under the pernicious influence of their parents example, and their many vices made familiar thereby.

10. I have found by experience, there may be a thorough and effectual exercise of government in such a school, and as severe as shall be necessary, without opposition from, or offence taken by, any. And who does not know, that evils so obstinate as those we may reasonably expect to find common in the children of savages, will require that which is severe? Sure I am, they must find such as have better natures, or something more effectually done to subdue their vicious inclinations, that most I have been concerned with, if it be not so. And moreover, in such a school, there will be the best opportunity to know what has such a genius

and disposition, as most invite to bestow extraordinary expence to fit them for special usefulness.

11. We have the greatest security we can have, that when they are educated and fitted for it, they will be employed in that business. There is no likelihood at all that they will, though ever so well qualified, get into business, either as school-masters or mistresses, among the English; at least till the credit of their nations be raised many degrees above what it is now, and consequently they can't be employed as will be honorable for them, or in any business they will be fit for, but among their own nation. And it may reasonably be supposed, their compassion towards their "bretheren according to the flesh" will most naturally incline them to, and determine them upon such an employment as they were fitted and designed for. And besides all this, abundant experience has taught us, that such a change of diet, and manner of living as missionaries must generally come into, will not consist with the health of many Englishmen. And they will be obliged on that account to leave the service, though otherwise well disposed to it. Nor can this difficulty be avoided at present (certainly not without great expence.) But there is no great danger of difficulty in this respect as to Indians, who will only return to what they were used to from their mother's womb.

And there may also be admitted into this school, promising English youth of pregnant parts, and who from the best principles, and by the best motives, are inclined to devote themselves to that service; and who will naturally care for their state.

A BOSTON MERCHANT DESCRIBES ELEAZER WHEELOCK'S INDIAN SCHOOL (1764)   From James Dow McCallum, ed., *The Letters of Eleazer Wheelock's Indians* (Hanover, N.H., 1932), pp. 73-75.

Boston May 18, 1764

SIR

In rideing last week to new London I turned some miles out of my way to see Mr Wheelocks Indian School; nor do I repent my Trouble I had heard in general that it consisted of Twenty or more Indian Boys & Girls of the Mohawks & other Tribes of Indians And that a number of the Ministers of that Province had spoken well of Mr Wheelock & of this undertaking of his, But this I thought was seeing with the Eyes of others & therefore Chose to use my own.

My first observation in travelling through the Towns was the Different acceptation of both Mr Wheelock & his Enterprize there, from what some in Boston had entertained.

Here because of his lively adhering to the Doctrines of Grace he was not accepted by *some;* & when this is the Case you are sensible both Enterprize & Executior of it are too apt to be viewed by an Eye of Surmize & sometimes of Carping: But in Connecticut I found Charity & Candor & every where in passing Mr Wheelock had the Reverence of a Man of God, & his School was had in high Esteem.

I reached his House a little before the Evening Sacrafice & was movingly

Touched on giveing out the Psalm to hear an Indian Youth set the Time & the others following him, & singing the Tenor, & Base, with remarkable Gravity & Seirousness, & tho' Mr Wheelock, The Schoolmaster & a minister from our Province (called as I was by Curiosity) joined in Praise; yet they unmoved seemed to have nothing to do but to sing to the Glory of God.

I omit Mr Wheelocks Prayer & pass to the Indians in the morning when on Ringing the School house Bell they Assemble at Mr Wheelocks House about 5 oClock with their Master; who named the Chapter in Course for the Day & called upon the near Indian who read 3 or 4 Verses til the Master said *Proximus*, & then the next Indian read some Verses & so on till all the Indians had read the whole chapter. After this Mr Wheelock Prayes And then they each Indian perse a Verse or two of the Chapter they had read. After this they entered Successively on Prosodia & then on Disputations on some Questions propounded by themselves in some of the Arts & Sciences. And it is really charming to see Indian Youths of Different Tribes & Languages in pure English reading the Word of God & speaking with Exactness & accuracy on points (either chosen by themselves or given out to them) in the Severall arts & Sciences, And especially to see this done with at Least a seeming Mixture of Obedience to God; a fillial Love & Reverence to Mr Wheelock, & yet with great Ambittion to Excell each other And indeed in this Morning Exercies I saw a Youth Degraded one lower in the Class who before the Exercises were finished not only recovered his own place but was advanced two Higher.

I learnt hear that my surprize was common to ministers & other persons of Litterature who before me had been to visit this School or rather Colledge for I doubt whither in Colledges in General a better Education is to be expected & in mentioning this to a Gentleman in this Town who had visited this Seminary, He acquainted me that he intended at his own Charge to send his Son to obtain his Education in Mixture with these Indians. There were 4 or 5 of these Indians from 21 to 24 years of age who did not mix with the youth in these Exercies—These I learnt were Perfected in their Literature & stand ready to be sent among the Indians to keep Scools & occasionally to preach as doors open.

On my return Mr Wheelock accompanied me a few Miles & on passing by one House he said here lives one of my Indian Girls who was I hope Converted last week; & calling to the Farmer he unperceiv'd to her brought the Young Girl into our Sight & the pleasure was exquisite to see the Savageness of an Indian moulded into the Sweetness of a follower of the Lamb.

In passing some Days after this through the Mohegan Country I saw an Indian Man on Horseback whom I challenged as Mr *Occum* & found it so. There was something in his mein & Deportment both amiable & venerable & though I had never before seen him I must have been sure it was he.—He certainly does Honour Mr Wheelocks indefatigable, judicious, pious Intentions to send the Gospel among the Indians. I heard Mr Ashpo was then among them but at a Distance & I being hurried & tired Lost the opportunity of seing Mr Wheelock in him & more especially of seeing Christs Image in this Tawney Man but I wont tire you

       & am your most
          Humble Servant
          JOHN SMITH

INDIAN REFUSAL OF OFFER OF EDUCATION (1744) From "A Treaty with the Indians of the Six Nations, June, 1744," quoted in Carl Van Doren, ed., *Indian Treaties Printed by Benjamin Franklin, 1736-1762* (Philadelphia, 1938), pp. 72-73, 76.

After a little Pause the Commissioners of Virginia Spoke as follows:

Sachems and Warriors of the Six Nations,

The Way between us being made smooth by what passed Yesterday, we desire now to confirm all former Treaties made between *Virginia* and you our Brethren of the *Six Nations*, and to make our Chain of Union and Friendship as bright as the Sun, that it may not contract any more Rust for ever; that our Childrens Children may rejoice at, and confirm what we have done; and that you and your Children may not forget it, we give you One Hundred Pounds in Gold, and this Belt of Wampum.

Which was received with the usual Ceremony.

* * *

Brethren,

Our Friend, *Conrad Weiser*, when he is old, will go into the other World, as our Fathers have done; our Children will then want such a Friend to go between them and your Children, to reconcile any Differences that may happen to arise between them, that, like him, may have the Ears and Tongues of our Children and yours.

The Way to have such a Friend, is for you to send three or four of your Boys to *Virginia*, where we have a fine House for them to live in, and a Man on purpose to teach the Children of you, our Friends, the Religion, Language and Customs of the white People. To this Place we kindly invite you to send some of your Children, and we promise you they shall have the same Care taken of them, and be instructed in the same Manner as our own Children, and be returned to you again when you please; and, to confirm this, we give you this String of Wampum.

Which was received with the usual Ceremony.

* * *

Brother Affaragoa,

You did let us know Yesterday, that tho' you had been disappointed in your Endeavours to bring about a Peace between us and the *Catawbas*, yet you would still do the best to bring such a Thing about. We are well pleased with your Design, and the more so, as we hear you know what sort of People the *Catawbas* are, that they are spiteful and offensive, and have treated us contemptuously. We are glad you know these Things of the *Catawbas*; we believe what you say to be true, that there are, notwithstanding, some amongst them who are wiser and better; and, as you say, they are your Brethren, and belong to the Great King over the Water, we shall not be against a Peace on reasonable Terms, provided they will come to the Northward to treat about it. In Confirmation of what we say, and to encourage you in your Undertaking, we give you this String of Wampum.

Which was received with the usual Ceremonies.

Brother Affaragoa,

You told us likewise, you had a great House provided for the Education of Youth, and that there were several white People and *Indians* Children there to learn Languages, and to write and read, and invited us to send some of our Children amongst you, &c.

We must let you know we love our Children too well to send them to great a Way, and the *Indians* are not inclined to give their Children Learning. We allow it to be good, and we thank you for your Invitation; but our Customs differing from yours, you will be so good as to excuse us.

. . . In Token of our Thankfulness for your Invitation, we give you this String of Wampum.

Which was received with the usual Ceremony.

BENJAMIN FRANKLIN ON THE EDUCATION OF INDIAN CHILDREN

(1735)   From Benjamin Franklin to Peter Collinson, May 9, 1753, as quoted in Leonard W. Labaree, ed., *The Papers of Benjamin Franklin* (New Haven, 1959-   ), vol. IV, pp. 481-83.

The proneness of human Nature to a life of ease, of freedom from care and labour appears strongly in the little success that has hitherto attended every attempt to civilize our American Indians, in their present way of living, almost all their Wants are supplied by the spontaneous Productions of Nature, with the addition of very little labour, if hunting and fishing may indeed be called labour when Game is so plenty, they visit us frequently, and see the advantages that Arts, Sciences, and compact Society procure us, they are not deficient in natural understanding and yet they have never shewn any Inclination to change their manner of life for ours, or to learn any of our Arts; When an Indian Child has been brought up among us, taught our language and habituated to our Customs, yet if he goes to see his relations and make one Indian Ramble with them, there is no perswading him ever to return, and that this is not natural [to them] merely as Indians, but as men, is plain from this, that when white persons of either sex have been taken prisoners young by the Indians, and lived a while among them, tho' ransomed by their Friends, and treated with all imaginable tenderness to prevail with them to stay among the English, yet in a Short time they become disgusted with our manner of life, and the care and pains that are necessary to support it, and take the first good Opportunity of escaping again into the Woods, from whence there is no reclaiming them. One instance I remember to have heard, where the person was brought home to possess a good Estate; but finding some care necessary to keep it together, he relinquished it to a younger Brother, reserving to himself nothing but a gun and a match-Coat, with which he took his way again to the Wilderness.

Though they have few but natural wants and those easily supplied. But with us are infinite Artificial wants, no less craving than those of Nature, and much more difficult to satisfy; so that I am apt to imagine that close Societies subsisting by Labour and Arts, arose first not from choice, but from necessity: When numbers being driven by war from their hunting grounds and prevented by seas or by other nations were crowded together into some narrow Territories, which without labour would not afford them Food. However as matters [now] stand with us, care and industry seem absolutely necessary to our well being; they should therefore have every Encouragement we can invent, and not one Motive to diligence be subtracted, and the support of the Poor should not be by maintaining them in Idleness, But by employing them in some kind of labour suited to their Abilities of body &c. as I am informed of late begins to be the practice in many parts of England, where work houses are erected for that purpose. If these were general I should think the Poor would be more careful and work voluntarily and lay up something for themselves against a rainy day, rather than run the risque of being obliged to work at the pleasure of others for a bare subsistence and that too under confinement. The little value Indians set on what we prize so highly under the name of Learning appears from a pleasant passage that happened some years since at a Treaty between one of our Colonies and the Six Nations; when every thing had been settled to the Satisfaction of both sides, and nothing remained but a mutual exchange of civilities, the English Commissioners told the Indians, they had in their Country a College for the instruction of Youth who were there taught various languages, Arts, and Sciences; that there was a particular foundation in favour of the Indians to defray the expense of the Education of any of their sons who should desire to take the Benefit of it. And now if the Indians would accept of the Offer, the English would take half a dozen of their brightest lads and bring them up in the Best manner; The Indians after consulting on the proposal replied that it was remembered some of their Youths had formerly been educated in that College, but it had been observed that for a long time after they returned to their Friends, they were absolutely good for nothing being neither acquainted with the true methods of killing deer, catching Beaver or surprizing an enemy. The Proposition however, they looked on as a mark of the kindness and good will of the English to the Indian Nations which merited a grateful return; and therefore if the English Gentlemen would send a dozen or two of their Children to Onondago the great Council would take care of their Education, bring them up in really what was the best manner and make men of them.

PROPOSAL BY THE SOCIETY FOR THE PROPAGATION OF THE GOSPEL IN FOREIGN PARTS FOR INDIAN EDUCATION IN NEW YORK

(1771)   From William Kemp, *The Support of Schools in Colonial New York by the Society for the Propagation of the Gospel in Foreign Parts* (New York, 1913), pp. 231-33.

I. That two Missionaries, men of good character, abilities, and prudence, and in the orders of the established Church of England, be sent to the Iroquois, one to reside at Conajohare, the other at the old Oneida Town. Most of the Indians at both these villages have been baptised, and even profess Christianity; all are willing to be further instructed. Each of these Missionaries should have a Salary of £150 sterling a year at least, to enable them to shew some marks of favor to the more deserving Indians, by making small Presents to them from time to time. This will be expected from them, and if judiciously managed, will have a good effect in conciliating the affections of the Indians. If these Missionaries have some knowledge of Physic, so as to be able to assist the Indians in sickness, it would also increase their influence, and make their Spiritual Labours more successful.

II. That a Schoolmaster be fixed at each of those villages, viz.: Conajohare, and the old Oneida Town; another at Onondaga; one at the principal village of the Cayugas, and two among the Senekas. These Schoolmasters, for whom admission and protection may be easily procured, should be prudent, and virtuous young men, and such as have had a liberal education. Their business will be to teach the Indians, to read and write. They ought also to apply themselves diligently to learn the Indian Language, by which they will be better qualified to act as Missionaries afterwards, should their behaviour and merit entitle them to that office. Schools, if properly conducted, will be of infinite service. The Indians are all willing that their Children should be taught to read and write; and Youth is the properest season to instill principles of Morality and Religion, which the Schoolmasters will have constant opportunities of doing. Of these they ought to avail themselves; and gradually unfold the Principles of the Christian Systems to their pupils. Each of those Schoolmasters ought to have a salary of £40 Sterl. a year, which might be increased according to their industry and success. They also, as well as the Missionaries, should be furnished with Prayer-books, and such other Tracts in the Indian language as can be procured; which will be necessary to teach the Indians to read, and instruct them in the principles of Religion.

III. That Smiths be placed at some of the most convenient Indian Villages. These would be of great service to the Indians, and therefore very acceptable; and probably some of the Indians, from a sense of their utility might be induced to learn their Trade. Their wives might also be engaged to teach such of the Indian women as are willing to learn Spinning, Sewing, and other Branches of female Industry. The Government formerly allowed Smiths at several of the Indian Villages, with a competent salary. These Mechanics would now be of much service in promoting the general design, and might be had at a trifling expense. The Spaniards have employed mechanics, and do still, for the same purpose to great advantage.

IV. That the Missionaries and Schoolmasters employed in this Scheme be appointed, or at least approved, by the Society for the Propagation of the Gospel in Foreign Parts. The Superintendency of those matters naturally belongs to that Venerable Body, not only by reason that they coincide with the design of their Incorporation, and with their connections on this Continent, but also because the Society have with great fidelity discharged the important trust reposed in them, and have already done much towards Converting and Civilising the Iroquois. It is therefore proposed that they have the Care and Direction of the Missions specified in this plan; that the Missionaries and Schoolmasters shall regularly transmit to them accounts of their respective charges from time to time, in the same manner as those Missionaries and Schoolmasters in the Society's service do at present; to be annually laid before the Public; with their other Transactions. That the Missionaries, Schoolmasters and Mechanics however, be under the immediate inspection of His Majesty's Superintendent of Indian Affairs for the time being. His Station and Authority among the Indians will enable him to promote the execution of this Scheme. He will be the properest Person to direct the several Measures that shall be necessary on any new emergencies; and through him, in conjunction with the Society, applications to Government should be made, in matters relative to those Missions. It will be proper that the Superintendent of Indian Affairs should be thus concerned in the Management of those Matters, because it will be of Utility to the general Design; and also that he may see that such steps be taken as are consistent with the Interests of Trade, and the Views of Government respecting the Indians.

V. That a set of Rules and Instructions be prepared by the Society for the Regulation of the Missionaries and Schoolmasters in the Discharge of their Respective Duties, which Rules and Instructions however shall, for the reasons already mentioned be inspected and approved by His Majesty's Superintendant of Indian Affairs, previous to their Establishment. In drawing up these Instructions, particular Care should be taken to caution the Missionaries and Schoolmasters to be prudent in their Conduct, and to avoid whatever might give offence to the Indians, or awaken their Jealousy. Diligence in their Station, Sobriety, Gentleness, Condescension, and a disinterested Regard to the Welfare of the Indians, should be recommended, and that they sedulously inculcate Principles of Loyalty among their Hearers, Converts and Pupils.

VI. The last Article I shall mention as necessary to compleat this Plan, and make it more extensively useful, is the erecting a College or Seminary in the old Oneida Town, where the Young Indians who are distinguished for their Genius, may repair for a more enlarged Education, and be fitted for the Ministry. Very few of the Indians can be prevailed on to let their Children go to any great Distance for Instruction, and when they are persuaded to it, the Children always go with Reluctance. They are continually anxious to return to their Parents and Brethren, which is an Obstruction to their literary Progress; and when they return to their own People they generally run into the greater Excesses for their former Restraints.

It is therefore a mistaken Notion that Seminaries at a Distance from the Indians and only among Christians, are fittest for the Education of Indian Youths. Besides the Difficulty of bringing them to such Seminaries, and the small Degree of Improvement they carry from them, it serves to raise their Jealousy, and the Transition is too great and too sudden, from their former mode of Life, to that which they must hereby enter upon. Any Change in the Manners of a Savage People, who have an high Sense of liberty, like the Iroquois, should be gradually effected. It should in some measure be the Result of their own Choice, as being apparently expedient, not of any Violence; which will not fail to rivet them firmly to their Customs, and shut their Minds against Reason and Conviction. The Indian Country is evidently the properest Place to fix a Seminary for this Purpose, where the Parents can frequently see their Children; by which all Uneasiness would be removed from both, and those other Inconveniences avoided. It would also be pleasing to the Indians in general. They would look upon it as a Mark of our Regard, and Confidence in them. This would serve to reconcile them to the Instructions and Discipline of a College; and induce them to encourage the Institution, even from a Principle of Gratitude. But I shall not enlarge on this Head, as this Seminary is not immediately necessary. It must be the Work of Time; after the other Parts of the preceding Plan are carried into Execution, and a considerable Progress is made in each.

The German Immigrant

BENJAMIN FRANKLIN ON THE GERMAN IMMIGRATION TO PENNSYLVANIA (1751) From letters to James Parker and Peter Collinson, March 20, 1751, May 9, 1753, as quoted in Leonard W. Labaree, ed., *The Papers of Benjamin Franklin* (New Haven, 1959-   ), vol. IV, pp. 117-18, 483-85.

The Observation concerning the Importation of Germans in too great Numbers into Pennsylvania, is, I believe, a very just one. This will in a few Years become a German Colony: Instead of their Learning our Language, we must learn their's, or live as in a foreign Country. Already the English begin to quit particular Neighbourhoods surrounded by Dutch, being made uneasy by the Disagreeableness of disonant Manners; and in Time, Numbers will probably quit the Province for the same Reason. Besides, the Dutch under-live, and are thereby enabled to under-work and under-sell the English; who are thereby extreamly incommoded, and consequently disgusted, so that there can be no cordial Affection or Unity between the two Nations. How good Subjects they may make, and how faithful to the British Interest, is a Question worth considering.

*   *   *

I am perfectly of your mind, that measures of great Temper are necessary with the Germans: and am not without Apprehensions, that thro' their indiscretion or Ours, or both, great disorders and inconveniences may one day arise among us; Those who come hither are generally of the most ignorant Stupid Sort of their own Nation, and as Ignorance is often attended with Credulity when Knavery would mislead it, and with Suspicion when Honesty would set it right; and as few of the English understand the German Language, and so cannot address them either from the Press or Pulpit, 'tis almost impossible to remove any prejudices they once entertain. Their own Clergy have very little influence over the people; who seem to take an uncommon pleasure in abusing and discharging the Minister on every trivial occasion. Not being used to Liberty, they know not how to make a modest use of it; and as Kolben says of the young Hottentots, that they are not esteemed men till they have shewn their manhood by beating their mothers, so these seem to think themselves not free, till they can feel their liberty in abusing and insulting their Teachers. Thus they are under no restraint of Ecclesiastical Government; They behave, however, submissively enough at present to the Civil Government which I wish they may continue to do: For I remember when they modestly declined intermeddling in our Elections, but now they come in droves, and carry all before them, except in one or two Counties; Few of their children in the Country learn English; they import many Books from Germany; and of the six printing houses in the Province, two are entirely German, two half German half English, and but two entirely English; They have one German News-paper, and one half German. Advertisments intended to be general are now printed in Dutch and English; the Signs in our Streets have inscriptions in both languages, and in some places only German: They begin of late to make all their Bonds and other legal Writings in their own Language, which (though I think it ought not to be) are allowed good in our Courts, where the German Business so encreases that there is continual need of Interpreters; and I suppose in a few years they will be also necessary in the Assembly, to tell one half of our Legislators what the other half say; In short unless the stream of their importation could be turned from this to other Colonies, as you very judiciously propose, they will soon so out number us, that all the advantages we have will not [in My Opinion] be able to preserve our language, and even our Government will become precarious. The French who watch all advantages, are now [themselves] making a German settlement back of us in the Ilinoes Country, and by means of those Germans they may in time come to an understanding with ours, and indeed in the last war our Germans shewed a general disposition that seems to bode us no good; for when the English who were not Quakers, alarmed by the danger arising from the defenceless state of our Country entered unanimously into an Association within this Government and the lower Countries [Counties] raised armed and Disciplined [near] 10,000 men, the Germans except a very few in proportion to their numbers refused to engage in it, giving out one among another, and even in print, that if they were quiet the French should they take the Country would not molest them; at the same time abusing the Philadelphians for fitting out Privateers against the Enemy; and representing the trouble hazard and Expence of defending the Province, as a greater inconvenience than any that might be expected from a change of Government. Yet I am not for refusing entirely to admit them into our Colonies: all that seems to be necessary is, to distribute them more equally, mix them with the English, establish English Schools where they are now too thick settled, and take some care to prevent the practice lately fallen into by some of the Ship Owners, of sweeping the German Goals to make up the number of their Passengers. I say I am not against the Admission of Germans in general, for they have their Virtues, their industry and frugality is exemplary; They are excellent husbandmen and contribute greatly to the improvement of a Country.

LETTER REGARDING THE ORGANIZATION OF A "SOCIETY FOR THE RELIEF AND INSTRUCTION OF POOR GERMANS" (1753) From William Smith to Benjamin Franklin, February 1754, as quoted in Leonard W. Labaree, ed., *The Papers of Benjamin Franklin* (New Haven, 1959-   ), vol. V, pp. 214-17.

[December 13, 1753]

ABSTRACT: He is gratified to learn that a society has been formed in London to propagate Christian knowledge and the English language among the Germans of

Pennsylvania. He will not propose any scheme for the more equal distribution, in the future, of foreigners among the British colonies, or inquire whether British America might not grow as fast by the natural increase of population without the admission of additional foreigners. He will consider here only "the most probable method for incorporating these foreigners with ourselves, who are already settled among us." What he submits to the Society is essentially what he has already laid before Proprietor Thomas Penn on the same subject.

Imagine "upwards of 100,000 strangers settled in our territory, chiefly by themselves, and multiplying fast; strangers . . . to our Laws and manners; strangers to the sacred sound of liberty in the land where they were born, and uninstructed in the right use and Value of it in the country where they now enjoy it; utterly ignorant and apt to be misled by our unceasing enemies, . . . and what is worst of all, in danger of sinking deeper and deeper every day into these deplorable circumstances, as being almost entirely destitute of instructors and unacquainted with our language, so that it is hardly possible for us to warn them of their danger, or remove any prejudices they once entertain." Indeed, these prejudices may actually be increased by designing men, for in Pennsylvania many German books are imported, there are as many German printing houses as English, of late legal documents are often made in German, interpreters are constantly needed in courts "and will probably be soon wanted in the assembly itself to tell one half the legislature what the other says." These circumstances should awaken both our compassion and our vigilance. The Germans are not themselves blamable. They simply lack the means to prevent themselves from falling into ignorance or being seduced from their religion, for they have neither preachers nor teachers to instruct them or their children in the gospel or in English, which is the qualification for all posts of honor, used in all writings, the courts of justice, and the like. For commiserating their circumstances, "the whole British nation, nay the whole protestant interest, and the interest of liberty" are all obliged to the Society. This is not the work of any party, but *"A British work"*; nor does it concern a particular denomination, but aims to keep a vast multitude of fellow Protestants from falling into deeper ignorance, being seduced by the enemy, living in a separate body, turning trade out of its proper channels, and at last giving us their laws and language.

He proposes the following measures:

1. That faithful clergymen be supplied to preach the gospel among the Germans, for their principles, and keep them to their duty.

2. That English common schools be established in the German communities, which German and English children may attend free. Such institutions "could hardly fail of incorporating them in process of time," for there they will form acquaintances and connections, learn the common language, like manners, and the meaning of liberty, a common weal, and a common country. Intermarriage will follow, which will further unite them in a common interest, as Roman history shows. More important, this common education will promote such a spirit through all ranks as is best suited to the particular genius of every colony.

He then takes up the following practical questions:

1. The method of education "should be calculated rather to make good citizens than what is called good scholars." English "together with a short system of truths and duties, in the *socratic* method by way of catechism," writing and arithmetic are all the education necessary for the vulgar; but at the same time they must be instructed in the principles of our common Christianity, the use and end of society, the differences between forms of government, and the excellency of our

own, for "the virtue of the active vulgar is the strength of the state." But this is such a large topic he will enlarge on it in a separate letter.

2. The government of the schools should be under the direction of six or seven of the principal gentlemen living in Pennsylvania where the need for English schools is greatest; these may be called trustees-general. One or more of them should visit all the schools annually to examine the students and award prizes to those who speak or read English best and give the best answers to questions on religious and civil duties. The trustees-general should be empowered to appoint at least six deputy trustees or visitors for each school, three English and three German, who should visit the schools monthly, present premiums, and transmit monthly or quarterly reports to the trustees-general at Philadelphia. The appointment of trustees-general should be the first step taken to put the schools into operation.

3. Supplying proper instructors is "something difficult." They must know English and German and be able to teach mathematics, geography, drawing, history, ethics, "with the constitution and interests of the several colonies with respect to the mother country and one another." They should be natives of the countries where they will teach, whose genius they will therefore know, and where they will therefore exert a natural leadership. Fortunately in Pennsylvania there is a flourishing seminary, "on the most catholic and manly bottom," for educating such teachers; and the Proprietor of the province has agreed to endow the education of three or four poor English and German youths in the academy each year, which should amply supply the German schools.

4. Maintenance. The Germans could not support these instructors; but the English in America, though with difficulty providing for their own children, would do what they could toward erecting schoolhouses, churches, and housing with a few acres for the teachers. For the rest, they must depend on the charity of the Society. Twenty pounds to a schoolmaster and forty to one who is both minister and schoolmaster (together with a glebe "and the perquisites of some of the most substantial Scholars") would enable them to live decently.

He prays for success in their undertaking. The propagation of such knowledge is the only way to preserve good government and advance the interests of the mother country in America. "Commerce is the child of Industry and an unprecarious Property; but these depend on virtue and liberty, which again depend on knowledge and Religion." A free people can be governed only by reason, virtue, glory, honor, and the like, which are the results of education, without which, therefore, they cannot be governed at all. Where men are free to speak and act they must be instructed how to speak and act rightly, otherwise they will use their liberty against those from whom they received it.

But there are other lights than the merely political in which to consider this matter. The fate of a considerable branch of the Protestant interest in this part of the world is important, and the plight of the children is most affecting of all, for they are "coming forward into the world like grasshoppers in multitude," liable to remin in ignorance, an easy prey for the designing. In their hands is the fate of a great part of the new world: whether it shall fall under the dread reign of popery or sink back into original barbarism, or flourish long in all that exalts and embellishes society.

The churches of the Netherlands and of Scotland will help as they have done in the past. But the English have the most immediate obligation "to incorporate these foreigners with themselves; to mingle them in equal privileges with the Sons of freedom, and teach their conscious bosoms to exult at the thoughts of an unprecarious property, a home and social endearments; to contrive Laws for making them flourish long in a well-ordered Society, and make a provision for improving their natures and training them up for eternal scenes!"

He hopes to be "a pleased spectator of part of this happiness," and assures his correspondents that he will "decline no labor as often as you honor me with any opportunity of forwarding your grand Scheme to effect it."

DESCRIPTION OF THE WORK OF THE SOCIETY FOR THE RELIEF AND INSTRUCTION OF POOR GERMANS IN PENNSYLVANIA

(1755)   From William Smith. *A Brief History of the Charitable Scheme Carrying On by a Society of Noblemen and Gentlemen in London, for the Relief and Instruction of Poor Germans, . . . in Pennsylvania* (Philadelphia, 1755), pp. 3-17.

For several years past, the small Number of reformed Protestant Ministers settled among the German Emigrants in Pennsylvania, finding the Harvest great, but the Labourers few, have been deeply affected with a true Christian Concern for the Welfare of their distressed Countrymen, and the Salvation of their precious Souls. In Consequence of this, they have, from Time to Time, in the most solemn and moving manner, entreated the Churches of Holland, to commiserate their unhappy Fellow-Christians, who mourn under the deepest Affliction, being settled in a remote Corner of the World, where the Light of the blessed Gospel has but lately reached, and where they are very much destitute of the Means of Knowledge and Salvation.

The Churches of Holland being accordingly moved with friendly Compassion, did, from Time to Time, contribute to the support of Religion in these remote Parts. But in the year 1751 a very moving Representation of their State having been made by a Person, whose unwearied Labors for the Benefit of his dear Countrymen have been for some years conspicuous, the States of Holland, and West Friesland, granted 2,000 Guilders per annum for 5 Years from that Time, to be applied towards the Instruction of the said Germans and their Children in Pennsylvania. A considerable Sum was also collected in the City of Amsterdam, and elsewhere; and upon a Motion made by the same zealous Person, the Rev. Mr. Thomson [a minister of one of the English churches in Amsterdam] was commissioned by the Synods of Holland and Classis of Amsterdam to solicit the friendly assistance of the Churches of England and Scotland.

When Mr. Thomson arrived in Great Britain, he found the readiest Encouragement among Persons of the first Rank, both in Church and State. It is the peculiar Glory of the British Government equally to consult the Happiness of all who live under it, however remote, wherever born, or of whatsoever Denomination. . . . Considered in this Light, Mr. Thomson's Design could not fail to be encouraged in our Mother Country, since it was so evidently calculated to save a vast Multitude of Industrious People from the Gloom of Ignorance, and qualify them for the Enjoyment of all those noble Privileges, to which it is now their good Fortune to be admitted, in common with the happy Subjects of a free Protestant Government.

Mr. Thomson, having thus made his Business known in England and prepared the Way for Encouragement there, he, in the meantime, went down to Scotland and . . . . represented the Case to the General Assembly of the Church, then sitting at Edinburgh, upon which a national Collection was made, amounting to upwards of 1,200 pounds sterling. Such an Instance of Generosity is one out of many, to shew how ready that Church has always been to contribute towards the Advancement of Truth, Virtue and Freedom.

Mr. Thomson . . . . saw that it would be absolutely necessary to have some Persons in London, not only to manage the Monies already collected, but also to solicit and receive the Contributions of the Rich and Benevolent in England, where nothing had yet been collected, and where much might be hoped for. With this view, he begged a certain number of Noblemen and Gentlemen of the first Rank, to take the Management of the Design upon themselves.

This Proposal was readily agreed to by these noble and worthy Persons. They were truly concerned to find that there were any of their Fellow-Subjects, in any Part of the British Dominions, not fully provided with the Means of Knowledge and Salvation. They considered it as a matter of the greatest Importance to the Cause of Christianity in general, and the Protestant Interest in particular, not to neglect such a vast Body of useful People, situated in a dark and barren Region, with almost none to instruct them and their helpless Children who are coming forward into the World in Multitudes. . . . .

The first thing the said Society did was to agree to a liberal Subscription among themselves; and, upon laying the Case before the King, his Majesty, like a true Father of his People, granted 1,000 Pounds towards it . . . . and the honorable Proprietories of this Province, willing to concur in every Design for the Ease and Welfare of their People generously engaged to give a considerable yearly Sum for promoting the most essential Part of the Undertaking. . . . . In the meantime the honorable Society have come to the following general Resolutions, with regard to the Management of the Whole:

I. To assist the People in the Encouragement of pious and industrious Protestant Ministers that are, or shall be, regularly ordained and settled among the said Germans, or their Descendants in America; beginning first in Pennsylvania, where the want of Ministers is greatest. . . . .

II. To establish some charitable Schools for the Pious Education of German Youth of all Denominations, as well as those English youth that may reside among them. . . . .

III. The said Honorable Society . . . . have devolved the general Management of the whole upon Us, under the names of Trustees General for the management of their Charity among the German Emigrants in North America. And as our Residence is in this Province where the chief Body is settled, and where we may acquaint ourselves with the Circumstances of the People, the generous Society hope that we cannot be imposed upon, or deceived, in the Direction or Application of their Excellent Charity.

IV. And lastly, the said honorable Society have, out of their true fatherly Care appointed the Rev. Mr. Schlatter to act under our Direction as Visitor or Supervisor of the Schools, knowing that he has already taken incredible Pains in this whole Affair, and being acquainted with the People in all Parts of the Country can converse with them on the spot and bring us the best advices, from Time to Time concerning the measures fit to be taken. . . . .

As to the important Article of establishing Schools, the following general Plan is proposed, which may be from Time to Time improved and perfected:

First, it is intended that every School to be opened upon this Charity, shall be equally for the Benefit of Protestant Youth of all Denominations, and therefore the education will be in such Things as are generally useful to advance industry and true Godliness. The Youth will be instructed in both the English and German Languages; likewise in writing, keeping of Common Accounts, Singing of Psalms, and the true Principles of the holy Protestant Religion, in the same Manner as the Fathers of these Germans were instructed, at the Schools in the Countries from which they came.

Secondly, as it may be of great Service to Religion and Industry, to have some Schools for Girls also we shall use our Endeavours with the honorable Society to have some few schoolmistresses encouraged to teach Reading and the Use of the Needle. . . . .

Thirdly, that all may be induced, in their early Youth, to seek the Knowledge and Love of God, in that manner which is most agreeable to their own Consciences, the Children of all Protestant Denominations, English and Dutch, shall be instructed in any Catechism of sound Doctrine which is approved of and used by their own Parents and Ministers. . . . .

Fourthly, for the Use of the Schools, the several Catechisms that are now taught to Children among the Calvinists, Lutherans and other Protestant Denominations will be printed in English and Dutch and distributed among the Poor, together with some Bibles and other good Books at the Expence of the Society. . . . .

With regard to the Number of Schools to be opened, that will depend partly on the encouragement given by the People themselves, and partly on the Increase of the Society's Funds. A considerable number of Places are proposed to fix schools in; but none are absolutely determined upon but New-Hanover, New-Providence, and Reading. These Places were first fixed upon, because People of all Persuasions, Lutherans, Calvinists, and other Protestants moved with a pious and fatherly concern for the illiterate state of their helpless children did, with a true Christian Harmony, present their Petitions, praying that their numerous Children of all Denominations in these Parts, might be made the Common Object of the intended Charity. And for this benevolent purpose they did farther agree to offer School houses in which their Children might be instructed together as dear Fellow-Christians redeemed by the same common Lord and Saviour, and travelling to the same heavenly Country, through this Valley of Tears, notwithstanding they may sometimes take Roads a little different in Points of smaller Moment.

. . . . And if the Petitioners shall recommend school masters, as was the case at New-Hanover, New-Providence, and Reading, such school masters will have the Preference; provided they are men of sufficient Probity and Knowledge, agreeable to all Parties and acquainted with both the English and Dutch Languages or willing to learn either of those Languages which they may not then be perfectly acquainted with.

These are essential qualifications; and unless the generous Society had made a Provision for teaching English as well as Dutch, it would not have answered their benevolent Design, which is to qualify the Germans for all the Advantages of *native English subjects*. But this could not have been done, without giving them an opportunity of learning English, by speaking of which they may expect to rise to Places of Profit and Honor in the Country. They will likewise be enabled to buy or sell to the greater Advantage in our Markets; to understand their own Causes in Courts of Justice where Pleadings are in English; to know what is doing in the Country round them; and, in a Word, to judge and act entirely for themselves, without being obliged to take Things upon the Word of others, whose Interests it may be to deceive and mislead them. . . . .

A Design for instructing a People and adorning the minds of their children with useful knowledge, can carry nothing in it but what is friendly to Liberty, and auspicious to all the most sacred Interests of Mankind. Were it otherwise, why are so many of the greatest and best Men, both of the British and German Nations engaged in the Undertaking? Why have they, as it were, stooped from their high Spheres and condescended to beg from House to House in order to promote it? Is not all this done with the glorious Intention of relieving you from the distressful ignorance that was like to fall upon you? . . . .

You shall know how to make the true Use of all your noble Privileges, and instead of mourning, in a dry and barren Land, where no Water is, you and your Posterity shall flourish, from age to age in all that is valuable in human Life. A barren Region shall be turned into a fruitful Country, and a thirsty Land into Pools of Water.

COMMENTS OF BENJAMIN FRANKLIN AND OTHERS ON THE "GERMAN SOCIETY" (1756) From Pennsylvania Trustees of the German Society to the Society, as quoted in Leonard W. Labaree, ed., *The Papers of Benjamin Franklin* (New Haven, 1959-), vol. VI, pp. 533-35.

Philada, 24th Sepr, 1756.

To the Right Honourable and worthy Members of the Society for promoting religious Knowledge and the English Language among the German Emigrants in Pennsylvania, &c.

MOST WORTHY LORDS AND GENTLEMEN,

We have been duly honoured with your several Letters thro' the Hands of your worthy Secretary and Fellow Member, the Reverend Dr. Chandler, part of which have been directed to Us jointly, and part to the Reverend Mr. Smith. We have, from Time to Time, faithfully endeavoured to follow your Orders and Instructions, and beg Leave to assure You of the sensible Pleasure it gives Us to find our Conduct approved by such an honourable Body of Men, in the Management of so useful and excellent a Charity. But nothing, in this whole Business, gives Us more real Satisfaction than to be so strongly assured in your Letter of January 28, 1755, "That the whole of what you aim at is, not to proselyte the Germans to any particular Denomination, but (leaving all of them to the entire Liberty of their own Judgments in speculative and disputed Points) to spread the knowledge of the avowed uncontroverted Principles of Religion and Morality among them, to render them acquainted with the English Language and Constitution, to form them into good Subjects to his Majesty King George whose protection they enjoy, and make them Friends to the Interests of that Nation which hath received them into her Bosom, blessed them with Liberty and given them a Share in her invaluable Privileges."

Such a noble and generous Declaration is truly worthy of the noble and generous Spirits from whence it comes. It is worthy of Men who have embarked on a Principle of Doing Good for its own Sake, and who by their Birth, Education, and liberal Turn of Mind, are elevated far above the narrow Distinctions that blind the

Vulgar. We have likewise the Honour to assure You, that such a Declaration is also perfectly agreeable to our Sentiments, who, by Reason of our Publick Situation in this Country, could never have engaged in the Management of any partial Scheme. Nor indeed would such Scheme have answered, in any Shape, your pious and noble Design. For whatever is proposed for the Benefit of the German Emigrants must, in its Nature and Plan, be as Catholic and General as their Denominations are various; especially as far as regards the Education of their Children; in which Point they are exceeding jealous and tenacious of their respective *Dogmas* and *Notions*.

*　　*　　*

Permit Us to assure You that we shall at all Times think Ourselves happy in contributing every Thing in our power, under so illustrious a Society of Men, to the forwarding such an excellent Design, for the Honour of Great Britain, and the Benefit of those poor People who have taken Refuge under her Wings, and with due Care may be preserved as his Majesty's most faithful Subjects, and zealous Defenders of the Protestant Cause.

We have the Honour to be Your most obedient and most humble Servants,

Signed as follows:　Benjamin Franklin,　James Hamilton,
　　　　　　　　　　Conrad Weiser,　　 William Allen,
　　　　　　　　　　William Smith,　　　Richard Peters,

MICHAEL SCHLATTER, Supervisor.